P9-DFX-750

Fodor's

AUSTRALIA

21st Edition

Fodor's Travel Publications   New York, Toronto, London, Sydney, Auckland
www.fodors.com

FODOR'S AUSTRALIA

Writers: Melanie Ball, Fleur Bainger, Tim Baker, Johanna Castro, Tess Curran, Barry Lorne Freedman, Caroline Gladstone, Amy Taylor-Kabbaz, Merran White

Editor: Margaret Kelly

Production Editor: Carrie Parker
Maps & Illustrations: David Lindroth and Mark Stroud, *cartographers;* Bob Blake, Rebecca Baer, *map editors;* William Wu, *information graphics*
Design: Fabrizio La Rocca, *creative director;* Guido Caroti, *art director;* Tina Malaney, Nora Rosansky, Chie Ushio, Jessica Walsh, *designers;* Melanie Marin, *associate director of photography*
Cover Photo: (Pinnacles Desert, Nambung National Park): Frank Krahmer/Masterfile
Production Manager: Angela L. McLean

21st Edition

ISBN 978–0–307–92844–3

ISSN 1095–2675

SPECIAL SALES

This book is available at special discounts for bulk purchases for sales promotions or premiums. Special editions, including personalized covers, excerpts of existing books, and corporate imprints, can be created in large quantities for special needs. For more information, write to Special Markets/Premium Sales, 1745 Broadway, MD 3-1, New York, NY 10019, or e-mail specialmarkets@randomhouse.com.

AN IMPORTANT TIP & AN INVITATION

Although all prices, opening times, and other details in this book are based on information supplied to us at press time, changes occur all the time in the travel world, and Fodor's cannot accept responsibility for facts that become outdated or for inadvertent errors or omissions. So **always confirm information when it matters**, especially if you're making a detour to visit a specific place. Your experiences—positive and negative— matter to us. If we have missed or misstated something, **please write to us**. Share your opinion instantly through our online feedback center at fodors.com/contact-us.

PRINTED IN COLOMBIA

10 9 8 7 6 5 4 3 2

CONTENTS

Fodor's Features

ABOUT THIS BOOK

Our Ratings

At Fodor's, we spend considerable time choosing the best places in a destination so you don't have to. By default, anything we recommend in this book is worth visiting. But some sights, properties, and experiences are so great that we've recognized them with additional accolades. Orange **Fodor's Choice** stars indicate our top recommendations; black stars highlight places we deem **Highly Recommended**; and **Best Bets** call attention to top properties in various categories. Disagree with any of our choices? Care to nominate a new place? Visit our feedback center at www.fodors.com/feedback.

For expanded hotel reviews, visit **Fodors.com**

Hotels

Hotels have private bath, phone, TV, and air-conditioning, and do not offer meals unless we specify that in the review. We always list facilities but not whether you'll be charged an extra fee to use them.

Restaurants

Unless we state otherwise, restaurants are open for lunch and dinner daily. We mention dress only when there's a specific requirement and reservations only when they're essential or not accepted—it's always best to book ahead.

Credit Cards

We assume that restaurants and hotels accept credit cards. If not, we'll note it in the review.

Budget Well

Hotel and restaurant price categories from ¢ to $$$$ are defined in the opening pages of the respective chapters. For attractions, we always give standard adult admission fees; reductions are usually available for children, students, and senior citizens.

Listings
- ★ Fodor's Choice
- ★ Highly recommended
- ⊠ Physical address
- ⊹ Directions or Map coordinates
- ⌂ Mailing address
- ☎ Telephone
- 🖷 Fax
- ⊕ On the Web
- ✉ E-mail
- 🎫 Admission fee
- ◷ Open/closed times
- Ⓜ Metro stations
- ⊟ No credit cards

Hotels & Restaurants
- 🏨 Hotel
- ↴ Number of rooms
- ₺ Facilities
- ⱺ Meal plans
- ✗ Restaurant
- ✍ Reservations
- 🕴 Dress code
- ↘ Smoking

Outdoors
- 🏌 Golf
- ⛺ Camping

Other
- ⊙ Family-friendly
- ⇨ See also
- ⊠ Branch address
- ☞ Take note

Experience Australia

WHAT'S WHERE

Numbers refer to chapters.

2 Sydney. One of the most naturally beautiful cities in the world, Sydney blends beachside cool with corporate capitalism and Victorian-era colonial architecture. Arts, tourism, and business interests thrive around spectacular Sydney Harbour.

3 New South Wales including Canberra and A.C.T. Southeastern Australia displays most of the continent's rural and coastal variations: historic towns, mountains, dramatic beaches, and world-class vineyards. The nation's spacious and immaculately landscaped capital showcases myriad Australian national monuments.

4 Melbourne. Melbourne is Australia's most European city and a cultural melting pot and you can see that in its fantastics food scene.

5 Victoria. Rugged Coastline, fairy penguins, wineries, historic towns, and national parks are reason enough to explore the Victorian countryside.

6 Tasmania. From Freycinet Peninsula to wild South West National Park, Tasmania's intoxicating natural beauty testifies to Australia's topographic diversity. Don't miss the numerous relics of the island's volatile days as a penal colony.

7 Brisbane and Its Beaches. Name your pleasure (or poison) and you'll find it in Queensland: mini-Miamis, nearly deserted beaches, and lush rain forests, great restaurants, and easy access to family-friendly adventure parks.

8 The Great Barrier Reef. Queensland's crown jewel is the 2,600-km-long (1,616-mi-long) Great Barrier Reef. More than 3,000 individual reefs and 900 islands make up this vast aquatic universe. There are countless ways to experience this quickly disappearing natural wonder.

9 Adelaide and South Australia. Well-planned and picturesque Adelaide has many charms, including its famous biennial festival of the arts. Be sure to take a tour of the renowned wine country, and then unwind on a Murray River cruise.

10 Outback Adventures. Outback Australia stuns with its diversity. In the country's vast, central desert region are Uluru and Kata Tjuta, monoliths of deep significance to the local Aboriginal people. Closer to Asia than to any other Australian city, Darwin is the gateway to World-Heritage wetlands, monster cattle ranches, and rock art.

AUSTRALIA PLANNER

Visitor Information

Tourism Australia's Web site is one of the best places to start planning your trip. As well as general information, they have package deals and searchable listings for U.S. travel agents who specialize in Australia.

Tourism Australia
⊕ www.australia.com.

Regional Information

Each Australian state has its own tourism Web site where you can find state-specific maps, thematically organized listings, travel information, and links to accommodation and transport. Some have free state travel guides that they'll send to you. In general, they handle queries online.

Australian Capital Tourism
⊕ www.visitcanberra.com.au.
Northern Territory ⊕ www.travel.nt.com. **South Australian Tourism Commission**
⊕ www.southaustralia.com.
Tourism New South Wales
⊕ www.visitnsw.com.
Tourism Queensland
⊕ www.queenslandholidays.com.au. **Tourism Tasmania**
⊕ www.discovertasmania.com.
Tourism Western Australia
⊕ www.westernaustralia.com.
Welcome to Victoria
⊕ www.visitvictoria.com.

Safety

Given Australia's relaxed lifestyle, it's easy to be seduced into believing that crime is nonexistent. In fact, Australia has its share of poverty, drugs, and crime, but rates aren't high by world standards, so be wary and you should have no problems. Wearing jewelry in public isn't a risk, and using ATMs in daylight hours is usually fine. Theft—especially pickpocketing—is a problem only in major tourist areas such as Sydney's Bondi or Queensland's Gold Coast. Try to avoid leaving valuables on the beach when you go for a swim or in your car when you park. Australia has had enough cases of children going missing in public places for parents to want to be vigilant on beaches and in malls.

Traveling in Australia is generally safe for women, provided you take a few commonsense precautions. Avoid isolated areas such as empty beaches and quiet streets at night. Single women usually receive attention entering pubs or clubs alone, but a few firm, polite words are normally enough to put a stop to it, if it's unwanted.

Emergencies

Australian emergency services are extremely efficient. Local people usually help each other unquestioningly, too. For theft, wallet loss, small road accidents, and minor emergencies, contact the nearest police station. In a medical or dental emergency, ask your hotel staff for information on and directions to the nearest hospital or clinic; taxi drivers should also know how to find one.

Pack a basic first-aid kit, especially if you're venturing into more remote areas. If you'll be carrying any medication, bring your doctor's contact information and prescription authorizations. Most Australian pharmacies only fill prescriptions from Australian doctors, so bring enough medication for your trip.

Pharmacies usually open between 9 and 5, but most towns have a 24-hour pharmacy system so that one pharmacy is always open. In an emergency, the local police station can tell you which pharmacy is open, as can hospitals.

Eating Out

These days fusion food is what's putting Australia on the foodie map—indeed, many claim that the very term was invented Down Under. The huge Asian communities in cities like Sydney and Melbourne have brought their traditional condiments and cooking styles to bear on local staples: the resulting combinations are what many of the country's most famous eateries specialize in.

Bush tucker, or indigenous Australian food, was once something you came across only on bushwalking expeditions in the Outback. Suddenly it's become fashionable, and uniquely Australian ingredients like lemon myrtle, wattle seed, and rosella (not to mention kangaroo meat) are appearing on fancy restaurant menus all over the country. Food is an international language, but your English may fail you in Australian restaurants. "Entrée" means appetizer, and "main courses" are what American entrées go by. The term "silver service" indicates upscale dining. French fries are called "chips," chickens are "chooks," sausages are known as "snags," and if you want ketchup, ask for "tomato sauce."

Accommodations

Australia's state capitals run the gamut of lodging options. But that's doesn't mean *all* the interesting accommodation is in town. Family-run bed-and-breakfasts, farmstays, country hotels, and even small-town pubs are some of the alternatives Australia has to offer. Sleeping Down Under is generally cheaper than in North America, and money-saving accommodation is particularly varied—be it a serviced apartment, a well-appointed caravan, or a bed at a backpackers' dorm.

⇨ *For more detailed information on accommodations, see the Travel Smart chapter at the end of the Guide.*

Wines, Beer, and Spirits

Beer and wine are an important part of Australian life. Australia is the world's 10th-largest wine producer, and Australian wine is gaining considerable respect worldwide. Australia's most famous wine-producing areas are the Hunter Valley in New South Wales, the Barossa Valley in South Australia, and Western Australia's Margaret River region. Although there are no native grape varietals in Australia, Shiraz (also known as Syrah) is a local specialty. Cabernet Sauvignon and Pinot Noir are common reds; popular whites include Chardonnay, Sauvignon Blanc, and Pinot Grigio. Australia produces a wide range of beers. As well as big national brands like Fosters, each state has its own brew: Victoria Bitter in Victoria and XXXX (called four-ex) in Queensland, for example.

If you're invited to an Australian's home, it's common—indeed, expected—practice to take a bottle of wine at dinnertime or a case of beer for a barbecue. When drinking at pubs, Australians always drink in rounds, British-style.

Tipping

Australians don't expect tips, and hotels and restaurants rarely add service charges. That said, a small tip for good service is common practice and appreciated. Room service and housemaids are only tipped for special services. Taxi drivers don't expect a tip, but leaving small change will win you a smile. Guides, tour-bus drivers, and chauffeurs don't expect tips either, though they're grateful if someone in the group takes up a collection for them. No tipping is necessary—indeed, it would cause confusion—in hair salons or for theater ushers.

AUSTRALIA
WORLD HERITAGE SITES

Australia has more cultural and natural treasures than is fair to many other countries. It also, fortunately, has the wealth and resolve to protect them as best it can. Eighteen sites across the country, including two offshore territories in sub-Antarctic waters, have been World Heritage listed.

Tasmanian Wilderness

(A) Harsh glacial action over millions of years has put the wild in the Tasmanian Wilderness. Remote and subject to extreme weather, this vast World Heritage area—it covers a fifth of Australia's island state—protects one of the few expanses of temperate rain forest on Earth. Here, too, are stunning landforms fashioned by complex geology, diverse habitats for flora and fauna found nowhere else, and evidence of tens of thousands of years of Aboriginal occupation. Angling, white-water rafting, and hiking national park walking trails, most of which are suited only to experienced hikers, are some favorite activities in the Tasmanian Wilderness World Heritage Area.

Fraser Island

(B) Remnant rain forest, shifting sand dunes, and half of the world's perched lakes (lakes that are isolated above the groundwater table by rock or organic material) contributed to Fraser Island's World Heritage listing in 1992. The largest sand island on Earth, Fraser lies just off Queensland's coast, about 200 km (124 mi) north of Brisbane. This exquisite island is both ecologically precious and extremely popular for soft-adventure holidays—a sometimes problematic combination. Fraser's dingo population is one of Australia's purest, but be aware that visitors have had fatal interactions with these wild dogs. Humpback whales frequent Fraser's west-coast waters June to November, and the spring tailor fish run lures anglers to the island's wilder ocean

shore. Four-wheel-drives barrel along the 76-mi ocean beach, which is Fraser Island's unofficial main highway.

Sydney Opera House

(C) One of Australia's recent World Heritage properties is the country's most recognizable building. A realization of visionary design and 20th-century technological innovation, the Sydney Opera House was listed in 2007 as a masterpiece of human creative genius. It is also a structure of extraordinary beauty. Danish architect Jorn Utzon's interlocking vaulted "shells" appear to hover like wind-filled sails on their Sydney Harbour promontory. Flood lighting at night increases the sense of movement.

Awarded the project in 1957 by an international jury, Jorn Utzon never saw his creation finished. Utzon resigned and left Australia in 1966, amid funding controversies and political change, and his architectural sculpture was completed by others. Familiar to people around the world, the Sydney Opera House is a world-class performing arts venue.

Greater Blue Mountains Area

(D) Sunlight refracting off a mist of eucalyptus oil gives the Blue Mountains, west of Sydney, their distinctive hue. The variety of eucalypts (commonly called gum trees) across this mountain range's varied habitats was integral to its World Heritage listing. The 1.03 million hectares of sandstone country encompasses the Blue Mountains National Park. Ninety-one varieties of eucalypts grow here. So, too, do significant numbers of rare species and "living fossils" such as the Wollemi pine, which was discovered in 1994.

Great Barrier Reef

(E) While its name suggests otherwise, Australia's most famous World Heritage site is not a single reef. The 2,600-km-long (1,616-mi-long) Great Barrier Reef is actually the world's largest collection of

reefs. This fragile natural wonder contains 400 types of coral and 1,500 fish species of every size and almost every conceivable color combination. The giant clam, with its voluptuous purple, green, or blue mantle (algae dictate the color) is one of the 4,000 mollusks the reef supports.

Uluru-Kata Tjuta National Park

(F) What you see projecting from the sandy plains of Australia's Red Centre is just the tip, but this majestic monolith still packs a physical and spiritual punch well above its weight. Uluru (also called Ayers Rock) and Kata Tjuta, the seemingly sculpted rock domes clustered 55 km (34 mi) to the west, are deeply significant to the park's traditional owners, the Anangu Aboriginal people.

The Anangu ask visitors not to climb Uluru. Some controversy continues, however, about whether this is because the climb is the traditional route of the ancestral Mala men or because the Anangu think the ascent

is just too dangerous. At least 35 people have died on the steep, exposed climb. Independent walks, ranger-guided walks, and Anangu-guided walks (fees apply) offer fascinating cultural perspectives of Uluru and Kata Tjuta from the ground.

Wet Tropics of Queensland

(G) Verdant and ancient, the Wet Tropics of Queensland are the hothouse of Australian flora and fauna. Three thousand plant species, hundreds of mammal types, and over half the country's recorded birds inhabit the tangled rain forests north, south, and west of Cairns, on Australia's far north-eastern coast. The remarkable tree kangaroo and the green possum are found only in this World Heritage area. Reptile residents of the Wet Tropics vary in size from inches-long geckos to 7-meter-long (23-foot-long) amethystine pythons. A shorter but considerably meaner local is the estuarine crocodile, or saltie as it is commonly called.

Purnululu National Park

(H) Geological history is written large across this World Heritage site in Australia's northwest Kimberley region. Twenty million years of erosion and weathering have deeply dissected the Bungle Bungle Range into banded, beehive-shape sandstone towers. Other examples of cone karst in sandstone, as this remarkable phenomenon is called, are found around the world. None of these sites rival Purnululu for the diversity, size, and grandeur of formations.

Purnululu means sandstone in the Kija aboriginal language, and spectacularly sculpted sandstone is the highlight of the park. Hard-edged gorges softened by fan palms separate the orange-and-black striped towers, however. Wild budgerigars are among the 100-plus bird species in the park. Wallabies, too, are sometimes spotted among the rocks.

Kakadu National Park

(I) X-ray paintings of barramundi, long-necked turtles, and other animals festoon the main gallery at Ubirr Rock in Kakadu National Park. This menu-in-ocher is one of more than 5,000 art sites in the park that collectively date back 20,000 years. Archaeologists have put human habitation at twice that long. Ongoing and uninterrupted connection with Top End Aboriginal peoples was a key factor in Kakadu's World Heritage listing. So were the park's diverse habitats. Estuarine crocodiles prowl the Alligator River. Red-billed jabiru, Australia's only stork, stroll the flood plains. Waterfalls cannon off the Arnhem Land escarpment. Nowhere else in Australia are cultural and ecological significance so richly intertwined.

IF YOU LIKE

Beautiful Beaches

Whether you want to bake in the sun, see and be seen, or try body- or board-surfing in the white-capped waves, Australia has an abundance of beautiful beaches. Miles and miles of pristine sand line the coastline, so you can choose to join the crowd or sunbathe in blissful solitude.

■ **Bondi Beach.** On the edge of the Tasman Sea, Bondi Beach is the most famous perhaps in all of Australia. You can take a surfing lesson here or just immerse yourself in the delights of suburban sand and water. Don't miss the Coast Walk from Bondi to Bronte Beach—it's a breathtaking 2.5-km (1.5-mi) path that will take you along dramatic coastal cliffs to a string of eastern beaches. The walking track continues beyond Bronte Beach to Waverley Cemetery, where many famous Australians are buried in cliff-top splendor.

■ **Queensland's Gold Coast and Islands.** Warm, moderate surf washes the 70-km (43-mi) stretch of Gold Coast beaches, which are perfect for board riding, swimming, or just collecting shells at sunset. Beach bums, however, know to head north to the Great Barrier Reef islands for less crowded, tropical stretches of sand.

■ **West Coast.** Fringing the Indian Ocean between Perth and South Fremantle are 19 wide beaches with good breaks, but head down to the south coast for a dip in the crystal-clear waters of the deserted, sandy white beaches around Margaret River.

■ **Whitehaven.** The Whitsunday Islands are home to arguably Australia's most beautiful beach. The near-deserted arc of Whitehaven Beach has some of the whitest and most powdery sand on earth.

Wine

Australian wines are among the best in the world, a judgment that international wine shows consistently reinforce. Australians are very proud of their wine. You'll be hard-pressed to find anything but Australian wines on the menus at most places, so take this opportunity to expand your palate beyond the export brands you may have tried at home, like Rosemount, Jacob's Creek, and Penfolds.

■ **Hunter Valley.** The largest grape-growing area in New South Wales, Hunter Valley has more than 120 wineries and a reputation for producing excellent wines. Expect some amazing Semillons and Cabernets.

■ **Margaret River.** In Western Australia the Margaret River region produces just 1% of the country's total wine output. Yet 25% of Australia's premium and ultrapremium wines come from this small area. Margaret River's Bordeaux-like climate helps producers grow excellent Cabernet-Merlot blends, since these grapes originally came from that region.

■ **South Australia.** The Barossa Valley, about an hour's drive northeast of Adelaide, produces some of Australia's most famous Syrah (or Shiraz, as they call it Down Under). You might recognize the Penfolds label, as makers of the renowned Grange Shiraz blend. In the nearby Clare Valley, German immigrants planted Riesling many decades ago and the grape has met with great success there.

■ **Yarra Valley.** More than 70 wineries fill the floor of the Yarra Valley, where Pinot Noir thrives.

Incredible Wildlife

Australia's diverse habitats are home to countless strange and amazing creatures.

■ **Birds.** Australia has many wild and wonderful creatures of the nonmarsupial variety. The waterholes at Kakadu National Park in the Northern Territory attract more than 280 species of birds, including the stately jabiru, Australia's only stork, and the fluorescent rainbow bee-eater, as well as crocodiles, the ubiquitous creatures of Australia's Top End. The much friendlier and cuter fairy penguins draw nighttime crowds at **Philip Island** in Victoria.

■ **Camels.** Don't be surprised if you catch the eye of a camel wandering the desert of the Red Centre. These are descendants of dromedaries shipped in during the 19th century for use on exploratory expeditions and Outback construction projects and for desert transport.

■ **Creatures of the Deep.** The Great Barrier Reef gets plenty of attention for underwater wildlife, but Western Australia has two phenomenal spots of its own. The dolphins at Shark Bay in Monkey Mia, Western Australia, can be hand-fed. Ningaloo Reef, off the Exmouth Peninsula, is home to humpback whales and whale sharks.

■ **Koalas and Kangaroos.** No trip to Australia would be complete without an encounter with Australia's iconic animals: kangaroos and koalas. The Lone Pine Koala Sanctuary in Brisbane is one of many wildlife parks around Australia that let you take a picture with a cuddly koala or hand-feed a mob of kangaroos.

Water Sports

With 36,735 km (22,776 mi) of coast bordering two oceans and four seas, Australians spend a good deal of their time in and on the water. Opportunities abound for scuba diving, snorkeling, surfing, waterskiing, windsurfing, sailing, and just mucking about in the waves. Prime diving seasons are September–December and mid-March–May.

■ **Diving.** Avid divers will want to visit the resort islands of the Great Barrier Reef, which provide upscale accommodation and access to some of the country's top diving spots. Cod Hole, off the Lizard Island reef, in far north Queensland, ranks highly among them. You can do a one-day introductory or resort dive, and four-day open water dive certification courses, or if fins and oxygen tanks aren't your speed, opt for snorkeling off the island beaches. Diving expeditions are a specialty of the Cairns area, with carriers like Quicksilver and Tusa Dive running day trips to the reef for diving and snorkeling.

■ **Sailing.** Sailors love the Whitsunday Islands off the mid-north Queensland coast. Almost all the 74 islands in this group are national parks, and only seven have resorts on them, making this an ideal spot to drop anchor and moor for a few days, or to try a vacation on a live-aboard boat or yacht. You can also experience the swashbuckling romance of olden-day sailing on multiday tall ship cruises.

QUINTESSENTIAL AUSTRALIA

Go Bush

When Aussies refer to the bush, they can mean either a scrubby patch of ground a few kilometers outside the city or the vast, sprawling desert Outback. In most cases it's a way to describe getting out of the daily routine of the city and getting in touch with the natural landscape of this incredibly diverse country.

With 80% of its population living on eastern shores, and with all of its major cities (except Canberra) on or near the coast, most of Australia's wild, wonderful interior is virtually empty. Whether you find yourself watching the sun rise (or set) over Uluru, taking a camel trek through the Kimberley, or sleeping under the stars in a swag (traditional Australian camping kit), there are countless ways to go bush and see Australia's most natural, rural, and stunning sights.

Aussie! Aussie! Aussie! Oi! Oi! Oi!

From world-class sporting events like the Australian Open tennis to national obsessions like the Australian Football League Grand Final, Aussies love their sports. The calendar is chock-full of sporting events that give Aussies good reason to drink a cold beer and gather with mates to barrack for (cheer on) their favorite team.

Aussie Rules Football (or footy) is a popular, fast-paced, and rough-and-tumble sport that's played without padding and uses what looks like an American football through four 25-minute quarters. Rugby League Football is a 13-a-side game that is played internationally. Cricket test matches are the sport of summer, though much less happens during these games than in footy matches. Spectators get to soak up the sun and drink a lot of beer while watching the Australians duel international teams in matches that can go for one to five days.

Aussies refer to authentic or genuine things as *fair dinkum.* The folks down under are a fun-loving bunch, so don't be shy. Here are a few ways to experience Australia like the locals do.

Swimming Between the Flags

Australians love their beaches as much as they love their barbies, so put on your bathers or your cossie (slang for bathing costume) and slather on good sunblock—the damage to the ozone layer above Australia is very, very severe.

Many Australian beaches are patrolled by volunteer members of the Surf Lifesaving Association (SLSA), who post red and yellow flags to demarcate the safest areas to swim on any beach. The SLSA was formed in 1907, and its tan, buff lifesavers make the *Baywatch* team look like amateurs—it's rumored that no one has ever drowned while swimming in the areas that they patrol. Of course, these hunky heroes can't be everywhere all the time, so use caution when swimming on those picturesque deserted beaches you're bound to come across in your travels. The undertow or rip can be strong and dangerous.

The Barbie

Paul Hogan, aka Crocodile Dundee, showed the world laid-back Australian hospitality by inviting visitors to say "G'day," then throw another shrimp on the barbie, or barbecue. But it's unlikely you'll find shrimp on a barbie in Australia. What you will find is Aussies cooking up steak, sausages (often called snags), beef, chicken, and lamb on gas grills all over the country.

Barbies are so ubiquitous in Australia that almost every public park or beach will have a barbecue area set up for people to come and grill at will. The tools required for "having a barbie" the traditional Aussie way are newspaper and butter. The newspaper helps wipe the barbie clean from the previous grilling, and butter greases it back up again before putting the meat on. Sometimes an onion instead of a newspaper is used to clean off the grill—a slightly more hygienic system.

AUSTRALIA TODAY

Government

Australia is a constitutional monarchy, and the Queen of England is still officially Australia's Queen as well. Her only role under the constitution, however, is to appoint her representative in Australia, the Governor General, which she does on advice from Australia's Prime Minister. In 1975 the then Governor General caused a political crisis when he sacked the Prime Minister and his government and installed the Opposition minority as caretaker until new elections could be held. Today the Governor General still retains that power, but his or her duties are primarily ceremonial. Australia's government is elected for three-year terms, with no limit on how many terms a Prime Minister can serve. Voting is compulsory for all citizens 18 years and older, and failure to vote can result in a fine.

Economy

Australia is a major exporter of wheat and wool, iron-ore and gold, liquefied natural gas and coal. The major industries are mining, industrial and transport equipment, food processing, chemicals, and steel manufacturing. The services sector dominates the domestic economy. Abundant natural assets and massive government spending have softened the short-term impact of the recent global financial crisis as compared with many other countries.

Tourism

On- and offshore wonders, unique wildlife, beach culture, indigenous history, and multicultural cuisines help maintain Australia's multibillion-dollar tourism industry. The major challenges are keeping Australia on travelers' radars as other countries gain popularity, and protecting the most fragile attractions.

Climate change has already affected the Great Barrier Reef, a World Heritage site on most visitors' must-see lists, and programs are in place to try to minimize the impact of rising sea temperatures. Contentious logging of old-growth forests for pulp, particularly in Tasmania, continues, and the opening of new mines rarely fits comfortably with conservation and cultural issues.

Religion

Australia's first settlers were predominantly English, Irish, and Scottish Christians. Two centuries later, almost two thirds of Australians call themselves Christians, with Buddhism a distant second (2%), and Islam third (1.7%), however nearly a fifth of the population ticked "no religion" on the last census. Active church worship has declined over recent decades, and many religious orders struggle to attract members.

Literature

Life Down Under has bred contemporary writers who speak with distinctly Australian voices. Tim Winton's book *Breath* brilliantly evokes the power of surfing and the angst of adolescence. Look out for Kate Grenville, Richard Flanagan, Peter Carey, Alex Miller, and Peter Corris, among others. Morris Gleitzman and Paul Jennings write (mostly) laugh-out-loud books for children and the young at heart.

MANAGING THE WATER CRISIS

If you were to suggest that World War III will be fought over water, not oil, many Australians might agree. Rainfall was below average for years in many places before record rains—and consequent devastating floods—across the eastern states in late 2010 to early 2011. The country's major river system remains in trouble, and some rural water storages, especially in the west, are extremely low or empty. The subject of water—its supply, collection, and use—is on almost everyone's lips.

The Impact

Australians are learning to live with the water restrictions that are in force across much of the country; limits on watering gardens and lawns, washing vehicles, and hosing paved areas are mandatory, and fines are levied for breaking them. Everyone in Australia is affected by the water crisis, but rural communities dependent on irrigation are feeling the brunt of it. The Murray and its main tributary, the Darling, are Australia's longest river system and the lifeblood of its crop farms. In the two years before the 2011 floods the volume of water flowing into the Murray from the rivers that feed it in NSW and Queensland was the lowest since records began in 1892. The farms and towns taking water from the Murray-Darling river system have become a huge threat to its survival. In 2009 a heat wave and wildfires in southeast Australia wreaked devastation on wine harvests. Faced with another drought, or a potentially new, dryer climate, some farmers walked away. Australia's native flora and fauna also face dwindling water supplies. Wetlands (and the wildlife they support) are most at risk.

Taking Action

Australia's federal and state governments are implementing measures to reduce the impact of climate change and improve and supplement existing water sources, but critics complain that it's too little, too late. South Australia and Victoria are, controversially, following Western Australia's example and building desalination plants. Authorities are also treading warily around the idea of recycling wastewater for consumption. The grand schemes for piping Top End floodwaters to the thirsty south pop up every few years, despite expert opinion that this is financially unviable—it would, apparently, be cheaper to ship the water south in bulk carriers. More practically, a revamped water trading and buy-out system based on water access entitlements promises to reallocate precious Murray-Darling water. Businesses, schools, and private homes are installing tanks to harvest rainwater, installing water-saving shower heads, and landscaping with heartier indigenous plants.

What You Can Do

Limit showers to 3 minutes and turn off taps while soaping up in the shower or brushing teeth.

Use a sink plug when rinsing food or dishes, and when washing hands.

Ask hotel staff to not change your towels and bed linen until you leave.

Bring or buy a reusable drinking bottle and fill it from the tap—tap water around Australia is safe, and the production of bottled water uses huge amounts of water and energy.

GREAT ITINERARIES

THE INDIAN PACIFIC RAILROAD JOURNEY

Australia's longest rail journey snakes 4,352 km (2,720 mi) across mountains, plains, and deserts between Sydney and Perth. Named after the oceans on either side of the country, the Indian Pacific dates back to the late 19th century, when Australia was pushing toward Federation. The independent British colonies of Queensland, New South Wales, Victoria, Tasmania, and South Australia enticed the isolated colony of Western Australia into federation with the promise of an east-west rail link. Construction of the final 1,996-km (1,248-mi) link in the transcontinental line, between Kalgoorlie in the west and Port Augusta in South Australia, was completed in 1917. Even though passenger services started that year, the Indian Pacific only made its first unbroken journey in 1970. Before then, travelers had to change trains several times to ride narrow-, standard-, and broad-gauge track, and the line was standardized only in 1969.

The Route

The Indian Pacific traverses dramatically diverse Australian landscapes on its 65-hour journey. You have the option of making the whole trip in one sitting or breaking it—for A$200 you can stop off in Adelaide.

The Eastern Leg (from Sydney to Adelaide)

East–west passengers leave Sydney in midafternoon and kick off the journey by traveling over the sandstone escarpments and through the villages of the Blue Mountains as the train scales the Great Dividing Range. Dinner is served as the Western Plains unfurl. After a good

night's rest, tuck into breakfast as the train rolls through Outback New South Wales toward Broken Hill. Morning and afternoon light on the gnarled hills, mulga scrub, and red-soil plains out here inspires artists, many of whom have galleries in Broken Hill. Look out for emus and kangaroos.

The Western Leg (from Adelaide to Perth)

Your second Indian Pacific dinner is served as the train backtracks through Adelaide's northern suburbs to the railway junction at Crystal Brook. Darkness covers the run up Spencer Gulf and into salt-lake country, and dawn finds you on the Nullarbor Plain. Nullarbor is a Latin-based name meaning no trees. There is little to see for mile after mile, and that's the appeal. This is prime hunting ground for the wedge-tailed eagle, symbol of the Indian Pacific, and train drivers sometimes slow down so passengers can see eagle chicks in a nest beside the train.

Whistle-Stop Tours—Broken Hill

All Whistle-Stop tours can be arranged through the bar staff or the Onboard Hospitality Attendant in each carriage. Three tours are offered during your 70- to 90-minute stop in Broken Hill. We like the Silver City tour (A$24), which explores the town's rich mining history.

Whistle-Stop Tours—Adelaide

If you want to stay on the train, then you've only 3½ hours to explore the city. The one-hour Adelaide–Festival City tour (A$23) shows you Adelaide Oval (arguably Australia's prettiest cricket ground), splendid sandstone buildings, and Rundle Street's famous café scene. If you decide to break up your journey, then your time depends on which Indian Pacific service you rejoin; the train runs weekly year-round, with a second departure each week from early September to late November and early January to late March. A three-day itinerary allows for one day in Adelaide, and the next day can be spent exploring the villages and wineries in the Adelaide Hills. On Day 3, head north to Barossa or south to McLaren Vale for some serious wine appreciation. The trains depart at 6:40 pm on Wednesdays (and Saturday in high season).

Whistle-Stop Tours—Kalgoorlie

Around breakfast time the following day, the Indian Pacific starts its run on the world's longest straight stretch of railway. After 90 minutes along this 478-km (300-mi) stretch of track, in the middle of nowhere, the train stops in Cook to take on water and change drivers. Step off and wander around this virtual ghost town. Around nightfall you'll roll into Kalgoorlie for a 3½-hour stop. This is Australia's largest Outback city, and it sits on the world's highest concentration of gold. Join the 75-minute Gold Capital Tour (A$30) and learn about the hardships of early mining and the unique cast of characters that came here to strike it rich. Weather permitting, you also see the 1,090-foot-deep, 3-km-long (2-mi-long) flood-lit Super Pit. From Kalgoorlie, the

NUTS AND BOLTS

■ Red Service: Daynighter seat A$399, sleeper cabin A$1,460 per person.

■ Gold Service: Twin or single sleeper cabin A$2,080 per person.

■ Chairman's Carriage (private, sleeps eight) A$17,120; Sir John Forest Carriage (private, accommodates six), A$15,240; Prince of Wales Carriage (private, sleeps ten) A$15,300 (The Prince of Wales operates only between Adelaide and Perth).

■ You can book your motor vehicle (up to 5.5 meters long) on the Indian Pacific for A$849.

■ Train Amenities: Restaurant and dining cars, bar service, lounge cars, tour bookings.

■ Duration of Trip: 65 hours.

■ Distance Traveled: 2,720 mi.

Indian Pacific continues west through the night, and the journey ends in Perth around 9 am. Take the All About Perth tour (A$44) and get a feel for Western Australia's riverside capital before checking into your hotel.

GREAT ITINERARIES

THE *GHAN* RAILROAD JOURNEY

The *Ghan* is one of the world's great train journeys. Named after the Afghan cameleers whose animals were crucial to central Australia's exploration, settlement, and development, this train rides 2,979 km (1862 mi) of track between Adelaide, in South Australia, and Darwin, on the country's north coast. Roughly halfway between these two cities the *Ghan* pulls into Alice Springs, the desert city in Australia's aptly named Red Centre. A north–south transcontinental Australian railway was mooted as early as 1858, but it took 20 more years for track to start creeping northward. Alice Springs consisted of just 100 people and one hotel when a steam engine hauled the first *Ghan* train into town in 1929. Unfortunately, extreme desert conditions and termites wreaked havoc on the track and train services for years to come. Finally, the rerouted *New Ghan* was launched in 1980, but stories about the old service live on: one tells of a woman who complained to the conductor about the delays because she was due to give birth. When the conductor rebuked her for making a rail journey while pregnant she replied, "I wasn't when I got on!" In contrast to the long, stop-start construction of the Adelaide-Alice line, the northern extension to Darwin was completed in just four years, and the inaugural Darwin-bound *Ghan* service left Adelaide on February 1, 2004.

The Route

On its 53-hour journey, the *Ghan* traverses some of Australia's most unforgiving and surprisingly beautiful country. Book the whole trip, or break it into northern and southern legs—you pay a negligible premium to split the fare—and explore Alice Springs and the ancient landscape surrounding it.

The Southern Leg (from Adelaide to Alice)

South–north passengers leave Adelaide at lunchtime. Watch South Australia roll by as the *Ghan* motors up Spencer Gulf to Port Augusta. From there the train turns inland, passing through ephemeral saltlake country into darkness. Dawn finds the *Ghan* deep in desert, with red earth flat to the horizon or occasionally gathered into ancient ranges. Enjoy the play of pastel colors on the plains from your cabin's picture window.

The Northern Leg (from Alice to Darwin)

The train leaves Alice for Darwin just in time for dinner. The next morning, after a brief whistle stop in Katherine, you'll spend your final day rolling through the desert and lonely scrubland of the Top End toward the lush tropical city of Darwin. Once in Darwin, celebrate your journey's end with Thai-style barramundi at Hanuman Darwin, one of the Top End's best restaurants.

Whistle-Stop Tours—Alice Springs

The *Ghan* rolls into Alice Springs around lunchtime on Day 2 for a four-hour stop. If you're up for a little adventure, a helicopter flight (A$195 per person) over the ancient MacDonnell Ranges might be to your liking. We especially like the Desert Park Tour (A$62) for its fascinating insights into Australia's desert country and the remarkable plants and animals that inhabit it. Passengers breaking their train journey in Alice Springs have three or seven days, depending on which service you rejoin (the *Ghan* operates weekly November to March and twice a week over winter, early April to end

October). With three days, explore Alice's museums, wildlife parks, and Aboriginal art galleries, then do a self-drive or group tour of the gorges, waterholes, and Aboriginal sites in the MacDonnell Ranges. If you have a week, explore Alice Springs and surrounds and then experience the geological and spiritual wonder of Uluru (Ayers Rock) and Kata Tjuta, which are 457 km (285 mi) southeast of Alice Springs by road or an hour by commercial flight.

Whistle-Stop Tours—Katherine

You're spoiled for choice with the selection of Whistle-Stop tours during your four-hour stay in Katherine. A passenger favorite—and one of Katherine's main attractions—is the Katherine Gorge boat cruise (A$85) in Nitmiluk National Park. Passengers can cruise between the gorge's soaring sandstone walls or hire a canoe and paddle on this Northern Territory landmark (careful of the crocs!). Double canoes are A$33.50 per person, single canoes A$45 per person.

NUTS AND BOLTS

- Red Service: Daynighter seat A$716, sleeper cabin A$1,312.

- Gold Service: Twin or single sleeper cabin A$1,973.

- Platinum Service: Sleeper cabin A$3,090 per person.

- Chairman's Carriage (private, sleeps eight) A$17,520; Sir John Forest Carriage (private, accommodates six), A$13,740; Prince of Wales Carriage (private, sleeps ten) A$21,300.

- You can book your motor vehicle (up to 5.5 meters long) on the *Ghan* for A$799. Train Amenities: Restaurant and dining car, bar service, lounge car, tour bookings.

- Duration of Trip: 53 hours.

- Distance Traveled: 1,862 mi.

GREAT ITINERARIES

ROAD TRIP: FROM SYDNEY TO BRISBANE

Drive along one of the most glorious and seductive stretches of land in northern New South Wales. It's a big trip—1,100 km (687.5 mi)—so allow a minimum of seven days if you decide to drive the entire route.

Day 1—175 km (109 mi):

Frame the Harbour Bridge in your rear-vision mirror and head north out of Sydney. Take the Sydney–Newcastle (F3) Freeway about 75 km (47 mi) north to the Peats Ridge Road exit, and wind through the forested hills to Wollombi, a delightful town founded in 1820. Browse the antiques shops, sandstone courthouse, and museum. Next, head northeast to Cessnock and Pokolbin, the hub of the Lower Hunter, and spend the day tasting—and buying—fine wines and artisanal cheeses. Know that Australia has a zero tolerance policy for driving and drinking. Be sure to choose a designated driver or, better yet, take one of our recommended wine-tasting tours.

Day 2—271 km (168 mi):

Get up with the birds and drive east via Cessnock to the Pacific Highway. Turn north for the long drive to Port Macquarie, Australia's third-oldest settlement. Have a well-earned lunch break in the café at Sea Acres Rainforest Centre and then stroll the elevated boardwalk—or take a guided tour—through centuries-old cabbage tree palms. Now it's into Port Macquarie for a lazy afternoon on a beach, but which of the 13 regional beaches do you laze on?

Day 3—260 km (162.5 mi)

Visit Port Macquarie's Koala Hospital for feeding time (8 am). Then resume driving up the Pacific Highway. Leave the highway 140 km (87.5 mi) north at the exit to Bellingen, one of the prettiest towns on the New South Wales north coast. It's a nice place to stop for lunch and a quick peek into a few galleries. Continue inland up onto the Dorrigo Plateau. Dorrigo National Park is one of about 50 reserves and parks within the World Heritage–listed Gondwana Rainforests of Australia. Stopping into the Dorrigo Rainforest Centre to learn about the area is gratifying, as is the forest canopy Skywalk. Back in your car, drive on to Dorrigo town and turn right onto the winding, partly unsealed, but scenic road to Corumba and Coffs Harbour. Now you've earned a two-night stay in Coffs.

Day 4—no driving

Scuba-dive on the Solitary Isles? Whitewater raft the Nymboida River? Or kick back on a beach? However you spend your day, don't miss an evening stroll to Muttonbird Island from Coffs Harbour marina. From September to April you can watch muttonbirds (or shearwaters) returning to their burrows. When the whales are about, it's also a good humpback viewing spot.

Day 5—247 km (154 mi)

North again, past Coffs Harbour's landmark Big Banana and up the coast to Byron Bay.

There is just too much to do in Byron: kayak with dolphins; dive with grey nurse sharks; go beachcombing and swimming; tread the Cape Byron Walking Track; or tour the lighthouse atop Cape Byron, which is mainland Australia's easternmost point. It's best to decide over lunch

Brisbane

QUEENSLAND

GOLD COAST

Mt. Warning ◆ ○Murwillumbah

Byron Bay

SOLITARY ISLANDS

Dorrigo
Dorrigo National Park ◆ ○○Coffs Harbour
Bellingen

Port Macquarie
◆Sea Acres Rainforest Centre

NEW SOUTH
WALES

Pokolbin
Wollombi ○○Cessnock

Sydney

at open-air Byron Bay Beach Café, a local legend. When the sun sets, wash off the salt and head out for some great seafood and then overnight in Byron Bay—there's everything from hostels to high-end villas.

Day 6—53 km (33 mi)

Catch up on the Byron Bay you missed yesterday before driving north to Murwillumbah and its remarkable natural landmark. Mt. Warning is the 3,800-foot magma chamber of an extinct shield volcano. From the top, on a clear day, there is a 360-degree view of one of the world's largest calderas, with mountainous rims on three sides and the Tweed River running through its eroded east rim. Climb this mountain (four hours return), then reward yourself with a night at Crystal Creek Rainforest Retreat (bookings essential).

Day 7—50 km (31 mi)

Relaxed and reinvigorated, it's over the New South Wales border to Queensland and Australia's most developed stretch of coastline. With Brisbane just 90 minutes' drive farther north, you can spend as much or as little time as you want on the Gold Coast. Visit theme parks; toss dice at the casino; ride waves in gorgeous sunshine. Don't miss feeding the lorikeets at Currumbin Wildlife Sanctuary before Brisbane beckons.

TIPS AND LOGISTICS

■ Unleaded petrol, diesel, and LPG are available at gas stations along most of this route.

■ Motel rooms are easy to find, except during school holidays and long weekends. To avoid driving around after a day at the wheel, book ahead. The staff at your previous night's accommodation should be able to help you arrange the next night.

■ If hiring a car for the trip, check that it contains a street directory. Pick up a good road map or touring atlas heading out of Sydney.

■ Mobile speed radars are used throughout Australia, and fines are high. Stick to the speed limits.

GREAT ITINERARIES

ROAD TRIP: GREAT OCEAN ROAD

Arguably one of the country's most spectacular drives, the iconic Great Ocean Road hugs the windswept, rugged coastline just west of Melbourne. Allow six days for this 900-km (562-mi) road trip and be prepared to enjoy some of Victoria's best.

Day 1 — 187 km (117 mi)

Having escaped Melbourne, drive down the Princes Freeway for about 75 km (47 mi) to the Torquay/Great Ocean Road turnoff. A quarter hour more at the wheel brings you to Torquay, Australia's premier surfing and windsurfing resort town. On your way out of town, detour to Bell's Beach, the setting for Australia's premier surfing competition each Easter. The renowned Great Ocean Road officially starts 30 km (19 mi) beyond Bell's Beach, but the dramatic splendor of Victoria's southwest coast reveals itself sooner. Stop in Lorne, at the foot of the lush Otway Ranges, for lunch. Once you're back on the road, slow down and enjoy it. The winding Great Ocean Road is narrow; don't pass unless you can see far ahead, and don't pull onto the shoulder to admire the view! There are designated pullover areas where you can safely enjoy the vista.

Drive the 45 km (28 mi) to Apollo Bay for dinner and the night.

Day 2 — 234 km (146 mi)

The 91-km (57-mi) Great Ocean Walk starts just west of Apollo Bay in Marengo. Here the Great Ocean Road heads inland. Stay on the main road to Lavers Hill; then detour about 17 km (11 mi) east to the Otway Fly. This 1,969-foot-long elevated treetop walk takes you up into the rain-forest canopy for a bird's-eye view of giant myrtle beech, blackwood, and mighty mountain ash. Backtrack to Lavers Hill and the Great Ocean Road. The road's most famous landmarks lie along a 32-km (20-mi) stretch of coast within Port Campbell National Park. First stop is the Twelve Apostles—there are now only seven of these offshore limestone stacks, but who's counting? Take a helicopter flight for a jaw-dropping view of the eroded and indented coast. Next stop is Loch Ard Gorge, named after the iron-hulled clipper that hit a reef and sank here in 1878. Loch Ard is a natural gallery of sea sculpture, where you could wander for hours on a sunny day. Don't stay in your car if the sun doesn't show, though. Only when a howling wind is roughing up the Southern Ocean will you fully appreciate why this is called the Shipwreck Coast. Leaving the Great Ocean Road now, drive to the maritime village of Port Fairy for the night. In whale season (June–November), divert to Logan's Beach, in Warrnambool, where southern right cows and calves often loll just off the beach.

Day 3 — 146 km (91 mi)

Take a leisurely post-breakfast promenade around Port Fairy, Victoria's second-oldest town and widely considered to be its prettiest. Then backtrack 7 km (4.4 mi) to the Penshurst/Dunkeld Road and drive 74 km (46 mi) north to Dunkeld, on the edge of the Grampians National Park. Stop for lunch before undertaking the 60-km (37-mi) drive to Halls Gap, the main accommodation base. Be sure to slow down and enjoy one of the most picturesque drives in the Grampians; pull in at the Brambuk Cultural Centre, just before Halls Gap, and learn about the park's rich Aboriginal history.

Check into your Halls Gap accommodation for two nights.

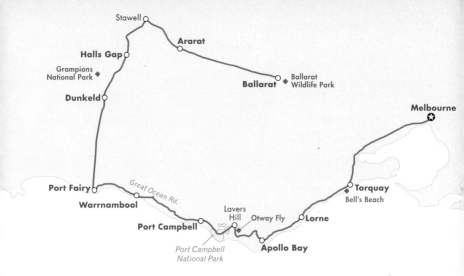

Day 4—No driving

Spend a day exploring on foot. Walks of varied grades showcase the Grampians' extraordinary geology; don't miss the Pinnacle Walk, just out of Halls Gap, the valley and ranges view from Chatauqua Peak, and Hollow Mountain in the park's north.

Day 5—140 km (87.5 mi)

Drive out of Halls Gap to Ararat, on the Western Highway, and follow the highway east to the famous gold town of Ballarat. Spend the rest of the morning among the gold-rush-era Victorian architecture on Sturt and Lydiard streets. Visit the Ballarat Fine Art Gallery, if only to see the tattered remains of the Southern Cross flag that the rebels flew during the 1854 Eureka uprising over mine license fees. Spend the afternoon at Sovereign Hill, where you can pan for gold, ride a horse-drawn stagecoach through dusty streets, and stick your teeth together with old-fashioned candy.

Day 6—111 km (69 mi)

Have close and not-so-close encounters with saltwater crocodiles, snakes, wombats, kangaroos, and other Australian fauna at Ballarat Wildlife Park. After that, continue your journey or head back to Melbourne.

TIPS AND LOGISTICS

■ Unleaded petrol, diesel, and LPG are available at gas stations in major centers; however, LPG is rare in small country towns.

■ There is a petrol price cycle in Victoria, which authorities can't—or won't—explain; try to fill up on Tuesday and Wednesday, and avoid buying fuel on Friday.

■ Choosing accommodation as you go gives you flexibility in when and where you stop. For peace of mind, though, you might prefer to prebook.

ABORIGIN
PAST

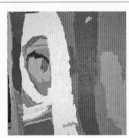

Today's Australian Aboriginals are guardians of the world's oldest living culture. Most experts agree that it was about 50,000 years ago (possibly as many as 80,000) when the continent's first inhabitants migrated south across a landmass that once connected Australia to Indonesia and Malaysia. These first Australians brought with them a wealth of stories, songs, tribal customs, and ceremonies—many of which are still practiced today.

By Sarah Gold

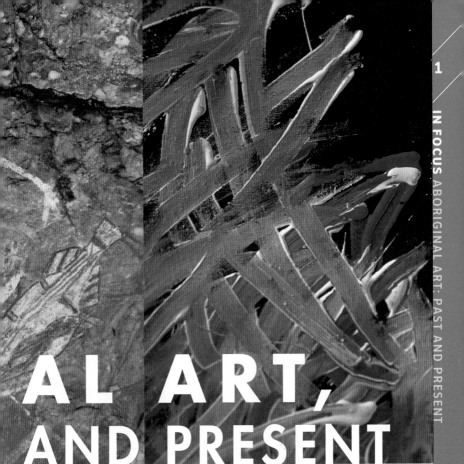

AL ART,
AND PRESENT

All Aboriginal ideology is based upon the creation period known as The Dreaming. During this primordial time, totemic ancestors (who were associated with particular animals, plants, and natural phenomena) lived on and journeyed across the earth. The legends of these ancestors—what they did, where they traveled, who they fought and loved— are considered sacred, and have been passed down among Aboriginal tribes for thousands of years. Though these stories are largely shared in secret rituals, they have also been documented through the creation of unique, highly symbolic artworks.

This is why Aboriginal art, despite humble beginnings as simple rock carvings and ochre paintings on bark, now hang in some of the world's finest museums. These works aren't just beautiful; they're also profound cultural artifacts—and a window onto humanity's oldest surviving civilizaion.

(top right) Nourlangie Rock, Kakadu;
(top left) Art by Emily Kame Kngwarreye;
(bottom left) Work from Papunya Tula;
(bottom right) Maningrida Art
and Culture, Darwin

EARLY ABORIGINAL ART

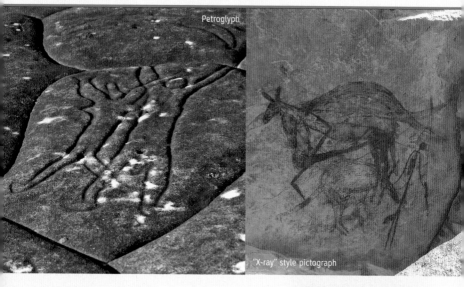

Petroglyph

"X-ray" style pictograph

While dot paintings are the most widely recognized Aboriginal artworks today, they're only the latest incarnation of a creative output that stretches back thousands of years. The achievements of Australia's earliest artists can still be seen—etched right onto the sacred landscapes that inspired them.

PETROGLYPHS

The earliest Aboriginal artworks were petroglyphs— engravings carved into flat rock surfaces or faces of cliffs (most likely using pointed stones or shards of shell). Some surviving etchings show lines and circles similar to those in modern-day paintings; others depict animals, fish, birds, and human or spirit figures. The oldest known engravings on the continent, at Pilbara in Western Australia and Olary in South Australia, are estimated to be 40,000 years old. Perhaps the most visited, though, are those in Ku-rin-gai Chase National Park, less than an hour's drive north of Sydney.

PROTECTING ROCK-ART SITES

Given the centuries of weathering they've endured, it's remarkable that so many ancient rock art sites remain intact. In many places, the longevity of the artworks can be attributed to local Aboriginal tribes, who consider it a sacred responsibility to preserve and repaint fading images. Help preservation efforts by staying on marked paths, not touching the artwork, and taking a tour of the site with an indigenous guide.

Freehand pictograph

Stencil painting

PICTOGRAPHS

Other early Aboriginal artists chose to paint images rather than etch them. Using ochres and mineral pigments, and employing sticks, feathers, and their own fingers as brushes, these ancient painters chose sheltered spots—like the insides of caves and canyons—for their mural-like images. Protection from the elements allowed many of these ancient rock paintings to survive; today they're still found all over Australia.

REGIONAL STYLES

The styles of painting varied by region. In the Northern Territory, in Arnhem Land and what is now Kakadu National Park, early Aboriginals painted "X-ray" portraits of humans and animals with their skeletons and internal organs clearly displayed. The Kimberley and Burrup Peninsula in Western Australia are rich repositories of elegant freehand paintings portraying human, animal, and ancestral Dreaming figures. And Queensland, especially the area that is now Carnarvon National Park, is known for its stencil paintings, in which the artists sprayed paint from their mouths.

EARTH TONES (LITERALLY)

Early Aboriginal artists used the earth to make pigments. Red, yellow, and brown were made from mineral-rich clays. Black was created with charcoal or charred tree bark; white from crushed gypsum rock; and grey from ashes left over from cooking fires. Modern artists may mix their pigments with oil or acrylic, but the traditional palette remains the same.

DECIPHERING "DOT PAINTINGS"

An artist uses a small, straight stick dipped in paint to create a dot painting. Ancient symbols and intricate dot motifs combine to create powerful works of art.

To a visitor wandering through a gallery, Aboriginal artwork can seem deceptively simple. Many traditional paintings feature basic designs—wavy lines, concentric circles—comprised of myriad tiny dots. They look as though they were created with the end of a paint-covered stick (and indeed, most were).

But the swirling motifs in these "dot paintings" aren't just abstractions—they're visual representations of ancestral legends.

According to Aboriginal beliefs, as the ancestors lived their lives during the Dreaming, they also gave shape to the landscape. In each spot where the ancestor shot an arrow, danced, or gave birth, an enduring mark was left on the topography: a hill, a ravine, a rock spire. As they conjured these geographical features, they sang out their names—composing singing maps of the territory they covered. Each is known as a "songline," and they criss-cross the entire continent.

Now thousands of years old, these songs are still memorized and sung by today's Aboriginals. Songlines are the basis of all indigenous traditions and tribal laws; learning and teaching the songs are considered sacred—and very secret—duties. Over many centuries, however, artists have revealed parts of the songlines through the symbology of dot paintings.

The symbols may seem cryptic, but many are recurring and give clues to the ancestral stories they depict. Shapes punctuating dot paintings usually correspond to landmarks: bodies of water, rock formations, campsites, or resting places. The lines that surround the shapes and connect them represent the tracks of the ancestors as they moved from place to place. Each dot painting is, in effect, a sacred walking map that plots an ancestor's journey.

COMMON SYMBOLS IN ABORIGINAL ART

woman

emu tracks

four women sitting around a campfire

ants, fruits, flowers, or eggs

well or main campsite

water, fire, smoke, lightning, or bushfire

holes, clouds, or nests

Honey ant

Coolamon (wooden dish)

kangaroo tracks

star

meeting place

traveling paths or heavy rain

running water connecting two waterholes

man

Witchetty grub

possum tracks

boomerang

snake

spear

cloud, rainbow, sandhill, or cliff

people sitting

THE DAWNING OF ABORIGINAL ART APPRECIATION

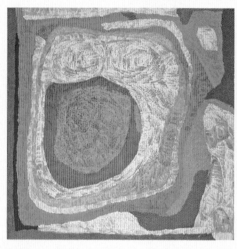
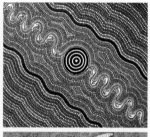

(left) Contemporary painting done in earth tones by a member of the Papunya Tula Artists collective; (top right) artwork from the Warlukurlangu Artists Aboriginal Corporation; (bottom right) Papunya Tula artwork.

IN THE BEGINNING...

It took a long time for Aboriginal art to gain the recognition it enjoys today. Australia's first European colonists, who began arriving in the late 18th century, saw the complex indigenous cultures it encountered as primitive, and believed that, as "nomads," Aboriginals had no claim to the land. Consequently, expansion into tribal lands went unchecked; during the 19th and early 20th centuries, most Aboriginals were forced onto white-owned cattle stations and missionary outposts.

Aboriginal land rights weren't formally acknowledged until 1976, when the first legislation was passed granting claim of title to natives with "traditional association" to the land. This watershed decision (called the Aboriginal Land Rights Act) allowed for the establishment of tribal land councils, which—in partnership with the Australian government—today manage many of the country's national parks and sacred ancient sites.

BREAKING GROUND

The growing awareness of Aboriginal heritage brought with it an increased interest in indigenous art. Before the 1970s, there had been only one celebrated Aboriginal artist in Australia—Albert Namatjira, who grew up on a Lutheran mission in Hermannsburg (in what is now the Northern Territory). In the 1930s, Namatjira studied under a white Australian artist and learned to paint sophisticated watercolor landscapes. Though these had almost nothing in common with traditional indigenous artworks, they won Namatjira enormous fame (by the 1950s, he was listed in *Who's Who*)

Curators often provide relevant historical context.

which reinforced an idea that was already burgeoning in the country: that Aboriginal creativity should receive the same attention and scholarship as non-Aboriginal forms of art.

ABORIGINAL ART CENTERS

Perhaps the single most significant event in modern Aboriginal art history occurred in 1973, with the formation of the Aboriginal Arts Board. The advent of this agency, as part of the government-funded Australia Council for the Arts, heralded a new level of respect for indigenous art. Its aim was to establish a standardized support system for Aboriginal artists through grant money.

But early board members (who came from both white and Aboriginal backgrounds) found this to be another challenge. Aboriginal artists were scattered all over the continent, many of them in isolated, far-flung camps surrounded by vast desert or impenetrable rainforests. How was the organization to find these artists, decide which of them deserved funds, and then dispense those funds in an organized way?

The solution was to set up art centers at specific Aboriginal settlements around

Renouned artist David Malangi, Central Arnhem Land

the country—helmed by art-industry specialists who could both cultivate connections with local artists and manage their nuts-and-bolts requirements (like arranging for deliveries of art supplies, and for transport of finished artworks to exhibitors and buyers).

The plan worked, and is still working. There are some 50 Aboriginal art centers in Australia today (most in the Northern Territory and Western Australia), and they collectively represent more than a thousand artists. These centers are the conduit by which most modern Aboriginal works get to art dealers—and then on to galleries, museums, auction houses, and private collectors.

PAPUNYA TULA

Brenda Nungarrayi Lynch, well-known Western Desert artist

The founding members of the Aboriginal Arts Board were inspired by the example of a particular Northern Territory desert settlement, Papunya Tula. Here, with the help of a white Australian art teacher, residents had begun to create and then sell "Dreaming paintings" (what are known today as dot paintings) to nearby galleries. By 1972, the community had established its own thriving and successful art collective, Papunya Tula Artists.

Today Papunya Tula Artists (which has never been government-subsidized) is the most famous Aboriginal art center in the country. The highly acclaimed dot paintings of its artists have hung in New York's Metropolitan Museum of Art and Paris's Musée du Quai Branly; their annual dollar sales are in the millions.

ABORIGINAL ART TODAY

 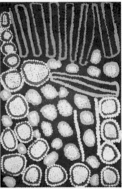

(left) Art by Emily Kame Kngwarreye, Utopia Central Australia; (right) Papunya Tula

Over the past 30 years, the art world's regard for Aboriginal works has skyrocketed—not just in Australia, but all over the world. Ancient etchings and modern dot paintings now hang in museums from London's British to the Chicago Art Institute; gallerists and art dealers vie to represent rising Aboriginal art stars; and many artists who got their start at art centers in the 1980s (such as Dorothy Napangardi, Michael Nelson Tjakamarra, and Paddy Stewart Tjapaljarri) are near-celebrities today. A few of these pioneers of the modern Aboriginal art movement (like Rover Thomas and David Malangi) were in their seventies and eighties by the time their canvases began decorating exhibit halls and commanding six-figure auction bids.

Some of Australia's most celebrated Aboriginal artists, though, never got to see just how popular their work became. Clifford "Possum" Tjapaltjarri, for example, whose painting *Warlugulong* sold at a Sotheby's auction in 2007 for $2.4 million—the highest price ever paid for a piece of Aboriginal art—died five years beforehand. And Emily Kame Kngwarreye died in 1996, a dozen years before the National Museum of Australia mounted a huge solo exhibition of her work.

The new generation of Aboriginal artists faces its own set of obstacles. The appetite among art dealers for a steady supply of works to sell has led some of them to cut exploitative deals directly with artists (rather than working through the relative safety net of art centers). Other opportunists have mass-produced paintings and then sold them as "authentic"—thus tainting the integrity of the real Aboriginal art market.

But even these problems, unsavory though they are, can be seen from a certain angle as signs of positive change. It was only decades ago, after all, that the phrase "Aboriginal artist" seemed oxymoronic for many Australians. Today, those "primitive" assemblages of lines, circles, and dots account for almost 75 percent of the country's art sales. They have, in effect, helped put Australia on the map.

Today, symbols might be just half the story: colors can range from calm and subdued to bright and vibrant.

TIPS FOR WHERE AND HOW TO BUY ART

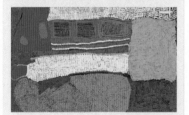

The most easily accessible sources for buying Aboriginal art are galleries. When considering a purchase, ascertain the art's authenticity and ethicality. The Australian Indigenous Art Trade Association recommends asking:

■ Is the artwork documented with a certificate of authenticity from a reputable source, or by photos of the artist with the art?

■ How did the artwork get to the gallery? Is the artist represented by a recognized art center, cooperative, or respected dealer?

■ Is it clear that the artist was treated fairly and paid a fair price for putting the artwork on the market?

MUSEUM AND GALLERY COLLECTIONS

Australia has hundreds of galleries and museums at least partially devoted to Aboriginal artworks. Here are some of the best:

PERMANENT COLLECTIONS

The Australian Museum, Sydney
australianmuseum.net.au

The National Gallery of Australia, Canberra
nga.gov.au

Queensland Art Gallery, Brisbane
qag.qld.gov.au

National Gallery of Victoria, Melbourne
www.ngv.vic.gov.au

ROTATING EXHIBITIONS

Gallery Gondwana, Alice Springs
www.gallerygondwana.com.au

Aboriginal Fine Arts Gallery, Darwin
www.aaia.com.au

Gallery Gabrielle Pizzi, Melbourne
www.gabriellepizzi.com.au

WHEN TO GO

Australia is in the southern hemisphere, so the seasons are reversed. It's winter Down Under during the American and European summer.

The ideal time to visit the north, particularly the Northern Territory's Kakadu National Park, is early in the dry season (around May). Birdlife remains profuse on the drying floodplains, and waterfalls are still spectacular and accessible. The Dry (April–October) is also a good time to visit northern Queensland's beaches and rain forests. You can swim off the coast without fear of dangerous stinging box jellyfish, which infest ocean waters between November and March. In rain forests, heat and humidity are lower than later in the year, and crocodile viewing is at its prime, as the creatures tend to bask on riverbanks rather than submerge in the colder water.

During school holidays, Australians take to the roads in droves. The busiest period is mid-December to the end of January, which is the equivalent of the U.S. and British summer break.

Climate

Australia's climate is temperate in southern states, such as Victoria and Tasmania, particularly in coastal areas, and tropical in Australia's far north. The Australian summer north of the Tropic of Capricorn is a steam bath. From September through November (the Australian spring), or from February through April (late summer–autumn), southern regions are generally sunny and warm, with only occasional rain in Sydney, Melbourne, and Adelaide. Perth and the south of Western Australia are at their finest in springtime, when wildflowers blanket the land.

Here are the average daily maximum and minimum temperatures for some major Australian cities.

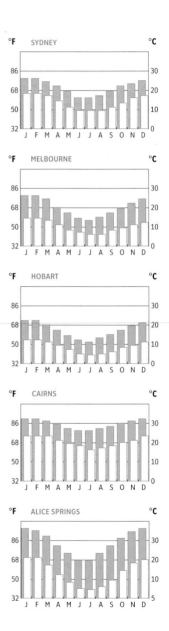

Sydney

WORD OF MOUTH

"The city of Sydney is situated on one of the most beautiful harbors in the world. There are lot many amazing places to go."

—Jeniekrag

WELCOME TO SYDNEY

TOP REASONS TO GO

★ **A Harbor Sail:** Take a ferry, sail a yacht, or paddle a kayak, but make sure you get out into Sydney Harbour. It's a glorious sight. Check out the Sydney Harbour section for tours of the harbor by boat.

★ **Exquisite Dining:** Sydney restaurants are among the finest eateries in the world. The harbor shines with gems like Aria and Guillaume at Bennelong, and mouthwatering smells waft though the air in the trendy food burbs of Surry Hills and Darlinghurst.

★ **Glorious Beaches:** Sydneysiders are besotted by the beach, and you'll be, too. With 40 to choose from, including world-famous Bondi, you can watch surfers ride the waves or paddle around the calmer waters of a sheltered harbor beach.

★ **National Parks and Wildlife:** Sydney's untamed beauty is close at hand. See native birds and colorful wildflowers just a few miles from the city; you may even spot a kangaroo in the Royal National Park.

1 Sydney Harbour. This spectacular waterway has a 240-km (149-mi) shoreline of bays, headlands, and quiet beaches. It's the city's jewel.

2 The Rocks. Sydney's oldest area, The Rocks, is full of restored 19th-century warehouses and pubs with great views of the famous bridge.

3 Domain and Hyde Park. This stately quarter of town contains Parliament House, formal gardens, and the Domain, where rallies and concerts are staged.

4 The Opera House and the Domain North. The white "sails" of the Opera House dominate the harbor; the neighboring Royal Botanic Gardens are an oasis on the harbor's edge.

5 Darling Harbour. Occupying a former goods yard on the city's western edge, Darling Harbour now houses museums, the aquarium, restaurants, and hotels.

6 Sydney City Center. Dominated by 880-foot Sydney Tower, the city center is packed with historic and modern shopping arcades.

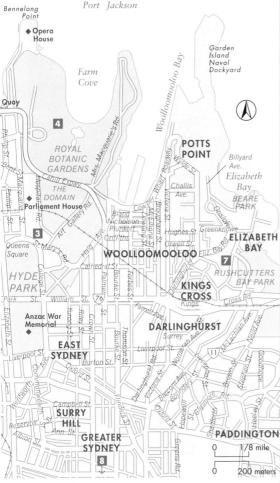

Bennelong
Point

Port Jackson

◆ Opera
House

Farm
Cove

Quay

4

ROYAL
BOTANIC
GARDENS

THE
DOMAIN
◆ Parliament House

3

Queens
Square

WOOLLOOMOOLOO

HYDE
PARK

Park St.   William St.

Anzac War
Memorial

EAST
SYDNEY

Campbell St.

SURRY
HILL

Reservoir St.

Albion St.

GREATER
SYDNEY

8

Garden
Island
Naval
Dockyard

POTTS
POINT

Billyard
Ave.
Elizabeth
Bay

Challis
Ave.

BEARE
PARK

Bland

Nicholson
Plunkett
Griffiths

Hughes St.

Orwell St.

Greenknowe

ELIZABETH
BAY

7

RUSHCUTTERS
BAY PARK

KINGS
CROSS

Kings   Cross Rd.

DARLINGHURST

Surrey

Liverpool St.

Burton St.

11

PADDINGTON

0   1/8 mile

0   200 meters

Woolloomooloo Bay

GETTING ORIENTED

Sydney is built around its huge harbor. The city center and main attractions are on the south shore. Harbour Bridge connects The Rocks on the south side with Milson's Point on the north side. Greater Sydney is vast, some 80 km (50 mi) from north to south and 70 km (43 mi) from east to west; however, the city center is relatively small. From the Opera House and Circular Quay the city stretches south for about 3 km (1.8 mi), and east to west for about 2 km (1 mi). It's relatively flat, making it easy to walk around. Beyond the harbor, the city center is essentially a business and shopping precinct, with colonial and modern buildings. The restaurant and nightlife suburbs of Kings Cross, Darlinghurst, and Surry Hill flank the city's eastern and southern edges.

7 The Eastern Suburbs.
A few miles east of the city you'll find palatial harborside homes, beaches, and café-culture, bohemian-chic enclaves.

8 Greater Sydney.
National parks, beautiful beaches, and relics of Sydney's colonial past can all be explored within an hour of the city center.

TOP SYDNEY SIGHTS

Ringed with world-class beaches and some of the most spectacular nature on the continent, Sydney is the continent's cosmopolitan hub, and home to two renowned architectural icons—the Opera House and the Harbour Bridge.

No one ever tires of Sydney's magnificent nature and its two landmark structures. The Sydney Opera House is both awe-inspiring and utterly welcoming. Its stunning "sail" design was the brainchild of Danish architect Joern Utzon, who won an international design competition from 233 submissions. Sydney Harbour Bridge is equally loved, especially when the city comes out to see the fireworks explode over it for New Year's Eve celebrations. Opened in 1932, it can be experienced by car or train, but we recommend taking it slower and walking across it. Adventure seekers can even climb up and over the arch to the top. Sydney Harbour's shoreline is dotted with large swaths of national park perfect for hiking and picnics. On the north side of the harbor is the ultimate zoo with a view, Taronga Zoo.

NEED A BREAK

The historic Harbour View Hotel is the place to sit with a drink and watch the folks in their special jumpsuits begin their climb up the Sydney Harbour Bridge. The pub is so close to the bridge that you feel you could reach out and touch it! The bar menu includes snacks of salt-and-pepper calamari and chicken schnitzel (¢); the more upscale restaurant menu features sizzling steaks, slow-cooked lamb shanks, and decadent desserts ($). It's near the south pylon of the bridge, at 18 Lower Fort Street and Cumberland Street (☎ *02/9254–4111* ⊕ *www.harbourview.com. au*).

2

FODOR'S CHOICE SIGHTS

SYDNEY HARBOUR BRIDGE
Despite its nickname "the coat hanger," the bridge has a fond place in all Sydneysiders' hearts. Its opening on March 19, 1932 (during the height of the Great Depression), lifted the spirits of citizens and provided some very unexpected theater. As NSW Premier Jack Lang waited to cut the ribbon, Captain Francis de Groot, a member of the paramilitary New Guard, galloped up on his horse, drew his sword, and slashed the ribbon first.

SYDNEY HARBOUR NATIONAL PARK
This national park is a collection of separate areas of native bush land flanking both sides of the harbor and dotted with walking tracks. Miles of paths wind through the bush and up and down rocky outcrops and headlands. One of the best walks is the 9.5-km (6-mi) Manly Scenic Walkway, which travels from Manly Beach to the Spit Bridge via pockets of rain forest, several little beaches, ancient Aboriginal sites, and the historic Grotto Point Lighthouse.

SYDNEY OPERA HOUSE
Sydney's most famous landmark, listed as a World Heritage site in 2007, had such a long and troubled construction phase that it's almost a miracle it was ever completed. Architect Joern Utzon's concepts were dazzling, and so far ahead of their time that the soaring "sails" that formed the walls and roof could not be built by existing technology.

TARONGA ZOO
Sydney's major wildlife sanctuary occupies one of the most prized positions on the north shore of Sydney Harbour. Daily shows, such as the seal and the birds of prey show, are included in the admission price of A$44. A Zoo Pass, using Sydney Ferries, is an excellent deal at A$49.50.

TIMING

THE HARBOR
Sydney Harbor and its many sites are best visited in spring (September–November) and autumn (March–May). Summers can be hot and sticky and crowded with kids on school break. Winters (June–August) can be mild, and you may even find some lunch bargains at nice restaurants. Midweek visits are always recommended.

THE OPERA HOUSE AND BRIDGE
A guided Opera House tour takes one hour, while the backstage tour, complete with a full breakfast, takes two hours. If you're exploring sans guided tour, allot about 30 minutes to walk around the outside of the building and into some of the interior areas. The two sites are about 1 km (½ mi) apart, which is a leisurely 30- to 45-minute stroll. It takes three hours to do the Bridge Climb tour and around 30 minutes if you do your own walk across the Harbour Bridge from the south to the north side.

DINING ALFRESCO

Grab an outdoor table by the harbor or beach— in an elegant restaurant or beachside burger shack—and savor all that Sydney has to offer; dining alfresco is the Aussie version of heaven!

Two Sydney Harbour areas are chock-full of outstanding outdoor dining spots: the Overseas Passenger Terminal where cruise ships dock, and East Circular Quay on the concourse leading from the ferry terminal to the Opera House. They're almost smack opposite each other and are packed with indoor-outdoor upscale eateries. For a cheap snack and an amazing view, stop by the Boathouse Café and Restaurant in Nielsen Park.

Another favorite option is one of the many casual cafés around Bondi and Manly Beach. The Woolloomooloo Finger Wharf has several alfresco restaurants, the most popular—and a celebrity haunt—being Otto.

The Middle Harbor beach of Balmoral has some lovely cafés and restaurants with great views out to the Sydney Heads.

DRINKING ALFRESCO

Glenmore Hotel.
Everyone loves The Rocks on a sunny Sunday afternoon. Check out the sensational harbor views from the rooftop bar of the Glenmore Hotel. The stairs to the roof are a bit ricketty. ✉ *96 Cumberland St., The Rocks* ☎ *02/9247-4794* ⊕ *www. glenmorerooftophotel. com.au.*

Manly Wharf Hotel.
Manly Wharf Hotel has four bars, the Jetty Bar perched right on the water with superb views. Outside heaters make it perfect even for winter drinks. ✉ *Manly Wharf, East Esplanade* ☎ *02/9977-1266.*

TOP SPOTS

✕Aquarium Bistro & Bar. The view and the price are just right at this popular casual bistro and bar at Coogee Beach. Housed in the heritage-listed Beach Palace Hotel, the bistro draws a younger crowd with the sensational views of Coogee Beach, as well as the burgers, king prawn chili spaghetti, and an array of sharing plates, known as boards. ⊠ *169 Dolphin St., Coogee* ☎ *02/9664-2900* ⊕ *www.beachpalacehotel.com.au* ⊗ *Closed Mon., Tues., and Thurs.*

✕Nielsen Park Restaurant and Café. This is a great place to laze, picnic in the park, or swim year-round in the roped-off harbor pool. The café and restaurant are housed in a heritage 1914 sandstone building. The herb-and -Parmesan-crusted king prawn cutlets make a tasty starter, followed by the spanner crab linguine with chili, garlic and white wine. ⊠ *Nielsen Park, Greycliffe Ave., Vaucluse* ☎ *02/9337-7333* ⊕ *www.nielsenpark.com.au* ⊗ *No dinner in the café or restaurant; restaurant closed Mon.–Friday. Cafe open Mon-Sunday.*

✕Pellegrini's Seafood Restaurant. Location, location, location are the draw at this quaint Italian restaurant. Perched right on the harbor at west Balmain you'll have a unique view of Cockatoo Island and all the comings and goings of water traffic. Barramundi fillets are popular, as are salt and pepper squid and soft-shell crab. ⊠ *107 Elliot St., Balmain* ☎ *02/9810-4551* ⊕ *www.pellegrinis.com.au* ⊗ *Closed Mon.–Tues., no dinner Sun.*

✕Pilu at Freshwater. If you love traditional Italian food, and enjoy dining right on the beach then this is the place. Chef Giovanni Pilu's specialty is Sardinian fare, and his signature dish is a feast that takes several hours to slow-cook—oven-roasted roasted suckling pig, served on the bone with traditional farmhouse suckling-pig sausages and condiments. ⊠ *On The Beach, Moore Rd., Harbord* ☎ *02/9938-3331* ⊕ *www.piluatfreshwater.com.au.*

DINING BY CUISINE

Chinese
BBQ King ¢
Billy Kwong $
Golden Century ¢–$
French
Bécasse $$
Bistro Moncur $–$$
Mere Catherine $$
Marque $$–$$$
Italian
Buon Ricordo $$$
Icebergs Dining Room and Bar $$
North Bondi Italian Food ¢–$
Japanese
Galileo $$$$
Malaysian
The Malaya ¢–$
Modern Australian
Altitude $$
The Deck $
Quay $$$
Rockpool $$$$
Swell $
Tetsuya's $$$$
Wharf Restaurant $
Seafood
Fishface ¢–$
Nick's Bondi Beach Pavilion ¢–$
Pier $$$

Updated
by Caroline
Gladstone

Sydney belongs to the exclusive club of cities that generate excitement. At the end of a marathon flight there's renewed vitality in the cabin as the plane circles the city, where thousands of yachts are suspended on the dark water and the sails of the Opera House glisten in the distance. Blessed with dazzling beaches and a sunny climate, Sydney is among the most beautiful cities on the planet.

With 4 million people, Sydney is the biggest and most cosmopolitan city in Australia. A wave of immigration in the 1950s has seen the Anglo-Irish immigrants who made up the city's original population joined by Italians, Greeks, Turks, Lebanese, Chinese, Vietnamese, Thais, and Indonesians. This intermingling has created a cultural vibrancy and energy—and a culinary repertoire—that was missing only a generation ago.

Sydneysiders embrace their harbor with a passion. Indented with numerous bays and beaches, Sydney Harbour is the presiding icon for the city, and urban Australia. Captain Arthur Phillip, commander of the 11-ship First Fleet, wrote in his diary when he first set eyes on the harbor on January 26, 1788: "We had the satisfaction of finding the finest harbor in the world."

Although a visit to Sydney is an essential part of an Australian experience, the city is no more representative of Australia than Los Angeles is of the United States. Sydney has joined the ranks of the great cities whose characters are essentially international. What Sydney offers is style, sophistication, and great looks; an exhilarating prelude to the continent at its back door.

PLANNING

WHEN TO GO

The best times to visit Sydney are in late spring and early fall (autumn). The spring months of October and November are pleasantly warm, although the ocean is slightly cool for swimming. The summer months of December through February are typically hot and humid, February being the most humid. In the early-autumn months of March and April weather is typically stable and comfortable, outdoor city life is still in full swing, and the ocean is at its warmest. Even the coolest winter months of July and August typically stay mild and sunny, with average daily maximum temperatures in the low 60s.

GETTING HERE AND AROUND
AIRPORT INFORMATION
Sydney's main airport is Kingsford–Smith International, 8 km (5 mi) south of the city. Kingsford–Smith's international (T1) and domestic terminals (T2 and T3) are 3 km (2 mi) apart. To get from one to the other, take a taxi for about A$12, use the Airport Shuttle Bus (called the TBus) for A$5.50 (it takes 10 minutes), or take the Airport Link train, A$5, which takes 2 minutes. Tourism New South Wales has two information counters in the arrival level of the international terminal. One provides free maps and brochures and handles general inquiries. The other books accommodations and tours, and sells travel insurance. Both counters are open daily from approximately 6 am to 11 pm. You can convert your money to Australian currency at the Travelex offices in both the arrival and departure areas.

AIRPORT TRANSFERS
Airport Link rail travels to the city center in 15 minutes. A one-way fare is A$15.80. Taxis are available outside the terminal buildings. Fares are about A$38 to city and Kings Cross hotels. There are a couple of shuttle-bus services from the airport that drop passenger at hotels in the city center, Kings Cross, and Darling Harbour for around A$14 to A$17 one-way and A$23 return.

BUS, CAR, AND TAXI INFORMATION
Bus travel in Sydney is slow due to congested streets and the undulating terrain. Fares are calculated in sections; the minimum section fare (A$2) applies to trips in the inner-city area, such as between Circular Quay and Kings Cross, or from Bondi Junction railway station to Bondi Beach. Bus information can be found at ⊕ *www.sydneybuses.info*.

With the assistance of a good road map you shouldn't have too many problems driving in and out of Sydney, thanks to the decent freeway system. However, driving a car around Sydney is not recommended because of congestion and lack of parking space. If you decide to drive a rental car, it will cost between A$75 and A$85 per day. Local operator Bayswater Car Rental has cars from as little as A$27 per day (on a seven-day rental plan) for a one-year-old vehicle. Campervans that sleep two people can be hired from operator Jucy Rentals for A$65 a day and A$125 in the January peak season

Taxis charge A$1.99 per kilometer, plus a flag fall (hiring charge) of A$3.30. Extra charges apply to baggage weighing more than 55 pounds, telephone bookings, and Harbour Bridge and tunnel tolls. Fares are 20% higher between 10 pm and 6 am, when the numeral "2" will be displayed in the tariff indicator on the meter.

TRAM AND TRAIN INFORMATION

Sydney Monorail links the city center, Darling Harbour, and China-town. The fare is A$4.90 one-way; the A$9.50 Day Pass is a better value if you intend to use the monorail to explore. It runs every five minutes from 7 am to 10 pm—and from 8 am on Sunday. The Sydney Light Rail is an efficient link between Central Station, Darling Harbour, the Star City casino/entertainment complex, Sydney fish markets, and two inner western suburbs. The modern trams operate at 10- to 30-minute intervals 24 hours a day. One-way tickets are A$3.40; the A$9 Day Pass is good value. The main terminal for long-distance, intercity, and Sydney suburban trains is Central Station. There are a number of good-value train passes including the Backtracker Pass, which at A$232 (for 14 days) allows unlimited travel between Sydney and Melbourne (and back to Brisbane), a trip to the Blue Mountains, and one day's unlim-ited travel on Sydney buses, trains, and ferries. Sydney's suburban train network, City Rail, links the city with dozens of suburbs as well as Blue Mountains and South Coast towns. Tickets start from A$3.20 one-way and are sold at all City Rail stations.

DISCOUNTS AND DEALS

For the price of admission to two or three main attractions, the **See Sydney Attractions Pass** (☎ *1300/366476* ⊕ *www.seesydneycard.com*) gets you into 40 Sydney sights and attractions—including the Opera House, Sydney Aquarium, and Koala Park Sanctuary. Several different cards are available, including two-, three-, and seven-day versions. Some cards can even include public transportation. Prices start at A$155 for a two-day adult card without transportation. Cards are available from the Sydney Visitor Centre at The Rocks.

NSW Transport operates all of the Sydney trains, buses, and ferries. They offer the **MyZone tickets** (☎ *13–1500* ⊕ *www.131500.com.au*), which include MyBus, MyTrain, MyFerry, and MyMulti tickets. The latter provides unlimited travel on buses, trains, and ferries (but not the light-rail or monorail systems) for a day, a week, a month, and longer. A daily ticket is A$20; a weekly is A$41 for Zone 1. The AirportLink rail service and sightseeing buses are not included in the price. MyMulti tickets can be bought at various kiosks and newsstands in the city (and suburbs) and at railway stations.

HOTELS

Sydney hotels range from the international five-star properties with stunning views over Sydney Harbour to boutique hotels in heritage buildings and historic pubs in The Rocks. Harbour-side hotels are mod-ern and large with executive levels, pools, and day spas. Smaller hotels and apartment hotels are located on the city fringes, in Surry Hills, Darlinghurst, and Kings Cross/Potts Point with easy access to the city center and harbor and in the thick of restaurant precincts.

DINING AND LODGING PRICE CATEGORIES (IN AUSTRALIAN DOLLARS)				
	¢	$	$$	$$$	$$$$
Restaurants	under A$25	A$25–A$35	A$36–A$45	A$46–A$65	over A$65
Hotels	under A$150	A$150–A$200	A$201–A$300	A$301–A$450	over A$450

Restaurant prices are based on the median main-course price at dinner. Hotel prices are for two people in a standard double room in high season, excluding service and tax (Goods and service tax [GST] is 10 percent).

TOURS

SIGHTSEEING TOURS

Harbour Jet. Harbour Jet runs high-speed jet-boat tours of the harbor, racing around at 75 kph (47 mph) and performing 270-degree spins. Trips range from 35 minutes to 1½ hours, and start at A$65 per person. ☎ *1300/887373* ⊕ *www.harbourjet.com.*

Mount 'n Beach Safaris. Mount 'n Beach Safaris operates tours to the Blue Mountains and minicoach tours around Sydney's northern beaches and to NSW's North and South Coast areas. The Blue Mountains 4WD Canyon and Wildlife Discovery tour provides opportunity to see koalas and kangaroos, have morning tea in the bush, see the highlights of the Blue Mountains, and have lunch at a historic pub. ☎ *02/9439–3010* ⊕ *www.mountnbeachsafaris.com.au.*

City Sightseeing Sydney. This fleet of brighly colored double-decker buses (with open tops) operates two routes: the Sydney route has 25 stops, and the Bondi and Bays has 10 stops. Both trips take 90 minutes. Sydney trips depart from Circular Quay at 8:30 am daily (last bus departs at 7:30 pm), the Bondi bus departs from Eddy Avenue, Central Station at 9 am daily (last bus at 7:30 pm). ☎ *02/9567–8400* ⊕ *www.citysightseeing.com.au.*

SPECIAL-INTEREST TOURS

Aboriginal Heritage Tour. The Aboriginal Heritage Tour (A$33) is a tour of the Royal Botanic Gardens' display of plants that were growing before Europeans arrived on Sydney's shores in 1788. The tour, which operates Friday at 10 am (1½ hours duration) is led by an Aboriginal guide who explains the plants and their uses, and Aboriginal bush foods. ☎ *02/9231–8134* ⊕ *www.rbgsyd.nsw.gov.au.*

Bass and Flinders Cruises. You can go whale-watching from Sydney Harbour with Bass and Flinders Cruises and **Captain Cook Cruises.** Boats leave from mid-May to early December, venturing a few miles outside Sydney Heads. ☎ *02/9583–1199* ⊕ *www.whalewatchingsydney.net.*

Bonza Bikes. Bonza Bikes lets you see the best Sydney sights without having to worry about heavy traffic. The half-day Classic Sydney Tour cruises past the Opera House, winds around the harbor, and cycles through the Royal Botanic Gardens. Trips start from A$99 for a half day (bike and helmet included). ☎ *02/9247–8800* ⊕ *www.bonzabiketours.com.*

BridgeClimb. BridgeClimb is a unique tour that affords the ultimate view of the harbor and city center from Sydney Harbour Bridge. The hugely popular tours take 3½ hours and cost from A$198 per person. Another option is the Discovery Climb, which takes climbers within the bridge's structure on their way to the top. Tours depart from 5 Cumberland Street, The Rocks. ☎ *02/8274–7777* ⊕ *www.bridgeclimb.com.*

Easyrider Motorbike Tours. Easyrider Motorbike Tours conducts exciting chauffeur-driven (you ride as a passenger) Harley-Davidson tours to the city's landmarks, and to the Blue Mountains and rural areas. A 15-minute ride is A$35, a two-hour tour is A$190 per person; full-day excursions start at A$410. ☎ *02/9247–2477, 1300/882065* ⊕ *www. easyrider.com.au.*

Sydney Seaplanes. A flight on Sydney Seaplanes is a wonderful way to see Sydney's sights and soar over beaches. Short flights taking in the harbor, Bondi Beach, and Manly cost from A$185 per person. The seaplanes take off from Rose Bay. ☎ *02/9388–1978, 1300/732752* ⊕ *www.seaplanes.com.au.*

SYDNEY BY BOAT

Captain Cook Cruises. Captain Cook Cruises runs a number of good tours, but the best introduction to Sydney Harbour is Captain Cook's two-hour Coffee Cruise, which follows the southern shore to Watsons Bay, crosses to the north shore to explore Middle Harbour, and returns to Circular Quay. ☎ *02/9206–1111* ⊕ *www.captaincook.com.au/sydney.*

Darling Harbour Water Taxis. A fun, fast, but somewhat expensive way to get around is by water taxi. (Circular Quay to Manly, for example, costs A$160 for four people, and A$10 for each extra person.) One company, Aussie Water Taxis, runs a taxi shuttle between Darling Harbour and the Opera House for A$15 one-way, A$25 return. Mini-tours of the harbor in these little yellow taxi boats begin at A$35 per person for 45 minutes. ☎ *02/9211–7730* ⊕ *www.aussiewatertaxis.com.*

Manly Ferry. There is no finer introduction to the city than a trip aboard one of the commuter ferries that ply Sydney Harbour. The hub of the ferry system is Circular Quay, and ferries dock at the almost 30 wharves around the harbor between about 6 am and 11:30 pm. One of the most popular sightseeing trips is the Manly Ferry, a 30-minute journey from Circular Quay that provides glimpses of harborside mansions and the sandstone cliffs and bushland along the north shore. The one-way Manly Ferry fare is A$6.60, and the Manly Fast Ferry, operated by a private company (www.manlyfastferry.com.au), costs A$8.50, although cheaper if a SmartCard is purchased. ☎ *13–1500* ⊕ *www.sydneyferries.info.*

WALKING TOURS

Ghost Tours. The Rocks' dark alleyways can be scary, and The Rocks Ghost Tours make sure people are suitably spooked, as the guides, dressed in long black cloaks and carrying lanterns, regale them with stories of the murders and other nasty goings-on in the early days of the colony. Tours depart nightly at 6.45 (April–September) and 7:45 (October–March) from Cadman's Cottage; A$42. ☎ *1300/731971* ⊕ *www.ghosttours.com.au.*

Rocks Pub Tour. You can literally drink in Sydney's history during The Rocks Pub Tour, where you wander the narrow streets with a guide and stop in for drinks at three pubs. The 2-hour tours depart from Cadman's Cottage on George Street (near the Museum of Contemporary Art) at 5 pm daily (except public holidays, New Year's Eve, and St. Patrick's Day); A$44. ☎ *02/9252–5505, 1300/458437* ⊕ *www.therockspubtour.com.*

Rocks Walking Tours. The Rocks Walking Tours introduce you to Sydney's first European settlement, with an emphasis on the buildings and personalities of the convict period. The 1½-hour tour costs A$32. Tours leave weekdays at 10:30, 12:30, and 2:30 (in January 10:30 and 2:30 only), and weekends at 11:30 and 2. ✉ *23 Playfair St., The Rocks* ☎ *02/9247–6678* ⊕ *www.rockswalkingtours.com.au.*

WORD OF MOUTH

"Five days in Sydney will give you a good opportunity to explore the city, its surrounds and perhaps even a day or so somewhere a little further afield. You could rent a car, see the Blue Mountains, some lovely country towns, and wine country."
—Bokhara2

VISITOR INFORMATION

There are information kiosks at locations throughout the city, including Circular Quay (corner of Alfred and Pitt streets), Martin Place (at the corner of Elizabeth Street), and Town Hall (corner of George and Bathurst streets). The Sydney Harbour Foreshore Authority, which manages The Rocks, Darling Harbour, and other harbor precincts, also has an informative Web site.

The Sydney Visitor Centre is the major source of information for Sydney and New South Wales. There are two locations: The Rocks and Darling Harbour.

Contacts Sydney Harbour Foreshore Authority. Sydney Harbour Foreshore Authority. ☎ *02/9240–8500* ⊕ *www.shfa.nsw.gov.au.* **Sydney Visitor Centre** ✉ *Level 2, The Rocks Centre, Argyle and Playfair Sts., The Rocks* ☎ *02/9240–8788, 1800/067676* ⊕ *www.sydneyvisitorcentre.com* ✉ *33 Wheat Rd., near IMAX Theatre, Darling Harbour.*

EXPLORING SYDNEY

Sydney is a giant, stretching nearly 80 km (50 mi) from top to bottom and about 70 km (43 mi) across. The harbor divides the city into northern and southern halves, with most of the headline attractions on the south shore. Most travelers spend their time on the harbor's south side, within an area bounded by Chinatown in the south, Harbour Bridge in the north, Darling Harbour to the west, and the beaches and coastline to the east. North of Harbour Bridge lie the important commercial center of North Sydney and leafy but somewhat bland suburbs. Ocean beaches, Taronga Zoo, Ku-ring-gai Chase National Park, and great shopping in the village of Mosman are the most likely reasons to venture north of the harbor. Within a few hours' drive of Sydney are the World Heritage–listed Blue Mountains and the renowned Hunter Valley vineyards. Although both these spots are worthy of an overnight stay, they're also close enough to visit on day trips from the city.

GREAT ITINERARIES

You really need three days in Sydney to see the essential city center, while six days would give you time to explore the beaches and inner suburbs. A stay of 10 days would allow trips outside the city and give you time to explore a few of Sydney's lesser-known delights.

IF YOU HAVE 3 DAYS

Start with an afternoon Harbour Express Cruise for some of the best views of the city. Follow with a tour of The Rocks, the nation's birthplace, and take a sunset walk up onto the **Sydney Harbour Bridge**. The following day, take a Sydney Explorer tour to the famous **Sydney Opera House** and relax in the afternoon in the **Royal Botanic Gardens and Domain park**. On the third day, explore the city center, with another spectacular panorama from the **Sydney Tower**. Include a walk around Macquarie Street, a living reminder of Sydney's colonial history, and the contrasting experience of futuristic Darling Harbour, with its museums, aquarium, and cafés.

IF YOU HAVE 6 DAYS

Follow the three-day itinerary *above*, then visit Kings Cross, Darlinghurst, and Paddington on the fourth day. You could continue to **Bondi**, Australia's most famous beach. The next day, catch the ferry to **Manly** to visit its beach and the historic Quarantine Station. From here, take an afternoon bus tour to the northern beaches, or return to the city to shop or visit museums and galleries. Options for the last day include a trip to a wildlife or national park, **Taronga Zoo**, or the **Sydney Olympic Park** west of the city.

IF YOU HAVE 10 DAYS

Follow the six-day itinerary *above*, and then travel beyond the city by rental car or with an organized tour. Take day trips to the Blue Mountains, Hunter Valley, **Ku-ring-gai Chase National Park**, the Hawkesbury River, or the historic city of Parramatta to Sydney's west. Or travel on the Bondi Explorer bus to **Vaucluse** or the charming harborside village of **Watsons Bay**. You could take a boat tour to the historic harbor island of **Fort Denison**, play a round of golf, or just shop or relax on the beach.

SYDNEY HARBOUR

On a bright sunny day there's no more magical sight than glistening Sydney Harbour. The white sails of the Opera House are matched by the dozens of sailing boats skimming across the blue expanse. It's both a hive of activity and blissfully peaceful: It's easy to get away from the bustle in one of this area's many remote little corners. Explore by taking a ferry, walking across the bridge, or hiking around its native bushland edges. But whatever you do, get up close and enjoy the view.

GETTING HERE AND AROUND

Sydney is well served by public transport. Buses travel from a base in Circular Quay through the city center to the inner suburbs of Kings Cross, Darlinghurst, and Surry Hills and to the eastern suburb beaches. Trains travel from Central Station through the city on a circle line (calling at Circular Quay and Town Hall), out to Bondi Junction, over the bridge to the north shore and out to the west. Ferries leave Circular Quay for Manly, Balmain, Darling Harbor, and other suburbs, while the free 555 shuttle bus does a circuit through the city, calling at the main sights.

TOP ATTRACTIONS

Farm Cove. The original convict-settlers established their first gardens on this bay's shores, now home to the **Royal Botanic Gardens.** The enterprise was not a success: the soil was too sandy for agriculture, and most of the crops fell victim to pests, marauding animals, and hungry convicts. The long seawall was constructed from the 1840s onward to enclose the previously swampy foreshore. ⊕ *You can enter the Botanic Gardens through gates near the Opera House and in Macquarie Street. From the Opera House, turn right and walk along the harbor foreshore (the seawall will be on your left, the Botanic Gardens on your right). To enter the Macquarie Street gates, take a train to Martin Place railway station, exit the station, turn left, and walk a few hundred yards down Macquarie Street.*

Fort Denison. For a brief time in the early days of the colony, convicts who committed petty offenses were kept on this harbor island, where they existed on such a meager diet that the island was named Pinchgut. Fortification of the island began in 1841, but was abandoned when cash ran out. It was finally completed in 1857, when fears of Russian expansion in the Pacific spurred the government on. Today the firing of the fort's cannon doesn't signal imminent invasion, but merely the hour—one o'clock. New South Wales National Parks run half-hour tours at Fort Denison. Purchase tickets from Cadman's Cottage, which include ferry transport from Jetty 6 at Circular Quay. ⊠ *Cadman's Cottage, 110 George St., The Rocks, Sydney Harbour* ☎ *02/9247–5033* 📧 *A$27* ⊙ *Tours run daily at 12:15 and 2:30, additional tours Wed.– Sun. at 10:45.*

Quarantine Station. From the 1830s onward, ship passengers who arrived with contagious diseases were isolated on this outpost in the shadow of North Head until pronounced free of illness. You can access the station as part of a guided tour, and now stay overnight in the newly opened four-star hotel and cottage accommodation known as Q Station. There are day tours and three different evening ghost tours (the station reputedly has its fair share of specters) that depart from the visitor center at the Quarantine Station. Tours are led by rangers from NSW National Parks and involve a fair bit of walking, so good shoes are a must. Reservations are essential. ⊠ *North Head, North Head Scenic Dr., Manly* ⊕ *Take the ferry to Manly from Circular Quay, then Bus 135 to site. Or catch Q Station's daily complimentary shuttle near the taxi rank in Belgrave Street opposite Manly Wharf. See Web site for shuttle times.* ☎ *02/9466–1500* ⊕ *www.qstation.com.au* 📧 *Day tour A$35, ghost tours A$34–A$44* ⊙ *The visitor center and museum open daily 10 am (with varying closing hours, check Web site); the Quarantine Story tour takes place on weekends only (A$35), call ahead for times. Adult ghost tours Wed., Thurs., and weekends 8 pm; family ghost tour Fri. and Sat. at 6:30 pm.*

"Hands down, these giraffes have the best view."—photo by Carly Miller Fodors.com member.

Fodor's Choice
★ **Sydney Harbour National Park.** This massive park is made up of 958 acres of separate foreshores and islands, most of them on the north side of the harbor. To see the best areas, put on your walking shoes and head out on the many well-marked trails. The Hermitage Foreshore Walk skirts through bushland around Vaucluse's Nielsen Park. On the north side of the harbor, Bradleys Head and Chowder Head Walk is a 5-km (3-mi) stroll that starts from Taronga Zoo Wharf. The most inspiring trail is the 9½-km (6-mi) Manly Scenic Walkway, which joins the Spit Bridge with Manly by meandering along sandstone headlands, small beaches, and pockets of rain forest, and past Aboriginal sites and the historic Grotto Point Lighthouse. You can take day tours of two harbor islands, Fort Denison and Goat Island, which have interesting colonial history and buildings. They depart from Cadman's Cottage, at The Rocks, with prices starting at A$27. You can also visit Shark Island (off Rose Bay) on a cruise with Captain Cook Cruises (A$20) departing daily from Wharf 6 at Circular Quay. The other two islands in the harbor park—Rodd and Clark—are recreational reserves that can be visited with permission from the New South Wales National Parks and payment of a landing fee of A$7. Visitors are allowed on these islands in small groups only, between 9 am and sunset or until 8 pm in summer. As there is no public transport, access is via private vessel, or water taxi. Water taxi fares are around A$70 to A$120 for 6 passengers one-way. Contact New South Wales National Parks by telephone, or visit Cadman's Cottage to pay the landing fee or organise tours. ■TIP→ The landing fee is included when you book a tour or a Captain Cook cruise. ⊠ *Cadman's Cottage, 110 George St., The Rocks* ☎ *02/9247–5033* ⊕ *www.nswnationalparks.com.au.*

☺ **Taronga Zoo.** Sydney's zoo, in a natu-
★ ral bush area on the harbor's north
shore, houses an extensive collection of Australian fauna, including
everybody's favorite marsupial, the
koala. The zoo has taken great care
to create spacious enclosures that
simulate natural habitats. The hillside setting is steep in parts, and
a complete tour can be tiring, but
you can use the map distributed
free at the entrance gate to plan
a leisurely route. The views of the
harbor are stunning. Use of children's strollers (the basic model) is
free. The best way to get here from

WORD OF MOUTH

"I love Taronga Zoo, it's in a beautiful location right on the Harbour
and the ferry ride across is great.
I particularly like the nocturnal
house as well as the platypus and
echidna viewing areas and the
bird house. Just one cautionary
note, avoid the zoo during the
summer school holidays when the
crowds make the experience fairly
unpleasant."

—Susan7

the city is by ferry from Circular Quay or Darling Harbour. From
Taronga Wharf a bus or the cable car will take you up the hill to the
main entrance. The ZooPass, a combined ferry-zoo ticket (A$49.50)
is available at Circular Quay. You can also stay overnight at the zoo in
what's billed as the "wildest slumber party in town." The "Roar and
Snore" program includes a night tour, two behind-the-scenes tours,
drinks, dinner, breakfast, and luxury tent accommodation from A$260
per adult. Other special programs include being a "Keeper for a Day."
✉ *Bradleys Head Rd., Mosman* ☎ *02/9969–2777* ⊕ *www.taronga.org.
au* 🎫 *A$44* ☉ *Daily 9–5.*

**NEED A
BREAK?**

Hikers completing the Hermitage Foreshore Walk can pull up a chair at the
newly-refurbished Beach House Café and Restaurant at beautiful Nielsen
Park, soak in fabulous harbor views, and watch the sailing boats. The
casual café is open daily 8–6, serving coffees, breakfast, including treats
such as blueberry pancakes, and light lunches such as BLTs and fish-and-
chips. The upscale restaurant is open for weekend breakfast and lunch
only. Take the 325 bus from Circular Quay (which will be signposted to Watsons Bay) and tell the driver where you want to get off. ✉ *Greycliffe Ave.,
Vaucluse* ☎ *02/9337–7333* ⊕ *www.nielsenpark.com.au.*

Vaucluse. The palatial homes in this glamorous harbor suburb provide
a glimpse of Sydney's high society. The small beaches at Nielsen Park
and Parsley Bay are safe for swimming and provide wonderful views.
Both beaches are packed with families in summer.

Vaucluse House. The suburb takes its name from the 1803 Vaucluse
House, one of Sydney's most illustrious remaining historic mansions.
The 15-room Gothic Revival house and its lush gardens, managed by
the Historic Houses Trust, are open to the public. The tearooms, built
in the style of an Edwardian conservatory, are popular spots for lunch
and afternoon tea on weekends. ✉ *Wentworth Rd., Vaucluse* ⊹ *Take
bus 325 from Circular Quay bus stand* ☎ *02/9388–7922* ⊕ *www.hht.
nsw.gov.au* 🎫 *A$8* ☉ *Fri.–Sun. 9:30–4; daily in Jan.*

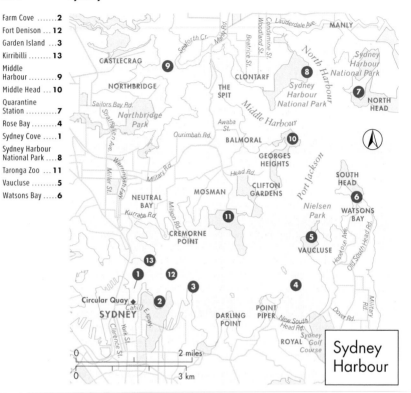

WORTH NOTING

Garden Island. Although it's still known as an "island," this promontory was connected with the mainland in 1942. During the 1941–45 War of the Pacific (WWII and a number of preceding conflicts), Australia's largest naval base and dockyard was a frontline port for Allied ships. Part of the naval base is now open to the public. Access to the site is via ferry from Circular Quay. ⊕ *You can take the ferry from Circular Quay to Watsons Bay and get off at Garden Island. No buses go directly to Garden Island. To walk, catch the train from Central or Town Hall to Kings Cross station, then walk all the way down either Macleay or Victoria streets toward the harbour (or north). At the very end of Victoria Street is a flight of stone steps that leads down to Woolloomooloo, near Garden Island.*

Kirribilli. Residences in this attractive suburb opposite the city and Opera House have million-dollar views—and prices to match. Two of Sydney's most important mansions stand here. The more modest of the two is **Kirribilli House,** the official Sydney home of the prime minister, which along with Admiralty House is open to the public once a year.

Admiralty House. Next door and far more prominent is Admiralty House—the Sydney residence of the governor-general, the Queen's representative in Australia. This impressive residence is occasionally open for inspection. Both houses can be viewed (from the water) during harbor cruises. ✥ *Both Kirribilli and Admiralty House are at the harbor end of Kirribilli Avenue; to get there you can take a ferry from Circular Quay to either Kirribilli Wharf or Milson's Point Wharf, or take the train from Town Hall to Milson's Point Station. The No. 267 bus does a loop from McMahon's Point to North Sydney via Kirribilli. There is no public access to either of these grand houses.*

Middle Harbour. Except for the yachts moored in the sandy coves, the upper reaches of Middle Harbour are almost exactly as they were when the first Europeans set eyes on Port Jackson more than 200 years ago. Tucked away in idyllic bushland are tranquil suburbs just a short drive from the city. ✥ *The focal point of Middle Harbour is Spit Bridge. To get there, take a train from either the Central or Town Hall station to Milson's Point then take Bus 229 to Spit Bridge. From Spit Bridge you can walk to Manly and view most of beautiful Middle Harbour.*

Middle Head. Despite its benign appearance today, Sydney Harbour once bristled with armaments. In the mid-19th century, faced with expansionist European powers hungry for new colonies, the authorities erected artillery positions on the headlands to guard harbor approaches. One of Sydney's newest open spaces, Headland Park, has opened on a former military base. A walking track winds past fortifications, tunnels, and heritage buildings, several of which are now used as cafés, including the Tea Room Gunners' Barracks. ✥ *Several buses travel from central Sydney to Mosman, Balmoral, and Chowder Bay, which are all suburbs within the Middle Head area and close to Headland Park. They include buses 244, 245, 246, and 247.*

NEED A BREAK? Housed in a beautiful sandstone building that served a number of military purposes for over 130 years, the Tea Room Gunners Barracks offers breathtaking views of the harbor and the surrounding gardens and bushland. Their traditional afternoon tea (A\$40) is a great way to relax after exploring the armaments of Middle Head. ✉ *202 Suakin Dr., Mosman* ☎ *02/8962–5900* ⊕ *www.thetearoom.com.au.*

Rose Bay. This large bay, the biggest of Sydney Harbour's 66 bays, was once a base for the Qantas flying boats that provided the only passenger air service between Australia and America and Europe. The last flying boat departed from Rose Bay in the 1960s, but the "airstrip" is still used by floatplanes on scenic flights connecting Sydney with the Hawkesbury River and the central coast. It's a popular place for joggers, who pound the pavement of New South Head Road, which runs along the bay. ✥ *Take Bus 325 from Circular Quay, or take the ferry to Watsons Bay (it stops at Rose Bay).*

Sydney Cove. Bennelong Point and the Sydney Opera House to the east and Circular Quay West and The Rocks to the west enclose this cove, which was named after Lord Sydney, the British home secretary at the time the colony was founded. The settlement itself was to be known as New Albion, but the name never caught on. Instead, the city took its name from this tiny bay. ✥ *Take the train from Central or Town Hall to Circular Quay railway station; or take any number of buses to*

The boardwalk around Sydney Cove on a typical sunny day.

Circular Quay from all over Sydney. Ferries travel to Circular Quay from many different parts of Sydney, including the north side of the harbor, Rose Bay, Balmain, and Parramatta. Circular Quay is right in the middle of Sydney Cove.

Watsons Bay. Established as a military base and fishing settlement in the colony's early years, Watsons Bay is a charming suburb, with a popular waterfront pub, that has held on to its village ambience despite the exorbitant prices paid for tiny cottages here. Unlike Watsons Bay's tranquil harbor side, the side that faces the ocean is dramatic and tortured, with the raging sea dashing against the sheer, 200-foot sandstone cliffs of The Gap.

Macquarie Lighthouse. When the sun shines, the 15-minute cliff-top stroll along South Head Walkway between The Gap and the Macquarie Lighthouse affords some of Sydney's most inspiring views. Convict-architect Francis Greenway (jailed for forgery) designed the original lighthouse here, Australia's first, in 1818. ⊠ *Old South Head Rd., Vaucluse ⊹ To reach Watsons Bay either take the ferry or buses 324 or 325 from Circular Quay. Bus 324 goes past the lighthouse.*

2

THE ROCKS

The Rocks is the birthplace not just of Sydney, but of modern Australia. Here the 11 ships of the First Fleet, the first of England's 800-plus ships carrying convicts to the penal colony, dropped anchor in 1788. This stubby peninsula enclosing the western side of Sydney Cove became known simply as The Rocks.

Most of the architecture here dates from the Victorian era, by which time Sydney had become a thriving port. Warehouses lining the waterfront were backed by a row of tradesmen's shops, banks, and taverns, and above them, ascending Observatory Hill, rose a tangled mass of alleyways lined with the cottages of seamen and wharf laborers. By the late 1800s The Rocks was a rough and squalid area. Conditions were so bad that as late as 1900 the black plague swept through The Rocks, prompting the government to offer a bounty for dead rats in an effort to exterminate their disease-carrying fleas.

> **MOVIES UNDER THE STARS**
>
> **Bondi Beach.** Bondi Beach screens movies at the 1928 Pavilion in summer.
> ⊕ www.bondiopenair.com.au.
>
> **Centennial Park.** Centennial Park is where film buffs relax on rugs or rented beanbags. It's the only time you're allowed in the park after sunset. Movies run from early January to mid-March.
> ⊕ www.moonlight.com.au.
>
> **Mrs. Macquarie's Point.** The best place for outdoor movies is at Mrs. Macquarie's Point. Films are screened at the Royal Botanic Gardens from mid-January to mid-February.
> ⊕ www.stgeorgeopenair.com.au.

Today The Rocks is hardly the ghetto it once was. Since the 1970s it's been transformed into a hot spot of cafés, restaurants, and quaint boutiques, and it's one of the city's most popular destinations. And because it's Sydney's most historic area, the old architecture has been beautifully maintained.

GETTING HERE AND AROUND

You can take the train or any number of buses to Circular Quay and then walk to The Rocks. From Bondi and Paddington, take the 380, 382, or 333 bus to Circular Quay via Elizabeth Street. From Clovelly, take the 339 bus all the way to The Rocks, via Central Station. The 431, 432, and 433 buses travel the inner western suburbs and terminate in The Rocks. Once there, the best way to get around is on foot—there are quite a few sandstone steps and narrow alleyways to navigate, and your feet are your best friends.

TOP ATTRACTIONS

Argyle Cut. Argyle Street, which links Argyle Place and George Street, is dominated by the Argyle Cut and its massive walls. In the days before the Cut (tunnel) was made, the sandstone ridge here was a major barrier to traffic crossing between Circular Quay and Millers Point. In 1843 convict work gangs hacked at the sandstone with hand tools for 2½ years before the project was abandoned due to lack of progress. Work restarted in 1857, when drills, explosives, and paid labor completed the

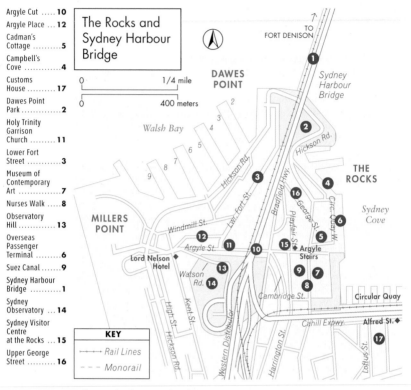

The Rocks and
Sydney Harbour
Bridge

0   1/4 mile

0   400 meters

DAWES POINT

TO
FORT DENISON

Sydney
Harbour
Bridge

THE ROCKS

Sydney
Cove

Walsh Bay

MILLERS POINT

Windmill St.

Argyle St.

Lord Nelson Hotel

Watson Rd.

Cambridge St.

Argyle Stairs

Circular Quay

Cahill Expwy.   Alfred St.

KEY

⊢————⊣ Rail Lines

- - - Monorail

job. On the lower side of the Cut an archway leads to the **Argyle Stairs,** which begin the climb from Argyle Street up to the Sydney Harbour Bridge walkway. There's a spectacular view from the South East Pylon.

Campbell's Cove. Robert Campbell was a Scottish merchant who is sometimes referred to as the "father of Australian commerce." Campbell broke the stranglehold that the British East India Company exercised over seal and whale products, which were New South Wales's only exports in those early days. The cove's atmospheric sandstone **Campbell's Storehouse,** built from 1838 onward, now houses waterside restaurants. The pulleys that were used to hoist cargoes still hang on the upper level of the warehouses. The cove is also the mooring for Sydney's fully operational tall ships, which conduct theme cruises around the harbor. ⊠ *Campbell's Storehouse, 7–27 Circular Quay West, The Rocks* ☎ *No phone.*

Holy Trinity Garrison Church. Every morning, redcoats would march to this 1840 Argyle Place church from Dawes Point Battery (now Dawes Point Park), and it became commonly known as the Garrison Church. As the regimental plaques and colors around the walls testify, the church still retains a close military association. ⊠ *Argyle Pl., Argyle and Lower Fort Sts, The Rocks* ☎ *02/9247–1268* ☉ *Daily 9–5.*

EXPLORING THE ROCKS ON FOOT

Begin at Circular Quay, the lively waterfront ferry terminal, and walk west toward Harbour Bridge, passing the Museum of Contemporary Art, and climb the few stairs into George Street. Pass the historic Fortune of War pub, then as you round the corner head down the sandstone stairs on the right to **Campbells Cove** and its warehouses. The waterfront restaurants and cafés are pleasant spots for a drink or meal. Continue along Hickson Road toward the Sydney Harbour Bridge until you are directly beneath the bridge's massive girders. Walk under the bridge to **Dawes Point Park** for excellent views of the harbor, including the Opera House and the small island of Fort Denison. Now turn your back on the bridge and walk south and west, via Lower Fort Street. Explore Argyle Place and continue walking south, past the **Sydney Observatory**. While you're in the neighborhood, be sure to pick up brochures and city information at the **Sydney Visitor Centre at The Rocks**, on the corner of Argyle and Playfair streets. Turn right at **Nurses Walk**, another of the area's historic and atmospheric backstreets, then left into Surgeons Court, and left again onto George Street. On the left is the handsome sandstone facade of the former Rocks Police Station, now a crafts gallery. From this point, Circular Quay is only a short walk away.

Fodor's Choice

★

Sydney Harbour Bridge. There are several ways to experience the bridge and its spectacular views. One is to walk to the midpoint of the bridge to take in the views free of charge, but be sure to take the eastern footpath, which overlooks the Sydney Opera House. Access is via the stairs on Cumberland Street, close to the Shangri-La Hotel.

South East Pylon. Another is to follow the walkway from its access point near the Argyle Stairs to the South East Pylon. This structure houses a display on the bridge's construction, and you can climb the 200 steps to the lookout and its unbeatable harbor panorama. The fee is A$11 and the display is open daily 10–5. ☎ 02/9240–1100

BridgeClimb Tour. A third (more expensive) option—not for those afraid of heights—is the BridgeClimb tour, which takes you on a guided walking tour to the very top of Harbour Bridge, 439 feet above sea level. The cost is A$198 per person. ☎ 02/8274–7777 ⊕ www.bridgeclimb.com.

NEED A BREAK?

While in the west end of Argyle Place, consider the liquid temptations of the Lord Nelson, which with at least one other contender claims to be Sydney's oldest hotel. (It has been licensed to serve alcohol since 1841). The sandstone pub has its own brewery on the premises. One of its specialties is Quayle Ale, named after the former U.S. vice president, who "sank a schooner" (drank a beer) here during his 1989 visit to Australia. ✉ 19 Kent St., at Argyle St., Millers Point, the Rocks ☎ 02/9251–4044 ⊕ www. lordnelsonbrewery.com.

WORTH NOTING

Argyle Place. With all the traditional requirements of an English green—a pub at one end, a church at the other, and grass in between—this charming enclave in the suburb of Millers Point is unusual for Sydney. Argyle Place is lined with 19th-century houses and cottages on its northern side and overlooked by Observatory Hill to the south.

Cadman's Cottage. Sydney's oldest building, completed in 1816, has a history that outweighs its modest dimensions. John Cadman was a convict who was sentenced for life to New South Wales for stealing a horse. He later became superintendent of government boats, a position that entitled him to live in the upper story of this house. The water once practically lapped at Cadman's doorstep, and the original seawall still stands at the front of the house. The small extension on the side of the cottage was built to lock up the oars of Cadman's boats, since oars would have been a necessity for any convict attempting to escape by sea. The upper floor of Cadman's Cottage is now a NSW National Parks bookshop and information center for Sydney Harbour National Park. ⊠ *110 George St., The Rocks* ☎ *02/9253–0888* ⊕ *www.environment.nsw.gov.au* ⏱ *Weekdays 9:30–4:30, weekends 10–4:30.*

Customs House. The last surviving example of the elegant sandstone buildings that once ringed Circular Quay, this former customs house now features an amazing model of Sydney under a glass floor. You can walk over the city's skyscrapers, all of which are illuminated by meters of fiber-optic lights. There's an excellent two-level library and plenty of art galleries. The rooftop Café Sydney, the standout in the clutch of restaurants and cafés in this late-19th-century structure, overlooks Sydney Cove. The building stands close to the site where the British flag was first raised on the shores of Sydney Cove in 1788. ⊠ *Customs House Sq., 31 Alfred St., Circular Quay* ☎ *02/9242 8551* ⊕ *www.cityofsydney.nsw.gov.au/customshouse.*

Dawes Point Park. The wonderful views of the harbor (and since the 1930s, the Harbour Bridge) have made this park and its location noteworthy for centuries. Named for William Dawes, a First Fleet marine officer and astronomer who established the colony's first basic observatory nearby in 1788, this park was also once the site of a fortification known as Dawes Battery. The cannons on the hillside pointing toward the Opera House came from the ships of the First Fleet. ⊠ *Hickson Road, The Rocks.*

Lower Fort Street. At one time the handsome Georgian houses along this street, originally a rough track leading from the Dawes Point Battery to Observatory Hill, were among the best addresses in Sydney. Elaborate wrought-iron lacework still graces many of the facades.

Museum of Contemporary Art. This ponderous art deco building houses one of Australia's most important collections of modern art, as well as two significant collections of Aboriginal art and continually changing temporary exhibits. ⊠ *140 George St., The Rocks* ☎ *02/9245–2400* ⊕ *www.mca.com.au* ⊠ *Free* ⊗ *Daily 10–5.*

Nurses Walk. Cutting across the site of the colony's first hospital, Nurses Walk acquired its name at a time when "Sydney" and "sickness" were synonymous. Many of the 736 convicts who survived the voyage from Portsmouth, England, aboard the First Fleet's 11 ships arrived suffering from dysentery, smallpox, scurvy, and typhoid. A few days after he landed at Sydney Cove, Governor Phillip established a tent hospital to care for the worst cases.

Observatory Hill. The city's highest point, at 145 feet, was known originally as Windmill Hill, since the colony's first windmill occupied this breezy spot. Its purpose was to grind grain for flour, but soon after it was built the canvas sails were stolen, the machinery was damaged in a storm, and the foundations cracked. The signal station at the top of the hill was built in 1848. This later became an astronomical observatory. This is a great place for a picnic with a view. ⊠ *Upper Fort St, The Rocks.*

Overseas Passenger Terminal. Busy Circular Quay West is dominated by this multilevel steel-and-glass port terminal, which is often used by visiting cruise ships. There are several excellent waterfront restaurants in the terminal, all with magnificent harbor views. Even if you're not dining in the terminal, it's worth taking the escalator to the upper deck for a good view of the harbor and Opera House.

Suez Canal. So narrow that two people can't walk abreast, this alley acquired its name before drains were installed, when rainwater would pour down its funnel-like passageway and gush across George Street. Lanes such as this were once the haunt of the notorious late-19th-century Rocks gangs, when robbery was rife in the area.

Sydney Observatory. Originally a signaling station for communicating with ships anchored in the harbor, this handsome building on top of Observatory Hill is now an astronomy museum. During evening observatory shows you can tour the building, watch videos, and get a close-up view of the universe through a 16-inch mirror telescope. Reservations are required for the evening show. ⊠ *Watson Rd., Millers Point* ☎ *02/9921–3485* ⊕ *www.sydneyobservatory.com.au* ⊠ *Museum free, daytime show A$7, evening show A$17* ⊗ *Daily 10–5.*

Sydney Visitor Centre at the Rocks. Known as The Rocks Centre, this ultramodern space is packed with free maps and brochures, and the friendly staff dispenses valuable information and will book tours, hotel rooms, and bus travel. It's near the popular Löwenbräu Keller, where

HISTORIC WATERING HOLES

Harbour View Hotel. You can get a close-up view of climbers on the Harbour Bridge from a bar stool at the aptly named Harbour View Hotel. ⊠ *19 Lower Fort St., at Cumberland St., The Rocks* ☎ *02/9252–4111.*

Hero of Waterloo. You're sure to get involved in a sing-along when bands take to the stage at the historic Hero of Waterloo. The pub has a maze of cellars and tunnels said to have been used by smugglers in Sydney's early days. ⊠ *81 Lower Fort St.* ☎ *02/9252–4553.*

2

DID YOU KNOW?

Listed in the *Guinness Book of Records* as the widest long span bridge in the world, the Sydney Harbour Bridge was the tallest structure in the city until 1967. It's the fourth longest single-span steel arch bridge in the world, behind Bayonne Bridge in New York and the New River Gorge Bridge in West Virginia. The very longest is the Lupu Bridge in Shanghai.

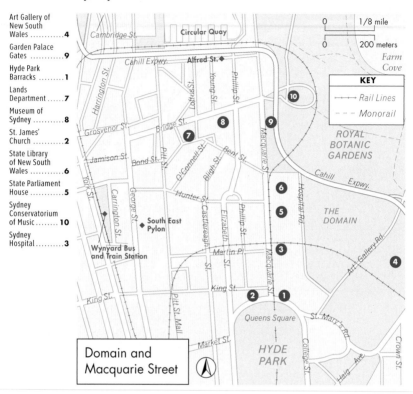

Domain and
Macquarie Street

many tourists gather for a beer. ⊠ *The Rocks Centre, Argyle and Play-fair Sts., The Rocks* ☎ *02/9240–8788* ⊕ *www.sydneyvisitorcentre.com* ⊙ *Daily 9:30–5:30.*

Upper George Street. The restored warehouses and Victorian terrace houses that line this part of George Street make this a charming section of the Rocks. The covered **Rocks Market** takes place here on weekends.

DOMAIN AND MACQUARIE STREET

Some of Sydney's most notable Victorian-era public buildings, as well as one of its finest parks, can be found in this area. In contrast to the simple, utilitarian stone convict cottages of The Rocks, these build-ings were constructed at a time when Sydney was experiencing a long period of prosperity thanks to the gold rushes of the mid-19th century and an agricultural boom. The sandstone just below the surface of many coastal areas proved an ideal building material—easily honed into the ornamentation so fashionable during the Victorian era. Macquarie Street is Sydney's most elegant boulevard. It was shaped by Governor Macquarie, who planned the transformation of the cart track leading to Sydney Cove into a stylish street of dwellings and government buildings. An occasional modern high-rise breaks up the streetscape, but many of the 19th-century architectural delights here escaped demolition.

Building Sydney

Descended from Scottish clan chieftains, Governor Lachlan Macquarie was an accomplished soldier and a man of vision. Macquarie, who was in office from 1810 to 1821, was the first governor to foresee a role for New South Wales as a free society rather than an open prison. He laid the foundations for that society by establishing a plan for the city, constructing significant public buildings, and advocating that reformed convicts be readmitted to society.

Macquarie's policies of equality may seem perfectly reasonable today, but in the early 19th century they marked him as a radical. When his vision of a free society threatened to blur distinctions between soldiers, settlers, and convicts, Macquarie was forced to resign. He was later buried on his Scottish estate, his gravestone inscribed with the words "the Father of Australia."

Macquarie's grand plans for the construction of Sydney might have come to nothing had it not been for Francis Greenway. Trained as an architect in England, where he was convicted of forgery and sentenced to 14 years in New South Wales, Greenway received a ticket of prison leave from Macquarie in 1814 and set to work transforming Sydney. Over the next few years he designed lighthouses, hospitals, convict barracks, and many other government buildings, several of which remain to bear witness to his simple but elegant eye. Greenway was eventually even depicted on one side of the old A$10 notes, which went out of circulation early in the 1990s. Only in Australia, perhaps, would a convicted forger occupy pride of place on the currency.

GETTING HERE AND AROUND

The area is served by two train stations—Martin Place and St. James—but they are not on the same line. You can catch train trains to both stations from Central and Town Hall. St. James is right next to Hyde Park, and Martin Place has an exit on Macquarie Street. From Macquarie Street it's a short walk to the Domain via the passageway that cuts through Sydney Hospital. A number of buses (including the 380/382 and 333 from Bondi Beach and 555 free shuttle) travel along Elizabeth Street.

TOP ATTRACTIONS

Art Gallery of New South Wales. Apart from Canberra's National Gallery, this is the best place to explore the evolution of European-influenced Australian art, as well as the distinctly different concepts that underlie Aboriginal art. All the major Australian artists of the last two centuries are represented in this impressive collection. The entrance level, where large windows frame spectacular views of the harbor, exhibits 20th-century art. Below, in the gallery's major extensions, the Yiribana Gallery displays one of the nation's most comprehensive collections of Aboriginal and Torres Strait Islander art. ■TIP➔ The gallery is open until 9 pm on Wednesdays. ✉ *Art Gallery Rd., Sydney, The Domain* ☎ *02/9225–1700* ⊕ *www.artgallery.nsw.gov.au* 💲 *Free; fee for special exhibits* ☉ *Daily 10–5.*

Sydney has enough museums and art galleries to appeal to just about every taste.

Hyde Park Barracks. Before Governor Macquarie arrived, convicts were left to roam freely at night. Macquarie was determined to establish law and order, and in 1819 he commissioned convict-architect Francis Greenway to design this restrained, classically Georgian-style building. Today the Barracks houses compelling exhibits that explore behind the scenes of the prison. For example, a surprising number of relics from this period were preserved by rats, which carried away scraps of clothing and other artifacts for their nests beneath the floorboards. A room on the top floor is strung with hammocks, exactly as it was when the building housed convicts. ⊠ *Queens Sq., Macquarie St., The Domain* 🕾 *02/8239–2311* ⊕ *www.hht.nsw.gov.au* 🖾 *A$10* ⊙ *Daily 9:30–5.*

★ **Museum of Sydney.** This museum built on the site of the original Government House documents Sydney's early period of European colonization. Aboriginal culture, convict society, and the gradual transformation of the settlement at Sydney Cove are woven into an evocative portrayal of life in the country's early days. A glass floor in the lobby reveals the foundations of the original structure. One of the most intriguing exhibits, however, is outside: the striking *Edge of the Trees* sculpture, the first collaborative public artwork in Sydney between an Aboriginal and a European artist. ⊠ *Bridge and Phillip Sts., The Domain* 🕾 *02/9251–5988* ⊕ *www.hht.nsw.gov.au* 🖾 *A$10* ⊙ *Daily 9:30–5.*

WORTH NOTING

Garden Palace Gates. These gates are all that remain of the Garden Palace, a massive glass pavilion that was erected for the Sydney International Exhibition of 1879 and destroyed by fire three years later. On the arch above the gates is a depiction of the Garden Palace's dome. Stone pillars on either side of the gates are engraved with Australian wildflowers. ✉ *Macquarie St. between Bridge and Bent Sts., The Domain.*

On a sunny day the courtyard tables of the Hyde Park Barracks Café provide one of the city's finest places to enjoy an outdoor lunch or morning or afternoon tea. The café and indoor restaurant serve light fare, full meals, and delicious desserts such as the warm Belgian chocolate pudding with orange sauce and white Belgian chocolate gelato. There's also an extensive Australian wine list. ✉ *Queens Sq., Macquarie St.* ☎ *02/9222–1815.*

ART AND ANGST

If you like a bit of controversy with your culture, head to the Art Gallery of New South Wales to view the finalists in the annual **Archibald Prize** (⊕ *www. thearchibaldprize.com.au*). Each year since 1921, the competition has attracted plenty of drama as everyone debates the merits of the winners. Prizes are announced in early March, and the exhibition hangs until mid-May.

Lands Department. The figures occupying the niches at the corners of this 1890 sandstone building are early Australian explorers and politicians. James Barnet's building stands among other fine Victorian structures in the neighborhood. ✉ *23–33 Bridge Street, near intersection of Macquarie Pl., The Domain.*

St. James' Church. Begun in 1822, the colonial Georgian–style St. James' is Sydney's oldest surviving church, and another fine Francis Greenway design. Now lost among the skyscrapers, the church's tall spire once served as a landmark for ships entering the harbor. Plaques commemorating Australian explorers and administrators cover the interior walls. Free guided tours are given weekdays at 2:30 pm. Lunchtime concerts are presented every Wednesday from late February to late December. ✉ *Queens Sq., 173 King St., Hyde Park* ☎ *02/9232–3022* ⊕ *www.sjks. org.au* ⊘ *Weekdays 9–5, Sat. 9–3.*

State Library of New South Wales. This large complex is based around the Mitchell and Dixson libraries, which make up the world's largest collection of Australiana. Enter the foyer through the classical portico to see one of the earliest maps of Australia, a copy in marble mosaic of a map made by Abel Tasman, the Dutch navigator, in the mid-17th century. Through the glass doors lies the vast Mitchell Library reading room, but you need a reader's ticket (establishing that you are pursuing legitimate research) to enter. You can, however, take a free escorted history and heritage tour Tuesday and Thursday at 10.30 am. The library continuously runs free exhibitions, and the opulent Shakespeare Room is open to the public Tuesday 10 am–4 pm. Inquire at the reception desk of the general reference library on Macquarie Street. ✉ *Between the Royal Botanic Gardens and Parliament House, Macquarie St.* ☎ *02/9273–1414, 02/9273–1768* ⊕ *www.sl.nsw.gov. au* ⊘ *Mon.–Thurs. 9–8, Fri. 9–5, weekends 10–5 (Mitchell Library closed Sun.).*

State Parliament House. The simple facade and shady verandas of this Greenway-designed 1816 building, formerly the Rum Hospital, typify Australian colonial architecture. From 1829, two rooms of the old hospital were used for meetings of the executive and legislative councils, which had been set up to advise the governor. These advisory bodies grew in power until New South Wales became self-governing in the 1840s, at which time Parliament occupied the entire building. The Legislative Council Chamber—the upper house of the parliament, identifiable by its red color scheme—is a prefabricated cast-iron structure that was originally intended to be a church on the goldfields of Victoria.

State Parliament generally sits between mid-February and late May, and again between mid-September and late November. You can visit the public gallery and watch the local version of the Westminster system of democracy in action. When parliament is not sitting, you can take a free escorted tour (there are several every day) or walk around at your leisure and view the large collection of portraits and paintings. You must reserve ahead for tours and to sit in the public gallery. ✉ *6 Macquarie St.* ☎ *02/9230–2111* ⊕ *www.parliament.nsw.gov.au* ☼ *Weekdays 9–5; hrs. vary when Parliament is in session—call ahead.*

Sydney Conservatorium of Music. Providing artistic development for talented young musicians, this institution hosts lunchtime concerts (entry by small donation) on Wednesday, free student performances throughout the year, and other musical events. The conservatory's turreted building was originally the stables for nearby Government House. The construction cost caused a storm among Governor Macquarie's superiors in London, and eventually helped bring about the downfall of both Macquarie and the building's architect, Francis Greenway. ✉ *Bridge & Macquarie Streets* ☎ *02/9351–1222.*

Sydney Hospital. Completed in 1894 to replace the main Rum Hospital building which stood on the site since 1811, this institution offered an infinitely better medical option. By all accounts, admission to the Rum Hospital was only slightly preferable to death itself. Convict nurses stole patients' food, and abler patients stole from the weaker. The kitchen sometimes doubled as a mortuary, and the table was occasionally used for operations.

In front of the hospital is a bronze figure of a boar. This is *Il Porcellino,* a copy of a statue that stands in Florence, Italy. According to the inscription, if you make a donation in the coin box and rub the boar's nose, "you will be endowed with good luck." Sydney citizens seem to be a superstitious bunch, because the boar's nose is very shiny indeed. ✉ *8 Macquarie St.* ☎ *02/9382–7111.*

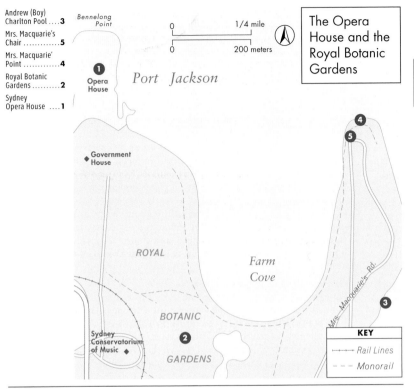

THE OPERA HOUSE AND THE ROYAL BOTANIC GARDENS

Bordering Sydney Cove, Farm Cove, and Woolloomooloo Bay, this section of Sydney includes the iconic Sydney Opera House, as well as extensive and delightful harborside gardens and parks.

The colony's first farm was established here in 1788, and the botanical gardens were laid out in 1816. The most dramatic change to the area occurred in 1959, however, when ground was broken on the site for the Sydney Opera House at Bennelong Point. This promontory was originally a small island, then the site of 1819 Fort Macquarie, later a tram depot, and finally the Opera House, one of the world's most striking modern buildings. The area's evolution is an eloquent metaphor for Sydney's own transformation.

GETTING HERE AND AROUND

The best way to get to the Opera House is to take one of the many ferries, buses, or trains that go to Circular Quay and then walk the pedestrian concourse. Some buses travel down Macquarie Street to the Opera House, which involves a slightly shorter walk. To get to the Royal Botanic Gardens, take the CityRail suburban train from the Town Hall, Central, or Bondi Junction stations to Martin Place station, exit on the Macquarie Street side, and walk a few hundred yards.

TOP ATTRACTIONS

★ **Royal Botanic Gardens.** More than 80 acres of sweeping green lawns, groves of indigenous and exotic trees, duck ponds, greenhouses, and some 45,124 types of plants—many of them in bloom—grace these gardens. The elegant property, which attracts strollers and botany enthusiasts from all over the country, is a far cry today from what it once was: a failed attempt by convicts of the First Fleet to establish a farm. Though their early attempts at agriculture were disastrous, the efforts of these first settlers are acknowledged in the Pioneer Garden, a sunken garden built in their memory.

Among the many other feature gardens on the property are the Palm Grove—home to some of the oldest trees in Sydney, the Begonia Garden, and the Rare and Threatened Plants Garden. Not to be missed is a cutting from the famous Wollemi Pine, a plant thought to be extinct until it was discovered in a secluded gully in the Wollemi National Park in the Blue Mountains in 1994. Plants throughout the gardens have various blooming cycles, so no matter what time of year you visit, there are sure to be plenty of flowers. The gardens include striking sculptures and hundreds of species of birds (along with a large colony of flying foxes, also known as fruit bats). There are spectacular views over the harbor and the Opera House from the two lovely restaurants.

Government House. Completed in 1843, this Gothic Revival building in the Royal Botanic Gardens served as the residence of the Governor of New South Wales—who represents the British crown in local matters—until the government handed it back to the public in 1996. Prominent English architect Edward Blore designed the two-story building without ever having set foot in Australia. The sandstone house's restored stenciled ceilings are its most impressive feature. Paintings hanging on the walls bear the signatures of some of Australia's best-known artists. You are free to wander on your own around Government House's gardens, which lie within the Royal Botanic Gardens, but you must join a guided tour to see the house's interior. Tours leave from the visitor center, near the Art Gallery of New South Wales. There are also maps available for a variety of themed, self-guided walks. ⊠ *Mrs. Macquaries Rd., The Domain* ☎ *02/9231–8111* ⊕ *www.rbgsyd.nsw.gov.au* ⊒ *Free* ☉ *Royal Botanic Gardens daily 7–dusk; tours at 10:30 am.*

Fodor's Choice   **Sydney Opera House.** Sydney's most famous landmark (listed as a World
★   Heritage site in 2007) had such a long and troubled construction phase that it's almost a miracle that the building was ever completed. In 1954 the state premier appointed a committee to advise the government on the building of an opera house. The site chosen was Bennelong Point (named after an early Aboriginal inhabitant), which was, until that time, occupied by a tram depot. The premier's committee launched a competition to find a suitable plan, and a total of 233 submissions came in from architects the world over. One of them was a young Dane named Joern Utzon.

His plan was brilliant, but it had all the markings of a monumental disaster. The structure was so narrow that stages would have minuscule wings, and the soaring "sails" that formed the walls and roof could not be built by existing technology.

"The Opera House as seen from The Rocks side of Circular Quay."—photo by Gary Ott, Fodors.com member.

Nonetheless, Utzon's dazzling, dramatic concept caught the judges' imagination, and construction of the giant podium began in 1959. From the start, the contractors faced a cost blowout; the building that was projected to cost A$7 million and take 4 years to erect would eventually require A$102 million and 15 years. Construction was financed by an intriguing scheme. Realizing that citizens might be hostile to the use of public funds for the controversial project, the state government raised the money through the Opera House Lottery. For almost a decade, Australians lined up to buy tickets, and the Opera House was built without depriving the state's hospitals or schools of a single cent.

Initially it was thought that the concrete exterior of the building would have to be cast in place, which would have meant building an enormous birdcage of scaffolding at even greater expense. Then, as he was peeling an orange one day, Utzon had a flash of inspiration. Why not construct the shells from segments of a single sphere? The concrete ribs forming the skeleton of the building could be prefabricated in just a few molds, hoisted into position, and joined together. These ribs are clearly visible inside the Opera House, especially in the foyers and staircases of the Concert Hall.

In 1966 Utzon resigned as Opera House architect and left Australia, reportedly embittered by his dealings with unions and the government. He never returned to see his masterpiece, although he had been invited on several occasions.

A team of young Australian architects carried on, completing the exterior one year later. Until that time, however, nobody had given much thought to the *interior*. The shells created awkward interior spaces, and conventional performance areas were simply not feasible. It's a tribute to the architectural team's ingenuity that the exterior of the building is matched by the aesthetically pleasing and acoustically sound theaters inside. Joern Utzon died in Denmark on November 29, 2008, aged 90. Then Prime Minister Kevin Rudd paid tribute to Utzon's genius in speeches, while the lights of the Opera House sails were dimmed and flags on the Harbor Bridge were flown at half-mast as a mark of respect.

Sydney Opera House showcases all the performing arts in its five theaters, one of which is devoted to opera. The Australian Ballet, the Sydney Dance Company, and the Australian Opera Company also call the Opera House home. The complex includes two stages for theater and the 2,700-seat Concert Hall, where the Sydney Symphony Orchestra and the Australian Chamber Orchestra perform. The box office is open Monday to Saturday 9–8:30.

Guided tours include the one-hour Essential Tour, departing daily from the lower forecourt level between 9 and 5, and a two-hour backstage tour departing daily at 7 am. Call in advance for bookings (☎ 02–9250–7250). Visitors are free to walk around inside the building throughout the day and night. ⊠ 2 Macquarie Street, Circular Quay ☎ 02/9250–7111 ⊕ www.soh.nsw.gov.au ✉ General tour A$35, backstage tour A$155.

WORTH NOTING

Ⓒ **Andrew (Boy) Charlton Pool.** This heated saltwater 8-lane swimming pool overlooking the navy ships tied up at Garden Island has become a local favorite. Complementing its stunning location is a radical design in glass and steel. The pool also has a chic terrace café above Woolloomooloo Bay. It's open from September 1 until April 30. ⊠ 1C Mrs. Macquarie's Rd., The Domain ☎ 02/9358–6686 ⊕ www.abcpool.org ✉ A$5.50 ⊙ 6 am–7 pm (until 8 pm from Oct to late March).

Mrs. Macquarie's Chair. During the early 1800s, Elizabeth Macquarie often sat on the point in the Domain at the east side of Farm Cove, at the rock where a seat has been hewn in her name. The views across the harbor are sensational. ⊠ Mrs. Macquaries Rd..

| NEED A BREAK? | Botanic Gardens Restaurant is a lovely place to have lunch during the week or brunch on the weekend. Wide verandas provide tranquil views over the gardens, and the sound of birdsong fills the air. The menu changes seasonally and may include starters such as grilled quail with roast quince, and main dishes of fettuccini with pine-forest mushrooms and macadamia nuts. The downstairs café serves lighter, more casual fare, and is open daily from 8:30 am to 4 (and later in summer). The restaurant is open for lunch from noon weekdays and brunch on the weekends from 9:30, where decadent eggs Benedict is best accompanied by a glass of bubbly. ⊠ Royal Botanic Gardens, Mrs. Macquarie's Rd. ☎ 02/9241–2419 ⊕ www.rbgsyd.nsw.gov.au. |

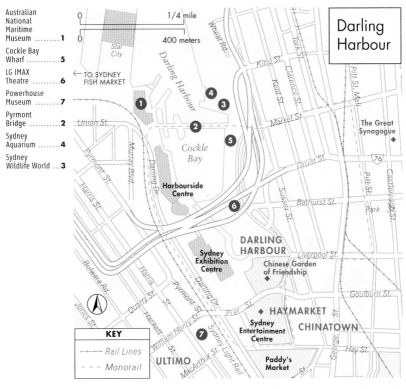

Australian National Maritime Museum **1**

Cockle Bay Wharf **5**

LG IMAX Theatre **6**

Powerhouse Museum **7**

Pyrmont Bridge **2**

Sydney Aquarium **4**

Sydney Wildlife World ...**3**

Mrs. Macquarie's Point. The inspiring views from this point combine with the shady lawns to make this a popular place for picnics. The views are best at dusk, when the setting sun silhouettes the Opera House and the Harbour Bridge. ⊠ *Mrs. Macquaries Rd..*

DARLING HARBOUR

Until the mid-1980s this horseshoe-shape bay on the city center's western edge was a wasteland of disused docks and railway yards. Then, in an explosive burst of activity the whole area was redeveloped and opened in time for Australia's bicentenary in 1988. Now there's plenty to take in at the Darling Harbour complex: the National Maritime Museum, Sydney Aquarium, Sydney Wildlife World, and the gleaming Exhibition Centre, whose masts and spars recall the square-riggers that once berthed here. At the harbor's center is a large park shaded by palm trees. Waterways and fountains lace the complex together.

The Powerhouse Museum is within easy walking distance of the harbor, and to the south are Chinatown and the Sydney Entertainment Centre. The Star City entertainment complex, based around the Star City Casino, lies just to the west of Darling Harbour.

GETTING HERE AND AROUND

Take the train to either Town Hall or Central Station. From Town Hall it's a short walk down Druitt Street; from Central you walk through Haymarket and Chinatown, passing by the Sydney Entertainment Centre. The monorail (A$4.90 one-way; A$9.50 day pass) travels in a loop from the city center to Darling Harbour, stopping on both sides of Cockle Bay. The Light Rail tram (A$3.40 one-way; day pass A$9) connects Central Station with Darling Harbour and the Star City Casino a little farther to the west.

TOP ATTRACTIONS

Ⓒ **Australian National Maritime Museum.**
★ The six galleries of this soaring, futuristic building tell the story of Australia and the sea. In addition to figureheads, model ships, and brassy nautical hardware, there are antique racing yachts and the jet-powered *Spirit of Australia,* current holder of the world water speed record, set in 1978. The USA Gallery displays objects from such major U.S. collections as the Smithsonian Institution, and was dedicated by President George Bush Sr. on New Year's Day 1992. An outdoor section showcases numerous vessels moored at the museum's wharves, including the HMAS *Vampire,* a retired Royal Australian Navy destroyer, and the historic tall ship the *James Craig.* You can also climb to the top of the 1874 Bowling Green Lighthouse for free. ⊠ *Wharf 7, Maritime Heritage Centre, 2 Murray St., Darling Harbour* ☎ *02/9298–3777* ⊕ *www.anmm.gov.au* ⊠ *Free* ⊙ *Daily 9:30–5 (until 6 in Jan.).*

Ⓒ **Sydney Aquarium.** The larger and more modern of Sydney's public
★ aquariums presents a fascinating view of the underwater world, with saltwater crocodiles, giant sea turtles, and delicate, multicolor fish. Excellent displays highlight Great Barrier Reef marine life and Australia's largest river system, the Murray-Darling. The latest exhibition, Shark HO, features the world's largest animatronic Great White Shark and live videos that track shark movements in Sydney Harbour and coast waters. Two show-stealing transparent tunnels give a fish's-eye view of the sea, while sharks and stingrays glide overhead. Although the adult admission price is high, family tickets are a good value, as is the "combo pass" that includes nearby Sydney Wildlife World (A$50). ⊠ *Aquarium pier, 1–5 Wheat Rd., Darling Harbour* ☎ *02/8251–7800* ⊕ *www.sydneyaquarium.myfun.com.au* ⊠ *A$35* ⊙ *Daily 9 am–8 pm.*

WORTH NOTING

Bounded by the Entertainment Centre, George Street, Goulburn Street, and Paddy's Market, Chinatown takes your senses on a galloping tour of the Orient. Within this compact grid are aromatic restaurants, traditional

VILLAGE VIBE

London Hotel. If you're seeking a taste of village life, take a ferry to Balmain. The left-of-center community spirit makes it one of Sydney's special places. On the western side of the harbor, Balmain is home to narrow streets, sandstone cottages, and good pubs, including one that welcomes dogs at the London Hotel. To get here, take the ferry from Circular Quay to Balmain Wharf and connect with buses that climb up Darling Street hill. ⊠ *234 Darling St., Balmain* ☎ *02/9555–1377.*

VISIT
CHINA

The Maritime Museum at Darling Harbour.

apothecaries, Chinese grocers, clothing boutiques, and shops selling Asian-made electronics. The best way to get a sense of the area is to take a stroll along Dixon Street, now a pedestrian mall with a Chinese Lion Gate at either end. Sydney's Chinese community was first established here in the 1800s, in the aftermath of the gold rush that originally drew many Chinese immigrants to Australia. For the next few years the area will be getting a major face-lift that will include new lighting, artwork, and more pedestrian walkways. Most Sydneysiders come here regularly to dine, especially on weekends for dim sum (called *yum cha*).

Cockle Bay Wharf. Fueling Sydney's addiction to fine food, most of this sprawling waterfront complex is dedicated to gastronomy. This is also the site of Sydney's biggest nightclub, Home. If you have a boat you can dock at the marina—and avoid the hassle of parking a car in one of the city's most congested centers. ⊠ *201 Sussex St., Darling Harbour* ☏ *02/9269–9800* ⊕ *www.cocklebaywharf.com.*

NEED A BREAK? Blackbird Café is an affordable place for lunch or dinner, and has great views across Cockle Bar if you nab a balcony table. There are A$12 lunch specials and A$10 cocktails daily. The menu includes burgers, pizza, soups, and Asian dishes. ⊠ *Balcony level, Cockle Bay Wharf, 201 Sussex St., Darling Harbour* ☏ *02/9283-7385* ⊕ *www.blackbirdcafe.com.au.*

LG IMAX Theatre. Both in size and impact, this eight-story-tall movie screen is overwhelming. One-hour presentations take you on astonishing, wide-angle voyages of discovery under the oceans and to the summit of the world's highest mountains. ⌧ *Southern Promenade, 31 Wheat Rd., Darling Harbour* ☎ *02/9281–3300* ⊕ *www.imax.com.au* ⤢ *A$19.50– A$28.50* ☉ *Daily 10–10.*

☼ **Powerhouse Museum.** Learning the principles of science is a painless process with this museum's stimulating, interactive displays ideal for all ages. Exhibits in the former 1890s electricity station that once powered Sydney's trams include a whole floor of working steam engines, space modules, airplanes suspended from the ceiling, state-of-the-art computer gadgetry, and a 1930s art deco–style movie-theater auditorium. ⌧ *500 Harris St., Ultimo, Darling Harbour* ☎ *02/9217–0111* ⊕ *www. powerhousemuseum.com* ⤢ *A$10* ☉ *Daily 10–5.*

Pyrmont Bridge. Dating from 1902, this is the world's oldest electrically operated swing-span bridge. The structure once carried motor traffic, but it's now a walkway that links Darling Harbour's western side with Cockle Bay. The monorail runs above the bridge, but the center span still swings open to allow tall-masted ships into Cockle Bay, which sits at the bottom of the horseshoe-shaped shore.

OFF THE BEATEN PATH

Sydney Fish Market. Second in size only to Tokyo's giant Tsukiji fish market, Sydney's is a showcase for the riches of Australia's seas. An easy 10-minute walk from Darling Harbour (and with its own stop on the Metro Light Rail network), the market is a great place to sample sushi, oysters, octopus, spicy Thai and Chinese fish dishes, and fish-and-chips at the waterfront cafés overlooking the fishing fleet. Guided tours of the auctions begin at 6:50 am and run until 8:30 am on Monday, Thursday, and Friday ($A20). They also offer cooking classes. Call ahead for advance reservations. ⌧ *Pyrmont Bridge Rd. at Bank St., Pyrmont West* ☎ *02/9004–1100* ⊕ *www.sydneyfishmarket.com.au* ☉ *7 am–4 pm.*

☼ **Sydney Wildlife World.** This new Sydney attraction brings 6,000 native Australian animals right to the heart of Sydney. Kangaroos, koalas, and dozens of other species come together under the one huge roof— in nine separate habitats—next door to the Sydney Aquarium. A huge wire-mesh dome covers Flight Canyon, an aviary where dozens of birds fly freely overhead as you stroll the 1-km (½-mi) walkway. You'll find koalas in Gum Tree Gully, and endangered bilbies, together with other nocturnal creatures, in the After Dark habitat. The latest exhibit is Kakadu Gorge Habitat, named after the lush park in the Northern Territory. It has red sandstone cliffs, a billabong (lagoon), waterfalls and the star attractons—Rex, a 5-meter (16.4 foot) saltwater crocodile. Each day you can watch a different animal being fed (including

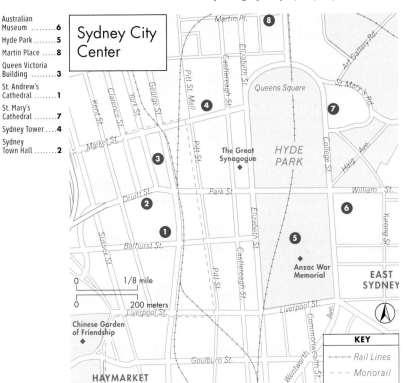

Sydney City Center

the snakes). A combined ticket with Sydney Aquarium costs A$50, or you can also combine this attraction with Sydney Tower for the same price. ✉ *Aquarium Pier, Wheat Rd., Darling Harbour* ☎ *02/9333–9288* ⊕ *www.sydneywildlifeworld.com.au* 🎫 *A$35* ⊙ *Daily 9–5.*

SYDNEY CITY CENTER

Shopping is the main reason to visit Sydney's city center, but there are several buildings and other places of interest among the office blocks, department stores, and shopping centers.

GETTING HERE AND AROUND

Buses from the eastern suburbs run along Elizabeth Street on the western side of Hyde Park; buses from the inner western suburbs such as Balmain travel to and from the Queen Victoria Building. The main train stations are Town Hall and Martin Place, while Hyde Park is served by both St. James and Museum Station on the City Circle rail line. The monorail has two stops in the city center. The free shuttle bus (No. 555) completes a circuit around the city center, stopping at the main attractions.

TOP ATTRACTIONS

☺ ★ **Australian Museum.** The strength of this natural-history museum, a well-respected academic institution, is its collection of plants, animals, geological specimens, and cultural artifacts from the Asia-Pacific region. Particularly notable are the collections of artifacts from Papua New Guinea and from Australia's Aboriginal peoples. One of the most popular exhibits is "Dinosaurs" on Level 2, containing 10 complete skeletons, 8 life-size models and interactive displays. There are behind-the-scene tours (A$110–A$130 per person), an excellent shop, and a lively café. ⊠ *6 College St., near William St., Hyde Park* ☎ *02/9320–6000* ⊕ *www.amonline.net.au* ⊠ *A$12* ☻ *Daily 9:30–5.*

Hyde Park. Declared public land by Governor Phillip in 1792 and used for the colony's earliest cricket matches and horse races, this area was turned into a park in 1810. The gardens are formal, with fountains, statuary, and tree-lined walks, and its tranquil lawns are popular with office workers at lunchtime.

Anzac Memorial. In the southern section of Hyde Park (near Liverpool Street) stands the 1934 art deco Anzac Memorial, a tribute to the Australians who died in military service during World War I, when the acronym ANZAC (Australian and New Zealand Army Corps) was coined. The 120,000 gold stars inside the dome represent each man and woman of New South Wales who served. The lower level exhibits war-related photographs. It's open daily 9–5. ☎ *02/9267–7668* ⊠ *Elizabeth, College, and Park Sts., Hyde Park.*

WORTH NOTING

NEED A BREAK?

Stop in at the Marble Bar to experience a masterpiece of Victorian extravagance. The 1890 bar was formerly in another building that was constructed on the profits of the horse-racing track, thus establishing the link between gambling and majestic public architecture that has its modern-day parallel in the Sydney Opera House. Threatened with demolition in the 1970s, the whole bar was moved—marble arches, color-glass ceiling, elaborately carved woodwork, paintings of voluptuous nudes, and all—to its present site. There is live music at night from Wednesday to Saturday. ⊠ *Hilton Sydney, 259 Pitt St., City Center* ☎ *02/9265–6026* ⊕ *www.marblebarsydney.com.au* ☻ *Closed Sun.*

Martin Place. Sydney's largest pedestrian precinct, flanked by banks, offices, and shopping centers, is the hub of the central business district. There are some grand buildings here—including the beautifully refurbished Commonwealth Bank and the 1870s Venetian Renaissance–style General Post Office building with its 230-foot clock tower (now a Westin hotel). Toward the George Street end of the plaza the simple 1929 cenotaph war memorial commemorates Australians who died in World War I. ⊠ *Between Macquarie and George Sts., City Center.*

Queen Victoria Building (QVB). Originally the city's produce market, this huge 1898 sandstone structure was handsomely restored with sweeping staircases, enormous stained-glass windows, and the 1-ton Royal Clock, which hangs from the glass roof. The clock chimes the hour from 9 am to 9 pm with four tableaux: the second shows Queen Eliza-beth I knighting Sir Frances Drake; the last ends with an executioner chopping off King Charles I's head. The complex includes more than 200 boutiques and restaurants including the lovely Tea Room on level 3. Boutiques on the upper floors are generally more upscale. ⊠ *455 George St., City Center* ☎ *02/9264–9209* ⊕ *www.qvb.com.au* ⊙ *Daily 8 am–6 pm; Thurs. 9 pm.*

St. Andrew's Cathedral. The foundation stone for Sydney's Gothic Revival Anglican cathedral—the country's oldest—was laid in 1819, although the original architect, Francis Greenway, fell from grace soon after work began. Edmund Blacket, Sydney's most illustrious church architect, was responsible for its final design and completion—a whopping 50 years later in 1868. Notable features of the sandstone construction include ornamental windows depicting Jesus's life and a great east window with images relating to St. Andrew. ⊠ *George and Bathurst Sts., next to Town Hall, City Center* ☎ *02/9265–1661* ⊙ *Mon.–Sat. 10–4, Sun. for services only 8:30 am, 10:30 am; Wed. healing service 6pm; tours by arrangement.*

St. Mary's Cathedral. The first St. Mary's was built here in 1821, but fire destroyed the chapel. Work on the present cathedral began in 1868. The spires weren't added until 2000, however. St. Mary's has some particularly fine stained-glass windows and a terrazzo floor in the crypt, where exhibitions are often held. The cathedral's large rose window was imported from England.

At the front of the cathedral stand statues of Cardinal Moran and Arch-bishop Kelly, two Irishmen who were prominent in Australia's Roman Catholic Church. Due to the high proportion of Irish men and women in the convict population, the Roman Catholic Church was often the voice of the oppressed in 19th-century Sydney, where anti-Catholic feel-ing ran high among the Protestant rulers. Call ahead to check for tours. ⊠ *College and Cathedral Sts., Hyde Park, City Center* ☎ *02/9220–0400* ⊑ *Tour free* ⊙ *Weekdays 6:30 am–6:30 pm, Sat. 8–7:30, Sun. 6:30 am–7:30 pm; tour Sun. at noon.*

Sydney Tower. Short of taking a scenic flight, a visit to the top of this 1,000-foot golden-turret-topped spike is the best way to see Sydney's spectacular layout. This is the city's tallest building, and the views from its indoor observation deck encompass the entire Sydney metropolitan area. You can often see as far as the Blue Mountains, more than 80 km (50 mi) away. You can view it all from Observation Deck 820 feet above the city streets, or for the real adrenaline don a saftety harness and do the Sky Walk, a guided walk around the outside of the golden turret some 880 feet above the city. Walkers are attached to the tower's superstructure by harness lines.

For those who work up an appetite, the building houses two restaurants in the turret. ⊠ *100 Market St., between Pitt and Castlereagh Sts., City Center* ☎ *02/9333–9222* ⊕ *www.sydneytower.com.au* ⊑ *Observation deck A$25, with SkyWalk A$65* ⊙ *Tower Daily 9 am–10:30 pm. Sky-walk daily 9:30 am–8:45 pm.*

The fountain in Hyde Park with the Australian Museum in the background.

Sydney Town Hall. Sydney's most ornate Victorian building—an elaborate sandstone structure—underwent a A$60 millon upgrade in 2009 to spruce up its grand interior spaces, especially the vestibule and large Centennial Hall. A centerpiece of the building is the massive 8,000-pipe Grand Organ, one of the world's most powerful, which is used for lunchtime concerts. Tours, conducted by the "Friends of Town Hall" for A$5, can be booked through the Web site. Mingle with locals on the marble steps of the front entrance. ⊠ *483 George St., City Center* ☏ *02/9265–9198 general inquiries* ⊕ *www.cityofsydney.nsw.gov.au* ✉ *Free* ⊙ *Weekdays 8:30–6.*

THE EASTERN SUBURBS

Sydney's inner city and eastern suburbs are truly the people's domain. They are the hip zones of Sydney featuring the foodie precincts as well as some of the most expensive real estate, great shopping, and the most accessible beaches. Architecture ranges from the mansions of the colonial aristocracy and the humble laborers' cottages of the same period to the modernized terrace houses of Paddington, one of Sydney's most charming and most desirable suburbs. A good way to explore the area is to take the Bondi and Bays Explorer bus that stops at 10 sites including Bondi Beach, Double Bay, Paddington, and Rose Bay.

GETTING HERE AND AROUND

The inner city and eastern suburbs are well served by buses, although the journey out to the eastern suburbs beaches can be quite long in peak hour. Most depart from Circular Quay (Alfred Street). Travel to Paddington and Bondi is on Nos. 380, 333, and 382; and to Watsons

Bay and Vaucluse (via Double Bay and Rose Bay) on Nos. 323, 324, and 325. Buses 380, 382 and 333 travel along Oxford Street, the main artery of the alternative (and gay) neighborhood of Darlinghurst. It is quicker to take the train to Edgecliff or Bondi Junction stations to connect with buses traveling to many of the eastern suburbs including Coogee and Clovelly. A ferry operates between Circular Quay and Watsons Bay, calling at Garden Island, Darling Point, Double Bay, and Rose Bay. It is an easy walk to Darlinghurst and Surry Hills from the city center, while Kings Cross has its own train station, just one stop from the city center.

TOP ATTRACTIONS

Elizabeth Bay. Much of this densely populated but still-charming harborside suburb was originally part of the extensive Elizabeth Bay House grounds. Wrought-iron balconies and French doors on some of the older apartment blocks give the area a Mediterranean flavor. During the 1920s and 1930s this was a fashionably bohemian quarter, and it remains a favorite among artists and writers.

Elizabeth Bay House. The Elizabeth Bay House was regarded in its heyday as the "finest house in the colony." This 1835–39 mansion retains little of its original furniture, although the rooms have been restored in Georgian style. The most striking feature is an oval-shaped salon with a winding staircase, naturally lighted by glass panels in the domed roof. The view from the front-facing windows across Elizabeth Bay is stunning. ⊠ *7 Onslow Ave., Elizabeth Bay* ☎ *02/9356–3022* ⊕ *www.hht.net.au* ☒ *A$8* ☯ *Fri.–Sun. 9:30–4; daily in January.*

★ **Sydney Jewish Museum.** Artifacts, interactive displays, and audiovisual displays chronicle the history of Australian Jews and commemorate the 6 million killed in the Holocaust. Exhibits are brilliantly arranged on eight levels, which lead upward in chronological order, from the handful of Jews who arrived with the First Fleet in 1788 to the 30,000 concentration-camp survivors who came after World War II—one of the largest populations of Holocaust survivors to be found anywhere. A 40-minute guided tour starts at noon on Monday, Wednesday, Friday, and Sunday. ⊠ *148 Darlinghurst Rd., Darlinghurst* ☎ *02/9360–7999* ⊕ *www.sydneyjewishmuseum.com.au* ☒ *A$10* ☯ *Sun.–Thurs. 10–4, Fri. 10–2.*

WORTH NOTING

Centennial Park. More than 500 acres of palm-lined avenues, groves of Moreton Bay figs, paperbark tree–fringed lakes, and cycling and horse-riding tracks make this a popular park and Sydney's favorite workout circuit. In the early 1800s the marshy land at the lower end provided Sydney with its fresh water. The park was proclaimed in 1888, the centenary of Australia's founding as a colony. The Centennial Park Café is often crowded on weekends, but a mobile canteen between the lakes in the middle of the park serves snacks and espresso. Bikes and blades can be rented from the nearby Clovelly Road outlets, on the eastern side of the park. The Moonlight Cinema screens movies during the summer months. ⊠ *Oxford St. at Centennial Ave., Centennial Park* ☎ *02/9339–6600* ⊕ *www.centennialparklands.com.au* ☯ *Daily dawn–dusk.*

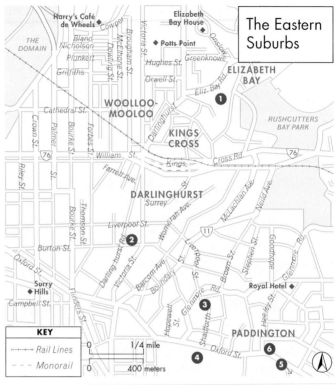

The Eastern
Suburbs

**OFF THE
BEATEN
PATH**

Harry's Café de Wheels. The attraction of this all-day dockyard food
stall is not so much the delectable meat pies and coffee served as the
clientele. Famous opera singers, actors, and international rock stars
have been spotted here rubbing shoulders with shift workers and taxi
drivers. This "pie cart" has been a Sydney institution since 1945, when
the late Harry "Tiger" Edwards set up his van to serve sailors from the
nearby Garden Island base. Drop in any time from 8:30 am (9 am on
weekends) until the wee hours for a Tiger Pie, made with mushy peas,
mashed potatoes, and gravy. ⊠ *1 Cowper Wharf Rd., Woolloomooloo*
☎ *02/9357–3074* ⊕ *www.harryscafedewheels.com.au.*

Paddington. Most of this suburb's elegant two-story terrace houses were
built during the 1880s, when the colony experienced a long period of
economic growth following the gold rushes that began in the 1860s.
The balconies are trimmed with decorative wrought iron, sometimes
known as Paddington lace, which initially came from England and later
from Australian foundries. Rebuilt and repainted, the now-stylish Paddington terrace houses give the area its characteristic village-like charm.
The Oxford Street shopping strip is full of upscale and funky boutiques,
cafés, and several good pubs.

Shadforth Street. Built at about the same time as Elizabeth Bay House, the tiny stone houses in this street were assembled to house the workers who built and serviced the Victoria Barracks, which are across the street.

NEED A
BREAK?

The Royal Hotel is an enjoyable Victorian pub with leather couches and stained-glass windows. It's a good place to stop for something cool to drink. The top floor has a balcony restaurant that's popular on sunny after-noons. ⊠ 237 Glenmore Rd., Paddington ☎ 02/9331–2604.

Victoria Barracks. If you're curious about the Australian military, you'll enjoy the free tours of this Regency-style barracks (built from 1841), which take place every Thursday at 10 am sharp. The tour includes entry to the Army Museum, which has exhibits covering Australia's military history from the days of the Rum Corps to the Malayan conflict of the 1950s. ⊠ *Oxford St. at Oatley Rd., Paddington* ☎ *02/8335–5330* ⊕ *www.army.gov.au/Army Museum of NSW/Victoria Barracks* ⊡ *Tours free, museum only A$2* ⊙ *Museum Thurs. 10–1, Sun. 10–4.*

GREATER SYDNEY

The Greater Sydney area has numerous attractions that can be easily reached by public transport. These include historic townships, the Sydney 2000 Olympics site, national parks where you can experience the Australian bush, and wildlife and theme parks that appeal to children.

Other points of interest are the northside beaches, particularly Manly, and the historic city of Parramatta, founded in 1788 and 26 km (16 mi) to the west; and the magnificent Hawkesbury River, which winds its way around the city's western and northern borders. The waterside suburb of Balmain has pubs and restaurants, an atmospheric Saturday flea market, and backstreets full of character.

GETTING HERE AND AROUND

Trains travel from Central Station to Parramatta daily, and directly to Sydney Olympic Park on weekdays. On weekends you take the train to Lidcombe and then change trains for the short ride to Olympic Park station. The RiverCat travels from Circular Quay to Parramatta, calling at Sydney Olympic Park on the way. Trains depart from Central Station for the Hawkesbury River (alight at Hawkesbury River station in the town of Brooklyn). They also travel to the Royal National Park (alight at Engadine or Heathcote stations, or Loftus, where a tram travels from the station to the park on Sundays only).

TIMING

Each of the sights here could easily fill the better part of a day. If you're short on time, try a tour company that combines visits within a particular area—for example, a day trip west to the Olympic Games site, Featherdale Wildlife Park, and the Blue Mountains.

TOP ATTRACTIONS

★ **Parramatta.** This bustling satellite city 26 km (16 mi) west of Sydney is one of Australia's most historic precincts. Its origins as a European settlement are purely agrarian. The sandy, rocky soil around Sydney Cove was too poor to feed the fledgling colony, so Governor Phillip

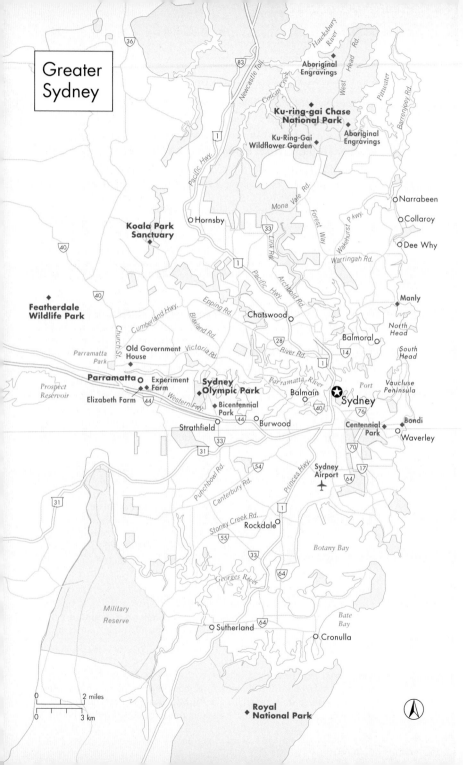

looked to the banks of the Parramatta River for the rich alluvial soil they needed. In 1789, just a year after the first convicts-cum-settlers arrived, Phillip established Rosehill, an area set aside for agriculture. The community developed as its agricultural successes grew, and several important buildings survive as outstanding examples of the period. The two-hour Harris Park Heritage Walk, which departs from the River-Cat Ferry Terminal, connects the key historic sites and buildings. The ferry departs at frequent intervals from Sydney's Circular Quay, and is a relaxing, scenic alternative to the drive or train ride from the city.

Experiment Farm. The site of the first private land grant in Australia, Experiment Farm was settled in 1789 by James Ruse, a former convict who was given 1½ acres by Governor Phillip on condition that he become self-sufficient—a vital experiment if the colony was to survive. Luckily for Phillip, his gamble paid off. The bungalow, with its wide verandas, was built by colonial surgeon John Harris in the 1830s; it contains a fine collection of Australian colonial furniture, and the cellar now houses an exhibition on the life and work of James Ruse. The surrounding ornamental garden is most beautiful in early summer, when the floral perfumes are strongest. ⊠ *9 Ruse St., Harris Park* ☎ *02/9635–5655* ⊕ *www.nsw.nationaltrust.com.au/placestovisit/ efc* ⊡ *A$7* ⊙ *Tues.–Fri. 10:30–3:30, weekends 11–3:30.*

Old Government House. On the bank of the Parramatta River, Old Government House is Australia's oldest surviving public building, and a notable work from the Georgian period. Built by governors John Hunter and Lachlan Macquarie, the building has been faithfully restored in keeping with its origins, and contains the nation's most significant collection of early Australian furniture. In the 260-acre parkland surrounding the house are Governor Brisbane's bathhouse and observatory and the Government House Dairy. ⊠ *Inside Parramatta Park, Parramatta* ☎ *02/9635–8149* ⊕ *www.nsw.nationaltrust.org.au* ⊡ *A$9; A$13 combined ticket with Experiment Farm* ⊙ *Tues.–Fri. 10–4.30, weekends 10:30–4.30*

Elizabeth Farm. The oldest European building in Australia, Elizabeth Farm was built by John and Elizabeth Macarthur in 1793. With its simple but elegant lines and long, shady verandas, the house became a template for Australian farmhouses that survives to the present day. It was here, too, that the merino sheep industry began, since the Macarthurs were the first to introduce the tough Spanish breed to Australia. Although John Macarthur has traditionally been credited as the father of Australia's wool industry, it was Elizabeth who largely ran the farm while her husband pursued his official and more lucrative unofficial duties as an officer in the colony's Rum Corps. Inside are personal objects of the Macarthur family, as well as a re-creation of their furnishings. ⊠ *70 Alice St., Rosehill* ☎ *02/9635–9488* ⊕ *www. hht.net.au/museums* ⊡ *A$8* ⊙ *Fri.–Sun. 9:30–4 or by group appointment weekdays*

★ **Royal National Park.** Established in 1879 on the coast south of Sydney, the Royal has the distinction of being the first national park in Australia and the second in the world, after Yellowstone National Park in the United States. Several walking tracks traverse the grounds, most of them

A bird's eye view of the boats in Parramatta River.

requiring little or no hiking experience. The Lady Carrington Walk, a 10-km (6-mi) trek, is a self-guided tour that crosses 15 creeks and passes several historic sites. Other tracks take you along the coast past beautiful wildflower displays and through patches of rain forest. You can canoe the Port Hacking River upstream from the Audley Causeway; rentals are available at the Audley boat shed on the river. The Illawarra train line stops at Loftus, Engadine, Heathcote, Waterfall, and Otford stations, where most of the park's walking tracks begin. There are three campsites in the park. *Box 44, Sutherland 1499 ✛ Royal National Park Visitor Centre, 35 km (22 mi) south of Sydney via Princes Hwy. to Farnell Ave., south of Loftus, or McKell Ave. at Waterfall ☎ 02/9542–0648, 02/9542–0666 National Parks and Wildlife Service district office, 02/9542–0683 Campsite reservations ⊕ www.nationalparks.nsw.gov.au ✍ A$11 per vehicle per day, overnight camping A$5–A$20; booking required ⊗ Daily 7 am–8:30 pm.*

WORTH NOTING

⟳ **Featherdale Wildlife Park.** This is the place to see kangaroos, dingoes, wallabies, and echidnas (and even feed some of them) in native bush settings 40 km (25 mi) west of Sydney. You can have your picture taken with a koala for free. The daily crocodile feeding sessions are very popular. Take the train to Blacktown station and then board the 725 bus for the park. ⊠ *217 Kildare Rd., Doonside ☎ 02/9622–1644 ⊕ www.featherdale.com.au ✍ A$25 ⊗ Daily 9–5.*

⟳ **Koala Park Sanctuary.** At this private park in Sydney's northern outskirts you can feed a kangaroo or cuddle a koala. (Koala presentations are daily at 10:20, 11:45, 2, and 3.) The sanctuary also has dingoes, wombats, emus, and wallaroos. There are sheep-shearing and boomerang-throwing demonstrations. ✉ *84 Castle Hill Rd., West Pennant Hills* ☎ *02/9484–3141* ⊕ *www.koalaparksanctuary.com.au* ☝ *A$22* ☼ *Daily 9–5.*

Ku-ring-gai Chase National Park. Nature hikes here lead past rock engravings and paintings by the Guringai Aboriginal tribe, the area's original inhabitants for whom the park is named. Created in the 1890s, the park mixes large stands of eucalyptus trees with moist, rain-forest-filled gullies where swamp wallabies, possums, goannas, and other creatures roam. The delightful trails are mostly easy or moderate, including the compelling 3-km (2-mi) Garigal Aboriginal Heritage Walk at West Head, which takes in ancient rock-art sites. From Mt. Ku-ring-gai train station you can walk the 3-km (2-mi) Ku-ring-gai Track to Appletree Bay, while the 30-minute, wheelchair-accessible Discovery Trail is an excellent introduction to the region's flora and fauna. Leaflets on all of the walks are available at the park's entry stations and from the Wildlife Shop at Bobbin Head.

The park is 24 km (15 mi) north of Sydney. Railway stations at Mt. Ku-ring-gai, Berowra, and Cowan, close to the park's western border, provide access to walking trails. On Sunday, for example, you can walk from Mt. Ku-ring-gai station to Appletree Bay and then to Bobbin Head, where a bus can take you to the Turramurra rail station. By car, take the Pacific Highway to Pymble. Then turn into Bobbin Head Road or continue on the highway to Mt. Colah and turn off into the park on Ku-ring-gai Chase Road. You can also follow the Pacific Highway to Pymble and then drive along the Mona Vale Road to Terry Hills and take the West Head turnoff.

For more information on the park, contact Ku-ring-gai Chase National Park Visitors Centre.

Basin. Camping in the park is permitted only at the Basin on Pittwater (near Palm Beach). Sites with access to barbecues and picnic tables must be booked in advance. The rate is A$14 per adult per night. Supplies can be purchased in Palm Beach. ☎ *02/9974–1011* 🗐 *Box 834, Hornsby 2077* ☎ *02/9472–8949* ⊕ *www.basincampground.com.au.*

NEED A BREAK? After visiting Old Government House, amble down to the bank of the river and pull up a seat in this shady spot, which was the park's former visitors' center. It's open for brunch and lunch daily with a menu of gourmet burgers, soup, pastas, and sweet treats. ✉ *Parramatta Park, Byrnes Ave, Parramatta* ☎ *02/9630–0144.*

Sydney Olympic Park. The center of the 2000 Olympic and Paralympic Games lies 14 km (8½ mi) west of the city center. Sprawling across 1,900 acres on the shores of Homebush Bay, the site is a series of majestic stadiums, arenas, and accommodation complexes. Among the park's sports facilities are an aquatic center, archery range, tennis center, and the centerpiece: the 85,000-seat ANZ Olympic Stadium. Since the conclusion of the 2000 Games it has been used for major sporting events like the 2003 Rugby World Cup and concerts for international acts including The Rolling Stone. The Explore interactive stadium tour, costing A$28.50 per person, takes you behind the scenes to sit in the media room and have your photo taken on the winners' dais. The new Gantry Tour (A$49) also includes a trip to the gantry (where the sound equipment and spotlights are kept, 140 feet above the stadium).

Don't miss the adjacent Bicentennial Park, made up of 247 acres of swamps, lakes, and parks dotted with picnic grounds and bike trials. The area, a former quarry, was developed to commemorate Australia's bicentennial celebrations in 1988. There's a visitor center outlining the history of the park, as well as a café (Lillies on the Park). The most scenic and relaxing way to get to Sydney Olympic Park is to take the RiverCat from Circular Quay to Homebush Bay. You can also take a train from Central Station, Sydney, to Olympic Park. ⊠ *1 Herb Elliot Ave., Homebush Bay* ☎ *02/9714–7888* ⊕ *www. sydneyolympicpark.com.au* ☉ *Daily during daylight hrs.*

> ### RUN FOR YOUR LIFE
>
> Pack your jogging shoes for the biggest footrace in the country. City to Surf (⊕ *city2surf. sunherald.com.au*) attracts more than 50,000 people each August— some taking it very seriously, others donning a gorilla suit or fairy outfit. The race starts at Hyde Park and winds through the eastern suburbs 14 km (9 mi) to Bondi Beach, via the notorious "Heartbreak Hill" at Rose Bay. For some reason, it never rains on the second Sunday in August.

BEACHES

Sydney is paradise for beach lovers. Within the metropolitan area there are more than 30 ocean beaches, all with golden sand and rolling surf, as well as several more around the harbor with calmer water for safe swimming. If your hotel is on the harbor's south side, the logical choice for a day at the beach is one of the southern ocean beaches between Bondi and Coogee. On the north side of the harbor, Manly is easily accessible by ferry, but beaches farther north involve a longer trip by car or public transportation.

Lifeguards are on duty at most of Sydney's ocean beaches during summer months, and flags indicate whether a beach is being patrolled. "Swim between the flags" is an adage that is drummed into every Australian child, with very good reason: the undertow can be very dangerous. If you get into difficulty, don't fight the current. Breathe evenly, stay calm, and raise one arm above your head to signal the lifeguards.

Although there's no shortage of sharks inside and outside the harbor, the risk of attack is very low. These species are not typically aggressive toward humans, and shark nets protect many Sydney beaches. A more common hazard is jellyfish, known locally as bluebottles, which inflict a painful sting—with a remote risk of more serious complications (including severe allergic reactions). The staff at most beaches will supply a spray-on remedy to help relieve the pain, which generally lasts about 24 hours. Many beaches will post warning signs when bluebottles are present, but you can also determine the situation yourself by looking for the telltale bright-blue, bubblelike jellies washed up along the waterline.

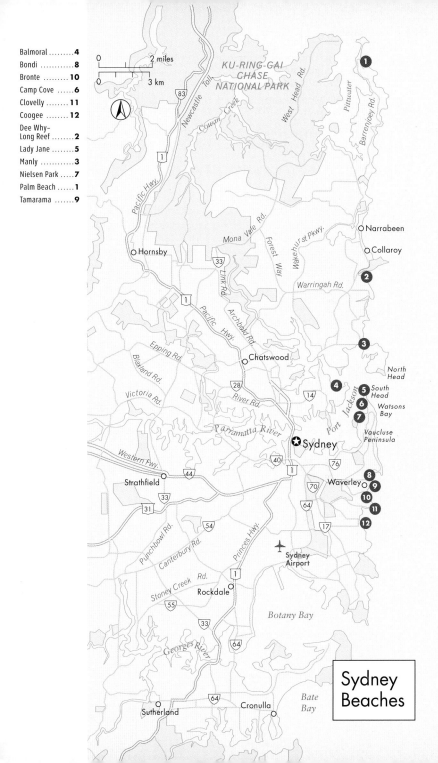

Sydney
Beaches

Topless sunbathing is common at many Sydney beaches, but full nudity is permitted only at a couple of locations, including Lady Jane Beach, close to Watsons Bay on the south side of the harbor.

Details of how to reach the beaches by bus, train, or ferry are provided below.

INSIDE THE HARBOR

★ **Balmoral.** This 800-yard-long, rarely crowded beach—among the best of the inner-harbor beaches—is in one of Sydney's most exclusive northern suburbs. There's no surf, but it's a great place to learn to windsurf (sailboard rentals are available). The Esplanade, which runs along the beachfront, has a handful of upscale restaurants, as well as several snack bars and cafés that serve award-winning fish-and-chips. In summer you can catch performances of Shakespeare on the Beach. You could easily combine a trip to Balmoral with a visit to Taronga Zoo. To reach Balmoral, take the ferry from Circular Quay to Taronga Zoo and then board Bus 238. ⊠ *Raglan St., Balmoral.*

Camp Cove. Just inside South Head, this crescent beach is where Sydney's fashionable people come to watch and be seen. The gentle slope and calm water make it a safe playground for children. A shop at the northern end of the beach sells salad rolls and fresh fruit juices. The grassy hill at the southern end of the beach has a plaque to commemorate the spot where Captain Arthur Phillip, the commander of the First Fleet, first set foot inside Port Jackson. Parking is limited; arrive by car after 10 on weekends, and keep in mind it's a long walk to the beach. Dive company Abyss (02/9588-9662) operates an easy dive off the beach here. Take Bus 324 or 325 from Circular Quay. ⊠ *Cliff St., Watsons Bay.*

Lady Jane. Lady Jane—officially called Lady Bay—is the most accessible of the nude beaches around Sydney. It's also a popular part of Sydney's gay scene. Only a couple of hundred yards long and backed by a stone wall, the beach has safe swimming with no surf. From Camp Cove, follow the path north and then descend the short, steep ladder leading down the cliff face to the beach. Take bus 234 or 25 from Circular Quay. ⊠ *Watsons Bay, Sydney.*

Nielsen Park. By Sydney standards, this beach at the end of the Vaucluse Peninsula is small, but behind the sand is a large, shady park that's ideal for picnics. The headlands at either end of the beach are especially popular for their magnificent views across the harbor. The beach is protected by a semicircular net, so don't be deterred by the beach's correct name, Shark Bay. The Beachhouse Cafe is open daily and sells drinks, snacks, and meals; there is also a more upscale restaurant open on weekends. Parking is often difficult on weekends. Historic Greycliffe House—built in 1840 and now used as National Park offices—is in the park, while the more elaborate and stately Vaucluse House is a 10-minute walk away. Take Bus 325 from Circular Quay. ⊠ *Greycliffe Ave. off Vaucluse Rd., Vaucluse.*

SOUTH OF THE HARBOR

Fodor'sChoice **Bondi.** Wide, wonderful Bondi (pronounced *bon*-dye) is the most famous
★ and most crowded of all Sydney beaches. It has something for just about everyone, and the droves that flock here on a sunny day give it a

Sydneysiders have more than 30 beaches to choose from.

bustling, carnival atmosphere unmatched by any other Sydney beach. Facilities include toilets, showers, and a kiosk on the beach that rents out sun lounges, beach umbrellas, and even swimsuits. Cafés, ice-cream outlets, restaurants, and boutiques line Campbell Parade, which runs behind the beach. Families tend to prefer the calmer waters of the northern end of the beach. Surfing is popular at the south end, where a path winds along the sea-sculpted cliffs to Tamarama and Bronte beaches. Take Bus 380, 382, or the new 333 all the way from Circular Quay, or take the train from the city to Bondi Junction and then board Bus 380, 381, 382, or 333. ⊠ *Campbell Parade, Bondi Beach.*

★ **Bronte.** If you want an ocean beach that's close to the city, has both sand and grassy areas, and offers a terrific setting, this one is hard to beat. A wooded park of palm trees and Norfolk Island pines surrounds Bronte. The park includes a playground and sheltered picnic tables, and excellent cafés are in the immediate area. The breakers can be fierce, but swimming is safe in the sea pool at the southern end of the beach. Take Bus 378 from Central Station, or take the train from the city to Bondi Junction and then board Bus 378. ⊠ *Bronte Rd., Bronte.*

★ **Clovelly.** Even on the roughest day it's safe to swim at the end of this long, keyhole-shaped inlet, which makes it a popular family beach. There are toilet facilities but no snack bars or shops in the immediate area. This is also a popular snorkeling spot that usually teems with tropical fish. Take Bus 339 from Argyle Street, Millers Point (the Rocks), or Wynyard bus station; Bus 341 from Central Station; or a train from the city to Bondi Junction, then board Bus 329. ⊠ *Clovelly Rd., Clovelly.*

🐚 **Coogee.** A reef protects this lively beach (pronounced *kuh*-jee), creating calmer swimming conditions than those found at its neighbors. A grassy headland overlooking the beach has an excellent children's playground. Cafés in the shopping precinct at the back of the beach sell ice cream, pizza, and the ingredients for picnics. Take Bus 373 and 374 from Circular Quay or Bus 372 from Central Station. ⊠ *Coogee Bay Rd., Coogee.*

★ **Tamarama.** This small, fashionable beach—aka "Glam-a-rama"—is one of Sydney's prettiest, but the rocky headlands that squeeze close to the sand on either side make it less than ideal for swimming. The sea is often hazardous here, and surfing is prohibited. A café in the small park behind the beach sells sandwiches, fresh juices, and fruit whips. Take the train from the city to Bondi Junction and then board Bus 360 or 361, or walk for 10 minutes along the cliff path from the south end of Bondi Beach. ⊠ *Tamarama Marine Dr., Tamarama.*

> ### CUTE COSSIES
>
> **The Big Swim.** Finding great bathing suits (or cossies, as they're called in Sydney) can be a dilemma. If you want a perfectly fitting cossie—and a matching sarong—that you'll wear for years, check out The Big Swim. This Bondi Beach favorite stocks women's cossies for all shapes and sizes. Check out the Australian brand, Jets, which has a huge selection of terrific designs. ⊠ *74 Campbell Parade, Bondi Beach* ☎ *02/9365–4457.*

NORTH OF THE HARBOR

Dee Why–Long Reef. Separated from Dee Why by a narrow channel, Long Reef Beach is remoter and much quieter than its southern neighbor. However, Dee Why has better surfing conditions, a big sea pool, and several good restaurants. To get here, take Bus 136 from Manly. ⊠ *The Strand, Dee Why.*

Fodor's Choice   **Manly.** The Bondi Beach of the north shore, Manly caters to everyone
★   except those who want to get away from it all. On sunny days Sydneysiders, school groups, and travelers from around the world crowd the 2-km-long (1.25-mi-long) sweep of white sand and take to the waves to swim and ride boards. The beach is well equipped with changing and toilet facilities and lockers. The promenade that runs between the Norfolk Island pines is great for people-watching and rollerblading. Cafés, souvenir shops, and ice-cream parlors line the nearby shopping area, the Corso. Manly also has several non-beach attractions, including Oceanworld, an aquarium about 200 yards from the ferry wharf. The ferry ride from the city makes a day at Manly feel more like a holiday than just an excursion to the beach. Take a ferry or Manly Fast Ferry from Circular Quay. From the dock at Manly the beach is a 10-minute walk. ⊠ *Steyne St., Manly.*

Palm Beach. The golden sands of Palm Beach glitter as much as the bejeweled residents of the stylish nearby village. The beach is on one side of the peninsula separating the large inlet of Pittwater from the Pacific Ocean. Bathers can easily cross from the ocean side to Pittwater's calm waters. You can take a circular ferry trip around this waterway from the wharf on the Pittwater side. The view from the lighthouse at the northern end of the beach is well worth the walk. Shops and cafés sell light snacks and meals. Take Bus 190 and L90 from Wynyard bus station. ⊠ *Ocean Rd., Palm Beach.*

WHERE TO EAT

Sydney's dining scene is as sunny and cosmopolitan as the city itself, and there are diverse and exotic culinary adventures to suit every appetite. Mod-Oz (modern-Australian) cooking flourishes, fueled by local produce and guided by Mediterranean and Asian techniques. Look for such innovations as tuna tartare with flying-fish roe and wasabi; emu prosciutto; five-spice duck; shiitake mushroom pie; and sweet turmeric barramundi curry. A meal at Tetsuya's, Bécasse, or Rockpool constitutes a crash course in this dazzling culinary language. A visit to the city's fish markets at Pyrmont, five minutes from the city center, will also tell you much about Sydney's diet. Look for rudderfish, barramundi, blue-eye, kingfish, John Dory, ocean perch, and parrot fish, as well as Yamba prawns, Balmain and Moreton Bay bugs (shovel-nose lobsters), sweet Sydney rock oysters, mud crab, spanner crab, yabbies (small freshwater crayfish), and marrons (freshwater lobsters).

There are many expensive and indulgent restaurants in the city center, but the real dining scene is in the inner city, eastern suburbs, and inner-western suburbs of Leichhardt and Balmain. Neighborhoods like Surry Hills, Darlinghurst, Paddington, and beachside suburb Bondi are dining destinations in themselves. Plus, you're more likely to find a restaurant that will serve on a Sunday night in one of these places than in the central business district (the city center)—which can become a bit of a ghost town after offices close during the week. Circular Quay and The Rocks are always lively, and the Overseas Passenger Terminal (on the opposite side of the harbor from the Opera House) has several top-notch restaurants with stellar views.

Use the coordinate (⊹ 1:B2) at the end of each listing to locate a site on the corresponding map.

SYDNEY HARBOUR AND THE ROCKS

$$
MODERN
AUSTRALIAN
✕**Altitude.** The lure of this decadent restaurant, perched high above Sydney Harbour on the 36th floor of the luxurious Shangri-La Hotel, is the view through the floor-to-ceiling windows, but the food is equally impressive. Chef Steve Krasicki presents an enticing menu of Mod-Oz dishes with a definite European influence. Seafood lovers will find ample selection among such dishes as ceviche of pink snapper and Hervey Bay scallops with pork belly. For a special occasion, gather a dozen friends to dine in the opulent, egg-shaped private dining room. On weekends the adjoining bar attracts a crowd that loves the thumping music, so it might be a good idea to beat it early or join in the fun. ⊠ *Shangri-La Hotel, 176 Cumberland St., The Rocks* ☎ *02/9250–6123* ⊕ *www.36levelsabove.com* ⌂ *Reservations essential* ☉ *Closed Sun. No lunch Mon.–Sat.* ⊹ *1:B2.*

Surf Lifesaving Clubs

In 2007 the Australian Surf Lifesaving Association celebrated its 100-year anniversary. The world's first Surf Lifesaving club was formed at Bondi Beach on February 21, 1907. Other clubs formed in quick secession, and today there are more than 300 clubs in Australia, with 36 in Sydney and 129 in New South Wales.

In the last century more than 500,000 swimmers have been rescued from patrolled beaches around the country, and more than 1 million swimmers have received first aid.

Lifesavers are Australian icons; volunteers undertake their five-hour beach patrols on a rostered basis during the summer season from September to April. In addition to the thousands of volunteers across Australia, there are also permanent, paid lifeguards who are employed by the local councils and are on duty year-round.

Lifesavers arrive at the beach bright and early, check the beach conditions, erect the red and yellow flags to indicate the safe swimming areas, and keep an eye on swimmers throughout their patrol. It's easy to spot a surf lifesaver—he or she wears the bright red-and-yellow cap and matching red-and-yellow uniform.

Bondi Beach lifesavers are the busiest in Australia. Each year about 2.5 million people come for a swim: some 2,500 rescues take place in an average year. The worst day in Bondi's history was February 6, 1938, known as Black Sunday. Lifesavers plucked 300 people from the huge surf. Five lives were lost.

It's not all work for Surf Lifesaving clubs. They hold competitions and surf carnivals throughout the summer months at numerous beaches. Events include surf swims, crew boat races (man-powered by oarsmen), surf ski races, and the macho-named "iron man" races where men (and women in separate events) perform all manner of endurance tests. Surf Lifesaving clubs opened their doors to women and children several decades ago.

$$$
AUSTRALIAN
★

✕ **Aria.** With windows overlooking the Opera House and Harbour Bridge, Aria could easily rest on the laurels of its location. Instead, chef Matthew Moran creates a menu of extraordinary dishes that may be your best meal in the antipodes—and a steep bill to show for it. Make a reservation before you even get on the plane and look forward to the Peking Duck consomme with duck dumplings, shaved abalone, and mushrooms. Whether you dine à la carte, sample the seasonal tasting menu, or order the pretheater menu, don't skip taking a look at the dessert list—the passion-fruit soufflé with white chocolate ripple ice cream is well worth the 20-minute wait. ⊠ *1 Macquarie St., East Circular Quay* ☎ *02/9252–2555* ⊕ *www.ariarestaurant.com* ⊗ *No lunch weekends* ✢ *1:C1.*

$
AUSTRALIAN

✕ **Bathers' Pavilion Cafe.** Balmoral Beach is blessed. Not only does it have an inviting sandy beach and great water views, but it also has one of the best eating strips north of Harbour Bridge. Queen of the strip is Bathers' Pavilion, which includes a restaurant, café, and lavish private dining room. Serge Dansereau cooks with one hand on the seasons and the other on the best local ingredients at the acclaimed restaurant, but for a casual breakfast, lunch, afternoon tea, or dinner it's hard to beat the café (¢). There's a choice of salad, wood-fired pizzas, and seafood dishes such as seared ocean trout fingers with fennel, orange segments, and white beans for around A$27.50. Breakfast dishes are a little on the expensive side, with most around A$21. No reservations taken for the café. ⊠ *4 the Esplanade, Balmoral* ☏ *02/9969–5050* ⊕ *www. batherspavilion.com.au* ⌲ *Reservations essential* ✛ *2:C1.*

$ ✕ **The Deck.** If you've wanted to know just what's inside that giant face
MODERN on the north side of the harbour under the bridge, well this is your
AUSTRALIAN chance. The Deck is located in a swanky refurbished space just as you step through the giant mouth of Luna Park, Sydney's long-established fun park. The stunning view, however, across the harbour with the Opera House right in your sights, is the real draw. The restaurant and cocktail bar are above a live venue that cranks up on the weekend, so expect a fun night out rather than a quiet tête-à-tête. There's a selection of seafood and non-seafood tasting plates to share, while wonderful classics such as paella and bouillabaisse are on the menu. Sweet treats include rich Belgian chocolate terrine and pistachio filo wafers with fresh strawberries, honey cream, and berry coulis. ⊠ *Luna Park, 1 Olympic Dr., Milsons Point* ☏ *02/9033–7670* ⊕ *www.thedecksydney. com.au* ✛ *2:A2.*

$$ ✕ **Galileo.** This gracious, salon-style restaurant within the Observatory
JAPANESE Hotel at the Rocks will have you thinking you've been transported to Paris, as will the French menu created by new executive chef Masahiko Yomonda. À la carte selections include champagne- and beer-brasied pork ribs, ginko nuts, chestnuts, and chicken jus. The chocolate souf- flé and lychee oolong milk ice cream uses produce from the famous French chocolatier, Valrhona. There are several degustation menus to choose from: the 8-course is $118, with matching wines an extra $80. Menus are good value from Tuesday to Thursday, when three courses from the à la carte menu cost $60. ⊠ *89–113 Kent St., City Center* ☏ *02/8248–5252* ☉ *No lunch* ✛ *1:B2.*

$$$ ✕ **Guillaume at Bennelong.** Chef Guillaume Brahimi rattles the pans at
AUSTRALIAN possibly the most superbly situated dining room in town. Tucked into the side of the Opera House, the restaurant affords views of Sydney Harbour Bridge and the city lights. Brahimi's creations soar: try the marron on a bed of seared foie gras, duck confit, and smoked duck consomme, and continue perhaps with the slowly cooked blue-eye trevalla with a lemon emulsion and Sterling caviar. Better yet, work your way through the eight-course degustation menu (A$180). ⊠ *Bennelong Point, Circular Quay* ☏ *02/9241–1999* ⊕ *www.guillaumeatbennelong.com.au/* ⌲ *Reservations essential* ☉ *Closed Sun. No lunch Sat.–Wed.* ✛ *1:C1.*

$$ ✕ **Longrain.** Fans of this popular Thai restaurant are loving its new look.
ASIAN The cocktail bar has moved to a new basement level (complete with a new canteen called Shortgrain and an Asian grocery store), leaving more room upstairs for new separate tables for six (groups of six must book to secure one), along with the traditional communal table. The generous-size mains are meant to be shared. Begin with a simple starter of either betel-nut leaf with prawn-toasted coconut or a freshly shucked

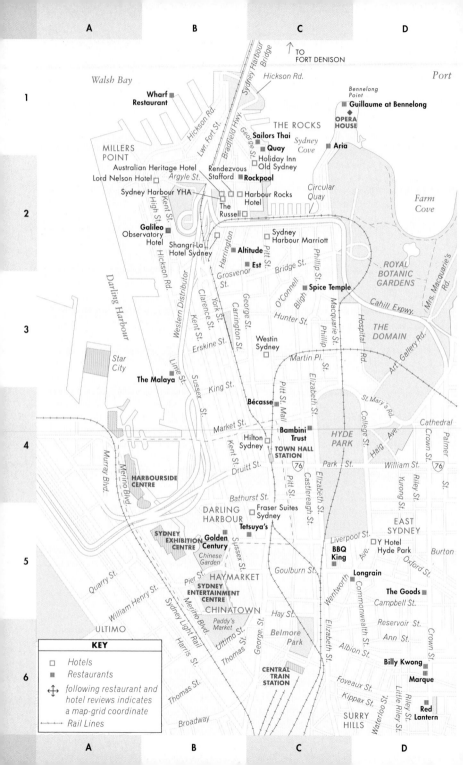

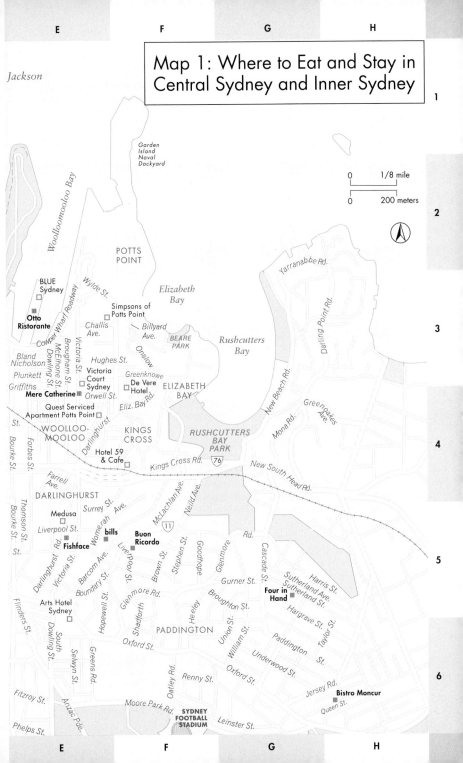

Map 1: Where to Eat and Stay in Central Sydney and Inner Sydney

E   F   G   H

Jackson

Garden
Island
Naval
Dockyard

0   1/8 mile
0   200 meters

POTTS
POINT

Yarranabbe Rd.

Woolloomooloo Bay

BLUE
Sydney

Wylde St.

Elizabeth
Bay

Darling Point Rd.

Otto
Ristorante

Cowper Wharf Roadway

Simpsons of
Potts Point

Brougham St.

McElhone St.

Dowling St.

Victoria St.

Challis
Ave.

Billyard
Ave.

BEARE
PARK

Rushcutters
Bay

Bland
Nicholson

Hughes St.

Onslow

Greengates
Ave.

Plunkett

Victoria
Court
Sydney

Greenknowe

De Vere
Hotel

ELIZABETH
BAY

New Beach Rd.

Griffiths

Mere Catherine

Orwell St.

Eliz. Bay Rd.

Mona Rd.

Quest Serviced
Apartment Potts Point

Eliz. Bay Rd.

St.

Bourke St.

Forbes St.

WOOLLOO-
MOOLOO

Darlinghurst

KINGS
CROSS

RUSHCUTTERS
BAY
PARK

New South Head Rd.

Hotel 59
& Cafe

Kings Cross Rd.   76

Farrell
Ave.

DARLINGHURST

Surrey St.

Womerah Ave.

McLachlan Ave.

Nerid Ave.

Thomson St.

Medusa

Liverpool St.

11

Bourke St.

Fishface

bills

Buon
Ricordo

Brown St.

Stephen St.

Goodhope

Rd.

Cascade St.

Harris St.

Sutherland Ave.

St.

Darlinghurst

Victoria St.

Barcom Ave.

Liverpool St.

Glenmore Rd.

Gurner St.

Four in
Hand

Sutherland St.

Flinders St.

Arts Hotel
Sydney

Boundary St.

Hopewell St.

Shadforth

Heeley

Broughton St.

Union St.

William St.

Paddington

Hargrave St.

Taylor St.

South
Dowling St.

Selwyn St.

Greens Rd.

PADDINGTON

Oxford St.

Oxford St.

Underwood St.

Fitzroy St.

Anzac Pde.

Oatley Rd.

Renny St.

Moore Park Rd.

SYDNEY
FOOTBALL
STADIUM

Leinster St.

Jersey Rd.

Bistro Moncur

Queen St.

Phelps St.

E   F   G   H

1
2
3
4
5
6

oyster with red chili and coriander. The standout main dish is the pricey (A$41) kingfish curry with baby corn and eggplant, while eggnets—lacy omelets filled with prawns, pork, peanuts, and beansprouts—are also a popular choice. Longrain's cocktails are legendary for their lethalness; try the ping pong, a luscious mix of passion-fruit, lychee, and vodka. ⊠ *85 Commonwealth St., Surry Hills* ☎ *92/9280–2888* ⊕ *www. longrain.com* ⌕ *Reservations not accepted* ✛ *1:C5.*

$$$$
MODERN
AUSTRALIAN
★

✕ **Quay.** In his take on Mod-Oz cuisine, chef Peter Gilmore masterfully crafts a four-course à la carte menu including such dishes as mud crab congee with Chinese-inspired split rice porridge; quail breasts with eschallots and truffle-infused milk custard; and 24-hour slow-cooked suckling pig ($155). Desserts are sublime—Gilmore's "snow egg," which changes with the seasons and can include white nectarine, apple, and jackfruit, had fans lining up to try it just hours after it stole the show on Australia's Masterchef. Glass walls afford wonderful views of the bridge and Opera House. The restaurant has moved up toward the top of the S. Pellegrino World's 50 Best Restaurants list; it came in at 26 in 2011, making it the highest-rated Australian restaurant in the world. ⊠ *Upper Level, Overseas Passenger Terminal, West Circular Quay, The Rocks* ☎ *02/9251–5600* ⊕ *www.quay.com.au* ⌕ *Reservations essential* ⊙ *No lunch Sat.–Mon.* ✛ *1:C1.*

$
VIETNAMESE

✕ **Red Lantern.** Owned by Vietnamese TV chef Luke Nguyen, this little restaurant with bright red walls and lanterns is popular with his legions of TV fans. Diners should always start with the country's great export, rice paper rolls. Here you can have them filled with roast duck, enoki mushrooms and herbs, or prawns and pork. A recommended main is the ultratasty *go chien don*—crispy-skinned chicken slowly poached in master stock with ginger, shallot, and oyster sauce. An unusual but yummy dessert is the black-sesame-seed dumplings with black-seasame-seed ice cream. For the full range of flavors, there's a tasting menu of nine dishes for A$60 per person (desserts an extra A$10). ⊠ *545 Crown St., Surry Hills* ☎ *02/9698–4355* ✛ *1:D6.*

$$$$
MODERN
AUSTRALIAN
Fodor's Choice
★

✕ **Rockpool.** A meal at Rockpool is a crash course in what Mod-Oz cooking is all about, conducted in a glamorous, long dining room with a catwalk-like ramp. The iconic Rocks restaurant celebrated 22 years in 2011. Chefs Neil Perry and Phil Wood weave Thai, Chinese, Mediterranean, and Middle Eastern influences into their repertoire with effortless flair and originality. The seasonal four-course menu (A$145) constantly dazzles and may feature Muscovy duck pastrami with mustard bread, duck egg *en cocotte* and sea-urchin butter, and the lotus-leaf wrapped burrong chicken with Szechuan dauphine, tempura, broccolini, and black garlic. Don't miss the date tart for dessert, which has graced the menu for 20 years; or hang on for 20 minutes as they prepare the passion-fruit soufflé with passion-fruit ice cream. ⊠ *107 George St., The Rocks* ☎ *02/9252–1888* ⊕ *www.rockpool.com* ⌕ *Reservations essential* ⊙ *Closed Sun. and Mon. No lunch Sat.* ✛ *1:B2.*

$
THAI

✕ **Sailors Thai.** Aussies love their Thai food, and this stylish restaurant has been delivering some of the best in the city for 16 years. In a charming mid-19th-century sandstone building in The Rocks, there's a dining room on the lower level and a casual canteen on the top. Start with the

2

crisp-skinned salmon and peanut salad with chili and lime dressing to get the tastebuds into gear, and then move on to whatever duck curry is on the menu that day—they're all good. The delicious candied coconut dumplings dessert takes 20 minutes but it's easy to while the time away with a spot of people-watching. You won't be disappointed in either. ☒ *Lower level, 106 George St., The Rocks* ☏ *02/9251–2466* ⊕ *www.sailorstahi.com* ✛ *1:C1.*

$
MODERN
AUSTRALIAN

✕ **Wharf Restaurant.** At one time only the Wharf's proximity to the Sydney Theatre Company (they share Pier 4) attracted diners, but with the restaurant now in the hands of two of Sydney's legendary chefs, Aaron Ross and Tim Pak Poy, the emphasis is firmly on the food. Fish dominates the menu, befitting the restaurant's name and locale, and there is a theme of Japanese-Western fusion in the flavoring, with the salt-and-pepper squid, for example, served with cucumber, mint, and red-pepper relish. You can see Sydney Harbour Bridge from some tables, but it's North Sydney and the ferries that provide the real show. Meal times and sizes are flexible to accommodate theatergoers. ☒ *End of Pier 4, Hickson Rd., Sydney Harbor* ☏ *02/9250–1761* ⊕ *www.thewharfrestaurant. com.au* ⌀ *Reservations essential* ☾ *Closed Sun.* ✛ *1:B1.*

DARLING HARBOUR AND CITY CENTER

$
CHINESE

✕ **BBQ King.** You can find better basic Chinese food elsewhere in town, but for duck and pork, barbecue-loving Sydneysiders know that this is the place to come. The poultry hanging in the window are the only decor at this small Chinatown staple, where the food is so fresh you can almost hear it clucking. Barbecued pork is the other featured dish, and the suckling pig is especially delicious. It's open until late at night, when the average customers are large groups of mates sprawled at the Formica tables feeding their drunken munchies, or Chinatown chefs kicking back after a day in the kitchen. The service can be a little brusque, but it's all part of the low-budget charm. ☒ *18–20 Goulburn St., Haymarket* ☏ *02/9267–2586* ✛ *1:C5.*

$
CHINESE
★

✕ **Golden Century.** For two hours—or as long as it takes for you to consume delicately steamed prawns, luscious mud crab with ginger and shallots, and *pipis* (triangular clams) with black-bean sauce—you might as well be in Hong Kong. This place is heaven for seafood lovers, with wall-to-wall fish tanks filled with crab, lobster, abalone, and schools of barramundi, parrot fish, and coral trout. You won't have to ask if the food is fresh: most of it is swimming around you as you eat. Come for the big-ticket seafood or a simple meal of deep-fried duck. Supper is served until 4 am, so it's popular with late-night revelers. ☒ *393–399 Sussex St., Haymarket* ☏ *02/9212–3901* ⊕ *www.goldencentury.com.au* ✛ *1:B5.*

$
MALAYSIAN
★

✕ **The Malaya.** The cocktails (all A$16.50) are legendary, the view is captivating, and the food, a traditional Chinese/Malay fusion, is extraordinary. After 48 years in the business, in different venues around Sydney, this modern Asian restaurant still does a roaring trade. Signature dishes include beef Rendang (Indonesian-style beef curry), and marinated, sticky-sweet, and crunchy Szechuan eggplant that's so good it may just be the food of the gods. Try one of the four set menus (for a minimum of three people and A$48 per person) for a true feast on the extensive menu's flavor combinations. ☒ *39 Lime St., King Street Wharf, Darling Harbour* ☏ *02/9279–1170* ⊕ *www.themalaya.com.au* ✛ *1:B3.*

Continued on page 112

MOD OZ

Australia's Modern Cuisine

By Erica Watson

It may be referred to as the land down under, but the culinary movement that's sweeping Australia means this country has come out on top. Modern Australian cuisine has transformed the land of Vegemite sandwiches and shrimp-on-the-barbie into a culinary Promised Land with unique flavors, organic produce, and bountiful seafood, fashioned by chefs who remain unburdened by restrictive traditions.

Australia is fast proving to be one of the most exciting destinations in the world for food lovers. With its stunning natural bounty, multicultural inspirations, and young culinary innovators, it ticks off all the requisite foodie boxes.

In Sydney, chefs are dishing up new twists on various traditions, creating a Modern Australian (Mod Oz) cuisine with its own compelling style. Traditional bush tucker, for example, has been transformed from a means of survival into a gourmet experience. Spicy Asian flavors have been borrowed from the country's neighbors to the north, and homage has been paid to the precision and customs brought by Australia's early European settlers.

The diversity of the modern Australian culinary movement also means that it is more than just flavors: it's an experience. And one that can be obtained from the award-winning luxury restaurant down to the small Thai-style canteens, pubs, and outdoor cafés.

While purists might argue that Mod Oz cuisine is little more than a plagiarism of flavors and cultures, others will acknowledge it as unadulterated fare with a fascinating history of its very own. Either way, it still offers a dining experience that's unique from anywhere else in the world.

MENU DECODER

Barbie: barbeque | Snags: sausages | Chook: chicken | Vegemite: salty yeast spread | Lamington: small chocolate sponge cake with coconut | Pavlova: meringue dessert filled with cream and fruit | Floater: meat pie with mushy peas and gravy | Damper: simple bread cooked on a campfire | Sanga: sandwich | Cuppa: cup of tea | Tucker: food | Chips: French fries | Tomato sauce: ketchup | Muddy: mud crab | Prawn: shrimp

Seared tuna with avocado, cilantro, and black sesame seeds, topped with caviar

BUSH TUCKER

Bush Tucker food; Tropical rainforest fruits on paper bark

BACK THEN

Native Australian plants and animals have played a vital role in the diets of the Aboriginal people for more than 50,000 years. Generally referred to as bush tucker, these native fruits, nuts, seeds, vegetables, meats, and fish are harvested around the country—from arid deserts to coastal areas and tropical rainforests.

Once little more than a means of survival, today they're touted as gourmet ingredients. And you certainly don't need to go "walkabout" to find them.

RIGHT NOW

Bush tucker has undergone much transformation over the decades, experiencing a renaissance in recent years. Heavily influenced by multicultural cooking techniques, game meats such as emu and wallaby have been elevated from bush-stew ingredients to perfectly seared cuts of meat garnished with seasonal herbs and vegetables. Kangaroo is making its way into stir-fries

and curries, while crocodile—once cooked over coals on the campfire—is now served as carpaccio, tempura, or curry, among the many preparations. Seafood, like rock lobster and barramundi can be found in humble fish-and-chips shops and top-notch eateries.

Of course, bush tucker isn't just about the protein. Native spices, wild fruits, and indigenous nuts have found favor in countless culinary applications. Lemon myrtle leaves lend a lemony flavor to baked goods and savory dishes. Alpine pepper, a crushed herb, gives foods a fiery zing. Quandong is a wild plum-like fruit with subtle apricot flavor. It once was dried as a portable energy source but now is made into jams and pie fillings. Kakadu plums are made into "super" juices with enormous vitamin C content. Bush tomatoes also have become popular in jams and sauces, and are available in supermarkets. Native nuts include bunya bunya, which is chestnut-like with pine notes, the shells of which are

Witchitty grub

Tandoori kangaroo

INDIGENOUS MEATS

CAMEL: With some one million camels in Australia, camel is fast being served up on many menus, though most are in the Northern Territory. The meat is often compared to mutton and has a similar taste and texture to beef.

CROCODILE: The meat may be fish-like in texture and appearance, but it tastes similar to chicken. The most popular cut is the tail, however legs and meat from the body are also consumed. Crocodile is growing in popularity because of its delicate flavor and versatility. It is often fried and grilled, but may be served raw in carpaccio or sushi rolls.

EMU: Although it's fowl, emu meat is similar in texture and flavor to beef with a light flavor and slight gamey tones on the palate. The meat is high in iron and very low in fat and cholesterol. Typical cuts include rump, strip loin, and oyster filet. It may be served pan-seared or lightly grilled.

KANGAROO: A dark red meat, it is extremely lean with only about 2% fat. The filet or rump is best eaten rare to medium rare, and is typically seared, barbecured, or stir-fried. Young kangaroo meat tastes like beef, while aged cuts take on a gamier flavor.

WALLABY: A cousin to the kangaroo, this meat has a somewhat milder flavor. It is a rich burgundy color and is best prepared with simple, delicate cooking styles, such as barbecuing or pan frying.

WITCHETTY GRUB: The larvae of ghost moths, these grubs are eaten raw or barbecued. People describe the taste as similar to egg, with the texture of a prawn.

used for smoking meat. Macadamia nuts, meanwhile, are among the country's biggest exports.

Despite the presence of numerous bush ingredients in Sydney restaurants, the modern bush tucker dining experience is more prominent in the northern parts of the country with Queensland and Northern Territory being leaders in the culinary movement.

You are most likely to find dishes such as kangaroo, and occasionally crocodile, on the menu of restaurants in the city's main tourist precincts of The Rocks and Circular Quay. The Australian Heritage Hotel (⊕ www.australianheritagehotel.com) has saltwater crocodile pizza and a kangaroo pizza on the menu, and very occasionally offers an emu pizza. Wolfie's Grill (⊕ www.wolfiesgrill.com.au), one of several large function-style tourist restaurants at Campbell's Cove in the Rocks, features kangaroo steak and crocodile tail medallions on the menu from time to time.

Simple meal of grilled camel with vegetables

UPDATED EUROPEAN FARE

Cuisine at Sean's Panaroma

BACK THEN

Although the foundation of Mod Oz cuisine stems from the arrival of early British settlers, the food scene has certainly steamed ahead since the days of boiled beef and damper.

The real progression of modern Australian food came after World War II when European immigrants brought a new wave of cooking to the country. It was the French and Italians who really opened the eyes of Australians with their distinguished flavors, commitment to freshness, and masterful culinary techniques. They also laid the foundations for some of the finest vineyards and cheese makers in the country.

RIGHT NOW

Though small, there are still degrees of British influence in modern Australian cooking, albeit slightly updated. The quintessential English meat pie is now filled with ingredients such as Murray cod, lamb, bush tomato, and kangaroo. Traditional Sunday roasts and fish-and-chips spring up in pubs and cafes, but often with a twist. And tea is still a staple on the breakfast table with a true Aussie favorite, Vegemite on toast.

Poaching, roasting, and braising are now popular methods to cook everything from reef fish and yabbies to lamb, suckling pig, and rabbit. Omelettes, cassoulets, and soufflés as well as pasta, risotto, and gnocchi are very well suited to the country's prize-winning meats, vegetables, and seafood. And the rigorous use of garlic, saffron, basil, and tarragon is common in many kitchens.

Greeks, Germans, and Spaniards have also greatly influenced dining, especially in Sydney with tapas bars, tavernas, and schnitzel houses well represented throughout the country. Middle Eastern and North African flavors are also beginning to leave their marks.

Even casual pubs are updating dishes to reflect ethnic influences

Aussie meat pie

AUSTRALIA'S NATURAL BOUNTY

CHEESE FRUIT: Grown in tropical areas, it's high in vitamin C and has long been used for medicinal purposes. The fruit is eaten while still green since it has a distinct rotting cheese smell when ripe. Leaves can also be eaten raw or cooked.

ILLAWARRA PLUMS: Usually used in jams and chutneys or as a rich sauce to accompany kangaroo, venison, or emu. High in antioxidants, they have a subtle plum flavor with a hint of pine.

LEMON MYRTLE: A native tree with a citrus fragrance and flavor. Leaves can be used fresh or dried and ground in sweet and savory styles of cooking.

MACADAMIA NUTS: Known as Kindal Kindal by native Australians, the macadamia is a round white nut with a hard brown shell and creamy flavor.

MUNTRIES: Small berry-like fruit that have a distinct apple flavor. Also known as emu apples, they can be eaten fresh in salads or added to desserts.

PAPER BARK: Papery leaves from the Mellaluca tree, used to cook meat and seafood.

QUANDONG: A bright red fruit similar to a native peach. It's commonly used to make jams and sauces.

WARRIGAL GREENS: A herb-like vegetable with a flavor similar to spinach. They must be well cooked to eliminate their toxic oxalate content.

WATTLESEED: Also known as acacia seeds. They have a nutty to coffee-like flavor and are very high in protein. Often ground down and used in baking.

and local products. It's not unusual to see menu items like spicy chorizo pizza and Peking Duck pizza featured at The Australian Heritage Hotel, a popular pub in the Rocks area.

Another hallmark of Mod Oz cuisine—and one that parallels America's current culinary trends—is its fascination with seasonal vegetables and organic meats. Specialist farms raising free-range poultry and livestock have become extremely popular with many restaurants throughout Sydney. Menus often cite an ingredient's producer, i.e. "Blackmore's wagyu bresaola," and also note whether ingredients are "pasture-raised" or "locally grown."

Taking the trend one step further is Bondi Beach establishment Sean's Panaroma (⊕ www.seanspanorama.com.au). There, owner Sean Moran grows produce for the restaurant on his Blue Mountains farm, which is harvested, prepared, and served to guests the same day. In terms of freshness, it really doesn't get much better than that.

Meringue topped with fresh fruit

ASIAN FUSION

Thai-style kangaroo curry

BACK THEN

Much has changed in the way of Asian food in Australia. Sixty years ago sushi didn't exist in the vocabulary, now there are Japanese restaurants on almost every street.

The Gold Rush of the mid-19th century brought an influx of Chinese immigrants to Australia, prompting Asian cuisine's humble beginnings here. Thai, Vietnamese, Indian, Malaysian, and Japanese migrants followed in various waves in the 20th century. Before long, a cuisine that had started out in family-run restaurants in the outer suburbs of Sydney had become a burgeoning new trend. And by the late 1990s the children of the first wave of immigrants had formed the new guard.

RIGHT NOW

Traditional Chinese, Thai, and Japanese restaurants are very popular in Australia. But Asian fusion restaurants are leading the charge in creating Australia-specific taste innovations. Asian fusion cuisine combines the traditional flavors of Thai, Chinese, Japanese, and Vietnamese cooking, using local Australian ingredients and western culinary techniques. Chic contemporary interiors, often with long communal tables and shared dishes are the latest trend. Robust herbs such as mint and coriander, fiery chili, zesty black vinegar, ginger, and pickled vegetables are core ingredients, often wok-fried with fresh Australian ingredients such as Barossa Valley chicken, Thirlmere duck, or Bangalow pork.

Leading the charge is world-renowned chef Tetsuya Wakuda of Tetsuya's Restaurat, in Sydney. His signature dish, a confit of Petuna Tasmanian Ocean Trout with konbu, apple, daikon, and wasabi is a prime example of Asian fusion, uniquely blending French techniques with his Japanese heritage and excellent Australian products.

Yet, smaller modern canteen-style eateries are also serving up contemporary Asian fare that pro-

Red chile peppers

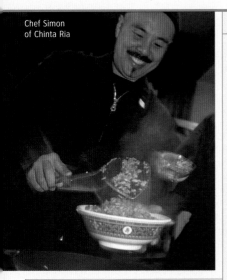
Chef Simon
of Chinta Ria

LOCAL FISH AND SEAFOOD

ABALONE: A large sea snail with an edible muscular foot. It has a firm, rubbery texture with a very delicate flavor and can retail for about $100 per kilogram. Abalone are often seared or fried.

BALMAIN OR MORETON BAY BUGS: A smaller relative of the rock lobster with a short tail, flat head, and bug-like eyes. They have a sweet taste and a medium texture. A favorite served cold in salads and seafood platters, or split down the middle and grilled.

BARRAMUNDI: A member of the perch family, it's a highly versatile fish with a medium to firm flesh and white to light pink tones. Native to Australia, it lives in both fresh and salt waters and is farmed as well as caught in the wild.

ROCK LOBSTERS: A spiny lobster with long antennae and no claws. The four main types—eastern, southern, western, and tropical—each offer slightly different flavours and textures. The tropical are excellent as sashimi, while the eastern, southern and western lend themselves to baking and barbecue.

SYDNEY ROCK OYSTERS: Despite their name, these bivalves are commonly found throughout the east coast. They're prized for their distinct rich and creamy flavor, and are smaller in size than Pacific oysters. Try eating them raw with a squirt of lemon.

YABBIES: A fresh-water crayfish with firm white flesh and a sweeter taste than rock lobster. Small in size, they can be tricky to eat but are worth the effort. They're often cooked simply in a pot of salted, boiling water.

vides excellent quality at a fraction of the price. Some of Sydney's best Asian fusion restaurants include Spice Temple (⊕ www.rockpool.com.au), led by top Australian chef Neil Perry, and the Thai-meets-Southern China concept Longrain Restaurant & Bar (⊕ www.longrain.com.au). The inventive Vietnamese canteen Red Lantern (⊕ www.redlantern.com.au) and inspired Sailors Thai (⊕ www.sailorsthai.com.au) are also among Sydney's best. It's in these bustling restaurants that flavors and dishes such as shucked oyster with chili and galangal vinaigrette, roasted duck in coconut curry, wagyu-beef hotpot, soft-shell crab with chili jam, and green curry of barramundi bounce off their plates.

While the majority of Asian fusion food in Australia relies heavily on light cooking styles and fresh ingredients, clay pot cooking as well as and heavier-style Malaysian and Indian curries, such as rendang and vindaloo made with local lamb and beef, are also becoming popular.

Neil Perry's salad of yabby tails

CITY CENTER

$ ✕ **Bambini Trust.** It's hidden behind huge black doors in one of the city's
AUSTRALIAN historic sandstone buildings, but once you're inside you'd swear you
were in Paris. Dark-wood paneling, black-and-white photographs, and
mirrors bearing the day's specials in flowing script lend a bistro feel.
The fare is a little French, a little more Italian, and a fair sprinkling of
Mod-Oz. We love to start with Alaskan king crab pannacotta, mizuna
salad and gazpacho and follow with the popular cracked pepper spa-
ghettini with a sautée of Yamba prawns, chili, and garlic. The Italian ice
cream or dark chocolate and raspberry tart are a lovely way to round
off a meal. A pre- or postmeal drink in the marble-lined, chandelier-
adorned Bambini Wine Room is a must. ✉ *185 Elizabeth St., City Center* ☎ *02/9283–7098* ⊗ *Closed Sun.* ✛ *1:C4.*

$$$ ✕ **Bécasse.** Sydney's darling chef Justin North has not only relocated
FRENCH Bécasse to the heart of Sydney but embraced the entire gastromic expe-
rience with a new venture on the fifth level of Sydney's newly revi-
talized Westfield Shopping Centre. Although fine food and shopping
malls don't usually go hand-in-hand, North has turned this theory on
its head. Bécasse has been slimmed down to an elegant 25-seat res-
taurant with an 8-seat chef's table and placed adjacent to North and
wife Georgina's new food emporium, cooking school, Bécasse Bakery,
and another casual-style eatery called Quarter 21. Diners who takethe
express elevator on Pitt Street up to the fifth floor will notice that prices
have gone up, too. Dinner is now a three-course à la carte menu ($120),
a five-course degustation ($150) or a nine-course degusation ($190)
with matching wines at extra cost. Starters may include an exotic dish
of spanner crab, chamomile, and custard apple, crab jelly, and expect
to see Blackmore Wagyu, white asparagus, nameko, and ginger as a
main ✉ *Level 5, Westfield Shopping Centre, Pitt and Market Sts., City
Center* ☎ *02/9283–3440* ✍ *Reservations essential* ⊗ *Closed Sun. No
lunch Sat.* ✛ *1:C4.*

$$$$ ✕ **Est.** This elegant, pillared dining room is the perfect setting for show-
MODERN ing off chef Peter Doyle's modern, light touch with Mod-Oz cuisine.
AUSTRALIAN Anything Doyle cooks with scallops is divine, and his zucchini flowers
★ with confit cherry tomatoes, mushooms, and chickpea are wonderful,
as is the panfried John Dory fillet with diamond clams. The warm
caramelized peach tart with peach-pistachio-nougat ice cream will test
any dieter's resolve. The six-course tasting menu (A$175) is a heavenly
experience and a bit more bang for your buck than the four-course
chef's menu (A$150). There is no à la carte menu. ✉ *Establishment
Hotel, 252 George St., City Center* ☎ *02/9240–3000* ✍ *Reservations
essential* ⊗ *Closed Sun. No lunch Sat.* ✛ *1:C2.*

$$ ✕ **Spice Temple.** The culinary focus of chic basement eatery—another
CHINESE of the restaurants owned by Neil Perry of Rockpool fame—is regional
China. There are dishes from far-flung Yunnan, Hunan, and Sichuan
provinces, and as the names suggest they all have a kick. The food is
meant to be shared, so pass around the crisp pork belly and smoked
tofu with spicy ginger and garlic dressing to start or the cutely named
spiced fried chicken wings with heaven-facing chilies. The caramelized
spare pork ribs are great down to the last finger lick, and for those

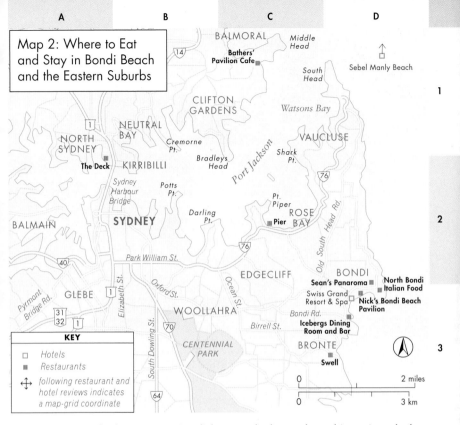

who love extra spicy dishes, try the hot and numbing crispy duck. ✉ *10 Bligh St., City Center* ☎ *02/8078–1888* ⊕ *www.spicetemple. com.au* ✛ *1:C3*.

$$$$

MODERN AUSTRALIAN

Fodor's Choice

★

✕ **Tetsuya's.** It's worth getting on the waiting list—there's *always* a waiting list—to sample the unique blend of Western and Japanese-French flavors crafted by Sydney's most applauded chef, Tetsuya Wakuda. The serene, expansive dining room's unobtrusive Japanese aesthetic leaves the food as the true highlight. Confit of ocean trout served with unpasteurized ocean-trout roe is a signature item on the set 11-course degustation menu (A$210 and A$95 extra for matching wines), while other dishes may include sashimi of king fish or slow-roasted breast of duck with smoked leeks. The menu changes often but never fails to dazzle. Views of a Japanese garden—complete with bonsai and a waterfall— make this place feel miles from the city center. ✉ *529 Kent St., City Center* ☎ *02/9267–2900* ⊕ *www.tetsuyas.com* ⌛ *Reservations essential* ☾ *Closed Sun. and Mon. No lunch Tues.–Fri.* ✛ *1:B5*.

One of the mouthwatering dishes at Bécasse.

INNER SYDNEY AND THE EASTERN SUBURBS

DARLINGHURST

¢
CAFÉ
Fodor's Choice
★

✕**bills.** Named after celebrity chef and cookbook author Bill Granger, this sunny corner café is so addictive it should come with a health warning. It's a favorite hangout of everyone from local nurses to semi-disguised rock stars, and you never know who you might be sitting next to at the newspaper-strewn communal table. If you're not interested in the creaminess of what must be Sydney's best scrambled eggs, try the ricotta hotcakes with fresh banana and honeycomb butter or the corn fritters. Dinner selections, at the Surry Hills location, are similarly gourmet comfort food. ✉ *433 Liverpool St., Darlinghurst* 🕾 *02/9360–9631* ⊕ *www.bills.com.au* ⊗ *No dinner* ✉ *352 Crown St., Surry Hills* 🕾*02/9360–4762* ✉ *118 Queen St., Woollahra* 🕾 *02/9328–7997* ✛ *1:E5.*

$
SEAFOOD
★

✕**Fishface.** Get here early, score one of the tiny tables, and you'll be able to dig into some of the most scrumptious seafood in Australia. The best sashimi-grade fish in the country—which is as good as it comes—is served up here to discerning locals. Menu highlights include the salmon pastrami (thinly sliced, cured salmon) with lemon on toast, and the blue-eyed trevalla. The fish-and-chips redefine the nation's favorite takeout order. Reservations aren't accepted after 7 pm. ✉ *132 Darlinghurst Rd., Darlinghurst* 🕾*02/9332–4803* 🍴*BYO, corkage fee A$7 per person* ☞ *Lunch on Sunday* ✛ *1:E5.*

¢
CAFÉ

✕**The Goods.** This friendly organic café and food store is the perfect place to stop for a wholesome salad, homemade cakes, or a savory griddle meal such as the tasty tomato, spinach, and haloumi cheese combo. It's a perfect break after shopping in nearby trendy Darlinghurst. Much of the produce on the shelves isused in the meals, and the tea and coffee are grown on organic or biodynamic farms. Here's a place you can happily (and healthily!) browse. ⊠ *253 Crown St., Darlinghurst* 🕾 *02/9357–6690* ⊘ *No dinner* ✛ *1:D5.*

KINGS CROSS AND POTTS POINT

$$ ✕ **Mere Catherine.** You won't find the number of this little hole-in-the-
FRENCH   wall restaurant in any trendy young thing's speed dial, but it is beloved by legions of fans who rejoiced when it reopened a couple of years ago. The decor is retro 1970s, and the dishes are classic French—onion soup, pâté, escargots, duck a l'orange, tarragon chicken, chateaubriand, and crème caramel for dessert. It only seats 14 in a tiny space that is akin to dining in some French family's home. The windows have lace curtains, the tables are candlelit, so come with someone you love and soak in the romantic atmosphere to the strains of Edith Piaf in the background. ⊠ *166 Victoria St., Potts Point* 🕾 *02/9358–2000* ⊟ *No credit cards* ⊘ *No lunch Sun. Mon.* ✛ *1:E4.*

WOOLLOOMOOLOO

$$ ✕ **Otto Ristorante.** Few restaurants have the magnetic pull of Otto, a
ITALIAN   place where radio shock jocks sit side by side with fashion-magazine editors and confirmed foodies. Yes, it's a scene, but fortunately one with good Italian food prepared by chef Richard Ptacnik. The homemade pastas are menu standouts; try the strozzapreti pasta with prawns or the saffron fettucine with rabbit ragout. The slow-cooked duck legs with extra virgin oil, quince, and chestnuts are delicious, too. The selection of Italian wines is expensive but rarely matched this far from Milan. ⊠ *Wharf at Woolloomooloo, Area 8, 6 Cowper Wharf Rd., Inner City and Eastern Suburbs* 🕾 *02/9368–7488* ⊕ *www.ottoristorante.com.au* ⩘ *Reservations essential* ✛ *1:E3.*

PADDINGTON

$$$ ✕ **Buon Ricordo.** Walking into this happy, bubbly place is like turning
ITALIAN   up at a private party in the backstreets of Naples. Host, chef, and sur-
Fodor's Choice   rogate uncle Armando Percuoco invests classic Neapolitan and Tuscan
★   techniques with inventive personal touches to produce such dishes as warmed figs with Gorgonzola and prosciutto, truffled egg pasta, and scampi with saffron sauce and black-ink risotto. The snapper fillet on a bed of zucchini flowers, mint, and zucchini is heaven for seafood lovers. Everything comes with Italian-style touches that you can see, feel, smell, and taste. Leaving the restaurant feels like leaving home, especially if you've partaken of the wonderful six-course degustation menu (A$125). ⊠ *108 Boundary St., Paddington* 🕾 *02/9360–6729* ⊕ *www. buonricordo.com.au* ⩘ *Reservations essential* ⊘ *Closed Sun. and Mon. No lunch Tues.–Thurs.* ✛ *1:F5.*

$$ ✕ **Four in Hand.** At this cute, popular little pub in Paddington, chef Colin
AUSTRALIAN   Fassnidge has been wowing patrons for years with his shared dish for two of slow-braised lamb shoulder with kipfler potatoes, baby carrots, and salsa verde. His starters and mains change monthly, and the restaurant's popularity has seen it open for lunch and dinner six days a week. You, too, can try cooking these dishes back home after you've

attended one of his cooking classes held on the first Monday of the month. ⊠ *105 Sutherland St., Paddington* ☎ *02/9362–1999* ⊘ *Closed Mon.* ✛ *1:G5*

WOOLLAHRA

$$
FRENCH

✕**Bistro Moncur.** Archetypically loud and proud, this bistro in the Woollahra Hotel spills over with happy-go-lucky patrons—mostly locals from around the leafy suburb of Woollahra—who have been coming back for more than 18 years now. The best dishes are inspired takes on Parisian fare, like the grilled Sirloin Café de Paris, french onion soufflé gratin, and port sausages with potato puree and Lyonnaise onions. Chef Damien Pignolet focuses on fresh, high-quality ingredients. The casual café and bar, Moncur Terrace, offers mains such as Wagyu beef burgers (A$23.90) and gourmet pizzas (A$24.50). ⊠ *Woollahra Hotel, 116 Queen St., Woollahra* ☎ *02/9327–9713* ⊘ *No lunch Mon.* ✛ *1:H6.*

SURRY HILLS

$
CHINESE
★

✕**Billy Kwong.** Locals rub shoulders while eating no-fuss Chinese food at TV chef Kylie Kwong's trendy drop-in restaurant. Kwong prepares the kind of food her family cooks, with Grandma providing not just the inspiration but also the recipes. The prawn wontons with brown rice vinegar are always popular, but the standout dish is the poached chicken with a dressing of tamari, chili, and coriander. If you have a big appetite, indulge in a variety of dishes with Kylie's banquet (A$95). A table for six to eight can be booked for 6 pm and 8:30 pm, otherwise it's turn up and wait with the other keen diners. ⊠ *3/355 Crown St., Surry Hills* ☎ *02/9332–3300* ⛚ *BYO, corkage fee A$12 per bottle* ⊘ *No lunch* ✛ *1:D6.*

$$$$
FRENCH

✕**Marque.** Chef Mark Best insists on exemplary service and great food at this elegant Surry Hills restaurant, awarded Sydney's best restaurant in 2011 by the well-thumbed "Sydney Morning Herald Good Food Guide." Few chefs approach French flavors with such passion and dedication (and stints alongside three-star demigods Alain Passard in Paris and Raymond Blanc in England haven't done any harm either). Best's creative fare includes blue swimmer crab with almond jelly, almond gazpacho, and sweet corn, and roasted Muscovy duck with carrots, Kimchi pear, and nori. The eight course-degustation (A$150) will transport you to foodie heaven, as will the three-course à la carte meal (A$95). The best deal in town, though, is the Friday-only set-menu three-course lunch for A$45. There are no individual à la carte prices and a minimum of three courses. ⊠ *355 Crown St., Surry Hills* ☎ *02/9332–2225* ⊜ *Reservations essential* ⊘ *Closed Sun. No lunch Sat.–Thurs.* ✛ *1:D6.*

EASTERN SUBURBS

$$
ITALIAN
Fodor's Choice
★

✕**Icebergs Dining Room and Bar.** The fashionable and famous (including celebrities like Mick Jagger) just adore perching like seagulls over the swimming pool at the south end of Australia's most famous beach. After nine years it is still one of the must-visit restaurants in Sydney, for both the sensational view and the exquisite food. Take a seat on a low-back suede chair, check your reflection in the frosted glass, and prepare to indulge in sophisticated Mediterranean creations like

2

buffalo mozzarella air-freighted from Campania, wood-fried artichole hearts, aged Sicilian salted anchovies, and Ligurian olives served with brushetta. If you're a hearty party of eight, tuck into the whole roasted suckling pig on bay leaves with grilled peppers (with 48 hours notice). ⊠ *1 Notts Ave., Bondi Beach* ☎ *02/9365–9000* ⌕ *Reservations essential* ☯ *Closed Mon.* ✛ *2:D3.*

$ ✕ **Nick's Bondi Beach Pavilion.** Sydney restaurateur Nick Manettas likes
SEAFOOD to grab the waterfront locations; his latest venture is a glass-encased modern space attached to the vintage-1928 pavilion on the beach's pedestrian promenade. Although it is a bit touristy for some diners, no one can dismiss the great location, and the classic seafood staples— including the three-tiered platter (designed for two diners at A\$130) bulging with oysters, shellfish, blue swimmer crab, Tasmanian salmon, and mussels—are sure to please. The Sunday and Monday night barbecue and seafood feast is a steal at A\$25. ⊠ *Queen Elizabeth Dr., Bondi Beach* ☎ *02/1300–989–989* ✛ *2:D3.*

$ ✕ **North Bondi Italian Food.** This popular spot is more casual and less
ITALIAN expensive than Icebergs (both are owned by stylish restaurateur Maurice Terzini), yet the trendy interior and great balcony overlooking the beach are sure to dazzle. The broad menu has more than 60 dishes (appetizers, entrées, and desserts) and is best described as home-style Italian, with comforting plates like lasagne with four cheeses, silverbeet, and spinach. The restaurant does not accept reservations, so arrive early to snag a table as it gets very busy. ⊠ *118–120 Ramsgate Ave., Bondi Beach* ☎ *02/9300–4400* ☯ *No lunch Sun.–Thurs. in winter, Mon. and Tues. in summer* ✛ *2:D3.*

$$ ✕ **Pier.** The wharf restaurant, with its wraparound harbor views and
SEAFOOD shipshape good looks, made foodie headlines in 2010 when owner and chef Greg Doyle renounced the restaurant's Three Hats (the top award given by the annual Sydney *Good Food* guide and the *Sydney Morning Herald* newspaper food writers). Although the quality of dining is still the same and seafood just as delicious, dishes are simpler—instead of 20 ingredients (or elements) to a dish, there are now around six. Start with freshly shucked oysters or pastrami of king salmon, follow with seared yellowfin tuna or the delectable pot-roasted lobster with chili and Thai basil. For something a little simpler but very tasty, the spanner crab omelet with Asian greens. A set three-couse lunch menu is A\$65 and the new fish-and-chip Sunday-only lunches are A\$35. ⊠ *594 New South Head Rd., Rose Bay* ☎ *02/9327–6561* ✛ *2:C2.*

$ ✕ **Swell.** When you finish the famous Bondi-to-Bronte coastal cliff walk,
MODERN this is a great place for a meal. By day it's a casual café, but at night
AUSTRALIAN it becomes more formal, thanks to white linen tablecloths and tea lights. The crispy soft-shell crab with green mango salad makes a great light lunch. When the sun goes down, listen to the surf and order a cocktail as you ponder seasonal menu delights such as Alaskan king crab with tortellini sweet corn, Avruga caviar, and crispy pancetta. If you'd prefer to sup in nearby Bronte park, the new adjacent Bronte Cucina serves casual dine-in or dine-out meals (such as homemade gnocchi with Gorgonzola sauce) from 5 to 9. ⊠ *465 Bronte Rd., Bronte* ☎ *02/9386–5001* ✛ *2:D3.*

$$ ✕ **Sean's Panaroma.** North Bondi Beach wouldn't be the same without
AUSTRALIAN Sean's Panaroma, perched on a slight rise a stone's throw from the
famous beach. It's been there since the mid-1990s, and owner Sean
Moran now graces his table with fresh produce grown on his farm in the
Blue Mountains, aptly named "Farm Panorama." Dishes change regu-
larly and are only featured on a blackboard: they may include baked
snapper with red capsicum (bell pepper), olives, eggplant, and tomanto,
or a ravioli of zucchini, mozzarella, and lemons. There are many fans
in Sydney, but also a few that say the service is hit-and-miss (if not a bit
arrogant), so be warned. A good way to while away a lazy day is the
five-course degustation for A$95 and A$145 with wine. ⊠ *270 Camp-
bell Parade, Bondi Beach* ☎ *02/9365–4924* ⊕ *www.seanspanaroma.
com.au* ⊗ *No dinner Sun.–Tues. No lunch Mon.–Thurs.* ✛ *2:D2.*

WHERE TO STAY

For expanded hotel reviews, visit Fodors.com.

From grand hotels with white-glove service to tucked-away bed-and-
breakfasts, there's lodging to fit all styles and budgets in Sydney. The
best addresses in town are undoubtedly in The Rocks, where the tranquil
setting and harbor views are right near major cultural attractions, res-
taurants, shops, and galleries. The area around Kings Cross is another
hotel district, with a good collection of boutique properties as well as a
backpacker magnet. Keep in mind, however, that this is also the city's
major nightlife district, and the scene can get pretty raucous after sunset.

*Use the coordinate (✛ 1:B2) at the end of each listing to locate a site
on the corresponding map.*

SYDNEY HARBOUR AND THE ROCKS

¢ ⊡ **The Australian Heritage Hotel.** This is the hotel for bargain hunters who
want to be right on the city's doorstep, don't mind sharing bathrooms,
and like the busy pub scene (meaning it could be noisy at night). **Pros:**
great location; excellent price; free Wi-fi. **Cons:** basic rooms; few ameni-
ties; can be noisy. ⊠ *100 Cumberland St., The Rocks* ☎ *02/9247–2229*
⊕ *www.australianheritagehotel.com* ⤳ *9 rooms sharing 5 bathrooms*
⌂ *In-room: no a/c, Wi-Fi. In-hotel: restaurant, bar* ❑ *Breakfast* ✛ *1:B2.*

$$$ ⊡ **Harbour Rocks Hotel.** Formerly a wool-storage facility, this four-story
hotel provides good value for its location, although its historic char-
acter is confined to the exterior of the 150-year-old building. **Pros:**
Great location, excellent in-room entertainment systems, suave modern
decor **Cons:** rooms could be larger. ⊠ *34 Harrington St., The Rocks*
☎ *02/8220–9998* ⊕ *www.harbourrocks.com.au* ⤳ *55 rooms* ⌂ *In-
room: safe, Internet. In-hotel: restaurant, bar* ❑ *Breakfast* ✛ *1:B2.*

$$$ ⊡ **Holiday Inn Old Sydney.** Even though it's been around for a few
decades, this hotel with its low-key facade is still a bit of a secret. **Pros:**
great location; good value. **Cons:** still has a dated look. ⊠ *55 George
St., The Rocks* ☎ *1800/669–562* ⊕ *www.holidayinn.com* ⤳ *174 rooms*
⌂ *In-room: safe, Internet, Wi-Fi. In-hotel: restaurant, bar, pool, laundry
facilities, business center, parking* ❑ *No meals* ✛ *1:C2.*

2

$ ⊞ **Lord Nelson Hotel.** If your idea of heaven is sleeping above a pub that brews its own boutique beers (or ales, as they're rightly called), then this is the place. **Pros:** great location, fun pub, cheap rates. **Cons:** may be noisy, expensive WiFi ⊠ *19 Kent St., The Rocks* ☎ *02/9251–4044* ⊕ *www.lordnelsonbrewery. com* ⟿ *9 rooms* ⌂ *In-room: no TV, Wi-Fi. In-hotel: restaurant, bar, business center, parking* ⦿ *Breakfast* ⊹ *1:B2.*

$$$$
Fodor'sChoice
★
⊞ **Observatory Hotel.** More English country manor than inner-city hotel, this gorgeous property feels like a decadent, luxurious sanctuary. **Pros:** sumptuous, good location; excellent in-house restaurant. **Cons:** lack of views. ⊠ *89–113 Kent St., The Rocks* ☎ *02/9256–2222* ⊕ *www.observatoryhotel.com.au* ⟿ *79 rooms, 21 suites* ⌂ *In-room: safe, Internet. In-hotel: restaurant, bar, pool, gym, parking* ⦿ *Breakfast* ⊹ *1:B2.*

$$$ ⊞ **Rendezvous Stafford Hotel Sydney.** Situated in the heart of the historic Rocks precinct, the lodging has a boutique-hotel style. **Pros:** boutique feel, great location, in-house movies, free Internet for hours; good breakfast/Internet package. **Cons:** simply appointed rooms. ⊠ *75 Harrington St., The Rocks* ☎ *02/9251–6711* ⊕ *www.rendezvoushotels.com/ sydney* ⟿ *61 apartments, 7 terrace houses* ⌂ *In-room: safe, kitchen, Internet. In-hotel: pool, gym, spa, laundry facilities, parking* ⊹ *1:B2.*

$$ ⊞ **The Russell.** For charm, character, and central location, it's hard to beat this ornate Victorian hotel. **Pros:** personal service; warm decor; includes breakfast. **Cons:** near a pub and busy area, so can be noisy. ⊠ *143A George St., The Rocks* ☎ *02/9241–3543* ⊕ *www.therussell. com.au* ⟿ *30 rooms, 16 with bath; 1 suite; 1 apartment* ⌂ *In-room: no a/c. In-hotel: restaurant* ⦿ *Breakfast* ⊹ *1:B2.*

$$$$
★
⊞ **Shangri-La Hotel Sydney.** Towering above Walsh Bay from its prime position alongside the Sydney Harbour Bridge, this sleek hotel is *the* place for a room with a view. **Pros:** breathtaking views; soothing decor; great in-house restaurant. **Cons:** impersonal and busy feel at times. ⊠ *176 Cumberland St., The Rocks* ☎ *02/9250–6000* ⊕ *www.shangri-la. com* ⟿ *523 rooms, 40 suites* ⌂ *In-room: safe, Internet. In-hotel: restaurant, bar, pool, gym, spa, business center, parking* ⊹ *1:B2.*

$ ⊞ **Sydney Harbour YHA.** Sydney's newest hostel occupies a brand-new building on the Big Dig, an an active late-18th- and early-19th-century archaeological site, first discovered in 1994. **Pros:** great location, budget prices for harbour views, history at your fingertips. **Cons:** few room amenities, little privacy. ⊠ *110 Cumberland St., The Rocks* ☎ *02/8272–0900* ⊕ *www.sydneyharbouryha.com.au* ⟿ *106 rooms* ⌂ *In-room: a/c, no TV, Wi-Fi. In-hotel: laundry facilities, business center* ⊹ *1:B2.*

CIRCULAR QUAY

$$$$ 🏨 **Sydney Harbour Marriott.** This modern high-rise hotel is a minute's walk from Circular Quay, a two-minute stroll from The Rocks, and a short distance from Pitt Street's best shopping. **Pros:** hip bar; good location and views; free Wi-Fi when guests join the free Marriott Rewards program. **Cons:** Busy, corporate feel. ⊠ *30 Pitt St., City Center* 🕿 *02/9259–7000* ⊕ *www.sydneyharbourmarriott.com.au* ⤴ *550 rooms, 42 suites* ♿ *In-room: Internet. In-hotel: restaurant, bar, pool, gym, parking* ✛ *1:C2.*

DARLING HARBOUR AND THE CITY CENTER

$$$ 🏨 **Fraser Suites Sydney.** This serviced-apartment hotel is one of Sydney's swankiest places to stay. **Pros:** cutting-edge design, well priced for longer stays. **Cons:** minimalist design may not be everyone's taste, costly Wi-Fi. ⊠ *488 Kent St., Sydney Center* 🕿 *02/8823–8888* ⊕ *www. sydney.frasershospitality.com* ⤴ *201 rooms* ♿ *In-room: safe, kitchen, Internet. In-hotel: pool, gym, laundry facilities, business center, parking* ❄ *No meals* ✛ *1:C5.*

$$$ 🏨 **Hilton Sydney.** At this landmark hotel in downtown Sydney you enter a spacious, light-filled lobby displaying a stunning four-story sculpture. **Pros:** excellent service, lavishly appointed rooms, hip bar. **Cons:** impersonal, at-times busy feel. ⊠ *488 George St., City Center* 🕿 *02/9266– 2000* ⊕ *www.hiltonsydney.com.au* ⤴ *550 rooms, 27 suites* ♿ *In-room: Wi-Fi. In-hotel: restaurant, pool, gym, spa* ✛ *1:C4.*

$$$$ 🏨 **Westin Sydney.** The Westin hotel chain is renowned for its heavenly
★ beds—in Sydney it offers heavenly service, too. **Pros:** in-room entertainment systems, great service, free Wi-Fi in public areas. **Cons:** slightly corporate feel. ⊠ *1 Martin Pl., City Center* 🕿 *02/8223–1111* ⊕ *www. westin.com/sydney* ⤴ *400 rooms, 16 suites* ♿ *In-room: safe, Internet. In-hotel: restaurant, bar, pool, gym, business center, parking* ✛ *1:C3.*

$$ 🏨 **Y Hotel Hyde Park.** Comfortable, recently renovated, and affordable lodgings in a prime city location means that rooms here are often booked months in advance. **Pros:** great value, lots of unexpected extras. **Cons:** have to book far ahead of time. ⊠ *5–11 Wentworth Ave., near corner of Hyde Park and Oxford St., City Center* 🕿 *02/9264–4251* ⊕ *www.yhotel. com.au* ⤴ *11 dorm rooms with shared baths, 6 studios, 104 rooms* ♿ *In-room: no TV, Wi-Fi. In-hotel: restaurant* ❄ *Breakfast* ✛ *1:D5.*

INNER CITY AND THE EASTERN SUBURBS

PADDINGTON

$ 🏨 **Arts Hotel Sydney.** On a quiet stretch in the trendy shopping precinct
★ of Paddington, this small, friendly, family-run hotel has simple accommodations at an outstanding price. **Pros:** great value; personal service; warm feel. **Cons:** simply appointed rooms. ⊠ *21 Oxford St., Paddington* 🕿 *02/9361–0211* ⊕ *www.artshotel.com.au* ⤴ *64 rooms* ♿ *In-room: Internet. In-hotel: restaurant, pool, parking* ✛ *1:E6.*

There's no shortage of luxurious accommodations in Sydney.

DARLINGHURST

$$$ 🛏 **Medusa.** If you're tired of the standard travelers' rooms, this reno-
★ vated Victorian terrace house may be just the tonic. **Pros:** flashy decor;
warm service; kichenettes in every room; entry to off-site pool and
gym. **Cons:** urban location may get noisy ⊠ *267 Darlinghurst Rd.,
Darlinghurst* ☎ *02/9331–1000* ⊕ *www.medusa.com.au* ⤵ *18 rooms*
⌂ *In-room: safe, kitchen. In-hotel: some pets allowed* ⊹ *1:E5.*

KINGS CROSS

¢ 🛏 **Hotel 59 & Cafe.** In its character as well as its dimensions, this friendly
B&B on a quiet part of a bar- and club-lined street is reminiscent of
a European *pensione*. **Pros:** comfortable rooms, recently repainted
Cons: Half-hour to the city center ⊠ *59 Bayswater Rd., Kings Cross*
☎ *02/9360–5900* ⊕ *www.hotel59.com.au* ⤵ *9 rooms* ⌂ *In-hotel: res-
taurant* ❢⊙❢ *Breakfast* ⊹ *1:F4.*

POTTS POINT

$$ 🛏 **De Vere Hotel.** "Simply comfortable and affordable" is the slogan at
this 1920s-style hotel at the leafy end of Potts Point, and it's hard to
disagree on either count. **Pros:** good value; spacious rooms; friendly
staff. **Cons:** breakfast, although available on-site, is no longer included
in rate. ⊠ *44–46 Macleay St., Potts Point* ☎ *02/9358–1211* ⊕ *www.
devere.com.au* ⤵ *117 rooms* ⌂ *In-room: kitchen. In-hotel: restaurant,
laundry facilities, parking* ❢⊙❢ *No meals* ⊹ *1:F3.*

$$ 🛏 **Simpsons of Potts Point.** This luxurious boutique hotel is the gem of
Fodor'sChoice inner Sydney. **Pros:** friendly, elegant, and cozy; free Wi-Fi and use of
★ computers; limited free parking; 20-minute walk to city center. **Cons:**

no elevator. ⊠ *8 Challis Ave., Potts Point* ☎ *02/9356–2199* ⊕ *www. simpsonshotel.com.au* ↜ *12 rooms* ⚘ *In-room: a/c. In-hotel: parking* ⎥⊙⎢ *Breakfast* ✛ *1:E3.*

$ ⛳ **Quest Serviced Apartments Potts Point.** This gorgeous, early 1920s-style boutique hotel is a find in the hip Potts Point on the eastern fringe of the city, an ideal base for exploring the eastern suburbs. **Pros:** funky rooms, some with amazing views; good location. **Cons:** neighboring parts of Kings Cross can be seedy and noisy. ⊠ *15 Springfield Ave., Potts Point* ☎ *2/8988–6999* ⊕ *www.questapartments.com.au* ↜ *69 rooms* ⚘ *In-room: safe, kitchen, Wi-Fi. In-hotel: restaurant, laundry facilities* ✛ *1:E4.*

¢   ⛳ **Victoria Court Sydney.** A small, smart hotel on a Potts Point street lined with budget accommodations, the Victoria Court is appealing for more than just its reasonable rates. **Pros:** heritage feel, comfortable rooms, free Wi-Fi **Cons:** simple amenities. ⊠ *122 Victoria St., Potts Point* ☎ *02/9357–3200* ⊕ *www.victoriacourt.com.au* ↜ *25 rooms* ⚘ *In-room: a/c, safe, Wi-Fi* ⎥⊙⎢ *Breakfast* ✛ *1:E3.*

WOOLLOOMOOLOO

$$$$ ⛳ **BLUE Sydney.** This ultrahip hotel, part of the prestigious Taj Hotel
★   group of India, occupies a former warehouse. **Pros:** DVDs and iPod docking stations in all rooms; trendy bar, trendier location. **Cons:** Wi-Fi is A$9 per day, per device. ⊠ *Wharf at Woolloomooloo, 6 Cowper Wharf Rd., Woolloomooloo* ☎ *02/9331–9000* ⊕ *www.tajhotels.com/ sydney* ↜ *100 rooms, 36 suites* ⚘ *In-room: safe, Internet. In-hotel: restaurant, bar, pool, gym, business center, parking* ✛ *1:E3.*

BONDI BEACH

$$$ ⛳ **Swiss Grand Resort & Spa.** With the beach just across the road, a rooftop pool, and a relaxing day spa, a stay at the Swiss Grand makes it easy to forget that you're just 15 minutes away from the action of Sydney. **Pros:** good spa, great beachside location. **Cons:** sometimes busy, public feel, street-facing rooms are noisy. ⊠ *Campbell Parade at Beach Rd., Bondi Beach* ☎ *02/9365–5666* ⊕ *www.swissgrand.com.au* ↜ *203 suites* ⚘ *In-hotel: restaurant, bar, pool, gym, spa, business center, parking* ✛ *2:D3.*

GREATER SYDNEY

MANLY

$$$ ⛳ **Sebel Manly Beach.** Right on the beachfront of beautiful Manly, this boutique hotel is a mixture of studios and one- and two-bedroom suites, all with private balconies; the more spacious accommodations have hot tubs, kitchenettes, and high-tech goodies. **Pros:** beachside locale; well-appointed rooms. **Cons:** busy place; expect crowds in summer. ⊠ *8–13 S. Steyne, Manly* ☎ *02/9977–8866* ⊕ *www.mirvachotels.com. au* ↜ *83 rooms* ⚘ *In-room: kitchen, Internet. In-hotel: restaurant, bar, pool, beach, laundry facilities, parking* ✛ *2:D1.*

NIGHTLIFE AND THE ARTS

THE ARTS

Although Sydney's contemporary theater pays tribute to the giants of drama, it's also driven by distinctly Australian themes: multiculturalism, relating to the troubled relations between Aboriginal and white Australia, and the search for national identity, characterized by the famous Australian irreverence. Dance, music, and the visual arts are celebrated with equal enthusiasm. At their best, Sydney's artists and performers bring a new slant to the arts, one that reflects the unique qualities of their homeland and the city itself. Standouts on the Sydney arts scene include the Sydney Dance Company, the Museum of Contemporary Arts, the Sydney Opera House, and Belvoir Street Theatre. The most comprehensive listing of upcoming events is in the "Metro" section of the *Sydney Morning Herald,* published on Friday. On other days, browse through the entertainment section of the paper.

Ticketek Phone Box Office. Ticketek Phone Box Office is the major ticket reservations agency, covering most shows and performances. ☎ *13–2849* ⊕ *premier.ticketek.com.au.*

DANCE

Bangarra Dance Theatre. Bangarra Dance Theatre, the acclaimed Aboriginal dance company, celebrated its 22nd anniversary in 2011. They stage dramatic productions based on contemporary Aboriginal social themes. ⊠ *Pier 4, 5 Hickson Rd., The Rocks* ☎ *02/9251–5333* ⊕ *www.bangarra.com.au.*

★ **Sydney Dance Company.** Sydney Dance Company is an innovative contemporary dance troupe with an international reputation. Spanish choreographer Rafael Bonachela is the artistic director. The company performs in Sydney at the Wharf Theatre, the Sydney Opera House, and the new Sydney Theatre. ⊠ *The Wharf, Pier 4, Hickson Rd., The Rocks* ☎ *02/9221–4811* ⊕ *www.sydneydance.com.au.*

THEATER

Belvoir Street Theatre. Belvoir Street Theatre has two stages that host innovative and challenging political and social drama. The smaller downstairs space is the home of "B Sharp," which showcases a lineup of brave new Australian drama. The theater is a 10-minute walk from Central Station. ⊠ *25 Belvoir St., Surry Hills* ☎ *02/9699–3444* ⊕ *www.belvoir.com.au.*

Capitol Theatre. This century-old city landmark was refurbished with such modern refinements as fiber-optic ceiling lights that twinkle in time to the music. The 2,000-seat theater specializes in Broadway blockbusters, such as *The Lion King* and *Mary Poppins.* ⊠ *13 Campbell St., Haymarket* ☎ *02/9320–5000* ⊕ *www.capitoltheatre.com.au.*

Lyric Theatre. Lyric Theatre, at the Star City Casino complex, is one of Sydney's most spectacular performing-arts venues. Despite its size, there's no better place to watch big-budget musicals. Every seat in the lavishly spacious, 2,000-seat theater is a good one. ⊠ *20–80 Pyrmont St., Pyrmont, Darling Harbour* ☎ *02/9777–9000* ⊕ *www.starcity.com.au.*

★ **State Theatre.** State Theatre is the grande dame of Sydney theaters. It operates as a cinema in June each year, when it hosts the two-week-long Sydney Film Festival; at other times this beautiful space hosts local and international performers. Built in 1929 and restored to its full-blown opulence, the theater has a vaulted ceiling, mosaic floors, marble columns and statues, and brass and bronze doors. A highlight of the magnificent theater is the 20,000-piece chandelier that is supposedly the world's second largest, which actor Robin Williams once likened to "one of Imelda Marcos's earrings." ✉ *49 Market St., City Center* ☎ *02/9373–6655* ⊕ *www. statetheatre.com.au.*

SWB Stables Theatre. SWB Stables Theatre is a small 120-seat venue and home of the Griffin Theatre Company, which specializes in new Australian writing. ✉ *10 Nimrod St., Kings Cross* ☎ *02/8019–0292* ⊕ *www.griffintheatre.com.au.*

Wharf Theatre. Wharf Theatre, on a redeveloped wharf in the shadow of Harbour Bridge, is the headquarters of the Sydney Theatre Company (STC), one of Australia's most original and highly regarded performance groups: Cate Blanchett and husband Andrew Upton are the artistic directors. Contemporary British and American plays and the latest offerings from leading Australian playwrights such as David Williamson and Nick Enright are the main attractions. The company also performs at the Sydney Opera House and at the new Sydney Theatre just opposite Pier 6/7 on Hickson St. ✉ *Pier 4, Hickson Rd., The Rocks* ☎ *1300–087–348* ⊕ *sydneytheatre.com.au.*

A SEA OF TALENT

Sculpture by the Sea. A steel whale's tail sticking out of the ocean and retro kettles cunningly disguised as penguins strapped to a huge rock being lashed by waves are some of the imaginative artworks that have wowed visitors to the annual show called Sculpture by the Sea. Since 1996, artists from more than 15 countries have positioned their sculptures on and under rocky outcrops and on hilltops along the much-trodden Bondi-to-Bronte Coastal Walk. This free exhibition, which runs for two weeks beginning in late October or early November, attracts thousands of visitors. ⊕ *www.sculpturebythesea.com.*

NIGHTLIFE

The *Sydney Morning Herald*'s daily entertainment section is the most informative guide to the city's pubs and clubs. For club-scene coverage—who's been seen where and what they were wearing—pick up a free copy of *Drum Media,* available at just about any Oxford Street café or pub or via the Internet (⊕ *www.drummedia.com.au*). The CitySearch (⊕ *www.sydney.citysearch.com.au*) and Sydney Gig Guide (⊕ *www. yourgigs.com.au6/Sydney*) are other good online sources of entertainment information.

All bars and clubs listed here are open daily unless noted. Entry is free unless we list a cover charge.

Inside Sydney's renowned Opera House

BARS AND DANCE CLUBS

The Arthouse Hotel. A former School of the Arts building, the Arthouse Hotel has been renovated into a modern, Belle Époque–style hot spot, with four bars and a restaurant spread over three cavernous floors. Art is the focus here, whether it's visual—life-drawing classes are given on Monday, a burlesque drawing class biweekly on Tuesday—aural, or comestible, and there is a full-time curator dedicated to programming events and installing exhibitions. ⊠ *275 Pitt St., City Center* ☎ *02/9284–1200* ⊕ *www.arthousehotel.com.au.*

★ **Bambini Wine Room.** Bambini Wine Room is a sparkling little jewel box encased in marble-clad walls and topped with lovely chandeliers. You can sip cocktails (A\$16) and any number of fine wines late into the night and feast on affordable bar snacks. ⊠ *185 Elizabeth St., City Center* ☎ *02/9283–7098.*

Beach Road Hotel. The Beach Road Hotel, a Bondi institution, is famous for its Sunday Sessions, when locals come to drink and dance all day in one of several pub rooms There's music every night (except Monday), good affordable food, and A\$10 pizzas on Thursday nights. ⊠ *71 Beach Rd., Bondi Beach* ☎ *02/9130–7247* ⊕ *www.beachroadbondi.com.au.*

Blu Bar on 36. Blu Bar on 36 has a stellar view! Situated on the 36th floor of the Shangri-La Hotel, this is a sophisticated place to relax after work or enjoy a late-night drink while taking in the sweeping views of Sydney Harbour and the Opera House. Get here early for a ringside seat. ⊠ *176 Cumberland St., The Rocks* ☎ *02/9250–6000.*

★ **Bungalow 8.** With its primo waterside location at the northern end of King Street Wharf, and famous mussels from its open kitchen,

Bungalow 8 invites a night of posing and partying. This is the place to be seen bobbing your head to the spinning of several ultra-cool resident DJs. Tuesday is especially packed for the all-you-can-eat mussel extravaganza. ✉ *8 The Promenade, King Street Wharf* ☎ *02/9299–4660* ⊕ *www.bungalow8sydney.com.*

★ **Hemmesphere.** One of a string of swanky venues in the area, Hemmesphere is still drawing a hip crowd 10 years after it first opened. Named for Justin Hemmes, son of iconic 1970s fashion designers Jon and Merivale Hemmes, this is where Sydney's hippest pay homage to cocktail culture from low, leather divans. The mood is elegant and sleek, and so are the well-dressed guests, who often include whichever glitterati happen to be in town. Closed Sunday. ✉ *Level 4, 252 George St., City Center* ☎ *02/9240–3104.*

Home. Sydney's largest nightclub is a three-story colossus that holds up to 2,000 party animals. The main dance floor has an awesome sound system, and the top-level terrace bar is the place to go when the action becomes too frantic. The venue houses various bars, including the Tokio Hotel with Bona Fides Cafe, which has live blues, roots, and jazz music every night. Arrive early or prepare for a long wait. Cover charges can be as high as A$55 for international DJs in the main dance area. Stays open until 4 am on Friday and Saturday. ✉ *101 Cockle Bay Wharf, Darling Harbour* ☎ *02/9266–0600* ⊕ *www.homesydney.com.*

Hugo's Lounge. This is the place that transformed Kings Cross from a seedy crossroads of sex shops and smut to a must-be-seen-here destination for Sydney's beautiful people. Red lamps are a nod to the neighborhood's skin trade, but the deep couches, opulent ottomans, and decadent cocktail menu are purely upmarket. The downstairs pizza bar is part of the Hugo's stable of eateries. Closed Monday–Wednesday. ✉ *Level 1, 33 Bayswater Rd., Kings Cross* ☎ *02/9357–4411.*

Ivy. The latest offering by Sydney's party prince Justin Hemmes (owner of Establishment and Hemmesphere), Ivy is in the same multilevel venue as the Ivy Lounge, the Den, the Pool Club (complete with swimming pool), the Royal George pub, and the newly opened Ash Street Cellar bistro. Add to all these watering-hole options A$12 jugs of beer, music most nights, and all you can eat promos (at around A$20). ✉ *330 George St., City Center* ☎ *02/9240–3000.*

Jimmy Liks. This small, sexy Asian street-food restaurant serves up drink concoctions with subtle flavors (like watermelon magaritas) and cocktails with names like Kyoto Protocol and Bangok Iced Teatea, which you can sip under a honeycomb-like lantern that flatters with its golden light. ✉ *186–188 Victoria St., Potts Point* ☎ *02/8354–1400.*

The Oaks. For a northern Sydney landmark, The Oaks encapsulates the very best of the modern pub. The immensely popular watering hole is big and boisterous, with a beer garden, a restaurant, and several bars offering varying levels of sophistication. It's packed on Friday and Saturday nights. ✉ *118 Military Rd., Neutral Bay* ☎ *02/9953–5515.*

Opera Bar. Perched beneath the concourse of the Opera House and at eye level with Sydney Harbour, Opera Bar has the best location in all of Sydney. Cozy up for a drink in the enclosed bar area or grab a waterside umbrella table and take in the glimmering skyline. Live music plays under the stars nightly from 8.30 pm on weeknight, and from 2 pm on weekends. The bar has a full menu, though the attraction here is the scenery, not the cuisine. ⊠ *Sydney Opera House, Circular Quay* ☎ *02/9247–1666.*

Orbit Lounge Bar and Tapas. On Level 47 of the Australia Square building, Orbit has been a Sydney icon for more than 40 years. It has floor-to-ceiling windows and, like Sydney Tower, it revolves. The design, to match the name, is Space Age, inspired by the Stanly Kubrick movie *2001: A Space Odyssey*, with white retro furniture and plush red carpet. This is a dressed-up bar perfect for a pre- or postdinner drink. It's open weekdays from 10 am for coffee and lunch and from 5 pm until late every night for tapas (from A$13 a plate) and cocktails. ⊠ *Australia Square, Level 47, 264 George St., City Center* ☎ *02/9247–7777* ⊕ *www.summitrestaurant.com.au.*

Soho Bar. Swank-looking Soho Bar is housed in a retro-style (1939-built) pub in the nightlife hub of Potts Point. There's free entry on Friday nights (and even A$5 drinks) and a A$20 charge on Saturday nights when you'll catch top name DJs and live bands . . . and maybe spy a celebrity or two. ⊠ *Piccadilly Hotel, 171 Victoria St., Kings Cross* ☎ *02/9358–6511.*

Trademark Hotel. This fun club is named for its unique position under the neon lights of the southern hemisphere's biggest billboard—the iconic Coca-Cola sign at the "top of the Cross," the highest point in Kings Cross. There's no chance of getting lost, as everyone knows the billboard, which is heritage listed, and has beamed out its message since 1974. Trademark consists of two bars; the Lounge (an elegant venue for after work, and the Piano Room (jazz nights and late-night dancing). Cover charges apply to special DJ party events. ⊠ *1 Bayswater Rd., Kings Cross* ☎ *02/8324–4500* 🍴 *A$10–A$30 for events.*

Tone. Decorated with plenty of street art, this is Sydney's newest small bar and performance space. It's a favorite among the city's keen nightclubbers thanks to its lineup of international and local DJs and its underground music policy. There are also "niche" nights such as Twist and Shout, which pay homage to the 1960s. It's open into the wee hours and has an affordable tapas menu. ⊠ *16 Wentworth Ave., Surry Hills* ☎ *02/9267–6440.*

COMEDY CLUBS

Sydney's Comedy Store. Sydney's Comedy Store, the city's oldest comedy club, is in a plush 300-seat theater in the Entertainment Quarter, which most people still refer to as Fox Studios (its former name). The

---

HAVE A GAY OLD TIME

If you're in Sydney in late February and early March, you'll think the whole city has gone gay. The Sydney Gay and Lesbian Mardi Gras parade, which celebrated its 33rd anniversary in 2011 is one of Australia's major events. Dozens of floats covered with buff dancers make their way from College Street, near St. Mary's Cathedral, up Oxford Street to Taylor's Square. Thousands of spectators watch this amazing party parade.

difficult-to-find theater is at the rear of the complex, close to the parking lot. Shows are Tuesday–Saturday at 8:30 pm, and admission runs A$20 to A$30. There's a second venue at 302 Church Street in Parramatta. ⊠ *Entertainment Quarter, Bent St. off Driver Ave., Centennial Park* ☎ *02/9357–1419* ⊕ *www.comedystore.com.au.*

GAY AND LESBIAN BARS AND CLUBS

Most of the city's gay and lesbian venues are along Oxford Street, in Darlinghurst. The free *Sydney Star Observer,* available along Oxford Street, has a roundup of Sydney's gay and lesbian goings-on, or check the magazine's Web site (⊕ *www.ssonet.com.au*). A monthly free magazine, *Lesbians on the Loose* (⊕ *www.lotl.com*), lists events for women, and the free *SX* (⊕ *www.sxnews.com.au*) lists bars and events.

★ **ARQ.** Sydney's biggest, best-looking, and funkiest gay nightclub, ARQ attracts a clean-cut crowd who like to whip off their shirts as soon as they hear the beat. (Some women head here, too.) There are multiple dance floors, a bar, and plenty of chrome and sparkly lighting. It's open from 9 pm until whenever Thursday through Sunday; a Thursday night drag contest is free, while shows have a cover charge ranging from A$15 to A$25 (and sometimes a little more) depending on when you arrive. ⊠ *16 Flinders St., Darlinghurst* ☎ *02/9380–8700* ⊕ *www. arqsydney.com.au.*

The Midnight Shift. The Midnight Shift is Sydney's hard-core party zone, a living legend on the gay scene for its longevity and its take-no-prisoners approach. If anything, the upstairs nightclub, with drag acts and shows three nights a week and DJs every other night, is a little quieter than the ground-floor bars, where most of the leather-loving men go to shoot pool. Brainiacs will love the Tuesday night trivia quizzes. Opening hours are Sunday to Thursday from about midday to 2 am and Friday and Saturday from 2 pm to 6 am. ⊠ *85 Oxford St., Darlinghurst* ☎ *02/9360–4463.*

JAZZ CLUBS

★ **The Basement.** The Basement is a Sydney legend, the city's premier venue for top local and international jazz, rock, and blues musicians. Lunch is available weekdays, dinner Monday–Saturday. Expect a cover charge starting at A$15. ⊠ *7 Macquarie Place, Circular Quay* ☎ *02/9251–2797* ⊕ *www.thebasement.com.au.*

The Vanguard. The Vanguard is Sydney's answer to a New Orleans jazz joint, and purposely built by its music-loving owners to mimic the U.S. model. Australian and international jazz, blues, and roots performers love this intimate venue with its 1920s decor and friendly vibe. Ticket prices range from around A$30 (some performances are free); it's advised to book a dinner and show package to get the best seats in the house. ⊠ *42 King St., Newtown* ☎ *02/9550–3666.*

PUBS WITH MUSIC

Mercantile Hotel. Mercantile Hotel, in the shadow of Harbour Bridge, is Irish and very proud of it. Fiddles, drums, and pipes rise above the clamor in the bar, and lilting accents rejoice in song seven nights a week and on weekends from 3 pm. ⊠ *25 George St., The Rocks* ☎ *02/9247–3570.*

Unity Hall Hotel. This quaint pub in the left-of-center suburb of Balmain declares itself the "spiritual home of jazz and live music for the past 40 years." Its resident jazz band has been playing there since 1972, and you can hear them for free each Sunday at 4 pm. A variety of live music including pop, rock, swing, and blues is also on the bill. Music cranks up on Friday nights from 9:30 pm. The pub attracts a friendly, unpretentious crowd and supports up and coming bands. ⊠ *292 Darling Street, Balmain* ☎ *02/9810–1331* ⊕ *www.unityhallhotel.com.au.*

SPORTS AND THE OUTDOORS

Given its climate and its taste for the great outdoors, it's no surprise that Sydney is addicted to sports. In the cooler months rugby league dominates the sporting scene, although these days the Sydney Swans, the city's flag bearer in the national Australian Rules Football (AFL) competition, attract far bigger crowds. In summer cricket is the major spectator sport, and nothing arouses more passion than international test cricket games—especially when Australia plays against England, the traditional enemy. Sydney is well equipped with athletic facilities, from golf courses to tennis courts, and water sports come naturally on one of the world's greatest harbors.

Ticketek Phone Box Office. Ticketek Phone Box Office is the place to buy tickets for major sports events, though these days most bookings are made via its Web site. ☎ *13–2849* ⊕ *www.premier.ticketek.com.au.*

AUSTRALIAN RULES FOOTBALL

Sydney Cricket Ground. A fast, demanding game in which the ball can be kicked or punched between teams of 22 players, Australian Rules Football has won a major audience in Sydney, even though the city has only one professional team—the Sydney Swans—compared to the dozen that play in Melbourne—the home of the sport. Sydney Cricket Ground hosts games April to September. ⊠ *Moore Park Rd., Centennial Park, Paddington* ☎ *02/9360–6601* ⊕ *www.sydneycricketground.com.au.*

BICYCLING

Sydney's favorite cycling track is Centennial Park's Grand Parade, a 3¾-km (2¼-mi) cycle circuit around the perimeter of this grand, gracious eastern suburbs park.

Centennial Park Cycles. Centennial Park Cycles rents bicycles for around A\$16 per hour, A\$50 per day. ⊠ *50 Clovelly Rd., Randwick* ☎ *02/9398–5027* ⊠ *Grand Dr.(inside the park), Centennial Park.*

Clarence Street Cyclery. Clarence Street Cyclery is a major store for all cycling needs. They rent bikes for A\$50 for four hours. ⊠ *104 Clarence St., City Center* ☎ *02/9295–0000* ⊕ *www.cyclery.com.au.*

BOATING AND SAILING

EastSail. EastSail rents bareboat sailing and motored yachts from about A\$655 per half day (four hours); a manned yacht costs around A\$915 for four hours and includes nine sailors and the skipper. ⊠ *D'Albora Marine, New Beach Rd., Rushcutters Bay, Darling Point* ☎ *02/9327–1166* ⊕ *www.eastsail.com.au.*

Surf school at Bondi Beach.

Northside Sailing School. Northside Sailing School at Middle Harbour teaches dinghy sailing to individuals and children's groups. You can learn the ropes in a two-hour, one-on-one private lesson from A$110. ⊠ *The Spit, 77 Parriwi Road, Mosman* ☎ *02/9969–3972* ⊕ *www.northsidesailing.com.au.*

Sydney Harbour Kayaks. Sydney Harbour Kayaks rents one- and two-person kayaks. The location beside Spit Bridge offers calm water for novices, as well as several beaches and idyllic coves. Prices per hour start from A$20 for a one-person kayak and A$40 for a double. Guided 4-hour tours depart every Saturday and Sunday at 8:30 am ($A99 per person). ⊠ *81 Parriwi Rd., Mosman* ☎ *02/9969–4590* ⊕ *www.sydneyharbourkayaks.com.au.*

CRICKET

Cricket is Sydney's summer sport, and it's often played in parks throughout the nation. For Australians the pinnacle of excitement is the Ashes, when the national cricket team takes the field against England. It happens every other summer, and the two nations take turns hosting the event. Cricket season runs from October through March.

Sydney Cricket Ground. International test series games are played at the Sydney Cricket Ground. ⊠ *Moore Park Rd., Centennial Park, Paddington* ☎ *02/9360–6601* ⊕ *www.sydneycricketground.com.au.*

HIKING

Fine walking trails can be found in the national parks in and around Sydney, especially in **Royal National Park** and **Ku-ring-gai Chase National Park** (32 km [20 mi] south and 25 km [15 mi] north of the city center, respectively) and **Sydney Harbour National Park**, which hugs the harbor shores.

The **Bondi-to-Bronte Coast Walk** is a lovely 3½-km (2-mi) cliff walk, popular with just about everyone in the eastern suburbs. Signage explains the flora and Aboriginal history, and the area is the venue for the hugely popular Sculpture by the Sea outdoor art display (held every October and November). The **Federation Cliff Walk** from Dover Heights (north of Bondi Beach) to Vaucluse, and on to Watsons Bay, winds past some of Sydney's most exclusive suburbs. At Diamond Bay you can soak in great views of the 20-million-year-old sandstone cliffs from the steps and boardwalks.

RUGBY LEAGUE

Sydney Football Stadium. Known locally as football (or footy), rugby league is Sydney's winter addiction. This is a fast, gutsy, physical game that bears some similarities to North American football, although the action is more constant and the ball cannot be passed forward. The season falls between March and September. Sydney Football Stadium is the home stadium of the Sydney Roosters. Other games are played at ANZ Stadium (Sydney Olympic Park) and stadiums throughout the suburbs. ⊠ *Moore Park Rd., Centennial Park, Paddington* ☎ *02/9360–6601* ⊕ *www.scgt.nsw.gov.au.*

SCUBA DIVING

Dive Centre Manly. Dive Centre Manly, at the popular northern Sydney beach, runs all-inclusive shore dives each day, which let you see weedy sea dragons and other sea creatures. PADI certification courses are also available. The cost for two shore dives starts at A$95. ⊠ *10 Belgrave St., Manly* ☎ *02/9977–4355* ⊕ *www.divesydney.com.*

Pro Dive. Pro Dive is a PADI operator conducting courses and shore- or boat-diving excursions around the harbor and city beaches. Some of the best dive spots—with coral, rock walls, and lots of colorful fish—are close to the eastern suburb beaches of Clovelly and Coogee. The company also has a center in Manly. A four-hour boat dive with a guide costs around A$189, including rental equipment; a four-dive learn-to-dive course is A$397. ⊠ *27 Alfreda St., Coogee* ☎ *1800/820820* ⊕ *www.prodive.com.au.*

SURFING

All Sydney surfers have their favorite breaks, but you can usually count on good waves on at least one of the city's ocean beaches.

Lets go Surfing. Lets go Surfing is a complete surfing resource for anyone who wants to hang five with confidence. Lessons are available for all ages, and you can rent or buy boards and wet suits. The basic three-class package of two-hour Surf Easy lessons costs A$195. ⊠ *128 Ramsgate Ave., North Bondi* ☎ *02/9365–1800* ⊕ *www.letsgosurfing.com.au.*

Manly Surf School. Manly Surf School conducts courses for adults and children, and provides all equipment, including wet suits. Adults can join a two-hour group lesson (four per day) for A$60. Private instruction costs A$90 per hour. ⊠ *North Steyne Surf Club, Manly Beach, Manly* ☎ *02/9977–6977* ⊕ *www.manlysurfschool.com.*

Rip Curl. This store has a huge variety of boards and surfing supplies. It's right at Bondi Beach. ⊠ *82 Campbell Parade, Bondi Beach* ☎ *02/9130–2660* ⊕ *www.ripcurl.com.au.*

Surfection Bondi Beach. Here is every surfer's idea of retail heaven–surfboards and cool clothing all housed in one huge sparkling new store. ✉ *31 Hall Street, Bondi Beach* ☎ *02/9130–1051.*

Swellnet. A Web site with surf reports and weather details. ⊕ *www. swellnet.com.au.*

SWIMMING

Sydney has many heated Olympic-size swimming pools, some of which go beyond the basic requirements of a workout. Many Aussies, however, prefer to do their "laps" in ocean pools at Bondi and Manly.

Andrew (Boy) Charlton Pool. Andrew (Boy) Charlton Pool isn't just any heated Olympic-size saltwater pool. Its stunning outdoor location overlooking the ships at Garden Island, its radical glass-and-steel design, and its chic terrace café above Woolloomooloo Bay make it an attraction in itself. Admission is A$5.70, and it's open September–April, daily 6 am–7 pm. ✉ *Mrs. Macquarie's Rd., The Domain* ☎ *02/9358–6686* ⊕ *www.abcpool.org.*

Cook and Phillip Park Aquatic and Fitness Centre. Cook and Phillip Park Aquatic and Fitness Centre includes wave, hydrotherapy, children's, and Olympic-size pools in a stunning high-tech complex on the eastern edge of the city center near St. Mary's Cathedral. There's also a complete fitness center and classes. Admission is A$6.20 to swim and A$17 for the gym, which includes pool entry. Open weekdays 6 am–10 pm, weekends 7 am–8 pm. ✉ *College St., City Center* ☎ *02/9326–0444* ⊕ *www.cookandphillip.org.au.*

TENNIS

Cooper Park Tennis Centre. Cooper Park Tennis Centre is a complex of eight synthetic-grass courts and a café in a park surrounded by native bushland, about 5 km (3 mi) east of the city. Court fees are A$25 per hour from 6 am to 5 pm and A$29 per hour from 5 pm to 10 pm (weekends) and A$30 all day on Saturday 6–7, and Sunday 6–8. ✉ *Off Suttie Rd., Cooper Park, 1 Bunna Place, Woollahra* ☎ *02/9389–3100* ⊕ *www.cptennis.com.au.*

Parklands Sports Centre. Parklands Sports Centre has 11 courts in a shady park approximately 2½ km (1½ mi) from the city center. The weekday cost is A$18.50 per hour 9–5 and A$28 per hour 5 pm–10:30 pm; it's A$28 per hour 8 am–6 pm on weekends. ✉ *Lang Rd. at Anzac Parade, Moore Park, Centennial Park* ☎ *02/9662–7033* ⊕ *www. parklandssportcentre.citysearch.com.au.*

WINDSURFING

Balmoral Windsurfing, Sailing, and Kayak School. Balmoral Windsurfing, Sailing, and Kayak School runs classes from its base at this north-side harbor beach. Windsurfing lessons start from A$120 per hour, sailing from A$285 for four hours of lessons over a two-day period. ⊠ *The Esplanade, Balmoral Beach* ☎ *02/9960–5344* ⊕ *www.sailboard.net.au.*

Rose Bay Aquatic Hire. Rose Bay Aquatic Hire has joined forces with kayak operator Oz Paddle. They now rent motorboats, kayaks, and catamarans. The cost is from A$50 per hour for a catamaran; some sailing experience is required to rent these boats. Kayaks are also available for rent from A$20 for the first hour; motorboat rentals cost A$60 per hour for the first hour, other prices apply thereafter. ⊠ *1 Vickery Ave., Rose Bay* ☎ *04/1623–9543, 04/1612–3339.*

SHOPPING

Sydney's shops vary from those with international cachet (Tiffany's, Louis Vuitton) to Aboriginal art galleries, opal shops, craft bazaars, and weekend flea markets. If you're interested in buying genuine Australian products, look carefully at the labels. Stuffed koalas and didgeridoos made anywhere but in Australia are a standing joke.

Business hours are usually 9 or 10 to 5:30 on weekdays; on Thursday stores stay open until 9. Shops are open Saturday 9–5 and Sunday 11–5. Prices include the 10% Goods and Services Tax (GST).

FLEA MARKETS

Balmain Market. Balmain Market, in a leafy churchyard less than 5 km (3 mi) from the city, has a rustic quality that makes it a refreshing change from city-center shopping. Crafts, handmade furniture, plants, bread, toys, tarot readings, and massages are among the offerings at the 140-odd stalls. Inside the church hall you can buy international snacks. Every Saturday 8:30–4. Take Bus No. 442 from the Queen Victoria Building in York Street. ⊠ *St. Andrew's Church, Darling St., Balmain* ☎ *02/9555–1791* ⊕ *www.balmainmarket.com.au.*

Fodor's Choice
★ **Paddington Markets.** Paddington Markets (sometimes called Paddington Bazaar) is a busy churchyard market with about 200 stalls crammed with clothing, plants, crafts, jewelry, and souvenirs. Distinctly New Age and highly fashion conscious, the market is an outlet for a handful of avant-garde clothing designers. Every Saturday from 10–4. ⊠ *Paddington Uniting Church, 395 Oxford St., Paddington* ☎ *02/9331–2923* ⊕ *www.paddingtonmarkets.com.au.*

Paddy's Market. Paddy's Market is a huge fresh produce and flea market held under the Market City complex near the Sydney Entertainment Centre in the Chinatown precinct. There has been a market on this site since 1834, and much of the historic exterior remains. The Metro Light Rail and Monorail stop at the door. Open Wednesday to Sunday 9 to 5. ⊠ *9–13 Hay St., Haymarket* ⊕ *www.paddysmarkets.com.au.*

The Rocks Market. This sprawling covered bazaar transforms the upper end of George Street into a multicultural collage of music, food, arts, crafts, and entertainment. Open weekends 10–5. Be sure to check out the new Rocks Foodies Market with delicious fare on Fridays from 10–4. ⊠ *Upper George St. near Argyle St., The Rocks* ⊕ *www.therocks. com/sydney-Shopping-The_Rocks_Markets.htm.*

SHOPPING CENTERS AND ARCADES

Birkenhead Point. A factory outlet with more than 100 clothing, shoe, and housewares stores and on the western shores of Iron Cove about 7 km [4 mi] west of Sydney, it's a great place to shop for discounted labels including Alannah Hill, Witchery, Bendon (Elle Macpherson's lingerie range), Rip Curl, and David Jones warehouse. Take Bus 504, 506, 518 or the M52 (a new red metro bus) from Druitt Street near Town Hall station and also Circular Quay. ⊠ *Roseby St. near the Iron Cove Bridge, Drummoyne* ☎ *02/9182–8800* ⊕ *www.birkenheadpoint.com.au.*

Oxford Street. Paddington's main artery, from South Dowling Street east to Queen Street, Woollahra, is dressed to thrill. Lined with boutiques, home-furnishings stores, and cafés, it's a perfect venue for watching the never-ending fashion parade. Take Bus No. 380, 382 and 333 from Circulary Quay.

Pitt Street Mall. The heart of Sydney's shopping area includes the Mid-City Centre, the newly redeveloped and huge Westfield Sydney Shopping Centre, Skygarden, Myer, and the charming and historic Strand Arcade—five multilevel shopping plazas crammed with more than 500 shops, from mainstream clothing stores to designer boutiques. ⊠ *Between King and Market Sts., City Center.*

Queen Victoria Building. This is a splendid Victorian-era building with more than 200 boutiques, cafés, and antiques shops. The building is open 24 hours, so you can window-shop even after the stores have closed. ⊠ *George, York, Market, and Druitt Sts., City Center* ☎ *02/9264–9209* ⊕ *www.qvb.com.au.*

SPECIALTY STORES

ABORIGINAL ART

Aboriginal art includes historically functional items, such as boomerangs, wooden bowls, and spears, as well as paintings and ceremonial implements that testify to a rich culture of legends and dreams. Although much of this artwork remains strongly traditional in essence, the tools and colors used in Western art have fired the imaginations of many Aboriginal artists. Works on canvas are now more common than works on bark. Much of the best work of Arnhem Land and the Central Desert Region (close to Darwin and Alice Springs, respectively), finds its way into Sydney galleries.

Cooee Aboriginal Art. This gallery, open Tuesday–Saturday 10–5, exhibits and sells high-end Aboriginal paintings, sculptures, and limited-edition prints. ⊠ *31 Lamrock Ave., Bondi Beach* ☎ *02/9300–9233* ⊕ *www. cooeeart.com.au.*

Kate Owen Gallery + Studio. This gallery showcases quality indigenous art over three levels in Rozelle, a suburb about 15 minutes west of the city center. ⊠ *680 Darling St, Rozelle* ☎ *02/9555–5283* ⊕ *www. kateowengallery.com.*

BOOKS

Ariel Booksellers. This is a large, bright browser's delight, and the place to go for literature, pop culture, avant garde, and art books. Both branches are open daily 9 am–midnight. ⊠ *42 Oxford St., Paddington* ☎ *02/9332–4581* ⊕ *www.arielbooks.com.au* ⊠ *103 George St., The Rocks* ☎ *02/9241–5622.*

Dymocks. This big, bustling bookstore is packed to its gallery-level coffee shop and is the place to go for all literary needs. It's open Monday to Wednesday and Friday 9 to 6, Thursday 9 to 8, Saturday 9:30 to 5:30, and Sunday 10:30 to 5. ⊠ *424 George St., City Center* ☎ *02/9235–0155* ⊕ *www.dymocks.com.au.*

BUSH APPAREL AND OUTDOOR GEAR

Mountain Designs. In the middle of Sydney's "Rugged Row" of outdoor specialists, this store sells camping and climbing gear and dispenses the advice necessary to keep you alive and well in the wilderness. ⊠ *499 Kent St., City Center* ☎ *02/9267–3822* ⊕ *www.mountaindesigns.com.au.*

Paddy Pallin. This should be the first stop for serious bush adventurers heading for wild Australia and beyond. Maps, books, and mounds of gear are tailored especially for the Australian outdoors. ⊠ *507 Kent St., City Center* ☎ *02/9264–2685* ⊕ *www.paddypallin.com.au.*

★ **R. M. Williams.** The place to go for riding boots, Akubra hats, Drizabone riding coats, and moleskin trousers—the type of clothes worn by Hugh Jackman and Nicole Kidman in the movie *Australia.* ⊠ *389 George St., City Center* ☎ *02/9262–2228* ⊕ *www.rmwilliams.com.au.*

CLOTHING

Belinda. This is where Sydney's female fashionistas go when there's a dress-up occasion looming. From her namesake store that scores high marks for innovation and imagination, former model Belinda Seper sells nothing but the very latest designs off the catwalks. ⊠ *8 and 14 Transvaal Ave., Double Bay* ☎ *02/9328–6288, 02/9327–8199* ⊕ *www. belinda.com.au.*

Collette Dinnigan. One of the hottest names on Australia's fashion scene, Collette has dressed Nicole Kidman, Cate Blanchett, and Sandra Bullock. Her Paddington boutique is packed with sensual, floating, negligee-inspired fashions crafted from silks, chiffons, and lace in soft pastel colors accented with hand-beading and embroidery. Her clothes are also available at the David Jones women's store in the city center. ⊠ *33 William St., Paddington* ☎ *02/9360–6691* ⊕ *www. collettedinnigan.com.au.*

Country Road. The fashion here stands somewhere between Ralph Lauren and Timberland, with an all-Australian assembly of classic, countrified his 'n' hers, plus an ever-expanding variety of soft furnishings in cotton and linen for the rustic retreat. ⊠ *142–144 Pitt St., City Center* ☎ *02/9394–1818* ⊕ *www.countryroad.com.au.*

Aboriginal paintings are visual representations of ancestral stories from "The Dreaming."

Marcs. The clothing here is located somewhere close to Diesel-land in the fashion spectrum, with a variety of clothing, footwear, and accessories for the fashion-conscious. Serious shoppers should look for the Marcs Made in Italy sub-label for that extra touch of class. ⊠ *Shop 1, QVB, 455 George St., City Center* ☎ *02/9267–0823* ⊕ *www.marcs. com.au.*

Orson & Blake. This feels like an art gallery dedicated to great modern design, with eclectic housewares, fashions, handbags, and accessories. ⊠ *83–85 Queen St., Woollahra* ☎ *02/9326–1155* ⊕ *www.orsonandblake. com.au.*

Scanlan & Theodore. This is the Sydney outlet for one of Melbourne's most distinguished fashion houses. Designs take their cues from Europe, with superbly tailored women's knitwear, suits, and stylishly glamorous evening wear. ⊠ *122 Oxford St., Paddington* ☎ *02/9380–9388* ⊕ *www. scanontheodore.com.au.*

CRAFTS
Collect. Come here for beautiful glass, wood, and ceramic creations. Its attached gallery, Object, displays a larger selection of Australian-made crafts. ⊠ *417 Bourke St., Surry Hills* ☎ *02/9361–4511* ⊕ *www. object.com.au.*

MUSIC
Birdland Records. This institution for music lovers has an especially strong selection of jazz, blues, African, and Latin American music, as well as an authoritative staff ready to lend some assistance. It's open Monday to Wednesday and Friday 10–5:30, Thursday 10–6, and Sat-

2

urday 9–4:30. ⊠ *Level 4, Dymocks Building, 428 George Street, City Center* ☎ *02/9231–1188* ⊕ *www.birdland.com.au.*

OPALS AND JEWELRY

Australia has a virtual monopoly on the world's supply of opals. The least expensive of these fiery gemstones are triplets, which consist of a thin shaving of opal mounted on a plastic base and covered by a plastic, glass, or quartz crown. Doublets are a slice of mounted opal without the capping. The most expensive stones are solid opals, which cost anywhere from a few hundred dollars to a few thousand. You can pick up opals at souvenir shops all over the city, but if you want a valuable stone you should visit a specialist. Sydney is also a good hunting ground for other jewelry, from the quirky to the gloriously expensive.

Dinosaur Designs. This fun store sells luminous bowls, plates, and vases, as well as fanciful jewelry crafted from resin and Perspex in eye-popping colors. ⊠ *Shop 77, Strand Arcade, George St., City Center* ☎ *02/9223–2953* ⊕ *www.dinosaurdesigns.com.au* ⊠ *339 Oxford St., Paddington* ☎ *02/9361–3776.*

Hathi Jewellery. Here you'll find a beautiful collection of handmade jewelry including earrings, necklaces, and bracelets. Most pieces are one of a kind. ⊠ *19 Playfair St., The Rocks* ☎ *02/9252–4328* ⊕ *www. hathijewellery.com.au.*

The National Opal Collection. The National Opal Collection is the only Sydney opal retailer with total ownership of its entire production process—mines, workshops, and showroom—making prices very competitive. In the Pitt Street showroom you can prearrange to see artisans at work cutting and polishing the stones or visit the on-site museum and learn about the process of opal development and opalised fossils. Hours are weekdays 9 to 6 and weekends 10 to 4. ⊠ *60 Pitt St., City Center* ☎ *02/9247–6344* ⊕ *www.gemtec.com.au.*

★ **Paspaley Pearls.** The jewelers here order their exquisite material from pearl farms near the remote Western Australia town of Broome. Prices start high and head for the stratosphere, but if you're serious about a high-quality pearl, this gallery requires a visit. ⊠ *Paspaley Building, 2 Martin Pl., City Center* ☎ *02/9232–7633, 1300/888–080* ⊕ *www. paspaleypearls.com.*

Percy Marks Fine Gems. Here you'll find an outstanding collection of high-quality Australian gemstones, including dazzling black opals, pink diamonds, and pearls from Broome. ⊠ *62–70 Elizabeth St., City Center* ☎ *02/9233–1355* ⊕ *www.percymarks.com.au.*

Rox Gems and Jewellery. Come here for serious one-off designs at the cutting edge of lapidary chic. ⊠ *Shop 31, Strand Arcade, George St., City Center* ☎ *02/9232–7828* ⊕ *www.rox.com.au.*

T-SHIRTS AND BEACHWEAR

Done Art and Design. This is a great place to find the striking artworks of prominent artist Ken Done, who catches the sunny side of Sydney with vivid colors and bold brushstrokes. His shop also carries a line of bed linens, sunglasses, beach towels, beach and resort wear, and

T-shirts. ✉ *123–125 George St., The Rocks* ☎ *02/9251–6099* ⊕ *www.done.com.au.*

Rip Curl. Rip Curl, the well-known Australian surfing company that has been making surfboards since 1967, sells gear from this flagship store. The two levels are packed with the latest board shorts, surf clothes, wet suits, swimsuits, T-shirts, and accessories. ✉ *105 George St., The Rocks* ☎ *02/9252–4551* ⊕ *www.ripcurl.com.au.*

New South Wales

WITH CANBERRA AND THE A.C.T.

WORD OF MOUTH

"If you like museums, you've got the Australian War Memorial (a must), the National Gallery of Australia, Questacon. The Parliament House and Old Parliament House are both worth a visit as well. If you like the outdoors, there's great hiking/scenery/wildlife at Tidbinbilla Nature Reserve and Namadgi National Park."

—longhorn55

WELCOME TO NEW SOUTH WALES

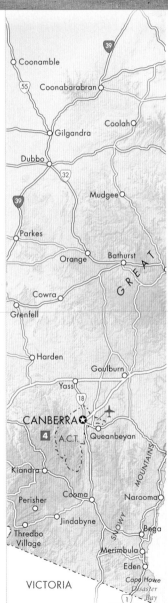

TOP REASONS TO GO

★ **Getting in Touch with Nature:** Exotic birds are prolific in the Blue Mountains and North Coast regions, and Canberra isn't known as the "Bush Capital" for nothing.

★ **The Great Australian Bite:** Fine restaurants have taken root in the Hunter Valley, as well as in the North Coast towns of Coffs Harbour and Byron Bay. Seafood can be excellent, and don't miss fish-and-chips on the beach.

★ **Outdoor Adventure:** The region's mountains and national parks offer opportunities for walks and hikes, horseback riding, rappelling, canyoning, and rock climbing. Outdoorsy folks will enjoy Canberra's wide-open spaces and cycling or walking around the city's Lake Burley Griffin.

★ **World-Class Wineries:** The Hunter Valley has an international reputation for producing excellent Chardonnay, Shiraz, and a dry Semillon.

1 The Blue Mountains. Sydneysiders flock to this UNESCO-protected wilderness region with its majestic mountain peaks and deep green valleys sprinkled with charming country guesthouses. The famous sandstone rock formations known as the Three Sisters are the area's best-known attraction.

2 Hunter Valley Wine Region. This is one of the oldest and best-known wine regions in Australia, with vineyards dating back to the 1830s. Oenophiles shouldn't miss a trip to this thriving and perennially busy destination. We also like the food, historic towns, and tranquil countryside.

3 The North Coast. This region has some of the most glorious and seductive stretches of beach in Australia—and that's saying something when you consider the competition. The almost continuous line of beaches is interspersed with lively towns and harbors, with the Great Dividing Range rising to the west.

Coffs Harbour
Armidale
Macksville
South West Rocks
Gunnedah
Walcha
Kempsey
Tamworth
Scone
Gloucester
Taree
Forster
Bulahdelah
Singleton
2
HUNTER VALLEY
Cessnock
Nelson Bay
Newcastle
1
3
Lithgow
Gosford
Katoomba
Three Sisters Parramatta **☆SYDNEY**
Camden
Seacliff Bridge
Wollongong
Bowral Kiama
Nowra
Jervis Bay
Wreck Bay
Ulladulla
Batemans Bay
Batemans Bay

NEW ENGLAND RANGE
DIVIDING   RANGE
BLUE MOUNTAINS

Pacific Ocean

0   100 mi
0   100 km

GETTING ORIENTED

3

New South Wales, with the country's capital city Canberra and the A.C.T. carved out in an area half the size of Rhode Island, covers the southeast corner of the country. Despite this being Australia's most populous state, the rich variety of landscapes is its biggest selling point. The Blue Mountains, a World Heritage site, lie approximately 100 km (60 mi) to the west of Sydney; the Hunter Valley is about 160 km (100 mi) or two hours north of Sydney. The North Coast is exactly where its name suggests, while Lord Howe Island is offshore, 700 km (435 mi) northeast of Sydney. Canberra is 288 km (180 mi) southwest of Sydney.

4 Canberra and the A.C.T. The nation's capital and its environs may be quiet and a little too well-mannered for some, but its museums and galleries are the best in the country, and its diverse range of parks and gardens is a major draw.

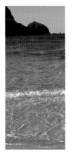

Updated
by Caroline
Gladstone

For many travelers Sydney is New South Wales, and they look to the other, less-populous states for Australia's famous wilderness experiences. However, New South Wales has many of Australia's natural wonders within its borders. High on the list are the subtropical rain forests of the North Coast, lush river valleys, warm seas, golden beaches, the World Heritage areas of Lord Howe Island, and some of Australia's finest vineyards. Many travelers overlook Canberra, but history buffs and art aficionados will love its selection of galleries and museums that are ranked as the nation's finest.

Today, with approximately 7.2 million people, New South Wales is Australia's most populous state. Although this is crowded by Australian standards, it's worth remembering that New South Wales is larger than every U.S. state except Alaska. In the state's east, a coastal plain reaching north to Queensland varies in width from less than a mile to almost 160 km (100 mi). This plain is bordered on the west by a chain of low mountains known as the Great Dividing Range, which tops off at about 7,300 feet in the Snowy Mountains in the state's far south. On this range's western slopes is a belt of pasture and farmland. Beyond that are the western plains and Outback, an arid, sparsely populated region that takes up two-thirds of the state.

PLANNING

WHEN TO VISIT
For visitors from the northern hemisphere the Australian summer (approximately December–February) has great pull. The best times to visit the Hunter Valley are during the February–March grape harvest season and the June Hunter Food and Wine Festival. Spring and autumn

are also ideal times to visit Canberra; from March to May, autumn leaves paint the city with amber hues. The spring flower celebration, Floriade, lasts from mid-September to mid-October. The North Coast resort region is often booked solid between Christmas and the first half of January, but autumn and spring are good times to visit.

GETTING HERE AND AROUND

AIR TRAVEL

New South Wales is peppered with airports, so flying is the easiest way to get around if you're traveling long distances. Prices are generally low, thanks to the budget airlines. From Sydney, REX (Regional Express) Airlines services Ballina and Lismore (both about ½ hour from Byron Bay). Qantas flies into Canberra, Port Macquarie, and Coffs Harbour, while Virgin Australia (formerly Virgin Blue) flies into Canberra, Port Macquarie, Ballina, and Coffs Harbour.

Information **Qantas Airways** ☎ 13–1313 ⊕ www.qantas.com.au. **REX Airlines** ☎ 13–1713 ⊕ www.regionalexpress.com.au. **Virgin Australia** ☎ 13–6789 ⊕ www.virginaustralia.com.

CAR RENTAL

Hiring your own car is the most convenient way of getting around the region. The scenic Blue Mountains and Hunter Valley routes and attractions are outside the towns, so having your own set of wheels is helpful. When visiting the wine country, be aware that Australia has very strict rules against drunk driving. Most towns have major car-rental companies. You can pick up a car at one point and drop off at another for an extra fee.

TRAIN TRAVEL

As in the States, most people drive here, so train services aren't brilliant and can often cost more than other options. It is possible to travel by train to the Blue Mountains with Sydney's Cityrail commuter trains. CountryLink trains link Sydney to towns in the Hunter Valley and towns along the North Coast. Canberra is not a convenient destination to get to by train, so unless you're a rail enthusiast, it's quicker to drive or catch a bus.

Information **Cityrail** ☎ 13–1500 ⊕ www.cityrail.info. **CountryLink** ☎ 13–2232 ⊕ www.countrylink.info.

HEALTH AND SAFETY

In an emergency, dial **000** to reach an ambulance, the police, or the fire department. If you decide to hike off the beaten track in the Blue Mountains, tell someone where you're headed. There is an emergency rescue service, which can be reached at ☎ 13/2500.

In summer, bush fires are a perennial worry—always obey the no-fire zones and make sure you have enough water to avoid dehydration.

RESTAURANTS

Dining varies dramatically throughout New South Wales, from superb city-standard restaurants to average country-town fare. As popular weekend retreats for well-heeled Sydneysiders, the Blue Mountains and Southern Highlands have a number of fine restaurants and cozy tea rooms that are perfect for light lunches or afternoon teas. In the

Hunter Valley several excellent restaurants show off the region's fine wines. Unsurprisingly seafood dominates on the North Coast, and again, thanks to holidaying Sydneysiders with high standards, you should be able to tuck into some excellent meals. The eclectic selection of eateries in Canberra reflects the city's cosmopolitan residents, so despite the city's size, Canberra's dining spots hold their own against the restaurants of Sydney and Melbourne, although the feeling is generally more casual.

HOTELS

Accommodations include everything from run-of-the-mill motels and remote wilderness lodges to historic, cliff-perched properties and expansive seaside resorts. Rates are often much lower on weekdays, particularly in the Blue Mountains and the Hunter Valley, as traffic from Sydney is heavier on weekends. The North Coast is popular during school holidays, so book as far ahead as possible. Hotels in Canberra, with one or two notable exceptions, don't have the character that other places do. But there are plenty of four-star chain hotel options and self-catering apartments. Smoking is banned in all public places in NSW and the A.C.T.

WHAT IT COSTS IN AUSTRALIAN DOLLARS					
	¢	$	$$	$$$	$$$$
Restaurants	under A$10	A$10–A$20	A$21–A$35	A$36–A$50	over A$50
Hotels	under A$100	A$100–A$150	A$151–A$200	A$201–A$300	over A$300

Meal prices are per person for a main course at dinner. Hotel prices are for two people in a standard double room in high season, including tax and service, based on the European Plan (with no meals) unless otherwise noted.

THE BLUE MOUNTAINS

Sydneysiders have been doubly blessed by nature. Not only do they have a magnificent coastline right at their front door, but a 90-minute drive west puts them in the midst of one of the most spectacular wilderness areas in Australia—World Heritage Blue Mountains National Park. This rippling sea of hills is covered by tall eucalyptus trees and dissected by deep river valleys—the area is perfect terrain for hiking and adventure activities. Standing 3,500-plus feet high, these "mountains" were once the bed of an ancient sea. Gradually the sedimentary rock was uplifted until it formed a high plateau, which was etched by aeons of wind and water into the wonderland of cliffs, caves, and canyons that exists today. Now the richly forested hills, crisp mountain air, cool-climate gardens, vast sandstone chasms, and little towns of timber and stone are supreme examples of Australia's diversity. The mountains' distinctive blue coloring is caused by the evaporation of oil from the dense eucalyptus forests. This disperses light in the blue colors of the spectrum, a phenomenon known as Rayleigh Scattering.

GREAT ITINERARIES

It's wise to decide in advance whether you'd like to cover a lot of ground quickly or choose one or two places to linger a while. If you have less than four days, stick close to Sydney. The most compelling choice would be the Blue Mountains, followed by the Hunter Valley. In a busy week you could visit the Blue Mountains plus the Hunter Valley. Two weeks would allow a Blue Mountains–North Coast–Lord Howe circuit, or brief stops in most of the region's top destinations.

IF YOU HAVE 4 DAYS

Start with a visit to the Blue Mountains. You could arrange a round-trip itinerary from Sydney in a fairly hectic day or, preferably, spend a night in Katoomba, Blackheath, or Leura and make it a two-day excursion. Return to Sydney, and then head north to the Hunter Valley. A two-day/one-night driving visit here would allow you enough time to see the main sights and spend time touring the wineries before traveling back to Sydney on the second day. An alternative would be a quick visit to the Blue Mountains, then two days in Canberra to see the city's excellent museums and galleries.

IF YOU HAVE 7 DAYS

Go to the Blue Mountains and Hunter Valley as described above, then if beach life is appealing, continue to the North Coast. In three days of driving you wouldn't get much farther than Coffs Harbour (with overnights there and in Port Macquarie), and this would be rushing it, but it's possible to fly back to Sydney from Coffs. Alternatively, or if you're looking for something more cerebral, travel southwest to sedate Canberra and have a leisurely few days exploring gems like the National Portrait Gallery, Parliament House, and the Australian War Memorial, while stretching your legs walking or biking around Lake Burley Griffin.

The Blue Mountains Visitor Information Centre is at the foot of the mountains on the Great Western Highway at Glenbrook, the town you'll encounter when driving from Sydney. There is another information office at Echo Point in Katoomba.

Visitor Information **Blue Mountains Visitor Information Centre** ⊠ *Great Western Hwy., Glenbrook* ☎ *1300/653408* ⊗ *Daily 9–5.* **Blue Mountains Visitors Centre–Katoomba** ⊠ *Echo Point, Echo Point Rd and Panorama Dr., Katoomba, New South Wales* ☎ *1300/653408.*

WENTWORTH FALLS

95 km (59 mi) west of Sydney.

This attractive township is home to the Blue Mountains' most stunning natural waterfalls and bush walking trails. The Falls themselves straddle the highway, but most points of interest and views of the Jamison Valley and Blue Mountains National Park are south of the road.

GETTING HERE AND AROUND

If you are driving from Sydney, head west onto Parramatta Road, then take the M4, following signs to the Blue Mountains. There is a toll to pay at the end of the motorway. Wentworth Falls is clearly signposted and is 95 km (59 mi) from Sydney. It's also easy to catch a train to Wentworth Falls; the journey from Sydney Central Station takes 1¾ hours, with trains leaving roughly every hour. The Blue Mountains Bus Company (☎ 02/4751–1077 ⊕ www.bmbc. com.au) connects towns within the region with routes 685 and 695, connecting Wentworth Falls to Leura and Katoomba.

ARTIST HAVEN

The Blue Mountains harbor a wealth of talent. You'll find artists, writers, composers, and performers living in this vibrant cultural community. Check out the galleries, browse in the bookshops, or pop into a café or pub to catch some good music.

Blue Mountains Music Festival. The Blue Mountains Music Festival, held every March in Katoomba, showcases folk, blues, and roots music. ⊕ www.bmff.org.au.

EN ROUTE

Norman Lindsay Gallery and Museum. If driving from Sydney, be sure to stop at the National Trust–listed Norman Lindsay Gallery and Museum, dedicated to the Australian artist and writer. Considered one of the cultural highlights of the Blue Mountains, Lindsay lived in this house during the latter part of his life until he died in 1969. Lindsay is best known for his paintings, etchings, and drawings (many of voluptuous nudes), but he also built model boats, sculpted, and wrote poetry and children's books, among which *The Magic Pudding* has become an Australian classic. The delightful landscaped gardens contain several of Lindsay's sculptures, and you can also take a short but scenic bushwalk beyond the garden or take refreshments in the café. Daily tours of Lindsay's studios run from 10:30 am to 2:30 pm and are included in the price, while dedicated art fans can stay in the cottage on the grounds for A$150 a night mid-week or A$200 a night Friday, Saturday, and Sunday. ⊠ *14 Norman Lindsay Crescent, Faulconbridge* ☎ *02/4751–1067* ⊕ *www.normanlindsay.com.au* ⊠ *A$12* ☉ *Daily 10–4.*

OUTDOOR ACTIVITIES

HIKING ★ **Falls Reserve.** From a lookout in Falls Reserve, south of the town of Wentworth Falls, you can take in magnificent views both out across the Jamison Valley to the Kings Tableland and of the 935-foot-high **Wentworth Falls** themselves. To find the best view of the falls, follow the trail that crosses the stream and zigzags down the sheer cliff face, signposted "national pass." If you continue, the trail cuts back across the base of the falls and along a narrow ledge to the delightful Valley of the Waters, where it ascends to the top of the cliffs, emerging at the Conservation Hut. The complete circuit takes at least three hours and is a moderately difficult walk. ⊠ *End of Falls Rd.*

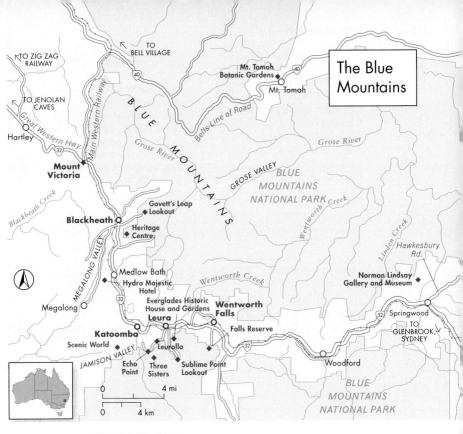

WHERE TO EAT

$$ ✕ **Conservation Hut.** From its prime spot in Blue Mountains National
AUSTRALIAN Park, on a cliff overlooking the Jamison Valley, this spacious, mud-
brick bistro serves simple, savory fare. Lovely breakfast dishes include
herbed mushrooms with a poached egg and roast tomatoes on toast.
For lunch and dinner, dig into hearty soups, beef pies, or seared ocean
trout with chervil and potato rosti. Be sure to save room for the dessert
cakes. An open balcony is a delight on warm days, and a fire blazes
in the cooler months. A hiking trail from the bistro leads down into
the Valley of the Waters, one of the splendors of the mountains. It's a
wonderful pre- or post-meal walk. ⊠ *88 Fletcher St.* ☎ *02/4757–3827*
⊕ *www.conservationhut.com.au* ⌑ *BYOB* ⊘ *No dinner Mon.–Thurs.*
in summer months.

LEURA

5 km (3 mi) west of Wentworth Falls.

Leura, the prettiest and chicest of the mountain towns, is bordered
by bush and lined with excellent cafés, restaurants, and gift shops.
From the south end of the main street (the Mall), the road continues
past superb local gardens as it winds down to the massive cliffs over-
looking the Jamison Valley. The dazzling 19-km (12-mi) journey along

Cliff Drive skirts the rim of the valley—often only yards from the cliff edge—providing truly spectacular Blue Mountains views.

GETTING HERE AND AROUND

The train station at Leura is one stop further on from Wentworth Falls on the same line from Sydney, and the station is walking distance from all the town's shops and galleries. In a car, Leura is a few kilometers further west from Wentworth Falls on the Great Western Highway. Alternatively, catch a Blue Mountains Bus Company bus—Routes 685 and 695 connect the town with Wentworth Falls and Katoomba.

EXPLORING

Everglades Historic House and Gardens. Everglades Gardens, a National Trust–listed, cool-climate arboretum and nature reserve established in the 1930s, is one of the best public gardens in the Blue Mountains region. This former home of a Belgian industrialist is surrounded by 5 hectares (13 acres) of native bushland and exotic flora, a rhododendron garden, an alpine plant area, and formal European-style terraces. The views of the Jamison Valley are magnificent. ✉ *37 Everglades Ave.* ☏ *02/4784–1938* ⊕ *www.evergladesgardens.com.au* ✉ *A$8* ☾ *Oct.– Mar., daily 10–5; Apr.–Sept., daily 10–4.*

Leuralla. Leuralla is an imposing 1911 mansion, and still belongs to the family of Dr. H. V. ("Doc") Evatt (1894–1965), the first president of the General Assembly of the United Nations and later the leader of the Australian Labor Party. A 19th-century Australian art collection and a small museum dedicated to Dr. Evatt are inside the home. Baby boomers and their children (and grandchildren) will love the collection in the New South Wales Toy and Railway Museum, which is both inside the house and in the gardens. The museum is comprised of an extensive collection of railway memorabilia, antique curios from yesteryear (including lots of dolls depicting Alice in Wonderland scenes), and exhibitions on iconic dolls like Barbie. Directly across the street from the mansion are the Leuralla Public Gardens (entry A$2), with spectacular views of the Jamison Valley. ✉ *36 Olympian Parade* ☏ *02/4784–1169* ⊕ *www.toyandrailwaymuseum.com.au* ✉ *A$14, A$10 for gardens only* ☾ *Daily 10–5.*

★ **Sublime Point Lookout.** Sublime Point Lookout, just outside Leura, lives up to its name with a great view of the Jamison Valley and the generally spectacular Blue Mountains scenery. It's a quiet vantage point that provides a different perspective from that of the famous **Three Sisters** lookout at nearby Katoomba. ✉ *Sublime Point Rd.*

Continued on page 157

BLOOMIN' BEAUTIFUL

Leura Garden Festival. When spring is in the air in the mountains, one of the most beautiful places to be is Leura. Dozens of cherry blossoms line the main street, and private gardens are open for viewing. Make a date for the weeklong Leura Garden Festival in early October. The gardens are adorned with the work of local artists keen to win the annual art prize. A village fair caps off the celebrations. One ticket (A$20) buys entrance to all the gardens on show. ☏ *0431/095-279* ⊕ *www.leuragardensfestival.com.au.*

HIKING THE BLUE MOUNTAINS

Kanangra Falls

Head west of Sydney along the M4, or simply hop a bus or train, and within an hour you'll be on a gradual climb along a traditional Aboriginal pathway into the heart of the Blue Mountains—a sandstone plateau formed 150 million years ago that tops out at 3,600 feet. Dramatic valleys, canyons, and cliff faces to the north and south of the main road have been carved by wind and water over millennia. And the blue? That's light refracting off the fine oil mist from the world's most ecologically diverse tract of eucalypt forest.

(top) Looking out over the Jamison Valley.

A WORLD HERITAGE WONDERLAND

Part of the Greater Blue Mountains World Heritage Area, Blue Mountains National Park encompasses 2,678 sq km (1,034 sq ft) of prime hiking country. Most tracks skirt the cliff edges or run along the bottom of the canyons; paths that connect the two levels are often at points along the cliff that offer breathtaking panoramas of the Jamison, Megalong, or Grose Valleys.

While the geological landscape is worth the trip alone, the flora and fauna are some of the country's most unique. Within just a few square miles, the world's widest variety of eucalypts in one contiguous forest have evolved to thrive in everything from open scrub plains to dense valley rainforests. The Wollami pine, a tree that grew alongside dinosaurs, can only be found in a few small areas

here. Then there are the rare or threatened creatures like the Blue Mountains water skink, the yellow-bellied glider, and the long-nosed potoroo. It seems only fitting that both Charles Darwin and John Muir visited here. In 1932 it became one of the first formally protected tracts of land in Australia.

Towns dot the main highway through the Blue Mountains, but Katoomba is the unofficial capital, fully outfitted with resources for visitors and the starting point for some of the most iconic walks. Less-bustling Blackheath, minutes up the road from Katoomba, has our favorite eco-lodges and is closest to the best walks of the Grose Valley. You can get a feel for the region on a day trip from Sydney, but if your schedule permits, stay a night (or three) to fit in a few different hikes.

HIKING LITE: THREE WAYS TO SEE THE JAMISON VALLEY WITHOUT BREAKING A SWEAT

Scenic Skyway

SCENIC CABLEWAY
Less crowded than the Scenic Railway, the world's steepest cable car feels gentle in comparison. The enclosed gondola glides between the valley floor and the cliff rim with views of the Three Sisters.

SCENIC SKYWAY
This Swiss-style, glass-bottom cable car takes you on a 720 m (1/2 mi) long journey 270 m (886 ft) above the gorge for great 360 degree views across the Jamison Valley, the Katoomba Falls, and the famous Three Sisters.

KATOOMBA SCENIC RAILWAY
An incline of 52 degrees makes this former coal-haul railway the world's steepest. Grab a seat in the front. Be prepared for lines at peak visiting times. The railway runs every 10 minutes until 4:50 pm.

Claustral Canyon

BLUE MOUNTAIN TRAIL OVERVIEW

Lookout at Echo Point

KATOOMBA-ECHO POINT	TRAIL TIPS	HIGHLIGHTS
ECHO POINT TO SCENIC RAILWAY: This may not be a long walk, but thanks to the 861 steps of the Giant Staircase, don't underestimate it.	This route is very popular, especially on weekends, so set off early. Be aware that the last railway and cable car up leave at 4:50 pm. If you miss them, you'll have to walk.	• Expansive views across the Jamison Valley and beautiful forest vistas. • Brings you right up against the Three Sisters. • Scenic Railway boarding area is at the end of the trail, so you don't have to walk back up.
PRINCE HENRY CLIFF WALK: Start at the Leura Cascades picnic area and head up the mountain to Echo Point. This is a tough hike and not for the faint of heart.	Olympian Rock and Elysian Rock are perfect spots to picnic.	• Thanks to the level of difficulty, you'll be able to escape the crowds at Katoomba. • Spot lyre birds, kookaburras, and glossy black cockatoos.
BLACKHEATH	**TRAIL TIPS**	**HIGHLIGHTS**
GRAND CANYON WALK: Possible for anyone who's reasonably fit (though there are some steps) and well worth the effort.	A great choice for hot days: the canyon's cool temperatures will come as welcome relief.	• A winding path through lush vegetation and around plummeting waterfalls. • Spectacular views of gorges, forest, and cliff lines at Evans lookout.
PERRY'S LOOKDOWN TO BLUE GUM FOREST: This track starts at Perry's Lookdown parking lot, 9 km (5.5 mi) northeast of Blackheath, and takes you down a steep track into the lovely Blue Gum Forest.	Stop by the Heritage Centre in nearby Blackheath for excellent information on historic sites and hiking trips.	• Experience for yourself why the ecologically unique Blue Gum Forest attracted conservationists' attention in Australia. • You might spot possums, gliders, bandicoots, brown antechinuses, and swamp wallabies.
GLENBROOK	**TRAIL TIPS**	**HIGHLIGHTS**
RED HANDS CAVE TRACK: This moderately difficult circuit walk goes up the Red Hands Creek Valley along a creek and through the rainforest.	It's best to park at the Visitors Centre on Bruce Road and then walk for 10 minutes following the signs to the Glenbrook causeway, as there is no easy parking at the causeway itself.	• Bring your binoculars, because there are many birdwatching opportunities. • See the Blue Mountains' most sacred Aboriginal site, Red Hands Cave. The cave is named after the displays of Aboriginal hand stencils on its walls.

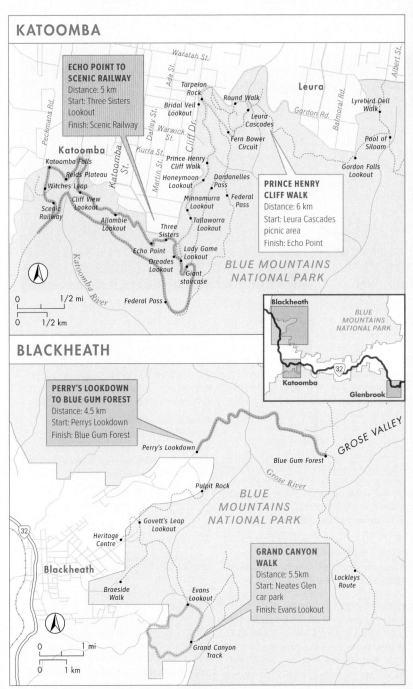

KATOOMBA

ECHO POINT TO SCENIC RAILWAY
Distance: 5 km
Start: Three Sisters Lookout
Finish: Scenic Railway

PRINCE HENRY CLIFF WALK
Distance: 6 km
Start: Leura Cascades picnic area
Finish: Echo Point

BLACKHEATH

PERRY'S LOOKDOWN TO BLUE GUM FOREST
Distance: 4.5 km
Start: Perrys Lookdown
Finish: Blue Gum Forest

GRAND CANYON WALK
Distance: 5.5km
Start: Neates Glen car park
Finish: Evans Lookout

KATOOMBA

View of Three Sisters from Echo Point lookout

ECHO POINT TO SCENIC RAILWAY

In the 1930s, the **Giant Staircase** was hewn out of the cliff by teams of park rangers. The top of the steps are near **Three Sisters Lookout** and the walk down is very steep and narrow in places. It's difficult going but the views make it all worthwhile. Look out for the encouraging half way sign. At the bottom, keep your eyes peeled for echidnas, brush-tailed and ring-tail possums, bandicoots, quolls, and grey-headed flying foxes. If you're keen for more exertion once you've reached the Railway, take the **Furber Steps**. It's a challenging but rewarding track that offers great views of **Katoomba Falls** and **Mt. Solitary** across the valley.

PRINCE HENRY CLIFF WALK

If you prefer to hike in the mountains rather than along the forest floor, you'll enjoy this section of the Cliff Walk with its superb vistas across the valley. From the picnic area, the trail descends beside Leura Cascades creek towards **Bridal Veil lookout**. Be sure to slow down and take in the great views over the **Leura Forest**. Continue on Prince Henry Drive; at **Tarpeian Rock** you can see Mt. Solitary.

Keep going uphill towards Olympian Rock and Elysian Rock. From here, follow the cliff line to **Millamurra** and **Tallawarra Lookouts**. The last part of the climb to the **Three Sisters** is perhaps the most challenging but also the most rewarding. Take a few minutes and savor the sweeping views of the valley.

QUICK BITES/SUPERMARKETS FOR PICNIC GOODIES

You can stock up at either Coles or ALDI supermarkets in Katoomba or Woolworths supermarket in Leura. Scenic World has two restaurants. For gourmet treats visit Carrington Cellars at the rear of the Carrington Hotel, or stop at Brown's Siding Store & Café at Medlow Bath for breakfast, lunch, and goodies.

STAY HERE IF:

On weekends tour buses descend on the town, but once they've headed back to Sydney, the place isn't over-run with vistors. Katoomba has a very relaxed feel helped in no small part by a small hippy community. It also has plenty of nice old pubs and cafés, cute vintage shops, and rural versions of big department stores.

BLACKHEATH

Mount Hay, Grose Valley

GRAND CANYON WALK

From the parking lot, 4.5 km (2.8 mi) from Blackheath, follow the Grand Canyon track signs as the path zig-zags down the hillside and the vegetation becomes more like a rainforest. The trail takes you down into the canyon and over a creek. It winds past a few overhanging rocks, then starts a steep decline towards a sandy overhang called the **Rotunda**. After a break here, follow the signs to **Evans Lookout**, which will lead you through a tunnel and past two waterfalls. You eventually reach the 10-meter-tall (33 ft) **Beauchamp Falls** in the center of the creek. From here head up through a gap in the cliffs, weaving through boulders, again following signs to Evans Lookout. From Evans Lookout, you can do a 6.5 km (4 mi) Cliffside walk to **Pulpit Rock** along the Cliff Top Track.

PERRYS LOOKDOWN
TO BLUE GUM FOREST

From the parking lot, follow the signs pointing out the trail down the hill to **Perrys Lookdown**. You'll have fine views over the **Grose Valley** with its sheer sandstone cliffs with the Blue Gum Forest below. Next, head down the hill and do

a quick detour to **Docker's Lookout** with its view of Mt. Banks to the north. Head back following the Perrys Lookdown–Blue Gum Forest walk signs. The descent to **Blue Gum Forest** will take about 90 minutes. Once you've explored the forest floor and it's dense canopy, head back up the steep track to Perrys Lookdown.

QUICK BITES/SUPERMARKETS
FOR PICNIC GOODIES

Blackheath has something of a gourmet reputation. For a quick pre-walk bite, we recommend **Denise's Pies** at the New Ivanhoe Hotel (corner of Great Western Hwy and Govetts Leap Rd, 02/4787–6156). It's considered by some connoisseurs as Australia's finest pie place. There's also a small IGA supermarket.

STAY HERE IF:

Blackheath is smaller and less-visited than Katoomba, but the old weatherboard houses give it a similar feel. There's also enough quirky shops and quaint cafes and restaurants to keep it entertaining. Several Sydney restaurateurs relocated here, so there's a breadth of excellent dining venues.

GLENBROOK

Glenbrook Gorge

An echidna

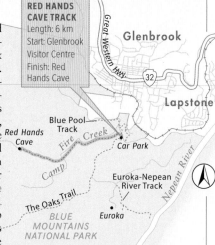

Kookaburras

RED HANDS CAVE TRACK

Red Hands Cave has some well preserved Aboriginal hand stencillings. The stencils are behind Plexiglas (called Perspex here) to protect them from graffiti. There are a few good placards explaining the history and describing the artifacts found in the area. The walk starts on the southern side of the causeway, and after about 2 km (1.2 mi) of gentle steps down the gully, the well-defined track forks: take the right-hand path just after a large rocky outcrop near the edge of a gully. ■**TIP**➔ Take care near the edge, there's a significant dropoff. Up the hill near **Camp Fire Creek**, keep an eye out for axe grinding grooves (oval-shaped indentations in sandstone outcrops that Aboriginals used to shape and sharpen stone axes). The trail passes through several types of forest, including dry eucalypt forest, so there's a good variety of birds in the area. Watch for echidnas in the open forest and chestnut-rumped heathwrens and rock warblers in the sandstone area near the Red Hands Cave.

RED HANDS CAVE TRACK
Length: 6 km
Start: Glenbrook Visitor Centre
Finish: Red Hands Cave

Glenbrook

Great Western Hwy

32

Lapstone

Blue Pool Track

Red Hands Cave

Fire Creek

Camp

Car Park

Euroka-Nepean River Track

Nepean River

The Oaks Trail

BLUE MOUNTAINS NATIONAL PARK

Euroka

QUICK BITES/SUPERMARKETS FOR PICNIC GOODIES

Glenbrook doesn't have the same variety of food and lodging options as Katoomba and Blackheath, but there's a small IGA supermarket on Park Street. Ross Street has a few nice cafes; check out **Mash Café's** delicious breakfasts.

WHERE TO EAT AND STAY

For expanded hotel reviews, visit Fodors.com.

$$
AUSTRALIAN
Fodor'sChoice
★

✕ **Silk's Brasserie.** Thanks to its Sydney-standard food, wine, and service, Silk's rates as one of the finest Blue Mountains restaurants. The menu here changes seasonally, but might include pan-seared scallops on avocado with cress, pancetta, and honey-mustard-seed dressing for a starter, or a main dish of confit of duck Maryland served with a salad of duck sausage, pickled pear, beet, and watercress. The locals' favorite dessert is the warm bittersweet chocolate fondant served with vanilla-bean Chantilly cream and black cherries. The restaurant is housed in a Federation-era building, and in colder months a log fire warms the century-old simple but

THE SWEET LIFE

Josophan's. This gorgeous chocolate boutique in Leura's main shopping street has fast become *the* place to stop for luscious handmade chocolates and drinking chocolate. You can also take part in classes (how does making chocolate truffles sound?) and take away lovely gift boxes of sweets. For a light snack and yummy chocolate desserts, walk across the road to Cafe Madeline (at 187a The Mall), which is also owned by Josophan's proprietor and chocolatier Jodie Van der Velden. ⊠ *132 The Mall, Leura, New South Wales* ☎ *02/4784–2031.*

elegant interior, where yellow ocher walls reach from black-and-white checkerboard floor to sky-high ceiling. ⊠ *128 The Mall* ☎ *02/4784–2534* ⊕ *www.silksleura.com.*

$$$$
🏨 **Bygone Beautys Cottages.** These six country cottages, scattered around Wentworth Falls and in the nearby village of Bullaburra, provide self-contained accommodations for couples, families, and small groups. **Pros:** antiques collectors will love the decor and the connected tea room (at Leura); very romantic surrounds. **Cons:** if olde worlde leaves you cold, this isn't the place for you; bathrooms can be chilly in winter. ⊠ *Main office:, Grose and Megalong Sts.* ☎ *02/4784–3117* ⊕ *www.bygonebeautys.com.au* ⊃ *6 cottages* △ *In-room: no a/c, kitchen. In-hotel: laundry facilities.*

$$
🏨 **Leura House.** This guesthouse, which dates back to 1890, is said to be Leura's first. **Pros:** free Wi-Fi access; freshly cooked breakfasts; lots of history. **Cons:** some areas still need an update; sometimes groups book the B&B out. ⊠ *7 Britain St., Leura* ☎ *02/4784–2035* ⊕ *www.leurahouse.com.au* ⊃ *11 rooms, 1 cottage* △ *In-room: Wi-Fi. In-hotel: restaurant, parking, some pets allowed* ⦿ *Breakfast.*

KATOOMBA

2 km (1 mi) west of Leura.

The largest and busiest town in the Blue Mountains, Katoomba developed in the early 1840s as a coal-mining settlement, turning its attention to tourism later in the 19th century. The town center on Katoomba Street has shops, restaurants, and cafés, but most travelers are keen to see the marvels at the lower end of town and don't linger here.

GETTING HERE AND AROUND

The 110-km (68-mi) journey to Katoomba takes between 90 minutes and two hours from Sydney via Parramatta Road and the M4 Motorway, which leads to Lapstone at the base of the Blue Mountains. From there, continue on the Great Western Highway and follow the signs to Katoomba. The town has its own train station, and is also connected to the rest of the Blue Mountains by the Blue Mountains Bus Company. A good deal is the Blue Mountains Explorer Link ticket, which can be purchased at Sydney railway stations. The A$48.80 pass combines a same-day return train ticket from Sydney to Katoomba and a day's access to the red double-decker Explorer buses that travel around Katoomba and Leura stopping at 26 stops (⊕ *www.explorerbus.com. au*). The same travel pass but for three days (instead of one) is available for A$64.80.

Another economical sightseeing option is the Blue Mountains Trolley bus, which provides a similar hop-on, hop-off tour, visiting 29 stops, in a vehicle that resembles a San Francisco streetcar. The cost is A$25, and tickets are available at the Trolley Shoppe near Katoomba railway station. There is a Blue Mountains Visitor Information Centre at Echo Point in Katoomba. Sydney Visitor Centre has information on Blue Mountains hotels, tours, and sights.

TOURS

Blu Cruzin' Harley Davidson Tours. Nothing beats zooming along Cliff Drive and through the Megalong Valley on the back of a Harley Davidson. You'll feel like one of the boys from *Easy Rider* on a "soft tail" Harley (the same bike as in the movie) or a Fat Boy. The shop is owned by locals who know the area well. The most popular two-hour ride is a round-trip from Katoomba to the towns of Blackheath, Mount Victoria, and historic Hartley. The two-hour ride costs A$180 per bike for one bike, or Ar A$165 per bike for two bikes. There are also 1-, 1.5-, 3-, and 4-hour rides. ⊠ *Katoomba, New South Wales* ☎ *0403 413 714, 0409 404 055.*

Blue Mountains Adventure Company. The well-established Blue Mountains Adventure Company (which operates in partnership with Wild at Heart Safaris) runs abseiling, rock-climbing, canyoning, bushwalking, and mountain-biking trips. A full-day abseiling adventure is A$150, while bushwalking is A$130, and both include lunch, snacks, and all equipment needed. There are both introductory and intermediate levels of canyoning from A$165; you'll visit such places as Empress Falls or Serendipity Canyon. ⊠ *84A Bathurst Rd.* ☎ *02/4782–1271* ⊕ *www. bmac.com.au.*

Blue Mountains Explorer Bus. This company operates the signature red buses coming out of Katoomba and running at regular intervals throughout the region. Different pass types are available that are tailored to everything from single rides to week-long passes. ⊠ *283 Main St., Katoomba, New South Wales* ☎ *1300/300–915* ⊕ *www. explorerbus.com.au.*

High n Wild. High n Wild conducts rappelling, canyoning, rock-climbing, and mountain-biking tours throughout the year. One-day rappelling trips cost A$150; combination rappelling and canyoning tours cost A$165. ⊠ *3/5 Katoomba St.* ☎ *02/4782–6224* ⊕ *www.high-n-wild.com.au.*

Trolley Tours. These purple hop-on, hop-off trolleys operate on a convenient circuit throughout Katoomba and Leura, stopping at the major points of interest. ⊠ *Main St., Katoomba, New South Wales* ☎ *1800/ 801–577* ⊕ *www.trolleytours.com.au.*

ESSENTIALS

Hospital Blue Mountains District Anzac Memorial Hospital ⊠ *Great Western Hwy., 1 km [½ mi] east of town center* ☎ *02/4784-6500* ⊙ *Daily 9–5.*

Visitor Information Blue Mountains Visitor Information Centre ⊠ *Echo Point Rd.* ☎ *1300/653-408* ⊕ *www.visitbluemountains.com.au.*

EXPLORING

Fodor's Choice
★

Echo Point. Echo Point, which overlooks the densely forested Jamison Valley and three soaring sandstone pillars, has the best views around Katoomba. The formations—called the Three Sisters—take their name from an Aboriginal legend that relates how a trio of siblings was turned to stone by their witch-doctor father to save them from the clutches of a mythical monster. The area was once a seabed that rose over a long period and subsequently eroded, leaving behind tall formations of sedimentary rock. From Echo Point—where the visitor center is located—you can clearly see the horizontal sandstone bedding in the landscape. There is a wide viewing area as well as the start of walks that take you closer to the Sisters. At night the Sisters are illuminated by floodlights. There are cafes and a visitor information center near the site. ⊠ *Follow Katoomba St. south out of Katoomba to Echo Point Rd., or take Cliff Dr. from Leura.*

The Edge cinema. The screen at The Edge cinema is the height of a six-story building. Specially filmed for this giant format, *The Edge,* shown six times daily starting at 10:20 (the last show is at 5:30), is an exciting 40-minute celebration of the region's valleys, gorges, cliffs, waterfalls, dramatic scenery, and the mysterious Wollemi Pine (thought to be extinct until it was discovered in the region in the early 1990s). The complex includes a café and gift shop, and regular feature films (A$14) are also screened here. ⊠ *225 Great Western Hwy.* ☎ *02/4782–8900* ⌨ *A$15.*

☾ **Scenic World.** If you'd like to check out the scenery but don't want to break a sweat, be sure to take one of the three rides at Scenic World: the Scenic Railway, the Cableway, or the Scenic Skyway. If you're going to pick one, the railway provides the best thrill. ⊠ *Cliff Dr. at Violet St.* ☎ *02/4780–0200* ⊕ *www.scenicworld.com.au* ⌨ *Scenic Pass round-trip Railway, Cableway, or Skyway A$28* ⊙ *Daily 9–5.*

OUTDOOR ACTIVITIES

A good hiking brochure can be picked up at Echo Point Tourist Information Centre, which lists walks varying in length from ½ hour to 3 days.

FOUR-WHEEL
DRIVES

Tread Lightly Eco Tours. Tread Lightly Eco Tours operates small-group tours of the Blue Mountains National Park and guided day and night walks as well as four-wheel-drive tours. Half- or full-day walking tours take in itineraries such as Fern Bower, Blue Gum Forest, and the

Ruin Castle, starting at A$135 per person with lunch. ✉ *100 Great Western Hwy., Medlow Bath* ☎ *02/4788–1229, 0414/976752* ⊕ *www. treadlightly.com.au.*

HIKING **Blue Mountains Walkabout.** Experience the Blue Mountains from an
★ Aboriginal perspective with the Blue Mountains Walkabout. These challenging one-day walks follow a traditional walkabout song line. Indigenous guides take you on a 7-km (4.5 mi) off-track walk through rain forests while giving some background on Aboriginal culture. You'll also taste bush tucker. The walk involves some scrambling, so you need to be fit. ✉ *Box 519, Springwood* ☎ *0408/433822* ⊕ *www. bluemountainswalkabout.com* ✉ *A$95.*

Blue Mountains Guides. Seven-day odysseys and easier walks are offered by Blue Mountain Guides. The half-day Grand Canyon Walk near Blackheath (A$135) is a great way to experience the rain forest if time is short. ✉ *2/187 Katoomba St., Katoomba* ☎ *02/4782–6307* ⊕ *www. bluemountainsguides.com.au.*

HORSEBACK **Werriberri Trail Rides.** At the foot of the Blue Mountains, 10 km (6 mi)
RIDING south of Blackheath, Werriberri Trail Rides conducts reasonably priced rides at A$99 for two hours and A$190 for a full-day ride through the beautiful Megalong Valley, as well as the Hartley Historic Ride (A$230). These guided rides are good for adults and children. ✉ *Megalong Rd., Megalong Valley* ☎ *02/4787–9171* ⊕ *www. australianbluehorserides.com.au.*

WHERE TO EAT

$ ✗ **Paragon Cafe.** With its chandeliers, gleaming cappuccino machine, and
CAFÉ bas-relief figures above the booths, this wood-paneled 1916 art deco café was a favorite Blue Mountains eatery in its heyday. Today visitors come more for the 52 varieties of homemade chocolates and the Devonshire Teas (a spread of scones, jam, cream, and a pot of tea). New owners took over mid-2011, and locals are hoping they will restore the place to a more meal-focused establishment. ✉ *65 Katoomba St.* ☎ *02/4782–2928* ☉ *No dinner Sun.–Thurs.*

WHERE TO STAY

For expanded hotel reviews, visit Fodors.com.

$$$ ⊞ **The Carrington.** Established in 1880, this is one of the grandes dames of the Blue Mountains, a Victorian-era relic that in its heyday was considered one of the four great hotels of the British Empire. **Pros:** drinks on their veranda are a pleasant way to end the day, breakfast included in the rate. **Cons:** the newer rooms lack character ✉ *15–47 Katoomba St.* ☎ *02/4782–1111* ⊕ *www.thecarrington.com.au* ↘ *59 rooms, 49 with bath; 6 suites; 1 apartment* ⏚ *In-room: no a/c, kitchen, Wi-Fi. In-hotel: restaurant, bar* ⍾ *Multiple meal plans.*

$$$$ ⊞ **Echoes Boutique Hotel & Restaurant.** Perched on the edge of the Jamison
★ Valley, this stylish boutique hotel has one of the best views in the Blue Mountains. **Pros:** spectacular views from the terrace; slick and funky accommodation. **Cons:** a little overpriced. ✉ *3 Lilianfels Ave.* ☎ *02/4782–1966* ⊕ *www.echoeshotel.com.au* ↘ *14 suites* ⏚ *In-room: Wi-Fi. In-hotel: restaurant, bar, spa, business center* ⍾ *Breakfast.*

$$$$
★
Lilianfels Blue Mountains Resort & Spa. Teetering close to the brink of Echo Point, this glamorous boutique hotel adds a keen sense of manor-house style to the standard Blue Mountains guesthouse experience. **Pros:** luxurious and restful bathrooms; staff give friendly five-star service. **Cons:** 19th-century style is not for everyone; restaurant prices are very expensive. ⊠ *Lilianfels Ave. at Panorama Dr.* ☎ *02/4780–1200* ⊕ *www.lilianfels.com.au* ⌖ *Reservations essential* ⌁ *81 rooms, 4 suites* ⌂ *In-room: safe, Internet. In-hotel: restaurant, bar, pool, tennis court, gym, spa, business center* ¡○¡ *Breakfast.*

$$
Fodor's Choice
★
Lurline House. This historic little B&B is considered the town's best. **Pros:** all rooms have four-poster beds; warm and welcoming. **Cons:** younger trendsetters might find the place not to their taste. ⊠ *122 Lurline St., Katoomba* ☎ *02/4782–4609* ⊕ *www.lurlinehouse.com.au* ⌁ *7 rooms, 1 cottage* ⌂ *In-room: Wi-Fi. In-hotel: restaurant, parking* ¡○¡ *Breakfast.*

$$$
Fodor's Choice
★
Melba House. If Dame Nellie, Dame Joan, and Dame Edna are new to you, you'll certainly be well acquainted with the ladies after a stay in beautiful Melba House. **Pros:** genial host; located minutes away from great walking trails. **Cons:** no year-round dining area (except in summer when the veranda is an option, breakfast is served in rooms). ⊠ *98 Waratah St.* ☎ *02/4782–4141* ⊕ *www.melbahouse.com* ⌁ *3 suites* ⌂ *In-room: Wi-Fi* ¡○¡ *Breakfast.*

$$$
Mountain Heritage Hotel & Spa. This hotel overlooking the Jamison Valley is steeped in history: it served as a "coffee palace" during the temperance movement, a rest-and-relaxation establishment for the British navy during World War II, and a religious retreat in the 1970s. **Pros:** friendly service, manicured gardens, public areas are charming with great valley views **Cons:** Furniture is a little dated. ⊠ *Apex and Lovel Sts.* ☎ *02/4782–2155* ⊕ *www.mountainheritage.com.au* ⌁ *37 rooms, 4 suites* ⌂ *In-room: kitchen, Internet. In-hotel: restaurant, bar, pool, gym, spa, laundry facilities.*

BLACKHEATH

12 km (7½ mi) north of Katoomba.

Magnificent easterly views over the Grose Valley—which has outstanding hiking trails—delightful gardens, good restaurants, and antiques shops head the list of reasons to visit the village of Blackheath, at the 3,495-foot summit of the Blue Mountains.

GETTING HERE AND AROUND
Blackheath is an easy drive north from Katoomba, traveling on the Great Western Highway, passing Medlow Bath on the way. There's also a train station on the Blue Mountains line and it's also serviced by Blue Mountains Bus Company on Route 698 between Katoomba and Mount Victoria.

ESSENTIALS
Visitor Information **Heritage Centre** ⊠ *End of Govett's Leap Rd., Blackheath* ☎ *02/4787–8877* ⊕ *www.nationalparks.nsw.gov.au* ☾ *Daily 9–4:30.*

EXPLORING

★ **Govett's Leap Lookout.** Blackheath's most famous view is from the Govett's Leap Lookout, with its striking panorama of the Grose Valley and Bridal Veil Falls. Govett was a surveyor who mapped this region extensively in the 1830s. This lookout is the start or finish of several excellent bushwalks. Brochures are available at the Heritage Centre. ⊠ *End of Govett's Leap Rd.*

OUTDOOR ACTIVITIES

HIKING   **Auswalk.** This environmentally conscious company, which also offers walks in other parts of Australia, has 3-, 5-, and 7-day self-guided or guided hiking tours through the region, staying at historic inns along the way. They ask that you be in reasonable shape before you start. ⊕ *www.auswalk.com.au* ✉ *From A\$1,000.*

HORSEBACK   **Megalong Australian Heritage Centre.** The Megalong Australian Heritage
RIDING   Centre, in a deep mountain valley off the Great Western Highway, is the place to saddle up and explore a country property. Both adults and children can go horseback riding around the farm's 2,000 acres, with prices ranging from A\$50 for an hour's wilderness ride to A\$195 for a day ride with lunch provided. There are pony rides for younger children. The on-site farm is closed for renovations at this writing. ⊠ *Megalong Rd., Megalong Valley* ⊹ *15 km (9 mi) south of Blackheath* ☎ *02/4787–8188* ⊕ *www.megalongcc.com.au* ✉ *Free for heritage center, horse riding for day A\$195* ☉ *Daily 9–5.*

WHERE TO EAT AND STAY

For expanded hotel reviews, visit Fodors.com.

\$\$ ✗ **Vulcan's.** Some people travel to the Blue Mountains just to dine here,
CAFÉ   so make sure you book ahead at this cozy café that revolutionized din-
Fodor's Choice   ing in rural New South Wales. Operated by Phillip Searle (formerly
★   one of the leading lights of Sydney's dining scene) and Barry Ross, Vulcan's specializes in slow-roasted dishes, cooked in a century-old baker's oven and flavored with Asian or Middle Eastern spices The duckling sausage and glazed pork dishes are locals' favorites. The restaurant's checkerboard ice cream—with star anise, pineapple, licorice, and vanilla flavors—is a favorite that tastes as good as it looks. Dinner is served at two sittings, so diners at the 6 pm sitting have little time to linger before they must vacate their tables for the 8 pm sitting. ⊠ *33 'Govetts Leap Rd.* ☎ *02/4787–6899* ⌁ *BYO* ☉ *Closed Mon.–Thurs. and Feb.*

\$\$\$ 🏠 **Jemby Rinjah Eco Lodge.** Designed for urbanites seeking a wilderness experience, these rustic, self-contained wooden cabins and lodges are set deep in the bush. **Pros:** cabins and lodges are private and tranquil, hearty and healthy mountain fare is served at the restaurant. **Cons:** some might find the eco-toilet disconcerting, the lodges can be booked out by groups. ⊠ *336 Evans Lookout Rd.* ☎ *02/4787–7622* ⊕ *www. jembyrinjahlodge.com.au* ↪ *10 cabins, 3 lodges* ⌂ *In-room: no a/c, kitchen. In-hotel: restaurant, laundry facilities.*

One of the hundreds of vineyards that dot the Hunter Valley.

MOUNT VICTORIA

7 km (4½ mi) northwest of Blackheath.

The settlement of Mount Victoria is the highest point in the Blue Mountains, and has a Rip Van Winkle air about it—drowsy and only just awake in an unfamiliar world. A walk around the village reveals many atmospheric houses, stores, and a couple of stately old hotels with the patina of time spelled out in their fading paint. Mount Victoria is at the far side of the mountains at the western limit of this region, and the village serves as a good jumping-off point for a couple of out-of-the-way attractions.

GETTING HERE AND AROUND

Mount Victoria is an easy drive north of Blackheath on the Great Western Highway, and it's also on the main Blue Mountains railway line linking Sydney with Lithgow. The 698 bus route connects the village with Katoomba.

EXPLORING

Hotel Imperial. The pink circa-1878 Hotel Imperial was one of several historic Blue Mountains inns built a few years after the railway line was opened from Sydney. It's worth popping in for a drink to have a look at the fading grand old lady, but its accommodations get mixed reviews at best. ⊠ *1 Station St.* ☎ *02/4787–1878* ⊕ *www.hotelimperial.com.au.*

Trains, Planes and Automobiles. Children and adults will enjoy a browse around Trains, Planes and Automobiles, which bills itself as the best antique toyshop in the world. ⊠ *86-88 Great Western Hwy.* ☎ *02/4787–1590* ⊕ *www.antiquetoys.com.au* ☉ *Daily 10–5.*

Jenolan Caves. Stalactites, stalagmites, columns, and lacelike rock on multiple levels fill the fascinating Jenolan Caves, a labyrinth of vast limestone caverns sculpted by underground rivers. There are as many as 320 caves in the Jenolan area. Three caves near the surface can be explored on your own, but a guide is required to reach the most intriguing formations. Standard tours lead through the most popular caves—many say that Orient Cave is the most spectacular, while the more rigorous adventure tours last up to seven hours. The one- to two-hour walks depart every 15 to 30 minutes, on weekends less frequently. Prices range from A$30 for a standard tour to A$75 for the adventurous two-hour "plug hole" tour, where you squeeze through ancient passegways, There's even a A$200 full-day abseiling cave adventure. Cave House, on the same site, is a nostalgic retreat and has been providing lodging since 1887. To get here, follow the Great Western Highway north out of Mount Victoria, then after Hartley turn southwest toward Hampton. ⊠ *59 km (37 mi) from Mount Victoria, Jenolan Caves Rd, Jenolan Caves* ☎ *1300/763311* ⊕ *www.jenolancaves.org.au* ☉ *Daily 9:30–5:30.*

☺
Fodor's Choice
★
Zig Zag Railway. You'll be wiping the soot from your face after a ride on the huff-and-puff vintage steam engine, but that's part of the fun of this cliff-hugging 16-km (10-mi) round-trip experience on the Zig Zag Railway. Built in 1869, this was the main line across the Blue Mountains until 1910. The track is laid on the cliffs in a giant "Z," and the train climbs the steep incline by chugging back and forth along switchback sections of the track—hence its name. The steam engine operates on weekends, public holidays, and Wednesday, and weekdays during school holidays. A vintage self-propelled diesel-powered railcar is used at other times. During selected Saturdays in winter (June to September) there's a special two-hour Wizard's Express ride for lovers of Harry Potter books. ⊠ *Bells Line of Rd., 19 km (12 mi) northwest of Mount Victoria, Clarence* ☎ *02/6355–2955* ⊕ *www.zigzagrailway. com.au* ☑ *A$28 return, A$18 one-way* ☉ *Departures from Clarence Station daily at 11, 1, and 3.*

WHERE TO EAT

$$
AUSTRALIAN
✕**Apple Bar.** Bilpin is the apple capital of New South Wales, and this friendly little roadside restaurant is set among the orchards. Wood-fired pizzas are a popular choice here, while the ever-changing specials blackboard may feature wood-grilled locally raised Black Angus eye fillet and the wood-grilled pork shoulder with caramelized applies (local of course). This is a great place for lunch or dinner either going to or on your way home from Mount Tomah Botanic Garden, which is about 10 km (6 mi) farther west on the same road. ⊠ *2488 Bells Line of Rd., Bilpin, New South Wales* ☎ *02/4567–0335* ⊕ *www.applebar.com.au.*

OFF THE
BEATEN
PATH
Mount Tomah Botanic Garden. This is the cool-climate branch of Sydney's Royal Botanic Gardens (30 km [19 mi] northeast of Mount Victoria). The garden is 3,280 feet above sea level, and is a spectacular setting for native and imported plants. You'll find beautiful rhododendrons and European deciduous trees, as well as plants that evolved in isolation for millions of years in the Gondwana Forest. The famous Wollemi Pine (once thought to be extinct) is also here. There are picnic grounds, a café with views of the ranges, and a daily guided tour at

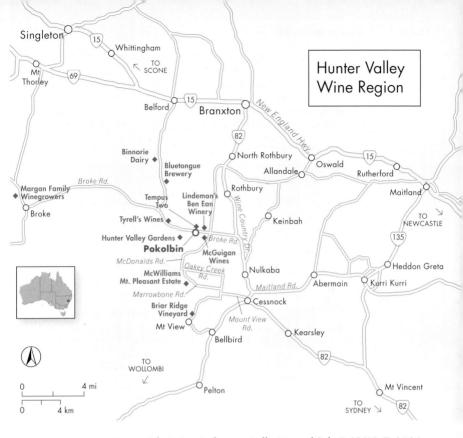

Hunter Valley
Wine Region

11:30 am. Admission is free. ✉ *Bells Line of Rd.* ☎ *02/4567–2154*
⊕ *www.mounttomahbotanicgarden.com.au* ⊙ *Mon.–Fri. 9–5:30, Sat.
and Sun. 9:30–5:30.*

THE HUNTER VALLEY WINE REGION

To almost everyone in Sydney, the Hunter Valley conjures up visions
of one thing: wine. The Hunter is the largest grape-growing area in
the state, with more than 120 wineries producing excellent varieties.
The Hunter is divided into seven subregions, each with its own unique
character. The hub is the Pokolbin/Rothbury region, where many of
the large operations are found, along with several boutique wineries.

The Hunter Valley covers an area of almost 25,103 square km (9,692
square mi), stretching from the town of Gosford north of Sydney to 177
km (110 mi) farther north along the coast, and almost 300 km (186 mi)
inland. The meandering waterway that gives this valley its name is also
one of the most extensive river systems in the state.

OFF THE
BEATEN
PATH

Wollombi. Nothing seems to have changed in the atmospheric town
of Wollombi, 24 km (15 mi) southwest of Cessnock, since the days
when the Cobb & Co. stagecoaches rumbled through town. Founded
in 1820, Wollombi was the overnight stop for the coaches on the

second day of the journey from Sydney along the convict-built Great Northern Road—at that time the only route north. The town is full of delightful old sandstone buildings and antiques shops, and there's also a museum in the old courthouse with 19th-century clothing and bushranger memorabilia.

Wollombi Tavern. Wollombi's local pub, the Wollombi Tavern, serves its own exotic brew, which goes by the name of Dr. Jurd's Jungle Juice. The pub also scores high marks for its friendliness and local color. ⊠ *Old North Rd.* ☎ *02/4998–3261* ⊕ *www.wollombitavern.com.au.*

Avoca House. The century-old Avoca House, set on a 67-acre farm a mile out of Wollombi, is the perfect place to spend a night. ⊠ *2683 Wollombi Rd.* ☎ *02/4998–3233* ⊕ *www.avocahouse.com.au*

POKOLBIN AND ENVIRONS

163 km (100 mi) north of Sydney.

The Lower Hunter wine-growing region is centered on the village of Pokolbin, where there are antiques shops, good cafés, and dozens of wineries. In peak season, wineries are very busy with tour groups, so if you can visit mid-week or off-season, all the better.

GETTING HERE AND AROUND

A car is the best way to visit the wineries and off-the-beaten-path attractions unless you are on a guided tour. Leave Sydney via the Harbour Bridge or Harbour Tunnel and get onto the Pacific Highway (keep following the signs for Newcastle). Just before Hornsby the road joins the Sydney–Newcastle Freeway, known as the F3. Take the exit from the freeway signposted "Hunter Valley vineyards via Cessnock." From Cessnock, the route to the vineyards is clearly marked. Allow 2½ hours for the journey.

TOURS

Any tour of the area's vineyards should begin at Pokolbin's **Hunter Valley Wine Country Visitors Information Centre**, which has free maps of the vineyards, brochures, and a handy visitor's guide.

From Sydney, AAT Kings operates a daylong wine-tasting bus tour of the Hunter Valley and another to Hunter Valley Gardens. Buses collect passengers from hotels, then make a final pickup from the Star City (Sydney Casino) bus terminal, departing at 8 am. The tour returns to the casino at 6:15 pm. Tours cost from A$170, including lunch and wine tasting.

To avoid driving after sampling too many wines, hop aboard one of the Wine Rover buses, which will pick you up from Pokolbin or Cessnock. These minibuses travel between restaurants and about a dozen wineries, allowing you to hop on and off during the day. A day pass with unlimited stops is A$45 during the week and A$55 on weekends.

Local operator Heidi's Hunter Valley operates personalized day tours to the wineries and restaurants in a sleek four-wheel-drive vehicle. Heidi Duckworth, who worked for the Hunter Valley Wine Tourism organization for 12 years, knows all the best places in the valley.

ESSENTIALS

Bus Contacts **AAT Kings** ☎ *1300/228–546* ⊕ *www.aatkings.com.au.*
Heidi's Hunter Valley ☎ *0408/623–136* ⊕ *www.heidishuntervalley.com.au.*
Rover Coaches ☎ *02/4990–1699, 0427/001–100* ⊕ *www.rovercoaches.com.au.*

Hospital **Cessnock District Hospital** ✉ *View St., Cessnock* ☎ *02/4991–0555.*

Visitor Information **Maitland Hunter Valley Visitor Information Centre**
✉ *New England Hwy. at High St., Maitland* ☎ *02/4931–2800*
⊕ *www maitlandhuntervalley. com.au* ⊗ *Daily 9–5.* **Hunter Valley Wine Country Visitors Information Centre** ✉ *455 Wine Country Drive* ☎ *02/4990–0900*
⊕ *www.winecountry.com.au* ⊗ *Mon.–Thurs. 9–5, Fri. and Sat. 9–6, Sun. 9–4.*

EXPLORING

Binnorie Dairy. Drop into Binnorie Dairy (at Tuscany Wine Estate) to sample and buy—few can resist—Simon Gough's handcrafted soft cow and goat cheeses made from locally sourced milk. You'd be hard-pressed to find a tastier marinated feta outside Greece—or even in it. ✉ *Hermitage Rd. at Mistletoe La.* ☎ *02/4998–6660* ⊕ *www.binnorie. com.au* ⊗ *Tues.–Sat. 10–5, Sun. 10–4.*

Hunter Valley Gardens. Garden lovers and those who admire beauty in general should flock to the **Hunter Valley Gardens**, in the heart of the Pokolbin wine-growing district. The 12 separate gardens occupy 50 acres and include European formal gardens, a Chinese Moongate garden, and a delightful children's storybook garden featuring characters such as the Mad Hatter and Jack and Jill. The adjacent complex houses restaurants, a popular pub, a hotel, a cute wedding chapel, the underground **Hunter Cellars,** and a selection of boutiques selling gifts as well as wonderful chocolates and fudge. ✉ *Broke and McDonalds Rds.* ☎ *02/4998–4000* ⊕ *www.hvg.com.au* 🎫 *A$23.50 for gardens* ⊗ *Daily 9–5.*

EXPLORING THE WINERIES

Eighteen Hunter Valley wineries are part of the Cellar Door Pass Scheme, which is a bargain if you are looking to stock up while visiting. A pass costs A$99 and gives you a host of benefits, including VIP premium tastings, guided tours to some of the region's best wineries, and six free bottles up to the value of A$120 from big name wineries like Tempus Two. Other famous names like Wyndham Estate, Binnorie Dairy, and Hunter Valley Gardens are also part of the scheme. See ⊕ *www.cellardoorpass.com.au* for more details.

Briar Ridge Vineyard. In a delightful rural corner of the Mount View region, Briar Ridge Vineyard is one of the Hunter Valley's outstanding small wineries and won a prestigious wine award in 2011. It produces a limited selection of sought-after reds, whites, and sparkling wines. The Semillon, Chardonnay, Shiraz, and intense Cabernet Sauvignon are highly recommended. The vineyard is on the southern periphery of the Lower Hunter vineyards, about a five-minute drive from Pokolbin. Drop in for a daily tasting or for lunch from Wednesday to Sunday. If you want to extend your stay, they have B&B accommodation suitable for up to six people. ✉ *593 Mt. View Rd., Mount View* ☎ *02/4990–3670* ⊕ *www.briarridge.com.au* ⊗ *Daily 10–5.*

★ **Lindeman's Ben Ean Winery.** The Lindemans Hunter River Winery has been one of the largest and most prestigious winemakers in the country since the early 1900s. In addition to its Hunter Valley vineyards, the company owns property in South Australia and Victoria, and numerous outstanding wines from these vineyards can be sampled in the tasting room. Try the Shiraz, Semillon, or Chardonnay. The winery has its own museum, displaying vintage winemaking equipment, as well as two picnic areas, one near the parking lot and the other next to the willow trees around the dam. ✉ *McDonalds Rd. just south of DeBeyers Rd.* ☎ *02/4998–7684* ⊕ *www.lindemans.com.au* ⊙ *Daily 10–5.*

Margan Family Winegrowers. A leading light in the new wave of Hunter winemakers, Margan Family Winegrowers produces some of the valley's best small-volume wines. Try their full-bodied Verdelho, rosé-style Saignée Shiraz, and Certain Views Cabernet Sauvignon. A riper-than-most Semillon is the flagship, and the 2004 Decanter World Wine Awards rated Margan's botrytis Semillon the world's best sweet wine at its price point (around A$20)—it's delicious. The ultramodern rammed-earth-design cellar door and restaurant is in the tiny village of Broke, 20 km (12 mi) from Pokolbin. Many items on the fine-dining Margan restaurant lunch menu are sourced from the chef's vegetable and herb garden on-site, along with fresh eggs. Tasting plates are a great way to sample many of the dishes on offer, such as panetta-wrapped quail. ✉ *1238 Milbrodale Rd., Broke* ☎ *02/6579–1372* ⊕ *www.margan.com. au* ⊙ *Daily 10–5.*

McGuigan Wines. Adjoining the Hunter Valley Gardens is the cellar-door complex of McGuigan Wines. Here you can taste wines and at the adjacent **Hunter Valley Cheese Company**'s (www.huntervalleycheese. com.au) superb cheeses—look out for the washed-rind Hunter Valley Gold and the deliciously marinated soft cows'-milk cheese. You can also see the cheeses being made by hand. There is a cheese talk daily at 11. ✉ *Broke and McDonalds Rds.* ☎ *02/4998–7402, 02/4998–7744* ⊕ *www.mcguiganwines.com.au.*

★ **McWilliams Mount Pleasant Estate.** At McWilliams Mount Pleasant Estate, part of Australia's biggest family-owned wine company, chief winemaker Phil Ryan (only the third since the winery was founded in 1921), continues the tradition of producing classic Hunter wines. The flagship Maurice O'Shea Shiraz and Chardonnay, and the celebrated Elizabeth Semillon, are among the wines that can be sampled in the huge cellar door. You can also enjoy a tasting plate of seasonal delicacies on the terrace of Elizabeth's Café, best savored with three vintages of Elizabeth Semillon and one of premium Lovedale Semillon. Guided winery tours run daily at 11 am. ✉ *401 Marrowbone Rd.* ☎ *02/4998–7505* ⊕ *www. mcwilliams.com.au* 🖃 *Tours A$5, tastings free* ⊙ *Daily 10–4:30.*

Tempus Two. You can't miss the ultramodern Tempus Two in the heart of Pokolbin. This futuristic winery is a joint venture between two leading Hunter Valley families: the Roches (owners of Hunter Valley Gardens) and the McGuigans, who have made wine for four generations. The winery is best known for its Pinot Gris; however, you can sample a wide variety, including Semillon, Sauvignon Blanc, Chardonnay, and Shiraz in the stylish tasting room. There's also a Goldfish Wine Bar and Oishii, an on-site fine-dining Japanese-Thai restaurant. If you can, stop in at the winery's branch of the Hunter Valley Smelly Cheese Shop. In the summer the winery hosts major concerts in its 10,000-seat ampithe-atre—past performers have included Elton John, Rod Stewart, and the Beach Boys. ⊠ *Broke and McDonalds Rds.* ☎ *02/4993–3999* ⊕ *www. tempustwo.com.au* ☾ *Daily 9–5.*

Tyrrell's Wines. Founded in 1858, Tyrrell's Wines is the Hunter Valley's oldest family-owned vineyard. This venerable establishment crafts a wide selection of wines, and was the first to produce Chardonnay com-mercially in Australia. Its famous Vat 47 Chardonnay is still a winner. Enjoy the experience of sampling fine wines in the rustic tasting room, or take a picnic lunch to a site overlooking the valley. Guided tours (A$5) are given daily at 1:30. ⊠ *Broke Rd., 2½ km (1½ mi) west of McDonalds Rd.* ☎ *02/4993–7000* ⊕ *www.tyrrells.com.au* ☾ *Mon.–Sat. 9–5, Sun. 10–4.*

OUTDOOR ACTIVITIES

Although most people's idea of activity in the Hunter is raising a glass, it is possible to expend more energy and still enjoy a glass or two.

BICYCLING **Hunter Valley Cycling.** You supply the pedal power, and for A$245 Hunter Valley Cycling will supply you with all the all the support (bikes, helmet, maps, luggage transfer, a three-course dinner, and accommodation) for a two-day, 50-km (31-mi) self-guided tour (mid-week only). If that's sounds too hardcore, the company also rents bikes for A$30 a day. Call ahead and they'll deliver a bike to your hotel. ☎ *0418/281480* ⊕ *www. huntervalleycycling.com.au.*

HELICOPTER TOURS **Slattery Helicopter Charter.** Soaring over a patchwork of wineries and the dramatic Brokenback Range is a thrilling experience–and can be a rela-tively inexpensive one (as helicopter rides go) when three people share a chopper for a 15-minute ride (A$250 for 3 people). A great experience is the winery tour and three-course-lunch flight with the helicopter picking you up at and delivering you back to your Hunter Valley accommo-dation (A$300 per person). ⊠ *230 Old Maitland Rd., Hexham, New South Wales* ☎ *0408/649 696,* ⊕ *www.slatteryhelicoptercharter.com.au.*

HORSEBACK RIDING **Hunter Valley Horse Riding and Adventures.** These friendly folks welcome equestrians of all levels and ages, and have a nice selection of guided rides around the valley. A favorite is the the sunset ride, when your most likely to see wildlife. ⊠ *288 Talga Rd., Rothbury* ☎ *02/4930–7111* ⊕ *www.huntervalleyhorseriding.com.au.*

HOT-AIR BALLOONS **Balloon Aloft Hunter Valley.** Drifting above the valley while the vines are still wet with dew is an unforgettable way to see the Hunter Val-ley. The award-winning Balloon Aloft has been operating for over 30 years, and runs hour-long sunrise flights for A$335. ☎ *02/4991–1955, 1800/028568* ⊕ *www.balloonaloft.com.*

WHERE TO EAT

$$$ ✕ **Bistro Molines.** Local French-born
FRENCH celebrity chef Robert Molines, who
Fodor'sChoice used to run Roberts Restaurant, has
★ a restaurant on the grounds of the
lovely Tallavera vineyard, which
might just have one of the best views
in the valley. Make sure you nab a
table on or near the veranda. Food
isn't overly complicated or styled,
which fits nicely with the relaxed
(but professional) service. The rack
of veal with roasted Jerusalem arti-
choke and porcini cream is delicious,
while seafood fans will love the fillet
of blue-eyed cod with saffron risotto
and baby clam. At lunch there's a
set menu that includes a glass of
local wine. ✉ *Tallavera Grove,
749 Mount View Rd., Mount
View* ☎ *02/4990–9553* ⊕ *www.
bistromolines.com.au* ◷ *Closed Tues., Wed., no lunch Mon., Thurs.*

> ### FOR BEER LOVERS
>
> Here's the dilemma: one of you
> likes wine, while the other pre-
> fers beer.
>
> **Bluetongue Brewery.** Pop into
> Bluetongue Brewery, Hunter Val-
> ley's only brewery. Named after a
> lizard with a bright blue tongue,
> the brewery makes premium lager,
> pilsner, and a very spicy ginger
> beer. You can watch it all happen-
> ing, and sample the goods, too.
> The brewery and cafe are part
> of the Hunter Resort, which also
> has accommodation. ✉ *Hermit-
> age Rd.* ☎ *02/4998–7777* ⊕ *www.
> huntervalley.com.au).*

$$ ✕ **Cafe Enzo.** This breakfast and lunch café is at Peppers Creek Village,
CAFÉ a charming little shopping and dining enclave in Pokolbin with a vil-
lage green atmosphere. Housed in a sandstone building, with a lovely
attached sun-drenched courtyard overlooking a fountain, this is a great
spot for a hearty lunch after a visit to neighboring David Hooks winery
and the clothing and antiques shops. Meals are substantial and may
include handmade linguini with tiger prawns and fresh chili or zucchini
and corn fritters with beetroot-cured Atlantic salmon. It's a popular
place in the warmer months. ✉ *Peppers Creek Village, at Broke and
Ekerts Rds., Pokolbin, New South Wales* ☎ *02/4998 7233* ⊕ *www.
enzohuntervalley.com.au.*

$$ ✕ **Leaves & Fishes.** A rustic boathouse-style café with a deck that projects
AUSTRALIAN over a fish-stocked dam and a lovely garden, this is the place to savor
delicious seafood and share antipasto dishes. Fish comes straight from
farm to plate, and wines are from local vineyards. You could start with
the mussels and prawn hot pot with chorizo or go straight to the hearty
seafood chowder. Those who are not fans of seafood can tuck into the
crispy-skin duck with steamed asparagus and confit of potato. Desserts
from the specials board might include mango and coconut pudding with
fresh papaya. Reservations are recommended, especially on weekends.
✉ *737 Lovedale Rd., Lovedale* ☎ *02/4930–7400* ◷ *Closed Mon. and
Tues. No dinner Wed., and Thurs.*

$$$ ✕ **Roberts Restaurant.** This restaurant in grapevine-covered, 1876-built
AUSTRALIAN Pepper Tree Cottage wins the ambience award hands down. Although
chef Robert Molines departed a few years ago to start his own restaurant, Robert's had such a loyal following that the name stayed
with the cute cottage. The seasonal Mod-Oz menu draws inspiration
from regional recipes of France and Italy and applies it to local game,

Many of the wineries also have excellent restaurants.

seafood, beef, and lamb. A good choice is the boned, crisp-skinned Hunter Valley quail, followed by the star-anise-glazed duck breast and confit leg with duck jus. The cozy fireside lounge is perfect for enjoying after-dinner liqueurs, or another wine from the extensive wine list, many of which come from nearby Tower Estate, which owns the restaurant. ⊠ *Halls Rd.* ☎ *02/4998–7330.*

WHERE TO STAY
For expanded hotel reviews, visit Fodors.com.

$$$ 🏨 **Carriages Country House.** On 36 acres at the end of a quiet country lane, this rustic-looking but winsome guesthouse, set on a small vineyard, is all about privacy. **Pros:** romantic in winter with roaring fireplaces in some rooms, lovely verandas overlooking the grounds **Cons:** no children allowed, wedding groups sometimes book out most of the place. ⊠ *Halls Rd.* ☎ *02/4998–7591* ⊕ *www.thecarriages.com.au* ⤵ *10 suites* ⌂ *In-room: kitchen. In-hotel: pool, tennis court, business center, some age restrictions* ⦿❘ *Breakfast.*

$$$$ 🏨 **Cedars Mount View.** This property, nestled in the hills above the valley, ★ might tempt you to forget about wine tasting for a few days. **Pros:** private and luxurious; the bathrooms have decadent sunken baths. **Cons:** the location may be a bit too remote for some. ⊠ *60 Mitchells Rd., Mount View* ☎ *0414/533070, 02/4959–3072* ⊕ *www.cedars.com.au* ⤵ *3 villas, 2 cottages* ⌂ *In-room: kitchen* ⦿❘ *Breakfast.*

$$$ 🏨 **The Cooperage Bed and Breakfast.** This lovely B&B is in the heart of Kelman Vineyards Estate, a working vineyard with a cellar door just a stone's throw from the rooms. **Pros:** big comfy beds; guesthouse rooms have private decks; free Wi-Fi. **Cons:** Not suitable for children under 10;

can be booked out months ahead. ⊠ *41 Kelman Vineyards, Oakey Creek Rd., Pokolbin* ☎ *02/4990–1232* ⊕ *www.huntervalleycooperage.com* ⤳ *5 rooms* ⚴ *In-room: kitchen, Wi-Fi. In-hotel: parking* ❘○❘ *Breakfast.*

$$$$ ☷ **Peppers Convent.** This former convent, built in 1909 and transported
★   605 km (375 mi) from its original home in western New South Wales, is ideal for those who love traditional guesthouses. **Pros:** romantic and secluded; balconies are a superb place to watch the sunset. **Cons:** standard rooms are on the small side; some noise audible from rooms. ⊠ *Halls Rd.* ☎ *02/4993–8999* ⊕ *www.peppers.com.au* ⤳ *17 rooms* ⚴ *In-room: Internet. In-hotel: pool, tennis court, spa* ❘○❘ *Breakfast.*

$$$$ ☷ **Tower Lodge.** This imposing lodge, a cross between a castle and a Tuscan villa, is the place for an indulgent getaway. ⊠ *Halls Rd., Pokolbin, New South Wales* ☎ *02/4998–7022* ⊕ *www.towerestate.com* ⤳ *12 rooms* ⚴ *In-room: a/c, Wi-Fi. In-hotel: restaurant, pool, parking.*

THE NORTH COAST

The North Coast is one of the most glorious and seductive stretches of terrain in Australia, stretching almost 600 km (373 mi) up to the Queensland border. An almost continuous line of beaches defines the coast, with the Great Dividing Range rising to the west. These natural borders frame a succession of rolling green pasturelands, mossy rain forests, towns dotted by red-roof houses, and waterfalls that tumble in glistening arcs from the escarpment.

A journey along the coast leads through several rich agricultural districts, beginning with grazing country in the south and moving into plantations of bananas, sugarcane, mangoes, avocados, and macadamia nuts. Dorrigo National Park, outside Bellingen, and Muttonbird Island, in Coffs Harbour, are two parks good for getting your feet on some native soil and for seeing unusual birdlife.

The tie that binds the North Coast is the Pacific Highway, but despite its name, this highway rarely affords glimpses of the Pacific Ocean. You can drive the entire length of the North Coast in a single day, but allow at least three—or, better still, a week—to properly sample some of its attractions.

PORT MACQUARIE

390 km (243 mi) northeast of Sydney.

Port Macquarie was founded as a convict settlement in 1821, and is the third-oldest settlement in Australia. Set at the mouth of the Hastings River, the town was chosen for its isolation to serve as an open jail for prisoners convicted of second offenses in New South Wales. By the 1830s the pace of settlement was so brisk that the town was no longer isolated, and its usefulness as a jail had ended. Today's Port Macquarie has few reminders of its convict past, and is flourishing as a vacation area. With its pristine rivers and lakes and 13 regional beaches, including beautiful Town Beach and Shelley Beach, which both have sheltered swimming, it's a great place to get into water sports, catch a fish for dinner, and watch migrating humpback whales in season, usually May to July and September to November.

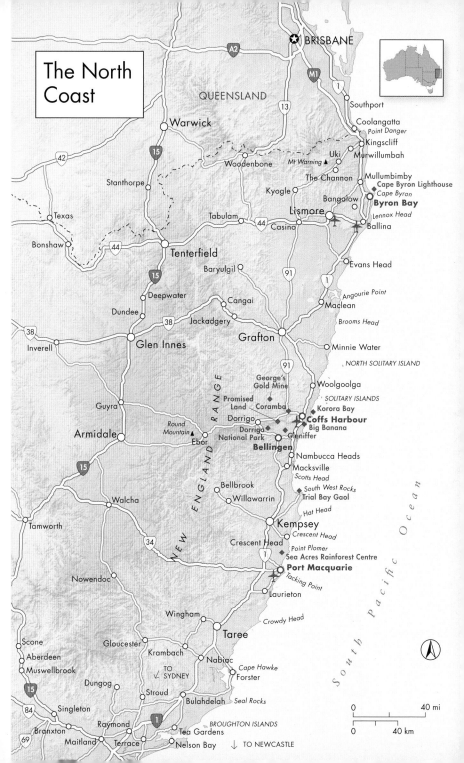

The North Coast

Brisbane

QUEENSLAND

Southport
Coolangatta
Point Danger
Kingscliff
Murwillumbah

Warwick

Woodenbone
Mt Warning ▲
Uki

The Channon
Mullumbimby
Cape Byron Lighthouse
Cape Byron
Byron Bay

Stanthorpe

Kyogle
Bangalow

Lismore
Lennox Head
Ballina

Texas

Tabulam
Casina

Bonshaw

Tenterfield
Baryulgil

Evans Head

Deepwater
Cangai
Angourie Point
Maclean
Brooms Head

Dundee
Jackadgery
Grafton

Inverell
Glen Innes
Minnie Water

NORTH SOLITARY ISLAND

George's
Gold Mine
Woolgoolga

SOLITARY ISLANDS

Guyra
Promised
Land
Coramba
Korora Bay
Coffs Harbour

*Round
Mountain* ▲
Dorrigo
Dorriga
National Park
Gleniffer
Big Banana

Armidale
Ebor
Bellingen

Nambucca Heads
Macksville
Scotts Head

Bellbrook
Willawarrin
South West Rocks
Trial Bay Gaol

Walcha
Hat Head

Tamworth
Kempsey

Crescent Head
Crescent Head
Point Plomer
Sea Acres Rainforest Centre

Nowendoc
Port Macquarie
Tacking Point

Laurieton

Wingham
Crowdy Head

Gloucester
Taree

Scone
Krambach
Nabiac
Cape Hawke
Forster

Aberdeen
Muswellbrook

TO
SYDNEY

Dungog
Stroud
Bulahdelah
Seal Rocks

Singleton

BROUGHTON ISLANDS

Branxton
Raymond
Tea Gardens
Maitland
Terrace
Nelson Bay
↓ TO NEWCASTLE

NEW ENGLAND RANGE

South Pacific Ocean

0 ——— 40 mi
0 ——— 40 km

GETTING HERE AND AROUND

It's a 5½-hour drive from Sydney heading north on the Pacific Highway. Greyhound and Premier Motor Service run coaches from Sydney Central Station. CountryLink trains operate three services daily between Sydney and the North Coast, though there is no direct train to Port Macquarie. Passengers have to take the train to Wauchope station and then a bus to Port Macquarie, which makes the journey seven hours long. Busway Buses travel from Port Macquarie to nearby towns and also to Coffs Harbour and Grafton. Timetables are available at the Greater Port Macquarie Visitor Centre or online. Qantas and Virgin Australia have flights from Sydney.

> **THAR SHE BLOWS!**
>
> Whales travel up and down the New South Wales coast by the hundreds, so book a whale-watching cruise to catch all the action at close range. Southern right whales and humpbacks travel up from Antarctica from May to August and down again from September to November. Dolphins can be seen almost any time of the year—you never know when an agile pair will shoot through a wave or bob up near your boat.

ESSENTIALS

Visitor Information Visitor Information Centre ⊠ *Corner of Clarence and Hay Sts., Port Macquarie* ☎ *1300/303155, 02/6581-8000* ⊕ *www.portmacquarieinfo.com.au.*

EXPLORING

☾ ★ **Koala Hospital.** Operated by the Koala Preservation Society of New South Wales, the town's Koala Hospital is both a worthy cause and a popular attraction. The Port Macquarie region supports many of these extremely appealing marsupials, and the hospital cares for 250 to 300 sick and injured koalas each year. The staff is passionate about their furry patients, and will happily tell you about the care the animals receive. You can walk around the grounds to view the recuperating animals; you can even adopt one (but you can't take it home). Try to visit during feeding times—8 in the morning or 3 in the afternoon. There are guided tours daily at 3. ⊠ *Macquarie Nature Reserve, Lord St.* ☎ *02/6584–1522* ⊕ *www.koalahospital.org.au* ⊉ *Donation requested* ⊗ *Daily 8–4:30.*

Port Macquarie Historical Museum. Housed in a two-story shop dating from 1836, the eclectic Port Macquarie Historical Museum displays period costumes, memorabilia from World Wars I and II, farm implements, antique clocks and watches, and relics from the town's convict days. ⊠ *22 Clarence St.* ☎ *02/6583–1108* ⊕ *www.port-macquarie-historical-museum.org.au* ⊉ *A\$5* ⊗ *Mon.–Sat. 9:30–4:30.*

Fodor's Choice ★ **Sea Acres Rainforest Centre.** The Sea Acres Rainforest Centre comprises 178 pristine acres of coastal rain forest on the southern side of Port Macquarie. There are more than 170 plant species here, including 300-year-old cabbage-tree palms, as well as native mammals, reptiles, and prolific birdlife. An elevated boardwalk allows you to stroll through the lush environment without disturbing the vegetation. The center has informative guided tours, as well as a gift shop and a pleasant

Orange fungi growing on the Rainforest Tree at Dorrigo National Park.

rain-forest café. ✉ *Pacific Dr. near Shelley Beach Rd.* ☎ *02/6582–3355* ⊕ *www.environment.nsw.gov.au* 🖃 *A$8.50* ⊙ *Daily 9–4:30.*

St. Thomas Church. The 1828 St. Thomas Church, the country's third-oldest house of worship, was built by convicts using local cedar and stone blocks cemented together with powdered seashells. ✉ *Hay and William Sts.* ☎ *02/6584–1033* ⊙ *Weekdays 10–noon and 2–4.*

OUTDOOR ACTIVITIES

Unsurprisingly, most of the outdoor activities in this area revolve around the town's crystal-clear waters.

FISHING **Ocean Star.** Deep-sea anglers will enjoy the day-long trips on this 40-foot custom Randel charting boat. Typical catches include snapper, pearl perch, dolphin fish, and jewfish. If you have cooking facilities, the crew is happy to clean, ice, and pack your catch. ✉ *Town Wharf, Port Macquarie* ☎ *0416/240–877* ⊕ *www.oceanstarfishing.com.*

HORSEBACK RIDING **Bellrowan Valley Horseriding.** Thirty minutes outside of Port Macquarie, Bellrowan welcomes experts and beginners, and offers short trail rides and overnight treks. The two-day Great Aussie Pub Ride ends the day's ride in some of the region's most interesting pubs. ✉ *Crows Rd., Beechwood* ☎ *02/6587–5227* ⊕ *www.bellrowanvalley.com.au.*

SURFING **Port Macquarie Surf School.** Head back to school and learn to ride the waves from some very competent coaches, all of whom are fully accredited, licensed, and insured with Surfing Australia. There are daily group lessons at 9 am, 11 am, and 2 pm (A$40 for two hours), or you can opt for one-on-one tutoring (A$60 per hours). Surf boards, wet suits, rashvests, and sunscreen are provided. ✉ *46 Pacific Dr., Port Macquarie* ☎ *02/6584-7733* ⊕ *www.portmacquariesurfschool.com.au.*

WHALE-
WATCHING

Port Macquarie Cruise Adventures. Majestic humpback whales migrate past Port Macquarie nonstop from May to the end of November, and Cruise Adventures offers great-value cruises on their fast 12-seater boats (A$30) for 1½ hours and cruises on a larger boat, the *Discovery* (A$35), for 2 hours. The company also has both long and short cruises to see local bottlenose dolphins that can be spotted year-round. ✉ *Short St. Wharf, Port Macquarie* ☎ *1300/555890* ⊕ *www.cruiseadventures.com.au.*

WHERE TO EAT AND STAY

For expanded hotel reviews, visit Fodors.com.

$$

AUSTRALIAN

★

✕ **The Restaurant at Cassegrain.** This restaurant, in the lovely Cassegrain winery 20-minutes south of Port Macquarie, has changed its name (from Ça Marche) and taken on a French Brasserie feel. Lunches are always popular as diners gaze out over the sundrenched vines. You may want to go all French and start with the escargots (snails cooked in their shells with garlic, parsley butter, and Pernod), or try the local Camden Haven oysters instead. Starters include exceptional confit duck salad and steak tartare, while a hearty main is the local eye fillet of beef with brandy sauce. The vineyard produces a wide variety of wines, including Chardonnay, Verdelho, and Rose, and the cellar door offers daily tastings from 9 to 5. The restaurant will open at night if there are bookings for 20 or more. ✉ *764 Fernbank Creek Rd.* ☎ *02/6582-8320* ⊕ *www. cassegrainwines.com* ☾ *No dinner.*

$$

AUSTRALIAN

✕ **The Corner.** This stylish café has been packed with happy diners since it opened in early 2007. The reason is clear—they serve fabulously tasty and inexpensive meals, though you have to be patient, as service can be a bit slow at times. Try the Corner Breakfast (A$19), which has just about everything from eggs the way you like them to ham-hock-braised beans. Return for dinner to sample the Yamba jewfish, baby beetroot, corn puree, and jamon. As the name suggests, it sits on a corner; it's part of the Macquarie Waters Hotel & Apartments complex. ✉ *Clarence and Munster Sts.* ☎ *02/6583-3300* ⊕ *www.mwaters.com.au.*

$

Beachcomber Resort. Spacious family-friendly accommodation can be tough to find in Port Macquarie, which is why this self-catering resort opposite Town Beach garners high praise for its service and price. **Pros:** well-maintained BBQ area and spotless accommodation. **Cons:** no elevators, so can be a pain if you're lugging children up stairs; if you don't have kids, you might feel outnumbered. ✉ *54 William St., Port Macquarie* ☎ *02/6584-1881, 1800/001-320* ⊕ *www.beachcomberresort. com.au* ⇶ *22 apartments* ⚐ *In-room: kitchen, Wi-Fi. In-hotel: pool, spa, parking* †○| *No meals.*

$$

Quality Inn HW Boutique Hotel. Although the building dates from the late 1960s—when its sawtooth shape was considered very stylish—it's filled with up-to-the-minute amenities: designer furnishings, luxurious linens, marble bathrooms, and private balconies with ocean and river views. **Pros:** a good continental breakfast is brought to your room; toasters in rooms; beautiful breakfast room on the top floor with ocean views. **Cons:** some street noise; a few rooms overlook car park. ✉ *1 Stewart*

St. ☎ *02/6583–1200* ⊕ *www.hwmotel.com.au* ↪ *45 rooms* ⬦ *In-room: kitchen, Internet. In-hotel: pool, laundry facilities, business center.*

EN ROUTE

Trial Bay Gaol. Trial Bay Gaol, a jail dating from the 1870s, occupies a dramatic position on the cliffs overlooking the seaside village of South West Rocks, 100 km (62 mi) north of Port Macquarie. The building, now partly in ruins, was used to teach useful skills to the prisoners who constructed it, but the project proved too expensive and was abandoned in 1903. During World War I the building served as an internment camp for some 500 Germans. The A$7.50 admission includes entry to a small museum. Discovery tours are run during the school holidays in December and January, April or May (usually around the Easter holiday), July, and October. Make sure you climb the tower for a stunning view of the coast. To get there, travel north through Kempsey and turn off to South West Rocks and follow the signs. ☎ *02/6566–6168* ⊕ *www.trialbaygaol.com.*

BELLINGEN

210 km (130 mi) north of Port Macquarie, 520 km (323 mi) from Sydney.

In a river valley a few miles off the Pacific Highway, artsy Bellingen is one of the prettiest towns along the coast. Many of Bellingen's buildings have been classified by the National Trust, and the museum, cafés, galleries, and crafts outlets are favorite hangouts for artists, craft workers, and writers. You'll find food, entertainment, and 250 stalls at the community markets that take place on the third Sunday of every month.

GETTING HERE AND AROUND

It's a seven-hour drive from Sydney along the Pacific Highway, but the town is just 30 minutes from Coffs Harbour and its airport. CountryLink trains run from Sydney three times a day and from Brisbane twice daily, stopping at Urunga, which is 10 km (6 mi) away. Both Greyhound and Premier Motor Service also run buses between Sydney and Urunga. From Urunga, either catch a taxi or a local Busways bus to Bellingen—though the bus is quite infrequent. There is also a Busways bus service from Coffs Harbour to Bellingen. The local tourist office is open 9–4.

ESSENTIALS

Visitor Information Waterfall Way Visitor Centre ✉ *29–31 Hyde St, Bellingen* ☎ *02/6655–1522, 1800/705-75* ⊕ *www.bellingermagic.com.*

EXPLORING

★ **Dorrigo National Park.** From Bellingen a meandering and spectacular road leads inland to Dorrigo before reaching the Pacific Highway, close to Coffs Harbour. This circular scenic route, beginning along the Bellinger River, climbs more than 1,000 feet up the heavily wooded escarpment to the Dorrigo Plateau. At the top of the plateau is Dorrigo National Park, a small but outstanding subtropical rain forest that is included on the World Heritage list. Signposts along the main road indicate walking trails. The Satinbird Stroll is a short rain-forest walk, and the 6-km (4-mi) Cedar Falls Walk leads to the most spectacular of the park's many waterfalls. The national park is approximately 31 km (19 mi) from Bellingen.

Dorrigo Rainforest Centre. The excellent Dorrigo Rainforest Centre, open daily 9–4:30, has information, educational displays, and a shop, and from here you can walk out high over the forest canopy along the **Skywalk** boardwalk. ☏ *02/6657–2309* ⊕ *www.dorrigo.com* ✉ *02/6657–2309* ⊕ *www.dorrigo.com.*

OUTDOOR ACTIVITIES

CANOEING   **Bellingen Canoe Adventures.** Hire a canoe or join an organized expedition on the Bellinger River, which meanders its way through some of the most spectacular and picturesque areas in the area. This company, which emphasises safety above everything else, offers a wide range of options, including one-hour sunset tours (A$25) and full-day tours that promise the thrill of rapids and provide lunch as well (A$90). ☏ *02/6655–9955* ⊕ *www.canoeadventures.com.au.*

HIKING   **Gambaarri Tours.** If you are interested in local Aboriginal culture, join one of these half-day tours led by local elder Wiruunngga. You'll learn about local history and look for bush tucker as you visit the Promised Land and the Never Never River. Morning or afternoon tea is provided. Wiruunngga also offers tours out of Coffs (A$45). ☏ *02/6655–5195* ⊕ *www.heartlanddidgeridoos.com.au.*

HORSEBACK RIDING   **Valery Trails.** This large horse-riding center is 10 km (6 mi) from Bellingen on the edge of Bongil Bongil National Park. They have 60 horses, and offer a variety of treks through the local rain forests. Choose from one-hour treks (A$45) to two-day rides that include accommodation (A$350). ✉ *758 Valery Rd., Valery* ☏ *02/6653–4301* ⊕ *www.valerytrails.com.au.*

WHERE TO STAY

For expanded hotel reviews, visit Fodors.com.

$$ **Koompartoo Retreat.** These self-contained hardwood cottages on a hillside overlooking Bellingen are superb examples of local craftsmanship, particularly in their use of timbers from surrounding forests. **Pros:** from the chalet verandas you can see kookaburras and black cockatoos; each cottage has small library. **Cons:** no wheelchair access; heating is noisy. ✉ *Rawson and Dudley Sts.* ☏ *02/6655–2326* ⊕ *www.koompartoo.com.au* ⤴ *4 cottages* ⚑ *In-room: kitchen. In-hotel: laundry facilities.*

COFFS HARBOUR

35 km (22 mi) northeast of Bellingen via the Pacific Hwy., 103 km (64 mi) from Bellingen via the inland scenic route along the Dorrigo Plateau, 534 km (320 mi) from Sydney.

The area surrounding Coffs Harbour is the state's "banana belt," where long, neat rows of banana palms cover the hillsides. Set at the foot of steep green hills, the town has great beaches and a mild climate. This idyllic combination has made it one of the most popular vacation spots along the coast. Coffs is also a convenient halfway point on the 1,000-km (620-mi) journey between Sydney and Brisbane.

GETTING HERE AND AROUND

Coffs Harbour is a comfortable 7½-hour drive from Sydney and a six-hour drive from Brisbane. Regular Greyhound and Premier Buses connect the town to Sydney. There is a train station with daily CountryLink services to and from Sydney and Brisbane. And the local airport, 6 km (4 mi) from the central Ocean Parade, is served by Qantas, Virgin Australia, and Brindabella Airlines (the latter between Coffs Harbour and Brisbane only). For more information, contact the visitor center, which is open 9–5 daily.

TOURS
ESSENTIALS

Airport Coffs Harbour Airport ⊠ *Hogbin Dr., Coffs Harbour* ☎ *02/6648–4837.*

Hospital Coffs Harbour Base Hospital ⊠ *345 Pacific Hwy.* ☎ *02/6656–7000.*

Visitor Information Coffs Coast Visitors Information Centre ⊠ *Pacific Hwy. at McLean St.* ☎ *02/6648–4990, 1300/369070* ⊕ *www.coffscoast.com.au.*

EXPLORING

☺ **The Big Banana.** Just north of the city, impossible to miss, is the Big Banana—the symbol of Coffs Harbour. This monumental piece of kitsch has stood at the site since 1964. It welcomes visitors to the Big Banana complex, which takes a fascinating look at the past, present, and future of horticulture. There's a multimedia display called "World of Bananas" and a walkway that meanders through the banana plantations and banana packing shed. A lookout high on the plantation hill provides great views to the coast, and is a good whale-watching vantage point July–November. The park also includes toboggan rides (A$5), a waterslide (A$16 for 1.5 hours), and an ice-skating rink (A$14.50). There's a café on the premises, as well as the Banana Barn, which sells the park's own jams, pickles, and fresh tropical fruit. ⊠ *351 Pacific Hwy.* ☎ *02/6652–4355* ⊕ *www.bigbanana.com* 🖭 *A$12 for movie & plantation tour* ☉ *Daily 9–4:30.*

Muttonbird Island. The town has a lively and attractive harbor in the shelter of Muttonbird Island, and a stroll out to this nature reserve is delightful in the evening. To get here, follow the signs to the Coffs Harbour Jetty, then park near the marina. A wide path leads out along the breakwater and up the slope of the island. The trail is steep, but the views from the top are worth the effort. The island is named after the muttonbirds (also known as shearwaters) that nest here between September and April. Between June and September Muttonbird Island is also a good spot for viewing migrating humpback whales.

☺ **Pet Porpoise Pool.** Near the port in Coffs Harbour, the Pet Porpoise Pool aquarium includes colorful reef fish, turtles, seals, and dolphins. Two new shows take place daily at 10 and 1, and visitors are advised to arrive 30 minutes earlier to get a good seat and receive "dolphin kisses" from the cute critters. Children may help feed and "shake hands" with dolphins, as well as interact with the seals. You can swim, pat, and play ball with the dolphins in special group encounters if you book in advance. These sessions vary in price, depending on time of year, from A$180 (low season) to A$220 (should season) or A$270 (in the peak school holiday season). ⊠ *Orlando St. beside Coffs Creek* ☎ *02/6659–1900* ⊕ *www.dolphinmarinemagic.com.au* ⊠ *A$32* ⊙ *Daily 9–4.*

OUTDOOR ACTIVITIES

SCUBA DIVING   The warm seas around Coffs Harbour make this particular part of the coast, with its moray eels, manta rays, turtles, and gray nurse sharks, a scuba diver's favorite. Best are the Solitary Islands, 7–21 km (4½–13 mi) offshore.

Jetty Dive Centre. Jetty Dive Centre also rents gear, schedules scuba and snorkeling trips, and hosts certification classes. There are whale- and dolphin-watching cruises from June to October. ☎ *02/6651–1611* ⊕ *www.jettydive.com.au.*

WHITE-WATER RAFTING   **Wildwater Rafting.** The highly regarded Wildwater Rafting conducts half-day, one-day, and two-day rafting trips down the Nymboida River. Trips begin from Bonville, 14 km (9 mi) south of Coffs Harbour on the Pacific Highway, but pickups from the Coffs Harbour and Bellingen region can be arranged. Half-day trips are A$80, one-day trips are A$185, and two-day trips cost A$430 per person including snacks and meals. Overnight trips feature camping on the river bank, breakfas,t and dinner. ⊠ *16 Prince St.* ☎ *02/6653–2067* ⊕ *www.coffscentral.com/wildwater.*

WHERE TO EAT AND STAY

For expanded hotel reviews, visit Fodors.com.

$$
ECLECTIC   ✕ **Shearwater Restaurant.** This waterfront restaurant with views of Coffs Creek (which is spotlighted at night—look for stingrays swimming by) is open for breakfast, lunch, and dinner, and leaves no culinary stone unturned in its search for novel flavors. The menu in the open-air dining room includes lunch dishes like prawn and scallop red curry. If you want a table on the deck in summer, book ahead. Service is friendly and attentive. The restaurant operates on a limited winter timetable (June–August) and only opens on Sunday to Tuesday nights if there are table bookings of 15 or more. ⊠ *321 Harbour Dr.* ☎ *02/6651–6053* ⌁ *BYOB.*

$$$
★   ⌂ **BreakFree Aanuka Beach Resort.** Teak furniture and antiques collected from Indonesia and the South Pacific fill the one-bedroom suites at this resort, which sits amid palms, frangipani, and hibiscus. **Pros:** brilliant setting in a private beachfront cove, great value for families. **Cons:** Some rooms need updating, kid-phobes might not appreciate all the families. ⊠ *11 Firman Dr.* ☎ *02/6652–7555* ⊕ *www.breakfreeaanukabeachresort. com.au* ⊠ *32 studio rooms, 38 suites* ⊘ *In-room: kitchen. In-hotel: restaurant, bar, pool, tennis court, gym, spa, children's programs, laundry facilities, business center* ⍦ *Breakfast.*

$$$$
⌂ **Smugglers on the Beach.** Five minutes' drive north of Coffs Harbour's busy city center is this small resort with just 16 self-contained 1- to 3-bedroom apartments spread out among tropical gardens. **Pros:** resort has fishing equipment and a BBQ, so you can catch your dinner, beautiful beachside location. **Cons:** minimum stay of two nights, check-out is at 9:30 am. ⊠ *36 Sandy Beach Rd., Coffs Harbour* ☎ *02/6653–6166* ⊕ *www.smugglers.com.au* ⊠ *16 apartments* ⊘ *In-room: kitchen, Wi-Fi. In-hotel: pool, tennis court, beach, water sports, laundry facilities, parking* ⍦ *No meals.*

EN
ROUTE
An hour or so north of Coffs Harbour is the historic town of Grafton, set on the banks of the Clarence River. The town is famous for the **Jacaranda Festival**, which has taken place the last week of October since 1935. A parade is held in the streets—lined with the beautiful purple flowering trees—and a new Jacaranda Queen is crowned each year. Between Grafton and the far North Coast, the Pacific Highway enters sugarcane country, where tiny sugarcane trains and thick, drifting smoke from burning cane fields are ever-present. The highway passes the fishing and resort town of **Ballina**, where beaches are the prime feature.

BYRON BAY

247 km (154 mi) north of Coffs Harbour, 772 km (480 mi) north of Sydney.

Byron Bay is the easternmost point on the Australian mainland, and perhaps earns Australia its nickname the "Lucky Country." Fabulous beaches, storms that spin rainbows across the mountains behind the town, and a sunny, relaxed style cast a spell over practically everyone who visits. For many years Byron Bay lured surfers with abundant sunshine, perfect waves on Watego's Beach, and tolerant locals who allowed them to sleep on the sand. These days a more upscale crowd frequents Byron Bay.

Byron Bay is also one of the must-sees on the backpacker circuit, and the town has a youthful energy that fuels late-night partying. There are many art galleries and crafts shops, a great food scene, and numerous adventure tours. The town is at its liveliest on the first Sunday of each month, when Butler Street becomes a bustling market.

GETTING HERE AND AROUND

Byron is the North Coast's most popular destination, and is well served by buses and trains from Sydney and Coffs Harbour. If driving, the journey takes 11 hours from Sydney and 3½ hours from Coffs Harbour. The closest airports are at Ballina and Lismore, both a 30-minute drive away. Virgin Australia and Jetstar both fly to Ballina, while REX flies from Sydney to Lismore. All the usual car companies are there, or you could get a taxi into Byron or take a Ballina-Byron shuttle bus (operated by Byron Easy Bus) for A$15 one-way. For tourist information, the Byron Visitor Centre is open daily 9–5.

ESSENTIALS

Airport Shuttle Byron Easy Bus ☎ *02/6685-7447* ⊕ *www.byronbayshuttle.com.au.*

Hospital Byron Bay District Hospital ✉ *Shirley St.* ☎ *02/6685-6200.*

Visitor Information Byron Visitor Centre ✉ *Transit Centre, 80 Jonson St.* ☎ *02/6680-8558* ⊕ *www.visitbyronbay.com.*

EXPLORING

Cape Byron Lighthouse. Cape Byron Lighthouse, the most powerful beacon on the Australian coastline, dominates the southern end of the beach at Byron Bay and attracts huge numbers of visitors. You can tour the lighthouse (no children under 5) on Tuesday and Thursday

There's no shortage of activities in Byron Bay.

year-round, and on Saturdays during the summer holidays. Whale-watching is popular between June and September, when migrating humpback whales come close to shore. Dolphins swim in these waters year-round, and you can often see pods of them from the cape. You can stay in the 6-person assistant tlighkeeper's cottage from A$1,600 a week during non holiday periods, and from A$3,600 a week in the peak Christmas/New Year and Easter holidays, but reservations should be made at least six months in advance. ⊠ *Lighthouse Rd.* ☏ *02/6685–5955* ⊕ *www.environment.nsw.gov.au* ✉ *Free, lighthouse tours A$8* ☉ *Lighthouse grounds daily 8–5:30. Lighthouse tours Tues. and Thurs. at 11, 12, and 2; Sat. 10, 11, 12:30, 2, and 3:30 in summer holidays.*

Cape Byron Walking Track. Cape Byron Walking Track circumnavigates a 150-acre reserve, passes through grasslands and rain forest, and offers sensational seas views as you circle the peninsula and the lighthouse. From several vantage points along the track you may spot dolphins in the waters below. The track begins east of the town on Lighthouse Road.

OFF THE
BEATEN
PATH

Byron Bay Hinterland. Inland from Byron Bay is some of the most pictur-esque country in Australia. Undulating green hills that once boasted a thriving dairy industry are dotted with villages with a New Age vibe. There are small organic farms growing avocados, coffee, fruits, and macadamia nuts, and cafés in most villages. The best way to discover this gorgeous part of the world—nicknamed the Rainbow Region—is to grab a map and drive. From Byron, take the road toward the regional town of Lismore for about 15 km (9 mi) to the pretty vil-lage of **Bangalow.** Walk along the lovely main street lined with 19th-century storefronts and native Bangalow palms. Carefully follow your map and wind your way northwest for about 20 km (13 mi) to **Federal**. Meander, via the cute towns of **Rosebank** and **Dunoon**, to **The Channon**, where on the second Sunday of every month you'll find a wonderful market with dozens of stalls and entertainment.

Eternity Springs Art Farm. You may want to relax for a few days at the town's Eternity Springs Art Farm, a groovy B&B that also offers art classes and yoga. ⊠ *483 Tuntable Creek Rd.* ☎ *02/6688–6385* ⊕ *www.eternitysprings.com*

> ### HIPPY DAYS
>
> You'll think you've traveled back in time when you arrive in Nimbin, northwest of Byron Bay. There are psychedelic storefronts, a hemp museum, and stores such as Hippy High Herbs and Nimbin Apothecary. The annual "Mardi Grass" Fiesta, which advocates the legalization of cannabis, is held on the first weekend of May, and is a sight to behold.

BEACHES

Several superb beaches lie in the vicinity of Byron Bay. In front of the town, Main Beach provides safe swimming, and Clarks Beach, closer to the cape, has better surf. The most famous surfing beach, however, is Watego's, the only entirely north-facing beach in the state. To the south of the lighthouse Tallow Beach extends for 6 km (4 mi) to a rocky stretch of coastline around Broken Head, which has a number of small sandy coves. Beyond Broken Head is lonely Seven Mile Beach. Topless sunbathing is popular on many Byron Bay beaches.

OUTDOORS ACTIVITIES

KAYAKING **Dolphin Kayaking.** Dolphin Kayaking has 2.5 hour trips (at 9:30 and 2) for A$65 that, weather permitting, take paddlers out to meet the local bottlenose dolphins and surf the waves. ☎ *02/6685–8044* ⊕ *www. dolphinkayaking.com.au.*

SCUBA DIVING The best local diving is at Julian Rocks Marine Reserve, some 3 km (2 mi) offshore, where the confluence of warm and cold currents supports a profusion of marine life.

Byron Bay Dive Centre. Byron Bay Dive Centre has snorkeling and scuba-diving trips for all levels of experience, plus gear rental and instruction. ⊠ *9 Marvel St.* ☎ *02/6685–8333, 1800/243483* ⊕ *www. byronbaydivecentre.com.au.*

Sundive. Sundive is a PADI dive center with courses for all levels of divers, as well as boat dives and snorkel trips. ⊠ *8 Middleton St.* ☎ *02/6685–7755, 1800/008755* ⊕ *www.sundive.com.au.*

WHERE TO EAT

$$ × **Byron Bay Beach Café.** A Byron Bay legend, this open-air café is a
CAFÉ perfect place to sit in the morning sun and watch the waves. Breakfast runs the gamut from wholesome (award-winning locally-produced Brookfarm Macadamia muesli with yogurt and banana) to hearty (corned beef hash, sautéed spinach, fried egg with Béarnaise sauce). For lunch, try the steamed mussels in Thai broth or the mini Wagyu burgers. The cafe is open for cocktails and dinner during the summer months of December and January and has an attached take-away section for those who want to have light meals on the run. Reservations

are recommended during the summer. ⊠ *Clarks Beach off parking lot at end of Lawson St.* ☎ *02/6685–8400* ⊕ *www.byronbeachcafe.com. au* ⊘ *No dinner Feb.–Nov.*

$$ × **Fig Tree Restaurant & Rooms.** In this century-old farmhouse with distant
AUSTRALIAN views of Byron Bay the draw is upmarket Mod-Oz cuisine blending
★ Asian and Mediterranean flavors. Produce fresh from the owners' farm is featured on the menu, along with locally produced Bangalow duck, Bangalow pork belly, and Binna Burra sirlion steak. À la carte choices also include field and forest mushroom risotto and slow-roasted shoulder of lamb. There are inexpensive set menus throughout the week, including the four-course farmer's market menu on Thursday (A$45 for four courses; A$65 for six courses). As the name suggests, the restaurant also has accommodation: the Dairy and the House, two cottages that have wonderful views and can both sleep up to eight people. The restaurant and rooms are 5 km (3 mi) inland from Byron Bay at Ewingsdale. ⊠ *4 Sunrise La., Ewingsdale* ☎ *02/6684–7273* ⊕ *www.figtreerestaurant. com.au* ⑅ *BYO (A$5 corkage fee)* ⊘ *Closed Sun.–Wed.*

WHERE TO STAY

For expanded hotel reviews, visit Fodors.com.

$$$$ 🏨 **Byron Bay Beach Bure.** Three luxury bures—the Fijian word for cabin—may be only 200 meters from the city center, but the lush, peaceful setting makes it feel like a private oasis. **Pros:** perfect accommodation for a romantic getaway; two elevated bures have beach views. **Cons:** Little to complain about here, so book early to secure a beach-view bure. ⊠ *36 Lawson St.* ☎ *02/6680–8483* ⊕ *www.byronbaybeachbure.com. au* ⑅ *3 bures* ⚗ *In-room: Wi-Fi. In-hotel: beach, parking, some age restrictions* ⊘⏹ *Breakfast.*

$$ 🏨 **Julian's Apartments.** These studio apartments just opposite Clarks Beach are neat, spacious, and well equipped. **Pros:** perfect for families (cots and baby supplies can be rented), this is the quiet end of Byron Bay town. **Cons:** Taxi, or hike into town required; popular, so early booking is required . ⊠ *124 Lighthouse Rd.* ☎ *02/6680–9697* ⊕ *www. juliansbyronbay.com* ⑅ *11 apartments* ⚗ *In-room: kitchen, Internet. In-hotel: laundry facilities.*

$$$$ 🏨 **Rae's on Watego's.** If a high-design boutique hotel is your cup of tea, you'd be hard-pressed to do better than this luxurious Mediterranean-style villa surrounded by a tropical garden. **Pros:** perfect for a romantic break, superb international-class spa. **Cons:** breakfast prices too high, you need your own transport or you'll have to catch a taxi into town. ⊠ *Watego's Beach, 8 Marina Parade* ☎ *02/6685–5366* ⊕ *www. raes.com.au* ⑅ *7 suites* ⚗ *In-room: kitchen, Wi-Fi. In-hotel: restaurant, pool, spa, business center, some age restrictions.*

NIGHTLIFE

For a small town, Byron rocks by night. Fire dancing—where bare-chested men dance with flaming torches—is a local specialty. Bars and clubs are generally open until about 2 am on weekends and midnight on weekdays.

Arts Factory Village. Head to the legendary Arts Factory Village—also known as the Piggery—to catch a movie at the Pighouse Flicks, grab a bite, have a beer brewed at the onsite Byron Bay Brewery, or see a live band at the Buddha Bar. A backpackers' lodge is attached to the venue, so expect a lively crowd—especially at the weekly talent show. ✉ *1 Skinners Shoot Rd., corner of Gordon St.* ☎ *02/6685–7709, 02/6685–583.*

Beach Bar. The Beach Bar in the Beach Hotel often hosts live bands. ✉ *Bay La. and Jonson Sts.* ☎ *02/6685–6402.*

Cocomangas. Lively bar-restaurant-nightclub Cocomangas is a favorite of carousing backpackers. ✉ *32 Jonson St.* ☎ *02/6685–8493* ⊕ *www.cocomangas.com.au.*

> ## NO BULL
>
> If there's one place that has milked its name for all its worth, it's Mooball, a blink-and-you-miss it village about 20 minutes north of Byron Bay. Follow the black-and-white cow prints painted on telegraph poles to the Moo Moo Café, which serves Moo Moo Burgers, Moo Moo shakes, and lots of kitschy souvenirs. If you find cow puns udderly annoying, then it's best to graze in other pastures.

Great Northern Hotel. Bands perform most evenings at the old-school Great Northern Hotel. ✉ *Jonson and Byron Sts.* ☎ *02/6685–6454.*

Railway Friendly Bar. Live music rocks the Railway Friendly Bar every night. ✉ *Jonson St. Railway Station* ☎ *02/6685–7662.*

SHOPPING

Byron Bay is one of the state's arts-and-crafts centers, with many innovative and high-quality articles for sale, such as leather goods, offbeat designer clothing, essential oils, natural cosmetics, and ironware. The community market, held on the first Sunday of every month, fills the Butler Street reserve with more than 300 stalls selling art, crafts, and local produce.

Byron Bay Hat Co. The Byron Bay Hat Co. is an institution with great hats and bags perfect for the beach. ✉ *4 Jonson St.* ☎ *02/6685–8357.*

Colin Heaney. Colin Heaney, a prolific artist based in Byron Bay who for many years was involved in sculpture and glass design, is now producing a luxurious range of women's wear, including silk kaftans, scarves, and bathing suits. His showroom also carries a number of glass goblets and sculpture pieces. The boutique is open from 10 am to 4 pm on weekdays, and by appointment at other times. ✉ *1a/81 Centennial Circuit* ☎ *02/6685–7044* ⊕ *www.colinheaney.com* ☉ *Weekdays 10–4.*

EN
ROUTE

Fifty-three km (33 mi) northwest of Byron Bay is the towering, conical **Mt. Warning**, a 3,800-foot extinct volcano that dominates the pleasant town of Murwillumbah. Its radical shape can be seen from miles away, including the beaches at Byron.

A well-marked **walking track** winds up Mt. Warning, which is a World Heritage national park, from the Breakfast Creek parking area at its base. The 4½-km (2½-mi) track climbs steadily through fern forest and buttressed trees where you can often see native brush turkeys and pademelons (small wallaby-like marsupials). The last 650 feet of the ascent is a strenuous scramble up a steep rock face using chain-link handrails. The local Aboriginal name for the mountain is Wollumbin, which means "cloud catcher," and the metal walkways on the summit are sometimes shrouded in clouds. On a clear day, however, there are fabulous 360-degree views of the massive caldera, one of the largest in the world: national parks crown the southern, western, and northern rims, and the Tweed River flows seaward through the eroded eastern wall. Many people undertake the Mt. Warning ascent before dawn, so they can catch the first rays of light falling on mainland Australia.

World Heritage Rainforest Visitors Information Centre. For information about the walk and Mt. Warning National Park, visit the World Heritage Rainforest Visitors Information Centre in Murwillumbah. From here it is a 16½-km (10-mi) drive to the start of the walking track. Fill your water bottles in Murwillumbah; there is no drinking water in the park or on the mountain. Allow at least four hours up and back, and don't start the walk after 2 pm in winter. ⊠ *Corner of Tweed Valley Way and Alma St.* ☎ *02/6672–1340* ⊕ *www.tweedtourism.com.au* ⊗ *Mon.–Sat. 9–4:30, Sun. 9:30–4.*

CANBERRA AND THE A.C.T.

As the nation's capital, Canberra is often maligned by outsiders, who see the city as lacking the coolness of Melbourne or the glamour of Sydney. But Canberra certainly has charms of its own, with its world-class museums (the majority of which are free), leafy open spaces, and the huge Lake Burley Griffin.

When Australia federated in 1901, both Sydney and Melbourne vied to be the nation's capital. But in the spirit of compromise, it was decided that a new city would be built, and Canberra and the Australian Capital Territory (A.C.T) were created when New South Wales ceded land to build a federal zone, based on the model of America's District of Columbia.

From the beginning this was to be a totally planned city. Walter Burley Griffin, a Chicago architect and associate of Frank Lloyd Wright, won an international design competition. Griffin arrived in Canberra in 1913 to supervise construction, but progress was slowed by two world wars and the Great Depression. By 1947 Canberra, with only 15,000 inhabitants, was little more than a country town.

Development increased during the 1950s, and the current population of more than 358,400 makes Canberra by far the largest inland city in Australia. The wide, tree-lined avenues and spacious parklands of present-day Canberra have largely fulfilled Griffin's original plan. The major public buildings are arranged on low knolls on either side of Lake Burley Griffin, the focus of the city. Satellite communities—using the same radial design of crescents and cul-de-sacs employed in Canberra—house the city's growing population.

GETTING HERE AND AROUND
AIR TRAVEL
Canberra Airport is 7 km (4½ mi) southeast of the city center. Flights are about a half-hour to Sydney, an hour to Melbourne, and two hours to Brisbane. Qantas, Tiger Airways, and Virgin Australia fly

Lord Howe Island

A tiny crescent of land in the Pacific Ocean 600 km (373 mi) northeast of Sydney, Lord Howe Island is the most remote and arguably the most beautiful part of New South Wales. With the sheer peaks of Mt. Gower (2,870 feet) and Mt. Lidgbird (2,548 feet) richly clad in palms, ferns, and grasses; golden sandy beaches; and the clear turquoise waters of the lagoon, this is a remarkably lovely place. Apart from the barren spire of Ball's Pyramid, a stark volcanic outcrop 16 km (10 mi) across the water to the southeast, the UNESCO World Heritage listed island stands alone in the South Pacific.

Not only is the island beautiful, but its history is fascinating. The first recorded sighting was not until 1788, by a passing ship en route to the penal settlement on Norfolk Island, which lies to the east. And evidence, or lack of it, suggests that Lord Howe was uninhabited by humans until three Europeans and their Maori wives and children settled it in the 1830s. By the 1870s the small population included a curious mixture of people from America (including whalers and former slaves), England, Ireland, Australia, South Africa, and the Gilbert Islands (now called Kiribati). Many of the descendants of these early settlers still live on Lord Howe.

Lord Howe is a remarkably safe and relaxed place for its 350 inhabitants, where cyclists and walkers far outnumber the few cars. No one locks their doors, the speed limit is a mere 25 kph (15 mph), and there's no cell-phone service. There are plenty of walking trails, both flat and rather precipitous, and fine beaches. Among the many bird species is the

unexpectedly high quality.

Visitor numbers are limited to 400 at any given time to protect the island's unique natural habitat, and if you want to experience the place, book well ahead. Getting there is part of the fun on Qantaslink's 32-seat Bombardier Dash 8 aircraft. The journey takes 2 hours from Sydney and 90 minutes from Brisbane, and a strict 14-kg (31-lb) luggage limit per person applies on all flights. Fares are expensive, costing from A$380 each way.

Also be aware that it's an expensive destination once you arrive, with most accommodation options more upmarket boutique than bucket and spades. Many of the lodges, restaurants, and tour operators close in winter—generally from June through August—and accommodation prices in the open establishments are reduced considerably during that period. Five- or seven-night flight-and-accommodation packages are the most economic way to visit Lord Howe. To plan your trip, your first port of call should be the Lord Howe Island's visitor center Web site (⊕ www.lordhoweisland.info).

...nod-
...ls, red-
...and sooty
...ore than just
...nes of feathered
...ter a few days on
...s the locals call Lord
...we Island). The skies are
full of birds gliding and
swooping on the warm cur-
rents, while at ground level
Lord Howe wood hens will
be picking at your feet. It's a
bird-lover's paradise.

to and from the capital, but there are no direct international flights. A taxi into the city is about A$25. A shuttle bus operated by Deane's Buslines runs every half hour between the airport and the city for A$9 per person, A$16.20 return.

BUS TRAVEL

Canberra is served by two major bus lines, Greyhound Australia and Murrays Australia. One-way fares to Sydney start from A$37, and the trip takes just over three hours.

The ACTION bus network operates weekdays 6:30 am–11:30 pm, Saturday 7 am–11:30 pm, and Sunday 8–7. There's a flat fare of A$4 per ride. A one-day ticket costs A$7.60, which allows unlimited travel.

ACTION Buses ✉ *Canberra City, Canberra, Australian Capital Territory*
⊕ *www.action.act.gov.au.* **Greyhound Australia** ☎ *1300/473–946.*
Murrays Australia ☎ *13–2251* ⊕ *www.murrays.com.au.*

CAR TRAVEL

Canberra is difficult to negotiate by car, given its radial roads, erratic signage, and often large distances between suburbs. Still, because sights are scattered about and not easily connected on foot or by public transportation, a car is a good way to see the city itself, as well as the sights in the Australian Capital Territory. If you're not a good map reader, think about getting a rental car with GPS.

Taxis and Shuttles Canberra Cabs ☎ *13–2227.*
Deane's Buslines ☎ *02/6299–3722* ⊕ *www.deanesbuslines.com.au.*

TRAIN TRAVEL

The Canberra railway station is about 6 km (4 mi) southeast of the city center. CountryLink trains make the four-hour trip between Canberra and Sydney twice daily. A daily bus-rail service by CountryLink makes the nine-hour run between Canberra and Melbourne.

Canberra Railway Station ✉ *Corner of Wentworth Ave. and Bourke Cres.,*
Kingston, Canberra ☎ *02/6208–9700.* **CountryLink** ☎ *13–2232*
⊕ *www.countrylink.info.*

TOURS

A convenient (and fun!) way to see the major sights of Canberra is with the Canberra Explorer Bus, operated by Canberra Day Tours, which makes a regular circuit around the major attractions. Tickets are A$35, and you can hop on and off all day. Destiny Tours offers ghost tours and other outings that explore the weirder side of the nation's capital.

The impressive Canberra and Region Visitor Centre, open weekdays 9–5 and weekends 9–4, is a convenient stop for those entering Canberra by road from Sydney or the north. The staff makes accommodation bookings for Canberra.

Visitor Information **Canberra Day Tours** ☎ *0418/455–099*
⊕ *www.canberradaytours.com.au.* **Destiny Tours** ☎ *02/9487–2895*
⊕ *www.destinytours.com.au.*

ESSENTIALS

Hospitals **Canberra Hospital** ✉ *Yamba Dr., Garran, Canberra, Australian Capital Territory* ☎ *02/6244–2222* ⊕ *www.canberrahospital.act.gov.au.*

Pharmacies **Capital Chemist** ✉ *O'Connor Shopping Centre, Sargood St., O'Connor, Canberra, Australian Capital Territory* ☎ *02/6248–7050, 02/6239-4800.*

Visitor Information **Canberra and Region Visitor Centre** ✉ *330 Northbourne Ave., Dickson, Canberra, Australian Capital Territory* ☎ *02/6205–0044* ⊕ *www.visitcanberra.com.au.*

EXPLORING CANBERRA

Canberra's most important public buildings stand within the Parliamentary Triangle. Lake Burley Griffin wraps around its northeast edge, while Commonwealth and Kings avenues radiate from Capital Hill, the city's political and geographical epicenter, to form the west and south boundaries. The triangle can be explored comfortably on foot, but a vehicle is required to see the rest of this area. The monuments and other attractions within the Parliamentary Triangle and around Lake Burley Griffin are not identified by street numbers, but all are clearly signposted.

CENTRAL CANBERRA

You can visit virtually all of central Canberra's major attractions by car, but in some places parking and walking may be more convenient. Around town you can use the local ACTION buses, which stop at most of the other sights, or join the hop-on, hop-off Canberra Day Tours bus.

TOP ATTRACTIONS

Fodor's Choice ★ **Australian War Memorial.** Both as a moving memorial to Australians who served their country in wartime and as a military museum, this is a shrine of great national importance and the most popular attraction in the capital. The museum explores Australian military involvement from the late 19th century through the 1970s and Vietnam up to Iraq and Afghanistan today. Displays include a Lancaster bomber, a Spitfire, tanks, landing barges, and sections of two of the Japanese midget submarines that infiltrated Sydney Harbour during World War II, as well as more interactive displays in the new Anzac Hall. One of the most moving places is the domed Tomb of the Unknown Soldier that stands above the Pool of Reflection and the Roll of Honour, which are two walls of names commemorating the thousands of Australians who have died in all military conflicts. You can best appreciate the impressive facade of the War Memorial from the broad avenue of **Anzac Parade.** Anzac is an acronym for the Australian and New Zealand Army Corps, formed during World War I. The avenue is flanked by several memorials commemorating the Army, Navy, Air Force, and Nursing Corps,

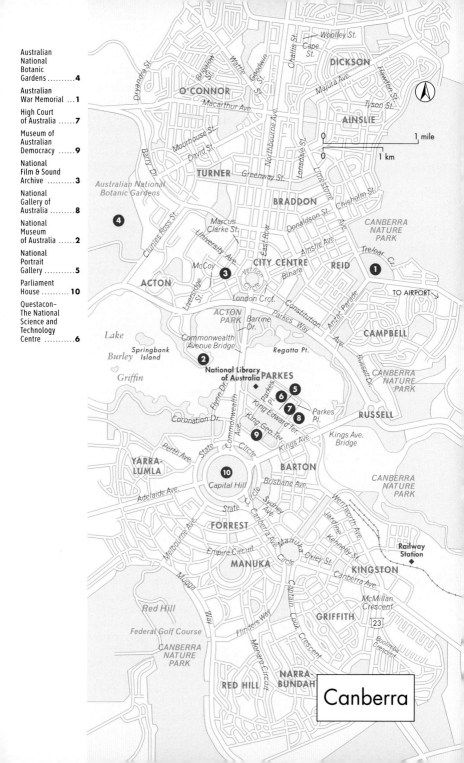

Canberra

as well as some of the campaigns in which Australian troops have fought, including the Vietnam War. ■TIP➔ At closing time a bugler or bagpiper plays the emotive Last Post outside the Tomb of the Unknown Soldier. ⊠ *Treloar Cresc., Campbell* ☎ *02/6243–4211* ⊕ *www.awm.gov. au* 🖃 *Free* ⊙ *Daily 10–5.*

Museum of Australian Democracy at Old Parliament House. This new museum is inside the Old Parliament House. In 1988 politicians moved to their more modern digs, and in 2009 the building was transformed into this highly interactive

LAKE BURLEY

Many of the main sights of Canberra are on the edge of Lake Burley Griffin. The Central Basin between Commonwealth and Kings Avenue bridges is a great place to begin a stroll, as it's close to such attractions as the National Library, the National Gallery of Australia, and the National Capital Exhibition. A bike ride or a boat cruise are other great ways to see the lake.

museum. Curators use stories of real people and events to trace the history of democracy both in Australia and abroad. The museum was three years in the making, and features five exhibits, as well as the opportunity to see the original chambers and prime minister's office. There are free 45-minute guided tours every day staring at 9:45 am, with the last at 3:45 pm. While you're in the area, take a stroll through the delightful **Rose Gardens** on both sides of the Old Parliament House building. Across the road from the entrance, visit the controversial **Aboriginal Tent Embassy,** established in 1972 to proclaim the Aboriginals as Australia's "first people" and to promote recognition of their fight for land rights. ⊠ *18 King George Terr., Parkes* ☎ *02/6270–8222* ⊕ *www.moadoph.gov.au* 🖃 *A$2* ⊙ *Daily 9–5.*

★ **National Film & Sound Archive.** Housed in one of Canberra's most beautiful art deco builidngs, this museum displays Australia's audio-visual cultural history. Among the many exhibits are costumes from films including *Muriel's Wedding, The Adventures of Priscilla Queen of the Desert,* and *Ned Kelly,* along with vintage film, sound equipment, and a film still collection of more than 300,000 images. You can relax in the small theatrette (designed along early 20th-century theater lines) and watch some of the country's early newsreels and short films (some are very funny). Watch art-house movies (extra cost usally around A$11) in the beautiful Arc cinema, which regularly screens classic movies and other non-mainstream cinematic gems. ⊠ *McCoy Circuit, Acton* ☎ *02/6248–2000* ⊕ *www.nfsa.gov.au* 🖃 *Free.*

★ **National Gallery of Australia.** The most comprehensive collection of Australian art in the country is on exhibit in the nation's premier art gallery, including superlative works of Aboriginal art and paintings by such famous native sons as Arthur Streeton, Sidney Nolan, and Arthur Boyd. The gallery also contains a sprinkling of works by European and American masters, including Rodin, Picasso, Pollock, and Warhol, as well as art and artifacts from closer to home, Southeast Asia. Free guided tours on a variety of topics with excellent guides begin in the foyer each day—check the Web site for details. A new wing, dedicated to indigenous art and containing 13 galleries, opened in

October 2010. The gallery extends outside into the Sculpture Garden, and the innovative Fog Sculpture takes place (outdoors) from 12:30 to 2 pm daily. ⊠ *Parkes Pl., Parkes* ☎ *02/6240–6502* ⊕ *www.nga.gov. au* ☜ *Free* ⊗ *Daily 10–5.*

NEED A BREAK?

Bookplate. A good spot to catch your breath amid the Parliamentary Triangle's mix of history, culture, and science is Bookplate, in the foyer of the National Library; It has lovely stained-glass windows and extends out onto a patio overlooking the lake. Sandwiches, salads, cakes, warming soup and curry in the winter, and tea and coffee are served weekdays 8:30–6 and weekends 11–3. ⊠ *Parkes Pl., Parkes* ☎ *02/6262-1154.*

Fodor's Choice
★

National Museum of Australia. This unstuffy museum is spectacularly set on Acton Peninsula, thrust out over the calm waters of Lake Burley Griffin. The museum highlights the stories of Australia and Australians by exploring the key people, events, and issues that shaped and influenced the nation. Memorabilia include a carcass of the extinct Tasmanian tiger, the old Bentley beloved by former Prime Minister Robert Menzies, and the black baby garments worn by dingo victim Azaria Chamberlain (whose story was made famous in the Meryl Streep film *A Cry in the Dark*). ⊠ *Lennox Crossing, Acton Peninsula* ☎ *02/6208–5000, 1800/026–132* ⊕ *www.nma.gov.au* ☜ *Free* ⊗ *Daily 9–5.*

National Portrait Gallery. This terrific space opened in 2009 is dedicated to portraits of people who have shaped Australia and who in some way reflect the national identity. Look out for famous faces like pop star Kylie Minogue and Olympic champion Cathy Freeman, as well as priceless portraits of Captain James Cook. The building on the south shore of Lake Burley Griffin caused some controversy, but most architecture fans like its simple, clean design. The gallery also has a good arts program offering talks and film screenings, and the café's outdoor terrace has lovely views. ⊠ *King Edward Terr., Parkes* ☎ *02/6102–7000* ⊕ *www.portrait.gov.au* ☜ *Free* ⊗ *Daily 10 am–5 pm.*

Fodor's Choice
★

Parliament House. Much of this vast futuristic structure is submerged, covered by a domed glass roof that follows the contours of Capital Hill. You approach the building across a vast courtyard with a central mosaic titled *Meeting Place*, designed by Aboriginal artist Nelson Tjakamarra. Native timber has been used almost exclusively throughout the building, and the work of some of Australia's finest contemporary artists hangs on the walls.

Question Time. The best time to observe the House of Representatives is during Question Time, starting at 2, when the government and the opposition are most likely to be at each other's throats. To secure a ticket for Question Time, contact the sergeant-at-arms' office until 12:30 pm on the day you require a ticket. ☎ *02/6277–4889 sergeant-at-arms' office* ⊠ *Capital Hill* ☎ *02/6277–5399* ⊕ *www.aph.gov.au* ☜ *Free* ⊗ *Daily 9–5, later when Parliament is sitting.*

The Australian War Memorial, Canberra.

WORTH NOTING

Australian National Botanic Gardens. Australian plants and trees have evolved in isolation from the rest of the world, and these delightful gardens on the lower slopes of Black Mountain display the continent's best collection of this unique flora. The rain forest, rock gardens, Tasmanian alpine garden, and eucalyptus lawn—with more than 600 species of eucalyptus—number among the 125-acre site's highlights. Two self-guided nature trails start from the rain-forest gully, and free guided tours depart from the visitor center daily at 11 and 2. Prebooked and more individualized guided tours cost A$4 per person. ⊠ *Clunies Ross St., Acton* ☎ *02/6250–9540* ⊕ *www.anbg.gov.au* *Free* ☉ *Jan., weekdays 8:30–6, weekends 8:30–8; Feb.–Dec.,daily 8:30–5. Visitor center daily 9:30–4:30.*

High Court of Australia. As its name implies, this gleaming concrete-and-glass structure is the ultimate court of law in the nation's judicial system. The court of seven justices convenes only to determine constitutional matters or major principles of law. Inside the main entrance, the public hall contains a number of murals depicting constitutional and geographic themes. Each of the three courtrooms over which the justices preside has a public gallery, and you can observe the proceedings when the court is in session. ⊠ *Parkes Pl. off King Edward Terr., Parkes* ☎ *02/6270–6811* ⊕ *www.hcourt.gov.au* *Free* ☉ *Mon.–Fri. 9:45–4:30.*

☾ **Questacon—The National Science and Technology Centre.** This interactive science facility is the city's most entertaining museum, especially for kids. About 200 hands-on exhibits in seven galleries including spaces on sport and music use high-tech computer gadgetry and anything from pendulums to feathers to illustrate principles of mathematics, physics, and human perception. There are daily stage shows (about such things as rockets and natural disasters), puppet shows, and talks. Staff members explain the scientific principles behind the exhibits. ⊠ *King Edward Terr., corner of Mall Rd. W, Parkes* ☎ *02/6270–2800, 1800/020–603* ⊕ *www.questacon.edu.au* ⊡ *A$20* ⊘ *Daily 9–5.*

AROUND CANBERRA AND THE A.C.T.

Cockington Green Gardens. You'll feel like Gulliver walking through this miniature village and gardens 15 km (9 mi) northwest of the center of Canberra. Named after a small town in England, this site is a big hit with children who love wandering past the football stadium and hearing the roar of the crowd, and seeing classic structures such as Stonehenge, a miniature turf maze, windmills, and a cricket match on the village green. They'll also love taking a ride on the miniature train through the gardens. Cockington Green began as a miniature museum for all things English (country cottages, village church, etc) more than 30 years ago; however, many international miniature buildings—such as the Tenochtitian Temple in Mexico, the Chateau Bojnice in Slovakia, and India's Red Fort—have been added over the years. It is near Gold Creek Village shopping center; take the Barton Highway and head toward Yass. ⊠ *11 Gold Creek Rd., Nicholls* ☎ *02/6230–2273* ⊕ *www.cockingtongreen. com.au* ⊡ *$17.50* ⊘ *Daily 9:30 am–4:15 pm.*

WINE TOURING AROUND CANBERRA

Wineries began popping up everywhere around Canberra in the late 1990s, once it was discovered that the cool climate was optimal for producing Chardonnays, Rieslings, Cabernets, Shirazes, Merlots, and Pinots. There are now about 140 vineyards, 30 of which have cellar doors, set in the peaceful rural countryside surrounding the city—mostly small operations, where visiting the cellar door usually involves sampling the wines in the tasting room. There is no charge for tastings, although the vintners hope you'll be impressed enough with the wine to make some purchases.

Most are a maximum of 30 minutes from the city and are concentrated in the villages of Hall and Murrumbateman and in the Lake George area and Bungendore. Many are open to visits on weekends only. If you want to explore the wineries on your own, pick up a copy of *The Canberra District Wineries Guide* from the Canberra and Region Visitor Centre, or check out the Web site (⊕ *www.yassvalley.com.au*), which focuses on the wine region.

Wine Wisdom Winery Tours. Wine Wisdom Winery Tours specializes in personally tailored wine-tour itineraries in the region; a luxury day tour costs A$290 person when two people are traveling together. ☎ *02/6260–7773* ⊕ *www.winewisdom.com.au.*

WINERIES ALONG THE BARTON HIGHWAY

From Canberra take the Barton Highway (25) in the direction of Yass. After 20 km (12 mi) you'll pass the village of Hall and reach a handful of wineries, several of which are quite impressive.

Brindabella Hills Winery. It's worth heading to their cellar door (weekends only) to taste the award-winning 2008 Reserve Shiraz, one of the varieties that this family-run operation specializes in. The vineyard is ringed by the lovely Brindabella ranges, providing a gorgeous setting on a sunny day for a picnic or BBQ. Lunches, provided by local gourmet caterer Food for Friends, are served on weekends, often accompanied by a jazz band. The vineyard is 25 km north of Canberra. ⊠ *156 Woodgrove Close, via Hall* ☎ *02/6230–2583* ⊕ *www.brindabellahills.com.au* ⊗ *Cellar door weekends only 10–5, weekdays for purchases only 10–5.*

Surveyors Hill Winery. Stop here to taste the Riesling, Chardonnay, Sauvignon Blanc, rosé, and some dessert and sticky wines. In addition to the simple cellar door, the owners offer light meals to go with their wines. They make ample use of olives from their trees and other produce sourced from the property's gardens. Guests can also stay overnight at their B&B, which can accommodate up to 12 people in both the original family homestead and the new, more modern units. ⊠ *215 Brooklands Rd., Wallaroo* ☎ *02/6230–2046.*

★ **Poachers Pantry & Wily Trout Winery.** This favorite among gourmands is 25 minutes from Canberra. Here you'll find a tasting room offering good examples of Pinot Noir and Shiraz, and fabulous food offered by Poachers Pantry and the award-winning Smokehouse Café. Stock up on picnic-style smoked meats, poultry, and vegetables at the Pantry, or visit the Café for a memorable countryside dining experience in a historic cottage. Poachers Panty is one of the 25 operators who make up the Poacher's Way (⊕ *www.thepoachersway.com.au*), a collective of food emporiums, wineries, restaurants, galleries, and experiences that are loosely linked by a trail and that provide memorable regional experiences. ⊠ *431 Nanima Rd., Hall* ☎ *02/6230–2487* ⊕ *www.poacherspantry.com.au* ⊗ *Daily 10–5.*

WINERIES ALONG THE FEDERAL HIGHWAY

From Canberra take the Federal Highway (23) for about 30 km (19 mi) north toward Sydney. There are a few wineries off the highway between Canberra and Lake George and a few not far from the lake.

Lambert Vineyards. You either like the style of this modern complex with cellar door and café or you don't—it provokes strong opinions on the Canberra wine trail. Its wines are generally popular, however. As it is more than 800 m above sea level, it produces mostly red cool-climate varieties. After your tasting, don't miss the barrel room, which holds approximately 250 barrels of maturing wine, or dine by the fireplace in winter or on the terrace in summer. ⊠ *810 Norton Rd., Wamboin* ☎ *02/6238–3866* ⊕ *www.lambertvineyards.com.au* ⊗ *Cellar door Fri.–Sun. 10–5, café Fri.–Sun. lunch and dinner, Thurs. dinner only.*

Lark Hill Winery. This family-run enterprise overlooking (the usually bone-dry) Lake George specializes in biodynamic Riesling, Chardonnay, and Pinot Noir varieties. After your tasting, be sure to try the renowned fine-dining restaurant (weekends only) and sit out on the deck that looks out over the vines. ⊠ *Bungendore Rd. and Joe Rocks Rd., Bungendore* ☎ *02/6238–1393* ⊕ *www.larkhillwine.com.au* ⊗ *Wed.–Mon. 10–5, restaurant Sat.–Sun. lunch only.*

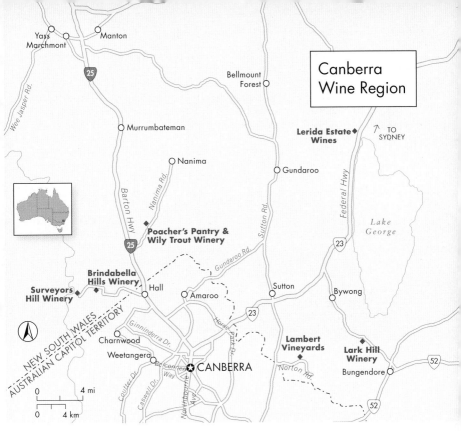

Lerida Estate Wines. Forty-five km (28 mi) out of Canberra, this award-winning winery is as famous for its design by Pritzker Prize–winning architect Glenn Murcutt as it is for its mid-price bottles. Try the Proprietor's Selection if 'its available at the cellar door—the 2006 Chardonnay is excellent. The tasting room and adjoining café, which offers light seasonal meals, enjoy lovely views over the often dry Lake George. Visitors, in groups of 6 or more, who make an appointment in advance can take either a 40-minute or 60-minute tour of the winery followed by tutored wine tasting priced from A$7.50 per person. ⊠ *Federal Hwy., Lake George* ☎ *02/6295–6640* ⊕ *www.leridaestate.com* ☉ *Cellar door daily 10–5, café weekends 10–5.*

WHERE TO EAT

The main restaurant precincts are around the city center and in the trendy suburbs of Manuka and Kingston. However, many fine eateries are tucked away in such suburban centers as Griffith, Ainslie, Belconnen, and Woden. In Dickson, Canberra's Chinatown, a line of inexpensive, casual eateries along Woolley Street includes many little spots serving Vietnamese, Malaysian, Chinese, Turkish, and Italian cuisine.

Use the coordinate (✛ B2) at the end of each listing to locate a site on the corresponding map.

The Australian Federal Parliament, Canberra.

CENTRAL CANBERRA AND NORTHERN SUBURBS

$$ ✕ **Bicicletta.** Its name is Italian for bicycle and the motif is carried through
ITALIAN this funky restaurant housed in the ultrahip Diamant Hotel, with two-
wheeled images on the big umbrella-shape light fittings and pieces of
memorabilia. The popular dining spot, open all day from 7:30 am until
10 pm, was once a student dormitory, and the interior's distressed look
(featuring old bathroom tiles and shabby walls) has been left to add to
the venue's funky feel. The menu features antipasti, pasta, a long list
of pizzas, salads, and only a light smattering of meat and fish dishes.
Start with the yummy large olives stuffed with savory mince, crumbed
and lightly fried; or try the slow-cooked pork and veal meatballs. Thin-
crust pizzas include the "fantasia": mozzarella, spinach, sausage, cherry
tomatoes, and Gorgonzola. Pop in early for great pastries and good
coffee, and use the free Wi-Fi while you eat. ✉ *15 Edinburgh Ave., City
Center* ☎ *02/6262–8683* ⊕ *www.bicicletta.com.au.* ✛ *B3.*

$$ ✕ **The Chairman and Yip.** The menu at this longtime fusion favorite gar-
ECLECTIC ners universal praise for its innovative mix of Asian and Western flavors
★ against a backdrop of artifacts from Maoist China. Menu standouts
include the duck pancakes and the pork chops with red dates, ginseng,
and honey. Finish with a delicious dessert, such as cinnamon-and-star-
anise crème brûlée. There are various specials, such as two-course lunch
for A$25 and an two-course early-bird dinner for $28.50. The service
and wine list are outstanding, but you can still bring your own bottle
of wine if you like. ✉ *108 Bunda St., Canberra City* ☎ *02/6248–7109*
⊕ *www.thechairmanandyip.com* ✐ *Reservations essential* ⛟ *BYO*
☾ *Closed Sun. No lunch Sat.* ✛ *C2.*

3

$$$
AUSTRALIAN
✕**Courgette.** Creative food served in spacious, sedate surroundings is the specialty of this popular restaurant on the city's outer edge. The seasonal menu has such dreamy dishes as cprosiutto-wrapped pan-seared scallops for a starter, or, for a main, the crispy-skin snapper, fennel puree and Balmain-bug-filled zucchini (also known as courgette) flower. Leave room for the decadent warm Belgian chocolate fondant with raspberries and vanilla-bean ice cream. There's a five-course degustation menu for A$120, and an impressive wine list. ⊠ *54 Marcus Clarke St., Canberra City* ☏ *02/6247–4042* ⊕ *www.courgette.com.au* ☽ *Closed Sun. No lunch Sat.* ✛ *B2.*

$$$$
AUSTRALIAN
Fodor's Choice
★
✕**The Ginger Room.** A regular haunt of politicians and journalists, the sensitively restored private members' dining room of old Parliament House is comfortable and elegant, and offers fine dining at affordable prices. The contemporary seasonal menu offers Asian-influenced dishes like chili crab, coconut, kaffir lime, and betel leaf. The high quality of the food makes the two-course (A$59) and three-course (A$69) options particularly good deals. The seven-course degustation (A$99) is also good value. The wine list is judged to be Canberra's best. ⊠ *Old Parliament House, King George Terr, Parkes* ☏ *02/6270–8262* ⊕ *www.gingercatering.com. au* ⚐ *Reservations essential* ☽ *Dinner Tues.–Sat.* ✛ *B4.*

$$
ITALIAN
✕**Italian and Sons.** This new, lively restaurant calls itself a modern version of the traditional Roman trattoria. It serves regional Italian cuisine using local produce, much of it from the owner's farm. Sit among the hanging salamis at tables covered in white paper and feast on antipasti such as chili and garlic prawns. Move on to one of the delicious pizzas (Sicilian anchovy, black olive, and baby caper are standouts), or one of the dishes of the day, like wood-roast suckling pig with apple and sage. Finish with Ligurian honey panna cotta, or one of the imported Italian cheeses. Buon appetito! ⊠ *7 Lonsdale St., Kuranda* ☏ *02/6162–4888* ✛ *B2.*

$$
THAI
✕**Thirst Wine Bar & Eatery.** This busy Thai restaurant in the heart of Canberra draws its inspiration from the street-food stalls of Thailand. Waitstaff does an excellent job of suggesting just the right wines for your meals. The crispy fish salad is a specialty, mixing the crisp fried-fish pieces with green mango, coriander, mint, roasted peanuts, and a chili dressing (have it with the Thirst Reisling). The main-course dish of red curry pork, baby corn, and cherry tomatoes is also delicious, and can be savored with a Shiraz or Chablis. The "two dishes for the price of one" deal on Monday and Tuesday nights is popular with the locals, so arrive early or expect a wait. ⊠ *Melbourne Bldg., 20 West Row, Canberra City* ☏ *02/6257–0700* ⊕ *www.thirstwinebar.com.au* ☽ *Closed Sun.* ✛ *B3.*

SOUTHERN SUBURBS

$$
AUSTRALIAN
✕**Rubicon.** Everything about this cozy romantic restaurant speaks of attention to detail. For instance, savor the melded flavors of chermoula-spiced lamb fillets with tangerine yoghurt and Parmesan and rosemary polenta chips. Later you can linger over such delicious desserts as honey and rum panna cotta with baby figs and ginger ice cream. For a lighter meal, sample the very popular char-grilled octopus with chili-whipped feta, or the cheese board and a few choice picks from the extensive collection of wines. ⊠ *6A Barker St., Griffith* ☏ *02/6295–9919* ☽ *Closed Sun. No lunch Mon., no dinner Sat.* ✛ *C6.*

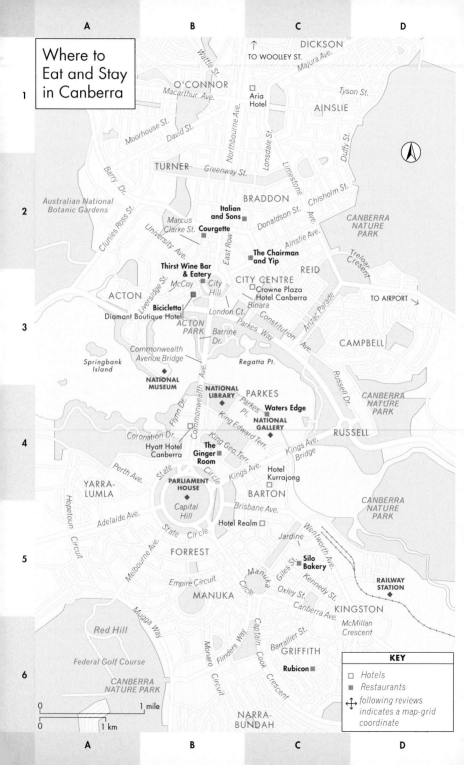

3

$$ ✕**Silo Bakery.** It's not unusual to find a queue of hungry Canberrians
CAFÉ waiting to take away some of the delectable homemade pastries (try
the black-currant and Cabernet tart) and breads. It's also possible to sit
down for breakfast, brunch, or lunch at one of the few tables. The eggs
with chili jam are popular, while the thin, crisp sourdough pizza topped
with a mixture of mushrooms and hint of blue cheese is mouthwater-
ing. Many people complain about the rude staff, but don't let it keep
you from going here; the food is so good that their brusqueness is easy
enough to ignore. ⊠ *36 Giles St., Kingston* ☎ *02/6260–6060* ⊕ *www.
silobakery.com.au* ⊗ *Closed Sun. and Mon. No dinner* ✛ *C5.*

$$$ ✕**Waters Edge.** At this swanky spot tables are set with fine linens and
ECLECTIC crystal, and huge windows look out over the sparkling waters of Lake
Burley Griffin. The menu cleverly blends French and Mod-Oz influences
with dishes such as duck breast and pressed leg confit with potatoes
and rosemary gratin and sautéed sweet cabbage, or a luscious dessert
of cherry soufflé and sour cherry jus served with coconut sorbet. For a
special night out, try the tasting menu (A$130 and A$170 with matching wines). An impressive wine list has many by-the-glass vintages.
⊠ *Commonwealth Pl. off Parkes Pl., Parkes* ☎ *02/6273–5066* ⊗ *No
lunch Mon.–Tues.* ✛ *C4.*

WHERE TO STAY

For expanded hotel reviews, visit Fodors.com.

CENTRAL CANBERRA AND NORTHERN SUBURBS

$$$$ ⌂ **Aria Hotel.** This is Canberra's newest hotel (opened in late 2010)
and everything is spic and span. **Pros:** brand new; good Internet rates
make apartments affordable. **Cons:** outside city center. ⊠ *45 Dooring
St., Dickson* ☎ *02/6279–7000* ⊕ *www.ariahotel.com.au* ↪ *128 rooms*
⌂ *In-room: a/c, kitchen, Internet, Wi-Fi. In-hotel: restaurant, pool,
gym, laundry facilities, business center, parking* ✛ *C1.*

¢ ⌂ **Crowne Plaza Hotel Canberra.** In a prime location between the city center and the National Convention Centre, this atrium-style hotel has a
touch of luxury. **Pros:** excellent gym and pool; gambling fans will enjoy
being next door to the casino. **Cons:** hotel bars can be noisy; expensive
parking. ⊠ *1 Binara St., Canberra City* ☎ *02/6247–8999, 1300/662–
218* ⊕ *www.crowneplaza.com.au* ↪ *287 rooms, 6 suites* ⌂ *In-room:
Internet. In-hotel: restaurant, bar, pool, gym, parking* ✛ *C3.*

$$$ ⌂ **Diamant Boutique Hotel.** In a city lacking in funk factor, the Diamant
Fodor'sChoice stands out thanks to its groovy blend of art-deco chic exterior and quirky
★ interior. **Pros:** great array of restaurants and bars for a hotel of this size;
beautifully landscaped modern gardens. **Cons:** bar and restaurants close
early; cheaper rooms are on the small side. ⊠ *15 Edinburgh Ave., City
Center* ☎ *02/6175–2222* ⊕ *www.diamant.com.au* ↪ *80 rooms* ⌂ *In-
room: safe, Wi-Fi. In-hotel: restaurant, bar, spa, parking* ✛ *B3.*

SOUTHERN SUBURBS

$$ ⌂ **Hotel Kurrajong.** If you want to immerse yourself in Canberra's
politcial history and be within walking distance of Parliament House,
the Hotel Kurrajong is the place; this boutique hotel built in 1925–26
was designed in the early Commonwealth style (influenced by both

Frank Lloyd Wright and lWater Burley Griffin). **Pros:** stylish; lots of history. **Cons:** doesn't offer the same facilities as larger hotels. ⊠ *8 National Circuit, Barton* ☎ *02/6234–4444* ⊕ *www.hotelkurrajong.com.au* ⤳ *26 rooms* ⌂ *In-room: a/c, Internet. In-hotel: restaurant* ⊕ *C4.*

$$$$ ⊡ **Hotel Realm.** This new kid on the block is an ultramodern hotel set amid a new development of residential apartments and trendy eateries. **Pros:** modern; good location; trendy dining options. **Cons:** has a real business feel to it. ⊠ *18 National Circuit, Barton* ☎ *02/6163–1888* ⊕ *www.hotelrealm.com.au* ⤳ *158 rooms* ⌂ *In-room: a/c, kitchen, Wi-Fi. In-hotel: restaurant, bar, pool, gym, business center, parking* ⊕ *C5.*

$$$$
Fodor's Choice
★

⊡ **Hyatt Hotel Canberra.** Occupying a National Heritage building dating from 1924, this elegant hotel has been restored to its original art deco splendor. **Pros:** friendly and unobtrusive service, superb location. **Cons:** Expensive breakfasts; can be very busy. ⊠ *Commonwealth Ave., Yarralumla* ☎ *13–1234, 02/6270–1234* ⊕ *www.canberra.hyatt.com* ⤳ *231 rooms, 18 suites* ⌂ *In-room: safe, Wi-Fi. In-hotel: restaurant, bar, pool, tennis court, gym, spa, parking* ⊕ *B4.*

NIGHTLIFE AND THE ARTS

Canberra's nightlife has had an adrenalin injection in recent years, and there are great wine bars, pubs, and music venues. Most venues are clustered in the city center and the fashionable southern suburbs of Manuka and Kingston. Except on weekends, few places showcase live music.

The Thursday edition of the *Canberra Times* has a "What's On" section (in the *Times Out* supplement) listing performances around the city. The Saturday edition's Arts pages also list weekend happenings.

THE ARTS

Canberra Theatre Centre. The Canberra Theatre Centre is the city's main live performance space. The center has two different theaters, which host productions by the Australian Ballet Company, touring theater companies, and overseas and local artists.

Canberra Ticketing. The theater's ticketing agency, Canberra Ticketing, is in the space joining the two main theaters in Civic Square. ⊠ *Civic Sq., Canberra City* ☎ *02/6275–2700, 1800/802025* ⊕ *www. canberraticketing.com.au* ⊠ *Civic Sq., Canberra City* ☎ *02/6275-2700* ⊕ *www.canberratheatrecentre.com.au.*

Erindale Theatre. Smaller stage and musical companies perform at neighborhood venues like the Erindale Theatre. ⊠ *McBryde Crescent, Wanniassa* ☎ *02/6207–2703* ⊕ *www.erindale.act.edu.au.*

Llewellyn Hall. The Australian National University's School of Music has classical recitals and modern-style concerts on campus at Llewellyn Hall. ⊠ *Childers St., Acton* ☎ *02/6125–2527* ⊕ *www.anu.edu.au.*

Street Theatre. The Street Theatre, near the Australian National University campus, showcases the best in local talent with excellent productions ranging from musicals to avant-garde plays. ⊠ *15 Childers St. at University Ave., Canberra City* ☎ *02/6247–1223* ⊕ *www.thestreet.org.au.*

Interior of the National Museum of Australia, Canberra.

ART GALLERIES

Apart from the major galleries, Canberra has a wealth of smaller private art galleries showcasing and selling the works of Australian artists. You can find paintings, sculpture, woodworking, glassware, and jewelry at these spots. Entry to most galleries is free, and it is always advisable to call ahead for business hours.

Beaver Galleries. Beaver Galleries has four exhibition galleries and a sculpture garden, where works by contemporary Australian artists are showcased. There is also a café. ⊠ *81 Denison St., Deakin* 🕾 *02/6282–5294* ⊕ *www.beavergalleries.com.au* ⊗ *Tues.–Fri. 10–5, Sat., Sun. 9–5.*

Chapman Gallery. Chapman Gallery has rotating exhibits by leading Australian artists, with a special emphasis on Aboriginal art. ⊠ *1/11 Murray Crescent, Manuka* 🕾 *02/6295–2550* ⊕ *www.chapmangallery. com.au* ⊗ *Closed Mon. and Tues.*

Solander Gallery. Solander Gallery displays a range of paintings and sculpture by leading Australian artists. ⊠ *10 Schlich St., Yarralumla* 🕾 *02/6285–2218* ⊕ *www.solander.com.au* ⊗ *Closed Mon.–Thurs.*

NIGHTLIFE

Canberra's nightspots offer everything from thumping house music to dance and comedy clubs. Many waive cover charges except for special events.

Academy Club and Candy Bar. Canberra's liveliest nightspot draws the hip crowd to its stylish, glitzy premises. The main room, which hosts DJs and live bands, attracts a young crowd. Upstairs, Candy Bar serves innovative cocktails in a chic lounge setting. ⊠ *Centre Cinema Bldg.,*

Experiencing Aboriginal Culture

The Ngunnawal people were the first inhabitants of the area now known as Canberra and the A.C.T., and the name Canberra comes from the Ngunnawal word "Kambera." In NSW the Cammeraygal, Eora, Kamilaroi, Tharawal, Wiradjuri, and Wonnarua peoples were some of the original inhabitants, each grouping speaking a different language and practicing a culture that stretched back thousands of years.

Muru Mittigar Aboriginal Cultural Centre near Penrith, an hour's drive from Sydney, tells the story of the Dharug people. You can try bush tucker and boomerang throwing, or learn about the native plants used for medicine and food. (⊠ *89–151 Old Castlereagh Rd., Castlereagh, NSW* ☎ *02/4729–2377* ⊕ *www. murumittigar.com.au*).

Bunda St., Canberra City ☎ *02/6257–3355* ⊕ *www.academyclub.com. au* ⌑ *A$5–A$40* ☉ *Academy Thurs.–Sat. 9 pm–late; Candy Bar Wed.– Sat. 5 pm–late.*

Casino Canberra. The European-style gaming room forgoes slot machines in favor of more sociable games like roulette, blackjack, poker, and keno. There are 40 gaming tables here, and the complex includes a restaurant (which has live music) and two bars. The Galaxy Night-club, above the main gaming floor, is open on Saturday nights from 9. ⊠ *Glebe Park, 21 Binara St., Canberra City* ☎ *02/6257–7074* ⊕ *www. casinocanberra.com.au* ⌑ *Free* ☉ *Daily noon–6 am.*

Tilley's Devine Café Gallery. This 1940s-style club was once just for women, but now anyone can sit at the wooden booths and enjoy a relaxing meeting with friends or a meal at this arty café that does a great breakfast; in fact, the kitchen is open all day from 9 am to 10 pm (except Sundays). Established in 1984, the café stages a full range of cultural events from poetry readings to live music, particularly jazz and blues. Check the Web site for details. ⊠ *Wattle and Brigalow Sts., Lyneham* ☎ *02/6247–7753* ⊕ *tilleys.com.au* ☉ *Mon.–Sat. 9 am–10 pm, Sun. 9–6.*

OUTDOOR ACTIVITIES

BICYCLING Canberra has almost 160 km (100 mi) of cycle paths, and the city's relatively flat terrain and dry, mild climate make it a perfect place to explore on two wheels. One of the most popular cycle paths is the 40-km (25-mi) circuit around Lake Burley Griffin.

Mr. Spokes Bike Hire. Mr. Spokes Bike Hire rents several different kinds of bikes, as well as tandems and baby seats. Bikes cost A$15 for the first hour, including helmet rental, locks, and a map of cycle routes. Half-day hire (4 hours) is A$25, while a full day (from 9 am to 5 pm) is A$35. ⊠ *Acton Ferry Terminal, Barrine Dr., Acton Park* ☎ *02/6257–1188* ⊕ *www.mrspokes.com.au* ☉ *Daily 9–5; closed Tues in school term; closed weekdays in winter months.*

BOATING **Burley Griffin Boat Hire.** You can rent paddleboats, kayaks, and canoes daily (except May–August) for use on Lake Burley Griffin from Burley Griffin Boat Hire. Rates start at A$15 an hour for kayaks and A$20 an hour for canoes; paddleboats are A$18 for 30 minutes. ⊠ *Acton Ferry Terminal, Barrine Dr., Acton Park* ☎ *02/6249–6861* ⊕ *www. actboathire.com.* ☽ *Closed in winter.*

Southern Cross Cruises. Southern Cross Cruises has daily one-hour sailings (A$15) around Lake Burley Griffin on the MV *Southern Cross* at 3 pm. During summer there's a 2-hour cruise (Thursdays only) that also takes in a tour of Government House Gardens (A$23). ⊠ *Southern Cross Club, Lotus Bay, 1 Mariner Pl. off Alexandrina Dr., Yarralumla* ☎ *02/6273–1784.*

HIKING **Namadgi National Park.** Covering almost half the total area of the Australian Capital Territory's southwest, this national park has a well-maintained network of walking trails across mountain ranges, trout streams, and some of the most accessible subalpine forests in the country. Some parts of the park were severely burned in the January 2003 bushfires, but the recovery powers of the native bush have been truly remarkable. The park's boundaries are within 35 km (22 mi) of Canberra, and its former pastures, now empty of sheep and cattle, are grazed by hundreds of eastern gray kangaroos in the early morning and late afternoon. Car-based tent camping is permitted in three designated campgrounds: Orroral, Honeysuckly Creek, and Mount Clear. Bookings are essential and can be done online (⊕ *www.bookings.act. gov.au*) or by phone. Snow covers the higher altitudes June–September. ⊠ *Visitor center: Naas–Boboyan Rd., 3 km (2 mi) south of Tharwa* ☎ *02/6207–2900, 13–2281* ⊕ *www.tams.act.gov.au* ✉ *Free* ☽ *Park daily 24 hrs; visitor center weekdays 9–4, weekends 9–4:30.*

Tidbinbilla Nature Reserve. The walking trails, wetlands, and animal exhibits within this reserve, many of which were badly damaged in the bushfires of 2003, have recovered beautifully since then. The park is 40 km (25 mi) southwest of Canberra. ⊠ *Paddy's River Rd., Tidbinbilla* ☎ *02/6205–1233, 13–2281* ⊕ *www.tams.act.gov.au* ✉ *Free* ☽ *Visitor center weekdays 9–4:30, weekends 9–5. Reserve Grounds standard time 9–6, daylight savings time weekdays 9–5, weekends 8:30–6:30.*

HOT-AIR **Balloon Aloft.** Balloon Aloft provides spectacular sunrise views over
BALLOONING Canberra from around A$290 on weekdays and A$340 on weekends. ☎ *02/6285–1540* ⊕ *www.balloonaloft.com.*

SHOPPING

Canberra has quite a diverse range of shopping opportunities, including the large 300-store Canberra Centre on Bunda Street in the heart of the city, and the well-to-do inner suburbs of Manuka and Kingston, where designer clothes and home wares can be had. There are also a number of high-quality arts-and-crafts outlets where you are likely to come across some unusual gifts and souvenirs. The galleries and museums sell interesting and often innovative items designed and made in Australia.

Gold Creek Village. The charming streets of this shopping complex on the city's northern outskirts are lined with all sorts of fun little places to explore. Peek into art galleries and pottery shops, browse through clothing boutiques and gift stores, and nosh at several eateries. ⊠ *O'Hanlon Pl., Nicholls* ⊕ *www.goldcreekvillage.com* ⊗ *Daily 10–5.*

Old Bus Depot Markets. South of Lake Burley Griffin, this lively Sunday market is in the former Kingston bus depot. Handmade crafts are the staples here, and buskers and inexpensive exotic food enliven the shopping experience. When you've had your fill, wander across the road to the Canberra Glassworks to watch artisans at work. ⊠ *Wentworth Ave., Kingston Foreshore, Kingston* ☎ *02/6239–5306, 02/6295–3331* ⊕ *www.obdm.com.au* ⊗ *Sun. 10–4.*

Melbourne

WORD OF MOUTH

Go look at the marvelous renovation of the beautiful Reading Room Dome at the State Library for an example of the sort of public building built when Melbourne was one of the richest cities in the world, at the height of its Gold Rush in the 1800s.

—Libretto

WELCOME TO MELBOURNE

TOP REASONS TO GO

★ **Fabulous Markets:**
Melbourne has nearly a dozen major markets. The huge Queen Victoria Market (the Vic) has more than 1,000 stalls. Others include the "foodie heaven" Prahran Market, and St. Kilda's Sunday market, awash with pottery and all things arty.

★ **International Cuisine:**
Melbourne's dining scene is a vast smorgasbord of cuisines: Chinese restaurants on Little Bourke Street are the equal of anything in Hong Kong. Richmond's Victoria Street convincingly incarnates Vietnam.

★ **Sizzling Nightlife:**
Melbourne's nightlife centers on King Street and Flinders Lane, with dozens of retro-style bars and clubs. Crown Casino's two nightclubs and the numerous bars along Southgate add life to the city center.

★ **Sports Galore:**
Melburnians, like Aussies in general, do love a good match. The Melbourne Cup horse race in November brings the entire city to a standstill. The same is true of Australian Rules Football.

1 City Centre. Why come? For arts, funky laneways, shopping and Australia's best food. Explore the Southgate development, the arts district around the National Gallery of Victoria, and the King's Domain

2 Richmond. Heaven for foodies and fashionistas in need of retail therapy. Come here for a new wardrobe, a Vietnamese soup kitchen, a Korean barbecue, a Laotian banquet, or a Thai hole-in-the-wall.

3 East Melbourne. The harmonious streetscapes in this historic enclave of Victorian houses, which date from the boom following the gold rushes of the 1850s, are a great excuse for a stroll.

4 St. Kilda. Dozens of alfresco restaurants overflow into the streets and the cafés and bars are buzzing with the young fashionistas.

5 Fitzroy. Come here if you're looking for an Afghan camel bag or a secondhand paperback, or yearn for a café where you can sit over a plate of tapas.

GETTING ORIENTED

Melbourne, the capital of Victoria, is in the south of the state on Port Phillip Bay. With a population of almost 4 million people, it is the fastest-growing major city in Australia. The Yarra River cuts through the city center; the main business district is on the northern side, the southern side has arts, entertainment, and restaurant precincts. Several exclusive suburbs hug the southeastern shore of the bay. The Yarra Valley wineries and the Dandenongs Ranges are an hour's drive to the east, while the beaches and vineyards of the Mornington Peninsula are a 90-minute drive south of Melbourne. The Great Ocean Road begins at Torquay, southwest of Melbourne, and continues along the Southern Ocean coast to Portland, a distance of about 350 km (217 mi). The goldfields, spa country, and Grampians are between one and two hours northwest of Melbourne; the Murray River Region and its wineries are about a three-hour drive north to northeast of Melbourne.

Updated by
Melanie Ball

Consistently rated among the "world's most livable cities" in quality-of-life surveys, Melbourne is built on a coastal plain at the top of the giant horseshoe of Port Phillip Bay. The city center is an orderly grid of streets where the state parliament, banks, multinational corporations, and splendid Victorian buildings that sprang up in the wake of the gold rush now stand. This is Melbourne's heart, which you can explore at a leisurely pace in a couple of days.

In Southbank, one of the newer precincts south of the city center, the Southgate development of bars, restaurants, and shops has refocused Melbourne's vision on the Yarra River. Once a blighted stretch of factories and run-down warehouses, the southern bank of the river is now a vibrant, exciting part of the city, and the river itself is finally taking its rightful place in Melbourne's psyche. Just a hop away, Federation Square—with its host of galleries—has become a civic landmark for Melburnians. Stroll along the Esplanade in the suburb of St. Kilda, amble past the elegant houses of East Melbourne, enjoy the shops and cafés in Fitzroy or Carlton, rub shoulders with locals at the Victoria Market, nip into the Windsor for afternoon tea, or rent a canoe at Studley Park to paddle along one of the prettiest stretches of the Yarra—and you may discover Melbourne's soul as well as its heart.

PLANNING

WHEN TO GO

Melbourne and Victoria are at their most beautiful in autumn, from March to May. Days are crisp, and the foliage in parks and gardens is glorious. Melbourne winters can be gloomy, although the wild seas and leaden skies from June to August provide a suitable backdrop for the dramatic coastal scenery of the Great Ocean Road. By September the weather begins to clear, and the football finals are on. Book early to visit Melbourne during the Spring Racing Carnival and the Melbourne

International Festival (late October/early November) and during mid-January when the Australian Open Tennis is staged.

GETTING HERE AND AROUND

Melbourne is most easily reached by plane, as it's hours by car from the nearest big city. International airlines flying into Melbourne include Air New Zealand, British Airways, United, Singapore Airlines, Emirates, Thai Airways, Malaysia Airlines, V Australia, and Qantas.

BY BUS AND TRAM

Melbourne is divided into two zones. Zone 1 is the urban core, where most travelers spend their time. There are two types of ticket: Metcard (paper tickets) and myki (a stored-money smartcard system being slowly introduced across the public transport network). The basic ticket (the Metcard) is the one-zone ticket, which can be purchased onboard the bus or tram (or purchased at 7-11 stores, Melbourne Town Hall, and the Melbourne Visitors Centre at Federation Square) for A$3.80. It's valid for travel within a specific zone on any bus, tram, or train for two hours after purchase. For travelers, the most useful ticket is probably the Zone 1 day ticket, which costs A$7. Trams run until midnight, and can be hailed wherever you see a green-and-gold tram-stop sign.

BY CAR

Melbourne's regimented layout makes it easy to negotiate by car, but two unusual rules apply because of the tram traffic. Trams should be passed on the *left,* and when a tram stops to allow passengers to disembark, the cars behind it also must stop. Motorists using various tollways have 72 hours to pay the toll after using the highway. To pay by credit card, call ☎ 13–2629. Alternatively, you can buy passes at the airport before using the tollways. A weekend pass is around A$10.

BY TRAIN

Southern Cross Railway Station is at Spencer and Little Collins streets. From here the countrywide V-Line has 11-hour trips to Sydney, as well as services to many regional centers in Victoria. V-Line buses connect with the trains to provide transport to coastal towns; take the train to Marshall (one stop beyond Geelong) to connect with a bus to Lorne, Apollo Bay, and Port Campbell, or travel by train to Warrnambool and take a bus to Port Fairy.

HEALTH AND SAFETY

There are medical centers around the city, but for medical emergencies, contact the city hospitals. Melbourne is generally a safe city, although people should avoid deserted dark areas at night and be aware that the nightlife areas around King Street and St. Kilda can get unruly and drugs can be prevalent. There are 23 CCTV surveillance areas in the city, and safe weekend taxi ranks are located at 55 King Street, Flinders Street Station, and at 50 Bourke Street.

ABOUT THE RESTAURANTS

Melbourne teems with top-quality restaurants, particularly in St. Kilda, South Yarra, and the Waterfront City precinct, including Docklands. Lygon Street is still a favorite with those who love great coffee, al-dente pasta, and Italian bakeries, while the city center also has many back alleys (known as laneways) with popular cafés. Reservations are generally advised, and although most places are licensed to sell alcohol, the few that aren't usually allow you to bring your own. Lunch is served noon–2:30, and dinner is usually 7–10:30. A 10% tip is customary for exemplary service, and there may be a corkage fee in BYO restaurants.

ABOUT THE HOTELS

Staying in the heart of Melbourne, on Collins or Flinders Streets and their nearby laneways, or at Southbank, is ideal for those who like dining and shopping. Another trendy area, a little out of town, is South Yarra, which also has excellent shopping. Wherever you stay, make sure you're near a tram, bus, or train line.

DINING AND LODGING PRICE CATEGORIES (IN AUSTRALIAN DOLLARS)					
	¢	$	$$	$$$	$$$$
Restaurants	under A$10	A$10–A$20	A$21–A$35	A$36–A$50	over A$50
Hotels	under A$100	A$100–A$150	A$151–A$200	A$201–A$300	over A$300

Restaurant prices are based on the median main-course price at dinner. Hotel prices include taxes, and are for two people in a standard double room in high season, excluding service.

TOURS

A free City Circle tram run by Metropolitan Transit operates every 10 minutes 10–6 Sunday–Wednesday and 10–9 Thursday–Saturday on the fringe of the Central Business District, with stops on Flinders, Spencer, La Trobe, Victoria, and Spring streets. Look for the burgundy-and-cream trams. A free orange tourist bus (the Melbourne City Tourist Shuttle) does a loop around central and inner Melbourne suburbs daily, every 30 minutes between 9:30 and 4:30, stopping at 13 destinations including Federation Square, Docklands, South Yarra, and the Botanic Gardens. Metropolitan buses operate daily until around 9 pm to all suburbs, while the NightRider bus service runs between 1:30 am and 4:30 am on Saturday and 1:30 am and 5:30 am on Sunday.

Boat Tours. One of the best ways to see Melbourne is from the deck of a boat on the Yarra River. Melbourne River Cruises' fleet of modern, glass-enclosed boats operate 1- and 2½-hour Yarra River cruises daily (A$23 and A$29, respectively), traversing either west through the commercial heart of the city or east through the parks and gardens, or a combination of the two. Cruises run roughly every half hour from 10 to 4.

Bus Tours. Gray Line has guided tours of Melbourne and environs by bus and boat. The City Tour visits the city center's main attractions and some of the surrounding parks. The 3½-hour, A$65 tour departs daily at 8:10.

AAT Kings, Australian Pacific Tours, and Melbourne's Best Day Tours all have similar city highlight tours.

Food Tours. Foodies Dream Tours (A$40) and cooking classes (2½ hours, A$90–A$180) are conducted at Queen Victoria Market.

Chocoholic Tours offers several Saturday tours for chocolate lovers: the Chocoholic Brunch Walk (10–noon) and the Chocoholic Indulgence Walk (12:15–2:15), among others. Each offers a different combination of chocolate-fueled tastings and activities (A$37 each). Bookings are essential and departure points vary.

Vietnam on a Plate runs a guided walking tour of the Asian precincts, visiting traditional Chinese herbalists, food stalls, spice and herb specialists, and the "Little Saigon" shopping districts of Footscray and Springvale. The tour includes lunch and food tasting. Tours are usually given Saturday 9:30–12:30, and cost A$66. Reservations essential.

Walking Tours. The Melbourne Greeter service, a Melbourne Information Centre program, provides free two- to four-hour tours by pairing you with a local volunteer who shares your interests. Melbourne's Golden Mile Heritage Trail runs guided walking tours of the city's architectural and historic sites. Tours, which cost A$20 and take two hours, depart daily at 10 am from Federation Square and finish at the Melbourne Town Hall weekdays and the Melbourne Museum on weekends.

Tour Operators AAT Kings ✉ *Federation Square E, Flinders and Russell Sts., City Centre* ☎ *1300/228546.* **Australian Pacific Touring (APT)** ✉ *475 Hampton St., Hampton* ☎ *03/9277–8555, 1300/336932* ⊕ *www.aptouring.com.au.* **Chocoholic Tours** ✉ *145/28 Southgate Ave., Southbank* ☎ *03/9686–4655* ⊕ *www.chocoholictours.com.au.* **Foodies Dream Tours** ✉ *Queen Victoria Market, Queen and Elizabeth Sts., City Center* ☎ *03/9320–5822* ⊕ *www.qvm. com.au.* **Golden Mile Heritage Trail** ☎ *03/9928–0000* ⊕ *www.visitvictoria. com.* **Gray Line** ✉ *Federation Square E, Flinders and Russell Sts., City Center* ☎ *1300/858687* ⊕ *www.grayline.com.au.* **Melbourne's Best Day Tours** ✉ *Federation Square, Flinders and Russell Sts., City Center* ☎ *1300/130550* ⊕ *www.melbournetours.com.au.* **Melbourne Greeters** ✉ *Federation Sq., Flinders and Swanston Sts., City Center* ☎ *03/9658–9658 (weekdays), 03/9658–9942 (weekends)* ✍ *greeter@melbourne.vic.gov.au* ⊕ *www.thatsmelbourne.com.au.* **Melbourne River Cruises** ✉ *Vault 11, Banana Alley, 367 Flinders St., City Center* ☎ *03/8610–2600* ⊕ *www.melbcruises.com.au.* **Vietnam on a Plate** ✉ *Footscray Market, Hopkins and Leeds Sts., Footscray* ☎ *03/9332–6848* ⊕ *www.vietnamonaplate.com.au.*

VISITOR INFORMATION

The Melbourne Visitor Centre at Federation Square provides touring details in six languages. Large-screen videos and touch screens add to the experience, and permanent displays follow the city's history. Daily newspapers are available, and there's access to the Melbourne Web site (⊕ *www.visitmelbourne.com*). The center is open daily 9–6. The Best of Victoria Booking Service here can help if you're looking for accommodations. It also has cheap Internet access.

City Ambassadors—usually mature men and women easily spotted by their red uniforms—are volunteers for the City of Melbourne, and rove the central retail area providing directions and information for people needing their assistance (Monday–Saturday 10–4, Sunday noon–3).

A free bus route map is available from the Melbourne Visitor Centre.

Visitor Information Best of Victoria Booking Service ☎ *03/9928–0000, 1300/780045.* **City of Melbourne Ambassadors Program** ☎ *03/9658–9658.* **Melbourne Visitor Centre** ✉ *Federation Sq., Flinders and Swanston Sts., City Center* ☎ *03/9658–9658* ⊕ *www.melbourne.vic.gov.au or www.thatsmelbourne.com.au.*

EXPLORING

CITY CENTER

GETTING HERE AND AROUND

Melbourne and its suburbs are well served by trams, trains, and buses. The free loop tram is perfect for sightseeing, but crowded on weekends. Trams run east–west and north–south across the city, and travel to the popular St. Kilda and Docklands. The Metro train network operates a City Loop service with stops at Flinders Street, Parliament, and Southern Cross Station, where you'll find connections with a network of trains to outer areas, including the Dandenong Ranges.

TOP ATTRACTIONS

Block Arcade. Melbourne's most elegant 19th-century shopping arcade dates from the 1880s, when "Marvelous Melbourne" was flush with the prosperity of the gold rushes. A century later, renovations scraped back the grime to reveal a magnificent mosaic floor. Tours (A$9) operate on Tuesday and Thursday at 1 pm and conclude with afternoon tea in the Charles Dickens Tavern. ⊠ *282 Collins St., City Center* ☏ *03/9654–5244.*

★ **Federation Square.** Encompassing a whole city block, the bold, abstract-style landmark was designed to house the second branch of the National Gallery of Victoria, which exhibits only Australian art. The square also incorporates the Australian Centre for the Moving Image; the BMW Edge amphitheater, a contemporary music and theater performance venue; the Melbourne Visitor Centre; and restaurants, bars, and gift shops. ⊠ *Flinders St. between Swanston and Russell Sts., City Center* ☏ *03/9655–1900* ⊕ *www.fedsquare.com* ✉ *Free* ☾ *Daily 10–5; National Gallery of Victoria closed Mon.*

Fitzroy Gardens. This 65-acre expanse of European trees, manicured lawns, garden beds, statuary, and sweeping walks is Melbourne's most popular central park. Among its highlights is the **Avenue of Elms,** a majestic stand of 130-year-old trees that is one of the few in the world that has not been devastated by Dutch elm disease. ⊠ *Lansdowne St. at Wellington Parade, East Melbourne* ✉ *Free* ☾ *Daily sunrise–sunset.*

Flinders Street Station. Melburnians use the clocks on the front of this grand Edwardian hub of Melbourne's suburban rail network as a favorite meeting place. When it was proposed to replace them with television screens, an uproar ensued. Today there are both clocks and screens. ⊠ *Flinders St. at St. Kilda Rd., City Center.*

★ **The Hotel Windsor.** Not just a grand hotel, the Windsor is home to one of Melbourne's proudest institutions—the ritual of afternoon tea (A$59 mid-week), which is served daily 2:30–4:30, with an additional session noon–2 on Friday. An even more indulgent dessert buffet (A$79), complete with chocolate fountain and other goodies, is served on weekends noon–2 and 2:30–4:30. Although the Grand Ball Room—a belle epoque extravaganza with a gilded ceiling and seven glass cupolas—is reserved for private functions, occasionally afternoon tea is served there, so it's best to call first to check. ⊠ *111 Spring St., City Center* ☏ *03/9633–6000* ⊕ *www.thewindsor.com.au.*

GREAT ITINERARIES

IF YOU HAVE 1 DAY

The free City Circle Tram is a hop-on and hop-off way to see many of the city's sights in a short time without exhausting yourself. The Parliament House tram stop gives access to the Princess Theatre, the grand Windsor Hotel, Parliament House, the "Paris End" of Collins Street, and St. Patrick's Cathedral. Get off at Flinders Street to take a peek at the infamous *Chloe* painting in Young and Jackson's pub, and then walk over the Princes Bridge. There you can stroll along the banks of the Yarra, looking back at Federation Square, and then wander along Southbank while checking out the restaurants and shops and the Crown Casino. A trip to the new Eureka Skydeck, the southern hemisphere's highest viewing platform, will put the city into perspective, and up there you can decide whether to head northeast to Fitzroy for an amble along groovy Brunswick Street, or north to Carlton to immerse yourself in Little Italy.

IF YOU HAVE 3 DAYS

You might squeeze in a bit more exploring on Day 1 with a stroll through Treasury Gardens and over to Fitzroy Gardens for a look at Captain Cook's Cottage, or see the sharks at the Melbourne Aquarium opposite Southbank. On your second day, stroll through the Royal Botanic Gardens and see the Shrine of Remembrance. Then take a tram along St. Kilda Road to the hip Acland Street area, in the suburb of St. Kilda, for dinner. On Day 3, tour Chapel Street's shops, restaurants, and bars; it's Melbourne's hippest district.

IF YOU HAVE 5 DAYS

Head east to the Yarra Valley on an organized winery tour, or go to the Dandenong Ranges for a ride on the Puffing Billy steam railway from Belgrave through the fern gullies and forests of the Dandenong ranges. On the way back, stop at a teahouse in Belgrave or Olinda and browse the curio stores. Or take an evening excursion to Phillip Island for the endearing sunset Penguin Parade. A trip to the Mornington Peninsula wineries and Arthurs Seat, just 90 minutes south of Melbourne, is another great day out. There you can rest and recuperate with a soak in the Peninsula Hot Springs.

IF YOU HAVE 7 DAYS

Hang out in Melbourne for two days, and on Day 3 drive to the Dandenong Ranges and poke around the cute towns and fabulous gardens, or visit one or two wineries in the Yarra Valley.

On Day 4 head south, either to the Mornington Peninsula or Phillip Island; the former promises beaches and wines, the latter beaches and wildlife.

On Day 5 make your way to the Mornington Peninsula town of Sorrento and take the car ferry across to Queenscliff. Check out the old fort in town before heading west to join the Great Ocean Road. Choose Princetown or Port Campbell for an overnight stop and spend the afternoon exploring the Twelve Apostles. On Day 6 either head north to Ballarat and the goldfields or northwest to the Grampians. Then take the Western Highway back to Melbourne.

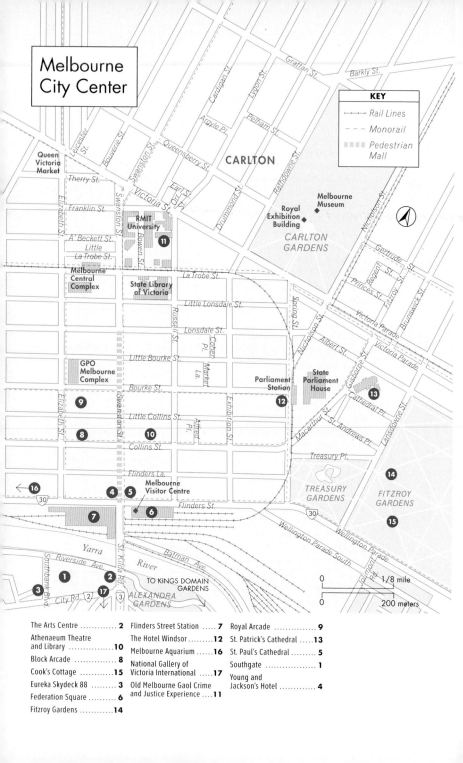

Melbourne City Center

CARLTON

Queen Victoria Market

Leicester St.

Therry St.

Bowerie St.

Queensberry St.

Franklin St.

Elizabeth St.

A' Beckett St.

Little La Trobe St.

Swanston St.

Victoria St.

Earl St.

Cardigan St.

Argyle Pl.

Lygon St.

Pelham St.

Grattan St.

Barkly St.

RMIT University **11**

Bowen St.

Drummond St.

Rathdowne St.

Melbourne Museum

Royal Exhibition Building ◆

CARLTON GARDENS

Nicholson St.

Gertrude St.

Melbourne Central Complex

State Library of Victoria

La Trobe St.

Little Lonsdale St.

Russell St.

Princes St.

Regent St.

Fitzroy St.

Brunswick St.

Victoria Parade

Lonsdale St.

Spring St.

Albert St.

Victoria Parade

GPO Melbourne Complex

Little Bourke St.

Cohen Pl.

Market La.

Bourke St.

Parliament Station

State Parliament House

Nicholson St.

Gisborne St.

Cathedral Pl.

13

Elizabeth St.

9

8

Swanston St.

Little Collins St.

10

Alfred Pl.

Exhibition St.

12

Macarthur St.

St. Andrews Pl.

Lansdowne St.

Collins St.

Flinders La.

Melbourne Visitor Centre

Treasury Pl.

14

16

30

4 **5**

St. Paul's

6

Flinders St.

TREASURY GARDENS

FITZROY GARDENS

15

7

Wellington Parade

Wellington Parade

Yarra

Riverside Ave.

St. Kilda Rd.

River

Batman Ave.

30

Wellington Parade South

1

2

TO KINGS DOMAIN GARDENS

Jolimont Rd.

Southbank Blvd.

3

City Rd.

2

17

3

ALEXANDRA GARDENS

0 ————— 1/8 mile

0 ————— 200 meters

OFF THE BEATEN PATH

King's Domain Gardens. This expansive stretch of parkland includes Queen Victoria Gardens, Alexandra Gardens, the Shrine of Remembrance, the Pioneer Women's Garden, the Sidney Myer Music Bowl, and the Royal Botanic Gardens. The temple-style **Shrine of Remembrance** is designed so that a beam of sunlight passes over the Stone of Remembrance in the Inner Shrine at 11 am on Remembrance Day—the 11th day of the 11th month, when in 1918 the armistice marking the end of World War I was declared. ⊠ *Between St. Kilda and Domain Rds., Anderson St., and Yarra River, City Center.*

Melbourne Aquarium. Become part of the action as you stroll through a transparent tunnel surrounded by water and the denizens of the deep on the prowl. Or press your nose to the glass in the Antarctica exhibition and watch King and Gentoo penguins waddling around on ice and darting through water. You can also don snow gear and sit among the penguins. If you're feeling brave, do a shark dive—they're held daily, include scuba equipment, and are led by an instructor. The aquamarine building illuminates a previously dismal section of the Yarra River bank, opposite Crown Casino. ⊠ *Flinders and King Sts., City Center* ☎ *03/9620–0999* ⊕ *www.melbourneaquarium.com.au* ✉ *A$33.50, shark dives from A$183, Penguin Passport A$290* ⊙ *Feb.–Dec., daily 9:30–6; Jan., daily 9:30–9 (last admission at 8).*

National Gallery of Victoria International. This massive, moat-encircled, bluestone-and-concrete edifice houses works from renowned international painters, including Picasso, Renoir, and van Gogh. It also hosts international blockbuster exhibitions, such as "Vienna: Art & Design" in 2011. An interactive Kids Space opened in 2011. A second branch of the National Gallery, in Federation Square in the city center, exhibits only Australian art. ⊠ *180 St. Kilda Rd., South Melbourne* ☎ *03/8620–0222* ⊕ *www.ngv.vic.gov.au* ✉ *Free* ⊙ *Wed.–Mon. 10–5; closed Tues. except public holidays.*

Royal Arcade. Opened in 1870, this is the country's oldest shopping arcade, and despite alterations it retains an airy, graceful elegance. Walk about 30 feet into the arcade to see the statues of Gog and Magog, the mythical monsters that toll the hour on either side of **Gaunt's Clock.** ⊠ *355 Bourke St., City Center* ☎ *03/9670–7777* ⊕ *www.royalarcade.com.au.*

EXPLORING THE THEATERS

Melburnians love their theater, and major shows often open in Melbourne first. If you want to take in Broadway or West End–style theater in grand surroundings, check out what's playing at the Regent and the Princess. Both are owned by Marriner Theatres, which lovingly restored the Regent for its reopening in the mid-1990s. You can tread the boards (i.e., act on stage) with a theater-loving tour guide on the Historic Rambles tour. Contact Wilma Farrow (☎ *03/9820–0239*) for details. For performances, check out ⊕ *www.marrinertheatres.com.au.*

4

St. Patrick's Cathedral. Ireland supplied Australia with many of its early immigrants, especially during the Irish potato famine in the mid-19th century. A statue of the Irish patriot Daniel O'Connell stands in the courtyard. Construction of the Gothic Revival building began in 1858 and only finished 82 years later. ⊠ *Cathedral Pl., East Melbourne* ☎ *03/9662-2233* ☉ *Weekdays 7-5, Sat. 8-7, Sun. 8-7:30.*

St. Paul's Cathedral. This 1892 headquarters of Melbourne's Anglican faith is one of the most important works of William Butterfield, a leader of the Gothic Revival style in England. In 2006 the cathedral underwent a massive restoration. Outside is a statue of Matthew Flinders, the first seaman to circumnavigate Australia, between 1801 and 1803. ⊠ *Flinders and Swanston Sts., City Center* ☎ *03/9653-4333* ☉ *Mon.–Fri. 8-6, Sat. 9-4, Sun. 7:30-7.*

> ### WHERE THE WILD THINGS ARE
>
> For most visitors Melbourne is a genteel, highly cultivated experience. However, you can get a taste of the wilds on a Slumber Safari at Werribee Open Range Zoo, a 45-minute drive southwest of Melbourne. Kick off the night with a gourmet barbecue while watching African animals roam freely, then bunk down under canvas listening to the wild night sounds of Africa. Great fun for city slickers! ⊕ *www.zoo.org.au.*

★ **Southgate.** On the river's edge next to the Arts Center, the development is a prime spot for lingering—designer shops, classy restaurants, bars, and casual eating places help locals and visitors while away the hours. The promenade links with the forecourt of Crown Casino and its hotels. ⊠ *Maffra St. at City Rd., Southbank* ☎ *03/9686-1000* ⊕ *www.southgate-melbourne.com.au.*

WORTH NOTING

Athenaeum Theatre and Library. The first talking picture-show in Australia was screened in 1896 at this beautiful theater. Today it houses three venues—a membership library, a theater for live performances, and the Last Laugh Comedy Club (see separate listing in Nightlife and the Arts). ⊠ *188 Collins St., City Center* ☎ *03/9650-3100* ⊕ *www.melbourneathenaeum.org.au* ☉ *Mon., Tues., Thurs., and Fri. 9:30-5, Wed. 11-7, Sat. 9:30-1.*

NEED A BREAK?	**Journal.** Journal, next to the City Library, has leather couches, bookcases filled with magazines and newspapers, and communal tables where you can enjoy bruschetta, salads, antipasto platters, and selections from an excellent wine list from A$8 a glass. Journal Canteen, upstairs, offers a short lunch and dinner selection of delicious Sicilian courses. There is no obvious sign giving the café's name, but you will hear the buzz as you near it. ⊠ *253 Flinders La., City Center* ☎ *03/9650-4399.*

Transport Hotel. At the Transport Hotel there's a choice of a public bar with casual meals, a cocktail lounge, and the upscale Taxi restaurant, with views across the Yarra River. ⊠ *Federation Sq., City Center* ☎ *03/9654-8808.*

"What a wonderful city! I had fun shopping, visiting museums and eating out." —photo by Carly Miller, Fodors.com member

Cook's Cottage. Once the on-leave residence of the Pacific navigator Captain James Cook, this modest two-story home, built in 1755 by Cook senior, was transported stone by stone from Great Ayton in Yorkshire, England, and rebuilt in the lush Fitzroy Gardens in 1934. It's believed that Cook lived in the cottage between his many voyages. The interior is simple, a suitable domestic realm for a man who spent much of his life in cramped quarters aboard sailing ships. ⊠ *Fitzroy Gardens near Lansdowne St. and Wellington Parade, East Melbourne* ☎ *03/9419–4677* 🖂 *A$5* ☙ *Daily 9–5.*

Eureka Skydeck 88. Named after the goldfields uprising of 1854, the Eureka Tower (which houses the 88th-level Eureka Skydeck 88) is the tallest residential building in the southern hemisphere. The funky-shaped blue glass building, with an impressive gold cap, opened in May 2007. The Skydeck is the place to get a bird's-eye view of Melbourne and overcome your fear of heights. An enclosed all-glass cube, known as The Edge (A$12 additional charge), projects 3 meters (9.84 feet) out from the viewing platform—here you can stand, seemingly suspended, over the city on a clear glass floor. ⊠ *7 Riverside Quay, Southbank* ☎ *03/9693–8888* ⊕ *www.eurekaskydeck.com.au* 🖂 *A$17.50* ☙ *10–10.*

Old Melbourne Gaol Crime and Justice Experience. The city's first jail is a museum run by the Victorian branch of the National Trust. The bluestone building—rumored to be haunted—has three tiers of cells with catwalks around the upper levels. Its most famous inmate was the notorious bushranger Ned Kelly, who was hanged here in 1880. The Hangman's night tours (reservations essential) are a popular, if macabre, facet of Melbourne nightlife. Museum entry now includes

"being arrested" next door at the City Watchhouse, where guides walk visitors through the experience of being incarcerated. ✉ *Russell between LaTrobe and Victoria Sts., City Center* ☎ *03/8663–7228, 13–2849 (Ticketek, for night tours)* ⊕ *www.oldmelbouregaol.com.au* ✉ *A$22, night tours A$35* ☉ *Daily 9:30–5. Night tours Oct.–Mar., Mon., Wed., Fri., and Sat. at 8:30; at 7:30 Apr.–Sep.*

WORD OF MOUTH

"It was a last minute decision to go to Melbourne, as I was told by many that I shouldn't miss it! I'm glad I went. It's much different than Sydney and I liked it better. Very multicultural city with tons of restaurants and just a great energy overall. Lots to do downtown and lots of shopping!"

—Celine

The Arts Centre. Melbourne's most important cultural landmark is the venue for performances by the Australian Ballet, Opera Australia, Melbourne Theatre Company, and Melbourne Symphony Orchestra. It encompasses Hamer Hall (formerly the Melbourne Concert Hall), which is due to reopen in 2012 after extensive refurbishment, the Arts Complex, the original National Gallery of Victoria, and the outdoor Sidney Myer Music Bowl. One-hour tours begin from the information desk at 11 am Monday through Saturday. On Sunday a 90-minute backstage tour (no children under 12) begins at 12:15 pm. At night, look for the center's spire, which creates a magical spectacle with brilliant fiber-optic cables. ✉ *100 St. Kilda Rd., Melbourne* ☎ *03/9281–8000* ⊕ *www.theartscentre.com.au* ✉ *Tour A$15, backstage tour A$20* ☉ *Mon.–Sat. 9 am–11 pm, Sun. 10–5.*

Young and Jackson's Hotel. Pubs are not generally known for their artwork, but climb the steps to the top-floor bar here to see *Chloe*, a painting that has scandalized and titillated Melburnians for many decades. The larger-than-life nude, painted by George Lefebvre in Paris in 1875, has adorned the walls of Young and Jackson's Hotel (which now specializes in Australian microbrewed beers) since 1909. ✉ *1 Swanston St. (opposite Flinders Street Station), City Center* ☎ *03/9650–3884* ⊕ *www.youngandjacksons.com.au.*

RICHMOND

Home of Victoria Street—Melbourne's "little Vietnam"—and the lively discount shopping stretch of Bridge Road, Richmond is 2 km (1 mi) east of the city center (take Tram 48 from Flinders St.). If you're looking for a new wardrobe, a Vietnamese soup kitchen, a Korean barbecue, a Laotian banquet, or a Thai hole-in-the-wall, this is the place to come.

GETTING HERE AND AROUND
Several tram lines connect central Melbourne with Richmond. Take Tram 70 from Flinders Street Station to Swan Street, Richmond; or take No. 109 from Bourke Street to Victoria Street. Tram 48 will take you from Flinders Street to Bridge Road, while Nos. 78 and 9 travel from Chapel Street (in South Yarra) to Richmond. Trains connect Flinders Street Station with Richmond Station. If driving, or even walking, proceed east along Flinders Street, which becomes Wellington Parade, past the Hilton and the Park Hotel to Hoddle Street.

Victoria Street. Fast becoming one of Melbourne's most popular "eat streets," this 2-km (1-mi) stretch has restaurants ranging from simple canteens (eat until you drop for A$10) to tablecloth-and-candlelight dining spots. The street also features Vietnamese grocers, kitchenware stores, several art galleries, and several chichi drinking spots. Once a year at Tet, Vietnamese New Year (in January and February, but the exact date varies from year to year), the street comes to life with a daylong Lunar Festival, with dragon dances, music, and more food! ⊠ *Victoria St., Richmond.*

Bridge Road. Once a run-down area of Richmond, this street is now a bargain shopper's paradise. It's chockablock with clothing shops, cafés, and factory outlets selling leather goods, shoes, and gourmet foods. Take Tram 48 or 75 from the city. ⊠ *Bridge Rd., Richmond.*

> **WALTZING MATILDA**
>
> Shopping mixes with history and a touch of patriotism at Melbourne Central shopping center. The main attraction, apart from the stores, is the historic brick shot tower, rising 165 feet above the center and encased in a glass cone. Built in 1890, the shot tower was used to make "shot" or bullets. Also suspended from the roof is a hot-air balloon and a huge fob-watch that entertains shoppers on the hour with a musical rendition of Australia's unofficial national anthem, "Waltzing Matilda." You'll find this huge shopping center on the corner of La Trobe and Swanston streets.

EAST MELBOURNE

The harmonious streetscapes in this historic enclave of Victorian houses, which date from the boom following the gold rushes of the 1850s, make East Melbourne a great neighborhood for a stroll.

GETTING HERE AND AROUND

East Melbourne's attractions are an easy walk from the city center. The Free City Circle tram travels along Spring Street, stopping at Parliament House and the City Museum at Old Treasury Melbourne. The new, free, orange-colored Melbourne City Tourist Shuttle bus also does a city loop and stops at the Sports and Entertainment Precinct, which is a short walk from the MCG and Fitzroy Gardens. Trams 48 and 74 travel along Flinders Street and Wellington Parade to East Melbourne sights: Fitzroy Gardens is on the north side of Wellington Parade, and the MCG is on the south side.

Melbourne Cricket Ground (MCG). A tour of this complex is essential for an understanding of Melbourne's sporting obsession. You can get the stories behind it all at the new National Sports Museum. The site is a pleasant 10-minute walk from the city center or a tram ride (Nos. 48 and 75) to Jolimont Station. ⊠ *Jolimont Terrace, Jolimont, East Melbourne* ☎ *03/9657–8888* ⊕ *www.mcg.org.au* ⊠ *A$15* ☉ *Tours daily every half hr 10–3, except on event days. Museum open 10–5 on non-event days.*

ST. KILDA

It often seems that every Melburnian heads to St. Kilda on Saturday night. The dozens of alfresco restaurants overflow into the streets, and the cafés and bars buzz with young fashionistas. The holiday atmosphere continues on Sunday with open-air markets and people enjoying the beach. The seaside suburb still has a Victorian-era atmosphere—the tree-lined promenade and the classic pier extending out into Port Phillip Bay are perfect for strolling and people-watching. The quaintly named St. Kilda Sea Baths (now a modern swimming pool and spa complex) are housed in a turn-of-the-20th-century building. Although no one wanted to live there in the 1970s and '80s, it is now a very smart address, and many visitors choose to stay in St. Kilda and hop on the tram for a short scenic ride into the city.

GETTING HERE AND AROUND

Several trams travel to St. Kilda from central Melbourne. Trams 96 and 112 traverse the city centre from its northern borders and go all the way south to St. Kilda. Tram 79 travels from North Richmond and No. 16 runs from Melbourne University along Swanston Street. A good place to get on a St. Kilda tram is at Flinders Street Station, or in Collins Street. It's a pleasant ride down St. Kilda Road, into Fitzroy Street and on to St. Kilda Beach.

Acland Street. An alphabet soup of Chinese, French, Italian, and Lebanese eateries—along with a fantastic array of cake shops—lines the sidewalk of St. Kilda's ultrahip restaurant row. The street faces Luna Park. ⊠ *Acland St. between Barkly St. and Shakespeare Grove, St. Kilda.*

Luna Park. Luna Park is a five-minute stroll southeast of St. Kilda pier. A much-photographed Melbourne landmark, the park's entrance is a huge, gaping mouth, swallowing visitors whole and delivering them into a world of ghost trains, pirate ships, and carousels. Built in 1912, the Scenic Railway is the park's most popular ride. It's said to be the oldest continually operating roller coaster in the world, and was renovated in 2006. The railway is less roller coaster and more a relaxed loop-the-loop, offering stunning views of Port Phillip Bay between each dip and turn. Several music festivals are held within the park's grounds each year. ⊠ *Lower Esplanade, St. Kilda* ☎ *03/9525–5033, 1300/888272* ⊕ *www.lunapark.com.au* ✉ *Free entry, A$9.50 per ride, A$41.95 for unlimited rides* ☉ *Summer (late Sept.–Apr. 25), Fri. 7 pm–11, Sat. 11–11, Sun., school holidays, and public holidays 11–6; winter (Apr. 26–late Sept.), weekends (and public holidays) 11–6.*

FITZROY

Melbourne's bohemian quarter is 2 km (1 mi) northeast of the city center. If you're looking for an Afghan camel bag or a secondhand paperback, or yearn for a café where you can sit over a plate of tapas and watch Melbourne go by, Fitzroy is the place. Take Tram 11 or 86 from the city.

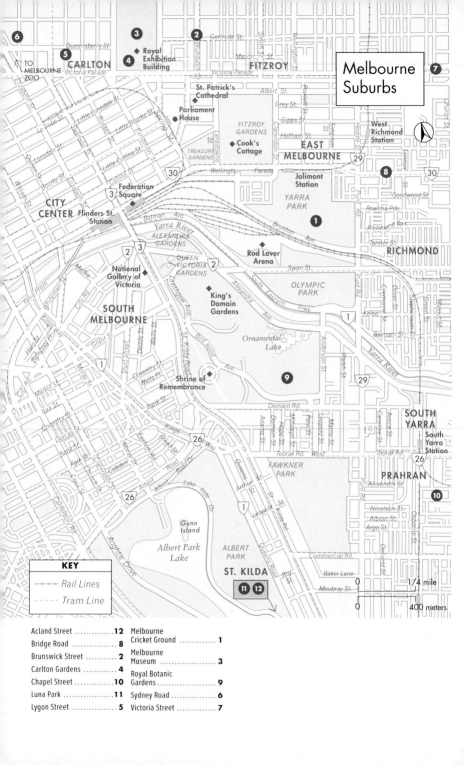

Melbourne Suburbs

CARLTON

Queensberry St.

TO MELBOURNE ZOO

Victoria Parade

Royal Exhibition Building

FITZROY

Gertrude St.

Mason St.

Victoria Parade

St. Patrick's Cathedral

Albert St.

Grey St.

Parliament House

Gipps St.

FITZROY GARDENS

Hotham St.

Cook's Cottage

EAST MELBOURNE

West Richmond Station

TREASURY GARDENS

Wellington Parade

Jolimont Station

YARRA PARK

Goodwood St.

RICHMOND

Rowena Pde.

CITY CENTER

Federation Square

Flinders St. Station

Yarra River

ALEXANDRA GARDENS

Batman Ave.

Brunton Ave.

Rod Laver Arena

Swan St.

Tanner St.

QUEEN VICTORIA GARDENS

National Gallery of Victoria

SOUTH MELBOURNE

King's Domain Gardens

OLYMPIC PARK

South Eastern Frwy.

Kelso St.

Batman St.

Yarra River

Ornamental Lake

Shrine of Remembrance

SOUTH YARRA

South Yarra Station

Domain Rd.

Toorak Rd. West

Toorak Rd.

FAWKNER PARK

PRAHRAN

Alexandra St.

Nicolson St.

Albion St.

Argo St.

Gunn Island

Albert Park Lake

ALBERT PARK

Queens Road

ST. KILDA

Commercial Rd.

Baker Lane

Moubray St.

KEY

+++ *Rail Lines*

--- *Tram Line*

0 ———— 1/4 mile

0 ———— 400 meters

GETTING HERE AND AROUND

Fitzroy is an easy place to access, both from the city and nearby suburbs. From the city, take the No. 112 from Collins Street (near Parliament House). It will take you all the way up Brunswick Street. In Bourke Street (also near Spring Street), hop on the No. 86 tram for a ride to Gertrude Street. Alternatively, you can take the Epping train line from Flinders Street Station and alight at Clifton Hill. From there you can walk west to Fitzroy or board the No. 86 tram to Gertrude Street.

Brunswick Street. Along with Lygon Street in nearby Carlton, Brunswick Street is one of Melbourne's favorite places to dine. You might want to step into a simple lunchtime café serving scrumptious crusty pizza for less than A$10, or opt for dinner at one of the stylish, highly regarded bar-restaurants. The street also has many galleries, bookstores, arts-and-crafts shops, and clothes shops (vintage fashion is a feature). ⊠ *Brunswick St. between Alexandra and Victoria Parades, Fitzroy.*

> **A DAY AT THE RACES**
>
> The usually serene atmosphere of Albert Park is turned into motorhead heaven every March, when Melbourne stages the Australian Grand Prix. It's the opening event of the Formula One season, with four full-throttle days of excitement on and off the track. Drivers scream around Albert Park Lake to the delight of fans and the horror of some nearby residents. Albert Park is 3 km (2 mi) south of the city center. It's on March 22–25, 2012. ⊕ *www.grandprix.com.au.*

BRUNSWICK

Just 4 km (2 mi) north of the city center, Brunswick is Melbourne's multicultural heart. Here Middle Eastern spice shops sit next to avant-garde galleries, Egyptian supermarkets, Turkish tile shops, Japanese yakitori eateries, Lebanese bakeries, Indian haberdasheries, and secondhand bookstores. Take Tram 19 from the city.

GETTING HERE AND AROUND

Tram 19 travels from Flinders Street Station in the city along Elizabeth Street all the way to Brunswick's main thoroughfare of Sydney Road. You can also catch a train to Brunswick; take the Upfield Railway Line from Flinders Street Station and alight at either Jewell or Brunswick stations—they're both in Brunswick.

Sydney Road. There's nowhere in Melbourne quite like Sydney Road. Cultures collide as Arabic mingles with French, Hindi does battle with Bengali, and the muezzin's call to prayer argues with Lebanese pop music. Scents intoxicate and colors beguile. Cafés serving everything from pastries to *tagines* (Moroccan stews) to Turkish delight sit shoulder-to-shoulder along the roadside with quirky record shops, antiques auction houses, and Bollywood video stores. ⊠ *Sydney Rd. between Brunswick Rd. and Bell St., Brunswick.*

The groovy cafés of St. Kilda.

CARLTON

To see the best of Carlton's Victorian-era architecture, walk along Drummond Street, with its rows of gracious terrace houses (notably Rosaville at No. 46, Medley Hall at No. 48, and Lothian Terrace at No. 175), and Canning Street, which has a mix of workers' cottages and grander properties. Take Tram 1 or 8 from the city.

GETTING HERE AND AROUND

Carlton is served by the many of Melbourne's tram routes that run through and terminate at Melbourne University (located in Parkville, just north of Carlton). Tram routes 1 and 8 ride along Swanston Street in the city, and then turn into Lygon Street. Alternatively, you can take a train to Melbourne Central Station (on the City Loop line) and then walk north to Carlton, or catch a bus (Nos. 200, 201, 203, 207, 253) from that station to Carlton.

Carlton Gardens. Forty acres of tree-lined paths, artificial lakes, and flower beds in this English-style 19th-century park are the backdrop for the outstanding Melbourne Museum, and the World Heritage–listed Royal Exhibition Building, erected in 1880. ⊠ *Victoria Parade at Nicholson, Carlton, and Rathdowne Sts., City Center* ☏ *No phone.*

★ **Lygon Street.** Known as Melbourne's Little Italy, Lygon Street is a perfect example of the city's multiculturalism: where once you'd have seen only Italian restaurants, there are now Thai, Malay, Caribbean, and Greek eateries. The city's famous café culture was also born here, with the arrival of Melbourne's first espresso machine at one of the street's Italian-owned cafés in the 1950s. La Dolce Italia Festival in February gathers the neighborhood to celebrate four different Italian regions with food, music, and merriment. ✉ *Lygon St. between Victoria and Alexandra Parades, Carlton.*

🔆 **Melbourne Museum.** A spectacular postmodern building (in Carlton Gardens) houses displays of the varied cultures around Australia and the Pacific Islands. The Bunjilaka exhibit explores the traditions of the country's Aboriginal groups, while the Australia Gallery focuses on Victoria's heritage (and includes the preserved body of Australia's greatest racehorse, Phar Lap). There's plenty for kids, too, with the wooded Forest Gallery, Children's Gallery (housed in what looks like a giant Rubik's Cube), Mind and Body Gallery, and Science and Life Gallery. The museum regularly hosts touring blockbuster exhibitions (additional fee), such as "Titanic" in 2010 and "Tutankhamun" in 2011. ✉ *Carlton Gardens, 11 Nicholson St., Carlton* ☎ *13–1102, 03/8341–7777* ⊕ *www.museumvictoria.com.au/MelbourneMuseum* 🎟 *A$8, children free* ⊘ *Daily 10–5.*

4

SOUTH YARRA–PRAHRAN

One of the coolest spots to be on any given night is in South Yarra–Prahran. The area is chock-full of bars, eateries, and upscale boutiques.

GETTING HERE AND AROUND

Several trams, including Nos. 6, 8, 78, and 79, travel to either South Yarra or Prahran or both. No. 6 comes down St. Kilda Road from Flinders Street Station and turns into High Street, Prahran, while No. 8 turns into Domain Road (just south of the Royal Botanic Gardens) and then travels down Toorak Road. Trams 78 and 79 travel down Chapel Street from North Richmond. You can also catch a train to both South Yarra and Prahran; take the Sandringham Line from Flinders Street Station.

Fodor's Choice ★ **Chapel Street.** The heart of the trendy South Yarra–Prahran area, this long road is packed with pubs, bars, notable restaurants, and upscale boutiques—more than 1,000 shops can be found within the precinct. Australian designers showcase their original designs at the fashion-conscious, upscale Toorak Road end of the street (nearest to the city). Walk south along Chapel Street to Greville Street and visit a small lane of hip bars, clothing boutiques, and record stores. Past Greville Street, at the south end of Chapel Street, it's grungier, with pawnshops and kitschy collectibles stores. ✉ *Chapel St. between Toorak and Dandenong Rds., South Yarra–Prahran* ☎ *03/9529–6331* ⊕ *www.chapelstreet.com.au.*

🔆 ★ **Royal Botanic Gardens.** The present design and layout were the brainchild of W. R. Guilfoyle, curator and director of the gardens from 1873 to 1910. Within its 100 acres are 12,000 species of native and imported plants and trees, sweeping lawns, and ornamental lakes populated with ducks and swans that love to be fed. The Children's Garden is a fun and interactive place for kids to explore. Summer brings alfresco performances of classic plays, usually Shakespeare, and children's classics like *Wind in the Willows,* as well as the popular Moonlight Cinema series. ✉ *Birdwood Ave., South Yarra* ☎ *03/9252–2300* ⊕ *www.rbg. vic.gov.au* 🎟 *Free* ⊘ *Daily 7:30–sunset. Children's Garden Wed.–Sun. 10–sunset (closed mid-Jul.–late Sep. for maintenance).*

CLOSE UP

Australian Rules Football

This fast, vigorous game, played between teams of 18, is one of four kinds of football Down Under. Aussies also play Rugby League, Rugby Union, and soccer, but Australian Rules, widely known as "footy," is the one to which Victoria, South Australia, the Top End, and Western Australia subscribe. It's the country's most popular spectator sport.

Despite its name, novice observers frequently ask the question: "What rules?" The ball can be kicked or punched in any direction, but never thrown. Players make spectacular leaps vying to catch a kicked ball before it touches the ground, for which they earn a free kick. The game is said to be at its finest in Melbourne.

Melbourne Cricket Ground. The Melbourne Cricket Ground is the prime venue for AFL games. ⊠ *Brunton Ave., Yarra Park* ☎ *03/9657–8867.*

Ticketmaster7. Tickets for Australian Rules Football are available through Ticketek (MCG games) or Ticketmaster (Etihad Stadium) or at the playing fields. ☎ *1300–136122 (Ticketmaster, 13–2849 (Ticketek)* ⊕ *www.ticketmaster.com.au.*

OFF THE BEATEN PATH

Melbourne Zoo. Verdant gardens and open-environment animal enclosures are hallmarks of this world-renowned zoo, which is 4 km (2½ mi) north of the city center. A lion park, reptile house, and butterfly pavilion where more than 1,000 butterflies flutter through the rain-forest setting are on-site, as is a simulated African rain forest where a group of Western Lowland gorillas lives. The spectacular Trail of the Elephants, home of seven Asiatic elephants, including two youngsters, Mali and Ongard, born in 2010, has a village, tropical gardens, and a swimming pool. The orangutan sanctuary and baboon outlook are other highlights. It's possible to stay overnight with the Roar 'n' Snore package (A$195 per adult) and enjoy dinner, supper, breakfast, close encounters with animals, and a behind-the-scenes look at the zoo's operations. Twilight jazz bands serenade visitors on summer evenings. A series of events are planned for 2012 to celebrate the zoo's 150th birthday. Children are admitted free. ⊠ *Elliott Ave., Parkville* ☎ *03/9285–9300* ⊕ *www.zoo.org.au* ⊠ *A$24.80* ⊙ *Daily 9–5, select summer evenings to 9 or 9:30.*

OUTDOOR ACTIVITIES

BEACHES

Unlike Sydney, Melbourne is not known for its beaches. Nonetheless, there are several popular beaches on the shores of Port Phillip Bay. The best known are St. Kilda and Brighton Beach, the latter extremely picturesque, adorned with a colorful row of "bathing boxes" that runs along its shore. These vividly decorated little sheds are basically privately owned changing rooms, but can sell for as much as a house in some parts of the city, with many dating back to the 1940s.

The absence of waves fails to provide the conditions for surfing; however, the brisk winds that whip across Port Phillip Bay make most of these beaches ideal for windsurfing (particularly Elwood Beach) and kitesurfing.

BICYCLING

Melbourne and its environs contain more than 100 km (62 mi) of bike paths, including scenic routes along the Yarra River and Port Phillip Bay. The Beach Road Trail extends 19 km (12 mi) around Port Phillip Bay from Elwood Beach to Sandringham; the new Docklands area of Melbourne can be cycled around—start on the Southbank Promenade, travel west, and then cross over the new Webb Street to Docklands Park and Harbour Esplanade; you can join the Main Yarra Trail bicycle route at the mouth of the Yarra River, just north of the West Gate Bridge or at Southbank. You can then follow the Yarra River for 35 km (22 mi) until it meets up with the Mullum Mullum Creek Trail in Templestowe in Melbourne's eastern suburbs. Bicycle Victoria has all the details on biking trails.

Bicycle Victoria. Bicycle Victoria can provide information about area bike paths. Its excellent Web site has trail maps and descriptions as well as directions. ✉ *Level 10, 446 Collins St., City Center* ☎ *03/8636–8888* ⊕ *www.bv.com.au.*

Bikes can be rented for about A$25 per day from trailers alongside the bike paths.

Real Melbourne Bike Tours. Real Melbourne Bike Tours runs daily bike tours that promise to show the very best of Melbourne. The four-hour rides (which depart at 10 am) include coffee and cakes in Little Italy and lunch. The company also rents bicycles from A$15 an hour (A$35 per day), and provides a map of five top rides, with suggestions of where to eat and drink. It's on the edge of the Yarra River just near Princes Bridge and Federation Square. ✉ *Vault 14, Federation Square, City Centre* ☎ *0417/339203* ⊕ *www.rentabike.net.au* 🖃 *A$110 per person.*

BOATING

Studley Park Boathouse. Studley Park Boathouse, which opened in 1864, rents canoes, kayaks, and rowboats for journeys on a peaceful stretch of the lower Yarra River, about 7 km (4½ mi) east of the city center. Rentals are A$30 per hour for a two-person canoe or rowboat and A$40 per hour for a four-person rowboat. The boathouse is open daily 9–5 and has a café (lunch and weekend breakfast) and restaurant (weekends) with lovely river views. ✉ *Boathouse Rd., Kew* ☎ *03/9853–1828* ⊕ *www.studleyparkboathouse.com.au.*

CAR RACING

Australian Formula 1 Grand Prix. Australian Formula 1 Grand Prix is a popular—but increasingly controversial—fixture on Melbourne's calendar of annual events. It's held every March in the suburb of Albert Park, a small neighborhood 4 km (2½ mi) south of the city that encompasses the area surrounding Albert Park Lake. ✉ *220 Albert Rd., South Melbourne* ☎ *03/9258–7100* ⊕ *www.grandprix.com.au.*

GOLF

Melbourne has the largest number of championship golf courses in Australia.

Albert Park Golf Course. Four kilometers (2½ mi) south of the city, Albert Park Golf Course is an 18-hole, par-72 course beside Albert Park Lake, where the Formula 1 Grand Prix is held in March. Greens fees are A$20 (9 holes, weekdays only) and A$27–A$29 (18 holes). ⊠ *Queens Rd., Albert Park* ☎ *03/9510–5588.*

Brighton Public Golf Course. The 18-hole, par-67 Brighton Public Golf Course has lovely scenery, with trees and wetlands, but is quite busy on weekends and midweek mornings. Club rental is available. Greens fees are A$18 (9 holes), A$25.50 (18 holes). ⊠ *232 Dendy St., Brighton* ☎ *03/9592–1388* ⊕ *www.brightongolfcourse.com.au.*

Ivanhoe Public Golf Course. Ivanhoe Public Golf Course, an 18-hole, par-68 course, is well suited to the average golfer and is open to the public every day except holidays. Greens fees are A$20 (9 holes) and A$26 (18 holes). ⊠ *Vasey St., East Ivanhoe* ☎ *03/9499–7001* ⊕ *www.ivanhoegolf.com.au.*

Sandringham Golf Links. Five minutes from the beach, Sandringham Golf Course is one of the better public courses, and one of several in Melbourne's renowned (coastal) Sand Belt. Sandringham is an 18-hole, par-72 course. Greens fees are A$27 (18 holes) and A$16.80 (9 holes). ⊠ *Cheltenham Rd., Sandringham* ☎ *03/9598–3590* ⊕ *www.sandringhamgolfcourse.com.au.*

HORSE RACING

Melbourne is the only city in the world to declare a public holiday for a horse race—the Melbourne Cup—held on the first Tuesday in November since 1861. The Cup is also a fashion parade, and most of Melbourne society turns out in full regalia. The rest of the country comes to a standstill, with schools, shops, offices, and factories tuning in to the action.

The city has four top-class racetracks.

Betfair Park. Betfair Park (formerly Sandown Race Course), 25 km (16 mi) from the city, hosts the Sandown Cup in November. ⊠ *Corrigan Rd. and Princes Hwy., Springvale* ☎ *03/9518–1300* ⊕ *www.melbourneracingclub.net.au.*

Caulfield Race Course. Caulfield Race Course, 10 km (6 mi) from the city, runs the Blue Diamond Stakes in February and the Caulfield Cup in October. ⊠ *Station St., Caulfield* ☎ *03/9257–7200* ⊕ *www.melbourneracingclub.net.au.*

Champions: Thoroughbred Racing Gallery. Champions: Thoroughbred Racing Gallery in the National Sports Museum is chock-full of horse-racing information, displays, and a mini-shrine to Australia's most famous racehorse, Phar Lap. ⊠ *Melbourne Cricket Ground, Brunton Ave., Yarra Park* ☎ *03/9657–8879* ☐ *A$15* ⊘ *10–5 on non-match days.*

Flemington Race Course. Flemington Race Course, 3 km (2 mi) outside the city, is Australia's premier racecourse and home of the Melbourne Cup. ⊠ *448 Epsom Rd., Flemington* ☎ *03/9371–7171* ⊕ *www.vrc.net.au).*

Moonee Valley Race Course. Moonee Valley Race Course is 6 km (4 mi) from town and hosts the Cox Plate race in October. ⊠ *McPherson St., Moonee Ponds* ☎ *03/9373–2222* ⊕ *www.mvrc.net.au.*

TENNIS

Australian Open. The Australian Open, held in January, is one of the world's four Grand Slam tournaments. You can buy tickets at the event or from Ticketek.

Melbourne & Olympic Parks. ⊠ *Batman Ave., City Center* ☎ *03/ 9286–1600* ⊕ *www.mopt.com.au* ⊕ *www.australianopen.com.*

Powlett Reserve Tennis Centre. Powlett Reserve Tennis Centre has five synthetic-grass outdoor courts. ⊠ *Powlett Reserve, Albert St., East Melbourne* ☎ *03/9417–6511* ⊕ *www.powlettreservetenniscentre.com.au.*

Fawkner Park Tennis Centre. Fawkner Park Tennis Centre has six synthetic-grass outdoor courts. ⊠ *Fawkner Park, Toorak Rd. W, South Yarra* ☎ *03/9820–0611* ⊕ *www.fawknerparktenniscentre.com.*

Melbourne Park Tennis Centre. Brought your racket? Melbourne Park Tennis Centre has 22 outdoor and 4 hard indoor Rebound Ace courts. Play is canceled during the Australian Open in January. ⊠ *Batman Ave., City Center* ☎ *1300/836647* ⊕ *www.mopt.com.au.*

WHERE TO EAT

Melbourne has fabulous food, and is known in some circles as Australia's food capital. The restaurants themselves are often exceptionally stylish and elegant—or totally edgy and funky in their own individual way. Some are even deliberately grungy. The dining scene is a vast smorgasbord of cuisines and experiences that's constantly evolving. The swankiest (and most expensive) restaurants all have five- to eight-course degustation menus (with the opportunity to wine-match each course), but newer restaurants are opting for tapas-style or grazing plates. Flexibility is the new word in dining—restaurants are also funky bars and vice versa.

Use the coordinate (✛ B2) at the end of each listing to locate a site on the corresponding map.

CITY CENTER

$$
SPANISH
✕ **Añada.** There is a hum of bees around a honey pot at this Andalusian bar and restaurant. A chalkboard on the exposed brick wall lists eight dry and six sweet sherries to start (or finish), and there are Spanish and Portuguese wines to accompany your selection of tapas and *raciones* (larger shared plates). Seated at a table or on a stool at the bar, you could begin with rabbit *empanadilla* (pastry pockets) and melt-in-your-mouth black pudding topped with a fried quail egg, and follow with vine-leaf wrapped sardines with pistachio and orange-blossom sauce. But leave room for dessert; the *churros* (Spanish donuts) and chocolate are sinful, while the Pedro Ximenez and muscatel ice cream could make an Atheist believe in a culinary god. ⊠ *197 Gertrude St., Fitzroy* ☎ *03/9415–6101* ⊗ *No lunch weekdays* ✛ *1:D3.*

$ ✕ **Babka.** Food lovers in the know are often found loitering at this tiny,
CAFÉ bustling café. Try the excellent pastries, fresh-baked breads, or more
substantial offerings like the Russian borscht (beetroot and cabbage
soup) or menemen—scrambled eggs with chili, mint, tomato, and a
sprinkling of feta cheese. It's an all-day brunch-style café, and there are
often queues, so be prepared to wait for a table. Some complain that the
busy staff can be brusque. ⊠ *358 Brunswick St., Fitzroy* ☎ *03/9416–
0091* ⊘ *Closed Mon. No dinner* ✛ *1:D3.*

$$ ✕ **Becco.** Every city center needs a place like this, with a drop-in bar
ITALIAN and lively dining room. At lunchtime no-time-to-dawdle business types
tuck into papparadelle osso bucco with pancetta and gremolata, while
those with a sweet tooth will go weak at the knees over chocolate
crème brûlée with peanut-butter ravioli and raspberry jelly. Things get
a little moodier at night, when a Campari and soda at the bar is an
almost compulsory precursor to dinner. ⊠ *11–25 Crossley St., City Cen-
ter* ☎ *03/9663–3000* ⊕ *www.becco.com.au* ⌕ *Reservations essential*
⊘ *Closed Sun.* ✛ *1:B4.*

¢ ✕ **Bimbo Deluxe.** This bohemian bar, with deep comfy sofas and the feel
CAFÉ of a local hangout, has the cheapest and possibly the most delicious
pizzas in town. On weekdays between noon and 4 pm, Saturday 7 to
9 pm, and Sunday–Thursday from 7 to 11 pm you can order a dinner-
plate-size pizza (from 19 choices) for a mere A$4. The queues of stu-
dents and hungry lunchers start to form outside around 11:55. If you
miss the special, fear not: the same great pizzas are only A$6–A$8 at
other times. Try the Agnello (tomato, mozzarella, spiced lamb, arugula,
pine nuts, and sultanas). If you're hankering for a sugar rush, there are
also sweet pizzas such as Belgian chocolate with mascarpone. A range
of chilled infused vodkas—including watermelon and lychee—is avail-
able, and the bar's signature "Blonde Bimbo" beer is popular. ⊠ *376
Brunswick St., Fitzroy* ☎ *03/9419–8600* ✛ *2:B1.* ⊠ *179 Chapel St.,
Windsor* ☎ *03/9525–1288*

$$$$ ✕ **Brunetti.** This Romanesque bakery is just as heavenly as when it
CAFÉ opened in 1985; it's still filled with perfect biscotti and mouthwater-
★ ing cakes. Pastas, pizza slices, and foccacias have been added to the
menu, and you can finish off your lunch with a perfect espresso—or
European-style hot chocolate (thick)—and cornetto con crema (custard-
filled croissant). City workers can now enjoy all these tempting delights
with the opening of branches in Flinders Lane and Myer department
store in Bourke Street, while outlets in Fitzroy and Camberwell, a cou-
ple of miles east of Richmond, satisfy suburban sugar fiends and cof-
fee cravers. ⊠ *194–204 Faraday St., Carlton* ☎ *03/9347–2801* ⊕ *www.
brunetti.com.au* ✛ *1:C1.* ⊠ *City Square, 214 Flinders La., at Swanston
St.* ☎ *03/9663–8085* ⊠ *1/3 Prospect Hill Rd., Camberwell* ☎ *03/9882–
3100* ✛ *1:A5.* ⊠ *Myer Melbourne, Bourke St., btw Swanston & Eliza-
beth sts.* ☎ *03/9661–1380* ⊠ *89 Johnston St., Fitzroy* ☎ *03/9419–4081*

$$ ✕ **Charcoal Lane.** This young restaurant could be described as taking
AUSTRALIAN a leaf from celebrity chef Jamie Oliver's book, in that disadvantaged
people are given an opportunity to transform their lives by gaining a
traineeship in the restaurant business. Named after a song by acclaimed
Aboriginal singer/songwriter Archie Roach, Charcoal Lane is a joint

project between the charity Mission Australia and the Victorian Aboriginal Health Service. It is housed in the former health service community center, dubbed Charcoal Lane by the many Aboriginal people who for decades would drop in and swap stories and wisdom. The menu includes many Australian bushland ingredients, and the dishes have an Aboriginal influence. They might include starters of roasted marron (freshwater crayfish) fondue with angel hair, lemon myrtle, and baby basil, and hearty main courses such as kangaroo with broccoli puree, black trumpette (mushrooms), truffle gnocchi, and bitter chocolate. ✉ *136 Gertrude St., Fitzroy* ☎ *03/9418–3400* ⊕ *www.charcoallane. com.au* ⊗ *Closed Sun. and Mon.* ✛ *1:D3.*

$$ ✗ **The Commoner.** The street-facing dining room here is packed with
BISTRO young couples enjoying some of the town's best and most eclectic food. Chef Matt Donnelly's menu features "small food" taste sensations like *boccerones* (Sicilian white anchovies on crostina with sweet pepper and aioli), and more substantial offerings such as rabbit, prune, and pinot pie or grouper and wild mushrooms, rolled in Savoy cabbage with smoked cauliflower. There's a roast every Sunday lunch, and regular set-price theme nights, such as "A Duck's Tale." The wine list has depth in both Aussie and international selections. The space itself is cozy, featuring original art, and there's an enclosed garden out the back. ✉ *122 Johnston St., Fitzroy* ☎ *03/9415–6876* ⊕ *www.thecommoner.com.au* ⊗ *Closed Mon. and Tues. No lunch Wed. and Thurs.* ✛ *1:D3*

$$$$ ✗ **ezard.** Chef Teage Ezard's adventurous—and often exhilarating—take
MODERN on fusion pushes the boundaries between Eastern and Western flavors.
AUSTRALIAN Some combinations may appear unusual, like the anchovy-crusted
★ swordfsh with beetroot, ruby-red grapefruit, rhubarb, and Persian feta salad, but everything works deliciously at this spot in the funky Adelphi hotel. And as with all upscale restaurants these days, there's an eight-course tasting menu (A$140 per person) featuring mouth-watering steamed blue swimmer crab dumplings with butter, crisp taro, and mint salad. The dessert menu is a celebration of indulgence. ✉ *187 Flinders La., City Center* ☎ *03/9639–6811* ⊕ *www.ezard.com.au* ⚐ *Reservations essential* ⊗ *Closed Sun. No lunch Sat.* ✛ *1:A5.*

$$$ ✗ **Flower Drum.** Superb Cantonese cuisine is the hallmark of one of Aus-
CANTONESE tralia's truly great Chinese restaurants, which is still receiving awards
★ after 34 years in business. The restrained elegance of the decor, deftness of the service, and intelligence of the wine list puts most other restaurants to shame. Those in the know don't order from the menu at all but simply ask the waiter to bring the specials, which often change between lunch and dinner with the arrival of produce fresh from suppliers; the Cantonese roast duck is one of the highlights. A delicious finish to the meal is the sweetened double-boiled almond soup. ✉ *17 Market La., City Center* ☎ *03/9662–3655* ⊕ *www.flower-drum.com* ⚐ *Reservations essential* ⊗ *No lunch Sun.* ✛ *1:B4.*

$$$ ✗ **Grossi Florentino.** Since 1928, dining at Florentino has meant expe-
ITALIAN riencing the pinnacle of Melbourne hospitality. After taking a seat in
★ the famous mural room, with its huge chandeliers, wooden panels, and Florentine murals, you can sample dishes like venison loin with a juniper crust and heirloom vegetables, and crab ravioli. There is also an

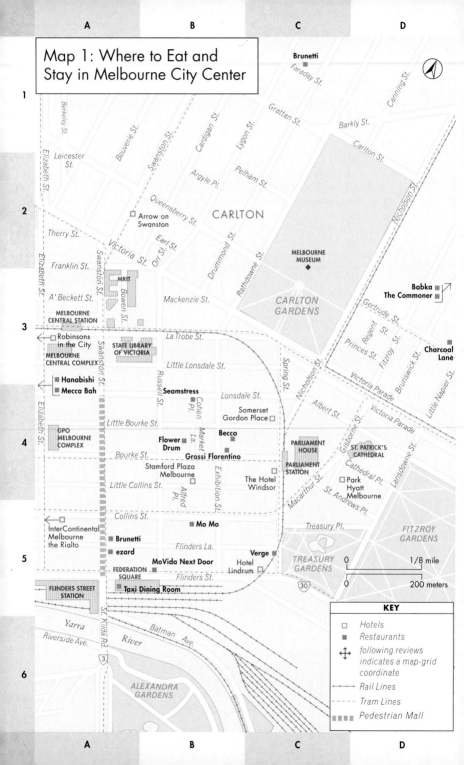

Map 1: Where to Eat and Stay in Melbourne City Center

A · **B** · **C** · **D**

1

Brunetti
Faraday St.
Berkeley St.
Grattan St.
Canning St.
Barkly St.
Carlton St.

2

Bouverie St.
Swanston St.
Cardigan St.
Lygon St.
Arrow on Swanston
Queensberry St.
Argyle Pl.
Pelham St.
CARLTON
Therry St.
Earl St.
Orr St.
Drummond St.
Rathdowne St.
Nicholson St.
MELBOURNE MUSEUM
Franklin St.
Victoria St.
Elizabeth St.
MRIT
A' Beckett St.
Mackenzie St.
CARLTON GARDENS
Gertrude St.
Babka
The Commoner

3

MELBOURNE CENTRAL STATION
La Trobe St.
Regent St.
St.
Princes St.
Fitzroy St.
Charcoal Lane
Robinsons in the City
STATE LIBRARY OF VICTORIA
Little Lonsdale St.
Spring St.
Nicholson St.
MELBOURNE CENTRAL COMPLEX
Hanabishi
Mecca Bah
Seamstress
Russell St.
Cohen Pl.
Lonsdale St.
Somerset Gordon Place
Victoria Parade
Albert St.
Victoria Parade
Brunswick St.
Little Napier St.

4

Elizabeth St.
Little Bourke St.
Flower Drum
Market La.
Becco
Grossi Florentino
PARLIAMENT HOUSE
Gisborne St.
ST. PATRICK'S CATHEDRAL
Lansdowne St.
GPO MELBOURNE COMPLEX
Bourke St.
Stamford Plaza Melbourne
Exhibition St.
PARLIAMENT STATION
Cathedral Pl.
Park Hyatt Melbourne
Little Collins St.
Alfred Pl.
The Hotel Windsor
Macarthur St.
St. Andrews Pl.

5

Collins St.
Mo Mo
Treasury Pl.
FITZROY GARDENS
InterContinental Melbourne the Rialto
Brunetti
ezard
Flinders La.
Verge
TREASURY GARDENS
0   1/8 mile
MoVida Next Door
Hotel Lindrum
0   200 meters
FEDERATION SQUARE
Flinders St.
30
FLINDERS STREET STATION
Taxi Dining Room

6

St. Kilda Rd.
Yarra
Riverside Ave.
Batman Ave.
River
Flinders St.
3
ALEXANDRA GARDENS

KEY

□	Hotels
■	Restaurants
↔	following reviews indicates a map-grid coordinate
┼┼┼	Rail Lines
---	Tram Lines
▪▪▪▪	Pedestrian Mall

eight-course tasting menu with food-matched wines (A$270). Downstairs, the Grill has more businesslike fare, while the Cellar Bar is perfect for a glass of wine and pasta of the day. ⊠ *80 Bourke St., City Center* ☎ *03/9662–1811* ⊕ *www.grossiflorentino.com.au* ⌖ *Reservations essential* ⊙ *Closed Sun.* ✛ *1:B4.*

$$ ✕ **Hanabishi.** Touted as the city's best Japanese restaurant, Hanabishi sits
JAPANESE   in slightly seedy King Street, an area known for its bars, club venues,
★   and occasionally unsavory clientele. With wooden floors, blue walls, and traditional ceramic serving trays, Hanabishi is the playground of Osakan chef Akio Soga, whose menu includes such gems as oven-grilled Patagonian toothfish wrapped in aromatic cedar wood. There are long lists of hot and chilled sake and wines, ranging from reasonable to pricey. The bento boxes, which are culinary works of art, feature sought-after Wagyu beef and are a favorite with the lunchtime crowd. ⊠ *187 King St., City Center* ☎ *03/9670–1167* ⌖ *Reservations essential* ⊙ *Closed weekends* ✛ *1:A3.*

$$ ✕ **Ladro.** Rita Macalli's stellar Italian bistro emphasizes flavor over
ITALIAN   starchy linen and stuffy attitude. Here eggplant is molded into gentle
★   round polpettes (meatball-like mounds), lamb rump is scented with garlic and parsley and slow-roasted to impossible tenderness, and the service is as upbeat as the wine list. Delicious wood-fired pizzas are yet another reason to visit this suburban gem (thankfully, it's only a short walk from the city). ⊠ *224 Gertrude St., Fitzroy* ☎ *03/9415–7575* ⌖ *Reservations essential* ⊙ *No lunch Mon.–Sat.* ✛ *2:B1.*

$$$ ✕ **Mo Mo.** This exotically lavish, crystal bedecked restaurant reopened
MIDDLE EASTERN   in early 2009 in the Grand Hyatt hotel. Against a backdrop of plush upholstery and veil-like curtains, chef Greg Malouf offers his upscale take on Middle Eastern dishes as family-style sharing menus (or small banquets) from A$120 per person. Dishes such as *kifta nayee* (Middle Eastern style beef tartare with basil, marjoram, and smoky chili) and Turkish fish doctors stew with stuffed mussels and roasted flounder fillets anchor the menu, while desserts like Persian saffron tart with passionfruit curd and marscapone elevate it heavenwards. À la carte dining is available only for pretheater reservations on Friday and Saturday. ⊠ *123 Collins St., City Center* ☎ *03/9650–0660* ⊙ *No lunch. Closed Sun. and Mon.* ✛ *1:B5.*

$ ✕ **MoVida Next Door.** As the name suggests, this popular Spanish tapas
SPANISH   restaurant is next door to something—in this case the grown-up parent restaurant called MoVida. This is the casual little sister (or daughter) for those who don't want to linger too long over their dinner. Dishes range from tapas (from $3.90 to $7), like chorizo-filled Catalan potato bomb with spicy sauce, to *racion* (bigger plates ranging from $8 to $15.50), which might include quail pan-seared with sherry and pomegranate. Finish the meal off with *churros con chocolate* (Spanish fried dough served with a hot, thick chocolate drink). If you're after a bigger meal, book table space at MoVida next door. Both eateries are owned by Frank Camoora, who's made a big splash in the Melbourne dining scene since 2003, and in 2010 opened his third installment, the big-space MoVida Aqui. ⊠ *1 Hosier La., City Center* ☎ *03/9663–3038* ⊕ *www.movida.com.au* ⊙ *No lunch Tues.–Thurs. Closed Mon.* ✛ *1:B5.*

Melbourne's restaurant scene is a global potpourri of ethnic influences.

$$
MODERN ASIAN

✕ **Seamstress Restaurant & Bar.** History and a prime Central Business District location are both draws for the Seamstress. This bar-restaurant occupies a Heritage-listed four-story building that has housed an undergarment manufacturer, a 1930s sweat shop, and even a brothel and a Buddhist temple (but not at the same time). Asian dishes, in small, medium, and large portions, are designed to be shared. Everything is served in an atmospheric brick-walled first-floor dining area decorated with swaths of fabric, and sewing machines; the wine selection is stored in battered metal luggage lockers. Small dishes include pods of snake bean and golden sweet kumaro poached in wanton pastry, green pea and coriander puree. Favorite medium dishes include the sublime crisp-fried fish of the day—perhaps hapuka—marinated in soybean and garlic paste, and served with a salad of dried guava and aromatic herbs. ✉ *113 Lonsdale St., City Center* ☎ *03/9663–6363* ⊕ *www.seamstress.com.au* ☯ *No lunch Sat. Closed Sun.* ✛ *1:B4.*

$$$
MODERN
AUSTRALIAN
★

✕ **Taxi Dining Room.** Occupying an innovatively designed steel-and-glass space above Federation Square, Taxi boasts both extraordinary food and spectacular views over Melbourne. East meets West on a menu that combines Japanese flavors—tuna tataki chased by udon noodles in a mushroom hot pot—with such European-inspired fare as pork hock with coconut caramel and apple puree. Tempura whiting, salt-and-pepper-fried duck, and an impressive list of New and Old World wines add to the mix. ✉ *Level 1, Transport Hotel, Federation Sq., Flinders St. at St. Kilda Rd., City Center* ☎ *03/9654–8808* ⊕ *www.transporthotel. com.au* ✍ *Reservations essential* ✛ *1:A5.*

$$$
FRENCH
★

✕ **Verge.** A favorite of the local arty set, and also of office workers dropping in for after-work drinks and dinner, this sharp-edged suit-gray eatery serves up modern French bistro food with a Japanese twist. Don't miss the Wagyu beef with beets, artichoke, and chicory. The bar, which stays open late, serves coffee from 10 am, and has a range of light meals including spiced crisp pig's ear with fresh apple and garlic chive. ✉ *1 Flinders La., City Center* ☎ *03/9639–9500* ⊕ *www.vergerestaurant. com.au* ☯ *Closed Sun.* ✛ *1:C5.*

ST. KILDA

$ ✗ **Café a Taglio.** Rarely has Roman-style pizza been this delicious—or
ITALIAN   this groovy. Although there's a blackboard menu of pastas and other Italian dishes, regulars prefer to cruise the counter, choosing from the giant squares of pizza on display. Toppings include ricotta, eggplant, and marinated mushrooms with truffle oil. It's open midday to late. ✉ *157 Fitzroy St., St. Kilda* ☎ *03/9534–1344* ✛ *2:A6.*

$$$ ✗ **Café di Stasio.** This upscale bistro treads a very fine line between
ITALIAN   mannered elegance and decadence. A sleek marble bar and modishly
Fodor's Choice   ravaged walls contribute to the sense that you've stepped into a scene
★   from *La Dolce Vita.* Happily, the restaurant is as serious about its food as its sense of style. Crisply roasted duck is now a local legend, and the pasta is always al dente. If the amazingly delicate crayfish omelet is on the menu, do yourself a favor and order it. ✉ *31 Fitzroy St., St. Kilda* ☎ *03/9525–3999* ⌕ *Reservations essential* ✛ *2:A6.*

$$$ ✗ **Circa the Prince.** A complete makeover has transformed this previously
AUSTRALIAN   intimate, silk- and organza-draped restaurant into a light-filled space featuring a central, glass-roofed courtyard complete with vertical vegetable and herb garden. There is a new head chef, too, and Jake Nicholson's imaginative use of fabulous, mostly Victorian produce keeps the tables full and the food reviewers happy. You could start with chestnut soup with rosemary-baked yabbies and ham hock, then move on to John Dory, mussel, and clam risotto with sea-urchin butter. There are also several dishes to share, including spiced honey-roasted duck stuffed with green raisins and walnuts, pumpkin, and fennel. A tapaslike menu is offered at the bar, where you can taste top-end wines by the glass. You can also go with the sommelier into the see-through cellar to select a bottle from the exhaustive and tempting wine list. ✉ *2 Acland St., St. Kilda* ☎ *03/9536–1122* ⌕ *Reservations essential* ☯ *No lunch Mon.– Thurs. and Sat.* ✛ *2:A6.*

$$ ✗ **Dog's Bar.** With its blazing fires, artfully smoky walls, and striking art
MEDITERRANEAN   deco–ish wrought-iron ceiling lights, this two-decade-old restaurant has a lived-in, neighborly look and is an institution for the artistic crowd that frequents it. The food is good, wine is taken very seriously—there are more than 200 wines on the list—and the kitchen is open until late each night. A new art show opens every Sunday and there's live jazz each Sunday night. Throughout the year there are caberet and comedy acts (admission from around $15). If you're in Kilda, it's definitely a place to visit. ✉ *54 Acland St., St. Kilda* ☎ *03/8534–3000* ⊕ *www. dogsbar.com.au* ✛ *2:A6.*

$$$ ✗ **Donovan's.** Grab a window table at this very popular bayside restau-
AUSTRALIAN   rant (housed in the former 1920s bathing pavilion), and enjoy wide-open
★   views of St. Kilda beach and its passing parade of in-line skaters, skateboarders, dog walkers, and ice-cream lickers. Chef Robert Castellani

4

serves wonderful pastas and risottos, a scrumptious fish soup, and a memorable steamed hazelnut and navel-orange pudding with Frangelico cream and blood-orange sorbet. Owners Kevin and Gail Donovan are such natural hosts you may feel like bunking down on the plush cushions near the cozy fireplace. ⊠ *40 Jacka Blvd., St. Kilda* ☎ *03/9534–8221* ⊕ *www.donovanshouse.com.au* ⚱ *Reservations essential* ✚ *2:A6.*

SOUTH YARRA–PRAHRAN

$$ ✕ **Caffe e Cucina.** It's easy to imagine you're in Italy when dining at
ITALIAN   this always-packed restaurant/café. If you're looking for a quintessen-
tial Italian dining experience, this is it. Fashionable, look-at-me types flock here for coffee and pastry downstairs, or for more-leisurely meals upstairs in the warm, woody dining room. Try the melt-in-your-mouth gnocchi, or calamari Sant' Andrea (lightly floured and shallow fried), but save room for dessert—the tiramisu is even better looking than the crowd. ⊠ *581 Chapel St., South Yarra* ☎ *03/9827–4139* ⊕ *www. caffeecucina.com.au* ✚ *2:D5.*

$$$$ ✕ **Jacques Reymond.** French and Asian flavors blend delightfully at this
MODERN   glamorous, century-old Victorian mansion turned eatery, which has col-
AUSTRALIAN   lected some prestigious awards in recent years. The wine list is the stuff
Fodor'sChoice   an oenophile dreams of, and the Burgundian-born chef uses the finest
★   Australian produce to create such new classics as wild kingfish with
a bread nougatine, Iberian ham, and saffron espuma, or tender octo-pus and dried miso, green pea, and ginger dressing. The eight-course degustation menu (A$175), which can be paired with wines (A$270), is justly famous; there's a vegetarian degustation menu too. You can also choose a three-, four-, and five-course menu (ranging from A$105 to A$160). Single à la carte dishes are not available. ⊠ *78 Williams Rd., Prahran* ☎ *03/9525–2178* ⊕ *www.jacquesreymond.com.au* ⚱ *Reserva-tions essential* ⊘ *Closed Sun. and Mon. No lunch Sat.* ✚ *2:D6.*

RICHMOND

¢   ✕ **I Love Pho 264.** Tucking into a steaming bowl of *phở* (traditional
VIETNAMESE   noodle soup) at this Victoria Street restaurant is like channeling the
★   backstreets of Hanoi and Saigon. While they also serve crunchy, deep-
fried spring rolls and flavour-packed ricepaper rolls, the mainstay of the menu (a blackboard on the wall) is various combinations of *bò* (beef) and *gà* (chicken) with noodles in aromatic stock. Each order comes with a piled plate of Vietnamese mint, bean shoots, and lemon wedges, and there are bottles of chili paste and fish sauce on every mock-marble plastic table. This restaurant is crowded with Vietnamese and other *phở* lovers on weekends, so you often have to queue on the footpath, but turnover is fast, so its never long before you are seated and eating some of Melbourne's best—and cheapest—food. ⊠ *264 Victoria St., Richmond* ☎ *03/9427–7749* ✚ *2:C1.*

$$$ ✕ **Pearl.** A change in owner and chefs seems to have only increased the
MODERN   luster of this decade-young restaurant, which remains a favorite hangout
AUSTRALIAN   for Melbourne's beautiful people, and continues to hover at the top of
the list in the annual *The Age* newspaper's *Good Food Guide*. Glamour

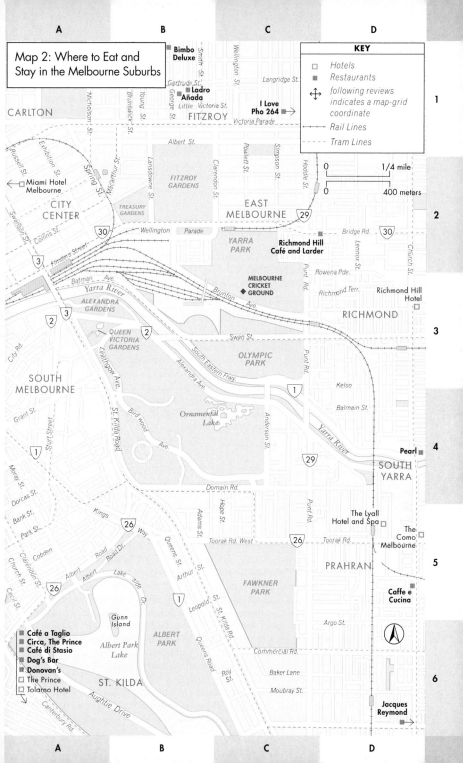

Map 2: Where to Eat and Stay in the Melbourne Suburbs

KEY

☐ Hotels
■ Restaurants
✥ *following reviews indicates a map-grid coordinate*
╌╌ Rail Lines
- - - Tram Lines

CARLTON

■ Bimbo Deluxe

Gertrude St.
■ Ladro
Añada

Smith St.
Young St.
George St.
Little Victoria St.

Wellington St.

Langridge St.

FITZROY

■ I Love
Pho 264 ➡

Victoria Parade

Nicholson St.
Brunswick St.

Albert St.

Lansdowne St.
Clarendon St.
Powlett St.
Simpson St.

Hoddle St.

FITZROY
GARDENS

Miami Hotel
Melbourne

Spring St.

CITY
CENTER

TREASURY
GARDENS

Macarthur St.

EAST
MELBOURNE

29

Russell St.
Exhibition St.
Swanston St.

Collins St.

30

Wellington Parade

Bridge Rd.

30

YARRA
PARK

■ Richmond Hill
Café and Larder

Lennox St.

Church St.

Flinders Street

3

Batman Ave.

Yarra River

Brunton Ave.

MELBOURNE
CRICKET
◆ GROUND

Rowena Pde.

Richmond Terr.

Richmond Hill
Hotel

Punt Rd.

ALEXANDRA
GARDENS

RICHMOND

2

3

QUEEN
VICTORIA
GARDENS

2

Swan St.

OLYMPIC
PARK

3

City Rd.

SOUTH
MELBOURNE

Linlithgow Ave.

St. Kilda Road

South Eastern Frwy.

Alexandra Ave.

Punt Rd.

Kelso

Yarra River

Balmain St.

3

Grant St.

Birdwood Ave.

Ornamental
Lake

Anderson St.

1

Moray St.
Dorcas St.
Bank St.
Park St.

1

Sturt Street

Domain Rd.

29

■ Pearl

SOUTH
YARRA

4

Kings

26

Hope St.

Adams St.

Toorak Rd. West

26

Toorak Rd.

The Lyall
Hotel and Spa ☐

The
Como ☐
Melbourne

5

Clarendon St.
Church St.
Cecil St.

Cobden

Albert
Albert
Lake
Road

26

Road Dr.
Lakeside Dr.

Queens St.
Arthur St.
Leopold St.
St. Kilda Rd.

FAWKNER
PARK

PRAHRAN

Commercial Rd.

■ Caffe e
Cucina

✥

5

Gunn
Island

Albert Park
Lake

ALBERT
PARK

Argo St.

■ Café a Taglio
■ Circa, The Prince
■ Café di Stasio
■ Dog's Bar
■ Donovan's
☐ The Prince
☐ Tolarno Hotel

ST. KILDA

Queens Road
Roy St.

Baker Lane

Moubray St.

■ Jacques
Reymond ➡

6

Canterbury Rd.

Aughtie Drive

0   1/4 mile
0   400 meters

aside, it's also home to some truly innovative (and excellent) dishes. There are strong Asian influences (wok-fried pearl meat with shiitake mushrooms and chive buds, and coconut-braised red duck curry) and hints of the Mediterranean (Harissa spiced lamb rump with preserved lemon, currant and pinenut couscous, tagine of eggplant and pickled watermelon rind). ⊠ *631–633 Church St., Richmond* ☎ *03/9421–4599* ⊕ *www.pearlrestaurant.com.au* ⌕ *Reservations essential* ✛ *2:D4.*

$$
CAFÉ

✕ **Richmond Hill Café and Larder.** This bright and buzzy café–cum–produce store is popular with those seeking a late breakfast and brunch that extends well into the day. It's so popular you might have to wait briefly if you haven't booked a table. The bistro fare brims with wonderful flavors, from the pie of the day (perhaps a tartlet of silverbeet and Taleggio cheese in a pumpkin and caraway crust) to the hand-cut pappardelle with belted Galloway short-rib ragu. Desserts are mouthwateringly simple and impossible to resist. After you've eaten, pick up some marvelous cheese and country-style bread from the adjoining cheese room and grocery. ⊠ *48–50 Bridge Rd., Richmond* ☎ *03/9421–2808* ⊕ *www.rhcl.com.au* ☽ *No dinner* ✛ *2:C2.*

DOCKLANDS

$$

MIDDLE EASTERN

✕ **Mecca Bah.** Chef Ben Azzopardi serves up delicious lamb and green-olive tagine, lemony grills, and sumac-dusted salads at this harborfront eatery. It's the sort of good, honest food that mum would've served—if she had been from Lebanon. In the evening you can enjoy splendid sunset views of the city skyline and the bay, or watch the hundreds of Melburnians who flock to Docklands every weekend. ⊠ *55A New Quay Promenade, Docklands* ☎ *03/9642–1300* ⊕ *www.meccabah.com.au* ⌕ *Reservations not accepted* ✛ *2:A4.*

WHERE TO STAY

CITY CENTER

For expanded hotel reviews, visit Fodors.com.

$$$

☷ **Arrow on Swanston.** Location and great value make up for the limited space in this CBD-edge hotel. **Pros:** easy walk to eateries and CBD attractions; inexpensive,. **Cons:** limited space. ⊠ *488 Swanston St., Carlton* ☎ *03/9225–9000* ⤢ *47 rooms, 38 apartments* ⌂ *In-room: a/c, kitchen, Internet. In-hotel: pool, gym, laundry facilities, parking* ✛ *1:A2.*

$$$

☷ **Crossley Hotel.** There's an unexpected sense of space and lots of light in this compact boutique hotel half a block from Chinatown. **Pros:** great location; good restaurant; reasonable price; **Cons:** redecorations planned over the next year. ⊠ *51 Little Bourke St., City Center* ☎ *03/9639–1639* ⤢ *84 rooms, 4 apartments* ⌂ *In-room: a/c, kitchen, Wi-Fi. In-hotel: restaurant, bar, gym, business center.*

$$$$

★

☷ **Hotel Lindrum.** Housed in the Heritage-listed Lindrum family billiards center, a short walk from Federation Square, this is one of Melbourne's savviest boutique properties. **Pros:** warm feel, exceptional service, full in-room entertainment systems. **Cons:** on busy thoroughfare. ⊠ *26*

Flinders St., City Center ☏ *03/9668–1111* ⊕ *www.hotellindrum.com. au* ⮑ *59 rooms* ♿ *In-room: safe, Internet. In-hotel: restaurant, bar, business center, parking* ✚ *1:C5.*

$$$$ 🏨 **The Hotel Windsor.** Built in 1883, this aristocrat of Melbourne hotels
★ combines Victorian-era character with modern comforts, and is a must for history lovers. **Pros:** elegant heritage feel, central location. **Cons:** heritage rooms are fittingly Old World in decor; a complete refurbishment is scheduled to begin 2013, during which they will not close, they will cater to the same market with a heritage feel. ✉ *111 Spring St., City Center* ☏ *03/9633–6000* ⊕ *www.thehotelwindsor.com.au* ⮑ *160 rooms, 20 suites* ♿ *In-room: safe, Internet. In-hotel: restaurant, bar, gym, parking* ✚ *1:C4.*

$$$$ 🏨 **InterContinental Melbourne The Rialto.** Unveiled late 2009 after a A$60 million upgrade, this luxury hotel occupies one of Melbourne's most historic sites. **Pros:** spectacular, historic facade, great bar and club lounge. **Cons:** slightly corporate feel, fee for in-room Wi-Fi. ✉ *495 Collins St., City Center* ☏ *03/8627–1400* ⊕ *www.intercontinental.com/melbourne* ⮑ *253 rooms* ♿ *In-room: safe, Internet. In-hotel: restaurant, bar, pool, gym, spa, laundry facilities, parking* 🍽 *No meals* ✚ *1:A5.*

$$$$ 🏨 **Park Hyatt Melbourne.** Set right next to Fitzroy Gardens and oppo-
Fodor's Choice site St. Patrick's Cathedral, this is one of Melbourne's most elegant
★ hotels. **Pros:** lavish appointments, new king-size beds, world-class service. **Cons:** slightly removed from the city center, fee for in-room Wi-Fi ✉ *1 Parliament Sq., East Melbourne* ☏ *03/9224–1234* ✉ *Melbourne@ hyatt.com.au* ⊕ *www.Hyatt.com* ⮑ *216 rooms, 24 suites* ♿ *In-room: safe, Internet, Wi-Fi. In-hotel: restaurant, bar, pool, gym, spa, business center, parking* ✚ *1:C4.*

$$ 🏨 **Robinsons in the City.** Melbourne's tiniest and possibly quaintest hotel occupies a converted 1850s bakery and 1906 baker's house. **Pros:** CBD-fringe location; great breakfast included; close to free city circle tram and free shuttle bus. **Cons:** a bit of a walk from the city center. ✉ *405 Spencer St., at Batman St., West Melbourne* ☏ *03/9329–2552* ⊕ *www. ritc.com.au* ⮑ *6 rooms* ♿ *In-room: no a/c, Wi-Fi. In-hotel: bar, laundry facilities, parking* 🍽 *Breakfast* ✚ *1:A3.*

$$ 🏨 **Somerset Gordon Place.** This National Trust-listed 1884 lodging house
★ is one of the most interesting and comfortable apartment hotels in the city. **Pros:** modern apartment-style furnishings, great location. **Cons:** homey feel. ✉ *24 Little Bourke St., City Center* ☏ *03/9663–2888* ⊕ *www.somerset.com* ⮑ *64 apartments* ♿ *In-room: safe, kitchen, Internet, Wi-Fi. In-hotel: pool, gym, laundry facilities, business center* ✚ *1:C4.*

$$$$ 🏨 **Stamford Plaza Melbourne.** Diamond-faceted glass elevators carry guests from the marble lobby of this "Paris-end," all-suite hotel to rooms decorated with plush, rich-hued velvets and art deco–ish crystal lamps. **Pros:** lush decor; great restaurant; central location, **Cons:** might not appeal to lovers of minimalist contemporary decor. ✉ *111 Little Collins St., City Center* ☏ *03/9659–1000* ⊕ *www.stamford.com. au* ⮑ *283 rooms* ♿ *In-room: a/c, kitchen, Internet, Wi-Fi. In-hotel: restaurant, bar, pool, gym, spa, laundry facilities, business center, parking* ✚ *1:B4.*

A delicatessen at Queen Victoria Market.

ST. KILDA

$$$ ⊞ **The Prince.** Cutting-edge design, contemporary artworks and sculptural furniture, and spare yet inviting luxury make this boutique hotel perfect for aficionados of unfussy elegance. **Pros:** super-comfortable rooms; gallery feel; great location. **Cons:** the modern shapes and neutral hues might not appeal to some. ⊠ *2 Acland St., St. Kilda* ☎ *03/9536–1111* ⊕ *www.theprince.com.au* ⤴ *40 rooms* ⬙ *In-room: a/c, Wi-Fi. In-hotel: restaurant, bar, spa* ✛ *2:A6.*

$$ ⊞ **Tolarno Hotel.** Set in the heart of St. Kilda's café, bar, and club precinct, Tolarno Hotel was once owned by artists who ran a gallery out of the space, and it still has an idiosyncratic artistic bent. **Pros:** great restaurant; cool vibe; heart of breezy St. Kilda location. **Cons:** area can have a dubious crowd; can be noisy late at night; no elevator. ⊠ *42 Fitzroy St., St. Kilda* ☎ *03/9537–0200* ⊕ *www.hoteltolarno.com.au* ⤴ *36 rooms* ⬙ *In-room: kitchen, Wi-Fi. In-hotel: restaurant, laundry facilities, parking* ✛ *2:A6.*

SOUTH YARRA–PRAHRAN

$$$$ ⊞ **The Como Melbourne.** With its opulence and funky modern furnish-
★ ings, this luxury hotel is as popular with business travelers as it is with visiting artists and musicians. **Pros:** lavishly appointed rooms; great shopping, restaurants nearby. **Cons:** outside the city center. ⊠ *630 Chapel St., South Yarra* ☎ *03/9825–2222* ⊕ *www.mirvachotels.com. au* ⤴ *107 suites* ⬙ *In-room: safe, kitchen, Internet. In-hotel: bar, pool, gym* ✛ *2:D5.*

$$$$ ☷ **The Lyall Hotel and Spa.** The spacious one- and two-bedroom suites at this exclusive hotel make an artform of understated elegance, and they come with all the luxuries: CD and DVD players, velour bathrobes and slippers, gourmet minibars, and a pillow "menu." **Pros:** an extravagant spa, 24-hour bistro, 24-hour gym. **Cons:** outside city center. ⊠ *14 Murphy St., South Yarra* ☎ *03/9868–8222* ⊕ *www.thelyall.com* ➴ *40 suites* ♨ *In-room: Internet, Wi-Fi. In-hotel: restaurant, bar, gym, spa, laundry facilities, business center, parking* ✛ *2:D5.*

RICHMOND

$ ☷ **Richmond Hill Hotel.** Just a short ride from the city center (on the No. 70 tram), this inexpensive boutique hotel occupies a garden-fronted 1918 mansion. **Pros:** city-fringe location, friendly service. **Cons:** somewhat Spartan digs, a bit maze-like, front rooms get peak-hour traffic noise ⊠ *353 Church St., Richmond* ☎ *03/9428–6501* ⊕ *www. richmondhillhotel.com.au* ➴ *42 rooms* ♨ *In-room: no a/c, Wi-Fi. In-hotel: bar, laundry facilities, parking* ¶◯¶ *Breakfast* ✛ *2:D3.*

WEST MELBOURNE

$$ ☷ **Miami Hotel Melbourne.** Like a Motel 6, only fancier, Miami Hotel is an excellent value option for the budget- and style-conscious. **Pros:** excellent service, great value, good location. **Cons:** basic amenities, fee for Wi-Fi. ⊠ *13 Hawke St., at King St., West Melbourne* ☎ *03/9321–2444, 1800/132333* ⊕ *www.themiami.com.au* ➴ *72 rooms (52 with bath)* ♨ *In-room: Internet, Wi-Fi. In-hotel: laundry facilities, parking* ✛ *2:A2.*

NIGHTLIFE AND THE ARTS

THE ARTS

Melbourne Events, available from tourist outlets, is a comprehensive monthly guide to what's happening in town. For a complete listing of performing-arts events, galleries, and films, consult the "EG" (Entertainment Guide) supplement in the Friday edition of *The Age* newspaper. Tourism Victoria hosts a fantastic Web site (⊕ *www.visitmelbourne. com*) detailing all of Melbourne's upcoming and current events. The free local music magazine *Beat* is available at cafés, stores, markets, and bars. *Brother Sister* is the local gay paper.

CITY CENTRE

Melbourne Park. Big-name, crowd-drawing contemporary artists perform at Melbourne Park. ⊠ *Batman Ave., City Center* ☎ *03/9286–1600.*

THEATER

Half-Tix. The Half-Tix ticket booth in the Melbourne Town Hall sells tickets to theater attractions at half price on performance days. It's open Monday 10–2, Tuesday–Thursday 11–6, Friday 11–6:30, and Saturday 10–4. Phone for information about shows on sale (recorded message).

No phone transactions, and sales are cash only. ⊠ *Melbourne Town Hall, Swanston and Collins Sts., City Center* ☎ *03/9650–9420.*

Comedy Theatre. Revues and plays are staged at the Comedy Theatre, which along with the Princess, Regent, and Forum theaters is owned by the Marriner Group and often uses the same telephone number. ⊠ *240 Exhibition St., City Center* ☎ *03/9299–9800, 1300/111011* ⊕ *www.marrinergroup.com.au.*

Regent Theatre. An ornate 1920s building, the Regent originally opened to screen movies, but nowadays presents mainstream productions, including Andrew Lloyd Webber's *Love Never Dies.* ⊠ *191 Collins St., City Center* ☎ *03/9299–9800, 1300/111011 box office* ⊕ *www.marrinergroup.com.au.*

ST. KILDA

THEATER

Theatre Works. This theater concentrates on contemporary Australian plays. ⊠ *14 Acland St., St. Kilda* ☎ *03/9534–3388* ⊕ *www.theatreworks.org.au.*

SOUTH MELBOURNE AND SOUTHBANK

MUSIC AND DANCE

Australian Ballet. In the 2,000-seat State Theatre at the Arts Centre, the Australian Ballet stages five programs annually, and presents visiting celebrity dancers from around the world. ⊠ *The Arts Centre, 100 St. Kilda Rd., Southbank* ☎ *03/9669–2700, 13–6100 Ticketmaster.*

Hamer Hall. The Hamer Hall (due to reopen in 2012 after extensive renovation) stages classy concerts. ⊠ *The Arts Centre, 100 St. Kilda Rd., Southbank* ☎ *03/9281–8000.*

Melbourne Symphony Orchestra. The Melbourne Symphony Orchestra performs year-round in the 2,600-seat Hamer Hall. ⊠ *The Arts Centre, 100 St. Kilda Rd., Southbank* ☎ *13–6100 Ticketmaster.*

Sidney Myer Music Bowl. Open-air concerts take place December through March at the Sidney Myer Music Bowl. ⊠ *King's Domain near Swan St. Bridge* ☎ *13–6100 Ticketmaster.*

THEATER

fortyfivedownstairs. Cutting-edge independent theatre, cabaret acts, and exhibitions are featured at fortyfivedownstairs. ⊠ *45 Flinders La., City Center* ☎ *03/9662–9966.*

Melbourne Theatre Company. Melbourne Theatre Company is Australia's oldest professional theater company. A brand-new theater opened in January 2009 with two performance spaces, the 500-seat Summer Theatre and the 150-seat Lawler Studio. Productions are also staged at the nearby Arts Centre in St. Kilda Road. ⊠ *140 Southbank Blvd., Southbank* ☎ *03/8688–0800 box office* ⊕ *www.mtc.com.au.*

Playbox at the CUB Malthouse Company. The city's second-largest company, the **Malthouse Theatre**, stages about 10 new or contemporary productions a year. The CUB Malthouse is a flexible theater space designed for drama, dance, and circus performances. ⊠ *113 Sturt St., Southbank* ☎ *03/9685–5111* ⊕ *www.malthousetheatre.com.au.*

NIGHTLIFE

Most of the central city's dance clubs are along the King Street strip or nestled in Little Collins Street. Clubs usually open at 9 or 10 weekends and some weeknights, and stay open until the early-morning hours. Expect to pay a small cover at most clubs—between A$10 and A$15.

CITY CENTRE

The Atrium Bar on 35. This cocktail bar on the 35th floor of the Sofitel Melbourne on Collins has spectacular views. ⊠ *25 Collins St., City Center* ☎ *03/9653–0000.*

Bennetts Lane. Bennetts is one of Melbourne's jazz mainstays. ⊠ *25 Bennetts La., City Center* ☎ *03/9663–2856.*

Last Laugh Comedy Club. A popular place to see top-class Australian and international acts. ⊠ *Athenaeum Theatre, 188 Collins St., City Center* ☎ *03/9650–6668.*

Comic's Lounge. Another good place for a laugh. ⊠ *26 Errol St., North Melbourne* ☎ *03/9348–9488.*

Cookie. Cookie, in a lofty warehouse-style space with exposed ceiling pipes and a balcony, focuses on imported beer and great Thai food. ⊠ *252 Swanston St., City Center* ☎ *03/9663–7660.*

Gin Palace. Reminiscent of Hollywood's golden era, Gin Palace has more than enough types of martinis to satisfy any taste. ⊠ *10 Russell Pl.(off Bourke St.), City Center* ☎ *03/9654–0533.*

The Hi-Fi. The Hi-Fi is a popular venue for live local and lesser-known international rock bands. ⊠ *125 Swanston St., City Center* ☎ *1300/843443 tickets.*

Kitten Club. Tony Starr's Kitten Club has a 1950s feel (Dean Martin songs are popular) and there's weekend jazz; the opulent ladies' powder room is a big hit with the girls. ⊠ *267 Little Collins St., City Center* ☎ *03/9650–2448.*

Melbourne Supper Club. Age-buffed leather sofas, cigars, and an exhaustive wine list characterize the classy Melbourne Supper Club. ⊠ *161 Spring St., City Center* ☎ *03/9654–6300.*

Pony. A diverse range of Australian and international acts, including rap, rock, funk, indie, and blues, plays at Pony. ⊠ *68 Little Collins St., City Center* ☎ *03/9662–1026.*

Silk Road. Silk Road is an exotic bar with lavish decor and a serious collection of chandeliers. Its themed Venetian Bar and Shahanshah Lounge are gorgeous places for a drink. ⊠ *425 Collins St., City Center* ☎ *03/9614–4888.*

RICHMOND

Corner Hotel. The Corner Hotel has alternative, reggae, rock, blues, and jazz acts with an emphasis on homegrown bands. ⊠ *57 Swan St., Richmond* ☎ *03/9427–7300 bar, 03/9427–9198 tickets.*

ST. KILDA

Esplanade Hotel. In addition to being a hallowed live music venue, the Esplanade, or "Espy," is a historic pub—built in 1878—listed with the National Trust. ⊠ *11 Upper Esplanade, St. Kilda* ☎ *03/9534–0211.*

Palais Theatre. This theater features film, music festival openings, and concerts by Australian and international acts such as the Soweto Gospel Choir and Joe Bonamassa. ⊠ *Lower Esplanade, St. Kilda* ☎ *03/9525–3240, 13–6100 Ticketmaster.*

Prince of Wales. For rock and roll, punk, and grunge, head to the Prince Bandroom at the Prince of Wales, which attracts a straight and gay crowd. ⊠ *29 Fitzroy St., St. Kilda* ☎ *03/9536–1168.*

The Saint. This is a glamorous hangout for the young and upwardly mobile. ⊠ *54 Fitzroy St., St. Kilda* ☎ *03/9593–8333.*

FITZROY

Night Cat. The Night Cat hosts bands and DJ's playing AfroCuban to disco dance music Thursday to Saturday evenings, and the Latin big band on Sunday nights is legendary. ⊠ *141 Johnston St., Fitzroy* ☎ *03/9417–0090.*

Polly. Mix with coloful and quirky clientele and enjoy a traditional or contemporary cocktail—there are 55 conconctions to choose from; Polly's decor is a blend of 1920s-style red-velvet lounges, gilt mirrors, and chandeliers. ⊠ *401 Brunswick St., Fitzroy* ☎ *03/9417–0880.*

SOUTH YARRA–PRAHRAN

Revolver Upstairs. Revolver Upstairs caters predominantly to the young. ⊠ *229 Chapel St., Prahran* ☎ *03/9521–5985.*

SOUTH MELBOURNE AND SOUTHBANK

Crown Casino. Melbourne's first gambling center has blackjack, roulette, and poker machines. The casino is part of the Crown Entertainment Complex, which also has dozens of restaurants, including branches of the famed Japanese chef Nobu and renowned Sydney chef Neil Perry's Rockpool, shops, bars, and two nightclubs open until late. The Palms at Crown hosts international and Australian headliners. The casino is on the south bank of the Yarra. ⊠ *8 Whiteman St., Southbank* ☎ *03/9292–8888* ⊕ *www.crowncasino.com.au* ⊘ *Daily 24 hrs.*

At the **Crown Casino** (⊠ *Level 3, Crown Entertainment Complex, Riverside Ave., Southbank* ☎ *03/9292–8888* ⊕ *www.crowncasino.com.au*) the Showroom and the Mercury Lounge attract big international and Australian headliners.

Seven. Melbourne's enduring nightspot Seven is a spot for chic young hipsters with fancy tastes in both fashion and cocktails. ⊠ *52 Albert Rd., South Melbourne* ☎ *03/9690–7877.*

Undertaker. Housed in a circa 1903 undertaker's parlor, the Undertaker is a good-looking bar, and the restaurant serves classy, upmarket pub grub. ⊠ *329 Burwood Rd., Hawthorn* ☎ *03/9818–3944.*

Melbourne is known for its top-notch live theater.

SHOPPING

Melbourne has firmly established itself as the nation's fashion capital. Australian designer labels are available on High Street in Armadale, on Toorak Road and Chapel Street in South Yarra, and on Bridge Road in Richmond. High-quality vintage clothing abounds on Greville Street in Prahran. Discount hunters will love the huge DFO (Discount Factory Outlet) right next door to Southern Cross Station on Spencer Street, with its many stores. Most shops are open Monday–Thursday 9–5:30, Friday until 9, and Saturday until 5. Major city stores are open Sunday until 5.

CITY CENTRE

Basement Discs. The Basement Discs has a exhaustive collection of country, blues, roots, jazz, folk, and world music. Midweek lunchtime performances feature local and international acts. Call ahead for show information. ⊠ *24 Block Pl., City Center* ☎ *03/9654–1110.*

Bourke Street Mall. Once the busiest east–west thoroughfare in the city, Bourke Street Mall is now a pedestrian zone—but watch out for those trams! Two of the city's biggest department stores are here.

Myer. An essential part of growing up in Melbourne is being taken to Myer at Christmas to see the window displays. ⊠ *314–336 Bourke St., between Elizabeth and Swanston Sts., City Center* ☎ *03/9661–1111*

David Jones. This is the other big department store that you may want to pop into. ⊠ *310 Bourke St., between Elizabeth and Swanston Sts., City Center* ☎ *03/9643–2222*

Block Arcade. Block Arcade, an elegant 19th-century shopping plaza with mosaic-tile floors, contains the venerable Hopetoun Tea Rooms, the French Jewel Box, Orrefors Kosta Boda, Dasel Dolls and Bears, and Australian By Design. ✉ *282 Collins St., City Center* ☎ *03/9654–5244.*

Craft Victoria. Craft Victoria fosters creativity with seminars and exhibits, and has a top-notch selection of Australian pottery, textile works, and jewelry. ✉ *31 Flinders La., City Center* ☎ *03/9650–7775.*

Discurio. Discurio carries a cross section of pop, rock, blues, jazz, classical, and contemporary music by international artists. ✉ *113 Hardware St., City Center* ☎ *03/9600–1488.*

A FUNNY NIGHT OUT

Melburnians love a laugh, and the annual comedy festival is the funniest place to be to catch top Australian and international performers. The month-long event takes place in the Town Hall and venues across town, and there are free events in open spaces. The festival also seeks out new talent and culminates with the Raw Comedy award for the best new Australian stand-up performer. If you're in town in April, you won't be laughing if you miss it.
⊕ *www.comedyfestival.com.au.*

Gallery Gabrielle Pizzi. Gallery Gabrielle Pizzi shows and sells the work of established and new Aboriginal artists from the communities of Balgo Hills, Papunya, Maningrida, Turkey Creek (Warmun), the Tiwi Islands, and others in the Central Desert, Top End, and Kimberley regions. ✉ *73–77 Flinders La., City Center* ☎ *03/9654–2944.*

★ **Little Collins Street.** A precinct of stores frequented by shoppers with perhaps more money than sense, Little Collins Street is still worth a visit. In between frock shops you'll find musty stores selling classic film posters, antique and estate jewelry, and Australian opals. At the eastern end of **Collins Street,** beyond the cream-and-red Romanesque facade of St. Michael's Uniting Church, is the **Paris End,** a name coined by Melburnians to identify the elegance of its fashionable shops as well as its general hauteur. Here you find big-name international designer clothing, bags, and jewelry.

Melbourne Central. Here you'll find a dizzying complex huge enough to enclose an 1880s redbrick shot tower (used to make bullets) in its atrium. ✉ *300 Lonsdale St., City Center* ☎ *03/9922–1100.*

Royal Arcade. Royal Arcade, built in 1846, is Melbourne's oldest shopping plaza. It remains a lovely place to browse, and it's home to the splendid Gaunt's Clock, which tolls away the hours. ✉ *355 Bourke St., City Center* ☎ *No phone.*

Sam Bear. Sam Bear, a Melbourne institution, sells everything from Aussie outerwear and footwear to Swiss Army knives. ✉ *225 Russell St., City Center* ☎ *03/9663–2191.*

★ **Southgate.** Southgate has a spectacular riverside location. The shops and eateries here are a short walk from both the city center across Princes Bridge and the Arts Center. There's outdoor seating next to the Southbank promenade. ✉ *4 Southbank Promenade, Southbank* ☎ *03/9699–4311.*

Queen Victoria Market. Queen Victoria Market has buzzed with food shoppers since 1878. With more than 1,000 mostly open-air stalls, this sprawling, spirited bazaar is the city's prime produce outlet—many Melburnians come here to buy strawberries, fresh flowers, imported cheeses, meat, and eye-bright fresh fish. On Sunday there is less food and more great deals on jeans, T-shirts, and souvenirs. It's open Tuesday and Thursday 6–2, Friday 6–5, Saturday 6–3, and Sunday 9–4. Market tours take you deep inside the labyrinth, and cooking classes are conducted by well-known chefs. Wandering entertainers and aromatic hot-food stalls add to the vibe at the Suzuki Night Market, open 5:30 to 10 pm on Wednesday from November to late-February; this market focuses on art, crafts, and gifts. ✉ *Elizabeth and Victoria Sts., City Center* ☎ *03/9320–5822* ⊕ *www.qvm.com.au.*

RICHMOND

Bridge Road. Bridge Road, in Richmond at the end of Flinders Street, east of the city, is a popular shopping strip for women's retail fashion that caters to all budgets.

ST. KILDA

The Esplanade Market St. Kilda. The Esplanade Market St. Kilda has up to 200 stalls selling contemporary paintings, crafts, pottery, jewelry, and homemade gifts. It's open Sunday 10–5. ✉ *Upper Esplanade, St. Kilda* ☎ *03/9209–6777.*

FITZROY

★ **Brunswick Street.** Brunswick Street, northeast of the city in Fitzroy, has hip and grungy restaurants, coffee shops, gift stores, and clothing outlets selling the latest look.

Brunswick Street Bookstore. Brunswick Street Bookstore specializes in art, design, and architecture publications, but also stocks modern Australian literature. ✉ *305 Brunswick St., Fitzroy* ☎ *03/9416–1030.*

SOUTH YARRA–PRAHRAN

Camberwell Sunday Market. Camberwell Sunday Market, about 6 km (3.75 mi.) northeast of Chapel Street, South Yarra, is a popular haunt for seekers of the old and odd. More than 300 stalls sell antiques, pre-loved clothing, books, and knickknacks. Food vans provide sustenance. ✉ *Station St., Camberwell* ✍ *manager@sundaymarket.com. au (no hone contact).*

Chapel Street. Chapel Street, in South Yarra-Prahran between Toorak and Dandenong roads, is where you can find some of the ritziest boutiques in Melbourne, as well as cafés, art galleries, bars, and restaurants.

Chapel Street Bazaar. Chapel Street Bazaar, open daily 10–6, has wooden cubicles and glass-fronted counters selling everything from estate jewelry and stylish secondhand clothes to porcelain and curios. ✉ *217–223 Chapel St., Prahran* ☎ *03/9529–1727.*

Collette Dinnigan. Collette Dinnigan is a household name in Australia, having dressed celebrities such as Nicole Kidman and Cate Blanchett. This is a great place to shop for limited-edition feminine dresses. ⊠ 553 Chapel St., South Yarra ☎ 03/9827–2111.

Dinosaur Designs. Dinosaur Designs sells a range of luminous bowls and vases, and funky resin and silver jewelry. ⊠ 562 Chapel St., South Yarra ☎ 03/9827–2600.

Greville Records. Greville Records is a Melbourne music institution. It carries rare releases in rock, alternative, and vinyl. ⊠ 152 Greville St., Prahran ☎ 03/9510–3012.

High Street. Located between the suburbs of Prahran and Armadale, to the east of Chapel Street, High Street has the best collection of antiques shops in Australia.

Jam Factory. The Jam Factory is a historic redbrick brewery-then-factory complex that house cinemas, fashion, food, and gift shops. ⊠ 500 Chapel St., South Yarra ☎ 03/9825–4699.

Prahran Market. Prahran Market sells nothing but food—a fantastic, mouthwatering array imported from all over the world. It's open Tuesday, Thursday, and Saturday dawn–5 pm, Friday dawn–6 pm, and Sunday 10–3. ⊠ 163 Commercial Rd., South Yarra ☎ 03/8290–8220 ⊕ www.prahranmarket.com.au.

South Melbourne Market. South Melbourne Market, established in 1867, is Melbourne's second-oldest market. You'll find a huge selection of fresh produce and foodstuffs. It's open Wednesday and weekends 8–4 and Friday 8–5. ⊠ Cecil and Coventry Sts., South Melbourne ☎ 03/9209–6295.

Flinders Lane. Dotted with chic boutiques, many of them selling merchandise by up-and-coming Australian designers, Flinders Lane will make fashionistas happy. Between Swanston and Elizabeth streets, look for shops such as the boudoir-like accessories outlet Christine and Alice Euphemia (in Cathedral Arcade), which stocks eclectic, sometimes whimsical, clothing by young designers.

Victoria

WORD OF MOUTH

The 12 Apostles seemed to be rising out of the mist while clouds and fog rolled and swirled behind them. I could barely believe how beautiful and mystical it was. I got some terrific photos but nothing that fully captured what we were treated to that morning.
—Songdoc

WELCOME TO VICTORIA

TOP REASONS TO GO

★ **The Amazing Outdoors:** Victoria has outstanding national parks. Bushwalking, canoeing, fishing, rafting, and horse riding are all on the menu. If you're pushed for time, there are organized day trips to Port Campbell and the outcrops of the Grampians National Park.

★ **Golden Country:** You can still pan for gold—and find it—in rivers about an hour northwest of Melbourne. Today's main attractions though are the beautiful 19th-century towns constructed from the riches of the goldfields. Walking trails outline the stories of lucky strikes and miners' fights for justice.

★ **Wonderful Wineries:** You'll find hundreds of wineries across the state, particularly in the Yarra Valley, Rutherglen, and on the Mornington Peninsula. Winery tours, departing from Melbourne, are a relaxing way to see four to five wineries in one day.

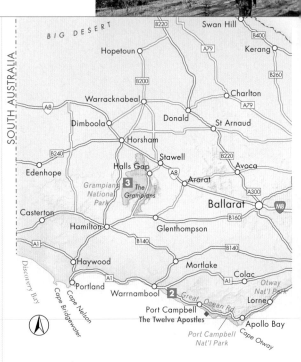

1 Side Trips from Melbourne. Dozens of wineries with fabulous restaurants, mist-swathed hills dotted with charming B&Bs and curio shops, forested walking trails noisy with multicolored parrots, gold-era towns flush with grand, boom-time buildings, and glorious beaches are right on Melbourne's doorstep. It's a breeze to visit the Yarra Valley, Mornington Peninsula, the Goldfields, or the Dandenong Ranges on day trips.

2 Great Ocean Road. This is the ultimate road trip along the wave-lashed Southern Ocean. From Melbourne it's a 450-km (280-mi) coastal journey, with occasional detours into wooded hills dotted with fern gullies. Lighthouses, surfing beaches, and lively towns punctuate the road, but the headline attractions are the amazing shapes carved from the coastline, including the Twelve Apostles and the smaller rock stacks on show in this amazing sculpture park.

GETTING ORIENTED

This compact state is a patchwork of spectacular landscapes just waiting to be explored. The Yarra Valley wineries and the Dandenong Ranges are an hour's drive east of Melbourne, while the beaches and vineyards of the Mornington Peninsula are a 90-minute drive south of the state's capital. The Great Ocean Road begins at Torquay, southwest of Melbourne, and continues along the Southern Ocean coast to Portland, a distance of about 350 km (220 mi). The Goldfields and spa country are between one and two hours northwest of Melbourne. The Grampians and the Murray River Region and its wineries are about a three-hour drive north to northeast of the city.

3 The Grampians. Encompassing a series of rugged sandstone ranges covered with native bushland, the Grampians National Park is a wilderness area three hours from the heart of Melbourne. Spectacular rock formations including the Balconies, the Pinnacle, and the Fortress can be visited via walking trails. The Wonderland Range forms a wall behind the township of Halls Gap, which is a popular hangout for kangaroos.

4 Murray River Region. The mighty Murray River forms the border between Victoria and New South Wales, and is a natural playground. Houseboats, speedboats, and old paddle-wheelers share the river, and golf courses, farms, historic towns, and stands of majestic eucalypt trees hug its banks. Wineries produce internationally acclaimed fortified wines and full-bodied reds.

OUTDOOR ADVENTURES

Victoria is blessed with amazing natural sculptures. Sandstone ridges and spires tower above country plains, and the ocean is littered with bizarrely shaped coastal sea stacks and cliff faces.

Two of the best places to experience Victoria's spectacular nature are Port Campbell National Park and the Grampians National Park. The first encompasses the "best of the best" of Victoria's dramatic Great Ocean Road coastline. Stretching for about 20 km (12 mi) between the towns of Princetown and Peterborough, the park contains the iconic Twelve Apostles—huge limestone rock stacks, measuring up to 45 meters (148 feet). The Grampians are a striking series of sandstone mountain ranges that rise dramatically from volcanic plains and harbor several waterfalls. More than 30 walking tracks (from easy to strenuous) wind through gullies, native bushland strewn with wildflowers, and up and over hills. It's possible to drive to the most popular lookout points. There are a dozen wineries within an easy drive of the park.

WHEN TO GO

The Great Ocean Road is a popular summer road trip, so it's best to visit Port Campbell National Park in winter, spring, or fall. Crowds thin out by the end of February, but holidaymakers return in force during Easter. Winter is suitably cold and windswept, giving an idea of the ferocious sea conditions that claimed hundreds of ships during the 19th century. Grampians National Park can be very hot and uncomfortable in summer, and fall can still be quite warm. Spring and winter are best for bushwalking and visiting cozy wineries. Campsites and hotels in Halls Gap fill up during Easter, and prices rise accordingly.

BEST WAYS TO EXPLORE

PORT CAMPBELL NATIONAL PARK

The Great Ocean Road is perfect for walking, so perfect that a long-distance walking track was opened a few years ago. The Great Ocean Walk begins at Marengo, just west of Apollo Bay. It stretches 100 km (62 mi) to Glenample Homestead (which is now closed), adjacent to the Twelve Apostles, hugging rugged coastline as it passes through national parks. You can set out on the walk on your own, do a few sections of it, or join an organized walking tour that has overnight stays in B&Bs and other comfortable accommodations. Parks Victoria's dedicated Great Ocean Walk Web site is ⊕ *www.greatoceanwalk.com.au*. It's easy to do something shorter as well. Walking trails wind past the iconic Twelve Apostles and nearby Loch Ard Gorge, each of which can be viewed from lookouts a few hundred yards from a car park. Loch Ard Gorge, a bay flanked by towering cliffs and with a narrow opening, is a spectacular sight. Other major landforms—the Arch, London Bridge, and the Grotto—have boardwalks and viewing platforms and are about a 10-minute drive (or a longer walk) from each other.

GRAMPIANS NATIONAL PARK

Bushwalking is by far the most popular activity in the national park. Some of the best walks include Mackenzie Falls, the walk to Mt. Abrupt (or Mt. Murdajoog in the Aboriginal language), the Hollow Mountain walk, and another to Silverband Falls. Even if you're not a big walker you can still see many of the best-known rock formations. Elephant Hide, the Balconies, the Pinnacle, and the Fortress are only a short walk from a car park. Canoeing is another great way to get away from the crowds and experience the lakes and rivers of the Grampians. And if you'd like a bit of education with your nature, we highly recommend a visit to the Brambuk Cultural Centre. Owned and operated by the Koori people (Aboriginal people of southeastern Australia), the center provides a unique living history of indigenous culture in this part of Victoria.

TIMING FOR PORT CAMPBELL

It is possible to visit Port Campbell National Park on an organized day trip from Melbourne, but a better alternative is to stay overnight at one of the nearby towns and explore the region over a half or full day. The 20-km (12-mi) coastal drive is crammed with amazing sea sculptures, and you'll be stopping in the car parks along the way to get out and walk along the boardwalks to viewing platforms and steps that lead down to the coast.

TIMING FOR THE GRAMPIANS

The most popular attractions of the central Grampians region can be visited in one day. However, if you want to visit the fascinating Bambuk Aboriginal Cultural Centre and take in a few wineries, allow yourself another day or two. From the town of Halls Gap it's a 15-km (9-mi) drive (plus a 100-yard walk from the car park) to the spectacular Boroka Lookout.

Updated by
Melanie Ball

Separated from New South Wales by the mighty Murray River and fronted by a beautiful coastline, Victoria boasts terrain as varied as any in the country. Sweeping landscapes are quilted together in this compact state.

Many of Victoria's best sights are within a day's drive of Melbourne. Without venturing too far from the city limits you can indulge in all sorts of pastimes—exploring the spectacular western coastline to the stunning Twelve Apostles; walking among the rocky outcrops, waterfalls, and fauna of the Grampians; visiting historic inland goldmining communities; toasting the sunrise over the Yarra Valley vineyards from the basket of a hot-air balloon; or taking in a Murray River sunset from the deck of a paddle steamer. Go farther afield and you can experience the high-country solitude of Alpine National Park.

PLANNING

WHEN TO GO

Victoria is at its most beautiful in fall, March through May, when days are crisp, sunny, and clear and the foliage in parks and gardens is glorious. Winter, with its wild seas and leaden skies, stretches May through August in this region, providing a suitable backdrop for the dramatic coastal scenery. It's dry and sunny in the northeast, however, thanks to the cloud-blocking bulk of the Great Dividing Range. Northeast summers, November through February, are extremely hot, so it's best to travel here and through Gold Country in spring and fall.

GETTING HERE AND AROUND

The best way to explore Victoria is by car. The state's road system is excellent, with clearly marked highways linking the Great Ocean Road to Wilson's Promontory, the Yarra Valley, the Murray River region, and the Mornington Peninsula. Distances are not as extreme as in other states. Many of the most scenic places (Bendigo, Ballarat, Beechworth, and Echuca, for instance) are less than three hours from Melbourne; the vineyards of the Yarra Valley and the Mornington Peninsula are an easy 90-minute drive. Buses and trains, which cost less but take more time, also run between most regional centers.

ABOUT THE RESTAURANTS

Chefs in Victoria take pride in their trendsetting preparations of fresh local produce. International flavors are found in both casual and upscale spots—and since prices are generally lower here than in Sydney, you can have your fill without breaking the bank. On Sunday be sure to join in the Victorian tradition of an all-day "brekky."

ABOUT THE HOTELS

Accommodations in Victoria include grand country hotels, simple roadside motels, secluded bushland or seaside cabins, friendly bed-and-breakfasts, and backpacker hostels. Although you won't find many sprawling resorts in this state, most of the grand old mansions and country homes have air-conditioning, home-cooked meals, and free parking. Rates are usually reduced after school and national holidays. Melbourne Visitor Centre (⊕ *www.visitvictoria.com*) has a list of the state's accommodations to help you plan.

5

DINING AND LODGING PRICE CATEGORIES (IN AUSTRALIAN DOLLARS)				
¢	$	$$	$$$	$$$$
Restaurants	under A$10	A$10–A$20	A$21–A$35	A$36–A$50	over A$50
Hotels	under A$100	A$100–A$150	A$151–A$200	A$201–A$300	over A$300

Restaurant prices are based on the median main-course price at dinner. Hotel prices include taxes, and are for two people in a standard double room in high season, excluding service.

SIDE TRIPS FROM MELBOURNE

Victoria's relatively compact size makes the state's principal attractions appealingly easy to reach, and the state's excellent road system makes driving the best option. There are a handful of enticing destinations within a 60- to 90-minute drive from Melbourne. Victoria is blessed with 21 distinct wine regions (and a total of 650 cellar doors where you can try and buy the product). The Yarra Valley, 40 km (25 mi) east of Melbourne, is Victoria's oldest wine region and a pleasant place to spend a day on an organized tour. About 35 km (22 mi) south of the Yarra Valley is Olinda, a cute village at the heart of the Dandenong Ranges. This area of beautifully forested hills and valleys is a favorite weekend escape for Melburnians. The Mornington Peninsula is famous for its wineries and beaches. On the western shore of Port Phillip Bay, the Bellarine Peninsula is also developing a winery industry, but it's the grand 19th-century hotels of Queenscliff that have been attracting day-trippers.

YARRA VALLEY AND HEALESVILLE

★ Healesville is a good base for travel to Yarra Valley wineries and the Dandenongs Region, as it's a short drive from both.

On February 7, 2009 (known as Black Saturday), ferocious bushfires ripped through forests and towns to the east and north of Healesville,

Side Trips From
Melbourne

Marysville

Dixon's Creek

Healesville
Yarra Glen
Coldstream   Maroondah Hwy.
Lilydale

MELBOURNE   Olinda   Warburton

Kallista

Werribee   Ferntree
                  Gully   Sherbrooke
                               Belgrave   The Dandenong
                                               Ranges
TO GREAT   Open Range   Port
OCEAN ROAD Zoo   Phillip Bay   Dandenong

Geelong   Frankston   Cranbumne   Princes Hwy.
                           Mount Eliza
Bellarine Hwy.   Mornington Peninsula
Bellarine   Queens-   Mornington   see detail map
Peninsula   cliff   Lang
              Pt.   Mount Martha   Lang
Torquay   Lonsdale Portsea Dromana Red   Hastings
              Rosebud McRae   Hill   Bittern French
Point Nepean Sorrento Rye   Balnarring Island
National Park   Arthurs Seat   Somers
                     State Park Shoreham Cowes   Leongatha
        Cape   Rhyll
        Schanck   Flinders   Phillip
                     Penguin   Island   San
                     Parade   Remo
        0   25 miles
                                    Bass Strait
        0   40 km

destroying more than 1,000 homes and claiming the lives of 173 people.
The historic town of Marysville (28 km [17 mi] east of Healesville)
was almost wiped out. Many of the clay sculptures at the town's major
attraction, Bruno's Art & Sculpture Garden, were later found to be
intact, and the garden was replanted and reopened late 2009, an act
of optimism and hope; the town itself is rebuilding more slowly. Several nearby national parks were burned and some areas remain closed.
Lake Mountain resort, a winter ski destination and a summer hiking
spot, 22 km (14 mi) from Marysville, is operational, and the 36-km
(22-mi) Acheron Way drive is open. Two popular areas within Yarra
Ranges National Park—Badger Weir Walk and Maroondah Reservoir—
are ideal for bushwalking and picnics. The Yarra Valley region and its
wineries were not damaged by the fires; the pretty town of Warburton, 30 km (19 mi) from Healesville was also untouched. ■ TIP→ We
encourage you to travel to the fire-affected areas, as your business will help
rebuild their communities.

🐾 **Healesville Sanctuary.** Come face-to-face with wedge-tailed eagles, grumpy
wombats, nimble sugar gliders, and shy platypuses at Healesville Sanctuary, a lovely, leafy wildlife sanctuary that houses Australian wildlife.
Don't miss the twice-daily Spirits of the Sky show, during which rap-
tors and parrots fly close overhead. You can pat a dingo (Australia's

wild dog) or feed an emu on a Magic Moments experience (A$10 extra). You can also book a behind-the-scenes tour of the animal hospital, where you may see wildlife recovering from injury or illness. Many native animals injured in the Black Saturday bushfires of 2009 were treated here. Take a break and refuel at the Sanctuary Harvest cafe, which serves delicious snacks and meals, many with a bush-tucker flavour. ⊠ *Badger Creek Rd.* ☎ *03/5957–2800* ⊕ *www.zoo.org.au* ✉ *A$25.40* ☉ *Daily 9–5.*

GETTING HERE AND AROUND

Healesville, on the eastern side of the Yarra Valley, is 65 km (40 mi) from Melbourne. Take the Eastern Freeway from Melbourne to its junction with the Maroondah Highway and follow the signs to Lilydale and on to Healesville. Trains, operated by Metro, travel from central Melbourne to Lilydale, and McKenzie's buses connect Lilydale with Yarra Glen and Healesville. It's advisable to have a car to explore the wineries, or take a half-day or full-day tour. Most tours will pick you up at your hotel.

TOURS

Several companies operate winery tours from Melbourne or the Yarra Valley itself. Tours generally include visits to four to five wineries and lunch. Wine Tours Victoria offers full-day tours departing from Melbourne and visiting four to five wineries and including lunch for A$147 per person. Yarra Valley Winery Tours runs public and private tours with flexible itineraries. Minibuses are the most common form of transport for most tours, but on weekends from 11 to 4 for A$100 per person Swans on Doongalla takes you out to four wineries along St. Huberts Road in a stretched horse-drawn carriage. A light lunch is served at Yering Farm winery. The meeting place is St. Huberts Winery. Rail enthusiasts can still enjoy the tracks even though passenger train services to Healesville ceased in 1980. You can travel along part of the track in railmotors (all-in-one motor and carriage) operated by the Yarra Valley Railway. The railmotors travel from Healesville through picturesque country, under bridges and through the historic TarraWarra brick tunnel and back again—a distance of about 8 km (5 mi) that takes about 45 minutes. Night Owl tours that include a buffet barbecue meal at the station are offered for groups of 12 or more.

ESSENTIALS

Tour Operators **Swans on Doongalla Horse Drawn Carriages** ⊠ *2A Doongalla Rd., The Basin* ☎ *03/9762–1910* ⊕ *www.swansondoongalla.com.au.* **Wine Tours Victoria** ⊠ *9 The Willows, Gisborne* ☎ *03/5428–8500* ⊕ *www.winetours.com.au.* **Yarra Valley Speciality Tours & Transport** ⊠ *30 Kelly's Rd., Warburton* ☎ *03/5966–2372* ⊕ *www.yarravalleyspecialtytours.com.au.* **Yarra Valley**

PRECIOUS RESOURCE

You won't be able to escape the "save water" signs as you travel around Victoria. Heavy rains and flooding in 2010 and 2011 ended the worst drought in more than a century, however, expectation is high that another long, dry stretch will come sooner than later. Some hotels ask guests to participate in water-saving practices, and may even provide buckets to catch the excess (nonsoapy) shower water to use it on the garden. It's a lot of fun to get involved and help feed those thirsty plants.

5

Railway ✉ *Healesville Station, Healesville Kinglake Rd.* ☎ *03/5962–2490 station* ⊕ *www.yarravalleyrailway.org.au* ✉ *A$13 motorrail rides; A$35 night tours with dinner* ☉ *10–4.* **Yarra Valley Winery Tours** ✉ *299 Maroondah Hwy., Healesville* ☎ *03/5966–2372* ⊕ *www.yarravalleywinerytours.com.au.*

Transportation Contacts **Metro** ☎ *131/638* ⊕ *www.metlinkmelbourne.com.au.* **McKenzie's Tourist Services.** ☎ *03/5962–5088* ⊕ *www.mckenzies.com.au.*

Visitor Information **Yarra Valley Visitor Information Centre** ✉ *Old Courthouse, Harker St.* ☎ *03/5962–2600* ⊕ *www.visityarravalley.com.au.*

EXPLORING THE WINERIES

The Yarra Valley is also known for its wonderful produce—fruit, vegetables, herbs, bread, and cheeses—on sale at the monthly regional farmers' markets, including one at Yering Station *(see listing below)*.

★ **De Bortoli.** A family winery for three generations, De Bortoli was established (in New South Wales) in 1928, four years after the founder Vittorio De Bortoli and his wife Giuseppina migrated to Australia from northern Italy. Chardonnays, Pinot Noir, and Rieslings are specialties of the Yarra Valley estate, and you'll have ample opportunity to sample a few—wine tastings are free, but a $7 charge charge applies for tasting stickies, including Noble One, De Bortoli's most awarded wine since its release in 1987. The restaurant, which has stunning views of the surrounding vines, landscaped gardens, and mountains, serves delectable dishes using Yarra Valley produce; a four-course chef's lunch is A$58 a head (A$70 weekends), you can also dine à la carte except on Sunday. You might like to start with a seasonal aperitif—perhaps a mandarin cocktail of aperol and Windy Peak Pinot Chardonnay (a sparkling wine). A popular feature is the cheese maturation and tasting room in the cellar-door area. Resident cheese maker Richard Thomas creates gourmet cheese-tasting plates with matching wines (prices vary depending on produce chosen). A Wine Adventure, which includes a wine tutorial, guided vineyard and winery tours, barrel tastings, hints on food and wine matching, and a three-course lunch, is held on the first Saturday of every month at $A140 per head. ✉ *Pinnacle La., Dixon's Creek* ☎ *03/5965–2271* ⊕ *www.debortoliyarra.com.au* ☉ *Daily 10–5; restaurant lunch Thurs.–Mon., dinner Sat. only.*

★ **Domaine Chandon.** Domaine Chandon has one of the most spectacular settings in the Yarra Valley; its Greenpoint tasting bar has enormous floor-to-ceiling windows providing fantastic views over the vineyards and to the Yarra Ranges in the distance. Apart from sparkling wines—including Australia's only Pinot Noir–Shiraz blend—the winery produces Shiraz, Pinot Noir, Chardonnay, Sauvignon Blanc, and rosé. Free guided tours, conducted daily at 11, 1, and 3, take visitors through the step-by-step production of sparkling wine, beginning among the vines and ending in the bottling area. Seasonal platters, tapas, and sharing plates (A$15–A$27) are served daily from 11 am in the Greenpoint brasserie, and each dish has a recommended accompanying wine (from A$9.50 a glass). Selections include flathead tacos with house-made tortilla washed down with Chandon Vintage Brut, and quail marinated in verjuice (made by pressing unripe grapes), accompanied by a salad of roquette, grapes,

GREAT ITINERARIES

IF YOU HAVE 3 DAYS

On the first morning after leaving Melbourne, head for the town of Belgrave. Here you can ride the **Puffing Billy** through the fern gullies and forests of the **Dandenongs.** In the afternoon, travel to **Phillip Island** for the endearing sunset penguin parade. Stay the night, and on the third morning meander along the coastal roads of the **Mornington Peninsula** through such stately towns as Sorrento and Portsea. Stop at a beach, or pick a Melbourne neighborhood or two to explore in the afternoon.

IF YOU HAVE 5 DAYS

Make your way west from Melbourne, stopping at Queenscliff on the Bellarine Peninsula, before setting off down the Great Ocean Road. (If you are starting from the Mornington Peninsula, you take the Sorrento-Queenscliff car and passenger ferry, which crosses Port Phillip

Bay in 45 minutes). The Great Ocean Road is one of the world's finest scenic drives, offering stops at some irresistible beaches. Overnight in **Lorne**, beneath the Otway Ranges, then drive west to **Port Campbell National Park.** Here you can view the Twelve Apostles rock formations and stroll along the beach. Continue to **Port Fairy** for the night, making sure that you check out the wonderful Bay of Islands and Bay of Martyrs rock stacks (in the sea) along the way. On Day 4 wander along the banks of Port Ferry's Moyne River and amble around Griffiths Island. You can then drive northeast to the Goldfields center of **Ballarat.** That evening you can explore the town's 19th-century streetscapes, then catch the sound-and-light show at Sovereign Hill. Spend the night here, and in the morning head to the wineries and spas around Daylesford before returning to Melbourne.

pecorino cheese, and a glass of Pinot Noir. ⊠ *727–729 Maroondah Hwy., Coldstream* ☎ *03/9738–9200* ⊕ *www.domainechandon.com.au.*

Rochford Wines. Rochford Wines occupies a striking-looking property; a building crafted almost entirely of glass overlooks the vineyards and rolling green paddocks. The family-owned winery produces renowned Pinot Noir and Chardonnay, and has in recent years become the most happening place in the Yarra Valley—its huge amphitheater plays host to international and local performers during the annual Day on the Green concert series (recent acts have included Leonard Cohen and Nora Jones); in summer it screens movies under the stars. The wine-tasting bar is open daily 10–5. A stylish restaurant (offering two courses for A$55 and three courses for $A65 per person) and a casual café are both open seven days a week for lunch; the café also serves all-day light meals. ⊠ *Maroondah Hwy. at Hill Rd., Coldstream* ☎ *03/5962–2119* ⊕ *www.rochfordwines.com.*

Stones of the Yarra Valley. A new addition to the Yarra Valley, Stones of the Yarra Valley is a restaurant and bar housed in an old weather-beaten barn that has been beautifully restored. Set amid 50 acres of Cabernet vines and surrounded by century-old oak trees, and with views of the Yarra Ranges, this is a great place to sit down to lunch, or just have a coffee or a wine at the casual Mezze Wine Bar. The weekend-only lunch menu might include slow-braised lamb shoulder with cracked-wheat pilaf, cucumber, and tzatziki, or blue-eye trevalla with dried forest mushrooms, salsa bianco, and crisp baby octopus (both A$35). Evening performances by well-known Australian artists, who have included jazz maestro James Morrison, take place throughout the year, and are excellent value at between A$100 to A$120 for a three-course meal (wine extra) and show. Sunday concerts featuring up-and-coming jazz and classical performers (A$15–A$30) are staged in the lovely hand-hewn stone chapel on the site on selected dates. ⊠ *14 St. Huberts Rd., Coldstream* ☎ *03/9739–0900* ⊕ *www.stonesoftheyarravalley.com* ☉ *No lunch weekdays; no dinner (except on musical evenings).*

WINE AND SONG

Catch a little jazz at lunch or spend the whole day watching great performances from local and international headline acts; Victoria's wineries provide an array of entertainment for music connoisseurs. Vineyards come alive in summer, so check out the events with local tourist offices. Make sure you book early for the popular Day on the Green concert series held in the Rochford Winery in the Yarra Valley, Seppelt Wines at Great Western, near the Grampians, All Saints Winery in Rutherglen, and two Melbourne theaters.

Yering Station. Yering Station shares grounds with the historic Chateau Yering boutique hotel. It's Victoria's first vineyard and it still has plenty of rustic charm. The 1859 redbrick building is home to the cellar door, a wine-and-produce store, and the casual upstairs Matt's Bar, where you can relax all day sipping wine and dining from a tasty menu beneath an arched timber ceiling. The property's architectural and gastronomical pièce de résistance is the winery building, which houses the Wine Bar Restaurant. It's a sweeping, hand-hewn stone building with floor-to-ceiling windows overlooking spectacular valley scenery. Enjoy a wonderful seasonal menu overseen by chef Laura Web-James. Main-course dishes (A$32–A$38) could include eye fillet, braised beef cheek, and corned-beef terrine with creamed spinach and red wine jus; you may want to finish the meal with a decadent goat's cheesecake with cashewnut tuille and truffled honey. Those who would prefer just to wander and sip wines at the cellar door are free to take the self-guided winery tour through the sculpture gardens. A farmers' market, where local growers sell their region's produce of olives, eggs, honey, cheese, coffee, flowers, and jams, takes place on the third Sunday of the month. ⊠ *38 Melba Hwy., Yarra Glen* ☎ *03/9730–0100* ⊕ *www yering.com* ☉ *Cellar door 10–5 weekdays, 10–6 weekends; restaurant: lunch daily from noon (no dinner).*

OUTDOOR ACTIVITIES

There are plenty of opportunities to get out in the fresh air in the Yarra Valley. Those with cash to spare can go ballooning; others may just like to walk or ride a bike along the trails or play golf at the three golf courses in the valley. Wine tasting is a given.

BALLOONING **Balloon Sunrise.** Balloon Sunrise was founded in 1986, and was the first commercial hot-air ballooning operation in Australia. From A$320 per

"Just a short drive from Melbourne is the captivating beauty of the Yarra Valley." —photo by lisargold, Fodors.com member

person you can take off at dawn and drift peacefully over the vineyards for an hour. A champagne breakfast is served after the flight at the Mercure Balgownie Estate Winery. ✉ *Bell St., Yarra Glen* ☎ *03/9735–0288, 1800/468247* ⊕ *www.hotairballooning.com.au.*

BIKING **Yarra Valley Cycles.** Yarra Valley Cycles will rent you a bike (and compulsory helmet) from A$40 a day and point you in the right direction for the best cycling routes in the valley and nearby scenic regions. ✉ *108 Main St., Lilydale ⊹ Across the road from Lilydale Railway Station* ☎ *03/9735–1483* ⊕ *www.yarravalleycycles.com* ⊗ *Mon.–Thu. 9–5:30, Fri. 9–7, Sat 9–5, Sun. 10–4 (May-August closed Sunday).*

BUSHWALKING **Yarra Ranges National Park.** A few sections of Yarra Ranges National Park remain closed after the devastating February 2009 bushfires, but these will be reopened gradually as reconstruction works are completed. Stop in the Yarra Valley Visitor Information Centre at Healesville for the best advice on which areas to hike; a free Walks and Riding Trails map is available. You can also check out Parks Victoria's Web site. ⊕ *www.parkweb.vic.au.*

GOLFING **Warburton Golf Club.** Warburton Golf Club is a gem of a course hidden among the Yarra Ranges. For A$30 for 18 holes on weekends (A$24 weekdays) you can golf over meandering streams and bushland blooming with wildflowers. Although it's called a semi-private club, visitors are very welcome to come and play 9 or 18 holes if they ring and book in advance. Rental clubs are available if you didn't pack your own. The course is hilly, and golf buggies can be hired for A$35. Warburton is 30 km (19 mi) southeast of Healesville. ✉ *17 Dammans Rd., Warburton* ☎ *03/5966–2306* ⊕ *www.warburtongolf.com.au.*

WHERE TO STAY
For expanded hotel reviews, visit Fodors.com.

$$$$
Fodor's Choice
★

🏯 **Chateau Yering.** Stockmen William, Donald, and James Ryrie built this homestead in the 1860s, and it was later one of the Yarra Valley's first vineyards. **Pros:** grand living and delicious food. **Cons:** this lifestyle comes at a high price. ⊠ *42 Melba Hwy., Yarra Glen* ☎ *03/9237–3333, 1800/237333* ⊕ *www.chateauyering.com.au* ⤺ *32 suites* ⚿ *In-room: safe, Internet. In-hotel: restaurant, bar, pool, tennis court* ⓞ *Some meals.*

$
★

🏯 **Healesville Hotel.** Housed in a restored 1910 pub, this famous local lodge has seven colorful, modern upstairs rooms (A$130 a night in high season) with high ceilings, tall windows, and genteel touches such as handmade soaps. **Pros:** funky accommodation; great food, historic hotel. **Cons:** limited facilities; share bathrooms. ⊠ *256 Maroondah Hwy.* ☎ *03/5962–4002* ⊕ *www.healesvillehotel.com.au* ⤺ *7 rooms, 2 cottages* ⚿ *In-hotel: restaurant, bar* ⓞ *Breakfast.*

$$$$

🏯 **Mercure Yarra Valley—Balgownie Estate Vineyard Resort and Spa.** This resort has it all—stylish suites and apartment-style accommodations with balconies overlooking the vineyards, plus a ton of other amenities. **Pros:** excellent facilities, on-site cellar door, great day spa. **Cons:** holds conferences, so may get busy at times. ⊠ *Melba Hwy. and Gulf Rd., Yarra Glen* ☎ *03/9730–0700* ⊕ *www.balgownieestate.com.au* ⤺ *14 rooms, 55 suites* ⚿ *In-room: safe, kitchen, Internet, Wi-Fi. In-hotel: restaurant, bar, pool, tennis court, gym, spa, parking* ⓞ *Breakfast.*

THE DANDENONG RANGES

Melburnians come to the beautiful Dandenong Ranges, also known simply as the Dandenongs, for a breath of fresh air, especially in autumn when the deciduous trees turn golden and in spring when the public gardens explode into color with tulip, daffodil, azalea, and rhododendron blooms. At Mt. Dandenong, the highest point (2,077 feet), a scenic lookout known as SkyHigh Mount Dandenong, affords spectacular views over Melbourne and the bay beyond. Dandenong Ranges National Park, which encompasses five smaller parks, including Sherbrooke Forest and Ferntree Gully, has dozens of walking trails. The many villages (which include Olinda, Sassafras, Kalorama, Sherbrooke, and Kallista) have curio shops, art galleries, food emporiums, cafés, and restaurants, and are dotted with lovely B&Bs. Visitors should be aware that the Dandenong Ranges and the high point of Mount Dandenong are completely different from Dandenong city (30 km [19 mi] southeast of Melbourne and on the Pakenham railway line), which is officially designated as an outer suburb of Melbourne.

GETTING HERE AND AROUND
Motorists can either take the Yarra Valley route *(see above)*, and turn off at Lilydale and head south to Montrose and on to Olinda, or take the South Eastern Freeway or M1 (a toll applies) and exit at Ferntree Gully Road. From there, take the Mt. Dandenong Tourist Road and follow it to Olinda, arriving from the south. Trains travel from Flinders Street Station to Belgrave on the Belgrave line. This town is on the southern edge of the Dandenongs and is the home of the steam train

called Puffing Billy. Other towns on the same railway line are Ferntree Gully and Upper Ferntree Gully. Bus 694 runs from Belgrave Station to the Mt. Dandenong Lookout, via the villages of Sherbrooke, Sassafras, and Olinda. Alternatively, take the train from Flinders Street Station to Croydon (on the Lilydale line), then take the 688 bus to Olinda and William Ricketts Sanctuary.

TOURS

Half- and full-day trips from Melbourne are run by local tour operators, including Gray Line and Melbourne's Best Day Tours. Tours of the Dandenongs, including afternoon tea and a ride on a steam-powered train known as Puffing Billy, cost A$93–A$95 (half day) or A$148 (full day with one or more winery stops).

ESSENTIALS

Tour Operators **Gray Line** ✉ *Federation Square, Flinders and Russell Sts., City Center* ☎ *1300/858687* ⊕ *www.grayline.com.au.* **Melbourne's Best Day Tours** ✉ *Federation Square, Flinders and Russell Sts., City Center, Melbourne* ☎ *1300/130550, 03/9397–4911* ⊕ *www.melbournetours.com.au.*

Visitor Information **Dandenong Ranges Information Centre** ✉ *1211 Burwood Hwy., Upper Ferntree Gully* ☎ *03/9758–7522* ⊕ *www.dandenongrangestourism.com.au.*

EXPLORING

Cloudehill Gardens & Nursery. These glorious gardens were first established in the late 1890s as commercial and cut-flower gardens by the Woolrich family (after whom the next door B&B cottage is named). They are divided into 20 "garden rooms" that include the Rhododendrom Woods, the Azalea Walk, and 80-year-old European beech trees. A central terraced area with manicured hedges and a sculpture of a huge vase is stunning, as is the view across the mountain ranges from the garden café. The café serves breakfast, lunch, and afternoon tea; a popular dish is the "Chatter Platter" for two with a selection of cheeses, dips, prawns, and salad. ✉ *89 Olinda-Monbulk Rd., Olinda* ☎ *03/9751–1009* ▢ *A$7.50* ☉ *Gardens daily 10–5; café daily 9:30–5.*

George Tindale Memorial Garden. Azaleas, camellias, and hydrangeas spill down the hillsides in this 6-acre garden. While it is most colorful in spring, when the flowers are in bloom, and in autumn, when the introduced trees turn gold and yellow, it is also beautiful in winter if there is a touch of snow. It's located just 8 km (5 mi) north of Belgrave in the little forest settlement of Sherbrooke, where whipbird calls echo through the trees. ✉ *Sherbrooke Rd., Sherbrooke* ☎ *13–1963* ☉ *Daily 10–5, last entry 4:30.*

National Rhododendron Gardens. Try to visit in October, when the thousands of rhododendrons, azaleas, and camellias put on a spectacular show of white, mauve, yellow, and pink blooms. Several kilometers of walking trails lead to vistas over the Yarra Valley; a small train also provides transportation around the property. The gardens are a short stroll from Olinda village. For a perfect afternoon, combine your visit with tea and scones in one of the many little cafés around town. ✉ *Georgian Rd. off Olinda-Monbulk Rd., Olinda* ☎ *13–1963* ☉ *Daily 10–5, last entry 4:30.*

All aboard the Puffing Billy steam train.

★ **Puffing Billy.** This gleaming narrow-gauge steam train (there are actually five heritage steam engines), based 40 km (25 mi) from Healesville in the town of Belgrave, runs on a line originally built in the early 1900s to open up the Dandenong Ranges to 20th-century pioneers. Today riding the train is a great way to see the foothill landscapes. Daily trips between Belgrave and Emerald Lake pass through picturebook forests and over spectacular wooden trestle bridges. The 13-km (8-mi) trip takes an hour; it's another hour if you continue to the historic town of Gembrook. There are also lunch and dinner trips. ⊠ *Old Monbulk Rd., Belgrave* ☎ *03/9754–6800* ⊕ *www.puffingbilly.com.au* ✉ *A$33; A$52 round-trip* ⊗ *Daily, but hrs vary.*

SkyHigh Mount Dandenong. This lookout at the top of Mt. Dandenong has breathtaking views over Melbourne to the Mornington Peninsula and Port Phillip Bay. You can picnic or barbecue on the grounds, eat at the bistro (lunch and dinner), or stroll along the pleasant English Garden Walk while the kids get lost in the hedge maze. Other fun attractions include a Wishing Tree and the Giant's Chair. ⊠ *26 Observatory Rd., Mt. Dandenong* ☎ *03/9751–0443* ⊕ *www.skyhighmtdandenong.com. au* ✉ *A$5 parking; maze A$6 adults, A$4 children* ⊗ *Daily from 10 am; 8 am on weekends, bistro open lunch and dinner daily.*

★ **William Ricketts Sanctuary.** Fern gardens, moss-covered rocks, waterfalls, towering mountain ash, and kiln-fired sculptures of Aborigines and Australian native animals fill this 4-acre property on Mt. Dandenong. William Ricketts, who established the sanctuary in the 1930s, meant it to stand as an embodiment of his philosophy: that people must act as custodians of the natural environment as the Aborigines did. ⊠ *Mt.*

Dandenong Tourist Rd., Mt. Dandenong ☎ *13–1963 Parks Victoria, 03/9751-1300 Sanctuary* ⊙ *Daily 10–4:30.*

OUTDOOR ACTIVITIES

GOLFING **Olinda Golf Course.** The Olinda Golf Course was originally built in 1952 to act as a firebreak. Today this 18-hole course has some pretty steep fairways and fabulous views. Stop by the on-site restaurant for a drink or light meal after a game. ⊠ *75 Olinda-Monbulk Rd., Olinda* ☎ *03/9751–1399* ⊕ *www.olindagolfcourse.com.au* ⟋ *A$20 18 holes; A$15 9 holes.*

HIKING **Danenong Ranges National Park.** Danenong Ranges National Park is made up of several reserves, including the Sherbrooke Forest, which contains Sherbrooke Falls. Trails include the Olinda Forest Trail (from Mt. Dandenong to Kallista), the Western Trail from the top of Mt. Dandenong to Ferntree Gully, the Sherbrooke Loop, and the Tourist Track from Sassafras to Emerald. Brochures and a trail map are available from the visitor information center at Upper Ferntree Gully and some cafés in the area. Trail maps can also be found on the park's Web site. ⊕ *www. parkweb.vic.gov.au.*

Heidelberg School Artists' Trail. Heidelberg School Artists' Trail is a great way to stay fit and brush up on Australian art. The trail commemorates famous Melbourne artists of the late 19th century, including Arthur Streeton, Tom Roberts, and Frederick McCubbin, who all painted around the Heidelberg area east of Melbourne. The Dandenongs section of this 40-km (25-mi) trail (which begins in Templestowe, Melbourne) displays 9 of the route's 57 interpretive signs explaining the artists' work. ☎ *13–1963 (Parks Victoria)* ⊕ *www.artiststrail.com.*

WHERE TO EAT AND STAY

For expanded hotel reviews, visit Fodors.com.

Olinda is the main village in the Dandenong Ranges region and a good base for exploring the area. It's actually two villages (Lower and Upper Olinda, the latter being the prettier) connected by Monash Road, where you'll find a lot of the town's B&Bs and self-catering cottages. Olinda has a handful of good restaurants and cafés, and 26 specialty boutique stores including curio shops and fashion and gift shops. It's a short drive from here to the National Rhododendrom Gardens, the golf course, Olinda Falls picnic grounds, Cloudehill Gardens, and various hiking trails.

$$ ✕ **Ranges.** This café-restaurant right in the heart of Olinda buzzes all
EUROPEAN day, and is the perfect place for a snack or meal after browsing the nearby curio shops or gardens. It's open daily for breakfast, lunch, and morning and afternoon tea, and dinner Tuesday to Saturday. Lunchtime fare includes slow-cooked lamb salad with pickled beetroot and Persian feta, and quince-glazed lamb backstrap wrapped in pancetta; at night you might want to begin with a cocktail while browsing the menu of hearty steaks and Asian-inspired specialties, such as curry-style bouillabaisse of mussels and prawns. ⊠ *5 Main St., Olinda* ☎ *03/9751–2133* ⊕ *www.ranges.com.au* ⊙ *No dinner Sun. and Mon.*

$ ✕ **Ripe.** With crackling open fires in winter and a covered deck for sum-
AUSTRALIAN mer grazing, this buzzy cottage café-cum-providore is the perfect place for a heartwarming casual lunch or afternoon tea. Savory offerings

5

might include carrot and ginger soup, or 18-hour pork hock slow-braised in sticky soy caramel with creamy parsnip mash. And while the Dandenongs have a long tradition of Devonshire teas, this café is proudly scone-free; temptation here comes in the shape of mouthwatering cakes, all made with free-range eggs. You can also buy relishes, cheeses, and fresh Yarra Valley pasta to cook yourself—the smoked trout and goat cheese ravioli is scrumptious. ⊠ *376–378 Mount Dandenong Tourist Rd., Sassafras* ☎ *03/9755–2100* ⊘ *No dinner.*

> **PERFECT PICNICS**
>
> The Dandenongs are heaven for fresh-air freaks and food-ies. Pick up some goodies at Olinda's Saturday morning market and work up an appetite taking the 2-km (1½-mi) loop walk to Sherbrooke Falls from Donohue Picnic Grounds. Ask the tourist office about other great walks and picnic spots.

$$
EUROPEAN
✕ **Wild Oak Restaurant and Bar.** A great way to warm up on the often crisp days and cool nights in the Dandenongs is with a bowl of New England–style clam chowder and house-baked sourdough bread at this popular restaurant in Lower Olinda village. A hearty winter dish is the pan-seared kangaroo fillet with native spice dukkah, parsnip tartlet, and roasted fig jus. Chef and owner Ben Higgs also conducts hands-on cooking classes with different themes for groups (minimum four people). Jazz performers play on the last Friday night of every month. ⊠ *232 Ridge Rd., at Mt. Dandenong Rd., Olinda* ☎ *03/9751–2033* ⊘ *Closed Mon. and Tues.*

$$$
⌅ **Candlelight Cottage.** Curl up with a book in front of the open fire in this 1880s cottage and you might be tempted not to do anything else in the Dandenongs. **Pros:** cozy rustic decor; good facilities and modern appliances. **Cons:** two night minimum stay on weekends, minibar treats cost extra. ⊠ *7–9 Monash Ave., Olinda* ☎ *03/9751–2464* 🖷 *03/9751–0552* ☎ *1300/553 011* ⊕ *www.candlelightcottages.com.au* ↬ *4 cottages* ⚴ *In-room: no a/c, kitchen, Wi-Fi. In-hotel: some pets allowed* ⎟⊘⎟ *Breakfast.*

MORNINGTON PENINSULA

The Mornington Peninsula circles the southeastern half of Port Phillip Bay. A much larger piece of land than it first appears, the peninsula is lapped by water on three sides and measures about 65 km (40 mi) by 35 km (22 mi). Along the Port Phillip Bay coast is a string of seaside villages stretching from the larger towns of Frankston and Mornington to the summer holiday towns of Mount Martha, Rosebud, Rye, Sorrento, and Portsea (which has one of the most dramatic beaches in the region). On the Western Port Bay side the smaller settlements of Flinders, Somers, and Hastings have quieter beaches without the crowds.

Together with Main Ridge and Merricks, Red Hill is one of the state's premium producers of cool-climate wines, particularly Pinot Noir and Shiraz. The majority of the peninsula's 60 wineries are clustered around Red Hill and Red Hill South; however, there are another dozen or more dotted around areas farther north, including Moorooduc, Dromana,

Artist sculptor William Ricketts (1898–1993) Mount Dandenong.

and Mount Martha. For an afternoon of fine wine, excellent seafood, and spectacular coastal views, plan a route that winds between vineyards. Red Hill has a busy produce and crafts market, which has been operating for 34 years and shows no signs of abating. It's held on the first Saturday morning of each month from September to May. A good Web site for getting all the lowdown on peninsular wineries is ⊕ *www. visitmorningtonvineyards.com.*

Sorrento is one of the region's prettiest beach towns and one of the most popular day-tripper spots on the peninsula. It's also the peninsula's oldest settlement, and thus is dotted with numerous historic buildings and National Trust sites (among them the Collins Settlement Historical Site, which marks the first settlement site at Sullivan Bay; and the Nepean Historical Society Museum, with its displays of Aboriginal artifacts and settlers' tools). In summer the town transforms from a sleepy seaside village into a hectic holiday hot spot. Sorrento Back Beach, with its rock pools and cliff-side trails, and Point King, with its piers and boathouses, are the two most popular hangouts.

GETTING HERE AND AROUND

Renting a car in Melbourne and driving south along the Nepean Highway is the most practical way of seeing the Mornington Peninsula. At Frankston you can take the Frankston-Moorooduc Highway or stay on the Nepean Highway—eventually they both merge into the Mornington Peninsula Highway, which continues south to the various bayside towns. A train runs from Flinders Street Station to Frankston. At Frankston, connect with a diesel-train service to towns on the east of the peninsula including Hastings, Bittern, Point Crib, and Stony Point.

Buses also run from Frankston to the bayside towns; the No. 781 bus goes to Mornington and Mount Martha and the No. 782 bus travels to Hastings and Flinders on the Western Port side.

Inter Island Ferries runs a passenger service from Stony Point (on the eastern side of the peninsula) to Phillip Island, while the Queenscliff–Sorrento car and passenger ferry is the best way to travel between these two towns on opposite sides of the bay. The Frankston and Peninsula airport shuttle bus runs from Melbourne Airport's international terminal to Frankstown and several other Mornington Peninsula towns.

TIMING

Set aside at least a day for a drive down the peninsula, planning time for lunch and wine tasting, an afternoon clifftop walk along the bluffs, or even a game of golf at Cape Schanck, one of 30 golf courses in the region. In summer pack a swimsuit and sunscreen for impromptu ocean dips as you make your way around the peninsula's string of attractive beaches. Be careful when driving along the tree-lined roads of the peninsula hinterland (the interior areas where most of the wineries are located). The wineries are tucked away and often hard to see, so slow down, as you may have to make a sudden turn into a driveway.

WINERY TOURS

Amour of the Grape. Set winery tours for groups of two to six passengers and personal tours for those who want to devise their own itinerary are this company's specialty. The day's outing includes tastings at four or five preselected cellar doors, and a gourmet lunch and a glass of wine at a boutique winery café. Passengers coming from Melbourne will be picked up and delivered back to the Frankston railway station. ⊠ *Box 529, Mt. Martha* ☎ *03/5974–3286* ⊕ *www.amourofthegrape.com.au* ✒ *A$142.50 per person Mornington Peninsula pickup; central Melbourne pickup A$165 per person (for 4 to 6 people).*

Wine Tours Victoria. This Melbourne-based company operates private tours of two to ten people using minivans. They visit four to five wineries that may include Box Stallion, Willow Creek, and Red Hill Estate. Lunch with wine and coffee are also on the menu. ⊠ *9 The Willows, Gisborne* ☎ *03/5428–8500, 1300/946386* ⊕ *www.winetours. com.au* ✒ *A$150.*

ESSENTIALS

Transportation **Frankston and Peninsula Airport Shuttle** ☎ *03/9783–1199* ⊕ *www.fapas.com.au.* **Inter Island Ferries** ☎ *03/9585–5730* ⊕ *www. interislandferries.com.au.* **Sorrento-Queenscliff Ferry** ☎ *03/5258–3244* ⊕ *www.searoad.com.au.*

Visitor Information **Mornington Community Information and Support Centre** ⊠ *320 Main St., Mornington* ☎ *03/5975–1644* ⊕ *www.morninfo.org.au.* **Mornington Peninsula Visitor Information Centre** ⊠ *359B Point Nepean Rd., Dromana* ☎ *03/5987–3078, 1800/804009* ⊕ *www.visitmorningtonpeninsula.org.*

EXPLORING

Arthurs Seat State Park. Sweeping views of the surrounding countryside, Port Phillip Bay, Port Phillip Heads, and—on a clear day—the city skyline, the You Yangs, and Mt. Macedon are the attractions at

Arthurs Seat State Park. The mountain, which gives the park its name, is the highest point on the Mornington Peninsula; it was named after Arthurs Seat in Edinburgh. A marked scenic drive snakes its way up to the summit, and walking tracks meander through the park's stands of eucalyptus. Seawinds, a public garden established by a local gardener in the 1940s, also forms part of the park and is a 10-minute walk or about 500 yards away. The road from Mornington is open at all times, so you can enjoy the spectacular mountaintop view by day or at night to see the lights. The once-popular chairlift at the state park has been idle since 2006, however there are plans to rebuild and reopen the ride in 2013. ⌧ *Arthurs Seat Rd. at Mornington Peninsula Hwy., Arthur's Seat* ☎ *13/1963* ⊕ *www.parkweb.vic.gov.au* ✉ *Free.*

WORD OF MOUTH

"I agree if you are going to visit wineries that it might be best to take a tour and then you don't need to watch what you drink. Australian police are very vigilant regarding drink driving, and the legal limit in Victoria is 0.05. Why not take a car for some of the day trips and a bus for the rest? Then you have the best of both worlds."
—lavandula

EXPLORING THE WINERIES

A small bus tour that visits four to five wineries is the best way to explore the region. Tours leave from Melbourne and from peninsula towns. Most of the wineries listed here also have excellent restaurants on-site, and many of the restaurants we list are located in wineries, so there's no need to go hungry or thirsty!

Box Stallion. Box Stallion winery and restaurant are housed in a rustic redbrick barn that once housed the Thoroughbred stallions of the illustrious Muranna Park racing stable. A visit is a reminder of the other important Mornington Peninsula industry—horse breeding. The winery, set on 100 acres, is not only full of country charm, but is said to be the peninsula's leading producer of varietal wine. The Shiraz is the stable's most awarded wine, while their Sauvignon Blanc and Pinot Noir have picked up a few medals as well. All wines are grown and made on the estate by winemaker Alex White. Tours can be arranged for the technically savvy visitor with advance notice. Meals, served either indoors in the barn Cellar Door (the former horse boxes have been retained as dining areas for small groups) or outside under big canvas umbrellas, will not break the bank. A grazing platter of many delicacies such as eggplant rolls filled with ricotta cheese, cheeses, olives, and dips suits two people (A$35), and the lemon, garlic, and parsley prawns on a risotto of celery and saffron is A$30. The starters (or entrées as they're called in Australia) are cheaper and are often quite large. On Sunday there's live music (blues and country folk) from 12:30 pm. Wine tastings are free, but there are no group tastings on Sunday during the busy hours of 11–3. ⌧ *64 Tubbarubba Rd., Merricks North* ☎ *03/5989–7444* ⊕ *www.boxstallion.com.au* ☉ *Daily 11–5.*

Crittenden Estate. Crittenden Estate is one of the area's most picturesque wineries, with a lovely lakeside setting. Run by Garry Crittenden and his son Rollo, it produces Chardonnay, Pinot Noir, Pinot Grigio, and

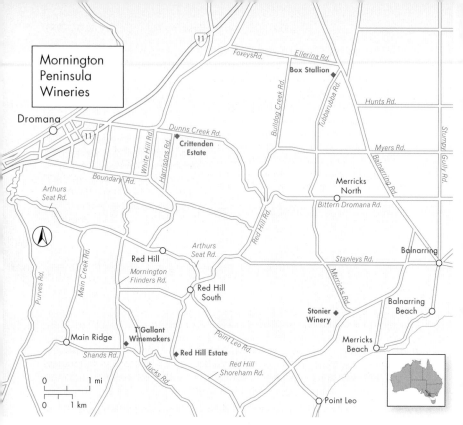

Mornington
Peninsula
Wineries

recently some Spanish styles under the new Los Hermanos label. The flagship Crittenden Estate Pinot Noir and Chardonnay are made from vines that are among the oldest on the peninsula. The cellar door is open for tastings daily; it doubles as a small area produce store selling olives, olive oil, dakka, and other morsels perfect to have while sipping wine. The tasting room is wonderfully warm in winter, and while you sip away you can admire the artworks that adorn the walls. The restaurant, Stillwater at Crittenden, is lovely year-round, and when the weather is fine diners sit out on a terrace under shady umbrellas while enjoying views over the lake. The braised pork belly with seared scallops is one of chef Zac Poulier's best dishes. It is open daily for lunch and weekends for dinner. ⊠ *25 Harrisons Rd., Dromana* ☎ *03/5981–8322 winery, 03/5981–9555 restaurant* ⊕ *www.crittendenwines.com.au* ☉ *Daily 11–4.*

Red Hill Estate. Red Hill Estate has picked up numerous medals for its Chardonnay, Pinot Noir, and Shiraz; and if they were giving out medals for location, it would claim them all. Not only are there sweeping views of the 22-acre vineyards, but the magnificent waters of Western Port Bay are spread out in the distance. On clear days you see right over to Phillip Island and beyond to Wilsons Promontory as you wander around the gardens. Be sure to stop at **Max's Restaurant**

(☎ *03/5931–0177, www.maxsrestaurant.com.au. No dinner Sun.–Thurs.).* Its award-winning cuisine and fabulous floor-to-ceiling windows make it the perfect place to while away at least half the day. You might start with Max's own antipasto, which could include a mini-soup of the day, baby calamari, house-cured scallop ceviche, carpaccio, and mini-herb, red wine, and garlic-marinated kangaroo. For dessert, don't miss the rhubarb crumble with house-made apple and white peppercorn ice cream. Although it may be a little chilly, winter is a good time to visit the winery, as several events are staged, including the Barrel Art Show, the Winter Winery Week in June, and a huge Tuscan feast in July. ✉ *53 Shoreham Rd., Red Hill South* ☎ *03/5989–2838* ⊕ *www.redhillestate.com.au* ⊙ *Daily 11–5.*

Stonier Winery. Established in 1978, Stonier Winery is considered a preeminent Mornington Peninsula producer of wines, made from the region's oldest vines. Owners Brian Stonier and his wife Noel have concentrated on Chardonnay and Pinot Noir (produced from vines first planted in 1978 and 1982, respectively) and more recently introduced a sparkling—the Stonier Pinot Noir Chardonnay. Although there's no restaurant, platters of local Red Hill cheeses accompany the daily tastings, and if time permits, visitors may be invited on an informal tour of the fermentation and barrel rooms. Several events take place during the year, such as the Pie and Pinot day in June (part of the regional Winter Wine Weekend), and Oyster Shucking and Sparkling in December. ✉ *Frankston–Flinders Rd. and Thompsons La., Merricks* ☎ *03/5989–8300* ⊕ *www.stoniers.com.au.*

★ **T'Gallant Winemakers.** T'Gallant Winemakers celebrates 15 years in business, and its Italian-theme winery and restaurant continue to grow in popularity. Winemaker Kevin McCarthy planted the first Pinto Grigio vines on the peninsula. If you're a stylist as well as an oenophile, you'll also admire the beautiful label artwork. He also produces Pinot Noir, Chardonnay, and Muscat à Petits Grains. La Baracca Trattoria and the alfresco Spuntino Bar are always buzzing (just close your eyes and think of Italy)—the food is exceptional, with dishes made from local ingredients, including from the house herb garden. Tuck into a crisp-based pizza or grilled sausages in the bar or try the trattoria's chicken braised with Pinot Gris, or gnocchi with slow-braised "sticky" duck. The cellar door and restaurant/bar are open seven days a week, there's live music every weekend at lunchtime and occasional cabaret nights. You can also sign up for the year-round Tre Gusti Cooking Classes. ✉ *1385 Mornington–Flinders Rd., at Shand Rd., Main Ridge* ☎ *03/5989–6565* ⊕ *www.tgallant.com.au* ⊙ *Daily 10–5.*

OUTDOOR ACTIVITIES

DIVING AND SNORKELING **Bayplay Adventure Tours.** Bayplay Adventure Tours is an operator that does it all—including diving, snorkeling, bike riding, and sea kayaking. Explore colonies of weedy seadragons, swim through an octupus's garden, or feel the wash when dolphins leap over your kayak. Dives start from A$55, while a three-hour sea kayaking tour to a dolphin sanctuary costs A$99 per person. ✉ *3755 Port Nepean Rd., Portsea* ☎ *03/5984–0888* ⊕ *www.bayplay.com.au.*

Continued on page 282

In recent decades Australia has emerged as an international wine powerhouse. The country's varied climate has proven favorable for growing high-quality grapes, and winemakers now produce some of the world's best Shiraz (Syrah) wines, as well as acclaimed Pinot Noirs and Rieslings. Wine sales currently contribute about $5.5 billion to the country's economy, and Australia is the third largest supplier to the United States behind France and Italy.

Touring wineries here is easy, as most properties have tasting rooms with regular hours. Whether you're sipping *in situ* at a winery or tasting wines at a shop in Sydney, here's how to get the most from your wine experience.

By Erica Watson

(top) Pinot noir grapes (right) Vineyard in One Tree Hill, South Australia

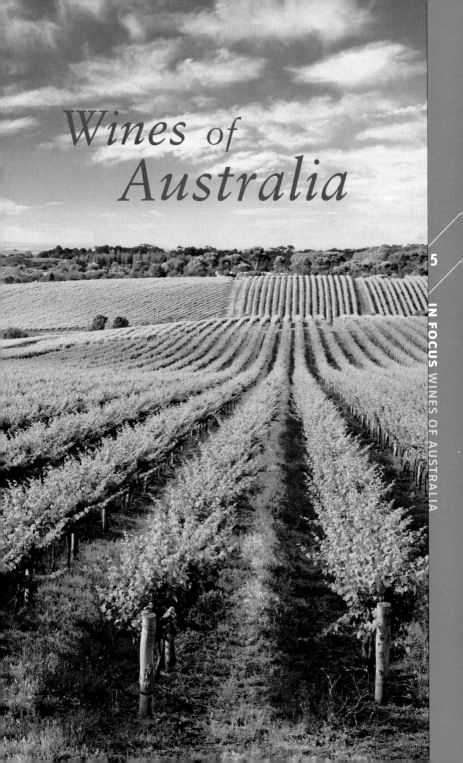

Wines of Australia

WINE TRENDS: THEN AND NOW

(top left) Wine bottles await labels, (bottom left) Hunter Valley vista, (right) tasting in Barossa Valley

Although the first grapes in Australia arrived with British settlers in 1787, it really wasn't until the mid 1960s that a more refined tradition of wine making began to take hold. Prior to 1960, Australia's wine repertoire extended little beyond sherry and port, but after WWII, an influx of European immigrants, notably from Germany and Italy, opened the country's eyes to new tastes and production methods.

Australia now produces many classic varietals at prices from A$10 to A$40,000 (for a 1951 Penfolds Grange Hermitage, made by Australian pioneer Max Schubert). There are more than 60 wine regions dotted across the country and many of the smaller producers in lesser-known areas are beginning to flourish.

Although the industry has experienced rapid growth, it hasn't been without its problems. The health of the global economy, international competition, global warming, disease, drought, and bushfire have each presented challenges along the way.

These days, Australian vintners are known for combining old traditions with new ideas and technical innovations. While oak barrels are still widely used, stainless steel and plastic tanks are now recognized as suitable fermentation and storage methods. Screw caps, introduced a decade ago, are becoming more popular with winemakers and consumers.

The industry's lastest trends also include a growing interest in environmental sustainability, with organic and biodynamic wines appearing from numerous producers. The internet has revolutionized business, giving even the smallest vintners access to an international stage.

Like well-cellared wine, the palate of modern Australia is continually maturing. Whether your taste is for robust reds from Coonawarra and Barossa or the delicate and versatile whites of the Hunter Valley and Margaret River, Australia's winemakers are producing beautiful wines perfect to enjoy now or later.

AUSTRALIA'S DOMINANT VARIETALS

REDS

SHIRAZ
Australia's classic varietal. A full-bodied wine that, in hot areas, makes an earthy expression with softer acidity. Cooler regions produce a leaner, peppery style.

CABERNET SAUVIGNON
Dark red with blackcurrant and black cherry flavors, often with firm tannins and more acidity than Shiraz.

MERLOT
Intensely purple colored, full-bodied wine characterized by moderate tannins, aromas of plum, and a velvety mouth-feel.

PINOT NOIR
Lighter-bodied with gentle tannins and fruity aromas of red berries.

WHITES

CHARDONNAY
Full-bodied wine that is often high in alcohol and low in acidity. Most Australian versions are oaked.

RIESLING
Lighter-bodied wines with citrus and honey notes. Most are unoaked and dry or slightly off-dry.

SAUVIGNON BLANC
Makes crisp, dry wines with high acid and aromas of peach and lime.

SEMILLON
Light-bodied wines that have crisp acidity and complex flavors, including herbs, nuts, and honey.

WHITE BLENDS
Chardonnay-Semillon and Sauvignon Blanc-Semillon blends are popular. Semillon adds bright notes.

5

IN FOCUS WINES OF AUSTRALIA

WINE TOURING TIPS

Large vintners like Rosemount, McGuigan Wines, Jacobs Creek, Yalumba, and Wolf Blass are well equipped for visitors and many offer vineyard tours, as well as restaurants or cafes. Some require appointments.

Many boutique producers also have "cellar doors," a.k.a. tasting rooms, open seven days a week, but it is advisable to check their websites for details. The average tastings cost around A$10 to A$15 for a flight of up to five different styles. Some include cheese, cracker, and fruit plates.

Winery in Clare Valley

AUSSIE WINE REGIONS

SOUTH AUSTRALIA

Barossa Valley

❶ BAROSSA VALLEY The country's best-known wine region, Barossa Valley has more than 550 grape growers, including some fifth- and sixth-generation families. Shiraz is highly celebrated, particularly the lauded Penfolds Grange. Cabernet Sauvignon, Grenache, Merlot, Riesling, Semillon, and Chardonnay are all well suited to Barossa's temperate climate, which is slightly cooler on its peaks and in neighboring Eden Valley. Big producers Jacobs Creek and Wolf Blass both have visitors centers with modern tasting rooms and restaurants. For a history lesson, take a tour at Langmeil Winery. An impressive property is Yalumba, with a stone winery and clock tower. So, too, is the well-established Peter Lehmann Estate on the banks of the North Para River.

❷ ADELAIDE HILLS For world-class Chardonnays, Sauvignon Blancs, Rieslings, and sparkling wines, look to the Adelaide Hills. Just 25 minutes from the center of Adelaide, this high-altitude region, amid Mount Lofty and down through the Piccadilly Valley, has nurtured elegantly refined white wines. The cooler climate also means that it's one of South Australia's leading producer of the temperamental Pinot Noir. There are about 25 cellars that offer tastings, including Petaluma Cellar, well known for its sparkling wines, Rieslings, and Chardonnays as well as its modern Bridgewater Mill restaurant. To try Italian varietals, head to Chain of Ponds. For excellent Sauvignon Blanc, stop into Shaw and Smith's 46-hectare estate.

Adelaide Hills

❸ MCLAREN VALE Situated in the Fleurieu Peninsula region, McLaren Vale is an easy 40-minute trip south of Adelaide. Uniquely located by the coast, it's regarded as one of the more unpretentious regions thanks to laid-back beach lifestyle, passionate vintners, and family-owned wineries. This fusion of ideals, together with its warm climate, has most likely sparked its interest in experimenting with more exotic varieties such as Tempranillo, Zinfandel, and Mourvedre, as well as Viognier and Sangiovese. There are more than 60 cellar tasting rooms, ranging from the large producers such as Rosemount Estate and Tintara Winery to boutique producers such as Wirra Wirra, D'Arenberg, and Gemtree, each offering sales and wine flights that include the chance to sample local foods.

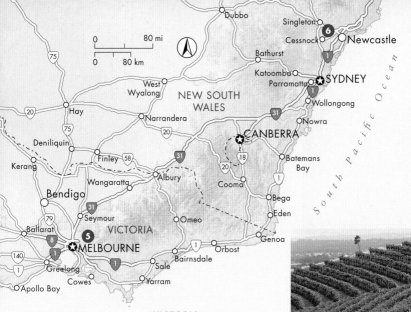

Hunter Valley

④ LIMESTONE COAST

Coonawarra's long ripening season coupled with the region's "terra rossa" soil atop rich limestone beds is responsible for some of Australia's most famed wines, most notably full-bodied reds. Often described as the Bordeaux of Australia, Coonawarra is a top spot for Cabernet Sauvignon, Cabernet blends, and spicy Shiraz. And they don't come any better than at places like Penley, Katnook Estate, Hollick, and Wynns Coonawarra Estate. Sixty kilometers to the north is Padthaway. While reds still prevail, the region's slightly warmer climate produces fruity Chardonnay and enjoyable Sauvignon Blanc, Verdelho, and Riesling. Built from limestone in 1882, the historic Padthaway Estate provides the perfect backdrop to sample some of the regions finest. Stonehaven and Henry's Drive are also worth a visit.

VICTORIA
⑤ YARRA VALLEY

Close proximity to Melbourne makes the Yarra an easy choice if your touring time is limited. A cool climate and diverse mix of volcanic and clay soils have allowed Chardonnay and Pinot Noir to flourish. Other notable varieties here include Viognier, Gewürztraminer, Pinot Gris, and Sauvignon Blanc, as well as Malbec, Sangiovese, and Nebbiolo. Sparkling wine is also a winner and Domaine Chandon is a magnificent spot to enjoy some perfect bubbly. For a laidback experience, Lillydale is also a good choice. But upping the style stakes is the magnificent Yering Station with its modern Australian restaurant and gallery space. Elsewhere, De Bortoli sells delicious top-end wines.

Yarra Valley

NEW SOUTH WALES
⑥ HUNTER VALLEY

Despite being a producer of award-winning Chardonnay, Verdelho, and Shiraz, it's the honeyed Semillon, which can mature for up to two decades, that Hunter Valley does best. Split into upper and lower regions, it has more that 150 years of winemaking up its sleeve and 120 cellar doors. It's safe to say the Hunter knows how to entertain. From large-scale music concerts at Bimbadgen Estate and Tempus Two to the annual Jazz in the Vines event and other small food and wine festivals year-round, the region is constantly buzzing. Pokolbin, Broke, Wollombi, Lovedale, Rothbury and Mt View are the main areas to sample the regions best offerings. Autumn is an excellent time to visit.

AUSSIE WINE REGIONS

Margaret River

WESTERN AUSTRALIA

7 MARGARET RIVER

REGION With the first vines planted in 1967, Margaret River might be one of the country's younger wine areas but that hasn't stopped it from producing exception-ally high quality vintages. Cool breezes from the Indian Ocean and a steady, Mediterranean-style climate offer perfect conditions for developing complex styles of Chardonnay and minty-toned Cabernet Sauvignons. Shiraz, Merlot, Semillon, Sauvignon Blanc, and Chenin Blanc also thrive. Although the area produces about 20% of Australia's premium wines, it only accounts for about 3% of the nation's grapes. Try the West Australian Marron—or crayfish—with a crisp glass of Leeuwin Estate chardonnay. Cape Mentelle and Evans & Tate are also among the region's highlights, with many of their special releases sold only through their cellar doors.

READING THE LABEL

According to Australia's Label Integrity Program, when a wine label states region, grape variety, or vintage, then 85% of the wine contained in the bottle must come from that region, variety, or vintage.

1 The producer of the wine.

2 The vintage year, meaning the year the grapes were picked, crushed, and bottled.

3 Australian GIs, or Geographic Indica-tions, identify the region where the wine grapes were grown.

4 The varietal, or type of grapes used to make the wine.

5 The wine in this bottle contains 12% alcohol content by volume.

6 The wine's country of origin.

7 The volume of wine in the bottle.

Art Series

1 LEEUWIN ESTATE

2 2006
3 MARGARET RIVER
4 RIESLING

5 12.0% vol **6** WINE OF AUSTRALIA **7** 750mL

MORE TASTING OPPORTUNITIES

Wine tasting at Mitchell Winery, Clare Valley

SIPPING IN SHOPS AND BARS

Even when you're not ensconced in the country's lush vineyards, high-quality wine isn't far away. The capital cities serve as a gateway for many of the wine country's top tastes.

In Sydney, try wine bars like the **Ivy's Ash Street Cellar**, **Glass Brasserie** wine bar at the Hilton Hotel and the **Gazebo Wine Garden** in Elizabeth Bay. The **Australian Wine Centre** in Circular Quay offers private tastings (with prior notice) and the **Ultimo Wine Centre** has free tastings each Saturday.

Heading south, visit **Melbourne's Prince Wine Store** at one of its three locations. Or soak up the atmosphere at **The Melbourne Supper Club** or **Melbourne Wine Room**. The bar of the award-winning **Press Club** restaurant also has an excellent Australian and international selection.

Apothecary 1878 on Adelaide's Hindley Street and **The Wine Underground**, just a few blocks away, both have a cosmopolitan ambience. Smaller vineyards are well represented at the city's **East End Cellars**.

In Perth, wine and dine alfresco at **Must Winebar** in Highgate. And **Amphoras Bar** in West Perth also has a long list of the country's best wines by the glass and bottle. No visit would be complete without heading to **East Fremantle's Wine Shop & Wine Liaisons**, for regular tastings and an extensive range of bottles. It also has an online store.

WINE FESTIVALS

Festivals offer chance to interact with the winemakers as well as sample local produce, especially cheese, fruit, and seafood. **The Barossa Vintage Festival** is one of the largest and longest running wine events in South Australia. Held in April each year it has everything from rare wine auctions to family friendly events. Other notables are **Adelaide's Tasting Australia** (April), **Coonawarra After Dark Wine Festival** (April), and **McLaren Vale Sea and Vines Festival** (June). In Western Australia, the **Margaret River Wine Region Festival** (April) celebrates wine with music and art.

RESEARCH & PLANNING

A little planning will allow you to make the perfect choices when it comes to deciding which regions to visit and where to taste. The websites of Australia's tourism commissions are filled with helpful planning informations. Not only do they offer winery information but also options for tours, accommodation and other sights to see while in the area. These include ⊕ www.visitvictoria.com, ⊕ www.southaustralia.com, www.winecountry.com.au, ⊕ www.westernaustralia.com

Once on the ground, visitors centers such as the **Margaret River Wine Centre**, **Adelaide's National Wine Centre of Australia**, and **Hunter Valley Wine Country Tourism** can offer sound advice, especially on the best varietals and history of the regions.

For further history, regional information, and primary producers, visit ⊕ www.wine.org.au or ⊕ www.australianwines.com.au

Barossa Vintage Festival

BE AMAZED

Victorians do love their mazes, and you'll find these quaint English-garden features dotted around the Mornington Peninsula. These maze complexes have topiary and sculptured creations, mystery lawn puzzles, and big garden chess sets.

Enchanted Maze Garden. Find your way through a traditional hedge maze or test your navigational skills in the indoor 3D maze at the Enchanted Maze Garden, which also has an "amazing" candy shop. ⊠ *55 Purves Rd., Arthur's Seat* ☎ *03/5981–8449* ⊕ *www.enchantedmaze.com.au* ✉ *A$25* ⊙ *10–6, last maze entry 4:30pm.*

Aschombe Maze & Lavender Gardens. Check out the world's first circular rose maze, two Cypress-hedge mazes and a lavender labyrinth at Aschombe Maze & Lavender Gardens, handily located not far from T'Gallant Winery. ⊠ *15 Shoreham Rd., Shoreham* ☎ *03/5989–8387* ⊕ *www.ashcombemaze.com.au* ✉ *A$17.50* ⊙ *10–5.*

GOLF **Rosebud Park Public Golf Course.** Situated on the steep slopes of Arthurs Seat overlooking Rosebud and Port Phillip Bay, Rosebud Park Public Golf Course provides spectacular views of hinterland farmland and down the coast to Sorrento. The 18-hole course has some extremely challenging holes, a resident teaching professional, plenty of parking, and excellent picnic facilities. ⊠ *Elizabeth Dr., Rosebud* ☎ *03/5981–2833* ⊕ *www.rosebudpark.com.au* ✉ *18-holes A$33 (A$22 on weekdays in winter).*

HIKING The Mornington Peninsula is a memorable walking destination. There are walks for all levels of fitness and interest from clifftop strolls to the ultimate 26-km (16-mi) Two Bays Walking Track. Stop in at the visitor information centers at Dromana or Mornington to see what walking maps they have on hand, or contact Parks Victoria, the government body that manages the state's national parks.

Here are some walks to get you started:

Arthurs Seat State Park: There is a one-hour circuit walk to Kings Falls, and the relaxing Seawinds Gardens walk is less than a mile in length and takes only about half an hour.

Bushrangers Bay Walk: An exhilarating 6-km (4-mi) return walk along Western Port Bay begins at Cape Schanck Lighthouse and winds past basalt cliffs and Bushranger Bay, to finish at Main Creek.

Coppin's Track: A pleasant 3-km (2-mi) round-trip walk that stretches from Sorrento ocean beach (or Back Beach as it's known) to Jubliee point along the Bass Strait coastline.

Two Bays Walking Track: A hard-core 26-km (16-mi) walking track that links Dromana, on Port Phillip Bay, with Cape Schnank on Western Port Bay.

MP Walking Tours. MP Walking Tours has half- and full-day guided outings, including one along the Millionaires Walk, viewing lovely vistas and expensive mansions in Sorrento and Portsea. A two-day coast-to-coast walk costs A$80 per person per day including packed lunch, and is cheaper if more people join the walk; you can stay overnight in a cottage at Cape Schanck Lighthouse at your own expense (about A$150 including breakfast). ⊠ *29 Hughes Rd.* ☎ *03/5984–4484, 0412/135142 mobile* ⊕ *www.mornpenwalks.com.au.*

Parks Victoria. Parks Victoria is the government agency that manages all of Victoria's national parks. Its informative Web site includes information on bushfire danger and park attractions. ☎ *13/1963* ⊕ *www. parkweb.vic.gov.au.*

HORSEBACK
RIDING

Ace-Hi Beach Rides. In addition to a lot of horses, Ace-Hi Beach Rides runs a 200-acre adventure park complete with a wildlife sanctuary and lots of activities for kids, including pony rides, rock wall climbing, and swinging through the air on a flying fox device. Horse rides start from A$44 for an hour. ⊠ *810 Boneo Rd., Cape Schanck* ☎ *03/5988–6262* ⊕ *www.ace-hi.com.au.*

WHERE TO EAT AND STAY
For expanded hotel reviews, visit Fodors.com.

$$$
FRENCH
Fodor'sChoice
★

✕ **Montalto Vineyard & Olive Grove.** Overlooking an established vineyard with vistas of rolling green hills, this place serves French-inspired cuisine. Chef Barry Davis prepares such creative dishes as Port Phillip Bay snapper fillet with confit fennel, kipfler potato, and mussel and saffron beurre blanc; the dish is best matched with a 2009 "The Eleven" Montalto Chardonnary. The menu changes daily, based on the local produce available. The wine list borrows from the best of the estate's vintages, as well as classic wines from other regions. The open-air Piazza café (open weekends) dishes up pizza, warming winter soups, and summer salads. If it's a nice day, you can picnic on the grounds from hampers prepared by the restaurant. Take a moment to check out the herb garden and admire the 17 sculptures on permanent display. If you're visiting from mid-February to late April you'll be able to see the entries in the Montalto Sculpture Prize and vote for your favorite. The expansive property also includes a natural wetlands and specially built boardwalks, so visitors have a chance of spotting more than 90 bird species. ⊠ *33 Shoreham Rd., Red Hill South* ☎ *03/5989–8412* ⊗ *Cellar door open 11–5* ⊗ *No dinner Sun.–Thurs. (No dinner Sun in Jan.).*

¢
DELI

✕ **Red Hill Cellar & Pantry.** This always-busy produce store-cum-deli is the perfect place to pick up the makings of a picnic lunch or a dinner in self-contained accommodation. It is packed full of crusty loaves, cured and fresh meats, fruits and vegetables, aromatic cheeses, olives, relishes and chutneys, and countless other goodies, most grown and/or made on the Mornington Peninsula. It is a popular spot for a delicious coffee, which you can drink on the veranda; coffee beans and local wines are also sold. ⊠ *141 Shoreham Rd. at Point Leo Rd., Red Hill* ☎ *03/5989–2411* ⊗ *Daily 7:30–7:30.*

$$$
AUSTRALIAN
★

✕ **Salix at Willow Creek.** Seasonal color changes along the vines make the vineyard view through the restaurant's floor-to-ceiling windows spectacular year-round. This is one of the two dining options at this popular winery; the more casual Salix Bistro is off the stylish downstairs cellar door. The restaurant, owned by Bernard McCarthy, makes much of the property's own produce. Try the confit duck leg, cotechino sausage, flageolet bean and hock ragout, garlic crumble, carrot puree, and preserved cherry jus. A star dessert is the Belgian chocolate tart served with pistachio and cinnamon doughnuts and caramel. The bistro, open noon–5 daily, serves such classic fare as boeuf bourguignon. The winery, known as Willow Creek Vineyard, opened in 1988 and concentrates on producing excellent Chardonnary and Pinot Noir from vines that have been tended by the same viticulturist since they were planted. In more recent times the owners have planted small quantities of Pinot Gris and Sauvignon Blanc. ✉ *166 Balnarring Rd., Merricks North* ☎ *03/5989–7640* ☯ *No dinner Sun.–Thurs.*

$$$ 🏨 **Hotel Sorrento.** Built in 1871, the Hotel Sorrento still commands a special place in town, and very funky interiors don't compromise its historic profile. **Pros:** great location; great views from some rooms. **Cons:** limited facilities. ✉ *5–15 Hotham Rd., Sorrento* ☎ *03/5984–8000* ⊕ *www.hotelsorrento.com.au* ⬦ *39 rooms* ♿ *In-room: safe, kitchen, Wi-Fi. In-hotel: restaurant, bar, beach, parking, some age restrictions* ⑂ *Breakfast.*

$$$$ 🏨 **Lakeside Villas at Crittenden Estate.** Wine and dine to your heart's content, then amble home to your accommodation projecting over a tranquil lake. **Pros:** fantastic position; stylish and snug. **Cons:** the nearby Stillwater Restaurant is open for dinner only on Friday and Saturday nights. ✉ *25 Harrisons Rd., Dromana* ☎ *03/5987–3275* ⊕ *www.lakesidevillas.com.au* ⬦ *3 rooms* ♿ *In-room: kitchen, Wi-Fi. In-hotel: restaurant, bar, tennis court, laundry facilities, business center, parking* ⑂ *Breakfast.*

PHILLIP ISLAND

Cowes. The seaside town of Cowes is the hub of Phillip Island; the pier is where you can board sightseeing cruises and the passenger ferry that travels across Western Port Bay to Stony Point on the Mornington Peninsula. It has a lively café scene and several quality gift shops interspersed with the traditionally cheaper tourist fare. Restaurant and hotel bookings are essential in the busy summer months.

★ **Penguin Parade.** A nightly parade of miniature little penguins, often called fairy penguins, waddling from the sea to their burrows in nearby dunes is this island's main draw, attracting onlookers year-round and crowds on summer weekends and holidays. But Phillip Island, a pleasant 1½-hour drive from Melbourne, has many other attractions. At low tide you can walk across a basalt causeway to the Nobbies (rugged coastal rocks); a boardwalk here takes you around the windswept coastline to a blowhole. Thousands of shearwaters (also known as muttonbirds) nest here from September to April, when they return north to the Bering Strait in the Arctic. Farther out, Seal Rocks host Australia's largest colony of fur seals; up to 20,000 creatures bask on the rocky platforms and cavort in the water here in midsummer. Boat tours cruise past these playful creatures in all but the coldest months.

There are several ways to view the Penguin Parade: general admission, with viewing from concrete bleachers; the Penguin Plus experience, which puts you on a smaller viewing platform that is closer to the action; and the Sky Box, an elevated tower where five adults join the ranger who is narrating the action. The Ultimate Penguin Tour, for private groups, includes headphones and night-vision equipment and a spot on the beach. The spectacle begins at around 8 pm each night; booking ahead is essential in summer and during public holidays. Bring warm clothing—even in summer—and rain protection gear. Make sure to arrive an hour before the tour begins. A good deal for visitors staying for a day is the 3 Park Pass, giving admission to the Penguin Parade, the Koala Conservation Centre, and Churchill Island. ⊠ *Summerland Beach, Phillip Island* ☎ *03/5951–2800* ✉ *General admission A$21.65; Penguin Plus viewing platform A$41.20; Sky Box A$62; Ultimate Penguin Tour A$76.30; Three Park Pass from A$36.85* ☉ *Daily.*

Phillip Island Grand Prix Circuit. The Phillip Island Grand Prix Circuit continues the island's long involvement with motor sports, dating back to 1928 when the Australian Grand Prix was run on local unpaved roads. The circuit was completely redeveloped in the 1980s, and in 1989 hosted the first Australian Motorcycle Grand Prix. The circuit holds regular races as well as big-ticket events, such as the MotoGP in October and Superbike World Championships in February. Speed freaks can buckle up for hot laps in a racing car (from A$295 for 30 minutes) driven by a professional driver year-round (dates and times vary, see Web site, or drive a go-kart (A$29 for 10 minutes) around a scale replica of the actual track .There are 45-minute guided walking tours of the track daily at 11 and 2, and a museum tracing the history of motor sports on the island. ⊠ *Back Beach Rd., Phillip Island* ☎ *03/5952–9400* ⊕ *www.phillipislandcircuit.com.au* ✉ *A$19 tours, A$13.50 museum* ☉ *Daily 9–7, tours run 11 and 2.*

GETTING HERE AND AROUND

Phillip Island is 124 km (78 mi) southeast of Melbourne or a 90-minute drive. To reach the island, take the Princes Freeway (M1) southeast to the South Gippsland Highway (M420), and follow this to the Bass Highway (A420). V/Line runs a combination train and bus service from Southern Cross Station to Cowes (with change at Dandenong railway station), a journey of three and a half hours. If you're on the Mornington Peninsula, there's a regular daily passenger ferry service from Stony Point to Cowes.

TOURS

Day trips from Melbourne are run by local tour operators, including Gray Line. Tours of the Phillip Island Penguin Parade cost A$145 (penguins and koalas only) to A$186 (with an island tour and lunch). Wildlife Coast Cruises runs two-hour cruises from Cowes Jetty to the Nobbies and Seal Rocks, spending 20–30 minutes viewing the seal colony. Cruises run year-round except August to mid-September with varying frequency depending on the season. The company also runs half-day cruises to French Island October to March.

ESSENTIALS

Tour Operators Gray Line ⊠ *Federation Sq., Flinders and Russell Sts., City Center, Melbourne* ☎ *1300/858687* ⊕ *www.grayline.com.* **Melbourne's Best Day Tours** ⊠ *Federation Sq., Flinders and Russell Sts., City Center, Melbourne* ☎ *1300/130550, 03/9397–4911* ⊕ *www.melbournetours.com.au.* **Wildlife Coast Cruises** ⊠ *The Rotunda, Jetty Carpark, The Esplanade, Cowes* ☎ *1300/763739* ⊕ *www.wildlifecoastcruises.com.au* ▱ *A$70.*

Transportation Inter Island Ferries ☎ *03/9585-5730 24-hour info line* ⊕ *www.interislandferries.com.au.* **V/Line** ⊠ *Southern Cross Railway Station, Spencer St., City Center, Melbourne* ☎ *13–6196* ⊕ *www.vline.com.au.*

Visitor Information Phillip Island Information Centre ⊠ *895 Tourist Rd., Newhaven* ☎ *03/5956–7447, 1300/366422* ⊕ *www.visitphillipisland.com.*

WHERE TO EAT AND STAY

For expanded hotel reviews, visit Fodors.com.

$$ ✕ **Harry's on the Esplanade.** Spilling onto an upstairs terrace above the
ECLECTIC main Cowes beach, Harry's is something of a Phillip Island institution. Its menu, which changes regularly, draws heavily on seafood bought fresh from the trawlers and locally raised beef and lamb. Don't pass up the crayfish if it's on the menu. The wine list has an Australian emphasis and includes local wines. The bread is made on the premises, as are the pastries and ice cream. ⊠ *Upper level, 17 The Esplanade, Cowes* ☎ *03/5952–6226* ☉ *Closed Mon.*

$$$ 🏠 **Glen Isla House.** A beautiful, safe swimming beach is right at the doorstep of this luxurious B&B, which has six individually themed rooms in one lodge. **Pros:** gorgeous furnishings, on a pristine beach, short drive to penguins. **Cons:** the heritage feel may not suit some. ⊠ *230–232 Church St., Cowes* ☎ *03/5952–1882* ⊕ *www.glenisla.com* ⤵ *1 king suite, 6 house rooms, 1 2-story gate cottage* 🕭 *In-room: safe, kitchen, Wi-Fi. In-hotel: restaurant, business center, parking, some age restrictions* ⵏⵍ *Breakfast.*

QUEENSCLIFF

103 km (64 mi) southwest of Melbourne.

In the late 19th century Queenscliff was a favorite weekend destination for well-to-do Melburnians, who traveled on paddle steamers or by train to stay at the area's grand hotels. Some, like the Vue Grand and the Queenscliff Hotel, welcome tourists to this day. Be sure to check out Fort Queenscliff, another landmark from bygone days. Good restaurants and quiet charm are also traits of Queenscliff. The best beach is at Lonsdale Bay, where a long stretch of golden sand and gentle surf make a great place to wade, walk, or swim in summer. The playground of families during the day and dog walkers come dusk, Queenscliff is a restful alternative to the resort towns of Sorrento and Portsea on the other side of the bay. On the last weekend in November the annual Queenscliff Music Festival (⊕ *www.qmf.net.au*) draws thousands of visitors to town.

GETTING HERE AND AROUND

The lovely coastal village of Queenscliff and nearby smaller sibling Point Lonsdale make for a worthy—and well-signposted—detour on the drive from Melbourne to the start of the Great Ocean Road.

It's about a 60- to 90-minute drive from Melbourne to Geelong via the Princes Freeway (M1), then to Queenscliff via the Bellarine Highway (B110). Trains run from Melbourne's Southern Cross Station to Geelong, where buses (Nos. 75 and 76) continue on to Queenscliff. The Queenscliff–Sorrento Ferry departs on the hour (in both directions) from 7 am to 6 pm and to 7 pm in the summer months. The journey takes 40 minutes and costs A$10 for pedestrians, A$69 for cars including two passengers in the high season.

> ### LIGHT UP YOUR TRIP
>
> If you're into lighthouses, then this coast is a must-see. Here you can find seven historic lighthouses of varying shapes and sizes—from Point Lonsdale in the east to Portland in the west. Don't miss the tall red-capped white **Split Point lighthouse** at Aireys Inlet, while **Cape Otway lighthouse**, the oldest on mainland Australia, marks the point where the Southern Ocean and Bass Strait collide. Farther west at Portland is majestic **Cape Nelson Lighthouse**, high above ferocious seas. Guided tours are available.

It's easy to walk around Queenscliff's main attractions; ask at the visitor center in Hesse Street for maps. The Bellarine Railway, a narrow gauge tourist train, runs between the towns of Queenscliff and Drysdale (a distance of 10 mi) several times a week, while on Saturday nights, and occasional Friday nights, between August and May the hugely popular Blues Train mixes dinner and live blues entertainment; tickets are A$89.50 per person.

ESSENTIALS

Transportation Bellarine Railway ⊠ *Queenscliff Railway Station, 20 Symonds St.* 🕾 *03/5258-2069 (recorded information)* ⊕ *www.bpr.org.au.* **Queenscliff–Sorrento Ferry** 🕾 *03/5258-3244* ⊕ *www.searoad.com.au.* **V/Line** ⊠ *Southern Cross Railway Station, Spencer St., City Center, Melbourne* 🕾 *13-6196* ⊕ *www.vline.com.au.*

Visitor Information Queenscliff Visitor Information Centre ⊠ *55 Hesse St.* 🕾 *03/5258-4843, 1300/884843* ⊕ *www.queenscliffe.vic.gov.au.*

WHERE TO STAY

For expanded hotel reviews, visit Fodors.com.

$$$ 🏨 **Queenscliff Hotel.** If you're after period charm rather than spacious modernity, this gloriously restored 19th-century beauty, with soaring, pressed-metal ceilings, stained-glass windows, and antique furnishings, is the place for you. **Pros:** grandly charming, good location, excellent on-site restaurants. **Cons:** limited room facilities. ⊠ *16 Gellibrand St.* 🕾 *03/5258-1066* ⊕ *www.queenscliffhotel.com.au* ⬚ *15 rooms* ⬚ *In-room: no a/c, no TV. In-hotel: restaurant, bar, laundry facilities* ⦿ *Breakfast.*

$$$ 🏨 **Vue Grand Hotel.** Built in 1881, the Vue Grand blends Old World ele-
★ gance with modern touches. **Pros:** grand experience; wonderful dining room. **Cons:** not on the seaside. ⊠ *46 Hesse St.* 🕾 *03/5258-1544* ⊕ *www.*

vuegrand.com.au ⤴ *29 rooms, 3 suites* ⤴ *In-room: Wi-Fi. In-hotel: restaurant, bar, parking* ❚◯❚ *Breakfast.*

**EN
ROUTE**
From Queenscliff, follow Great Ocean Road signs for 45 km (28 mi) to **Torquay,** Australia's premier surfing and windsurfing resort, and Bell's Beach, famous for its Easter surfing contests and its October international windsurfing competitions. The Great Ocean Road, a positively magnificent coastal drive, officially begins at Eastern View, 10 km (6 mi) east of Lorne. The seaside towns of Anglesea, Aireys Inlet, and Fairhaven are other good warm-weather swimming spots.

GREAT OCEAN ROAD

The Great Ocean Road, which snakes along Victoria's rugged and windswept southwestern coast, is arguably the country's most spectacular coastal drive. The road, built during the Great Depression along majestic cliffs, occasionally dips down to sea level. Here, in championship surfing country, some of the world's finest waves pound mile after mile of uninhabited, golden, sandy beaches and rocky headlands.

Although this region is actually on the southeast coast of the Australian mainland, it lies to the west of Melbourne, and so Melburnians refer to it as the "West Coast." From the city, you should allow two or more days for a West Coast sojourn.

Driving is the most convenient way to see the region, and the only way to really enjoy the Great Ocean Road. Although the Great Ocean Road is officially deemed to be 243 km (152 mi), and run between the towns of Torquay in the east and Allansford (near Warnambool) in the west, most people think of it as the much longer route that continues farther west to Port Fairy and Portland. Its many twists and turns and wonderful sights along the way take many hours to explore.

The going may be slow on the most scenic routes, especially during the summer holiday period. The winding road is notorious for its motor accidents, so take care on the bends and slow down.

TOURS

12 Apostles Helicopter rides are an exciting way to appreciate the awesome force of the Southern Ocean and this amazing natural sculpture park. Ten-minute flights take in the Twelve Apostles and Loch Ard Gorge; longer flights travel farther up the coast to the west and inland. Prices start at A$95 per person.

AAT Kings has a six-day tour from Melbourne to Adelaide that travels the length of the Great Ocean Road and also includes visits to Mount Gambier and Kangaroo Island. The tour is A$2,285.

Absolute Outdoors is a one-stop shop for kayak, bike, abseiling, and surfing tours around southwest Victoria; there's also a surf school. All equipment is provided.

Adventure Tours Australia has two three-day tours that include both the Great Ocean Road and the Grampians National Park. Young backpackers are their target market, however anyone can join the tours, and a choice between dorm accommodation and singles or doubles is

Sea kayaking in Apollo Bay.

available. You can choose a round-trip tour from Melbourne or one that continues on to Adelaide. Both tours spend one night in Princetown (just east of the Twelve Apostles) and another night in Halls Gap. It's A$395 for dorm accommodation and A$485 for a double or twin room, with two dinners and two breakfasts.

Auswalk. Auswalk offers guided (five nights) and self-guided Great Ocean Walk tours; the self-guided walk takes you from Apollo Bay to the Twelve Apostles over eight days (seven nights), or the trip can be divided into two four-night segments. Walkers carry a day pack only; a support vehicle carries the luggage by car from hotel (or B&B) to hotel. Most tours include at least one night in the 19th-century Cape Otway Lighthouse cottages, and most meals are provided. Both guided and self-guided tours can be arranged year-round and require a minimum of two people. Auswalk also offers a set-date group guided walk of six nights including pickup and drop-off from Melbourne Airport. The six-night group guided tour ranges from A$2,395 per person (double) depending on the season. Self-guided tours are about A$1,000 less. Daily walks can range from five to seven hours, although the support vehicle can drive those who feel they have had enough walking for one day. ✉ *4 Red Gum Lease Track, Halls Gap* ☎ *03/5356–4971* ⊕ *www.auswalk.com.au.*

Great Ocean Road Adventure Tours or GORATS as it's called, runs mountain-bike tours across the region. Many tours run to the town of Forrest, considered a mountain-bike mecca, with 15 trails showcasing the natural beauty of the Otway Ranges. GORATS specializes in school groups but can tailor-make trips for a minimum of two people. Prices start from $85 per person for a two-hour trip, including bike, helmet, map, transport, and guide; pickups from local accommodation can be arranged. They also operate flatwater canoe tours on the Barwon, Anglesea. and Aire rivers.

Lighthouse Tours explore the majestic, and still operational, Split Point Lighthouse at Aireys Inlet, also known as the White Queen. You can see her for miles as you approach this section of the Great Ocean Road west of Anglesea—just look for the huge white tower with the red cap—and the views from the top are amazing. The 45-minute tours operate year-round, but bookings are required on weekdays. Tour cost is $A12.

Melbourne's Best Day Tours has a 4WD tour of the Great Ocean Road from Melbourne. Starting at 7:30 am, it includes breakfast and lunch, a lighthouse tour, rain-forest walks, the Otway. Fly treetop walk, and sightseeing in Port Campbell National Park. The 12-hour tour takes a maximum of six people and costs $A364.

Mulloka Cruises give half-hour cruises around the Port Fairy Bay—a quick way to set your sea legs and see Port Fairy from a different angle. Boat owner Jane Grimshaw dispenses interesting information about the area. Cruises cost from A$10.

Port Campbell Boat Charters operates diving tours to the famous wreck sites as well as scenic cruises and fishing trips.

Southern Exposure Adventure Sports runs mountain-bike tours along the coast and in the nearby Great Otway National Park, kayaking tours, and surfing lessons. Surfing lessons are A$65 for two hours, and combined bike and kayaking tours can be arranged. Bookings are essential.

Spring Creek Horse Rides take you through the beautiful Otway National Park. It's a leisurely way to spend an hour or two. Located at Bellbrae, just a few miles inland from Torquay, rides are A$40 for one hour and A$60 for two.

ESSENTIALS

Tour Operators **12 Apostles Helicopters** ✉ *Twelve Apostles Information Centre, Great Ocean Rd. at Booringa Rd., Port Campbell* ☎ *03/5598–8283* ⊕ *www.12apostleshelicopters.com.au.* **AAT Kings** ✉ *Melbourne Day Tour Centre, Federation Sq., Flinders and Russell Sts., City Center, Melbourne* ☎ *03/9663–3377, 1300/228546* ⊕ *www.aatkings.com.au.* **Absolute Outdoors** ✉ *67 Bentinck St., Portland* ☎ *03/5521–7646* ⊕ *www.absoluteoutdoors.com.au.* **Adventure Tours Australia** ✉ *72 The Parade, Norwood, South Australia* ☎ *1300/654604, 0008132–8200* ⊕ *www.advenutretours.com.au.* **Auswalk** ✉ *4 Red Gum Lease Track, Halls Gap* ☎ *03/5356–4971* ⊕ *www.auswalk.com.au.* **Great Ocean Road Adventure Tours** ✉ *P.O. Box 325, Lorne* ☎ *0417/576973* ⊕ *www.gorats. com.au.* **Lighthouse Tour** ✉ *Split Point lighthouse, Reserve Rd., Aireys Inlet* ☎ *1800/174045, 03/5263–1133* ⊕ *www.splitpointlighthouse.com.au* 💷 *A$12.* **Melbourne's Best Day Tours** ✉ *Federation Square, Flinders and Russell Sts., City Center* ☎ *1300/130550* ⊕ *www.melbouretours.com.au.* **Mulloka Cruises** ✉ *Martins Point, end of wharf, Port Fairy* ☎ *0408/514382 mobile* ✍ *janegrimshaw@ bigpond.com.* **Port Campbell Boat Charters** ✉ *32 Lord St., Port Campbell* ☎ *03/5598–6366, 0428/986366 mobile* ⊕ *www.portcampbellboatcharters.com. au.* **Southern Exposure Adventure Sports** ✉ *38 Bell St., Torquay* ☎ *03/5261– 9170* ⊕ *www.southernexposure.com.au.* **Spring Creek Horse Rides** ✉ *245 Portreath Rd., Bellbrae* ☎ *03/5266–1541, 0403/167590 mobile* ⊕ *www.springcreekhorserides.com.au.*

Visitor Information Geelong and Ocean Road Visitor Information Centre.
The Geelong and Great Ocean Road Visitor Information Centre is open daily 9–5.
✉ *Princes Hwy(at the gas station, 20 km before Geelong), Little River, Geelong*
☏ *03/5283-1735, 1800/620888* ⊕ *www.visitgeelongbellarine.com.* **Torquay Visitor Information Centre.** Torquay Visitor Information Centre is open daily 9–5.
✉ *Surf Walk* ☏ *1300/614219, 03/5261–4219* ⊕ *www.visitsurfcoast.com.au.*

LORNE

148 km (92 mi) southwest of Melbourne, 95 km (59 mi) southwest of Queenscliff, 50 km (31 mi) southwest of Torquay.

Located between sweeping Loutit Bay and the Otway Mountain Range, Lorne is one of the main towns on the Great Ocean Road, but one that has a definite surf-and-holiday feel. It's the site of both a wild celebration every New Year's Eve and the popular Pier-to-Pub Swim held on the first weekend in January. Some people make their reservations a year or more in advance. It's also the starting point for the Great Ocean Road International Marathon held each May (the foot race ends in Apollo Bay). The town has a lively café and pub scene, as well as several upscale restaurants, trendy boutiques, and a day spa.

GETTING HERE AND AROUND

You really need a car to get to Lorne and other Great Ocean Road towns; the next best option is to take an organized tour. Public transport is available, but it's a long process: take the V/Line train to Geelong, then transfer to a bus to Apollo Bay, which stops at Lorne (about five hours). If driving, take the Princes Highway west from Melbourne across the Westgate Bridge to Geelong. From there, follow signs along the Surf Coast Highway to Torquay, where you'll connect with the Great Ocean Road.

ESSENTIALS

Emergencies Lorne Community Hospital ✉ *Albert St., Lorne* ☏ *03/5289–4300* ⊕ *www.lornecommunityhospital.com.au.* **Lorne Police Station** ✉ *5 Charles St., Lorne* ☏ *03/5289–2712.*

Visitor Information Lorne Visitor Information Centre ✉ *15 Muntjoy Parade, Lorne* ☏ *1300/89–1152* ⊕ *www.visitsurfcoast.com.*

OUTDOOR ACTIVITIES

HIKING AND WALKING The Great Ocean Road and the "Surf Coast" section of it around Torquay, Lorne, and Airleys Inlet have fantastic walks providing great clifftop views, while inland a little way there are waterfalls and picnic grounds to explore.

The 30-km (19-mi) Surf Coast Walk, which begins near Jan Juc car park (1 mi west of Torquay) and ends around Moggs Creek Picnic Area at Aireys, can be done in short segments.

Inland from the towns of Fairweather and Eastern View is the vast Great Otway National Park, which has many picturesque walks, including the 12-km (7.5-mi) walk from Aireys Inlet to Distillery Creek, which can be quite strenuous. There are also shorter and easier walks to Erskine Falls and Sheaoak Falls just inland from Lorne. The Torquay and Lorne visitor centers have trail maps.

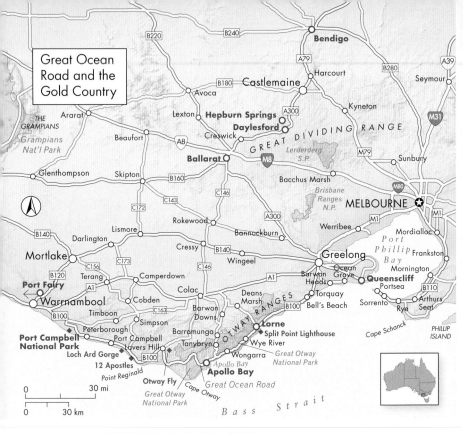

Great Ocean
Road and the
Gold Country

WHERE TO EAT AND STAY

For expanded hotel reviews, visit Fodors.com.

$$
SEAFOOD
★

✕ **Marks.** Fresh seafood—from fried calamari to roasted flathead—is the draw at this Lorne institution, which has been going strong since 1989 and now counts third-generation customers among regulars. The decor is "funky seaside," with bright walls, blue chairs, and a smattering of local art and sculpture for sale. The menu changes daily depending on what the fishermen have caught and what's growing in the restaurant's garden, but you'll always find oysters and steak on the menu, along with Atlantic salmon, and perhaps Sicilian seafood soup. To finish there's nothing more delicious than the house-churned ice cream. It's open for dinner only and located on the main road across from the beach. ⊠ *124 Mountjoy Parade* ☎ *03/5289–2787* ⊙ *Closed Sun. and Mon. Easter–mid-Jul.; closed mid-Jul.–Sept. No lunch.*

$$$

🏨 **Mantra Erskine Beach Resort.** You can fall asleep listening to waves rolling ashore at this huge complex on 12 acres near the water's edge. **Pros:** close to the beach; lots of facilities. **Cons:** fee for Internet. ⊠ *Mountjoy Parade* ☎ *03/5228–9777* ⊕ *www.mantraerskinebeachresort.com.au* ⇲ *142 rooms, 135 apartments* ⟐ *In-room: kitchen, Internet, Wi-Fi. In-hotel: restaurant, bar, pool, tennis court, gym, spa, beach, laundry facilities, business center, parking* ⦿ *Breakfast.*

**EN
ROUTE**

Otway Fly. About an hour's drive and 70 km (43 mi) from Lorne (follow the Great Ocean Road until it joins Skenes Creek Road, then take Forrest Apollo Bay Road to Beech Forest Road, then Colac Lavers Hill Road until you reach the signed turnoff to Phillips Track) you'll find the entrance to the Otway Fly. The Fly is a 1,969-foot-long elevated treetop walk, where you can stroll a steel walkway (one section is springboard-cantilevered, and gently bounces as you pass over Young's Creek) above the rain-forest canopy. You'll see the tops of giant myrtle beech, blackwood, and mountain ash trees, as well as spectacular views of the surrounding region. It's open daily 9–5 (last entry 4 pm); tickets are A$24. ☎ *03/5235–9200, 1800/300477* ⊕ *www.otwayfly.com.*

APOLLO BAY

GETTING HERE AND AROUND

Apollo Bay is 45 km (28 mi) west of Lorne. Driving is the most convenient way to get here. Otherwise take the combined V/Line train-bus option, which involves riding a train from Melbourne's Southern Cross Station to Geelong and then a bus along the Great Ocean Road to Apollo Bay, via Lorne and other Surf Coast towns.

OUTDOOR ACTIVITIES

DIVING

The Twelve Apostles Marine National Park and the nearby Arches Marine Sanctuary both provide fantastic diving opportunities. Local wrecks that can be explored with experienced guides include the *Napier* at Port Campbell, the famous *Loch Ard* (off Muttonbird Island), the *Schomberg* at Peterborough, and the *Fiji* near Moonlight Head. All wrecks are protected by federal law, and are not to be disturbed in any way. (⇨ *See Port Campbell boat charters in Tours, above.)*

HIKING AND
WALKING

The Port Campbell National Park area, which is home to the Twelve Apostles, Loch Ard George, and other amazing landforms, has many good walks. Most are along wooden boardwalks; some also include steep stairs down to the beach. The Visitor Centre at Port Campbell has all the details.

Inland from Port Campbell is the Camperdown-Timboon Rail Trail (also known as the Coast to Crater Rail Trail). It passes by lakes and streams and open volcanic plains. It is suitable for walkers and mountain bikers. The 36-km (22-mi) trail has good signage. Ask at the tourist offices for details.

WHERE TO STAY

For expanded hotel reviews, visit Fodors.com.

$$$$
Fodor'sChoice
★

☆ **Chris's Beacon Point Restaurant and Villas.** Set high in the Otway Ranges overlooking the Great Ocean Road and the sea, this is a wonderful place to dine or bed down for the night. **Pros:** sensational views. **Cons:** pricey; steep walk to rooms. ⊠ *280 Skenes Creek Rd.* ☎ *03/5237–6411* ⊕ *www.chriss.com.au* ⤴ *4 villas, 5 studios* ⚐ *In-room: kitchen, Wi-Fi. In-hotel: restaurant, laundry facilities, parking* ❏ *Breakfast.*

PORT CAMPBELL NATIONAL PARK

283 km (75 mi) southwest of Melbourne via the Great Ocean Rd., 90 km (56 mi) west of Apollo Bay, 135 km (83 mi) west of Lorne.

Fodor'sChoice **Port Campbell National Park.** Stretching some 30 km (19 mi) along Victo-
★ ria's southern coastline, Port Campbell National Park is the site of some of the most famously beautiful geological formations in Australia. The ferocious Southern Ocean has gnawed at the limestone cliffs along this coast for aeons, creating a sort of badlands-by-the-sea, where strangely shaped formations stand offshore amid the surf. The most famous of these formations is the Twelve Apostles, as much a symbol for Victoria as the Sydney Opera House is for New South Wales. (The name has always been a misnomer, as there were only nine of these stone columns or sea stacks as they are correctly termed. Then in July 2005 one of them collapsed into the sea, leaving behind just eight.) If you happen to be visiting the Twelve Apostles just after sunset, you're likely to see bands of little penguins returning to their burrows on the beach. There's a population of around 3,000 of these cute creatures in the area.

Loch Ard Gorge, named after the iron-hulled clipper that wrecked on the shores of nearby Muttonbird Island in 1878, is another spectacular place to walk. Four of the *Loch Ard*'s victims are buried in a nearby cemetery, while a sign by the gorge tells the story of the ship and its crew. This stretch of coast is often called the Shipwreck Coast for the hundreds of vessels that have met untimely ends in the treacherous waters. The Historic Shipwreck Trail, with landmarks describing 25 of the disasters, stretches from Moonlight Head to Port Fairy.

The best time to visit the park is late September to April, when you can also witness the boisterous birdlife on nearby Muttonbird Island. Toward nightfall, hundreds of hawks and kites circle the island in search of baby muttonbirds emerging from their protective burrows. The birds of prey beat a hasty retreat at the sight of thousands of adult shearwaters approaching with food for their chicks as the last light fades from the sky. Other amazing sea stacks and stone formations farther west along the Great Ocean Road are also not to be missed. These include the Grotto, the Arch, London Bridge, and the spectacular Bay of Islands and Bay of Martyrs.

The Twelve Apostles Information Centre is open daily 9 to 5. A self-guided, 1½-hour Discovery Walk begins near Port Campbell Beach, where it's safe to swim. The pounding surf and undertow are treacherous at other nearby beaches.

GETTING HERE AND AROUND
The scenic route to Port Campbell National Park (which is actually a few miles east of the town of Port Campbell) is via the Great Ocean Road from Torquay, via Lorne and Apollo Bay. A car is the best way to go. A shorter drive is via the Princes Highway (M1) from Melbourne to Warrnambool, then the Great Ocean Road east to Port Campbell. A V/Line train operates to Warrnambool, and then a bus can be taken to Port Campbell. The journey takes about five hours.

Loch Ard Gorge in Port Campbell National Park, Great Ocean Road.

ESSENTIALS

Transportation V/Line ⊠ *Southern Cross Railway Station, Spencer St., City Center, Melbourne* ☎ *13–6196* ⊕ *www.vline.com.au.*

Visitor Information Parks Victoria Twelve Apostles Information Centre ⊠ *26 Morris St., Port Campbell* ☎ *03/5598–6089, 1300/137–255* ⊕ *www. visit12apostles.com.au.* ⊠ *Parks office: Tregea St., Port Campbell* ☎ *13–1963* ⊕ *www.parkweb.vic.gov.au.*

WHERE TO EAT AND STAY

For expanded hotel reviews, visit Fodors.com.

$$
AUSTRALIAN
✕ **Waves.** You won't see any waves from this relaxed main-street eatery even though it's only yards from the water. You will find enormous breakfasts and fireside seafood dinners, a spacious sundeck, and a friendly staff. The menu changes weekly based on locally available ingredients; there might be such dishes as a half-chicken cooked in Asian masterstock, and blue swimmer crab, while meat eaters can tuck into sizzling steaks and pork loin with caramelized apple. ⊠ *29 Lord St., Port Campbell* ☎ *03/5598–6111* ⊕ *www.wavesportcampbell.com.au.*

$$
🏠 **Daysy Hill Country Cottages.** Set in manicured gardens with lavender-lined walkways, these five sandstone-and-cedar cottages look over the Newfield Valley. **Pros:** good price; good location. **Cons:** limited facilities; minimum stay required. ⊠ *7353 Timboon/Port Campbell Rd., Port Campbell* ☎ *03/5598–6226* ⊕ *www.greatoceanroad.nu/daysyhill* ⊅ *5 cottages, 4 suites, 3 cabins* ⚒ *In-room: a/c, kitchen. In-hotel: laundry facilities.*

$$$ ⊞ **Southern Ocean Villas.** Ideally situated on the edge of Port Campbell National Park, within short walking distance of the town center and beach, these villas are stylishly furnished and fitted with polished-wood floors, picture windows, and high ceilings. **Pros:** good location near Twelve Apostles. **Cons:** located in sleepy town, difficult to find. ⊠ *2 McCue St., Port Campbell* ☎ *03/5598–4200* ⊕ *www.southernoceanvillas. com* ⇥ *20 villas* ⅄ *In-room: kitchen. In-hotel: laundry facilities.*

EN
ROUTE

■ **Warrnambool.** About 66 km (41 mi) west of Port Campbell, Warrnambool is Victoria's southern right whale nursery. Platforms at Logan's Beach, about 3 km (2 mi) east of the city, provide views of an amazing marine show from June to September. Whales return to this beach every year to calve, with the females and young staying close to the shore and the males playing about 150 yards out to sea.

Warrnambool Visitor Information Centre ⊠ *Flagstaff Hill, 89 Merri St., Warrnambool* ☎ *03/5559–4620, 1800/637725* ⊕ *www.visitwarrnambool. com.au.*

PORT FAIRY

377 km (215 mi) southwest of Melbourne via the Great Ocean Road; it is shorter if you take the Princes Highway (M1).

Port Fairy is widely considered to be the state's prettiest village. The second-oldest town in Victoria, it was originally known as Belfast, and there are indeed echoes of Ireland in the landscape and architecture. More than 50 of the cottages and sturdy bluestone buildings that line the banks of the River Moyne have been classified as landmarks by the National Trust, and few towns repay a leisurely stroll so richly. Huge Norfolk Island pines line many of the streets, particularly Gipps Street, and the town is dotted with good cafés, a few pubs, and art galleries.

The town still thrives as the base for a fishing fleet, and as host to the Port Fairy Folk Festival, one of Australia's most famous musical events, held every March. The town has a large colony of short-tailed shearwaters that nest on Griffiths Island. Amazingly, these birds travel here from the Aleutian Islands near Alaska, always arriving within three days of September 22. You can take a 45-minute walk around the island on marked trails to the historic lighthouse.

GETTING HERE AND AROUND

The most convenient form of transport is by car; the 377-km (234-mi) trip along the Great Ocean Road from Melbourne takes about six and a half hours, and it's advisable to break the journey, as there's so much to see along the way. It's a shorter trip if you take the Princes Highway (M1). V/Line trains travel from Melbourne's Southern Cross Station to Warrnambool (3 hours), and V/Line buses then make the short distance (29-km) to Port Fairy.

ESSENTIALS

Transportation **V/Line** ⊠ *Southern Cross Railway Station, Spencer St., City Center, Melbourne* ☎ *13–6196* ⊕ *www.vline.com.au.*

Visitor Information **Port Fairy Visitor Information Centre** ⊠ *Railway Place, Bank St.* ☎ *03/5568–2682* ⊕ *www.visitportfairy-moyneshire.com.au.*

EXPLORING

Port Fairy Historical Society. Founded in the 1830s, Port Fairy was once a whaling station with one of the largest ports in Victoria. The Port Fairy Historical Society museum contains relics from whaling days and from the many ships that have foundered along this coast. ⊠ *Old Courthouse, 30 Gipps St.* ☎ *03/5568–2263* ⊕ *www.historicalsociety. port-fairy.com* ⊿ *A$3* ⊘ *Sept. 1–mid-July, Wed. and weekends 10–5; mid-July–Aug., Sat. 2–4.*

Mott's Cottage. National Trust-listed Mott's Cottage is a restored limestone-and-timber cottage built by Sam Mott, a member of the 1830s whaling crew from the cutter *Fairy* who founded the town. ⊠ *5 Sackville St.* ☎ *03/5568–2682, 03/5568–2632* ⊿ *Gold coin donation* ⊘ *Wed. and Sat. 2–4, or by appointment, Closed late July–Aug.*

OUTDOOR ACTIVITIES

HIKING AND WALKING There are several walks around Port Fairy that highlight the town's historical aspects and and the area's great beauty. Pick up a Historic Walks map from the visitor center and follow a trail past some 30 beautiful buildings; it takes about an hour. The Port Fairy Maritime & Shipwreck Heritage Walk is a 2-km (1.2-mi) trail that passes the sites of several shipwrecks: the bark *Socrates*, which was battered by huge seas in 1843; the bark *Lydia*, which wrecked off the coast in 1847; the schooner *Thistle*, which went down in 1837; and the brigantine *Essington*, which sank while moored at Port Fairy in 1852. Other historic attractions en route include the town port, the lifeboat station, riverside warehouses, cannons and gun emplacements at Battery Hill, and Griffiths Island Lighthouse. The walk is well marked.

Griffiths Island is another good place to walk. You can stroll around the entire island in about an hour, visiting the lighthouse and perhaps spotting a black wallaby along the way.

Ten minutes or 14 km (9 mi) east of Port Fairy is Tower Hill State Game Reserve, nested in an extinct volcano. There are several walking trails and plenty of chances to see emus and kangaroos. About 40-minutes northeast is Mount Eccles National Park, another extinct volcano. Here there are four walks, including one to the crater rim and lava caves.

Tower Hill State Game Reserve. Parks Victoria, the national park body, manages Tower Hill State Game Reserve with the Worn Gundidj Aboriginal Co-Operative, an organization that conducts cultural interpretative walks. Take one of their one-hour personalized bush and nature walks to learn about indigenous lifestyles, bush food, and medicine, and hear about the local inhabitants, which include emus, sugar gliders, koalas, kangaroos, various birdlife, and reptiles. There are also evening tours on which you may see nocturnal native animals and view the crater rim under the stars. Tours start from A$18.95. Parks Victoria's Web site also has a map of the reserve and walking trails. ⊠ *Tower Hill State Game Reserve, Princes Hwy, between Port Fairy and Warrnambool, Tower Hill* ☎ *03/5565–9202, 0428/318876 mobile* ⊕ *www.parkweb. vic.gov.au.*

WHERE TO EAT AND STAY

For expanded hotel reviews, visit Fodors.com.

$$$ ✕ **time&tide.** "High Tea by the High Sea" is the star of this luscious café, CAFÉ which—fortunately—has an appetite stimulating Southern Ocean view! Take a seat on a high-backed chair and indulge in three tiers of frittata, finger sandwiches, brownies, filled meringues, and more. The Grand High Tea (A$45 per person) and Mini Grand (two tiers, A$29) include tea or coffee and a glass of sparkling rosé. Also available are three share plates (A$25 each); all food on the Regional Taste Plate, which features buffalo cheeses and olives, comes from within 45 km (28 mi) of the café. ⊠ *21 Thistle Pl.* ☎ *03/5568–2134* ⊗ *Closed weekdays. No dinner.*

$ ⊡ **Merrijig Inn.** One of Victoria's oldest inns, this beautifully restored 1841 Georgian-style building looks over Port Fairy's working wharf from King George Square. **Pros:** cute and cozy; great food. **Cons:** upstairs rooms have character, but they're very small. ⊠ *1 Campbell St., at Gipps St.* ☎ *03/5568–2324* ⊕ *www.merrijiginn.com* ⌲ *4 rooms, 4 suites* ⚙ *In-room: no a/c, no TV, Wi-Fi. In-hotel: restaurant, bar* ⊙ *Breakfast.*

$$$ ⊡ **Oscars Waterfront Boutique Hotel.** Overlooking the waterfront and a ★ marina of yachts, Oscar's gives French provincial style an Australian edge. **Pros:** fantastic location; great breakfasts. **Cons:** town is dead in the off season. ⊠ *41B Gipps St.* ☎ *03/5568–3022* ⊕ *www.oscarswaterfront. com* ⌲ *6 rooms, 1 suite* ⚙ *In-room: Wi-Fi. In-hotel: bar* ⊙ *Breakfast.*

THE GOLD COUNTRY

Victoria was changed forever in the early 1850s by the discovery of gold in the center of the state. News of fantastic gold deposits caused immigrants from every corner of the world to pour into Victoria to seek their fortunes as "diggers"—a name that has become synonymous with Australians ever since. Few miners became wealthy from their searches, however. The real money was made by those supplying goods and services to the thousands who had succumbed to gold fever.

Gold towns like Ballarat, Castlemaine, Maldon, and Bendigo sprang up like mushrooms to accommodate these fortune seekers, and prospered until the gold rush receded. Afterward, they became ghost towns or turned to agriculture to survive. However, many beautiful buildings were constructed from the spoils of gold, and these gracious old public buildings and grand hotels survive today and make a visit to Bendigo and Ballarat a pleasure for those who love architecture. Victoria's gold is again being mined in limited quantities, while these historic old towns remain interesting relics of Australia's past.

Although Victoria was not the first Australian state to experience a gold rush, when gold was discovered here in 1851 it became a veritable El Dorado. During the boom years of the 19th century, 90% of the gold mined in Australia came from the state. The biggest finds were at Ballarat and then Bendigo, and the Ballarat diggings proved to be among the richest alluvial goldfields in the world.

This region of Victoria is now considered a center for modern-day rejuvenation. Between Ballarat and other historic gold towns to the north are the twin hot spots of Daylesford and Hepburn Springs—which together constitute the spa capital of Australia.

For leisurely exploration of the Gold Country, a car is essential. Public transportation adequately serves the main centers, but access to smaller towns is less assured and even in the bigger towns attractions are spread out.

TOURS

Gray Line, Australian Pacific Tours, and AAT Kings cover the Gold Country; all three depart from the New Day Tour Centre in Federation Square at the corner of Flinders and Russell Streets, Melbourne.

Contacts **AAT Kings** ☎ *1300/228546* ⊕ *www.aatkings.com.au.* **Australian Pacific Touring** ☎ *1300/336932* ⊕ *www.aptouring.com.au.* **Gray Line** ✉ *Federation Square E, Flinders and Russell Sts., City Center* ☎ *1300/858687* ⊕ *www.grayline.com.au.*

> ### BRUSH STROKES
>
> The riches of Victoria's goldfields are reflected in beautiful Victorian buildings and in the treasures of the art galleries of Ballarat, Bendigo, and Castlemaine. Among Australia's top five regional galleries, they show the works of famous artists such as Arthur Boyd and Sidney Nolan. Take advantage of the opportunity to view the masterpieces away from the big-city crowds.

BALLARAT

106 km (66 mi) northwest of Melbourne.

In the local Aboriginal language, the name Ballarat means "resting place." In pre-gold-rush days nearby Lake Wendouree provided the area with a plentiful supply of food. Once the gold boom hit, however, the town became much less restful; in 1854 Ballarat was the scene of the Battle of the Eureka Stockade, a skirmish that took place between miners and authorities over gold license fees that miners were forced to pay. More than 20 men died in the battle. Today their flag—the Southern Cross—is a symbol of Australia's egalitarian spirit.

Despite the harsh times, fortunes made from the mines (and from the miners) resulted in the grand Victorian architecture on Sturt and Lydiard streets—note the post office, the town hall, Craig's Royal Hotel, and Her Majesty's Theatre. The Old Colonists' Hall and the Mining Exchange (at 20 and 26 Lydiard Street, respectively) now house shops and cafés. The visitor center has a self-guided heritage walk.

GETTING HERE AND AROUND

It's an easy 80-minute drive to Ballarat along the Western Highway (M8) from Melbourne. The road, however, is the main artery between Melbourne and Adelaide, and many huge trucks also use the road. Take care and drive within the speed limit. From Ballarat you can easily drive north to the spa-country towns of Daylesford–Hepburn Springs and Bendigo on the Midland Highway. The city itself is well signposted. The city center is built around a well-planned grid and has ample parking. Lock bus services run from Sturt Street, the main thoroughfare, to most of Ballarat's attractions.

V/Line operates trains to Ballarat and Bendigo from Melbourne.

ESSENTIALS

Transportation V/Line. ✉ *Southern Cross Railway Station, Spencer St., City Center, Melbourne* ☎ *13–6196* 🌐 *www.vline.com.au.*

Visitor Information Ballarat Visitor Information Centre ✉ *43 Lydiard St.* ☎ *1800/446633* 🌐 *www.visitballarat.com.au.*

EXPLORING

Art Gallery of Ballarat. The Art Gallery of Ballarat has a large collection of contemporary Australian art. It also has some impressive historical exhibits, the showpiece being the tattered remains of the Eureka Flag (sometimes known as the Southern Cross) which was flown defiantly by the miner rebels at the Eureka Stockade in 1854. ✉ *40 Lydiard St.* ☎ *03/5320–5858* 🌐 *www.artgalleryofballarat.com.au* ⏲ *Daily 9–5.*

Ballarat Wildlife Park. All sorts of native animals, including kangaroos and emus (which roam free), saltwater crocodiles, snakes, lizards, wombats, and echidnas can be found at Ballarat Wildlife Park. Daily tours of the park are led at 11, with a koala show at 2, a wombat show at 2:30, and a crocodile feeding at 3. The park also has a café and picnic areas. ✉ *Fussel and York Sts., East Ballarat* ☎ *03/5333–5933* 🌐 *www.wildlifepark.com.au* 🎟 *A$24* ⏲ *Daily 9–5:30.*

Ballarat Botanical Gardens. On the shores of Lake Wendouree, the Ballarat Botanical Gardens are identifiable by the brilliant blooms and classical statuary. At the rear of the gardens, the Conservatory is one focus of events during the town's Begonia Festival held each March (the other is Lake Wendouree). ✉ *Wendouree Parade* ☎ *03/5320–5135* 🎟 *Free* ⏲ *Daily 7–6, conservatory 9–5.*

★ **Sovereign Hill.** Sovereign Hill, built on the site of the Sovereign Hill Quartz Mining Company's mines, is a replica town that provides an authentic look at life, work, and play in this area during the gold rush. The main street features a hotel, blacksmith's shop, bakery, and post office—all perfectly preserved relics of their time. You can have your photo taken in period costumes, take a mineshaft tour, pan for gold (and find some), ride in a stagecoach, or head to the "lolly shop" to taste old-fashioned candy. You can return at night for "Blood on the Southern Cross," a 90-minute sound-and-light spectacular that tells the story of the Eureka Uprising. Your entry ticket also gets you into the **Gold Museum,** across Bradshaw Street, which displays an extensive collection of nuggets from the Ballarat diggings. ✉ *Bradshaw St.* ☎ *03/5337–1100* 🌐 *www.sovereignhill.com.au* 🎟 *A$42.40; A$94 (entry and Blood on the Southern Cross show)* ⏲ *Daily 10–5; two show sessions, times vary.*

WHERE TO EAT AND STAY

For expanded hotel reviews, visit Fodors.com.

$$ MEDITERRANEAN ✕ **Europa Cafe.** The all-day breakfast at this hip yet relaxed dining spot is legendary, but the lunches and dinners are also worth a trip. Lunch includes such savory treats as smoked-salmon bruschetta. For dinner, go for the lamb cutlets on mashed chats or the honey-and-mustard Western Plains pork roasted with pear, apple, and onion. ✉ *411 Sturt St.* ☎ *03/5331–2486* ⏲ *No dinner Mon.–Wed.*

Typical architecture from the gold rush era on a main street in Ballarat.

$ ✕**L'espresso.** Meals at this low-lighted local institution taste like they're
ITALIAN from your grandmother's kitchen. It's open for breakfast and lunch daily
★ and dinner (more expensive) on Friday, with specials like rolled and
roasted pork belly with an orange, fennel, and parsley salad, or slippery
jack and pine mushroom bruschetta with goat's cheese, chorizo, and
aged balsamic. The zucchini and corn fritters with bacon, roasted tomatoes, and tomato jam are a great way to start the day. This was a popular
record shop back in the 1970s, and after 35 years co-owner Greg Wood
is still selling his blues, jazz, and interesting contemporary music CDs
here. ⊠ *417 Sturt St.* ☏ *03/5333–1789* ⊗ *No dinner Sat.–Thurs.*

$$ ⊞ **The Ansonia.** Built in the 1870s as professional offices—and rescued
★ by new owners who refurbished it completely—the Ansonia is now an
excellent boutique hotel. **Pros:** cozy; arty; free parking. **Cons:** rooms
opening onto the atrium lack privacy. ⊠ *32 Lydiard St.* ☏ *03/5332–
4678* ⊕ *www.Ansonia.com.au* ⤴ *16 rooms, 3 apartments* ⌂ *In-room:
Wi-Fi. In-hotel: restaurant, parking.*

DAYLESFORD AND HEPBURN SPRINGS

*109 km (68 mi) northwest of Melbourne, 45 km (28 mi) northeast
of Ballarat.*

Nestled in the slopes of the Great Dividing Range, Daylesford and its
nearby twin, Hepburn Springs, are a spa lover's paradise. The water
table here is naturally aerated with carbon dioxide and rich in solu-
ble mineral salts, making it ideal for indulging in mineral baths and
other rejuvenating treatments. The natural springs were first noted
during the gold rush, and Swiss-Italian immigrants established a spa

at Hepburn Springs in 1875. There are now about 70 natural springs in the area. The best time to visit the area is autumn, when the deciduous trees turn bronze and you can finish up a relaxing day next to an open fire with a glass of local red.

GETTING HERE AND AROUND

The twin towns of Daylesford and Hepburn Springs are easily reached by car from Melbourne. Take the Western Highway (M8) to Ballarat, then take the Midland Highway for another 40 km (25 mi) to Daylesford (via Creswick). Hepburn Springs is a mile or two from Daylesford. V/Line operates trains from Southern Cross Station, Melbourne, to Ballarat or Woodend (near Mount Macedon), and V/Line buses connect with the trains to take passengers to Daylesford.

LIQUID GOLD

The promise of gold "in them thar hills" drew mobs of prospectors in the 1850s, but today's visitors aren't looking to quench their thirst for riches. The "Great Grape Touring Route" (⊕ *www. greatgraperoute.com.au*) and the "Vine to Vintage Trail" (⊕ *www. bendigotourism.com*) are wonderful itineraries for those who love fine wine and food. Ballarat's climate produces great Pinot Noir and Chardonnay, while the Grampians is the birthplace of Great Western, Australia's first and best-known sparkling wine. The Pyrenees region is known for its classic Shiraz.

ESSENTIALS

Transportation **V/Line** ⊠ *Southern Cross Railway Station, Spencer St., City Center, Melbourne* ☎ *13–6196* ⊕ *www.vline.com.au.*

Visitor Information **Daylesford Regional Visitor Information Centre** ⊠ *98 Vincent St.* ☎ *03/5321–6123* ⊕ *www.visitdaylesford.com.*

EXPLORING

Convent Gallery. Perched on a hillside overlooking Daylesford, the Convent Gallery is a former nunnery that has been restored to its lovely Victorian state. It houses three levels of fine art and a nun's museum. At the front of the gallery is Bad Habits, a sunny café that serves light lunches and snacks. Altar Bar is a hip place for a drink. The second-story penthouse suite is the ultimate in decadence, with its own hydrotherapy bath and a boudoir-style bedroom ($$$). ⊠ *Hill and Daly St.* ☎ *03/5348–3211* ⊕ *www.theconventy.com.au* ⊠ *A$5* ☺ *Daily 10–5.*

Fodor'sChoice ★ **Hepburn Bathhouse & Spa.** The Hepburn Bathhouse & Spa is the centerpiece of Australia's premier spa destination, and one of the largest and most spectacular spas in the country. The complex encompasses the original Edwardian Bathhouse (circa 1895), which houses private mineral baths and more than 30 wet-and-dry treatment rooms, and a stunning, contemporary building, where you find the public Bathhouse and private, more indulgent Sanctuary. Patrons can buy two-hour passes for the Bathhouse or the Sanctuary. The Bathhouse includes a relaxation mineral pool and a spa pool (A$25, Tuesday–Friday and A$35 Saturday–Monday), while the Sanctuary has underwater spa couches (for the ultimate in hydrotherapy), an aroma steam room, and a salt therapy pool (A$55 Tuesday–Friday and A$75 Saturday–Monday). There is also the day spa area, where you can choose from a long list of therapies, including body wraps and polishes, facials, and other treatments using the mineral waters. Products used in the spa include La Gaia, Emminence, and Thalgo, as well as a Hepburn Collection range specifically designed for Hepburn Bathhouse & Spa. ⊠ *1 Mineral Springs Crescent, Hepburn Springs* ☎ *03/5321–6000* ⊕ *www.hepburnbathhouse.com.au* ⊙ *Daily 9–6:30.*

Mineral Springs Reserve. Above the Hepburn Bathhouse and Spa a path winds through a series of mineral springs at the Mineral Springs Reserve. Each spring has a slightly different chemical composition—and a significantly different taste. You can bring empty bottles, if you like, and fill them for free with the mineral water of your choice.

WHERE TO STAY

For expanded hotel reviews, visit Fodors.com.

$$ **Dudley House.** This fine example of timber Federation architecture sits behind a neat hedge and picket gate on the main street of Hepburn Springs. **Pros:** tranquil garden setting; great heritage character. **Cons:** limited facilities. ⊠ *101 Main St., Hepburn Springs* ☎ *03/5348–3033, 0407/866–733* ⊕ *www.dudleyhouse.com.au* ⊅ *4 rooms* ⌂ *In-room: no a/c. In-hotel: restaurant, parking, some age restrictions* ¶⊙| *Breakfast.*

$$$$

Fodor's Choice

★

Lake House. Consistently rated one of Victoria's best restaurants, this rambling lakeside pavilion brings glamour to spa country. **Pros:** renowned food; tranquil garden setting. **Cons:** two-night minimum stay at weekends. ⊠ *King St.* ☎ *03/5348–3329* ⊕ *www.lakehouse.com.au* ⊅ *21 rooms, 12 suites* ⌂ *In-room: no a/c. In-hotel: restaurant, bar, pool, tennis court, parking* ¶⊙| *Breakfast.*

BENDIGO

150 km (93 mi) northwest of Melbourne, 92 km (57 mi) south of Echuca.

Gold was discovered in the Bendigo district in 1851, and the boom lasted well into the 1880s. The city's magnificent public buildings bear witness to the richness of its mines. Today Bendigo is a bustling, enterprising small city, with distinguished buildings lining both sides of Pall Mall in the city center. These include the Shamrock Hotel, General Post Office, and Law Courts, all majestic examples of late-Victorian architecture. Although these glorious relics of a golden age dominate the landscape, the city is far from a time warp. You'll also find a lively café and restaurant scene, 30 boutique wineries, some of which can be visited on organized winery tours, and one of the best regional art galleries in Australia.

GETTING HERE AND AROUND

To reach Bendigo, take the Calder Highway northwest from Melbourne; the trip takes about 1 hour and 40 minutes. V/Line operates trains to Bendigo from Melbourne's Southern Cross Station, a journey of about two hours.

TOURS

Bendigo Goldfields Experieces. This company, based in the grounds of Ironbark Riding Centre, runs personalized gold-prospecting tours, as well as do-it-yourself gold-panning. The half- or full-day tours include a guide, prospecting permit, transport, food and drinks, and the use of a Minelab metal detector. It's A\$350 for a full day (two people sharing one detector) or A\$290 for half a day (two people). Gold panning (groups only) costs A\$15 per person for an hour, including a 15-minute lesson, and you get to keep all the gold you find. If you like the idea of striking it rich, you can also buy your own metal detector at the company's shop. ⊠ *Lot 2, Watson St., Bendigo* ☎ *03/5448–4140* ⊕ *www. bendigogold.com.au* ➩ *A\$290 half day; A\$350 full day (for two people)* ☉ *Mon.–Sat. 8:30–5, Sun. by appointment.*

Vintage Talking Tram. A good introduction to Bendigo is a tour aboard the Vintage Talking Tram, which includes a taped commentary on the town's history. The half-hourly tram runs on its 8-km (5-mi) circuit between the Central Deborah Gold Mine and the Tram Museum, making five stops at historic sites. ☎ *03/5442–2821* ⊕ *www.bendigotramways.com* ➩ *A\$15* ☉ *Daily 10–4:20.*

ESSENTIALS

Transportation V/Line ⊠ *Southern Cross Railway Station, Spencer St., City Center, Melbourne* ☎ *13–6196* ⊕ *www.vline.com.au.*

Visitor Information Bendigo Visitor Information Centre ⊠ *51–67 Pall Mall* ☎ *03/5434–6060, 1800/813153* ⊕ *www.bendigotourism.com.au.*

EXPLORING

Fodor's Choice ★

Bendigo Art Gallery. The beautiful Bendigo Art Gallery houses a notable collection of contemporary Australian paintings, including the work of Jeffrey Smart, Lloyd Rees, and Clifton Pugh. (Pugh once owned a remote Outback pub infamous for its walls daubed with his own pornographic cartoons.) The gallery also has some significant 19th-century French realist and impressionist works, bequeathed by a local surgeon. It also hosts international exhibitions such as the world exclusive "The White Wedding Dress: 200 Years of Wedding Fashions" in 2011, featuring dresses from the the London Victoria and Albert Museum's superb collection. There's a free guided tour every day at 2 pm. ⊠ *42 View St.* ☎ *03/5434–6088* ⊕ *www.bendigoartgallery.com.au* ➩ *Free or donation* ☉ *Daily 10–5.*

Bendigo Pottery. Australia's oldest working pottery turns out the distinctive brown-and-cream style that many Australians have in their kitchens. Founded in 1858, the historic workshop offers demonstrations. You can even get your hands dirty creating your own clay piece during a wheel-throwing lesson (bookings essential during school holidays); there's also a clay play area for small children. Impressive beehive brick kilns, which you can step inside, are star exhibits in the museum. It's 6½ km (4 mi) northeast of Bendigo on the way to Echuca. ⊠ *146 Midland Hwy., Epsom* ☎ *03/5448–4404* ⊕ *www.bendigopottery.com.au* ➩ *Free, museum A\$8, wheel-throwing lessons A\$12 for half hr, A\$18 for hr* ☉ *Daily 9–5.*

Central Deborah Gold Mine. Central Deborah Gold Mine, with a 1,665-foot mine shaft, yielded almost a ton of gold before it closed in 1954. Aboveground you can pan for gold, see the old stamper battery, and climb up the poppet head, but the thrill of mining is felt below ground. Three underground tours explore different mine levels; on the Mine Experience you descend 200 feet to widened tunnels, while the Underground Adventure puts you another 78 feet deeper. Nine Levels of Darkness is the ultimate adventure here; over 4½ hours you sign on as a "new chum" and ride a tiny cage lift 748 feet down to dripping original tunnels, where you work a drill, "set" explosives, and climb ladders. ⊠ *76 Violet St.* ☎ *03/5443–8322* ⊕ *www.central-deborah.com* ⛱ *A$14 (above ground area only); tours (including entry): Mine Expeience A$26.50; Underground Adventure A$75; Nine Levels of Darkness A$275* ☉ *Daily 9:30–5 (last tour at 4).*

Golden Dragon Museum. The superb Golden Dragon Museum evokes the Chinese community's important role in Bendigo life past and present. Its centerpieces are the century-old Loong imperial ceremonial dragon and the Sun Loong dragon, which, at more than 106 yards in length, is said to be the world's longest. When carried in procession, it requires 52 carriers and 52 relievers; the head alone weighs 64 pounds. Also on display are other ceremonial objects, costumes, and historic artifacts. The lovely Yi Yuan Gardens, opposite, with ponds and bridges, are part of the museum. ⊠ *5–11 Bridge St.* ☎ *03/5441–5044* ⊕ *www.goldendragonmuseum.org* ⛱ *A$10* ☉ *Daily 9:30–5.*

Joss House. An active place of worship on the outskirts of the city, the Joss House was built during the gold-rush days by Chinese miners. At the height of the boom in the 1850s and 1860s, about a quarter of the miners were Chinese. These men were usually dispatched from villages on the Chinese mainland, and they were expected to work hard and return as quickly as possible with their fortunes. The Chinese were scrupulously law-abiding and hardworking—qualities that did not always endear them to other miners—and anti-Chinese riots were common. ⊠ *Finn St., Emu Point* ☎ *03/5442–1685* ⊕ *www.bendigotrust.com.au* ⛱ *A$5.50* ☉ *11–4.*

WHERE TO EAT AND STAY

For expanded hotel reviews, visit Fodors.com.

$$　✕ **Whirrakee.** One of Bendigo's most decorative old buildings is the
FRENCH　perfect setting for this restaurant's fine French-accented food, starched white tablecloths, and exemplary, yet friendly, service. The menu reflects the best of local produce, and you might start with ravioli of organic pumpkin served with whipped goat's curd, roasted pinenuts, and a currant and balsamic vinegar dressing, or the seared Coffin Bay scallops with marinated potato and yabbie salad, creme fraiche dressing, and baby sorrel. The Berkshire pork rib cutlet with potato fondant, braised cabbage, crackling, and sauce charcuterie is a highlight of the entrées. But leave room for navel-orange mousse with blood orange sorbet or an indulgence in chocolate. The wine list showcases local wineries. ⊠ *17 View Point* ☎ *03/5441–5557* ☉ *Closed Mon.*

$$ ⬛ **The Hotel Shamrock.** The lodgings at this landmark Victorian hotel in the city center range from traditional guest rooms to spacious suites. **Pros:** historic gold-era building, central position. **Cons:** limited facilities. ⬛ *Pall Mall at Williamson St.* ☎ *03/5443–0333* ⊕ *www.hotelshamrock. com.au* ⬛ *24 rooms, 4 suites* ⬛ *In-room: Wi-Fi. In-hotel: restaurant, bar, parking.*

$$ ⬛ **Langley Hall.** A circa-1903 Edwardian mansion, Langley Hall was
★   built as a residence for the Anglican archbishop of Bendigo. **Pros:** lovely garden; good price; 19th century furnishings. **Cons:** few amenities; breakfast is a tad expensive; not walking distance from town. ⬛ *484 Napier St.* ☎ *03/5443–3693* ⊕ *www.innhouse.com.au/langleyhall.html* ⬛ *6 rooms* ⬛ *Breakfast.*

THE GRAMPIANS

About 93 km (79 mi) north of Port Fairy are the Grampians, sometimes referred to by their Aboriginal name Gariwerd. This 415,000-acre region combines stunning mountain scenery, abundant native wildlife, and invigorating outdoor activities. The sharp sandstone peaks here were long ago forced up from an ancient seabed, and sculpted by aeons of wind and rain. Today the park has more than 160 km (100 mi) of walking trails, as well as some 900 wildflower species, 200 species of birds, and 35 species of native mammals. The best time to visit is October–December, when wildflowers carpet the landscape, the weather is mild, and summer crowds have yet to arrive. There are several wineries in the region, including the historic Seppelt vineyard and winery at Great Western about 38 km (24 mi) east of Halls Gap, which offers fascinating tours of its underground wine cellars.

THE GRAMPIANS NATIONAL PARK

260 km (162 mi) west of Melbourne, 100 km (62 mi) north of Hamilton.

Fodor'sChoice **Grampians National Park.** Comprising four mountain ranges—Mt. Dif-
★   ficult, Mt. William, Serra, and Victoria—the Grampians National Park spills over 412,000 acres. Its rugged peaks, towering trees, web of waterfalls and creeks, and plethora of wildlife attract bushwalkers, rock climbers, and nature lovers. Spectacular wildflowers carpet the region in spring, while a number of significant Aboriginal rock-art sites make it an ideal place to learn about Victoria's indigenous history. The township of Halls Creek (population 300) is in the national park, and with its 10,000 tourist beds becomes quite a busy place in summer and at Easter. If you're staying in a self-catering accommodation, it is very wise to stock up on groceries and wine in the big towns of Ballarat, Arafat, Hamilton, or Horsham, since prices at the Halls Gap general store are inflated. One of the most picturesque drives in the park is the 60-km (37-km) stretch from Halls Gap to Dunkeld.

Heavy rain in early 2011 caused extensive damage to the park, including multiple landslides, and much of the park was closed. Walking tracks are steadily reopening as restoration works are completed.

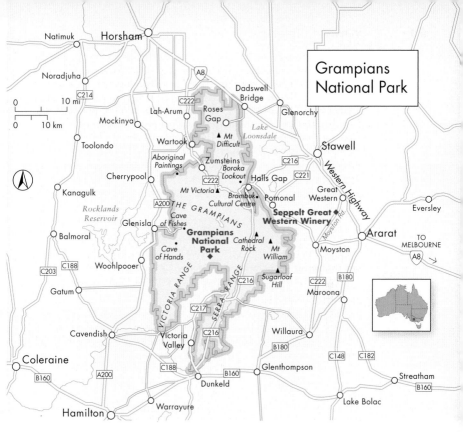

Brambuk National Park & Cultural Centre. Owned and operated by Aboriginal people, the Brambuk National Park and Cultural Centre provides a unique living history of indigenous culture in this part of Victoria. Displays of artwork, weapons, clothes, and tools here provide a glimpse into the life of Koori people (Aboriginal people of southeastern Australia). A film screened in the Dreaming Theatre tells the Creation legends of the Grampians mountains. Educational programs, including boomerang throwing, painting, and didgeridoo workshops, are presented daily, and there is a bushtucker discovery walk and tasting most days at 2 pm. Ceremonial music and dances are performed weekly during school holidays. Visitors can learn the significance of paintings at nearby Bunjil's Shelter on rock-art tours conducted on weekdays at 9:30 am. ⊠ *Grampians Tourist Rd., Halls Gap* ☎ *03/5361-4000* ⊕ *www. brambuk.com.au* ⊠ *Free; rock-art tours A$35, films and activities A$5, bushtucker walks A$9* ⊙ *Daily 9–5*

GETTING HERE AND AROUND

Halls Gap (the base town for the Grampians National Park) is reached via Ballarat and Ararat on the Western Highway (Highway 8). The town is 260 km (162 mi) northwest of Melbourne, 97 km (60 mi) northeast of Hamilton, 140 km (87 mi) west of Ballarat. V/Line operates trains to Ballarat from Melbourne. V/Line buses connect with the trains to take passengers to Halls Gap. For timetables and fares, contact V/Line.

TOURS

For those who love experiencing the great outdoors from different angles, Hangin' Out runs rock climbing and abseiling tours to suit beginners and more experienced climbers; they also have an all-day guided adventure walk (A$135) from Mt. Stapylton to Hollow Mountain in the north of the Grampians. A four-hour taste of real rock climbing and abseiling costs A$75 (minimum two people); a full-day introduction to the rope sports is A$130. Private guided single- and multipitch climbs can be arranged.

ESSENTIALS

Tour Operators **Hangin' Out** ✉ *PO Box 75, Halls Gap* ☎ *03/5356–4535, 0407/684–831.* **V/Line** ✉ *Southern Cross Railway Station, Spencer St., City Center, Melbourne* ☎ *13–6196* ⊕ *www.vline.com.au.*

Visitor Information **Halls Gap Visitor Information Centre** ✉ *Grampians Rd., Halls Gap* ☎ *03/5356–4616, 1800/065599* ⊕ *www.visithallsgap.com.au.* **Stawell and Grampians Visitor Information Centre** ✉ *50–52 Western Hwy., Stawell* ☎ *03/5358–2314, 1800/330080* ⊕ *www.visitgrampians.com.au.*

OUTDOOR ACTIVITIES

CANOEING **Absolute Outdoors.** If you want to experience the Grampians wilderness from its serene lakes, a half- or full-day canoeing trip is the answer. This company has outings on Lake Bellfield, a little to the southeast of the township. They also offer rock climbing, abseiling, and mountain-bike adventures within the park. They operate from a shop that sells outdoor equipment in Halls Gap, and have another shop/office in Portland on the Great Ocean Road. ✉ *Shop 4, Stony Creek Stores, Halls Gap* ☎ *03/5356–4556* ⊕ *www.absoluteoutdoors.com.au* 🛶 *Canoeing tours A$60 half day; from A$100 full day (depending on numbers).*

HIKING AND WALKING **Auswalk.** This long-established walking specialist is based at Halls Gap, and its guides know the area like the backs of their hands. It operates guided and self-guided five-night inn-to-inn hikes with a mix of B&B and motel accommodation; Auswalk transports your luggage between accommodation stops. Maps and other information are provided for self-guided walkers, and only two participants are needed for a tour to take place. The terrain is graded "moderate" for 55% of the walk, with about 25% rated strenuous. Wildlife, particularly kangaroos and wallabies, is abundant in many areas and wildflowers festoon the park from August to November. Trips usually run year-round, with the exception of July, however torrential rain and consequent landslides in early 2011 closed parts of the park and standard tours could not run. At this writing walks were resuming, but call ahead to be safe. Self-guided walks start at A$1,395 per person, and guided walks from A$2,195. ✉ *4 Red Gum Lease Track, Halls Gap* ☎ *03/5356–4971* ⊕ *www.auswalk.com.au.*

OFF THE BEATEN PATH **Seppelt Great Western Winery.** Although many Australians may have never visited Seppelt Great Western winery, it's a good bet that most of them have sampled Great Western "champagne" at some point in their lives. Today it's referred to as "sparkling," and the winery makes a Salinger and a Fleur de Lys sparkling as well as a Sparkling Shiraz and still wines. Beneath the winery is an underground labyrinth of tunnels, known as the Drives, dating back to 1868 and originally built by goldminers.

Sitting on edge of Boroka Lookout in the Grampians National Park.

This is where the best sparklings are kept. You can take a day tour of these tunnels and the nearby shaft house and taste 20 Seppelt wines, or a candlelight evening tour (minimum 10 people) on the last weekend of every month, which includes wine tasting and a cheese platter. ⊠ *Moyston Rd., Great Western* 🕾 *03/5361–2239* ⊕ *www.seppelt.com. au* ⊇ *Cellar door free (premium wine tasting $5); tours A$16, night tour A$30* ⊗ *Tastings daily 10–5; tunnel tours Mon.–Sat. at 11 and 2.*

WHERE TO EAT AND STAY

For expanded hotel reviews, visit Fodors.com.

$$
AUSTRALIAN

✗ **Kookaburra Bar & Bistro.** In the heart of Halls Gap, this is one of the best dining options you'll find in the park area. You can graze on a crispy squid salad and spinach crepes or tuck into a risotto of duck slow roasted with star anise. The mains range from sea to paddock, with blackened barramundi, kangaroo fillet, and sizzling steaks. Kookaburra's own ice cream, made daily with pure ingredients, is a great way to finish a meal. ⊠ *125 Grampian Rd., Halls Gap* 🕾 *03/5356–4222* ⊗ *Closed Mon., no lunch Tues.–Sat.*

$$
MODERN
AUSTRALIAN
Fodor's Choice
★

✗ **Royal Mail Hotel.** Expansive views of the southern Grampians peaks are almost an unwelcome distraction from the extraordinary food plated up at the only hotel in the tiny town of Dunkeld, 64 km (40 mi) south of Halls Gap. The fare is all about seasonality, locality, and creativity, with chef Dan Hunter drawing on organic and heirloom produce from the hotel garden, local farms, and the wild. His 10-course degustation dinner menu (A$160), featuring such culinary wonders as southern rock lobster with prosciutto, sea lettuce, and quinoa, and eel and bone marrow with pickled vegetables, earned the hotel Restaurant of the

Year in *The Age's Good Food Guide 2011*. There is also an à la carte bistro ($$$), and an excellent bar menu ($). With fine accommodation on-site too ($$–$$$), after dinner you can stroll to a spacious Mountain View or Garden View room, or apartment, all fitted with every modern convenience, or drive the 3 km (1.86 mi) to the hotel's historic Mt. Sturgeon farm, and sleep in a luxurious, period-furnished homestead bedroom or cozy stone cottage. ✉ *98 Parker St. (Glenelg Hwy.), Dunkeld* ☎ *03/5577–2241* ⊕ *www.royalmail.com.au* ⌖ *Reservations essential* ☉ *Restaurant: closed Sun. and Mon., no lunch. Bar: closed Mon., no dinner Sun.*

$$$$
Fodor'sChoice
★

☲ **Boroka Downs.** On 300 acres of bush, scrub, and grassland, bordering the national park, Boroka's six villas are nothing short of spectacular. **Pros:** luxurious and eco-friendly. **Cons:** all of this beauty comes at a steep price. ✉ *51 Birdswing Rd., Halls Gap* ⌂ *Box 77, Halls Gap 3382* ☎ *03/5356–6243* ⊕ *www.borokadowns.com.au* ⤴ *6 villas* ⌖ *In-room: safe, kitchen. In-hotel: laundry facilities, parking, some age restrictions* ⑩ *Breakfast.*

MURRAY RIVER REGION

From its birthplace in the folds of the Great Dividing Range in southern New South Wales, the Mighty Murray winds 2,574 km (1,596 mi) northwest and then south before it empties into Lake Alexandrina, south of Adelaide. But it is not as mighty as it once was. Despite flooding rains in early 2011, the decade-long drought which preceded the deluge, and many more years than that of reliance on—and exploitation of— the Murray and its tributaries by irrigators, river towns and the city of Adelaide threaten the river's health and the livelihoods of the people who rely on it.

Water—its supply, collection, and use—is a subject on almost everyone's lips. A revamped but still controversial water-trading and buy-out system based on water access entitlements, which promises to reallocate precious Murray-Darling water, is one of a range of measures being implemented by Australia's federal and state governments to reduce the impact of climate change and improve and supplement existing water sources. Making the right decisions for the river and those dependent on it is a challenging balancing act.

Some farmers walked off the land during the most recent dry stretch, and the floods tested many more, but the Murray River still waters vast acreages of pastures, orchards, and vineyards.

Victoria exports more than A$100 million worth of wine annually, and the Murray River muscats and ports are legendary. The Rutherglen area, in particular, produces the country's finest fortified wine (dessert wine or "stickies").

Steeped in history and natural beauty, the eastern Murray River valley and High Country region is a gourmet foodies' heaven known for its fruit, olives, honey, and cheeses, as well as a renowned wine region. The lovely town of Beechworth is an ideal place to break the drive between Sydney and Melbourne.

GETTING HERE AND AROUND

The wide-open spaces of the region surrounding the Murray River make driving the most sensible and feasible means of exploration. Rutherglen is 274 km (170 mi) north of Melbourne, about a 3½- to 4-hour drive up the Hume Highway; Echuca is 204 km (127 mi) northwest of Melbourne, about a 2½-hour drive. These two Murray River towns are 194 km (121 mi) apart. V/Line trains (☏ 13–6196 ⊕ *www. vline.com.au*) run to most of the major towns in the region, including Echuca and Rutherglen, but not Beechworth; this reasonable access is useful if you do not have a car or want to avoid the long-distance drives. As with most country Victorian areas, direct train access from Melbourne to the main centers is reasonable, but getting between towns isn't as easy.

BEECHWORTH

271 km (168 mi) northeast of Melbourne, 96 km (60 mi) northwest of Alpine National Park, 44 km (26 mi) south of Rutherglen.

One of the prettiest towns in Victoria, Beechworth flourished during the gold rush. When gold ran out, the town of 30,000 was left with all the trappings of prosperity—fine banks, imposing public buildings, breweries, parks, and hotels wrapped in wrought iron—but with scarcely two nuggets to rub together. However, poverty protected the town from such modern improvements as aluminum window frames, and many historic treasures that might have been destroyed in the name of progress have been brought back to life.

GETTING HERE AND AROUND

Beechworth and Rutherglen are on opposite sides of the Hume Freeway, the main Sydney–Melbourne artery. The 44-km (26-mi) Rutherglen-Beechworth Road (C377) connects both towns. Beechworth is about a four-hour drive from Melbourne, twice that from Sydney.

ESSENTIALS

Visitor Information Beechworth Tourist Information Centre ⊠ *Old Town Hall, 103 Ford St.* ☏ *03/5728–8065, 1300/366321* ⊕ *www.beechworthonline.com.au.*

EXPLORING

Ford Street. A stroll along Ford Street is the best way to absorb the town's character. Among the distinguished buildings are **Tanswell's Commercial Hotel,** the **Town Hall,** and the **Courthouse.** It was in the latter that the committal hearing for the famous bushranger Ned Kelly took place in August 1880. His feisty mother, Ellen Kelly, was also sentenced to three years in jail at this court.

Burke Museum. The Burke Museum takes its name from Robert O'Hara Burke who, with William Wills, became one of the first white explorers to cross Australia from south to north in 1861. Burke served as superintendent of police in Beechworth from 1856 to 1859. Not surprisingly, the small area and few mementos dedicated to Burke are overshadowed by the Ned Kelly exhibits, including letters, photographs, and memorabilia that give genuine insight into the man and his misdeeds. The museum also displays a reconstructed streetscape of Beechworth

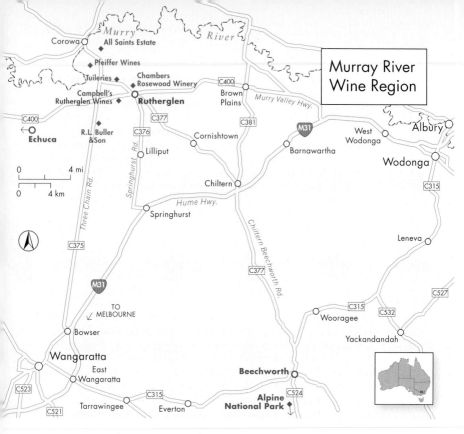

in the 1880s. ⊠ *Loch St.* ☎ *03/5728–8067* ⊕ *www.beechworth.com/ burkemus* 🖾 *A$8* ☉ *Daily 10–5.*

Murray Breweries Beechworth. Murray Breweries Beechworth brewed beer in the 1860s, but now concentrates on nonalcoholic cordials produced using old-time recipes and seasonal flavors, like Sicilian blood orange. You'll find a display of antique brewing equipment, worldwide beer labels, and rare bottles. On the same site is the Beechworth Carriage Museum, a collection of 20 horse-drawn vehicles and Australian Light Horse Infantry memorabilia from World War I. Tastings are free. ⊠ *29 Last St.* ☎ *03/5728–1304* ⊕ *www.murraybreweries.com.au* 🖾 *Free* ☉ *Weekdays 10–4.*

OUTDOOR ACTIVITIES

BICYCLING The area from the Murray River to the mountains of North-East Victoria are ideal for mountain bike enthusiasts.

Beechworth Cycle & Saws. Beechworth Cycle & Saws on Beechworth's main street rents for A$25 for half a day and A$35 for a full day. ⊠ *17 Camp St., Beechworth* ☎ *03/5728–1402* ☉ *9–5:30 Mon. to Fri., 9–1 Sat., open Sun only during school holidays.*

Ned Kelly

The English have Robin Hood, the Americans Jesse James. Australians have Ned Kelly, a working-class youth whose struggles against police injustice and governmental indifference captured the country's heart. The best way to learn about the local legend is to visit the town of Beechworth, where a Ned Kelly Guided Walking Tour (A$10) departs from the visitor information center every day at 1:15 pm. You'll see the courthouse where he was tried and the jail where he was imprisoned during his many scrapes with the law. The Burke Museum displays one of his death masks, made shortly after he was hanged at Melbourne Gaol. If you long to hear more, visit Glenrowan (40 km [25 mi], southwest of Beechworth), the scene of his famous "last stand." It was here that Kelly, dressed in his legendary iron armor, walked alone down the main street fending off police bullets. He was shot in the leg and arrested. A huge statue, and a sound-and-light show that has received rather mixed reviews and is said to be "quite loud," commemorate Australia's most infamous outlaw.

Murray to Mountains Rail Trail. The Murray to Mountains Rail Trail is a 98-km (61-mi) paved trail that travels from Wangaratta to Bright, with a branch line to Beechworth. Bicycle hire is available at Wangaratta, Beechworth, Bright, and Myrtleford. A trail map is available from the visitor centers at each of these towns, and can be downloaded from the trail Web site. ☎ *1800/991–044* ⊕ *www.murraytomountains.com.au.*

HIKING AND WALKING There are several national parks within easy reach of Beechworth: Chiltern-Mt. Pilot National Park, Beechworth Historic Park, Mount Buffalo National Park, Mount Granya State Park, and Warby Range State Park. The Beechworth visitor center and Parks Victoria have information on bushwalks. The town of Beechworth is the perfect place to get out and about and stretch your legs while admiring late 19th-century architecture. You can pick up a copy of "Echoes of History," a self-guided walking tour of the town from the visitor information center.

Parks Victoria. Parks Victoria has information on Victoria's National Parks and walking trails. ☎ *13–1963* ⊕ *www.parkweb.vic.gov.au.*

WHERE TO STAY

For expanded hotel reviews, visit Fodors.com.

$$$ Country Charm Swiss Cottages. Landscaped gardens overlooking the Beechworth Gorge surround these charming pine and cedar cottages. **Pros:** tranquil setting; great views. **Cons:** two-night stay on weekends. ✉ *22 Malakoff Rd.* ☎ *03/5728–2435* ⊕ *www.swisscottages.com.au* ⌐ *4 cottages* ⚘ *In-room: kitchen. In-hotel: laundry facilities.*

The mighty Murray River is the life-blood of the region.

RUTHERGLEN

274 km (170 mi) northeast of Melbourne, 40 km (25 mi) northwest of Beechworth.

The surrounding red-loam soil signifies the beginning of the Rutherglen wine district, the source of Australia's finest fortified wines. If the term conjures up visions of cloying ports, you're in for a surprise. In his authoritative *Australian Wine Compendium*, James Halliday says, "Like Narcissus drowning in his own reflection, one can lose oneself in the aroma of a great old muscat."

The main event in the region is Tastes of Rutherglen, held over two consecutive weekends in March. The festival is a celebration of food, wine, and music—in particular jazz, folk, and country. Events are held in town and at all surrounding wineries. Another popular day in the vineyards is the Rutherglen Winery Walkabout held in June, when wine, food, and music are again on the menu.

GETTING HERE AND AROUND

See Beechworth above. Rutherglen is 274 km (170 mi) north of Melbourne, about a 3½- to 4-hour drive along the Hume Highway. A V/Line train and bus service operates daily from Melbourne's Southern Cross Station via Seymour and Wangaratta, a journey of about 3 hours and 15 minutes.

TOURS

Grapevine Getaways offers winery tours for a minimum of four people, with visits to five to six wineries on half-day tours and eight to nine estates on day tours. Day tours cost from A$50 per person (with pickup from Rutherglen accommodation only), and from A\$95 including a gourmet picnic hamper lunch at one of the wineries. The tour vehicle is a distinctive purple minibus.

ESSENTIALS

Transportation **V/Line** ✉ *Southern Cross Railway Station, Spencer St., Melbourne* ☎ *13–6196* ⊕ *wwwvline.com.au.*

Visitor Information **Grapevine Getaways** ✉ *72 Murray St.* ☎ *02/6032-8577* ⊕ *www.grapevinegetaways.com.au.* **Rutherglen Wine Experience and Visitor Information Centre** ✉ *57 Main St.* ☎ *02/6033–6300, 1800/622871* ⊕ *www.rutherglenvic.com.*

EXPLORING THE WINERIES

★ **All Saints Estate.** All Saints Estate has been in business since 1864. A splendid, turreted castle built in the 1880s houses the winery, storage areas, and cellar door, while the old bottling hall and cellar have been revamped as a cheese tasting room. (A corrugated-iron Chinese dormitory is the property's third heritage-listed building.) A guided tour of the winery can be arranged on request. The winery produces muscat and tokay made from 50-year-old vines and a range of crisp whites and full-bodied reds. The Indigo Cheese Co., with its resident cheesemaker Paula Jenkin, produces premium handmade treats, and wine and cheese tasting sessions are available by appointment. The menu at the Terrace restaurant changes daily, but might include starters like roated Milawa (local) quail with truffled polenta, Calabrese sausage, and chestnuts, and entrées such as durif-braised suckling lamb with buttermilk mashed potato, zucchini, and capsicum. Desserts are excellent, especially when combined with a formidable northeast fortified wine. The cellar door and cheese room are open daily; the restaurant is open for lunch from Wednesday to Sunday and for dinner on Saturday only. ✉ *All Saints Rd., Wahgunyah* ✛ *9 km (5½ mi) southeast of Rutherglen* ☎ *02/6035–2222* ⊕ *www.allsaintswine.com.au* 🎫 *Free* ☉ *Cellar door: Mon.–Sat. 9–5:30, Sun. 10–5:30; cheese room: weekdays 10–4, weekends 10–5.*

R.L. Buller & Son. Established by Reginald Langdon Buller in 1921, R.L. Buller & Son produces delicious fortified wines (muscuts and sherries) and gutsy, full-bodied reds, the flagship being the Shiraz. As the old Shiraz vines are not irrigated, the annual yields are low, but the fruit produced has intense flavor, which winemaker Andrew Buller crafts into wines of great depth and elegance. There are also small plantings of rarer varieties such as Mondeuse. There are tastings and sales at the cellar door, but no restaurant. This is a winery for those who like their reds. Also on the winery's grounds is **Buller Bird Park,** an aviary of rare parrots and native Australian birds. ✉ *Three Chain Rd. at Murray Valley Hwy.* ☎ *02/6032–9660* ⊕ *www.rlbullerandson.com.au* 🎫 *Free* ☉ *9–5.*

Campbell's Rutherglen Wines. Campbell's Wines is a fifth-generation family business that dates back to 1870. Brothers Colin and Malcolm Campbell, the winemaker and viticulturist, respectively, have been at the helm for the past 40 years. Famed for its award-winning Bobbie Burns Shiraz and Merchant Prince Rare Rutherglen Muscat, the property spills over a picturesque 160 acres. You can wander freely through the winery on a self-guided tour and taste wines at the cellar door, including rare and aged vintages. Vintage Reserve wines are available only at the cellar door. The winery does not have a restaurant, but takes part in the annual Tastes of Rutherglen wine festival, when food and music are on the agenda. It's 3 km (1 mi) from Rutherglen. ⊠ *Murray Valley Hwy.* ☏ *02/6033–6000* ⊕ *www.campbellswines.com.au* ☕ *Free* ⊘ *Mon.–Sat. 9–5, Sun. 10–5.*

Chambers Rosewood Winery. Chambers Rosewood Winery was established in the 1850s and is one of Australia's heavyweight producers of fortified wines. Stephen Chambers's muscats are legendary, with blending stocks that go back more than a century. Stephen runs a very relaxed winery, which is rustic in the real sense of the word, being just a few corrugated-iron sheds in an off-the-beaten track laneway. The cellar door is renowned for offering great value and plenty of tastings; you can take home reasonably priced red and white wines, sherries, ports, muscat, and tokays—from the clean skin variety (no label stock) to big two-liter flagons. There's no restaurant, just a cellar door, which also sells homemade jams, gourmet dressings, pickles, olive oil, and even chocolate-infused wine. ⊠ *Barkly St. off Corowa Rd.* ☏ *02/6032–8641* ⊕ *www. chambersrosewood.com.au* ☕ *Free* ⊘ *Mon.–Sat. 9–5, Sun. 10–5.*

Pfeiffer Wines. Pfeiffer Wines is another winery with a long history, the first vines having been planted on the bend of Sunday Creek, near Wahgunyah, in 1895. The Pfeiffers bought it in the 1980s and have continued the tradition of making exceptional fortified wines and varietal wines, including Chardonnay. It also has one of the few Australian plantings of gamay, the classic French grape used to make Beaujolais. At this small rustic winery you can pre-order (24 hours notice) spring/summer picnic baskets stuffed with crusty bread, smoked trout, marinated lamb fillets, chicken-breast slices, kipfler potato salad, cheese, fresh fruit, and a bottle of table wine, or autumn/winter hampers with treats such as soup, curry, and all the other trimmings for A$80 for two including plates and cutlery. Vegetarian baskets are A$72, and children's are A$12.50. Cheese platters are available any time. Winemaker Jen Pfeiffer makes an aperitif called Pfeiffer Seriously Pink, along with a Chardonnay-Marsanne, Shiraz, Merlot, and fortifieds such as muscadelle and tawnies (which one can no longer call "ports"). ⊠ *Distillery Rd., Wahgunyah* ✛ *9 km (5½ mi) southeast of Rutherglen* ☏ *02/6033–2805* ⊕ *www.pfeifferwinesrutherglen.com.au* ☕ *Free* ⊘ *Mon.–Sat. 9–5, Sun. 10–5.*

WHERE TO STAY

For expanded hotel reviews, visit Fodors.com.

$$ 🏨 **Tuileries.** Incorporating a vineyard, olive groves, and a renowned
★ restaurant, Tuileries feels like an exclusive retreat. **Pros:** beautifully appointed suites. tranquil country setting. **Cons:** next-to-no nighlife in Rutherglen. ⊠ *13–35 Drummond St.* ☏ *02/6032–9033* ⊕ *www. tuileriesrutherglen.com.au* ⇴ *16 suites* ⌂ *In-room: Wi-Fi. In-hotel: restaurant, pool, tennis court, gym, parking* ❢⏐ *Breakfast.*

ALPINE NATIONAL PARK

323 km (200 mi) northeast of Melbourne, 40–50 km (25–31 mi) south to southeast of Mt. Buffalo.

Alpine National Park. The name Alpine National Park actually applies to three loosely connected areas in eastern Victoria that follow the peaks of the Great Dividing Range. One of these areas, formerly called Bogong National Park, contains some of the highest mountains on the continent. Accordingly, it is a wintertime destination for skiers who flock to the resorts at Falls Creek, Mt. Buller, and Mt. Hotham.

The land around here is rich in history. *Bogong* is an Aboriginal word for "big moth," and it was to Mt. Bogong that Aborigines came each year after the winter thaw in search of bogong moths, considered a delicacy. Aborigines were eventually displaced by cattle ranchers who brought their cattle here to graze. The main townships in the area are Bright and Mount Beauty, both of which have visitor information centers.

GETTING HERE AND AROUND

Bus services to Alpine National Park operate from Albury on the New South Wales border in the north. In ski season Pyles Coaches depart from Melbourne for Falls Creek via Mt. Beauty. V/Line's combined train and bus operates from Melbourne's Southern Cross Station to Wangaratta, with a connection on to Bright.

ESSENTIALS

Transportation **Pyles Coaches** ☎ *03/5754–4024* ⊕ *www.pyles.com.au.* **V/Line** ✉ *Southern Cross Station, Spencer St., City Center, Melbourne* ☎ *13–6196* ⊕ *www.vline.com.au.*

Visitor Information **Parks Victoria.** For information on walks and parks in the area, contact Parks Victoria. ☎ *13–1963* ⊕ *www.parkweb.vic.gov.au.*

OUTDOOR ACTIVITIES

The Alpine National Park really has two seasons—winter (from June to September) and the rest of the year. In winter the main activities are skiing, snowboarding, and tobogganing at Falls Creek, Mt. Buller, Mt. Hotham, and Dinner Plain. In spring, summer, and autumn these areas are perfect for bushwalking, cycling, horseback riding, and kayaking. The visitor centers and Parks Victoria have walking and cycling trail maps.

5 Star Adventure Tours. Bright-based 5 Star Adventure Tours can hook you up with bushwalking, kayaking, 4WD and camping tours, as well as half- and full-day ski and snowboarding trips. Kayaking takes place on the Buffalo, Ovens, or Kiewa rivers from spring to autumn, with all-day trips including 90 minutes of training. ✉ *PO Box 470 3741* ☎ *03/5759–2555, 0438/339–030 bookings* ⊕ *www.5staradventure.com.au.*

WHERE TO EAT AND STAY

For expanded hotel reviews, visit Fodors.com.

$$$ ✕ **Simone's of Bright.** Made a Melbourne Food and Wine Festival Leg-
ITALIAN end in 2009, Patrizia Simone heads the family team behind this two-decades-old restaurant in a 19th-century cottage in the middle of town. The menu shows off Patrizia's passion for cooking rustic Italian food and using seasonal local produce: you might try stuffed zuccini flowers,

roasted goat, or saltbush lamb. The rhubarb comes fresh from "Joe's garden." Tables and chairs spill out onto the front patio or the rear atrium over summer. ⊠ *98 Gavan St., Bright* 🕾 *03/5755–2266* ⊕ *www. simonesrestaurant.com.au* ⌲ *Reservations essential.*

$$$ 🍴 **Villa Gusto.** Everything in Colin McLaren's Tuscan-inspired lodging
Fodor's Choice   has been imported from Italy: cast-iron fountains, marble fittings, 17th-
★   century antiques, exquisite tapestries—even the retro movie posters above the bar. **Pros:** luxury accommodations; superb food; tranquil country setting. **Cons:** minimum two-night booking on weekends. ⊠ *630 Buckland Valley Rd., Buckland, Bright* 🕾 *03/5756–2000* ⊕ *www.villagusto.com. au* 🛏 *8 suites* ⌂ *In-hotel: restaurant, bar, some age restrictions* ⊗ *No lunch in restaurant. No dinner Mon.–Wed.* 🍴 *Breakfast.*

ECHUCA

206 km (128 mi) north of Melbourne, 194 km (120 mi) west of Rutherglen, 92 km (57 mi) north of Bendigo.

The name Echuca comes from a local Aboriginal word meaning "meeting of the waters," a reference to the town's location at the confluence of the Murray, Campaspe, and Goulburn rivers. In the second half of the 19th century Echuca was Australia's largest inland port. Many reminders of Echuca's colorful heyday remain in the restored paddle steamers, barges, and historic hotels, and in the Red Gum Works, the town's sawmill, now a working museum.

GETTING HERE AND AROUND

Echuca is a three-hour drive from Melbourne, reached most directly by the Northern Highway (Highway 75). The V/Line train and bus combination takes three hours and 20 minutes from Melbourne's Southern Cross Station to Echuca, via Bendigo. At Bendigo station, a bus connects for the onward bus journey.

ESSENTIALS

Visitor Information Echuca Moama Visitor Information Centre ⊠ *2 Heygarth St.* 🕾 *1800/804446* ⊕ *www.echucamoama.com.*

EXPLORING

Historic River Precinct. A tour of the Historic River Precinct begins at the Port of Echuca office on Murray Esplanade, where you can purchase a ticket that gets you into several historic buildings. The **Bridge Hotel** was built by Henry Hopwood, ex-convict father of Echuca, who had the foresight to establish a punt, and then to build a bridge at this commercially strategic point on the river. The **Star Hotel,** built in the 1860s, has an underground bar and escape tunnel, which was used by after-hours drinkers in the 19th century to evade the police. The **Historic Wharf** displays the heavy-duty side of the river trade, including a warehouse, old railroad tracks, and riverboats. Among the vessels docked at the wharf is the PS *Adelaide,* the world's oldest operating wooden-hulled paddle steamer.

One-hour river excursions aboard the *Adelaide* (built in 1866*),* the historic *Pevensey, Canberra,* and *Alexander Arbuthnot,* and the *Emmylou,* a 19th-century-style boat built in 1980–82 for a television series, are a

Snow Gum trees on the Bogong High Plains in Alpine National Park.

refreshing treat at the end of a hot summer's day. The paddle wheelers depart regularly from 10 am to 4 pm; tickets are available from the port office or Bond Store on Murray Esplanade; a one-hour cruise on the PS *Emmylou* costs A$25. ⊕ *www.echucapaddlesteamers.net.au, www. emmylou.com.au.*

OUTDOOR ACTIVITIES

BOATING **Murray River Houseboats.** It seems that everyone who visits the Murray hires a houseboat and drifts slowly down the river. Today's houseboat is a five-star floating experience with Jacuzzis, state-of-the-art kitchen, and the latest appliances. They can sleep from two to 12 people and can be hired from three days to a week and longer. This operator has six boats for hire. Prices start from A$1,450 for three nights in the peak late-December/January period for 2 to 6 people. ⊠ *Riverboat Dock, Echuca* ☏ *03/5480–2343* ⊕ *www.murrayriverhouseboats.com.au.*

CANOEING **River Country Adventours.** If you want to canoe up a lazy river—the Goulburn, which is a tributary of the Murray—you can for a half or full day with this company run by Rob and Joan Asplin. Tours are from A$55 per person. ☏ *03/5852–2736, 0428/585227 mobile* ⊕ *www.adventours.com.au.*

HIKING AND BIKING There are many popular hiking and bicycling trails in the area, including the Banyule River Village Forest Trail, which travels upstream under the Echuca Moama Bridge for up to 30 km (20 mi); another ventures along the Campaspe River esplanade, while another travels into the Moama bush riverside reserve. The visitor center has all the details and maps.

WHERE TO EAT AND STAY

For expanded hotel reviews, visit Fodors.com.

$$
ECLECTIC
Fodor's Choice
★

✕ **Oscar W's Wharfside.** Named after the last paddle steamer ever built in Echuca, Oscar W's is one of the port's finest restaurants. With a beautiful, tree-fringed view of the Murray River, it's a comfortable, relaxed establishment with a casual Deck Bar and upscale Redgum Grill, the latter serving such treats as spicy boned quail with warm bean chorizo salad, coriander, and lime yoghurt dressing. Pavlova and little laimington's (Australia's own chocolate and coconut–dipped sponge cakes) are stars of the dessert menu. Have a drink and watch the paddle steamers cruise by. ✉ *101 Murray Esplanade* ☎ *03/5482–5133* ⊕ *www. oscarws.com.au.*

$$$

▦ **PS *Emmylou*.** Departing from Echuca around sunset, this paddle steamer chugs downriver, fueled by redgum logs, taking passengers on one-, two-, or three-night cruises with all meals. **Pros:** fabulous sense of history; lots of birdlife; lovely scenery. **Cons:** limited facilities. ✉ *57 Murray Esplanade* ☎ *03/5480–2237* ⊕ *www.emmylou.com.au* ⤳ *9 rooms without bath* ♨ *In-room: no a/c, no TV. In-hotel: restaurant, bar* ⊙ *Closed June–Aug.* ⦵ *Some meals.*

$$

▦ **River Gallery Inn.** A 19th-century building just a stone's throw from the port houses this boutique hotel. **Pros:** historic atmosphere; room themes; great location. **Cons:** Wi-Fi patchy in some rooms. ✉ *578 High St.* ☎ *03/5480–6902* ⊕ *www.rivergalleryinn.com* ⤳ *8 rooms* ♨ *In-room: Wi-Fi. In-hotel: bar, parking, some age restrictions* ⦵ *Breakfast.*

Tasmania

WORD OF MOUTH

"Tasmania ... Australia's best kept secret! Australia, mainland, is of course great and there are so many lovely places to see, trouble is the distances between them are vast. Tasmania is so much smaller and although you are never that far away from anywhere (compared with mainland) you will be doing a lot of travelling on your itinary in that timeframe."

—mikandsue

WELCOME TO TASMANIA

TOP REASONS TO GO

★ **Beautiful Walks:** Tasmania has some of Australia's best walking terrain. The stunning mountains and coastlines of Mt. Field, South West, and Franklin-Gordon Wild Rivers national parks are a mecca for serious trekkers. Less strenuous but equally stunning walks can be taken around Cradle Mountain or on Freycinet Peninsula.

★ **Colonial Homes and Cottages:** Many of the Georgian mansions and charming cottages built during Tasmania's early days as a colony have been turned into unusual and hospitable accommodation options.

★ **Tassie Tastes:** While Tasmania's unspoiled surrounds make it hiking heaven, foodies are also well served, thanks to its beautiful produce and excellent wine.

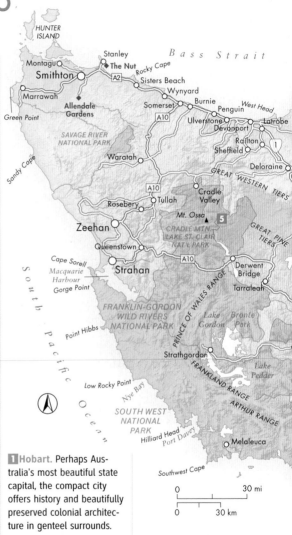

1 Hobart. Perhaps Australia's most beautiful state capital, the compact city offers history and beautifully preserved colonial architecture in genteel surrounds.

2 Port Arthur and the Tasman Peninsula. The horrors of Tasmania's convict past are there to discover in the notorious penal settlement, which has been sensitively converted into an absorbing museum.

3 Freycinet National Park and East Coast Resorts. Deserted white-sand beaches, including the legendary Wineglass Bay, as well as some superb wineries, make the east coast a must-visit.

323

GETTING
ORIENTED GETTING ORIENTED

About the size of West Virginia, and with a population of less than a half-million, the island of Tasmania offers geographical diversity in stunning, easily navigable scenery. Surrounded by sea, the climate is of course maritime, with the west coast the wettest thanks to the roaring forties winds. On the other hand, the island's capital of Hobart, a proud port city that is Australia's second oldest settlement, is Australia's second-driest city. The beautiful east coast is nearly always warmer and milder than the rest of the isle. This diversity has contributed to an amazing variety of vegetation, from eucalypt forest and alpine heathlands tolarge areas of cool temperate rain forests and moorlands.

4 Launceston. Tasmania's second biggest city is a pleasant place to while away time thanks to its attractive parks and historic colonial mansions.

5 Northwest Cradle Mountains—Lake St. Clair National Park. A nearly deserted rugged coastline and the dramatic landscapes of Cradle Mountain National Park make this area a must-visit for walkers.

6

OUTDOOR ADVENTURES

Tasmania's pristine national parks are a national treasure. Freycinet, with its picture-perfect sandy bays, and the dramatic mountain peaks of Franklin-Gordon Wild Rivers National Park are two of the island's highlights.

Freycinet National Park, with its pristine beaches, eucalypt forests, and jagged granite peaks known as the Hazards is a must for fans of the great outdoors. Set on 169 square km (65 square mi) on the Freycinet Peninsula on the east coast, the park makes for a rewarding visit for a few hours or for a few days. If you visit one beach in Tasmania, make it the iconic Wineglass Bay.

More remote but equally beguiling is Franklin-Gordon Wild Rivers National Park in the west of the island. Stretching from the source of the Franklin River to the sea, it has spectacular mountain scenery. Although the park is known to most visitors as the location of the popular Gordon River cruises, hardy walkers can explore the alpine scenery of the Upper Franklin region or attempt the four-day trek up Frenchmans Cap, while daredevil rafters can test their limits on the wild and ferocious river.

WHEN TO GO

Freycinet is popular with travelers, but remember, this is Tasmania. It's never overcrowded. In summer, the park's peak season, accommodation can be more difficult to come by, so book ahead. Even so, the trails are never congested. Spring is also a good time to visit to see all the wildflowers in bloom.

The best time to visit Franklin-Gordon Wild Rivers National Park is between October and April, but even then visitors should be aware that the weather is temperamental: it rains frequently, and it can snow even in summer. But because of the size of the park, it never feels crowded no matter when you go.

FREYCINET NATIONAL PARK

Magnificent Freycinet National Park draws visitors because of its birdlife, wildflowers, bushwalking, and spectacular coastal scenery. It's probably Tassie's most user-friendly park, with near-endless options for hiking and bushwalking, ranging from 30 minutes in length to multiday treks. Two of the more popular shorter walks are to the lookouts above Wineglass Bay and the Friendly Beaches, which are usually deserted. The pink granite peaks known as the Hazards are also a major attraction. Most people base themselves in accommodation in Coles Bay, the gateway to the park and the start of many walks. While it is possible to get to Coles Bay by public transport—Tassielink buses run from Hobart or Launceston to Bicheno, where passengers can use the Bicheno Bus Service to Coles Bay—it's much easier to get around if you have your own vehicle.

FRANKLIN-GORDON WILD RIVERS NATIONAL PARK

Untamed and perfect for the adventurous, the Franklin-Gordon Wild Rivers National Park has a rich and remarkable heritage. Best known to most visitors as the location of the popular Gordon River cruises, the park also contains many Aboriginal sites bearing witness to a heritage that extends back more than 36,000 years. Resilient walkers who aren't put off by the initial steep climb to Frenchmans Cap are rewarded by stunning eucalyptus forests before scrambling up the Cap's snow-topped dome at 1,446 meters to enjoy views over the peaks of Cradle Mountain, Barn Bluff, and Ossa. There are basic free campsites at the Collingwood River. If this sounds too adventurous, do as most day visitors do and stay in Strahan and drive along the meandering Lyell Highway, which winds for 56 km (35 mi) through the park.

TIMING FOR FREYCINET

Freycinet is equally rewarding for quick visits as well as multiday stays. If time is short, head to Coles Bay and do the short walk to Wineglass Bay, or spot wallabies on Friendly Beaches. However, if you decide you have all the time in the world, you can trek the entire length of the Freycinet Peninsula on a three-day walk.

6

TIMING FOR FRANKLIN-GORDON

Much of the Franklin-Gordon Wild Rivers National Park is remote and rugged, and serious walkers would get the most out of a few days' stay (the Frenchmans Cap walk can be extended to five days). If time is short, the Franklin River Nature Trail is a quick and easy 20-minute trek, while the Donaghys Lookout walk takes 40 minutes.

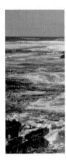

Updated by
Barry Lorne
Freedman

Wild and dramatic landscapes, empty white beaches, heavenly food and wine—Tasmania's charms have been overlooked for too long by international travelers. Hikers have always known about the island's wilderness trails, which lead you through deserted forests and national parks, but now gourmands are discovering Tassie's superb local produce, making it a world-class gourmet destination, too.

Tasmania's attractions encompass the historic, the healthy, and the hedonistic. Although Tasmania now is an unspoiled reminder of a simpler, slower lifestyle away from the rat race, its bloody history is never far from the surface. Today, walking through the lovely grounds in Port Arthur, the notorious penal colony, or the unhurried streets of Hobart with its profusion of Georgian buildings, it's difficult to picture Tasmania as a land of turmoil and tragedy. But the destruction of the Aboriginal population, who are thought to have crossed into Tasmania approximately 36,000 years ago, is a dark stain on the island's memory.

In many ways Tasmania is still untamed, making it a hiker's delight. Twenty-eight percent of the land is preserved in national parks, where impenetrable rain forests and deep river gorges cut through the massive mountain valleys. The coastlines are scalloped with endless desolate beaches—some pristine white, fronting serene turquoise bays, and some rugged and rocky, facing churning, choppy seas.

These beautiful surrounds have led to Tasmania's newest claim to fame as a gourmet haven. Thanks to the island's many microclimates, you can grow or harvest virtually anything from superb dairy produce to wonderful meat, and its clear seas abound in wonderful seafood. Oenophiles have also discovered the island's wines, and the island's wine routes are well worth a slow meander.

PLANNING

WHEN TO GO

Cold weather–phobes beware: Tasmanian winters can draw freezing blasts from the Antarctic, so this is not the season to explore the highlands or wilderness areas. It's better in the colder months to enjoy the cozy interiors of colonial cottages and the open fireplaces of welcoming pubs.

Summer can be surprisingly hot—bushfires are common—but temperatures are generally lower than on the Australian mainland.

The best times to visit are autumn and spring; early autumn is beautiful, with deciduous trees in full color. Spring, with its splashes of pastel wildflowers and mild weather, is equally lovely.

Tasmania is a relaxing island with few crowds, except during the mid-December to mid-February school holiday period and at the end of the annual Sydney-to-Hobart yacht race just after Christmas. Most attractions and sights are open year-round.

GETTING HERE AND AROUND

Tasmania is compact—the drive from southern Hobart to northern Launceston takes little more than two hours. The easiest way to see the state is by car, as you can plan a somewhat circular route around the island. Begin in Hobart or Launceston, where car rentals are available from the airport and city agencies, or in Devonport if you arrive on the ferry from Melbourne. Allow plenty of time for stops along the way, as there are some fabulous views to be seen. Bring a sturdy pair of shoes for impromptu mountain and seaside walks; you'll most often have huge patches of forest and long expanses of white beaches all to yourself.

In some cases the street addresses for attractions may not include building numbers (in other words, only the name of the street will be given). Don't worry—this just means either that the street is short and the attractions are clearly visible or that signposts will clearly lead you there.

If you are exploring several national parks in the space of a few weeks or months it is recommended to buy a Holiday Park Pass that is valid for two months for A$56 in the National Parks of Tasmania.

AIR TRAVEL

Hobart International Airport is 22 km (14 mi) east of Hobart, one hour by air from Melbourne or two hours from Sydney. Although most interstate flights connect through Melbourne, Qantas, Jetstar, and Virgin Blue also run direct flights to other mainland cities. Launceston airport is at Western Junction, 16 km (10 mi) south of central Launceston. It's served by Jetstar, Tiger Airways, and Virgin Blue.

On the island, Tasair can get you to the northwest and King Island. Tickets can be booked through the airlines or through the Tasmanian Travel and Information Centre. Tasmanian Redline Coaches has airport shuttle service for A$15 per person between the airport and its downtown depot. Metered taxis are available at the stand in front of the terminal. The fare to downtown Hobart is approximately A$40.

CAR TRAVEL

Port Arthur is an easy 90-minute drive from Hobart via the Arthur Highway. A private vehicle is essential if you want to explore parts of the Tasman Peninsula beyond the historic settlement. A vehicle is absolutely essential on the west coast. The road from Hobart travels through the Derwent Valley and past lovely historic towns before rising to the plateau of central Tasmania. Many of the northwest roads are twisty and even unpaved in the more remote areas, but two-wheel drive is sufficient for most touring. Be prepared for sudden weather changes: snow in the summertime is not uncommon in the highest areas. Lake St. Clair is 173 km (107 mi) northwest of Hobart, and can be reached via the Lyell Highway, or from Launceston via Deloraine or Poatina. Cradle Mountain is 85 km (53 mi) south of Devonport, and can be reached by car via Claude Road from Sheffield or via Wilmot. Both lead 30 km (19 mi) along Route C132 to Cradle Valley.

DISCOUNTS AND DEALS

If you're planning to explore all of the island, the See Tasmania Smart-visit Card (☏ 1300/661771 ⊕ www.seetasmaniacard.com) provides unbeatable convenience and value. Three-, 7-, and 10-day cards give you free (or greatly reduced) admission at more than 60 of Tasmania's most popular attractions.

RESTAURANTS

Although there are elegant dining options in the larger towns—especially Hobart—most eateries serve meals in a casual setting. Fiercely proud of their local produce, Tasmania's restaurateurs have packed their menus with home-grown seafood, beef, and cheeses, washed down with their famous cold-climate wines. Tasmanian wine is nearly unknown in the rest of the world, but that's not a comment on its quality; it's because Tasmanians tend to drink the vast majority of it themselves, leaving next to nothing to export.

HOTELS

The hospitality industry is thriving in Tasmania, so in popular areas you'll find a wide range of accommodation options, from inexpensive motels to genteel B&Bs, rustic lodges to luxury hotels. Most hotels will have air-conditioning, but bed-and-breakfast lodgings often do not. Apart from a few hotels right in the main city center, most Hobart accommodations have free parking. In many smaller places, especially the colonial-style cottages, no smoking is allowed inside.

DINING AND LODGING PRICE CATEGORIES (IN AUSTRALIAN DOLLARS)				
	¢	$	$$	$$$	$$$$
Restaurants	under A$10	A$10–A$20	A$21–A$35	A$36–A$50	over A$50
Hotels	under A$100	A$100–A$150	A$151–A$200	A$201–A$300	over A$300

Meal prices are per person for a main course at dinner. Hotel prices are for two people in a standard double room in high season, including tax and service, based on the European Plan (with no meals) unless otherwise noted.

GREAT ITINERARIES

IF YOU HAVE 3 DAYS

Spend your first morning in Hobart, where you can stroll around the docks, Salamanca Place, and Battery Point, and have some caught-that-morning fish-and-chips from the harbor's floating chippies. After lunch, drive to Richmond and explore its 19th-century streetscape, then stay in a local B&B. On the second day head for Port Arthur, and spend the morning exploring the town's historic park, the site of the island's former penal colony. Take the afternoon to drive through the dramatic scenery of the Tasman Peninsula, noting the tessellated pavement and Tasman Arch blow-hole near Eaglehawk Neck. Return to Hobart for the night, then on the third morning take a leisurely drive around the scenic Huon Valley. On return to Hobart, finish your tour with a trip to the summit of Mt. Wellington.

IF YOU HAVE 5 DAYS

Explore Hobart on foot the first morning, stopping for lunch at one of the waterfront restaurants at Elizabeth Street Pier, and then wander through historic Richmond. Spend the night in Hobart, then on the second day drive through the scenic Huon Valley. Return to Hobart for the night, and on the Day 3 drive to Port Arthur, taking in the beauty of the Tasman Peninsula on the way. Spend the night in Port Arthur, then drive early on the fourth day to Freycinet National Park. Climb the steep path to the outlook over Wineglass Bay, then descend to the sands for a picnic and swim. Stay the night in the park, then on Day 5 meander back through the east coast wine regions. Return to the capital, topping off the day with city views from Mt. Wellington.

IF YOU HAVE 10 DAYS

Take a walking tour of Hobart on the first morning, then take an afternoon drive to Richmond before returning for the night. On the second day, drive to the Tasman Peninsula, enjoying the scenic back roads before heading to Port Arthur for the night. On the third day, head back southwest through Hobart toward the bucolic orchards of the Huon Valley and the Tahune Forest Airwalk. Depart early on the fourth morning for Strahan, stopping at Lake St. Clair. Spend the night, take an all-day cruise on the Gordon River, and stay another night. On Day 6 make the long drive north via Zeehan and Marrawah to Stanley, a village set beneath the Nut. Have lunch here, then head back east to Devonport and stay the night. On Day 7, turn inland via Sheffield or Wilmot to reach Cradle Mountain National Park. Stay two nights, using Day 8 to explore the region's natural beauty. On the ninth day, leave early for Launceston, spend the night, then head back to Hobart.

6

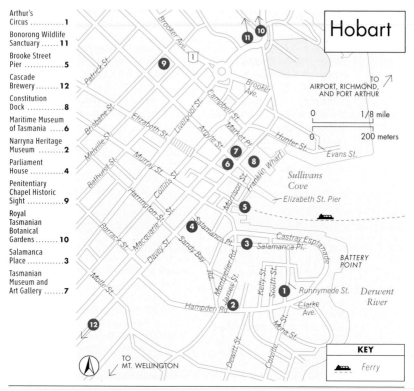

HOBART

Straddling the Derwent River at the foot of Mt. Wellington's forested slopes, Hobart was founded as a penal settlement in 1803. It's the second-oldest city in the country after Sydney, and it certainly rivals its mainland counterpart as Australia's most beautiful state capital. Close-set colonial brick-and-sandstone shops and homes line the narrow, quiet streets, creating a genteel setting for this historic city of 200,000. Life revolves around the broad Derwent River port, one of the deepest harbors in the world. Here warehouses that once stored Hobart's major exports of fruit, wool, and corn and products from the city's former whaling fleet still stand alongside the wharf today.

Hobart sparkles between Christmas and New Year's—summer Down Under—during the annual Sydney-to-Hobart yacht race. The event dominates conversations among Hobart's citizens, who descend on Constitution Dock to welcome the yachts and join in the boisterous festivities of the crews. The New Year also coincides with the Tastes of Tasmania Festival, when the dockside area comes alive with the best of Tasmanian food and wine on offer in numerous cafés, bars, and waterfront stalls. Otherwise, Hobart is a placid city whose nightlife is largely confined to excellent restaurants, jazz clubs, and the action at the Wrest Point Casino in Sandy Bay.

The Hobart Tasmanian Travel and
Information Centre hours are weekdays 8:30–5:30 and Saturday 9–5.

GETTING HERE AND AROUND

Hobart, being teeny-tiny, is emi-
nently walkable; once you're in the
city center, no attraction is more
than 15 minutes' walk away, apart
from the Cascade Brewery. Because
of the many one-way streets, it's
best to park a car and leave it for
the day as you explore. If you prefer two wheels to two legs, you can
hire trendy electric bicycles from
the Henry Jones Art Hotel on Hunter Street for A$24 for five hours.

> ## DISAPPEARING DEVILS
>
> Tasmanian devils are becom-
> ing extremely rare because of a
> deadly cancer that is devastat-
> ing the devil population—in 2009
> they were officially listed on the
> endangered species list. Experts
> estimate that 70% of the popula-
> tion has already succumbed, and
> unless a cure is found the species
> faces extinction.

ESSENTIALS

Visitor Information Tasmanian Travel and Information Centre
✉ *20 Davey St., at Elizabeth St., Hobart City* ☎ *1800/990–440, 03/6238–4222*
⊕ *www.hobarttravelcentre.com.au.*

6

EXPLORING HOBART

TOP ATTRACTIONS

Cascade Brewery. This is Australia's oldest and most picturesque brewery,
producing fine beers since 1824. You can see its inner workings only on
the one- and two-hour tours, which require lots of walking and climbing, but you're rewarded with three free drinks at the end. Note that
appropriate attire (long pants and closed-toe shoes only) is required,
and tour reservations are essential. It's a 30-minute walk from the city
center, or buses leave from Franklin Square every 35 minutes from
9:15 am. ✉ *140 Cascade Rd., South Hobart* ☎ *03/6224–1117* ⊕ *www.
cascadebreweryco.com.au* 🍴 *A$20 Tours every day at 11 and 1.*

Constitution Dock. Yachts competing in the annual Sydney-to-Hobart race
moor at this colorful marina dock from the end of December through
the first week of January. Buildings fronting the dock are century-old
reminders of Hobart's trading history. Nearby Hunter Street is the original spot where British ships anchored. ✉ *Argyle and Davey Sts., Hobart
City* ☎ *No phone* 🍴 *Free* ☉ *Daily 24 hrs.*

Fodor'sChoice
★
Salamanca Place. Old whaling ships used to dock at Salamanca Place.
Today many of the warehouses that were once used by whalers along
this street have been converted into crafts shops, art galleries, and restaurants. At the boisterous Saturday market, which attracts all elements
of Tasmanian society from hippies to the well-heeled, dealers in Tasmanian arts and crafts, antiques, old records, and books—and a fair bit
of appalling junk—display their wares between 8:30 and 3. Keep an
eye open for items made from beautiful Tasmanian timber, particularly
Huon pine. ⊕ *www.salamanca.com.au.*

WORTH NOTING

Arthur's Circus. Hobart's best-preserved street is a charming collection of tiny houses and cottages in a circle around a village green on Runnymede Street, in the heart of historic Battery Point. Most of these private houses, which were built in the 1840s and 1850s, have been nicely restored.

Brooke Street Pier. The busy waterfront at Brooke Street Pier is the departure point for harbor cruises. Nearby **Elizabeth Street Pier** has trendy restaurants and bars. ⊠ *Franklin Wharf, Hobart City.*

Maritime Museum of Tasmania. The old state library building houses one of the best maritime collections in Australia, including figureheads, whaling implements, models, and photographs dating from as far back as 1804. It's only a small museum though, so don't plan on spending more than an hour. ⊠ *Carnegie Bldg., Argyle and Davey Sts., Hobart City* ☎ *03/6234–1427* ⊕ *www.maritimetas.org* ☞ *A$7* ⊙ *Daily 9–5.*

Narryna Heritage Museum. Exhibits in this gracious old Georgian town house, surrounded by a lovely rose-filled garden, depict the life of Tasmania's upper-class pioneers. Of particular interest are the collections of colonial furniture, clothes, paintings, and photos. ⊠ *103 Hampden Rd., Battery Point* ☎ *03/6234–2791* ⊕ *www.narryna.com.au* ☞ *A$6* ⊙ *Tues.–Fri. 10:30–5 (closed for lunch 12:30–1), weekends 2–5.*

Parliament House. Built by convicts in 1840 as a customs house, this building did not acquire its present function until 1856. Although it's closed to the general public, tours run on weekdays. ⊠ *Morrison St. between Murray St. and Salamanca Pl., Hobart City* ☎ *03/6233–2288* ⊕ *www.parliament.tas.gov.au* ☞ *Free* ⊙ *Guided tours weekdays 10–2.*

OFF THE
BEATEN
PATH

Bonorong Wildlife Sanctuary. About 25 km (16 mi) north of Hobart on the highway toward Launceston, this sanctuary hosts a diverse selection of Australian species—many of which have been rescued—including koalas, wombats, quolls, and the adorable Tasmanian devil. Free feeding tours take place daily at 11:30 and 2. The private dusk tours are highly recommended, and provide a rare opportunity to experience Tassie's beautiful nocturnal animals at their most active. ⊠ *Briggs Rd., 593, Brighton* ☎ *03/6268–1811* ⊕ *www.bonorong.com.au* ☞ *A$22, Night Tours $149* ⊙ *Daily 9–5.*

Penitentiary Chapel Historic Sight. Built and used during the early convict days, these buildings vividly portray Tasmania's penal, judicial, and religious heritage in their courtrooms, old cells, and underground tunnels. If you want to get spooked, come for the nighttime ghost tour (reservations necessary). ⊠ *Brisbane and Campbell Sts., Hobart City* ☎ *03/6231–0911, 0417/361–392* ⊕ *www.penitentiarychapel.com* ☞ *A$10, ghost tour A$10* ⊙ *Tours weekdays at 10, 11.30, 1, and 2.30 and Saturday at 1 and 2:30; ghost tour daily at 8:30 pm.*

Royal Tasmanian Botanical Gardens. The largest area of open land in Hobart, these well-tended gardens are rarely crowded and provide a welcome relief from the city. Plants from all over the world are here—more than 6,000 exotic and native species in all. The collection of Tasmania's unique native flora is especially impressive. ⊠ *Lower Domain Rd., Queen's Domain* ☎ *03/6236–3075* ⊕ *www.rtbg.tas.gov.au* ☞ *Free* ⊙ *Daily 8–5:30 (Oct.–Mar. until 6:30).*

Tasmanian Museum and Art Gallery. This building overlooking Constitution Dock houses is a good starting point for uncovering Tasmania's history. It's a great place in Hobart to learn about the island's Aboriginal culture and unique wildlife. There are free guided tours Wednesday to Sunday at 2:30 pm. ⊠ *5 Argyle St., Hobart City* ☎ *03/6211–4177* ⊕ *www.tmag.tas. gov.au* ⊠ *Free* ⊙ *Daily 10–5.*

> ### BELLERIVE VILLAGE
>
> Take the ferry across the River Derwent to Bellerive, a lovely little villagelike suburb that will make you feel as if you've stepped back in history. There are great restaurants, and the view back to the city with Mt. Wellington looming in the background is impressive.

OUTDOOR ACTIVITIES

Hobartians are an outdoorsy lot who make the most of the city's waterfront location by fishing, cruising, and sailing or heading inland to Mt. Wellington to explore the many trails that start there.

BOAT TOURS **Peppermint Bay Cruises.** Their catamaran zips through the majestic waterways of the Derwent River and the D'Entrecasteaux Channel to Peppermint Bay at Woodbridge. Wildlife is abundant, from sea eagles and falcons soaring above the weathered cliffs to pods of dolphins swimming alongside the boat. Underwater cameras explore kelp forests and salmon in the floating fish farms. ⊠ *Peppermint Bay, 3435 Channel Hwy., Woodbridge* ☎ *03/6267–4088* ⊕ *www. peppermintbay.com.au.*

Captain Fell's Historic Ferries. Travelers love the old-fashioned ferries that take you on a leisurely cruise around the harbor as friendly tour guides point out the sights. ⊠ *Franklin Wharf Pier, Hobart Waterfront* ☎ *03/6223–5893* ⊕ *www.captainfellshistoricferries.com.au.*

BICYCLING Although most of Hobart and its surrounding areas are too hilly to make for easy cycling, some old railway lines along the western bank of the Derwent River (which are quite flat) have been transformed into bicycle paths. These offer a relaxing way to explore parts of the city. Electric bikes can be rented from the Henry Jones Art Hotel on Hunter Street.

Derwent Bike Hire. Bikes can be rented from Derwent Bike Hire. ⊠ *Regatta Grounds, Queens Domain* ☎ *0428/899169* ⊕ *www. derwentbikehire.com.*

FISHING Tasmania's well-stocked lakes and streams are among the world's best for trout fishing. The season runs from August through May, and licensed trips can be arranged through the Tasmanian Travel and Information Centre.

Several professional fishing guides are based on the island. For information on these guides, as well as related tours, accommodations, and sea charters, check out ⊕ *www.troutguidestasmania.com.au* or inquire at the Tasmanian Travel and Information Centre for a professional guide in the area you are visiting.

Rod & Fly Tasmania. Tasmania offers some world-class fishing, and if you'd like to catch some local trout in the local wonderfully clear rivers, the friendly tour guides here have over thirty years of experience. ☎ *03/6266–4480* ⊕ *www.rodandfly.com.au.*

Mr Flathead. If you'd rather take to the ocean, this company will take you on half- or full-day tours to local fishing hot spots, where you'll find flathead, whiting, and salmon. All rods, reels, and equipment are supplied. ☎ *0439/617–200* ⊕ *www.mrflathead.com.au.*

HIKING Pick up a Mt. Wellington Walk Map from the tourist office on Elizabeth Street in Hobart to make the most out of the park that towers over Hobart. Although shops around town stock outdoor equipment, you should bring your own gear if you're planning any serious bushwalking. Sneakers are adequate for walking around Mt. Wellington and along beaches. A car is necessary to access several of the trails around the peak.

Adventure Seekers. Go hiking with Adventure Seekers and they will take care of all the details. Their 9-day South Coast track starts in Hobart and explores the wild south coast, but they do shorter trips, too. See their Web site for dates. ⊕ *www.adventureseekers.com.au.*

WALKING Hobart Historic Tours offers guided walks through old Hobart, around
TOURS the waterfront and maritime precinct, and a historic pub tour. A minimum of three people is required for all walks.

Hobart Historic Tours ✉ *20 Davey St., Hobart* ☎ *03/6278–3338* ⊕ *www. hobarthistorictours.com.au.*

WHERE TO EAT

Constitution Dock is the perfect place for yacht-watching, as well as for gobbling fresh fish-and-chips from one of the punts (floating fish-and-chips shops) moored on the water. Ask for the daily specials, such as local blue grenadier or trevally, which cost A$7–A$12, or go for some freshly shucked oysters. The city's main restaurant areas include the docks and the streets around Salamanca Place.

$$$$ ✕ **Annapurna.** In the bustling restaurant strip of North Hobart, this local
INDIAN favorite has maintained an enviable reputation for many years thanks to its consistently good-value food. Tandoori, curries (take care, they can be searingly hot), and a wide selection of other Indian delicacies keep people coming back. Inexpensive lunch boxes are available. ✉ *305 Elizabeth St, North Hobart* ☎ *03/6236–9500.*

$ ✕ **Ethos Eat Drink.** Ethos is the newest restaurant by one of Hobart's most
AUSTRALIAN trusted fine-dining restaurateurs. This time it is slow-food Australian
Fodor's Choice tapas and high-quality Hobart-style comfort food. Housed in a historic
★ building (it was formerly a stable) in the heart of the city, the dining rooms have serious charm and the food is outstanding. Much of the menu is made from local produce and dishes are simply prepared—think slow-cooked lamb belly with roasted artichoke and celeriac remoulade. Don't miss a thing, from the excellent wine list to housemade chocolates and tea mixes. ✉ *100 Elizabeth St., Hobart* ☎ *03/6231 1165.*

Continued on page 340

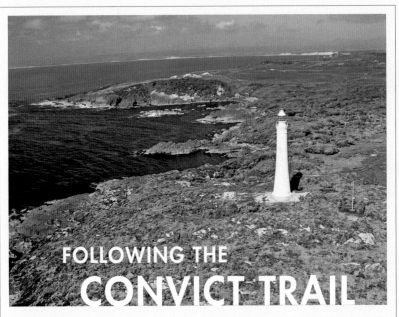

FOLLOWING THE
CONVICT TRAIL

For many, Tasmania conjures up grim images of chain-ganged prisoners: British convicts banished from the motherland to languish on a distant island in a faraway colony.

This humble (and brutal) beginning as a penal colony is a point of pride for many Australians. It's no small feat that a colony comprised of, among others, poor Irish, Scottish, and Welsh convicts—many imprisoned for crimes as petty as stealing a loaf of bread—were able to build what is now Australia. It epitomizes a toughness of character that Australians prize. Many here can accurately trace their lineage back to the incarcerated. Kevin Rudd, the country's Prime Minister, is himself descended from six convicts, including Mary Wade, the youngest female prisoner transported to Australia at the age of 11.

Tasmania has a number of remarkably well-preserved convict sites, most of which are set on the isolated Tasman Peninsula, some 75 km (47 mi) southeast of Hobart. Here, the region's beautifully rugged landscape belies the horrors of the past. Exploring Tasmania's convict heritage and the dramatic beauty of the island are two sides of the same coin. The region's isolation, impenetrable rain forests, and sheer cliffs falling into the sea made it a perfect island prison. By following signs on what's called the Convict Trail, you'll go home with provocative insight into what life was like for the almost 75,000 souls sent to Tasmania between 1803 and 1853.

by Helena Iveson

The rugged and beautiful Tasmanian Coast.

TASMANIA'S CONVICT PAST

Port Arthur Historic Site

"It is impossible to convey, in words, any idea of the hideous phantasmagoria of shifting limbs and faces which moved through the evil-smelling twilight of this terrible prison-house. Callot might have drawn it, Dante might have suggested its horrors, but a minute attempt to describe its horrors would but disgust. There are depths in humanity which one cannot explore, as there are mephitic caverns into which one dare not penetrate."

—Marcus Clarke's description of Port Arthur's Separate Prison in his famous novel *For the Term of his Natural Life.*

They came in chains to this hostile island, where the seasons were all the wrong way around and the sights and smells were unfamiliar. In the 50 years following the establishment of the first settlement in Tasmania (Van Diemen's Land) in 1803, 57,909 male and 13,392 female prisoners were sent to the island. From 1830 on, many ended up at the newly built penal settlement at Port Arthur, where the slightest infraction would be punished by 100 lashes or weeks of solitary confinement on a diet of bread and water. Life was spent in chains, breaking up rocks or doing other menial tasks—all meant to keep criminal tendencies at bay.

The location of the settlement on the Tasman Peninsula was ideal. Joined to the rest of the island by a narrow neck of land with steep cliffs pounded by surging surf, it was easy to isolate and guard with half-starved dogs on the infamous dogline. Even though convicts were sentenced for a specific number of years, conditions were so brutal that even a few years could become a life sentence. With no chance of escape, some prisoners saw suicide as the only way out.

As the number of prisoners increased, more buildings went up. In time, the penal colony became a self-sufficient industrial center where prisoners sawed timber, built ships, laid bricks, cut stone, and made tiles, shoes, iron castings, and clothing.

A sculpture representing the infamous dogline at Eaglehawk Neck, Tasman Peninsula

HOW TO EXPLORE

GETTING HERE

To fully experience the trail, you'll need a car. It's possible to get to Port Arthur via operators such as Tassielink, but you can't access the whole trail by public transportion.

From Hobart head north to the well-preserved village of Richmond before continuing southeast on the Arthur Highway (A9) to the small town of Sorrell. Not far from here is the infamous Eaglehawk neck, marking the start of the Tasman Peninsula. The Convict Trail runs in a circle around the peninsula, with signs clearly marking the many sites along the way.

TIMING

Port Arthur is 120 km (75 mi) or an hour and a half away from Hobart, but will take longer if you intend on making stops at Richmond and Sorell (which you should).

This trip can be done in one long day, but if you want to thoroughly explore the Tasman Peninsula, allow for two or three days. The Convict Trail booklet is available from visitor information centers across Tasmania for $2.50 and details the key sites and attractions along the route.

Isle of the Dead

Richmond Bridge and Church

EXPLORING

It's easy to forget that Port Arthur wasn't an isolated settlement. The whole of the Tasman Peninsula was part of a larger penal colony, so, for the full experience, don't overlook the smaller sights. There are plenty of cafés and accommodations along the way, so take your time.

STUNNING VIEWS

Don't miss the vistas at the Tasman National Park Lookout. The walk along dramatic sea cliffs, which are among the highest and most spectacular in Australia, is easy and rewarding. The views of Pirates Bay, Cape Hauy, and the two islands just off the coast called The Lanterns are spectacular.

EN ROUTE

Take a break at the famous Sorell Fruit Farm where from November to May it's pick-you-own-berry season (✉ *174 Pawleena Road, Sorell* ☎ *03/6265–2744* ⊕ *www.sorellfruitfarm.com* ⊙ *Oct., Mar., Apr., and May 10–4; Nov., Dec., Jan., and Feb. 8:30–5*). For something more savory, a meal at The Mussel Boys is worth the drive from Hobart alone. Unsurprisingly, this casual restaurant's claim to fame are the mollusks. (*5927 Arthur Highway, Taranna, 03/6250–3088, closed Mon.–Tues.*)

TOURING THE CONVICT TRAIL

It's hard to absorb this disturbing story of human suffering. Around 73,000 convicts were transported here, and about 1 in 5 served time in Port Arthur, on Tasmania's southernmost tip.

Stone bridge at Richmond

outlaws who lived in the bush. A walk around the town reveals some interesting heritage buildings; there are also plenty of antiques shops and cafes to keep you occupied.

❶ RICHMOND BRIDGE. Australia's oldest bridge was built by convict labor in 1825 and is a lasting symbol of the island's convict heritage. Don't miss the village's gaol, which predates Port Arthur by five years.

❷ SORELL. This early settlement is where bloody bushranger battles were fought in the colony's formative years. Bushrangers were actually

Sorell Berry Farm

❸ THE DOGLINE. Statues of snarling hounds represent the dogs that prevented the convicts from escaping and mark the infamous dogline along the narrow strip of land linking the Tasman Peninsula with the rest of Tasmania.

Old wooden jetty in Norfolk Bay

❹ NORFOLK BAY. This is the site of a human-powered tramway. Goods were unloaded from ships at the Convict Station and then transported to Port Arthur by a tram dragged by convicts across the peninsula. This saved the ship a dangerous journey across the peninsula's stormy bays.

❺ PORT ARTHUR. Walking among the peaceful ruins and quiet gardens, it's difficult to imagine that this place was hell-on-earth for the convicts. When the settlement closed in 1877, the area was renamed Carnarvon in an attempt to disconnect the land from the horrors associated with its former name. However, in 1927 it was reinstated as Port Arthur and opened to a public keen to embrace this aspect of the Australian story.

TRAIL MARKERS

The Convict Trail is marked with a broad arrow symbol that was stamped on convict-made goods. It's framed in yellow to reference the color of convict clothing.

Sandstone church at Port Arthur

7 ISLE OF THE DEAD CONVICT CEMETERY. A small island in the harbor near Port Arthur is the final resting place for about a thousand people, most of them convicts and ex-convict paupers who were buried mostly in unmarked graves.

8 NUBEENA was established as an outstation of Port Arthur and for many years was an important convict farming community. It was also the sight of a semaphore station, used to raise the alarm if a convict made a bid for freedom.

9 SALTWATER RIVER. Exploring the abandoned mines reveals the terrible conditions in which the convicts suffered: restored tiny underground cells, totally without light and filled with fetid air give horrifying insight.

10 KOONYA. The probation station here was once an important convict outpost known as the Cascades. It operated between 1843 and 1846 and you'll find a few isolated houses and a well-restored penitentiary that once held 400 men, at least a quarter of them in chains.

6 POINT PUER BOYS PRISON. More than 3,000 boys, some as young as age nine, passed through here from 1834 to 1849. Located just across the harbor from the main Port Arthur settlement, this was the first jail in the British Empire built exclusively for juvenile male convicts. But just because they were young doesn't mean they were spared from hard labor like stone-cutting and construction. The prison was also infamous for its stern discipline—solitary

The Penitentiary Block

confinement, days at a time on a tread wheel, and whipping were standard punishments for even a trivial breach of the rules.

The extremely popular Saturday Salamanca Market

$$$
ECLECTIC

✕ **Henry's Harbourside.** Part of the Henry Jones Art Hotel, this small restaurant offers some of Hobart's best fine dining in arty surrounds. The food isn't overshadowed by the contemporary art on the walls thanks to the focus on seasonal produce in hearty dishes like slow-cooked pork belly with braised red cabbage, pickled apple, and daikon. The wine list features selections from only the finest Tasmanian, mainland Australian, and overseas wineries. ✉ *25 Hunter St., Hobart City* ☎ *03/6210–7706* ⊕ *www.thehenryjones.com.*

$$$
AUSTRALIAN

✕ **Lebrina.** Elegant surroundings in an 1840 brick colonial home inspire classic Tasmanian cooking in Hobart's most formal dining room. The best of the island's fresh produce is well utilized in such dishes as the twice-cooked Gruyère soufflé appetizer, or the seared loin of venison with fresh horseradish, served with red cabbage salad. Leave room for the superb Tasmanian cheese plate. The wine list includes many fine Tasmanian vintages. ✉ *155 New Town Rd., New Town* ☎ *03/6228–7775* ☻ *Closed Sun and Mon. No lunch.*

$$$
SEAFOOD
★

✕ **Mures Fish Centre.** On the top floor of this complex on the wharf, Mures Upper Deck Restaurant has superb indoor and alfresco views of the harbor. Try the pan-fried kingfish with carrot puree, confit fennel, olive, almond cream, wild rocket, star anise and vanilla butter if it's on the seasonal menu. Downstairs, Mures Lower Deck is a bistro-style alternative, where you can order, take a number, pick up your food, and eat at tables outside. Also in the complex is Mures Sushi Bar, where you can find fresh-out-of-water sushi and sashimi. ✉ *Victoria Dock, Hobart City* ☎ *03/6231–1999 Upper Deck, 03/6231–2009 Lower Deck, 03/6231–1790 Sushi Bar* ⊕ *www.muresupperdeck.com.au.*

$$ **✕ Restaurant 373.** Those who enjoy a little culinary creativity shouldn't
ECLECTIC miss this casual little bistro in fashionable North Hobart. It's very
popular, and you often have to wait for a table, but well worth it
for its ambience and modern feel. The duck breast with red cabbage,
foie gras dumplings and duck consommé is delicious, but be sure to
leave room for the truly inspired desserts. ⊠ *373 Elizabeth St., North
Hobart* ☎ *03/6231–9031* ⊕ *www.restaurant373.com.au* ☉ *Closed Sun.
and Mon. No lunch.*

WHERE TO STAY

For expanded hotel reviews, visit Fodors.com.

Hobart has some lovely lodgings in old, historic houses and cottages,
most of which have been beautifully restored. If you're seeking more
modern conveniences, there are plenty of newer hotels, too.

$$ **Corinda's Cottages.** This charming residence was built in the 1880s
★ for Alfred Crisp, a wealthy timber merchant who later became Lord
Mayor of Hobart. **Pros:** wonderfully restored historic accommodation,
generous buffet breakfast. **Cons:** no leisure facilities. ⊠ *17 Glebe St.,
Glebe* ☎ *03/6234–1590* ⊕ *www.corindascottages.com.au* ⋍ *3 cottages*
⌂ *In-room: kitchen. In-hotel: laundry facilities, parking* ⎮◯⎮ *Breakfast.*

$$$ **Hotel Grand Chancellor.** Across the street from the old wharves and
★ steps from some of the best restaurants in Hobart, this imposing glass-
and-stone building seems a bit out of place amid Hobart's colonialism.
Pros: steps away from the city's museums, offers familiar chain com-
forts. **Cons:** some traffic noise, stark lobby, Wi-Fi in lobby only, fee
for parking and valet. ⊠ *1 Davey St., Hobart City* ☎ *03/6235–4535,
1800/753379* ⊕ *www.ghihotels.com* ⋍ *240 rooms, 12 suites* ⌂ *In-
room: Internet, Wi-Fi. In-hotel: restaurant, bar, pool, gym, parking.*

$$$$ **Islington Hotel.** Built in 1847, this elegant Regency mansion was con-
Fodor's Choice verted to a five-star luxury boutique hotel, and is now considered to be
★ one of the finest in Australia. **Pros:** fully-tailored hospitality experience,
sophisticated service from staff. **Cons:** 20-minute walk to city center,
not family-friendly. ⊠ *321 Davey St., South Hobart* ☎ *03/6220–2123*
⊕ *www.islingtonhotel.com* ⋍ *11 suites* ⌂ *In-room: Wi-Fi. In-hotel:
parking, some age restrictions* ⎮◯⎮ *Breakfast.*

$ **Lodge on Elizabeth.** This opulent grand manor, convict-built in 1829
and home over the years to many Hobart notables, is within walk-
ing distance of the city center, but far enough removed to feel like a
sanctuary. **Pros:** bargain-priced Internet, convenient option for groups.
Cons: a few bedrooms are on the small side, some street noise. ⊠ *249
Elizabeth St., Hobart City* ☎ *03/6231–3830* ⊕ *www.thelodge.com.au*
⋍ *14 rooms* ⌂ *In-room: Internet. In-hotel: laundry facilities, parking*
⎮◯⎮ *Breakfast.*

$$$$ **MONA Pavilions.** These eight high-style pavilions are Tasmania's most
cutting-edge accommodations experience. **Pros:** access to the breathtak-
ing indoor infinity pool with views of the Derwent. **Cons:** lots of high-
tech features that are confusing to operate. ⊠ *655 Main Rd., Berridale*
☎ *03/6277–9900* ⊕ *mona.net.au/visit/sleep/the-pavilions/pavilions* ⋍ *8
chalets* ⌂ *In-room: safe, kitchen, Wi-Fi. In-hotel: restaurant, parking.*

6

NIGHTLIFE AND THE ARTS

Although Hobart has the only true nightlife scene in Tasmania, it's extremely tame compared to what's in Melbourne and Sydney. There are few dance clubs, but evenings out tend to revolve around a bottle of excellent local wine. Consult the Friday or Saturday editions of the *Mercury* newspaper before heading out. *This Week in Tasmania*, available at most hotels, is a comprehensive guide to current stage performances and contemporary music concerts.

BARS AND DANCE CLUBS

The waterfront area is lined with bars that cater to the local, very thirsty after-work crowds.

T42. T42 is a lively waterfront spot popular for both dining and drinking. The food is excellent, too. ⊠ *Elizabeth St. Pier, Hobart City* ☎ *03/6224–7742.*

Atrium Bar. Hotel Grand Chancellor's relaxing piano bar is popular with local professionals. ⊠ *1 Davey St., Hobart City* ☎ *03/6235–4535.*

Grape. Grape is Tasmania's go-to wine and tapas bar, with a wonderful shop where you can pick up one of its 300 types of Tasmanian wines and a cheese platter for an impromptu picnic. It serves all its wines in trendy Reidel O tumblers, and the excellent staff are keen to advise from behind the bar decorated with thousands of corks. There is live music in the evening toward the end of the week. ⊠ *55 Salamanca Pl., Battery Point* ☎ *03/6224–0611.*

Republic Bar and Cafe. The cool kids go for the raucous, art deco Republic Bar and Cafe,which has live music most nights. ⊠ *299 Elizabeth St., North Hobart* ☎ *03/6234–6954.*

Round Midnight. Round Midnight is a blues spot and has a mix of youngish live bands and DJs. ⊠ *39 Salamanca Pl., Battery Point* ☎ *03/6223–2491.*

SHOPPING

Tasmanian artisans and craftspeople work with diverse materials to fashion unusual pottery, metalwork, and wool garments. Items made from regional timber, including myrtle, sassafras, and Huon pine, are popular. The wonderful scenery around the island is an inspiration for numerous artists.

Along the Hobart waterfront at Salamanca Place are a large number of shops that sell arts and crafts. On Saturday (between 8 and 3) the area turns into a giant market, where still more local artists join produce growers, bric-a-brac sellers, and itinerant musicians to sell their wares.

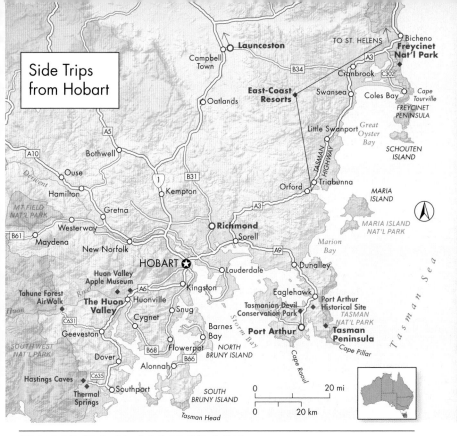

Side Trips
from Hobart

SIDE TRIPS FROM HOBART

Hobart is a perfect base for short trips to some of Tasmania's most historic and scenic places. Although you can visit them in a day; if you can, stay a night or two and experience their delights at a leisurely pace.

THE HUON VALLEY

★ *40 km (25 mi) south of Hobart.*

En route to the vast wilderness of South West National Park is the tranquil Huon Valley. Sheltered coasts and sandy beaches are pocketed with thick forests and small farms. William Bligh planted the first apple tree here, founding one of the region's major industries. Salmon and trout caught fresh from churning blue rivers are also delicious regional delicacies.

The valley is also famous for the Huon pine, much of which has been logged over the decades. The trees that remain are strictly protected, so other local timbers are used by the region's craftspeople.

EXPLORING

Huon Valley Apple Museum. En route to Huonville, the Huon Valley Apple Museum is in a former apple-packing shed. Over 500 varieties of apples are grown in the valley, and the museum displays farming artifacts, picking and processing equipment, and early-settler memorabilia from the area's orchards. There's also an art gallery. ⊠ *2064 Huon Hwy., Grove* ☎ *03/6266–4345* ⊕ *www.applemuseum.huonvalley.biz* ⊠ *A$5.50* ⊙ *Sept.–May, daily 9–5; June–Aug., daily 10–4.*

Tahune Forest AirWalk. Beyond Geeveston, the cantilevered, 1,880-foot-long Tahune Forest AirWalk rises to 150 feet above the forest floor, providing a stunning panorama of the Huon and Picton rivers and the Hartz Mountains. The best views are from the platform at the end of the walkway, and if you have time, follow one of the trails that lead from the center through the surrounding forests. ⊠ *Tahune Forest AirWalk and Visitor Centre, Tahune Forest Reserve, Arve Rd.* ☎ *03/6297–0068* ⊕ *www.forestrytas.com.au* ⊠ *A$25* ⊙ *Daily 9–5 in summer, 10-4 winter.*

Hastings Caves and Thermal Springs. Spectacular cave formations and thermal pools amid a fern glade await at the Hastings Caves and Thermal Springs. The caves are about 125 km (78 mi) south of Hobart, past Huonville and Dover. You can take a tour of the chambers, or just relax at the well-equipped picnic areas and make use of the thermal pool. The route to the site is well marked from the town of Dover. ☎ *03/6298– 3209,* ⊕ *www.parks.tas.gov.au* ⊠ *A$24* ⊙ *Apr.–Sept., cave tours 11–3, thermal spring 10–4; Sept.–Dec., cave tours 10–4, thermal springs 9–5; Mar. and Apr., cave tours 10–5, thermal springs 9–5.*

WHERE TO EAT AND STAY

For expanded hotel reviews, visit Fodors.com.

$$
AUSTRALIAN
✕ **Home Hill Winery Restaurant.** Large plate-glass windows here open to the Home Hill winery's endless hillside vineyards. The seasonal menu includes delicacies such as pan-seared Huon aquaculture Atlantic salmon served on potato croquettes garnished with spinach and poached egg. After dinner you can head down to the cellar to enjoy a complimentary sampling of the winery's excellent cool-climate wines. ⊠ *38 Nairn St., Ranelagh* ☎ *03/6264–1200* ⊕ *homehillwines.com.au* ⊙ *No dinner Sun.–Thurs.*

$
☲ **Heron's Rise Vineyard.** Mornings in any of the vineyard's three self-contained cottages are bucolic and gorgeous; you'll wake to glorious water views out over the flower gardens, where you might see rabbits nibbling. **Pros:** peaceful surrounds, owners pride themselves on their eco-friendly accommodation. **Cons:** no leisure facilities, smoke from fireplaces might be a problem for the asthmatic. ⊠ *Saddle Rd., Kettering* ☎ *03/6267–4339* 🖷 *03/6267–4245* ⊕ *www.heronsrise.com.au* ⤵ *3 cottages* ☒ *In-room: kitchen. In-hotel: laundry facilities, parking* ⨿⦾⦿ *Breakfast.*

RICHMOND

★ *24 km (15 mi) northeast of Hobart.*

Twenty minutes' drive from Hobart and a century behind the big city, this colonial village in the Coal River valley is a major tourist magnet. Visitors stroll and browse through the craft shops, antiques stores, and cafés along the main street. Richmond is also home to a number of vineyards, all of which produce excellent cool-climate wines.

WHERE TO EAT AND STAY

For expanded hotel reviews, visit Fodors.com.

¢ ✕ **Ashmore on Bridge Street.** Once you've perused all of Richmond's cute
CAFÉ shops and historic sights, be sure to recharge in this surprisingly trendy café with an open roaring fire and a friendly owner. The creamy scrambled eggs on sourdough toast with Tasmanian cold smoked salmon and house relish is delicious for breakfast, and in the afternoon the huge and delectable Devonshire teas will have you sighing with pleasure. Dinner with a changing menu is offered Tuesday and Wednesday from 6. ✉ *34 Bridge St., Richmond* ☎ *03/6260–2238* ⊕ *www. ashmoreonbridge.com.au.*

$$ ✕ **Meadowbank Estate.** Wine tasting and two art galleries complement
AUSTRALIAN this unpretentious fine-dining restaurant with floor-to-ceiling windows leading out to views over the vineyards of Meadowbank Estate and the waters of Barilla Bay. The à la carte menu emphasizes food and wine pairings. Try the seared venison with spiced pumpkin puree and cassis jus, and make sure to save room for the passion-fruit soufflé with vanilla-bean ice cream. ✉ *699 Richmond Rd., Cambridge* ☎ *03/6248–4484* ⊕ *www.meadowbankestate.com.au* ☾ *No dinner.*

$ ⊡ **Mrs Currie's House B&B.** This gracious Georgian house, built between
★ 1820 and 1860, is set in a peaceful garden with lovely views over the village of Richmond and the surrounding countryside. **Pros:** quaint accommodation and friendly owners. **Cons:** not particularly child-friendly, showers are on the historic side. ✉ *4 Franklin St.* ☎ *03/6260–2766* ⊕ *www.mrscurrieshouse.com.au* ⇆ *4 rooms* ⟁ *In-hotel: parking* ⊺⊙⊺ *Breakfast.*

PORT ARTHUR AND THE TASMAN PENINSULA

102 km (63 mi) southeast of Hobart.

When Governor George Arthur, Lieutenant-Governor of Van Diemen's Land (now Tasmania), was looking for a site to dump his worst convict offenders in 1830, the Tasman Peninsula was a natural choice. Joined to the rest of Tasmania only by the narrow Eaglehawk Neck, the spit was easy to isolate and guard. Between 1830 and 1877 more than 12,000 convicts served sentences at Port Arthur in Britain's equivalent of Devil's Island. Dogs patrolled the narrow causeway, and guards spread rumors that sharks infested the waters. Reminders of those dark days remain in some of the area names—Dauntless Point, Stinking Point, Isle of the Dead.

Historic buildings from Tasmania's convict past can be seen in Port Arthor.

EXPLORING

Fodor's Choice **Port Arthur Historic Site.** This property, formerly the grounds of the Port
★ Arthur Penal Settlement, is now a lovely—and quite large—histori-
cal park. Be prepared to do some walking between widely scattered
sites. Begin at the excellent visitor center, which introduces you to the
experience by "sentencing, transporting, and assigning" you before
you set foot in the colony. Most of the original buildings were damaged by bushfires in 1895 and 1897, shortly after the settlement was
abandoned, but you can still see the beautiful church, round guard-
house, commandant's residence, model prison, hospital, and government cottages.

The old **lunatic asylum** is now an excellent museum, with a scale model
of the Port Arthur settlement, a video history, and a collection of tools,
leg irons, and chains. Along with a walking tour of the grounds and
entrance to the museum, admission includes a harbor cruise, of which
there are eight scheduled daily in summer. There's a separate twice-daily
cruise to and tour of the **Isle of the Dead,** which sits in the middle of
the bay. It's estimated that 1,769 convicts and 180 others are buried
here, mostly in communal pits. Ghost tours (reservations are essential) leave the visitor center at dusk and last about 90 minutes. ⊠ *Arthur Hwy.* ☏ *03/6251–2300, 1800/659101* ⊕ *www.portarthur.org.au*
🎟 *1-day entry ticket A$30; Isle of the Dead tour only A$12; 2-day Gold
pass A$100, ghost tour only A$20; After Dark pass A$61 (which also
includes a 2-course dinner).* ⊗ *Daily 8:30–dusk.*

Tasmanian Devil Conservation Park. This is a prime site to see tasmanian
devils (burrowing carnivorous marsupials about the size of a small

dog), as well as quolls, boobooks (small, spotted brown owls), masked owls, eagles, and other native fauna. The devils are fed six times throughout the day; ring the office for exact hour. ⊠ *Arthur Hwy., Taranna ⊹ 11 km (7 mi) north of Port Arthur* ☎ *03/6250–3230* ⊕ *www. tasmaniandevilpark.com* 🔊 *A$30* ⊗ *Daily 9–5.*

WHERE TO EAT AND STAY

For expanded hotel reviews, visit Fodors.com.

$$
AUSTRALIAN

✕ **Felons Bistro.** This restaurant at the Port Arthur Historic Site serves fresh Tasmanian seafood and game. Standout appetizers include fresh local oysters. If it's teatime (dinner), pop in for one of the rich desserts. There is also an inexpensive café in the visitor center. ⊠ *Port Arthur Historic Site, Port Arthur* ☎ *03/6251–2314, 1800/659–101* ⊗ *No lunch.*

$$

⌸ **Cascades Colonial Accommodation.** Part of a onetime convict outstation that dates to 1841, the original buildings here have been transformed into luxury accommodations. **Pros:** beautifully modernized rustic chic, private beach is stunning. **Cons:** kitchens aren't big enough to whip up a gourmet feast, in peak seasons there is a minimum stay. ⊠ *533 Main Rd., Koonya ⊹ 20 km (12 mi) north of Port Arthur* ☎ *03/6250–3873* ⊕ *www.cascadescolonial.com.au* ⤳ *4 cottages* ⌂ *In-room: kitchen. In-hotel: laundry facilities, parking* ⫴ *Breakfast.*

FREYCINET NATIONAL PARK AND EAST-COAST RESORTS

The east coast enjoys Tasmania's mildest climate, pristine beaches, and excellent fishing spots. The stretches of white sand here are often so deserted that you can pretend you're Robinson Crusoe. The towns in this region are quiet but historically interesting; in Louisville, for example, you can catch a ferry to the Maria Island National Park, which was a whaling station and penal settlement in the mid-19th century. Farther north, the town of Swansea has numerous stone colonial buildings that have been restored as hotels and restaurants, as well as the unusual Spiky Bridge (so named because of its vertically placed sandstone "spikes") and the convict-built Three Arch Bridge, both of which date from 1845.

The jewel of the eastern coast is Freycinet National Park, renowned among adventure seekers and those who appreciate stunning scenery. The spectacular granite peaks of the Hazards and the idyllic protected beach at Wineglass Bay have been dazzling visitors to this peninsula since it became a park in 1916.

EAST-COAST RESORTS

★ From Hobart the east-coast Tasman Highway travels cross-country to Orford, then passes through beautiful coastal scenery with spectacular white-sand beaches, usually completely deserted, before reaching Swansea. Bicheno, just north of Freycinet National Park, and St. Helens, which is farther north, are both fishing and holiday towns with quiet, sheltered harbors.

Bay of Fires Walk. Taking the four-day guided Bay of Fires Walk along the coast north of St. Helens is a wonderful way to enjoy the rugged beauty and tranquillity of the coast. The walk, which is about 27 km (18 mi) long, winds along the edge of Mt. William National Park, and allows you to visit stunning beaches, heathlands, Aboriginal sites, and peppermint forests, where a profusion of plant and animal life flourishes. During part of the relatively easy walk you'll stay at an ecologically sound campsite which is as luxurious as it can get, with timber floors and kitchen facilities, and two nights at the dramatic, remote, and ecologically sustainable **Bay of Fires Lodge.** All meals are provided. For details and prices, check out ⊕ *www.bayoffires.com.au.*

OUTDOOR ACTIVITIES

If you're sporty, you'll love Freycinet with its glut of outdoor adventures on land and sea, but even if you're not athletically inclined it's possible to let someone else do the work as you cruise or fly over the bay.

DIVING **Bicheno Dive Centre.** The spectacular coastline and clear, cool-temperate waters make this a great place to go diving. This well-established company offers boat dives twice daily at 9:00 am and 1:00 pm. They also offer fishing charters targeting flathead, morwong, the elusive Tasmanian striped trumpeter, and tuna when in season. ⊕ *www.bichenodive.com.au.*

HIKING **Wineglass to Wineglass.** This exceptional tour run by Freycinet Lodge is a 8-km (5-mi) guided walk to Wineglass Bay and then through pristine forests, and it would convert even the most vehement exercise-phobe. The guide is not only informative about the area's history and local animals, he also whips up a mean cup of coffee and brings out morning cakes and biscuits. At the end of the walk you're led to a clearing, where a table beautifully laid out with a white tablecloth is laden with local crayfish and oysters as well as some fine local Pinot Noir and Chardonnay. As if that weren't hedonistic enough, you're then whisked back to the start on a boat, ending the trip in style. ⊕ *www.puretasmania.com.au* ✉ *A$380.*

KAYAKING Freycinet is Tasmania's premier sea-kayaking destination, and it's possible to do guided tours or hire your own kayak and cruise around at your own pace.

Freycinet Adventures. This family-run company offers half-day tours around the peninsula, slowly exploring this spectacular coastline while guides point out local marine life like sea eagles and seals. ⊕ *www.freycinetadventures.com.au* ✉ *A$95.*

WILDLIFE WATCHING **Bicheno Penguin Tour.** At Bicheno, a very popular tour is the nightly hour-long vigil to see the penguins emerge from the water and clamber up to their nesting area. ⊕ *www.bichenopenguintours.com.au* ✉ *A$25* ☾ *Dusk.*

"We had driven from Friendly Beach further into the Park when we came across this beautiful area."
—photo by Gary Ott, Fodors.com member

WHERE TO STAY

For expanded hotel reviews, visit Fodors.com.

$
Fodor's Choice
★

🏨 **Avalon Coastal Retreat.** This three-bedroom house is the ultimate in exclusivity: it sits entirely alone on Tasmania's east coast. Pros: unadulterated privacy; gorgeous views; fully-stocked. Cons: There's only one house, and it books up quickly. ⊠ *11922 Tasman Hwy., Rocky Hills* ☎ *1300–361–136* 🛏 *3 rooms.*

$$$

🏨 **Diamond Island Resort.** Located 1½ km (1 mi) north of Bicheno, this property overlooks the Tasman Sea and has direct beach access. **Pros:** minutes from a superb beach; kitchenettes in all units. **Cons:** no Wi-Fi. ⊠ *69 Tasman Hwy., Bicheno* ☎ *03/6375–0100, 1800/030299* ⊕ *www. diamondisland.com.au* 🛏 *27 rooms* 🛏 *In-room: kitchen. In-hotel: restaurant, pool, tennis court, laundry facilities, parking.*

$$
★

🏨 **Meredith House.** Exquisite red-cedar furnishings and antiques decorate this 1853 refurbished residence in the center of Swansea. **Pros:** excellent service from affable hosts, superb freshly cooked breakfasts. **Cons:** gets lots of repeat visitors, so you have to book ahead, the mews rooms are not as charming as the ones in the main house. ⊠ *15 Noyes St., Swansea* ☎ *03/6257–8119* ⊕ *www.meredith-house.com.au* 🛏 *11 rooms* 🛏 *In-room: kitchen, Wi-Fi. In-hotel: parking* 🍽 *Breakfast.*

$$$

🏨 **Wagners Cottages.** These five charming stone cottages, two of which date from the 1850s, sit amid rambling gardens. **Pros:** open fires are a treat in winter; cozy feel to rooms. **Cons:** not ideal for children; no leisure facilities. ⊠ *Tasman Hwy. near Francis St., 3 km (2 mi) south of town, Swansea* ☎ *03/6257–8494* ⊕ *www.wagnerscottages.com* 🛏 *5 cottages, 2 rooms* 🛏 *In-room: kitchen. In-hotel: laundry facilities, parking* 🍽 *Breakfast.*

FREYCINET NATIONAL PARK

238 km (149 mi) north of Port Arthur, 214 km (133 mi) southwest of Launceston, 206 km (128 mi) northeast of Hobart.

The road onto the Freycinet Peninsula ends just past the township of Coles Bay; from that point the Freycinet National Park begins and covers 24,700 acres.

EXPLORING

Fodor'sChoice ★

Freycinet National Park. Highlights of the dramatic scenery here include the mountain-size granite formations known as the **Hazards.** On the ocean side of the peninsula there are also sheer cliffs that drop into the deep-blue ocean; views from the lighthouse at Cape Tourville (reached by a narrow dirt road) are unforgettable. A series of tiny coves called the Honeymoon Bays provide a quieter perspective on the Great Oyster Bay side. **Wineglass Bay,** a perfect crescent of dazzling white sand, is best viewed from the lookout platform, about a 30-minute walk from the parking lot; if you're feeling energetic, though, the view from the top of Mt. Amos, one of the Hazards, is worth the effort. A round-trip walk from the parking lot to Wineglass Bay takes about 2½ hours. The park's many trails are well signposted.

Daily entry to the park costs A$12 per person and A$24 per vehicle.

ESSENTIALS

Contact **Freycinet National Park** ⊠ *Park Office* ☎ *03/6256–7000.*

WHERE TO STAY

For expanded hotel reviews, visit Fodors.com.

$$ 🛏 **Edge of the Bay.** The views from these modern, minimalist-style water-view suites and cottages stretch across Great Oyster Bay to the Hazards. **Pros:** animals wander freely around the resort, idyllic setting. **Cons:** minimum stay of two nights, restaurant menu is limited and no breakfast is served. ⊠ *2308 Main Rd.* ☎ *03/6257–0102* ⊕ *www.edgeofthebay. com.au* ➭ *14 suites, 7 cottages* ⚒ *In-room: kitchen, Wi-Fi. In-hotel: restaurant, bar, tennis court, beach, laundry facilities, parking.*

$$$ 🛏 **Freycinet Lodge.** These 60 plush cabins are scattered through the densely wooded forest of Great Oyster Bay. **Pros:** superb food in fine-dining restaurant, perfect for getting away from it all; no TVs, phones, or cell reception. **Cons:** utilitarian furniture for the price, rooms can be on the cold side. ⊠ *Freycinet National Park* ☎ *03/6225–7000, 1800/420155* ⊕ *www.freycinetlodge.com.au* ➭ *60 cabins* ⚒ *In-room: no TV. In-hotel: restaurant, bar, tennis court, laundry facilities, parking.*

Fodor'sChoice ★

LAUNCESTON

200 km (124 mi) north of Hobart.

Nestled in a fertile agricultural basin where the South Esk and North Esk rivers join to form the Tamar, the city of Launceston (pronounced *Lon*-sess-tun), or Lonie to locals, is the commercial center of Tasmania's northern region. Its abundance of unusual markets and shops is concentrated downtown (unlike Hobart, which has most of its stores in the historic center, set apart from the commercial district).

Launceston is far from bustling, and has a notable number of pleasant parks, late-19th-century homes, historic mansions, and private gardens. The sumptuous countryside that surrounds the city—rolling farmland and the rich loam of English-looking landscapes—set off by the South Esk River meandering through towering gorges, is also appealing.

EXPLORING

Queen Victoria Museum and Art Gallery. The Queen Victoria Museum and Art Gallery, opened in 1891, offers insights into the city's history including its Aboriginal and colonial past. There's also a large natural-history collection of stuffed birds and animals (including the now-extinct thylacine, or Tasmanian tiger). ⊠ *2 Invermay Rd.* ☎ *03/6323–3777* ⊕ *qvmag.tas.gov.au* ✉ *Free* ⊙ *Daily 10–5.*

Cataract Gorge. Almost in the heart of the city, the South Esk River flows through the exceptionally beautiful Cataract Gorge on its way toward the Tamar River. A 1-km (.5-mi) path leads along the face of the precipices to the Cliff Gardens Reserve, where there are picnic tables, a pool, and a restaurant. Take the chairlift in the first basin for a thrilling aerial view of the gorge—at just over 900 feet, it's the longest single span in the world. Self-guided nature trails wind through the park, and it's a great place for a picnic. ⊠ *Basin Rd.* ☎ *03/6331–5915* ⊕ *www.launcestoncataractgorge.com.au* ✉ *Gorge free, chairlift A$15* ⊙ *Daily 9–4:30 winter/6:00 summer.*

Franklin House. Built in 1838 by convicts, this fine late-Georgian house was built by a local brewer but is now owned by the National Trust. It's notable for its beautiful cedar architecture and its collection of period English furniture, clocks, and fine china. Morning and afternoon teas are served in the tearoom. ⊠ *413 Hobart Rd., Franklin Village* ☎ *03/6344–7824* ✉ *A$8* ⊙ *Daily 9–5 summer, 9–4 winter.*

Fodor's Choice ★ **Tamar Valley Wine Route.** Along both sides of the Tamar River north of Launceston the soil and cool weather are perfect for grape growing. Outstanding varieties to try are Pinot Noir, Riesling, and Chardonnay; the sparkling wines produced here are world-leading. A map of the route, available for download at their Web site, will help you to plan your visit. Noteworthy stops along the route are Moores Hill, Hollyman wines at Stoney Rise, Clovery Hill, and Jansz. To help pace yourself, pop into Strathlynn Restaurant at Ninth Island for an unbelievable rustic lunch inspired by the microculture of the Tamar. ⊕ *www.tamarvalleywineroute.com.au.*

OUTDOOR ACTIVITIES

There are plenty of opportunities to spot wildlife, fish, or birds in the lovely countryside surrounding Launceston and the Tamar Valley.

BIRD-WATCHING **Tamar Island Wetlands.** This bird sanctuary on the banks of the Tamar River just outside Launceston is the place to see purple swamp hens and black swans from boardwalks over the wetlands while scanning the sky for white-breasted sea eagles or forest ravens. ⊠ *West Tamar Hwy., Riverside* ☎ *03/6327–3964* ⊕ *www.parks.tas.gov.au* ✉ *A$3* ⊙ *Daily dawn to dusk.*

CANOPY
TOURS
Fodor's Choice
★

Hollybank Treetops Adventure. A new and very popular attraction of particular appeal to kids has visitors gliding along wires on harnesses on this three-hour tour led by guides through the treetops and above the Pipers River. ✉ *66 Hollybank Rd., Launceston* ☎ *03/6395–1390* ⊕ *www.treetopsadventure.com.au* 🖃 *A$100 bookings are essential* ⏱ *Daily 9–7:30 (times vary depending on the season).*

RIVER CRUISES

Tamar River Cruises. This company conducts relaxing trips on the Tamar, past many wineries and into Cataract Gorge. ☎ *03/6334–9900* ⊕ *www. tamarrivercruises.com.au.*

WALKING

Launceston Historic Walks. This professional outfit conducts a leisurely stroll through the historic heart of the city. Walks leave from the 1842 Gallery. ✉ *Corner St. John and Cimitiere Sts., Launceston* ☎ *03/c* ⊕ *www.1842.com.au* 🖃 *A$15* ⏱ *Tues.–Sat. at 10, Mon. at 4.*

WILDLIFE-
WATCHING

Pepperbush Adventures. This husband-and-wife team runs tours out of Launceston covering Tasmania's northeast and looking at local wildlife in its natural habitat. The full-day Quoll Patrol takes you to view the "bandit of the Bush," as well as wallabies, platypuses, and, if you're lucky, some devils. ⊕ *www.pepperbush.com.au.*

WHERE TO EAT AND STAY

For expanded hotel reviews, visit Fodors.com.

$
STEAKHOUSE

✕ **Jailhouse Grill.** If you have to go to jail, this is the place to do it, in a 130-year-old historic building. Despite being furnished with chains and bars, it was never actually a place for incarceration, so relax and feast on prime beef cuts (or fish and chicken), and an all-you-can-eat salad bar. The wine list is comprehensive. ✉ *32 Wellington St.* ☎ *03/6331–0466* ⊕ *www.jailhousegrill.com.au.*

$$$
AUSTRALIAN
Fodor's Choice
★

✕ **Stillwater.** Part of Ritchie's Mill (a beautifully restored 1830s flour mill beside the Tamar River), this multi-award-winning restaurant serves wonderfully creative seafood dishes, usually with an Asian twist, such as the confit of Macquarie Harbour ocean trout with wasabi mash, trout crackle, and citrus and flying fish roe emulsion. The seven-course tasting menu can include wine pairings from the great selection of Tasmanian wines. A produce shop, café, wine bar, and art gallery are part of the same complex. Open for breakfast, lunch and dinner. ✉ *2 Paterson St.* ☎ *03/6331–4153* ⊕ *www.stillwater.net.au.*

$

🏠 **Alice's Cottages.** Constructed from the remains of three 1840s buildings, this delightful B&B is full of whimsical touches. **Pros:** perfect for a romantic getaway, especially the "boudoir"-themed room; spa bathrooms are luxurious and decadent. **Cons:** extra charge for open fires, not child-friendly. ✉ *129 Balfour St.* ☎ *03/6334–2231* ⊕ *www. alicescottages.com.au* ⤴ *8 rooms* ⚐ *In-room: kitchen. In-hotel: laundry facilities, parking* ⟐ *Breakfast.*

¢

🏠 **Old Bakery Inn.** History comes alive at this colonial complex made up of a converted stable, the former baker's cottage, and the old bakery. **Pros:** quaint and sensitively restored rooms, great value for money. **Cons:** some noise from busy road; breakfast ends at 9 am sharp. ✉ *York and Margaret Sts.* ☎ *03/6331–7900, 1800/641264* ⊕ *www. oldbakeryinn.com.au* ⤴ *24 rooms* ⚐ *In-room: Internet. In-hotel: restaurant, laundry facilities, parking.*

$$$ 🏨 **TwoFourTwo.** Three contemporary apartments and a town house built within a historic Launceston property have all modern conveniences including espresso machines and iPod docks, and feature the wonderful timber design work of Alan Livermore, one of the owners. **Pros:** rooms are stylish and well laid out; plenty of personal touches like fresh flowers and a thoughtfully stocked in-room wine selection. **Cons:** not particularly child-friendly, no leisure facilities. ⊠ *242 Charles St.* ☎ *613/6331–9242 from U.S., 0437/242–942 cell* ⊕ *www.twofourtwo. com.au* 🛏 *4 apartments* ⚲ *In-room: kitchen. In-hotel: laundry facilities, parking.*

$ 🏨 **Waratah on York.** Built in 1862, this grand Italianate mansion has been
★ superbly restored. **Pros:** complimentary port in guest sitting rooms is a nice touch, helpful staff. **Cons:** a lot of stairs to climb, rooms are on the dark side. ⊠ *12 York St.* ☎ *03/6331–2081* ⊕ *www.waratahonyork.com. au* 🛏 *9 rooms* ⚲ *In-hotel: business center, parking, some age restrictions* ⊙| *Breakfast.*

THE NORTHWEST

Tasmania's northwestern region is one of the most beautiful and least explored areas of the state. For its sheer range of landscapes, from jagged mountain contours to ancient rain forests and alpine heathlands in the Cradle Mountain area alone, the northwest can't be matched. The region's beauty saw it designated the Tasmanian Wilderness World Heritage Area, protecting one of the last true wilderness regions on earth. These regions are a major draw for hikers and sightseers. The western side of the northwest tip of Tasmania bears the full force of the roaring forties winds coming across the Indian Ocean, and this part of Tasmania contains some of the island's most dramatic scenery. Mining was a major industry a century ago, and although some mines still operate, the townships have a rather forlorn look.

GETTING HERE AND AROUND

This region is not the easiest to get to (the nearest airport is two hours away at Launceston) but the destination is certainly rewarding enough to make the journey worthwhile. Driving to Cradle Mountain from Launceston takes 2 hours, and 1½ hours from Devonport. It is possible to take public transport through coach operator Tassie Link, which connects the major transportation hubs with Cradle Mountain and Strahan, but for convenience, nothing beats renting your own car. It should be noted that the northern part of the Cradle Mountain–Lake St. Clair National Park (that is, Cradle Mountain itself) is accessed by roads inland from Devonport and the nearby town of Sheffield. The southerly Lake St. Clair end of the park, though, is reached by the Lyell Highway between Hobart and Queenstown at Derwent Bridge.

6

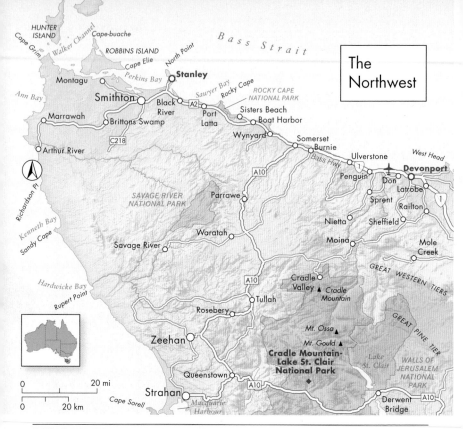

DEVONPORT AND ENVIRONS

89 km (55 mi) northwest of Launceston, 289 km (179 mi) northwest of Hobart.

In the middle of the North Coast, Devonport is the Tasmanian port where ferries from Melbourne dock. Visitors often dash off to other parts of Tasmania without realizing that the town and its surroundings have many interesting attractions.

ESSENTIALS

Contact **Devonport Visitor Centre** ⊠ 92 Formby Rd. ☏ 03/6424–4466.

WHERE TO EAT AND STAY

For expanded hotel reviews, visit Fodors.com.

$$$$ ✕ **Pedro's.** Despite the Spanish-sounding name, there's nothing Latin
SEAFOOD or Iberian about this menu. Instead, expect seafood caught fresh and cooked up daily in this restaurant on the edge of the Leven River. You can relax above the flowing water while sampling local crayfish, calamari, Tasmanian scallops, flounder, or trevally. The take-out fish-and-chips window lets you make a picnic of your feast in a nearby park. ⊠ *Wharf Rd., Ulverstone* ☏ *03/6425–6663 restaurant, 03/6425–5181 take-out counter.*

$ ⊞ **Westella House.** This charming 1885 homestead has stunning sea views. **Pros:** lovely gazebo in the garden to sit in and enjoy the views, complimentary sherry goes down well in winter. **Cons:** on the twee side, far from any restaurants or shops. ⊠ *68 Westella Dr., Ulverstone* ☎ *03/6425–6222* ⊕ *www.westella.com* ⇥ *3 rooms* ⌂ *In-hotel: laundry facilities, parking* ⦙⊙⦙ *Breakfast.*

STANLEY

140 km (87 mi) northwest of Devonport, 430 km (267 mi) northwest of Hobart.

Stanley is one of the prettiest villages in Tasmania, and a must for anyone traveling in the northwest. A gathering of historic cottages at the foot of the Nut, Tasmania's version of Uluru (Ayers Rock), it's filled with friendly tearooms, interesting shops, and old country inns.

EXPLORING

Highfield Historic Site. At the atmospheric Highfield Historic Site you can explore the town's history at the fully restored Regency house and grounds where Van Diemen's Land Company, who settled the estate in 1824, once stood. Guides in period costumes are on hand to answer any questions. ⊠ *Just outside Stanley, Box 74* ☎ *03/6458–1100* ⊕ *www. historic-highfield.com.au* ⛴ *A$10* ☉ *Sept.–mid June, daily 9:30–4:30; late June–Aug., weekdays 10–4.*

★ **The Nut.** The Nut, a sheer volcanic plug some 12.5 million years old, rears up right behind the village. It's almost totally surrounded by the sea. You can ride a chairlift to the top of the 500-foot-high headland, where the views are breathtaking; or, you can make the 20-minute trek on a footpath leading to the summit, where walking trails lead in all directions. ☎ *03/6458–1286 Nut chairlifts* ⛴ *Chairlift A$10* ☉ *Chairlift daily 9:30–5.*

OUTDOOR ACTIVITIES

FISHING **Murray's Day Out.** The exuberant owner will take you on a full day's fishing expedition, providing everything you need including lunch and refreshments. Some of their recommended common fishing spots include Stanley Wharf, Beauty Point, and Garden Island. ☎ *03/6424–5250* ⊕ *www.murraysdayout.com.au.*

WILDLIFE- **Stanley Seal Cruises.** Twice a day, animal lovers can take a 75-minute
WATCHING journey on the motor cruiser *Sylvia C.* The cruiser takes you offshore to Bull Rock to see Australian fur seals in their natural habitat in Bass Strait. ⊠ *Dockside* ☎ *0419/550–134* ⊕ *www.stanleysealcruises.com.au* ⛴ *A$49* ☉ *No tours July–Aug.*

♻ **Wing's Wildlife Park.** This park, 50 minutes drive from Devonport, has one of the larger collections of Tasmanian wildlife in Australia, which as well as all the usual suspects includes an aquatic section where you can view albino rainbow trout and Atlantic salmon. Excellent guided tours can be tailored to your interests. ⊠ *137 Winduss Rd., Gunn's Plains* ⊕ *wingswildlife.com.au* ⛴ *A$17* ☉ *Daily 10–4.*

Looking out across Cradle Mountain–Lake St. Clair National Park.

WHERE TO EAT AND STAY

For expanded hotel reviews, visit Fodors.com.

$$ \times$ **Stanley's on the Bay.** Set on the waterfront in the fully restored old

AUSTRALIAN Bond Store, this unpretentious restaurant specializes in fine steaks and

★ seafood. Try the eye fillet of beef—Australian terminology for the top-quality beef cut—topped with prawns, scallops, and fish fillets, served in a creamy white-wine sauce. ⊠ *15 Wharf Rd.* ☎ *03/6458–1404* ⊗ *Closed Sun. and all of Aug. No lunch.*

$$ ☷ **Beachside Retreat West Inlet.** These modern, environmentally friendly

★ cabins are set on waterfront sand dunes overlooking the sea. **Pros:** guests with special needs are well catered to, breathtaking views from cabins. **Cons:** two nights minimum, limited food availability on-site. ⊠ *253 Stanley Hwy.* ☎ *03/6458–1350* 🖷 *03/6458–1350* ⊕ *www. beachsideretreat.com* ↘ *5 cabins* ⚬ *In-room: kitchen. In-hotel: laundry facilities, business center, parking* ❏ *Breakfast.*

$ ☷ **Touchwood Cottages.** Built in 1840 right near the Nut, this is one of Stanley's oldest homes, and it's furnished with plenty of period pieces. **Pros:** relaxing and romantic play to stay. **Cons:** no baths in two of the cottages; no leisure facilities. ⊠ *31 Church St.* ☎ *03/6458–1348* ⊕ *www. touchwoodstanley.com.au* ↘ *3 rooms* ⚬ *In-hotel: parking* ❏ *Breakfast.*

CRADLE MOUNTAIN–LAKE ST. CLAIR NATIONAL PARK

173 km (107 mi) northwest of Hobart to Lake St. Clair at the southern end of the park, 85 km (53 mi) southwest of Devonport, 181 km (113 mi) from Launceston, 155 km (97 mi) northeast from Strahan to Cradle Mountain at the northern end of the park.

Cradle Mountain–Lake St. Clair National Park. Cradle Mountain–Lake St. Clair National Park contains some of the most spectacular alpine scenery and mountain trails in Australia. Popular with hikers of all abilities, the park has several high peaks, including Mt. Ossa, the highest in Tasmania (more than 5,300 feet). The Cradle Mountain section of the park lies in the north. The southern section of the park, centered on Lake St. Clair, is popular for boat trips and hiking. Many walking trails lead from the settlement at the southern end of the lake, which is surrounded by low hills and dense forest. Visitors are advised to park their cars in the free car park and then make use of the shuttle bus that runs from the Cradle Mountain Visitor Centre and makes stops at all the trails. In summer the bus runs every 15 minutes, in winter every 30 minutes. The entrance fee is A$16.5 per person.

One of the most famous trails in Australia, the **Overland Track** traverses 85 km (53 mi) between the park's northern and southern boundaries. The walk usually takes five to seven days, depending on the weather, and on clear days the mountain scenery seems to stretch forever. Hikers are charged A$180 to do the Overland during peak walking season (November to April), and Tasmania's Parks and Wildlife Service has provided several basic sleeping huts that are available on a first-come, first-served basis. Because space in the huts is limited, hikers are advised to bring their own tents. If you prefer to do the walk in comfort, you can use well-equipped, heated private structures managed by Cradle Mountain Huts ☎ *03/6492–1110* ⊕ *www.cradlehuts.com.au.*

ESSENTIALS

Contacts **Cradle Mountain Visitor Centre** ✉ *4057 Cradle Mountain Rd., Cradle Mountain* ☎ *03/6492–1110.* **Lake St. Clair Visitor Centre** ✉ *Lake St. Clair National Park, Derwent Bridge* ☎ *03/6289–1172.*

OUTDOOR ACTIVITIES

As well as the self-guided day and multiday walks you can do in Cradle Mountain, there are plenty of opportunities to see the sights from a horse, the air, or even a quad bike.

AIR TOURS **Cradle Mountain Helicopters.** Departing by helicopter from Cradle Mountain village, this flight provides spectacular views over Fury Gorge—Australia's deepest gorge—Cradle Mountain itself, and beautiful Dove Lake. ⊕ *www.adventureflights.com.au* ✉ *A$190.*

HIKING **Tiger Wilderness Tours.** This Launceston-based company offers afternoon guided walks to Cradle's glacial lakes and alpine forests with stunning views of Mt. Roland. ⊕ *www.tigerwilderness.com.au* ✉ *A$149.*

HORSEBACK RIDING **Cradle Country Adventures.** There are half-day, full-day, and multi-day rides through stunning natural vistas to choose from that are suitable for both novices and the experienced rider. All equipment, guides, and transfers are included. ⊕ *www.cradleadventures.com.au.*

QUAD BIKING   **Cradle Mountain Quad Bikes.** All year round you can hire a Suzuki Ozark 250 quake bike and ride it on a special track that winds up through ancient myrtle forest and alpine eucalypt forest. Four-wheel-drives are also available. ⊕ *www.cradlemountainquadbikes.com.au* ⌦ *From A$95 for two hours including morning tea.*

WHERE TO STAY

For expanded hotel reviews, visit Fodors.com.

$ Cradle Mountain Chateau.** Five minutes' drive from the entrance to the national park is this corporate-style place—don't be misled by the word chateau—think upmarket lodge. **Pros:** the excellent spotlight animal tour at dusk is unmissable, and the fine-dining restaurant offers delicious meals. **Cons:** can be packed with corporate events ⊠ *Cradle Mountain Rd., Cradle Mountain* ☎ *1800/420155* ⊕ *www.cradlemountainchateau. com.au* ⥅ *60 rooms* ♿ *In-room: a/c, Wi-Fi. In-hotel: restaurant, bar, spa, business center, parking.*

$$ Cradle Mountain Lodge.** This wilderness lodge with its collection of cabins is a comfortable place to stay at Cradle Mountain. **Pros:** good range of food options, open fires are a hit in winter. **Cons:** some might rue the lack of home comforts—no room service, TV, or Internet. ⊠ *4038 Cradle Mountain Rd., Cradle Mountain* ⊹ *60 km (37 mi) from Sheffield* ☎ *03/8296–8010* ⊕ *www.cradlemountainlodge.com.au* ⥅ *96 rooms* ♿ *In-room: no TV. In-hotel: restaurant, laundry facilities, parking* ⦿ *Breakfast.*

Brisbane and Its Beaches

WORD OF MOUTH

"The Gold Coast hinterland is really beautiful, so is the Gold Coast with some fabulous beaches [and] some great theme parks. There's an awful lot there to do and it really is a fun place. Tamborine Mountain is part of the scenic rim and that is very lovely . . . North Stradbroke Island will also offer whale watching as does Tangalooma—both are excellent choices."

—stormbird

WELCOME TO
BRISBANE AND ITS BEACHES

TOP REASONS TO GO

★ **Enjoying the Outdoors:** Choose from rain forests and reefs, unspoiled beaches and islands, rushing rivers, dramatic gorges, distinctive wildlife, hiking, and water sports.

★ **Experiencing the Laid-Back Vibe:** Queensland's communities have affable, relaxed locals, even at the upmarket hotels and fine-dining restaurants of Brisbane and resort areas.

★ **Releasing Your Inner Child:** Queensland's Gold Coast is abuzz with world-class theme parks—from thrill rides, watery attractions, to Outback-inspired extravaganzas.

★ **Seeing Wildlife:** Head out to the southern end of the Reef for millions of fish, rays, turtles, and cetaceans; on the mainland, watch for rare birds and mammals, endangered frogs, dingoes, and koalas.

1 Brisbane. Affectionately dubbed Brisvegas, Queensland's capital city is a breezily cheerful, increasingly sophisticated city with a thriving casino, a riverside cultural complex, and some terrific eateries, galleries, nightspots, and markets.

2 The Gold Coast. An hour's drive south of Brisbane, Queensland's first coastal resort has expanded into a busy strip of high-rise hotels, theme parks, casinos, bars, eateries, and nightclubs. If you need a break from the bustle, walk down to the beach and curl your toes in the sand; alternatively, drive west and spend a day (or several) exploring the lush, mountainous hinterland.

3 The Sunshine Coast. This stretch of coastline about an hour north of Brisbane is known for its glorious beaches, fine national parks, and a hinterland dotted with charming townships. In recent years new roads and infrastructure have spurred a boom in accommodations and eateries.

4 Fraser Island. A gigantic sand island off Hervey Bay, Fraser Island has much to offer the active visitor. What it lacks in luxe amenities it makes up for in scenery: miles of white-sand beaches, deep-blue lakes, and bushland bristling with wildlife—including some of the world's most purebred dingoes.

5 Mackay-Capricorn islands. This smattering of coral cays along the southern end of the Great Barrier Reef—including Heron, Wilson, Lady Musgrave, and Lady Elliot islands—shelters significant marine wildlife, including seabirds, turtles, rays, sharks, and millions of tropical fish.

GETTING ORIENTED

At 1,727,999 square km (667,180 square mi) and more than four times the size of California, Queensland has enormous geographic variety. Its eastern seaboard stretches 5,200 km (3,224 mi) from the subtropical Gold Coast to the wild and steamy rain forests of the far north. Away from the coastal sugar and banana plantations, west of the Great Dividing Range, Queensland looks as arid and dust-blown as any other part of Australia's interior. Not surprisingly, most of the state's 4 million or so inhabitants reside on the coast; Brisbane and the beach resorts, toward the south of the coast, have experienced dramatic expansion over the past decade. The region's main attractions (apart from the kitschy "Big Things" that dot its highways) are its glorious coastline, the fertile hinterland flanking it, and the reefs and islands that lie offshore.

7

GOLD COAST TOP AMUSEMENT PARKS

Queensland's Gold Coast is littered with large outdoor theme parks, collectively luring millions of visitors annually with multimillion-dollar thrill rides, waterslides, kids' zones, live shows, and animal attractions.

The Gold Coast's theme parks offer an array of attractions as vast as their acreage. Some, such as WhiteWater World and Wet 'n' Wild Water World, draw crowds with massive wave pools, tubes, and waterslides. At others, the attraction is "true-blue Aussie" experiences: Paradise Country has an Outback farm focus with kid-friendly activities, animals, and tours; the Australian Outback Spectacular, a nightly big-budget arena show, highlights jackeroo (Aussie cowboy) skills. Dreamworld excites folk of all ages with high-tech thrill rides and action-packed shows, while Seaworld, a little farther south, has daily dolphin and seal shows and a polar bear park. Some parks double as locations for movies and TV series; Warner Bros. Movie World also has a daily live-action stunt show, wandering cartoon characters, and movie memorabilia. At all six you'll find a glut of merchandising and snack outlets.

BEAT THE CROWDS

The Gold Coast's theme parks are often crowded, especially on weekends and during school holidays. To beat the crowds, arrive early, go midweek, visit on rainy days, or take theme-park excursions in winter, when crowds are thinner but days are often sunny (pools and water-rides are heated).

Prebuy tickets online (valid for a year), then use the e-ticket express gate. An Early Entry Pass (A$10 extra) lets you enter some parks an hour before opening time (these are limited; book early). Some parks hire out "virtual queueing" devices so you can explore the park while waiting for rides rather than standing in line.

DREAMWORLD

Dreamworld, near the Gold Coast town of Coomera, boasts a vast acreage and the "big six"–multimillion-dollar, state-of-the-art thrill rides claiming global superiority on various fronts. Here, among the kids' rides, souvenir stalls, and snack-food outlets, you'll find the world's fastest, highest thrill ride, the Tower of Terror; the southern hemisphere's tallest high-speed gravity roller coaster; a Guinness-Record-breaking free-fall ride; and what is allegedly the world's largest pendulum, the Claw. Dreamworld's latest attractions include the fast and furious Motocoaster race ride and the stomach-turning underwater adventure Shockwave. For a true Gold Coast experience, try the Flowrider, a mix of surfing and skateboarding, or a surfing lesson in the Cave of Waves. The park also shelters a group of endangered Bengal and Sumatran tigers, supports one of the largest koala populations in the state, and houses 800-plus native animals in a landscaped sanctuary, viewable up close on the Sunset Safari. Don't miss the daily sliming at Nickelodeon World.

WHITEWATER WORLD

Too hot to traipse around Dreamworld? Pack bathing suits and head to its cooler neighbor, WhiteWater World. The focus of the Gold Coast's latest theme park is aquatic rides and water slides, including the BRO, a twisting eight-lane racer slide named after deadly Australian marine critter, the blue ringed octopus, as well as Australia's largest corkscrew-cored whirlpool ride, the A\$1.4 million, 26-second Rip ride. You can also take a trip on an inner-tube "aquacoaster" known as the Temple of Huey; hang five in the Green Room, a 65-foot-high "tube" simulating a monster wave's innards; or face your fears on the park's newest power slide, the Wedgie. Ankle-biters will enjoy Nickelodeon's Pipeline Plunge, and toddlers can play safely at Wiggle Bay. You can even learn to surf here three mornings a week.

TIMING

It's tempting to pack both park visits into one day, but unless you're on a super-tight schedule, don't. You'll need a full day to do justice to White-Water World's dozens of slides, wave pools, fun zones, and attractions; an equal amount of time to enjoy Dreamworld. Fitting in everyone's activities of choice, queueing, changing, and showering all take time.

Virtual queueing with Q4U saves your spot in line for WhiteWater World and Dreamworld's most popular rides, leaving you free to explore (the device gives little reminder beeps). Rides can't be queued for simultaneously, but Q4U still saves you hours. It's A\$10 (plus A\$7.50 per person using it) and well worth it.

Prebook early-bird tickets, Q4U devices, surf lessons, and Flowrider sessions online, as all are limited and sell out fast. A two-day World Pass, permitting second visits to Dream-world and WhiteWater World within a fortnight, is a smart idea for rainy-day (and cranky-kid) flexibility.

7

SUNSHINE COAST'S TOP BEACHES

Queensland's Sunshine Coast stretches from Caloundra in the south to Noosa Heads in the north. Along it you'll find everything from family-friendly beaches to thundering surf breaks to pretty sheltered coves ideal for snorkeling.

The Sunshine Coast has been developed more slowly and sensitively than its southern counterpart, the Gold Coast. Although it has its share of shops, cafés, and resorts, there are still dozens of clean, uncrowded beaches where you can sunbathe, stroll, cast a line, or take the plunge and get in the water to swim, snorkel, and surf.

Some beaches are perfect for water sports such as sailing, windsurfing, kayaking, or wakeboarding. Others are known for their reliable surf breaks. You'll find secluded rocky coves where you can "fossick" (Australian for beachcomb) among rockpools, or don a mask and snorkel and duck beneath the surface to see colorful fish, rays, sea stars, and squid. There are also safe, lifeguard-patrolled swimming beaches with playgrounds, skate parks, kiosks, change rooms, and picnic facilities ideal for families.

WHEN TO GO

The Sunshine Coast is renowned for sunny skies and year-round balmy temperatures, but you can still optimize your experience with some good timing. Beaches can get crowded at peak season, and prices are higher. The most ideal time to visit is November and early December or March and April (except Easter week, which usually includes Queensland's week-long fall school break), when crowds are fewer but the weather is still summery. Note that many beaches are only patrolled during peak times. January and February bring the most rain.

SUNSHINE BEACH

Lovely Sunshine Beach, the last easterly facing beach before Noosa, is patrolled year-round. Beach breaks, reliable swell, a rocky headland sheltering it from winds, and clear, glassy water make Sunshine popular with surfers. When northeasterlies blow, surf the northern pocket. Fish off the beach year-round for dart, bream, and flathead, or cast a long line into deep water to hook numerous seasonal species. Use covered picnic areas, BBQs, toilets, and parking. From here, hike past nudist-friendly Alexandria Bay to Noosa.

MOOLOOLABA BEACH

This super-safe swimming beach, patrolled year-round, has just enough swell to make it fun. Surfers might want to check out the left-hand break that sometimes forms off the rocks at the northern end. There are shady picnic areas with BBQs, playgrounds, showers, toilets, public phones, exercise areas, and parking—as well as the local meeting point, the Loo with a View. Stroll south along the coastal path to the river mouth and rock wall (off which you can fish, year-round, for bream); north to Alexandra Headland for views of the bay; or along Mooloolaba Esplanade, lined with casual eateries.

COOLUM BEACH

Coolum Beach is family-friendly with a surf club, skate park, playgrounds, change rooms, toilets, kiosk, shorefront parks, and picnic areas. Across David Low Way lie shops, cafés, and restaurants. A long, white-sand beach, Coolum is patrolled year-round, and offers a nice beach break and some decent, uncrowded waves off the headland. Fish from the beach in the evening for jewfish, tailor, bream, and dart; catch bream around the headland, especially in winter. Walk south along the boardwalk to the headland park for magnificent coastal views, or north to quieter Peregian Beach with its patrolled surf, playground, and adjacent Environmental Park.

SAFETY

Most popular Sunshine Coast beaches are patrolled by lifeguards in school holiday and peak periods and on weekends throughout the warmer months. On some Sunshine Coast beaches, sandbanks, strong currents, and riptides make surf conditions challenging. Even on patrolled beaches, swimming unaccompanied is not recommended. Swim between the red-and-yellow flags, and follow lifeguards' directives. Locals are often the best sources of advice on where and when to dive in.

Sharks are rarely a problem; however, lifeguards keep watch and issue warnings if they're sighted. A more constant hazard is the harsh Queensland sun: apply SPF30-plus sunscreen at regular intervals. Get information on local beaches at ⊕ *coastalwatch.com,* and surf reports on Surf Life Saving Queensland's Web site, ⊕ *www.lifesaving.com. au.* Contact the SLSQ Lifesaving Services Manager at ☎ *07/3846–8021.*

7

COASTAL AND WILDERNESS WALKS

Southeast Queensland lays claim to some of the world's most superb wilderness areas, and the best way to explore them is on foot. Behind the Gold and Sunshine coasts are national parks, forests, and nature reserves dense with trails. Several also trace scenic sections of the coastline.

Coastal trails wind along the beachfront, trace rainforest-clad headlands, and meander through waterfront reserves from the Gold Coast to the national parkland north of Noosa.

A string of national parks and wilderness areas connects the Gold and Sunshine coast hinterlands, laced with trails of varying lengths and degrees of difficulty. Walkers are rewarded with memorable sights: dramatic waterfalls and pristine pools, tracts of ancient rain forest, and glowworm caves; wildflowers, wildlife, and exceptional views, some stretching as far as the coast.

SAFETY

For bushwalking you'll need sturdy shoes with grip, a hat, sunscreen, insect repellent, wet- and cold-weather gear, drinking water, food, camping equipment and permits (if overnighting), and a map and compass. Leech-proof yourself by wearing long socks over your pant legs and carrying a lighter to burn off any hitchhikers. Let others know your planned route and timing, even for day hikes.

Over summer's wetter months trails may be muddy or closed. January to March, conditions can be hot. Watch for snakes. The EPA (⊕ *www.epa.qld.gov.au*) provides trail maps and up-to-date information.

QUEENSLAND'S GREAT WALKS

If your schedule allows it, tackle one of Queensland's Great Walks. A A$10 million state government initiative, the Great Walks aim to allow visitors of all ages and of average fitness to explore significant wilderness areas in a safe, eco-sensitive way.

A standout is the 54-km (34-mi) **Gold Coast Hinterland Great Walk**, linking the species-rich, Gondwana Rainforests of Australia World Heritage Area of Lamington and Springbrook plateaus via the glorious Numinbah Valley. En route, you'll traverse ancient volcanic terrain and pristine rain forest, passing torrential streams and waterfalls and 3,000-year-old hoop pines. Allow three days for the full walk, camping at designated sites en route, or trek just one section.

The **Sunshine Coast Hinterland Great Walk**, a 58-km (36-mi) hike traversing the Blackall Range northwest of Brisbane, includes sections of Kondalilla and Mapleton Falls national parks, Maleny Forest Reserve, and Delicia Road Conservation Park. The four- to six-day hike takes you past waterfalls and through open eucalypt and lush subtropical rain forest teeming with native birds, reptiles, and frogs.

The **Cooloola Great Walk** meanders through Great Sandy National Park north of Noosa. A 90-km (55-mi) network of graded walking tracks passes the spectacular multihue sand dunes of Rainbow Beach, and covers walks of varying distances and difficulty.

Fraser Island Great Walk rewards hikers with exceptional scenery—wide, white-sand beaches, pristine deep-blue lakes, rain-forest tracts, and plenty of birds, reptiles, wallabies, and dingoes.

For downloadable trail maps and detailed information, visit ⊕ *www.epa.qld.gov.au.* For camping information and permits, go to ⊕ *www.qld.gov.au/camping* or phone ☎ *13–1304.*

SHORTER OPTIONS

Coastal Trails. Compact Burleigh Head National Park (☎ *07/5535–3032*), midway between Surfer's Paradise and Coolangatta, includes coastal rain forest and heath that's home to wallabies, koalas, lizards, snakes, and brush turkeys. Trek the 2.8-km (1.75-mi) coastal circuit for excellent views, or the shadier, shorter, 1.2-km (0.75-mi) rain-forest circuit.

Hinterland Trails. Mt. Tamborine, Springwood, Witches Falls-Joalah, and Lamington national parks in the Gold Coast hinterland are all ideal for exploring on foot. Several wilderness retreats in the region offer guided bushwalks as part of the package.

West of the Sunshine Coast, short scenic walking trails in Kondallilla National Park, near Montville, take you past waterfalls, boulder-strewn streams, and lush rain forest teeming with wildlife. Or stroll along easy trails through Mary Cairncross Scenic Reserve, near Montville.

7

Updated by
Tess Curran

A fusion of Florida, Las Vegas, and the Caribbean, southern Queensland attracts crowd-lovers and escapists alike. Whether you want to surf or soak in the Pacific Ocean, stroll from cabana to casino with your favorite cocktail, hike through subtropical rain forests, or join seabirds and turtles on some pristine coral isle—it's all here.

Local license plates deem Queensland "The Sunshine State," a sort of Australian Florida—a laid-back stretch of beaches and sun where many Australians head for their vacations. The state has actively promoted tourism, and such areas as the Gold Coast, an hour south of Brisbane, and the Sunshine Coast, a roughly equivalent distance north of the capital, have expanded exponentially in recent years, with high-rise buildings, casinos, and beachfront amusements popping up on every block. These thriving coastal strips are the major attraction of southern Queensland for Australians and foreign tourists alike—along with a scattering of islands, notably Fraser Island, off Hervey Bay, and the Mackay-Capricorn islands lying on the southern end of the Great Barrier Reef.

Queensland was thrust into the spotlight when Brisbane hosted the Commonwealth Games in 1982. The World Expo '88 and the 2001 Goodwill Games have ensured that it's remained there. Such big-name competitions exposed Brisbane to the wider world and helped to bring the city, along with other provincial capitals, to social and cultural maturity. Consequently, Queensland is a vibrant place to visit, and Sunshine Staters are far more likely to be city slickers than stereotypical "bushies" who work the land. And, as it is in many regions blessed with abundant sunshine, the lifestyle here is relaxed.

PLANNING

WHEN TO GO

Temperatures average 15.6°C (60°F) between May and September with chillier nights, and 20°C (68°F) to 29°C (80°F) December to February. From December through March, expect heavy rains. Temperatures run slightly cooler inland. Sea- and reef-side Queensland tends to fill up from mid-December through January, and can also be heavily booked in July, September, and throughout Easter. There's no Daylight Saving Time in the state.

HEALTH AND SAFETY

In an emergency, dial **000** to reach an ambulance, the police, or the fire department.

Outdoors, wear a hat and sunscreen whatever the season. Water can be rough; resist anything more than getting your ankles wet without a lifeguard present and always swim between the red-and-yellow flags.

Medical and emergency facilities are basic offshore on the Moreton Bay islands, Fraser Island, and the Mackay-Capricorn Islands. All tour operators recommended here have contingency plans for major medical situations.

GETTING HERE AND AROUND

AIR TRAVEL

Qantas (⊕ *www.qantas.com.au*), V Australia (⊕ *www.vaustralia.com.au*), and a number of other carriers fly direct from U.S. cities to Australian capitals and regional tourist hubs. Qantas, Virgin Australia (⊕ *www.virginaustralia.com.au*), and Jetstar (⊕ *www.jetstar.com.au*) link several regional centers throughout Queensland. Budget carrier Tiger Airways (⊕ *www.tigerairways.com*) also covers most major centers, including the Sunshine Coast, Cairns, and Rockhampton.

BOAT TRAVEL

Ferries and charter boats ply the waters between the South-East Queensland mainland and its various islands and offshore resorts. Most make daily or more frequent return trips; some carry vehicles as well as passengers.

BUS TRAVEL

Buses service most major towns and tourist areas around South-East Queensland, and are reliable and affordable—though on many routes it's as cheap, and faster, to fly. During holiday periods on popular routes buses are often heavily booked; buy tickets in advance, and don't expect to stretch out, even on overnight services. Tourist offices can advise on which companies go where.

CAR TRAVEL

Traveling outside of cities is often simplest and most comfortable by car. Roads are generally good, but signage varies in clarity; study maps and work out highway exits in advance (although most hire cars will have GPS systems installed). Be prepared for heavy traffic between Brisbane and the Gold and Sunshine coasts in peak periods. Expect temporary road closures and detours after heavy rains. Roads are narrow and winding in some parts of the hinterlands. You'll need a 4x4 to

7

get around Fraser Island, the sand islands of Moreton Bay, and some national park roads and Outback tracks. You can rent a small runabout from about A$35 per day; a decent touring car from about $45 a day, and a 4x4 from about A$90 per day. Gas costs vary, and tend to be pricier away from major towns and highways.

TRAIN TRAVEL

Frequent trains service routes between the capital and the Gold and Sunshine coasts. The Queensland Rail network links regional towns and tourist centers, and is a scenic way to travel (though on longer routes it's often cheaper to fly). The *Sunlander* and high-speed *Tilt Train* ply the coast between Brisbane and Rockhampton or Cairns, servicing towns that serve as launching pads for island resorts.

RESTAURANTS

The concept of specialized rural cuisines is virtually unknown in Queensland. Steak, seafood, and the occasional Chinese restaurant predominate, apart from tourist hubs. Brisbane, however, has its share of modern Australian, Mediterranean, and Asian-influenced menus capitalizing on fresh regional produce, and the cuisine at many of Queensland's high-end resorts now rivals the standards of big-city fine-dineries. Coastal tourist towns are full of casual open-air restaurants that take advantage of the tropical climate—an increasing number of them helmed by city-class chefs.

HOTELS

Accommodations in this state run the gamut from rain-forest lodges, outback pubs, backpacker hostels, and colonial "Queenslander" bed-and-breakfasts—beautiful timber houses built above the ground on stilts, with wraparound verandas and character windows—to deluxe beachside resorts and big-city hotels. The luxury resorts are clustered around the major tourist areas of the Gold and Sunshine coasts and nearby islands such as Heron and Wilson. In smaller coastal towns accommodation is mostly in motels, apartments, and B&Bs. There are an increasing number of eco-friendly accommodations utilizing green technologies, including waste recycling and water conservation systems, to minimize the impact on their environs: many of Queensland's island resorts fall into this category.

DINING AND LODGING PRICE CATEGORIES (IN AUSTRALIAN DOLLARS)				
	¢	$	$$	$$$	$$$$
Restaurants	under A$10	A$10–A$20	A$21–A$35	A$36–A$50	over A$50
Hotels	under A$100	A$100–A$199	A$200–A$299	A$299–A$400	over A$400

Restaurant prices are based on the median main-course price at dinner. Hotel prices are for two people in a standard double room in high season, excluding service and tax (10%).

GOOD TOURS

Guided day tours are a simple way to see Brisbane if your schedule is tight. View the city's vast sprawl from the comfort of a chauffeured coach, with a driver offering insider information. *Buses are also*

GREAT ITINERARIES

IF YOU HAVE 3 DAYS

If you're after a Miami Beach–style holiday, fly into **Brisbane** and head straight for the glitzy **Gold Coast**, overnighting in **Surfers Paradise**. You could end the spree with a final night and day in **Lamington National Park** for its subtropical wilderness and birdlife.

IF YOU HAVE 5 DAYS

Do three days on shore and two days on the reef. Stay a night in **Brisbane**, then head to the **Sunshine Coast** for a hike in the **Glasshouse Mountains** on the way to **Noosa Heads**. Apart from beaches and surf, take in the Sunshine Coast's monument to kitsch, the **Big Pineapple**, and indulge in one of their famous sundaes. Then make your way north to Bundaberg or Gladstone for a flight to **Lady**

Elliot, Heron, or Wilson islands to wildlife-watch, dive, and snorkel; or a ferry to Fraser Island, off Hervey Bay, where you can swim in pristine lakes, 4WD along beaches stretching 50 mi, and see wild dingoes.

IF YOU HAVE 7 OR MORE DAYS

Unless you're keen to see everything, limit yourself to a few areas— **Brisbane**, its surrounding **Sunshine and Gold coasts**, Fraser Island or the coral isles of the Mackay-Capricorn group—taking three to four days to explore each. Extended stays also allow for bushwalking expeditions in national parks, trips to resorts on the reef, traipsing around the wineries of Queensland's **Southern Downs**, and enjoying the state's many theme parks.

7

great for covering the relatively short distances between Brisbane and nearly all of the mainland attractions covered in the chapter. Within an hour or two you can be taste-testing your way through the Tambourine or Scenic Rim wineries, or practicing your poker face at a Gold Coast casino.

Most day tours include admission to sights, refreshments, and on full-day tours lunch, as well as commentary en route and time to explore. Australian Day Tours/JPT conducts half- and full-day tours of Brisbane and nearby Moreton Island; one- and two-day trips to and around the Gold Coast, Noosa Heads, and the Sunshine Coast, from A$93 to A$529; and a two-day Fraser Island tour for A$477 per person. Greyhound Australia runs daily express coaches to the Gold Coast, as well as day trips that cover southeast Queensland and beyond.

Australian Day Tours/JPT ✉ *Level 1, Olympia Court, 3059 Surfers Paradise Blvd, Surfers Paradise* ☎ *1300/363–436, 07/5512–6444* ⊕ *www.daytours.com.au.*

Greyhound Australia ✉ *Transit Centre, Level 3, Roma Street* ☎ *1300–473946, 07/3236–3035* ⊕ *www.greyhound.com.au.*

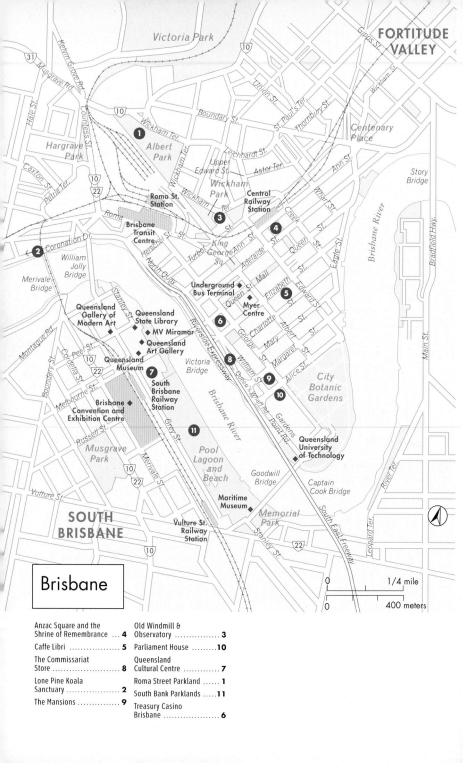

Brisbane

BRISBANE

Founded in 1824 on the banks of the wide, meandering Brisbane River, the former penal colony of Brisbane was for many years regarded as just a big country town. Many beautiful timber Queenslander homes, built in the 1800s, still dot the riverbanks and suburbs, and in spring the city's numerous parks erupt in a riot of colorful jacaranda, poinciana, and bougainvillea blossoms. Today the Queensland capital is one of Australia's up-and-coming cities: glittering high-rises mark its polished business center, fashion boutiques abound, and numerous outdoor attractions beckon. In summer, temperatures here are broilingly hot and days are often humid, a reminder that this city is part of a subtropical region: wear SPF 30-plus sunscreen and a broad-brimmed hat outdoors even on overcast days.

Brisbane's inner suburbs, a 5- to 10-minute drive or 15- to 20-minute walk from the city center, have a mix of intriguing eateries and quiet accommodations. Fortitude Valley combines Chinatown with a cosmopolitan influx of clubs, cafés, and boutiques. Spring Hill has several high-quality hotels, and Paddington, New Farm, and West End are full of an eclectic mix of restaurants and bars. Brisbane is also a convenient base for trips to the Sunshine and Gold coasts, the mountainous hinterlands, and the Moreton Bay islands.

GETTING HERE AND AROUND

AIR TRAVEL   Brisbane is Queensland's major transit hub. Qantas and Virgin Australia fly to all Australian capital cities and regional hubs around Queensland. Jetstar links Brisbane with the Fraser, Gold, and Sunshine coasts and regional cities farther north.

Brisbane International Airport is 9 km (5½ mi) from the city center. Coachtrans operates a bus service to meet all flights and drops passengers door to door at major hotels throughout Brisbane and the Gold Coast. The one-way fare is A$15 to Brisbane, A$43.50 to Gold Coast hotels, with cheaper deals available for families.

Airtrain has rail services to stations throughout Brisbane and the Gold Coast. The one-way fare is A$15 per person, or A$28 round-trip from the airport to City Central. Trains depart up to four times an hour, taking 20 minutes to reach the city center. Kids travel free. Taxis to downtown Brisbane cost A$35 to A$50, depending on time of day.

BOAT AND   Speedy CityCat boats and City Ferries dock at 23 points along the
FERRY TRAVEL   Brisbane River from Apollo Road to the University of Queensland, running half-hourly between 5:30 am and 11:30 pm. The ferries are terrific for a quick survey of the Brisbane waterfront from the city skyline to luxury homes. Due to flood damage, some terminals are temporary but still very useable.

BUS TRAVEL   Greyhound Australia, the country's only nationwide bus line, travels to around 1,100 destinations. Bus stops are well signposted, and vehicles usually run on schedule. It's 1,716 km (1,064 mi), a 30-hour journey, between Brisbane and Cairns. Book in person at Greyhound's Roma Street office, by phone, or online. Purchase point-to-point tickets or flexible passes that allow multiple stops.

Crisps Coaches operates a daily service from Brisbane to the Southern Downs and towns to the city's south and west.

TransLink's help line and Web site can help you find bus lines that run to your destination.

RENTAL CAR TRAVEL
Most major car-rental companies have offices in Brisbane, including Avis, Thrifty, Budget, and Hertz. Four-wheel-drive vehicles, motor homes, and camper vans (sleeping two to six people) are available from Britz, Maui Rentals, and KEA Campers. If you're heading north along the coast or northwest into the bush, you can rent in Brisbane and drop off in Cairns or other towns. One-way rental fees usually apply.

Brisbane is 1,002 km (621 mi) from Sydney, a 12-hour drive along the Pacific Highway (Highway 1). Another route follows Highway 1 to Newcastle, then heads inland on the New England Highway (Highway 15). Either drive can be made in a long day, although two days or more are recommended for ample time to rest and sightsee.

TAXI TRAVEL
Taxis are metered and relatively inexpensive. They are usually available at designated taxi stands outside hotels, downtown, and at Brisbane Transit and Roma Street stations, although it is often best to phone for one.

TRAIN TRAVEL
CountryLink trains make the 14-hour journey between Sydney and Brisbane. Rail services from Brisbane city and airport to the Gold Coast run regularly from 5:30 am until midnight. The *Sunlander* plies Queensland's coast from Brisbane to Cairns three times weekly, taking 31 hours. All trains include the option of luxurious *Queenslander*-class carriages with twin-berth sleeping cabins and fine food and wine. The speedy, state-of-the-art *Tilt Train* runs from Brisbane to Rockhampton daily except Saturday; to Bundaberg Monday–Thursday; and to Cairns (a 24-hour trip) Monday and Friday nights, stopping at Mackay, Proserpine, and Townsville as well as other towns.

Other long-distance passenger trains from Brisbane include the *Westlander,* to and from Charleville (twice weekly); and the *Spirit of the Outback,* to and from Longreach, via Rockhampton (twice weekly). Trains depart from Roma Street Station

TOURS

Australian Day Tours/JPT conducts half- and full-day tours of Brisbane and nearby Moreton Island. CitySights, run by the Brisbane City Council, operates air-conditioned hop-on, hop-off tour buses that make circuits of city landmarks and other points of interest, including South Bank and Chinatown. They leave from Post Office Square every 45 minutes, starting at 9 am; last departure is 3:45 pm. You can buy tickets on the bus and get on or off at any of the 19 stops for A$35. At the Brisbane City Council office, pick up a self-guided BrisbaneCityWalk map (also available from tourist information offices and online), as well as brochures and maps detailing other designated Brisbane walking trails.

Kookaburra River Queens are paddle wheelers that run lunch, dinner, tea, and jazz cruises on the Brisbane River. Lunch cruises include scenic and historic commentary; live entertainment and dancing are highlights of dinner cruises. The weekend seafood and carvery buffet dinner cruise is especially popular. Tours run A$10–A$89 per person.

Energetic visitors might want to scale Brisbane's Story Bridge for a 360-degree city overview; a climbing tour with Story Bridge Adventure Climb takes 2½ hours and costs A$89–A$99 per person, extra for twilight climbs.

ESSENTIALS

Airport Information and Transfers Airtrain ☎ 07/3216–3308 ⊕ www.airtrain. com.au. **Brisbane International Airport** ✉ Airport Dr., Eagle Farm ☎ 07/3406–3191, 07/3406–3000 ⊕ www.bne.com.au. **Coachtrans Australia** ☎ 07/3358–9700 ⊕ www.coachtrans.com.au.

Boat and Ferry Information CityCat ferries ☎ 13–1230 ⊕ www.translink.com.au.

Bus Information Crisps Coaches ✉ 78 Grafton Street, Warwick ☎ 07/4661–8333 ⊕ www.crisps.com.au. **Greyhound Australia** ✉ Level 3, Brisbane Transit Centre, Roma St., City Center ☎ 1300/473946 ⊕ www.greyhound.com.au. **TransLink** ☎ 13–1230 ⊕ www.transinfo.qld.gov.au.

Currency Exchange Commonwealth Bank of Australia ✉ 240 Queen St., City Center ☎ 13–2221 ⊕ www.commbank.com.au.

Rental Cars Britz Australia Campervan Hire and Car Rentals ✉ 647 Kingsford Smith Dr., Eagle Farm ☎ 07/3868–1248, 1800/331454 ⊕ www.britz.com. au. **KEA Campers** ✉ 348 Nudgee Rd., Hendra ☎ 1800/252555, 07/3868–4500 ⊕ www.keacampers.com. **Maui Australia Motorhome Rentals and Car Hire** ✉ 647 Kingsford Smith Dr., Eagle Farm ☎ 1300/363800, 07/3630–1153 ⊕ www.maui.com.au.

Taxis Black and White Cabs ☎ 13–3222 ⊕ www.blackandwhitecabs.com.au. **Yellow Cab Co** ☎ 13–1924 ⊕ www.yellowcab.com.au.

Tour Operators Australian Day Tours/JPT ✉ Level 3, Brisbane Transit Centre, Roma St., City Center ☎ 07/3489–6444, 1300/363436 ⊕ www.daytours.com. au. **Kookaburra River Queens** ✉ Eagle Street Pier, 1 Eagle St., City Center ☎ 07/3221–1300 ⊕ www.kookaburrariverqueens.com. **Story Bridge Adventure Climb** ☎ 1300/254–627 ⊕ www.storybridgeadventureclimb.com.au.

Trains Queensland Rail (QR) Travel Centre Traveltrain Holidays ✉ 305 Edward St., City Center ☎ 07/3235–1323, 1300/131–722 ⊕ www.qr.com.au.

Visitor Information Brisbane City Council ✉ 266 George St., City Center ☎ 07/3403–8888, 13/0013–4199 ⊕ www.brisbane.qld.gov.au.

EXPLORING BRISBANE

Brisbane's city-center landmarks—a mix of Victorian, Edwardian, and slick contemporary architecture—are best explored on foot. Most lie within the triangle formed by Ann Street and the bends of the Brisbane River. Hint: streets running toward the river are named after female British royalty; those parallel to the river after male royalty. The well-tended South Bank precinct has riverfront parklands and cultural centers, al fresco cafés, and weekend markets. Upriver, the quiet, leafy suburb of Fig Tree Pocket is home to Brisbane's best-known koala sanctuary.

7

TOP ATTRACTIONS

Lone Pine Koala Sanctuary. Queensland's most famous fauna park,
founded in 1927, is recognized by the *Guinness Book of World Records*
as the world's first and largest koala sanctuary. The attractions for most
people are the koalas (more than 130 in all), although emus, wombats,
crocs, bats, and lorikeets also reside here. You can hand-feed baby
kangaroos in the free-range 'roo and wallaby enclosure, have a snake
wrapped around you, or cuddle a koala (and have your photo taken
with one for A$15, until 4:30). There's also a thrice-daily sheepdog
show and regular barn animal feedings.

Fodor's Choice ★

MV *Mirimar*. The MV *Mirimar*, a historic 1930s ferry, travels
daily to Lone Pine Koala Sanctuary from the Cultural Centre pontoon
beside Victoria Bridge, departing at 10 sharp (board from 9:30 am),
departing from Lone Pine at 1:30 and returning to the city at 2:45
(A$60 round-trip, including entrance to the sanctuary). Bus 430 from
Platform B4, Queen Street Bus Station, and Bus 445 from Stop 40
on Adelaide Street also stop at the sanctuary. Taxis cost about A$35
from the city center, from which it's around 11 km (6.5 mi) to the
sanctuary. ☏ 07/3221–0300, 0412/749–426 ✉ 708 Jesmond Rd., Fig
Tree Pocket ☏ 07/3378–1366, 1300/729–742 ferry ⊕ www.koala.net
⤳ A$32 ⊗ Daily 8:30–5.

Queensland Cultural Centre. This really is a collection of centers and facilities: the Queensland Museum South Bank and Sciencentre, the architecturally renowned State Library of Queensland, and the Queensland
Performing Arts Centre (QPAC) are all here, as well as the Queensland
Art Gallery, and, a short stroll away, the world famous Gallery of Modern Art (GoMA). There's also a host of restaurants, cafés, shops selling
quality gifts, art posters, books and cards, a ticketing agent (within
QPAC), public-access computer terminals, and various interesting public spaces. The Centre houses significant art, cultural, indigenous, and
historic collections, most of which can be viewed free of charge and
without advance bookings. Green Cabs (modern rickshaws) are a fun
and unique way to get around and sightsee. From the Cultural Centre
forecourt they'll ferry passengers anywhere between West End and Fortitude Valley. ✉ Melbourne St. at Grey St., Southbank, South Brisbane
☏ 07/3840–7303 (galleries), 07/3840–7555 (museum), 07/3840–7810
(library), 07/3840–7482 (performing arts center) ⊕ www.qag.qld.gov.
au ⤳ Free ⊗ Galleries weekdays 10–5, weekends 9–5; museum daily
9:30–5; library Mon.–Thurs. 10–8, Fri.–Sun. 10–5.

Fodor's Choice ★

Roma Street Parkland. The world's largest subtropical garden within a
city is a gentle mix of forest paths and structured plantings surrounding a fish-stocked lake. Spot birds, lizards, and unique artworks along
the walkways. Highlights include the Lilly Pilly Garden, with native
evergreen rain-forest plants; and interesting children's play areas. Pack
a picnic, take advantage of the free grills, or stop for lunch at on-site
café Melange. Free hour-long guided garden tours begin daily at 10
and 2, or on weekends hop on the Parkland Explorer, a trackless train
that gives guests a full tour of the gardens for only $3. There are also
specialist art, heritage, curator's, or sensory tours (pre-book these) and
brochures for self-guided walks available online or from the Spectacle

Lone Pine Koala Sanctuary, Brisbane.

Garden Infobooth. ⊠ *1 Parkland Blvd., City Center* ☎ *07/3006–4545* ⊕ *www.romastreetparkland.com* ✉ *Free* ⊘ *Daily 24 hrs.*

☪ **South Bank Parklands.** One of the most appealing urban parks in Australia, this massive complex includes parklands, shops, a maritime museum, walking and cycling paths, a sprawling man-made beach and luxurious lagoons, a carved-wood pagoda, and excellent city views. The Friday-night Market by Moonlight and weekend South Bank Lifestyle Market bristle with handmade goods, live entertainers, buskers, artists, and New Age pundits. The Wheel of Brisbane, a giant Ferris wheel at the northern entrance of South Bank, is also a must for travelers wanting a spectactular view of the city for A$15 per person. South Bank Parklands stretches along the riverbank south of Queensland Cultural Centre. ⊠ *Grey St. south of Melbourne St.* ☎ *07/3867–2051 (parklands), 07/3844–3464 (Wheel of Brisbane)* ⊕ *www.visitsouthbank.com. au* ✉ *Parklands free, museum A$8* ⊘ *Parklands daily 5 am–midnight; info center daily 9–5; museum daily 9:30–4:30 (last entry 3:30); markets Fri. 5 pm–10 pm, Sat. 10–5, Sun. 9–5.*

Fodor's Choice ★

WORTH NOTING

Anzac Square and the Shrine of Remembrance. Paths stretch across manicured lawns toward the Doric Greek Revival shrine made of Queensland sandstone. An eternal flame burns here for Australian soldiers who died in World War I. In the Shrine of Remembrance, a subsurface crypt stores soil samples from key battlefields. On April 25, Anzac Day, a moving dawn service is held here in remembrance of Australia's fallen soldiers. ⊠ *Adelaide St. between Edward and Creek Sts., City Center* ✉ *Free* ⊘ *Shrine weekdays 9–2.*

Modern sculpture at the Queensland Cultural Centre, South Bank, Brisbane.

NEED A BREAK?

Caffe Libri. Duck down Elizabeth Street to the locally owned American Book Store. In the back, Caffe Libri serves coffee, cakes, and extravagant sandwiches. The bookstore carries literary fiction, academic, design, and foreign-language titles, and has been run by the same family for more than 50 years. ✉ *195 Elizabeth St., City Center* 🕾 *07/3229–4677, 1800/177395* ⊕ *www.americanbookstore.com.au.*

The Commissariat Store. Convict-built in 1829 on the site of the city's original timber wharf, this was Brisbane's first stone building. It has served variously as a customs house, storehouse, and immigrants' shelter, and is currently the headquarters of the Royal Historical Society of Queensland. The RGSQ library and museum, open to visitors, hold exhibitions, historical documents, manuscripts, and artifacts dating back to Brisbane's early colonial days. At this writing, the store is operating out of a temporary location due to the 2010–2011 Queensland floods, but is expected to be back in its original location by early 2012. ✉ *115 William St., City Center* 🕾 *07/3221–4198* ⊕ *www.queenslandhistory. org.au* 🖾 *A$5* 🕑 *Tues.–Fri. 10–4.*

The Mansions. Constructed in 1889, these Victorian terrace homes are a good place to cool off in warm weather. Few buildings like this were built this far north (more of this type of architecture prevailed in the southern capitals, especially Melbourne); elegant, wrought-iron lace trim garnishes the exterior. Inside is the upmarket Augustine's on George restaurant. ✉ *40 George St., City Center* 🕾 *07/3221–9365, 07/3229–0014 Augustine's* ⊕ *www.brisbanelivingheritage.org.*

Old Windmill & Observatory. This 1824 construction is the oldest remaining convict-built structure in Brisbane, dubbed the "Tower of Torture" by convicts forced to power a treadmill to crush the colony's grain on windless days. When fire razed part of the city in 1864 the windmill survived, later repurposed as an observatory. Stripped of its blades, the tower now resembles a lighthouse. ⊠ *Wickham Park, Wickham Terr., City Center* ☎ *07/3403–5048.*

Parliament House. Opened in 1868, this splendid, stone-clad, French Renaissance building with a Mount Isa copper roof earned its colonial designer a meager 200-guinea (A$440) fee. A legislative annex was added in the late 1970s. The interior is fitted with polished timber, brass, and frosted and engraved glass. There are free half-hour tours weekdays on demand, when Parliament is not in session (when it is, you're welcome to watch from the public gallery). High tea is offered in the elegant Strangers' Dining Room from 10:30 am to noon the first Friday of every month (A$39 per person). The adjacent, kid-friendly City Botanic Gardens have native and exotic plants and theme areas, including the Bamboo Grove and Weeping Fig Avenue, along with sculptures and ponds. ⊠ *George and Alice Sts., City Center* ☎ *07/3406–7562* ⊕ *www. parliament.qld.gov.au/home.asp* ☞ *Free* ☉ *Parliament House weekdays 9–5 (last tour 4:15 pm), gardens daily 24 hrs.*

Treasury Casino Brisbane. This Edwardian baroque edifice overlooking the river stands on the site of military barracks from the original penal settlement, flanked by bronze statuary. Constructed between 1885 and 1889, the former treasury reopened as a **hotel, casino, and entertainment complex.** In addition to three floors of gaming, the casino houses six eateries and five bars. ⊠ *Queen St. Mall, William and Elizabeth Sts., City Center* ☎ *07/3306–8888, 1800/506–888* ⊕ *www.treasurybrisbane. com.au* ☞ *Free* ☉ *Daily 24 hrs.*

OUTDOOR ACTIVITIES

ADVENTURE Kangaroo Point cliffs, near the city center, are ideal for climbing and abseiling. You can canoe or kayak on the Brisbane River; and numerous scenic bushwalking, climbing, and abseiling sites lie less than 90 minutes' drive from Brisbane. Government-run Outdoors Queensland (⊕ *www.qorf.org.au*) gives regional information and lists businesses offering adventure activities from hiking to horse riding.

Adventures Around Brisbane. Adventures Around Brisbane runs daily rock-climbing and abseiling sessions off Kangaroo Point cliffs, day and moonlight canoe tours along the Brisbane River, and bushwalks and adventure day trips to the scenic Glass House Mountains and Mt. Tinbeerwah. ☎ *1800/689–453, 0421/152–147* ⊕ *www.adventuresaroundbrisbane. com.au* ☞ *A$79 3-hour rock-climbing session or A$35 nighttime introductory climb, A$69 2-hour sunset abseil, A$99–A$109 day tours.*

BIKING An extensive network of bicycle paths crisscrosses Brisbane. One of the best paths follows the level, recently upgraded Bicentennial Bikeway southeast along the Brisbane River, across the Goodwill Bridge, then along to South Bank Parklands or Kangaroo Point cliffs. The new Kuripla Bridge and Go Between Bridge are also both cyclist-friendly ways to cross the river between the city and South Brisbane.

Brisbane City Council. The Brisbane City Council Web site includes downloadable maps and lets you search for bikeways. Visitors can pick up free Council-operated CityCycle bikes from 150 designated points around the inner city, returning them when they're done. ⊕ *www.brisbane.qld.gov.au.*

Gardens Cycle Hire. Gardens Cycle Hire, on Alice Street, hires out bicycles for A$15 for an hour or A$35 a day, or A$55 if you want the bike for a whole week (all prices include helmets). For A$10 extra they'll deliver a rental bike to your hotel. Tandem bikes are also available. ☎ *0408/003198* ⊕ *www.brisbanebicyclehire.com* ⊙ *Closed Tues. and in bad weather.*

Riverlife Adventure Centre. Riverlife Adventure Centre runs guided rock-climbing and abseiling sessions off Kangaroo Point cliffs, cycling tours around Brisbane attractions, day and night kayaking trips on the Brisbane River (followed by prawns and drinks or a barbecue), skate lessons and rollerblade hire, and indigenous culture experiences. A highlight is the Mirrabooka Aboriginal Cultural Experience, which includes a traditional performance by the Yuggera Aboriginal Dancers and hands-on instruction in fire-starting, instrument-playing, boomerang-throwing, and painting, plus food-tasting. ✉ *Naval Stores, via Lower River Terr. or River Terr., Kangaroo Point* ☎ *07/3891–5766* ⊕ *www.riverlife.com. au* 🍴 *A$49–A$79.*

GOLF **St. Lucia Golf Links and Golf World.** One of Brisbane's oldest golf courses, St. Lucia Golf Links and Golf World is an 18-hole, par-70 course open to visitors; greens fees are A$29 for 18 holes on weekdays, A$35 weekends, and two-for-one on Monday. Dine on-site at the Clubhouse or 100 Acre Bar (☎ *07/3870–3433)* overlooking the 18th green. ✉ *Indooroopilly Rd. at Carawa St., St. Lucia* ☎ *07/3403–2556.*

OUTDOOR
GEAR
OUTFITTERS **Paddy Pallin.** Australian-owned Paddy Pallin sells quality outdoor and travel gear, including hats, footwear, clothing, backpacks, and equipment. On staff are dedicated bushwalkers, rockclimbers, and travelers. The store is open Monday–Friday 9 am–5:30 pm, Saturday 9–5, and Sunday 10–4. ✉ *108 Wickham St., Fortitude Valley* ☎ *07/3839–3811* ⊕ *www.paddypallin.com.au.*

TENNIS **Tennis Queensland.** Contact Tennis Queensland for information about court hire, guided tours of the adjacent, ultra-modern **Queensland Tennis Centre,** and details on tournaments. ✉ *190 King Arthur Terr., Tennyson* ☎ *07/3120–7900* ⊕ *www.queenslandtenniscentre.com.au.*

WATER
SPORTS **Moreton Bay.** A half-hour's drive east of Brisbane city brings you to Moreton Bay, stretching 125 km (78 mi) from the Gold Coast to the Sunshine Coast. A number of operators based in Brisbane's bayside suburbs—Manly, Redcliffe, Sandgate—run sailing, diving, sightseeing, and whale- and dolphin-watching trips around the Bay, and trips to its various islands. Some cruises include tours of St. Helena Island's historic prison ruins; others visit Moreton Island, where you can toboggan down massive white sand-dunes.

Moreton Bay Escapes. Moreton Bay Escapes runs tours and charters around Moreton Bay Marine Park and Moreton Island National Park that might include sailing, 4WD-driving, snorkeling, and sand-boarding. They'll also tailor excursions to incorporate hiking, scuba-diving, sea-kayaking, bird-watching, and swimming with dolphins. ☎ *1300/559–355* ⊕ *www.moretonbayescapes.com.au.*

WHERE TO EAT

In the past decade Brisbane has transformed from a culinary backwater into a city full of inventive dining options. Top chefs have decamped to Brisbane's best eateries, and are busy putting put a fresh subtropical spin on Modern Australian, pan-Asian, and Mediterranean cuisine.

Imaginative dishes capitalize on abundant regional produce: fine fresh seafood—notably the local delicacy, Moreton Bay bug (a sweet-fleshed crustacean)—premium steak, Darling Downs lamb, cheeses, macadamia nuts, avocadoes, olives, and fruit, matched with fine regional wines.

Most of the city's hip cafés and smart fine-dineries are clustered in West End, Fortitude Valley, New Farm, and Petrie Terrace; you'll also find some excellent eateries in the city center and the riverfront South Bank precinct, and a smattering around the suburbs, particularly Rosalie, Paddington, Milton, and Ascot. For terrific fresh seafood, head for Brisbane's bayside suburbs, such as Manly, Redcliffe, and Sandgate, or to South Stradbroke Island.

Typically, dining ambience is relaxed, seating is alfresco, and well-mannered children are welcomed.

Use the coordinate (✛ B2) at the end of each listing to locate a site on the corresponding map.

$$
STEAKHOUSE
✕ **Breakfast Creek Hotel.** A Brisbane institution, this enormous hotel is perched on the wharf at Breakfast Creek. National Heritage–listed interiors and a lush tropical beer garden are as much of a draw as its superb trademark steaks. Non-steak eaters also have plenty of options, including vegetarian dishes and terrific fresh oysters. ✉ *2 Kingsford Smith Dr., Albion* ☎ *07/3262–5988* ⊕ *www.breakfastcreekhotel.com* ✛ *C1.*

$
THAI
✕ **Caxton Thai.** This unassuming restaurant, where you dine flanked by Thai art and sculpture, is popular with locals and tourists. The most requested dish is the pork chop stir-fried with chili and basil; or try the coral trout fillet with chili-tamarind sauce. Other than these, it's mostly traditional; find curries, soups, plenty of vegetarian options, and many noodle dishes, including a warm Thai salad (a mix of chicken, prawns, glass noodles, and vegetables). ✉ *47B Caxton St., Petrie Terr.* ☎ *07/3367–0300* ⊕ *www.caxtonthai.com.au* ⊗ *No lunch* ✛ *A1.*

$$$
AUSTRALIAN
Fodor's Choice
★
✕ **e'cco.** Consistently ranked among the best restaurants in town, this petite eatery serves innovative food to a loyal following. The white-columned entry leads into a warm-toned dining room with an open kitchen and bar. Seasonally changing Mediterranean and Asian-inspired dishes incorporate premium local produce. One recent season patrons could start with with grilled quail or duck terrine, and follow it with seared ocean trout or Wagyu rump steak. Each seasonal dessert selection

is equally delectable: lemon and ricotta torte, passion-fruit panna cotta, and chocolate assiette are just a sampling of one recent selection. There's no sommelier, but waiters can suggest accompanying wines. ✉ *100 Boundary St., City Center* ☎ *07/3831–8344* ⊕ *www.eccobistro.com* ⌾ *Reservations essential* ☾ *Closed Sun. and Mon. No lunch Sat.* ✛ *D1.*

$$ CAFÉ ★

✕ **Freestyle Tout.** Tucked away in an inner-city suburb, this gallery-café is famous for its 21 beautiful, all-day desserts—including artfully designed sundaes, fruity tarts, sticky tortes, and a memorable white-chocolate raspberry brioche. The savoury dining menu now includes interesting Mod-Oz mains as well as café-style fare. You can also take high tea here. The local Australian artwork displayed is refreshed every month and often for sale. ✉ *Shop 50, 1000 Ann St., Fortitude Valley* ☎ *07/3252–0214* ⊕ *www.freestyletout.com.au* ✛ *D1.*

$$ AUSTRALIAN

✕ **The Gunshop Café.** Named for its previous business, this West End café is the place to go for breakfast on weekends (the potato-feta hash cakes with spinach, house-dried tomato, and herbed sour cream are locally famous). Unfinished brick walls where guns once hung lend a rustic ambience. Dine around wooden tables near the open kitchen or request a seat out on the sidewalk. A select but eclectic Mod-Oz menu fuses Mediterranean and Asian flavors in dishes featuring premium Margaret River lamb, Angus beef, duck, and seafood; they also do vegetarian dishes and exciting salads, with all produce sourced from local markets. Foodies flock here for lunch, dinner, or even just a coffee and dessert; the flourless chocolate cake is particularly memorable. ✉ *53 Mollison St., West End* ☎ *07/3844–2241* ⊕ *www.thegunshopcafe.com* ☾ *Closed Sun. except breakfast; no dinner Mon.* ✛ *A3.*

$ TIBETAN ★

✕ **The Himalayan Cafe.** Clusters of pendant lanterns and colorful Buddhist prayer flags welcome you to the Himalayan Cafe, one of Brisbane's most popular inner-city eats. At this Tibetan/Nepalese sanctuary, the homemade entrée breads are perhaps as famous as the restaurant itself—divinely moist and fluffy, each is served with a minted yogurt dipping sauce in the traditional Himalayan style. When it comes to mains, there's something for everyone, from vegans and vegetarians to the most unswayable meat lovers: spicy noodle soups, tofu and vegetable curries, and succulent, tender lamb, beef, chicken, and goat dishes in a range of flavors and intensities. For an extra treat, ask for a seat out back in one of the traditional Himalayan raised restaurant rooms. ✉ *640 Brunswick St., New Farm* ☎ *07/3358–4015* ✛ *D1.*

$$$ SEAFOOD

✕ **Jellyfish.** Red-meat restaurateur John Kilroy of Brisbane steak house Cha Cha Char turns his hand to fish at his latest eatery. Sit indoors on smart black-and-white chairs under low-slung, jellyfish-shaped lights, or outside at wooden tables, some dressed in nautical black-and-white-striped linens, and choose from a Modern Australian menu that changes daily but always features eight species of fish—panfried or oven-roasted, steamed, seared, or with your choice of six available batters (say, saffron or tempura, curry or beer). Try the signature tempura soft-shell mud crab with green chili, shallots, and wasabi mayo; or the butterfish with wasabi leaves, shaved coconut, and kaffir lime—a worthy contender. The fresh, interesting menu also includes eye fillet steak, lamb and vegetarian options, and more-ish desserts, such as white-chocolate and violet parfait. The attached bar offers several wines by the glass. ⊠ *Boardwalk, Riverside Centre, 123 Eagle St., Brisbane* ☎ *07/3220–2202* ⊕ *www.jellyfishrestaurant.com.au* ⌂ *Reservations essential* ⊙ *No lunch Sat., closed Sun.* ✛ *C2.*

$$
AUSTRALIAN

✕ **Luxe.** This casual restaurant-cum-bar serves delicious tapas-style starters and seasonally changing dishes with a Euro-Mediterranean edge. Sample the rib fillet with potato scone, braised shallots, house jus, and mustard leaves, or the tender Brazilian spiced chicken breast. The crème brûlée is delicious, and the wine and seasonal cocktail lists are impressive. In nice weather, try for a table on the sidewalk. ⊠ *1/39 James St., Fortitude Valley* ☎ *07/3854–0671* ⊕ *www.luxerestaurant.com.au* ✛ *C1.*

$
CAFÉ

✕ **Pancake Manor.** This elegant 24-hour pancake parlor is a Brisbane institution. Housed inside the historic, heritage-listed St. Luke's Cathedral, guests can take a seat in one of the Manor's converted church pew booths and chow down on a tempting menu of snacks, salads, steaks, and sweets beneath the building's elegant redbrick arches. For breakfast, try the simple eggs Benedict or the hearty Aussie Sunrise, while dinner patrons will find a range of savory crepes and pancake dishes to please the palette. But it's the desserts that Pancake Manor is really famous for: grilled bananas drizzled in creamy butterscotch sauce, set upon a fluffy short stack of pancakes with rich vanilla ice cream; or, for chocolate lovers, the Blackforest Cherry or Jaffa Orange will surely hit the note. The a bar downstairs has an all-day drinks menu of local and imported beers and wines; with its swift, attentive service, this is the place to venture when jet lag kicks in. ⊠ *18 Charlotte St.* ☎ *07/3221–6433* ⊕ *www.pancakemanor.com.au* ✛ *C2.*

$$$
AUSTRALIAN

✕ **Seasalt at Armstrongs.** Well-known local chef Russell Armstrong works seafood magic at this popular 45-seat restaurant. Choices include "freelance fish"—the day's freshest catch, generally pan-seared and served to suit the chef's mood. You can also enjoy the Queensland scallops with lemon and chili linguini or grilled eye fillet, sourced locally. ⊠ *73 Wickham Terr., City Center* ☎ *07/3832–4566* ⊙ *Closed Sun. except breakfast. No lunch weekends* ✛ *B2.*

$$
AUSTRALIAN

✕ **Tukka Restaurant.** Earth-tone walls lined with Aboriginal artworks are a fitting backdrop for chef-owner Bryant Wells's native-inspired Modern Australian cuisine, featuring a range of lean Australian meats (seared wallaby, kangaroo, emu, croc tail, and possum) and seasonal produce, deliciously fused with native Australian herbs and spices. One excellent option is the entrée platter of cured meats and flavorful indigenous berries and flowers, all served on a rustic wooden campher platter. The wine list showcases top vintages from boutique wineries around Australia. You can also buy Tukka's own line of spices, cured meats, glazed fruits and sorbets, or ask for a "taste and smell" tour of the restaurant's on-site back garden. ⊠ *145 Boundary St., West End* ☎ *07/3846–6333* ⊕ *www.tukkarestaurant.com.au* ⊙ *No dinner Sun.* ✛ *A3.*

7

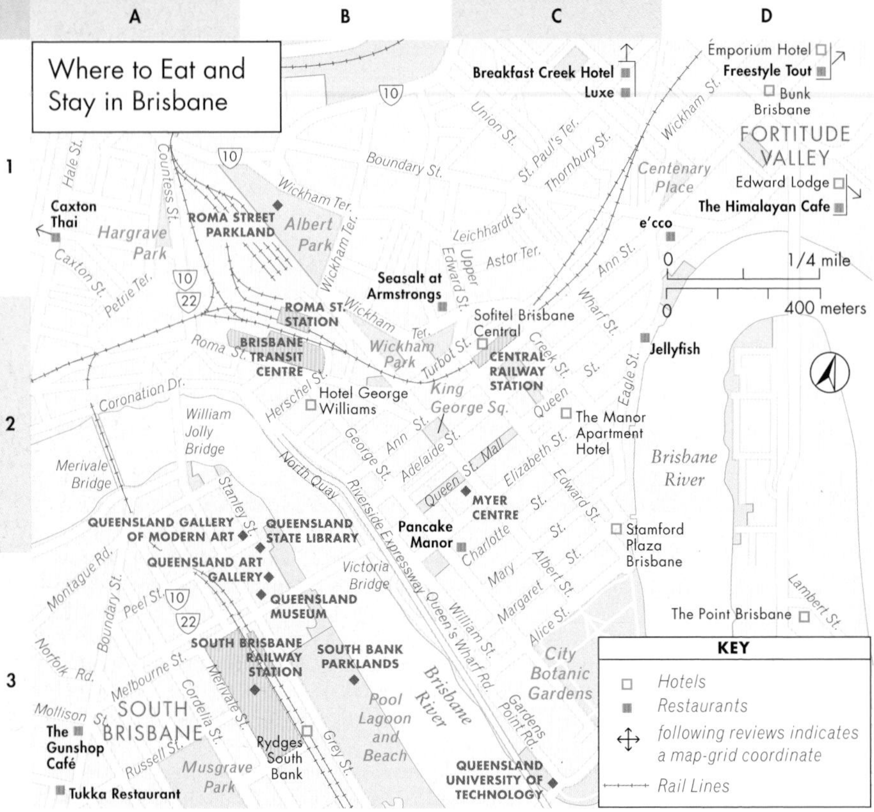

Where to Eat and Stay in Brisbane

Map labels (grid A–D, rows 1–3):

Breakfast Creek Hotel ■, Luxe ■, Emporium Hotel □, Freestyle Tout ■, Bunk Brisbane □, FORTITUDE VALLEY, Centenary Place, Edward Lodge □, The Himalayan Cafe ■, Caxton Thai ■, Hargrave Park, ROMA STREET PARKLAND, Albert Park, Boundary St., Wickham Ter., Union St., St. Paul's Ter., Thornbury St., Wickham St., Leichhardt St., Astor Ter., Upper Edward St., Ann St., e'cco ■, Seasalt at Armstrongs ■, Sofitel Brisbane Central ■, ROMA ST. STATION, BRISBANE TRANSIT CENTRE, Wickham Park, CENTRAL RAILWAY STATION, Jellyfish ■, Hotel George Williams □, King George Sq., The Manor Apartment Hotel □, Brisbane River, William Jolly Bridge, Merivale Bridge, Coronation Dr., Herschel St., George St., Ann St., Adelaide St., Queen St. Mall, Elizabeth St., Edward St., North Quay, Riverside Expressway, MYER CENTRE ◆, Pancake Manor ◆, Charlotte St., Mary St., Albert St., Stamford Plaza Brisbane □, QUEENSLAND GALLERY OF MODERN ART ◆, QUEENSLAND STATE LIBRARY ◆, QUEENSLAND ART GALLERY ◆, Victoria Bridge, Queen's Wharf Rd., William St., Margaret St., Alice St., The Point Brisbane □, Lambert St., QUEENSLAND MUSEUM ◆, Stanley St., SOUTH BRISBANE RAILWAY STATION, SOUTH BANK PARKLANDS ◆, City Botanic Gardens, Gardens Point Rd., SOUTH BRISBANE, The Gunshop Café ■, Rydges South Bank, Pool Lagoon and Beach, Grey St., Musgrave Park, Tukka Restaurant ■, QUEENSLAND UNIVERSITY OF TECHNOLOGY ◆, Mollison St., Norfolk Rd., Peel St., Boundary St., Montague Rd., Melbourne St., Merivale St., Cordelia St., Russell St.

Scale: 0 — 1/4 mile; 0 — 400 meters

KEY
□ Hotels
■ Restaurants
⊕ following reviews indicates a map-grid coordinate
⸺ Rail Lines

WHERE TO STAY

Twenty years ago Brisbane's accommodation options consisted of a few big hotels and some welcoming but nondescript motels and B&Bs. These days the inner-city area bristles with luxury hotels and smart serviced-apartment complexes. There are also a few excellent boutique hotels, some cut-above B&Bs, and modern backpacker hotels giving pricier digs a run for their money. Many have good-value packages and seasonal and last-minute specials: go online for the best deals.

Use the coordinate (⊕ B2) at the end of each listing to locate a site on the corresponding map.

For expanded hotel reviews, visit Fodors.com.

¢ ★ **Bunk Brisbane.** This award-winning backpacker joint is close to the cafés, bars, and attractions of Fortitude Valley. **Pros:** tight security; printing, CD-burning, iTunes and Skype services; cheap food on-site; free shuttle from Brisbane Transit Centre at Roma St. from 8 am to 7 pm daily. **Cons:** can be crowded. ⊠ Ann and Gipps Sts., Fortitude Valley ☎ 07/3257–3644, 1800/682865 ⊕ www.bunkbrisbane.com.au ⟁ In-room: kitchen, Internet. In-hotel: restaurant, bar, pool, laundry facilities, business center, parking, some age restrictions ⊕ D1.

$ ⊞ **Edward Lodge.** This affordable inner-suburban sanctuary is set in
★   Asian-style tropical gardens, close to cafés, New Farm Park, and the
CityCat ferry. **Pros:** free broadband Internet access; guest kitchen and
laundry; vibrant area; free continental breakfast. **Cons:** 20 minutes from
the city; no room service. ⊠ *75 Sydney St., New Farm* ☎ *07/3358–2680*
⊕ *www.edwardlodge.com.au* ➫ *9 rooms, 1 suite* ♻ *In-room: kitchen,
Wi-Fi. In-hotel: laundry facilities* ⑩ *Breakfast* ✢ *D1.*

$$ ⊞ **Emporium Hotel.** Billing itself as a luxury boutique hotel, this modern
Fodor's Choice establishment is furnished with distinctive pieces sourced from around
★   the world. **Pros:** superb decor; terrific facilities; exceptional service; inter-
connecting rooms available. **Cons:** downstairs restaurant not at the same
level of excellence; outside the city center. ⊠ *1000 Ann St., Fortitude
Valley* ☎ *07/3253–6999, 1300/883–611* ⊕ *www.emporiumhotel.com.
au* ➫ *102 suites* ♻ *In-room: kitchen, Wi-Fi. In-hotel: bar, pool, gym,
laundry facilities, business center, parking* ⑩ *No meals* ✢ *D1.*

$ ⊞ **Hotel George Williams.** This modern hotel is right in the heart of the
city, 150 yards from Brisbane Transit Center. **Pros:** close to Brisbane
Transit Centre; fast Internet; ecofriendly. **Cons:** small rooms; fee to use
adjoining YMCA gym; access to carpark difficult. ⊠ *317–325 George
St., City Center* ☎ *07/3308–0700, 1800/064858* ⊕ *www.hgw.com.au*
➫ *106 rooms* ♻ *In-room: Internet. In-hotel: restaurant, bar, laundry
facilities, parking* ⑩ *Breakfast* ✢ *B2.*

$ ⊞ **The Manor Apartment Hotel.** Good old-fashioned service and charm are
the hallmarks of Brisbane's heritage-listed Manor Apartment Hotel.
⊠ *289 Queen St.* ☎ *07/3319–4700* ⊕ *www.manorapartments.com.au*
➫ *45 studios, suites, and apartments* ♻ *In-room: a/c, kitchen, Internet*
⑩ *Breakfast* ✢ *C2.*

$ ⊞ **The Point Brisbane.** Across the river from the central business district,
★   this modern hotel on picturesque Kangaroo Point has great city sky-
line and river views from each balcony. **Pros:** terrific on-site facilities;
free secure parking; wheelchair- and women-friendly suites. **Cons:** a
commute from the city; fee (A$24.95 per day) for in-room Internet
access. ⊠ *21 Lambert St., Kangaroo Point* ☎ *07/3240–0888, 1800/088–
388* ⊕ *www.thepointbrisbane.com.au* ➫ *106 rooms* ♻ *In-room: safe,
kitchen, Internet, Wi-Fi. In-hotel: restaurant, bar, pool, tennis court,
gym, business center, parking* ✢ *D3.*

$$$ ⊞ **Rydges South Bank.** Sandwiched between South Bank Parklands and
★   the Brisbane Convention and Exhibition Centre, within walking dis-
tance of numerous attractions, this hotel is an excellent choice if location's your focus. **Pros:** friendly, helpful staff; good buffet breakfast.
Cons: steep fees for Internet and parking. ⊠ *9 Glenelg St., at Grey St.,
South Brisbane* ☎ *07/3364–0800* ⊕ *www.rydges.com/southbank* ➫ *240
rooms, 64 suites* ♻ *In-room: kitchen, Internet. In-hotel: restaurant, bar,
gym, spa, laundry facilities, business center, parking* ✢ *B3.*

$$ ⊞ **Sofitel Brisbane Central.** Despite its position above the city's main rail
★   station, this hotel is a quiet and pleasant place to stay. **Pros:** prompt,
pleasant service; great bathroom amenities; legendary high teas (A$38).
Cons: short-staffed front desk, especially in the morning. ⊠ *249 Tur-
bot St., City Center* ☎ *07/3835–4444* ⊕ *www.sofitelbrisbane.com.au*

7

⇗ *409 rooms, 20 suites* ⟡ *In-room: safe, kitchen, Internet. In-hotel: restaurant, bar, pool, gym, spa, business center, parking* ⊕ *C2.*

$$ ⌂ **Stamford Plaza Brisbane.** This refined riverfront hotel next to the City Botanic Gardens offers a retreat from the city. **Pros:** upmarket dining options; friendly service; bathroom LCD TVs. **Cons:** plumbing noise from adjacent rooms; expensive parking; pricey breakfasts with slow service. ✉ *Edward and Margaret Sts., City Center* ☎ *07/3221–1999, 1800/773–700* ⊕ *www.stamford.com.au/spb* ⇗ *232 rooms, 20 suites* ⟡ *In-room: safe, kitchen, Wi-Fi. In-hotel: restaurant, bar, pool, gym, spa, business center, parking* ⊕ *C3.*

NIGHTLIFE AND THE ARTS

The Saturday edition of *the Courier–Mail* newspaper lists live gigs and concerts, ballet, opera, theater, jazz, and other events in its ETC section. Friday's paper includes a free *Ultimate Weekend Guide,* Brisbane's most comprehensive entertainment guide. Or go to ⊕ *www.news.com.au/couriermail.*

Brisbane Powerhouse. The Heritage-listed Brisbane Powerhouse, built in a former power plant, hosts often-free live performances in flexible 200- and 400-seat theaters and art exhibits. Cafés, restaurants, bikeways, boardwalks, and picnic areas complement the funky art space. A 2007 renovation added a new café-bar, a roof terrace, and enlarged theater spaces. ✉ *119 Lamington St., New Farm* ☎ *07/3358–8600 box office, 07/3358–8622 reception* ⊕ *www.brisbanepowerhouse.org.*

Cloudland. Designed as an "urban oasis" with fanciful decor, a retractable glass roof, and street-front waterfall flowing over its contemporary architectural facade, Cloudland nightclub woos well-heeled locals and tourists alike with an extensive drinks menu, cut-above food, and an exciting, expensive ambience. ✉ *621 Ann St., Fortitude Valley* ☎ *07/3872–6600* ⊕ *www.cloudland.tv.*

Treasury Casino Brisbane. Treasury Casino Brisbane—with a "neat and tidy" dress code geared to securing an upscale clientele—is a European-style casino. Until recently, it was called Conrad Treasury Casino. Open 24 hours, the facility has more than 80 gaming tables with 60 games and more than 1,300 machines, as well as six restaurants and six bars. ✉ *Queen Street Mall at George St., City Center* ☎ *07/3306–8888.*

Cru Bar + Cellar. Cru Bar + Cellar is sleek and sophisticated, with leather ottomans, a long onyx bar, a French chandelier circa 1800, and a fine-wine-loving clientele. Cru's huge cellar houses hundreds of top Australian vintages, to drink on-site or later. Cheese tasting plates all day. ✉ *James St. Market, 22 James St., Fortitude Valley* ☎ *07/3252–2400* ⊕ *www.crubar.com.*

SHOPPING

DEPARTMENT
STORES

David Jones. The renowned David Jones department store, downtown in the Queen Street Mall, is open daily until 6 pm (7 pm Thurs., 9 pm Fri.). ✉ *Queens Plaza, 149 Adelaide St., City Center* ☎ *07/3243–9000* ⊕ *www.davidjones.com.au.*

Myer. Myer, in Queen Street Mall, is open daily until 5.30 pm (9 pm Fri.). ⊠ *Myer Centre, 91 Queen St., City Center* ☎ *07/3232–0121* ⊕ *www.myer.com.au.*

MALLS AND ARCADES

Queen Street Mall. Fun and lively Queen Street Mall, considered the best downtown shopping area, attracts numerous buskers and around 26 million visitors a year. Nearly a third of a mile long, the mall incorporates five major shopping centers, including the Myer Centre, Wintergarden, and Queens-Plaza, as well as two large department stores, Myer and David Jones, and four arcades: historic Tattersall's Arcade and MacArthur Central, Heritage-listed Brisbane Arcade, and Broadway on the Mall, all housing designer boutiques and specialty stores. ⊠ *City Center* ☎ *07/3229–5918* ⊕ *www.queenstreetmall.com.*

For more information on shopping in Brisbane, visit ⊕ *www.ourbrisbane. com/shopping.*

MARKETS

Brisbane Powerhouse. The Brisbane Powerhouse hosts a farmers' market (all produce) from 6 am to noon on the second and fourth Saturday of the month. Afterward, stroll through nearby New Farm Park. ⊠ *119 Lamington St., New Farm* ☎ *07/3358–8600* ⊕ *www.brisbanepowerhouse.org.*

Riverside Markets. At the Riverside Markets, an upscale arts-and-crafts bazaar, you can buy everything from pressed flowers to hand-painted didgeridoos and homemade treats. It's open Sunday 7–3. ⊠ *Riverside Centre, 123 Eagle St., City Center* ☎ *07/3780–2807* ⊕ *www.riversidemarkets.com.au.*

SPECIALTY STORES

AUSTRALIAN PRODUCTS

Woolloongabba Antique Centre. For something different, spend a morning at the vibrant Woolloongabba Antique Centre: a retro-theme warehouse of 60-plus different stalls, an on-site vintage café, and enough antiques and treats to get everyone's nostalgic juices flowing. From fine china, collectibles, and the kitschiest of curiosities, to clothing, records, prints, paintings, home wares, games, and a vast collection of Australiana, it's the perfect place to pick up something truly unique. It's open every day, 9 am–5 pm. ⊠ *22 Wellington Rd., Woolloongabba* ☎ *07/3392–1114* ⊕ *www.woolloongabbaantiquecentre.com.*

Woolloongabba Art Gallery. The Woolloongabba Art Gallery represents indigenous and contemporary artists. Works cost between A$50 and A$10,000, and come with certificates of authenticity. It's open Wednesday–Saturday 11 am–6 pm. ⊠ *613 Stanley St., Woolloongabba* ☎ *07/3891–5551* ⊕ *www.wag.com.au.*

EARTH'S FASTEST MOVING ISLAND

Moreton Island lies just 35 km (20 mi) offshore. This 38-km-long (23-mi-long) mass is shifting at an estimated 3¼ feet a year toward the Queensland coast. Attractions include tobogganing down sand dunes, bird-watching, water sports, and cetacean- and dugong-watching.

Tangalooma Island Resort. You can hand-feed wild dolphins after dusk at Tangalooma Island Resort. ☎ *07/3637–2118, 1300/652–250* ⊕ *www.tangalooma.com.*

Camping within Moreton Island National Park is possible (A$5.15 per person permit; information available at ⊕ www.qld.gov.au/camping).

7

State library, Queensland Cultural Centre.

WINERY TOURS FROM BRISBANE: SOUTHERN DOWNS

From Brisbane, Granite Belt is 225 km (140 mi) west, Mount Tamborine is 62 km (39 mi) southwest, and Scenic Rim wineries are around 135 km (85 mi) southwest.

If the Brisbane cityscape has given you a thirst for pastoral rolling hills—and fabulous wine—you're in luck, because some of Queensland's best viticultural regions lie within a two-hour drive of the city.

Drive two hours west on the Cunningham Highway and you'll reach the Southern Downs, where spring brings the scent of peach and apple blossoms; fall finds the region's 50-plus vineyards, concentrated around Stanthorpe, ripe for harvest; and winter is ideal for wine-country excursions. This area, extending from Cunninghams Gap in the east to Goondiwindi in the west, Allora in the north to Wallangarra in the south, is known as the Granite Belt.

The local Italian community pioneered viticulture here, planting the first Shiraz grapes in 1965. Today the Granite Belt is the state's largest wine region, with nearly 2,000 acres under vines and more than 50 cellar doors, most attached to family-run and boutique wineries. Thanks to its altitude (2,500–4,000 feet above sea level) and decomposed-granite soils, the region enjoys unique growing and ripening conditions, enabling the production of outstanding, full-bodied reds and extra-crisp whites.

Just over an hour's drive southwest of Brisbane, inland from the Gold Coast, you'll find the world's largest caldera and one of the state's most exciting emerging wine regions: the Scenic Rim. The region's rich volcanic soils, first planted with vines in the late 19th century, now produce fine red and white varieties. On the region's easterly edge, you'll find a dozen wineries and a distillery within a compact area around Mount Tamborine.

GETTING HERE AND AROUND

Driving yourself is an option but may not be the best idea if you plan to skip the spit bucket on your tasting stops. However, for the self-guiders out there, the Granite Belt and Scenic Rim tourism boards provide downloadable maps. Find Granite Belt winery and walking trails at ⊕ *www.granitebeltwinecountry.com.au*, and Scenic Rim winery and trail maps at ⊕ *www.ipswichtourism.com.au*.

Arguably, the safest way to sample the offerings of the region's wineries is via guided tour. More than half a dozen companies run tours of wineries in the Scenic Rim and Mount Tamborine areas, but most require groups of at least six people. Family-run Cork 'n Fork Winery Tours is an exception, running daily and overnight viticultural tours for couples and small groups to Mount Tamborine and the Scenic Rim. Their popular full-day tour (A$140 per person) includes hotel pickups from the Gold Coast or Brisbane, lunch, and five winery visits with guided tastings.

Local operators Granite Highlands Maxi Tours runs half-day, full-day, weekend, and customized tours of Granite Belt wineries.

ESSENTIALS

Guided Tours Cork 'n Fork Winery Tours ☎ 07/5543–6584 ⊕ www.corknfork. com.au. **Granite Highlands Maxi Tours** ✉ 19 Amosfield Rd., Stanthorpe ☎ 07/4681–3969 ⊕ www.maxitours.com.au.

WINERIES

Felsberg Winery. In the tiny town of Glen Aplin, 235 km (146 mi) southwest of Brisbane, is Felsberg Winery. Known for red and white wines (including an award-winning Merlot) made from hand-picked grapes grown at 850 meters, and honey mead, this Granite Belt winery has a tasting room inside a German-inspired château, with hilltop views over the Severn River valley and Granite Belt area. Guided tours are available on request. ✉ 116 Townsends Rd., Glen Aplin ☎ 07/4683–4332 💳 Free ⊙ Daily 9:30–4:30.

Ballandean Estate Wines. Just south of Glen Aplin is the town of Ballandean, home to award-winning Ballandean Estate Wines, the oldest family-owned and -operated vineyard and winery in Queensland. The first grapes were grown on the Granite Belt site in 1931, and the tasting room is the original brick shed built in 1950. The Barrel Room Café behind it—with massive, 125-year-old wooden barrels lining one wall—serves light lunches and coffee. There are 45-minute tours of the facility daily at 11, 1, and 3. ✉ 354 Sundown Rd., Ballandean ☎ 07/4684–1226 ⊕ www.ballandeanestate.com 💳 Free ⊙ Daily 9–5.

Normanby Wines. Normanby Wines is a friendly, family-run winery-vineyard established a decade ago. All its wines—including many medal winners—are made from grapes grown on the property. There are 14 from which to choose, including Verdelho, Shiraz, Durif, Chaumbourcin, Grenache, Veraz, Merlot, Viognier, and traditional fortified varieties. Taste and buy them at the cellar door, then wander through the vineyard and native gardens or enjoy a barbecue under the trees. Guided vineyard tours are available for a small extra charge, if staff are available. ⊠ *178 Dunns Ave., Harrisville* ☏ *07/5467–1214* ⊕ *www.normanbywines.com. au* ⊠ *A$3 (tasting fee)* ☉ *Daily 10–5; 10–7 (Dec.–Feb.).*

Sirromet Wines at Mount Cotton. Queensland's largest winery sits midway between Brisbane and the Gold Coast. Sirromet's much-lauded wines—distinctive reds, crisp whites, and some terrific blended varieties—can be sampled at their impressive cellar door, along with tasting plates for two. Award-winning on-site restaurant Lurleens, open for breakfast, lunch, morning and afternoon teas, and dinner (Thursday through Saturday), has an alfresco dining area with stupendous views to Moreton Bay. Live jazz livens things up on weekend afternoons. ⊠ *850–938 Mount Cotton Rd., Mount Cotton* ☏ *07/3206–2999* ⊕ *www.sirromet. com* ⊠ *Tastings (up to 8 wines) A$5; guided tours from A$20* ☉ *Cellar door daily 10–4.*

EXPLORING

⟳ **Girraween National Park.** One of the most popular parks in southeast Queensland, Girraween National Park sits at the end of the New England Tableland, a stepped plateau area with elevations ranging from 1,968 to 4,921 feet. The 17 km (11 mi) of walking tracks, most starting near the information center and picnic area, wind past granite outcrops, giant boulders, eucalyptus forests, and wildflowers in spring. Along the way you might encounter kangaroos, echidnas, brush-tailed possums, and turquoise parrots. To camp, you'll need a permit from the Queensland Parks and Wildlife Service. ⊠ *Ballandean* ⊹ *11 km (7 mi) north of Wallangarra or 26 km (16 mi) south of Stanthorpe, off the New England Hwy.* ☏ *1300/130–372 park info, 13–1304 permits* ⊕ *www.derm.qld.gov.au.*

OUTDOOR ACTIVITIES

GUIDED GOURMET BUSHWALKING

Hidden Peaks Walks. Hidden Peaks Walks operates small-group three- and four-day guided hikes through the World Heritage-listed national parks and private nature reserves of the Scenic Rim, camping for one or two nights and staying one night at Spicers Peak Lodge (complete with 7-course degustation dinner). This is a one-of-a-kind, upmarket, all-inclusive outdoor adventure, geared for eco-friendly appreciation of the Australian bush. A new, three-day "glamping" option has just been added for those more interested in a certain level of creature comforts throughout the journey. All trips include private coach to and from Brisbane. ⊠ *10613 Cunningham Hwy., Maryvale* ☏ *1300/773425* ⊕ *www. hiddenpeaks.com.au* ⊠ *A$1,540 per person (3 days), A$2,050 (4 days), $1,290 (3 days glamping)* ☉ *Depart Mon. and Sat., Mar.–Nov.*

WHERE TO STAY

For expanded hotel reviews, visit Fodors.com.

$$$$
ALL-INCLUSIVE
Spicers Peak Lodge. If you're looking for an exclusive, all-inclusive mountain retreat with an entire mountaintop to itself and the views to match, look no further. **Pros:** meals included in room rates; world-class restaurant with terrific wine list; Cordon Bleu breakfasts; thoughtful, impeccable service. **Cons:** pricey, albeit worth it; must book months ahead. ⊠ *Wilkinsons Rd., Maryvale* ☎ *1300/198–386, 07/4666–1083* ⊕ *www.spicersgroup.com.au* ⤢ *10 suites, 2 lodges* ⚬ *In-room: kitchen. In-hotel: restaurant, bar, pool, tennis court* ⦿ *All-inclusive.*

$$
Fodor'sChoice
★
Vineyard Cottages and Café. Built around a turn-of-the-20th-century church that's now the Vineyard Café, this property has four cottages and a row of two-story terrace houses set amid two acres of gardens, two blocks from Ballandean village. **Pros:** good food and wine; warm ambience; comfortable. **Cons:** far from city attractions. ⊠ *New England Hwy. near Bents Rd., Ballandean* ☎ *07/4684–1270* ⊕ *www. vineyardcottages.com.au* ⤢ *4 cottages, 3 terraces* ⚬ *In-room: no a/c, kitchen. In-hotel: restaurant, bar.*

THE GOLD COAST

Three hundred days of sunshine a year and an average temperature of 24°C (75°F) ensure the popularity of the Gold Coast, the most developed tourist destination and one of the fastest-growing regions in Australia, with plenty of amusement complexes and resorts. Easter weekend and December through the last week of January and Australian school holidays are peak seasons. Around 80 km (50 mi)—an hour's drive—south of Brisbane, the Gold Coast stretches some 70 km (43 mi) from Labrador in the north to Coolangatta-Tweed Heads in the south, and has now sprawled as far inland as Nerang. It has around three dozen patrolled beaches and 446 km (277 mi) of canals and tidal rivers, nine times the length of the canals of Venice.

GETTING HERE AND AROUND

Gold Coast Airport, also known as Coolangatta Airport, is the region's main transit point.

Access Hope Island via bridges from the west (Oxenford and Coomera) or from the eastern, coastal side (via Paradise Point, Hollywell, and Runaway Bay). Route 4, the Oxenford–Southport Road, begins in Oxenford at the Pacific Motorway's (M1's) Exit 57 and travels through Hope Island on its way to Hope Harbour, on the coast.

Driving distances and times from the Gold Coast via the Pacific Highway are 859 km (533 mi) and 12–13 hours to Sydney, 65 km (40 mi) and less than an hour to Brisbane's outskirts, and 1,815 km (1,125 mi) and 22 hours to Cairns.

The Gold Coast begins 65 km (40 mi) south of Brisbane. The Pacific Motorway, or M1, bypasses Gold Coast towns, but well-marked exits guide you to your destination. If you're coming from Brisbane International Airport by car, take the toll road over Gateway Bridge to avoid traversing Brisbane, then follow the signs to the Gold Coast.

Queensland Rail service connects Brisbane to Coomera, Helensvale, Nerang, Robina, and Varsity Lakes stations on the Gold Coast from 5:30 am until midnight. Alight at Coomera or Helensvale for the theme parks and northern suburbs; Nerang for Surfer's Paradise; and Robina or Varsity Lakes for Main Beach and all suburbs south of it. From rail stations, cabs and shuttle buses ferry visitors to nearby beaches, tourist centers, theme parks, and the airport. From any of these stations, it's a short (A$20–A$30) cab ride to the nearest Gold Coast town.

Long-distance buses traveling between Sydney and Brisbane stop at Coolangatta and Surfers Paradise. Surfside Buslines' Gold Coast Tourist Shuttle runs around the clock between Gold Coast attractions, theme parks, and the airport, along the strip between Tweed Heads, and Southport. Services run at five-minute intervals during the day and at least half-hourly after dark. Buy single tickets or a 3-, 5-, 7-, or 10-day Gold Pass (A$54–A$118) or Freedom Pass (A$70–A$135), which give you unlimited shuttle travel and theme park transfers; the Freedom Pass also includes a return Gold Coast airport transfer.

Approximate taxi fare from Gold Coast Airport to Currumbin is A$30; to Burleigh Heads, A$38; to Broadbeach, A$55; to Surfers Paradise, A$60; to Main Beach, A$65; and to the northern suburbs, more than A$95. Shuttle buses can be cheaper than cabs at A$5–A$35, depending on your destination: before boarding, confirm that the bus stops near your accommodation.

At Gold Coast Airport the Transport and Information Desk just outside International Arrivals sells tickets for Surfside Buslines, the Gold Coast Shuttle Bus, and Con-x-ion coaches. They'll also direct you to the free Airport Link shuttle that takes you to the Gold Coast Highway, where public transport is readily available. You can also buy tickets for the Gold Coast Shuttle Bus and flexible Go Cards (allowing multiple trips on council buses, trains, and ferries) available at newsagencies, 7-11 stores, and train stations. You can top up your Go Card as needed online.

Rental cars are a cost-effective option if you plan to tour the area. Most major car-rental agencies have offices in Brisbane, Surfers Paradise, and at Gold Coast Airport. Companies operating on the Gold Coast include Avis, Budget, and Thrifty. Four-wheel-drive vehicles are available. It's strongly recommended that you prebook.

It's essential to book ahead for private coach or limo transfers; both can be cost-effective options, especially if you're traveling in a group.

Zane's Water Taxi runs up to six campers plus gear from Runaway Bay Marina to Currigee (A$50, one-way) and Tipplers (A$90, one-way); bookings are essential.

From the Gold Coast it's 30 minutes' flying time to Brisbane, 2 hours 10 minutes to Melbourne, and 1 hour 25 minutes to Sydney. Qantas, Virgin Australia, Jetstar, and Tiger Airways operate domestic flights from the Gold Coast to Australian capital cities and some regional centers.

ESSENTIALS

Airport **Gold Coast Airport** (*Coolangatta Airport*). ✉ *1 Eastern Ave., Bilinga* ☎ *07/5589–1100.*

Car Rental **Avis** ✉ *Ferny and Cypress Ave., Surfers Paradise* ☎ *07/5539–9388, 13–6333 reservations* ⊕ *www.avis.com.au.* **Budget** ✉ *Palm and Ferny Ave., Surfers Paradise* ☎ *07/5538–1344, 1300/362–848 international reservations* ⊕ *www. budget.com.au.* **Thrifty** ✉ *Enderly Ave. and Surfers Paradise Blvd., Surfers Paradise* ☎ *07/5570–9999, 1300/139–009 reservations* ⊕ *www.rentthrifty.com.*

Ferry **Zane's Water Taxi** ✉ *Runaway Bay Marina, 247 Bayview St., Runaway Bay* ☎ *0404/905970* ⊕ *www.zaneswatertaxis.com.au.*

Limousine **Hughes Chauffeured Limousines** ☎ *1300/306–644* ⊕ *www. hugheslimousines.com.au.*

Public Bus and Train **Con-x-ion** ☎ *07/5556–9888* ⊕ *www.con-x-ion.com.* **Gold Coast Tourist Shuttle** ☎ *07/5574–5111, 1300/655655* ⊕ *gcshuttle.com. au.* **Greyhound Australia** ✉ *Surfers Paradise Transit Centre, 10 Beach Rd., Surfers Paradise* ☎ *1300/473–946, 07/5531–6677* ⊕ *www.greyhound.com.au.* **Queensland Rail** ☎ *13–1617* ⊕ *www.qr.com.au.* **Surfside Buslines** ✉ *1–10 Mercantile Ct., Ernest* ☎ *07/5539–9388, 13–1230 translink* ⊕ *www.surfside.com. au.* **Translink** ☎ *13–1230* ⊕ *www.translink.com.au.*

Taxi **Gold Coast Cabs** ☎ *13–1008* ⊕ *www.gccabs.com.au.*

Visitor Information **Gold Coast Tourism Information & Booking Centres** ✉ *2 Cavill Ave., Surfers Paradise* ☎ *1300/309–400, 07/5569–3830 international* ⊕ *www.verygc.com.au* ✉ *Shop 22, Showcase on the Beach, Griffith Ave., Coolangatta* ☎ *07/5569–3380.*

COOMERA AND OXENFORD

48 km–51 km (30 mi–32 mi) south of Brisbane.

The biggest draws of these two northern Gold Coast suburbs are their family-oriented theme parks—Dreamworld, Warner Bros. Movie World, Wet 'n' Wild Water World, Paradise Country, the Australian Outback Spectacular, and WhiteWater World. The sprawling complexes have many attractions: each takes about a day for a leisurely visit.

EXPLORING

☾ **Australian Outback Spectacular.** The Australian Outback Spectacular, one of six Warner Village theme parks in the area, lets visitors experience "the heart and soul of the Australian Outback." The exciting evening show features state-of-the-art visual effects and performances from top local stunt riders, a pig race, and live country music. Guests get a three-course "Aussie barbecue" dinner and complimentary drinks during the 90-minute, A$23 million extravaganza, plus a souvenir stockman's hat. Doors open at 6:30 pm; showtime is at 7:30 pm. A special Sunday matinee show takes place at 12.30 pm once a month, more frequently in high season. Return transfers from Gold Coast hotels cost A$20; on-site parking is free. This park (and neighboring theme parks Paradise Country, Warner Bros. Movie World, and Wet 'n' Wild Water World) is a short taxi ride from Helensvale station; if driving, take Exit 60 at

The Gold Coast

Oxenford off the M1 Pacific Motorway. ⊠ *Pacific Motorway, Oxenford* ☎ *13-3386, 07/5519-6200 bookings* ⊕ *outbackspectacular.myfun. com.au* ✉ *A$99.99* ⊘ *Closed Mon.*

Dreamworld. At Coomera's Dreamworld the big draws are the "big six": high-tech thrill rides including the aptly-named Giant Drop, a 120-meter vertical plummet akin to skydiving; an outsized pendulum, the Claw; a high-speed gravity roller coaster, the Cyclone; the turbulent Wipeout and screamingly fast, scarily high Tower of Terror; and new Mick Doohan's Motocoaster, a fluid bike-race track with high-speed corners. You can also watch Bengal tigers play and swim with their handlers on Tiger Island, cuddle a koala in Koala Country, see more than 800 native animals at the Wildlife Sanctuary, cool off in an artificial lagoon, or cruise the park's waterways on a paddle wheeler. Bring swimwear, book ahead, and you can also try the Flowrider, an amalgam of surfing and skateboarding. A guided, two-hour Sunset Safari (A$25) promises close-up encounters with tigers and native wildlife from 4:45 pm in season. Beat the queues by buying an Earlybird Pass (A$10 extra) and hiring a Q4U virtual queueing device, preferably well ahead of your visit. The park is 45 minutes outside Brisbane and 25-30 minutes from Surfers Paradise along the M1 Pacific Motorway: take Exit 54 at Coomera. ⊠ *Dreamworld Pkwy., Coomera* ☎ *07/5588-1111,*

Fodor's Choice
★

1800/073300 ⊕ dreamworld.com.au ✉ A$74 single park entry; A$5 per half-hr Flowrider session with Dreamworld entry, or A$20 per hr NightRider pass; A$89 1-day World Pass (entry to Dreamworld and WhiteWater World); A$109 2-day World Pass (2 entries each to Dreamworld and WhiteWater World; 2nd visits within 14 days) ⊗ Daily 10–5; Flowrider 10–4:30; NightRider Thurs. and Fri. 5–10.

☺ **Paradise Country.** Billed as "an authentic Australian farm experience," the park appeals to families with half-day farm tours beginning at 9:30 am, 11:45 am, and 2:15 pm (bookings essential). You'll see displays of horsemanship, sheep shearing, boomerang throwing, and whip cracking. Kids will enjoy koala cuddling and kangaroo feeding. An optional barbecue lunch is accompanied by bush dancing and Aussie-theme live entertainment. The park is directly behind the Australian Outback Spectacular. Car parking spaces are limited. ⊠ *Pacific Motorway, Oxenford* ☎ *13–3386, 07/5519–6200* ⊕ *paradisecountry.myfun.com. au* ✉ *A$32.99 (tour and lunch)* ⊗ *Daily 9:30–4.*

☺ **Warner Bros. Movie World.** Warner Bros. Movie World, one of the few movie theme parks outside the United States, lets you share virtual space with an animated ogre in the eye-popping *Shrek* 4D Adventure, accelerate to 96 km (60 mi) an hour in two seconds on the awesome Superman Escape ride, or get airborne on the Batwing Spaceshot. You can also check out vehicles, props, and costumes from the Batman blockbuster *Dark Knight*; enter a custom-built "immersive" movie set to watch precision driving and action-film-style stunts in the new Hollywood Stunt Riders show; and rocket through the spine-tingling Scooby-Doo Spooky Coaster. Little kids will want to see the daily Main Street Star Parade, visit Bugs Bunny and friends in the WB! Fun Zone and Looney Tunes River Ride, and catch the live show What's Up Rock? (daily at 11:30 am). You can also indulge yourself at numerous outlets selling Warner Bros. souvenirs. With a large portion of its area now covered by a 4,000-square-meter (43,055-square-foot) roof, this park is a smart choice in inclement weather. It's adjacent to Australian Outback Spectacular. ⊠ *Pacific Motorway, Oxenford* ☎ *07/5573–8495* ⊕ *www.movieworld.com.au* ✉ *A$74.99; VIP pass $109.99 (unlimited entry into Seaworld, Movie World, and Wet'n'Wild for 12 months).* ⊗ *Daily 10–5.*

☺ **Wet 'n' Wild Water World.** Oxenford's Wet 'n' Wild Water World has magnificent waterslides, including the aptly named Mammoth Falls, Terror Canyon II, and Super-8 Aqua Racer; a giant whirlpool; a wave pool with 3-foot-high surf; tandem, entwined-tube and family-friendly water slides; and the new Surfrider that simulates the sensation of surfing the world's biggest waves, plummeting you 30 meters (over 100 feet) while you spin on a giant board. In the Extreme H20 zone, you can plunge down pitch-black spirals of water in the Black Hole, hang on through the churning Tornado, or survive the scary Kamikaze, a giant, U-shaped, friction-free slide with a near-vertical 11-meter (36-foot) drop. Enough aquatic thrills? Take it easy on Calypso Beach, a "tropical island" fringed with white-sand beaches and a lazy river; or chill out at a Dive'n'Movie. Keep kids entertained at Buccaneer Bay, a state-of-the-art aquatic playground with multiple levels. All pools and slides are heated May through September. The park is ½ km (¼ mi) down the Pacific Highway from Warner Bros. Movie World. ⊠ *Pacific Hwy., Oxenford* ☎ *07/5573–2255* ⊕ *www.wetnwild.com.au* 🖃 *A$54.99 single entry; A$29.99 afternoon only; VIP Pass $109.99 (unlimited entry to SeaWorld, Movie World, and Wet'n'Wild for 12 months).* ⊙ *Feb.–Apr. and Sept.–Dec., daily 10–5; May–Aug., daily 10–4.30; Jan., daily 10–9.*

🐾 **Fodor's Choice** ★ **WhiteWater World.** Directly adjacent to Dreamworld, and under the same management, is the Gold Coast's latest thrill-seeker's theme park, WhiteWater World. Here you'll find state-of-the-art water rides including the Blue Ringed Octopus (BRO), a convoluted eight-lane racer slide; The Rip, Australia's biggest corkscrew-cored whirlpool; the dual-bowl Little Rippers ride; an inner-tube "aquacoaster" ride known as the Temple of Huey; and the Green Room, a 65-foot-high "tube" simulating the inside of a monster wave; and the mat-free "doom drop" of The Wedgie. Small kids will enjoy Nickelodeon's Pipeline Plunge, an aquatic activity zone; deposit toddlers at shady, supervised Wiggle Bay, complete with mini waterslides and water cannons. Learn to surf before or after public park hours with Get Wet Surf School for only A$75, including photos, transfers, and a guranteed board stand up. Beat the queues with a pre-booked Q4U device and early-bird entry. The park is close to Coomera rail station; from there, catch a Surfside bus to the park. ⊠ *Dreamworld Pkwy., Coomera* ☎ *07/5588–1111, 1800/073300* ⊕ *www.dreamworld.com.au* 🖃 *A$46 park entry, A$109 2-day World Pass (2 entries each to Dreamworld and WhiteWater World; 2nd visits within 14 days)* ⊙ *Daily 10–4; surf lessons Mon., Wed., and Sat; open nights 6:30 pm–10 pm in Jan.*

HOPE ISLAND

This isn't your average island. Like several Gold Coast islands, it is actually a mile or two inland, and is circled by the Coomera River and a series of canals. The resort has a marina full of luxury launches and yachts, two golf courses, a swanky hotel, beautiful condos, and upscale restaurants, nightclubs, and shops. Stop by if you're passing through for a glimpse into jet-set culture, Queensland style.

Hope Island is accessed via bridges from the west or east. Route 4, also known as the Oxenford–Southport Road, passes straight through.

WHERE TO STAY

For expanded hotel reviews, visit Fodors.com.

$$$$ ★ 🛏 **Peppers Ruffles Lodge.** The immaculate, architect-designed luxury lodge is 5 km (3 mi) from Dreamworld, but its tranquil location makes it seem worlds away. **Pros:** architecturally superb; feels luxurious; terrific food. **Cons:** must book well ahead; off the beaten track; fees for using AmEx. ⊠ *423 Ruffles Rd., Willow Vale* ☎ *07/5546–7411* ⊕ *www.ruffleslodge.com.au* 🖃 *10 villas (including 3 tree houses and 1 suite)* ⚲ *In-room: safe, no TV, Wi-Fi. In-hotel: restaurant, bar, pool, spa, business center, parking, some age restrictions* ⦿ *Breakfast.*

Main beach in Byron Bay, Queensland's Gold Coast.

SOUTH STRADBROKE ISLAND

1 km (½ mi) east of the Gold Coast.

White-sand beaches, diverse flora and fauna, and a peaceful interior draw visitors to South Stradbroke Island, which is just 22 km (12 mi) long and 2 km (1 mi) wide. The island and its northern neighbor, North Stradbroke Island, were once connected, but in 1896 a fierce storm separated them at a narrow neck called Jumpinpin. Unlike its northern namesake, South "Straddie" is less populated, and does not have a public ferry service. It's a good spot for fishing, boating, and camping.

GETTING HERE AND AROUND

Zane's Water Taxi runs up to six campers plus gear from Runaway Bay Marina to Currigee (A$50, one-way) and Tipplers (A$80, one-way) campgrounds on the island; to book, phone ☎ *0404/905970.*

From Gold Coast Airport, Coolangatta, it's a 50-km (30-mi), 50-minute drive northeast on the Pacific Motorway, then the Oxenford–Southport Road (take Exit 57 at Oxenford) to Hope Harbour.

SOUTHPORT AND MAIN BEACH

16 km (10 mi) southeast of Oxenford.

South of Southport, look for the turnoff to the **Spit,** a natural peninsula that stretches 4 km (2½ mi) north, almost to the tip of South Stradbroke Island. Sea World Drive runs the full length of the Spit, from Mariner's Cove (a popular covered area with affordable restaurants and fast-food outlets) to a nature reserve. This narrow peninsula is bordered by the

Pacific Ocean to the east and the calm waters of the Broadwater (a long lagoon) to the west. Two of the Gold Coast's best hotels face each other across Sea World Drive and are connected to Marina Mirage, arguably the most elegant shopping precinct on the Gold Coast. Farther up the road is Sea World itself.

Sea World. Sea World, Australia's largest marine theme park, has daily shows that highlight the resident dolphins and sea lions, and water-skiing displays. You can also check out the park's polar bears in their state-of-the-art home, fairy penguin and endangered dugong exhibits, and various other marine creatures, including 100-plus eagle, manta, and sting rays at Ray Reef. Don't miss Shark Bay, the world's largest artificial lagoon system for sharks, an innovative dual enclosure with dangerous tiger sharks in one section and harmless reef sharks, rays, and fish in another. Patrons can dive in the latter, and get close-up views of the former through the massive windows that separate the lagoons. Rides include Jet Ski and corkscrew coasters, a monorail, waterslides, the Sky High Skyway cable car, and Sea World Eye, a 95-foot-high observation wheel offering bird's-eye views of the action. ⊠ *Seaworld Dr. (at oceanside end of this long street), The Spit, Main Beach* ☎ *13–3386, 07/5588–2205* ⊕ *www.seaworld.com.au* ✉ *A$74.99; VIP Pass A$109.99 (unlimited entry to SeaWorld, Movie World, and Wet'n'Wild for 12 months).* ☉ *Daily 10–5.*

OUTDOOR ACTIVITIES

SURFING   **Get Wet Surf School.** The Gold Coast, renowned for long, sandy beaches and reliable breaks, is a terrific place to surf. Of the patrolled beaches, Main Beach, Surfer's Paradise, Broadbeach, Mermaid, Miami, and Nobby are the most popular; Kirra Beach, in the south, is arguably the area's best surf beach. Though the challenging break at Kirra is perhaps best left to the pros, most Gold Coast beaches are suitable for grommets (beginners). There are plenty of local surf schools happy to teach you, and board and wet-suit hire outlets flank popular beaches. Local surfers and lifeguards are good sources of information about surf conditions and hazards.

Get Wet Surf School holds daily group lessons (up to 6 students per coach) at a sheltered, crowd-free beach off the Spit, just north of Surfer's Paradise; and lessons before and after park hours three times a week in the controlled environment of WhiteWater World's large wave pool, heated in winter. They also host private lessons and multi-day surf tours. ☎ *1800/438–938, 07/5532–9907 international* ⊕ *www.getwetsurf.com* ✉ *A$55 (beach); A$95 (private); A$75 (wave pool)* ☉ *Daily 10 am and 1 pm (beach); Mon., Wed., Fri. 8 am and 5 pm (wave pool).*

WHERE TO EAT AND STAY

For expanded hotel reviews, visit Fodors.com.

$$ ✕ **Omeros Bros Seafood Restaurant.** The Omeros brothers, who arrived
SEAFOOD   from Greece in 1953, have run seafood restaurants in Australia for more than 40 years. This one on the waterfront at the lovely Marina Mirage center offers dishes spanning the seafood spectrum—from bouillabaisse, barbecued prawns, mussels, and barramundi to classic surf-and-turf, lobster, mud crab, and Moreton Bay bugs. There are

SURFERS PARADISE

Before the Gold Coast existed as a tourism entity, there was Surfers Paradise, a 3-km (2-mi) stretch of beach with great surf, 5 km (3mi) south of Southport. Now overrun with high-rises, it's still a vibrant beachside town. Nightlife is the main draw; head to Orchid, Elkhorn, and Cavill avenues. Or, for stunning 360-degree views of the entire coast and hinterland, venture up to the SkyPoint observation deck located on the 77th and 78th floor of Surfers' famous Q1 Tower: the tallest building in the southern hemisphere.

Surfers Paradise Beachfront Markets. Twice weekly, crowds flock to haggle for handmade crafts and gifts at Surfers Paradise Beachfront Markets. ⊠ *The Esplanade between Hanlan St. and Elkhorn Ave.* ◻ *Free* ☉ *Wed. and Fri. 5:30 pm–10 pm.*

also meat, vegetarian, and pasta dishes. ⊠ *4 Marina Mirage, Seaworld Dr.* ☎ *07/5591–7222* ⊕ *www.omerosbros.com.*

$$ **✕ Saks.** Located alongside Broadwater, only a short boardwalk removed
AUSTRALIAN from Palazzo Versace, is this hip restaurant and bar with wood floors, floor-to-ceiling windows, and indoor and outdoor areas. Relax on faux-suede lounge seats and ottomans while nibbling tapas, or nab a waterside table. Savor a steak or seafood dish, share a platter or pizza, or go for broke with the Saks Sensation: Moreton Bay bugs, king prawns, scallops, and eye fillet. There's also a celiac-friendly gluten-free menu. Live music and DJs on Friday and Saturday nights and Sunday afternoons attract a crowd. ⊠ *Marina Mirage, 74 Seaworld Dr., Main Beach* ☎ *07/5591–2755* ⊕ *www.saksrestaurantandbar.com.*

$$$$ **⌂ Palazzo Versace.** Sink into one of the sofas, armchairs, or circular
Fodor'sChoice banquettes in the sensational, recently-refurbished lobby, and watch the
★ beautiful people walk by. **Pros:** fine dining, five-star service, free Internet. **Cons:** pricey. ⊠ *94 Seaworld Dr., adjoining Marina Mirage, Main Beach* ☎ *07/5509–8000* ⊕ *www.palazzoversace.com* ⇥ *151 rooms, 54 suites* ⌂ *In-room: safe, Internet. In-hotel: restaurant, bar, pool, gym, spa, business center, parking* †◻ *Breakfast.*

SHOPPING

★ **Marina Mirage Gold Coast.** Marina Mirage Gold Coast is perhaps the most beautiful shopping and dining complex on the Gold Coast. Among its 60-plus stores are high-end gift and homewares, jewelry and designer fashion boutiques, including Nautica, Louis Vuitton, Hermès, Christiansen Copenhagen, Max&Co, La Perla, MoMA Store, and Calvin Klein, along with famous Australian brands, fine waterfront restaurants, and marina facilities. On the first and third Saturday of each month, buy fresh gourmet produce between 7 and noon at the Marina Mirage Farmers' Markets. Surfside buses 750 and 715 stop at the door. ⊠ *74 Seaworld Dr., Main Beach* ☎ *07/5555–6400, 07/3103–2325 market* ⊕ *www.marinamirage.com.au.*

BROADBEACH

8 km (5 mi) south of Southport.

With clean beaches, great cafés, and trendy nightspots, Broadbeach is one of the most popular areas on the Gold Coast, especially with locals. It's also home to mega-shopping mall Pacific Fair, and is a good base for visiting the wildlife parks south of town.

EXPLORING

Ⓒ ★ **Currumbin Wildlife Sanctuary.** A Gold Coast institution and perhaps the most ecologically-minded wildlife facility in the region, Currumbin Wildlife Sanctuary is a 70-acre, not-for-profit National Trust Reserve. Established in 1947 as a lorikeet sanctuary, it now shelters many Australian species, including crocodiles, snakes, wombats, dingoes, Tasmanian devils, kangaroos, and endangered frogs. There are more than a dozen daily animal shows, informative talks, Aboriginal dance and didgeridoo sessions, 'roo feedings, and koala cuddling. Come at 8 am or 4 pm when the lorikeets are fed, or book a nifty Segway Safari guided tour of the park (A$10 for 40 min.). You can also take a treetops ropes course (A$20, weekends and holidays). The nightly guided Wildnight Adventure includes a "Wild Buffet" from 5:30, a tour of the sanctuary's nocturnal inhabitants from 7, and Aboriginal dancing by firelight afterward (reservations essential). Tickets are much cheaper if bought online in advance, especially in low season. There's a gourmet produce market in the carpark on Saturday mornings. Return transfers to and from the Gold Coast can be booked with **Surfside Bus Lines** (⊕ *www.surfsidebuslines.com*). ⊠ *28 Tomewin St., off Gold Coast Hwy., 14 km (8½ mi) south of Broadbeach, Currumbin* ☎ *07/5534–1266, 1300/886511* ⊕ *www.cws.org.au* ⌦ *general admission A$49; ropes course A$10; Wildnight Adventure $89* ⊙ *Daily 8–5, grounds close 5:30 for Wildnight Adventure.*

Ⓒ **David Fleay Wildlife Park.** Located in the town of Burleigh Heads and named for an Australian wildlife naturalist, the park features a boardwalk trail through pristine wetlands and rain forests. Koalas, kangaroos, dingoes, platypuses, and crocodiles, grouped together in separate zones according to their natural habitat, are just some of the creatures you might see. A state-of-the-art nocturnal house displays threatened species and the elusive platypus. Daily presentations are free. There's also a café and a gift shop. Family passes offer a significant admission discount. ⊠ *7 km (4½ mi) south of Broadbeach, Tallebudgera Creek Rd. near W. Burleigh Rd., Burleigh Heads* ☎ *07/5576–2411* ⊕ *www.derm.qld.gov.au* ⌦ *A$17.60* ⊙ *Daily 9–5.*

WHERE TO STAY

For expanded hotel reviews, visit Fodors.com.

$$ 🏨 **Jupiters Hotel & Casino.** This massive resort is always bustling. **Pros:** modern furnishings and facilities, great on-site entertainment options; close to shopping centers. **Cons:** no in-room Wi-Fi, fee for parking. ⊠ *Broadbeach Island, Casino Dr., off Gold Coast Hwy.* ☎ *07/5592–8100, 1800/074–344* ⊕ *www.jupitersgoldcoast.com.au* ⌦ *563 rooms,*

29 suites, 2 penthouses & *In-room: safe, Internet. In-hotel: restaurant, bar, pool, tennis court, gym, spa, business center, parking* ⦿ *Breakfast.*

$$ ▦ **The Wave Resort.** This award-winning high-rise apartment resort is
★ one of Broadbeach's newest and most luxurious. **Pros:** helpful staff; babysitting service; well soundproofed; clean and secure. **Cons:** minimum three-day (or, in peak periods, five-day) stay. ⊠ *89–91 Surf Parade, Broadbeach* ☏ *07/5555–9200* ⊕ *www.thewavesresort.com.au* ↵ *53 rooms* & *In-room: kitchen, Internet. In-hotel: pool, gym, beach, laundry facilities, parking* ⦿ *No meals.*

NIGHTLIFE

Jupiters Casino. Jupiters Casino provides flamboyant round-the-clock entertainment. There are 70-plus blackjack, baccarat, craps, sic bo, Texas Hold'em poker, and keno tables, and more than 1,300 'round-the-clock slot machines on one level. There's also a members' gaming club. Since the casino's A$53 million expansion over 2006–2008 there are even more dining, drinking, and entertainment options, including seven restaurants and eight bars. The 950-seat showroom hosts glitzy Las Vegas–style productions. ⊠ *Casino Dr., off Gold Coast Hwy., Broadbeach* ☏ *07/5592–8100* ⊕ *www.conrad.com.au/jupiters.*

Howl at the Moon. Howl at the Moon is fun if you like sing-alongs and know the words to hits from the '80s, '90s, and today. Every night two pianists with vocal skills belt out a medley of tunes (some requested by patrons) on baby grands to an appreciative crowd of thirty- and fortysomethings. Grab a Cosmopolitan and hit the dance floor (come weekends for the fun crowds). ⊠ *Level 1, Neicon Plaza, Victoria Ave.* ☏ *07/5538–9911* ⊕ *www.howlatthemoon.com.au.*

SHOPPING

Fodor's Choice **Pacific Fair.** Pacific Fair, a sprawling outdoor shopping center, is
★ Queensland's largest, featuring a Myer department store, major retailers, and around 300 specialty stores and services (including travel agencies, fashion outlets, and sports and outdoor gear stores). This place should satisfy even die-hard shoppers. There's even the requisite cinema complex. For a breather, head to the landscaped grounds with three small lakes, a children's park, and village green. It's open daily until 5 and until 9 on Thursdays. ⊠ *Hooker Blvd. at Gold Coast Hwy., opposite Jupiters Casino* ☏ *07/5581–5100* ⊕ *www.pacificfair.com.au.*

GOLD COAST HINTERLAND

Hinterland. No visit to the Gold Coast would be complete without an excursion to the region's verdant Hinterland. The natural grandeur of the area lies in dramatic contrast to the human-made excesses of the coastal strip. The Gold Coast Hinterland's superb national parks and nature reserves protect magnificent waterfalls, natural rock pools, mountain lookouts with expansive views of the surrounding terrain and coast, and an array of wildlife. Walking trails traverse rain forest dense with ancient trees. Among the parks lie boutique wineries and quaint villages where high-rise is anything over one story. The parks form part of a unique, ancient geological region known as the Scenic

Rim, a chain of mountains running parallel to the coast through southeast Queensland and northern New South Wales. Because it rises to 3,000 feet above sea level, some parts of the hinterland are 4°C–6°C (7°F–11°F) cooler than the coast.

GETTING HERE AND AROUND

The Hinterland's main areas—Tamborine Mountain, Lamington National Park, and Springbrook—can be reached from the Pacific Highway or via Beaudesert from Brisbane, and are a 30- to 40-minute drive inland from the Gold Coast. To reach Tamborine, around 80 km (50 mi) south of Brisbane and 36 km (24 mi) from Southport, take Exit 57 off the Pacific Motorway to the Oxenford–Tamborine Road; or take Exit 71 off the Pacific Motorway, the Nerang–Beaudesert Road, to Canungra. From Canungra, follow the signs to Tamborine, 4 km (2½ mi) along Tamborine Mountain Road. The Gold Coast Hinterland is ideal for touring by car: rent a vehicle, arm yourself with local maps, fill the tank, and take to the hills.

TOURS

From the Gold Coast, Mountain Coach Company buses pick passengers up from the major bus depots, most of the major hotels, and from Coolangatta Airport for O'Reilly's Rainforest Retreat in the Gold Coast Hinterland (A$69 round-trip day tour or individual transfer, departing at 8 am).

Australian Day Tours/JPT leaves the Brisbane Transit Centre daily at 8:30, or 8:45 am for Gold Coast passengers, and travels via Tamborine Mountain to the Hinterland. Day tours stop at O'Reilly's Rainforest Retreat, returning to the Gold Coast at 4:30, Brisbane at 6. The cost—A$93 round-trip—is for a full-day tour, but Retreat guests can use it for transfers. Two-day Hinterland tours, with accommodation, dinner, and breakfast at O'Reilly's included, are A$399.The company also runs nightly tours and guided night walks through local Hinterland caves which, when the sun is down, light up spectacularly with populations of glowworms. Departing from the Gold Coast at 5.30 pm, the tours run for four hours with dinner included in the $A147 ticket price.

Hinterland accommodations, including O'Reilly's, Binna Burra Mountain Retreat, and Spicers Peak Lodge, shuttle guests to and from the coast. Various smaller coach tour companies, including winery tour operator Cork 'n Fork *(see Winery Tours)*, also visit Hinterland destinations.

ESSENTIALS

Coach Tours and Transfers **Australian Day Tours/JPT** ⊠ *Level 1, Olympia Ct., 3059 Surfers Paradise Blvd., Surfers Paradise* ☎ *07/5512–6444* ⊕ *www.daytours.com.au.*

Tours **Mountain Coach Company** ☎ *1300/762–665* ⊕ *www.mountaincoach.com.au.*

EXPLORING

Tamborine National Park. More than 20 million years ago, volcanic eruptions created rugged landscapes, while fertile volcanic soils produced the luxuriant tracts of rain forest that make up enchanting Tamborine National Park. This is the most developed region of the Gold Coast

Luke's Bluff Lookout on O'Reilly's Plateau, Lamington National Park.

Hinterland, and it's worth spending a day or two here. Apart from the natural environment, there are wineries, lodges, restaurants, and the famed Gallery Walk, a 1-km-long (½-mi-long) street lined with art galleries. Some of the simplest (under two hours) and best trails here are the Cedar Creek Falls Track, with waterfall views; Palm Grove Rainforest Circuit; and Macdonald Rainforest Circuit, a quieter walk popular with bird-watchers. Start your visit with a stop at Tamborine Mountain Visitor Information Centre, open 10 am to 3 pm daily.

Several fragmented parks make up Tamborine National Park. To the east of Witches Falls is **Joalah National Park,** where a 1½-km (1-mi) circuit takes you to a rocky pool at the base of Curtis Falls.

Witches Falls. Queensland's first national park, Witches Falls, has excellent picnic facilities and a 3-km (2-mi) walk that snakes downhill through open rain forest and past lagoons.

MacDonald National Park. MacDonald National Park has a flat, easy 1½-km (1-mi) walk. ☎ 07/5538–4419 *(Gold Coast Tourism)* ⊕ *www.derm.qld.gov.au* ✉ *Free* ☙ *Daily dawn–dusk.* ✉ *Doughty Park, Geissman Dr. at the corner of Main Western Rd., North Tamborine* ☎ *13/7468* ⊕ *www.derm.qld.gov.au.*

Springbrook National Park. The peaks of Springbrook National Park rise to around 3,000 feet, dominating the skyline west of the Gold Coast. The World-Heritage-listed park has four regions: scenic Springbrook plateau, Mt. Cougal, Natural Bridge, and Numinbah. Waterfalls and cascades, Jurassic-Age hoop pines, ancient rain forest, and teeming wildlife are highlights. Thanks to steep, winding roads and longish distances between sections, it takes at least a full day to explore this large park. It's about 30 km (19 mi) from the tiny hamlet of Spring-brook to Natural Bridge—a waterfall that cascades through a cavern roof into an icy pool (reach it via a half-mile circuit track, an hour's round-trip). This cavern is home to Australia's largest glowworm colony, which at night illuminates the rock walls to stunning effect. Several waterfalls, including the area's largest, Purling Brook Falls, can be reached via a steepish 4-km (2½-mi) path (allow 15 minutes for each half-mile). The 54-km Gold Coast Hinterland Great Walk extends from the Settlement campground to Green Mountains camp-site in Tamborine National Park. For those short on time or energy, the lookout near the parking lot has waterfall views. Camping is per-mitted only in designated private campgrounds. ☎ 13/7468 ⊕ www.derm.qld.gov.au 🖃 Free ☉ Daily dawn–dusk.

Lamington National Park. Lamington National Park is a subtropical-temperate ecological border zone sheltering abundant plant and ani-mal life. Its 50,600-acre expanse comprises two sections: Binna Burra and Green Mountains. Lamington National Park is listed as a World Heritage Area, which protects its varied rain forest, including Ant-arctic beech trees dating back 3,000 years. Lamington has 160 km (100 mi) of bushwalking tracks ranging from 1.2 km (3/4 mi) to 54 km (34 mi), as well as waterfalls, mountain pools, exceptional views, and some 120 native bird species. The Gold Coast Hinterland Great Walk begins at the Green Mountains campsite. All park camping areas require nightly permits (A\$5.15), obtained in advance. ⊠ Binna Burra Rd. ☎ 07/5543–4501 (Beaudesert Tourism), 13–7468 permits and camping ⊕ www.derm.qld.gov.au 🖃 Free ☉ Daily 24 hrs; park offices open limited weekday hours.

OUTDOOR ACTIVITIES

BUSHWALKING Bushwalking is a popular pastime in the national parks and nature reserves of the Gold Coast Hinterland, where an extensive network of well-maintained scenic trails caters to recreational walkers, serious hikers, campers, and wildlife lovers. The region's many protected wil-derness tracts, including World Heritage–listed Gondwana Rainforests of Australia (within Springbook National Park), contain hundreds of well-marked trails that vary from easy half-hour strolls to steep half-day hikes and multi-day treks. Most Hinterland walks offer spectacular views and sights.

Conditions can be challenging and changeable, however: before set-ting out on longer hikes, get suitably equipped. Download local trail maps and detailed park info from DERM's Web site or regional visitor information offices and follow DERMguidelines.

When walking, wear sturdy shoes, sunscreen, and protective gear, carry maps and a compass, and pack drinking water, emergency food supplies, and a well-charged mobile phone. If possible, walk in a group, espe-cially on long hikes. Check local weather conditions with the Bureau of Meterology and trail conditions on DERM's Web site before you go.

If exploring the national parks by car, check road conditions with the RACQ's Web site and be sure you have local maps, good tires, sound brakes, water, and a full tank of gas before setting out.

Contacts **Department of Environment and Resource Management (DERM)**
☎ *13–7468 camping permits and information* ⊕ *www.derm.qld.gov.au.* **RACQ**
☎ *13–1905 information* ⊕ *www.racq.com.au.*

WHERE TO STAY
For expanded hotel reviews, visit Fodors.com.

$ ☂ **Binna Burra Mountain Lodge & Campsite.** Founded in 1933, this group of
☺ hilltop cabins has sweeping views across Heritage-listed rain forest and
★ the Hinterland to the Gold Coast. **Pros:** good facilities and kids' programs;
gorgeous setting; abseiling sites nearby. **Cons:** multi-night minimum stays
in peak periods. ⊠ *Binna Burra Rd., Lamington National Park, via
Beechmont* ☎ *07/5533–3622, 1300/246–622* ⊕ *www.binnaburralodge.
com.au* ➳ *35 cabins (9 with shared bath), 2 suites* ⚏ *In-room: no a/c,
no TV. In-hotel: restaurant, bar, children's programs, laundry facilities,
business center, parking* ⦿ *Multiple meal plans.*

$$ ☂ **O'Reilly's Rainforest Retreat, Villas & Lost World Spa.** Since 1926 the
☺ O'Reilly family has welcomed travelers into their forested world. **Pros:**
★ excellent outdoor activities, great facilities, kids under 11 stay free.
Cons: 2-3 night minimum stays on weekends, Easter, and Christmas;
inconsistent mobile phone coverage; fees for many activities; surcharge
for credit-card transactions. New Birds of Pray & Wildlife Shows. Seg-
way tours ⊠ *Lamington National Park Rd., via Canungra* ☎ *07/5502–
4911, 1800/688–722* ✉ *reservations@oreillys.com.au* ⊕ *www.oreillys.
com.au* ➳ *67 rooms, 5 suites, 48 villas* ⚏ *In-room: no a/c, no TV, Wi-Fi.
In-hotel: restaurant, bar, pool, spa, laundry facilities, business center*
⦿ *Multiple meal plans.*

$$$ ☂ **Pethers Rainforest Retreat.** On 12 acres of privately owned rain forest,
★ this couples-only resort comprises 10 spacious tree houses with tim-
ber floors, French doors opening onto verandas, fireplaces, hot tubs,
and open-plan interiors furnished with Asian antiques. **Pros:** luxurious appointments, glorious environs, no kids. **Cons:** no on-site dinner Sunday to Wednesday; limited mobile phone coverage; minimum
2-night stay. ⊠ *28B Geissmann St., North Tamborine* ☎ *07/5545–4577*
✉ *retreat@pethers.com.au* ⊕ *www.pethers.com.au* ➳ *10 tree houses*
⚏ *In-room: no a/c. In-hotel: restaurant, bar, gym, parking, some age
restrictions* ⦿ *Breakfast.*

SUNSHINE COAST

60 km (37 mi) north of Brisbane.

The Sunshine Coast is a 60-km (37-mi) stretch of white-sand beaches,
inlets, lakes, and mountains that begins at the Glass House Mountains,
an hour's drive north of Brisbane, and extends to Rainbow Beach in the
north. Kenilworth is its inland extreme, 40 km (25 mi) from the ocean.
For the most part, the Sunshine Coast has avoided the high-rise glitz of
its southern cousin, the Gold Coast. Although there are plenty of stylish
restaurants and luxurious hotels, this coast is best loved for its national
parks, secluded coves, and relaxed beachside towns.

GETTING HERE AND AROUND

From Brisbane, drive 60 km (35 mi) north on the Bruce Highway, taking the Caloundra Road exit to get to the Sunshine Coast's southernmost beach town, Caloundra. Another five 5 km (3 mi) along the highway, there's a well-marked exit to the Sunshine Motorway, which funnels you through to Sunshine Coast towns farther north via a series of large roundabouts (stay tuned for the appropriate exit). Follow the motorway north for 9.5 km (6 mi) to get to the Brisbane Road–Mooloolaba exit; 15 km (9 mi) to reach the turn-off to Maroochydore; 29 km (18 mi) to the Yandina-Coolum Road exit for Coolum Beach; and 34 km (21 mi) to reach the Noosa turnoff.

Sunshine Coast Regional Council, Maroochy Tourist Information Centre has branches at the Sunshine Coast airport, Maroochydore, Mooloolaba, Coolum, and Montville.

AIR TRAVEL   The revamped Sunshine Coast Airport is the main airport for the Sunshine Coast area, servicing several flights a day by Jetstar and Virgin Australia from Sydney and Melbourne. By air from Maroochydore it's 2 hours 25 minutes to Melbourne, 2 hours 15 minutes to Adelaide, and 1 hour 35 minutes to Sydney. Park at the airport for around A\$13 a day, A\$65 a week.

BUS TRAVEL   SunAir Bus Service runs daily buses from Brisbane Airport and the Roma Street Transit Centre in Brisbane to all the main Sunshine Coast towns. Distances between towns are short (10 to 30 minutes drive). SunAir also runs hourly services from Brisbane International Airport to Sunshine Coast and Hinterland towns (A\$35–\$54), meeting every flight into and out of Sunshine Coast Airport and shuttling prebooked, prepaid passengers to and from Sunshine Coast towns south of the airport, including Maroochydore, Mooloolaba, and Caloundra (A\$13–\$37 one-way).

Henry's Transport Group meets all flights, running buses from Maroochy Airport to the northern Sunshine Coast (A\$25 to Noosa) and, on market days, to Eumundi.

CAR TRAVEL   A car is a virtual necessity on the Sunshine Coast. The traditional route to the coast from Brisbane is along the Bruce Highway (Highway 1) to the Glass House Mountains, with a turnoff at Cooroy. Taking the Sunshine Motorway may be faster, however: after 65 km (40 mi), turn off the Bruce Highway at Tanawha (toward Mooloolaba) and follow the signs. On either route, allow 1½ hours to get to the central coastal town of Coolum, a further half-hour to reach Noosa, on the northern Sunshine Coast. The most scenic route is to turn off the Bruce Highway at the exit to Caloundra, then follow the coast to Noosa Heads.

TRAIN TRAVEL   Trains leave regularly from Roma Street Transit Centre in Brisbane en route to Nambour, the business hub of the Sunshine Coast. They continue on to Yandina, Eumundi, and other non-coastal towns. Once in Nambour, however, a car is a virtual necessity unless you're a keen cyclist, so it may make more sense to drive from Brisbane.

ESSENTIALS

Airports **Sunshine Coast Airport** ⊠ *Runway Dr. off David Low Way, Marcoola* ☎ *07/5453–1500* ⊕ *www.sunshinecoastairport.com.au.*

Bus Contacts Henry's Transport Group ☎ 07/5474–0199 ⊕ www.henrys.com.
au. **SunAir Bus Service** ☎ 07/5477–0888, 1800/804–340 ⊕ www.sunair.com.au.

Medical Services Coolum Beach Medical Centre ✉ 21 Birtwill St., Coolum
☎ 07/5446–1466. **Medifirst Noosa 7 Day Medical Centre** ✉ 81 Noosa Dr.,
Noosa Junction Plaza, Noosa Heads ☎ 07/5473–5488.

Train Contacts Queensland Rail ☎ 13–1617 ⊕ www.qr.com.au.

**Visitor Information Sunshine Coast Regional Council Visitor Informa-
tion Centre—Maroochydore** ✉ 6th Ave. at Melrose Parade, Maroochydore ☎ 07/5459–9050, 1800/644969 ⊕ www.discovermaroochy.com.au.
Sunshine Coast Tourist Information Centre ☎ 1800/330–142 ⊕ www.
sunshinecoastinformation.com.au. **Tourism Sunshine Coast** ✍ Box 9325,
Paradise Palms 4564 ☎ 07/5458–8888 ⊕ www.visitsunshinecoast.com.au.
Tourism Noosa ✉ 61 Hastings St., near the Surf Club, Noosa Heads4567
☎ 07/5430–5000, 1800/002–624 ⊕ www.visitnoosa.com.au ✉ Noosa Marina,
2 Parkyn Ct., Tewantin4566.

NOOSA

*39 km (24 mi) northeast of Nambour, 17 km (11 mi) north of Coolum,
140 km (87 mi) north of Brisbane.*

Set along the calm waters of Laguna Bay at the northern tip of the Sunshine Coast, Noosa is one of Australia's most stylish resort areas. Until
the mid-1980s the town consisted of little more than a few shacks: then
surfers discovered the spectacular waves that curl around the sheltering
headland of Noosa National Park. Today Noosa is a beguiling mix of
surf, sand, and sophistication, with a serious reputation for distinctive,
evolving cuisine. Views along the trail from Laguna Lookout to the
top of the headland north of Main Street take in miles of magnificent
beaches, ocean, and dense vegetation.

EXPLORING

Teewah Coloured Sands. About 3 km (2 mi) east of Noosa Heads you'll
find the Teewah Coloured Sands, an area of multicolored dunes created
in the Ice Age by natural chemicals in the soil. Teewah's sands stretch
inland from the beach to a distance of about 17 km (11 mi); some of
the 72 distinctly hued sands form cliffs rising to 600 feet. A four-wheel-
drive vehicle is essential for exploring this area and interesting sites to
the north, such as Cooloola National Park, home to 1,300-plus species
of plants, 700 native animals, and 44 percent of Australia's bird species; Great Sandy National Park; the wreck of the *Cherry Venture*, near
beachside hamlet Freshwater; and Rainbow Beach. Access is by ferry
across the Noosa River at Tewantin.

Tour operators run day trips via cruise boat and four-wheel drive that
take in these sights; some include visits to Fraser Island, north of Rainbow Beach. You can also explore the area on foot: one of Queensland's
latest Great Walks winds through Cooloola National Park.

CRUISING **Noosa Everglades Discovery.** Eco-accredited Noosa Everglades Discovery
runs day-trip river cruises around the Noosa Everglades and a combined
cruise and four-wheel-drive tour to Cooloola National Park, Teewah

Coloured Sands, and Rainbow Beach. ☏ *07/5449–0393* ⊕ *www. noosaeverglades.com.au* ⊠ *A$75, Everglades Discovery afternoon tea cruise; A$155 full-day Cruise 'n' Coast* ☻ *Everglades Discovery: noon–4 daily; Cruise 'n' Coast: 9–4:30, Sun. and Thurs.*

WHERE TO EAT

$$
AUSTRALIAN

✘ **Berardo's Bistro on the Beach.** Expatriate New Yorker Jim Berardo came to Noosa to retire, but he ended up with two restaurants and a kiosk. Berardo's Bistro, the more casual of the restaurants, has a prime location right on Noosa's beach, and attracts a constant stream of customers. Quirky fish sculptures line the walls; handblown chartreuse carafes are on every table. The menu lists fresh juices, cocktails, Berardo's Wagyu Burger (at lunch), and light meals that focus on seafood: have the fish of the day with a garnish of your choice; or linguine with prawns, scallops, mussels, chili, parsley, and garlic. There's also a gourmet deli bar with takeout options. ⊠ *49 Hastings St., beachfront* ☏ *07/5448–0888* ⊕ *www.berardos.com.au.*

$$
MODERN
AUSTRALIAN

✘ **Bistro C.** Spectacular views of the bay from the open dining area make a stunning backdrop for this restaurant's Mod-Oz cuisine. The fresh, tropical menu highlights seafood, though landlubbers can partake of several meat and vegetarian dishes. Try the signature fresh medley of local seafoods, served in the pan, or seafood antipasto. Coffin Bay oysters are also a delicious way to indulge, or try the local favorite: beer-battered flathead with lemon and tartar sauce. Book ahead for Thursday night's "seafood platter": for A$85 you get cold then hot platters for two, brimming with Moreton Bay bugs, prawns, squid, mussels, salmon, and more (except in peak season). There's also a kids' menu. ⊠ *On the Beach Complex, 49 Hastings St.* ☏ *07/5447–2855* ⊕ *www.bistroc.com.au.*

$$
CAFÉ

✘ **Ricky's River Bar + Restaurant.** A dining room overlooking the Noosa River makes this restaurant perfect for a relaxed lunch or a romantic dinner. The menu features "modern Noosa cuisine," in which Mediterranean flavors mingle with Australian ingredients. Sip a mojito or a mango daiquiri and polish off a plate of tapas before moving on to a main course of fresh reef fish. There's also a kids' menu. On Thursdays from 5 to 8 pm Ricky's hosts wine tastings (A$2 per taste; A$6 cheese platters). ⊠ *Noosa Wharf, Quamby Pl.* ☏ *07/5447–2455* ⊕ *www.rickys.com.au.*

WHERE TO STAY

For expanded hotel reviews, visit Fodors.com.

¢

⊞ **Halse Lodge.** This National Heritage–listed 1880s guesthouse with colonial-style furnishings sits in 2 acres of gardens on the edge of Noosa National Park. **Pros:** fantastic setting, good breakfasts, free use of surfboards. **Cons:** must book ahead, can be noisy on weekends. ⊠ *2 Halse La., at Noosa Dr., near Lions Park* ☏ *07/5447–3377, 1800/242–567* ✉ *backpackers@halselodge.com.au* ⊕ *www.halselodge.com.au* ⌘ *26 rooms without bath* ⚑ *In-room: no a/c, safe, no TV. In-hotel: restaurant, bar, beach, water sports, laundry facilities, business center, parking.*

$$$
★

⊞ **Sheraton Noosa Resort & Spa.** You can't miss this stepped, six-story, horseshoe-shaped complex as you drive into Noosa Heads. **Pros:** sleek decor; terrific on-site day spa; Cato's Restaurant. **Cons:** pricey, no in-room Wi-Fi; fees for Internet and parking. ⊠ *14–16 Hastings St.*

"We were walking along the beach in Noosa at sunset when we came across this guy building the sand castle. He was amazing!" —photo by jenwhitby, Fodors.com member

☎ 07/5449–4888 ⊕ *www.sheraton.com/noosa* ⤳ *140 rooms, 29 suites, 7 spa studios* ⅄ *In-room: safe, kitchen, Internet. In-hotel: restaurant, bar, pool, gym, spa, laundry facilities, business center, parking.*

SUNSHINE BEACH

4 km (2½ mi) south of Noosa.

Ten minutes away from the bustle and crowds of Hastings Street and Noosa Beach, south of the headland and Noosa National Park, is the serene suburb of Sunshine Beach. It's home to a number of good restaurants, a small shopping village, and, as the name suggests, 16 km (10 mi) of beachfront that stretches north to the national park.

PEREGIAN AND COOLUM

Peregian is 11 km (7 mi) south of Noosa, with Coolum 17 km (11 mi) south of Noosa and 25 km (16 mi) northeast of Nambour.

At the center of the Sunshine Coast, Coolum makes an ideal base for exploring the countryside. It has one of the finest beaches in the region, a growing reputation for good food and quality accommodation, and all the services you might need: banks with ATMs, medical centers, gas stations, pharmacies, supermarkets, gyms, beauty salons, and day spas—even a beachfront playground, kiosk, and skate park. Ten minutes north of Coolum is Peregian, a quaint little seaside town with numerous shops, eateries, and facilities, a string of stunning beaches, and a local produce and crafts market on the second and forth Sunday of the month.

OUTDOOR ACTIVITIES

SURFING **Coolum Surf School.** Coolum Surf School is run by an expert surfer and local lifeguard who offers 90-minute group and private lessons as well as board and gear hire. It's the only surf school in the area: find it 50 meters north of Coolum Surf Lifesaving Club, next to the skate park. ⊠ *Coolum Boardriders Clubhouse, Tickle Park, David Low Way, Coolum Beach* ☎ *07/5446–5279* ⊕ *www.coolumsurfschool.com. au* ⌦ *A$90 single, A$55 per person in a group of 4 or more; prices include gear* ⊗ *Daily, dawn–dusk, by appointment; Sat. 9–11 during school holidays.*

WHERE TO EAT AND STAY

For expanded hotel reviews, visit Fodors.com.

$$ ✗ **Pitchfork.** Positioned within the café and shopping strip along Pere-
MODERN gian Beach, this new restaurant is drawing crowds with its delectable
AUSTRALIAN Mod-Oz menu. But Pitchfork's rustic-feel furnishings, indoor and out-
door dining, BYO alcohol and a change-by-the-season menu aren't its only draws. It also caters specifically to gluten-free and vegetarian diners. Top dishes include the lightly fried stuffed zucchini flowers or braised beef cheeks to start, and the wild-mushroom and truffle-oil risotto for main. However, keep an eye out for their specials board—their duck pie is one to request. Booking in advance is highly recommended. ⊠ *5/4 Kingfisher Dr., Peregian Beach* ☎ *07/5471–3697* ⊗ *Closed Mon.*

$$$ ⛱ **Coolum Seaside Holiday Apartments.** These sleek and spacious studios and one- to four-bedroom apartments are just around the corner from Coolum's restaurants, shops, and beach. **Pros:** all modern conveniences, good on-site facilities, close to beach. **Cons:** seven-night minimum stay, except in peak season. ⊠ *23 Beach Rd.* ☎ *07/5255–7200* 🖷 *07/5455–7288* ⊕ *www.coolumseaside.com* ⛵ *44 apartments* ♿ *In-room: safe, kitchen, Internet. In-hotel: pool, tennis court, gym, laundry facilities, business center.*

MAROOCHYDORE

18 km (11 mi) south of Coolum, 18 km (11 mi) east of Nambour.

Maroochydore, at the mouth of the Maroochy River, has been a popular beach resort town for years, and has its fair share of high-rise towers. Its draw is excellent surfing and swimming beaches.

WHERE TO EAT AND STAY

For expanded hotel reviews, visit Fodors.com.

$$ ✗ **Beach Break Cafe at the Maroochy Surf Club.** Head to this relaxed beach-
SEAFOOD side eatery for lunch or dinner post-surf. The gourmet burgers, steaks, and hearty surf-and-turf—grilled rump with scallops and prawns—are hugely popular; the fresh oysters, chili calamari, pistachio-stuffed chicken breast, and grilled barramundi are also excellent. There are also salads, vegetarian dishes, and good-value kids' dishes. Beachwear is fine by day; smart-casual is the rule after dark. There's a bar, a gam-ing area, karaoke on Thursday nights, and live bands on weekends. A courtesy bus shuttles patrons to and from local hotels. ⊠ *34–36 Alex-andra Parade* ☎ *07/5443–1298* ⊕ *www.maroochydoresurfclub.com.au.*

$$$
AUSTRALIAN

✕ **ebb Waterfront.** Faux-suede sofas and ottomans in varying shades of cool blue set the mood at this riverside restaurant specializing in top-quality regional produce, particularly sustainably farmed local seafood. Floor-to-ceiling windows line one side of the long, open dining room, and there's a large outdoor dining area. Start with the oysters, perhaps, moving on to duck, lamb, or locally farmed barramundi or Spanner crab; finish with the delectable chocolate fondant. Menus change with the season; there's a kids' menu year-round. Open Thursday through Sunday for lunch; Thursday through Saturday for dinner. ⊠ *6 Wharf St.* ☎ *07/5452–7771* ⊕ *www.ebbwaterfront.com.*

$

⊡ **Twin Waters Resort.** About 9 km (5½ mi) north of Maroochydore, this hotel was built around a 15-acre saltwater lagoon bordering Maroochy River and Mudjimba Beach. **Pros:** great lawns and lagoon; free use of water-sports equipment; terrific kids' programs. **Cons:** housekeeping standards vary; buffet dinners pricey; lackluster spa. ⊠ *Ocean Dr., Twin Waters* ☎ *07/5448–8000, 1800/072277* ⊕ *www.twinwatersresort. au* ⤳ *234 rooms, 126 suites* ⚉ *In-room: kitchen, Internet, Wi-Fi. In-hotel: restaurant, bar, pool, tennis court, gym, spa, beach, water sports, children's programs, laundry facilities, business center, parking* ⵏ⊙⎮ *Breakfast.*

$$

⊡ **The Sebel Maroochydore.** Each one- or two-bedroom apartment in this stylish hotel has a curved feature wall and a kitchen bristling with European appliances. **Pros:** 25-meter (82-foot) pool and separate kids pool; stylish decor; good service. **Cons:** noise from pool area and traffic at night; beach is across a four-lane road; soft furnishings showing wear. ⊠ *20 Aerodrome Rd.* ☎ *07/5479–8000, 1800/137–106* ⊕ *www. mirvachotels.com/sebel-maroochydore* ⤳ *70 apartments, 6 penthouses* ⚉ *In-room: safe, kitchen, Internet. In-hotel: pool, laundry facilities, business center, parking.*

7

MOOLOOLABA

5 km (3 mi) south of Maroochydore.

Mooloolaba stretches along a lovely beach and riverbank, both an easy walk from town. The Esplanade has many casual cafés, upscale restaurants, and fashionable shops. Head to the town outskirts for picnic spots and prime coastal views.

EXPLORING MOOLOOLABA

🜃 **Underwater World.** Underwater World has back-to-back marine presentations, including stingray feedings, guided shark tours, and seal and otter shows, all accompanied by informative talks. A clear underwater tunnel lets you get face-to-face with creatures from the deep. You can also swim with seals for A$90, play with otters for A$150 (including photo), and scuba dive with resident sharks: the cost, including training and 30 minutes underwater, is A$225 for beginners, A$195 for certified divers. The twice-daily behind-scenes tour, taking in the nursery, oceanarium, and marine turtle rehab center, is well worth it at A$15: pre-booking is a must. A souvenir shop and a café are on-site. The aquarium is part of Mooloolaba's Wharf Complex, which also has a marina, restaurants, and a tavern. ⊠ *10 Parkyn Parade, The Wharf* ☎ *07/5458–6280 Sat/Sun, 07/5458–6226 Mon.–Fri.* ⊕ *www.underwaterworld.com.au* ⊠ *A$33* ☉ *Daily 9–5.*

WHERE TO EAT AND STAY

For expanded hotel reviews, visit Fodors.com.

$$
ITALIAN
★

✕ **Bella Venezia Italian Restaurant & Bar.** A large mural of Venice, simple wooden tables, and terra-cotta floor tiles decorate this popular restaurant in an arcade off the Esplanade, You can eat in or take out traditional and modern Italian cuisine, such as the *filetto chianti* (a 250g [8.8 oz], grain-fed eye fillet with field mushrooms, mash, and a Chianti jus); *anatra puccini* (an oven-roasted organic duck with a rich orange–white wine glaze); or panfried fish of the day. There's an extensive selection of pizza, pasta, and risotto, as well as wine and cocktails. They'll also deliver to local hotels. ✉ *Shop 1, Pacific Beach Resort, 95 The Esplanade* ☎ *07/5444–5844* ⊕ *www.bellav.com.au.*

$$

⌂ **Mantra Sirocco.** The futuristic curves of this apartment complex loom above Mooloolaba's main drag. **Pros:** fantastic views from big balconies; friendly staff; DVD players in every room **Cons:** no Wi-Fi; occasional housekeeping lapses; minimum five-night stay late December through January. ✉ *59–75 The Esplanade* ☎ *07/5444–1400, 1800/811–454 reservations* ⊕ *www.mantrasirocco.com.au* ⤴ *41 apartments* ⌂ *In-room: kitchen, Internet. In-hotel: pool, gym, laundry facilities, parking.*

CALOUNDRA

29 km (18 mi) south of Maroochydore, 63 km (39 mi) south of Noosa, 91 km (56 mi) north of Brisbane.

This unassuming southern seaside town has nine beaches of its own, which include everything from placid wading beaches (King's Beach and Bulcock Beach are best for families) to bays with thundering surf, such as Dicky, Buddina, and Wurtulla beaches.

WHERE TO EAT AND STAY

For expanded hotel reviews, visit Fodors.com.

$$
SEAFOOD

✕ **mooo char + bar.** Owned by legendary (and now retired) Queensland Rugby League footballer Allan "Alfie" Langer, this steak-centric restaurant has an ideal setting right on Bulcock Beach, overlooking the sheltered inlet known as Pumicestone Passage. The decor and design are light and bright, and there's both indoor and outdoor dining. Try the restaurant's deservedly popular steak, wild barramundi, champagne lobster morney, or local king prawns. ✉ *30/100 Bulcock Street* ☎ *07/5492–0800* ⊕ *www.alfies.net.au.*

$$

⌂ **Rolling Surf Resort.** The white sands of Kings Beach front this resort enveloped in tropical gardens. **Pros:** huge pool, good on-site eatery; right on the beach. **Cons:** no Wi-Fi; 5-night minimum stay in high season. ✉ *10 Levuka Ave., Kings Beach* ☎ *07/5491–9777, 1800/775559* ⊕ *www.rollingsurfresort.com.au* ⤴ *74 apartments* ⌂ *In-hotel: restaurant, pool, gym, beach, laundry facilities, business center, parking.*

The Sunshine Coast and Sunshine Coast Hinterlands

SUNSHINE COAST HINTERLAND

The Sunshine Coast Hinterland, extending from the Glass House Mountains just northwest of Brisbane to Eumundi and Yandina, west of the northern Sunshine Coast town of Noosa, is ideal terrain for day-trippers. Tracts of subtropical rainforest and mountainous areas linked by scenic drives and walking trails are interspersed with pretty hillside villages, their main streets lined with cafés, galleries, gift shops, and guesthouses. Here you'll also find thriving markets, renowned restaurants and cooking schools, ginger, nut, and pineapple farms, theme and wildlife parks, and luxury B&Bs.

The Hinterland's southerly extent is the nine distinctive conical outcrops of the Glass House Mountains—the eroded remnants of ancient volcanoes—rising dramatically from a flattish landscape 45 km (27 mi) northwest of Brisbane. Get a great view of the mountains from Glass House Mountains Lookout, also the starting point for a scenic, 25-minute walk. Several longer trails begin from nearby vantage points, such as Mount Beerburrum and Wild Horse Mountain Lookout. Nearby, you'll find Aussie World amusement park, the Ettamogah Pub, and the late Steve Irwin's famous Australia Zoo.

Fishing at Bulcock Beach, Caloundra, Sunshine Coast.

Meander north through the mountains to reach the arty village of Maleny, quaint, European-style Montville, and food-friendly Mapleton. Nearby, you'll find tranquil Baroon Lake and easy walking trails in Kondalilla National Park and Mary Cairncross Scenic Reserve.

Continue north to Yandina, where you'll find much-lauded restaurant Spirit House and the Ginger Factory, and Eumundi, known for its thriving twice-weekly markets. Hinterland hub Nambour, east of Mapleton, has shops, banks, and local attractions.

GETTING HERE AND AROUND

To get to the Sunshine Coast Hinterland from Brisbane, follow the Bruce Highway north for around 35 km (22 mi), taking the Glass House Mountains Road exit. A 10 km (6 mi) drive along Glass House Mountains Road brings you to the quaint Glass House Mountains Village. Access Glass House Mountains Lookout, 10 km (6 mi) from the village, via Glass House Mountains Tourist Route. Drive 10 km (6 mi) north along Glass House Mountains Road from the village to reach Maleny.

From Maleny, take the Landsborough-Maleny Road for 10 km (6 mi), turning right at Maleny–Montville Road, to get to Montville. From Montville it's a 5-minute drive west on Western Avenue to Kondallila National Park. A further 10 km (6 mi) drive northwest brings you to Mapleton, from which it's a 12 km (7 mi), 15-minute drive east to Nambour, en route to the Sunshine Coast.

From Nambour, a 20-minute drive east along Petrie Creek Road and David Low Way brings you to the mid-Sunshine Coast town of Maroochydore. Or drive 20 minutes north along the Bruce Highway to reach Eumundi, 20 km (12 mi) away. From here it's a half-hour, 20 km (12 mi) drive east along the Eumundi–Noosa Road to Noosa, the northernmost town on the Sunshine Coast.

From Nambour it's an 8-km (5-mi) drive north along the Nambour Connection Road, then Old Bruce Highway, to reach Yandina. From Brisbane, it's an hour's drive north along the Bruce Highway: take the Coolum/Yandina exit.

It's around 60 km (35 mi) to Glass House Mountains Village; just under 100 km (60 mi) to Montville; and nearly 110 km (65 mi) to Maleny from Brisbane. Driving time is 90 minutes to the Glasshouse Mountains; around 1½ hours to Maleny and Montville, and a further 15-minute drive to Nambour and another 12-minute drive to Yandina. From the Sunshine Coast most parts of the Hinterland are less than an hour's drive inland.

You'll find few banks and money exchanges around the Sunshine Coast Hinterland: ■ TIP➔ Get cash in advance from ATMs in larger coastal towns such as Noosa. Alternatively, there is one in Nambour and several are available at service stations along the Bruce Highway.

ESSENTIALS

Banks Bank of Queensland Nambour ⊠ *15 Ann St., Nambour* ☎ *07/5476–2003.*

Visitor Information Maleny Hinterland Visitor Information Centre ⊠ *787 Landsborough-Maleny Rd., Maleny* ☎ *07/5499–9788.* **Montville Visitors Information Centre** ⊠ *198 Main St., Montville* ☎ *07/5459–9050.*

GLASS HOUSE MOUNTAINS AREA

35 km (22 mi) north of Brisbane on Bruce Highway to the Glass House Mountains Road exit; 4 km (2.5 mi) south of Beerwah.

More than 20 million years old, the Glass House Mountains consist of nine conical outcrops—the eroded remnants of volcanoes—that rise dramatically from a flattish landscape northwest of Brisbane. Get a great view of the mountains from Glass House Mountains Lookout. Access is 10 km (6 mi) from the village via Glass House Mountains Tourist Route. The lookout is also the starting point for a scenic 25-minute walk. Several longer walks begin from nearby vantage points, such as Mount Beerburrum and Wild Horse Mountain Lookout.

EXPLORING GLASS HOUSE MOUNTAINS AREA

Australia Zoo. Australia Zoo, made famous by the late Steve Irwin, has all manner of Australian animals: koalas, kangaroos, wallabies, dingos, Tasmanian devils, snakes and lizards—and, naturally, crocodiles. There are also otters, lemurs, tigers, red pandas, and a giant rain-forest aviary. Daily shows feature crocs, birds of prey, and koalas. Don't miss hand-feeding the Asian elephants (A$145) and red pandas (A$80). A courtesy bus shuttles visitors to and from Beerwah station; get around the park on foot or on free hop-on, hop-off mini-trains. ⊠ *1638 Steve Irwin Way, 5 km (3 mi) north of Glass House Mountains, Beerwah* ☎ *07/5436–2000* ⊕ *www.australiazoo.com.au* ⊑ *A$59* ☉ *Daily 9–5 (last entry 4:30).*

Ettamogah Pub. The Ettamogah Pub, whose name (allegedly, Aboriginal for "place of good drink") and quirky design are based on the fictitious pub made famous by Aussie cartoonist Ken Maynard, looms 18 meters (55 feet) over the Bruce Highway just north of Palmview (21 km [13 mi] north of Glass House Mountains). The much-photographed watering hole, its furniture constructed mainly from wood logged on the site, has an upstairs bistro, a beer garden, and a bar, and is open daily 9 am–8 pm. Kitschy Australiana and Maynard's cartoons adorn the walls. ☎ *07/5494–5444.*

☺ **Aussie World.** The Aussie World amusement area, adjacent to the Ettamogah Pub, has a large shed with pool tables, a hall for the Funnybone Flicks, and a fairground with 30-plus "old-school" rides, including dodgems, a retro merry-go-round, a Ferris wheel, a roller coaster, minigolf—even a sideshow alley. ⊠ *Bruce Hwy. at 73 Frizzo Rd.* ☎ *07/5494–5444* ⊕ *www.aussieworld.com.au* ☜ *A$25 unlimited rides, or A$10 mini-golf, flicks, and Ferris wheel* ☽ *Daily 9–5.*

MONTVILLE

16 km (10 mi) northwest of Forest Glen.

This charming mountain village, settled in 1887, is known as the creative heart of the Sunshine Coast, as many artists live here. There are panoramic views of the coast from the main street, an oddly charming mix of Tudor, Irish, and English cottages constructed of log or stone; Bavarian and Swiss houses; quaint B&Bs; and old Queenslander homes. Shops are a browser's delight, full of curiosities and locally made crafts; galleries showcase more serious pieces by local artists. Note that the nearest banks (and thus ATMs) are in Nambour.

☺ **Kondalilla National Park.** Kondalilla National Park, with its swimming hole, 295-foot waterfall, picnic grounds, and walking trails, is a popular local attraction. Three bushwalks begin near the grassy picnic area: Picnic Creek Circuit, Rock Pools Walk, and the Kondalilla Falls Circuit. They're all rated easy to moderate and range from 2 km (1 mi) to 5 km (3 mi) in length. The **Sunshine Coast Hinterland Great Walk** (58 km [34 mi]) is accessible from the Falls Loop track, and links with parks farther north. Download maps from the Department of Environment and Resource Management Web site. Camping is not permitted within the park. ⊠ *Kondalilla Falls Rd. off Montville–Mapleton Rd., near Flaxton* ☎ *07/5494–3983, 07/5459–6110* ⊕ *www.derm.qld.gov.au* ☜ *Free.*

WHERE TO EAT AND STAY

For expanded hotel reviews, visit Fodors.com.

$$ ✕ **Poets Cafe.** Pictures of famous poets adorn the walls, and French
CAFÉ doors open onto a balcony shaded by tall rain-forest trees. An eclectic menu includes gourmet open sandwiches, seafood risotto, barramundi, eye fillet steak, pasta dishes, cakes, and desserts (save room for the caramel macadamia tart). The Main Street Gallery below sells contemporary Australian artwork, including glassware. ⊠ *167 Main St.* ☎ *07/5478–5479 café, 07/5478–5050 gallery* ⊕ *www.weddingsatpoets. com.au* ☽ *No dinner Sat.–Thurs.*

$$ ⊞ **The Falls Rainforest Cottages.** Adjacent to Kondalilla Falls National Park, these secluded Queenslander-style accommodations make for a romantic getaway. **Pros:** beautiful location; quiet (no restaurants, shops, bushwalks nearby). **Cons:** A$25 single-night-stay surcharge; minimum 2-night stay; longish walk to the cottages at night (you'll need the provided flashlight). ⊠ *20 Kondalilla Falls Rd.* ☎ *07/5445–7000* ⊕ *www. thefallscottages.com.au* ⇆ *6 cottages* ⟨⟩ *In-room: kitchen. In-hotel: parking, some age restrictions* ⊤⊙⊦ *Breakfast.*

$$ ⊞ **The Spotted Chook & Amelie's Petite Maison.** This newly-built ⟳ Queenslander home has a delightful French provincial ambience. **Pros:** delicious French-style country breakfasts included in tariff; bicycles available for exploring the beautiful area, wheelchair-friendly cottage, ramps, and walkways. **Cons:** two-night minimum stay on weekends; no in-room Internet. ⊠ *176 Western Ave.* ☎ *07/5442–9242* ⊕ *www. spottedchook.com* ⇆ *4 suites, 1 cottage* ⟨⟩ *In-room: kitchen. In-hotel: restaurant, business center, some age restrictions* ⊙ *Closed Christmas Day, Boxing Day* ⊤⊙⊦ *Breakfast.*

$$$$ ⊞ **Treetops Montville.** These cutting-edge-design treehouses perched on an escarpment are the ideal location for a romantic escape. **Pros:** stunning views; quiet; close to town. **Cons:** minimum two-night stay; no Wi-Fi. ⊠ *4 Cynthia Hunt Dr., off Kondalilla Falls Rd.* ☎ *07/5478–6618, 1800/087330* ⊕ *www.treetopsmontville.com.au* ⇆ *10 cabins.*

MALENY

14 km (8½ mi) west of Montville.

The Hinterland village of Maleny is a lively mix of rural life, the arts, wineries, cafés, and cooperative ventures. First settled around 1880, Maleny is now a popular tourist resort with a strong community spirit, as well as a working dairy town. The annual Great Walks Festival takes place here in August and September.

EXPLORING MALENY

Mary Cairncross Scenic Reserve. Mary Cairncross Scenic Reserve, one of the area's most popular picnic spots, is 5 km (3 mi) southeast of Maleny at the intersection of the Landsborough–Maleny Road and Mountain View Road. The 130 acres of subtropical rain forest shelter an array of wildlife that includes bandicoots, goannas, echidnas, wallabies—and even pythons. There's an excellent information center and two easy walks. Eat in the café or at picnic tables for magnificent views of the Glass House Mountains. It's open daily from dawn to dusk, the info center 9–5. ☎ *07/5429–6122* ⊕ *www.mary-cairncross.com.au.*

WHERE TO EAT AND STAY

For expanded hotel reviews, visit Fodors.com.

$ ✕ **Maple 3 Café.** A covered veranda and courtyard surround this local **CAFÉ** favorite. The menu changes daily, but there are always salads, focaccias, salmon steaks, and many dessert options, including terrific cheesecake. Come in for breakfast or brunch, grab a sandwich and a huge slice of homemade cake, and head down to Lake Baroon for a picnic. Or just

Eumundi Market, Eumundi, Sunshine Coast

sit out front on the deck and watch affable Maleny townsfolk go about their day. ⌷ *3 Maple St.* ☎ *07/5499–9177.*

$$$ ⬚ **Maleny Tropical Retreat.** At the end of a steep driveway lies a misty rain-forest valley and this lovely B&B. **Pros:** huge DVD and CD library; good breakfasts; no kids. **Cons:** two-night minimum stay on weekends, not wheelchair-friendly. ⌷ *540 Maleny–Montville Rd.* ☎ *07/5435–2113* ⊕ *www.malenytropicalretreat.com* ⬚ *3 rooms, 1 cabin* ⬚ *In-hotel: some age restrictions* ⎜⎜*Breakfast.*

YANDINA, EUMUNDI, AND COOROY

Yandina is 110 km (68 mi) north of Brisbane on the Bruce Highway; Eumundi is 12 km (7.5 mi) north of Yandina.

Yandina and Eumundi, just 12 km (7.5 mi) apart, are home to some of the most iconic attractions in the area. Don't miss the Ginger Factory in Yandina, where you can learn—and eat—lots while enjoying the mini-amusement park-like attractions; or stop in at the tranquil Spirit House for a meal or cooking class. The Eumundi Market (on Wednesday and Saturday) are also a must.

EXPLORING YANDINA, EUMUNDI, AND COOROY

Big Pineapple. Sunshine Plantation in Nambour, just over 100 km (63 mi) north of Brisbane, is home to the impossible-to-miss Big Pineapple. You'll pass it on your way west if you head inland to Eumundi, Maleny, or Montvale. The 50-foot fiberglass monster towers over the highway. It's currently closed and under new ownership, with no open attractions yet, but if you're interested in Australia's "Big" things (a series of large fiberglass roadside attractions that dot the country's road system) and are passing through anyway, it's worth a quick stop for a photo. ⊠ *Nambour Connection Rd., 6 km (4 mi) south of Nambour, Woombye, Nambour* ☎ *07/5442–1333* ⊕ *www.bigpineapple.com.au* ☒ *Free, rides/nursery extra (A$22 all-inclusive)* ⊙ *Daily 9–5.*

Fodor'sChoice **Eumundi Market.** The big attraction of this area is the twice-weekly
★ Eumundi Market —the best street market on the Sunshine Coast. More than 300 stall-holders gather along Memorial Drive in the picturesque town of Eumundi to sell arts, crafts, clothing, accessories, and fresh and gourmet produce, from 6:30 am to 2 pm on Saturday and 8 am to 1:30 pm on Wednesday. Buses run to Eumundi from Noosa on market days, when the town swells to near-cosmopolitan proportions. Live musicians, poets, and masseurs keep the crowd relaxed. ☎ *07/5442–7106* ⊕ *www.eumundimarkets.com.au.*

☺ **The Ginger Factory.** The Ginger Factory, a legendary Queensland establishment, goes far beyond its original factory-door sale of ginger. You can still take a 40-minute guided tour of the world's only publically accessible ginger processing plant. A cafe and shop sell ginger in all forms—incorporated into jams, cookies, chocolates, ice cream, wine, and herbal products. There's a train trip and a boat ride, both with animated puppetry en route, and a live beehive tour that includes a honey tasting. You can even take cooking classes. ⊠ *50 Pioneer Rd., 1 km (½ mi) east of Bruce Hwy., 9 km (5½ mi) north of Nambour* ☎ *07/5446–7100, 1800/067–686* ⊕ *www.gingerfactory.com.au* ☒ *Free; A$31–A$38 (3-hour tour package)* ⊙ *Daily 9–5.*

WHERE TO EAT

$ ✕ **Maison de Provence.** Run by French couple Eric and Francoise Per-
BISTRO noud, Maison de Provence is one part patisserie/café, one part French homewares shop. All the food is made on-site by chef Eric, with light meals like quiches and baguettes to the most delectable tartes aux fruits, eclairs, and other cakes and pastries. They also make their own tempting range of chocolates and macaroons. At the back of a large corner balcony, this little café is a great spot to soak up some sun and fresh Hinterland air while treating yourself to a little bit of French delight. ⊠ *9/13 Garnet St., Cooroy* ☎ *07/5472–0077* ✎ *maisondeprovence@bigpond.com* ⊙ *Closed Sun.*

$$ ✕ **Spirit House.** Mention that you're looking for a place to eat in Yandina,
THAI and even Brisbane foodies say "Spirit House." The restaurant's trio of
Fodor'sChoice credentialed chefs, who travel annually to Asia to get inspiration and
★ skills, do a remarkable job re-creating contemporary Asian cuisine on Queensland soil. The menu, designed around plates to share, changes seasonally, with most ingredients sourced locally; a worthy signature dish is the whole crispy reef fish with tamarind-chili sauce. Save room for delectable desserts, best sampled in the tasting plate for two. The lush garden setting has a lagoon and Buddhist shrines. A hydroponic farm and cooking school with daily lessons are on-site. ⊠ *20 Ninderry Rd., Yandina* ☎ *07/5446–8994* ⊕ *www.spirithouse.com.au* ⊜ *Reservations essential* ⊙ *No dinner Sun.–Tues.*

MACKAY–CAPRICORN ISLANDS

Despite its name, this group of islands lying offshore between Bundaberg and Rockhampton is closer to the southern half of Queensland than it is to the city of Mackay. The Mackay–Capricorn Islands comprise the section of the Great Barrier Reef known as Capricorn Marine Park, which stretches for 140 km (87 mi) and cuts through the Tropic of Capricorn, Heron Island being the closest point. This is a great area for wildlife: turtles use several of the islands as breeding grounds; seabirds nest here; and humpback whales pass through on their migration to Antarctica each spring—generally between July and October.

LADY ELLIOT ISLAND

Fodor's Choice ★   **Lady Elliot Island.** Lady Elliot Island is a 104-acre coral cay on the southern tip of the Great Barrier Reef, positioned 80 km (50 mi) off the Queensland coast, within easy reach of Bundaberg and Hervey Bay. One of just six island resorts actually on the reef, it's a high-level Marine National Park Zone. Wildlife here easily outnumbers the guests (a maximum of 100 can visit at any one time)—and that reality is underscored by the ammoniacal odor of hundreds of nesting seabirds and, in season, the sounds and sights of them courting, mating, and nesting.

Divers will enjoy the easy access to the reef and the variety of diving sites around Lady Elliot. Fringed on all sides by coral reefs and blessed with a stunning white-sand, coral-strewn shore, this oval isle seems to have been made for diving. There's a busy dive shop and a reef education center with marine-theme exhibits (plus an educational video library—great for rainy days). Inclement weather and choppy waves can lead to canceled dives and washed-out underwater visibility. When the waters are calm, you'll see turtles, morays, sharks, rays, and millions of tropical fish. Many divers visit Lady Elliot specifically to encounter the resident population of manta rays that feed off the coral.

From October to April, Lady Elliot becomes a busy breeding ground for crested and bridled terns, silver gulls, lesser frigate birds, and the rare red-tailed tropic bird. Between November and March, green and loggerhead turtles emerge from the water to lay their eggs; hatching takes place after January. During the hatchling season, staff biologists host guided turtle-watching night hikes. From about July through October, pods of humpback whales are visible from the beachfront restaurant.

Lady Elliot is one of the few islands in the area where camping—albeit modified—is part of the resort, and a back-to-basics theme pervades the accommodations.

GETTING HERE AND AROUND

Lady Elliot is the only coral cay with its own airstrip. Small aircraft generally make the flight from Hervey Bay (40 minutes) or Bundaberg (30 minutes), though pickups can be arranged from as far south in Queensland as Coolangatta, on the Gold Coast (2 hours). You can day-trip to Lady Elliot with Seair Pacific, too. The cost includes scenic flight, buffet lunch, reef walking, glass-bottom boat ride, snorkeling, and island tour.

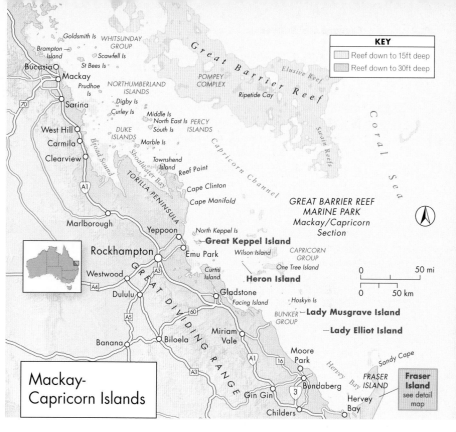

Tours require a minimum of 2 passengers and use planes that can carry up to 12. Strict luggage limits for both hand and checked baggage allow 10 kilograms (22 pounds) per person (for A$20 extra, divers can take an extra 10 kg in dive gear). If you exceed this limit, you can repack at the ticket-counter scale or wave goodbye to the plane.

ESSENTIALS

Airlines Seair Pacific ☎ 07/5599–4509 ⊕ www.seairpacific.com.au.

OUTDOOR ACTIVITIES

At the resort dive shop you can rent equipment and arrange dive courses to more than a dozen excellent sites, including Lighthouse Bommie, home to a 40-strong manta ray colony, and the Blow Hole and Hiro's Cave. Refresher pool dives, a shore snorkeling trip, and guided reef, nature, and historical walks are free for resort guests. Off-boat snorkeling and glass-bottom boat rides are A$30. Boat dives and night dives start at A$50, but all guests are entitled to one complimentary combined tour during their stay. Open-water certification courses cost A$525; "Discover Scuba Diving" short courses are A$150; and referral courses, available to those who've completed the classroom and pool portions of a certification course prior to arrival, are A$400. Diving here is weather-dependent, so plan accordingly if you intend doing a dive course over multiple days. Four-night packages, including seven dives, flights (from

Hervey Bay, Fraser coast), Bundaberg, the Gold and Sunshine coasts, or Brisbane), guest activities, meals, reef tax, and accommodation, start at A$1,281; all-inclusive seven-night packages, with 15 dives, start at A$1,671. Other special deals are available. There is a one-time A$15 environmental management charge for all nonpackage guests.

WHERE TO STAY

For expanded hotel reviews, visit Fodors.com.

$$$$ ⛆ **Lady Elliot Island Eco Resort.** Here you're more like a marine biologist at an island field camp than a tourist enjoying a luxury resort. **Pros:** eco-friendly, proximity to nature; friendly, knowledgable staff. **Cons:** few in-room modern conveniences; limited leisure options for rainy, non-diving days. ✑ *Box 348, Runaway Bay 4216* ☎ *07/5536–3644 (head office), 07/4156–4444 (resort), 1800/072200* ⊕ *www.ladyelliot.com.au* ⤶ *15 reef rooms, 6 garden units, 3 shearwater rooms, 5 suites, 12 tents* ⌂ *In-room: no a/c, no TV. In-hotel: restaurant, bar, pool, beach, water sports, children's programs, laundry facilities, business center* ¦◎¦ *Some meals.*

LADY MUSGRAVE ISLAND

★   **Lady Musgrave Island.** Lady Musgrave Island sits at the southern end of the Great Barrier Reef Marine Park, about 40 km (25 nautical mi) north of Lady Elliot Island and 96 km (53 nautical mi) northeast of Bundaberg. The cay has a 2,945-acre surrounding reef, about one-third of which is a massive yet calm lagoon, a true coral cay of 39.5 acres. Here day-trippers, yachties, divers, and campers converge, and the island has some of the best diving and snorkeling in Queensland. Campers have a chance to view the myriad sea life surrounding this tiny speck of land in the Pacific.

From October through April the island is a bird and turtle rookery, with black noddies, wedge-tailed shearwaters, bridled terns, more timid black-naped and roseate terns, and green and loggerhead turtles. There's also an abundance of flora, including casuarina and pisonia trees.

GETTING HERE AND AROUND

Lady Musgrave Barrier Reef Cruises is the only carrier servicing Lady Musgrave Island. It primarily operates as a day-cruise service, but also ferries campers to the Island. Boats depart daily at 8:30 am from the Town of 1770 marina on Captain Cook Drive, arriving around 75 minutes later (board from 8 am). Baggage is limited to about a cubic foot per person, as space on board is tight. You'll be expected to load most of your gear the evening prior to sailing; on the island, use wheelbarrows to haul it to the campground from the island drop-off point, 250 meters (275 yards) away. If you're carrying a dinghy for getting around the island, it costs an extra A$120 round-trip (hire dinghies from Burnett Boat Hire (☎ *0414/721883)*. Campers must have a DERM permit at time of boarding (A$5.15 per person, per night). If you're camping, you get substantial discounts on boat transfers April through June.

Coral and Lighthouse, Lady Elliot Island

ESSENTIALS

Cruise **Lady Musgrave Barrier Reef Cruises** ☎ *07/4974–9077*
⊕ *www.lmcruises.com.au.*

OUTDOOR ACTIVITIES

WATER **Lady Musgrave Barrier Reef Cruises.** Lady Musgrave Barrier Reef Cruises
SPORTS operates a pontoon in the vast deep-water coral lagoon off Lady Musgrave Island, with an underwater observatory, snorkeling deck, changing rooms, and sheltered seating. Their Lady Musgrave day cruises get
you out to the reef in 75 minutes. Day Cruise passengers can enjoy more
than 5 hours on the reef, including a buffet lunch and a 90-minute stop-
over on the Outer Reef, at a pontoon within a sheltered lagoon where
you can snorkel, view 350 varieties of colorful live coral and 1,300
species of tropical fish year-round from a submersible or glass-bottom
boat, take a guided island walk, see migrating whales in season, or do
some scuba diving or reef fishing before the boat cruises back to the mainland in the afternoon. Reef fishing and scuba diving are extra (for
novice and certified divers, with or without gear). There's a per-person
reef tax of A$10. Cruises depart daily from the Town of 1770 and
include a tropical buffet lunch, morning and afternoon tea, activities on
the reef, and most gear. The day trip, including most extras, is A$175
per person; visitors staying on-island pay A$160 each way—but get to
take the cruise twice. ⊠ *Town of 1770 marina, 535 Captain Cook Dr.,
Town of 1770* ☎ *07/4974–9077* ⊕ *www.lmcruises.com.au* ✉ *A$175
day cruise; A$20 reef fishing; A$50 or $60 for 1 or 2 dives, certified
diver (A$60 or $90 including gear); A$85 introductory lesson and 1
dive with gear* ⊙ *Daily 8–5, except Wed.*

Camping on Lady Musgrave Island

Camping here can be isolated: take first-aid supplies, food, water, and all gear—including, if possible, an emergency marine radio (mobile phone coverage is limited on the cays). Hurricanes (cyclones) may necessitate emergency evacuation in the wet season. In an emergency, tune in to VMR477 Round Hill or VMR488 Bundaberg, 7 am–6 pm on channel 81 marine VHF; or Queensland Police Service, Bundaberg, monitors channel 81 marine VHF day and night. Be aware of local hazards, including large centipedes and bird ticks; and follow DERM guidelines to minimize your impact on island vegetation, nesting seabirds, turtle hatchlings, and the fragile reef. The island is generally closed from after the Australia Day weekend (around January 27) until Easter (March or early April), to minimize impact on emerging turtle hatchlings, breeding seabirds, and sensitive vegetation.

The island, part of the Capricornia Cays National Park, is uninhabited and has only basic facilities (one toilet block and emergency radio equipment) for campers. Commercial tour operators from the Town of 1770 on the mainland have all camping equipment and necessary provisions available for rent. More information on the national park can be obtained from the Gladstone office of the **Queensland Parks and Wildlife Service** (☎ 07 4971–6500) or the **Great Barrier Reef Marine Park Authority** (☎ 07 4750–0700 ⊕ www.gbrmpa.gov. au). The **Environmental Protection Agency** (⊕ www.derm.qld.gov.au) is a good source of information on camping in Capricornia Cays National Park. Contact the Queensland government's 24-hour info line (☎ 13–1304) for camping permits (A$5.15 per person per night). Reservations can be made 11 months in advance. Book early, as school breaks and holidays fill up fast; no more than 40 campers may visit the island at any one time.

HERON ISLAND

Fodor's Choice ★   **Heron Island.** Most resort islands lie well inside the shelter of the distant reef, but Heron Island, some 72 km (45 mi) northeast of the mainland port of Gladstone, is actually part of the reef. The waters off this 18 hectare (20 acre) island are spectacular, teeming with fish and coral, and ideal for snorkeling and scuba diving. The water is generally clearest in June and July and cloudiest during the rainy season, January and February. Heron Island operates on "island time"—an hour ahead of Eastern Standard Time—and at its own leisurely pace. You won't find much in the way of nightlife, as the island's single accommodation accepts a cozy maximum of 250 people—and there are no day-trippers. But these might be reasons why you decide to come here.

GETTING HERE AND AROUND

Once in Gladstone, passengers can board the high-speed, 34-meter *Heron Islander* from the city's marina. The launch makes the two-hour run to Heron Island from Gladstone, on the Queensland coast, for A$100 one-way, departing at 11 am daily and arriving at 2 pm in time for a late lunch. The return boat departs from Heron Island for the mainland at 2:30 island time (1:30 EST). This can be a rough journey: take ginger or anti-nausea medicine ½ hour before departure. A courtesy shuttle bus transfers guests from Gladstone Airport, leaving at 10:15 am daily, and meets all afternoon boats. (Fly to Gladstone from Brisbane, Mackay, Rockhampton, Townsville, and Cairns with Qantas or Virgin Australia.) You can also arrange transfers to and from Gladstone Station; get here on Queensland Rail's fast *Tilt Train* or *Sunlander* from the north or south (⊕ *www.qr.com.au*).

Australian Helicopters makes 30-minute helicopter flights to Heron Island from Gladstone for A$370 one-way, with more services October through April. The baggage restriction is 15 kilograms (33 pounds) per person. Lockup facilities for excess baggage are free (or get it brought over on the daily launch for free). You can charter a helicopter to the island from Gladstone for A$2,191 (maximum 5 adults, 1 infant).

ESSENTIALS

Air Travel Australian Helicopters ⊠ *Gladstone Airport, Aerodrome Rd., Gladstone* ☎ *07/4978–1177* ⊕ *www.austheli.com.*

EXPLORING

Wilson Island. Only guests of the Heron Island Resort can visit uninhabited Wilson Island, a coral cay 15 km (9 mi) north of (and a 45 minute launch trip from) Heron Island. In January and February Wilson Island becomes the breeding ground for roseate terns and green and loggerhead turtles. The island also has its own exclusive, six-suite, premium tented resort, catering to a maximum of 12 guests (and no children under 13), with all meals included in the rate—from A$671 per tent, per night (more nights mean lower rates). Combination packages allow for nights at both Heron and Wilson islands, including meals. The island closes in February to protect nesting birds. ☎ *1300/863–248* ⊕ *www. wilsonisland.com.*

OUTDOOR ACTIVITIES

You can book snorkeling, scuba diving, and fishing excursions as well as turtle-watching tours and sunset cruises through Heron Island Marine Centre and Dive Shop. Snorkeling lessons and refresher dive courses are free. Snorkeling trips are A$45.

DIVING Various diving options include a resort diving course for beginners, including training and one guided dive, for A$165 (subsequent dives, A$130). For certified divers it's A$65 per dive, and just A$45 per dive upward of four dives. Referral dive courses cost A$490. A full-day tour of neighboring islands including up to three dives among pristine reefs is A$360 per person (minimum six divers), including lunch and drinks. A half-day, two-dive trip is A$250. Dive charter packages are also available, and you can get a dive package with a two-day or longer stay, including five dives, for A$275.

For all dives, prebooking's essential, and gear costs you extra. Children under 7 aren't permitted on snorkeling trips, under-10s can't go diving, and under-14s must be accompanied by an adult (and if diving, must be certified).

Scuba diving off Heron Island.

FISHING **Heron Island Marine Centre & Dive Shop.** In addition to diving, snorkeling, and semisubmersible trips, Heron Island Marine Centre & Dive Shop runs three-hour fishing trips and half- and full-day guided reef-fishing charters for up to four passengers, with gear, tackle, and optional stops for snorkeling. Toast the sunset on an hour-long wine-and-cheese cruise or book a charter cruise for up to eight people. Heron Island resort can pack you a sandwich lunch for A$19, or a Mediterranean beach picnic for A$29. ☎ 07/4972–9055 ⊕ *www.heronisland.com* ✉ *A$45 semisubmersible tour, A$130 snorkeling tour, A$40–A$450 per-person scuba diving, A$90 3-hr fishing, A$850 (half-day, up to 4) to A$1,200 (full-day, up to 4, including snorkeling), reef-fishing, A$70 sunset cruise, A$500 (max. 4) or A$700 (max. 8) sunset charter, A$10 stargazing* ⊘ *Daily, hrs. vary, closed Feb.*

SNORKELING AND SEMISUBMERSIBLE Nondivers wanting to explore their underwater environs can take a half-day snorkeling tour of Heron, Wistari, and Bloomfield reefs, or an hour-long, naturalist-guided semisubmersible tour. Interpretive nature walks, guided reef walks, and visits to the island's Marine Research Station are free.

WHERE TO STAY
For expanded hotel reviews, visit Fodors.com.

$$$ 🛏 **Heron Island Resort.** Set among palm trees and connected by sand paths, this secluded, eco-certified resort offers six accommodation types, from the deluxe Beach House with private outdoor shower and beach boardwalk to the comparatively compact, garden-level Turtle Rooms. **Pros:** lots of activities; eco-friendly; under-12s stay and eat free. **Cons:** inconsistent mobile phone coverage; public dial-up Internet only; no TVs (though these could be pluses too). ⌂ *Heron Island Resort, via*

Gladstone, Gladstone 4680 ☎ 1300/863–248 ⊕ www.heronisland.com ⬳ 32 rooms, 76 suites, 1 house ⚿ In-room: no a/c, Internet. In-hotel: restaurant, bar, pool, tennis court, spa, beach, water sports, children's programs, laundry facilities ꙮ Multiple meal plans.

GREAT KEPPEL ISLAND

Great Keppel Island. Although Great Keppel is large, at 8 km (5 mi) by 11 km (7 mi), it lies 40 km (25 mi) from the Great Barrier Reef, which makes for a long trip from the mainland. There's lots to do, with walking trails, 17 stunning safe swimming beaches, excellent coral gardens in many sheltered coves, and dozens of beach and water-sports activities available. A refurbished underwater observatory at nearby Middle Island lets you stay dry while viewing the local marine life from six meters below the ocean surface. A confiscated Taiwanese fishing boat has been deliberately sunk alongside the observatory to shelter tropical fish. An abundance of bushwalking tracks allows visitors to explore the island's interior and access secluded beaches.

GETTING HERE AND AROUND

AIR TRAVEL Peace Aviation can arrange the scenic 20-minute flight to the island, which has its own airstrip, from Rockhampton, on request. One to three people can charter a one-way flight for A$275 (or two trips A$500); four to six people for A$385 (two trips A$700) including GST.

Low-cost carrier **Virgin Australia** flies to Rockhampton from Brisbane, with connections to all major Australian cities. **Qantas** has direct flights to Rockhampton from Brisbane, Townsville, and Mackay, connecting to other capitals.

BOAT AND FERRY TRAVEL Freedom Fast Cats ferries transfer guests to the island from Pier 1 at Rosslyn Bay Harbour, near Yeppoon (across the bay from the marina). Departures are mid-morning (check schedules) daily, with an additional departure Friday afternoon. Return trips back to the mainland Tuesday to Sunday early- to mid-afternoon, and an additional departure Friday morning. The cost is A$49 per person, round-trip. Depending on the time of your flight arrival, you may need to stay overnight in Rockhampton or Yeppoon before and after your island stay.

Keppel Bay Marina also runs day cruises to secluded coves and beaches: choose a short glass-bottom-boat coral-viewing and fish-feeding cruise for A$23, a scenic winter cruise for A$69, or two full-day cruises: one includes a 1½-hour sail and optional snorkeling, kayaking, fishing, and coral-viewing, on *Grace*, plus refreshments and a buffet lunch, including local prawns, for A$115 per person, including reef tax and gear; a similar cruise with boom-netting is A$130.

ESSENTIALS

Airlines Peace Aviation ☎ 07/4927–4355, 0429/616758 ⊕ www.peaceaviation.com.au. **Virgin Australia** ☎ 13–6789 ⊕ www.virginaustralia.com. **Qantas** ☎ 13–1313 ⊕ www.qantas.com.au.

Ferries Freedom Fast Cats ☎ 07/4933–6888 ⊕ www.freedomfastcats.com. **Keppel Bay Marina** ☎ 07/4933–6244, 1800/336–244 ⊕ www.keppelbaymarina.com.au.

OUTDOOR ACTIVITIES

WATER SPORTS **The Watersports Activities Hut.** The Watersports Activities Hut at Great Keppel Island Holiday Village offers guided kayak and motorized canoe trips, and water taxi drop-offs to and pickups from surrounding beaches and islands. They also hire out water-sports equipment, including kayaks and catamarans, and offer banana and tube rides. ⊠ *Fisherman's Beach, Great Keppel Island* ⊕ *www.gkiholidayvillage. com.au* ☎ *From A$35* ☉ *Daily.*

WHERE TO STAY

For expanded hotel reviews, visit Fodors.com.

¢ **Great Keppel Island Holiday Village.** In the welcome shade of gum trees, this is a modest, quiet alternative for travelers looking to get back to basics without a party scene. **Pros:** tranquillity; good value; rates drop with longer stays. **Cons:** patchy mobile phone coverage (OK for Telstra and Optus phones), no Internet, no meals provided. ⊠ *Community Mailbag* ☎ *07/4939–8655, 1800/537–735* ⊕ *www.gkiholidayvillage. com.au* 📞 *4 rooms, 2 houses, 2 cabins, 9 tents* ⚐ *In-room: no a/c, kitchen, no TV. In-hotel: beach, water sports, laundry facilities.*

FRASER ISLAND

Some 200 km (125 mi) north of Brisbane, Fraser Island, at 1,014 square km (391 square mi), is the largest of Queensland's islands and the most unusual. Originally known as K'gari to the local Butchulla Aboriginal people, the island was later named after Eliza Fraser, who in 1836 was shipwrecked here and lived with local Aborigines for several weeks.

Fraser is the world's largest sand island—instead of coral reefs and coconut palms, it has wildflower-dotted meadows, 100-plus freshwater lakes, dense, tall stands of rain forest, towering dunes, and sculpted, multicolor sand cliffs, up to 40,000 migratory shorebirds, and rare and endangered species including dugongs, turtles, Illidge's ant-blue butterfly, and eastern curlews—a lineup that won the island a place on UNESCO's World Heritage list.

The surf fishing is legendary, and humpback whales and their calves winter in Hervey Bay between May and September. The island also has Aboriginal sites dating back more than a millennium.

Hervey Bay is the name given to the expanse of water between Fraser Island and the Queensland coast, and to four nearby coastal towns—Urangan, Pialba, Scarness, and Torquay—that have merged into a single settlement. Hervey Bay and Rainbow Beach are the main jumping-off points for offshore excursions. (Maps and road signs usually refer to individual town names.)

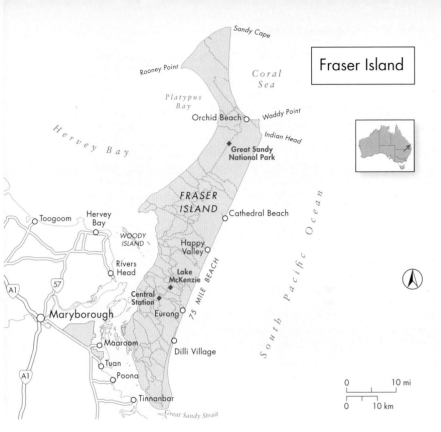

Fraser Island

GETTING HERE AND AROUND

AIR TRAVEL   Several direct air services on Jetstar, Qantas, and Virgin Australia connect Sydney and Fraser Coast (Hervey Bay) Airport. Wide Bay Shuttle buses link the airport to Urangan (A$8), meeting all flights.

BOAT AND FERRY TRAVEL   Numerous vehicular ferries service Fraser Island from Rainbow Beach and Hervey Bay. The *Rainbow Venture* and *Fraser Explorer* ferries run continuously 6 am–5:30 pm between Inskip Point, near Rainbow Beach, and Hook Point at the island's southern end.

The *Fraser Venture* barge makes the half-hour trip between River Heads, 20 minutes' drive south of Hervey Bay, and Wanggoolba Creek, opposite Eurong Bay Resort on the island's west coast, three times a day. The *Fraser Dawn* ferry departs from Urangan Boat Harbour for the 55-minute journey to Fraser Island's Moon Point twice a day. The thrice-daily Kingfisher vehicle barge connects River Heads with Kingfisher Bay Resort in 45 minutes. Fares for these services are interchangeable; tickets must be prebooked.

Kingfisher Bay also runs passenger catamarans from Urangan marina to Kingfisher Bay Resort on Fraser Island four times daily. The trip takes 45 minutes.

Manta Ray's two barges go between Inskip Point and Hook Point, making up to 40 round-trips daily, on demand, from 6:30 am to 5:30 pm.

It's a short trip, so if you miss one barge the next will be along soon. Buy tickets online (recommended) or as you board.

CAR AND BUGGY TRAVEL Fraser's east coast favors two Australian passions: beaches and vehicles. Unrestricted access has made this coast a giant sandbox for four-wheel-drive vehicles, busiest in school-holiday periods.

The southernmost tip of Fraser Island is just more than 200 km (125 mi) north of Brisbane. The simplest access is via barge from Rainbow

GETTING HELP

Fraser Island does not have a resident doctor. Emergency medical assistance can be obtained at the ranger stations in Eurong, Waddy Point, and Dundubara, but these have variable hours—if no answer, phone the base station at Nambour on the mainland. Kingfisher Bay Resort has first-aid facilities and resident nursing staff.

Beach or Hervey Bay, 90 km (56 mi) farther north. For Rainbow Beach, take the Bruce Highway toward Gympie, then follow signs to Rainbow Beach. For Hervey Bay, head to Maryborough, then follow signs to Urangan.

Every vehicle entering the island by barge from the mainland must have a one-month Vehicle Access Permit (A$39.35). To obtain these and island camping permits (A$5 per person, per night), contact DERM.

You can rent four-wheel-drive vehicles at Kingfisher Bay Resort and Village for upward of A$275 a day, or from Budget car rentals at Urangan on the mainland for considerably less.

Four-wheel-drive rentals may be cheaper on the mainland, but factoring in the ferry ticket makes rental on-island a viable option. Most commodities, including gas, are pricier on-island.

Wet weather and sandy surfaces can make island driving challenging and hazardous. Consult DERMs Web site for detailed information on safe driving and local hazards. Basic mechanical assistance and tow-truck services are available from Eurong (☎ 07/4127–9449). Orchid Beach has emergency towing only. If you can't get the mechanical assistance you need, phone Eurong Police.

If you prefer your wilderness *sans* dune-buggying, head for the unspoiled interior of the island, where they're not allowed. They're a necessity everywhere else, unless you're a fit walker or cyclist or can ride a motorcycle pretty well.

ESSENTIALS

Airport Fraser Coast (Hervey Bay) Airport ⌧ *Don Adams Dr., Hervey Bay* ☎ *07/4194–8100* ⊕ *www.frasercoastairport.com.au.*

Boat and Ferry Contacts Fraser Island Barges (*Fraser Dawn, Fraser Venture, Rainbow Venture,* and *Fraser Explorer*) ☎ *07/4194–9300, 1800/227–437* ⊕ *www.fraserislandferry.com.au.* Kingfisher Bay Ferry & Vehicle Barge ☎ *1800/072–555* ⊕ *www.kingfisherbay.com.* Manta Ray ☎ *0418/872–599, 07/5486–3935* ⊕ *www.fraserislandbarge.com.au.*

Car Rental Budget Car Rental ☎ *07/4124–4064* ⊕ *www.budget.com.au.* Fraser Island Wilderness Co. Tour Desk ☎ *1800/249–122*

⊕ *www.fraserexplorertours.com.au.* **Kingfisher Bay Resort and Village**
☎ *07/4194–9300, 1800/072–555* ⊕ *www.kingfisherbay.com.*

Shuttle Bundaberg and Wide Bay Shuttle Service ☎ *0421/413–446*
⊕ *www.bundabergshuttleservice.com.au.*

Tours Air Fraser Island/OzHorizons ☎ *07/4125–3600, 07/4214–9943*
⊕ *www.ozhorizons.com.au.* **Kingfisher Bay Resort** ☎ *1800/072–555* ⊕ *www.*
kingfisherbay.com.

Vehicle Permits Environmental Protection Agency (EPA) ☎ *1300/130–372*
info, 13–7468 permits ⊕ *www.epa.qld.gov.au.*

Visitor Information Hervey Bay Tourist & Visitors Information Centre
✉ *401 The Esplanade, Hervey Bay* ☎ *07/4124–4050, 1800/649–926*
⊕ *www.herveybaytouristinfo.com.au.*

EXPLORING

Note that swimming in the ocean off the island is not recommended
because of the rough conditions and sharks that hunt close to shore.
Stick to the inland lakes. For more detail, head to ⊕ *www.derm.qld.gov.*

Highlights of a drive along the east coast, which is known as Seventy-
Five Mile Beach for its sheer distance, include **Eli Creek**, a great freshwater swimming hole. North of this popular spot lies the rusting hulk
of the *Maheno*, half buried in the sand, a roost for seagulls and a
prime hunting ground for anglers when the tailor are running. Once a
luxury passenger steamship that operated between Australia and New
Zealand (and served as a hospital ship during World War I), it was
wrecked during a cyclone in 1935 as it was being towed to Japan to be
sold for scrap metal. North of the wreck are the **Pinnacles**—dramatic,
deep-red cliff formations. About 20 km (12 mi) south of Eli Creek, and
surrounded by massive sand-blow (or dune), is **Lake Wabby,** the deepest
of the island's lakes.

Fraser Island, Great Sandy National Park. Fraser Island, Great Sandy
National Park covers the top third of the island. Beaches around Indian
Head are known for their shell middens—shell heaps that were left
behind after Aboriginal feasting. The head's name is another kind of
relic: Captain James Cook saw Aborigines standing on the headland
as he sailed past, and he therefore named the area after inhabitants he
believed to be "Indians." Farther north, past Waddy Point, is one of
Fraser Island's most magnificent variations on sand: wind and time
have created enormous dunes. Nearby at Orchid Beach are a series of
bubbling craters known as the Champagne Pools. ☎ *1300/130–372*
⊕ *www.derm.qld.gov.au/fraser.*

Wanggoolba Creek. A boardwalk heads south from Central Station to
Wanggoolba Creek, a favorite spot for photographers. The little stream
snakes through a green palm forest, trickling over a bed of white sand
between clumps of rare angiopteris fern. The 1 km (½ mi) circuit takes
30 minutes to an hour.

OUTDOOR ACTIVITIES

FISHING   **Offshore, Fraser Island.** All freshwater fish are protected on Fraser Island, so you can't fish in lakes or streams, but just offshore is one of Australia's richest, most diverse fishing areas, with whiting, flathead, trevally, red emperor, snapper, sea perch, coronation trout, cod, and, in summer, mackerel, cobia, amberjack, and more. This is partly due to the diversity of habitat; choose between estuary, surf beach, reef, sport, and game fishing. On reef-fishing trips dolphins are commonly sighted, as are whales in season.

When angling off Fraser Island beaches and jetties, follow EPA guidelines. To discourage dingoes and other undesireable visitors, clean fish away from campsites and dispose of scraps carefully (bury fish scraps at least 30 cm, about a foot, below the tide line). Bag and size limits apply to some species: for details, go to ⊕ *www.dpi.qld.gov.au.*

Hervey Bay Fishing Charters. Contact Hervey Bay Fishing Charters to set up a fishing trip off Fraser Island. ✉ *15 Tristania Cr., Urangan* ☎ *07/4125–3958* ⊕ *www.herveybayfishingcharters.com.au.*

HIKING   **Central Station.** The island's excellent network of walking trails converges at Central Station, a former logging camp at the center of the island. Services here are limited to a map board, parking lot, and campground. It's a promising place for spotting dingoes. Comparative isolation has meant that Fraser Island's dingoes are the most purebred in Australia. They're also wild animals, so remember: don't feed them, watch from a distance, don't walk alone after dark, and keep a close eye on children, especially between late afternoon and early morning. Dingo alerts are in force around Eurong and Happy Valley.

Most of the island's well-marked trails are sandy tracks. Guides advise wearing sturdy shoes, wearing sunscreen, and carrying first-aid supplies and drinking water on all walks.

Pile Valley. One trail from Central Station leads through rain forest—growing, incredibly enough, straight out of the sand—to Pile Valley, which has a stand of giant satinay trees. Allow two hours to walk this 4½-km (2¼-mi) circuit.

SWIMMING   **Lake McKenzie.** The center of Fraser Island is a quiet, natural garden of paperbark swamps, giant satinay and brush box forests, wildflower heaths, and 40 freshwater lakes. The spectacularly clear Lake McKenzie, ringed by a beach of incandescent white sand, is arguably the most stunning of the lakes and is the perfect place for a refreshing swim.

WHERE TO STAY

For expanded hotel reviews, visit Fodors.com.

$ 🏠 **Eurong Beach Resort.** This east-coast resort has the best of Fraser Island at its doorstep. **Pros:** on-site general store; great location. **Cons:** spotty mobile phone reception; slow Internet. ✉ *75 Mile Beach* ⌖ *Box 7332, Hervey Bay 4655* ☎ *07/4127–9122, 1800/111808* ⊕ *www.eurong.com. au* ⇆ *124 rooms, including 16 apartments* ⌂ *In-room: no a/c, kitchen. In-hotel: restaurant, bar, pool, tennis court, beach, laundry facilities, business center, parking.*

CLOSE UP

Camping on Fraser Island

You can pitch a tent anywhere you don't see a "no camping" sign; there are four main public campgrounds—Central Station, Dundubara, and two at Waddy Point—that require you to book in advance. These campgrounds have fenced sites (advised if you have kids under 14), toilet blocks, drinking water, hot showers (some coin-operated), gas grills, phones, and other amenities. There are also smaller designated camping areas along Fraser Island's Great Walk, and a number of established beach campsites, all run by Queensland Parks and Wildlife Service. They have toilet blocks, picnic tables, and walking trails. Most lack drinking water, so bring plenty with you. Because the entire island is a World Heritage site, permits for camping (A$5 per person, per night) are required, and there's a maximum stay of 22 nights.

Dilli Village Campground. The University of the Sunshine Coast runs Dilli Village Campground, just south of Eurong, where a 2-bedroom cabin for up to five is A$100, a 4-person bunkhouse is A$40, and camping is A$10 per night. ☎ 07/4127–9130 ⊕ www.dillivillage.com.au.

Frasers at Cathedral Beach. The island's only official private campground, Frasers at Cathedral Beach, 10 km (6 mi) north of Eurong, costs A$29–A$49 per night. Cabins with two and three bedrooms are A$135–A$220 nightly, depending on the season. Booking well ahead is essential. ☎ 07/4127–9177, 1800/444–234 ⊕ www.frasers-cathedral-beach.qld.big4.com.au.

The Queensland Parks and Wildlife Service manages the island, and maintains ranger bases at Dundubara, Eurong, and Waddy Point.

7

$$
☾
Fodor's Choice
★

☷ **Kingfisher Bay Resort and Village.** This stylish, high-tech marriage of glass, stainless steel, dark timber, and corrugated iron nestles in tree-covered dunes on the island's west coast. **Pros:** terrific facilities and activities; eco-friendly; food is a cut above. **Cons:** west-coast beaches unsuitable for 4WD vehicles. ⊠ *North White Cliffs, 75 Mile Beach ⌖ PMB 1, Urangan 4655* ☎ *07/4194–9300, 1800/072–555* ⊕ *www.kingfisherbay.com* ↝ *152 rooms, 109 villas, 184 beds in lodges (for 18–35s)* ⌂ *In-room: kitchen, Internet. In-hotel: restaurant, bar, pool, tennis court, spa, beach, water sports, children's programs, laundry facilities, business center.*

The Great Barrier Reef

INCLUDING CAIRNS AND THE NORTH COAST

WORD OF MOUTH

"We took an all day excursion to the outer reef. The highlights: snorkeling with countless fish swimming around us, often just inches from our masks . . . and seeing two turtles."

—GregY2

WELCOME TO GREAT BARRIER REEF

TOP REASONS TO GO

★ **Cultural Immersion:** The Kuku Yalanji have lived in the area stretching roughly from Port Douglas to Cookdown for thousands of years. A highlight of visiting northern Queensland is experiencing this unique landscape from their perspective. Try to get on a multiday tour to see some of the region's most spiritual places.

★ **Reef Explorations:** There are thousands of spectacular dive sites scattered along the coral spine of the Great Barrier Reef. Some draw hundreds of divers and snorkelers a day with clouds of fish and coral formations.

★ **Wildlife Watching:** Flora and fauna on the islands themselves can be fascinating: rain forests, hills and rocky areas, and postcard-perfect beaches might be home to everything from turtles, birds, and lizards to echidnas and bandicoots. On the mainland, Daintree National Park is home to the endangered southern cassouary.

1 Cairns. A laid-back tropical tourist hub built around a busy marina and swimming lagoon, Cairns bristles with hotels, tour agencies, dive-cruise boats, and travelers en route to the rain forest and reef. It has some fine retail precincts and markets, plus a waterfront casino.

2 North of Cairns. The pristine coastline north of Cairns is punctuated by charming villages and tourist towns, including Palm Cove, with its European Riviera ambience, and bustling Port Douglas, with its busy marina, sprawling resorts, and laid-back café scene. North of the Daintree River, World Heritage–listed wilderness extends to Cape Tribulation and beyond; here you'll find few services but some fantastic, eco-friendly rain-forest retreats.

3 Whitsundays/Airlie Beach. The glorious Whitsunday Islands, just off the mid-north-Queensland coast, lure holidaymakers with world-class water sports, sheltered yacht anchorages, and resorts catering to every taste. Airlie Beach, the closest mainland town, buzzes with backpackers, who flock to its manmade lagoon, markets, bars, and budget digs. Well-heeled travelers might prefer the boutique retreats and resorts hugging the hillsides behind the main drag.

4 North Coast islands. The eco-conscious resorts on Hinchinbrook and Orpheus islands, off Cardwell and Ingham, respectively, are tailored to nature-loving travelers, while Bedarra Island's upmarket retreat attracts honeymooners and sunbathers. Lizard and Fitzroy islands, off Cairns, offer ready access to world-class dive and game-fishing sites.

5 Townsville and Magnetic Island. Regional city Townsville has gracious heritage buildings, excellent museums and marine centers, and a well-maintained waterfront with a manmade swimming lagoon. Offshore, Magnetic Island is a popular holiday spot, with high-end and budget accommodation and an array of aquatic activities, including sea kayaking and scuba diving.

GETTING ORIENTED

A map linking all of northern Queensland's coastal ports and offshore resorts from the Whitsundays to as far north as Lizard Island would look like a lace-up boot 1,600 km (1,000 mi) long. However, you'd only see less than half the reef, which extends south as far as Lady Elliot Island and as far north as the roadless wilderness of Cape York and the shores of Papua New Guinea. If you're visiting the reef only briefly, it's easiest and most economical to day-trip from the mainland. Some reef-island resorts are accessible by boat; many others can be reached only by plane, and both airfare and lodging rates can be expensive. Day trips depart from major coastal cities including Cairns, Port Douglas, Townsville, and Airlie Beach. Some island resorts, such as Hamilton, let you visit and use their facilities for the day—then return you to the mainland to continue your travels.

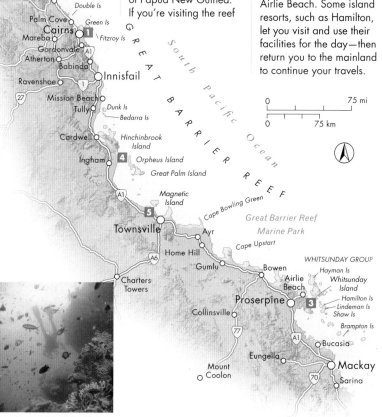

8

Cape Melville
Cape Melville Nat'l Park
HOWICK GROUP
Lizard Island
Jack River Nat'l Park
Cape Flattery
TURTLE GROUP
Cape Bedford
Lakefield National Park
Cooktown
Laura
Lakeland
Great Barrier Reef Marine Park
Cape Tribulation
Daintree
Mossman
Port Douglas
Double Is
Palm Cove
Green Is
Cairns
Fitzroy Is
Mareeba
Gordonvale
Atherton
Babinda
Innisfail
Ravenshoe
Mission Beach
Dunk Is
Tully
Bedarra Is
Cardwell
Hinchinbrook Island
Ingham
Orpheus Island
Great Palm Island
Magnetic Island
Townsville
Ayr
Cape Bowling Green
Cape Upstart
Home Hill
Great Barrier Reef Marine Park
Gumlu
Bowen
WHITSUNDAY GROUP
Airlie Beach
Hayman Is
Whitsunday Island
Charters Towers
Proserpine
Hamilton Is
Lindeman Is
Shaw Is
Collinsville
Brampton Is
Bucasia
Eungella
Mount Coolon
Mackay
Sarina

GREAT BARRIER REEF

South Pacific Ocean

0 ——— 75 mi
0 ——— 75 km

SAILING THE WHITSUNDAY ISLANDS

The Whitsundays, 74 islands and dozens of islets scattered off Queensland's central coast off Airlie Beach, are among yachties' and beach-lovers' favorite holiday destinations— and with good reason.

The Whitsunday Islands, protected from Coral Sea swells by sheltering reefs and cooled by trade winds, offer an abundance of yacht anchorages in close proximity, making this ideal cruising territory. The aquamarine waters shimmer and sparkle—a light-scattering effect that results when fine sediment run-off from river systems is stirred up by the 3- to 5-meter tides that sweep the coast.

Island resorts offer safe moorings for passing yachts and an array of water sports and facilities. Farther out, on the Barrier Reef, you'll find fine snorkeling, diving and fishing sites. Most Whitsunday islands are unspoiled national parks; just a few—Hayman, Hamilton, Daydream, South Molle, South Long and Lindeman—have resorts.

WHEN TO GO

With a climate moderated by cooling trade winds, the Whitsundays are balmy year-round, though summer days can sometimes exceed 100 degrees Fahrenheit. Over winter (June–August) it's warm, clear, and sunny by day and cool—even chilly—at night. Steer clear of summer holidays to avoid hordes of local families who, despite often wet and stormy weather, flock here December to February. Spring and fall weather can be perfect, and these seasons are often the quietest, if you avoid school and Easter holidays. Migrating southern right and humpback whales traverse these waters between July and September.

WHERE CAN I FIND . . .

Underwater adventure? Most Whitsundays resorts have dedicated dive shops offering scuba and snorkeling lessons and gear hire; all either run or can organize day trips to nearby dive and snorkeling spots. Highlights include Heart Reef and vast Knuckle Reef Lagoon, where a purpose-built pontoon floats in sheltered waters teeming with tropical fish, turtles, and rays. Not keen to get wet? Take a semi-submersible coral-viewing tour, guided reef walk, or scenic heli-flight.

Luxury? At Qualia, Hamilton Island's most lavish accommodation, sleek suites have infinity pools and alfresco areas, artfully lit after dark, and food and wine are brought in from Hamilton's best restaurants. Lizard Island Resort serves up gourmet meals and exclusive accommodations, while Paradise Bay Island Eco-Resort pampers its select group of guests with top-quality, all-natural furnishings and fabrics, Molton Brown toiletries, and cruises on the resort's own sailing cat. Recently revamped Hayman Resort, a magnificent sprawl of public areas and opulent suites, is solid enough to withstand a Category 5 cyclone and luxurious enough to satisfy the fussiest visitor, with a 1:1 staff-to-guest ratio. Here your needs are more than met: they're spookily anticipated.

Family-friendliness? Club Med Lindeman Island's jam-packed sports and activities program offers dozens of aquatic and land-based sports, most included in rates. Daydream and Hamilton islands have dedicated kids' clubs, playgrounds, and myriad kid-at-heart features and activities. At Fitroy Island Resort, children's activity programs mean parents can relax or join in the fun, while nature-based activities on Lizard Island are great for older kids.

TOP REASONS TO GO

Aquatic playground
This is a snorkelers' and divers' paradise and one of the world's top sailing and cruising areas. It's also great for kayaking, windsurfing, paragliding, and sailboarding—and most resorts include non-motorized water sports in their rates.

Tropical paradise
Enjoy a mild climate and warm, clear waters whatever the season, plus some of the most beautiful fine-white-sand beaches in the world.

Gourmet destination
Many Whitsunday island resorts now offer cuisine to rival that of high-end city establishments. Food runs the gamut from traditional four-star gourmet fare to fresh, regional food presented with inventive, site-specific twists.

Resort variety
You can easily divide your time between luxurious, leisurely resorts (such as Hayman, Lizard Island Resort, or Paradise Bay Eco-Resort on South Long Island) and a gregarious, activity-oriented isle (such as Hamilton, Lindeman, or Daydream).

8

OUTBACK ADVENTURES

Queensland's Outback is a vast and exhilarating place filled with real-life Crocodile Dundee types. Everyone lives in very isolated townships, so locals are used to relying on each other.

Heading west from Townsville along the Flinders Highway (aka Overlanders Highway), stop at once-prosperous gold-mining town **Charters Towers**—a beautiful city with 60 or so historically significant buildings. Farther west is Hughenden, showcasing significant ancient fossils found in the region. Continue via Cloncurry to Mount Isa, a surprisingly multicultural city of around 23,000 people, where you'll find the sprawling Xstrata Mount Isa Mines; Australia's deepest mine (at 6,234 feet), it's one of the world's largest producers of copper, zinc, silver, and lead. The drive takes about six days, one-way.

SAFETY FIRST

When traveling any of these routes by car, take practical precautions. Use a four-wheel-drive vehicle—many roads in the region are unpaved and become slippery after it rains. Always carry spare water, a first-aid kit, a good local map, and sufficient fuel to get to the next town (which may mean carrying spare gas cans). If you're traveling into remote areas, advise local police or other responsible persons of your travel plans and report back to them when you return. If you have an on-road emergency, call 000 from the nearest public phone (or 112 from mobile phones) to reach an ambulance or the police.

OVERLANDERS HIGHWAY TOP STOPS

Flinders Discovery Centre. In Hughenden, don't miss meeting "Hughie," a Muttaburrasaurus skeleton on display at Flinders Discovery Centre, alongside natural history, gem, and fossil exhibits, a multimedia sheep-shearing installation, and a shop with tour brochures, maps, and souvenirs. This is a great place for kids, young and old. ⊠ *37 Gray St., Hughenden* ☎ *07/4741–1021* ⊕ *www.hughenden.com* 🎫 *A$3.50* 🕙 *Daily 9–5 (Feb–Nov), 10–4 (Dec–Jan).*

McKinlay. If you're a fan of the movie *Crocodile Dundee*, head south from Cloncurry via Route 66 to McKinlay. This hamlet's claim to fame is **Walkabout Creek Hotel**. If you're a fan of the movie *Crocodile Dundee*, head south from Cloncurry via Route 66 to McKinlay. This hamlet's claim to fame is Walkabout Creek Hotel, which featured in the movie. ⊠ *Middleton St. at Kirby St., McKinlay* ☎ *07/4746–8424*

Boodjamulla (Lawn Hill) National Park. Mount Isa is a good jumping-off point for exploring the spring-fed rivers and gorges of **Boodjamulla (Lawn Hill) National Park**, where you can canoe amid freshwater crocodiles and camp in the wilderness for A$5.15 per person, per night (BYO tents, gear, and water). ☎ *13–7468 permits* ⊕ *www.derm.qld.gov.au.*

Mount Isa. The southern hemisphere's biggest rodeo takes place in Mount Isa each year in late July or August. ☎ *07/4743–2706* ⊕ *www.isarodeo.com.au.*

Outback at Isa. In addition to the rodeo at Mount Isa, another must-see in the region is Outback at Isa, an interpretive center housing fossil exhibits from the UNESCO World Heritage-listed Riversleigh Fossil Fields some 300 km (186 mi) away. Here you can take the miner-guided Hard Times Mine underground tour experience, where you'll dress in a hard hat, orange coveralls, and headlamp, and tour a "mock-up" mine 49½ feet below the surface. ⊠ *19 Marion St., Mount Isa* ☎ *1300/659660, 07/4749–1555* ⊕ *www.outbackatisa.com.au* 🎫 *Mine and all museums A$55, mine only A$45* 🕙 *Daily 8:30–5.*

WHY OVERLANDER?

The Overlander's Highway stretch of the Flinders Highway is a great drive for experiencing a small slice of the Australian Outback, but how did it come to be, exactly? The name gives it away; "overlander" is a term used to refer to someone who helps move cattle from one place to another, and this route used to be used for that purpose. The word has found its way into general usage to describe other distance-traversing feats; a small sampling includes *Overland* magazine which focuses on 4WD vehicles, the town of Overlander in Western Australia, the *Overland* train that runs between Adelaide and Melbourne, and of course this great drive.

8

OUTDOOR ADVENTURES IN DAINTREE

Cape Tribulation, Daintree National Park is an ecological wonderland. Here you can see several of the world's most ancient plants and some of Australia's rarest creatures, protected by the Daintree's traditional owners, the Eastern Kuku Yalanji, for thousands of years.

The park extends over approximately 22,000 acres, although the entire Wet Tropics region—which stretches from Townsville to Cooktown and covers 1,200 square km (463 square mi)—was declared a UNESCO World Heritage site in 1988. Within it, experts have identified several species of angiosperms, the most primitive flowering plants in existence, many of which are found nowhere else on the planet.

WHEN TO GO

Clear, sunny days, comfortably cool nights, no stingers in the ocean and mud-free rain forest and mangrove trails: "the Dry" season is the most pleasant time to visit.

"The Wet"—roughly November through April—can be wonderful, too: foliage is lush and green; buds turn to hothouse blooms. Drawbacks include high humidity, slippery tracks, and leeches and mosquitoes.

Spring and late fall can be a good compromise: the weather—and the water—are typically warm and clear, but accommodations, restaurants and activities are less heavily booked than in the dry season.

A SACRED SITE

With diverse plant and animal life, abundant fresh water, and tracts of fertile coastal lowland, the Daintree rain forest is rich terrain for the resourceful. Its traditional custodians are the Eastern Kuku Yalanji, a peaceable people who've been coexisting with and subsisting on the forest's abundant flora and fauna for tens of thousands of years Their tribal lands stretch north almost as far as Cooktown, south as far as Mossman and west to the Palmer River, with the Kuku Yalanji traveling seasonally throughout the region.

Designating five rather than four seasons in a year, the Eastern Kuku Yalanji used changes in weather and growth cycles to guide hunting and foraging expeditions into the rain forest: when the *jun jun* (blue ginger) came into fruit, they'd catch *diwan* (Australian brush-turkey); when *jilngan* (mat grass) flowered, they'd collect *jarruka* (orange-footed scrubfowl) eggs; and year-round, they'd track tree-dwelling animals—*yawa* (possum), *kambi* (flying fox), and *murral* (tree kangaroo). Even today, members of the Kuku Yalanji can tell you which local plants can be eaten, used as medicines, and made into utensils, weapons, and shelter.

The Daintree's indigenous inhabitants believe many of the area's natural sites have spiritual significance, attributing particular power to Wundu (Thornton Peak), Manjal Dimbi (Mount Demi), Wurrmbu (The Bluff), and Kulki (Cape Tribulation). Dozens of spots in the rain forest—waterfalls, crags, peaks and creeks—are deemed by the Kuku Yalanji to have spiritual, healing or regenerative powers. Take a walk with one of the area's traditional custodians to get an intimate, intriguing perspective on this extraordinary terrain.

Various indigenous-guided tours and experiences in the Daintree area focus on bush tucker and medicines, wildlife and hunting techniques, culture, history, and ritual. A waterhole just behind Daintree Eco Lodge & Spa is deemed a site of special significance for women: a dip in its healing waters is a female-only ritual.

TOP REASONS TO GO

Animals. Watch for the rare Bennett's tree kangaroo, believed to have evolved from possums; the endangered, spotted-tailed quoll, a marsupial carnivore; a giant white-tailed rat (prone to raiding campsites); and the Daintree River ringtail possum, found only around Thornton Peak and the upper reaches of the Daintree and Mossman rivers.

Birds. Daintree National Park shelters hundreds of bird species: azure kingfishers swoop on crabs in the creeks, white-rumped swiftlets dart above the canopy. The pied imperial pigeon flies south from Papua New Guinea to breed here—as does the glorious buff-breasted paradise kingfisher, distinguished by its orange underbelly, blue wings, and long white tail. Year-round, you'll see orange-footed scrubfowl foraging or building gigantic leaf-litter nest-mounds. If you're very lucky, you might even spot the six-foot-tall, flightless southern cassowary.

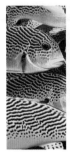

Updated by
Merran White

A maze of 3,000 individual reefs and 900 islands stretching for 2,600 km (1,616 mi), the Great Barrier Reef is one of the world's most spectacular natural attractions, and one of which Australia is extremely proud. Known as Australia's "Blue Outback," the reef was established as a marine park in 1975, and is a collective haven for thousands of species of sea life as well as turtles and birds.

In 1981 the United Nations designated the Great Barrier Reef a World Heritage Site. In 2004 strict legislation was enacted prohibiting fishing along most of the reef—a further attempt to protect the underwater treasures of this vast, delicate ecosystem. Any visitor over the age of four must pay an A$5.50 Environmental Management Charge ("reef tax") to support ongoing efforts to preserve the reef.

The Great Barrier Reef system began to form approximately 6,000–7,000 years ago, say marine scientists. It's comprised of individual reefs and islands, which lie to the east of the Coral Sea and extend south into the Pacific Ocean. Most of the reef is about 65 km (40 mi) off the Queensland coast, although some parts extend as far as 300 km (186 mi) offshore. Altogether, it covers an area bigger than Great Britain, forming the largest living feature on Earth and the only one visible from space.

Most visitors explore this section of Australia from one of the dozen-plus resorts strung along the coasts of islands in the southern half of the marine park; most of them in or north of the Whitsunday Islands group. Although most Barrier Reef islands are closer to the mainland than they are to the spectacular outer reef, all island resorts offer (or can organize) boat excursions to various outer-reef sites. Live-aboard dive boats ply remote sections of the northern reef and Coral Sea atolls, exploring large cartographic blank spots that on maritime charts simply read, in bold purple lettering, "Area unsurveyed."

PLANNING

WHEN TO GO

The majority of the Barrier Reef islands lie north of the tropic of Capricorn and have a distinctly monsoonal climate. In the hot, wet season (roughly December–April), expect tropical downpours that can limit outdoor activities and mar underwater visibility for days.

The warm days, clear skies, and pleasantly cool nights of the Dry season, especially June–August, are ideal for traveling around and above Cairns. In the Whitsundays, some winter days may be too cool for swimming and nights can be chilly (pack a sweater and long pants).

The islands are warm, even in winter; during the summer months, temperatures regularly top 35 degrees Celsius (95 degrees Fahrenheit), and the farther north you go, the hotter it gets. The water temperature is mild to cool, varying only by a few degrees between winter and summer; however, in jellyfish season (November through May or so) you'll need to wear a full-body stinger suit to swim anywhere but within patrolled, netted areas.

GETTING HERE AND AROUND

AIR TRAVEL

Jetstar, Virgin Blue, and Qantas have daily direct flights linking capital cities around Australia to Cairns Airport (which also handles international flights). These airlines also have flights to Townsville, Whitsundays Coast, Hamilton Island, Proserpine, and Mackay airports, linking with east coast capitals and major regional cities throughout Queensland. From these hubs, regular boat and charter air services are available to most of the Great Barrier Reef resorts. Generally, island charter flights are timed to connect with domestic flights, but double-check. ⇨ *For information about reaching the islands, see Getting Here and Around under each island's heading.*

BOAT TRAVEL

Generally, island launches are timed to connect with charter flights from island or mainland airports, but do ask. Crossings can be choppy; take ginger tablets for motion sickness ahead of time. If you're based on the mainland or in a hurry, many operators run day trips out to the reef and resort islands.

Several operators provide skipper-yourself (bareboat) and crewed charters to explore the Whitsundays. Almost all have five-day minimum charter periods; most offer discounts for multiday hire and optional extras such as catering. Packages start from around A$110 per person, per night, but can be several times that on crewed or luxury vessels.

BUS TRAVEL

Long-distance buses are an economical but often cramped way to travel along the North Queensland coast. Sleeping on them is uncomfortable. Shuttle buses transfer visitors from the airport, Cairns, and beaches and towns to as far north as Cape Tribulation. They link island ferry services departing from Mission Beach, Airlie Beach, and Shute Harbour. Hotel pickups are usually available; call ahead to confirm.

CAR TRAVEL

If you're visiting several North Queensland destinations, it may be simplest to drive. Most popular North Queensland routes are paved, though roads may be flooded in wet season. A 4WD vehicle is advised. Leave plenty of time if you're crossing the Daintree River or going between Port Douglas and Cairns. If you're heading farther north, fill up with gas at or before Wonga Beach, and carry water, tools, and supplies.

RESTAURANTS

Most restaurants on Barrier Reef islands are part of each island's main resort, so many resorts' rates include some or all meals. Some larger resorts have a range of restaurants, with formal dining rooms, outdoor barbecues, and seafood buffets; some have premium dining options for which you pay extra. Dress is generally "island casual." Some upscale restaurants—such as those on Hayman Island—require men to wear jackets for dinner and frown on flip-flop sandals. On the mainland you'll find plenty of casual, open-air restaurants, serving mainly steak and seafood dishes. Cairns is your best bet for upscale dining.

HOTELS

Most inhabited islands have just one main resort, usually offering a range of lodging types and prices. Choose island destinations based on your budget and the kind of vacation you want—active, relaxed, or a mix. Offerings range from white-glove service (Lizard, Orpheus, Hayman islands) to eco-focused island resorts (Long Island). All but the most rustic and zero-footprint resorts have modern conveniences such as air-conditioning, telephones, televisions, refrigerators, and Internet access—though on some Barrier Reef islands connections can be slow and mobile phone coverage limited or non-existent.

	¢	$	$$	$$$	$$$$
DINING AND LODGING PRICE CATEGORIES (IN AUSTRALIAN DOLLARS)					
Restaurants	under A$15	A$15–A$20	A$21–A$30	A$31–A$45	over A$45
Hotels	under A$100	A$101–A$200	A$201–A$300	A$301–A$450	over A$450

Restaurant prices are based on the median main course price at dinner. Hotel prices are for two people in a standard double room in high season, excluding service and tax (10%).

HEALTH AND SAFETY

You'll find large, well-equipped hospitals in Cairns, Townsville, and Mackay; doctors in Port Douglas and Airlie Beach. Emergency services are scarce between the Daintree River and Cooktown. Island resort front desk staff handle emergencies and can summon doctors and aerial ambulance services. Remote islands have "flying doctor" kits; Hamilton Island has its own doctor. Contact Cairns Health Online (www.cairnshealthonline.com) for a list of GPs, hospitals, and pharmacies in the region.

Avoid midday rays, even in winter, and wear a hat and SPF15+ sunscreen to prevent sunburn. Rehydrate often and take it easy in the heat.

Avoid touching coral: it is easily damaged, and can cut and sting. Clean cuts thoroughly, scrubbing with a brush and flushing the affected area with saline solution. Toxic and stinging jellyfish frequent waters off the mainland and some Barrier Reef islands over the warmer months. Avoid the ocean without a stinger suit at these times. If in doubt, ask a local.

Mosquitoes, midges, and leeches can be a problem in wet summer months. Wear insect repellent to avoid being bitten; remove leeches by applying a flame or salt.

Estuarine crocodiles live in rivers and coastal waters along the North Queensland coast and on some Barrier Reef islands. Don't swim where crocs live (ask a local), especially in breeding season, September to April—and never dangle your limbs over the sides of boats.

CAIRNS

Tourism is the lifeblood of Cairns (pronounced *Caans*). The city makes a perfect base for exploring the wild top half of Queensland, and tens of thousands of international travelers use it as a jumping-off point for activities such as scuba diving and snorkeling trips to the Barrier Reef, as well as boating, parasailing, and rain-forest treks.

It's a tough environment, with intense heat and fierce wildlife. Along with wallabies and grey kangaroos in the savannah and tree kangaroos in the rain forest, you'll find stealthy saltwater crocodiles, poisonous snakes, and jellyfish so deadly they keep the stunning beaches virtually unswimmable for half the year. Yet despite their formidable setting, Cairns and tropical North Queensland are far from intimidating. The people are warm and friendly, the sights spectacular, and the beachside lounging world-class—at the right time of year.

GETTING HERE AND AROUND

AIR TRAVEL   Cairns Airport is a major international gateway, and a connection point for flights to other parts of Queensland, including Townsville, Mackay, Rockhampton, Hamilton Island, and the Northern Territory, as well as all Australian capital cities.

Airport Connections runs coaches between the airport and town—an 8-km (5-mi) trip that takes about 10 minutes and costs A$12. The company also services Cairns's northern beaches, Palm Cove, Port Douglas, Silky Oaks Lodge (near Mossman), and Cape Tribulation (A$18 to upward of A$50), as well as Mission Beach to the south. Port Douglas–based Express Chauffeured Coaches and Limousines provides bus services from the airport to Palm Cove and Port Douglas, north of Cairns (A$18–A$34 by coach, A$75–A$165 in a limousine). Private taxis make these trips as well (A$18–A$22 to Cairns).

Airlines based at Cairns Airport include Air New Zealand, Cathay Pacific, Continental Micronesia, Qantas, Jetstar, Virgin Blue, Pacific Blue, and Skytrans.

BUS TRAVEL   Greyhound Australia operates daily express buses from major southern cities to Cairns. By bus, Cairns to Brisbane takes around 30 hours, to Sydney it's just under 48 hours, and to Melbourne it's a gargantuan trip of more than 66 hours, best broken into bearable segments.

GREAT ITINERARIES

Most visits to the Great Barrier Reef combine stays on one or more islands with time in Queensland's mainland towns and parks. With a week or more, you could stay at two very different Barrier Reef island resorts: perhaps at an activities-packed Whitsundays resort and one of the northerly islands, allowing a day or two to travel between them. If you want to resort-hop, opt for the Whitsundays, all relatively close to one another and well serviced by boat and air transport.

IF YOU HAVE 1 DAY

Take a boat from Cairns or Port Douglas to a pontoon on the outer reef for a day on the water. A helicopter flight back to the mainland will give you an astounding aerial view of the reef and its islands. Alternatively, catch an early boat from Cairns to Fitzroy Island or from Shute Harbour to Daydream Island. Spend a couple of hours snorkeling, take a walk around the island, then relax on a quiet beach for an idyllic afternoon.

IF YOU HAVE 3 DAYS

Pick one island with a variety of aquatic and land-based activities and attractions—flora and fauna, beaches and dive sites, sports and relaxation facilities, resort-style nightlife—and give yourself a taste of everything.

IF YOU HAVE 7 OR MORE DAYS

Planning to spend a full week on an island probably means you're a serious diver, a serious lounger, or both. Keen to scuba dive the reef? Hop on one of the Lizard Island–Port Douglas live-aboards for a multiday dive trip, then recuperate on an island that has fringing coral, such as Lizard Island. Or stay at any Whitsundays resort—most have fringing reefs and can arrange dive-boat excursions out to Barrier Reef pontoons. Live-aboard trips can be surprisingly affordable—typically, they run from two to 10 days. Beach lovers might prefer to focus on exploring one or two of the islands with outstanding beaches and hiking terrain, such as Orpheus, Lizard, or Hayman.

CAR TRAVEL Between Brisbane and Cairns, the Bruce Highway rarely touches the coast. Unless you're planning to stop off en route or explore the Great Green Way, fly or take the fast Tilt Train to Cairns, renting a vehicle on arrival. Avis, Budget, Hertz and Europcar all have rental cars and four-wheel-drive vehicles available. An economical, reliable alternative is Cairns Leisure Wheels, just off Captain Cook Highway; it offers free delivery and pickup.

TRAIN TRAVEL Trains arrive at the Cairns Railway Station in the city center. The *Sunlander*, with its coach seats, luxury Queenslander-class sleeping and fine-dining carriages, makes the 31-hour journey between Brisbane and Cairns thrice-weekly in each direction (A$180.68–A$453.10). The fast, modern Tilt Train plies the coast from Brisbane to Cairns twice-weekly each way, taking just under 24 hours (A$275.52–A$344.40). The *Savannahlander* links Cairns and Forsyth, traveling four days through rain forest, savanna land, and Outback (A$1,160). You can also take shorter segments of all these journeys.

TOURS

BOAT TOURS
🌀
Fodor's Choice
★

Ocean Spirit Cruises' streamlined four-hour and full-day tours aboard the *Ocean Spirit I*, a large catamaran, and the smaller *Ocean Spirit II and III*, cost from A$110 to A$195 per person, snorkeling gear included. *Ocean Spirit IV* takes up to 100 guests on a nightly, four-course dinner cruise along Trinity Inlet from 6:45 to 9:30 (A$89). Boats depart from Marlin Jetty, Cairns, and Palm Cove Jetty on demand. Transfers from Cairns, Northern Beaches, Palm Cove, and Port Douglas are available (A$25–A$66).

> **ATM LOGISTICS**
>
> Resorts on the following islands have money-changing facilities: Daydream, Fitzroy, Hamilton, Hayman, Lindeman, Lizard, Long and Orpheus. It's better to change money before arriving on any resort island, however, as rates are generally more favorable elsewhere.

NATURE
TOURS
🌀

BTS Tours & Transfers runs various trips out of Cairns and Port Douglas (and shuttle services between the two). From Cairns or Port Douglas, the popular full-day Kuranda tour includes the train, cable car, and around two hours exploring the township (A$132–A$138). You could also take an activity-packed day tour to the Daintree rain forest and Cape Tribulation (A$154), a half-day Mossman Gorge tour with a Ku Ku Yalanji guided walk (A$58), a quick trip to the Daintree (A$66) or a whistlestop tour of Mossman Gorge (A$20) from Port Douglas.

Advanced eco–certified Wilderness Challenge runs Daintree rain-forest day tours and multiday trips between the Daintree and the top of the Cape York Peninsula in the dry season, May through November, including off-the-tourist-track "advanced" safaris, and a 5-day, fly/drive rock-art and rain-forest camping safari between Cairns and Cape York for A$1,645 (twin-share) or A$1,745 (sole use) per person. Most tours visit the world-renowned Quinkan Aboriginal rock-art site near Laura and stay in bush cabins and/or safari tents.

Eco-certified Down Under Tours makes half- and full-day trips and four-wheel-drive excursions to Kuranda, Cape Tribulation, the Daintree, and the southern tablelands (A$88–A$252 per person). The company's luxury arm, Down Under By Appointment, takes small groups on customized journeys with expert driver-guides.

Blazing Saddles organizes half-day horse rides (A$105) and all-terrain vehicle tours (A$125) through bushland around Kuranda. A full day's horse-riding and ATV touring is A$215. All riders pay insurance of A$15.

CULTURAL
TOURS
★

The Eastern Kuku Yalanji people have called the Daintree area home for tens of thousands of years, and have an intimate understanding of the terrain. Today the Kubirri Warra brothers pass on a little of that boundless ancestral wisdom on a two-hour beach, mudflat, and mangrove walk (daily, 9:30 am and 1.30 pm, A$75) with Kuku Yalanji Cultural Habitat Tours. Learn techniques for throwing spears, tracking coastal food sources, and much more from your knowledgeable,

skillful guides. The tour company also offers two-hour night spearfishing walks (daily from 7:30 pm, A$150) as well as tour combinations and themed options, including multiday packages. Transfers between the Port Douglas area and Cooya Beach, a 25-minute drive north, are A$30.

ESSENTIALS

Airport and Transfers **Airport Connections** ☎ 07/4098–2800 ⊕ www.tnqshuttle.com. **Cairns Airport** ⊠ Mick Borzi Dr. off Airport Ave., Aeroglen ☎ 07/4080–6703 ⊕ www.cairnsairport.com.

Boat Information **Ocean Spirit Cruises** ⊠ Office 3–Level 1, Shangri-La Marina, Pierpoint Rd., CBD ☎ 07/4031–2920, 1800/644227 ⊕ www.oceanspirit.com.au.

Bus Information **Greyhound Australia** ☎ 1300/473–946 ⊕ www.greyhound.com.au.

Car Rental **Cairns Leisure Wheels** ⊠ 314 Sheridan St., CBD ☎ 07/4051–8988 ⊕ www.leisurewheels.com.au.

Medical Assistance **Cairns Base Hospital** ⊠ The Esplanade at Florence St., CBD ☎ 07/4050–6333.

Tour Operators **Blazing Saddles Adventures** ⊠ 2326 Kennedy Hwy., Kuranda ✑ PO Box 278, Edge Hill 4870 ☎ 07/4085–0197 ⊕ www.blazingsaddles.com.au. **BTS Tours & Transfers** ⊠ 49 Macrossan St. 4877 ☎ 07/4099–5665 ⊕ www.btstours.com.au. **Down Under Tours** ⊠ 26 Redden St., CBD4870 ☎ 07/4035–5566 ⊕ www.downundertours.com. **Kuku Yalanji Cultural Habitat Tours** ☎ 07/4098–3437 ⊕ www.bamaway.com.au. **Wilderness Challenge** ☎ 07/4035–4488, 1800/354486 ⊕ www.wilderness-challenge.com.au.

Train Information **Cairns Railway Station** ⊠ Bunda St. between Spence and Aplin Sts., CBD ☎ 07/4036–9250 ⊕ www.queenslandrail.com.au. **Queensland Rail** ☎ 07/3272–2222, 1800/872–467 ⊕ www.queenslandrail.com.au. **The Savannahlander** ☎ 1800/793–848, 07/4053–6848 ⊕ www.savannahlander.com.au.

Visitor Information **The Cairns & Tropical North Visitor Information Centre (TTNQ)** ⊠ 51 The Esplanade, between Spence and Shield Sts., CBD ☎ 07/4051–3588, 1800/093300 ⊕ www.cairnsgreatbarrierreef.org.au.

EXPLORING CAIRNS

Cosmopolitan Cairns, the unofficial capital of Far North Queensland, is Australia's 16th-largest city, with a burgeoning population pushing 170,000. Once a sleepy tropical town sprawled around Trinity Bay and Inlet, the city has expanded hugely in recent decades, and now extends north to Holloway's Beach, west to the Atherton Tablelands, and south along the Great Green Way as far as Edmonton.

TOP ATTRACTIONS

Australian Butterfly Sanctuary. More than 1,500 tropical butterflies—including dozens of the electric-blue Ulysses species—flutter within a rain-forest aviary environment, alighting on the foliage, interpretative signage, and feeding stations. The sanctuary is home to Australia's

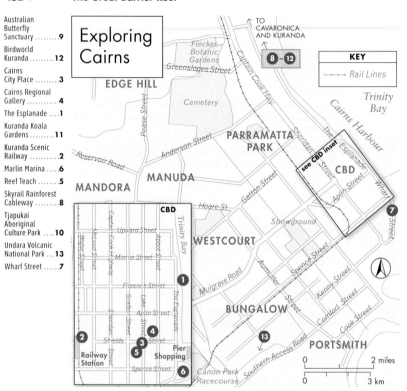

Exploring Cairns

largest butterfly, the green-and-gold Cairns birdwing. Free half-hour guided tours are full of fascinating tidbits. ⊠ *8 Rob Veivers Dr., Kuranda* ☏ *07/4093–7575* ⊕ *www.australianbutterflies.com* ⊠ *A\$18* ⊘ *Daily 10–4, tours 10:15–3:15.*

Ⓒ **Cairns Regional Gallery.** Occupying the impressive former Public Office
★ Building constructed in the 1930s, Cairns Regional Gallery houses a hodgepodge of local, national, international, and indigenous artworks, including a fine collection of Australian photography, in its wood-paneled rooms. The shop stocks high-quality Australian giftware, toys, jewelry, prints, books, and cards. Pre-book an hour-long guided tour; there are also kids' programs, classes, talks, and workshops. ⊠ *City Place, Shields and Abbott Sts., CBD* ☏ *07/4046–4800* ⊕ *www. cairnsregionalgallery.com.au* ⊠ *A\$5 (free, first Sat. of the month and for under-16s)* ⊘ *Mon.–Sat. 10–5, Sun. 1–5.*

Ⓒ **The Esplanade.** Fronting Cairns Harbour between Minnie and Spence
★ streets, this is the focal point of life in Cairns. A shallow, 4,800-square-meter (51,667-square-foot) saltwater lagoon-style swimming pool with a sandy shore, decking, and shelters, is open until well after sunset. It's patrolled by lifeguards (6 am–10 pm October–March, 7 am–9 pm April–September), and is a free, convenient place to seek relief rom the sticky air. Farther along the Esplanade are imaginative children's play areas and

SCENIC DRIVE: THE GREAT GREEN WAY

Great Green Way. Take a drive along a section of the Bruce Highway locals call the Great Green Way. The main road connecting Townsville to Cairns, it travels through sugarcane, papaya, and banana plantations, passing white-sand beaches and an island-dotted ocean. The 348-km (216-mi) drive takes about 4½ hours—longer if you get caught behind a tractor or if the sugarcane rail is running—plus stops to explore towns, parks, waterfalls, and rainforest tracts along the way.

Babinda Boulders. This is a popular swimming hole—and a sacred Aboriginal site. It's 7 km (5 mi) inland from Babinda, accessible via the Bruce Highway about 60 km (37 mi) south of Cairns. You can also hike to the boulders, taking the 19-km (12-mi) **Goldfield Track (Wooroonooran National Park)** that starts in Goldsborough Valley, southwest of Cairns, and ends in Babinda Boulders car park. ⊠ *Babinda Information Centre, Munro St., Babinda* ☎ *07/4067–1008 info center, 07/4067–6304 park ranger, 13–7468 camping* ☉ *Information center daily 9 am–4 pm.*

Paronella Park. A sprawling Spanish-style castle and gardens grace this offbeat National Trust site in the Mena Creek Falls rain forest. Explore the park on a self-guided botanical walk or 45-minute guided tour, enjoy Devonshire tea on the café's deck, and cool off under a 40-foot waterfall. On hour-long torch-lit evening tours you might spot eels, water dragons, fireflies and glowworms. Allow at least three hours to explore. It's about 1½ hours' (about 60 mi) drive south of Cairns via the Bruce Highway.

⊠ *1671 Japoonvale Rd. (Old Bruce Hwy.), Mena Creek* ☎ *07/4065–0000* ⊕ *www.paronellapark.com.au* 🎫 *A$36* ☉ *Daily 9 am–7:30 pm.*

Tully Gorge. Located in the wettest zone of the Wet Tropics World Heritage area, the mighty Tully River is a magnet for white-water rafters. Access the gorge via Tully, 141 km (88 mi) or about 2 hours' drive south of Cairns, then drive for 54 km (34 mi)—approximately 40 minutes—along Jarra Creek and Cardstone roads to Kareeya Hydroelectric Station parking lot and viewing platform. Other excellent vantage points are the Tully Falls lookout, 24 km (15 mi) south of Ravenshoe, and the Flip Wilson and Frank Roberts lookouts. September to February, the short, wheelchair-accessible Rainforest Butterfly walk is filled with fluttering creatures. ☎ *07/4068–2288* ⊕ *www. derm.qld.gov.au.*

Wooroonooran National Park. Extending south of Gordonvale to the Palmerston Highway near Innisfail, this is one of the most densely vegetated areas in Australia. Rain forest dominates Wooroonooran—from lowland tropical rain forest to the stunted growth on Mt. Bartle Frere—at 5,287 feet the highest point in Queensland. Tracks range from the easy, 30-minute circuits to hugely challenging, two day treks. You may camp throughout the park with permits (A$5.15 per person, per day), except at Josephine Falls; BYO drinking water and stove. Josephine Falls is 75 km (47 mi) south of Cairns off the Bruce Highway, near Miriwinni. 🚗 *Bartle Frere Rd., Box 93, Miriwinni 4871* ☎ *07/4067–1008, 13–7468 info and camping permits* ⊕ *www.derm.qld.gov.au.*

8

parklands, picnic grounds with BBQ facilities,volleyball courts, and Skate Plaza—Australia's largest, at just under 25,000 square feet. Some fine shops, hotels, galleries, and eateries can be found along the Esplanade; backpackers also tend to gather here, giving it a lively feel. ⊠ *The Esplanade, between Spence and Upward Sts., CBD* ☎ *07/4044–3715* ⊕ *www. cairnsesplanade.com.au* ⌑ *Free* ⊙ *Pool: Daily 6 am–10 pm (Oct.–Mar.), 7 am–9 pm (Apr.–Sept.), closed Wed. 6 am–noon; Muddy's playground: daily 8–8 (Oct.–Mar.), 9 am–7 pm (Apr.–Sept.), closed Tues. and Thurs. 7–11 am; volleyball courts: Thurs.–Tues. 9 am–9:30 pm, Wed. 4–9:30 pm.*

☼
★ **Kuranda Scenic Railway.** The Kuranda Scenic Railway makes a 115-minute ascent through rain forest and 15 hand-hewn tunnels to pretty Kuranda village, gateway to the Atherton Tableland, as excerpts from Kuranda's WWII history and narration on the railway's construction are broadcast throughout the historic railway car. Several tours are available, from full-day rain-forest safaris and visits to local Aboriginal centers and wildlife parks to simple round-trips combining rail and cable-car journeys. ⊠ *Cairns Railway Station, Bunda St., CBD* ☎ *07/4036–9333, 1800/079–033* ⊕ *www.ksr.com.au* ⌑ *1-way ticket A$47, round-trip A$71; Dreamtime package A$148* ⊙ *Departs from Cairns daily 8:30 am and 9:30 am, Kuranda at 2 and 3:30.*

☼
Fodor's Choice
★ **Reef Teach.** At Reef Teach, qualified marine biologists and conservationists present informative, entertaining lectures on the Great Barrier Reef, usually to packed houses. They use video, slides, and samples to teach about the reef's evolution and the inhabitants of this delicate marine ecosystem. The attached Marine Shop sells a wide array of reef-themed merchandise: T-shirts, DVDs, books, field guides, and souvenirs. Sign up for a Reef Teach seat by midday. ⊠ *2nd floor, Mainstreet Arcade, 81–85 Lake St., CBD* ☎ *07/4031–7794* ⊕ *www.reefteach.com. au* ⌑ *A$15* ⊙ *Shows Tues.–Sat. 6:30–8:30.*

☼
Fodor's Choice
★ **Skyrail Rainforest Cableway.** From the remarkable Skyrail Rainforest Cableway, six-person cable cars carry you on a 7½-km (5-mi) journey across the rain-forest canopy to the highland village of Kuranda, where you can visit local attractions and shop for Aboriginal art. At two stations along the way you can hop off and explore (the Skyrail ticket price includes a short ranger-guided rain-forest tour at Red Peak, and there's an info center and lookout at Barron Falls). The cableway base station is 15 km (9 mi) north of Cairns. Many visitors take the Scenic Railway to Kuranda, the cableway on the return trip. ⊠ *Captain Cook Hwy. at Cairns Western Arterial Rd., Smithfield* ☎ *07/4038–1555* ⊕ *www.skyrail.com.au* ⌑ *1-way A$44, round-trip A$66 (self-drive); A$86–A$108 (with transfers)* ⊙ *Daily 9–5:15, last round-trip boards at 2:45; last 1-way trip at 3:30.*

☼
★ **Tjapukai Aboriginal Cultural Park.** Located at the base of the Skyrail Rainforest Cableway, this park offers many opportunities to learn about the history and lifestyle of the indigenous Djabugay people. One of Australia's most informative cultural attractions, it's also one of the few that returns profits to the indigenous community. Watch a dance performance, try your hand at traditional fire-making, throw a spear or boomerang, have a didgeridoo lesson, or learn about bush tucker and

The Skyrail Rainforest Cableway outside of Cairns.

medicines from friendly, knowledgeable staff. There are also Aboriginal artworks, artefacts, and instruments (including didgeridoos) for sale, and buffet lunches are available. Ticket options include Tjapukai by Day (A$35, A$58 from Cairns or Northern Beaches transfers) and Tjapukai by Night, a nightly buffet dinner and performance package (A$99, A$121 with transfers). ✉ *Cairns Western Arterial Rd., Cavaronica ✛ 15 km (9 mi) north of Cairns* ☎ *07/4042–9900* ⊕ *www.tjapukai.com.au* ☾ *Daily 9–5, night show 7–9:30 pm.*

WORTH NOTING

Birdworld Kuranda. One of your best chances to see the endangered cassowary, a prehistoric emu-like bird, is at Birdworld Kuranda. It's also home to around 500 or so birds from 75 species, more than 25 of them native to vanishing rain-forest areas—all flying freely in a giant aviary, and many of them tame enough to perch on your shoulders. ■TIP➔ Wear a hat and sleeved shirt: birds' claws are scratchy. ✉ *Kuranda Heritage Village, Kuranda* ☎ *07/4093–9188* ⊕ *www.birdworldkuranda.com.au* ☒ *A$16.50* ☾ *Daily 9–4.*

Cairns City Place. Cairns' center is City Place, a pedestrian mall bordered by Lake and Shields streets. Some of the town's few "authentic" pubs and its major shopping area flank this square. The plaza regularly hosts entertainment and community-based events, including free live entertainment on Thursday and Friday at lunchtime. ✉ *Lake and Shield Sts., CBD* ☎ *07/4044–3715.*

Kuranda Koala Gardens. All kinds of Australian wildlife are housed here, but the namesake marsupials are star attractions. The compact park is ideal for time-strapped visitors: a half-hour stroll takes you past koalas, wombats, wallabies, fresh-water crocs, lizards, and snakes in open walk-through enclosures. For A$16.50, have your photo taken with a tame koala. ⊠ *Kuranda Heritage Village, Kuranda* ☎ *07/4093–9953* ⊕ *www.koalagardens.com* ✉ *A$16.50; Friends in the Rainforest Pass (Birdworld/Koala Gardens): A$28* ☼ *Daily 9–4.*

Marlin Marina. Up to 214 charter fishing, diving, and private vessels can moor along Marlin Marina. Big-game fishing is a big business here; fish weighing more than 1,000 pounds have been caught in the waters off the reef. Most of the dive boats and catamarans that ply the Great Barrier Reef dock here or at nearby Trinity Wharf. ⊠ *1 Spence Street, CBD* ☎ *07/4052–3866* ⊕ *www.portsnorth.com.au.*

> **KURANDA WILDLIFE PASS**
>
> Tropical Kuranda offers several nature-oriented attractions, including the Australian Butterfly Sanctuary, Birdworld Kuranda, and Kuranda Koala Gardens. See these sites individually, visit on a Kuranda Wildlife Experience pass (A$44), which gives entry to all three, or buy a Wildlife Day-tripper's package that includes Skyrail and/or Scenic Railway tickets (A$157).

Wharf Street. Cairns can trace its beginnings to the point where the Esplanade becomes Wharf Street. In 1876 this was a port for gold and tin mined inland. Chinese and Malaysian workers and other immigrants, lured by the gold trade, settled here, and Cairns grew into one of the most multicultural cities in Australia. As the gold rush receded and the sugarcane industry around the Atherton Tableland grew, Cairns turned its attention to fishing. It is still a thriving port. ⊠ *Wharf St., south end of the Esplanade, CBD.*

OFF THE BEATEN PATH

Undara Volcanic National Park. The lava tubes here are a fascinating geological oddity in the Outback. A volcanic outpouring 190,000 years ago created the hollow basalt, tubelike tunnels, many of which you can wander through on tours led by trained guides. Undara is the Aboriginal word for "a long way," and it's apt: one of the original lava tubes extended for 100 miles in total, and several sections of it can still be explored on guided tours. The lava tubes extend over an area of 580-odd square miles; some are 62 feet high and half a mile long.

Undara Experience. Vintage railway cars have been converted into comfortable (if compact) motel rooms (A$80–A$125) at the Undara Experience. You can also camp; unpowered or powered sites are A$20 and A$30 per night, respectively. The lodge, 275 km (171 mi) or a four-hour drive from Cairns, has 12 three-person dorm rooms (A$50 per person) and is set amid savanna and woodlands. It supplies the complete Outback experience: bush breakfasts, campfire activities, lava-tube tours (A$47.50–A$132), snake shows (A$22), and guided evening wildlife walks (A$47.50). Two- and three-night Outback Experience packages that incorporate tours, campfire activities, some meals, and accommodation cost A$356 (3 nights) or A$246 (2 nights) if you self-drive; pricing available from A$368 (two nights) if they arrange transportation (options include coach or *Savannahlander* train transfers to and from Cairns). You can also make various daytrips to Undara, including a lava tubes tour, by plane or helicopter from Cairns or Port Douglas for A$540–A$1,935, or by air (some include a GBR scenic flight en route. Alternatively, take a three-day photography tour for A$550, including meals and tours but not transfers or accommodation. ⊠ *Undara Volcanic Park, Savannah Way, Mt. Surprise* ☎ *07/4097–1900, 1800/990–992* ⊕ *www.undara.com.au* ☎ *07/4097–1485* ⊕ *www. derm.qld.gov.au* ⌑ *Free* ⊗ *Daily dawn–dusk.*

WHERE TO EAT

Use the coordinate (⊕ B2) at the end of each listing to locate a site on the corresponding map.

$$$
SEAFOOD

✕ **Barnacle Bill's Seafood Inn.** Complete with netting and mounted, shellacked fish on the walls, Barnacle Bill's serves fresh, delicious seafood: mud crabs, crayfish, prawns, oysters, wild barramundi, and coral trout—cooked various ways. The kitchen also dabbles in Aussie specialties: try the Taste of Australia plate, with grilled barramundi, kangaroo, and crocodile. The wine list favors quality mid-range Australian and New Zealand vintages. Early diners get a 20% discount. ⊠ *103 The Esplanade, near Aplin St., CBD* ☎ *07/4051–2241* ⊕ *www.barnaclebills. com.au* ⊗ *No lunch* ⊕ *B2.*

$$
INDONESIAN
Fodor's Choice
★

✕ **Bayleaf Balinese Restaurant.** Dining in the open-sided restaurant or alfresco under the glow of tiki torches, you can enjoy some of the most delicious, innovative cuisine in North Queensland. An expansive menu combines traditional Balinese spices with native Australian ingredients—this may be the only place where you'll have the opportunity to try crocodile satay. The pork in sweet soy sauce sounds simple, but is mouthwatering. The classic rijsttafel feast for two—rice with lots of curries, salads, fish dishes, stews, and pickle sides (and if you can squeeze them in, desserts)—is the best way to sample the Bali-trained chefs' masterly cooking. ■ **TIP**➡ Don't eat lunch if you're planning to order the rijsttafel at dinner—it's huge. ⊠ *Bay Village Tropical Retreat, 227 Lake St. at Gatton St., CBD* ☎ *07/4047–7955* ⊕ *www.bayvillage.com. au/bayleaf* ⊗ *No lunch weekends* ⊕ *A1.*

¢
FAST FOOD
☖

✕ **Cairns Night Markets Food Court.** The food court in these night owl–friendly markets offers something for every palate, from spicy Malaysian *laksa* (coconut-milk soup) to sushi, kebabs, sweet-and-sour chicken, crepes, and ice cream. Officially, it's open daily with the markets, 5 to 11 pm, but many outlets start serving at 11 am or earlier. ⊠ *71–75 The Esplanade, between Shield and Spence Sts., CBD* ☎ *07/4051–7666* ⊕ *www.nightmarkets.com.au* ⌑ *Reservations not accepted* ═ *No credit cards* ⊕ *B3.*

$$$
MODERN FRENCH
★

✕ **M Yogo.** Occupying a prime spot on the pier, M Yogo could be Cairns's best-placed restaurant. Here chef and co-owner Masa puts a deft modern spin on classic French dishes: enjoy his creamy seafood risotto with tiger prawns, squid, and scallops; roasted duck breast in orange sauce; pan-seared market-fresh fish; or premium grain-fed Wagyu tenderloin. Or tuck into a half-lobster as you take in 180-degree views of the marina, inlet, mountains, and ocean. Waitstaff can help you select the perfect match from a well-chosen Antipodean wine list. If

8

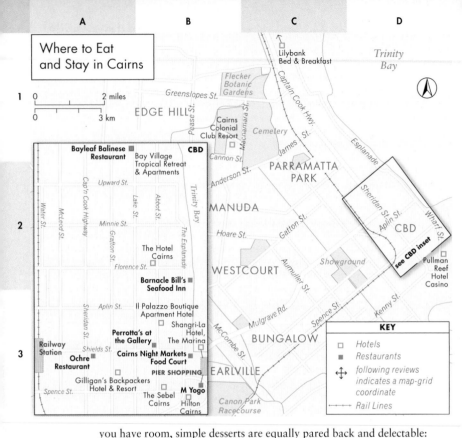

Where to Eat and Stay in Cairns

you have room, simple desserts are equally pared back and delectable: Grand Marnier ice cream, mango mousse or sorbet, "opera" cake, or cheesecake soufflé. The four-course set menu featuring a lobster main is good value at A$99. This is refined dining in relaxed environs, perfect for special occasions. ⊠ *Shop G9, Pier Shopping, Pierpoint Rd.* ☎ *07/4051–0522* ⊕ *www.matureyogo.com* ✛ *B3.*

$$$
AUSTRALIAN
Fodor's Choice
★

✕ **Ochre Restaurant.** Local seafood and native ingredients have top billing at this upscale yet casual spot that specializes in bush dining. Try the Australian antipasto platter: 'roo terrine, emu pâté, and crocodile wontons. Most dishes employ native foods and seasonal ingredients: sample wild-caught barramundi or emu fillet with bush tomato, or order a vegetarian, Australian game, or seafood platter to share (A$29–A$66 per person, min. 2). Ochre's signature dessert, wattle-seed pavlova with Davidson plum sorbet and macadamia biscotti, makes a fine finish; or settle into a velvet booth and quaff a glass of Australian wine. ⊠ *43 Shields St. at Sheridan St., CBD* ☎ *07/4051–0100* ⊕ *www.ochrerestaurant.com.au* ⌨ *Reservations not accepted* ☉ *No lunch weekends* ✛ *A3.*

$$
AUSTRALIAN

✕ **Perrotta's at the Gallery.** This outdoor café with galvanized-steel tables and chairs at the Cairns Regional Gallery also has a wine bar. Sumptuous breakfasts are served here from 7:30 am, including French toast with vanilla poached pear, King Island yoghurt and raspberry caramel, baked eggs, frittata, and eggs Benedict with lime hollandaise; lunch fare includes warm chicken salads, pasta dishes, and a variety of sandwiches. Tuck into Italian and modern Australian mains—perhaps slow-cooked lamb shoulder or roast pepper, tomato, and basil soup with red-claw yabbies (crayfish)—and desserts, such as vanilla-bean panna cotta with seasonal fruits. ⊠ *Gallery Deck, Cairns Regional Gallery, 38 Abbott St. at Shield St., CBD* ☎ *07/4031–5899* ⊕ *www.cairnsregionalgallery.com.au* ⊹ *B3.*

WHERE TO STAY

For expanded hotel reviews, visit Fodors.com.

$ 🖫 **Bay Village Tropical Retreat & Apartments.** Resident managers Klaus and Lyn Ullrich have translated years of expertise in high-end Sydney hospitality into this family-friendly accommodation complex. **Pros:** disabled-friendly room and wheelchair-friendly public areas; free airport pickups 7 am to 7 pm. **Cons:** bland decor; some rooms lack Internet access, old-fashioned TVs in standard rooms/studios. ⊠ *227 Lake St. at Gatton St., CBD* ☎ *07/4051–4622* ⊕ *www.bayvillage.com.au* ⤶ *62 suites, 28 apartments* ⌂ *In-room: a/c, safe, kitchen, Internet. In-hotel: restaurant, bar, pool, laundry facilities, business center, parking* ⊹ *A1.*

$ 🖫 **Cairns Colonial Club Resort.** Though it's just a few minutes outside the
Ⓒ city center, this resort's 11 acres of tropical gardens make you feel a world away from the hubbub of Cairns. **Pros:** cheap city shuttle till 10 pm; many facilities; free pool towels; hearty dinners. **Cons:** dated decor and facilities; distance from CBD; resort bars close at 10 pm. ⊠ *18–26 Cannon St., Cairns* ☎ *07/4053–5111* ⊕ *www.cairnscolonialclub.com. au* ⤶ *342 rooms, 3 suites* ⌂ *In-room: a/c, safe, kitchen, Internet, Wi-Fi. In-hotel: restaurant, bar, pool, tennis court, gym, laundry facilities, business center, parking* ⊹ *B1.*

¢ 🖫 **Gilligan's Backpackers Hotel & Resort.** If you're in Cairns for an active
Fodor's Choice vacation and don't need spa-level silence, this upscale budget property
★ is ideal. **Pros:** fun, friendly guests; good gym; comfy beds; guest freebies. **Cons:** noisy dorm rooms; nondescript food; dodgy washing machines. ⊠ *57–89 Grafton St., CBD* ☎ *07/4041–6566, 1800/556–995* ⊕ *www. gilligans.com.au* ⤶ *120 rooms* ⌂ *In-room: no TV. In-hotel: restaurant, bar, pool, gym, beach, laundry facilities, business center, parking* ⊹ *A3.*

$$ 🖫 **Hilton Cairns.** This attractive, modern hotel has an enviable location near the waterfront—just a short walk from the reef cruise pier—and is a convenient spot for a short stay in Cairns. **Pros:** Modern, renovated rooms with nice amenities; expansive breakfast buffet; convenient location. **Cons:** Internet access very expensive; some reports of noise; big tour groups coming in and out frequently. ⊠ *34 Esplanade, Cairns* ☎ *7/4050–2000* ⤶ *264 rooms* ⌂ *In-room: a/c, safe, Internet, Wi-Fi. In-hotel: restaurant, bar, pool, gym, business center, parking* 🍴⊜ *Multiple meal plans* ⊹ *B3.*

$$ 🖫 **The Hotel Cairns.** One of the region's best examples of the Queenslander heritage style, the Hotel Cairns retains a genteel ambience despite extensive remodeling and refurbishment. **Pros:** free cable channels and daily newspapers; in-room Wi-Fi; bicycle hire and courtesy Smart cars. **Cons:** some rooms are dated and lack views (ask); noisy air-conditioning; small, chilly pool. ⊠ *Abbott St. at Florence St., CBD* ☎ *07/4051–6188*

8

07/4051–1806 ⊕ *www.thehotelcairns-queensland.com* ⊃ *89 rooms, 3 suites △ In-room: a/c, Wi-Fi. In-hotel: restaurant, pool, gym, laundry facilities, business center, parking ⊹ B2.*

$ **Il Palazzo Boutique Apartment Hotel.** Cairns is a long way from Europe but you can imagine yourself on the Riviera at this intimate, centrally located continental-style hotel. **Pros:** free Austar cable channels and movies; helpful staff; clean, quiet rooms. **Cons:** dated decor; slow in-room Internet; free Wi-Fi only in public areas (bring a laptop). ⊠ *62 Abbott St., CBD* ☎ *07/4041–2155, 1800/813–222* ⊕ *www.ilpalazzo. com.au* ⊃ *38 suites △ In-room: a/c, safe, kitchen, Internet. In-hotel: pool, laundry facilities, business center, parking ⊹ B3.*

$ **Lilybank Bed & Breakfast.** Built in the 1887, this two-story Queenslander became the home of the mayor of Cairns in the early 1900s, and was the homestead attached to North Queensland's first tropical-fruit plantation. **Pros:** helpful hosts, warm atmosphere; big breakfasts. **Cons:** a fair distance from the CBD; common areas lack air-conditioning; must love animals. ⊠ *75 Kamerunga Rd., Stratford* ☎ *07/4055–1123* ⊕ *www. lilybank.com.au* ⊃ *4 suites △ In-room: a/c, Internet. In-hotel: pool, laundry facilities, business center, parking* ❘○❘ *Breakfast ⊹ C1.*

$$$$ **Pullmann Reef Hotel Casino.** Part of an entertainment complex in the
★ heart of Cairns, this high-end hotel has spacious rooms and suites—as well as gaming tables, bars, a cabaret show, and a nightclub. **Pros:** great on-site entertainment and dining options; helpful, high-end service (call ahead for a firmer mattress and they'll even remove the down topper). **Cons:** chilly pool; soft furnishings showing wear. ⊠ *35–41 Wharf St., CBD* ☎ *07/4030–8888* ⊕ *www.pullmannhotels.com* ⊃ *128 rooms and suites △ In-room: a/c, safe, Internet, Wi-Fi. In-hotel: restaurant, bar, pool, gym, business center, parking ⊹ D2.*

$$$ **The Sebel Cairns.** The Sebel Cairns is one of two Mirvac apartment-hotels in the CBD (the other is the Sebel Harbour Lights—equally salubrious but minus a day spa). **Pros:** central location; good on-site day spa, bar, and dining. **Cons:** thin walls; old-style TVs; fees for Internet access and parking; main pool is chilly. ⊠ *17 Abbot St., at Spence St., CBD* ☎ *07/4031–1300, 1800/079100* ⊕ *www.mirvachotels.com/ sebel-cairns* ⊃ *321 rooms/suites △ In-room: a/c, safe, Internet, Wi-Fi. In-hotel: restaurant, bar, pool, gym, spa, laundry facilities, business center, parking ⊹ B3.*

$$$ **Shangri-La Hotel, The Marina.** With a minimalist lobby, golden-orb
Fodor's Choice chandeliers, and suede chaise longues, this resort is among Cairns's hip-
★ pest. **Pros:** great views; free Wi-Fi and Internet; free use of beach towels and umbrellas. **Cons:** service can be offhand; room-to-room plumbing noise; over-chlorinated Jacuzzi. ⊠ *Pierpoint Rd., CBD* ☎ *07/4031– 1411, 1800/222–448* ⊕ *www.shangri-la.com* ⊃ *230 rooms, 25 suites △ In-room: a/c, safe, kitchen, Wi-Fi. In-hotel: restaurant, bar, pool, gym, business center, parking ⊹ B3.*

OUTDOOR ACTIVITIES

It's no surprise that lots of tours out of Cairns focus on the Great Barrier Reef. Half-day snorkeling, diving, and fishing trips out of Cairns, most departing from Marlin Marina, start from around A$125; full-day trips start from about A$185. Scuba dives and gear generally cost extra, and often you'll pay an additional A$5.50 reef tax and a Port Authority charge of around A$15 per day.

Ask a few pertinent questions before booking diving tours: dive trips vary in size, and some cater specifically to, say, sightseers; others to experienced divers. If you're a beginner or Open Water diver, ensure tht you book excursions that visit suitable dive sites, with certified staff on hand to assist you.

Cairns is also a great base for adventure activities and horse riding on the Atherton Tableland, ballooning over the Mareeba Valley, and day tours to the UNESCO World Heritage–listed Daintree rain forest. The offices of adventure-tour companies, tourist offices and booking agents are concentrated around the Esplanade.

> ## BEACHES
>
> Since Cairns lacks city beaches, most people head out to the reef to swim and snorkel. North of the airport, neighboring areas including **Machans Beach, Holloways Beach, Yorkey's Knob, Trinity Beach,** and **Clifton Beach** are perfect for swimming from June through September and sometimes even October; check local weather reports. Avoid the ocean at other times, however, when deadly box jellyfish (marine stingers) and invisible-to-the-eye Irukandji jellyfish float in the waters along the coast.

ADVENTURE TOURS

Fodor's Choice
★

Raging Thunder. Raging Thunder has various adventure packages: dive and snorkel on the Barrier Reef; glide over the Mareeba Valley in one of the world's largest hot-air balloons; horseback ride or white-water raft through the hinterland's rugged gorges; hike and bungee-jump on the Atherton Tablelands; or sea kayak around Fitzroy Island. Some tours can be combined with a visit to Tjapukai Aboriginal Cultural Park or Cairns Wildlife Safari Reserve. Pricing varies vastly by activity, season, and other factors, but the Web site makes it relatively simple to plug in your proposed dates to learn the price points for the activities you're interested in. ⊠ *52–54 Fearnley St., Portsmith* ☎ *07/4030–7990* ⊕ *www.ragingthunder.com.au.*

RnR White Water Rafting. This operator runs white-water expeditions on the North Johnstone and Tully rivers for adults of all skill levels, as well as reef and rain-forest trips, horse rides, ATV tours, balloon rides, and more. Prices start at A$130 for a half-day's Barron River rafting tour, and there's an additional A$25 rafting charge on white-water excursions. They will pick you up from your accommodation. ⊠ *CBD* ☎ *07/4041–9444* ⊕ *www.raft.com.au.*

SNORKELING AND DIVING

Deep Sea Divers Den. Long-established, PADI-5-star-rated Deep Sea Divers Den has a roaming permit that allows guides to visit any part of the Great Barrier Reef, including 14 permanent moorings on the outer reef. Day trips include up to three dives, gear, and lunch. Pricing schemes are reasonable: from A$175 for a reef day trip with two dives, A$195 with three; from A$395 for a 2-day, 5-dive live-aboard trip; and A$110 for a day's unlimited snorkeling, gear and guided tour included. ⊠ *319 Draper St., CBD* ☎ *07/4046–7333* ⊕ *www.diversden.com.au.*

8

"This was taken at Steve's Bommie. This fish struck me as really angry that fate had made him tough-looking, yet pink." —Photo by Rowanne, Fodors.com member

Fodor'sChoice
★ **Mike Ball Dive Expeditions.** Mike Ball Dive Expeditions has been diving the Great Barrier Reef since 1969, and is credited with many underwater "firsts." Ball, an enthusiastic American, runs multiday, multidive trips along the Queensland coastline on which experienced divers get to set their own bottom times and dive their own plans—or be expertly guided. Custom-built, twin-hulled live-aboard boats loaded with top-end gear, serious divers, and qualified chefs depart twice-weekly to visit renowned dive sites and spot minke whales and sharks. Prices start at A$1,547 for a three-night fly/dive trip; allow for standard gear hire fees (A$40 per day) and nitrox, guides and reef tax (A$18 per trip). Dive courses cost extra, but the quality of instruction's high. ⊠ *143 Lake St., CBD* ☎ *07/4053–0500* ⊕ *www.mikeball.com.*

Ocean Spirit Cruises. Ocean Spirit Cruises offers daily trips that include four hours at Michaelmas Cay on the Great Barrier Reef (A$190) or coral viewing at Oyster and Upolo reefs (A$110-A$140); reef tax and port charges are included. The cost of both trips also includes guided snorkeling, optional dives, and a fresh buffet lunch with plenty of seafood, cold meats, salads, and dessert options. For guided introductory dives, you'll pay an extra A$120–A$175; for certified dives, it's A$60–A$100, gear included. If you're a beginner or aren't a strong swimmer, this might be the best operator for you. ⊠ *Office 3/Level 1, Shangri-La Marina, Pierpoint Rd., CBD* ☎ *07/4031–2920, 1800/644227* ⊕ *www.oceanspirit.com.au.*

Fodor'sChoice **Tusa Dive.** Among Cairns' best dive boats are the custom-built fast cats run
★ by Tusa Dive, which zoom up to 64 passengers out to sites on the Great Barrier Reef. On board, there's space aplenty. Get dive briefs and info en route to the sites, and continual refreshments including a big lunch. In the

water, people of all ages and experience levels can dive (A$190–A$265) or snorkel (A$165) under the watchful gaze of guides. Get your photo taken with marine critters for posterity. Three-day multi-dive live-aboard trips cost between A$510 and A$645 per person. ⊠ *Shield St. at The Esplanade, CBD* ☎ *07/4047–9100* ⊕ *www.tusadive.com.*

NIGHTLIFE

Cairns's Esplanade and the CBD streets leading off it come alive at night, with most restaurants serving until late, and wine a staple with evening meals. Several rowdy pubs catering to backpackers and younger travelers line the central section of City Place; a few bars and hotel venues manage to be upscale while remaining true to the city's easygoing spirit. Unless noted, bars are open nightly and there's no cover charge.

Casa de Meze. If you're looking for a feast—or a fiesta—Casa de Meze, with its tapas bar, Latin music, pasta, pizza, steaks, and signature seafood paella (A$29.90), is the place to be. Platters for two loaded with premium oysters, barbequed prawns, barramundi and coral trout, panfried chili mussels, steamed sand crab, Greek-style octopus, calamari fritti, and barbequed Moreton Bay Bugs (A$130) are practically reason enough to head here. On Friday and Saturday nights there are also DJs spinning Latin music and dancing till 2 am, and free hour-long salsa lessons from 9:30. (Friday, with topless barmen and free entry for ladies, is the Casa's "Girls' Night Out.") Other nights, the bar's open till around midnight. ⊠ *Level 1, Aplin St. at the Esplanade, CBD* ☎ *07/4051–5550* ⊕ *www.casademeze.com.au* ☉ *Daily, 5 pm till late.*

PJ O'Brien's Irish Pub. PJ O'Brien's, part of a nationwide chain of traditional Irish pubs, buzzes with backpackers swapping travel tales over pints and generally enjoying the *craic* (Gaelic for "good time"). It has good-value meal deals (A$12) at lunch and dinner, Coyote Ugly-style bar-dancing contests on Wednesday and Saturday nights, and is open until around 3 am. ⊠ *87 Lake St., CBD* ☎ *07/4031–5333* ⊕ *www.pjobriens.com.au.*

Vertigo Cocktail Bar & Lounge. Vertigo, on the ground floor of the Pullman Reef Hotel Casino, has live bands (including big-name acts) Wednesday through Saturday, karaoke on Sunday, and big production shows two or three nights a week, followed by DJs and dancing. It's open from 4 pm until 11 pm Monday and Tuesday, midnight Wednesday and Sunday, 1 am Thursday, and 2 am Friday and Saturday nights; entry is free. ⊠ *Pullmann Reef Hotel Casino, 35–41 Wharf St., CBD* ☎ *07/4030–8888, 1800/808883* ⊕ *www.reefcasino.com.au/vertigo.*

SHOPPING

MALLS

Cairns Central. Cairns Central, adjacent to Cairns Railway Station, houses 180-plus specialty stores, a Myer department store, a food court, and a six-screen cinema complex. The folks who represent the property claim it's the largest shopping center in Far North Queensland, and that might just be the case. Stroller hire is available. ⊠ *McLeod and Spence Sts., CBD* ☎ *07/4041–4111* ⊕ *www.cairnscentral.com.au.*

The Pier at the Marina. The Pier at the Marina houses the outlets of top Australian and international designers as well as a newsagent, bookstore, Internet café, salons, fitness facilities, and a visitor information center. Many of its bars and restaurants open onto waterfront verandas and the marina boardwalk. ⊠ *Pierpoint Rd., CBD* ☎ *07/4051–7244* ⊕ *www.thepier.com.au.*

MARKETS

The Cairns Night Markets. If you're looking for bargain beachwear, local jewelry, art and crafts, a massage, a meal, a coffee, or souvenirs, The Cairns Night Markets, open 5–11 pm weekdays, are the place to go. Bring cash—many of the 70-plus merchants charge additional fees for credit cards. ⊠ *71–75 The Esplanade, at Aplin St., CBD* ☎ *01/4051–7666* ⊕ *www.nightmarkets.com.au.*

Rusty's Markets. Cairns's best "street" market is Rusty's, with 180-plus stallholders selling homegrown produce, art and crafts, jewelry, clothing, natural health and skincare products, and even massages, as well as all sorts of food. The market is covered (so come escape the sun if needed); it's open Friday 5 am–6 pm, Saturday 6–3, and Sunday 6–2. ⊠ *Spence and Sheridan Sts., CBD* ☎ *07/4051–5100* ⊕ *www.rustysmarkets.com.au.*

SPECIALTY STORES

Jungara Aboriginal Art Gallery. Established in 1998, Jungara stocks authentic Aboriginal arts and artifacts from artists Australia-wide, plus pieces from Torres Strait Island, and is open daily from 10:30 am–10:30 pm. Jungara also has a gallery on Williams Esplanade in Palm Cove. ⊠ *Shop 8, 99 The Esplanade, CBD* ☎ *07/4051–5355* ⊕ *www.jungaraaboriginalart.com.au.*

Tusa Dive Shop. Tusa Dive Shop stocks a wide range of big-name dive gear as well as stinger and wet suits, swimwear, kids' gear, and accessories such as snorkels and sunscreen. ⊠ *The Esplanade at Shields St., CBD* ☎ *07/4047–9120* ⊕ *www.tusadive.com* ☉ *Daily 7:30 am–9 pm.*

NORTH OF CAIRNS

The Captain Cook Highway runs from Cairns to Mossman, a relatively civilized stretch known mostly for the resort towns of Palm Cove and Port Douglas. Past the Daintree River, wildlife parks and sunny coastal villages fade into sensationally wild terrain. If you came to Australia seeking high-octane sun, pristine coral cays, steamy jungles filled with exotic birdcalls and riotous vegetation, and a languid beachcomber lifestyle, head for the coast between Daintree and Cooktown.

The southern half of this coastline lies within Cape Tribulation, Daintree National Park, part of the Greater Daintree Wilderness Area, a region named to UNESCO's World Heritage list because of its unique ecology. To experience the area's natural splendor, there's no need to go past Cape Tribulation. However, the Bloomfield Track continues on to Cooktown, a frontier destination that tacks two days onto your itinerary. This rugged country breeds some maverick personalities offering fresh perspectives on Far North Queensland.

Prime time for visiting is May through September, when daily maximum temperatures average around 27°C (80°F) and the water is comfortably warm. During the wet season, November through April, expect rain, humidity and lots of bugs. Highly poisonous box and Irukandji jellyfish make the coastline unsafe for swimming from October through May, but "jellies" hardly ever drift out as far as the reefs, so you're safe to get wet there.

PALM COVE

23 km (14 mi) north of Cairns.

Fodor's Choice
★
A 35-minute drive north of Cairns, Palm Cove is one of Queensland's jewels: an idyllic, albeit expensive base from which to explore the far north. It's a quiet place, sought out by those in the know for its magnificent trees, calm waters, exceptionally clean beach, and excellent restaurants.

GETTING HERE AND AROUND
Getting here from Cairns is a cinch: by car, follow the signs from the city center to Captain Cook Highway, then head north, taking the Palm Cove turn-off after about 25 km (16 mi). Regular shuttle buses service Palm Cove from the airport and Cairns. Around this compact beach area, though, most people walk or cycle.

ESSENTIALS
Medical Clifton Beach Medical and Surgical ⊠ *Shop 12, Clifton Village Shopping Center, Captain Cook Hwy., Clifton Beach* ☎ *07/4059–1755* ⊕ *www.cbms.com.au.*

EXPLORING PALM COVE
A charming beachside village that sprawls back toward the highway, Palm Cove is easily navigated on foot. Many of the best accommodations, bars and eateries are strung along the oceanfront strip of Williams Esplanade, fronting what has been dubbed Australia's cleanest beach. At its far north end, a five-minute stroll from the "village," there's a jetty and small marina.

TOP ATTRACTIONS
☾ **Cairns Tropical Zoo.** The 10-acre Cairns Tropical Zoo is home to many species of Australian wildlife, including kangaroos, wombats, dingoes, emus, southern cassowaries, and reptiles including saltwater crocodiles. Most distinguished among its residents is Sarge, a 17-foot, 660-pound centenarian croc. The park has daily snake, crocodile, and bird shows. You can handle and hand-feed koalas and tame kangaroos, and have your photo taken with a koala, boa, or baby croc for A$16, or with all three for A$35. Daily Breakfast Time at the Zoo (from A$53, self-drive, including park entry) includes a wildlife presentation on the deck. The sanctuary incorporates Cairns Night Zoo (⊕ *www.cairnsnightzoo.com*) where, five evenings a week, up to 100 guests tuck in to a big barbecue dinner, then get close-up glimpses of Australia's fascinating nocturnal creatures on a guided tour (reservations essential). ⊠ *Captain Cook Hwy.* ⊕ *PO Box 214, Clifton Beach 4879* ☎ *07/4055–3669* ⊕ *www. cairnstropicalzoo.com.au* ☎ *A$33, A$99 night zoo, A$13–A$46 coach transfers* ⊙ *Daily 8:30–4; Night Zoo Mon.–Thurs. and Sat. 6:50–10.*

8

Palm Cove is one of many pristine beaches along the tropical Queensland coast.

Hartley's Crocodile Adventures. 13.5 km (8 mi) or 15 minutes' drive north of Palm Cove, Hartley's houses dozens of crocodiles, as well as koalas, wallabies, snakes, lizards, southern cassowaries and other tropical birds in natural environs, accessible via boardwalks and boats. Lagoon boat cruises and crocodile-farm tours (where the crocs are farmed for meat and skin) guarantee you close-up views of crocs, and there are daily cassowary and koala feedings, croc and snake shows, and more. Lilies Restaurant showcases local delicacies, including crocodile and 'roo. The education center has useful info on how to avoid croc attacks. If you don't feel like driving, **Down Under Tours** (☎ 07/4035–5566), **BTS Tours** (☎ 07/4099–5665), and many other operators include Hartley's on their day-tour itineraries. ⊠ *Captain Cook Hwy., Wangetti Beach* ✆ *P.O. Box 171 4879* ☎ *07/4055–3576* ⊕ *www.crocodileadventures. com* ✉ *A$33* ⊗ *Daily 8:30–5.*

Fodor'sChoice
★
Mareeba Tropical Savanna & Wetlands Reserve. Drive 70 km (44 mi) west of Palm Cove along the Kennedy Highway, past Mareeba, and you'll encounter another world: giant termite mounds dot savanna scrub, and vast reclaimed wetlands give refuge to hundreds of bird species, including Australia's only stork, the jabiru. The reserve runs a raft of nature-based excursions on and around the vast, lily-littered lagoons. A great-value 2½-hour Sunset Reserve Safari combines a bird-watching cruise, a ranger-guided savanna drive on which you'll spot wallabies and kangaroos, a "billy" tea and bird-hide stop, and fine Aussie wine and cheese. Advanced eco-certified luxury safari-tent accommodation comes with breakfast baskets (A$98–A$159) and, if you like, all meals—including self-catering BBQ fixings (A$198–A$260 per night)—as well

as wildlife-spotting and bird-watching walks. You can also paddle canoes or fly-fish for ancient species in the lagoons. Consider signing up for the Wetlands' fantastic four-day package including rainforest, reef, and outback trips, for A$815 per person (half that for kids); the price also includes accommodation and some meals. Daily transfers to and from Cairns are A$48 one-way. All proceeds feed back into the Wetlands' environmental work; you're not just paying for an experience, you're supporting a great not-for-profit organization and their strong, respected conservation efforts. ⊠ *142 Pickford Rd., Biboohra* ☎ *07/4093–2514* ⊕ *www.mareebawetlands.org.*

WORTH NOTING

Outback Opal Mine. At this opal infocenter and showroom, see huge specimens of Australia's unique gemstone as well as opalized seashells and fossils. A short documentary shows how an opal is formed, cut, and polished; the walk-through simulated mine has natural opals embedded in its walls. An on-site jewelry store showcases opals (naturally) as both unset stones and in jewelry (pricing ranges from less than A$10 to more than A$5,500). The mine is adjacent to Cairns Tropical Zoo. ⊠ *Captain Cook Hwy., Clifton Beach* ☎ *07/4055–3492* ⊕ *www.outbackopalmine. com.au* ✉ *Free* ☉ *Daily 9–6.*

OUTDOOR ACTIVITIES

Palm Cove makes a great base for rain-forest and reef activities—hiking, biking, horseback riding, rafting, ballooning, and ATV adventures on the Atherton Tableland; snorkeling, diving, and sailing around the Low Isles and Barrier Reef; sea kayaking just offshore; and scenic flights over just about anywhere a small plane can get on a tank of gas.

SEA KAYAKING · **Palm Cove Watersports.** Paddling around history-rich Double Island, 100 meters (33 feet) from Palm Cove Jetty, is a tranquil, eco-friendly way to get close to local marine life: you'll often spot dolphins, stingrays, turtles, and colorful fish on this local operator's sunrise sea-kayaking tours and half-day excursions, with stops for refreshments, snorkeling (May–November), and stretching en route. Helpful guides impart labor-saving tips on technique and safety briefings. Not that you're likely to capsize: the single and double kayaks are super-stable. Half-day trips circumnavigate Double Island, stopping off on the fringing reef about 600 meters (½ mi) from shore and on a secluded beach. Transfers from Cairns (A$25 per person) and Port Douglas (A$30 per person) available; bookings essential. Gear provided, but bring sunglasses, a hat, and sunscreen. ⊠ *100 meters south of Palm Cove Jetty, Williams Esplanade (north end)* ☎ *0402/861011* ⊕ *www. palmcovewatersports.com* ✉ *A$48, sunrise tour; A$88, half-day tour; A$10 reef tax/insurance* ☉ *Daily 6–7:30 am, sunrise tour; 8:30–12:30 and 1:30–5, half-day tour.*

WHERE TO EAT

$$ ✕ **Casmar Restaurant.** The ocean's bounty is the focus at this innovative,
AUSTRALIAN intimate waterfront restaurant. Try the seafood platter for two (A$90) with oysters, prawns, Moreton Bay bugs, chili-salt squid, scallops, reef fish, and various dipping sauces. Fresh barramundi-and-chips, roast lamb rump, and beef sirloin on mash are other crowd-pleasers. Leave

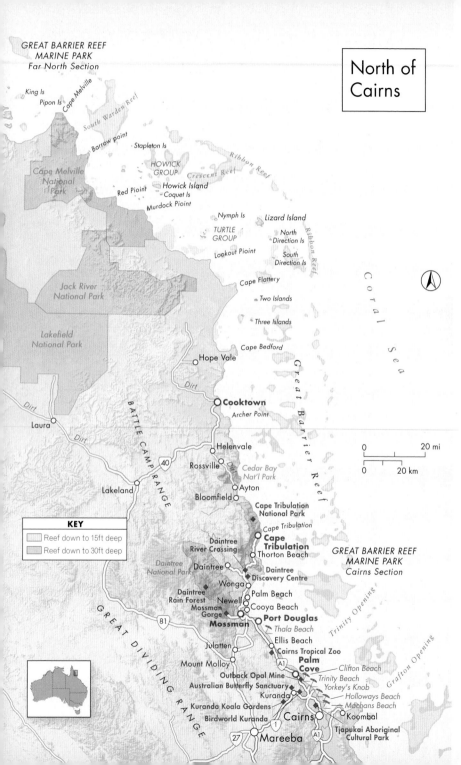

North of Cairns

GREAT BARRIER REEF
MARINE PARK
Far North Section

King Is
Pipon Is
Cape Melville
South Warden Reef
Barrow point
Stapleton Is
HOWICK GROUP
Crescent Reef
Ribbon Reef
Cape Melville National Park
Howick Island
Red Pioint
Coquet Is
Murdock Pioint
Nymph Is
Lizard Island
TURTLE GROUP
North Direction Is
South Direction Is
Lookout Pioint
Jack River National Park
Cape Flattery
Two Islands
Lakefield National Park
Three Islands
Cape Bedford
Hope Vale
Dirt
Laura
Dirt
BATTLE CAMP RANGE
Cooktown
Archer Point
Helenvale
40
Rossville
Dirt
Cedar Bay Nat'l Park
Lakeland
Ayton
Bloomfield
Cape Tribulation National Park
Cape Tribulation
Cape Tribulation
Daintree River Crossing
Thorton Beach
Daintree National Park
Daintree
Daintree Discovery Centre
Wonga
Daintree Rain Forest
Newell
Palm Beach
Cooya Beach
Mossman Gorge
81
Mossman
Port Douglas
Thala Beach
Julatten
Ellis Beach
Cairns Tropical Zoo
Mount Molloy
A1
Palm Cove
Clifton Beach
Outback Opal Mine
Trinity Beach
Australian Butterfly Sanctuary
Yorkey's Knob
Kuranda
Holloways Beach
Kuranda Koala Gardens
Machans Beach
Birdworld Kuranda
Koombal
27
Cairns
Mareeba
A1
Tjapukai Aboriginal Cultural Park
1

Coral Sea

Great Barrier Reef

GREAT BARRIER REEF
MARINE PARK
Cairns Section

Trinity Opening

Grafton Opening

GREAT DIVIDING RANGE

KEY
Reef down to 15ft deep
Reef down to 30ft deep

0   20 mi
0   20 km

space for a post-prandial coffee or liqueur and one of Casmar's divine desserts (A$10), best enjoyed by candlelight on the balcony. The food is a pleasure, as are the creative cocktails. You can also order take-out feasts, perfect for beach picnics. ⊠ *Level 1, 73 Williams Esplanade at Harpa St.* ☎ *07/4059–0013* ⊘ *No lunch.*

$$$
MODERN
AUSTRALIAN
Fodor's Choice
★

✕ **Nu Nu Restaurant.** Sexy suede lounges, intimate banquettes, and an uninterrupted view of Palm Cove beach make lingering easy at this top-nosh eatery next to the Beach Club (vanilla-ginger mojitos and lime-coconut daiquiris help). The chef, decamped from Melbourne, prides himself on an ever-changing Asia-meets-Mediterranean-inspired Mod-Oz menu. Dishes have a cutting-edge, flavorful twist, with seafood center stage: fresh-shucked Pacific oysters and roasted Hervey Bay scallops, wok-fried mud crab (A$70), line-caught reef fish and baby barramundi. You'll also find prime Victorian lamb and alpine goat, cardamom roast chicken, duck curry, and interesting vegetarian options on the menu—try the millionaires' salad of shaved palm hearts, baby herbs, and chili—as well as decadent, tropically inspired desserts. Splurge on the five- or eight-course tasting menu, with or without matched wines from an extensive list (A$90–A$200). Nu Nu's big breakfasts feature organic produce, fresh-baked sourdough, and pastries (daily 8–noon). ⊠ *123 Williams Esplanade* ☎ *07/4059–1880* ⊕ *www.nunu.com.au* ⊘ *Closed Tues.*

$$$
ECLECTIC

✕ **Vivo Bar and Grill.** Diners at this classy eatery enjoy dress-circle Coral Sea views framed by palms and melaleucas. Those views, plus tropical cocktails, vibrant decor, and fresh Mod-Oz-meets-Mediterranean dishes, draw food-loving locals and travelers in the know. House muesli and freshly baked breads make this a favorite breakfast spot, and panini, pasta, salads, and calamari pack in the crowds at lunch. At dinner, head chef Russell Molina transforms fine fresh seasonal produce, especially seafood, into inventive contemporary food in Vivo's gleaming open kitchen. Try his popular crispy-skin barramundi with mango-midori dressing or the king-prawn risotto, then indulge in the wattleseed bombe Alaska with flaming Sambuca. A chic sunken bar forms the hub of this sociable haunt; between meals, Vivo's a popular spot for city-strong coffee, tapas, and cocktails. It's a good idea to book ahead, especially on weekend evenings and in holiday periods. ⊠ *Williams Esplanade* ☎ *07/4059–0944* ⊕ *www.vivo.com.au* ⊘ *Daily from 7 am.*

WHERE TO STAY

For expanded hotel reviews, visit Fodors.com.

$$$$
★

🛏 **Angsana Resort & Spa.** Fine landscaping, pools, barbecues, and sunny areas in which to relax enhance this classy colonial-style vacation apartment complex fronting a palm-shaded white-sand beach. **Pros:** helpful staff; terrific location; good on-site bar-restaurant. **Cons:** no elevators; pools on the chilly side. ⊠ *1 Veivers Rd.* ☎ *07/4055–3000, 1800/050019* ⊕ *www.angsana.com* ⤵ *67 apartments* ⌂ *In-room: a/c in bedroom only (for rentals only), kitchen, Wi-Fi. In-hotel: restaurant, bar, pool, spa, beach, laundry facilities, business center, parking.*

⊞ **Kewarra Beach Resort & Spa.** This true beachfront property just south of Palm Cove has its priorities right: the sensitively designed, sleekly appointed bungalows and restored pioneer's cottage have silky wood floors, custom furnishings, and high-tech appointments (flat-screen LCD TVs, free VOIP-enabled Wi-Fi). **Pros:** high-end facilities and service; eco-friendly ethos; spectacular grounds; free Wi-Fi (even on the beach—though please don't be that guy who makes work phone calls from there). **Cons:** a drive from Palm Cove's cafés; no on-site gym. ⊠ *Kewarra St., Kewarra Beach* ☎ *07/4058–4000* ⊕ *www.kewarra.com* ⇆ *44 rooms* ☾ *In-room: a/c in bedroom only (for rentals only), no TV, Wi-Fi. In-hotel: restaurant, bar, pool, spa, beach, water sports, laundry facilities, parking* ❘○❘ *All-inclusive.*

⊞ **Peppers Beach Club & Spa.** The open-air reception area of this gorgeous beachfront resort opens onto landscaped grounds and one of the Club's three pools, fed by a soothing cascade of water. **Pros:** terrific dining options; laptops for hire; lovely pool. **Cons:** spa standards vary; gym equipment basic; pool area can be noisy. ⊠ *123 Williams Esplanade* ☎ *07/4059–9200, 1300/737–444* ⊕ *www.peppers.com.au* ⇆ *140 rooms and suites* ☾ *In-room: a/c, safe, kitchen, Internet, Wi-Fi. In-hotel: restaurant, bar, pool, tennis court, gym, spa, laundry facilities, business center, parking.*

⊞ **Reef House Resort & Spa.** This centrally located small resort, which was once a private residence, feels positively quaint, and that's a good thing when you're looking for a low-key escape in this low-key resort area. **Pros:** large rooms; in-house spa; nice restaurant. **Cons:** pools can be cold; breakfast is pretty expensive but not very expansive; no Wi-Fi access in rooms. ⊠ *99 Williams Esplanade, Palm Cove* ☎ *07/4055–3633* ⊕ *www.reefhouse.com.au* ⇆ *69 rooms* ☾ *In-room: a/c, safe, Internet. In-hotel: restaurant, bar, pool, spa, parking* ❘○❘ *Multiple meal plans.*

PORT DOUGLAS

67.4 km (42 mi) northwest of Cairns.

Known simply as "Port" to locals, Port Douglas offers almost as broad a range of outdoor adventures as Cairns, but in a more compact, laid-back setting. In this burgeoning tourist town there's a palpable buzz, despite tropical haze and humidity. Travelers from all over the world base themselves here when making excursions to the north's wild rain forests and Great Barrier Reef. Varied lodgings, restaurants, and bars center on and around Port's main strip, Macrossan Street.

Like much of North Queensland, Port Douglas was settled after gold was discovered nearby. When local ore deposits dwindled in the 1880s it became a port for sugar milled in nearby Mossman until the 1950s. The town's many old "Queenslander" buildings give it the feel of a humble seaside settlement, despite its modern resorts and overbuilt landscape. The rain forests and beaches enveloping the town are, for the most part, World Heritage sites—so while Port's growing in popularity, the landscapes that draw people here should remain undeveloped.

Have "Breakfast With the Birds" at Wildlife Habitat.

GETTING HERE AND AROUND

By car, it's a scenic, 75-minute drive north to Port Douglas from Cairns: take Sheridan Street to the Captain Cook Highway, following it for around 60 km (35 mi) to the Port Douglas turnoff. North of Palm Cove, along the 30-km (19-mi) Marlin Coast, the road plays hide-and-seek with an idyllic stretch of shoreline, ducking inland through tunnels of tropical coastal forest and curving back to the surf to reach Port Douglas.

Around town, most people drive, walk, or cycle. It's about 5½ km (3½ mi), or an hour's level walk from the highway to the main street. Regular shuttle buses call in at major hotels and resorts day and night, ferrying travelers to and from Cairns, the airport, and nearby towns and attractions.

ESSENTIALS

Banks Commonwealth Bank of Australia ✉ *Shop 15, Saltwater Building, Macrossan St. at Grant St.* ☎ *13/2221* ⊕ *www.commbank.com.au.*

Medical Port Village Medical Centre ✉ *33 Macrossan St., Port Douglas* ☎ *07/4099–5276* ⊕ *www.portdoctors.com.au.* **Port Douglas Police** ✉ *31 Wharf St.* ☎ *07/4099–5220.*

EXPLORING PORT DOUGLAS

Port Douglas is actually an isthmus, bounded by Four Mile Beach on one side, Dickson Inlet on the other, with the town's main retail, café, and restaurant strip, Macrossan Street, running up the center. The town sprawls as far as the highway, 5.5 km (3.5 mi) to the west, along Port Douglas Road, lined with upmarket resorts and holiday apartment complexes. At the far end of Macrossan Street, on Wharf Street, there's a busy marina and shopping complex.

Wildlife Habitat. Don't miss an outing to Wildlife Habitat—previously the Rainforest Habitat Wildlife Sanctuary—on the road to Port Douglas from the highway. You'll have many creature encounters around Australia, but the Breakfast with the Birds experience here—with avian residents so tame they'll perch on your shoulders as you dine (and may steal your steak if you're distracted)—is delightful. The park houses more than 180 species of tropical native wildlife, including cassowaries, parrots, wetland waders, koalas, kangaroos, and crocodiles in eight acres of world-class "immersion" wetland, rain-forest, and grassland environs. The "tropical" buffet breakfast, served daily 8–10:30, is A$45 including sanctuary admission and a well-worth-it guided tour. You can also Lunch with the Lorikeets for A$45, noon–2 daily, tag along on one of the sanctuary's free expert-guided tours (or book a VIP behind-scenes version), and attend croc, snake, and koala shows. ⊠ *Port Douglas Rd. at Agincourt St.* ☎ *07/4099–3235* ⊕ *www.wildlifehabitat.com.au* ⊡ *A$32* ⊙ *Daily 8–5, last admission at 4.*

OUTDOOR ACTIVITIES

Port Douglas is a great base for activities on the mainland and reef. Several tour companies conduct day trips into the rain forest and beyond in four-wheel-drive buses and vans; most include river cruises for crocodile-spotting and stops at local attractions. Several reef operators either base vessels at or pick up from Meridien Marinas' Marina Mirage Port Douglas. You can also horseback ride, bungee jump, raft, go off-roading, hike, mountain-bike, and balloon on and around the Atherton Tablelands, or go Outback for excellent bird- and wildlife-watching west of Mareeba, less than two hour's drive from Port.

BOAT TOURS **Crocodile Express.** *Crocodile Express*, a flat-bottom boat run by operators who've been plying this waterway since 1979, cruises the Daintree River from two main access points on crocodile-spotting excursions—though you may also see birds, butterflies, snakes, and lizards en route. Sixty-minute cruises leave the Daintree Gateway, near the ferry crossing point, at regular intervals from 8:30 am to 2:30 pm (A$25 per person); alternatively, leave from Daintree Village Jetty from 10 to 3:30 (A$25). Extra cruises are scheduled in peak periods. ⊠ *5 Stewart St., end of Mossman–Daintree Rd., Daintree Village* ☎ *07/4098–6120* ⊕ *www. crocodileexpress.com.*

Tony's Tropical Tours. Tony's Tropical Tours gives entertaining small-group day tours in luxe land cruisers that take in rain-forest sights and attractions as far as Cape Tribulation (A$165) or, if you're prepared to get up earlier, the renowned and ruggedly beautiful Bloomfield Track (A$185). Well-informed, witty commentary from Tony and other local experts, and non-rushed, well-chosen stops and activities—from interpretative rain-forest walks and Daintree River wildlife (croc) cruises, to hand-made ice-cream and tropical-fruit tasting—make these trips crowd-pleasers. Refreshments, included in the cost, are a cut above the norm: think plunger (French press) coffee, rain-forest tea, and a satisfying BBQ lunch. There's also a terrific charter tour to the Crater Lakes, Atherton Tablelands, and Mareeba Wetlands (A$940 for 4 people). ⌂ *Box 206, Port Douglas 4877* ☎ *07/4099–3230* ⊕ *www.tropicaltours.com.au.*

DAY TOURS **Back Country Bliss Adventures.** Back Country Bliss Adventures is based
☺ in Port Douglas but ranges much farther afield. Its customised, cul-
Fodor'sChoice turally and eco-sensitive small-group day and multiday trips take you
★ to nature and adventure hot spots from the Atherton Tablelands and
Mareeba Wetlands to Cape Trib and Cooktown. Go sea kayaking,
wakeboarding, or kite-surfing, rafting and mountain biking, drift-
snorkelling in rain-forest streams, or "jungle surfing" over the canopy; or take a guided 4WD trip along the ruggedly scenic Bloomfield
Track. Well-chosen wilderness locations, quality equipment, excellent
staff including indigenous guides, and Wet Tropic World Heritage
Tour Operator accreditation give the Bliss team the edge. ⊕ *PO Box
9744877* ☎ *07/4099–3677* ⊕ *www.blissbackcountrytours.com.au.*

FISHING *Norseman.* Long-established MV *Norseman* is one of the best game-
fishing boats on the Great Barrier Reef. Novice and experienced anglers
can head out to the reef's edge on a 60-foot, purpose-designed high-tech
vessel to fish for large pelagic fish including Spanish mackerel, tuna,
wahoo, and the elusive giant trevally. Closer in, find sea perch, mangrove Jack, red and spangled emperor, and coral trout. ⊠ *Closehaven
Marina, Port St.* ☎ *07/4099–6668* ⊕ *www.mvnorseman.com.au.*

REEF TRIPS/ **Poseidon.** Poseidon conducts guided snorkeling and PADI-style diving
SNORKELING/ trips to sites at three separate parts of the Agincourt Ribbon Reef on a
DIVING small, usually uncrowded boat, and longer cruises to Outer Great Bar-
☺ rier Reef sites, with excellent pre-dive briefings by a marine naturalist,
Fodor'sChoice high safety standards, and a wider-than-average choice of dive sites. A
★ day's cruise is A$195.50, plus a rental fee for diving or snorkeling gear;
introductory diving, including tuition, cruise, all gear, and up to three
underwater forays, is A$250 (with one dive; subsequent dives are A$40
each). For certified divers, a full day in the water, including two or three
dives and a buffet lunch, is A$230–A$245. ⊠ *Grant and Macrossan
Sts.* ☎ *1800/085–674, 07/4099–4772* ⊕ *www.poseidon-cruises.com.
au* ⊴ *A$195.50–A$250 cruise, A$5.50 reef tax* ☉ *Daily 8:30–4:30.*

☺ **Quicksilver Connections.** Quicksilver Connections runs fast, modern cata-
★ marans from the Port Douglas marina to a large commercial activity
platform at Agincourt Reef on the Outer Great Barrier Reef (A$205),
where options include marine-biologist-guided snorkeling tours (A$47–
$67), scuba diving (A$99–A$149), 10-minute scenic heli-tours (A$148),
and "Ocean Walker" sea-bed tours (A$146). There's also a semisub-
mersible underwater observatory. A quieter sailing excursion to a Low
Isles coral cay, closer to shore (A$150), includes a biologist-guided
glass-bottom-boat trip and snorkeling. Everyone pays a A$5.50 reef
tax. The staff is patient, efficient, and knowledgeable. The trip includes
a lunch buffet. Transfers are available from Port Douglas accommodations, Palm Cove, the Northern Beaches, and Cairns (A$8-A420).
⊠ *Marina Mirage, 1 Wharf St.* ⊕ *P.O. Box 171 4877* ☎ *07/4087–2100*
⊕ *www.quicksilver-cruises.com.*

SIGHTSEEING **Daintree Tours by Deluxe Safaris.** Daintree Tours by Deluxe Safaris con-
TOURS ducts day-long, well-guided trips in top-of-the-line 4WD vehicles and
custom-built trucks. Visit the Atherton Tablelands, Mossman Gorge,
and Cape Tribulation (A$165), or take the rugged track to Bloomfield

8

Falls (A$185). All safaris stop for guided walks, swims, and croc-spotting cruises, and visit the Daintree Ice Cream Factory. You can also arrange a day-long private wildlife-spotting charter to the Outback, west of Mareeba. Ample lunch and refreshments, included in all excursions, ensure that you keep your strength up. ⊠ *Shop 3A, 23 Warner St.* ☎ *07/4099–6406, 1800/005–966* ⊕ *www.deluxesafaris.com.au.*

♻ **Reef and Rainforest Connections.** Reef and Rainforest Connections' day trips out of Port Douglas include visits to Kuranda's key attractions, including the Scenic Railway and Skyrail Rainforest Cableway, with add-ons such as Tjapukai Aboriginal Cultural Park, Hartley's croc farm, and Wildlife Habitat, an open-enclosure sanctuary. The company also runs excursions to Cape Tribulation, the Daintree, and Mossman Gorge, and out to the Great Barrier Reef with Quicksilver. ⊠ *40 Macrossan St.* ☎ *1300/780–455, 07/4035–5566* ⊕ *www.reefandrainforest.com.au.*

WHERE TO EAT

$$$ ✕ **Bistro 3.** This chic, colorful eatery has an unabashedly local focus,
MODERN   showing off the region's best in tasty Mod-Oz dishes and serving fine
AUSTRALIAN   Australian wines. The signature Daintree saltwater whole crispy baby
★   barramundi is farmed in Wonga Beach and delivered fresh daily. They also do a terrific spiced tempura soft-shell crab on green papaya salad, handmade pasta, Black Angus sirloin steak, and chocolate sapote and mandarin mousse cake. Bistro 3's Sunday brunch is the perfect hangover cure, and any time of day they'll mix you a mean specialty cocktail. A reservation isn't technically essential, but it's a very good idea. ⊠ *Wharf and Macrossan Sts.* ⌁ *P.O. Box 668 4877* ☎ *07/4099–6100* ⊕ *www.bistro3.com.*

$$$ ✕ **Harrison's Restaurant.** A classic "Queenslander" with a lovely outdoor
INTERNATIONAL   cocktails area shaded by century-old mango trees and fine-dining in the house itself, Harrison's occupies a prime position opposite the Port Douglas foreshore. New owners have given the old room a revamp—and a serious culinary upgrade. Think deftly executed French meets Modern Australian cuisine with the emphasis on fresh seafood and premium local produce. You might start with Moreton Bay bugs or yellowfin tuna sashimi; mains on offer could include a mouthwatering Chateaubriand of Victorian Black Angus steak with truffle mash, red wine jus, and sauce Béarnaise, or fish like roasted barramundi or line-caught coral trout. Desserts include classic French favorite, Grand-Marnier-flambeed crepes Suzette (A$30 for 2), or Harry's Eton mess, a divine mix of strawberries, puree, meringue, red fruit, and poppy-seed jelly with Chantilly cream. There's a delectable six-course "menu gourmande" for A$100 per person, A$150 with matched wines; a four-course one for the faint-hearted is A$75 or A$125 with wines. ⊠ *22 Wharf St.* ☎ *07/4099–4011* ⊕ *www.harrisonsrestaurant.com.au* ⌁ *Reservations essential* ☉ *Daily breakfast, lunch, and dinner.*

$$$ ✕ **On The Inlet Seafood Restaurant.** Choose your own live mud crab from
SEAFOOD   holding tanks at this much-lauded seafood restaurant fronting Dickson
♻   Inlet. Watch yachts dock as you sit on the deck and down the sunset
★   special: a generous bucket of prawns and a choice of beer, wine, or bubbly for A$18; arrive around 5 and you can watch resident giant 250-kilogram (550-lb) grouper, George, get fed. Modern Australian

dishes—chili-spiked salmon and seafood linguine with sundried tomato; pan-fried fish of the day—put the focus on fine, fresh North Queensland produce and seafood that's delivered direct from local fishing boats to the restaurant's pontoon. Non-pescophiles are well catered to with eye fillet steak, chicken, and vegetarian options. There's a good kids' menu (A$15, 2 courses), and a terrific wine and cocktail list. If you're planning to come during peak dinner hours, a reservation is highly recommended. ☒ *3 Inlet St.* ☎ *07/4099–5255* ⊕ *www.portdouglasseafood. com* ☉ *Daily from 10 am.*

$$
MODERN
AUSTRALIAN
★

✕ **Salsa Bar & Grill.** This lively waterside restaurant is a Port Douglas institution. The louver-windowed interior is bright and beachy; the large wooden deck overlooking Dickson Inlet becomes an intimate dining area after sunset. Seafood, steaks, salads, and light snacks grace the lunch menu; a tropical Modern Australian dinner menu includes kangaroo loin, smoked duck breast, eye fillet, herb-crusted barramundi, yellowfin tuna, a standout seafood linguine, and a house jambalaya loaded with yabbies (local crayfish), tiger prawns, squid, and croc sausage. There's an extensive Antipodean wine list, and happy hour comes daily between 3 and 5, just right for a tropical daiquiri or two. Prebooking is strongly advised. ☒ *26 Wharf St.* ☎ *07/4099–4922* ⊕ *www. salsaportdouglas.com.au.*

WHERE TO STAY

For expanded hotel reviews, visit Fodors.com.

$$$
★

🏠 **Coconut Grove Apartments Port Douglas.** These luxe three-bedroom apartments and penthouses perched above Port's main strip have state-of-the-art furnishings and appliances, deep free-standing spa baths, and large entertaining spaces including huge balconies or decks. **Pros:** immaculate, user-friendly living areas; central location; gourmet food options. **Cons:** extra fees for Wi-Fi use and servicing; standard-issue sheets; two-night minimum stay (longer in peak periods). ☒ *56 Macrossan St.* ☎ *07/4099–0600* ⊕ *www.coconutgroveportdouglas.com.au* ↪ *31 apartments, 2 penthouses* △ *In-room: safe, kitchen, Internet, Wi-Fi. In-hotel: pool, beach, laundry facilities, parking* ☉ *8 am–6 pm reception/concierge/tour desk* ⧦ *No meals.*

¢

🏠 **Global Backpackers.** This tidy budget accommodation above Rattle and Hum has modern dorms (from A$27 per person), simple yet well-kept doubles with en-suites (A$90), and clean, sleek public areas including a lounge with plasma TV. **Pros:** boutique decor and facilities at budget prices; clean rooms with better-than-average beds; central location. **Cons:** can be noisy; dorms smallish; no outdoor areas or pool. ☒ *Upstairs, 38 Macrossan St.* ☎ *07/4099–5641, 1800/682647* ⊕ *www. globalbackpackerscairns.com.au/portdouglas* △ *In-room: no TV. In-hotel: restaurant, bar, laundry facilities, business center* ⧦ *No meals.*

$$$
☾
★

🏠 **Mandalay Luxury Beachfront Apartments.** With beautiful Four-Mile Beach just outside the back gate and restaurants and shops within walking distance, you can't find a better location than these comfortable, expansive, fully-equipped apartments. **Pros:** reasonable rates, especially for two-bedroom units; plenty of space; close to the beach. **Cons:** the street outside is poorly lit at night; no reception in off-hours; closest restaurants are a 10-minute walk away. ☒ *Garrick and Beryl Sts., Port*

8

Douglas ⓓ *PO Box 251, Port Douglas 4877* ☎ *7/4099–0100* ⊕ *www.mandalay.com.au* ⤳ *16 2-bedroom apartments, 26 3-bedroom apartments* ⌂ *In-room: a/c, safe, kitchen, Internet, Wi-Fi. In-hotel: pool, tennis court, laundry facilities, parking* ⦿ *No meals.*

$$$ ⛫ **Sea Temple Resort & Spa.** A grand marble-columned lobby, flow-through public areas, well-tended grounds, and vast swimming pools flanked by sun-lounges and dramatically torch-lit at night lend a Riviera-meets-Phuket ambience to this exclusive resort. **Pros:** lovely environs and pools; school-holiday activities programs; generous discounts for multi-night stays. **Cons:** pricey food and drinks; sluggish Internet in Spa rooms; service standards vary. ⊠ *Mitre St.* ☎ *07/4084–3500, 1800/833-762* ⊕ *www.seatempleresorts.com* ⤳ *194 spa rooms, apartments, and penthouses* ⌂ *In-room: a/c, safe, kitchen, Internet, Wi-Fi. In-hotel: restaurant, bar, golf course, pool, gym, spa, beach, children's programs, laundry facilities, parking* ⦿ *Multiple meal plans.*

$$ ⛫ **Sheraton Mirage Port Douglas Resort.** One of the oldest beachfront resorts in Port Douglas has a stunning array of saltwater lagoon pools and an excellent 18-hole golf course, making it a good choice even though it's starting to show its age. ■**TIP**→ Always check into packages (particularly those that include the exceptional but expensive breakfast buffet) that can offer significant savings, especially for stays of over three nights. **Pros:** the saltwater lagoon pools are absolutely magnificent; the beach is steps away from the resort; plenty of facilities and programs to keep you occupied. **Cons:** rooms need updating; not close to off-site restaurants and shopping; cost of food and other extras can really add up; children's programs offered only during Australian school holidays. ⊠ *Davidson St., Port Douglas* ⓓ *PO Box 172, Port Douglas 4877* ☎ *7/4099–5888* ⊕ *www.starwoodhotels.com* ⤳ *291 rooms, 3 suites, 100 villas* ⌂ *In-room: a/c, safe, kitchen, Internet, Wi-Fi. In-hotel: restaurant, bar, golf course, pool, gym, spa, beach, children's programs, business center, parking* ⦿ *Multiple meal plans.*

$$
ALL-INCLUSIVE
★
⛫ **Thala Beach Lodge.** Set on 145 acres of private beach, coconut groves, and forest, this eco-certified nature lodge is about low-key luxury. **Pros:** interesting activities; beautiful property; eco-friendly ethos; multi-day packages (including tours) available. **Cons:** no in-room Internet acess; limited food available between meals; 20-minute drive to Port Douglas. ⊠ *Private Beach Rd. (off Bruce Hwy., 24 mi north of Cairns), Oak Beach* ☎ *07/4098–5700* ⊕ *www.thalabeach.com.au* ⤳ *45 rooms* ⌂ *In-room: a/c, safe. In-hotel: restaurant, bar, pool, spa, beach, water sports, business center, parking* ⦿ *All-inclusive.*

SHOPPING

Marina Mirage Port Douglas. Marina Mirage houses fashion, specialty, and souvenir shops; hair and beauty salons; a newsagency and an Internet café; the offices of various cruise, dive, and tour operators; and a handful of restaurants. ⊠ *65 Macrossan St., at Wharf St.* ☎ *07/4099–5775* ⊕ *www.meridienmarinas.com.au* ⊗ *Daily 8–5.*

Port Douglas Markets. At the waterfront Port Douglas Markets, local growers and artisans gather on Sunday mornings to sell fresh tropical produce and gourmet goodies, original art and crafts, hand-made garments, jewelry, books, and souvenirs by the shore. You can also get reflexology massages and hair-braiding and -beading. The atmosphere's relaxed, the crowd's colorful, and there's plenty of variety. ⊠ *Anzac Park, Wharf St. end of Macrossan St.* ☎ *0408/006–788* ☉ *Sun. 8 am–2 pm.*

MOSSMAN

14 km (8½ mi) northwest of Port Douglas, 75 km (47 mi) north of Cairns.

This sleepy sugarcane town of just a couple of thousand residents attracts few visitors: most merely pass through en route to Mossman Gorge, the Daintree, and rain-forest accommodations.

GETTING HERE AND AROUND

From Port Douglas it's 20 km (12 mi) or about 20 minutes' drive northwest to Mossman. From Cairns it's a 75-km (47-mi) drive along the Captain Cook Highway. There's little here to explore, but it's a good place to stop for supplies and has a few fine eateries.

ESSENTIALS

Medical **Mossman Medical Centre** ⊠ *37 Front St.* ☎ *07/4098–1248* ⊕ *www.portdoctors.com.au.*

Visitor Information **Tourism Daintree Region** ☎ *No phone* ⊕ *www.daintreevillage.asn.au.*

EXPLORING MOSSMAN

Daintree Village, a half-hour drive north along the Mossman-Daintree Road, has restaurants, cafés, galleries, and access to croc river cruises. Drive 20 minutes northeast of Mossman to reach Wonga Beach, where you can ride horses along the sand or go walkabout with indigenous guides.

Fodor's Choice ★ **Mossman Gorge.** Just 5 km (3 mi) out of town are the spectacular waterfalls and river that tumble through sheer-walled Mossman Gorge. Ice-cold water flows here year-round, and there are several boulder-studded, croc-free swimming holes. (Swimming in the river itself is hazardous, crocs or no, due to swift currents, slippery rocks, and flash flooding.) There's a suspension bridge across the Mossman River and a 2½-km (1½-mi) rain-forest walking track. Keep your eyes peeled for tree and musky rat-kangaroos, Boyd's water dragons, scrub fowl, turtles, and big, bright butterflies—and try to avoid stinging vines (plants with serrated-edge, heart-shaped leaves, found at rain-forest edges). If you intend hiking beyond the river and rain-forest circuits, inform one of the appropriate authorities: Queensland Parks & Wildlife Service (✑ *info@derm.qld.gov.au*), Cairns and Tropical North Visitor Information Centre (☎ *07/4051–3588* ✑ *info@ttnq.org.au*), or the area's local guardians, Kuku Yalanji Dreaming (✑ *tours@yalanji.com.au*). ⊠ *Kuku Yalanji Dreaming, Gorge Rd.* ☎ *07/4098–2595* ⊕ *www.derm. qld.gov.au.*

Shannonvale Tropical Fruit Winery. Call in at the cellar door, open daily 10–4:30, and taste up to a dozen fine single-fruit wines made from organic fruits grown on-site. With mango, pineapple, passionfruit, purple mangosteen, grapefruit, limecello, and more, there's a drop to suit every palate, from dry table varieties to dessert wines and ports. Try the medal-winning Black Sapote (chocolate pudding fruit) port;

8

then buy a bottle for the road (or get a case shipped home). Your $5 tasting fee comes off any purchase. ■ TIP→ It's best to phone ahead and arrange a time to stop by; make sure you have a decent map to get there with, as some find it difficult to locate (but your efforts will be rewarded). ⊠ *417 Shannonvale Rd., Shannon Valley,* ☎ *07/4098–4000* ⊕ *www. shannonvalewine.com.au.*

OUTDOOR ACTIVITIES

ABORIGINAL TOURS **Kuku Yalanji Dreamtime.** On this 1½-hour walk along easy, graded rainforest tracks, you'll visit culturally significant sites and traditional bark settlements with a Kuku Yalanji guide. He or she will demonstrate traditional plant use, explain the history of cave paintings, point out bush tucker ingredients, and share Dreamtime legends, conveying the indigenous owners' special relationship with this ancient tropical terrain. Afterwards, enjoy billy tea and damper, then browse the aboriginal art and artefacts at the gallery shop and info center. ⊠ *Mossman Gorge Rd., Mossman* ☎ *07/4098–2595* ⊕ *www.yalanji.com.au* ⚏ *A$35, Port Douglas transfers available* ⊙ *Gallery/infocenter, Daily 8:30–5. Tours, Mon.–Sat. 9, 11, 1, and 3.*

★ **Walkabout Cultural Adventures.** Daintree Eco Lodge & Spa offers a raft of Aboriginal-guided activities, mostly operated by Juan Walker, the owner of Walkabout Adventures. His hour-long Guided Aboriginal Rainforest Walk (A$40), offered several days a week, gives insights into the Kuku Yalanji culture, indigenous bush tucker, medicinal plants, and local wildlife, and takes in a waterfall important for women's healing. A two-hour hands-on, sociable Aboriginal Art and Cultural Workshop (A$68) takes place most afternoons on the bar/restaurant's airy deck. Both of these shorter experiences should be booked directly through Daintree Eco Lodge & Spa. But if you're looking for something a bit more adventurous, Juan also offers half- or full-day rain-forest safari and coastal hunting trips and is happy to create more unique, personalized itineraries. ⊠ *Daintree Eco Lodge & Spa, 20 Daintree Rd., 3 km (2 mi) past Daintree village, Daintree* ☎ *07/4098–6100 for Daintree Eco Lodge & Spa, 04/2947–8206 for Juan Walker* ⊕ *www.walkaboutadventures. com.au* ⚏ *Longer tours A$150 (half day)–A$190 (full day)* ⊙ *Daily, prebooking essential.*

HORSEBACK RIDING **The Australian Muster Experience.** Impressive displays of horsemanship and "jackeroo" (cowboy) skills are the draw at The Australian Muster Experience, 35 minutes' drive north of Port Douglas. Daily shows, staged in a 19th-century-inspired "Outback station shed" arena in rain-forest environs 12.5 km (8 mi) north of Mossman, include whip-cracking, cattle-driving, a bull catcher, quad bikes (ATVs), plus super-smart cattle dogs, stunt horses, and various other animals. It's all delivered with dry Outback humor and followed by a BBQ lunch or dinner, live music, and bush tales. Choose between the Stockmans Lunch Muster and the Grand Outback Experience (after which you can test your rodeo skills on a mechanical bull). There's a cash bar and combined gallery–giftshop on-site. ⊠ *Kingston Rd., Whyanbeel Valley* ☎ *07/4098–1149* ⊕ *www.australianmusterexperience.com* ⚏ *A$108, A$156 with transfers (Grand Outback); A$63, A$120 with transfers (Stockmans Lunch)* ⊙ *Daily 8:30 am, 2:30 pm.*

From their watery perch, two visitors survey a swimming hole at Mossman Gorge.

✺ **Wonga Beach Horse Rides.** This terrain is ideal for exploring on horse-
★ back, and one of the area's best guides is Wonga Beach Horse Rides.
Well-guided 2½-hour rides take you along Wonga Beach and pristine
Daintree rain-forest trails, crossing creeks in wet season. Keep an eye
out for rays, dolphins, and jumping cod in the ocean; birds, butterflies,
and reptiles in the forest. The cost includes gear, drinks, and Port Douglas pickups. You can also book two-hour sunset rides in season (A$90),
exclusive guided rides (A$170–A$210, min. 2 persons), and one-hour
lessons (A$60). ⊠ *Wonga Beach Equestrian Centre, Mossman-Dain-
tree Rd., Wonga Beach* ✆ *PO Box 2384873* ☎ *07/4099–1117* ⊕ *www.
beachhorserides.com.au* ⊠ *A$115 plus $A10 insurance* ⊗ *Daily 8:30
am, 2:30 pm; sunset rides 4 pm.*

WHERE TO STAY
For expanded hotel reviews, visit Fodors.com.

$$$$ 🏨 **Daintree Eco Lodge & Spa.** Dozens of stars have taken time out at
★ this 30-acre boutique eco-resort in the ancient Daintree rain forest;
elevated boardwalks protect the fragile environs, linking the spa, heated
pool, restaurant-bar-lounge-deck and 15 freestanding tree houses. **Pros:**
alfresco spa treatments; luxe, house-made bathroom amenities; eco-
friendly; lower rates with longer stays; no kids under 6. **Cons:** some
rooms lack seclusion; few rooms get Wi-Fi; rooms (particularly bathrooms) are pretty basic for the price; noise from public areas carries to
rooms and spa. ⊠ *20 Daintree Rd., 3 km (2 mi) past Daintree village,
110 km (68 mi) north of Cairns* ✆ *PMB 20 4873* ☎ *1800/808–010 toll-
free within Australia, 07/4098–6100* ⊕ *www.daintree-ecolodge.com.au*

Silky Oaks Lodge, near Daintree National Park.

🛏 *15 rooms* 🏊 *In-room: a/c, Internet, Wi-Fi. In-hotel: restaurant, bar, pool, spa, business center, parking, some age restrictions* 🍴 *Breakfast.*

$$$$
Fodor's Choice
★

🏆 **Silky Oaks Lodge.** Surrounded by national parkland, this Advanced Ecotourism-certified hotel is reminiscent of high-end African safari lodges. **Pros:** lovely spa; glorious location; top-notch food; French-press coffee at breakfast. **Cons:** no in-room TV or Internet; steep paths and long walks to some rooms; occasional critters; access road can flood after heavy rain. ✉ *Finlayvale Rd., Mossman Gorge* 📞 *07/4098–1666* 🌐 *www.silkyoakslodge.com.au* 🛏 *37 rooms, 13 suites* 🏊 *In-room: a/c, safe, no TV. In-hotel: restaurant, bar, pool, tennis court, gym, spa, water sports, laundry facilities, business center, parking, some age restrictions* 🍴 *Breakfast.*

CAPE TRIBULATION

35 km (22 mi) north of the Daintree River crossing, 140 km (87 mi) north of Cairns.

Set dramatically at the base of Mt. Sorrow, Cape Tribulation was named by Captain James Cook after a nearby reef snagged the HMS *Endeavour*, forcing him to seek refuge at the site of present-day Cooktown. Today the tiny settlement, little more than a general store and a few lodges, is the activities and accommodations base for the surrounding national park.

GETTING HERE AND AROUND

Daintree River. The turnoff for the Daintree River crossing is just under 30 km (18 mi) north of Mossman on the Daintree–Mossman Road, which winds through sugarcane plantations and towering green hills to the Daintree River, a short waterway fed by monsoonal rains that make it a favorite inland haunt for saltwater crocodiles. On the northerly side of the river, a sign announces Cape Tribulation National Park. There's just one ferry, carrying a maximum 27 vehicles, so although the crossing takes five minutes, the wait can be 15, especially between 11 am and 1 pm and in holiday periods. ☎ *07/4098–7536* ⊕ *www.capetribulation. com.au* ✉ *A$21 per car (round-trip), A$2 walk-on passenger, A$42 multiday car pass (5 return trips)* ☉ *Daily 6 am–midnight.*

North of the river, the road winds its way to Cape Tribulation, burrowing through dense rain forest and onto open stretches high above the coast, with spectacular views of the mountains and coastline. The 140-km (86-mi) drive from Cairns to Cape Trib takes just under three hours. If you're renting a car, it's simplest to do so in Cairns or Port Douglas.

This can be tough driving territory. The "highway" is narrow with just two lanes; many minor roads are rough and unpaved; and even major thruways in this area may be closed in the wet season due to flooding.

Mason's Cape Tribulation Tourist Information Centre & Shop and PK's Jungle Village, a little farther north on the opposite side of Cape Tribulation Road, are the last stops for food, supplies, and fuel as you head north. At PK's there's an IGA supermarket and the Cape Trib Pharmacy.

ATMs are scarce beyond Mossman. Get cash at the Caltex service station and convenience store at Wonga Beach or at PK's. North of the Daintree River, mobile phone coverage is limited (except in and around Mossman and Daintree Village), and you'll be lucky to get any signal once you get as far as Cape Tribulation.

Public transport is limited throughout the region. Coral Reef Coaches runs daily services between Cairns, Port Douglas, and Mossman/Silky Oaks Lodge. Sun Palm Transport Group's daily services link Cairns, Palm Cove, Port Douglas, Mossman, Daintree, Cow Bay, and Cape Trib: the full journey takes three to four hours, with stops at most resorts on request, and is A$78 ($A48 from Port Douglas; A$68 from Palm Cove).

ESSENTIALS

ATMs Caltex Wonga ✉ *Daintree Rd., Wonga Beach* ☎ *07/4098-7616.*

Bus Contacts Coral Reef Coaches ☎ *07/4098-2800*
⊕ *www.coralreefcoaches.com.au.* **Sun Palm Transport Group** ☎ *07/4087-2900*
⊕ *www.sunpalmtransport.com.*

Tours and Visitor Information Mason's Cape Tribulation Tourist Information Centre, Shop, & Mason's Tours ✉ *CMA 4, Cape Tribulation Rd.*
☎ *07/4098-0070* ⊕ *www.masonstours.com.au.* **PK's Jungle Village**
✉ *PMB 7, Cape Tribulation Rd.* ☎ *1800/232333, 07/4098-0040*
⊕ *www.pksjunglevillage.com.au.*

8

EXPLORING CAPE TRIBULATION

Cape Tribulation Road winds through rain forest north of Cow Bay, veering east to join the coast at Thornton Beach, then skirting a string of near-deserted beaches en route to Cape Trib. Accommodations, attractions, and access points for beaches, croc cruise boats, and mangrove and rain-forest boardwalks are well signposted from the main road.

These rugged-looking yet fragile environs, Kuku Yalanji tribal lands, are best explored with experienced, culturally sensitive and eco-conscious guides. Excursions by 4WD and on horseback, bicycle, boat, and foot are all offered by local operators and resorts.

If exploring off-road on your own, arm yourself with detailed local maps, supplies, and good information. Let a reliable person know your intended route and return time, and don't underestimate the wildness of this terrain.

HIKING **Cape Tribulation, Daintree National Park.** Cape Tribulation, Daintree

Fodor's Choice National Park—the world's oldest tropical rain forest—is an ecological
★ wonderland: 85 of the 120 rarest species on earth are found here, and new ones are still being discovered. The 22,000-acre park, part of the UNESCO World Heritage–listed Wet Tropics region, stretches along the coast and west into the jungle from Cow Bay, 40 km (25 mi) or around an hour's drive northwest of Mossman, to Aytor. Traditional owners, the Eastern Kuku Yalanji, who live in well-honed harmony with their rain-forest environs, attribute powerful properties to many local sites— so tread carefully. Prime hiking season here is May through September, and many local operators offer guided Daintree rain-forest walks, longer hikes, and nighttime wildlife-spotting excursions. Gather information and maps from local rangers or the **Queensland Parks & Wildlife Service** Web site before hiking unguided, and stay on marked trails and boardwalks to avoid damaging your fragile surroundings. Whatever season you go, bring insect repellent. ☎ *13/7468* ⊕ *www.derm.qld.gov.au.*

OUTDOOR ACTIVITIES

CANOPY **Daintree Discovery Centre.** This World Heritage-accredited Wet Tropics
TOURS Visitor Centre (a specific category of visitor center in Australia) provides detailed information on the rain forest and its ecosystem. There are four audio-guided trails, including the Bush Tucker Trail and the Cassowary Circuit. Take the Aerial Walkway across part of the bush, and climb the stairs to the top of the 76-foot-high Canopy Tower. Pre-book a guided group tour or take the detailed audio-self-guided one. The shop sells books, cards, souvenirs, and clothing. There's also a good on-site cafe. ⊠ *Tulip Oak Rd. off Cape Tribulation Rd., 10 km (6 mi) north of Daintree River ferry station, Cow Bay* ☎ *07/4098–9171* ⊕ *www. daintree-rec.com.au* ⊑ *A$28 (includes 48-page guidebook/ return entry for 7 days)* ☉ *Daily 8:30–5.*

↻ **Jungle Surfing Canopy Tours.** It's an exhilarating perspective on the rain for-
★ est and reef: suspended above the canopy on flying-fox ziplines, your speed controlled by guides, you whiz along (and if you like, flip upside-down) over lush rain forest and Mason's Creek, stopping at five tree platforms for killer bird's-eye views. Sessions last 1½ to 2 hours (A$90) and depart eight times a day starting at 7:45 am. Nightly guided Jungle Adventures

Nightwalks (A$30–A$40) explore the critter-filled 45-acre grounds, departing from PK's Jungle Village reception at 7:30 pm. Transfers from most local accommodations are free, or self-drive to the central departure point. Thrice-weekly day-tour packages from Port Douglas include lunch at Whet. ⊠ *From the Boardwalk Café (next to PK's), Cape Tribulation Rd.* ⌖ *PO Box 117, Port Douglas 4877* ☎ *07/4098–0043* ⊕ *www.junglesurfing.com.au.*

HORSEBACK RIDING **Cape Trib Beach Horse Rides.** Cape Trib Beach Horse Rides has 3½-hour rides (A$99–A$109) that meander through rain forest, along Myall Beach, and across open paddocks, with opportunities to swim in rainforest waterholes. The cost includes tea, instruction, gear, insurance, and transportation from Cape Tribulation accommodations. ⊕ *www.capetribhorserides.bookconfirm.com* ⊙ *Daily 8 am (year-round), 1:30 pm (Apr.–Nov.).*

REEF TOURS **Ocean Safari.** Eco-accredited Ocean Safari runs daily 3½-hour eco-tours that include snorkeling at two Great Barrier Reef sites off Cape Trib: magnificent MacKay and/or Undine reefs. The waters here teem with "Nemos" (clown anemone fish), turtles, rays, barracuda, potato cod, giant clams and nudibranchs, and an array of hard and soft corals. The rate includes wet suits and snorkeling gear, guidance, and marine park charges (reef tax); you can buy soft drinks, chocolate, and underwater cameras on board. Transfers from Cow Bay are A$10; pick-ups from Cape Trib accommodations are free. ⊠ *From the Boardwalk Café, opposite PK's, Cape Tribulation Rd.* ☎ *07/4098–0666* ⊕ *www.oceansafari.com.au* ⊠ *A$190* ⊙ *Daily 9 am and 1 pm, weather permitting.*

WHERE TO EAT

$$$ AUSTRALIAN ✕ **On The Turps Bar & Restaurant.** At this open-air restaurant in the Daintree rain forest, wallabies and musky rat-kangaroos might join you at the table as you tuck into fine Mediterranean food that highlights local, seasonal ingredients including fresh seafood, and wines from the well-stocked bar. Bundaleer also does "tropical continental" breakfasts and varied, good-value lunches as well as morning and afternoon Devonshire teas. Arrive early for a dip in the creek, rain-forest stroll, or spa treatment. ⊠ *Daintree-Cape Tribulation Heritage Lodge & Spa, Lot 236, R36, Turpentine Rd., 15 km (10 mi) north of Daintree River crossing* ⌖ *P.M.B. 14, Mossman 4873* ☎ *07/4098–9321.*

¢ CAFÉ ✕ **Café on Sea.** Half an hour's drive past the Daintree ferry crossing, on the rain forest–fringed Coral Sea shore, sits a rustic, beach shack–style café. Service can be surly, but you'll find unfussy, family-friendly fare—big fried breakfasts, burgers, beef-and-shiraz pies, Cajun chicken wraps, and feta-spinach flan with salad. Alternatively, just order an espresso and a slice of cake and contemplate the ocean. ■TIP➜ Make phone calls here: it's one of the few spots in the area that gets clear cell-phone reception. ⊠ *Beachfront, 90 Cape Tribulation Rd., Thornton Beach* ☎ *07/4098–9118.*

\$\$\$ ✕ **Whet Restaurant.** Stylish and hip yet comfortable, Whet's licensed
MODERN   eatery-bar attracts visitors and locals alike. The outdoor deck is per-
AUSTRALIAN   fect for cocktails; food, wine, and service would hold their own in
☺   most big cities. Fresh regional and seasonal ingredients, including lots
Fodor'sChoice   of local seafood, are deftly combined in fresh, simple Mod-Oz dishes
★   with Asian and Mediterranean influences. Gluten-free and vegetarian
meals are available, as are healthy options for kids. Booking ahead is
a good idea for peak times. Whet Flicks, a laid-back licensed 24-seat
cinema upstairs, runs daily sessions of pre-DVD-release movies. Relax
in air-conditioned comfort on beanbags, recliners, or leather lounges
and enjoy tapas-style snacks with the film. Meal-movie deals are available. ⊠ *Lot 1, Cape Tribulation Rd.* ☎ *07/4098–0007* ⊙ *Daily 10:30
am–late; 2, 4, and 8 pm (screenings).*

WHERE TO STAY

For expanded hotel reviews, visit Fodors.com.

Privately run campgrounds and small resorts can be found along Daintree Road at Myall Creek and Cape Tribulation.

\$ 🛏 **Cape Tribulation Farmstay B&B.** A handful of simple, solar-powered
cabins sit among rambutan, mangosteen, and breadfruit trees on this
40-hectare exotic fruit farm. **Pros:** clean, eco-friendly cabins; fresh
fruit; free Internet. **Cons:** few in-room modern conveniences. ⊠ *Cape
Tribulation Rd.* ✉ *Mail Service 20414873* ☎ *07/4098–0042* ⊕ *www.
capetribfarmstay.com* ↜ *5 cabins* ⌂ *In-room: a/c, no a/c, no TV, Wi-Fi.
In-hotel: water sports, laundry facilities, business center, parking, some
pets allowed* ⊠ *Breakfast.*

\$\$\$ 🛏 **Cockatoo Hill Retreat.** The simple but elegant treehouses at this impec-
★   cably-run, eco-friendly boutique retreat have king-size, handcrafted
Balinese-style beds, billowing white mosquito nets, romantic under-
floor lighting, and sea-breezy balconies overlooking the infinity-edge
pool (with pool bar), the Coral Sea, and a rain forest teeming with
wildlife—frogs, birds, and butterflies—with lots of walks nearby. **Pros:**
helpful, thoughtful hosts; good breakfasts; tranquil; fab views. **Cons:**
few modern conveniences; minimum three-night stay; must go offsite to
dine or (in the cottage) self-cater. ⊠ *13 Cape Tribulation Rd., Daintree*
☎ *07/4098–9277* ⊕ *www.cockatoohillretreat.com.au* ↜ *3 treehouses,
1 cottage* ⌂ *In-room: a/c, no a/c, kitchen, no TV. In-hotel: restaurant,
bar, pool, water sports, laundry facilities, parking.*

\$\$\$ 🛏 **Heritage Lodge & Spa.** Nestled in World Heritage–listed rain forest
☺   beside Cooper Creek, this secluded resort is an antidote to stress. **Pros:**
★   friendly fauna; lots of on-site facilities; rain-forest environs. **Cons:** limited cell-phone coverage; drive or longish trek to beach; occasional
critters. ⊠ *Lot 236, R96, Turpentine Rd., 15 km (10 mi) north of the
Daintree River, Diwan* ☎ *07/4098–9321* ⊕ *www.heritagelodge.net.au*
↜ *20 cabins* ⌂ *In-room: a/c, Wi-Fi. In-hotel: restaurant, bar, pool, spa,
water sports, laundry facilities, parking* ⊠ *Breakfast.*

\$ 🛏 **PK's Jungle Village.** This backpacker's haven attracts active, youth-
ful travelers who often settle in for multiday stays. **Pros:** central location; good facilities, food, and tours; a/c in cabins and dorms; fun bar.
Cons: generator power; basic in-room facilities; can be noisy. ⊠ *PMB*

"Taking a walk of faith across a rope bridge in Daintree Rainforest." —poimuffin, Fodors.com member

7, Cape Tribulation Rd. ☎ *07/4098–0040, 1800/232–333* ⊕ *www. pksjunglevillage.com.au* ⇆ *19 cabins, 8 with bath; 14 dorm rooms* ⌂ *In-room: a/c, no a/c, no TV. In-hotel: restaurant, bar, pool, beach, water sports, laundry facilities, business center, flush toilets, drinking water, running water (non-potable), guest laundry, showers, public telephone, general store, play area, swimming.*

COOKTOWN

103 km (64 mi), around 3.5-hours' drive, north of Cape Tribulation; 324 km (203-mi) or 5.5-hours' drive north of Cairns.

Traveling north, Cooktown is the last major settlement on the east coast of the continent, sitting at the edge of a difficult wilderness. Its wide main street consists mainly of two-story pubs with four-wheel-drive vehicles parked out front. Despite the frontier air, Cooktown has an impressive history. It was here in 1770 that Captain James Cook beached HMS *Endeavour* to repair her hull. Any tour of Cooktown should begin at the waterfront, where a statue of Cook gazes out to sea, overlooking the spot where he landed.

GETTING HERE AND AROUND

By car from Cairns, take the inland highway, Peninsula Developmental Road, a 200-odd-mi stretch of fully paved road that barrels you through Australia's Outback—watch for errant cattle and 'roos on the drive. From Cape Tribulation, head up the Cooktown Developmental Road, or take the 4WD-only Bloomfield Track, just 97 km (60 mi), but challenging and sometimes flooded in the Wet. The Bloomfield

Track journey, which roughly traces a series of indigenous story-line trails known as the Bama Way, takes around three hours, longer in wet weather; the Developmental Road is smoother but less scenic. Getting around Cooktown, a compact town, is a comparative cinch: drive, walk, or cycle.

ESSENTIALS

Medical **Cooktown Multi-Purpose Health Service (Cooktown Hospital)** ✉ *48 Hope St.* ☎ *07/4043–0100* ⊕ *www.myhospitals.gov.au.*

Rental Cars **Cooktown Car Hire** ✉ *Milkwood Lodge Rainforest Retreat, Annan Rd.* ☎ *07/4069–5007* ⊕ *www.cooktown-car-hire.com.*

EXPLORING COOKTOWN

Cooktown has some lovely old buildings and a cemetery dating from the 1870s Gold Rush. Stroll along botanic gardens trails and uncrowded beaches, check out the environment interpretative center and visitor info-hub Nature's Powerhouse, cool off in the public swimming pool, and scale Grassy Hill around sunset for stupendous views.

James Cook Museum. Cooktown, in its heyday, was a gold-mining port town, with 64 pubs lining the 3-km-long (2-mi-long) main street. A significant slice of this colorful history is preserved here at the National Trust–run James Cook Museum. The former convent houses relics of the Palmer gold-mining and pastoral eras along with Aboriginal artifacts, canoes, and mementos of Cook's voyage, including the anchor and one of six cannons jettisoned when the HMS *Endeavour* ran aground. The surprisingly nice shop sells books and souvenirs. ✉ *Helen St. at Furneaux St.* ✆ *P.O. Box 103 4895* ☎ *07/4069–5386* ⊕ *www. nationaltrustqld.org* ☑ *A$10* ⊗ *Daily 9:30–4, may close Feb.–Mar.*

OUTDOOR ACTIVITIES

There's plenty of outdoorsy fun to be had in and around Cooktown. Book a diving, snorkeling, or game-fishing cruise to the Outer Barrier Reef or Lizard Island; take a guided rock-art or rain-forest walk; go Outback on a multiday 4WD Cape York excursion; or charter a scenic heli-flight over both World Heritage Areas.

CULTURAL
TOURS
Ⓒ
Fodor'sChoice
★

Guurrbi Tours. An hour or so's drive inland of Cooktown lie ancient Aboriginal rock-art sites of immense significance. Their exact locations are a closely guarded secret—so who better to guide you than Nugal-warra elder Willie Gordon, a designated storyteller for the sites you'll visit? Willie guides guests around his ancestral rock-art sites, set high in the hills behind Hope Vale, on scheduled day tours that pick up from accommodations around Cooktown. The 5½-hour Rainbow Serpent tour takes in half a dozen sites, including the renowned Rainbow Serpent Cave. En route, Willie, an engaging raconteur, shares the Dreamtime stories and traditional lore behind this extraordinary cave art, some of which was painted by his own grandfather. If you're self-driving to the Guurrbi Meeting Point, near Hope Vale Aboriginal Community (about 45 minutes from town), and want a little extra navigational support, you can usually caravan with Willie if he's doing a pickup in town. Otherwise, collect a map and directions from **Cooktown Motel Pam's Place** on Boundary St. (*07/4069–6259*). Guurrbi also offers multi-day drive-tour packages. ⌂ *P.O. Box 417, Cooktown 4895* ☎ *07/4069–6043* ⊕ *www.guurrbitours.com.au* ☒ *A$85 (self-drive), A$120 (with transportation from Cooktown); min. 2 people (single supplement A$40)* ⊙ *Mon.–Sat. from 7:45 am (Rainbow Serpent tour); self-drivers 8:30 am at Guurrbi Meeting Point.*

FISHING The closest town on the Queensland coast to the Great Barrier Reef, Cooktown offers fast, easy access to some of the reef's best fishing (and dive) sites. Boats bristling with game-fishing gear depart from the marina daily, bound for famed fishing grounds on the Outer Reef, and at Egret and Boulder, 10 mi offshore. The likely catch: Spanish mackerel, sailfish, coral trout, red and spangled emperor, and black marlin.

Cooktown Fishing Adventures. Bottom-fish with handlines, troll for giant black marlin, or pop lures over the reef with Cooktown Fishing Adventures, an established local operator with a 56-foot, 900hp boat and energetic, safety-conscious crew. The company runs guided game-fishing excursions to local sites and specializes in multiday, live-aboard trips to renowned fishing areas off Lizard Island, Cod Hole, and Princess Charlotte Bay, with fishing equipment and tackle, snorkeling gear, galley-cooked meals, and more supplied. You can also fish the estuaries or go crabbing on the mangrove flats. ☎ *07/4069–5500, 0409/696–775* ⊕ *www.cooktownfishingcharters.com* ☒ *Prices vary according to charter* ⊙ *Daily, pre-booking essential.*

WHERE TO STAY

For expanded hotel reviews, visit Fodors.com.

$ 🏨 **Milkwood Lodge Rainforest Retreat.** Six pole cabins oriented for seclusion provide breezy, split-level accommodation overlooking rain forest and bushland at this user-friendly tropical retreat. **Pros:** free airport pickups; breakfast packs; discounts for on-site vehicle hire and longer stays. **Cons:** small TVs; some rooms lack Wi-Fi access; no restaurant; fair way out of town. ⌂ *Annan Rd.* ☎ *07/4069–5007* ⊕ *www.milkwoodlodge.com* ↪ *6 treehouses* ⌁ *In-room: a/c (some), safe, kitchen, Internet, Wi-Fi. In-hotel: bar, pool, water sports, laundry facilities, business center, parking, some pets allowed* ⊙ *Breakfast.*

$ 🏨 **Seaview Motel.** This clean, quiet seafront establishment has five categories of accommodation, some newer than others: standard rooms with older-style TVs and no kitchenettes; semi-self-contained rooms with microwave and sink; newer "deluxe" motel rooms with large flat-screen TVs and lounge/dining areas; a self-contained family unit; and split-level town houses that have two bedrooms, full kitchens with dishwashers, separate lounge and dining areas, and large flat-screen TVs. **Pros:** helpful staff, takeout drinks and breakfast packs/toasters (for a fee); scenic location. **Cons:** no screens on sliding doors to motel-room balconies; small pool; breakfast restaurant may close outside of peak periods. ⌂ *178 Charlotte St.* ☎ *07/4069–5377* ⊕ *www.cooktownseaviewmotel.com.au* ↪ *38 motel rooms, 1 family unit, 3 town houses* ⌁ *In-room: a/c, safe, kitchen, Internet, Wi-Fi. In-hotel: pool, beach, water sports, laundry facilities, business center, parking, some pets allowed* ⊙ *Breakfast.*

8

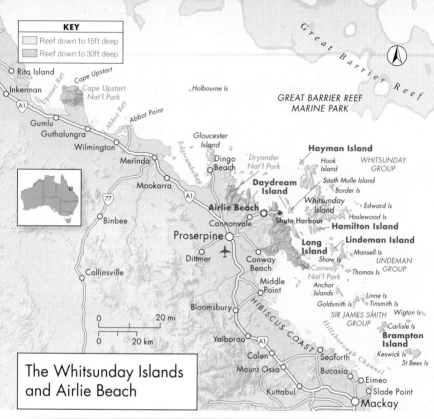

The Whitsunday Islands and Airlie Beach

$ 🏨 **The Sovereign Resort Hotel.** This attractive, two-story colonial-style
☻ hotel in the heart of town is the best bet in Cooktown. **Pros:** good-value
★ apartments (best is #201); free in-room Wi-Fi and sport/movie cable
channels; airport/wharf transfers; terrific gardens, BBQ area, and pool.
Cons: restaurant not open for dinner in wet season; continental breakfast buffet low on selection yet expensive. ✉ *128 Charlotte St., at Green
St.* ☎ *07/4043–0500* ⊕ *www.sovereign-resort.com.au* ➥ *31 rooms, 7
apartments* ↻ *In-room: a/c, kitchen, Wi-Fi. In-hotel: restaurant, bar,
pool, laundry facilities, business center, parking* ⊙ *Café closed Sun. No
dinner Sun. and Nov.–Mar.* 🄁 *No meals.*

THE WHITSUNDAY ISLANDS
AND AIRLIE BEACH

The Whitsundays are a group of 74 islands situated within 161 km
(100 mi) of each other and around 50 km (31 mi) from Shute Harbour, the principal mainland departure point, though some boats depart
from Airlie Beach marina nearby. Discovered in 1770 by Captain James
Cook of the HMS *Endeavour*—though in fact not on Whitsunday itself,
thanks to a time-zone change oversight on Cook's part—the Whitsundays are a favorite sailing destination and an easy-access base from

which to explore the midsection of the Great Barrier Reef. Some of the islands' beaches—notably, famous Whitehaven Beach—are picture-postcard gorgeous, though vegetation on the islands themselves looks more scrubby than tropical. In fact, the entire region is subtropical, making for moderate air and water temperatures year-round. Most of the Whitsunday Islands are national parks, and, although you'll spot few animals on them, birds are plentiful—more than 150 species make their homes here. Only a few of the islands have resorts; others serve as destinations for day trips, beach time, and bushwalks, or simply as backdrop at scenic moorings.

Camping is popular on the myriad islands of the Whitsunday group. To pitch a tent on islands lying within national parks you need a A$5.15 per-person, per-night permit from the Queensland Environmental Protection Authority (EPA). The Whitsunday Information Centre, on the Bruce Highway at Proserpine, is open weekdays 9–5, Saturday 9–3, Sunday 10–3.

AIRLIE BEACH

1,119 km (695 mi) or 13.5 hours' drive north of Brisbane; 623 km (387 mi) south of Cairns via the Bruce Highway.

Airlie Beach's balmy climate and its proximity to the Whitsunday Islands, a resort and water-sports playground, make it hugely popular with partying backpackers and holiday-makers en route to the islands and reef.

GETTING HERE AND AROUND

The Whitsunday Coast Airport near Proserpine, 36 km (23 mi) southeast of Airlie Beach, has direct daily flights to and from Brisbane and less frequent services to Sydney, on Virgin Blue and Jetstar. **Whitsunday Shuttle Service** and **Whitsunday Transit** buses connect the airport and Proserpine Railway Station to Airlie Beach and Shute Harbour, with services timed to meet all flights and passenger trains (drive time 30–40 minutes; A$11–A$15 one-way, bookings required). **Greyhound Australia** and **Oz Experience** offer daily services into Airlie Beach from Sydney, Brisbane, and towns between, and from Cairns. **Queensland Rail** operates around six northbound and six southbound trains weekly that stop at Proserpine Railway Station, about 25 km (15 mi) from Airlie Beach.

Koala Adventures is popular with the younger backpacker set, and runs three-day sailing trips around the Whitsundays on an 83-foot Whitbread round-world maxi racing yacht for A$469 or a luxury catamaran for A$349, including local charges, all meals, snorkeling gear, stinger suits, and two nights' accommodation on South Molle Island. **Whitsunday Sailing Adventures** runs several sailing, scuba, and snorkeling trips around the islands and Great Barrier Reef on a dozen-plus owner-operated vessels, including modern sailing cats and tall ships. Choose from dive and snorkeling trips, performance sailing, eco-friendly excursions, and two- and three-day sailing cruises with all meals, bedding, and snorkeling gear provided.

8

ESSENTIALS

Airlines Jetstar ☎ *13–1538* ⊕ *www.jetstar.com.* **Virgin Australia** ☎ *13–6789* ⊕ *www.virginaustralia.com.*

Airport Whitsunday Coast Airport ⊠ *Lascelles Ave., Sir Reginald Ansett Dr., Proserpine* ☎ *07/4945–0200.*

Boat Tour Contacts Cumberland Charter Yachts ⊠ *Abel Point Marina, Shingley Dve.* ☎ *07/4946–7500, 1800/075–101* ⊕ *www.ccy.com.au.* **Koala Adventures** ⊠ *Shute Harbour Rd.* ☎ *07/4946–9433, 1800/466444* ⊕ *www.koalaadventures.com.* **Queensland Yacht Charters** ⊠ *Abel Point Marina* ☎ *07/4946–7400, 1800/075013* ⊕ *www.yachtcharters.com.au.* **Whitsunday Rent A Yacht** ⊠ *6 Bay Terrace, Shute Harbour* ⬚ *PO Box 3574802* ☎ *07/4946–9232, 1800/075000* ⊕ *www.rentayacht.com.au.* **Whitsunday Sailing Adventures** ⊠ *Level 2, 293 Shute Harbour Rd.4802* ⬚ *PO Box 53584802* ☎ *07/4940–2000, 1300/653100* ⊕ *www.whitsundaysailingadventures.com.au.*

Buses Greyhound Australia ☎ *1300/473–946* ⊕ *www.greyhound.com.au.* **Oz Experience** ☎ *08/8132–8233, 1800/555–287* ⊕ *www.ozexperience.com.* **Whitsunday Shuttle Service** ☎ *07/4948–1515* ⊕ *www.whitsundayshuttle.com.au.*

Hospitals Doctors Airlie Beach ⊠ *283 Shute Harbour Rd.* ☎ *07/4948–0900* ⊕ *www.whitsundaydoctors.com.au.*

Trains Proserpine Railway Station ⊠ *Hinschen St., Proserpine* ☎ *13–1617* ⊕ *www.qr.com.au.* **Queensland Rail** ☎ *1800/872–467* ⊕ *www.qr.com.au.*

EXPLORING AIRLIE BEACH

Airlie's main street is packed with cafés, bars, tour agencies, and hotels—many catering to the backpacker crowd—with homes and higher-end accommodations extending up the steep hills behind it. The waterfront Esplanade, with its boardwalk, landscaped gardens, and weekend markets, is generally lively.

🕃 **Airlie Beach Lagoon.** Airlie Lagoon, a large, stinger-free swimming enclosure on the shorefront, is hugely popular. It's patrolled year-round by lifeguards and has dedicated lap-swimming lanes and two adjoining children's pools. There are toilets, showers, change rooms, picnic tables, BBQs, and a playground nearby. ⊠ *The Esplanade, at Broadwater Ave.* ⬚ *Whitsunday Regional Council, PO Box 104, Proserpine 4800* ☎ *07/4945–0200* ⊕ *www.whitsunday.qld.gov.au* 🎫 *Free* ☉ *Patrolled daily, 8 am–9 pm (summer), 9–7 (winter).*

🕃 **Conway National Park.** Conway National Park, 10 minutes' drive southeast of Airlie, is a 54,000-acre expanse of mangroves, woodlands, rocky cliffs, and tropical lowland rain forest that shelters the endangered Proserpine rock wallaby and other rare species, as well as plenty of sulphur-crested cockatoos, emerald doves, Australian brush-turkeys, and orange-footed scrubfowl. Most walking trails start at the park's picnic area off Shute Harbour Road, 6 km (3½ mi) from Airlie. Mount Rooper Walking Track, a 5.4-km (3-mi) circuit, meanders uphill through bushland to a lookout with breathtaking Whitsundays views. The 30-km (18.5-mi), three-day Whitsunday Great Walk starts at the Brandy Creek carpark and ends in Airlie Beach (with campsites en route). Swamp Bay track follows the creek to a coral-strewn beach with a bush camping area. Campers need permits (A$5.15 per person, per night), as well as water, fuel stoves (open fires prohibited), and all supplies. ⊠ *Shute Harbour Rd. at Mandalay Rd.* ☎ *07/4945–3711 (Whitsunday Visitor Information), 1800/801-252, 13–7468 permits* ⊕ *www.derm.qld.gov.au.*

> **BEWARE**
>
> From October to May the ocean off beaches north of Rockhampton is rendered virtually unswimmable by toxic-tentacled box jellyfish.

Shute Harbour. Shute Harbour, 10 km (6 mi) southeast from Airlie Beach, is the main ferry terminal and gateway to the islands and reef. The large, sheltered inlet bristles with boats—it's the second-busiest commuter port in Australia, after Sydney's Circular Quay. Though accommodation is available, the harbor is geared toward transferring visitors. For a great view over Shute Harbor and the Whitsunday Passage, drive to the top of Coral Point. ⊠ *Shute Harbour Rd., Shute Harbour* ⊕ *www.shuteharbour.net.*

WHERE TO EAT

$$$
MEDITERRANEAN
☙
Fodor's Choice
★

✕**Déjà Vu Restaurant.** Alfresco tables and Balinese-style dining pavilions flank an infinity-edge pool at this classy Airlie eatery. The usual surf'n'turf options are replaced by inventive, seasonally driven Mod-Oz–Mediterranean dishes. Follow an entrée of oysters, coconut-crusted prawns, or meze plates with crispy-skin mango chicken breast or bluefin tuna braised in white wine and brandy. Alternatively, go with the Moreton Bay bugs (crayfish) with a deconstructed Caesar salad, or kangaroo fillet with an Asian-style noodle salad. Freshly made desserts (such as a trio of seasonal fruit tarts or a gluten-free choc-strawberry soufflé) are delicious. Vegetarian and children's meals are available, the coffee's a cut above the norm, and the wine list is extensive. At lunch, tuck into fresh seafood dishes, interesting salads and gourmet panini for under A$25—preceded, perhaps, by a swim. Sunday's eight-course epicurean lunches with live entertainment are legendary (A$44.50, beverages additional). ⊠ *Water's Edge Resort, 4 Golden Orchid Dr.* ☎ *07/4948–4309* ⊕ *www.dejavurestaurant.com.au* ⊘ *Wed.–Sun., lunch noon–2:30 (Sun. noon–4), dinner 6–9:30 pm.*

$$
MODERN
AUSTRALIAN

✕**Easy Cafe.** Tucked away in an arcade just off the main strip, Easy Cafe is a terrific option for relaxed breakfasts, lunches, and suppers, drawing a sociable crowd of travelers and the odd local. Onsite Internet, board games, good music, and attentive, cheerful staff are part of its allure; the other is the very reasonably priced, tasty food. Join the crowd that flocks here Monday to Friday for the A$10 Easy Breakfast, pop in during the day for terrific coffee and cake or a few cold beers, or dine here from 5 pm till late on a small but varied menu of quality Modern Australian dishes. ⊠ *Pavilion Arcade, 287 Shute Harbour Rd., Airlie Beach* ☎ *07/4946–5559* ⊕ *www.easycafe.com.au* ⊘ *Daily for breakfast, lunch, and dinner.*

8

WHERE TO STAY

For expanded hotel reviews, visit Fodors.com.

$ ⚙ **Airlie Beach Hotel.** With the town's small beach at its doorstep, three eateries and bars downstairs, and the main street directly behind it, this hotel makes a convenient base. **Pros:** convenient location; free Wi-Fi and parking; on-site food and drink. **Cons:** no room service; small pool; Airlie's main drag can be noisy. ✉ *16 The Esplanade, at Coconut Grove* ☎ *07/4964–1999, 1800/466–233* ⊕ *www.airliebeachhotel.com. au* ⤶ *56 rooms, 4 suites* ☖ *In-room: a/c, Wi-Fi. In-hotel: restaurant, bar, pool, beach, laundry facilities, parking.*

¢ ⚙ **Beaches Backpackers.** With a big, lively bar on-site, this main-street hostel attracts a party crowd, which makes things noisy (but keeps dorms near-empty) until around midnight. **Pros:** good in-room and on-site facilities; cheap Internet including CD/DVD burning. **Cons:** noisy environs; tiny pool. ✉ *356 Shute Harbour Rd.* ☎ *07/4946–6244, 1800/636630* ⊕ *www.beaches.com.au* ⤶ *7 rooms, 24 dorms* ☖ *In-room: a/c. In-hotel: restaurant, bar, pool, laundry facilities, business center, parking, some age restrictions.*

$$ ⚙ **Peppers Coral Coast.** The expansive one-, two- and three-bedroom
★ apartments at this high-end hillside resort are tailored for comfort, with spa baths the size of small cars, designer decor, and premium appliances: flat-screen TVs (with Austar cable channels and pay movies) in the lounge and master bedroom, CD and DVD players and iPod docking stations. **Pros:** classy decor, food, and service; quiet location; culinary packages available. **Cons:** up a steep hill; limited room service; smallish pool area. ✉ *Mt. Whitsunday Dr.* ☎ *07/4962–5100, 1300/737–444* ⊕ *www.peppers.com.au* ⤶ *102 apartments* ☖ *In-room: a/c, safe, kitchen, Internet. In-hotel: restaurant, bar, pool, gym, spa, laundry facilities, business center, parking.*

$ ⚙ **Whitsunday Moorings B&B.** Overlooking Abel Point Marina, both self-
Fodor's Choice contained suites here have panoramic views from their patios. **Pros:**
★ charming, knowledgable hosts; fab breakfasts; upmarket toiletries; free Wi-Fi and cable channels. **Cons:** uphill walk from main street; open room plan best suited to couples. ✉ *37 Airlie Crescent* ✍ *PO BOX 394 4802* ☎ *07/4946–4692* ⊕ *www.whitsundaymooringsbb.com.au* ⤶ *2 rooms* ☖ *In-room: a/c, kitchen, Wi-Fi. In-hotel: pool, laundry facilities, business center, parking* ⧈ *Breakfast.*

NIGHTLIFE

Shute Harbour Road, the main strip, is where it all happens in Airlie Beach. Most main-street establishments cater to the backpacker crowd, with boisterous, college-style entertainment, live music, and late-opening dance-clubs. Older visitors gravitate to quieter establishments with pleasant outdoor areas, such as the bars attached to some of the hillside resorts.

Beaches Bar & Bistro. The crowd's gregarious at Beaches Bar & Bistro, part of the hostel of the same name. Here, you can catch live bands most nights, eat hearty food cheaply, play pool, mingle in the big beer garden, and watch games on big-screen TVs. ✉ *356 Shute Harbour Rd.* ☎ *07/4946–6244, 1800/636630* ⊕ *www.beaches.com.au.*

The Juice Bar and Nightclub. At the Juice Bar and Nightlub, the decor's arty, the temperature is chilled, the vibe's city-sleek but sociable. Flamboyant "flair-tenders" mix mean tropically-inspired cocktails, and DJs spin the latest club favorites till dawn. ⊠ *352 Shute Harbour Rd.* ☎ *07/4946–5055* ☉ *Nightly, 10 pm–5 am.*

Mama Africa. When the main-street watering-holes close around midnight, Airlie's party kicks on till late at hot, tribally-themed Mama Africa. ⊠ *263 Shute Harbour Rd.* ☎ *07/4948–0438.*

BRAMPTON ISLAND

Twelve coral-and-white-sand beaches encircle Brampton Island; kangaroos, rainbow lorikeets, and butterflies populate the rain forests of its hilly interior. This 1,137-acre island at the southern end of the Whitsunday Passage, 32 km (20 mi) northeast of Mackay and 50 km (31 mi) southeast of Hamilton Island, is one of the prettiest in the area. Most of the island is a designated national park, with seven secluded beaches accessible via walking trails and fringing hard and soft coral reefs sheltering countless marine creatures. Though the resort is lively after dark, the biggest attractions are on and under the water: the snorkeling over the reef between Brampton and the adjoining Carlisle islands is world-class.

GETTING HERE AND AROUND

Blue Fin, a high-speed catamaran, leaves Mackay Marina daily at 2, arriving at Brampton at 3:15. Fare is A$65 one-way, including coach transfer from Mackay Airport, departing at 1:30. Return boats leave Brampton marina at 3:45, connecting with the coach at 5 for a 5:15 pm arrival at Mackay Airport.

Virgin Blue and Qantas connect all Australian capitals with Mackay daily. Jetstar has flights from Brisbane; Tiger Airways from Melbourne. Some Virgin Blue flights tie in with Brampton boat transfers. Australasian Jet flies to Brampton Island from Mackay and Hamilton Island airports, taking 20–30 minutes, a minimum of two passengers, and a maximum 15 kg (33 lbs) of baggage each (plus 5 kg [11 lbs] hand luggage), preferably soft-sided. Fare is A$85 one-way from Mackay via scheduled, twice-daily transfer (departing from the mainland at 11:30 am and 5 pm, Brampton at 9 am and 2 pm); upward of A$175 per person, one-way, from Hamilton Island via charter flight.

OUTDOOR ACTIVITIES

Most folk are so busy getting on or under the water that they don't explore their island environs. But many Barrier Reef isles include significant tracts of national parkland, with trails often leading to or past spectacular views. Overcast days are perfect for trekking along island trails. Careful walkers may spot possums, goannas (iguanas), blue-tongued lizards, various birds, the odd wallaby, and nesting green and loggerhead turtles on beaches, in season. Carry a map, snacks, and plenty of water; wear a hat and sunscreen regardless of weather, and don't forget your camera.

8

Beaches on the Whitsunday Islands group are among the state's best.

LINDEMAN ISLAND

More than half of Lindeman Island—which at 2,000 acres is one of the largest in the Whitsunday group—is national park, with 20 km (12 mi) of walking trails that wind through tropical growth and up hills for fantastic views. Bird-watching is excellent here, though the blue tiger butterflies you might spot in Butterfly Valley are, arguably, even more impressive. With its natural and sporting attractions, the island draws lots of families. It lies 40 km (25 mi) northeast of Mackay, near the southern entrance to the Whitsunday Passage.

GETTING HERE AND AROUND

There are four direct 30-minute boat transfers daily to Lindeman Island from Hamilton Island, 17 km (11 mi) away. Transfers are included in Club Med guests' rate (or A$75 each way).

ESSENTIALS

Boat Contact Fantasea ☎ 07/4946–5455, 1800/650851 ⊕ www.fantasea.com.au.

OUTDOOR ACTIVITIES

WATER
SPORTS

🖰

Club Med Lindeman Island. Not far from Lindeman Island lie Barrier Reef sites ideal for introductory diving and snorkeling. Club Med Lindeman Island organizes day cruises for guests to Hook and Hardy reefs that include snorkeling, optional guided dives, and lunch. You can also arrange to take refresher scuba-diving courses, go deep-sea fishing, or book shorter boat excursions to snorkeling sites off nearby Whitehaven Beach. Dive trips to the outer reef by air are 30 minutes each way; by boat it's two hours each way, but considerably cheaper. On Lindeman itself, guided snorkeling trips are scheduled only once or twice a week, but if you bring your own gear you can snorkel off the pier for free. ☎ *07/4946–9333 ⊕ www.clubmed.com.au ☜ Cost varies ☉ Daily schedule varies, bookings essential.*

WHERE TO STAY
For expanded hotel reviews, visit Fodors.com.

$$$$
ALL-INCLUSIVE
☺

☷ **Club Med Lindeman Island.** This three-story, palm-tree-filled resort, Australia's only Club Med, sits on 1,750 acres on the southern end of the island; rooms are sparsely furnished, as is customary at Club Med (poolside rooms and those with hot tubs cost more). **Pros:** babysitting; circus school; kids under four stay free. **Cons:** inadequate equipment to meet demand; two overused computer terminals for public Internet access; slow bar service. ☜ *PMB 1, Mackay Mail Centre 4741 ☎ 1300/855–052, 07/4946–9333 resort ⊕ www.clubmed.com. au ⤴ 214 rooms ⚇ In-room: a/c, safe. In-hotel: restaurant, bar, golf course, pool, tennis court, spa, beach, water sports, children's programs, laundry facilities, business center* ❡☉❘ *All-inclusive.*

LONG ISLAND

This aptly named island lies south of Shute Harbour, 12 km (7 mi) west of Hamilton Island. Although it's 9 km (5½ mi) long and no more than 2 km (1.2 mi) wide—around 3,000 acres total—it has several walking trails through tracts of dense rain forest. Most of the island is national parkland, sheltering birds, butterflies, goannas, and wallabies. Some of its beaches are picturesque; others rocky and windblown. Though its waters are less clear than those off the outer reef islands, there are some excellent snorkeling spots on the island's fringing reef, where you'll share the balmy water with soft and hard corals, tropical fish, and turtles. You may also see dolphins and migrating humpback whales July through September.

GETTING HERE AND AROUND
You can reach Long Island (but not Paradise Bay Island Eco-Escape) several times a day via air-conditioned catamaran with Cruise Whitsundays from Shute Harbour, Abel Point Marina (Airlie Beach) via Daydream Island, or Hamilton Island. The 35-minute journey from Hamilton Island Airport costs A$60 one-way, or pay A$50 from Whitsunday Coast (Proserpine) Airport; reps meet passenger flights at both. From Shute Harbour or Abel Point Marina, the one-way fare is A$30. The transfer lands you at Long Island Resort, which can transfer you to Palm Bay for A$20 per person.

Air Whitsunday provides one-way charter plane connections between Hamilton Island's Whitsunday Airport and Long Island for A$280 (up to four passengers) or A$420 (up to 6); and from Whitsunday Coast (Proserpine) Airport for A$790 (up to four passengers) or A$950 (up to 6), each way. Flights are timed to coincide with domestic air services. Aviation Adventures can fly you by helicopter between Long Island and various other Whitsundays islands, including Hamilton Island (Whitsundays) Airport, and from Airlie Beach; however prices are steep, the trip requires minimum passenger numbers, and prebooking is essential.

8

Guests of Paradise Beach Island Eco-Escape can take a helicopter from Hamilton Island airport to Long Island (or back again) anytime between 7:30 am and 5 pm; or fly from Airlie Beach on the mainland, a 15-minute trip, between 9 and 5. The scenic flight is A$290 return, per person. Baggage is limited to 15 kilograms (30 pounds) per person, and should be in soft-sided bags. Excess luggage can be stored at the airport. Virgin, Qantas, and Jetstar schedule daily flights between Hamilton Island and Sydney, Brisbane, and Cairns.

ESSENTIALS

Air Contacts Air Whitsunday ✉ *Terminal 1, Air Whitsunday Airport, Airlie Beach* ☎ *07/4946–9111* ⊕ *www.airwhitsunday.com.au.* **Aviation Adventures** ☎ *07/4946–9988* ⊕ *www.av8com.au.*

Boat Contact Cruise Whitsundays ☎ *07/4946–4662, 1800/426–403* ⊕ *www.cruisewhitsundays.com.*

WHERE TO STAY

For expanded hotel reviews, visit Fodors.com.

$$ **Long Island Resort.** A short walk over the hill from Palm Bay, this
☺ family-focused resort might as well be on a different island. **Pros:** lots of activities; good value room-meal packages; sociable. **Cons:** noisy; kids run amok; heavy competition for equipment. *PO Box 1080, Airlie Beach 4802* ☎ *07/4946–9400, 1800/075–125* ⊕ *www.longislandresort. com.au* ↝ *161 rooms, 31 lodges without bath* ♿ *In-room: a/c, no a/c, safe, Internet. In-hotel: restaurant, bar, pool, tennis court, beach, water sports, children's programs.*

$$$$ **Paradise Bay Island Eco-Escape.** Talk about secluded—this intimate,
★ eco-friendly lodge on South Long Island's isolated southern tip is acces-
ALL-INCLUSIVE sible only by helicopter. **Pros:** quality food; biodynamic Jurlique bath-room amenities; pillow menu; eco-friendly. **Cons:** pricey; little variation in food; 15kg (30 lb) baggage limit. *PO Box 842, Airlie Beach 4802* ☎ *07/4946–9777* ⊕ *www.paradisebay.com.au* ↝ *8 bungalows* ♿ *In-room: no a/c, no TV. In-hotel: restaurant, bar, beach, water sports, some age restrictions* ❙❙ *All-inclusive.*

HAMILTON ISLAND

Though it's the most heavily populated and developed island in the Whitsunday group, more than 70% of Hamilton Island has been pre-served in its natural state. The 1,482-acre island abounds in beauti-ful beaches (such as long, curving, palm-dotted Catseye Beach), bush trails, and spectacular lookouts. Yet for all its natural beauty, Ham-ilton's is more an action-packed, sociable holiday isle than a place to get away from it all.

Around 35 minutes by ferry from Shute Harbour, Hamilton buzzes with activity. Guests of the resort, and its six types of accommodation, including hotel-style and self-catering establishments, make up most of the itinerant population, but there are private residences here—as well as throngs of day-trippers from the mainland, other islands, and cruising yachts, who wander the island's bustling marina and village each day.

In recent years the island has worked hard to improve the quality of its eateries, and its broad range of dining options includes everything from take-out pizza to upscale restaurants, but most on-island eateries still tend toward the "accessible" end of the culinary scale, though prices tend to be higher than those in comparable mainland restaurants.

For a family-friendly, one-stop Whitsundays experience, Hamilton Island is a good bet. They allow kids under age 13 to stay free, provided they stay with parents and use existing beds (no roll-aways or cribs). Under-13s can even eat free at some island restaurants when staying at resort hotels, choosing from kids' menus, and accompanied by their parents. It's set up as a small city, with its own school, post office and banking outlets, medical center, pharmacy, supermarket and DVD-hire store, plus shops, restaurants, bars, and a nightclub, all open to island guests and day-trippers. There's also a day spa/relaxation center (open daily 10–6), offering massage, aromatherapy treatments, and float-tank sessions. But little on Hamilton is free; prices—for food, activities, Internet use, even grocery items—can be steep. The ubiquitous golf carts that visitors hire to zip around the island are A$45 an hour, A$60 for 3 hours, and A$85 for 24 hours from Hamilton Island Buggy Rentals (7:30 am to 6 pm). Save a few bucks by using the free Island Shuttle service that runs around the island at regular intervals between 7 am and 11 pm.

GETTING HERE AND AROUND

Several carriers—Virgin, Qantas, Jetstar—fly directly to Hamilton Island from Sydney, Melbourne, and Brisbane. **Air Whitsunday** provides one-way seaplane connections between Airlie Beach on the mainland and Hamilton Island from A$550 (four to six passengers); and to other island and mainland destinations and yacht moorings on request. They also operate snorkeling tours and scenic flights over the Great Barrier Reef. **Aviation Adventures** transfers visitors from Hamilton Island airport to Long, Daydream, Hook, Hayman, and South Molle islands via helicopter, on request. **Fantasea** makes the 35-minute journey between Shute Harbour and Hamilton Island Marina 10 or 11 times daily between 6:30 am and 5:25 pm for A$45 each way. Fantasea also has several scheduled daily services coinciding with incoming and outgoing flights that link Shute Harbour and Hamilton Island airport, via Daydream Island and/or Hamilton Island Marina, for A$49 each way.

TOURS

Aviation Adventures. Aviation Adventures has helicopter flights over the Whitsunday Islands (A$109–A$299); private champagne picnics with heli-transfers (A$219–A$599); and a day trip to Whitehaven Beach and the Great Barrier Reef, flying over glorious Heart Reef and stopping near Langford Reef for snorkeling and a gourmet picnic lunch, returning over the Whitsunday Passage (A$669). They also transfer guests to various islands including Hayman, Hook, Long, Daydream, and South Molle. ✉ *2927 Shute Harbour Rd., Airlie Beach* ☎ *07/4946–9988* ⊕ *www.av8.com.au.*

8

⟲ **Fantasea.** Fantasea runs "island discovery" and reef trips daily from
★ Hamilton and Hook islands and Shute Harbour. From Hamilton Island
it's a 55-km (34-mi) trip to Fantasea's huge Reefworld pontoon inside
magnificent Hardy Reef Lagoon, where you can swim and snorkel
along easy coral trails teeming with thousands of tropical fish including 10-foot resident grouper George. You can also scuba dive, ride in
a semisubmersible, or simply relax. The cost is A$225, including gear,
Reefworld facilities, all taxes and charges, and a BBQ lunch. While
you're there, take a guided snorkel tour for A$40, a dive lesson and
introductory dive for A$115, or a certified dive for A$100. A scenic heli-
flight over famous Heart Reef starts from A$110 per person. There's a
kid-friendly safe snorkeling area and an on-reef child-minding service, a
massage hut with reef views (massages from A$20). Fantasea also runs
a daily high-speed catamaran cruise to Whitehaven Beach, a justifiably
famous stretch of pure white silica sand as fine as talcum powder. Find
a secluded spot on the 6½-km (4-mi) beach—and apply sunblock: the
sand acts as a reflector—or swim in the crystal-clear water. Trips on
the air-conditioned vessels, including onboard commentary, barbecue
lunch, afternoon tea, beach shelters, and games, costs A$150 from
Shute Harbour (including pick-ups from Airlie Beach), 8 am–5:25 pm;
A$110 from Hamilton Island, noon–4 pm.

   Reefsleep. Stay overnight on the Hardy Reef pontoon with a Reefworld host and up to five others on a Fantasea's terrific two-day Reefsleep
package: it includes restaurant-quality meals, sunset cocktails, and drinks
with dinner, a dive or a guided snorkeling tour (with gear), a reef appreciation presentation, unlimited access to the underwater viewing chamber,
accommodation in a king room or four-bed bunkroom, reef tax, and use
of Reefworld facilities during your stay (A$480–A$650 per person, min.
2 persons). ☎ 07/4967–5455, 1800/650–851 ⊕ *www.fantasea.com.au.*
Sunsail Australia. Sunsail Australia has various boats available for bareboat charter, with optional extras including professional skippers and
cook, kayaks, and dinghy. ✉ *Front St.* ☎ *07/4948–9509, 1800/803988*
⊕ *www.sunsail.com.au.*

ESSENTIALS

Buggy Rental Hamilton Island Buggy Rental ☎ *07/4946–8263*
⊕ *www.hamiltonisland.com.au.*

Ferry Fantasea ⌂ *PO Box 6164802* ☎ *07/4967–5455, 1800/650851*
⊕ *www.fantasea.com.au.*

Helicopter Aviation Adventures ☎ *07/4946–9988* ⊕ *www.av8.com.au.*

Medical Hamilton Island Medical Centre ✉ *Resort Dr.* ☎ *07/4946–8243.*

Seaplane Air Whitsunday ☎ *07/4946–9111* ⊕ *www.airwhitsunday.com.au.*

OUTDOOR ACTIVITIES

Clownfish Club. The Clownfish Club, for children aged six weeks to 4
years, has simple games and activities for the young ones: painting,
blocks, sand sculpting, dancing, and climbing, in three-hour and two
half-day sessions (conducted in two separate rooms—one for infants,
the other for 2–4-year-olds). For 5- to 14-year-olds, there are activities

Wind- and motor-powered water sports are popular on many Whitsunday Islands.

including swimming, mini-golf, beach sports, kite- and chocolate-making, drama, and craft, in morning and afternoon sessions.

Babysitting services (A$65-A$75 for 3 hours, A$20 an hour thereafter, plus a A$10 booking fee) must be arranged before 4 pm. You can also hire strollers and baby backpacks (A$15 per day), books and toys (A$5 per day). ☎ *07/4946–8941* ⊕ *www.clownfishclub.com.au* ⊗ *Daily 8:30–5:30.*

Hamilton Island Beach Sports. Hamilton Island Resort has the widest selection of activities in the Whitsundays: game fishing, snorkeling, scuba diving, waterskiing, parasailing, jet skiing, wakeboarding, sea kayaking, speedboat adventure rides and fish-feeding tours are all on the agenda, with staff from the resort's Beach Hut (Hamilton Island Beach Sports) on Catseye Beach ready to give assistance, tips, and—for a fee—lesssons. Many non-motorized water sports are free to resort guests. There are also bushwalks, go-karts, quad-bike (ATV) tours, an aquatic driving range, and a terrific 18-hole golf course (on its own island, a five-minute ferry-ride away), as well a flying fox, nine-pin bowling center, target-shooting range, wildlife sanctuary, and five public-access swimming pools. The island's sports and fitness complex incorporates a state-of-the-art gym (with daily classes), a whirlpool spa and sauna, squash and floodlit tennis courts, and a mini-golf course. You can also take twilight 4WD "bush safaris" and sign up for various tours, cruises, and special events.

  Tour Booking Desk. Reserve Hamilton Island tours, cruises, a table at a restaurant, and activities ahead of time through the Tour Booking Desk. ☎ *07/4946–8305* ⊕ *www.hamiltonisland.com.au* ☎ *07/4946–8305.*

CASTAWAY CUISINE

On Hamilton, the Whitsundays' largest inhabited island, guests can eat and drink at a variety of restaurants and bars. Virtually all of them are now managed by the Hamilton Island consortium, whose owners, the Oatley family, made their millions out of wine. The Oatleys are keen to further the island's reputation for quality wining and dining—recruiting big-city chefs, improving supply lines, scheduling epicurean events, and adding to the island's vast central cellar and produce store. Opportunities for young guns to work their way up through Hamilton's hierarchy, training under culinary heavyweights, bring a continuing stream of fresh talent to the island. The bad news? Staff don't always stay and as a result, food and service standards can be inconsistent—and as there's a virtual monopoly on dining options, prices tend to be steep.

GOLF ★ **Dent Island Golf Course.** This sleek Peter Thomson–designed, par 71, Hamilton Island-run golf course sits on Dent Island, a five-minute ferry ride from Hammo. The 6,083-meter (19,957-foot) course has sweeping Whitsundays views from all 18 holes. You can hire clubs, take lessons, and practice your swing on the golf driving range (A$15 for 50 balls). There's also a clubhouse, pro shop, restaurant, and bar. Ferries depart all day from 7:30 am from Hamilton Island Marina; allow five hours to play 18 holes (A$185) and half that to play nine (A$125). Prices include ferry transfers. ☎ 07/4949–9760 ⊕ *www.hamiltonislandgolfclub.com.au.*

FISHING **Hamilton Island fishing.** Staff can arrange half-day, full-day, share or private charter sportfishing trips with Renegade Sports Fishing & Charters for those looking to catch coral trout, mackerel, and tuna. Private charters cost A$2,750 for a full day, A$1,450 for a half day; shared charters are A$300 for a full day and A$160 for a half day. All equipment's included and catering can be arranged; the crew will even debone and fillet your catch so it's ready for barbecuing. You can take a half-day bottom-fishing excursion for coral trout using hand lines, or for giant trevally and Spanish mackerel using live bait and rods (A$135), from 8 am or 1 pm daily with Rapture Sport Fishing Charters; you can also hire dinghies for angling closer to shore. Arrange it all through Hamilton Island's Tour Booking Desk. ✉ *PO Box 124803* ☎ 07/4946–8305 ⊕ *www.renegadecharters.com.au* or *www.hamiltonisland.com.au.*

SCUBA DIVING **H2O Sportz Dive & Snorkel Shop.** The island has a free daily pool-based snorkeling lesson and scuba trial (prebooking is essential). If you sign up for an introductory dive course with H2O Sportz, the island's dive shop, you'll get instruction, equipment, and two guided dives, gear included. If you have three or four days, you can take a PADI Open Water or Advanced Diver course (run weekly). Already qualified? Rent scuba equipment and take a day trip to Bait Reef Marine Park, a Barrier Reef site rich in tropical marine life, including turtles and manta rays, and with a range of terrain, such as coral gardens, underwater canyons, walls, and swim-throughs. Hours are from 9:30–5 daily except Tuesday and Saturday. Gear, lunch, snacks, drinks, and reef tax are included (A$169, plus A$120–A$150 for two dives). Also available

are twice-weekly Whitsundays dive-snorkel day trips to three exceptional dive sites and Whitehaven Beach (A$175, plus A$80–A$110
for two dives, including buffet lunch, snacks, drinks, and gear), and
guided three-hour snorkeling safaris on *Reef Ryder* to Whitehaven
Beach and Chalkie's Beach (A$90, gear included). ⊠ *Hamiton Island
Marina, Front St., next to general store* ☎ *07/4946–9888 Dive Shop,
07/4946–8305 Tour Bookings Desk* ⊕ *www.h2osportz.com.au.*

WILDLIFE **Hamilton Island Wildlife Park.** The wildlife sanctuary houses koalas, kan-
PARK garoos, wallabies, wombats, birds, and reptiles, including a resident
⟲ croc. There are daily breakfasts (7:30–9:30) and lunches (11–2) with
the animals, as well as guided tours, talks, feedings, and koala-cuddling
photo sessions. ☎ *07/4946–8305, 13/7333* ⊒ *A$20, unlimited entry
for duration of HI stay.*

WHERE TO EAT

Hamilton Island Resort has lots of dining options, including casual cafés
and takeaway outlets, a pub serving counter meals, a dinner cruise boat
and several restaurants.

$$$$ ✗ **Bommies Restaurant.** In keeping with Hamilton Island Yacht Club's
MODERN modern design and upmarket ambience, Bommies has a luxuriously
AUSTRALIAN carpeted floor, polished-wood, sail-shape tables and comfortable
Eames chairs. Indeed, it's the ideal setting for fine Modern Australian
food. After a day out sailing, what could be more fitting than ceviche
(super-fresh raw fish marinated in lime and spices), just-caught pan-
fried reef fish, or a perfectly cooked seafood risotto? Ravenous yachties
might prefer to tuck into tender steaks or tasty 'roo fillets. Either way,
a sophisticated resort ambience is ensured by Bommies' smart-casual
dress code, no-kids-under-12 policy, and deliberately small tables.
There's also a private dining room seating up to 40 (minimum 24
hours' notice required). The island's classy new fine-dinery is justifiably popular, especially in peak season—book early to secure a coveted
table on the deck. ⊠ *Hamilton Island Yacht Club, Hamilton Island,
Whitsunday Islands* ☎ *07/4948–9433,* ⊕ *www.hamiltonisland.com.au/
yachtclub/dining* ⊙ *Daily, dinner 6 pm till late (last bookings 9 pm).*
⊙ *No lunch.*

$$$$ ✗ **Denison Star.** The *Denison Star*, a magnificent 107-foot motor cruiser
AUSTRALIAN hewn from Tasmanian Huon pine, glides out of Hamilton Island Marina
most evenings for a starlit dinner tour around the sheltered waters of
the island. It's all very civilized: canapes and welcome daiquiris are
served to a maximum 40 guests on the sundeck as night falls, then
the boat moors in some scenic, secluded spot. You order three courses
from a small à la carte selection, your complimentary bottle of wine
is uncorked (extra bottles available for purchase), and the food duly
emerges from the galley. Down a post-meal port, perhaps, and stargaze
from the upper deck as you cruise back to base. ⊠ *Hamilton Island
Marina* ☎ *07/4946–8305, 13/7333* ⊕ *www.hamiltonisland.com.au or
www.cruiseindigo.com.au.*

$$ ✗ **Manta Ray Café.** This could be the island's best all-rounder. Dine
ECLECTIC right by the marina on salads and pasta dishes, say, spaghetti Bolog-
⟲ nese or seafood risotto—or join the queue for gourmet, wood-fired
★ pizzas (also available as takeout, 6–9 pm). There's plenty on Manta

8

Ray's menu to suit all tastes. The wine list's a winner, too (though for a corkage charge of A\$15, you can BYO special bottle). ⊠ *Front St.* ☎ *07/4946–8536* ⊘ *Daily, 10:30-noon (coffee/cakes), noon–3 (lunch), 5:30–10 (dinner).*

\$\$\$

SEAFOOD

✕ **Mariners Restaurant.** Perched on the marina, this breezy, upscale eatery turns the local catch into fresh contemporary dishes: artfully arranged sashimi, seasonal crustaceans, reef fish, house-made tagliatelle marinara, Thai-style jumbo prawn curry, and hot and cold seafood platters. They also offer vegetarian and other non-seafood options, and there's a well-stocked bar. Book a balcony table and watch watercraft dock as you dine. ⊠ *Marina Village* ☎ *07/4946–8628* ⚱ *Reservations essential* ⊘ *No lunch.*

\$\$\$

ITALIAN

★

✕ **Romano's Waterfront Italian.** With polished wood floors and a wide balcony overlooking the marina, Romano's is the place to come for casual fine dining. The kitchen produces traditional Italian favorites such as pasta *marina* and Bolognese as well as more inventive dishes, such as the house-made ravioli with spiced pear, pumpkin, walnut gremolata, and pecorino, but the focus is on fresh produce and local seafood, as in the terrific Spring Bay mussels with a fresh tomato, fennel, and herb broth. Dessert (A\$17) might be gelato, pannacotta, or tiramisu. It's licensed, and there's a steep corkage charge (A\$25) if you BYOB. ⊠ *Marina Village, Harbourside* ☎ *07/4946–8212* ⊘ *No lunch.*

\$\$\$

BISTRO

☏

✕ **Sails Restaurant.** Set right on Catseye Beach, this airy beach shack bistro serves three good-quality meals daily with a choice of beachfront or poolside dining. The Modern Australian–International menu is a crowd-pleaser, with pasta, salads, and surf-and-turf dishes—perhaps pan-fried reef fish or Scotch fillet with beer-battered fries. The seafood platter is A\$70 per person. Dessert could be apple pie, cheesecake, mud cake, or a citrus tart with mixed berries. Breakfast, if it's not included in your room rate, is A\$34. There's also a good kids' menu and a giant chess set to keep older offspring occupied between courses. After dinner, catch some live jazz or a local band. ⊠ *Main resort complex* ☎ *07/4946–8536.*

WHERE TO STAY

For expanded hotel reviews, visit Fodors.com.

\$\$\$

☏

★

🏨 **Hamilton Island Holiday Homes.** Part of the Hamilton Island resort, Hamilton Island Holiday Homes manages more than 100 self-catered one- to four-bedroom holiday properties around the island, including studio, split-level, and two-story designs. **Pros:** all the amenities of home, great pool, money-saving kid's program. **Cons:** Restaurants where kids eat free can get crowded. ⊠ *Front St.* ☎ *02/9433–0444, 13/7333* ⊕ *www.hihh.com.au* ⚭ *In-room: a/c, kitchen, Internet, Wi-Fi. In-hotel: pool, gym, beach, laundry facilities, parking.*

\$\$\$\$

🏨 **Hamilton Island Beach Club.** The upscale amenities and no-kids policy mean that this hotel swarms with couples. **Pros:** cut-above breakfasts; beachside location; free Wi-Fi; no kids. **Cons:** service lacks attention to detail; four-night minimum stay in peak periods. ⊠ *Hamilton Island, Whitsunday Islands* ☎ *02/9433–0444, 13–7333* ⊕ *www.hamiltonisland.com.au* ⚓ *57 rooms* ⚭ *In-room: a/c, safe, Wi-Fi. In-hotel: restaurant, bar, pool, tennis court, gym, spa, water sports, business center, some age restrictions* ⊙❘ *Breakfast.*

$$$ ⊡ **Hamilton Island Palm Bungalows.** These steep-roofed, freestanding bun-
☺ galows resemble Polynesian huts; each has a private furnished balcony
with a hammock, cool tile or polished-wood floors, a basic kitchenette
with cutlery and bar fridge, king-size and sofa beds, and ceiling fans.
Pros: free use of the island's gym/sports complex and non-motorized
water-sports equipment; free airport transfers; close to main pool,
beach and wildlife park. **Cons:** unrefurbished rooms can be musty;
buggy hire not included; up a steepish hill. ⊠ *Hamilton Island, Whit-
sunday Islands* ☎ *02/9433–0444, 13–7333* ⊕ *www.hamiltonisland.
com.au* ⤴ *49 bungalows* ⅏ *In-room: a/c, Internet. In-hotel: gym, water
sports, children's programs.*

$$$ ⊡ **Hamilton Island Reef View Hotel.** Only rooms on higher floors of this
☺ hotel live up to the name—those on the fifth floor and above have spec-
★ tacular vistas of the Coral Sea, while rooms on lower levels overlook a
landscaped, tropical garden—but all are comfortable, with private balconies. **Pros:** good breakfasts (included with days of four or more days);
terrific outlook from higher floors, with beds facing the views; better-
than-usual service. **Cons:** lower-level rooms can be noisy; pricey in-house
food and drinks; cockatoos fly in open windows. ⊠ *Hamilton Island,
Whitsunday Islands* ☎ *02/9433–0444, 13–7333* ⊕ *www.hamiltonisland.
com.au* ⤴ *382 rooms and suites* ⅏ *In-room: a/c, safe, Internet. In-hotel:
restaurant, bar, pool, tennis court, gym, spa, beach, water sports, children's programs, laundry facilities, business center* ⓨ *Breakfast.*

$$$$ ⊡ **Qualia.** The latest addition to Hamilton Island's accommodations is eas-
★ ily its most luxurious. **Pros:** glorious, tranquil location; fine food and wine;
high-end everything. **Cons:** 2-night minimum stay in peak periods; slow
room service; pricey. ⊠ *20 Whitsunday Blvd.* ☎ *02/9433–0444, 13/7777*
⊕ *www.qualia.com.au* ⤴ *60 suites* ⅏ *In-room: a/c, safe, Internet, Wi-Fi.
In-hotel: restaurant, bar, golf course, pool, tennis court, gym, spa, beach,
water sports, children's programs, some age restrictions* ⓨ *Breakfast.*

$$$ ⊡ **Whitsunday Apartments.** These twin 13-story towers, overlooking Cats-
eye Beach and the Coral Sea, house one-bedroom apartments with comfy
wood-and-cane furniture, large furnished balconies, full kitchens, and din-
ing and sitting areas equipped with cable TV and DVD players. **Pros:** self-
catering; family-friendly; free water sports. **Cons:** lower-floor apartments
are a tad shabby; serviced only every four days; on-island supplies pricey
(BYO groceries from the mainland or order online from Coles supermar-
ket and have them delivered for A$15). ⊠ *Hamilton Island, Whitsunday
Islands* ☎ *08/9483–8600,* ⊕ *www.broadwaters.com.au* ⤴ *165 apartments*
⅏ *In-room: kitchen, Internet. In-hotel: water sports, children's programs.*

NIGHTLIFE

Hamilton Island has several resort bars as well as a handful of indepen-
dent ones: all except Qualia's are open to visitors. Find live music at the
Reef Lounge and Sails, harborside tables at the Marina Tavern, and sun-
downer cocktails on the Bommie Deck at Hamilton Island Yacht Club.

Boheme's Bar & Nightclub. At Boheme's Bar & Nightclub you can dance
to DJ-spun classic and contemporary music and shoot a round of pool.
Boheme's Balcony Bar is open Thursday–Saturday 9 pm–late; the night-
club is open Friday and Saturday 11 pm–late. ⊠ *Front St., Marina Vil-
lage* ☎ *07/4946–9999.*

SHOPPING

Hamilton Island's Marina Village, along Front Street, houses many shops selling resort wear, children's clothes, souvenirs and gifts. You'll also find an art gallery, florist, small supermarket, pharmacy, real-estate agent, bakery, bottle shop, DVD-hire store, day spa, and a hair salon on the island. In general, you'll pay more for goods and services here than for their equivalents on the mainland.

DAYDREAM ISLAND

The resort on this small, 42-acre island is especially welcoming to day-trippers. Around 30 minutes' boat ride from Shute Harbour, Abel Point Marina, or Hamilton Island, it's a perfect place to relax or pursue outdoor activities such as snorkeling and water sports—which are comparatively affordable here. The resort's lush gardens blend into a small tract of rain forest, frequented by tame wallabies and big-eyed, stilt-legged Stone curlews. The island is surrounded by clear blue water and coral reefs.

GETTING HERE AND AROUND

Cruise Whitsundays runs several daily services between Daydream Island and Great Barrier Reef (Hamilton Island) Airport Jetty (A$60), as well as from Whitsunday Coast (Proserpine) Airport and Proserpine Rail Station (A$50); and between the island and Abel Point Marina and (less frequently) Shute Harbour (A$30 each way). Transfers from Abel Point Marina to Hamilton Island Airport Jetty cost A$60 each way. Cruise Whitsunday Resort Connections offers direct island transfers from Hamilton Island Airport on modern, air-conditioned catamaran cruisers. Cruise Whitsundays also runs Island Escape Day Cruises, half- and full-day cruises to nearby islands and beaches: Single Island Escape tours take you to Daydream, Hook, or Long Island for the day (A$59—A$89, including lunch and use of the island resort's facilities); the Twin Island Escape (A$105) calls in at two of these three islands; and the Island Wanderer (A$55) is a relaxed scenic cruise around several of the Whitsunday islands; and the Island Hopper (A$79) allows you to visit various Whitsunday resort islands at your leisure.

Although most people arrive by boat from Great Barrier Reef (Hamilton Island) Airport, an alternative is to fly to Whitsunday Coast (Proserpine) Airport on the mainland, catch a bus to Shute Harbour, then take a boat to the island. Several major airlines operate flights between Hamilton Island and Proserpine airports and capital cities around Australia, and between the Whitsundays, Townsville, and Cairns. Check with each carrier for weight restrictions.

ESSENTIALS

Cruise Whitsundays ☎ 07/4946–4662 ⊕ www.cruisewhitsundays.com.

Fantasea Cruises ☎ 07/4967–5455 ⊕ www.fantasea.com.au.

OUTDOOR ACTIVITIES

At Daydream Island Resort & Spa many activities, such as water polo, beach volleyball, aquarobics, tennis, bocce, and the use of resort kayaks and catamarans, are included in room rates, as are marine talks and fish feeds, spa tours, scavenger hunts, rain-forest walks, and nightly outdoor cinema screenings. Guided fishing, snorkeling, and scuba diving day trips, parasailing, jet skiing, waterskiing, and wakeboarding sessions, guided sea kayak and ocean rafting excursions, glass-bottom boat tours, banana-boat tube rides, croc safaris, and more can be arranged through the resort's Tour Desk for an additional charge.

Daydream offers day trips to Whitehaven Beach on catamaran *Camira*, including snorkeling gear, a BBQ lunch, morning and afternoon tea, and all beverages (including alcoholic drinks) for A$175; snorkel and dive cruises to Knuckle Reef Lagoon with classy local operator Cruise Whitsundays for A$199; sailing excursions on maxi-yacht *Ragamuffin*; an introductory pool scuba training session and ocean dive for A$110 (or, if time permits, a multiday PADI Open Water dive course including training, six ocean dives, and all gear for A$325. Guided local dives for certified divers cost A$90 for the first dive, A$70 for an additional dive. To prebook on- or offshore activities prior to your arrival, phone ☎ *07/4948–8477* or email ✉ *discover@daydream.net.au.*

An ocean rafting excursion on fast, semi-rigid inflatable boats takes you to neighboring islands and gorgeous Whitehaven Beach, with stops to snorkel and stroll around. Half- and full-day sportfishing trips around the Whitsundays on *Sea Fever* (☎ *07/4984–2734 or 0427/524975* ⊕ *www.seafever.com.au*) include bait, tackle, and lines. Or take a helicopter flight to Fantasea's Reefworld pontoon, where you can snorkel, take semi-submersible tours, and try out the giant waterslide. Nonguests can also book activities through the resort.

WHERE TO STAY

For expanded hotel reviews, visit Fodors.com.

$$$$ ⬚ **Daydream Island Resort and Spa.** Colorfully decorated, with whimsical touches—starfish-and-shell-embedded toilet seats, mermaid and dolphin statues perched on rocks, a giant chess set, and outsize marine mobiles and murals—this family-friendly resort has youthful, cheerful staff, a well-run, albeit pricey kids' club (open daily for morning and afternoon sessions for 0- to 4-year-olds; fun school-holiday programs, including evening sessions, for 5- to 12-year-olds), a terrific pool, and a lovely day spa. **Pros:** family-friendly; classy spa (unfortunately sited above the kids' club); mini-golf and outdoor movie screenings; snorkeling off Lovers' Cove. **Cons:** teeming with kids; food lackluster; steep fees for kids' club, babysitting and PlayStation games. ⊠ *Daydream Island, Whitsunday Islands* ⬚ *Daydream Island, PMB 22, Mackay 4740* ☎ *07/3259–2350, 1800/075040* ⊕ *www.daydreamisland.com* ⬚ *280 rooms, 9 suites* ⬚ *In-room: a/c, safe, Wi-Fi. In-hotel: restaurant, bar, pool, tennis court, gym, spa, beach, water sports, children's programs, laundry facilities, business center* ⊠ *Breakfast.*

SHOPPING

The Boat House, at the southern end of the island, serves sandwiches, salads, wraps, pies, and cakes as well as hot beverages during the day, while Gilligan's Health Hut, near the south-end pool, sells ice-cream, smoothies, juices, and alcoholic drinks. A convenience store in the main resort complex, near Reception, sells essentials, candy, pharmacy goods, resort wear, cards, and gifts, and is open daily until 5.

NIGHTLIFE

As Daydream is primarily a family resort, there's little to do after dinner: live musical ensembles play nightly from 6:30 in the lobby Lagoon Bar but the ambience is low-key—think quiet conversation over a predinner or postprandial drink rather than dancing and carousing. Theme nights occasionally take place in the bar at the island's southern end, where you can also watch new-release movies on a gigantic beachfront screen (deck chairs and blankets provided), then stroll home along the coast-hugging boardwalk. Babysitting's not cheap here (and the cost escalates with every extra child), so staying in and watching pay-per-view movies may be your best option.

HAYMAN ISLAND

Fodor'sChoice
★

Hayman Island, in the northern Whitsunday Passage, is the closest of the Whitsunday resort isles to the Outer Barrier Reef. The island, a 900-acre crescent with a series of hills along its spine, has just one resort, one of the oldest and most opulent in the region and popular with jet-setters who take their leisure seriously. The service—understated yet attentive—merits the price you pay for it; staff members even traverse the resort via tunnels so they're less of a "presence." Reflecting pools, sandstone walkways, manicured tropical gardens, statuary, and waterfalls—meticulously recreated in 2011 under the guidance of celebrity landscape designer Jamie Durie (who also designed six additional garden areas for the resort) after substantial damage from Cyclone Larry—provide the feel of an exclusive club, while beautiful walking trails crisscross the island, leading to pristine coves and vantage points. The main beach sits right in front of the resort complex, but more secluded sands and fringing coral can be reached by boat or on foot.

GETTING HERE AND AROUND

Hayman doesn't have its own airstrip, but you can fly to Hamilton Island and from there transfer onto one of Hayman's luxury motor yachts or charter a helicopter or seaplane. From Hayman's wharf a shuttle whisks you to the resort about ½ km (¼ mi) away. Tea, coffee, and Australian sparkling wine are served during the 60-minute motor-launch trip to the island. On the return journey, you'll get full bar service, platters of food, tea, and espresso coffee. Make sure you're ticketed all the way to Hayman Island, including the motor-yacht leg, as purchasing the round-trip yacht journey from Hamilton Island to Hayman separately costs upward of A$300. Air Whitsunday provides seaplane connections from Whitsunday Airport, Airlie Beach to Hayman for A$490 each way (up to 4 passengers) or A$760 (up to 6) and from Great Barrier Reef (Hamilton Island) Airport for A$790 (up to 4 passengers) and A$1,590 (up to 6), on request, from mainland airports including Whitsunday Coast (Proserpine) and Mackay airports. They also run scenic flights around the Whitsundays and over the reef. Heli-reef Whitsundays can transfer guests (minimum 2) to Hayman Island from Hamilton Island or Airlie Beach for A$325 per person, and from Whitsunday Coast Airport at Proserpine for A$430 per person., Baggage weight limits apply.

TOURS

Hayman Island Guest Services provides information on all guided tours around the island and excursions offshore. All listed costs are per person.

An hour-long scenic seaplane flight over Whitehaven Beach and the Great Barrier Reef, including renowned Heart Reef, is A$340 per person—or get a bird's-eye glimpse of your environs on a 10-minute **Whitsundays scenic helicopter ride** (A$145). A half-day excursion with Helireef Whitsundays to Knuckle Reef pontoon with two hours to have lunch and enjoy the pontoon facilities and underwater environs, is A$699 per person.

Various half-day seaplane and helicopter excursions let you explore neighboring islands and the reef from aloft and underwater, and be back to Hayman for lunch. Fly to Whitehaven Beach for a morning's snorkeling, strolling, and sunbathing for A$300 by seaplane; A$399 by helicopter, refreshments and scenery included.

An **Air Whitsundays** seaplane excursion to an outer Barrier Reef pontoon, with an hour of snorkeling and an hour's semi-submersible coral viewing tour, is A$315 for three hours, with gear, tuition, Australian sparkling wine, and nibblies included.

Pick of the bunch is a three-hour seaplane tour to Fantasea Reefworld, where Hayman guests get exclusive use of the huge pontoon and its facilities, refreshments, scenic overflights, and commentary en route for A$480 per person.

Keen golfers can take a scenic 10-minute helicopter flight to Dent Island Golf Course, just off Hamilton Island, and play 18 holes for A$999. Anglers can take half- and full-day bottom-fishing excursions for coral trout, red emperor, sweetlip, and scarlet sea perch (A$250) and game-fishing trips for black marlin, tuna, mackerel, and giant trevally on Hayman's own 41-foot vessel *Sun Aura* (A$280, min. 2 persons). Various sailing options are offered, and most of Hayman's immaculate fleet is available for private charter.

Cruise Whitsundays runs a daily full-day dive-snorkel cruise on a 121-foot wave-piercer craft from Hayman (and the mainland and neighboring isles) to Knuckle Reef Lagoon pontoon on the outer Reef: the A$199 per person fare includes use of pontoon facilities (including a giant waterslide), snorkeling gear, buffet lunch and refreshments, and priority access to coral-viewing tours. Optional extras include guided snorkel safaris (A$35), introductory and certified diving (A$99–A$110, second dives A$55), scenic helicopter flights (A$129–A$199), even massages (A$25–A$105).

ESSENTIALS

Seaplane Air Whitsunday ☎ 07/4946–9111 ⊕ *www.airwhitsunday.com.au.* **HeliReef Whitsundays** ☎ 07/4946–9102 ⊕ *www.helireef.com.au.*

Tour Operators Cruise Whitsundays ☎ 07/4946–4662 ⊕ *www.cruisewhitsundays.com.* **Hayman Island Guest Services** ☎ 07/4940–1838, 1800/122–339 ⊕ *www.hayman.com.au.*

Parasailing off Hayman Island.

OUTDOOR ACTIVITIES

All nonmotorized water sports on Hayman Island—well-maintained catamarans, Windsurfers, and paddle skis—are included in the room rates, as are use of the well-equipped indoor-outdoor gym, five flood-lighted tennis courts, squash and basketball courts, badminton, Ping-Pong and croquet equipment, and a golf driving range and 9-hole putting green. Swim in the vast lagoon pools; take a self-guided art or garden walk; group fitness, yoga or meditation class (A$25) or personal training session; an exhilarating inflatable tube ride, waterskiing or wakeboarding session; or guided sea-kayak excurison to nearby beaches and islands. Or order a picnic hamper and set off to one of the island's secluded beaches.

The fully-accredited five-star PADI Hayman Diving and Snorkeling Centre at Hayman Marina has a training tank for diving lessons, and runs various dive courses, trips, and packages, including a signature Hayman night dive aboard the resort's dive vessel, *Sun Aura*, to nearby Castle Rock Wall, on which you'll see crabs, shrimp, crayfish, moray eels, parrot fish, and more (minimum 2 persons). It also sells everything from snorkel gear to wet suits and sports clothing.

Here you can book waterskiing, windsurfing, sailing, boating, game- and bottom-fishing, and snorkeling excursions as well as dive trips.

You can also arrange scenic flights to nearby beaches and over the reef as well as heli-golf tours to Dent Island Golf Course (off Hamilton Island) through the resort's Recreation Information Centre.

Recreation Information Centre ☎ *07/4940–1838.*

WHERE TO EAT

All restaurants are within the resort complex. Reservations are recommended and in some cases essential: they can be booked with ease through the resort's concierge. Dress for all Hayman's evening restaurants is "smart resort wear"—no singlets, shorts or flip-flops. Restaurant opening times are staggered so you always have at least two dining options; by day, eat at the Beach Pavilion or snack by the Pool Bar.

Hayman schedules various epicurean events, including weekly six-course degustation dinners and behind-scenes tours of its vast kitchens, impressive wine cellar, and chocolate room (A$245 per person); chef and wine-maker events; and Hayman Culinary Academy cooking classes (A$220–A$240 per person, including the resulting three-course meal).

> ### ONE WITH NATURE
>
> At Barrier Reef resorts, part of the fun is sharing your vacation with the local wildlife. On Orpheus Island, lace monitor lizards up to 3 feet long frequently wander into the resort grounds looking for food. Cute wallabies and doe-eyed, mournful-sounding Stone curlews roam the grounds of many Whitsunday resorts. Hayman supports a colony of endangered Proserpine rock wallabies; Hamilton has a small wildlife sanctuary at which you can breakfast with koalas. Unsuspecting Whitsundays resort guests may be subject to fly-by room raids from cheeky white cockatoos.

$$$$
AUSTRALIAN
★

✕ **Azure.** Right on the island's main beach, this casually elegant restaurant affords glorious views. Dine indoors or alfresco: seating extends onto the sand. There's a splendid buffet breakfast each morning, with à la carte options, freshly baked breads and pastries, tropical fruits and juices, and brewed coffee. A contemporary Australian menu showcasing seafood and sophisticated, romantically lit dining after dark are the draw cards. A lavish seafood grill is available on selected evenings. There's also a kids' menu.

$$$$
MODERN
AUSTRALIAN
★

✕ **La Fontaine.** Named for its central fountain, this elegant restaurant is the resort's culinary showpiece. In 2011 it received a complete re-fit, reopening with a fresh ambience and a revamped, Modern Australian menu. La Fontaine diners now have the option of sitting outside; book early and you can reserve a dining platform over the swan pool. A private dining room—with the option of designing your own menu, in consultation with the resort's executive chef—is available year-round (minimum 4 people). ⌕ *Reservations essential. Jacket required* ☾ *No lunch.*

$$$
ITALIAN

✕ **La Trattoria.** With its red-and-white-checked tablecloths, hand-beaten hanging lamps, and rustic furnishings, "Tratt's" is a classic provincial Italian restaurant. Sit inside or outdoors, and choose from an extensive list of pastas and traditional Italian dishes, a spectacular antipasto buffet, and a well-chosen wine list with some excellent reds. Live music adds to the sociable atmosphere. ⌕ *Reservations essential* ☾ *No lunch.*

8

$$$$ ✕ **Oriental Restaurant.** This lovely pan-Asian establishment, a Hayman
ASIAN staff favorite, overlooks a tranquil Japanese garden complete with
rock pools and waterfalls, a teahouse, and dining platforms. Menu
choices include exotic and classic Thai, Chinese, Japanese, and Indian
dishes, and there's a separate vegetarian menu. ⚞ *Reservations essential* ⊘ *No lunch.*

WHERE TO STAY

For expanded hotel reviews, visit Fodors.com.

$$$$ ⊡ **Hayman.** This magnificently solid resort is the grande dame of the
Whitsundays, attracting high-flying guests seeking precious down time.
Pros: meticulous, attentive service; terrific food, wine, and activities;
lovely public areas; well-stocked boutiques. **Cons:** pricey (albeit top-
notch) food, drinks, and spa treatments; room-raiding cockatoos; a fair
hike from some rooms to the restaurants. ⊠ *Hayman Island, Great Barrier Reef* ☎ *07/4940–1234 resort, 07/4940–1838, 1800/075175 reservations (toll-free), 1800/122339 resort (toll-free)* ⊕ *www.hayman.com.
au* ⤹ *210 rooms, suites, penthouses, beach houses, villa* ♿ *In-room:
a/c, safe, Wi-Fi. In-hotel: restaurant, bar, pool, tennis court, gym, spa,
beach, water sports, children's programs.*

SHOPPING

Hayman has its own chi-chi shopping arcade next to the spa. Prices
aren't cheap, but the merchandise is high-quality and well chosen. There
are a couple of lovely boutiques stocked with designer clothes and accessories, swimwear, and resort wear for men, women, and kids, including
enough stylish pieces to ensure you meet Hayman's "smart-resort-wear-
for-dinner" dress code. There's Depazzi, a small high-end jeweler, a
newsagency that also sells photographic accessories and prints images, a
medical center that fills pharmacy prescriptions, and a gift shop stocked
with quality Australian-made and Hayman-branded merchandise, art,
and crafts. If you're lucky, you'll visit during a sale: in the low season
you might snare a bargain designer swimsuit, kaftan, or beach bag.
Stores are open daily until 5 or 6, depending on the season.

NIGHTLIFE

Hayman's genteel ambience extends to its nighttime entertainment
options. After dinner, most folk are so busy digesting fine food and wine
that dancing's not an option—which is fortunate, perhaps, as unless
there's a wedding in progress, you'll find no loud, live entertainment or
obnoxiously intoxicated bar patrons here. Guests tend to gather in the
Club Lounge next to reception, where the ambience is warm but low-
key, to play billiards or chess, read books from the library, or converse
quietly over a cognac. You could also organize a private moonlight
cruise or join one of Hayman's popular local night dives.

NORTH COAST ISLANDS

ORPHEUS ISLAND

Volcanic in origin, this narrow island—11 km (7 mi) long and 1 km (½ mi) wide, 3,500 acres total—uncoils like a snake in the waters between Halifax Bay and the Barrier Reef. It's part of the Palm Island Group, which consists of 10 islands, 8 of which are Aboriginal reservations. Orpheus is a national park, occupied only by a marine research station and the island's resort, recently refurbished under its new, eco-conscious owners and scheduled to reopen in March 2012 with the addition of a large vegetable garden, a solar hot-water system, and a 21,134-gallon water tank, a brand-new infinity-edge pool, and several beachfront villas linked by a rear boardwalk. Although there are patches of rain forest in the island's deeper gullies and around its sheltered bays, Orpheus is a true Barrier Reef island, ringed by seven unspoiled sandy beaches and superb coral. Incredibly, 340 of the known 350 species of coral inhabit these waters, as well as more than 1,100 types of tropical fish and the biggest giant clams in the southern hemisphere. The marine life here is easily accessed and extraordinary—and the maximum 42 guests at the resort are virtually the only ones visiting it. You may occasionally see unfamiliar boats offshore, which is their right according to a marine park treaty, but you'll know everyone on Orpheus at any given time, maybe even by name.

GETTING HERE AND AROUND

Orpheus Island lies 24 km (15 mi) offshore of Ingham, about 80 km (50 mi) northeast of Townsville, and 190 km (118 mi) south of Cairns. The 25-minute seaplane flight from Domestic Gate Lounge 10 at Townsville Airport to Orpheus aboard a Nautilus Aviation seaplane costs A$550 per person round-trip; from Cairns it's A$950 including a connecting Qantas flight to Townsville; a mixed-port trip is A$750. Twice-daily scheduled flights depart from Townsville at 11:30 and 2:15, returning at 12:15 and 3. You can also charter flights from other mainland ports and islands. Baggage is limited to a maximum of 15 kilograms (33 pounds) per person. Excess baggage can be stored at Townsville Airport for free. Book flights with Orpheus Island Resort.

ESSENTIALS

Seaplane **Nautilus Aviation** ☏ 07/4725–6506, 0412/591–732 ⊕ www.nautilusaviation.com.au.

OUTDOOR ACTIVITIES

Orpheus Island Resort is surrounded by walking trails, and there are spectacular snorkeling and diving sites right off the beaches, with manta rays the highlight. Resort guests get complimentary use of snorkeling and light fishing gear, as well as canoes, paddle-skis, catamarans, and motorized dinghies in which to buzz from cove to cove. The coral around Orpheus is some of the best in the area, and cruises to the outer reef can be arranged through the resort for an additional fee. Whereas most of the islands are more than 50 km (31 mi) from the reef, Orpheus is just 15 km (9 mi) away. Dive operators on the island provide scuba courses and various boat-diving options.

8

Continued on page 522

WHAT LIVES ON THE REEF?

Equivalent to the Amazon Rainforest
in its biodiversity, the Reef hosts the
earth's most abundant collection of
sea life. Resident species include (but
aren't limited to):

- More than 1,500 species of fish
- 5,000 species of mollusk
- 400 species of hard and soft coral
- 30 whale and dolphin species
- More than 500 species of sea plants
  and grasses
- 14 sea-snake species
- Six sea-turtle species
- 200 sea-bird species
- More than 150 species of shark

DIVING THE REEF

To astronauts who've seen it from space, the Great Barrier Reef resembles a vast, snaking wall—like a moat running parallel to Australia's entire northeastern coast. Almost unimaginably long at 1,430-odd miles, it's one of the few organic structures that can be seen from above the earth's atmosphere without a telescope.

(left) purple anthias; (above) pink coral

Up close, though, what looks (and from its name, sounds) like a barrier is in fact a labyrinthine complex with millions of points of entry. Mind-boggling in size and scope, encompassing more than 4,000 separate reefs, cays, and islands, the Reef could rightly be called its own subaqueous country.

An undersea enthusiast could spend a lifetime exploring this terrain—which ranges from dizzying chasms to sepulchral coral caves, and from lush underwater "gardens" to sandy sun-dappled shallows—without ever mapping all its resident wonders. Not only is the Reef system home to thousands upon thousands of sea-life species, the populations are changing all the time.

So how is a visitor—especially one with only a week to spend—supposed to plan a trip to this underwater Eden? How to choose among the seemingly endless spots for dropping anchor, donning fins and tanks, and plunging in?

With this many options, figuring out what you want to experience on the Reef is essential. If you've dreamed of floating among sea turtles, you'll likely need to head to a different location than if you want to swim with sharks; if you're an experienced deep-water diver with a taste for shipwrecks, you'll probably need to make separate arrangements from your friends who prefer to hover near the surface. There really is a spot for every kind of diver on the Reef; the trick is knowing where they are.

Luckily, many veteran divers agree about some of the Reef's most reliably excellent sites (and the best ways to access them). The selection compiled here should help you to— ahem—get your feet wet.

by Sarah Gold

BEST DIVING EXPERIENCES

Potato Cod and diver at Cod Hole

BEST WRECK DIVE

The coral formations of the Reef, while dazzling for divers, have proved treacherous to ship captains for centuries. More than 1,500 shipwrecks have been found on the Reef thus far—and there are almost certainly more waiting to be discovered.

S.S. YONGALA

The hulk of this 360-foot steamship, which sank during a cyclone in 1911, is easily the most popular wreck dive on the Reef. Part of the appeal is its easy accessibility; the Yongala lies just a half-hour's boat ride off the coast of Townsville, and though some sections are fairly deep (around 90 feet), others are just 45 feet below the surface. The entire wreck is now encrusted with coral, and swarms with a profusion of species including giant grouper, sea snakes, green sea turtles, and spotted eagle rays.

Difficulty level: Intermediate. Divers should have some previous deep-water experience before visiting this site.

How to get there: Yongala Dive (www. yongaladive.com.au), based in Alva Beach (south of Townsville), runs trips to the wreck several times per week.

BEST SITE TO GET YOUR HEART RATE UP

For some thrill-seeking divers, the wonders of the Great Barrier Reef are even better when accompanied by an extra shot of adrenaline—and a few dozen sharks.

OSPREY REEF

More than 200 miles north of Cairns (and only accessible via a live-aboard dive trip), Osprey is peerless for divers hell-bent on a rendezvous with the ocean's most famous predators. The northernmost section of the reef, where two ocean currents converge (it's known as the North Horn) is an especially thronged feeding ground for white-tipped reef, gray reef, hammerhead, and tiger sharks.

Difficulty level: Intermediate. Though the North Horn's best shark-viewing areas are only at about 60 feet, even seasoned divers may feel understandably anxious.

How to get there: Both Taka Dive (www. takadive.com.au) and John Rumney's Marine Encounters (www.marineencounters.com.au) offer multi-day packages to Osprey Reef from Cairns and Port Douglas.

PAPUA
NEW GUINEA

Torres Strait

Cape York

Denham
Group

◪ Raine Island

Cape Grenville

Sir Charles Hardy
Group

CAPE YORK PENINSULA

Far North Section

Claremont
Isles

Cape Melville

◪ Osprey Reef

Howick
Group

Ribbon Reef #10

◪ Cod Hole

Lizard Island   Cape Flattery

Turtle
Group

Cooktown

GREAT BARRIER REEF
MARINE PARK

Cape Tribulation

Mossman

Port Douglas

◪ Cathedral

Cairns   Cape Grafton

Coral Sea

Innisfail

Cairns
Section

Flinders Reefs

Coral Sea
Islands

Cardwell

Ingham

Hinchinbrook
Island

A1

GREAT BARRIER REEF

KEY

Reef down to 15ft deep

Reef down to 30ft deep

Townsville

Ayr

◪ S.S. Yongala

Bowen

Whitsunday Island

Proserpine   Airlie   Whitsunday
             Beach   Group

Central Section

Mackay

Northumberland
Islands

Swain Reefs

Percy Islands

Duke Islands

A1

Marlborough

TORILLA PENINSULA

Cape Manifold

Macay/Capricorn
Section

Rockhampton

Capricorn
Group

Bunker
Group

◪ Blow
Hole

Lighthouse Bommies ◪   ◪

Bundaberg

Lady Elliot
Island

Fraser
Island

Hervey Bay

Maryborough

Gympie

A1

BRISBANE ★

Dwarf Minke Whale

Ribbon Reef

Cuttlefish

0   100 mi

0   100 km

8

IN FOCUS DIVING THE REEF

RAINE ISLAND

Thousands of green sea turtles migrate
each year to lay eggs on the protected
shores of Raine Island.

Scuba isn't the only option; snorkelers have plenty of opportunities to get up close to coral, too.

BEST CORAL-FORMATION SITES

Whether they're hard formations that mimic the shapes of antlers, brains, and stacked plates, or soft feathery Gorgonians and anemones, the building blocks of Reef ecology are compelling in their own right.

BLOW HOLE

Set off the eastern coast of Lady Elliot Island, this cavern-like coral tube is almost 60 feet in length. Divers can enter from either end, and swim through an interior festooned with Technicolor hard and soft corals—and swarming with banded coral shrimp, crayon-bright nudibranchs (sea slugs), and fluttery lionfish.

Difficulty level: Easy. Unless you're claustrophobic. Divers need only be Open-Water certified to visit this site, which ranges in depth from about 40 to 65 feet.

How to get there: The dive center at the Lady Elliot Island resort (www.ladyelliot.com.au) runs dives to the Blow Hole several times daily.

CATHEDRAL

Part of Thetford Reef, which lies within day-tripping distance of coastal Cairns, Cathedral is a wonderland of coral spires and swim-through chasms. The towering coral heads include thick forests of blue staghorn, sea fans, and sea whips; in between are sandy-bottomed canyons where shafts of sunlight play over giant clam beds.

Difficulty level: Intermediate. Though many coral peaks lie just 15 to 20 feet below the surface, the deeper channels (which go down to 85 feet) can be disorienting.

How to get there: Silverseries (www.silverseries.com.au) runs day-long trips from Cairns that visit several Thetford sites.

Divers explore a swim-through coral formation.

BEST GUARANTEED CLOSE-ENCOUNTER SITES

While just about any dive site on the Reef will bring you face-to-face with fantastic species, a few particular spots maximize your chances.

RIBBON REEF NUMBER 10

The northernmost of the Ribbon Reefs (a group that extends off the Cairns coast all the way to the Torres Strait) is home to some famously curious sea creatures. At Cod Hole, divers have been hand-feeding the enormous, 70-pound resident potato cod for decades. Ribbon Reef Number 10 is also one of the only places on earth where visitors can have breathtakingly close contact with wild dwarf minke whales. These small, playful baleen whales stop here every June and July —and they often approach within a few feet of respectful divers.

Sea turtle and diver

Difficulty level: Easy. Divers need only be Open-Water certified to dive at the 50-foot Cod Hole; dwarf minke encounters are open to snorkelers.

How to get there: Several dive operators run live-aboard trips to the Ribbon Reefs, including Mike Ball Expeditions (www.mikeball. com), ProDive Cairns (www.prodivecairns.com), and John Rumney's Marine Encounters (www. marineencounters.com.au).

LIGHTHOUSE BOMMIES

Part of the southerly Whitsunday group, Lady Elliott Island is surrounded by shallow, pristine waters that teem with life. In particular, the Lighthouse Bommies— freestanding coral formations set off the island's northwest coast—host a large population of manta rays, some of which have a wingspan twelve feet across.

Difficulty level: Easy. Divers need only be Open-Water certified to visit this site; the depth averages about 50 feet.

How to get there: The dive center at the Lady Elliot Island Resort (www.ladyelliot.com. au) runs dives to the Bommies daily.

RAINE ISLAND

Set in the far north reaches of the Coral Sea off Cape York, this coral cay is one of the Reef's greatest—and most inaccessible—treasures. Its beaches comprise the world's largest nesting ground for endangered green sea turtles; during November and December more than 20,000 turtles per week mob the shores to lay their eggs. Because Raine is a strictly protected preserve, seeing this annual phenomenon is an exceedingly rare privilege. In fact, only one dive operator, John Rumney, is currently sanctioned by the Marine Park Authority to visit the site—and only twice a year.

Difficulty level: Intermediate to Expert. Rumney's dive trips involve what he calls "a heavy research component;" participants not only dive among the turtles, but also collect data on them and fit them with satellite tags (some also tag tiger sharks, another rare endemic species).

How to get there: The 18 spots on these ten-day trips are in high demand; learn more at www.marineencounters.com.au.

SCUBA DIVING 101

(left) ProDive is one of several great dive companies on the Reef; (right) snorkelers receive instruction.

Visiting the Reef can be a snap even if you've never dived before; most local dive operators offer Open Water (entry-level) certification courses that can be completed in just three to five days. The course involves both classroom and pool training, followed by a written test and one or more open-water dives on the Reef. Once you're certified, you'll be able to dive to depths of up to 60 feet; you'll also be eligible to rent equipment and book dive trips all over the world.

TIGHT SCHEDULE?

If time is of the essence, ask about doing your Open Water class and in-pool training near home; some Reef operators may allow you to complete your certification (and get right to the good part—the actual ocean dives) once you arrive in Australia.

Though most serious divers insist that certification is necessary for scuba safety, if you're short on time you may find yourself tempted to take advantage of what are generally called "resort courses"—single-day instruction programs that allow you to dive at limited depths under strict supervision. As long as you choose a reputable operator

(like Mike Ball Dive Expeditions, www. mikeball.com) and do exactly as your dive guides say, you'll likely be fine.

FLYING

No matter how you get yourself underwater, you'll need to make sure you don't schedule a flight and a dive in the same day. Flying too soon after diving can lead to "the bends"—an excruciating buildup of nitrogen bubbles in the bloodstream that requires a decompression chamber to alleviate. Since that's not anything you'd want to develop at the beginning of a transatlantic flight, be sure to wait 12 hours before flying after a single dive, 18 hours after multiple dives, and 24 hours if your dive(s) required decompression stops.

Regulators up! Reef visitors learn Scuba basics.

LOGISTICS

CERTIFYING ORGANIZATIONS

You'll find that all reliable dive operators—on the Reef and elsewhere—are affiliated with one of the three major international dive-training organizations: PADI (www.padi.com), NAUI (www.naui.org), or SSI (www.divessi.com). The certification requirements for all three are similar, and most dive shops and outfitters consider them interchangeable (i.e., they'll honor a certification from any of the three).

COSTS

The price for taking a full Open Water certification course (usually over four or five days of training) averages around $400-$500—but in many cases, rental equipment, wetsuits, and instruction manuals cost extra. Some dive shops have relationships with hotels, and offer dive/stay packages. One-day scuba resort courses usually cost around $200-$300, with all gear included.

EMERGENCIES

Before diving on the Reef, it's a good idea to purchase divers' insurance through the Divers Alert Network (DAN), an international organization that provides emergency medical assistance to divers. (Learn more about the different plans at www.diversalertnetwork. org). DAN also has a 24-hour emergency hotline staffed by doctors, emergency medical technicians, and nurses; for help with diving injuries or immediate medical advice, call (001) 919-684-4326 from Australia.

SNORKELING TIPS

Snorkelers explore Fitzroy Reef Lagoon.

■ If you're a beginner, avoid snorkeling in areas where there's chop or strong currents.

■ Every few minutes, look up and check what's floating ahead of you—you'll want to avoid boats, jellyfish, and other surface-swimmers.

■ Give corals, plants, and sea creatures a wide berth—for their protection and yours.

■ Coat every part of your back with high-SPF, waterproof sunscreen; the water's reflection greatly intensifies the sun's rays.

DIVING TIPS

■ Before heading off on a dive trip, have your doctor rule out any possible health complications.

■ Be sure your dive operator is affiliated with an internationally known training organization, such as PADI or NAUI.

■ Stick to dive trips and sites that are within your expertise level—the Reef is not the place to push safety limits.

■ Remember that in Australia, depths and weights use the metric system—so bring a conversion table if you need to.

■ Always dive with a partner, and always keep your partner in sight.

■ Never dive when you're feeling ill—especially if you're experiencing sinus congestion.

■ Never dive after consuming alcohol.

■ If you feel unwell or disoriented while diving, signal to your partner that you need to surface so she or he can accompany you.

DANGERS OF THE REEF

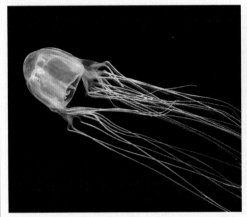 

(left) The Irukandji box jellyfish sting causes severe pain; (right) small sharks inhabit areas of the Reef.

Like any other wild natural habitat, the Reef is home to creatures that are capable of causing you harm—and possibly even killing you. But surprisingly, the most lethal Reef inhabitants aren't of the Shark Week variety. In fact, they're just about invisible.

THE DEADLIEST REEF DWELLER

Chironex fleckeri—better known as box jellyfish—are native to the same waters as the Reef. They also just happen to be the most poisonous sea creatures on the planet. Cube-shaped and transparent (which makes them almost impossible to see in the water), these jellies have tentacles whose stinging cells release an enormously potent venom on contact. A box-jelly sting causes excruciating pain, often followed very quickly (within three or four minutes) by death.

The good news about box jellies is that they're only rarely encountered on the outer Reef and islands (they're much more prevalent close to the mainland shore, especially in summer—which is why you may see beautiful North Queensland beaches completely empty

on a hot December day). While the only sure way to prevent a box jellyfish sting is to stay out of the sea altogether, there are measures you can take to lessen the already minimal risks. First, consider wearing a full-length Lycra "sting suit" when you dive. Second, make sure your dive operator carries a supply of Chironex antivenom onboard your dive boat, just in case.

OTHER (LESS DEADLY) DANGERS

Although box jellyfish are by far the most dangerous creatures on the Reef, there are other "biteys" and "nasties" to be aware of. In particular, you should try to stay clear of a smaller box-jelly variety called Irukandji (whose sting causes delayed but often intense pain); Millepora, or stinging coral (which causes irritation and welts when it touches bare skin); sea snakes (who seldom bite humans, but whose poison can cause paralysis); and, yes, sharks (although you'll likely only see small ones on the Reef—the much more hyped Hammerheads, Tiger Sharks, and Great Whites prefer deeper and colder waters).

PROTECTING THE REEF

(left) Even the tiniest coral can serve as protective habitat; (right) divers explore a large coral formation.

Enormous though it may be, the Great Barrier Reef's ecosystem is one that requires a delicate balance. The interdependence of species here means that harming even a single food source—like a particular type of plankton—can have wide-ranging and even devastating effects.

The majority of the Reef is an official marine preserve that's managed and protected by the Great Barrier Reef Marine Park Authority. This government agency has developed a series of long-range programs to help protect the Reef—including population-monitoring of sealife species, water-temperature and salinity studies, and screening of all commercial fishing and tourism/recreational operations.

Since almost 2 million tourists visit the Reef each year, even day-trippers should be mindful of their impact on this fragile environment. Specifically, if you're planning to dive and snorkel here, you should:

■ Make sure your dive gear is secure, with no loose straps or dangling hoses that might snag on corals.

■ Swim slowly to avoid brushing against corals (and be especially mindful when wearing swim fins).

■ Avoid picking up or touching any corals, plants, or creatures (for your protection and theirs). No souvenirs, even empty shells or dead-looking coral.

■ Keep clear of all free-swimming sea creatures like sea turtles, dolphins, dugongs, or whales.

VOLUNTEERING ON THE REEF

If you'd like to do more to protect the Reef, the following organizations offer volunteer programs that allow you to help collect study data and monitor the health of reef species:

■ The Australian Marine Conservation Society: http://www.amcs.org.au/

■ Reef Check Australia: http://www.reefcheckaustralia.org/

■ UNESCO (United Nations Educational, Scientific, and Cultural Organization): http://whc.unesco.org

8

IN FOCUS DIVING THE REEF

Outer Reef Dive & Snorkel Excursion. A true Great Barrier Reef island, Orpheus is surrounded by some of the reef's most diverse coral gardens, sheltering 340 of the world's 350 known species of reef coral and more than 1,100 species of fish. Orpheus Island Resort organizes Discover Scuba Training Sessions and first guided dives, half-day local dive trips around the Palm Islands, and full-day charter excursions to the Outer Barrier Reef that include two guided dives, the chance to swim and snorkel, and a generous smorgasbord. ⊠ *Pickups from Orpheus Island Resort jetty* ☎ *07/4777–7377* ⊕ *www.orpheus.com.au* ⊡ *Price on application* ☉ *Daily on demand (pre-booking essential, subject to weather conditions).*

Picnic & Snorkel Cruise. A dozen guests at a time can join a daily five-hour cruise around the nearby Palm Islands, stopping at two premium snorkeling sites. Travel is via the resort's purpose-built catamaran, with a gourmet seafood lunch and relaxation time mid-excursion. The resort also runs hour-long PADI Discover Snorkeling pool training sessions and 2½-hour marine-naturalist-led tours of snorkeling spots around the Palm Island group. ⊠ *Orpheus Island Resort jetty* ☎ *07/4777–7377* ⊕ *www.orpheus.com.au* ⊡ *Free for guests* ☉ *Daily 10–3 picnic cruise.*

WHERE TO STAY

For expanded hotel reviews, visit Fodors.com.

$$$$
ALL-INCLUSIVE
Fodor's Choice
★

⌂ **Orpheus Island.** Nestled amid lush tropical gardens, this intimate island sanctuary offers various types of beachfront accommodation: Nautilus Suites; Orpheus Retreats; new, two-bedroom beach villas suitable for families and groups; and three eco-friendly safari-style tents, each with a platform floor, balcony, and queen-sized bed. **Pros:** eco-conscious owners with scuba skills; cut-above food; free Wi-Fi in communal areas; good dive and snorkeling sites nearby. **Cons:** no in-room Internet access; limited Vodafone cell-phone access; occasional lizards and insects indoors; resort now takes kids and daytrippers. ⌖ *Orpheus Island, PMB 15, Townsville4810* ☎ *07/4777–7377* ⊕ *www.orpheus. com.au* ⤙ *17 rooms and suites, 3 eco-tents* ⌂ *In-room: a/c, safe, no TV. In-hotel: restaurant, bar, pool, tennis court, gym, beach, water sports, business center* ⦿ *All-inclusive.*

HINCHINBROOK ISLAND

This 97,000-acre national park is the largest island on the Great Barrier Reef. It's a nature lover's paradise, with dense tropical rain forests, mangroves, mountain peaks, and sandy beaches. When Captain Cook discovered it in 1770, he didn't realize it was an island and mistakenly named it Mt. Hinchinbrook—likely imagining that 3,746-foot Mt. Bowen, Australia's third-highest mountain, was part of the mainland. Dolphins, dugongs, tiger sharks, and sea turtles inhabit the surrounding waters, as do fish that you're permitted to catch (a rarity, given the strict protection of the reef's marine life). There are also estuarine crocodiles, adders, numerous birds, goannas, and small mammals. The island is virtually untouched save for a small resort on its northeast corner, now open only occasionally to prebooked groups, and a few toilets and campsites.

THORSBORNE TRAIL

The Thorsborne Trail runs the length of Hinchinbrook Island's east coast. The walk takes three to four days each way and includes some steep climbs—it's certainly not for the ill-prepared or faint-hearted. You'll need to bring a fuel stove, a first-aid kit, drinking water, and plenty of supplies, and it's strongly advised that you do some survival and fitness training in advance. Ferries depart from Lucinda, south of Cardwell on the mainland, to the island's southern end, then you follow the marked trail for 32 km (20 mi), winding up on the island's northeastern corner near the resort (currently closed). If you don't want to do the round-trip, you'll need to arrange a ferry pick-up at this end in advance via the Reef and Rainforest Information Centre in Cardwell. Only 40 walkers at a time are permitted to camp along the Thorsborne Trail (in groups of six, maximum); you should book as far in advance as possible. Contact the **Cardwell Rainforest and Reef Visitor Information Centre** (☏ *07/4066–8601 or 13–7468* ⊕ *www.derm.qld.gov.au*) at least eight weeks in advance for camping permits and to organize ferry transfers.

GETTING HERE AND AROUND

Hinchinbrook is a 50-minute ferry ride from mainland marina Port Hinchinbrook, near Cardwell, 190 km (118 mi) south of Cairns and 161 km (100 mi) north of Townsville. Since the island's resort closed, however, scheduled ferries no longer run from Port Hinchinbrook to the island. To charter a ferry from Port Hinchinbrook, you'll need to contact Cardwell Reef and Rainforest Visitor Information Centre in advance. Hikers wishing to trek the island's renowned Thorsborne Trail can take a ferry from Lucinda, farther south.

ESSENTIALS

Tours Port Hinchinbrook Resorts & Cruises ☏ *07/4066–2000* ⊕ *www.porthinchinbrook.com.au.*

OUTDOOR ACTIVITIES

The focus here is on the island's environment, not the one underwater, though snorkeling and swimming are both good here (do take the regular snorkeling trip, generally offered every second day).

Nature walks through varied and spectacular landscapes are the primary attraction. Conditions can be hot and, on some tracks, demanding: wear sturdy shoes and take drinking water, sunscreen, and a map of the island. The Hinchinbrook Island Wilderness Lodge has morning and afternoon beach and island drop-offs/pick-ups (you walk one way). All bushwalking guests must sign in and out, ensuring their safe return. Experienced walkers (preferably with prior training) can trek the famed but difficult **Thorsborne Trail.**

Hinchinbrook Island is a hiker's paradise.

DUNK ISLAND

A member of the Family Islands, this 2,397-acre island is divided by a hilly spine that runs its entire length. The eastern side consists mostly of national park, with dense rain forest and secluded beaches accessible only by boat. Beautiful paths have been created through the rain forest, where you might be lucky enough to glimpse a Ulysses butterfly—a beautiful blue variety with a wingspan that can reach 6 inches, Dunk is 4½ km (2 mi) from Mission Beach on the mainland, making it a pleasant spot for day-trippers, though now that the resort has closed, there are few on-island facilities; be sure to bring your own food, water, and sunscreen.

GETTING HERE AND AROUND

From Mission Beach on the mainland, take a Mission Beach-Dunk Island Water Taxi (A$62–A$95, one-way) to Dunk Island It's a choppy 10-minute ride but these days, the water Taxi is your best option for accessing the island. It's necessary to disembark in shallow waters, but staff are on hand to help. The round-trip fare is A$40.

ESSENTIALS

Transportation Hinterland Aviation ☏ *03/9854-5740* ⊕ *www.dunk-island. com.* **Mission Beach–Dunk Island Water Taxi** ☏ *07/4068-8310* ⊕ *www.missionbeachwatertaxi.com.* **Sun Palm Transport** ☏ *07/4087-2900* ⊕ *www.sunpalmtransport.com.*

OUTDOOR ACTIVITIES

In addition to reef cruises and fishing charters, the resort has many choices of land and water sports. Rates include a dozen-plus sports and outdoorsy activities, including tennis, squash, and fitness classes, and the use of paddle-skis, catamarans, and snorkeling gear.

You'll pay extra for beach and rain-forest horseback rides, kayak and mountain-bike tours, guided reef and bush walks, golf, and archery, as well as activities requiring fuel—skydiving, waterskiing, tube rides, wake boarding, and beach drop-offs. Prices range from A$5 to A$230. The resort also organizes sportfishing charters, snorkeling, and scuba-diving trips through local operators.

The resort provides a bushwalking map of the island's well-maintained trails. Kids will enjoy the farm, Coonanglebah; you can also visit the island's artists' colony.

BEDARRA ISLAND

This tiny, 247-acre island 5 km (3 mi) off the coast of Mission Beach has natural springs, dense rain-forest tracts, and eight unspoiled beaches. Bedarra Island Resort was damaged extensively in Cyclone Larry and is closed for the forseeable future.

GETTING HERE AND AROUND

Bedarra Island lies about 20 minutes by boat from Dunk Island. Boat transfers are included in the resort rate. To get to the Barrier Reef from Bedarra, you have to return to Dunk Island, from which all reef excursions depart.

OUTDOOR ACTIVITIES

Bedarra's geared for relaxation (a massage on the beach anyone?), but there's still plenty to engage active guests. Snorkeling is possible around the island, but it's not on the reef and the water can be cloudy during summer rains. You can also play tennis, scuba dive, paddle-ski, sail catamarans, explore local beaches in a motorized dinghy, or fish. Other sporting activities can be organized on nearby Dunk Island, along with transfers, and reef fishing, sailing, and diving charters can be arranged if you're prepared to rise early to do the transits needed to get you there.

FITZROY ISLAND

This ruggedly picturesque, heavily forested island is 94% national park, with vegetation ranging from rain forest to heath, and an extensive fringing coral reef. Only 6 km (4 mi)—less than an hour's cruise—from Cairns, the 988-acre island, once connected to the mainland, was a hunting, gathering, and ceremonial ground for the Gungandji people, who called it Kobaburra before Cook re-named it in 1770. Today it's popular with day-trippers and houses a newly-built resort and a water-sports hut. From June to September, migrating manta rays and humpback whales pass right by the island.

8

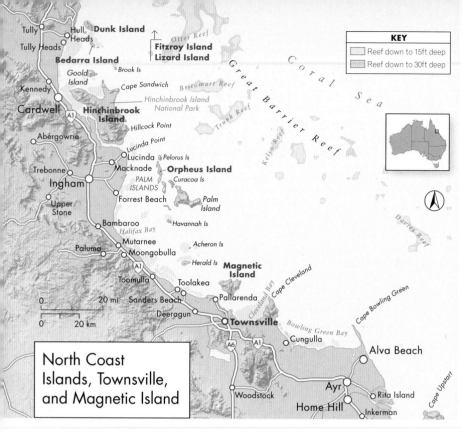

North Coast
Islands, Townsville,
and Magnetic Island

GETTING HERE AND AROUND
Various ferries service the island daily, taking around 45 minutes to reach the island, departing daily at 7:30 am and 2 pm (*Reefkist*, A$65 round-trip), 8:30 am (*Raging Thunder*, A$58) and 10 am (*Sunlover*, A$64). All depart from the Reef Fleet Terminal in Cairns, leaving the island for the return journey at 4:30 pm (*Raging Thunder*), 4:45 pm (*Sunlover*) and 5 pm (*Reefkist*). Cairns Dive Adventures and Sunlover Reef Cruises run daily transfers between Cairns and Fitzroy Island as part of snorkeling daytrips.

ESSENTIALS
Ferry Raging Thunder ☎ 07/4030–7907 ⊕ *www.ragingthunder.com.au.*

OUTDOOR ACTIVITIES
Half a dozen marked walking trails traverse Fitzroy Island National Park; they range from half-hour rain-forest strolls to steep, challenging three-hour hikes. Take drinking water, wear sturdy closed shoes, insect repellent, sunscreen, and a hat, and watch for snakes (and in estuaries and mangroves, crocs). For maps and detailed information, visit the **Queensland Government Department of Environment and Resource Management (DERM)** (⊕ *www.derm.qld.gov.au*).

Cairns Dive Adventures ☎ 07/5641–0112 ⊕ *www.cairnsdiveadventures.com.*

Fitzroy Island Dive and Activities Center. Day-trippers, resort guests, divers, and campers can rent paddle-skis, stinger suits, and diving and snorkeling gear from the resort-run Dive and Activities Center at the southern end of Fitzroy Island. Here you can also book everything from guided dive and snorkeling trips to windsurfing, sailing, and AquaJet excursions, sea-kayaking tours, glass-bottom boat tours,

and day trips on the resort's luxury 52-foot catamaran, *Eye Spy.* ☎ *07/4044–6700* ⊕ *www.fitzroyisland.com.*

Sunlover Reef Cruises ⊠ *Reef Fleet Terminal, Tenancy 3, 1 Spence St., Cairns* ☎ *07/4050–1333, 1800/810512* ⊕ *www.sunlover.com.au.*

WHERE TO STAY

For expanded hotel reviews, visit Fodors.com.

Fitzroy Island Resort (formerly Hunt Resort), the island's only accommodation, reopened late in 2009. Day-trippers can still get food and drinks at Foxy's Bar & Café at the southern end of the island, and can hire water-sports gear from the adjacent Dive and Activities Centre run by Raging Thunder. The old resort's dorm rooms have given way to a Cairns council-run campground, but it's not always open (⊕ *www.cairns.qld.gov.au*).

$$$ 🏨 **Fitzroy Island Resort.** The extensively redeveloped reef retreat has new accommodation in four categories and various configurations: self-contained one- and two-bedroom ocean suites, beach cabins, a resort studio, and a four-bedroom penthouse unit. **Pros:** sleek new decor; high-end facilities; easy access to and from Cairns. **Cons:** day-trippers. ☝ *Fitzroy Island Resort, PO Box 3058, Cairns 4870* ☎ *07/4044–6700* ⊕ *www.fitzroyisland.com* ⏎ *98 resort rooms, 11 budget/diver rooms, 28 tent sites* ⚃ *In-room: a/c, no a/c, safe, kitchen, Internet. In-hotel: restaurant, bar, pool, tennis court, gym, spa, beach, water sports, laundry facilities, business center, flush toilets, drinking water, running water (non-potable), guest laundry, showers, grills, picnic table, food service, electricity, general store, swimming.*

LIZARD ISLAND

★ The small, upscale resort on secluded Lizard Island, just under 150 mi off the North Queensland coast, is the farthest north of any Barrier Reef hideaway. At 2,500 acres, it's larger than and quite different from other islands in the region. Composed mostly of granite, Lizard has a remarkable diversity of vegetation and terrain; here grassy hills give way to rocky slabs interspersed with valleys of rain forest.

Ringed by two dozen white-sand beaches, the island is actually a national park with some of the best examples of fringing coral of any of the resort areas. Excellent walking trails lead to key lookouts with spectacular views of the coast. The highest point, Cook's Look (1,180 feet), is the historic spot from which, in August 1770, Captain Cook finally spied a passage through the reef that had held him captive for a thousand miles. Large monitor lizards, after which the island is named, often bask in this area.

GETTING HERE AND AROUND

Lizard Island has its own small airstrip served by Hinterland Aviation. Hour-long flights to the island depart up to twice a day from Cairns, at 11 and 2, returning at 12:30 and 3:25; taking an hour and costing A$255 per person each way. Allow two hour's transit time for connecting international flights, one for domestic flight transits: check-in is 30 minutes prior to flight time at the Hinterland Aviation Terminal. You can also arrange charter flights to the island (☎ *1300/233–432 or 03/9426–7550*).

ESSENTIALS

Plane Hinterland Aviation ☎ *07/4035–9323 24 hours* ⊕ *www.hinterlandaviation.com.au.*

EXPLORING LIZARD ISLAND

Fodor's Choice ★ **Cod Hole.** For divers and snorkelers, the usually crystal-clear waters off Lizard Island are a dream. Cod Hole, 20 km (12 mi) from Lizard Island, ranks among the best dive sites on Earth. Massive potato cod swim up to divers like hungry puppies; it's an awesome experience, considering that these fish can weigh 300 pounds and reach around two meters (6 feet) in length. The island lures big-game anglers from all over the world from September to December, when black marlin are running.

OUTDOOR ACTIVITIES

The lodge has catamarans, outboard dinghies, paddle-skis (including glass-bottomed ones), fishing supplies, snorkeling gear, and lessons. There is superb snorkeling around the island's fringing coral, or you can cruise over it on a glass-bottomed paddle-ski tour. Self-guided bushwalking trails and nature slide shows get guests in touch with the local flora and fauna. Arrange a picnic hamper with the kitchen staff and take a rowboat or sailboat out for an afternoon on your own private beach. All these activities are included in your room rate. Contact **Lizard Island Activities Desk** (☎ *1300/134044* ⊕ *www.lizardisland. com.au*) for details.

FISHING ★ Lizard Island is one of the big game-fishing centers in Australia, with several world records set here since the mid-1990s. Game fishing is generally best in spring and early summer, and giant black marlin weighing more than 1,000 pounds are no rarity. September through December, the folk from Lizard Island run full-day game-fishing trips to the outer reef on 51-foot Riviera Platinum Model Flybridge cruiser, *Fascination III*; the cost, including heavy tackle, lunch, and light refreshments for up to four people is A$2,950. January through August, the resort offers half-day bottom-fishing excursions on *Fascination III*, with bait, light tackle, and refreshments for up to four people, for A$1,800, and full-day trips for A$2,750.

SCUBA DIVING The reefs around Lizard Island have some of the best marine life and coral on the planet. The resort can arrange supervised scuba-diving and snorkeling trips to the inner and outer reef, as well as local dives.

Half- or full-day dive-snorkel reef trips are A$155/A$210, plus A$80 for an optional dive or on the full-day trip, A$145 for two dives, and A$19/A$30 for dive gear. You can also book a private guided dive for A$250 (half day) or A$400 (full day). If you have a queasy stomach, take ginger or seasickness tablets before heading out to the reef, as crossings between dive sites in the exposed ocean can make for a bumpy ride.

There's good diving, day and night, just offshore: scuba "refresher" courses are free; an introductory Discover Scuba Diving course is A$190, and a full day's follow-up diving is A$340 (with one dive) or A$460 (with two). A guided local day dive is A$160; a night dive is A$165; or do both for A$210; gear costs just A$15 extra. Guided day and twilight snorkeling tours (maximum 2 people) are A$85. You can even dive right off the beach for A$95 by day, A$105 by night. Need scuba skills? The resort can organize PADI-accredited introductory, referral and refresher scuba diving courses on request.

WHERE TO STAY

For expanded hotel reviews, visit Fodors.com.

$$$$ ☆ **Lizard Island.** One of Australia's premier resorts, this property has
★ simply but stylishly appointed beachside rooms, suites, and sumptuous villas with sail-shaded decks and views of the turquoise bay, as well as an elegant pavilion on the point. **Pros:** world-class location, superb diving and fishing; quality food and wine. **Cons:** critters sometimes invade the rooms; lighting inadequate for reading. ✉ *PMB 40, Cairns 4871* 🖀 *bookings, 07/4043–1999 resort, 1300/863–248 tollfree, within Australia* ⊕ *www.lizardisland.com.au* ⬎ *39 villas, 1 pavilion* 🛁 *In-room: a/c, safe, Internet. In-hotel: restaurant, bar, pool, tennis court, gym, spa, beach, water sports, laundry facilities, business center, some age restrictions* ❛O❜ *All meals.*

TOWNSVILLE AND MAGNETIC ISLAND

Townsville and adjacent twin city Thuringowa make up Australia's largest tropical city, with a combined population of around 190,000. It's the commercial capital of the north, and a major center for education, scientific research, and defense. Spread along the banks of Ross Creek and around the pink granite outcrop of Castle Hill, Townsville is a pleasant city of palm-fringed malls, historic colonial buildings, extensive parkland, and gardens. It's also the stepping-off point for Magnetic Island, one of the state's largest islands and a haven for wildlife.

GETTING HERE AND AROUND

Qantas flies frequently from Townsville Airport to Brisbane, Cairns, Cloncurry, Mount Isa, and Mackay, as well as to capital cities around Australia and overseas destinations. Jetstar has services to Brisbane, Sydney, and Melbourne; Virgin Blue connects Townsville with Cairns, Brisbane, the Gold Coast, Rockhampton, Sydney, Melbourne, and

Canberra. There are no air connections to Magnetic Island; you need to take a ferry from Townsville (A$15.50 one-way, A$29 round-trip). Townsville Taxis are available at the airport. The average cost of the ride to a city hotel is A$21, more after 7 pm.

Townsville is a flat, somewhat dull 1,358-km (844-mi), 16-hour drive from Brisbane. The 348-km (216-mi), 4½-hour journey from Townsville to Cairns, with occasional Hinchinbrook Island views, is more scenic. Greyhound Australia coaches travel regularly to Cairns, Mount Isa, Rockhampton, Brisbane, and other destinations throughout Australia from the Sunferries Terminal on the Breakwater in Townsville.

Traveling to and from Townsville via rail is a low-stress, scenic option. The *Sunlander* plies the coast between Brisbane and Townsville three times weekly in each direction, taking just under 24 hours. You have the choice of economy-class seats and single, twin, or economy sleeper berths, as well as chef-cooked meals, premium Australian wines, and informative commentary from the maître d'. From Brisbane to Townsville a one-way ticket is A$209 in an economy seat, A$375 in an economy sleeper berth, and A$406.70 in a first-class berth.

On the smooth, state-of-the-art *Tilt Train* business-class passengers can watch movies and kids' shows on individual TV screens during less scenic segments of the journey, and every second seat's passenger can plug laptops, chargers, and consoles into seat-side 240-volt AC sockets. From Brisbane to Townsville it's A$298, business class. The *Inlander* connects Townsville with Mount Isa twice weekly in each direction (from A$174.90 in an economy seat to A$357.90 in a first-class berth, one-way). Trains are operated by Queensland Rail.

Once in town, you can can flag Townsville Taxis on the street, find one at taxi stands, hotels, and the island's ferry terminal, or book one online.

TOURS

Coral Princess Cruises has three- and seven-night cruises that leave weekly or fortnightly, from the Breakwater Terminal in Townsville, bound for Cairns and Lizard Island. The company's two comfortable 115-foot, 50-passenger expedition-style ships stop for snorkeling, diving, fishing, beach BBQs, and rain-forest hikes (get dive gear or lessons on board). Onboard marine biologists give lectures en route and lead excursions. Prices start at A$1,546, twin-share (with no sole use discount) for a three-night, four-plus-dive live-aboard trip including 3–5 optional guided scuba dives and free snorkeling, glass-bottom boat tours, fish feeds, land tours, most gear, food, and entertainment; A$3,148 for a 7-night trip with 4–6 optional dives Your bar tab, reef taxes, and diving costs—A$60, A$70 with gear (certified divers); A$85 for the first two dives, A$70 thereafter (beginners)—are extra.

The Tropicana Guided Adventure Company runs expertly guided, small-group Magnetic Island expeditions to normally inaccessible bays and beaches in a converted, extra-long jeep. Bush-tucker adventures let you taste native foods; on other trips you get to meet and feed island wildlife. Day trips start from A$66 per person for a three-hour eco-orientation tour, departing daily at 11 from Nelly Bay near the taxi stand (catch the 10:30 Sunferry from the mainland). An 8½-hour sightseeing tour of the island, including its wildlife hot spots and remote and tourist areas, leaves daily at 11 am from Magnetic Harbour (A$198, including lunch and refreshments).

ESSENTIALS

Medical Emergencies **Townsville Hospital** ⊠ *100 Angus Smith Dr., Douglas, Townsville* ☎ *07/4796–1111* ⊕ *www.health.qld.gov.au/townsville.*

Police **Townsville District Police HQ** ⊠ *134 Stanley St., Townsville* ☎ *07/4579–9777* ⊕ *www.police.qld.gov.au.*

Taxi **Townsville Taxis** ☎ *13–1008* ⊕ *www.tsvtaxi.com.au.*

Tours **Coral Princess Cruises** ⊠ *Breakwater (Sunferries) Terminal, Sir Leslie Thiessen Dve., Townsville* ✆ *PO Box 20934870* ☎ *07/4040–9999, 1800/079545* ⊕ *www.coralprincess.com.au.* **Tropicana Guided Adventure Company** ☎ *07/4758–1800* ⊕ *www.tropicanatours.com.au.*

Transportation **SeaLink (Sunferries)** ☎ *07/4726–0800* ⊕ *www.sealinkqld.com. au.* **Queensland Rail** ☎ *1800/872–467* ⊕ *www.queenslandrail.com.au.*

Visitor Information **Townsville Enterprise Visitor Information Centre** ⊠ *Flinders Mall, near Stanley St., Townsville* ☎ *07/4721–3660, 1800/801902* ⊕ *www.townsvilleonline.com.au or www.townsvilleholidays.info.*

TOWNSVILLE

The Queensland Parks and Wildlife Service has an office on Magnetic Island, but Townsville Enterprise's Flinders Mall and Museum of Tropical Queensland (MTQ) information kiosks, on the mainland, are the best sources of visitor info about the island. The Mall kiosk is open weekdays 9–5, weekends 9–1; the Museum kiosk, 9–5 daily.

EXPLORING TOWNSVILLE

Castle Hill. The summit of pink-granite monolith Castle Hill, 1 km (½ mi) from the city center, provides great views of the city and Magnetic Island. While you're perched on top, think about the proud local resident who, with the aid of several scout troops, spent years in the 1970s piling rubble onto the peak to try to add the 23 feet that would make Castle Hill a mountain, officially speaking—which means a rise of at least 1,000 feet. Most people trek to the top along a steep walking track that doubles as one of Queensland's most scenic jogging routes.

Flinders Street. A stroll along Flinders Street will show you some of Townsville's turn-of-the-20th-century colonial architecture. **Magnetic House** and other buildings have been beautifully restored. The grand old **Queens Hotel** is built in early Victorian Classical Revival style, as is the 1885 **Perc Tucker Regional Gallery,** originally a bank. The **Tattersalls Hotel,** circa 1865, is typical of its era, with wide verandas and iron balustrades; today, it houses Molly Malone's Irish pub. The former post office, now **the Brewery,** had an impressive **masonry clock tower** when it was erected in 1889. The tower was dismantled in 1942 (so it wouldn't be a target during World War II air raids) and re-erected in 1964. The Exchange, Townsville's oldest pub, was built in 1869, burned down in 1881, and was rebuilt the following year.

8

⟳ **Museum of Tropical Queensland.** The Museum of Tropical Queensland displays relics of the HMS *Pandora* (sent by the British Admiralty to capture the mutinous *Bounty* crew), which sank in 1791 carrying 14 crew members of Captain Bligh's infamous ship. There's a fun introduction to North Queensland's culture and lifestyle, a shipwreck exhibit, and the fresh, ecology-focused Enchanted Rainforest. Also on display are tropical wildlife, dinosaur fossils, local corals, and deep-sea creatures. ⊠ *70–102 Flinders St. E* ☎ *07/4726–0600* ⊕ *www.mtq.qm.qld. gov.au* ⊡ *A$15* ⊘ *Daily 9:30–5.*

⟳ **Queens Gardens.** Queens Gardens, at the base of Castle Hill, is a lovely place to spend a cool couple of hours. The four-hectare (10-acre) park is bordered with frangipani and towering Moreton Bay fig trees, whose unique hanging roots veil the entry to the grounds; the gardens include two small hedge mazes, a formal rose garden, and a rain-forest walk. Don't miss the aviary, housing peacocks, lorikeets, and sulphur-crested cockatoos. ⊠ *Gregory St. near Warburton St. (enter off Paxton St.)* ☎ *07/4727–8330* ⊕ *www.townsville.qld.gov.au* ⊡ *Free* ⊘ *Daily dawn–dusk.*

⟳ **Reef HQ Aquarium.** Reef HQ Aquarium, on the waterfront, a few min-
★ utes' walk from the city center, casino, and ferry terminal, houses the world's largest live coral-reef aquarium, containing around 100 species of hard coral, 30 soft corals, and hundreds of fish, sea star, urchin and sponge species: open to the elements, it's a living slice of the Great Barrier Reef (the behind-the-scenes tour is fascinating). There's a 20-meter (65-foot) Perspex underwater walkway, a predator tank teeming with sharks, rays, turtles, and large pelagic fish, several daily talks, dives, feeds, and tours, and a theater, café and shop. ⊠ *2–68 Flinders St. E* ✉ *PO Box 1379 4810* ☎ *07/4750–0800* ⊕ *www.reefhq.com.au* ⊡ *A$26.50* ⊘ *Daily 9:30–5.*

⟳ **Townsville Town Common Conservation Park.** Townsville Town Common
★ Conservation Park, a seasonally changing wetlands, is home to a huge variety of birdlife including spoonbills, jabiru storks, pied geese, brolgas, herons and ibis, as well as occasional wallabies, goannas, echidnas, and dingoes. Most birds leave the wetlands in dry season, May–August, but they're back by October—around 280 species have been spotted here. The park is open daily 6:30 am–6:30 pm; entry is free. Take Cape Pallarenda Road north to Pallarenda, 6 km (4 mi) from Townsville's center. Most walking tracks begin from the Bald Rock carpark, 7 km (4½ mi) from the park entrance on unsealed (or unpaved) roads. ☎ *07/4721–3660 Townsville Tourist Information, 1800/801–902* ⊕ *www.derm.qld.gov.au/parks.*

OUTDOOR ACTIVITIES

BEACHES Townsville is blessed with a golden, 2-km (1-mi) beach that stretches
⟳ along its northern edge. Four man-made headlands jut into the sea, and a long pier is just the spot for fishing. There is no surf, as the beach is sheltered by the reef and Magnetic Island. The Strand's permanent swimming enclosure, known as the Strand Water Park and Rockpool (10–5 June–August, 10–6 April and May, and 10–8 December–March; closed Thursday), is fitted with temporary nets during box-jellyfish

Townsville's main beach features calm surf and jellyfish-free enclosures.

season, November–May. Townsville's beaches and waterfront pools are patrolled by lifeguards year-round on weekdays, as well as weekends in summer and over public and Australian school holidays. The surrounding area has picnic facilities, barbecues, toilets, formal gardens, and gazebos. ☎ 07/4727–9050 or 1300/87800 ⊕ *www.townsville.qld. gov.au/facilities/swimming.*

BOATING **Magnetic Island Sea Kayaks.** Magnetic Island Sea Kayaks organizes guided eco-kayaking trips to the quieter bays of Magnetic Island. The 4½-hour morning tour includes a tropical breakfast and costs A$85 per person in two-person kayaks or A$155 for single-person kayaks; the 2½-hour sunset tour is A$60 per person. The cost includes reef tax, gear, tuition, and breakfast or sunset drinks. Minimum group size is two; maximum is 12. Advance booking is recommended. ⊠ *Horseshoe Bay Rd., Horseshoe Bay* ⌖ *PO Box 130, Magnetic Island 4819* ☎ *07/4778–5424* ⊕ *www.seakayak.com.au* ⊗ *Morning tour: Daily from 8. Sunset tour: Wed, Fri and Sat. from 2 hours before sunset.*

SCUBA DIVING Surrounded by tropical islands and warm waters, Townsville is a top-notch diving center. Diving courses and excursions tend to be less crowded than those in the hot spots of Cairns or the Whitsunday Islands.

The wreck of the SS *Yongala*, a steamship that sank just south of Townsville in 1911, lies between 49 and 91 feet beneath the ocean surface about 16 km (10 mi) offshore, 60 km (37 mi) from Townsville. It teems with marine life and is considered one of Australia's best dive sites. It can be approached as a one- or two-day trip. All local dive operators conduct excursions to the wreck.

Adrenalin Dive. Adrenalin Dive has day trips to a number of popular sites in the region, including the wreck of the *Yongala*. Prices start at A$226 for a day trip to the *Yongala*, and A$186 to the Great Barrier Reef. The cost includes weight belt, tanks, two dives, and lunch; it's an extra A$40 for dive gear and A$20 for a guided dive (compulsory for novice divers—i.e. those with fewer than 10 dives logged for GBR dives, or fewer than 15 dives logged for *Yongala* dives). A three-day, three night live-aboard eco-dive trip including up to 10 dives (with two night dives) costs from A$720–A$785 for divers, A$600–A$665 for snorkelers; gear hire is an extra A$95, and guided dives (compulsory for novice divers) are an extra A$10 per dive. ⊠ *252 Walker St.* ☎ *07/4724–0600, 1300/664600* ⊕ *www.adrenalindive.com.au* ⊙ *GBR trip Tue., Thu., Fri., and Sun; Yongala trip Mon., Wed., and Sat. From 7 am (Townsville), 7:25 am (Magnetic Is.).*

WILDLIFE
WATCHING

ℭ

Billabong Sanctuary. This 22-acre nature park 17 km (11 mi) south of Townsville shelters crocodiles, koalas, wombats, dingoes, wallabies, snakes, and birds—including cassowaries, kookaburras, sulphur-crested white, and red-tailed black cockatoos. Educational shows throughout the day give you the chance to learn more about the native fauna; you can also take a behind-scene tour of the food prep area and snake house (A$10), and have your photo taken with a koala, wombat, or reptile (A$16), or all three (A$33). There's also a café on-site. The sanctuary, a 20-minute drive south of Townsville, is well signposted. ⊠ *Bruce Hwy., Nome* ☎ *07/4778–8344* ⊕ *www.billabongsanctuary.com.au* 🖼 *A$30* ⊙ *Daily 9–4.*

WHERE TO EAT

$$

MODERN
AUSTRALIAN

ℭ

★

✕ **Table 51.** This casually chic waterfront eatery specializes in fresh contemporary Australian food that makes the most of fine seasonal, regional produce. Your entrée might be oyster shooters, coconut prawns, seafood chowder, or braised pork belly; follow it with a delectable honey duck, Moroccan lamb, oven-baked Tasmanian salmon, the day's fresh catch, or a tender aged eye fillet. There are good vegetarian options, a kids' menu, and varied lunch offerings. Desserts are worth the calories: indulge in the raspberry and peach cream mille feuille or berry bombe Alaska. ⊠ *51 Palmer St.* ☎ *07/4721–0642* ⊕ *www.table51.com.au* ⊙ *No lunch weekends, closed Sun. and public holidays.*

WHERE TO STAY

For expanded hotel reviews, visit Fodors.com.

$$$

Oaks M on Palmer. This ultramodern 11-story establishment in Townsville's Palmer Street dining precinct is handy to cafés and restaurants, bars, and Jupiters Casino. **Pros:** smart modern facilities; in-room kitchenettes; central location. **Cons:** feels a tad clinical; service lackluster; fee for Wi-Fi. ⊠ *81 Palmer St.* ☎ *07/4753–2900 reception, 1300/559–129 toll-free within Australia* ⊕ *www.theoaksgroup.com.au* ⌨ *104 rooms* ♨ *In-room: a/c, safe, kitchen, Wi-Fi. In-hotel: pool, gym, laundry facilities, business center, parking, some age restrictions.*

$

Fodor's Choice

★

Yongala Lodge by the Strand. This late-19th-century lodge was originally the home of building magnate Matthew Rooney, whose family was shipwrecked off the Townsville coast on the SS *Yongala* in

1911. **Pros:** historic environs, top-notch food; welcoming ambience; Austar cable TV. **Cons:** few in-room modern conveniences; guestroom walls a tad thin. ⊠ *11 Fryer St., North Ward* ☎ *07/4772–4633* ⊕ *www. historicyongala.com.au* ⌗ *10 rooms, 10 apartments* ⚒ *In-room: a/c, kitchen, Internet, Wi-Fi. In-hotel: restaurant, bar, pool, beach, laundry facilities, parking.*

NIGHTLIFE

The Brewery. The Brewery, once the Townsville Post Office, now houses a bar serving light "tavern-style" meals and an award-winning micro-brewery. The owners have combined ultramodern finishes with the original design, incorporating old post office fittings, such as the bar—once the post office's stamp counter. The on-site restaurant is open for weekday lunches, and dinner is served Monday through Saturday; the bar has half-price "happy hour" pizzas from Monday to Thursday, 5-6 pm. ⊠ *Flinders Mall, 252 Flinders St.* ☎ *07/4724–2999* ⊕ *www. townsvillebrewery.com.au.*

Jupiters Townsville Hotel & Casino. Dominating Townsville's waterfront area, this casino and hotel complex is the city's entertainment center. The complex has a 195-room hotel (including well-appointed rooms, suites, and an apartment) as well as a day spa, pool, gym, lobby shop, complimentary business center, postal and currency exchange facili-ties, two restaurants, a cafe, a trio of bars, regular live shows, and of course the big draw: more than 320 slot machines and 20-plus gaming tables. Not surprisingly, it kicks on until late. ⊠ *Sir Leslie Thiess Dr., Box 1223* ⌂ *PO Box 12234810* ☎ *07/4722–2333* ⊕ *www. jupiterstownsville.com.au.*

Mad Cow Tavern. Centrally located and perennially popular, the Mad Cow attracts a youthful, boisterous crowd of locals and travelers with live music and DJs, good bar service, an upbeat atmosphere, and relaxed, friendly staff. Regular competitions keep patrons keen. ⊠ *129 Flinders St., Townsville* ☎ *07/4771–5727* ⊙ *Thurs.–Sat. 5 pm–2 am.*

Monsoons Bar & Grill. Monsoons Bar & Grill, a smart riverfront establish-ment on Flinders Street's dining and entertainment strip, draws a mixed, convivial crowd. Billiard tables, arcade games, plasma TVs screening sports matches, and live acoustic entertainment on weekends ensure that everyone's entertained. If it's nice out, drink and dine on the deck overlooking the Ross River, on surf and turf dishes—the house favorites. ⊠ *194 Flinders St. E* ⌂ *PO Box 19864810* ☎ *07/4772–0900* ⊕ *www. monsoons.com.au* ⊙ *Weekdays, noon till midnight; weekends, noon till 2 am.* ⊙ *Closed Mondays.*

MAGNETIC ISLAND

More than half of Magnetic Island's 52 square km (20 square mi) is national parkland, laced with miles of walking trails and rising to a height of 1,640 feet on Mt. Cook. The terrain is punctuated with huge granite boulders and softened by tall hoop pines, eucalyptus forest, and rain-forest gullies. A haven for wildlife, the island shelters rock wal-labies, echidnas, frogs, possums, fruit bats, nonvenomous green tree

8

DID YOU KNOW?

Bigeye trevally (Caranx Sexfasciatus), a type of jack, can form schools of up to 1,500 fish during the day. At night, these schools break up and individuals or small groups hunt sea-borne insects, crustacians, jellyfish, and smaller species of fish.

snakes, and Northern Australia's largest population of wild koalas. Its beaches, mangroves, sea-grass beds, and fringing reefs support turtles nesting, fish hatching, and a significant dugong population. You can escape to 23 beaches and dive nine offshore shipwrecks.

The 2,500-plus residents, who fondly call their island "Maggie," mostly live on the eastern shore at Picnic Bay, Arcadia, Nelly Bay, and Horseshoe Bay. Many locals are artists and craftspeople, and there are numerous studios and galleries around the island.

GETTING HERE AND AROUND

The 40-minute Fantasea Cruising Magnetic runs several departures daily, between 5:20 am weekdays (7:10 weekends) and 6:05 pm, from the mainland to Nelly Bay Ferry Terminal on Magnetic Island, 10 km (6 mi) offshore, with the last return ferries departing the island at 6:55 pm. Round-trip fares are A$169 for a vehicle with up to six people, A$35 for a motorbike and one rider, A$27 for a person without a vehicle (bicycles free). Sealink (Sunferries) has 25-minute catamaran service daily between Townsville and Nelly Bay on Magnetic Island. Bus and island transfers meet the ferry during daylight hours. There are up to 18 ferry departures daily from Townsville between 5:30 am (6:30 Sunday) and 10:30 pm (11:30 pm Friday and Saturday), returning between 6:20 am (7:10 Sunday) and 11 pm (12 midnight Friday and Saturday); a round-trip ticket costs A$29.

Magnetic Island Sunbus. Get an overview of Magnetic Island riding the Magnetic Island Sunbus. Single-fare tickets or unlimited-travel day and weekly passes are available from the driver. The bus departs at regular intervals between 5:55 am and 9:45 pm (Sun. to Wed.), 10:25 (Thu.) and midnight (Fri. and Sat.), linking Picnic Point, Nelly Bay, Arcadia, and Horseshoe Bay. Hail it between designated stops simply by standing at the roadside and raising your hand.

The tiny Mini Moke, a soft-top convertible version of the Minor Mini car, is an ideal means by which to explore Magnetic Island. **MI Wheels**, next to the IGA supermarket near Nelly Bay Ferry Terminal, rents out Mokes, including fuel; driver's license required.

Motorbikes or scooters are a cheap and easy way to get around. **Road Runner Scooter Hire** rents trail bikes for A$60 per day, scooters from A$35, and dual-seat scooters from A$50 (9 am–5 pm). The cost includes helmets and unlimited mileage; you top up the gas yourself.

ESSENTIALS

Transportation Fantasea Cruising Magnetic ⊠ Ross St. ⬧ P O Box 1612, Townsville 4810 ☎ 07/4796–9300 ⊕ www.fantaseacruisingmagnetic.com.au. Magnetic Island Sunbus ☎ 07/4778–5130 ⊕ www.sunbus.com.au. Magnetic Island Taxi Service ☎ 13/1008 24-hour hotline. MI Wheels ⊠ 138 Sooning St., Nelly Bay4819 ☎ 07/4758–1111 ⊕ www.miwheels.com.au. Road Runner Scooter Hire ⊠ 3/64 Kelly St., Nelly Bay4819 ☎ 07/4778–5222.

Visitor Information Queensland Parks and Wildlife Service, Magnetic Island ⊠ 22 Hurst St., Picnic Bay ☎ 07/4778–5378 ⊕ www.derm.qld.gov.au.

OUTDOOR ACTIVITIES

The island has 24 km (15 mi) of hiking trails, most of which are relatively easy. The popular Forts Walk leads to World War II gun emplacements overlooking Horseshoe and Florence bays. At a leisurely pace it takes 45 minutes each way from the Horseshoe–Radical Bay Road. Look up en route, and you may spot a sleepy koala.

The best views are on the 5-km (3-mi) Nelly Bay to Arcadia Walk. Look out for shell middens created over thousands of years by the island's Aboriginal owners, the Wulgurukaba, or "Canoe People."

Swimming and snorkeling are other popular activities, but from November to May stingers are a hazard: swim at Picnic and Horseshoe bays, which have stinger nets, and wear a protective suit. At other times, Alma Bay and Nelly Bay, as well as Picnic, Florence, Radical, Horseshoe, and Balding bays, are all suitable for swimming. Horseshoe has daily lifeguards; Alma and Picnic bays are patrolled over weekends and school holidays from September to May.

Geoffrey Bay has a well-touristed unofficial snorkel trail. Other good snorkeling spots include Nelly Bay, Alma Bay, and the northern ends of Florence and Arthur bays. Near the northeastern corner of the island, Radical Bay has a small, idyllic beach surrounded by tree-covered rock outcrops. Horseshoe Bay has the largest beach, with boat rentals.

HORSEBACK RIDING
🕙
★

Horseshoe Bay Ranch. With Horseshoe Bay Ranch, you can take a two-hour guided bush-and-beach ride with the chance to take the horses swimming (A$100), daily at 9 and 3. Half-day rides are also offered daily from 9–12 (A$130). Wear a swimsuit, long pants, socks, and closed shoes, and BYO drinking water and sunscreen; safety helmets are provided. ⊠ *38 Gifford St., Horseshoe Bay* ☎ *07/4778–5109* ⊕ *www.horseshoebayranch.com.au.*

SNORKELING AND SCUBA DIVING

Pleasure Divers. Pleasure Divers rents snorkeling and diving gear (including marine-stinger-proof suits), and runs trips to various sites off Magnetic Island. The company also runs dive excursions to the wreck of the SS *Yongala* and sites on the outer Barrier Reef: a full-day trip to pristine Wheeler Reef is A$186 for snorkelers, A$226 for divers, with optional introductory dive an extra A$80, subsequent dives A$40–A$50, and gear (A$40). Reef dive and snorkel trips run four days a week from Nelly Bay Ferry Terminal and Townsville. You can also do a refresher scuba course for A$125, or a three-day PADI Open Water dive course for A$339 per person, including gear, training, and four ocean dives. ⊠ *10 Marine Parade, Arcadia* ☎ *07/4778–5788, 1800/797–797* ⊕ *www.pleasuredivers.com.au.*

TOAD RACES

Arcadia Hotel. One of the more unusual evening activities on Magnetic Island is the weekly toad racing at the Arcadia Hotel. The event, which has been held every Wednesday night from 8 pm for nearly three decades, raises funds for local charities. The crowd's generally a mix of tourists and locals. After the race, the winner kisses his or her toad and collects the proceeds. ⊠ *7 Marine Parade, Arcadia* ☎ *07/4778–5177, 1800/663666.*

MIGALOO THE ALBINO WHALE

Migaloo, the world's only documented white humpback whale, was first spotted in 1991 as he made his way up the Queensland coastline. The albino humpback was named on the suggestion of an indigenous elder, who recommended he be dubbed Migaloo, an Aboriginal word for "white fella."

Every year thousands eagerly watch for a glimpse of Migaloo's distinctive pure-white dorsal fin, as the 14-meter (46-foot) humpback makes his annual migration from the Antarctic to tropical waters in June and July. He's been spotted all the way up Australia's east coast as far as Port Douglas, north of Cairns—usually from the decks of dive and cruise boats (which are forbidden by law from going within 500 metres of the rare cetacean).

Sometimes Migaloo travels alone; on other journeys he's accompanied by dolphins or fellow humpbacks.

Migaloo's not the only albino marine creature you might spot on your visit to Queensland: in early 2006 a tiny white sea turtle was found on Blacks Beach, Mackay, and shipped off to Reef HQ in nearby Townsville for rehab. Today he's doing well and has more than doubled in size.

Keen to know where Migaloo's heading? Go to the White Whale Research Centre's dedicated Web site, ⊕ *www.migaloo.com.au*, where whale-spotters document the migratory movements of this unique cetacean. To help to protect Migaloo and his mates, sign the onsite petition.

WATER SPORTS **Adrenalin Jet Ski Tours.** Adrenalin Jet Ski Tours provides three-hour guided, self-drive tours around Magnetic Island on SeaDoo luxury Jet Skis, as well as 90-minute "Top End" Jet Ski tours, with up to two people on each ski. ⊠ *46 Gifford St., Horseshoe Bay* ☎ *07/4778–5533, 0407/785533.*

Horseshoe Bay Watersports. Horseshoe Bay Watersports can take you parasailing, tube riding, wakeboarding, and waterskiing, and has a variety of water-sports equipment—cats, windsurfers, kayaks, surfskis, and paddleboats—for rent on weekends. ⊠ *Boat ramp, Horseshoe Bay* ☎ *07/4758–1336* ⊕ *www.sailsonhorseshoe.com.au.*

WHERE TO STAY

For expanded hotel reviews, visit Fodors.com.

Magnetic Island began "life" as a holiday-home getaway for Townsville residents, and has only recently attracted the kind of large-scale development that has transformed other islands near the Barrier Reef. Accommodations here are a mix of functional 1970s properties; small budget lodges; and newer, upmarket but relatively small apartment complexes and resorts. Luxurious Peppers Blue Resort, opened in 2007, is an exception to the rule.

¢ ★ **Bungalow Bay Koala Village.** Set in 6.5 acres of bushland adjoining national parkland, this eco-accredited YHA hostel has the air of a secluded campground. **Pros:** good food; fast Internet access; great facilities (24-hour ATM, public phone, book exchange, tour desk, jeep hire).

Cons: can be chilly in winter; rooms basic. ⊠ *40 Horseshoe Bay Rd., Horseshoe Bay* ☎ *07/4778–5577, 1800/285577* ⊕ *www.bungalowbay. com.au* ⤳ *30 bungalows and suites* ☖ *In-room: a/c, no a/c, no TV. In-hotel: restaurant, bar, pool, laundry facilities, business center, parking, some age restrictions, guest laundry, electricity.*

$$ ⛅ **Peppers Blue On Blue Resort.** This five-star waterfront resort adjacent to Nelly Bay Ferry Terminal overlooks the island's private marina. **Pros:** well-appointed rooms; lovely Endota day spa; terrific pool. **Cons:** service variable; breakfast buffet lackluster; marina-front rooms can be noisy. ⊠ *123 Sooning St., Nelly Bay* ☎ *07/4758–2400* ⊕ *www.peppers. com.au/Blue-On-Blue* ⤳ *60 dual-key (twin) rooms, 127 suites* ☖ *In-room: a/c, kitchen, Internet, Wi-Fi. In-hotel: restaurant, bar, pool, gym, spa, beach, laundry facilities, business center, parking.*

$$ ⛅ **Sails on Horseshoe.** As the name suggests, this modern complex is located at Horseshoe Bay, the biggest of Magnetic Island's 23 beaches. **Pros:** good location; lovely grounds; self-contained accommodation. **Cons:** dated furnishings; service can be offhand. ⊠ *13–15 Pacific Dr., Horseshoe Bay* ☎ *07/4778–5117* ⊕ *www.sailsonhorseshoe.com.au* ⤳ *2 studios, 2 villas, 10 town-house apartments* ☖ *In-room: a/c, no a/c, kitchen, Internet, Wi-Fi. In-hotel: pool, beach, laundry facilities, parking.*

Adelaide and South Australia

WORD OF MOUTH

If you like wine, I highly recommend a visit to the Barossa Valley, which is about 90 minutes from the city. You can easily spend your entire time there . . . There's so much to do in and around the Barossa, and the food is fantastic. We loved the German influence and the great German food.

—melnq8

WELCOME TO ADELAIDE AND SOUTH AUSTRALIA

TOP REASONS TO GO

★ **Arts and Music:** South Australia has fantastic festivals, from the Adelaide Festival of Arts, the internationally acclaimed Come Out festival, and the annual WOMADelaide celebration of world music.

★ **Bush Tucker:** The Australian palate has been reeducated in the pleasures of bush tucker—food that has been used for millennia by the Aboriginal people. Kangaroo, crocodile, emu, and other regional fare are now embraced by all.

★ **Historic Homes:** There are historic properties in both North Adelaide and in the Adelaide Hills, which have the best of both worlds: easy access to the city as well as to countryside vineyards and rustic villages.

★ **Wonderful Wines:** South Australia is considered Australia's premier wine state, and the top-notch wines of the Barossa Region, Clare Valley, McLaren Vale, Adelaide Hills, and Coonawarra are treasured by connoisseurs.

1 Adelaide. Heritage buildings line the small but perfectly formed center of South Australia's capital city. A diverse range of attractions, eateries, and bars makes the city a livelier option than its reputation would suggest.

2 The Barossa Region. One of the country's best-known wine regions—expect rolling hills, delicious local produce, and some of the best Shiraz in the world.

3 The Clare Valley. Less visited than the Barossa. Riesling fans should meander through the valley, tasting as they go while enjoying some spectacular views of the Flinders Ranges.

4 Fleurieu Peninsula. Wine buffs on a short time frame shouldn't miss beautiful McLaren Vale and its amenable cellar doors, while beautiful beaches and dramatic cliff walks are only a short drive away.

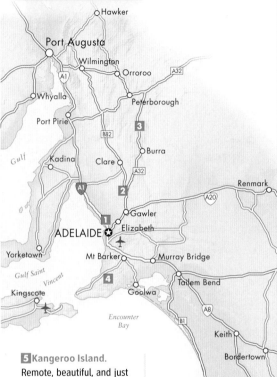

GETTING ORIENTED

South Australia encompasses both the dry hot north of the Outback and the greener, more temperate south coast. The green belt includes Adelaide and its surrounding hills and orchards, the Barossa and Clare Valley vineyards, the beautiful Fleurieu Peninsula, and the cliffs and lagoons of the mighty Murray, Australia's longest river. Offshore, residents of Kangaroo Island live at a delightfully old-fashioned pace, savoring their domestic nature haven.

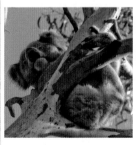

9

5 **Kangeroo Island.** Remote, beautiful, and just verging on the right side of isolated, Australia's third-largest island is a paradise for animal lovers, and also offers some of the world's coolest accommodation.

6 **The Outback.** Heading north, a trip to South Australia's Outback gives visitors a glimpse into an arid and dramatic landscape that is unmistakably Australian.

Updated by
Amy Taylor-
Kabbaz and
Tim Baker

Renowned for its celebrations of the arts, its multiple cultures, and its bountiful harvests from vines, land, and sea, South Australia is both diverse and divine. Here you can taste some of the country's finest wines, sample its best restaurants, and admire some of the world's most valuable gems. Or skip the state's sophisticated options and unwind on wildlife-rich Kangaroo Island, hike in the Flinders Ranges, or live underground like opal miners in the vast Outback.

Spread across a flat saucer of land between the Mt. Lofty ranges and the sea, the capital city of Adelaide is easy to explore. The wide streets of its 1½-square-km (½-square-mi) city center are organized in a simple grid that's ringed with parklands. The plan was laid out in 1836 by William Light, the colony's first surveyor-general, making Adelaide the only early-Australian capital not built by English convict labor. Today Light's plan is recognized as being far ahead of its time. This city of 1.1 million still moves at a leisurely pace, free of the typical urban menace of traffic jams thanks to Light's insistence that all roads be wide enough to turn a cannon.

Nearly 90% of South Australians live in the fertile south around Adelaide, because the region stands on the very doorstep of the harshest, driest land in the most arid of Earth's populated continents. Jagged hills and stony deserts fill the parched interior, which is virtually unchanged since the first settlers arrived. Desolate terrain and temperatures that top 48°C (118°F) have thwarted all but the most determined efforts to conquer the land. People who survive this region's challenges do so only through drastic measures, such as in the far-northern opal-mining town of Coober Pedy, where residents live underground.

Still, the deserts hold great surprises, and many clues to the country's history before European settlement. The ruggedly beautiful Flinders Ranges north of Adelaide hold Aboriginal cave paintings and fossil remains from when the area was an ancient seabed. Lake Eyre, a great salt lake, filled with water in the year 2000 for only the fourth

GREAT ITINERARIES

Many of the state's attractions are an easy drive from Adelaide. However, for a taste of the real South Australia a trip to a national park or to the Outback is definitely worth the extra travel time. Short flights between destinations make any journey possible within a day or overnight, but the more time you leave yourself to explore the virtues of this underrated state, the better.

IF YOU HAVE 3 DAYS

Spend a leisurely day in Adelaide enjoying the museums and historic sights, as well as the bustling Central Market. Take a sunset stroll along the Torrens, then have dinner and drinks at one of the city's vibrant restaurants or wine bars. Spend the night, then on Day 2 tour the Adelaide Hills, strolling the streets of 19th-century villages and taking in the panorama from atop Mt. Lofty. Stay the night in a charming bed-and-breakfast in one of the region's small towns, or come back down to North Adelaide and rest among the beautiful sandstone homes. Save Day 3 for wine tasting in the Barossa Region.

IF YOU HAVE 5 DAYS

After exploring Adelaide for a day, expand your horizons beyond the city and take a tram-car ride to the beach at touristy Glenelg or its posher neighbors Brighton or Henley Beach, where you can laze on the white sands and dine at tasty outposts. Spend the night here or at a B&B on the Fleurieu Peninsula, then take Day 3 to explore the vineyards and catch the ferry to Kangaroo Island. After a night here, use Day 4 to explore and appreciate the island's wildlife and untamed beauty. Return to Adelaide in the afternoon on Day 5 and drive up to the Adelaide Hills for sunset at Mt. Lofty.

IF YOU HAVE 7 DAYS

Spend Day 1 in Adelaide nosing through museums and picnicking in a park or on the bank of the River Torrens. After a night in the city, head into the leafy Adelaide Hills to meet nocturnal Australian wildlife at Cleland Wildlife Sanctuary. Stay the night in a local B&B, then on Day 3 travel to the Barossa Region, where German and English influences are strong and the dozens of wineries offer tempting free tastings. Spend the evening at a country house, then on Day 4 cross to Kangaroo Island. Stay two nights, giving you Day 5 to fully explore the island's remote corners and unwind. On Day 6, plunge into the Outback at extraordinary Coober Pedy (consider flying to maximize your time). There you can eat, shop, and stay the night underground as the locals do and "noodle" (rummage) for opal gemstones.

If you're a hiker, consider heading for Flinders Ranges National Park on Day 7 to explore one of the country's finest Outback parks.

9

time in its recorded history. The Nullarbor ("treeless") Plain stretches west across state lines in its tirelessly flat, ruthlessly arid march into Western Australia.

Yet South Australia is, perhaps ironically, gifted with the good life. It produces most of the nation's wine, and the sea ensures a plentiful supply of lobster and famed King George whiting. Cottages and guest-houses tucked away in the countryside around Adelaide are among the most charming and relaxing in Australia. Farther afield, unique experiences like watching seal pups cuddle with their mothers on Kangaroo Island would warm any heart. South Australia may not be grand in reputation, but its attractions are extraordinary, and after a visit you'll know you've indulged in one of Australia's best-kept secrets.

PLANNING

WHEN TO GO

Adelaide has the least rainfall of all Australian capital cities, and the midday summer heat is oppressive. The Outback in particular is too hot for comfortable touring during this time, but Outback winters are pleasantly warm. South Australia's national parks are open year-round. The best times to visit are in spring and autumn. In summer extreme fire danger may close walking tracks, and in winter heavy rain can make some roads impassable. Boating on the Murray River and Lake Alexandrina is best from October to March, when the long evenings are bathed in soft light. The ocean is warmest from December to March.

GETTING HERE AND AROUND

AIR TRAVEL

Adelaide Airport, 15 minutes from the city center, is a pleasant place to fly into and the state's main hub. The international and domestic terminals share a modern building complete with cafés, a tourist office, and free Wi-Fi.

International airlines serving Adelaide include Singapore Airlines, Malaysia Airlines, and Cathay Pacific. Qantas also connects Adelaide with many international cities (usually via Melbourne or Sydney). Domestic airlines flying into Adelaide include Jetstar, REX/Regional Express, Tiger Airways, and Virgin Blue. You can also fly to Coober Pedy and Kangaroo Island from here.

BUS TRAVEL

Adelaide's recently renovated Central Bus Station is the state's main hub for travel across the region as well as interstate services to Melbourne and Sydney. It's difficult and time-consuming to travel by bus to the wine regions, however; we recommend either renting a car or taking a tour.

CAR TRAVEL

The best way to experience this diverse state is by road. In general, driving conditions are excellent, although minor lanes are unpaved. It's two hours from Adelaide to the Barossa and Clare, the southern coast, and most other major sights, and less than an hour to McLaren

Vale's wineries. The most direct route to the Flinders Ranges is via the Princes Highway and Port Augusta, but a more interesting route takes you through the Clare Valley vineyards.

TRAIN TRAVEL

If you love train travel, you might find yourself stopping in Adelaide, as two classic train journeys also wind through this state: the *Ghan,* which runs north via Alice Springs to Darwin, and the *Indian Pacific,* which crosses the Nullarbor Plain to reach Perth. More prosaically, you can catch a train to Sydney or Melbourne, though often budget airlines are much cheaper.

HEALTH AND SAFETY

In an emergency, dial **000** to reach an ambulance, the police, or the fire department. Adelaide has the majority of the state's hospitals, though healthcare throughout the region is excellent. Summer 2009 saw temperatures of 43 degrees in Adelaide and even higher in the Outback, so be wary of sunstroke and dehydration.

ABOUT THE RESTAURANTS

Foodies are spoiled for choice in south Australia; the region is famous throughout the country for its excellent produce. Make sure you try some of Adelaide's Mod-Oz cuisine, with dishes showcasing oysters, crayfish, and King George whiting prepared with Asian and Mediterranean flavors. Bush foods are also available in some eateries; look for kangaroo, emu, and wattle seed.

Many restaurants close for a few days a week, so call ahead to check. Some upscale institutions require booking well in advance, and tables are tight during major city festivals and holidays.

ABOUT THE HOTELS

As well as all the standard chains, South Australia is packed with delightful lodgings in contemporary studios, converted cottages, and grand mansions. Modern resorts sprawl along the coastal suburbs, the Barossa Valley, and other tourist centers, but intimate properties for 10 or fewer guests can easily be found

There is plenty of competition in Adelaide, so shop around for great deals. Outside the city, weekday nights are usually less expensive and two-night minimum bookings often apply.

9

DINING AND LODGING PRICE CATEGORIES (IN AUSTRALIAN DOLLARS)				
¢	$	$$	$$$	$$$$
Restaurants	under A$10	A$10–A$20	A$21–A$35	A$36–A$50	over A$50
Hotels	under A$100	A$100–A$150	A$151–A$200	A$201–A$300	over A$300

Restaurant prices are based on the median main course price at dinner. Hotel prices are for two people in a standard double room in high season, excluding service and tax.

WINNING WINERIES

Oenophiles rejoice: in South Australia you've arrived in wine heaven. SA is the country's wine powerhouse, producing most of the nation's wine and boasting some of the oldest vineyards in the world. Thanks to its diverse geography and climate, the region produces a huge range of grape varieties—from cool-climate Rieslings in the Clare Valley to the big, full-bodied Shiraz wines of the world-famous Barossa. Less well known, McLaren Vale now punches above its weight with an exceptional variety of grapes, including Merlot, Chardonnay, and Cabernet Sauvignon, while just a 20-minute drive from Adelaide is Adelaide Hills, where temperatures are lower than the rest of the region, leading to great sparkling wines and Pinot Noir.

Although you can drive yourself to any of these regions, strict drunk driving laws mean that the unfortunate designated driver will be restricted to a few sips, if that. We highly recommend that you leave the driving to professionals. The most luxurious option is to go with Mary Anne Kennedy, the owner of A Taste of South Australia, who is one of the most knowledgeable regional food and wine guides. Her boutique tours of any region you choose (A$398; minimum 2 people, max 5) are a taste treat.

A Taste of South Australia (☎ *08/8271–7777 or 0419/861588* ⊕ *www. tastesa.com.au*).

ADELAIDE

Australians think of Adelaide as a city of churches, but Adelaide has outgrown its reputation as a sleepy country town dotted with cathedrals and spires. The Adelaide of this millennium is infinitely more complex, with a large, multiethnic population and thriving urban art and music scenes.

Bright and clean, leafy and beautiful Adelaide is a breeze to explore, with a grid pattern of streets encircled by parkland. The heart of the greenbelt is divided by the meandering River Torrens, which passes the Festival Centre in its prettiest stretch.

GETTING HERE AND AROUND

A car gives you the freedom to discover the country lanes and villages in the hills region outside the city, and Adelaide also has excellent road connections with other states. But South Australia is a big place, and we recommend flying if you're looking to save time. Adelaide has an excellent bus system, including the no-cost Adelaide FREE buses, which make about 30 downtown stops. Free guides to Adelaide's public bus lines are available from the Adelaide Metro Info Centre. The city's only surviving tram route now runs between the Entertainment Centre in Hindmarsh through the City to the beach at Glenelg. Ticketing is identical to that on city buses; travel between South Terrace and the Entertainment Centre on Port Road is free.

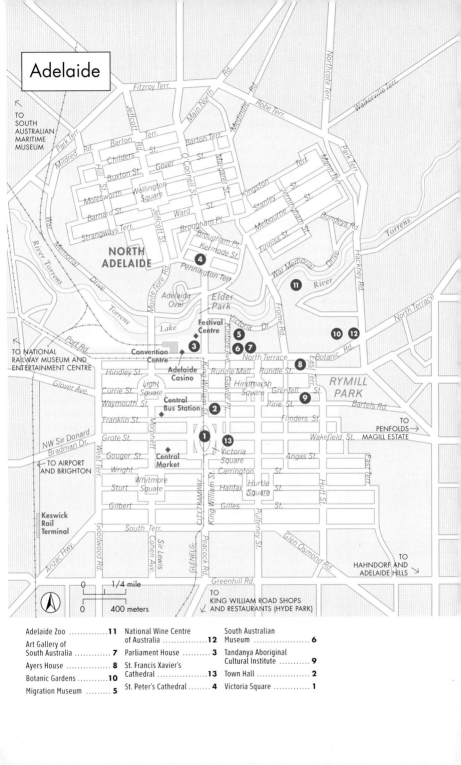

Adelaide

TO
SOUTH
AUSTRALIAN
MARITIME
MUSEUM

Fitzroy Terr.

Park Terr.

Mildred Rd.

Jeffcott Rd.

Barton Terr.

Childers St.

Buxton St.

Gover St.

O'Connell St.

Molesworth St.

Wellington Square

Barton Terr.

Margaret St.

Main North Rd.

Kingston Terr.

Martindale St.

Robe Terr.

Northcote Terr.

Walkerville Terr.

Ward St.

Stanley St.

Jerningham St.

Park Terr.

Barnard St.

Strangways Terr.

Brougham Pl.

Brougham Pl.

Melbourne St.

Finniss St.

Bundeys Rd.

Kermode St.

4

Pennington Terr.

War Memorial Drive

11

River Torrens

Torrens

Hackney Rd.

NORTH
ADELAIDE

Montefiore Rd.

Adelaide
Oval

Elder
Park

Victoria Dr.

Frome Rd.

North Terrace

Torrens

War
Memorial
Drive

Lake

Festival
Centre

Port Rd.

TO NATIONAL
RAILWAY MUSEUM AND
ENTERTAINMENT CENTRE

Convention
Centre

3

5

Kintore Ave.

6 **7**

10 **12**

Botanic Rd.

Glover Ave.

Hindley St.

Currie St.

Light
Square

Waymouth St.

Adelaide
Casino

Central
Bus Station

Rundle Mall

King William St.

Gawler Pl.

Hindmarsh
Square

Rundle St.

Grenfell St.

North Terrace

8

East Terr.

Botanic Rd.

9

RYMILL
PARK

Bartels Rd.

Franklin St.

Grote St.

NW Sir Donard
Bradman Dr.

TO AIRPORT
AND BRIGHTON

West Terr.

Morphett St.

2

Pirie St.

Flinders St.

Wakefield St.

Angas St.

East Terr.

TO
PENFOLDS →
MAGILL ESTATE

1

13

Central
Market

Gouger St.

Wright St.

Whitmore
Square

Sturt St.

Gilbert St.

Victoria
Square

Carrington St.

Halifax St.

Hurtle
Square

Gilles St.

King William St.

Hutt St.

CITY TRAMWAY

Keswick
Rail
Terminal

South Terr.

Goodwood Rd.

Anzac Hwy.

Sir Lewis
Cohen Ave.

GLENELG

Peacock Rd.

Pulteney St.

Glen Osmond Rd.

TO
HAHNDORF AND
ADELAIDE HILLS

Greenhill Rd.

TO
KING WILLIAM ROAD SHOPS
AND RESTAURANTS (HYDE PARK)

0   1/4 mile

0   400 meters

TOURS

Adelaide Sightseeing operates a morning city sights tour for A$62. The company also runs a daily afternoon bus tour of the Adelaide Hills and the German village of Hahndorf for A$62. For A$63, Gray Line Adelaide provides morning city tours that take in all the highlights. They depart from 85 Franklin Street at 9:30 am.

Tourabout Adelaide has private tours with tailored itineraries. Prices run from around A$40 for an Adelaide walking tour to A$360 for day-long excursions to the Barossa Valley. Jeff Easley, the owner and chief tour guide, can arrange almost anything.

Rundle Mall Information Centre hosts 30-minute free guided walks. The First Steps Tour points out the main attractions, facilities, and transportation in central Adelaide. Call for exact departure times. Bookings are not required.

ESSENTIALS

Banks and Currency Exchange ANZ ⊠ *13 Grenfell St, City Center* ☎ *13–1314.* **Commonwealth Bank** ⊠ *96 King William St., City Center* ☎ *13 2221.*

Taxi Suburban Taxis ☎ *13–1008.* **Yellow Cabs** ☎ *13–2227.*

Tour Operators Adelaide Sightseeing ⊠ *85 Franklin St, City Centre, Adelaide* ☎ *1300/769–762* ⊕ *www.adelaidesightseeing.com.au.* **Gray Line Adelaide** ☎ *1300/858–687* ⊕ *www.grayline.com.au.* **Rundle Mall Information Centre** ⊠ *Rundle Mall at King William St., City Center* ☎ *08/8203–7611.* **Tourabout Adelaide** ☎ *08/8365–1115, 0408/809–232* ⊕ *www.touraboutadelaide.com.au.*

EXPLORING ADELAIDE

The tiny city center is where you'll find most of Adelaide's sights, shops, and grand stately buildings. Staying here means you're in the heart of what action there is in Adelaide. North of the Torrens River is North Adelaide, which is dominated by the spires of St. Peter's Cathedral. This genteel suburb is where the city's yuppies live, and it has some great neighborhood restaurants. For fun in the sun, head to touristy Glenelg and its cooler near neighbors, Henley Beach and Brighton. Greater Adelaide has attractions encompassing delicious wines at Penfolds Magill Estate and views over the city at Mount Lofty and in Port Adelaide. Seafaring fans will enjoy the South Australian Maritime Museum.

TOP ATTRACTIONS

Adelaide Zoo. The second-oldest in Australia, Adelaide's zoo still retains much of its original architecture. Enter through the 1883 cast-iron gates to see such animals as Sumatran tigers, Australian rain-forest birds, and chimpanzees housed in modern, natural settings. The zoo

Dusky leaf monkey langurs at the Adelaide Zoo.

is world renowned for its captive breeding and release programs, and rare species including the red panda and South Australia's own yellow-footed rock wallaby are among its successes. In June 2008 the Australian government and Adelaide zoo signed a cooperative agreement to help secure the long-term survival of the giant panda, and in late 2009 Wang Wang and Funi arrived on loan from China to become the only giant pandas in the Southern Hemisphere, and the first to live permanently in Australia. Special VIP panda tours are now also available. Ask at the ticket office about tours and feeding times. ⊠ *Frome Rd. near War Memorial Dr., City Center* ☎ *08/8267–3255* ⊕ *www.zoossa. com.au* ✉ *A$31.50, kids under 14 A$18, families (2 adults, 2–3 kids) A$85* ☉ *Daily 9:30–5.*

Art Gallery of South Australia. Many famous Australian painters, including Charles Conder, Margaret Preston, Clifford Possum Tjapaltjarri, Russell Drysdale, and Sidney Nolan, are represented in here. Extensive Renaissance and British artworks are on display, and the atrium houses Aboriginal pieces. There is usually a visiting exhibition, too. A café and bookshop are also on-site. ⊠ *North Terr. near Pulteney St., City Center* ☎ *08/8207–7000* ⊕ *www.artgallery.sa.gov.au* ✉ *Free* ☉ *Daily 10–5.*

★ **Botanic Gardens.** These magnificent formal gardens include an international rose garden, giant water lilies, an avenue of Moreton Bay fig trees, acres of green lawns, and duck ponds. The Bicentennial Conservatory—the largest single-span glass house in the southern hemisphere—provides an environment for lowland rain-forest species such as the cassowary palm and torch ginger. Daily free guided

An exhibition at the Pacific Cultures Gallery, Adelaide.

tours leave from the Schomburgk Pavilion at 10:30. On weekends there's often a wedding ceremony taking place somewhere on the grounds. In summer the Moonlight Cinema series screens new, classic, and cult films inside the garden at sunset; bring a picnic blanket and a bottle of wine. Tickets sell fast, so plan ahead. More details at www.moonlight.com.au. ✉ *Plane Tree Dr., Botanic Park, City Center* ☎ *08/8222–9311* 🌐 *www.botanicgardens.sa.gov.au* 🎟 *Gardens free, conservatory A$4.50* ⏱ *Opens 8 am weekdays, 9 am weekends. Closing times vary seasonally.*

Migration Museum. Chronicled in this converted 19th-century Destitute Asylum, which later in the 19th century served as a school where Aboriginal children were forced to train as servants to the British, are the origins, hopes, and fates of some of the millions of immigrants who settled in Australia during the past two centuries. The museum is starkly realistic, and the bleak welcome that awaited many migrants is graphically illustrated. ✉ *82 Kintore Ave., City Center* ☎ *08/8207–7580* 🌐 *www.history.sa.gov.au* 🎟 *Free* ⏱ *Weekdays 10–5, weekends 1–5.*

Parliament House. Ten Corinthian columns are the most striking features of this classical parliament building. It was completed in two stages 50 years apart: the west wing in 1889 and the east wing in 1939. Alongside is **Old Parliament House,** which dates from 1843. There's a free guided tour of both houses weekdays at 10 and 2 during non-sitting days, and on Monday and Friday only when parliament is in session. The viewing gallery is open to the public when parliament is sitting. ✉ *North Terr. at King William St., City Center* ☎ *08/8237–9100* 🎟 *Free.*

South Australian Museum. This museum's Australian Aboriginal Cultures Gallery—the world's largest—houses 3,000 items, including ceremonial dress and paintings from the Pacific Islands. Old black-and-white films show traditional dancing, and touch screens convey desert life. Also in the museum are an exhibit commemorating renowned Antarctic explorer Sir Douglas Mawson, after whom Australia's main Antarctic research station is named; a Fossil Gallery housing the fantastic opalized partial skeleton of a 19-foot-long plesiosaur; and a biodiversity gallery. There's also a café overlooking a grassy lawn. If you are traveling during local school holidays, there are fantastic interactive craft and education activities for children for a small fee. ⊠ *North Terr., near Gawler Pl., City Center* ☎ *08/8207–7500* ⊕ *www.samuseum.sa.gov.au* ⊠ *Free* ⊙ *Daily 10–5; tours weekdays at 11, weekends at 2 and 3.*

Tandanya Aboriginal Cultural Institute. A must-see, Tandanya is the first major Aboriginal cultural facility of its kind in Australia. You'll find high-quality changing exhibitions of works by Aboriginal artists and a theater where you can watch didgeridoo performances (Tuesday to Friday at noon) and shows from Pacific Islanders at the same times at the weekend. There's a great gift shop, too, where you can buy CDs of local music. ⊠ *253 Grenfell St., City Center* ☎ *08/8224–3200* ⊕ *www. tandanya.com.au* ⊠ *Free* ⊙ *Daily 10–5.*

WORTH NOTING

Ayers House. Between 1855 and 1897 this sprawling colonial structure was the home of Sir Henry Ayers, South Australia's premier and the man for whom Uluru was originally named Ayers Rock. Most rooms—including the unusual Summer Sitting Room, in the cool of the basement—have been restored with period furnishings, and the state's best examples of 19th-century costumes are sometimes displayed in changing exhibitions. Admission includes a one-hour tour. ⊠ *288 North Terr., City Center* ☎ *08/8223–1234* ⊕ *www.ayershousemuseum.org.au* ⊠ *$8, kids under 16 A$4, Family of 2 adults and children $17* ⊙ *Tues.–Fri. 10–4, weekends 1–4.*

National Wine Centre of Australia. Timber, steel, and glass evoke the ribs of a huge wine barrel, and a soaring, open-plan concourse make this a spectacular showcase for Australian wines set in the Botanic Gardens. The Wine Discovery Journey takes you from neolithic pottery jars to a stainless-steel tank; you can even make your own virtual wine on a touch-screen computer. Some of the best vintages from more than 20 Australian wine-growing regions are also available for tasting at the Concourse Café (which offers a fantastic menu) from A$5. ⊠ *Hackney and Botanic Rds., City Center* ☎ *08/8303–3355* ⊕ *www.wineaustralia. com.au* ⊠ *Free* ⊙ *Weekdays 9–5, weekends 10–5.*

St. Francis Xavier's Cathedral. This church faced a bitter battle over construction after the 1848 decision to build a Catholic cathedral. It's now a prominent, decorative church with a soaring nave, stone arches through to side aisles with dark-wood ceilings, and beautiful stained-glass windows. ⊠ *Wakefield St. at Victoria Sq., City Center* ☎ *08/8231–3551* ⊠ *Free* ⊙ *Mass weekdays 8 am, 12:10, and 5:45 pm; Sat. 8 and 11:30 am; Sun. 7, 9, 11 am, and 6 pm.*

9

St. Peter's Cathedral. The spires and towers of this cathedral dramatically contrast with the nearby city skyline. St. Peter's is the epitome of Anglican architecture in Australia, and an important example of grand Gothic Revival. Free 45-minute guided tours are available Wednesday at 11 and Sunday at 12:30. ⊠ *1–19 King William St., North Adelaide* ☎ *08/8267–4551* ⊒ *Free* ⊙ *Services daily.*

Town Hall. An imposing building constructed in 1863 in Renaissance style, the Town Hall was modeled after buildings in Genoa and Florence. Tours visit the Colonel Light Room, where objects used to map and plan Adelaide are exhibited, and there are frequently traveling art exhibitions. The balcony of the Town Hall is famous for the appearance of the Beatles in 1964, which attracted the venue's largest crowd to date: approximately 300,000 screaming fans. If the guards aren't busy, they will show you around even when there isn't a tour scheduled. ⊠ *128 King William St., City Center* ☎ *08/8203–7203* ⊕ *www.cityofadelaide. com.au* ⊒ *Free* ⊙ *Tours by appointment Mon. at 10, 11, and noon.*

Victoria Square. The fountain in the square, which is floodlighted at night, celebrates the three rivers that supply Adelaide's water: the Torrens, Onkaparinga, and Murray are each represented by a stylized man or woman paired with an Australian native bird. Dominated by the huge Australian and Aboriginal flags overhead (the square is also known by its Aboriginal name Tarndanyangga), the park has benches that attract lunching office workers while shoppers and tourists come and go from the Glenelg-City Tram, which stops here. ⊠ *King William, Grote, and Wakefield Sts., City Center.*

GREATER ADELAIDE

☯ **National Railway Museum.** Steam-train buffs will love this collection of locomotives and rolling stock in the former Port Adelaide railway yard. The largest of its kind in Australia, the collection includes enormous "mountain"-class engines and the "Tea and Sugar" train, once the lifeline for camps scattered across the deserts of South and Western Australia. Great for the family, free train rides operate daily during local school holidays and on weekends. Train ride tickets are $7 for adults, $5 for children ages 3–15. ⊠ *Lipson St. near St. Vincent's St., Port Adelaide* ☎ *08/8341–1690* ⊕ *www.natrailmuseum.org.au* ⊒ *A$12, kids 5–16 A$6* ⊙ *Daily 10–5.*

★ **Penfolds Magill Estate.** Founded in 1844 by immigrant English doctor Christopher Rawson Penfold, this is the birthplace of Australia's most famous wine, Penfolds Grange, and one of the world's only city wineries. Introduced in 1951, Grange is the flagship of a huge stable of wines priced from everyday to special-occasion (collectors pay thousands of dollars to complete sets of Grange). Hour-long winery tours (A$15) leave daily at 11 and 3. The Great Grange Tour is the ultimate Magill Estate experience; over 2½ hours you visit the original Penfold family cottage, tour the winery, and enjoy a tasting of premium wines, including Grange, and a selection of gourmet cheeses. This tour departs at 1 pm on the first and third Sunday of every month and costs A$150 per person (minimum of four); reservations are essential. ⊠ *78 Penfold Rd., Magill* ☎ *08/8301–5400* ⊕ *www.penfolds.com.au* ⊒ *Free* ⊙ *Daily 10–5.*

☺ **South Australian Maritime Museum.** Inside a restored stone warehouse, this museum brings maritime history vividly to life with ships' figureheads, shipwreck relics, and intricate scale models. In the basement you can lie in a bunk bed aboard an 1840s immigrant ship and hear passengers telling of life and death on their journeys to South Australia. In addition to the warehouse displays, the museum includes a lighthouse (worth climbing the 75 steps up to see the view), restored steam tug, and a WWII tender at the nearby wharf. ⊠ *126 Lipson St., Port Adelaide* ☎ *08/8207–6255* ⊕ *www.history.sa.gov.au/maritime/maritime.htm* ☜ *A$8.50, A$3.50 for children (lighthouse entry included)* ☉ *Daily 10–5; lighthouse closed Sat.*

WHERE TO EAT

Melbourne, Gouger, O'Connell, and Rundle streets, along with the Norwood Parade and Glenelg neighborhoods, are the main eating strips. In any of these areas it's fun to stroll around until a restaurant or café takes your fancy. Chinatown is also lively, and if you feel like an alfresco picnic, pick some delicious local produce from Central Market.

Use the coordinate (✧ B2) at the end of each listing to locate a site on the corresponding map.

$$ ✕ **Amalfi Pizzeria Ristorante.** This place is rustic and noisy. If it weren't for

ITALIAN the Australian accents here, you'd swear you were in a regional Italian eatery. The terrazzo-tile dining room is furnished with bare wooden tables, around which sit professionals and university students in enthusiastic conversation. The paper place-mat menu lists traditional pizza and pasta dishes in two sizes—appetizer and entrée—a must-order is the spaghetti marinara. As this is one of the most popular (read: packed) restaurants in the East End of Rundle St, reservations are a good idea. Because the restaurant stays open late, it's also popular after a show or a movie. ⊠ *29 Frome St., City Center* ☎ *08/8223–1948* ☉ *Closed Sun. No lunch Sat.* ✧ *C2.*

$ ✕ **Big Table.** Simply the best breakfast choice in Adelaide, Big Table has

CAFÉ been at the Central Market for over 15 years, and regulars know to get there early for a chance at one of the few tables. Sitting up at the counter isn't too bad an option, however, especially when you have treats like fresh banana bread with rhubarb conserve and ricotta to look forward to. The enormous Big Brekkie lives up to its name, and offers quality as well as quantity with delicious thick-sliced local bacon and field mushrooms cooked with pesto and served on Turkish bread. ⊠ *Stall 39/40, Southern Roadway Adelaide Central Market, City Centre* ☎ *08/8212–3899* ▭ *No credit cards* ☉ *Closed Mon. and Sun. and evenings* ✧ *B3.*

$$ ✕ **The Brasserie.** The Brasserie's chef Simon Bryant has become somewhat

AUSTRALIAN of a local celebrity, having appeared on a national weekly TV program. Although his restaurant has a lively and relaxed atmosphere, Bryant is renowned for his insistence on top-quality local produce. The menu from the open kitchen changes every season, but always makes use of local specialties from the Fleurieu Peninsula, Kangaroo Island, and the local Central Market around the corner. If Australia's national animal is on the menu, give it a try here. ⊠ *Hilton Hotel, 233 Victoria Sq., City Center* ☎ *08/8237–0697* ☜ *Reservations essential* ☉ *No lunch weekends* ✧ *B3.*

9

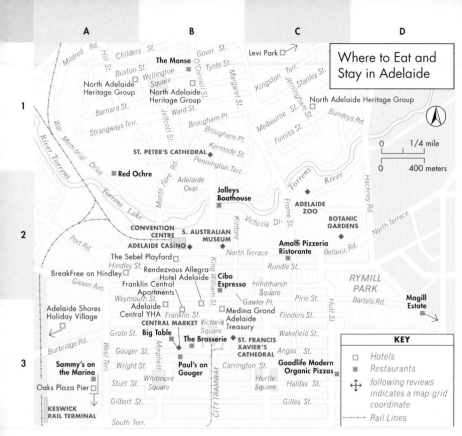

Where to Eat and Stay in Adelaide

KEY

☐	Hotels
■	Restaurants
⟡	following reviews indicates a map-grid coordinate
⊢⟶⊣	Rail Lines

¢

CAFÉ

✕ **Cibo Espresso.** Caffeine addicts head here for a little taste of Italy in stylish fun surroundings. The small local chain has branches dotted around the city, and in each one you are guaranteed a fabulous espresso from their Wega machines and irresistible sweet treats. If you're there at lunchtime, the freshly baked panini are good, too. All branches have free Wi-Fi. ⊠ *Shop 7, 82 King William St., City Center* ☎ *08/8410–4088* ⊗ *Closed Sat. after 1 pm* ⟡ *B2.*

$$

PIZZA

✕ **Goodlife Modern Organic Pizzas.** Forget about greasy pepperoni-loaded pizzas—the pies at this local trend-setting favorite are as different from the norm as you can get. It was the country's first pizzeria to be certified as organic, and the innovative toppings like kapunda free-range chicken are as tasty as they sound, especially with a glass of their well-priced local wine. The dessert pizzas are worth a try if you're not carb-ed out. You'll also find a Goodlife Pizza in Glenelg and North Adelaide. ⊠ *170 Hutt St., City Center* ☎ *08/8223–2618* ⊗ *No lunch weekends* ⟡ *C3.*

$$

MODERN
AUSTRALIAN

✕ **Jolleys Boathouse.** Blue canvas directors' chairs and white-clothed wooden tables create a relaxed, nautical air here—which perfectly suits the location on the south bank of the River Torrens. Sliding glass doors open onto a full-width front balcony for alfresco dining. The imaginative modern Australian menu changes seasonally, but might include a salad of grilled Kangaroo Island marron, green mango, basil and shallots, or sweet pork belly with red dates. Executives make up most lunch crowds, and warm evenings attract couples. There is an unfriendly minimum of A$23 per person, however. ✉ *Corner of Victoria Dr. and King William Rd., 1 Jolleys La., City Center* ☎ *08/8223–2891* ⚱ *Reservations essential* ☺ *No dinner Sun.* ✛ *B2.*

$$$$
ECLECTIC

✕ **Magill Estate.** Do you inhale deeply from your wine glass before drinking? Do you know your back palate from your front? Then you're ready to join the wine buffs at this pavilion-style vineyard restaurant. The restaurant overlooks vineyards and the distant city skyline and coast. The view alone makes eating here a memorable experience. The seasonal menu might include such European-flavor Oz delights as KI marron (a delicious lobster-looking creature typically harvested near Kangaroo Island), chick weed, young shoots, peas, wood sorrel, and organic honey. You can choose between a 4-, 7-, or 10-course meal. Opt to have accompanying wines selected for you; it costs extra but the experience is well worth it (this is a vineyard after all). ✉ *78 Penfold Rd., Magill* ☎ *08/8301–5551* ⚱ *Reservations essential* ☺ *Closed Sun. and Mon. No lunch Tues.–Thurs. and Sat.* ✛ *D3.*

$$$$
FRENCH

✕ **The Manse.** Tailcoats were de rigueur dinner attire when this Victorian church manse was built in the heart of North Adelaide, but the dress code for the modern French gem it houses now is thankfully more relaxed. Continental cuisine, such as the Storm Bay Salmon with sugared cereals and popcorn, apples, and soft herb cream, is prepared with flair, and special effort is made to add local ingredients to classic and contemporary dishes (try the South Australian Blue Crab with corn cream, onion consomme, and watercress). There is a degustation menu in case you can't choose. Wood-burning fireplaces and an outdoor terrace make dining a pleasure any time of year. The *Australian* newspaper recently picked this place as their fine-dining restaurant of the year. The same family also owns the trendy Sparrow Kitchen and Bar at 10 O'Connell Street, North Adelaide, and—new in 2011—Grace the Establishment on the Parade, Norwood. ✉ *142 Tynte St., North Adelaide* ☎ *08/8267–4636* ⚱ *Reservations essential* ☺ *No lunch. Closed Sun. and Mon.* ✛ *B1.*

$$
SPANISH

✕ **Mesa Lunga.** This tapas-inspired restaurant and adjacent bar is packed to the rafters most nights of the week. Head to the bar for the perfect ambience for enjoying smaller plates of delicious fine-sliced meats, white anchovies, or confit potato-and-onion Spanish omelet. Opt to be seated at a table with comfortable leather chairs for a heartier option such as marsala-braised ox tail and cheek, celeriac puree, and heirloom carrots and jus. There's a shared wall with the neighboring Sangria bar, which is also popular, especially for the wide variety of sangria cocktails on offer. Be prepared to share your drinking and eating space—all corners of this restaurant can get busy. ✉ *140 Gouger St., City Center, Adelaide* ☎ *08/8410–7617* ⚱ *Reservations essential.*

$$
CAFÉ

✕ **Paul's on Gouger.** It may look like your run-of-the-mill chippie, but this Gouger Street veteran of more than 60 years is the place to get hooked on King George whiting. It's been hailed as one of Adelaide's best—and best-priced—seafood restaurants. The salt-and-pepper squid is another local favorite. For a great view of the bustle in the open kitchen, request a table upstairs on the ship's-deck-like mezzanine floor. ✉ *79 Gouger St., City Center* ☎ *08/8231–9778* ✛ *B3.*

$$ ✕ **Red Ochre.** A sweeping view of Adelaide is the backdrop for contemporary workings of traditional bush meats, herbs, and fruits at this
MODERN
AUSTRALIAN   riverfront restaurant. The downstairs River Café, the restaurant's sister venue, is more informal, and offers a modern Italian menu for lunch weekdays, while Red Ochre is only open for dinner. For a splurge, head upstairs; if you like your steaks, you'll love their Premium steaks served with onion puree and brocolini, bush tomato chimmichurri, wattle-seeded mustard, pepper berry jam, and confit garlic. Don't miss the wattle-seed pavlova, Red Ochre's version of Australia's famous meringue dessert. ⊠ *War Memorial Dr., North Adelaide* ☎ *08/8211–8555* ⌂ *Reservations essential* ⊘ *Closed Sun.* ✛ *A2.*

$$ ✕ **Sammy's on the Marina.** Enormous fishbowl windows frame views of
SEAFOOD   million-dollar yachts at this restaurant—one of Adelaide's top seafood eateries—at the far end of Glenelg's glitzy Holdfast Marina. Watch the setting sun silhouette playing dolphins or a storm rolling across Gulf St. Vincent as you tuck into skewered scallops or crispy-skin Atlantic salmon wrapped in prosciutto and served over brocolini and baby carrots with salsa verde. The menu here charts South Australia's ocean bounty, and the hot seafood platter (for two people) would feed a school of sharks. ⊠ *1–12 Holdfast Promenade, Glenelg* ☎ *08/8376–8211* ⌂ *Reservations essential* ✛ *A3.*

WHERE TO STAY

At first glance, large international, business-style hotels seem to dominate Adelaide—there's a Hilton, a Hyatt, a Sebel, and a Crowne Plaza—but there's actually a wide choice of places to rest your head. Adelaide's accommodations are a mix of traditional mid-rise hotels, backpacker hostels, an abundance of self-contained apartments, and charming bed-and-breakfasts, many in century-old sandstone buildings. With a car you'll be within easy reach of a Glenelg beach house or an Adelaide Hills B&B.

For expanded hotel reviews, visit Fodors.com.

Use the coordinate (✛ 1:B2) at the end of each listing to locate a site on the corresponding map.

¢   🏠 **Adelaide Central YHA.** Mostly young people buzz around this purpose-built, city-center hostel like bees at a hive. **Pros:** extremely clean, friendly staff. **Cons:** sometimes impossible to book ahead during peak season, older people will feel outnumbered. ⊠ *135 Waymouth St., City Center* ☎ *08/8414–3010* ⊕ *www.yha.com.au* ⌂ *63 rooms* ⌂ *In-room: Wi-Fi. In-hotel: laundry facilities, business center, parking* ✛ *B3.*

$$ 🏠 **Adelaide Shores Holiday Village.** The breeze is salty, the lawns are green, and white sand is only a few lazy steps from this summery resort on the city's coastal fringe. **Pros:** very family-friendly, with plenty of activities for kids and well-planned family rooms. **Cons:** bad choice for a romantic break, in peak season service levels drop. ⊠ *Military Rd., West Beach* ☎ *08/8355–7360* ⊕ *www.adelaideshores.com.au/holidayvillage.htm* ⌂ *22 bungalows, 30 villas, 32 units* ⌂ *In-room: kitchen. In-hotel: pool, tennis court, beach, laundry facilities, business center, parking* ✛ *A3.*

$ 🏨 **BreakFree on Hindley.** Step out your door at this three-story redbrick complex and you might think you're in the tropics; open-air walkways and palm trees suggest you're closer to the beach than the western-parkland end of Hindley Street. **Pros:** great value for money; kitchens are fully equipped for self-catering. **Cons:** basic furnishings; bathrooms could do with a face-lift. ⊠ *255 Hindley St., City Center* ☎ *08/8217–2500* ⊕ *www.breakfree.com.au* ⤳ *48 studios, 94 2-bedroom apartments* ⚐ *In-room: kitchen, Internet. In-hotel: restaurant, bar, laundry facilities, business center, parking* ✣ *A2.*

$$$ 🏨 **Franklin Central Apartments.** Check in here and you'll have room to move in one of Adelaide's most crowded quarters. **Pros:** around the corner from foodie heaven, the Central Market, good-sized rooms. **Cons:** not much in the way of soundproofing, furnishings on the simple side. ⊠ *36 Franklin St., City Center* ☎ *08/8221–7050, 1300/662288* ⊕ *www. franklinapartments.com.au* ⤳ *62 apartments* ⚐ *In-room: kitchen, Internet. In-hotel: restaurant, laundry facilities, parking* ✣ *B3.*

¢ 🏨 **Levi Park.** Port Lincoln parrots and black ducks are regulars at this caravan park overlooking the River Torrens 5 km (3 mi) from central Adelaide. **Pros:** family-friendly, with a host of activities available; inexpensive. **Cons:** cabins can be close together; not the place for a romantic interlude. ⊠ *1A Harris Rd., Vale Park* ☎ *08/8344–2209, 1800/442209* ⊕ *www.levipark.com.au* ⤳ *20 unpowered sites, 66 powered sites, 30 cabins* ⚐ *In-hotel: flush toilets, partial hookups, dump station, drinking water, guest laundry, showers, grills, picnic table, electricity, public telephone, general store, play area* ✣ *C1.*

$$$ 🏨 **Medina Grand Adelaide Treasury.** Contemporary Italian furnishings in
★ white, slate-gray, and ocher are juxtaposed with 19th-century Adelaide architecture in this stylish Victoria Square hotel. **Pros:** beautiful and classic building with light and airy reception rooms. **Cons:** no close parking, reception staff get harassed at peak periods. ⊠ *2 Flinders St., City Center* ☎ *08/8112–0000, 1300/633462* ⊕ *www.medina.com.au* ⤳ *20 studio rooms, 59 apartments* ⚐ *In-room: safe, kitchen, Internet. In-hotel: restaurant, bar, pool, gym, laundry facilities, parking* ✣ *B3.*

$$$ 🏨 **North Adelaide Heritage Group.** Tucked into the city's leafy, oldest sec-
Fodor's Choice tion, these 18 lodgings are stunningly unique. **Pros:** historic properties
★ in Adelaide's most upscale suburb, friendly owners give helpful tips on what to do. **Cons:** some properties can be on the dark side, not child-friendly. ⊠ *Office:, 109 Glen Osmond Rd., Eastwood* ☎ *08/8272–1355* ⊕ *www.adelaideheritage.com* ⤳ *7 cottages, 3 suites, 8 apartments* ⚐ *In-room: kitchen, Internet, Wi-Fi. In-hotel: laundry facilities, parking* ✣ *A1, B1, C1.*

$$$ 🏨 **Oaks Plaza Pier.** Sea air wafts through open balcony doors in this all-apartment complex on Adelaide's favorite beach. **Pros:** steps from the beach, helpful reception staff who are full of advice. **Cons:** corporate feel to the lobby, the bars can get noisy and messy at peak times, expensive Internet. ⊠ *16 Holdfast Promenade, Glenelg* ☎ *08/8350–6688, 1300/551111* ⊕ *www.theoaksgroup.com.au* ⤳ *121 1-bedroom apartments, 34 2-bedroom apartments* ⚐ *In-room: safe, kitchen, Internet. In-hotel: restaurant, bar, pool, gym, beach, laundry facilities, parking* ✣ *A3.*

9

$$$
Fodor's Choice
★

⛬ **Rendezvous Allegra Hotel Adelaide.** Black-tile-and-timber columns frame the Hollywood-glamorous marble lobby of this ultrasleek upscale hotel. **Pros:** five-star facilities and an excellent wine list at the restaurant. **Cons:** tiny gym, and more corporate than boutique in feel. ⊠ 55 Waymouth St., City Center ☎ 08/8115–8888 ⊕ www.rendezvoushotels. com/adelaide/ ⌁ 166 rooms, 35 suites ⛬ In-room: Internet. In-hotel: restaurant, bar, pool, gym ✛ B2.

$$$
★

⛬ **The Sebel Playford.** Showy chandeliers illuminate a movie-set-like celebration of art nouveau in the lobby of this luxury hotel. **Pros:** excellent breakfast spread, convivial bar. **Cons:** expensive Internet and parking. ⊠ 120 North Terr., City Center ☎ 08/8213–8888 ⊕ www.sebelplayford. com.au ⌁ 110 rooms, 72 suites ⛬ In-room: safe, kitchen, Internet. In-hotel: restaurant, bar, pool, gym, laundry facilities, parking ✛ B2.

NIGHTLIFE AND THE ARTS

THE ARTS

Adelaide truly is the festival state, and with the majority of the major events running at the end of summer in "Mad March," this is the best time to visit, as the city takes on an extra festival feel. The three-week **Adelaide Festival of Arts** (⊕ www.adelaidefestival.com.au), Australia's oldest arts festival, takes place in February and March of even-numbered years. It's a cultural smorgasbord of outdoor opera, classical music, jazz, art exhibitions, comedy, a writer's festival, and cabaret presented by some of the world's top artists. Recent highlights include the critically acclaimed opera La Grande Macabre by Ligeti and the exuberant Good Morning Mr. Gershwin. The annual four-day **WOM-ADelaide Festival** (⊕ www.womadelaide.com.au) of world music, arts, and dance takes place in early March and attracts top musicians from all over the world to its stages in the picturesque Botanic Park. There's also an annual fringe festival (⊕ www.adelaidefringe.com.au), the southern hemisphere's biggest, with hundreds of shows around town.

For a listing of performances and exhibitions, look to the entertainment pages of the Advertiser, Adelaide's daily newspaper. The Adelaide Review, a free monthly arts paper, reviews exhibitions, galleries, and performances, and lists forthcoming events.

BASS Ticket Agency. Tickets for most live performances can be purchased from BASS Ticket Agency. ⊠ Adelaide Festival Centre, King William St., City Center ☎ 13–1246 ⊕ www.bass.net.au.

Adelaide Festival Centre. The Adelaide Festival Centre is the city's major venue for the performing arts. The State Opera, the State Theatre Company of South Australia, and the Adelaide Symphony Orchestra perform here regularly. Performances are in the Playhouse, the Festival and Space theaters, the outdoor amphitheater, and Her Majesty's Theatre at 58 Grote Street. The box office is open Monday–Saturday 9–6. ⊠ King William St. near North Terr., City Center ☎ 13–1246 ⊕ www. adelaidefestivalcentre.com.au.

The Art Gallery of South Australia.

NIGHTLIFE

BARS AND CLUBS There's something going on every evening in Adelaide, although clubs are especially packed on weekends. Cover charges vary according to the night and time of entry. Nightlife for the coming week is listed in "Adelaide (Scene)," a pullout section of Thursday's edition of the *Advertiser*. *Rip It Up* is a free Thursday music-and-club publication aimed at the younger market. *Onion*, published fortnightly on Thursday, is Adelaide's top dance music magazine. *dB*, a twice-monthly free independent publication, covers music, arts, film, games, and dance.

Bars along Rundle Street, the west end of Hindley Street, and Gouger Street are trendy, while Hindley and Waymouth streets are lined with traditional pubs. North Adelaide's O'Connell Street buzzes every night, and the popular Sunday-evening beer-and-banter sessions really pack in the crowds. There are also a number of vibrant pubs on The Parade at Norwood, especially popular on a Sunday afternoon in the sun.

Austral Hotel. Austral Hotel, the first bar in South Australia to put Coopers beer on tap, is a local favorite and a great place to drink outdoors. You can down shooters or sip cocktails from a long list while listening to a band play or a DJ spin groovy tunes. It's open daily 11 am–3 am. ✉ *205 Rundle St., City Center* ☎ *08/8223–4660.*

Botanic Bar. Botanic Bar, a cool city lounge, has cordovan banquettes encircling the U-shaped, marble-top bar. Muddlers (crushed ice drinks) are the specialty, and they bring in mostly young professionals, including off-duty medics from the hospital opposite. It's open until the wee hours Tuesday to Sunday. ✉ *310 North Terr., City Center* ☎ *08/8227–0799.*

★ **The Gov.** The Gov is the favorite venue of a mixed crowd. Young homeowners and long-term regulars come for Irish music sessions, all-weekend metal fests, and everything in between. Cabaret, comedy, Latin music—if you can name it, you can probably hear it here. There's good pub grub, too. It's open weekdays 11 am to late and Saturday noon to late. It's closed Sunday unless there is a show. ⊠ *59 Port Rd., Hindmarsh* ☎ *08/8340–0744.*

Grace Emily. Grace Emily, a multilevel music-lover's pub, has bartenders spouting the mantra "No pokies, no TAB, no food." (Pokies are the poker machines found in many pubs, and TAB, Australia's version of OTB, lets you place bets on horse races.) Instead, there's live music nightly, and a pool table. The beer garden is one of the city's best, with secluded spots for those wanting a quiet tipple and big round tables for groups to drink en masse and alfresco. It's open daily 4 pm–late. ⊠ *232 Waymouth St., City Center* ☎ *08/8231–5500.*

Supermild. The cavernous Supermild has a retro feel and is as unpretentious as they come, which fits in perfectly with the local nightlife scene. Grab a comfy sofa and chill out with a bunch of friends while listening to the local DJs going their thing—either indie, retro, or funk, depending on the night. ⊠ *182 Hindley St., City Center* ☎ *08/8212–8077* ☉ *Closed Mon. and Tues.).*

Wellington Hotel. The Wellington Hotel, first licensed in 1851, is hops lovers' heaven, with 32 Australian-brewed beers on tap. Line up six "pony" (sample) glasses on a taster tray, then enjoy a schooner (large glass) of your favorite. ⊠ *36 Wellington Sq., North Adelaide* ☎ *08/8267–1322.*

CASINO **SkyCity.** Head to SkyCity for big-time casino gaming, including the highly animated Australian Two-up, in which you bet against the house on the fall of two coins. Four bars, including the stylish venue Loco, and four restaurants are also within the complex. It's one of a handful of places in Adelaide that keep pumping until dawn. ⊠ *North Terr., City Center* ☎ *08/8212–2811* ☉ *24 hrs.*

OUTDOOR ACTIVITIES

PARTICIPANT SPORTS

BICYCLING Adelaide's parks, flat terrain, and uncluttered streets make it a perfect city for two-wheel exploring.

Linear Park Mountain Bike Hire. Linear Park Mountain Bike Hire rents 21-speed mountain bikes by the hour or for A$20 per day and A$80–A$100 per week, including a helmet, lock, and maps. They're open daily 9–5 in winter, 9–6 in summer, or by appointment. You can also hire paddleboats to use on the Torrens River from here, and buy tickets to ride on the Popeye—Adelaide's famous 40-minute cruise along the river. ⊠ *Elder Park adjacent to Adelaide Festival Centre, City Center* ☎ *0400/596065.*

GOLF **City of Adelaide Golf Links.** A 10-minute walk outside of the city, the City of Adelaide Golf Links—reputed to be one of the most picturesque golf settings in the country—runs one short (par 3) and two 18-hole courses. You can rent clubs and carts from the pro shop. Greens fees are from A$21 weekdays and A$24.50 weekends for the north course, A$25.00 weekdays and A$30.00 weekends for the south course. Playing hours are dawn to dusk daily. ⊠ *Entrance to par-3 course is off War Memorial Dr.; 18-hole courses are off Strangways Terr., North Adelaide* ☎ *08/8267–2171* ⊕ *www.cityofadelaide.com.au.*

WATER
SPORTS

The Beachhouse. The Beachhouse is a kid's dream come true, with an array of attractions like waterslides, fairground rides, and boats steps from the Glenelg beach. Entry requires purchasing a Fun Card for $2, and then buying credits for the games and rides you want for a two-hour limit. You can keep topping up your card throughout the day. ⊠ *Colley Terr., Glenelg* ☎ *08/8295–1511* ⊕ *www.thebeachhouse.com.au.*

The Dolphin Boat. Youngsters—and the young at heart—will love a cruise on the Dolphin Boat, which allows you to swim with the cute and friendly animals. The dolphins and tour guides have developed a close relationship over the years, so you're guaranteed to get up close. In fact, if you don't get into the water to swim with the dolphins, they will refund the difference between the watch and the swim. ⊠ *Holdfast Shores Marina, Glenelg* ☎ *0412/811–838* ⊕ *www.dolphinboat.com.au* ☒ *A$98 to swim, A$58 to watch.*

SPECTATOR SPORTS

Venue*Tix. Venue*Tix sells tickets for domestic and international one-day and test (five-day) cricket matches, other major sporting events, and concerts. ⊠ *Shop 24, Da Costa Arcade, Grenfell St. at Gawler Pl., City Center* ☎ *08/8225–8888* ⊕ *www.venuetix.com.au.*

CRICKET
★

Bradman Collection Museum. Cricket season is October–March, and the main venue for interstate and international competition is the Adelaide Oval. Two-hour tours (A$10) of the Oval and the Bradman Collection Museum, dedicated to the legendary Sir Donald Bradman, depart weekdays at 10 am (except on match days and public holidays). ⊠ *Adelaide Oval, War Memorial Dr. and King William St., North Adelaide* ☎ *08/8300–3800* ☉ *9:30–4:30 weekdays, closed weekends.*

FOOTBALL

AAMI Stadium. Australian Rules Football is the most popular winter sport in South Australia. Games are played at AAMI Stadium. Teams play in the national AFL competition on Thursday, Friday, Saturday, or Sunday. The season runs March to August. Finals are in September. ⊠ *Turner Dr., West Lakes* ☎ *08/8268–2088.*

SHOPPING

If you are wondering where everyone in Adelaide is, you'll find them at Rundle Mall, the city's main shopping area. Shops in the City Center are generally open Monday–Thursday 9–5:30, Friday 9–9, Saturday 9–5:30, and Sunday 11–5. Suburban shops are often open until 9 pm on Thursday night instead of Friday. As the center of the world's opal industry, Adelaide has many opal shops, which are around King William Street. Other good buys are South Australian regional wines, crafts, and Aboriginal artwork. The trendiest area to browse is King William Road in Hyde Park, a 20-minute walk south from Victoria

Square. Outside of the city, the Parade at Norwood and the Burnside Shopping Centre are packed with current trends, and Harbour Town next to Adelaide Airport is a great place to find a bargain.

MALLS

Rundle Mall. Adelaide's main shopping area is Rundle Mall, a pedestrian plaza lined with boutiques, department stores—including Australia's two best known stores, Myers and David Jones—and arcades. Heritage-listed Adelaide Arcade is a Victorian-era jewel, with a decorative tiled floor, skylights, and dozens of shops behind huge timber-framed windows. ⊠ *Rundle St. between King William and Pulteney Sts., City Center* ☎ *08/8203–7611.*

> **NICE VIEWS**
>
> There is no better view of Adelaide—day or night—than the city-and-sea sweep from atop 2,300-foot Mt. Lofty. There's an appropriately named glass-front restaurant here called the Summit, though prices at both the café and restaurant are sky-high.

MARKETS

★ **Central Market.** One of the largest produce markets in the southern hemisphere, and Adelaide's pride and joy, the Central Market is chock-full of stellar local foods, including glistening-fresh fish, meat, crusty Vietnamese and continental breads, German baked goods, cheeses of every shape and color, and old-fashioned lollies (candy). You can also buy souvenir T-shirts, CDs, books, cut flowers, and a great cup of coffee. Hours are Tuesday 7–5:30, Thursday 9–5:30, Friday 7 am–9 pm, and Saturday 7–3. The enthusiastic couple behind Adelaide's Top Food and Wine Tours (⊕ *www.topfoodandwinetours.com.au*) showcase Adelaide's food-and-wine lifestyle—as in the behind-the-scenes guided tour of the Central Market (A$46), which lets you meet stall holders, share their knowledge, and taste the wares. Tours are scheduled Tuesday and Thursday–Saturday at 9:30 am; reservations are essential. ⊠ *Gouger St., City Center* ☎ *08/8203–7494.*

SPECIALTY STORES

CHOCOLATE
★ **Haigh's Chocolates.** Haigh's Chocolates, Australia's oldest chocolate manufacturer, has tempted people with corner shop displays since 1915. The family-owned South Australian company produces exquisite truffles, pralines, and creams—as well as the chocolate bilby (an endangered Australian marsupial), Haigh's answer to the Easter bunny. Shop hours are Monday to Saturday 8:30–6, Sunday 10:30–5. Free chocolate-making tours at the visitor center run Monday–Saturday at 11, 1, and 2; bookings are essential. ⊠ *2 Rundle Mall at King William St., City Center* ☎ *08/8231–2844* ⊠ *Haigh's Visitors Centre, 154 Greenhill Rd., Parkside* ☎ *08/8372–7077.*

HOME WARES **Jam Factory.** The Jam Factory, a contemporary craft-and-design center at the Lion's Arts Centre, exhibits and sells unique Australian glassware, ceramics, wood, and metal work. Its fantastic gift shop offers buyers a chance to purchase a handmade piece, including a description from the artist. ⊠ *19 Morphett St., City Center* ☎ *08/8231–0005* ⊕ *www.jamfactory.com.au* ⊗ *Mon.–Sat. 10–5, Sun. 1–5.*

Urban Cow Studio. For quirky locally made jewelry, pottery, glass, and sculptures, visit Urban Cow Studio. ⊠ *11 Frome St., City Center* ☎ *08/8232–6126* ⊕ *www.urbancow.com.au* ⊘ *Mon.–Thurs. 10–6, Fri. 10–9, Sa.t 10–5, Sun. 12–5.*

JEWELRY AND GEMS
Adelaide Exchange. Adelaide Exchange, off Rundle Mall, sells high-quality antique jewelry. They can also be found in Glenelg and Modbury. ⊠ *10 Stephens Pl., City Center* ☎ *08/8212–2496.*

Australian Opal and Diamond Collection. The Australian Opal and Diamond Collection sells and manufactures superb handcrafted one-of-a-kind opal jewelry. ⊠ *14 King William St., City Center* ☎ *08/8211–9995.*

SIDE TRIPS TO THE ADELAIDE HILLS

With their secluded green slopes and flowery gardens, the Adelaide Hills are a pastoral vision in this desert state. The patchwork quilt of vast orchards, neat vineyards, and avenues of tall conifers resembles the Bavarian countryside, a likeness fashioned by the many German immigrants who settled here in the 19th century. In summer the Hills are consistently cooler than the city, although the charming towns and wineries are pleasant to visit any time of year. To reach the region from Adelaide, head toward the M1 Princes Highway or drive down Pulteney Street, which becomes Unley Road and then Belair Road. From here signs point to Crafers and the freeway.

MT. LOFTY
16 km (10 mi) southeast of Adelaide.

There are splendid views of Adelaide from the lookout atop 2,300-foot Mt. Lofty, the coldest location in Adelaide, where snow is not uncommon in winter months. The energetic can follow some of the many trails that lead from the summit, or alternatively, have a cup of coffee in the café and enjoy the view in the warmth.

GETTING HERE AND AROUND
By car from Adelaide, take the Crafers exit off the South Eastern Freeway and follow Summit Road or from the eastern suburbs via Greenhill Road. You can get to the summit as well as the Mt. Lofty Botanic Gardens and Cleland Wildlife Park in about 40 minutes by catching Bus 842, 865, or 865F from Currie or Grenfell Street in the city center. Alight at bus stop 24A and connect to Bus 823.

A 3½-km (2-mi) round-trip walk from the Waterfall Gully parking lot in Cleland Conservation Park (15-minute drive from Adelaide) takes you along Waterfall Creek before climbing steeply to the white surveying tower on the summit; the track is closed on Total Fire Ban days.

ESSENTIALS
Transportation Adelaide Metro Info Centre ⊠ *Currie and King William Sts., City Center* ☎ *08/8210–1000* ⊕ *www.adelaidemetro.com.au.*

EXPLORING
Cleland Wildlife Park. A short drive from Mt. Lofty Summit brings you to delightful Cleland Wildlife Park, where many animals roam free in three different forest habitats. Walking trails crisscross the park and

9

its surroundings, and you're guaranteed to see emus and kangaroos in the grasslands and pelicans around the swampy billabongs. There are also enclosures for wombats and other less sociable animals. Koala cuddling is a highlight of koala close-up sessions (daily 11–noon, 2–4). Monthly two-hour night walks (A$32 for adults, A$19.50 for children 3–14) let you wander among nocturnal species such as potoroos and brush-tailed bettongs. Private guided tours can be arranged for A$103 per hour weekdays, A$155 per hour on the weekends. Reservations are essential for tours. The park is closed when there's a fire ban (usually between December and February). ⊠ *Summit Rd.* ☎ *08/8339–2444* ⊕ *www.cleland.sa.gov.au* ✉ *A$18, A$11 children 3–14, A$49.50 family pass* ☉ *Daily 9:30–5.*

Mt. Lofty Botanic Gardens. Mt. Lofty Botanic Gardens, with its rhododendrons, magnolias, ferns, and exotic trees, is glorious in fall and spring; during these seasons, free guided walks leave the lower parking lot on Thursday at 10:30. ⊠ *Picadilly entrance off Lampert Rd.* ☎ *08/8370–8370* ⊕ *www.environment.sa.gov.au/botanicgardens* ✉ *Free* ☉ *Weekdays 8:30–4, weekends 10–5.*

WHERE TO EAT AND STAY

$$
ECLECTIC
★

✕ **Summit.** If you suffer from vertigo, think twice about dining here; this glass-front building atop Mt. Lofty is all about dining with altitude. The menu here is a frequently changing play of flavors; dishes might include spiced lamb rump with crushed minted peas and baby carrots. The wine list promotes Adelaide Hills vintages. While the food is good, you pay a premium for the view. ⊠ *Mt. Lofty Lookout* ☎ *08/8339–2600* ⚏ *Reservations essential* ☉ *No dinner Mon. and Tues.*

$$$

🍽 **Mt. Lofty House.** From very English garden terraces below the summit of Mt. Lofty, this refined country house overlooks a patchwork of vineyards, farms, and bushland. **Pros:** peaceful location in stunning surroundings. **Cons:** dated furniture in rooms, restaurant is overpriced. ⊠ *74 Summit Rd., Crafers* ☎ *08/8339–6777* 🖷 *08/8339–5656* ⊕ *www.mtloftyhouse.com.au* ➷ *25 rooms, 1 suite* ♿ *In-room: Wi-Fi. In-hotel: restaurant, bar, pool, tennis court* ⃓◯⃓ *Breakfast.*

BRIDGEWATER

6 km (4 mi) north of Mylor, 22 km (14 mi) southeast of Adelaide.

Bridgewater came into existence in 1841 as a refreshment stop for bullock teams fording Cock's Creek. More English than German, with its flowing creek and flower-filled gardens, this leafy, tranquil village was officially planned in 1859 by the builder of the first Bridgewater flour mill.

GETTING HERE AND AROUND

From the city center, drive onto the Mount Barker Expressway until you see the Stirling exit. From there, travel through lush countryside following the signs to Bridgewater. The town itself is small and walkable. By public transport, catch Bus 864 or 864F from Currie Street in the city to stop 45.

ESSENTIALS

Transportation Adelaide Metro Info Centre ✉ *Currie and King William Sts., City Center* ☎ *08/8210–1000* ⊕ *www.adelaidemetro.com.au.*

Bridgewater Mill. The handsome stone flour mill, built in 1860, stands at the western entrance to the town, where its waterwheel still churns away. These days the mill houses the first-class Petaluma's Bridgewater Mill Restaurant, where diners feast on fantastic local produce by the open fires in winter, or in the tree-covered beer garden in summer. The mill also serves as the shop front for Petaluma Wines, one of Australia's finest labels; try the Chardonnay and Viognier. The prestigious Croser champagne is matured on the building's lower level. ✉ *Bridgewater and Mt. Barker Rds.* ☎ *08/8339–9222* ✉ *Free* ☉ *Daily 10–5.*

WHERE TO EAT AND STAY

$$
✕ **Aldgate Pump Bistro.** You get a leisurely glimpse of local culture at this
ECLECTIC
friendly two-story country pub. There is an extensive, eclectic selection of hearty fare such as Pump platters with everything from chicken wings to spring rolls to oysters. Warmed by log fires in winter, the dining room overlooks a shaded beer garden. The place is 2 km (1 mi) from Bridgewater, in the delightful village of Aldgate. ✉ *Strathalbyn and Mt. Barker Rds., Aldgate* ☎ *08/8339–2015.*

$$$
✕ **Petaluma's Bridgewater Mill Restaurant.** A stylish and celebrated restau-
AUSTRALIAN
rant in a converted flour mill, this is one of the state's best dining spots.
Fodor's Choice
Using mostly local produce, new chef for 2011 Zac Ronayne creates an
★
imaginative contemporary menu; dishes might include organic chicken, black bean butter, radish, brocolini, and XO sauce. In summer, book ahead to get a table on the deck beside the waterwheel. If you're feeling flush, ask to see the special wine list. On Sunday and public holidays, eating here means a three-course set price (A$90 per person) menu. The mill also serves as the cellar door for Petaluma Wines, one of Australia's finest labels; the prestigious Croser champagne is matured on the building's lower level. ✉ *Mt. Barker Rd.* ☎ *08/8339–9200* ☉ *Closed Tues. and Wed. No dinner.*

$
✕ **Organic Market and Café.** Pram-wheeling parents, hikers resting their
CAFÉ
walking poles, and friends catching up on gossip keep this red-and-blue café and adjoining organic supermarket buzzing all day. Reasons to linger include focaccias, soups, home-baked muffins and cakes, and all kinds of purportedly healthy and unquestionably delicious drinks. While this establishment is in Stirling, about 3 km (2 mi) from Bridge-water, it's worth the short drive. ✉ *5 Druids Ave., Stirling* ☎ *08/8339–7131 café, 08/8339–4835 market* ☉ *No dinner.*

$$$$
🏨 **Thorngrove Manor Hotel.** This romantic Gothic folly of turrets and tow-
★
ers is *Lifestyles of the Rich and Famous* writ large. **Pros:** perfect for the archetypal romantic getaway. **Cons:** if you have to ask how expensive it is, you can't afford it. ✉ *2 Glenside La., Stirling* ☎ *08/8339–6748* ⊕ *www.slh.com/thorngrove* ⤙ *6 suites* ⚙ *In-room: safe, Internet. In-hotel: restaurant, business center* ⚑ *Breakfast.*

9

THE BAROSSA WINE REGION

Some of Australia's most famous vineyards are in the Barossa, just over an hour's drive northeast of Adelaide. More than 200 wineries across the two wide, shallow valleys that make up the region produce some of Australia's most celebrated wines, including aromatic Rhine Riesling, Seppelt's unique, century-old Para Port—and Penfolds Grange, which sells for more than A$600.

Cultural roots set the Barossa apart. The area was settled by Silesian immigrants who left the German–Polish border region in the 1840s to escape religious persecution. These farmers brought traditions that you can't miss in the solid bluestone architecture, the tall slender spires of the Lutheran churches, and the *kuchen*, a cake as popular as the Devonshire tea introduced by British settlers. Together, these elements give the Barossa a charm that is unique among Australian wine-growing areas.

Most wineries in the Barossa operate sale rooms—called cellar doors—that usually have 6 to 12 varieties of wine available for tasting. You are not expected to sample the entire selection; to do so would overpower your taste buds. It's far better to give the tasting-room staff some idea of your personal preferences and let them suggest wine for you to sample. Some cellar doors charge a A$5 tasting fee, refundable against any purchase.

There is also zero tolerance when it comes to drunk driving—the legal blood-alcohol limit is 0.05g/100ml—so the best advice is to get someone else to drive you round the wine regions if you're planning on tasting a glass or two.

GETTING HERE AND AROUND

The most direct route from Adelaide to the Barossa is via the town of Gawler. From Adelaide, drive north on King William Street. About 1 km (½ mi) past the Torrens River Bridge, take the right fork onto Main North Road. After 6 km (4 mi) this road forks to the right—follow signs to the Sturt Highway and the town of Gawler. At Gawler leave the highway and follow the signs to Lyndoch on the Barossa's southern border. The 50-km (31-mi) journey should take just more than an hour. A more attractive, if circuitous, route to Lyndoch takes you through the Adelaide Hills' Chain of Ponds and Williamstown.

Because the Barossa wineries are relatively far apart, a car is by far the best way to get around. But keep in mind that there are stiff penalties for driving under the influence of alcohol. Police in patrol cars can pull you over for a random breath test anywhere in the state, and roadside mobile breath-testing stations—locally known as "Booze Buses"—are particularly visible during special events, such as the biennial Barossa Vintage Festival, held over the Easter weekend in odd-numbered years. The best advice is to take a tour—**Barossa Epicurean Tours** (⊕ *www.barossatours.com.au*) are highly praised.

TOURS

Tracey and Tom Teichert have lived in the Barossa for 20 years and make excellent guides to the region's best wineries as well as where to buy some excellent local produce. They will make suggestions or they

The vineyards of the Barossa Valley.

will take you wherever you fancy. They can pick you up from Adelaide (A$160) or more cheaply, from anywhere in the Barossa. Gray Line Adelaide's full-day tour of the Barossa Region (A$128) leaves from Adelaide Central Bus Station. It includes lunch at a winery. Enjoy Adelaide runs a full-day (A$75) Barossa tour that visits four vineyards and includes lunch. Groovy Grape Getaways offers full-day (A$85) Barossa tours with a visit to the Adelaide Hills and a barbecue lunch.

9

ESSENTIALS

Tour Operators Barossa EpicureanTours ☎ 0402/989647 ⊕ www.barossatours. com.au. **Enjoy Adelaide** ☎ 08/8332–1401 ⊕ www.enjoyadelaide.com.au. **Gray Line Adelaide** ☎ 1300/858687 ⊕ www.grayline.com.au/adelaide. **Groovy Grape Getaways** ☎ 08/8440 1640, 1800/661177 ⊕ www.groovygrape.com.au.

Visitor Information Barossa Visitors Centre ✉ 66–68 Murray St., Tanunda ☎ 08/8563–0600, 1300/852–982 ⊕ www.barossa.com ☾ Weekdays 9–5, weekends 10–4.

LYNDOCH

58 km (36 mi) northeast of Adelaide.

This pleasant little town surrounded by vineyards was established in 1840 and is the Barossa's oldest settlement site. It owes the spelling of its name to a draftsman's error—it was meant to be named after the British soldier Lord Lynedoch.

Burge Family Winemakers. You can drink in a leafy vineyard view while tasting from the wine barrels in this understated cellar door. Winemaker

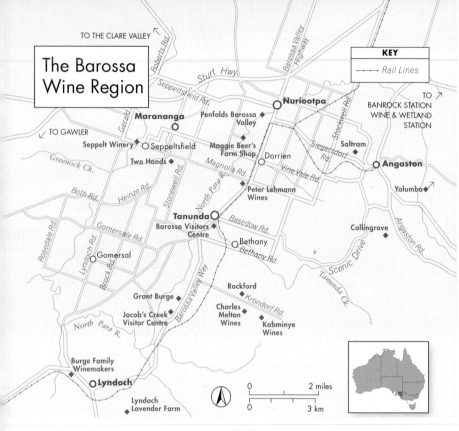

The Barossa Wine Region

TO THE CLARE VALLEY

TO GAWLER

KEY
Rail Lines

TO
BANROCK STATION
WINE & WETLAND
STATION

Roberts Rd.
Seppeltsfield Rd.
Sturt Hwy.
Barossa Valley Highway
Stockwell Rd.

Nuriootpa
Penfolds Barossa Valley
Marananga
Gerald
Seppelt Winery
Seppeltsfield
Two Hands
Maggie Beer's Farm Shop
Dorrien
Siegersdorf Rd.
Saltram
Vine Vale Rd.
Angaston
Yalumba
Greenock Ck.
Both Rd.
Heinze Rd.
Stonewell Rd.
Magnolia Rd.
North Para Rd.
Peter Lehmann Wines
Tanunda
Barossa Visitors Centre
Basedow Rd.
Collingrove
Bethany
Bethany Rd.
Scenic Drive
Angaston Rd.
Tanunda Ck.
Rosedale Rd.
Gomersale Rd.
Lyndoch Rd.
Brack Rd.
Gomersal
Rockford
Krondorf Rd.
Grant Burge
Barossa Valley Way
Jacob's Creek Visitor Centre
Charles Melton Wines
Kabminye Wines
North Para R.
Burge Family Winemakers
Lyndoch
Lyndoch Lavender Farm

0   2 miles
0   3 km

Rick Burge's best include the powerful yet elegant Draycott Shiraz and Olive Hill Shiraz-Grenache-Mourvedre blend. There is also sometimes A Nice Red—read the label! ⊠ *Barossa Valley Way near Hermann Thumm Dr.* ☎ *08/8524-4644* ⊕ *www.burgefamily.com.au* ☞ *Free* ⊗ *Fri., Sat., and Mon. 10–5 (call ahead).*

Lyndoch Lavender Farm. Lyndoch Lavender Farm, a family-friendly tribute to the purple flower that adorns the hills, grows more than 90 varieties on 6 lush acres high above Lyndoch. Light café meals are available, and the farm shop sells essential oils, creams, and other products, including wine from their adjacent vineyard. ⊠ *Corner of Hoffnungsthal and Tweedies Gully Rds.* ☎ *08/8524-4538* ⊕ *www. lyndochlavenderfarm.com.au* ☞ *A$2, children under 14 free* ⊗ *Open Feb.–July 10–4:30 weekends only, Aug.–Jan. daily 10–4:30.*

WHERE TO STAY
For expanded hotel reviews, visit Fodors.com.

$$$$
Fodor's Choice
★

Abbotsford Country House. Tranquillity reigns at this property on 50 acres of rolling beef farm with Barossa views. **Pros:** a serene and luxurious place to recover from all the wine tasting you will no doubt do, very welcoming hosts. **Cons:** dining in the restaurant is expensive, health nuts might rue the lack of gym and leisure facilities. ⊠ *Yaldara Dr. at Fuss Rd.* ✉ *Box 675, Lyndoch, SA5351* ☎ *08/8524-4662* ⊕ *www.*

abbotsfordhouse.com ⌐ 8 *rooms* ☐ *In-room: no TV, Wi-Fi. In-hotel: restaurant, some age restrictions* ❙◎❙ *Breakfast.*

$ ☐ **Belle Cottages.** Rose-filled gardens or sweeping rural acres surround these classic Australian accommodations. **Pros:** great discounts available for groups, comfortable and homely accommodation. **Cons:** not the place for an anonymous stay, some quirks to the plumbing. ☐ *Box 481, Lyndoch, SA5351* ☎ *08/8524–4825, 0411/108–800* ⊕ *www.bellescapes.com* ⌐ 11 *cottages, 3 suites* ☐ *In-room: kitchen. In-hotel: laundry facilities, some pets allowed* ❙◎❙ *Breakfast.*

> **TAKE IT SLOW**
>
> Allow yourself only one day in the Barossa and you'll regret it. Slow down and savor the food and wine and warm hospitality.

TANUNDA

13 km (8 mi) northeast of Lyndoch, 70 km (43 mi) northeast of Adelaide.

The cultural heart of the Barossa, Tanunda is its most German settlement. The four Lutheran churches in the town testify to its heritage, and dozens of shops selling German pastries, breads, and wursts (sausages)—not to mention wine—line the main street. Many of the valley's best wineries are close by.

Charles Melton Wines. At Charles Melton Wines tasting is relaxing and casual in a brick-floor, timber-wall cellar door, which is warmed by a log fire in winter. After making sure the resident cats have vacated it first, settle into a director's chair at the long wooden table and let the staff pour. Nine Popes, a huge, decadent red blend, is the flagship wine, and the ruby-red Rose of Virginia is arguably Australia's best rosé. You can enjoy a glass of either with a cheese platter or game pie on the veranda. ✉ *Krondorf Rd. near Nitschke Rd.* ☎ *08/8563–3606* ⊕ *www.charlesmeltonwines.com.au* ▧ *Free* ☽ *Daily 11–5.*

Grant Burge. Grant Burge is one of the most successful of the Barossa's young, independent wine labels. Wines include impressive Chardonnays, crisp Rieslings, and powerful reds such as Meshach Shiraz. Don't miss the Holy Trinity—a highly acclaimed Rhône blend of Grenache, Shiraz, and Mourvedre. The cellar door is at Jacob's Creek, 5 km (3 mi) south of Tanunda. Don't come hungry, as there isn't any food available here. ✉ *Barossa Valley Way near Koch Rd.* ☎ *08/8563–3700* ⊕ *www.grantburgewines.com.au* ▧ *Free* ☽ *Daily 10–5.*

Jacob's Creek Visitor Centre. An impressive block of glass, steel, and recycled timber, Jacob's Creek Visitor Centre overlooks the creek whose name is familiar to wine drinkers around the world, as they export to more than 60 countries. The informative staff makes the place well worth a visit—it's certainly more than your run-of-the-mill visitor center. Inside the building, plasma screens and pictorial displays tell the history of the label. Cabernet Sauvignon, Merlot, Chardonnay, and the Shiraz-rosé, served chilled, can be tasted at a 60-foot-long counter. There is a lunch-only restaurant with broad glass doors opening onto a grassy lawn edged with towering eucalyptus trees, and there are workshops and tours you can join. ✉ *Barossa Valley Way near Jacob's Creek* ☎ *08/8521–3000*

9

⊕ *www.jacobscreek.com* ✉ *Free* ⊙ *Daily 10–5.*

★ **Kabminye Wines.** Built from local mud brick and corrugated iron, with a winglike roof, the light-filled cellar door at Kabminye Wines was a controversial addition to the valley—but there's no argument about the wines and the food. Each wine has its own unique and surprising taste, particularly the excellent Ilona rosé and the full-frontal flagship Hubert Shiraz. The Krondorf Road Café cooks up traditional Silesian fare with a focus on locally produced products, and the staff are really passionate about the region. Changing art exhibitions are often displayed in the upstairs gallery. ✉ *Krondorf Rd. near Nitschke Rd.* ☎ *08/8563–0889* ⊕ *www.kabminye.com* ✉ *Free* ⊙ *Daily 11–5.*

Peter Lehmann Wines. Peter Lehmann Wines is owned by a larger-than-life Barossa character whose wine consistently wins international awards. Art-hung stonework and a wood-burning fireplace make the tasting room one of the most pleasant in the valley. This is the only place to find Black Queen Sparkling Shiraz. Wooden tables on a shady lawn encourage picnicking on Barossa platters. Served daily, it's full of local produce and big enough for two. They also offer VIP tastings in a private room with food matchings. But you must book in advance. ✉ *Para Rd. off Stelzer Rd.* ☎ *08/8563–2500* ⊕ *www.peterlehmannwines.com.au* ✉ *Free* ⊙ *Weekdays 9:30–5, weekends 10:30–4:30.*

★ **Rockford.** Nestled in a lovely cobbled stable yard, Rockford is a small winery with a tasting room in an old stone barn. The specialties are heavy, rich wines made from some of the region's oldest vines. Several notable labels have appeared under the Rockford name—be sure to try the Cabernet Sauvignon and the Basket Press Shiraz (at cellar door from March until sold out), outstanding examples of these most traditional of Australian varieties. The owners pride themselves on their old-school methods. The same equipment (you can see in the yard) has been used for over a century. ✉ *Krondorf Rd. near Nitschke Rd.* ☎ *08/8563–2720* ⊕ *www.rockfordwines.com.au* ✉ *Free* ⊙ *Daily 11–5.*

WHERE TO EAT AND STAY
For expanded hotel reviews, visit Fodors.com.

$$
AUSTRALIAN
✕ **1918 Bistro & Grill.** This rustic and whimsical restaurant in a restored villa makes exemplary use of the Barossa's distinctive regional produce in a seasonal Oz menu flavored with tastes from Asia and the Middle East. Local olive oil and seasonal fruits and vegetables influence dishes like the delicious char-grilled octopus with cauliflower skordalia, pancetta, ruby grapefruit, and truffle oil. Meals are served beside a two-sided fireplace in winter and alfresco in the garden in summer. The

mostly Barossa wine list includes rare classics and newcomers. ✉ *94 Murray St.* ☎ *08/8563–0405* ✍ *Reservations essential.*

¢

GERMAN ✕ **Die Barossa Wurst Haus & Bakery.** For a hearty German lunch at a reasonable price, no place beats this small, friendly café and shop. The wurst is fresh from local butchers, the sauerkraut is direct from Germany, and the potato salad is made on-site from a secret recipe. ✉ *86A Murray St.* ☎ *08/8563–3598* ▭ *No credit cards* ⊘ *No dinner.*

$ ⊡ **Blickinstal Barossa Valley Retreat.** Its name means "view into the valley," which understates the breathtaking panoramas from this lovely B&B. **Pros:** great-value rooms with superb views across the valley, complimentary port in the evening. **Cons:** don't expect corporate-style facilities or an anonymous stay. ✉ *Box 17, Rifle Range Rd.5352* ☎ *08/8563–2716, 0419/868–921* ⊕ *www.users.bigpond.com/blickinstal* ⋌ *4 studios, 2 apartments* ⚭ *In-room: kitchen. In-hotel: laundry facilities, business center* ⍾ *Breakfast.*

$$ ⊡ **Lawley Farm.** Amid 20 acres of grapes, in a courtyard shaded by
★ gnarled peppercorn trees, these delightful stone cottage-style suites were assembled from the remains of barns dating from the Barossa's pioneering days. **Pros:** original buildings have been lovingly preserved, the breakfasts are legendary. **Cons:** no exercise facilities for working off all the local wine and produce. ✉ *Krondorf and Grocke Rds., Box 103* ☎ *08/8563–2141* ⊕ *www.lawleyfarm.com.au* ⋌ *4 suites* ⚭ *In-room: Internet. In-hotel: business center* ⍾ *Breakfast.*

ANGASTON

16 km (10 mi) northeast of Tanunda via Menglers Hill Rd. Scenic Drive, 86 km (53 mi) northeast of Adelaide.

Named after George Fife Angas, the Englishman who founded the town and sponsored many of the German and British immigrants who came here, Angaston is full of jacaranda trees, and its main street is lined with stately stone buildings and tiny shops. Schulz Butchers has been making and selling wurst (German sausage) since 1939; 17 varieties hang above the counter. You can buy other delicious regional produce every Saturday morning at the Barossa Farmers Market, behind Vintners Bar & Grill.

Collingrove. Collingrove was the ancestral home of the Angas family, the descendants of George Fife Angas, one of South Australia's founders. At the height of its fortunes, the family controlled more than 14 million acres from this house. Today the property is administered by the National Trust, and you can inspect the Angas family portraits and memorabilia, including Dresden china, a hand-painted Louis XV cabinet, and Chippendale chairs, on guided tours. You can also stay overnight at Collingrove in evocative Old World B&B luxury. ✉ *Eden Valley Rd. near Collingrove Rd.* ☎ *08/8564–2061* ⊕ *www. collingrovehomestead.com.au* ⊟ *A$8* ⊘ *Tours weekdays 12–3, weekends 12–4; booking advised, as hotel guests get priority.*

Saltram. Low-beamed ceilings and ivy-covered trellises give Saltram an urbanized sort of rustic charm. The vineyard's robust wine list includes the Pepperjack Barossa Grenache Rosé, a delightful vintage available

9

only in summer. It's a delicious accompaniment to the Italian-influenced menu at the adjacent—and excellent—Salter's Kitchen restaurant. ⊠ *Murray St.* 📞 *08/8561–0200* ⊕ *www.saltramwines.com.au* ✉ *Free* ◷ *Daily 10–5.*

Yalumba. Australia's oldest family-owned winery, Yalumba sits within a hugely impressive compound resembling an Italian monastery. The cellar door is decorated with mission-style furniture, antique wine-making materials, and mementos of the Hill Smith family, who first planted vines in the Barossa in 1849. The Octavius Shirazes are superb, and the "Y Series" Viognier is thoroughly enjoyable. ⊠ *Eden Valley Rd. just south of Valley Rd.* 📞 *08/8561–3200* ⊕ *www.yalumba. com* ✉ *Free* ◷ *Daily 10–5.*

SHIPPING WINE

Wouldn't it be wonderful if international airlines showed some empathy for wine fanciers and stopped charging exorbitant excess baggage fees for cases of wine? In the meantime you can appeal to the better nature of the Barossa vignerons who sell overseas or can arrange shipping.

WHERE TO EAT

$$$
AUSTRALIAN
★

✕ **Vintners Bar & Grill.** The Barossa region is at its best in this sophisticated spot, where vivid contemporary artworks adorn the walls and wide windows look out on rows of vineyards. The short menu blends Australian, Mediterranean, and Asian flavors in such dishes as delicious truffled leek risotto with confit duck leg, roasted apple, and pinot jus. Scarlet and charcoal suede chairs and an upbeat jazz sound track make it easy to relax; top winemakers often come here to sample from the cellar's 160 wines. ⊠ *Nuriootpa Rd. near Stockwell Rd.* 📞 *08/8564–2488* ⌂ *Reservations essential* ◷ *No dinner Sun.*

NURIOOTPA

8 km (5 mi) northwest of Angaston, 74 km (46 mi) northeast of Adelaide.

Long before it was the Barossa's commercial center, Nuriootpa was used as a bartering place by local Aboriginal tribes, hence its name: Nuriootpa means "meeting place." Most locals call it Nurie.

★ **Maggie Beer's Farm Shop.** Renowned cook and food writer Maggie Beer is an icon of Australian cuisine. Burned-fig jam, ice cream, *verjuice* (a golden liquid made from unfermented grape juice and used for flavoring), and her signature Pheasant Farm Pâté are some of the delights you can taste and buy at Maggie Beer's Farm Shop. Treat-filled picnic baskets are available all day to take out or dip into on the deck overlooking a tree-fringed pond full of turtles. Don't miss the daily cooking demonstrations at 2 pm. ⊠ *End of Pheasant Farm Rd. off Samuel Rd.* 📞 *08/8562–4477* ⊕ *www.maggiebeer.com.au* ✉ *Free, but bookings are required for cooking demonstrations for groups of 10 or more* ◷ *Daily 10:30–5.*

Penfolds Barossa Valley. A very big brother to the 19th-century Magill Estate in Adelaide, this massive wine-making outfit in the center of Nuriootpa lets you taste Shiraz, Cabernet, Merlot, Chardonnay, and

Fish Tales

With nearly 4,800 km (3,000 mi) of coastline and hundreds of miles of rivers, South Australia has almost as many opportunities for fishing as it has varieties of fish. You can join local anglers of all ages dangling hand lines from a jetty, casting into the surf from coastal rocks, hopping aboard charter boats, or spending a day sitting on a riverside log.

The Murray River is the place to head for callop (also called yellow belly or golden perch) and elusive Murray cod. In the river's backwaters you can also net a feed of yabbies, a type of freshwater crayfish, which make a wonderful appetizer before you tuck into the one that didn't get away. In the ocean King George whiting reigns supreme, but there is also excellent eating with mulloway, bream, snapper, snook, salmon, and sweep. The yellowtail kingfish, a great fighter usually found in deep water, prefers the shallower waters of Coffin Bay, off the Eyre Peninsula.

Baird Bay Charters & Ocean Eco Experience. Baird Bay Charters & Ocean Eco Experience runs fishing charters to Coffin Bay and other top spots. ☎ 08/8626–5017 ⊕ www.bairdbay.com.

Another popular destination is the Yorke Peninsula.

S.A. Fishing Adventures. S.A. Fishing Adventures takes anglers to great spots around the Yorke Peninsula. ☎ 08/8854–4098 ⊕ www.safishingadventures.com.au.

Last, but certainly not least, is legendary Kangaroo Island.

Kangaroo Island Fishing Charters. You can spend from a few hours to a few days fishing the waters around Kangaroo Island with Kangaroo Island Fishing Charters. ☎ 08/8552–7000 ⊕ www.kifishchart.com.au.

–Melanie Ball

9

Riesling blends—but not the celebrated Grange—at the cellar door. To savor the flagship wine and other premium vintages, book a Taste of Grange Tour (A$150 per person, minimum of two). ⊠ *Barossa Valley Hwy. at Railway Terr.* ☎ *08/8568–9408* ⊕ *www.penfolds.com.au* 🖃 *Free* ☉ *Daily 10–5.*

OFF THE
BEATEN
PATH

Banrock Station Wine & Wetland Centre. The salt-scrub-patched Murray River floodplain 150 km (94 mi) east of Nuriootpa is an unlikely setting for a winery, but it is worth making the journey to this spot at Kingston-on-Murray. Within the stilted, mud-brick building perched above the vineyard and river lagoons you can select a wine to accompany an all-day grazing platter or lunch on the outdoor deck—try the pan-seared Murray Cod with corn puree, braised spring onions, and beetroot chips. Afterward, you can take an 8-km (5-mi) walk (A$5, bookings essential) to view the surrounding wetlands (which can be "drylands" during a drought), and learn about the ongoing wildlife habitat restoration and conservation work funded by Banrock Station wine sales. ⊠ *Holmes Rd. just off Sturt Hwy., Kingston-on-Murray* ☎ *08/8583–0299* ⊕ *www.banrockstation.com.au* 🖃 *Free* ☉ *Daily 9–5.*

Stomping the grapes at the Barossa Vintage Festival.

MARANANGA

6 km (4 mi) west of Nuriootpa, 68 km (42 mi) northeast of Adelaide.

The tiny hamlet of Marananga inhabits one of the prettiest corners of the Barossa. This area's original name was Gnadenfrei, which means "freed by the grace of God"—a reference to the religious persecution the German settlers suffered before they emigrated to Australia. Marananga, the Aboriginal name, was adopted in 1918, when a wave of anti-German sentiment spurred many name changes in the closing days of World War I.

★ **Seppelt Winery.** Joseph Seppelt was a Silesian farmer who purchased land in the Barossa after arriving in Australia in 1849. Under the control of his son, Benno, the wine-making business flourished, and today Seppelt Winery and its splendid grounds are a tribute to the family's industry and enthusiasm. Fortified wine is a Seppelt specialty; this is the only winery in the world that has ports for every year as far back as 1878. Most notable is the 100-year-old Para Liqueur Tawny. The Grenache, Chardonnay, Cabernet, and sparkling Shiraz are also worth tasting. Tours of the 19th-century distillery are run daily; you can also book 24 hours ahead for the Centenary Tour, where you get to taste four of the six paramount wines as well a 100 year-old wine and one that was 100 years old in your birth year. There's a small snack bar that offers delicious cakes and afternoon teas. ⊠ *Seppeltsfield Rd., 3 km (2 mi) west of Marananga, Seppeltsfield* ☎ *08/8568–6217* ⊕ *www.seppelt. com* ➲ *Free; Heritage Tour A$15, Centenary Tour A$79, Legend of Seppelt tour A$95* ☉ *10:30–5. Heritage Tours daily 11:30, 1:30, and 3:30; Centenary Tour daily (by appointment) 2:30; Legend of Seppelt weekends (by appointment) 10:30 and 2:30.*

★ **Two Hands.** The interior of this 19th-century sandstone cottage is every bit as surprising as the wines produced here. Polished wood and glass surround the contemporary counter where the excellent staff leads you through the tasting of several "out of the box" red and white varietals and blends. The main event is Shiraz sourced from six wine regions. Compare and contrast Shiraz from Victoria and Padthaway (South Australia); and try the Barossa-grown Bad Impersonator. From Thursday to Sunday you can join a structured Masterclass Tasting (maximum 8 people, bookings recommended) in the adjoining bakehouse, which has a glass floor over the original cellar. There are also fantastic tasting plates available in the adjoining dining area. ✉ *Neldner Rd. just off Seppeltsfield Rd.* ☎ *08/8562–4566* ⊕ *www.twohandswines. com* ✉ *General Tastings A$5 (refundable with purchase), Bakehouse Masterclass A$25* ⊘ *Daily 10–5.*

WHERE TO STAY

For expanded hotel reviews, visit Fodors.com.

$$$$ ⚏ **The Lodge Country House.** Rambling and aristocratic, this bluestone
★ homestead 3 km (2 mi) south of Marananga was built in 1903 for one of the 13 children of Joseph Seppelt, founder of the showpiece winery across the road. **Pros:** beautiful gardens, informative hosts who delight in telling guests about the history of the place. **Cons:** not particularly suitable for kids. ✉ *Seppeltsfield Rd., 3 km (2 mi) west of Marananga, Seppeltsfield* ☎ *08/8562–8277* ⊕ *www.thelodgecountryhouse.com.au* ⤳ *4 double rooms* ⚘ *In-room: no TV. In-hotel: restaurant, pool, tennis court, some age restrictions* �’⃝ *Breakfast.*

$$$$ ⚏ **The Louise.** Prepare for pampering and privacy at this country estate on a quiet back road with glorious valley views. **Pros:** stunning rooms with beautiful private gardens. **Cons:** extras like Internet access are annoyingly expensive, pool and spa could use a facelift. ✉ *Seppeltsfield and Stonewell Rds.* ☎ *08/8562–2722, 08/8562–4144 restaurant* ⊕ *thelouise.com.au, restaurant www.appellation.com.au* ⤳ *15 suites* ⚘ *In-room: safe, Internet, Wi-Fi. In-hotel: restaurant, bar, pool, business center* �’⃝ *Breakfast.*

9

THE CLARE VALLEY

Smaller and less well known than the Barossa, the Clare Valley nonetheless holds its own among Australia's wine-producing regions. Its robust reds and delicate whites are among the country's finest, and the Clare is generally regarded as the best area in Australia for fragrant, flavorsome Rieslings. On the fringe of the vast inland deserts, the Clare is a narrow sliver of fertile soil about 30 km (19 mi) long and 5 km (3 mi) wide, with a microclimate that makes it ideal for premium wine making.

The first vines were planted here as early as 1842, but it took a century and a half for the Clare Valley to take its deserved place on the national stage. The mix of small family wineries and large-scale producers, 150-year-old settlements and grand country houses, snug valleys and dense native forests, has rare charm.

GETTING HERE AND AROUND

The Clare Valley is about a 90-minute drive from Adelaide via Main North Road. From the center of Adelaide, head north on King William Street through the heart of North Adelaide. King William becomes O'Connell Street. After crossing Barton Terrace, look for Main North Road signs on the right. The road passes through the satellite town of Elizabeth, bypasses the center of Gawler, and then runs due north to Auburn, the first town of the Clare Valley when approaching from the capital. Main North Road continues down the middle of the valley to Clare.

As with the Barossa, a car is essential for exploring the Clare Valley in any depth. Taste wine in moderation if you're driving; as well as keeping yourself and others safe, you'll avoid paying the extremely high penalties for driving while intoxicated.

TOURS

Clare Valley Tours combines wine tasting with history and culture on its daylong tour of the region's major towns and sites (A$100 including lunch), departing from Clare. Barossa Epicurean Tours also offer a Clare option.

Contact **Clare Valley Tours** ☎ 0418/832–812, 08/8843–8066 ⊕ www.cvtours.com.au. **Barossa EpicureanTours** ☎ 0402/989647, 08/8564–2191 ⊕ www.barossatours.com.au.

ESSENTIALS

Visitor Information **Clare Valley Visitor Information Centre** ✉ Main North and Spring Gully Rds., 6 km (4 mi) south of Clare, Clare ☎ 1800/242–131, 08/8842–2131 ⊕ www.clarevalley.com.au ⊙ Weekdays 9–5, weekends and public holidays 10–4.

SEVENHILL

126 km (78 mi) north of Adelaide.

Sevenhill is the Clare Valley's geographic center, and the location of the region's first winery, established by Jesuit priests in 1851 to produce altar wine. The area had been settled three years earlier by Austrian Jesuits who named their seminary after the seven hills of Rome.

The Riesling Trail, a walking and cycling track that follows an old Clare Valley railway line, runs through Sevenhill. The 35-km (22-mi) trail passes wineries and villages in gently rolling country between Auburn and Clare, and three loop trails take you to vineyards off the main track.

Clare Valley Cycle Hire. Bikes can be rented from Clare Valley Cycle Hire. ✉ 32 Victoria Rd., Clare ☎ 0418/802–077, 08/8842–2782.

Kilikanoon Wines. A rising star of the Clare Valley, Kilikanoon is already renowned for multilayered reds, such as the dense, richly colored Oracle Shiraz (occasionally available for tasting); Prodigal Grenache is another beauty. ✉ Penna La., Penwortham, 2 km (1 mi) off Main North Rd. ☎ 08/8843–4206 ⊕ www.kilikanoon.com.au ⊡ Free ⊙ Thurs.–Mon. 11–5.

Fodor's Choice
★

Sevenhill Cellars. The area's first winery, Sevenhill Cellars was created by the Jesuits, and they still run the show, with any profits going to education, mission work, and the needy within Australia. In the 1940s the winery branched out from sacramental wine to commercial production, and today 21 wine varieties, including Riesling (try the St. Aloysius label), Verdelho, Grenache, and fortified wines, account for 75% of its business. Book a guided tour with the charming Brother John May, Jesuit winemaker emeritus, who takes you to the cellars, the cemetery, and the church crypt where Jesuits have been interred since 1865. You can also rent bicycles here to explore the rolling hills and vineyards. ✉ *College Rd. just off Main North Rd.* ☎ *08/8843–4222* ⊕ *www.sevenhillcellars.com.au* ✉ *Free; tours A$7.50* ⊙ *Weekdays 9–5, weekends 10–5; tours Tues. and Thurs. at 2.*

Skillogalee Winery. Skillogalee Winery is known for its excellent Riesling, Gewürztraminer, and Shiraz, as well as its wonderful restaurant. Wine tasting takes place in a small room in the 1850s cottage (the restaurant occupies the others). Don't miss the sparkling Riesling. ✉ *Hughes Park Rd.* ☎ *08/8843–4311* ⊕ *www.skillogalee.com* ✉ *Free* ⊙ *Daily 10–5.*

WHERE TO EAT

$$
AUSTRALIAN

✕ **Rising Sun.** People have watched the world go by from the veranda of this landmark hotel in Auburn, 16 km (10 mi) south of Sevenhill, since it was built in 1849. Pull up a chair overlooking the street and partake of the delicious modern Australian food, perhaps kangaroo fillet with quandong (a native fruit) and sweet-potato mash, or butterfish in a batter of Coopers Pale Ale (Adelaide's own beer). The wine list shows off the Clare Valley's best. ✉ *19 Main North Rd., Auburn* ☎ *08/8849–2015.*

$$
AUSTRALIAN
★

✕ **Skillogalee Winery.** The dining area here spills from a 1850s cottage onto a beautiful veranda overlooking a flower-filled garden and rows of grapevines. The menu changes seasonally, but you can't go wrong with the "vine pruner's lunch," chef Diana Palmer's spin on the British plowman's meal, a platter of rum-glazed local ham, cheddar cheese, chutney, and crusty bread. Entrées might include fish tagine with olives, apricots, and Skillogalee figs with saffron and lemon couscous or dukkah-crusted chicken breast. While most Clare restaurants have limited hours, Skillogalee is so popular it's open 7 days a week. Gourmet picnic baskets can be ordered, and group dinners are available by prior arrangement. Skillogalee also has self-contained cottage accommodation. ✉ *Hughes Park Rd.* ☎ *08/8843–4311* ⚑ *Reservations essential* ⊙ *No dinner.*

CLARE

10 km (6 mi) north of Sevenhill, 136 km (84 mi) north of Adelaide.

The bustling town of Clare is the Clare Valley's commercial center. Unusual for ultra-English South Australia, many of its early settlers were Irish—hence the valley's name, after the Irish county Clare, and place-names such as Armagh and Donnybrook.

★ **Tim Adams Wines.** The small, no-frills tasting room means there is nothing to distract you from discovering why Tim Adams Wines has a big reputation. The standout in an impressive collection of reds and whites, which includes a celebrated Riesling and delicious Pinot Gris, is the purple-red Aberfeldy Shiraz, made from hundred-year-old vines. You can buy wine by the glass and bottle to enjoy with a bring-your-own-picnic on the veranda. ⊠ *Warenda Rd. just off Main North Rd., 5 km (3 mi) south of Clare* ☎ *1800/356–326, 08/8842-2429* ⊕ *www. timadamswines.com.au* 🖾 *Free* ⊙ *Weekdays 10:30–5, weekends 11–5.*

WHERE TO STAY

For expanded hotel reviews, visit Fodors.com.

¢   🏨 **Bungaree Station.** Your journey back to colonial Australia begins at check-in at this family-owned farm; the reception area is in the original station store. **Pros:** fascinating insight into a working homestead, accommodation options for all budgets. **Cons:** city types might find it too rustic, food options are limited. ⊠ *Main North Rd., 12 km (7 mi) north of Clare* ☎ *08/8842-2677* ⊕ *www.bungareestation.com.au* 📑 *7 cottages, 3 rooms with shared bathrooms* ⌂ *In-room: no a/c, kitchen, no TV. In-hotel: pool, gym.*

$$$$ 🏨 **North Bundaleer.** The spoils of wealthy pastoral life await you at this
Fodor's Choice   century-old sandstone homestead 61 km (38 mi) north of Clare, on the
★   scenic route to the Flinders Ranges. **Pros:** relaxed and informal despite the grandeur, perfect for getting away from it all. **Cons:** city types might find it too secluded and intimate. ⊠ *Spalding–Jamestown Rd., Jamestown* ⬦ *Box 255, Jamestown 5491* ☎ *08/8665-4024* ⊕ *www. northbundaleer.com.au* 📑 *3 rooms, 1 suite* ⌂ *In-room: no a/c, no TV. In-hotel: restaurant, bar, pool* ¶⊙¶ *Multiple meal plans.*

FLEURIEU PENINSULA

The Fleurieu has traditionally been seen as Adelaide's backyard. Generations of local families have vacationed in the string of beachside resorts between Victor Harbor and Goolwa, near the mouth of the Murray River. McLaren Vale wineries attract connoisseurs, and the beaches and bays bring in surfers, swimmers, and sunseekers. The countryside, with its rolling hills and dramatic cliff scenery, is a joy to drive through.

Although the region is within easy reach of Adelaide, you should consider spending the night if you want to enjoy all it has to offer. You can also easily combine a visit here with one or more nights on Kangaroo Island. The ferry from Cape Jervis, at the end of the peninsula, takes less than an hour to reach Penneshaw on the island, and there are coach connections from Victor Harbor and Goolwa.

GETTING HERE AND AROUND

Renting a car in Adelaide and driving south is the best way to visit the Fleurieu Peninsula, especially if you wish to tour the wineries, which aren't served by public transportation.

The Fleurieu is an easy drive south from Adelaide. McLaren Vale itself is less than an hour away. Leave central Adelaide along South Terrace or West Terrace, linking with the Anzac Highway, which heads toward Glenelg. At the Gallipoli Underpass intersection with Main South Road,

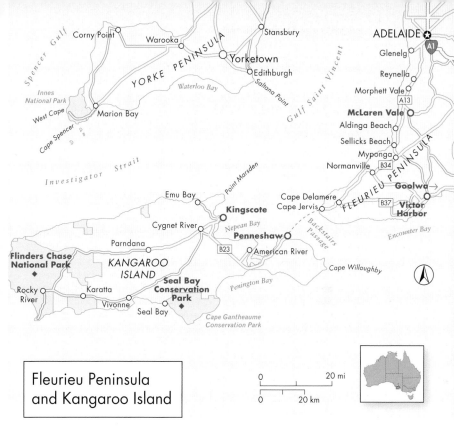

Fleurieu Peninsula
and Kangaroo Island

0 ———— 20 mi
0 ———— 20 km

turn left. This road takes you almost to McLaren Vale. After a detour to visit the wineries, watch for signs for Victor Harbor Road. About 20 km (12 mi) south the highway splits. One road heads for Victor Harbor, the other for Goolwa. Those two places are connected by a major road that follows the coastline. Drivers heading to Cape Jervis and the Kangaroo Island ferries should stay on Main South Road.

ESSENTIALS

Visitor Information **McLaren Vale and Fleurieu Visitor Centre** ⊠ *Main St., McLaren Vale* ☎ *08/8323-9944* ⊕ *www.mclarenvale.info* ⊘ *Mon–Fri 9–5, weekends and public holidays 10–4.* **Victor Harbor Visitor Information Centre** ⊠ *The Causeway, Victor Harbor* ☎ *08/8557-0777, 1800/557-094* ⊕ *www.tourismvictorharbor.com.au* ⊘ *Daily 9–5.*

MCLAREN VALE

39 km (24 mi) south of Adelaide.

The nearest wine region to Adelaide, this area has a distinctly modern, upscale look, even though many of the more than 80 wineries in and around town are as old as their Barossa peers. The first vines were planted in 1838 at northern Reynella by Englishman John Reynell, who had collected them en route from the Cape of Good Hope.

The McLaren Vale region has always been known for its big—and softer—reds, including Shiraz, as well as a few white varietals. Local microbrewed beer is also becoming an increasingly popular attraction in the region.

Coriole Vineyards. The 1860s stone cellar door at Coriole Vineyards sits among nasturtiums and hollyhocks on a hill with stunning St. Vincent Gulf views. From the surrounding vines, winemakers Simon White and Mark Lloyd make some of Australia's best Italian varietal wines, such as Sangiovese and Nebbiolo. Coriole grows olives, too, and you can taste olive oils as well as wine. Enjoy a platter of estate-grown and local produce—cheese, smoked kangaroo, roasted vegetables, and chutney—in the flagstone courtyard (Friday to Monday). The hosted tastings led by Tim Nicholls are excellent and should be booked ahead. ⊠ *Chaffeys Rd. near Kays Rd.* ☎ *08/8323–8305* ⊕ *www.coriole.com* ☞ *Free* ⊙ *Weekdays 10–5, weekends 11–5.*

d'Arenberg Wines. A fine restaurant complements excellent wine at d'Arenberg Wines, family-run since 1912. Winemaker Chester d'Arenberg Osborn is known for his quality whites, including the luscious Noble Riesling dessert wine, as well as powerful reds and fortified wines with equally compelling names. Reservations are essential for d'Arry's fine-dining Verandah restaurant, which overlooks the vineyards, the valley, and the sea. The tempting seasonal lunch-only menu uses local produce for its Mod-Oz dishes. ⊠ *Osborn Rd.* ☎ *1800/882–335 cellar door, 08/8329–4848 restaurant* ⊕ *www.darenberg.com.au* ☞ *Free* ⊙ *Daily 10–5.*

Pertaringa. On a quiet, unpaved back road, boutique winery Pertaringa (meaning "belonging to the hills") makes limited quantities of mouth-filling reds and several whites. At the cellar door, facing the vines, you can sip Two Gentlemen's Grenache and Scarecrow Sauvignon Blanc, a great accompaniment to a bring-your-own picnic. It is worth buying some of the premium Over the Top Shiraz even without tasting—you won't be disappointed. ⊠ *Hunt and Rifle Range Rd.* ☎ *08/8323–8125* ⊕ *www.pertaringa.com.au* ☞ *Free* ⊙ *Weekdays 10–5, weekends 11–5.*

WHERE TO EAT AND STAY

For expanded hotel reviews, visit Fodors.com.

¢ ✕ **Blessed Cheese.** It's hard to disappoint when cheese and chocolate are
AUSTRALIAN   your specialties, particularly when they're adeptly paired with local wines. Blessed cheese is a unique combination of cheese shop, licensed cafe, and provedore specializing in artisan cheeses, local and imported gourmet foods, and regional produce. You can pack a picnic for the day with platters for two available from A$30, dine in their licensed cafe with a regional breakfast or lunch, relax with cake and coffee, or sample their delicious range of cheese. ⊠ *150 Main Rd.* ☎ *08/8323–7958* ⊙ *Mon.–Thurs. 8–4:30, Fri.–Sun. 8–5* ⊙ *No dinner.*

$ ✕ **Market 190.** With its worn floorboards and pressed-metal ceilings,
AUSTRALIAN   this café feels like a country corner store. Bottled olive oil and local
★   jams line the shelves, and an assortment of cakes, savory baked goods, and cheeses fills the glass-front counter. Come early for a cup of coffee

and the best breakfast outside Adelaide. The menu shows off Fleurieu Peninsula produce: for a taste of McLaren Vale, order a regional platter, and for something spicier, tuck into gluten-free salt-and-pepper squid (in season). To finish, try the lemon-curd tart. Book ahead for weekends. Afterwards, check out the Almond Train next door, where everything nut-related can be bought from this converted railway carriage. ⊠ *190 Main Rd.* ☎ *08/8323–8558* ⊕ *www.market190.com. au* ☾ *No dinner.*

$$ ✕ **Star of Greece.** More for the linen-slacks-and-deck-shoes set than
AUSTRALIAN the board-shorts-and-sunscreen crowd, this extended weatherboard
★ kiosk on the cliffs at Port Willunga, 10 km (6 mi) southwest of McLaren Vale, is beach-ball bright and extremely popular. Wooden chairs painted in mandarin, lime, and sky-blue stripes sit at paper-draped tables, and windows frame the aqua sea. (The offshore buoy marks where the three-masted *Star of Greece* foundered in 1888.) Reading the menu nets mostly seafood. You could order seared scallops wrapped in octopus bacon, or crispy skinned ocean trout on prawn salsa, but every white-plated dish the hip staff carries past may make you question your choice. ⊠ *The Esplanade 1, Port Willunga* ☎ *08/8557–7420* ⊕ *www.starofgreececafe.com.au* ⚲ *Reservations essential* ☾ *No dinner Sun.–Thurs., no lunch Mon. and Tues.; kiosk open 7 days weather permitting.*

$$ ⊞ **Willunga House B&B.** Parquet floors, pressed-metal ceilings, and marble fireplaces are among the original features in this inviting 1850s Georgian-style residence. **Pros:** oodles of rustic charm, beautiful organic garden to wander around in. **Cons:** not ideal for an anonymous stay because of the size, two-day minimum stay at weekends. ⊠ *1 St. Peter's Terr., Willunga* ☎ *08/8556–2467* ⊕ *www.willungahouse.com.au* ⤴ *5 rooms* ⚘ *In-room: no a/c, Internet. In-hotel: restaurant, pool, business center, some age restrictions* �‖ *Breakfast.*

$$$ ⊞ **Wine and Roses B&B.** It may look like a regular residential house from the outside, but this luxury B&B has an interior that's far from ordinary. **Pros:** perfect for a romantic getaway, the complimentary port is delicious. **Cons:** if all four suites are booked it's a little cramped, not child-friendly. ⊠ *39 Caffrey St.* ☎ *08/8323–7654* ⊕ *www.wineandroses. com.au* ⤴ *4 suites* ⚘ *In-room: safe, kitchen, Wi-Fi. In-hotel: restaurant, some age restrictions* �‖ *Breakfast.*

GOOLWA

44 km (27 mi) southeast of McLaren Vale, 83 km (51 mi) south of Adelaide.

Beautifully situated near the mouth of the mighty Murray River, which travels some 2,415 km (1,594 mi) from its source in New South Wales, Goolwa grew fat on the 19th-century river paddle-steamer trade. Today, with its enviable position close to the sea and the combined attractions of Lake Alexandrina and Coorong National Park, tourism has replaced river trade as the main source of income.

☺ **Goolwa Wharf.** Goolwa Wharf is the launching place for daily tour cruises. The *Spirit of the Coorong,* a fully equipped motorboat, has both a four-and-a-half-hour (A$78) or six-hour cruise (A$92) to Coorong

National Park. Both include guided walks, lunch, and afternoon tea. ✉ *Goolwa Wharf* ☎ *08/8555–2203, 1800/442203 tour cruises* ⊕ *www. coorongcruises.com.au.*

Oscar W. Goolwa is also the home port of paddle-steamer *Oscar W.* Built in 1908, it's one of the few remaining wood-fired boiler ships. This boat holds the record for bringing the most bales of wool (2,500) along the Darling River, which flows into the Murray River. When not participating in commemorative cruises and paddleboat races, the boat is open for inspection. ✉ *Goolwa Wharf* ☎ *1300/466–592* ⊕ *www.oscar-w.info* 🕮 *Donation to inspect boat, fees charged for cruises.*

VICTOR HARBOR

18 km (11 mi) west of Goolwa, 83 km (51 mi) south of Adelaide.

As famous for its natural beauty and wildlife as for its resorts, Victor Harbor is South Australia's favorite seaside getaway. In 1802 English and French explorers Matthew Flinders and Nicolas Baudin met here at Encounter Bay, and by 1830 the harbor was a major whaling center. Pods of southern right whales came here to breed in winter, and they made for a profitable trade through the mid-1800s. By 1878 the whales were hunted nearly to extinction, but the return of these majestic creatures to Victor Harbor in recent decades has established the city as a premier source of information on whales and whaling history.

Ⓒ ★ **South Australian Whale Centre.** The South Australian Whale Centre tells the often graphic story of the whaling industry along South Australia's coast, particularly in Encounter Bay. Excellent interpretive displays spread over three floors focus on dolphins, seals, penguins, and whales—all of which can be seen in these waters. In whale-watching season the center has a 24-hour information hotline on sightings. There's a Discovery Trail and craft area for children. ✉ *2 Railway Terr.* ☎ *08/8551–0750, 1900/942–537 whale information* ⊕ *www. sawhalecentre.com* 🕮 *A8* ⊙ *Daily 9:30–5.*

Bluff. The Bluff, 7 km (4½ mi) west of Victor Harbor, is where whalers once stood lookout for their prey. Today the granite outcrop, also known as Rosetta Head, serves the same purpose in very different circumstances. It's a steep, 1,400-foot climb to the top, on a formed trail, to enjoy the bluff views.

Encounter Bikeway. For cycling enthusiasts, there's Encounter Bikeway, a paved track that runs 30 km (19 mi) from the Bluff along a scenic coastal route to Laffin Point (east of Goolwa). Almost flat, the bikeway is suitable for riders of most ages and experience levels.

Ⓒ **Granite Island.** Granite Island is linked to the mainland by a 650-yard causeway, along which Clydesdales pull a double-decker tram. Within Granite Island Nature Park a self-guided walk leads around the island, and guided walking tours to view the colony of about 500 fairy penguins are run from the penguin interpretive center. There is also an excellent restaurant (lunch only) with deck dining overlooking the harbor entrance. Look out for seals in the shallows. ✉ *Granite Island*

☎ *08/8552–7555* ⊕ *www.graniteisland.com.au* 🚊 *Round-trip tram A$7, penguin tours A$12.50, penguin interpretive center A$6* ⊙ *Daily; penguin tours at dusk.*

↻ **Cockle Train.** The Cockle Train travels the route of South Australia's first railway line. Originally laid between Goolwa and Port Elliot, and extended to Victor Harbor in 1864, the line traces the lovely Southern Ocean beaches on its 16-km (10-mi), half-hour journey. The train runs by steam power, subject to availability and weather conditions, daily during summer school holidays (late December to late January), on Easter weekend, and on the third Sunday of each month from June to November. A diesel locomotive pulls the heritage passenger cars (or a diesel railcar operates) on other Sundays and public holidays, and days of Total Fire Ban. ⊠ *Railway Terrace near Coral St.* ☎ *08/8552–2782 on days the train is operating, 1300/655–991* ⊕ *www.steamranger.org. au* 🚊 *Round-trip A$28.*

OFF THE BEATEN PATH

Coorong National Park. Coorong National Park, a sliver of land stretching southeast of the Fleurieu Peninsula and completely separate from it, hugs the South Australian coast for more than 150 km (94 mi). Many Australians became aware of the Coorong's beauty from the 1970s film *Storm Boy*, which told the story of a boy's friendship with a pelican. These curious birds are one reason why the Coorong is a wetland area of world standing. There's an A$11 charge per vehicle. ⊠ *32–34 Princes Hwy., Meningie* ☎ *08/8575–1200.*

WHERE TO STAY

For expanded hotel reviews, visit Fodors.com.

¢ 🏕 **The Port Elliott Holiday Park.** Six kilometers (4 mi) east of Victor Harbor, this grassy park fronts beautiful tree-lined Horseshoe Bay, one of South Australia's best swimming beaches. **Pros:** great location on the beach, wide range of accommodation options. **Cons:** overcrowded in peak season, not for kid-phobes. ⊠ *Off Goolwa Rd. near Hussey St., Port Elliot* ☎ *08/8554–2134* ⊕ *www.portelliotholidaypark.com.au* 🛏 *7 unpowered and 258 powered campsites, 9 villas, 4 cottages, 4 units, 4 cabins* ⚬ *In-hotel: flush toilets, partial hookups, dump station, drinking water, guest laundry, showers, picnic table, electricity, public telephone, general store, play area, swimming.*

$ 🏕 **Whalers Inn Resort.** The vibe is more tropical than maritime at Victor Harbor's upscale resort complex, with palm trees and spectacular surf as the backdrop for spacious, well-equipped rooms of varying configurations. **Pros:** stunning views of three islands, real "getaway" feel. **Cons:** expensive unless you get a last-minute deal, 15-minute drive from downtown. ⊠ *121 Franklin Parade* ☎ *08/8552–4400* ⊕ *www. whalersinnresort.com.au* 🛏 *12 suites, 14 apartments, 12 upper studios, 4 poolside studios* ⚬ *In-room: kitchen, Internet. In-hotel: restaurant, bar, pool, tennis court, laundry facilities, business center.*

KANGAROO ISLAND

Kangaroo Island, Australia's third-largest (after Tasmania and Melville), is barely 16 km (10 mi) from the Australian mainland. Yet the island belongs to another age—a folksy, friendly, less sophisticated time when you'd leave your car unlocked and knew everyone by name.

The island is most beautiful along the coastline, where the land is sculpted into a series of bays and inlets teeming with bird and marine life. The stark interior has its own charm, however, with pockets of red earth between stretches of bush and farmland. Wildlife is probably the island's greatest attraction; in a single day you can stroll along a beach crowded with sea lions and watch kangaroos, koalas, pelicans, and fairy penguins in their native environments.

Its towns and most of its accommodations are on the island's eastern third. The standout sights are on the southern coast, so if you've only one day—you could easily spend a week—it's best to tour the island in a clockwise direction, leaving the north-coast beaches for the afternoon. Before heading out, fill your gas tank and pack a picnic lunch. Shops are few and far between outside the towns, general stores being the main outlets for food and gas.

Department of Environment and Natural Resources Office. The Kangaroo Island Pass (A$61, A$166 families) is available from any National Parks and Wildlife site, or from the Department of Environment and Natural Resources Office or any Parks Pass outlet. The pass covers a selection of guided tours and park entry fees and is valid for a year. ⊠ *37 Dauncey St., Kingscote* ☎ *08/8553–4444* ⊕ *www.environment. sa.gov.au/parks.*

GETTING HERE AND AROUND

REX/Regional Express flies two times daily between Adelaide and Kingscote, the island's main airport. Ask about holiday packages in conjunction with SeaLink. Flights to the island take about 30 minutes.

SeaLink ferries allow access for cars through Penneshaw from Cape Jervis, at the tip of the Fleurieu Peninsula, a 90-minute drive from Adelaide. There are four daily sailings each way, with additional crossings at peak times. SeaLink operates the vehicular passenger ferry *Sea Lion 2000* and *Spirit of Kangaroo Island*, a designated freight boat with passenger facilities. These ferries make 45-minute crossings between Cape Jervis and Penneshaw. Ferries are the favored means of transportation between the island and the mainland, and reservations are advisable during the holidays. Adelaide Sightseeing operates coach tours of Kangaroo Island out of Adelaide in conjunction with the SeaLink ferry services from A$248 for a (very long) day trip.

Kangaroo Island's main attractions are widely scattered; you can see them best on a guided tour or by car. The main roads form a paved loop, which branches off to such major sites as Seal Bay and Admirals Arch and Remarkable Rocks in Flinders Chase National Park. Stretches of unpaved road lead to lighthouses at Cape Borda and Cape Willoughby, South Australia's oldest. Roads to the island's northern beaches, bays, and camping areas are also unpaved. These

"Bryson on top of a Remarkable Rock at Flinders Chase National Park." —photo by Rich_B_Florida, Fodors.com member

become very rutted in summer, but they can be driven carefully in a conventional vehicle. Be alert for wildlife, especially at dawn, dusk, and after dark. Slow down and dip your lights so you don't blind the animals you see.

TOURS

Exceptional Kangaroo Island has quality four-wheel-drive and bush-walking tours from A\$377 per person per day. Tailor-made itineraries, including bird-watching and photography, and flight-accommodation packages can also be arranged. Kangaroo Island Odysseys operates luxury four-wheel-drive nature tours from one to three days priced from A\$385 per person. Kangaroo Island Wilderness Tours has five personalized four-wheel-drive wilderness tours from one to four days and starting from A\$412 per person (tour only); a range of accommodation packages is available.

SeaLink Kangaroo Island operates one-day (A\$248) bus tours of the island, departing from Adelaide, in conjunction with the ferry service from Cape Jervis. They also can arrange fishing and self-drive tours and extended packages. Two-day/one-night tours are A\$399 and up per person; two-day/one-night self-drive tours start at A\$187 per person.

ESSENTIALS

Banks ANZ ✉ *62 Dauncey St., Kingscote* ☎ *13–1314.*

Tour Operators Exceptional Kangaroo Island ☎ *08/8553–9119* 🖷 *08/8553–9122* ⊕ *www.exceptionalkangarooisland.com.* **Kangaroo Island Odysseys** ☎ *08/8553–0386* 🖷 *08/8553–0387* ⊕ *www.kiodysseys.com.au.*

Kangaroo Island Wilderness Tours
☎ 08/8559–5033 🖷 08/8559–5088
⊕ www.wildernesstours.com.au.
SeaLink Kangaroo Island ⊠ 440 King
William St., Adelaide ☎ 13–1301
⊕ www.sealink.com.au.

Transportation Adelaide
Sightseeing ⊠ 85 Franklin St., City
Center, Adelaide ☎ 1300/769–762
⊕ www.adelaidesightseeing.com.au.
REX/Regional Express ☎ 13–1713
⊕ www.regionalexpress.com.au. SeaLink
☎ 13–1301 ⊕ www.sealink.com.au.

Visitor Information Gateway Visitor Information Centre ⊠ Howard Dr., Penneshaw ☎ 08/8553–1185 🖷 08/8553–1255 ⊕ www.tourkangarooisland.com.au ☉ Mon–Fri 9–5, weekends and public holidays 10–4.

KINGSCOTE

121 km (75 mi) southwest of Adelaide.

Kangaroo Island's largest town, Kingscote is a good base for exploring. Reeves Point, at the town's northern end, is where South Australia's colonial history began. Settlers landed here in 1836 and established the first official town in the new colony. Little remains of the original settlement except Hope Cottage, now a small museum; several graves; and a huge, twisted mulberry tree that grew from a cutting the settlers brought from England—locals still use the fruit to make jam. Today American River, about halfway between Kingscote and Penneshaw, the island's second-largest town, is another accommodation and restaurant hub.

☺ ★ **Pelican Feeding.** Make sure you catch the Pelican Feeding "show" at 5 pm daily on the rock wall beside Kingscote Jetty. A guide in fishing waders gives an informative and entertaining talk as he feeds handfuls of seafood to a comic mob of noisy pelicans. This is great fun. ⊠ *Kingscote Jetty* ☎ *08/8553–3112* 🖘 *A$4* ☉ *Daily 5 pm.*

WHERE TO STAY
For expanded hotel reviews, visit Fodors.com.

$$$ ⊞ **Acacia Apartments.** A huge movie collection in the reception area confirms that the self-contained one- and two-bedroom units at this Reeve's Point complex are family-friendly. **Pros:** kid-friendly, very amenable owner. **Cons:** slightly overpriced, 10 am check-out time. ⊠ *3–5 Rawson St., Reeve's Point* ☎ *08/8553–0088, 1800/247–007* ⊕ *www. acacia-apartments.com.au* 🛏 *10 apartments* ⟟ *In-room: a/c, kitchen, Internet, Wi-Fi. In-hotel: pool, spa, laundry facilities, business center* ˇ◯˙ *Breakfast.*

¢ ⊞ **Kangaroo Island Lodge.** The island's oldest resort faces beautiful Eastern Cove at American River. **Pros:** set in beautiful and peaceful surroundings, nearby trails lead to kangaroos and pelicans. **Cons:** dated

9

Lots of Remarkable Rocks, Flinders Chase National Park.

rooms and distinctly ordinary breakfast. *Box 232, American River 5221* ☎*08/8553–7053, 1800/355–581* ⊕ *www.kilodge.com.au* ⇗ *38 rooms* ⌂ *In-room: a/c, kitchen. In-hotel: restaurant, bar, pool, beach, laundry facilities, business center.*

$$ 🏨 **Aurora Ozone Hotel.** The original Victorian facade on this two-story 1920s hotel, directly opposite the new section across the road, hides surprisingly modern and spacious rooms that overlook Nepean Bay. **Pros:** across the street from the penguin colony, friendly staff. **Cons:** older rooms are old-fashioned, as is the breakfast. ⊠ *1, Commercial St.* ☎*08/8553–2011, 1800/083133* ✍ *reservations@ozone. auroraresorts.com.au* ⊕ *www.auroraresorts.com.au* ⇗ *75 rooms* ⌂ *In-room: safe. In-hotel: restaurant, bar, pool, gym, beach, laundry facilities, business center.*

$$$ 🏨 **Wanderers Rest.** Delightful local artworks dot the walls in this country inn's stylish units, all of which have king-size beds. **Pros:** simple, high-quality accommodation with stunning views. **Cons:** kids under 10 aren't allowed, tours and extras quickly add up. ⊠ *Lot 2, Bayview Rd., American River* ☎*08/8553–7140* ⊕ *www.wanderersrest.com.au* ⇗ *9 rooms* ⌂ *In-room: a/c, Wi-Fi. In-hotel: restaurant, bar, pool, some age restrictions* ❙◎❙ *Breakfast.*

PENNESHAW

62 km (39 mi) east of Kingscote.

This tiny ferry port has a huge population of penguins, which are visible on nocturnal tours. Gorgeous shoreline, views of spectacularly blue water, and rolling green hills are a few lovely surprises here.

🕙 **Penneshaw Penguin Centre.** Penneshaw Penguin Centre offers two ways to view the delightful fairy penguins indigenous to Kangaroo Island. From the indoor interpretive center, where you can read about bird activity—including mating, nesting, and feeding—a boardwalk leads to a viewing platform above rocks and sand riddled with burrows. Because the penguins spend most of the day fishing at sea or inside their burrows, the best viewing is after sunset. You can take a self-guided walk or an informative guided tour, which starts with a talk and video at the center. You might see penguins waddling ashore, chicks emerging from their burrows to feed, or scruffy adults molting. ⊠ *Middle and Bay Terraces* 🖀🖳 *08/8553–1103* 🖃 *Interpretive center free, guided tours A$10, self-guided walks A$8* ⊙ *Tours at 7:30 and 8:30 pm in winter, 8:30 and 9:30 pm in summer.*

Sunset Winery. Sip smooth Chardonnay while overlooking Eastern Cove at this calm, cool, and pristine addition to Kangaroo Island's thriving wine industry. You can sample wines for free at the cellar door, and opt for the Savoury Platter: a selection of Kangaroo Island and regional cheeses, KI Source Relish, South Rock Salami, local olives, crackers and more for A$25. Alternately, try a Dukkah Platter from the Fleurieu, served with local wild olive oil and delicious local bread for $15. ⊠ *Hog Bay Rd.* 🖀 *08/8553–1378* 🖳 *08/8553–1379* ⊕ *www.sunset-wines.com. au* 🖃 *Free* ⊙ *Daily 11–5.*

OFF THE BEATEN PATH

Australia's oldest lighthouse stands on Kangaroo Island's easternmost point, Cape Willoughby, 27 km (17 mi) from Penneshaw, on a mostly unpaved road. You can explore the property around the towering, white lighthouse, but only guided tours (A$13.50 or KI Pass) can enter the 1852 building itself. Tours depart from the National Parks office in one of the three 1920s lighthouse keepers' cottages. The other two cottages have been converted into self-contained accommodations that let you experience Kangaroo Island at its most remote and wildest—it's always windy here!

WHERE TO EAT AND STAY

For expanded hotel reviews, visit Fodors.com.

$$ ✕ **Fish.** Belly up to the counter in this tiny shop for cheap local sea-
SEAFOOD food—named by *The Australian* newspaper as some of the best in the
★ country—to take out or enjoy with a glass of wine in the seating area next door. Choose your fish—whiting, John Dory, garfish—from the blackboard menu and have it beer-battered, crumbed, or grilled. Or you might prefer a paper-wrapped parcel of scallops, prawns, lobster, and oysters (in season) shucked to order. The team behind the shop also runs 2 Birds & A Squid, which prepares seafood packs and cooked meals for pickup or delivery to your accommodation anywhere on the island. ⊠ *43 North Terr.* 🖀 *08/8553–1177 Fish, 08/8553–7406 2 Birds & A Squid* ⊕ *www.2birds1squid.com* 🖃 *No credit cards* ⊙ *Closed May–Sept. No lunch.*

$$ 🏨 **Kangaroo Island Seafront Resort.** This hotel has an ideal position near the ferry terminal and overlooking Penneshaw Bay. **Pros:** steps away from ferry terminal and penguin viewing, spacious rooms. **Cons:** older parts of the hotel are showing their age, no air-conditioning in rooms.

9

⊠ *49 North Terr.* ☎ *08/8553–1028, 1800/624–624* ⊕ *www.seafront. com.au* ⤳ *22 rooms* ⅏ *In-room: kitchen, Internet. In-hotel: restaurant, bar, pool, tennis court, laundry facilities* ⏀ *Breakfast.*

$$ ⌷ **Seaview Lodge.** Host Barbara Ewens welcomes you into her 1860s home at this elegant yet relaxing B&B. **Pros:** beautiful cottage-style gardens, stylishly furnished rooms. **Cons:** if full, the B&B can feel claustrophobic, limited views of the ocean. ⊠ *Willoughby Rd.* ☎ *08/8553–1132* ⊕ *www.seaviewlodge.com.au* ⤳ *5 rooms, 1 cottage* ⅏ *In-room: no TV. In-hotel: restaurant, bar* ⏀ *Breakfast.*

SEAL BAY CONSERVATION PARK

60 km (37 mi) southwest of Kingscote via South Coast Rd.

↻ **Seal Bay Conservation Park.** This top Kangaroo Island attraction gives
Fodor's Choice you the chance to visit one of the state's largest Australian sea-lion
★ colonies. About 300 animals usually lounge on the beach, except on stormy days, when they shelter in the dunes. You can only visit the beach, and get surprisingly close to females, pups, and bulls, on a tour with an interpretive officer; otherwise, you can follow the self-guided boardwalk to a lookout over the sand. Two-hour sunset tours depart on varied days in December and January; a minimum of four people is required, as is 24-hour advance booking. The park visitor center has fun and educational displays, and a touch table covered in sea-lion skins and bones. There is also a shop. ⊠ *End of Seal Bay Rd., Seal Bay* ☎ *08/8559–4207* ⊠ *Group tour A$28.50 per person, pre-sunset tour A$55, boardwalk A$13* ⊙ *Tours Dec. and Jan., daily 9–5:15, every 15–45 mins; Feb.–Nov., daily 9–4:15, every 45 mins.*

FLINDERS CHASE NATIONAL PARK

102 km (64 mi) west of Kingscote.

★ **Flinders Chase National Park.** Some of Australia's most beautiful coastal scenery is in Flinders Chase National Park on Kangaroo Island.

The effects of seas crashing mercilessly onto Australia's southern coast are visible in the oddly shaped rocks on the island's shores. A limestone promontory was carved from beneath at Cape du Couedic on the southwestern coast, producing what is known as **Admiral's Arch.** From the boardwalk you can see the New Zealand fur seals that have colonized the area around the rock formation. About 4 km (2½ mi) farther east are the aptly named **Remarkable Rocks,** huge, fantastically shaped boulders balanced precariously on the promontory of Kirkpatrick Point. This is a great place to watch the sun set or rise.

Much of Kangaroo Island has been cultivated since settlement, but after being declared a national treasure in 1919, a huge area of original vegetation has been protected in Flinders Chase. In December 2007 a bushfire burned a large part of Flinders Chase, and its destructive power and the various stages of regeneration are now on show.

Flinders Chase has several 1½-km to 9-km (1-mi to 5½-mi) loop walking trails, which take one to three hours to complete. The trails meander along the rivers to the coast, passing mallee scrub and sugar gum

"Naptime on the beach at Kangaroo Island." —photo by Istarr, Fodors.com member

forests, and explore the rugged shoreline. The 4-km (2½-mi) Snake Lagoon Hike follows Rocky River over and through a series of broad rocky terraces to the remote sandy beach where it meets the sea. The sign warning of freak waves is not just for show.

The park is on the island's western end, bounded by the Playford and West End highways. The state-of-the-art visitor center, open daily 9–5, is the largest National Parks and Wildlife office. Displays and touch screens explore the park's history and the different habitats and wildlife in Flinders Chase. The center provides park entry tickets and camping permits, and books stays at the Heritage cabins. A shop sells souvenirs and provisions, and there is also a café.

WHERE TO STAY

For expanded hotel reviews, visit Fodors.com.

¢ 🍴 **KI Regional Office.** Accommodations within the national park (and in Cape Willoughby Conservation Park at the other end of the island) are controlled by the KI Regional Office. ☎ 08/8553–4444 ⊕ www.environment.sa.gov.au ⤳ 8 cottages, 1 cabin, 1 hut, 46 campsites.

$$ 🍴 **Kangaroo Island Wilderness Retreat.** With wallabies and possums treating the grounds as their own domain, this eco-friendly retreat is everything a wildlife-loving traveler could want. **Pros:** wonderful experience for animal lovers, free Internet access and DVD rental. **Cons:** only two time slots for dinner, basic rooms might disappoint city slickers. ✉ 1 South Coast Rd., Flinders Chase ☎ 08/8559–7275 ⊕ www.kiwr.com ⤳ 18 courtyard rooms, 2 suites, 4 apartments, 7 lodge rooms ⚘ In-room: kitchen, Internet, Wi-Fi. In-hotel: restaurant, bar, laundry facilities, business center.

$$$$
ALL-INCLUSIVE
Fodor'sChoice
★

☞ **Southern Ocean Lodge.** This truly remarkable hotel might be the highlight of your trip—if money is no object. **Pros:** superb restaurant, simple but stunning decor exudes luxury and class. **Cons:** if you have to ask the price, you can't afford this place, sophisticated surroundings are not really suitable for children. ⊠ *Hanson Bay, Kingscote* ☎ *08/8559–7347* ⊕ *www.southernoceanlodge.com.au* ↬ *21 suites* ⚭ *In-room: a/c, safe, no TV, Wi-Fi. In-hotel: restaurant, bar, gym, spa* ☩ *All-inclusive.*

OUTDOOR ACTIVITIES

FISHING Fishing is excellent on Kangaroo Island's beaches, bays, and rivers. The island's deep-sea fishing fleet holds several world records for tuna. No permit is required for recreational fishing, but minimum lengths and bag limits apply. You can pick up a fishing guide from the information center in Penneshaw.

Cooinda Fishing Charters. Cooinda runs fishing, diving, and combined fishing and diving charters from half a day to three days out of American River. ☎ *0439/867–713, 08/8553–1072* ⊕ *cooindacharters.tripod.com.*

Grimshaw's Corner Store & Cafe. You can rent fishing equipment from Grimshaw's Corner Store & Cafe. ⊠ *3rd St. at North Terr., Penneshaw* ☎ *08/8553–1151.*

Kangaroo Island Fishing Charters. Kangaroo Island Fishing Charters has fast, clean boats and a live-aboard mother ship; the company takes groups in a 30-foot cruiser out in the Western River region (the island's north coast). ☎ *08/8559–3232* ⊕ *www.kangarooislandadventures.com.au.*

Kings. The Kings offer fishing tours (maximum six passengers) and personalized charters from half a day in American River waters. ☎ *08/8553–7003.*

Turner Fuel. Turner Fuel sells fishing tackle and bait. ⊠ *26 Telegraph Rd., Kingscote* ☎ *08/8553–2725.*

SCUBA DIVING Kangaroo Island waters also offer arguably the best temperate-water diving in Australia. Divers can explore some of the more than 50 shipwrecks around the coast, and swim among corals, sponges, and fish. The beautiful leafy sea dragon is endemic to the island's north-coast waters.

Kangaroo Island Diving Safaris. Kangaroo Island Diving Safaris runs day trips, live-aboard tours, and dive training courses. They promise interactions with seals and dolphins on most trips. ☎ *08/8559–3225* ⊕ *www.kidivingsafaris.com.*

THE OUTBACK

South Australia is the country's driest state, and its Outback is an expanse of desert vegetation. But this land of scrubby salt bush and hardy eucalyptus trees is brightened after rain by wildflowers—including the state's floral emblem, the blood-red Sturt's desert pea, with its black, olive-like heart. The terrain is marked by geological uplifts, abrupt transitions between plateaus broken at the edges of ancient, long-inactive fault lines. Few roads track through this desert wilderness—the main highway is the Stuart, which runs all the way to Alice Springs in the Northern Territory.

The people of the Outback are as hardy as their surroundings. They are also often eccentric, colorful characters who happily bend your ear over a drink in the local pub. Remote, isolated communities attract loners, adventurers, fortune-seekers, and people simply on the run. In this unyielding country, you must be tough to survive.

COOBER PEDY

850 km (527 mi) northwest of Adelaide.

Known as much for the way most of its 3,500 inhabitants live—underground in dugouts gouged into the hills to escape the relentless heat—as for its opal riches, Coober Pedy is arguably Australia's most singular place. The town is ringed by mullock heaps, pyramids of rock and sand left over after mine shafts are dug.

Opals are Coober Pedy's reason for existence. Australia has 95% of the world's opal deposits, and Coober Pedy has the bulk of that wealth; this is the world's richest opal field.

Opal was discovered here in 1915, and soldiers returning from World War I excavated the first dugout homes when the searing heat forced them underground. In midsummer temperatures can reach 48°C (118°F), but inside the dugouts the air remains a constant 22°C–24°C (72°F–75°F).

Coober Pedy is a brick-and-corrugated-iron settlement propped unceremoniously on a scarred desert landscape. It's a town built for efficiency, not beauty. However, its ugliness has a kind of bizarre appeal. There's a feeling that you're in the last lawless outpost in the modern world, helped in no small part by the local film lore—*Priscilla Queen of the Desert*, *Pitch Black*, *Kangaroo Jack*, and *Mad Max 3* were filmed here. Once you go off the main street, you get an immediate sense of the apocalyptic.

GETTING HERE AND AROUND

REX/Regional Express Airlines flies direct to Coober Pedy from Adelaide Sunday–Friday. Because it's the only public carrier flying to Coober Pedy, prices are sometimes steep. However, anyone holding a valid ISIC, YHA, or VIP card is eligible for unlimited air travel throughout Australia on the Backpackers Pass for a flat rate of A$499 for one month, or A$949 for two months. The airport is open only when a flight is arriving or departing. At other times, contact the Desert Cave Hotel.

Greyhound Australia buses leave Adelaide's Central Bus Station for Coober Pedy daily. Tickets for the 12-hour ride can cost between A$139–A$180 each way.

The main road to Coober Pedy is the Sturt Highway from Adelaide, 850 km (527 mi) to the south. Alice Springs is 700 km (434 mi) north of Coober Pedy. The drive from Adelaide to Coober Pedy takes about nine hours. From Alice Springs it's about seven hours.

A rental car enables you to see what lies beyond Hutchison Street, but an organized tour is a much better way to do so. Budget is the only rental-car outlet in Coober Pedy. Although some roads are unpaved—those to the Breakaways and the Dog Fence, for example—surfaces are generally suitable for conventional vehicles. Check on road conditions with the police if there has been substantial rain.

The most interesting route to Flinders Ranges National Park from Adelaide takes you north through the Clare Valley vineyards and Burra's copper-mining villages. For a more direct journey to Wilpena Pound, follow the Princes Highway north to Port Augusta, and then head east toward Quorn and Hawker. A four-wheel-drive vehicle is highly recommended for traveling on the many gravel roads around the national park.

> **PONY EXPRESS**
>
> The Coober Pedy–Oodnadatta Mail Run Tour is the most unusual experience you'll have anywhere. Former miner-turned-entrepreneur Peter Rowe and his brother Derek Rowe, a renowned horseman, run the tour, delivering mail and supplies to remote cattle stations and Outback towns. You also get a good look at the Dog Fence, and at the dingoes it was built to keep away.

ESSENTIALS

Banks ANZ ⊠ *11 Wilpena Rd., Hawker* ☎ *13–1314.* **Westpac** ⊠ *Lot 1, Hutchison St.* ☎ *13–2032.*

Emergencies Coober Pedy Hospital ⊠ *Hospital Rd.* ☎ *08/8672–5009.* **Hawker Memorial Hospital** ⊠ *Craddock St., Hawker* ☎ *08/8648–4007.*

Transportation Coober Pedy Airport ⊠ *Stuart Hwy., 2 km [1 mi] north of town* ☎ *08/8672–5688.* **Greyhound Australia** ☎ *1300/473946, 1300/GREYHOUND* ⊕ *www.greyhound.com.au.* **REX/Regional Express** ☎ *13–1713* ⊕ *www.regionalexpress.com.au.*

Visitor Information Coober Pedy Visitor Information Centre ⊠ *Coober Pedy District Council Bldg., Hutchison St.* ☎ *1800/637–076* ⊕ *www.cooberpedy.sa.gov. au* ⊙ *Weekdays 8:30–5, weekends 10–1.* **Wilpena Pound Visitor Centre** ⊠ *Wilpena Rd., Hawker* ☎ *08/8648–0048* ⊙ *Daily 8–5.*

EXPLORING

Fossicking for opal gemstones—locally called noodling—requires no permit at the Jewellers Shop mining area at the edge of town. Take care in unmarked areas, and always watch your step, as the area is littered with abandoned opal mines down which you might fall. (Working mines are off-limits to visitors.)

Although most of Coober Pedy's devotions are decidedly material in nature, the town does have its share of spiritual houses of worship. In keeping with the town's layout, they, too, are underground. **St. Peter and St. Paul's Catholic Church** is a National Heritage–listed building, and the Anglican **Catacomb Church** is notable for its altar fashioned from a windlass (a winch) and lectern made from a log of mulga wood. The **Serbian Orthodox Church** is striking, with its scalloped ceiling,

rock-carved icons, and brilliant stained-glass windows. The **Revival Fellowship Underground Church** has lively gospel services.

★ **Old Timers Mine.** The Old Timers Mine is a genuine opal mine turned into a museum. Two underground houses, furnished in 1920s and 1980s styles, are part of the complex, where mining memorabilia is exhibited in an extensive network of hand-dug tunnels and shafts. You can also watch demonstrations of opal-mining machines. Tours are self-guided. ⊠ *Crowders Gully Rd. near Umoona Rd.* ☎ *08/8672–5555* ⊕ *www. oldtimersmine.com* ☒ *A$10* ☉ *Daily 9–5.*

Umoona Opal Mine & Museum. Umoona Opal Mine & Museum is an enormous underground complex with an original mine, a noteworthy video on the history of opal mining, an Aboriginal Interpretive Centre, and clean, underground bunk camping and cooking facilities. Guided tours of the mine are available. ⊠ *14 Hutchison St.* ☎ *08/8672– 5288* ⊕ *www.umoonaopalmine.com.au* ☒ *Museum is free, tour A$10* ☉ *Daily 8–7; tours at 10, 12, 2, and 4.*

AROUND TOWN

Breakaways. Breakaways, a striking series of buttes and jagged hills centered on the Moon Plain, is reminiscent of the American West. There are fossils and patches of petrified forest in this strange landscape, which has appealed to makers of apocalyptic films. *Mad Max 3—Beyond Thunderdome* was filmed here, as was *Ground Zero*. The scenery is especially evocative early in the morning. The Breakaways area is 30 km (19 mi) northeast of Coober Pedy.

Fodor's Choice **Mail Run Tour.** The Coober Pedy–Oodnadatta Mail Run Tour, a 12-hour,
★ 600-km (372-mi) tour through the Outback (A$190), is one of the most unusual experiences anywhere, with stops at outback cattle stations, bush pubs, and the world's longest man-made structure, the Dingo Fence. Tours depart Monday and Thursday at 8:45 am from Underground Books on Post Office Hill Road. ⊠ *Post Office Hill Rd.* ☎ *08/8672–5226, 1800/069911* ⊕ *www.mailruntour.com.*

WHERE TO EAT AND STAY

For expanded hotel reviews, visit Fodors.com.

$ ✕ **Stuart Range Caravan Park Pizza Bar.** Locals swear that the pizzas at
PIZZA this popular Caravan Park are among Australia's best. The toppings combinations can be classic, creative, or gourmet, such as the Noon (with tomato, mushrooms, and onions) and the Garlic Prawn (with basil pesto and semi-dried tomatoes). ⊠ *Stuart Hwy. at Hutchison St.* ☎ *08/8672–5179, 1800/067 787* ☉ *No lunch.*

$$ ✕ **Umberto's.** Perched atop the monolithic Desert Cave Hotel, this eatery
AUSTRALIAN named after the hotel's founding developer is Coober Pedy's most urbane restaurant. The Mod-Oz menu takes you from the Outback (oven-baked kangaroo loin with grilled figs) to the sea (lemon sole). ⊠ *Hutchison St.* ☎ *08/8672–5688* ⊕ *www.desertcave.com.au* ☉ *No lunch.*

$$$ 🛏 **Desert Cave Hotel.** What may be the world's only underground hotel presents a contemporary, blocky face to the desert town. **Pros:** unique place to stay, pool is welcome relief in the heat. **Cons:** not for the claustrophobic, overpriced for what you get. ⊠ *Lot 1, Hutchison St. at Post Office Hill Rd.* ☎ *08/8672–5688, 1800/088521* ⊕ *www.desertcave.*

com.au ⤵ *50 suites incl. 19 underground* ☖ *In-room: no a/c, Internet, Wi-Fi. In-hotel: restaurant, bar, pool, gym, laundry facilities, business center.*

$ ⊞ **The Underground Motel.** The Breakaways sometimes seem close enough to touch at this hilltop motel, where you can lounge on a veranda watching the sun set on the rock formations 30 km (19 mi) across the desert. **Pros:** lovely patio to sit out on and watch the stars, very helpful owners. **Cons:** slightly out of town, which in the heat is a disadvantage. ✉ *1185 Catacomb Rd.* ☎ *08/8672–5324, 1800/622979* ⊕ *www.theundergroundmotel.com.au* ⤵ *6 rooms, 2 suites* ☖ *In-room: no a/c, kitchen, Internet, Wi-Fi. In-hotel: laundry facilities* ⓧ *Breakfast.*

FLINDERS RANGES NATIONAL PARK

690 km (430 mi) southeast of Coober Pedy, 460 km (285 mi) northeast of Adelaide.

Flinders Ranges National Park. Extending north from Spencer Gulf, the Flinders Ranges mountain chain includes one of Australia's most impressive Outback parks. These dry, folded and cracked mountains, once the bed of an ancient sea, have been sculpted by millions of years of rain and sun. Cypress pine and casuarina cover this furrowed landscape of deep valleys, which slope into creeks lined with river red gums. The area is utterly fascinating—both for geologists and for anyone else who revels in wild, raw scenery and exotic plant and animal life.

The numerous steep trails make the Flinders Ranges ideal for bushwalking, even though the park has few amenities. Water in this region is scarce, and should be carried at all times. The best time for walking is during the relatively cool months between April and October. This is also the wettest time of year, so you should be prepared for rain. Wildflowers, including the spectacular Sturt's desert pea, are abundant between September and late October.

The park's most spectacular walking trail leads to the summit of 3,840-foot **St. Mary's Peak,** the highest point on the Pound's rim and South Australia's second-tallest peak. The more scenic of the two routes to the top is the outside trail (15 km [9 mi] return); give yourself a full day to get up and back. The mid section of the ascent is steep and strenuous, but views from the summit—including the distant white glitter of the salt flats on Lake Frome—make the climb worthwhile.

Wilpena Pound. The scenic center of the Flinders Ranges is Wilpena Pound, an 80-square-km (31-square-mi) bowl ringed by hills that curve gently upward, only to fall away from the rims of sheer cliffs. The only entrance to the Pound is a narrow cleft through which Wilpena Creek sometimes runs.

Visitor Center. A mud-brick visitor center, part of the Wilpena Pound Resort, has information about hiking trails and campsites within the park. ✉ *End of Wilpena Rd., 156 km (97 mi) off Princes Hwy., via town of Hawker* ☎ *08/8648–6419* ⊕ *www.southaustralia.com/ FlindersRangesOutback.aspx.*

9

WHERE TO STAY

For expanded hotel reviews, visit Fodors.com.

$$

★

⊞ **Wilpena Pound Resort.** You couldn't ask for a more idyllic and civilized nature outpost than this popular resort at the entrance to Wilpena Pound. **Pros:** quiet and peaceful rooms; perfect for animal lovers. **Cons:** campsites can be overrun with school groups; permanent tents are overpriced. ⊠ *End of Wilpena Rd., Wilpena Pound ✛ 156 km (97 mi) off the Princes Hwy. via the town of Hawker* ☎ *08/8648–0004* ⊕ *www.wilpenapound.com.au* ⇆ *34 rooms, 26 units* ⚲ *In-room: kitchen. In-hotel: restaurant, bar, pool, laundry facilities, business center.*

Outback Adventures

WORD OF MOUTH

"We loved Darwin and the Top End and cannot wait to return. We could not believe how much we enjoyed the area, so relaxed and fascinatingly up close with nature. Don't panic about the snakes, we saw 3 in total whilst there, but they were in the open and did not make a move to bite us."

—Kasyorks

WELCOME TO OUTBACK ADVENTURES

TOP REASONS TO GO

★ **Beach Heaven:** Some of Australia's finest beaches are in Western Australia. Hundreds of kilometers of virtually deserted sandy coves and bays invite you to swim, surf, snorkel, or laze about.

★ **National Parks:** With spectacular terrain and one-of-a-kind plant and animal species, rugged national parks tell the story of Australia's ancient landforms, especially across the Top End and Kimberley regions.

★ **Old Culture:** The Red Centre, Top End, and the Kimberley are the best places to experience one of the oldest cultures in the world, that of Australia's Aborigines.

★ **Top End Cooking:** Innovative chefs blend immigrant Asian and European flavors with local produce to create distinctive plates.

★ **Wine Trails:** Follow the wine trails from Perth to the south coast to enjoy free tastings of internationally renowned wines at the cellar doors.

1 Red Centre. Uluru (Ayers Rock) is one of Australia's iconic images, and the main reason people visit the Red Centre. A striking sight, it is one of the world's largest monoliths, the last vestige of an ancient mountain range that looms 1,100 feet above the surrounding plain. But, there is more than just "the Rock" in the Red Centre—traditional Aboriginal "Dreamtime" stories overlie a region rich in geological wonders.

MELVILLE ISLAND

Arafura Sea Cape Wessel

DARWIN 2 ✪

Timor Sea

Cape Londonderry

Jabiru Nhulunbuy

Adelaide River

Pine Creek

Katherine

Wyndham Kununurra

Daly Waters Borroloola

Gulf of Carpentaria

Mataranka

Fitzroy Crossing

Halls Creek

BUCHANAN HILLS

Tennant Creek

NORTHERN TERRITORY

Barrow Creek

Hermannsburg

Alice Springs

Yulara

Uluru (Ayer's Rock) 1

SOUTH AUSTRALIA

QUEENSLAND

GREAT VICTORIA DESERT

0 200 mi

0 200 km

GETTING ORIENTED

Big, vast, expansive, huge—whichever way you cut it, Western Australia and the Northern Territory are daunting. Western Australia sprawls across nearly 1 million square mi—3.6 times the size of Texas—while the Northern Territory adds another 520,000 square mi, together accounting for half of Australia's landmass, but just about 11% of the population. This, in many respects, is the "real Australia" as you imagine it—remote, mostly uninhabited, the landscape ground down over millennia. Getting around by road will absorb days, if not weeks, but fortunately air services can cut the travel times between the gems of this vast area—the Red Centre, the Top End, and the Kimberley, and Perth and Western Australia's South West—to hours not days.

10

2 Darwin and the Kimberley. The "Top End" of Australia packs in some of the world's great natural environments—and with few people to crowd the views. Add in modern and ancient Aboriginal art and locals with a definite individualistic attitude, and you have an Australia so different from Sydney and Melbourne that you'll think you're in another country entirely.

3 Perth and Western Australia. Most trips to Western Australia begin and end in Perth. Here the major air, road, and rail transport links terminate in a city dubbed the most isolated in the world. But, don't expect some backward Hicksville—Perth is breezy, sophisticated, and culturally diverse, with an energetic outdoor lifestyle. Outside the city are untouched natural environments, plus exceptional food and wine.

ABORIGINAL CULTURE

When Europeans arrived to establish a permanent colony in what was to become New South Wales, Aboriginal people had been living across the continent for at least 50,000 years.

Perhaps 600 different "clan groups" or "nations"—each with its own distinctive culture and beliefs—greeted the new settlers in a clash of civilizations that remains largely unresolved today. Despite the efforts of governments of all persuasions and society at large, Aboriginal people by all measures—economic, health, social, education— remain an underprivileged group.

But Aboriginal culture as expressed in oral tradition, art, and lifestyle and by sacred sites such as Uluru is of growing interest to national and international travelers. Tours and experiences that promote Aboriginal culture and lifestyle are available throughout Western Australia and the Northern Territory. Experiences range from organized tours to dance performances, shopping for traditional Aboriginal artifacts and art, and the opportunity to stay on Aboriginal land to experience the daily lives of Aboriginal people. Tourism represents an important source of income ensuring that Aboriginal communities prosper and that their heritage is preserved.

COMMUNITY VALUES

Welcome to Country is an important ritual. Protocol dictates that people are welcomed when entering and learning about Country; for many this is simply good manners and respect. It's likely you will enjoy a Welcome to Country if you join any Aboriginal-guided tour.

In some cultures there were once strict rules about eye contact; you may find that some people follow this practice and won't make eye contact with you. This, or lowering the eyes are two actions that are often a show of respect toward older people.

SACRED SITES

Uluru (Ayers Rock) is probably Australia's best-known natural site, but it also has significant cultural meaning for the traditional owners, the Anangu people. They believe they are direct descendants of the beings—which include a python, an emu, a blue-tongue lizard, and a poisonous snake—who formed the land and its physical features during the Tjukurpa (the "Dreamtime," or creation period). Rising more than 1,100 feet from the surrounding plain, Uluru is one of the world's largest monoliths, though such a classification belies the otherworldly, spiritual energy surrounding it.

Kakadu National Park contains some of the best ancient rock art accessible to visitors in Australia. The Anbangbang Gallery has a frieze of Aboriginal rock painting dating back thousands of years, while among the six galleries at Ubirr there is a 49-foot frieze of X-ray paintings depicting animals, birds, and fish. Warradjan Aboriginal Cultural Centre's large display, developed by the local Bininj/Mungguy people, provides detailed information about Aboriginal culture in Kakadu.

Purnululu National Park (the Bungle Bungles) is an amazing geological wonder and a site for Aboriginal culture. Although the Bungle Bungle Range was extensively used by Aboriginal people during the wet season, when plant and animal life was abundant, few Europeans knew of its existence until the mid-1980s. The area is rich in Aboriginal rock art, and there are also many burial sites, although these are not typically open to visitors.

Farther west in the Kimberley Region the pearling town of Broome is the starting point for many adventure tours into the remote Outback, and visiting Aboriginal communities such as Bardi Creek, Biridu Community, and One Arm Point Community with local Aboriginal guides. Geickie Gorge, Windjana Gorge, and Tunnel Creek combine wilderness scenery with indigenous rock art, lifestyles, and stories from the Dreamtime.

TOP SIGHTS

By far the best way to experience Aboriginal culture is on foot and with an experienced guide, though at some national parks, interpretive centers, signage and—occasionally—self-guided audio equipment mean you can visit on your own. On foot generally requires a level of fitness and surefootedness for trails and pathways; even the best locations are uneven and stony, and can include steep climbs. Boats provide an alternative, such as at Geickie Gorge and Kakadu, where guided tours along the waterways include information about Aboriginal culture. In Margaret River you can canoe to Aboriginal sites and enjoy bush tucker as well. From Broome, four-wheel-drive safaris can get you into remote Aboriginal communities where you can meet the locals and listen to campfire stories. If mobility is an issue, there are easily accessible interpretive centers at places like Uluru and Kakadu national parks that have extensive displays describing Aboriginal life.

10

MARGARET RIVER WINE REGION

From humble beginnings more than 30 years ago, the Margaret River Wine Region now ranks as one of the premium wine-producing regions of the world.

Agronomist Dr. John Gladstones is credited with the birth of the area's wine industry—his 1965 report identified climate, soil, and weather conditions in the South West as similar to the Bordeaux region of France. A handful of pioneers took his advice, and by the mid-1970s were turning out outstanding wines. Today approximately 150 wineries claim Margaret River origins. At 120 or so on-farm cellar-door outlets you can taste and buy wines and often have a delicious meal as well.

Although the wine gives the region its cachet and is the prime reason for touring the area, there is more to explore. With gorgeous landscapes and seascapes, world-renowned surf breaks and swimming beaches, arts and crafts outlets, locally produced foods, and forest and beachside hiking trails, the region attracts some 1.5 million visitors a year.

WHEN TO GO

The region is a year-round destination. Most wineries are open seven days a week, but its popularity with visitors from Perth means that weekends are busiest and public holidays, such as Easter, can be crowded and accommodations booked solid. The summer school holidays in December and January are also popular times for Western Australians to visit, and accommodations can be at a premium. Vintage—when the grapes are picked and crushed—is usually between February and April, while in mid-winter from June through August the vines are bare and you'll see pruning teams in the vineyards.

Margaret River wineries are owned and run by international corporations, midsize companies, and families. This ownership structure influences your experience when visiting a cellar door—often, though not always, the family-run operations offer a friendlier welcome and a more authentic winery experience.

Cullen Wines is one of the region's founding wineries, established by the late industry patriarch Dr. Kevin Cullen (and his wife Diana) in 1971. His daughter Vanya now runs the operation, producing wines using biodynamic practices, one of the few such wineries in Australia. The tasting room is small, but the experience is archetypal Margaret River. Their flagship wines are named after mum and dad—the Kevin John Chardonnay and the Diana Madeline Cabernet Sauvignon Merlot.

Happs Winery is the product of another pioneer vigneron, Erl Happ, who hand-built his winery and adjoining pottery with mud bricks, recycled timbers, and stained glass, planting the first vines in 1978. The eclectic architecture of the cellar door is also reflected in Happ's passion for trying something new—the biggest choice in wines is found here. Daughter-in-law Jacquie runs the adjacent pottery.

Hayshed Hill has been through the circle of ownership. Established as a family operation—the first vines were planted in 1973—it was bought out in 2000 by a national wine investment company and then bought again by winemaker Michael Kerrigan in 2006, in a move he describes as "winemakers buying back the farm." The white-clapboard building that houses the cellar door and a small café is the perfect setting for tasting the wines and enjoying a light lunch.

Leeuwin Estate is one of the iconic wineries in the area, established by the entrepreneurial Denis Horgan in 1974 with the assistance of legendary American winemaker Robert Mondavi. Before you taste the wines in the stone-and-timber tasting room, head downstairs to view the art gallery of original commissioned works from Robert Juniper, Peter Cole, Sidney Nolan, and Clifton Pugh, among others.

TIMING

There are some 120 wineries with cellar-door outlets in the region, so deciding which ones to visit can be a challenge. We suggest that you don't try to visit more than four or five wineries in a day—this gives you time to appreciate the architecture and ambience of each cellar door, learn about and taste the wines on offer, talk with the staff (maybe even the winemaker), stop for a leisurely lunch at a vineyard restaurant, and avoid getting completely bamboozled. If you're driving, make sure you choose a "skipper," a nondrinking driver.

NEED A BREAK

One of the great pleasures of touring the Margaret River wineries is lunch, and there are some excellent winery restaurants to choose from. Vasse Felix's restaurant is set on top of the cellar door, shop, and winery complex with views over landscaped gardens, bushland, and a billabong. Chef Aaron Carr's menus include "trust the chef" options with two- and three-course set menus that spotlight fresh creations of the day.

10

Updated by
Fleur Bainger

A vast mass of the earth's surface—almost half the area of the United States—dating back millions of years, Western Australia and the Northern Territory combine to offer some of Australia's most fascinating and iconic natural attractions. Weathered down over the millennia, the region presents no snow-capped mountains. Instead, it offers deeply carved rock canyons, rock formations that leap up from surrounding plains, giant hardwood forests, tropical wetlands, deserts with unending horizons, mile upon mile of untrammeled white-sand beaches, and crystal-clear marine parks.

Indigenous peoples have been here for around 50,000 years, bringing with them legends and myths from their "Dreaming" to describe the land, animals, and plants. European settlement is *much* younger. Perth, in Western Australia, only dates back to inauspicious beginnings in 1829; Darwin, in the Northern Territory, dates to around the same time. Many other towns and villages have a history of less than 100 years. With a population of 2.4 million, and 1.6 million of those in Perth, only a scant human toehold exists here, making it one of the most lightly populated areas on earth.

And remote, too—it's close to a five-hour flight from Sydney to Perth, about the same to Darwin. Western Australians and Territorians bemoan and celebrate their isolation from the rest of Australia. On the one hand, there is what they call "over east," the Sydney, Canberra, and Melbourne triangle, where the nation's political, financial, and social decisions are made. On the other hand, their isolation engenders strong feelings of independence, and pride in what they regard as "the real Australia."

Residents of Western Australia—once dubbed the "Cinderella State"—now repeatedly point out that they are the nation's economic powerhouse, producing much of its export mineral, energy, and agricultural wealth. From a modest start when gold was discovered in the 1890s to the 1970s, and when other massive mineral deposits were discovered—notably iron ore—to today, the state has now become inextricably linked to global markets and regards Asia as a closer neighbor than Australia's eastern states. The mining boom has resulted in a strong inflow of people from around the world. Many have settled in Perth and southward, where the population growth rate is among the fastest in Australia. The Mediterranean climate fosters an easygoing outdoor lifestyle, the attractions of sport, superb local food and wine, beaches and bush married to an energetic, go-getting economic drive.

Territorians, living mainly in Darwin and Alice Springs, in the Red Centre, make the most of their isolation with a strongly independent and individualistic attitude. For thousands of years these areas have been home to Aboriginal communities who have undiminished ties to the land. With an art history dating back at least 20,000 years, Aboriginal artwork has now moved into Australia's mainstream art movement, and some expensive canvasses by Aboriginal artists decorate galleries, homes, and corporate boardrooms around the world. Across the state border in Western Australia, the Kimberley region is a largely untouched wilderness. Four-wheel-drive vehicles are de rigueur for this area with many unsealed (unpaved) roads, while between Derby and Wyndham there are some 1,000 km (625 mi) of glorious coastline unreachable except by sea.

PLANNING

WHEN TO GO

May through September (Australia's winter) are the best months to visit the Red Centre and the Top End; nights are crisp and cold and days are pleasantly warm. Summer temperatures in the Centre—which can rise above 43°C (110°F)—are oppressive, while the wet season (December–April) means that Darwin and surroundings are hot, humid, and, well, wet. Perth and the South West you can visit year-round, though the weather will influence your activities and sightseeing. Summer (December–February) in Perth is *hot* and temperatures can rise to 40°C (100°F) and higher. In the Kimberley May–November is the preferred season, with usually clear skies and balmy days and nights.

In the Top End the year is divided into the wet season (the Wet; December–April) and the dry season (the Dry; May–November). The Dry is a period of idyllic weather with warm days and cool nights, while the Wet brings monsoonal storms that dump an average of 52 inches of rain in a few months and result in widespread road closures. You can also catch spectacular electrical storms, particularly over the ocean. The "Build Up," in October, is the Top End's most oppressive weather period and should be avoided. The Kimberley has a similar wet season; however, the rainfall is less and generally comes in short, heavy storms. Cyclones also occur during this period and can disrupt travel arrangements.

10

GETTING HERE AND AROUND

AIR TRAVEL

Perth and Darwin are the main international arrival points, and both are serviced by a dozen or more airlines. Qantas is Australia's main domestic airline, and with its budget subsidiary Jetstar operates an extensive network and regular services crisscrossing the country from all the major cities to regional centers like Alice Springs and Broome. Virgin Australia competes with Qantas in major cities as well as some regional centers such as Broome, though not the Red Centre. Air North has an extensive network throughout the Top End and covers some WA legs, while Skywest flies from Perth to Broome, Kununurra, and Darwin.

CAR AND BUS TRAVEL

Driving around Western Australia and the Northern Territory is relatively easy, with mostly good paved roads and light traffic outside Perth and Darwin. But distances can be daunting. For example, Adelaide to Alice Springs via the Stuart Highway is 1,000 mi, and can take 24 hours. From Darwin to Broome is 1,152 mi, a tiring two-day drive. On the other hand, Perth to Margaret River in the South West is less than four hours along good roads. Greyhound Australia operates an extensive network of long-distance coaches. From Perth to Broome takes two days, with another day on to Darwin. From Perth to Adelaide, expect to be on the road for 36 hours.

TRAIN TRAVEL

Great Southern Railways operates the *Ghan* from Adelaide north to Alice Springs, then on to Darwin twice a week; return services from Darwin to Adelaide are also twice a week. The *Indian Pacific,* also operated by Great Southern, links Sydney and Perth via Adelaide with twice-weekly services each way. The trip takes around 60 hours.

From Perth, TransWA operates train services to Bunbury twice daily and to Northam and Kalgoorlie.

Getting around Perth by train is quick and easy, with lines to Armadale, Clarkson, Midland, Joondalup, Fremantle, Mandurah, and Rockingham.

ABOUT THE RESTAURANTS

Restaurants and cafés in Western Australia and the Northern Territory are largely reflective of their location: in the Red Centre you'll find "bush tucker" menus with crocodile, kangaroo, camel, and native fruits, berries, and plants; in Darwin and Broome locally caught seafood are prepared with flavor influences from Asia; in Perth—and the winery restaurants down south—fusion cuisines are influenced by the continual influx of immigrants from Europe and Asia. A small bar trend means tapas-style menus are now extremely popular.

Expect to find Western Australian wines on the wine list when dining in most licensed restaurants in Perth and, of course, in the Margaret River wine region, where first-class food is matched with highly regarded wines.

Many restaurants and cafés offer alfresco dining. Tips aren't expected, but an extra 10% for exceptional service is welcome.

ABOUT THE HOTELS

From five-star to basic, you'll find suitable accommodations throughout the region. The well-known international chains are largely in Perth and Darwin, but there are also sublime boutique accommodations set in wilderness or natural settings outside these centers. Both the Kimberley and Western Australia's South West are especially noted for these types of properties. You can also experience Outback Australia at homesteads and working cattle stations, while owner-run bed-and-breakfasts provide comfort, charm, and a glimpse of local life. In the cities and the Outback there are plenty of less-than-memorable motels where you can at least get a clean bed for the night. Popular options—especially for families and small groups—are self-contained apartments, villas, and chalets. With two or three bedrooms, living areas, and kitchens, they allow you to save on dining costs by cooking your own meals; these are best if staying more than one night.

DINING AND LODGING PRICE CATEGORIES (IN AUSTRALIAN DOLLARS)				
	¢	$	$$	$$$	$$$$
Restaurants	under A$10	A$10–A$20	A$21–A$35	A$36–A$50	over A$50
Hotels	under A$100	A$100–A$150	A$151–A$200	A$201–A$300	over A$300

Restaurant prices are based on the median main course price at dinner. Hotel prices are for two people in a standard double room in high season, excluding service and tax.

HEALTH AND SAFETY

If you are self-driving—especially in remote areas—make sure you have enough fuel, water, and food and carry a first-aid kit. Let others know where you are going and for how long. Going off bushwalking or hiking without adequate supplies, directions, and alone or without letting others know your plan is also risky and perhaps just stupid.

There are "critters" to avoid—snakes, crocodiles, and box jellyfish, for example. Mosquitoes can carry encephalitis, dengue fever, and Ross River fever, so cover up and use a good insect repellent; the worst times for mosquitoes are dawn and dusk.

Respect the Australian sun, especially in summer. Sunburn is a real danger if you don't do what the Australians are urged to do: slip, slap, slop—that is, slip on a hat, slap on sunglasses, and slop on sunscreen. On popular beaches around major cities and towns lifesavers (lifeguards) are usually on duty and put up flags to swim between, but generally most beaches are unguarded. Take extra care, especially where there are strong currents. Crocodiles are active in many of the Territory's waterways, so obey warning signs and check before swimming.

The emergency contact number for police, fire, and ambulance is *000*. From a GSM mobile (cell) phone the number is *112*.

10

TOURS

If you want to avoid the hassles of getting yourself around this vast region, then a tour group is certainly an option. Hundreds of tours and tour operators cover Western Australia and the Northern Territory, and can introduce you to the many experiences on offer here: four-wheel-drive treks, helicopter flights, bush-tucker-gathering expeditions, Aboriginal-guided walks, fishing safaris, and national park tours to name a few.

You can also take a day tour or shorter overnight tours up to, say, five days. Most of these operate from Darwin, Broome, Perth, and Alice Springs. The benefit is that all your transport, accommodation, meals, and sightseeing arrangements are preset, and you will get to see and do things you may otherwise miss if you try to organize them yourself.

To see a larger part of the country you can join an extended tour.

Australian Adventure Travel. Australian Adventure Travel has comfortable camping safaris for small groups through the Kimberley, using four-wheel-drive vehicles. Highlights of their nine-day Broome to Darwin safari (from A$2,255) include Gibb River Road, Cable Beach, Broome, Derby, Windjana Gorge, Tunnel Creek, Bells Gorge, the King Leopold Ranges, Aboriginal rock art, wildlife, El Questro Station, Kununurra, Bungle Bungles, and Darwin. ⊠ *39 Oxleigh Dr., Malaga* ☎ *08/9248–2355* ⊕ *www.australianadventuretravel.com.au.*

Bill Peach Journeys. Bill Peach Journeys runs Aircruising Australia, using 34-seat Dash 8 aircraft to fly you to the icon attractions of central Australia, staying overnight in best-available hotels and motels. Their 12-day Great Australian Aircruise departs from and returns to Sydney, and includes stops at Longreach (Queensland), Katherine, Kakadu, and Darwin in the Northern Territory, Kununurra and Broome in Western Australia, and finally Uluru and Alice Springs in the Northern Territory. The inclusive cost starts at A$12,995. ⊠ *Unit 20, 77 Bourke Rd., Alexandria* ☎ *02/9693–2233* ⊕ *www.billpeachjourneys.com.au.*

Casey Australia Tours. Casey Australia Tours has a range of extended tours departing from Perth, including a 16-day fly and coach tour that takes in Broome, Kununurra, Darwin, Kakadu, Alice Springs, and Uluru. Accommodation is in motels and cabins. The price is from A$3,490. ⊠ *63 Burwood Cr., Bicton* ☎ *08/9339–4291* ⊕ *www.caseytours.com.au.*

North Star Cruises. North Star Cruises operates the small luxury-expedition cruise ship *True North*, which takes just 36 passengers on 6- and 13-night cruises between Broome and Wyndham along the inaccessible Kimberley coastline. The cruises are adventure oriented, with daily activities including scenic walks, fishing, diving, snorkeling, and on-shore picnics. The ship has six expedition craft and its own helicopter for scenic flights. ⊠ *Shop 2, 25 Carnarvon St., Broome* ☎ *08/9192–1829* ⊕ *www.northstarcruises.com.au.*

The Red Centre

Trephina Gorge Nat'l Park

Ross River

Corroboree Rock

Santa Teresa

Ewoninga Rock Carvings

Conservation Reserve

Maryvale

Titjikala

Emily Gap

Alice Springs

John Flynn's Grave

Rainbow Valley Conservation Reserve

Chambers Pillar

Chambers Pillar Historical Reserve

Stuart Hwy.

TO DARWIN

Simpsons Gap

Hugh River

Standley Chasm

Owen Springs Reserve

Ellery Creek Big Hole

Camel Outback Safaris

Henbury

Serpentine Gorge

Wallace Rockhole

Stuart Hwy.

Impadna

TO ADELAIDE

Ormiston Gorge

Hermannsburg

Henbury Meteorites Conservation Reserve

Glen Helen Gorge

Glen Helen Resort

WEST MACDONNELL RANGES

Palm Valley

Finke Gorge Nat'l Park

West Macdonnell National Park

Mount Ebenezer

Lasseter Hwy.

Tnorala (Goose Bluff) Conservation Reserve

Tnorala (Goose Bluff)

Areyonga

KRICHAUFF RANGE

MIDDLE RANGE

Wallara Ranch

30 mi

30 km

IDIRRIKI RANGE

Watarka National Park

Kings Canyon

Curtin Springs

Mt. Conner

Uluru (Ayers Rock)

Ayers Rock Resort

Uluru-Kata-Tjuta National Park

Cultural Centre

Kata Tjuta (The Olgas)

RED CENTRE

The light in the Red Centre—named for the deep color of its desert soils—has a purity and vitality that photographs only begin to approach. For tens of thousands of years this vast desert territory in the south of the Northern Territory has been home to Australia's Aboriginal people. Uluru, also known as Ayers Rock, is a great symbol in Aboriginal traditions, as are many sacred sites among the Centre's mountain ranges, gorges, dry riverbeds, and spinifex plains.

The essence of this ancient land is epitomized in the paintings of the renowned Aboriginal landscape artist Albert Namatjira and his followers. Viewed away from the desert, their images of the MacDonnell Ranges may appear at first to be garish and unreal in their depiction of purple-and-red mountain ranges and stark-white ghost gum trees. Seeing the real thing makes it difficult to imagine executing the paintings in any other way.

Uluru (pronounced *oo*-loo-*roo*), that magnificent stone monolith rising from the plains, is but one focus in the Red Centre. Kata Tjuta (*ka*-ta *tchoo*-ta), also known as the Olgas, are another. Watarrka National Park and Kings Canyon, Mt. Conner, and the cliffs, gorges, and mountain chains of the MacDonnell Ranges are other worlds to explore.

The primary areas of interest are Alice Springs, which is flanked by the intriguing Eastern and Western MacDonnell Ranges; Kings Canyon; and Uluru–Kata Tjuta National Park, with neighboring Ayers Rock Resort. Unless you have more than three days, focus on only one of these areas.

ALICE SPRINGS

2,021 km (1,256 mi) northwest of Sydney, 1,319 km (820 mi) north of Adelaide, 1,976 km (1,228 mi) northeast of Perth.

Once a ramshackle collection of buildings on dusty streets, Alice Springs—known colloquially as "the Alice" or just "Alice"—is today an incongruously suburban tourist center with a population of more than 30,000 (including about 2,000 Americans, many employed at Pine Gap, a joint Australian and U.S. satellite tracking station) in the middle of the desert. Alice derives most of its income from tourism, and more than 300,000 tourists visit annually. The town's ancient sites, a focus for the Arrernte Aboriginal people's ceremonial activities, lie cheek-by-jowl with air-conditioned shops and hotels. The MacDonnell Ranges dominate Alice Springs, changing color according to the time of day from brick red to purple.

GETTING HERE AND AROUND

Alice Springs Airport is 15 km (9 mi) southeast of town. Qantas flies in and out of Alice Springs daily with direct flights from Brisbane, Sydney, Melbourne, Adelaide, Perth, Darwin, and Cairns, as well as Ayers Rock. Tiger Airways flies direct from Melbourne to Alice Springs twice daily on Tuesday, Thursday, and Saturday. It's three hours' flying time from Sydney, Melbourne, and Brisbane; two hours from Adelaide and Darwin; and about 40 minutes from Ayers Rock. Flights run less frequently in the "Wet" summer months. Alice Springs Airport Shuttle Bus meets every flight. The ride to all hotels and residential addresses in town costs A$19 each way. On request, the bus will also pick you up at your hotel and take you back to the airport, though you must give four hours notice (☎ 08/8953–0310). From the airport, taxi fare to most parts of town is about A$35.

The *Ghan* train leaves Adelaide at 12:20 pm Sunday and Wednesday, arriving in Alice Springs at 1:45 pm Monday and Thursday. Return trains leave Alice Springs at 12:45 pm Thursday and 3:15 pm Sunday, arriving in Adelaide at 1:10 pm on Friday and Monday. On Monday and Thursday at 6 pm the *Ghan* continues to Darwin via Katherine, arriving at 5:30 pm Tuesday and 6:30 pm Friday. Trains from Darwin depart Wednesday at 10 am and Saturday at 9 am. The Alice Springs railway station is 2½ km (1½ mi) west of Todd Mall.

Ghan ✉ *Great Southern Railway* ☎ *13–2147 bookings, 08/8213 4592 bookings outside Australia* ⊕ *www.gsr.com.au.*

The Stuart Highway, commonly called the Track, is the only road into Alice Springs. The town center lies east of the highway. The 1,693-km (1,000-mi) drive from Adelaide takes about 24 hours. The drive from Darwin is about 160 km (100 mi) shorter, and takes about 21 hours. Bus tours run between all Red Centre sites, as well as between Alice Springs and Ayers Rock Resort. Traveling by car will give you the most flexible itinerary—although the trade-off is that you'll travel many long, lonely stretches of one-lane highway through the red-dust desert. Vehicles can be rented at Alice Springs and Ayers Rock Resort. The Central Australian Tourism Industry Association in Alice Springs books tours and rental cars, and provides motoring information.

SAFETY AND PRECAUTIONS

Please note that many Aborigines living in or around Alice Springs have been asked to leave their native villages by tribal elders because of their problems with alcohol. Crime and violence stemming from alcohol abuse can make Alice unsafe at night, and it's recommended you travel only by taxi after dark. Sections of the dry Todd riverbed function as makeshift campsites for some Aborigines, so caution is advised when traversing it.

10

TIMING

The best time to visit is between May and August, when the weather is mild during the day, although often freezing at night; the summer months can be blisteringly hot, and some tourism services are less frequent or stop altogether. Alice Springs is pleasant enough, but most of the Red Centre's attractions are outside the town. If visiting Uluru is the main reason for your visit to the Red Centre, you can skip Alice Springs and go directly to Uluru–Kata Tjuta National Park.

TOURS

The *Alice Explorer* bus completes a 70-minute circuit (with narration) of 14 tourist attractions in and around Alice Springs 9–5 daily. You can leave and rejoin the bus whenever you like over two nonconsecutive days for a flat rate of A$44. Entry into attractions is extra. It's part of Alice Wanderer Centre Sightseeing, a company that also runs half-day

GREAT ITINERARIES

The sheer size of Western Australia and the Northern Territory—together making up half of Australia's landmass—means it is impossible to cover it all on a short visit. You will need to be selective.

For the most part, the major draws are clustered and accessible by air and road: in the Northern Territory Uluru and Kakadu National Park, for both an Aboriginal experience and the natural environment; in Western Australia Purnululu (Bungle Bungle) National Park for an amazing geological formation; Perth and Rottnest Island for a city-based trip and unique wildlife (quokkas); and the South West for wine-tasting trails, beaches, and forests.

IF YOU HAVE 3 DAYS

Don't even think about trying to do more than one of the major spots or you'll be spending all your time in airports or on the road.

If you choose one of Australia's great icons—Uluru—you could fly directly to Ayers Rock Airport and spend two days there, taking a hike around the rock followed by a look at the **Uluru–Kata Tjuta Cultural Centre** near its base.

The next day take a sightseeing flight by helicopter or fixed-wing aircraft, then visit **Kata Tjuta** (the Olgas) to explore its extraordinary domes and end the day with sunset at the rock. A flight will get you to Alice Springs, where you can tour out to either the Eastern or Western MacDonnell Ranges to explore the gorges and take a dip in a waterhole.

If you make **Darwin** your starting point, head east early on the Arnhem Highway to Fogg Dam to view the birdlife. Continue into **Kakadu National Park** and picnic at the rock-art site at Ubirr. Take a scenic flight in the afternoon, then a trip to the Bowali Visitors Centre, and you can overnight in **Jabiru**.

On the second day, head to Nourlangie Rock; then continue to the Yellow Water cruise at **Cooinda** and stay there for the night. The next day, drive to **Litchfield National Park** and visit Florence, Tjaynera, or Wangi Falls.

The easiest way to see **Purnululu's** amazing "beehive" rock formations is from the air. To do this you'll need to fly to **Kununurra** from Darwin or **Broome**, then take a sightseeing flight.

If you fly into **Perth**, spend most of the first day knocking around the city center. Take the train to pleasantly preserved **Fremantle** and stroll through the streets, stopping for breaks at sidewalk cafés. In the evening in either city, have dinner overlooking the water.

Next day, take a ferry to **Rottnest Island** and cycle around, walk on the beach, fish, or try to spot the small local marsupials called quokkas. A coach tour on the final day will get you to the **Margaret River** wine region.

IF YOU HAVE 5 DAYS

Five days allows you to spend more time at your preferred destination, or, indeed, combine two, though it will still be rushed.

In the Red Centre follow the three-day itinerary, finishing in Alice Springs, then fly to Darwin for a two-day trip to Kakadu National Park. Alternatively, start in Perth with the three-day itinerary then add on a return flight to Ayers Rock Airport to visit Uluru; you'll be there in time for sunset before departing the next morning.

Another option is to fly to Kununurra from Perth, then take a sightseeing flight over Purnululu's rock formations, though this is time-consuming, as the flight time to Kununurra is around three hours.

You could also spend a couple of days in Perth and Rottnest, then fly to Broome, a fascinating pearl producing town, for two days.

IF YOU HAVE 7 DAYS

Seven days will allow you to hop, skip, and jump around Western Australia and the Northern Territory. Start in Perth, spending half a day in the city, including King's Park, then take the bus or train to the heritage city of Fremantle for lunch of fish-and-chips by the water and a stroll through the heritage precinct.

The next day, fly to Ayers Rock and watch sunset at Uluru and spend the next day driving to Alice Springs, visiting the Aboriginal Australia Arts and Culture Centre before a late afternoon camel ride along the dry Todd River.

The next morning fly to Darwin and head to Kakudu National Park for two days before returning to Darwin and flying back to Perth. Alternatively, fly west to Kununurra for a night, taking in a sightseeing flight over the Bungle Bungles in Purnululu National Park before flying on to Perth; or, pass over Kununurra and fly on to Broome, where you can laze on the fabulous Cable Beach before taking a camel ride or checking out the locally crafted jewelry of pearls and diamonds. You could start this itinerary in the Red Centre, flying in from Sydney or Melbourne before returning there from Perth.

IF YOU HAVE 10 DAYS

If you follow the seven-day itinerary *above*, you can afford to spend an extra day in Perth, either taking the ferry to Rottnest Island, a lunch and wine-tasting cruise on the Swan River, or even a winery tour to Margaret River. You could also add in a two-day safari trip from Kununurra to Purnululu National Park, camping out in the bush camps there.

10

tours of the Alice Springs Desert Park. AAT Kings and Tailormade Tours operate three-hour guided trips that include visits to the Royal Flying Doctor Service Base, School of the Air, Telegraph Station, and Anzac Hill scenic lookout.

ESSENTIALS

Banks and Currency Exchange
ANZ, Commonwealth, National Australia, and Westpac all have branches and ATMs in Alice Springs, open 9:30–4 weekdays.

ART HUNT

If you're looking for Aboriginal art, galleries abound along Todd Mall (the main shopping street); they're filled with canvas and bark paintings, as well as handcrafted didgeridoos and other artifacts. You can also buy art directly from Aborigines on weekends outside Flynn Memorial Church in the mall.

Medical Emergencies Alice Springs Hospital ⊠ *Gap Rd. between Traeger Ave. and Stuart Terrace* ☎ *08/8951–7777.*

Police Police ☎ *08/8956–2166 Yulara, 08/8951–8888 Alice Springs.*

Taxi Alice Springs Taxis ☎ *08/8952–1877.*

Tour Operators AAT Kings ⊠ *74 Todd St.* ☎ *08/8952–1700, 1300/228546* ⊕ *www.aatkings.com.au.* **Alice Wanderer** ☎ *08/8952–2111, 1800/722111* ⊕ *www.alicewanderer.com.au.* **Tailormade Tours** ☎ *08/8952–1731, 1800/806641* ⊕ *www.tailormadetours.com.au.*

Visitor Information Tourism Central Australia. Tourism Central Australia dispenses information, advice, and maps and will book tours and cars. ⊠ *60 Gregory Terr.* ☎ *08/8952–5800, 1800/645199* ⊕ *www.centralaustraliantourism. com* ⊗ *Weekdays 8:30–5:30, weekends 9–4.*

EXPLORING ALICE SPRINGS

⟳ **Alice Springs Reptile Centre.** Thorny devils, frill-neck lizards, some of the world's deadliest snakes, and "Terry" the saltwater crocodile inhabit this park in the heart of town, opposite the Royal Flying Doctor Service. May to August (winter) the viewing is best from 11 to 3, when the reptiles are most active. There's also a gecko cave. Free talks are conducted daily at 11, 1, and 3:30, during which you can learn to pick up the pythons. ⊠ *9 Stuart Terr.* ☎ *08/8952–8900* ⊕ *www.reptilecentre. com.au* ⊗ *A$14* ⊗ *Daily 9:30–5.*

Royal Flying Doctor Service (RFDS). Directed from this RFDS radio base, doctors use aircraft to make house calls at settlements and homes hundreds of miles apart. The RFDS is a vital part of Outback life. The visitor center has historical displays, including replica planes, and an audiovisual show. Tours run every half hour throughout the year, and there's a good café at the back. ⊠ *8–10 Stuart Terr.* ☎ *08/8952–1129* ⊕ *www.flyingdoctor.net/Alice-Springs.html* ⊗ *A$8* ⊗ *Mon.–Sat. 9–4, Sun. 1–4.*

School of the Air. What do children who live hundreds of miles from the nearest school do for education? Find out at this informative visitor center, which harbors a working school within its walls. Uniquely Australian, discover how distance education has been delivered to the country's most remote parts since 1951; from telephone systems to

The Outback just outside of Alice Springs.

interactive online classes which are all on display, it's come a long way. ✉ *80 Head St.* ☎ *08/8951–6834* ⊕ *www.assoa.nt.edu.au* ✉ *$7.50* ⊙ *Mon.–Sat. 8:30–4:30, Sun. 1:30–4:30.*

OUTSIDE THE CITY

★ **Araluen Cultural Precinct.** The most distinctive building in this complex is the Museum of Central Australia, which charts the evolution of the land and its inhabitants—human and animal—around central Australia. Exhibits include a skeleton of the 10½-foot-tall duck relative *Dromornis stirtoni*, the largest bird to walk on earth, which was found northeast of Alice. Also in the precinct are the (free) Aviation Museum, Territory Craft, and Araluen Centre, home to the Araluen Art Galleries and the Namatjira Gallery, a collection of renowned Aboriginal landscapes. The precinct is 2 km (1 mi) southwest of town, and is on most tourist bus itineraries. The entry pass is good for two days. ✉ *61 Larapinta Dr.* ☎ *08/8951–1120* ✉ *A$15* ⊙ *Weekdays 10–4, weekends 11–4.*

☾ ★ **Alice Springs Desert Park.** Focusing on the desert, which makes up 70% of the Australian landmass, this 75-acre site contains 320 types of plants and 120 animal species in several Australian ecosystems—including the largest nocturnal-animal house in the southern hemisphere. An open-air habitat is also open at night, when animals are most active. Local Aboriginal guides share their native stories about the wildlife and the land. Don't miss the twice-daily birds of prey presentation. Allow about four hours to explore the park; it's 6½ km (4 mi) west of Alice Springs, and is on the Alice Wanderer and Tailormade bus itineraries. ✉ *Larapinta Dr.* ☎ *08/8951–8788* ⊕ *www.alicespringsdesertpark.com.au* ✉ *A$20* ⊙ *Daily 7:30–6.*

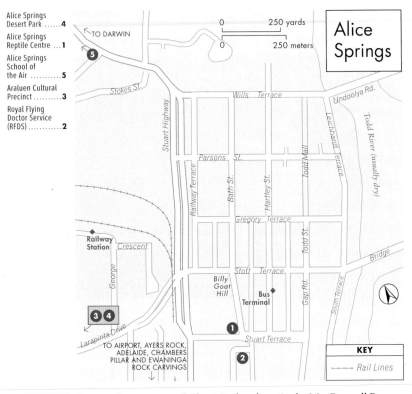

OFF THE BEATEN PATH   Spectacular scenery and Aboriginal rock art in the MacDonnell Ranges east of the Alice are well worth a day or more of exploration. Emily Gap (a sacred Aboriginal site), Jessie Gap, and Corroboree Rock, once a setting for important men-only Aboriginal ceremonies, are within the first 44 km (27 mi) east of Alice Springs. Beyond these are Trephina Gorge, John Hayes Rockhole, and N'Dhala Gorge Nature Park (with numerous Aboriginal rock carvings).

Arltunga Historical Reserve, 110 km (69 mi) northeast of Alice, contains the ruins of a 19th-century gold-rush site. If you fancy fossicking (prospecting) for your own semiprecious stones, you can take your pick—and shovel—at Gemtree in the Harts Ranges, 140 km (87 mi) northeast of Alice. Ranger stations (☎ 08/8956–9765) are at Trephina Gorge and John Hayes Rockhole.

OUTDOOR ACTIVITIES

CAMEL RIDING   **Pyndan Camel Tracks.** Pyndan Camel Tracks has daily one-hour camel rides at noon, 2:30, and sunset (each A$50) that explore a valley of diverse habitat about 15 km (9 mi) from Alice Springs and surrounded by the ancient MacDonnell Ranges. Half-day morning rides at 9 am (A$95) allow you to spend more time with your camel, discovering the Ilparpa Valley and stopping for morning tea in a sandy river bed. ☎ 0416/170164 ⊕ www.cameltracks.com.

HIKING/ BUSHWALKING The MacDonnell Ranges, the craggy desert mountains that frame Alice Springs, are rich with desert landscapes and Aboriginal significance. The **Emily and Jessie Gaps Nature Park**, located in the Eastern MacDonnells, just 10 km (6 mi) east of Alice Springs along the Ross Highway, contains registered sacred Aboriginal sites, including rock paintings depicting the caterpillar story of the Dreamtime—the Aboriginal stories of the world's creation.

The **Larapinta Trail** is a 223-km-long (145-mi-long) walking track that runs west from Alice Springs into the Western MacDonnell Ranges. It's a spectacular, though challenging, track that takes hikers through classically rugged and dry central Australian landscape. Hikers are encouraged to participate in the voluntary Overnight Walker Registration Scheme, designed to ensure that all trekkers on the trail can be tracked and accounted for in case of emergency. Contact the **Northern Territory Parks & Wildlife Service** (☏ *08/8951–8250*) for more information. **Tourism Central Australia** in Alice Springs (☏ *08/8952–5800*) can also advise you if you're interested in planning bushwalking itineraries.

> ### WORD OF MOUTH
>
> "I suggest two nights in Alice Springs, especially if you are flying in and out from either Sydney, Melbourne, or Adelaide. Most (but not all) flights to Alice Springs arrive and depart around mid-day, and after checking or fetching your baggage and checking into and out of your hotel, you may be left with barely one-half day of any travel day to sightsee."
> —AliceSprings

HOT-AIR BALLOONING **Outback Ballooning.** At dawn on most mornings hot-air balloons float in the sky around Alice Springs. Outback Ballooning makes hotel pickups about an hour before dawn and returns between 9 am and 10 am. The A$290 fee covers 30 minutes of flying time, insurance, and a champagne breakfast. A 60-minute flight costs A$385. ✉ *Box 2702* ☏ *1800/809–790* ⊕ *www.outbackballooning.com.au.*

QUAD-BIKE RIDING **Outback Quad Adventures.** Hop aboard a motorbike with four huge wheels and explore the Northern Territory's oldest working cattle station with Outback Quad Adventures. The company collects you from Alice Springs and takes you to the station, 17 km (10 mi) out of town on the edge of the MacDonnell Ranges. No special license is needed, and all tours are escorted by guides with two-way radios. Rides of 2½ hours (A$135) and 3½ hours (A$199) and overnight tours—which include barbecue dinner with wine, sleeping bags, and breakfast (A$399)—operate year-round. ✉ *Undoolya Station, Undoolya Rd.* ☏ *08/8953–0697.*

WHERE TO EAT

$$ ✗**Barra on Todd.** Northern Territory barramundi prepared five ways—
AUSTRALIAN char-grilled, herb and macadamia oven-roasted, grilled, panfried, and
★ more—is the highlight at this classy restaurant and bar at Chifley Alice Springs Resort. It's popular with locals, too. Other delicious dishes on offer include kangaroo fillet, mango-glazed pork cutlet, and prawns flambéed in Malibu. ✉ *34 Stott Terr.* ☏ *08/8952–3523.*

10

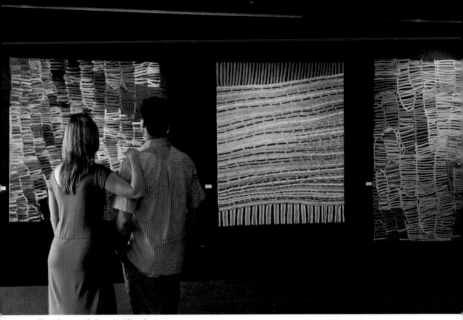

The Mbantua Gallery in Alice Springs.

$$ ✕ **Bojangles Saloon and Restaurant.** Cowhide seats, tables made from
AUSTRALIAN   old *Ghan* railway benches, and a life-size replica of bushranger Ned
Kelly give this lively restaurant true Outback flavor. Food is classic
Northern Territory tucker: barramundi, kangaroo, camel, emu, thick
slabs of ribs, and huge steaks—and the peanuts are free! Bojangles
also broadcasts its own live radio show across the Territory via Sun
FM radio, and around the world via the Internet, every night from
8:30 pm. Come along and be part of this unique concept, and wave
to family and friends on one, or all, of their four Webcams which are
featured on their Web site. ⊠ *80 Todd St.* ☎ *08/8952–2873* ⊕ *www.
bossaloon.com.au.*

$$ ✕ **Casa Nostra.** Red-and-white-checkered tablecloths, Chianti bottles,
ITALIAN   and plastic grapes festoon this family-run Alice old-timer. Locals crowd
in for traditional meat dishes, pizza, and pasta, including Al's Special,
a dish of chicken parmigiana paired with pasta in a cream-and-black-
pepper sauce that the chef took 15 years to perfect. Take a tip from the
regulars and preorder a serving of vanilla slice for dessert, or you might
miss out on this scrumptious cake of layered papery pastry and custard
cream. ⊠ *Undoolya Rd. at Stuart Terr.* ☎ *08/8952–6749* ⊘ *Closed Sun.
and late Dec.–mid-Jan. No lunch.*

$$ ✕ **Hanuman Thai.** With its Thai, Nonya (Malaysian), and Indian-
ASIAN   flavored menu, this lovely spot is the only place in the desert to
Fodor's Choice   offer a range of big-city-quality Southeast Asian food. The trumpet
★   mushrooms topped with prawn and pork mince are popular, as is the
barramundi poached in coconut sauce. Desserts include black-rice
brûlée, and banana spring rolls with butterscotch sauce. This place is
as popular with the locals as it is the tourists—which is always a good

sign. ✉ *Crown Plaza Alice Springs, 82 Barrett Dr.* ◧ *Box 16340871* ☎ *08/8953–7188* ⊕ *www.hanuman.com.au* ⊗ *No lunch weekends.*

WHERE TO STAY

For expanded hotel reviews, visit Fodors.com.

\$\$ ☷ **Chifley Alice Springs Resort.** This convenient spot might make you for-
★ get that you're surrounded by desert; the palm trees and broad, foliage-
fringed lawns provide respite from the region's red dirt. **Pros:** short walk
to shops; tour desk can book variety of tours; great beds. **Cons:** convention facilities attract tour groups; no views; reception staff often inex-
perienced; WiFi costs \$25 per day. ✉ *34 Stott Terr.* ☎ *08/8951–4545*
🖷 *08/8953–0995* ⊕ *www.alicespringsresort.com.au* ⤹ *139 rooms* ♿ *In-
room: a/c, safe, Internet, Wi-Fi. In-hotel: restaurant, bar, pool, gym,
laundry facilities, business center, parking.*

\$ ☷ **Crowne Plaza Resort Alice Springs.** Landscaped lawns with elegant euca-
★ lyptus and palm trees greet you at this upscale international chain about
a mile outside town. **Pros:** excellent restaurant; many rooms have views
of MacDonnell Ranges; winner of environmental awards. **Cons:** in suburban area; no shopping nearby; Internet \$27.50 per day. ✉ *82 Barrett
Dr.* ☎ *08/8950–8000, 1800 007 697 reservations* ⊕ *www.crowneplaza.
com.au* ⤹ *229 rooms, 7 suites* ♿ *In-room: safe, Wi-Fi. In-hotel: restaurant, bar, pool, tennis court, gym, laundry facilities, business center,
parking* ❘◎❘ *Multiple meal plans.*

\$ ☷ **Desert Palms Resort.** Although just a few minutes' walk from the cen-
ter of Alice Springs, this resort property feels a million miles away
from the red desert. **Pros:** villas are private, screened by foliage; palm
trees and bougainvillea create a tropical garden; golf course adjacent;
licensed mini mart. **Cons:** no restaurant; villas are adequate, not fancy.
✉ *74 Barrett Dr.* ☎ *08/8952–5977, 1800 678 037 reservations* ⊕ *www.
desertpalms.com.au* ⤹ *80 cabins* ♿ *In-room: kitchen, Wi-Fi. In-hotel:
pool, tennis court, laundry facilities, parking.*

\$ ☷ **Lasseters Hotel Casino.** There are great views of the MacDonnell
Ranges from your balcony or the courtyard. **Pros:** mountain bikes
are complimentary; excellent views of MacDonnell Ranges; casino
and nightlife on-site. **Cons:** nights can be noisy with casino open till
3 am; adjacent convention center attracts big groups. ✉ *93 Barrett Dr.*
☎ *08/8950–7777* 🖷 *08/8953–2422* ⊕ *www.hotel.lhc.com.au* ⤹ *127
rooms, 13 suites* ♿ *In-room: safe, Internet. In-hotel: restaurant, bar,
pool, tennis court, gym, laundry facilities, business center, parking*
❘◎❘ *Some meals.*

NIGHTLIFE AND THE ARTS

Lasseters Hotel Casino. Entry is free at Lasseters Hotel Casino, where the
action goes late into the night. More than 290 slot machines sit here,
plus blackjack, roulette, craps, and baccarat tables. The two bars have
entertainment most nights—the Juicy Rump is a favourite for its live
music. ✉ *93 Barrett Dr.* ☎ *08/8950–7777, 1800/808–975.*

Sounds of Starlight. Sounds of Starlight is the place to enjoy evocative
Outback theater performances and didgeridoo music accompanied by
a slide show of Red Centre images. Concerts (A\$30) are held at 8 pm
Tuesday, Friday, and Saturday April–November; call ahead to check

10

the schedule. A pretheater dinner-and-show package (with dinner at the Red Ochre Grill across the street on the mall) costs A$78; the food is fine but nothing really remarkable, and those with more sensitive palates tend to feel the package deal isn't good value. Free didgeridoo classes (definitely good value) are held at the venue during the day. ⊠ *40 Todd Mall* ☎ *08/8953–0826* ⊕ *www.soundsofstarlight.com.*

SHOPPING

Shopping in Alice Springs is all about Aboriginal art and artifacts. Central Australian Aboriginal paintings are characterized by intricate patterns of dots—and are commonly called sand paintings because they were originally drawn on sand as ceremonial devices.

Aboriginal Desert Art Gallery. The Aboriginal Desert Art Gallery is one of the best local galleries for Aboriginal art. ⊠ *87 Todd Mall* ☎ *08/8953–1005.*

Gallery Gondwana. Gallery Gondwana sells wonderful contemporary and traditional Aboriginal art, and also has a branch in Sydney's suburbs. ⊠ *43 Todd Mall* ☎ *08/8953–1577* ⊕ *www.gallerygondwana.com.au.*

Red Kangaroo Books. From bush poetry and traditional bush tucker recipes to anthropological texts on Aborigines and their culture, Red Kangaroo Books has an outstanding collection of literature pertaining to all things Australian. ⊠ *79 Todd Mall* ☎ *08/8953–2137.*

Todd Mall Markets. The Todd Mall Markets are held every other Sunday morning from 9 am, late February to early December (and every Sunday in July). More than 100 stalls of local arts, crafts, and food are displayed while musicians entertain. ⊠ *Todd St.* ☎ *0458555506* ⊕ *www.toddmallmarkets.com.au.*

Papunya Tula Artists. Be drawn into Papunya Tula Artists, where Aboriginal art from the western and central desert regions is beautifully displayed. ⊠ *63 Todd Mall* ☎ *08/8952–4731* 📠 *08/8953–2509* ⊕ *www.papunyatula.com.au.*

WEST MACDONNELL RANGES

The West MacDonnell Ranges—stretching westward from just a few kilometers outside Alice Springs for around 200 km (125 mi)—are a spectacular series of red-capped mountains interspersed by rocky canyons and narrow gorges. Each of the chasms and gorges has its own unique character, and in many there are waterholes where you can swim. Black-footed rock wallabies are among the wildlife to be spotted. The 223 km (139 mi) Larapinta Trail in the park is the showpiece of Central Australian bushwalking. The trail is broken into 12 sections, each a one- to two-day walk.

GETTING HERE AND AROUND

To reach all the major sights, the Red Centre Way follows Larapinta Drive (the western continuation of Stott Terrace) from Alice Springs and Namatjira Drive westward to Glen Helen, about 130 km (81 mi) from Alice Springs. Roads leading off it access the highlights.

SAFETY AND PRECAUTIONS

Take care when bushwalking or hiking, as paths are usually rocky and uneven. Snakes inhabit most areas, so be cautious when walking through tall grass. You should always carry and drink plenty of water; at least one liter of water for every hour of walking in very warm weather.

TIMING

Most of the best locations are within the West MacDonnell National Park, and can be visited on a half-day or one-day trip from Alice Springs.

TOURS

Emu Run Tours. Emu Run Tours has a one-day tour by air-conditioned bus to all the major sights in the park, including Simpsons Gap, Standley Chasm, the Ochre Pits, and Ormiston Gorge. The cost is from A$199. ✉ *25 Undoolya Rd., Alice Springs* ☎ *08/8953–7057* ⊕ *www.emurun.com.au.*

Trek Larapinta. Trek Larapinta has small-group guided bushwalks along the Larapinta Trail. Their six-day tour costs from A$1,690; a longer tour completing the whole trail is 18 days (A$4,800). ⊡ *Box 3317, Alice Springs 0871* ☎ *0428/402027* ⊕ *www.treklarapinta.com.au.*

Wayoutback Desert Safaris. Wayoutback Desert Safaris has a two-and-a-half day, four-wheel-drive tour to the West MacDonnells, camping out overnight. The cost is from A$445. ✉ *30 Kidman St., Alice Springs* ☎ *08/8952–4324* ⊕ *www.wayoutback.com.au.*

ESSENTIALS

Visitor Information Simpsons Gap Visitor Information Centre (☎ *08/8951–8250*) is 1 km from the turn-off into Simpsons Gap, 18 km from Alice Springs.

EXPLORING

These sights are organized by distance—from closest to farthest—from Alice Springs.

John Flynn's Grave. John Flynn's Grave memorializes the Royal Flying Doctor Service founder. It's on a rise with the stark ranges behind, in a memorable setting 6 km (4 mi) west of Alice Springs. ✉ *Larapinta Dr.* ☎ *No phone* ⊕ *www.flynntrail.org.au* ⛺ *Free* ⊙ *Daily 24 hrs.*

Simpsons Gap. Simpsons Gap isn't dramatic, but it's the closest gorge to town. Stark-white ghost gums, red rocks, and the purple-haze mountains provide a taste of the scenery to be seen farther into the ranges. The gap can be crowded in the morning and late afternoon, since these are the best times to see rock wallabies, but unlike Standley Chasm, it's only a short walk from the parking lot. ✉ *Larapinta Dr., 18 km (11 mi) west of Alice Springs, then 6 km (4 mi) on side road* ☎ *08/8951–8250* ⛺ *Free* ⊙ *Daily 5–8.*

★ **Standley Chasm.** Standley Chasm is one of the most impressive canyons in the MacDonnell Ranges. At midday, when the sun is directly overhead, the 10-yard-wide canyon glows red from the reflected light—this lasts for just 15 minutes. The walk from the parking lot takes about 20 minutes, and is rocky toward the end. There's a kiosk selling snacks and drinks at the park entrance. ✉ *Larapinta Dr., 40 km (25 mi) west of Alice Springs, then 9 km (5½ mi) on Standley Chasm Rd.* ☎ *08/8956–7440* ⛺ *A$8* ⊙ *Daily 8–6.*

10

The Heartland

For most Australians the Red Centre is the mystical and legendary core of the continent, and Uluru is its beautiful focal point. Whether they have been there or not, locals believe its image symbolizes a steady pulse that radiates deep through the red earth, through the heartland, and all the way to the coasts.

Little more than a thumbprint within the vast Australian continent, the Red Centre is harsh and isolated. Its hard, relentless topography (and lack of conveniences) makes this one of the most difficult areas of the country to survive in, much less explore. But the early pioneers—some foolish, some hardy—managed to set up bases that thrived. They created cattle stations, introduced electricity, and implemented telegraph services, enabling them to maintain a lifestyle that, if not luxurious, was at least reasonably comfortable.

The people who now sparsely populate the Red Centre are a breed of their own. Many were born and grew up here, but many others were "blow-ins," immigrants from far-flung countries and folk from other Australian states who took up the challenge to make a life in the desert and stayed on as they succeeded. Either way, folks out here have a few common characteristics. They're laconic and down-to-earth, canny and astute, and likely to try to pull your leg when you least expect it.

No one could survive the isolation without a good sense of humor: Where else in the world would you hold a bottomless-boat race in a dry riverbed? The Henley-on-Todd, as it is known, is a sight to behold, with dozens of would-be skippers bumbling along within the bottomless-boat frames.

As the small towns grew and businesses quietly prospered in the mid-1800s, a rail link between Alice Springs and Adelaide was planned. However, the undercurrent of challenge and humor that touches all life here ran through this project as well. Construction began in 1877, but things went wrong from the start. No one had seen rain for ages, and no one expected it; hence, the track was laid right across a floodplain. It wasn't long before locals realized their mistake, when intermittent heavy floods regularly washed the tracks away. The railway is still in operation today, and all works well, but its history is one of many local jokes here.

For some, the Red Centre is the real Australia, a special place where you will meet people whose generous and sincere hospitality may move you. The land and all its riches offer some of the most spectacular and unique sights on the planet, along with a sense of timelessness that will slow you down and fill your spirit. Take a moment to shade your eyes from the sun and pick up on the subtleties that nature has carefully protected and camouflaged here, and you will soon discover that the Red Centre is not the dead center.

—Bev Malzard

Standley Chasm, West MacDonnell Ranges near Alice Springs.

Ellery Creek Big Hole. Ellery Creek Big Hole is one of the coldest swimming holes in the Red Centre. It's also the deepest and most permanent water hole in the area, so you may glimpse wild creatures like wallabies or goannas (monitor lizards) quenching their thirst. Take the 3-km (2-mi) Dolomite Walk for a close-up look at this fascinating geological site. ⊠ *Namatjira Dr.* ⊹ *88 km (55 mi) west of Alice Springs* ☎ *08/8951–8250.*

Serpentine Gorge. Serpentine Gorge, is best seen by taking a refreshing swim through the narrow, winding gorge. According to an Aboriginal myth a fierce serpent makes its home in the pool, hence the name. ⊠ *Namatjira Dr. , 99 km (61 mi) west of Alice Springs* ☎ *08/8951–8250.*

Glen Helen Gorge. Glen Helen Gorge slices through the MacDonnell Ranges, revealing dramatic rock layering and tilting. The gorge was cut by the sporadic Finke River, often described as the oldest river in the world. Here the river forms a broad, cold, permanent water hole that's perfect for a bracing swim. ⊠ *Namatjira Dr 132 km (82 mi) west of Alice Springs* ☎ *08/8951–8250.*

Ormiston Gorge. Ormiston Gorge is truly breathtaking. A short climb takes you to Gum Tree Lookout, where you can see the spectacular 820-foot-high red gorge walls rising from the permanent pool below. There is a water hole suitable for swimming. Trails include the 7-km (4½-mi) Ormiston Pound Walk. ⊠ *Namatjira Dr.* ⊹ *135 km (84 mi) west of Alice Springs* ☎ *08/8956–7799.*

WHERE TO STAY
For expanded hotel reviews, visit Fodors.com.

$$
\begin{array}{ll}
\$\$ & \text{🔲 Glen Helen Resort. Better described as an Outback lodge, Glen Helen} \\
\bigstar
\end{array}
$$

$$ \text{🔲} $$ **Glen Helen Resort.** Better described as an Outback lodge, Glen Helen Resort earns its charm from its traditional bush welcome and atmosphere. **Pros:** traditional Outback Australia atmosphere; easy access to Larapinta Walking Trail; plenty of opportunities to see local fauna. **Cons:** one hour from Alice Springs; limited amenities in motel rooms; need your own transport. ✉ *Namatjira Dr.* 📫 *Box 2207, Alice Springs 0871* ✈ *135 km (84 mi) west of Alice Springs* ☎ *08/8956–7489* ⊕ *www. glenhelen.com.au* 🛏 *25 motel rooms, 10 bunkhouse rooms, 105 unpowered sites, 38 powered sites* ♿ *In-room: no TV. In-hotel: restaurant, bar, pool, laundry facilities.*

ULURU AND KATA TJUTA

It's easy to see why the Aborigines attach spiritual significance to Uluru (Ayers Rock). It rises magnificently above the plain and dramatically changes color throughout the day. The Anangu people are the traditional owners of the land around Uluru and Kata Tjuta. They believe they are direct descendants of the beings—which include a python, an emu, a blue-tongue lizard, and a poisonous snake—who formed the land and its physical features during the Tjukurpa (the "Dreamtime," or creation period). At more than 1,100 feet, Uluru is one of the world's largest monoliths, though such a classification belies the otherworldly, spiritual energy surrounding it. Historically, it's been a sacred site to the Aborigines, and from that a great controversy has arisen over whether it's appropriate to climb the rock. The Anangu people have politely requested that visitors not scale Uluru, but thousands of tourists wish to do so every year. If you want to make the climb, a well-marked path will help you do it.

Kata Tjuta (the Olgas), 53 km (33 mi) west, is a series of 36 gigantic rock domes hiding a maze of fascinating gorges and crevasses. The names Ayers Rock and the Olgas are used out of familiarity alone; at the sites themselves, the Aboriginal Uluru and Kata Tjuta are the respective names of preference. The entire area is called Yulara, though the airport is still known as Ayers Rock.

Uluru and Kata Tjuta have very different compositions. Monolithic Uluru is a type of sandstone called arkose, while the rock domes at Kata Tjuta are composed of conglomerate. Both of these intriguing sights lie within Uluru–Kata Tjuta National Park, which is protected as a World Heritage Site. The whole experience is a bit like seeing the Grand Canyon turned inside out, and a visit here will be remembered for a lifetime.

GETTING HERE AND AROUND
Qantas operates daily direct flights from Sydney, Perth, and Cairns, and Virgin Australia flies direct from Sydney to Ayers Rock Airport, which is 5 km (3 mi) north of the resort complex. Passengers from other capital cities fly to Alice Springs to connect with flights to Ayers Rock Airport. Qantas flies daily 40-minute flights from Alice Springs to Ayers Rock.

AAT Kings runs a complimentary shuttle bus between the airport and Yulara, which meets every flight. If you have reservations at the resort, representatives wait outside the baggage-claim area of the airport to whisk you and other guests away on the 10-minute drive.

If you're driving from Alice Springs, it's a five-hour-plus 440-km (273-mi) trip to Ayers Rock Resort. The road is paved, but lacks a shoulder, and is one lane in each direction for the duration, making it challenging and risky to overtake the four-trailer-long road trains. The unscenic route often induces fatigue.

> ### WATCH THE SKY
>
> More stars and other astronomical sights, such as the fascinating Magellanic Clouds, are visible in the southern hemisphere than in the northern, and the desert night sky shows off their glory with diamond-like clarity. Look out for the Southern Cross, the constellation that navigators used for many centuries to find their way—most Australians will proudly point it out for you.

From the resort it's 19 km (12 mi) to Uluru or 53 km (33 mi) to Kata Tjuta. The road to Kata Tjuta is paved.

If you prefer to explore Uluru and Kata Tjuta on your own schedule, then renting your own car is a good idea; the only other ways to get to the national park are on group bus tours or by chauffeured taxi or coach. Avis, Hertz, and Thrifty–Territory Rent-a-Car all rent cars at Ayers Rock Resort. Arrange for your rental early, since cars are limited.

Automobile Association of N.T. ☎ *08/8956–2188, 13–1111 emergency road assistance* ⊕ *www.aant.com.au.*

N.T. Road Report ☎ *1800/246–199* ⊕ *www.ntlis.nt.gov.au/roadreport/.*

Greyhound and AAT Kings coaches (which runs day and extended tours) make daily departures from Alice Springs to Ayers Rock.

AAT Kings ☎ *08/8956–2171, 1300/228–546* ⊕ *www.aatkings.com.*

Greyhound Australia ☎ *08/8952–7888, 1300/473–946* ⊕ *www.greyhound. com.au.*

SAFETY AND PRECAUTIONS

Water is vital in the Red Centre. It is easy to forget, but the dry atmosphere and the temperatures can make you prone to dehydration. If you are walking or climbing, you will need to consume additional water at regular intervals. You should carry at least two liters of water for every hour. Regardless of where you plan to travel, it is essential to carry plenty of water, 20 liters minimum.

TIMING

If seeing Uluru is your reason for visiting the Red Centre, there are tours that fly in and out, stopping just long enough to watch the rock at sunset. However, for a more leisurely visit, allow two days so you can also visit Kata Tjuta (the Olgas) nearby.

TOURS

AIR TOURS The best views of Uluru and Kata Tjuta are from the air. Light plane tours, with courtesy hotel pickup from Ayers Rock Resort hotels, include 40-minute flights over Ayers Rock and the Olgas, and day tours to Kings Canyon and a huge meteorite crater known as Gosses Bluff. Prices run from A$95 to A$695 per person; for options, contact Ayers Rock Scenic Flights. Helicopter flights are A$135 per person for 15 minutes over Ayers Rock, or $250 for 30 minutes over the Olgas and the rock.

Ayers Rock Helicopters ☎ 08/8956–2077 🖷 08/8956–2060 ⊕ www. helicoptergroup.com.

Ayers Rock Scenic Flights ☎ 08/8956–2345 🖷 08/8956–2060 ⊕ www. ayersrockflights.com.

Professional Helicopter Services ☎ 08/8956–2003 ⊕ www.phs.com.au.

ABORIGINAL TOURS
Owned and operated by local Aboriginal people, Anangu Tours organizes trips through the Uluru and Kata Tjuta region. Tours, which leave from the Ayers Rock Resort, include the Aboriginal Uluru Tour (A$139 with breakfast), led by an Aboriginal guide; the Kuniya Sunset Tour (A$116); and the Anangu Cultural Pass, which combines the first two tours and Kata Tjuta over 24 hours (A$229). You can drive to the trailhead of the Liru Walk (A$69). Guides are Aborigines who work with interpreters. Aboriginal art aficionados can attend dot-painting workshops (A$87).

Anangu Tours ☎ 08/8950–3030 ⊕ www.ananguwaai.com.au/anangu_tours/.

CAMEL TOURS
A great way to get out in the open and see the sights is from the back of one of the desert's creatures. Uluru Camel Tours, a subsidiary of Anangu Tours, has sunrise and sunset tours that last for 2½ hours for A$199; tours leave from the Ayers Rock Resort.

Camels Australia. En route from Alice Springs you'll find Camels Australia. Owners Neil and Jayne Waters offer everything from quick jaunts to whole-day safaris. Phone beforehand for all rides; 72 hours' notice for day treks is required. It's A$25 for a half-hour ride and A$45 for a one-hour ride, and A$175 for a day trek with lunch. Take-away food and gifts are also available at the farm shop. ✉ Stuarts Well, Stuart Hwy., 90 km (56 mi) south of Alice Springs ☎ 08/8956–0925 🖷 08/8956–0909 ⊕ www.camels-australia.com.au.

Uluru Camel Tours ☎ 08/8956–2444 ⊕ ulurucameltours.com.au.

WALKING TOURS
SEIT Outback Australia. SEIT Outback Australia specializes in small-group tours with guides who have extensive local knowledge. The Uluru Trek, a 14-km (8-mi) hike around the base, gives fascinating insights into the area's significance to the Aboriginal people (A$132). Book at least a day in advance. ☎ 08/8956–3156 ✎ bookings@seitoutbackaustralia.com. au ⊕ www.seitoutbackaustralia.com.au.

ESSENTIALS

Banks and Currency Exchange ANZ bank has a branch and ATM at Yulara Village at Ayers Rock Resort.

Emergencies Ayers Rock Medical Centre. The medical clinic at Ayers Rock Resort in Yulara is open for emergencies only. ✉ Yulara Dr. near police station, Ayers Rock Resort ☎ 08/8956–2286.

Police Yulara Police ☎ 08/8956–2166.

Taxi **Uluru Express** Uluru Express minibuses can whisk you from the lodgings at Ayers Rock Resort to the sights for much less than the cost of a guided bus tour—plus, you can go at your own convenience. ☎ 08/8956–2019 ⊕ www.uluruexpress.com.au.

Visitor Information **The Uluru–Kata Tjuta Cultural Centre** is on the park road just before you reach the rock. It also contains the park's ranger station. The Cultural Centre is open daily 7–6. The Ayers Rock Visitor Centre next to the Desert Gardens Hotel on Yulara Drive is open daily 9:30–4:30 and includes an interesting free museum. **Ayers Rock Visitor Centre** ☎ 08/8957–7377. **Uluru–Kata Tjuta Cultural Centre** ☎ 08/8956–1128.

OFF THE
BEATEN
PATH

The 440-km (273-mi) drive to Uluru from Alice Springs along the Stuart and Lasseter highways takes about five hours—or longer if you veer off the track to see some other impressive geological sites.

Ewaninga Rock Carvings Conservation Reserve. More than 3,000 ancient Aboriginal rock engravings (petroglyphs) are etched into sandstone outcrops in Ewaninga Rock Carvings Conservation Reserve, 39 km (24 mi) south of Alice on the road to Chamber's Pillar. Early-morning and late-afternoon light are best for photographing the lines, circles, and animal tracks. A 2-km (1-mi) trail leads to several art sites. The reserve is open all day year-round and is accessible by regular (rather than four-wheel-drive) cars. ⊠ *Old South Rd., 39 km (24 mi) south of Alice Springs* ☎ *08/8951–8250* ⛱ *Free.*

Henbury Meteorites Conservation Reserve. The Henbury Meteorites craters, 12 depressions between 6 feet and 600 feet across, are believed to have been formed by a meteorite shower about 5,000 years ago. One is 60 feet deep. To get here, you must travel off the highway on an unpaved road. ⊠ *Ernest Giles Rd., 114 km (71 mi) south of Alice Springs and 13 km (8 mi) west of Stuart Hwy.* ☎ *08/8951–8250.*

Rainbow Valley Conservation Reserve. Amazing formations in the sandstone cliffs of the James Range take on rainbow colors in the early-morning and late-afternoon light. The colors have been caused by water dissolving the red iron in the sandstone, and further erosion has created dramatic rock faces and squared towers. To reach the reserve, turn left off the Stuart Highway 75 km (46 mi) south of Alice. The next 22 km (13 mi) are on a dirt track, requiring a four-wheel-drive vehicle. ⊠ *Stuart Hwy.* ☎ *08/8951–8250* ⊕ *www.nt.gov.au/nreta/parks/find/rainbowvalley.html* ⛱ *Free.*

Fodor's Choice
★

Kings Canyon. Kings Canyon, in **Watarrka National Park,** is one of the most spectacular sights in central Australia. Sprawling in scope, the canyon's sheer cliff walls shelter a world of ferns and woodlands, permanent springs, and rock pools. The main path is the 6-km (4-mi) Canyon Walk, which starts with a short but steep climb to the top of the escarpment; the view 886 feet down to the base of the canyon is amazing. The trail then leads through a colony of beehive sandstone domes, known as the Lost City, to a refreshing waterhole in the so-called Garden of Eden, halfway through the four-hour walk. All this is visible during the half-hour scenic helicopter flight over the canyon and range from Kings Canyon Resort (A$250 or A$135 for 15 minutes). ⊠ *Luritja Rd., 167 km (104 mi) from turnoff on Lasseter Hwy.*

10

Kurrparru Tours. Run by a young man who has both Aboriginal and European heritage, this tour gives an insight not only into the Indigenous history of Kings Canyon, but also into the challenging duality of modern Aboriginal and white Australian communities. Being party to both, Micah Laughton is able to talk about the difficulties the two cultures regularly experience, and doesn't shy away from probing questions. Equipped with a great sense of humor, he also includes a few Aussie pranks along the way. Join him for a rim walk (A$55), 8 am daily, or the less challenging creek walk (A$45), 2 pm on demand. ⌂ *Alice Springs* ☎ *0404/326–527, 1800/011–144* ⊕ *www.kurrparru.com.au.*

WHERE TO STAY

$$$ 🏨 **Kings Canyon Resort.** The only place to stay within Watarrka National Park, this resort is 7 km (4½ mi) from the canyon. **Pros:** deluxe rooms offer floodlit views of adjacent ranges at night; bush entertainment at the Outback BBQ diner. **Cons:** room rates are pricey; room amenities are limited; Wi-Fi expensive at A$20/hr. ⌂ *Box 136, Alice Springs 0871* ☎ *08/8956–7442* ⊕ *www.kingscanyonresort.com.au* ⤳ *32 deluxe rooms, 96 standard rooms, 35 budget rooms, 72 powered caravan sites, unlimited tent sites* ♿ *In-room: a/c, Wi-Fi. In-hotel: restaurant, bar, pool, tennis court, laundry facilities, business center.*

¢ 🏨 **Kings Creek Station.** Although not everyone falls in love with this rus-
🕐 tic accommodation on a working cattle station, it is the most afford-
able option close to Kings Canyon. ⌂ *PMB 164, Alice Springs 0872* ✛ *Luritja Road via Lasseter Highway (from Alice Springs or Uluru), head towards Kings Canyon and see the large signs.* ☎ *08/8956–7474* ⊕ *www.kingscreekstation.com.au* ⤳ *25 cabins, 250 campsites* ♿ *In-room: no TV. In-hotel: bar, parking, flush toilets, drinking water, guest laundry, showers, picnic table, food service, electricity, public telephone, general store, service station (gas only)* ⏏ *Breakfast.*

ULURU

Fodor's Choice
★ **Uluru.** An inevitable sensation of excitement builds as you approach the great monolith. If you drive toward it in a rental car, you may find yourself gasping at the first glimpse of it through the windshield; if you're on a tour bus, you'll likely want to grab the person sitting next to you and point out the window as it looms larger and larger. Rising like an enormous red mountain in the middle of an otherwise completely flat desert, Uluru is a marvel to behold.

Uluru–Kata Tjuta Cultural Centre. The Uluru–Kata Tjuta Cultural Centre is the first thing you'll see after entering the park through a tollgate. The two buildings are built in a serpentine style, reflecting the Kuniya and Liru stories about two ancestral snakes who fought a long-ago battle on the southern side of Uluru. Inside, you can learn about Aboriginal history and the return of the park to Aboriginal ownership in 1983. There's also an excellent park ranger's station where you can get maps and hiking guides, as well as two art shops where you'll likely see indigenous artists at work. ⊠ *Off Lasseter Hwy.* ☎ *08/8956–1128*

The monumental Uluru as seen from the air.

EXPLORING

Uluru is circled by a road and walking trails. Two car parks—Mala and Kuniya—provide access for several of the walks, or you can choose to do the full circle of the Rock on the **Base Walk**.

As you work your way around Uluru, your perspective of the great rock changes significantly. You should allow four hours to walk the 10 km (6 mi) around the rock and explore the several deep crevices along the way. Some places are Aboriginal sacred sites and cannot be entered, nor can they be photographed. These are clearly signposted. Aboriginal art can be found in caves at the rock's base.

If you're looking for an easy walk that takes you just partway around the base, the **Mala Walk** is 2 km (1 mi) in length and almost all on flat land. The walk goes to the Kanju Gorge from the base of the climbing trail; park rangers provide free tours daily at 8 am from October to April and at 10 am from May to September.

The Liru Walk starts at the cultural center and takes you to the base of the Rock. Along the way are stands of mulga trees and—after rain—wildflowers. The track is wheelchair accessible, and the walk is an easy 1½ hours.

On the southern side of Uluru, the Kuniya Walk and Mutitjulu Water-hole trail starts of the Kuniya carpark and is an easy 45-minutes walk along a wheelchair-accessible trail to the waterhole, home of Wanampi, an ancestral snake. A rock shelter used by Aborigines houses rock art.

Another popular way to experience Uluru is far less taxing but no less intense: watching the natural light reflect on it from one of the two sunset-viewing areas. As the last rays of daylight strike, the rock positively glows as if lighted from within. Just as quickly, the light is extinguished and the color changes to a somber mauve and finally to black.

CLIMBING THE ROCK—OR NOT   There's only one trail that leads to the top of the rock. Though many people visit Uluru with the explicit intention of climbing it, there are a few things you should bear in mind before attempting this. First, Aboriginal people consider climbing the rock to be sacrilege—so if you believe in preserving the sanctity of sacred native sites, you may have to be content with admiring it from below. Your entry pass into the park even says, "It is requested that you respect the wishes of the Anangu by not climbing Uluru." The climb is not closed; the Aboriginal people prefer that you choose to respect their law and culture by not climbing because of your education and understanding. Second, if you do decide to make the climb, be aware that it's a strenuous hike, and not suitable for those who aren't physically fit. The ascent is about 1½ km (1 mi), and the round-trip climb takes about three hours. Sturdy hiking boots, a hat, sunscreen, and drinking water are absolute necessities. The climb is closed when temperatures rise above 36°C (97°F)—which means after 9 am most mornings in summertime.

SHOPPING

Cultural Centre. The Uluru–Kata Tjuta Cultural Centre not only has information about the Anangu people and their culture, it also houses beautiful art for purchase. The Ininti Cafe (08/8956–2214) carries souvenirs and light food. The nearby Maruku Arts (08/8956–2558) is owned by Aborigines, and sells Aboriginal paintings and handicrafts. Canvases drape the walls at Walkatjara Art Centre (08/8956–2537), where the stories of Anangu culture and heritage are told. The Cultural Centre itself is open daily 7–6 (information desk 8–5); Ininti Store is open daily 7–5; Maruku Arts is open daily 7:30–5:30; and Walkatjara art center is open daily 9–5.

    Ininti Cafe. Ininti Cafe carries souvenirs and light food. ☎ *08/8956–2214*
    Maruku Arts. Maruku Arts (08/8956–2558) is owned by Aborigines, and sells Aboriginal paintings and handicrafts. ☎ *08/8956–2558* 🖷 *08/8956–1128*.

KATA TJUTA

Fodor's Choice ★   **Kata Tjuta.** Many visitors feel that Kata Tjuta is more satisfying to explore than Uluru. Uluru is one immense block, so you feel as if you're always on the outside looking in. Kata Tjuta, as its Aboriginal name ("many heads") suggests, is a collection of huge rocks hiding numerous gorges and chasms that you can enter and explore.

EXPLORING

There are three main walks, the first from the parking lot into Walpa Gorge (formerly known as **Olga Gorge**), the deepest valley between the rocks. This is a 2-km (1-mi) walk, and the round-trip journey takes about one hour. The gorge is a desert refuge for plants and animals. The rocky track gently rises along a moisture-rich gully, passing inconspicuous rare plants and ending at a grove of flourishing spearwood.

More rewarding, but also more difficult, is the Valley of the Winds Walk. This 7.4-km (4.6-mi) walk is along a stony track to two spectacular lookouts—Karu and Karingana. Experienced walkers can complete this walk in about three hours. The Valley of the Winds walk is closed when temperatures rise above 36°C (97°F), which is after 11 am most days in summer.

The **Kata Tjuta Viewing Area,** 25 km (16 mi) along the Kata Tjuta Road, offers a magnificent vista, and is a relaxing place for a break. It's 600 meters from the car park, and interpretive panels explain the natural life around you.

AYERS ROCK RESORT

Officially known as the township of Yulara, Ayers Rock Resort is a complex of lodgings, restaurants, and facilities, and is base camp for exploring Uluru and Kata Tjuta. The accommodations and services here are the only ones in the vicinity of the national park. Uluru is about a 20-minute drive from the resort area (there's a sunset-viewing area on the way); driving to Kata Tjuta will take another 30 minutes. The park entrance fee of A$25 is valid for three days.

The resort "village" includes a bank, newsstand, supermarket, several souvenir shops, Aboriginal art gallery, hair salon, and child-care center.

The accommodations at the resort, which range from luxury hotels to a campground, are all run by Voyages Indigenous Tourism Australia and share many of the same facilities. Indoor dining is limited to each hotel's restaurants and the less-expensive Geckos Cafe, all of which can be charged back to your room. All reservations can be made through Voyages Indigenous Tourism Australia on-site, or their central reservations service in Sydney.

Central reservations service ☎ *02/8296–8010, 1300/134044* ⊕ *www. ayersrockresort.com.au.*

WHERE TO EAT

$$ ✕**Geckos Cafe.** Geckos Cafe in the resort's main shopping center is the
AUSTRALIAN most casual dining option on-site, and relative to other eateries, it's quite reasonably priced. The all-day dining options include affordable appetizers, hamburgers, pastas, and pizzas. ✉ *Town Sq., Yulara Centre, Yulara* ☎ *08/8957–7722.*

$$$ ✕**Kuniya Restaurant.** Kuniya Restaurant has the resort's best food. The
AUSTRALIAN decor reflects local legends, with images of Kuniya and Liru burned into two magnificent wooden panels at the entrance, and a Kuniya Dreaming mural covering the rear wall. Appetizers and main courses are named after the Australian states. Specialties include barramundi and duck, prepared with a combination of traditional and Mod-Oz flavors. ✉ *Sails in the Desert hotel, Yulara Dr., Yulara* ☎ *08/8957–7714* ⌕ *Reservations essential* ☯ *No lunch.*

$$ ✕**Pioneer BBQ and Bar.** You'll see why Australians love cooking and din-
AUSTRALIAN ing outdoors at the casual, although pricey, open-air Pioneer BBQ and Bar eatery at the hostel-style Outback Pioneer Hotel & Lodge. You can order steak, prawn skewers, or a kangaroo kebab from the server, and then cook it to your liking on huge barbecues. ✉ *Outback Pioneer Hotel & Lodge, Yulara Dr., Yulara* ☎ *08/8957–7605* ☯ *No lunch.*

10

$ ✕ **Tali Bar.** Tali Bar is a casual poolisde bar at Sails in the Desert hotel;
ECLECTIC   it offers an all-day menu, serving simple meals from 11 am to10 pm.
Cocktails are popular. ⊠ *Sails in the Desert hotel, Yulara Dr., Yulara*
☎ *08/8957–7417* ⚓ *Reservations essential.*

$$$$ ✕ **Sounds of Silence.** The most memorable group-dining experience in the
AUSTRALIAN   region is the unique, but expensive (A$164 including transfers) Sounds
★   of Silence, an elegant (although heavily attended) outdoor dinner served
on a dune that provides sunset views of either Uluru or Kata Tjuta
(though you can request to attend a dinner being held at the site that
allows you to view both). Champagne and Northern Territory specialty
dishes—including bush salads and Australian game—are served at a
lookout before you progress to a buffet meal devoured on tables covered
with crisp white linens, right in the desert. An astronomer takes you on
a stargazing tour of the southern sky while you dine.

WHERE TO STAY

¢   ⛺ **Ayers Rock Resort Campground.** Ayers Rock Resort Campground has
☾   220 tent sites. **Pros:** cheapest accommodations at Yulara; camper's
kitchen, mini mart and guest laundry. **Cons:** no private en suites available; limited shopping; need to catch resort shuttle to reach shops, no
dining outlets. ⊠ *Ayers Rock Resort, Yulara Dr., Yulara* ☎ *08/8957–
7001* ↴ *418 sites, 14 permanent tents, 14 cabins (all without bath)*
⚒ *In-room: a/c. In-hotel: pool, flush toilets, partial hookups, drinking
water, guest laundry, showers, fire grate, grills, picnic table, electricity,
public telephone, general store, play area.*

$$$$ ⛺ **Desert Gardens Hotel.** Extensive native gardens surround the clusters
of rooms in this one- and two-story hotel. **Pros:** central location for
resort facilities; shady gardens among gum trees. **Cons:** busy resort
entrance road passes hotel; rooms are pricey; Wi-Fi patchy and expensive at A$25/day. ⊠ *Yulara Dr., Yulara* ☎ *08/8957–7701* ↴ *218 rooms*
⚒ *In-room: a/c, safe, Wi-Fi. In-hotel: restaurant, bar, pool, business
center, parking.*

$$$$ ⛺ **Emu Walk Apartments.** Self-catering one- and two-bedroom apartments
with fully equipped kitchens, separate living rooms, and daily maid service are available at Emu Walk Apartments. **Pros:** extra beds ideal for
families or traveling companions; kitchen allows for self-catering; adjacent to resort dining options and shops. **Cons:** room rates are pricey;
rooms need refurbishment; limited amenities in rooms. ⊠ *Yulara Dr.,
Yulara* ☎ *08/8957–7701* ↴ *40 1-bedroom and 20 2-bedroom apartments* ⚒ *In-room: a/c, kitchen, Wi-Fi.*

$$$$ ⛺ **Longitude 131°.** Longitude 131° is set on its own in the desert 3 km
(2 mi) from Ayers Rock Resort and accessible only by private transfer.
Pros: luxury tented accommodation, some convertible to twin share;
dinner under the stars; touring included; attentive staff. **Cons:** isolated
location; taking all the tours can be tiring; no bathtubs; minimum
two-night stay. ⚑ *Yulara Dr., Yulara 0872* ☎ *08/8957–7131* ⊕ *www.
longitude131.com.au* ↴ *15 tents* ⚒ *In-room: safe, no TV, Wi-Fi. In-
hotel: restaurant, bar, pool, business center, some age restrictions*
🍽 *Multiple meal plans.*

"As we drove from Uluru (Ayers Rock), we approached Kata Tjuta. It consists of 36 domes and is as impressive and spiritual as Uluru." —Photo by Gary Ott, Fodors.com member

$$$$ Lost Camel Hotel. Blocks and splashes of lime, purple, and orange in boxy white rooms make the Lost Camel Hotel the funkiest for a thousand miles. **Pros:** brightly colored decor; unusual bathroom layout; Aboriginal-themed photographs on walls. **Cons:** Internet costs $25 per day and is slow; rooms in need of refurbishment. ⊠ *Yulara Dr., Yulara* ☎ *08/8957–5650* ⌦ *99 rooms* △ *In-room: a/c, safe, Internet, Wi-Fi. In-hotel: restaurant, bar, pool.*

$$$$ Outback Pioneer Hotel & Lodge. Outback Pioneer Hotel & Lodge is the most affordable hotel option at the resort and the most popular. **Pros:** lodge rooms are cheapest in the resort; swimming-pool area. **Cons:** resort shuttle bus to shops; hotel rooms somewhat dark. ⊠ *Yulara Dr., Yulara* ☎ *08/8957–7606* ⌦ *125 hotel rooms, 42 budget rooms (30 with bathroom, 12 without bathroom); 168 lodge bunk beds* △ *In-room: kitchen, no TV. In-hotel: restaurant, bar, pool, laundry facilities, business center.*

$$$$ Sails in the Desert. Architectural shade sails, ghost-gum-fringed lawns, Aboriginal art, and numerous facilities distinguish this upscale hotel option. **Pros:** Aboriginal artworks featured throughout; best restaurant at resort; distinctive architecture. **Cons:** pricey; rooms need refurbishment. ⊠ *Yulara Dr., Yulara* ☎ *08/8957–7417* ⌦ *214 rooms, 18 suites* △ *In-room: a/c, Wi-Fi. In-hotel: restaurant, bar, pool, tennis court, laundry facilities, business center.*

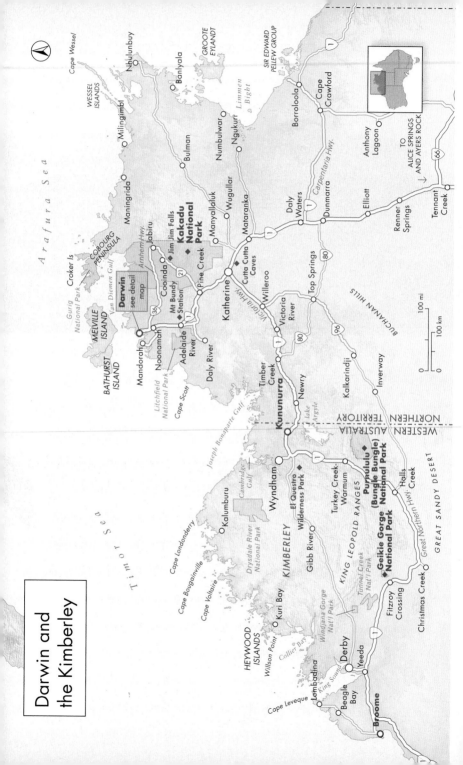

Darwin and
the Kimberley

DARWIN

The Top End is a geographic description—but it's also a state of mind. Isolated from the rest of Australia by thousands of miles of desert and lonely scrubland, Top Enders are different and proud of it. From Arnhem Land in the east—home to remote Aborigines—to the lush tropical city of Darwin and on to Broome in the west, the Top End is a region where individualistic people carve out their lives in what could be considered the real Australia.

The stark isolation of the Top End and Western Australia's Kimberley is reflected in its tiny population. Although the Northern Territory occupies one-sixth of Australia's landmass, its population of 275,000 makes up just more than 1% of the continent's citizenry—an average density of one person per 8 square km (3 square mi). The Kimberley, an area larger than the state of Kansas, is home to only 30,000 people. Traveling by road from Darwin to Broome is the best way to see the Kimberley, but you pass through only nine communities in 2,016 km (1,250 mi).

The region offers some of the most dramatic landscapes in Australia. A land of rugged ranges, tropical wetlands, and desert, of vast cattle stations and wonderful national parks, including the bizarre, beautiful, red-and-black-stripe sandstone domes and towers of Purnululu National Park and Kakadu National Park, a wilderness area that is one of Australia's natural jewels and the reason many people come to the Top End.

DARWIN

3,146 km (1,955 mi) northwest of Sydney, 2,609 km (1,621 mi) north of Adelaide.

No other city in Australia defines its history by a single cataclysmic event. For the people of Darwin—including the vast majority who weren't here at the time—everything is dated as before or after 1974's Cyclone Tracy, which hit on Christmas Eve. It wasn't just the death toll (65 people) that left a lasting scar in the area; it was the immensity of the destruction. More than 70% of Darwin's homes were destroyed or suffered severe structural damage; all services—communications, power, and water—were cut off. The resulting food shortage, lack of water, and concerns about disease moved government officials to evacuate the city; some 25,600 were airlifted out and another 7,200 left by road.

10

It's a tribute to those who stayed and to those who have come to live here after Tracy that the rebuilt city now thrives as an administrative and commercial center for northern Australia. Old Darwin has been replaced by something of an edifice complex—such buildings as Parliament House and the Supreme Court all seem too grand for such a small city, especially one that prides itself on its relaxed, multicultural openness.

The seductiveness of contemporary Darwin lifestyles belies a Top End history of failed attempts dating back to European attempts to establish an enclave in a harsh, unyielding climate in 1824. The original 1869

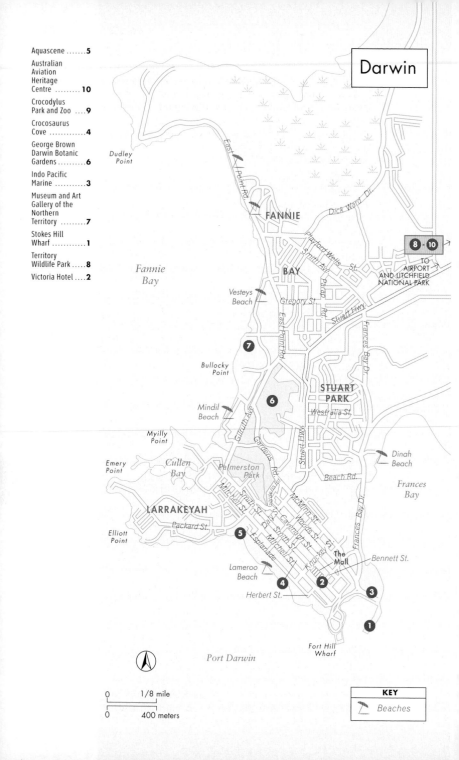

Darwin

Dudley
Point

East Point Rd.

Dick Ward Dr.

FANNIE

Playford
Wells
Smith Ave.
Parap Rd.

St.

8 · **10**

TO
AIRPORT
AND LITCHFIELD
NATIONAL PARK

BAY

Stuart Hwy.

Frances Bay Dr.

_Fannie
Bay_

Vesteys
Beach

Gregory St.

East Point Rd.

7

Bullocky
Point

**STUART
PARK**

6

Westralia St.

Mindil
Beach

Gilruth Ave.

Stuart Hwy.

Myilly
Point

Emery
Point

_Cullen
Bay_

Palmerston
Park

Gardens Rd.

The Esplanade

Dinah
Beach

Beach Rd.

_Frances
Bay_

LARRAKEYAH

Packard St.

Mitchell St.

Smith St.

Cavenagh St.

McMinn St.

Woods St.

Knuckey St.

Frances Bay Dr.

Elliott
Point

5

_Lameroo
Beach_

The Esplanade

Mitchell St.

**The
Mall**

Bennett St.

4

2

3

Herbert St.

1

Port Darwin

Fort Hill
Wharf

0   1/8 mile

0   400 meters

KEY
Beaches

settlement, called Palmerston, was built on a parcel of mangrove wetlands and scrub forest that had changed little in 15 million years. It was not until 1911, after it had already weathered the disastrous cyclones of 1878, 1882, and 1897, that the town was named after the scientist who had visited Australia's shores aboard the *Beagle* in 1839.

Today Darwin is the best place from which to explore Australia's Top End, with its wonders of Kakadu and the Kimberley region.

GETTING HERE AND AROUND

Darwin's International Airport is serviced from overseas by Qantas, Garuda, Royal Brunei, Jetstar, Tiger Airways, and Air North. Qantas and Garuda fly from Darwin to Bali several times a week, Tiger Airways and Jetstar connect Darwin with Singapore, and Air North flies to East Timor.

Qantas, Air North, Virgin Australia Airlines, Skywest, and Jetstar fly into Darwin regularly from other parts of Australia and operate regional flights within the Top End. Air North flies west to Kununurra and Broome, and east to Gove. The Darwin Airport Shuttle has regular service between the airport and the city's hotels. The cost is A$15 one-way, A$26 round-trip; book a day in advance. Taxis await at the airport's taxi rank. The journey downtown costs about A$25–A$30.

The *Ghan* train connects Darwin with Adelaide via Alice Springs on a two-night 2,979-km (1,861-mi) journey a couple of times a week.

Ghan ☎ *13–2147 bookings, 08/8213–4592* ⊕ *www.gsr.com.au.*

The best way to get around Darwin is by car. The Stuart Highway is Darwin's land connection with the rest of Australia. By road Darwin is 15 hours from Alice Springs (1,491 km [926 mi]), 2½ days from Broome via the Great Northern Highway (1,875 km [1,165 mi]), 4–5 days from Brisbane (3,387 km [2,105 mi]), and 5–6 days from Perth (3,981 km [2,474 mi]).

For drivers headed outside the Northern Territory, one-way drop-off fees for rental vehicles are often twice as much as a weekly rental. If you don't feel like driving, the bus network in Darwin links the city with its far-flung suburbs, and a choice of minibus operators, including the 24-hour Metro minibuses, run all over town for fixed prices starting at A$4. The main bus terminal (Darwin Bus) is on Harry Chan Avenue, near the Bennett Street end of Smith Street Mall. A minibus stand is also located at the front of Darwin's airport terminal.

SAFETY AND PRECAUTIONS

Swimming in the ocean is not recommended because of the box jellyfish. Salt and freshwater crocodiles are found in most Top End billabongs and rivers, and are occasionally seen on remote beaches. The accessible rivers and billabongs are generally signposted if saltwater crocodiles are known to inhabit the area, but if you are not sure, don't swim. If you are driving, avoid driving outside towns after dark due to the dangers presented by buffalo, cattle, horses, donkeys, and kangaroos on the road. If your vehicle breaks down, stay with it; it is easier to find a missing vehicle than missing people. If you are going for a bushwalk, always tells someone your plan and when you expect to return.

10

TIMING

Although Darwin has some attractions, many people view the city as the entry point to the Top End's national parks, in particular Kakadu and Litchfield. Two days in the city will be enough to see the main attractions, after which you will want to head to Kakadu.

TOURS

Every day but Sunday, Darwin Day Tours conducts afternoon trips for A$69, and for A$145 (April–November) you can take the afternoon tour and finish with a harbor cruise. Tours include historic buildings, the main harbor, the Botanic Gardens, the Northern Territory Museum of Arts and Sciences, East Point Reserve, and Stokes Hill Wharf. Alternatively, for A$45 you can hop on and off the Tour Tub "City Sights" bus. It picks up at Knuckey Street, at the end of Smith Street Mall, and runs daily 9–4. Quirkier is the Duck About tour, using an amphibious vehicle to deliver you from land to water while seeing the sights, for ($40). Daytime and sunset cruises explore a harbor five times the size of Sydney's. A two-hour cruise on the *Spirit of Darwin* begins at A$65. Trips depart daily from Cullen Bay Marina between April and October.

> ### CROCS BITE!
>
> The crocodile has long been a dominant predator in the wetland regions of Australia. Powerful and stealthy, the saltwater (estuarine) crocodile has little to fear—and that includes humans. More than 80,000 crocodiles are found in the coastal and tidal areas of rivers, as well as floodplains and freshwater reaches of rivers. In fact, they can be found in the larger rivers, lagoons, and billabongs right across northern Australia. Attacks on people are rare and deaths few (an average of one a year), but you should observe all no swimming and warning signs, and treat crocs with the respect.

Darwin Day Tours ☎ *1300/721–365* ⊕ *www.aussieadventure.com.au.*

✆ **Duck About Tours** ☎ *1300/382–522* ⊕ *www.duckabout.com.au.*

Spirit of Darwin ☎ *0417/381–977, 08/8942–3131* ⊕ *www.spiritofdarwin. net.*

Tour Tub ☎ *08/8985–6322* ⊕ *www.tourtub.com.au.*

ESSENTIALS

Banks and Currency Exchange The main banks with tourist services are Westpac and Commonwealth on the intersection of Smith and Bennett streets. Banking hours are Monday–Thursday 9:30–4 and Friday 9:30–5. Currency-exchange facilities are available on Smith Street Mall and Mitchell Street.

Medical Emergencies Royal Darwin Hospital ⊠ *Rocklands Dr. at Floreyr Ave., Tiwi* ☎ *08/8922–8888.*

Police Police ☎ *000 emergency, 08/8922–3344 general inquiries.*

Taxis City Radio Taxis ☎ *08/8981–3777.* **Dart Taxis** ☎ *08/8947–4300.* **Darwin Radio Taxis** ☎ *13–1008, 08/8985–0777.*

Visitor Information Top End Tourism. ⊠ *6 Bennett St., City Center* ☎ *08/8980–6000, 1300/138886* ⊕ *www.tourismtopend.com.au.*

EXPLORING: CITY CENTER
TOP ATTRACTIONS

Stokes Hill Wharf. The best views of Darwin Harbour are from this working pier, which receives cargo ships, trawlers, defense vessels, and, occasionally, huge cruise liners. It's also a favorite spot for Darwinites to fish, and when the mackerel are running you can join scores of locals over a few beers. The cluster of cafés and restaurants becomes crowded on weekends and when cruise ships arrive. Closest to the city, at the start of the Waterfront Precinct, you'll see the brand new Wave Lagoon (entry A$5 half day; $8 full day; open daily 10–6) and a free, sandy swimming beach. Both are understandably popular on hot days. ✉ *McMinn St., Darwin Harbour* ☎ *08/8981–4268.*

> **A TROPICAL SUMMER**
>
> Darwin's wet season—when the humidity rises and monsoonal rains dump around 52 inches—runs from December to April. The days offer a predictable mix of sunshine and afternoon showers, along with some spectacular thunder and lightning storms. There are fewer visitors at this time of the year, and Darwin slows to an even more relaxed pace. Across the Top End, waterfalls increase in size, floodplains rejuvenate to a lush green, and flowers bloom. Despite the rains, Darwinites still prefer the outdoors—eating, drinking, and shopping at the markets.

WORTH NOTING

NEED A BREAK?

Victoria Hotel. The balcony of the Victoria Hotel, overlooking the passing parade on Smith Street Mall, is a good place for a cool drink. A Darwin institution since its construction in 1890, the Vic has been hit by every cyclone and rebuilt afterward. ✉ *27 Smith St. Mall, City Center* ☎ *08/8981–4011* ⊕ *www.thevichotel.com.*

Indo Pacific Marine. This marine interpretive center houses a large open tank with one of the few self-contained coral-reef ecosystems in the southern hemisphere—and it's been growing on its own for 18 years. Other exhibits include a static display of rare, deepwater coral skeletons and an exhibit explaining the effects of global warming on the planet. Night tours, which begin at 7 on Wednesday, Friday, and Sunday, take you by ultraviolet flashlight to view the biodiversity of the fluorescing reef and live venomous animals; the colors the coral produce are astounding. The tours include a four-course seafood dinner, followed by a nocturnal coral reef tour of the exhibitions. Bookings are essential. ✉ *Stokes Hill Wharf, Wharf Precinct* ☎ *08/8981–1294* ⊕ *www.indopacificmarine.com. au* 🎫 *A$20, night tours A$110* ⊗ *Apr.–Oct., daily 10–5; Nov.–Mar., weekdays 9–1, weekends and public holidays 10–5.*

EXPLORING: AROUND DARWIN
TOP ATTRACTIONS

☺ ★ **Crocodylus Park and Zoo.** This world-renowned research facility has an excellent air-conditioned crocodile museum and education center. There are more than 1,200 crocodiles here, from babies to giants up to 5 meters long. A man-made creek is one of the newest features, and at

10

this writing it's expected to be ready to offer jumping crocodile boat experiences in 2012. The saurian section of the zoo includes the croc-infested Bellairs Lagoon and pens for breeding and raising. The park also has enclosures with lions, tigers, cassowaries, primates, and turtles, and it holds one of the biggest snakes in Australia: a Burmese python weighing 140 kg (308 lbs). Tours and feedings are at 10, noon, 2, and 3:30. ⊠ *815 McMillans Rd., opposite Berrimah Police Centre, Berrimah* ☎ *08/8922–4500* ⊕ *www.crocodyluspark.com* ☒ *A$35* ◷ *Daily 9–5.*

Ⓒ **Crocosaurus Cove.** Although not as information-rich as Crocodylus Park, this more modern croc haven wins on the convenience front, positioned right in the heart of town. Feeding times and the cage of death, where paying visitors are lowered into croc-infested pools in a perspex container, are the highlights. Feeding happens at different times throughout the day in the four main sections: fish, big crocs, turtles, and nocturnal reptiles. ⊠ *58 Mitchell St., Berry Springs* ☎ *08/8981–7522* ⊕ *www.croccove.com* ☒ *28* ◷ *8 am–6 pm daily in the Dry (Apr.–Sept.). Closed in the Wet.*

Ⓒ **George Brown Darwin Botanic Gardens.** First planted in 1886 and largely destroyed by Cyclone Tracy, the 92-acre site today displays rain forest, coastal fore dunes, mangroves, and open woodland environments. There are more than 450 species of palms growing in the gardens. A popular walk takes visitors on a self-guided tour of plants Aborigines used for medicinal purposes. The Children's Evolutionary Playground is an award-winning playground that traces the changes in plant groups through time, while the plant display house has tropical ferns, orchids, and other exotic plants. ⊠ *Gardens Rd. at Geranium St., Mindil Beach* ☎ *08/8981–1958* ⊕ *www.nt.gov.au/nreta/parks/botanic* ☒ *Free* ◷ *Geranium St. gates daily 7 am–7 pm, Gardens Rd. gates daily 7 am–7 pm; information center daily 8 am–4 pm.*

★ **Museum and Art Gallery of the Northern Territory.** Collections at this premier cultural institution encompass Aboriginal and Southeast Asian art and material culture, visual arts, crafts, maritime archaeology, Northern Territory history, and natural sciences. One gallery is devoted to Cyclone Tracy, and you can see "Sweetheart," a 16-foot 10-inch stuffed saltwater crocodile that attacked fishing boats on the Finniss River in the 1970s. The Cornucopia Museum Café overlooks tropical gardens and the Darwin harbor and is open all day for meals. ⊠ *19 Conacher St, Bullocky Point, Fannie Bay* ☎ *08/8999–8264* ☒ *Free* ◷ *Weekdays 9–5, weekends and public holidays 10–5.*

Ⓒ ★ **Territory Wildlife Park.** In 1,000 acres of natural bushland, this impressive park is dedicated to the Northern Territory's native fauna and flora. In addition to saltwater crocodiles, water buffalo, dingoes, and waterbirds, it also has an underwater viewing area for observing freshwater fish and a nocturnal house kept dark for late night creatures. The treetop-level walkway through the huge aviary allows you to watch native birds from the swamps and forests at close range. Daily events include feeding at 9 am and a birds of prey display at 11 am and 2:30 pm. ⊠ *Cox Peninsula Rd, 47 km (29 mi) south of Darwin, Berry Springs* ☎ *08/8988–7200* ⊕ *www.territorywildlifepark.com.au* ☒ *A$26* ◷ *Daily 8:30–4; exit open until 6.*

Enjoying an outdoor festival in Darwin.

WORTH NOTING

Aquascene. You can hand-feed hundreds of fish at this beach on the northwestern end of the Esplanade. At high tide people wade into the water with buckets of bread to feed the schools of batfish, bream, catfish, milkfish, and mullet that come inshore in a feeding frenzy. ⊠ *28 Doctor's Gully Rd., Doctor's Gully* ☏ *08/8981–7837* ⊕ *www. aquascene.com.au* ⊠ *A$11* ⊗ *Daily at high tide; check local publications or hotels for feeding times.*

Australian Aviation Heritage Centre. Due to its isolation and sparse population, the Northern Territory played an important role in the expansion of aviation in Australia, and this impressive museum traces the history of flight Down Under. Planes on exhibition include a massive B-52 bomber on permanent loan from the United States as well as a Japanese Zero shot down on the first day of bombing raids in 1942. ⊠ *557 Stuart Hwy., 8 km (5 mi) northeast of city center, Winnellie* ☏ *08/8947–2145* ⊕ *www.darwinsairwar.com.au* ⊠ *A$12* ⊗ *Daily 9–5.*

OUTDOOR ACTIVITIES

BICYCLING   Darwin is fairly flat and has a good network of bike paths, so cycling is a nice way to get around—although you might need something waterproof during the wet season. Rentals are available at some hotels.

FISHING   Barramundi, the best-known fish of the Top End, can weigh up to 110 pounds and are excellent fighting fish that taste great on the barbecue afterward.

Equinox Fishing Charters. Equinox Fishing Charters has half-day, day and extended fishing trips using the 38-foot *Tsar*, which is licensed to carry 12 passengers and two crew, and *Equinox II*, which can carry

18–20 people. Full-day fishing charters with all meals and tackle provided are from A$250 per person. ✉ *Shop 2, 64 Marina Blvd., Cullen Bay* ☎ *08/8942–2199* ⊕ *www.equinoxcharters.com.au.*

Northern Territory Fisheries Division's Recreational Fishing Office. The Northern Territory Fisheries Division's Recreational Fishing Office has information on licenses and catch limits. ✉ *Berrimah Research Farm, Makagon Rd., Berrimah* ☎ *08/8999–2144* ⊕ *www.nt.gov.au/dpifm/Fisheries.*

OFF THE BEATEN PATH

Litchfield National Park. This beautiful, relatively new park lies just 122 km (76 mi) south of Darwin off the Stuart Highway. Its 1,340 square km (515 square mi) are an untouched wilderness of monsoonal rain forests, rivers, and striking rock formations. The highlights are four separate, spectacular waterfalls—**Florence, Tjaynera, Wangi, and Tolmer Falls**—all of which have secluded plunge pools. ⚠ There are crocs here, so observe the "no swimming" signs. There is also a dramatic group of large, freestanding sandstone pillars known as the **Lost City**; and the **Magnetic Termite Mounds,** which have an eerie resemblance to eroded grave markers, dot the black-soiled plains of the park's northern area. You'll need to camp if you want to stay in the park; campgrounds and RV sites are near several of the major sights (call the Parks and Wildlife Service of the Northern Territory at ☎ *08/8976–0282* for information). There are also a few restaurants and a modest hotel (the Batchelor Resort [☎ *08/8976–0123*], which has comfortable hotel rooms, as well as RV and camping facilities) in the nearby town of Batchelor.

> **GONE FISHING**
>
> Joining a local tour guide is the best way to hook a big one. They know the best spots and techniques, and their local knowledge can make an enjoyable experience even better. In the estuaries you can catch threadfin and blue salmon, cod, queenfish, golden snapper, and the Top End's most famous fighting fish, the barramundi—barra in the local parlance. You don't have to go far—Darwin's harbor teems with fish.

WHERE TO EAT

$$
AUSTRALIAN

✕ **Buzz Café.** This is just one of many thriving waterfront eateries on the finger peninsula northwest of downtown, where Darwinites come to socialize. You can mingle at the bar with neighborhood millionaires, visiting boaties, and locals relaxing by the water, then dine on fresh seafood presented in a contemporary Australian style. There's air-conditioned comfort in the glass-walled dining room, or you can head out to the umbrella-shaded decks overlooking yachts and cruisers moored in the marina. One of the more curious panoramas is from the men's glass-sheeted urinal, which has one-way views over the restaurant. ✉ *The Slipway, 48 Marina Blvd., Cullen Bay* ☎ *08/8941–1141* ⊘ *Closed Sun. and Christmas Eve–New Year's Day.*

$$$
SEAFOOD

✕ **Crustaceans on the Wharf.** In a corrugated-iron storage shed at the end of a commercial pier, this large restaurant is dominated by a traditional Macassan fishing prau. Open to sea breezes, it's an ideal place to escape the city's summer heat. Seafood takes center stage here; standout choices include the Moreton Bay bugs (which are like small lobsters), calamari, and chili mud crabs, a specialty of the house. ⊠ *Stokes Hill Wharf, Wharf Precinct* ☎ *08/8981–8658* ⊗ *Closed Sun.*

$$ ✕ **Hanuman Darwin.** Excellent food
THAI
Fodor's Choice
★
and a wine list that includes the best from every grape-growing region in Australia are served against a backdrop of furnishings, tableware, and artworks from around the world in Hanuman's indoor and alfresco dining areas. By drawing on Thai, Nonya (Malaysian), and Indian tandoori culinary traditions, Hanuman's chefs turn local herbs, vegetables, and seafood into sumptuous and innovative dishes. Of special note are Hanuman oysters, lightly cooked in a spicy coriander-and-lemongrass sauce; Hanuman prawns; and any of the curries. ⊠ *93 Mitchell St., City Center* ☎ *08/8941–3500* ⊗ *No lunch weekends.*

$$ ✕ **Il Lido.** This polished Italian restaurant, owned by local celebrity chef,
ITALIAN
Jimmy Shu, sits in the outer curve of Darwin's new waterfront precinct, providing reflective views as you dine in the open air. The food is more modern Italian than traditional—recommended are the linguini with tiger prawns and the eight-hour roast lamb. Best suited to couples, there's a romantic atmosphere and a small bar next door. ⊠ *Wharf One, Kitchener Dr., Darwin Waterfront* ☎ *08/8941–0900* ⊕ *www. illidodarwin.com.au.*

$$ ✕ **Pee Wee's at the Point.** Uninterrupted views of Darwin Harbour at East
MODERN
AUSTRALIAN
★
Point Reserve make this restaurant a favorite with locals and visitors. Dine inside with views of the harbor through large glass doors, or out on the tiered timber decks beneath the stars. The cooking is modern Australian with a touch of Creole, and the carefully considered wine list has good values. Highlights include soft-shell mud crabs, Thai fried gold band snapper, and pan-roasted wild saltwater barramundi. ⊠ *Alec Fong Ling Dr., East Point Reserve, Fannie Bay* ☎ *08/8981–6868* ⊕ *www. peewees.com.au* ⌂ *Reservations essential* ⊗ *No lunch.*

$$ ✕ **Tasty House.** For made-to-order Chinese food with a distinctly Dar-
CHINESE
win flavor, including giant mud crab in sweet chili and salt and pepper prawns—make your way to this two-part restaurant. Part one is the à la carte section, though it's still relatively casual, while part two is called Roast and Noodle 328, and is found just around the corner in a covered arcade. It features cheaper and more basic roast meats eaten at plastic chairs and tables, food court style. If you've got more time, settle in at Tasty and choose their authentic dishes such as steamed prawn dumplings, Cantonese roast duck, pearl meat, and whatever local seafood is on the menu that day. ⊠ *Shop 9, Anthony Plaza, Smith St. Mall* ☎ *08/8981–2269* ⊗ *Weekdays 11 am–2:30 pm; Tues.–Sat. 5:30 pm–late, Sat. 10:30 am–2:30 pm, Sun. 9:30 am–2:30 pm.*

> **WORD OF MOUTH**
>
> "We went on to Wangi Falls [in Litchfield National Park]. There were many people there. We ate our picnic and then went to the pool below the Falls. It was such a large pool that there was plenty of room to swim, and I had a good swim over to the Falls and back. We then walked along the boardwalk and through the monsoon forest and up to the Treetop Platform. It was shady and very pleasant."
>
> —Suelynne

10

Tiwi islands sculptures at a gallery in Darwin.

WHERE TO STAY

For expanded hotel reviews, visit Fodors.com.

$$$$ 🏨 **Holiday Inn Esplanade Darwin.** With its colorful, round exterior, this five-story hotel is one of the city's most architecturally striking. **Pros:** city center location; large swimming pool; good breakfast. **Cons:** convention center attracts tour groups. ✉ *The Esplanade* ☎ *08/8980–0800, 1800/007697* ⊕ *www.holiday-inn.com/hidarwin* 🛏 *163 rooms, 34 suites* 🔧 *In-room: safe. In-hotel: restaurant, bar, pool, gym, parking.*

$ 🏨 **Mount Bundy Station.** This station near Adelaide River, 115 km (72 mi) south of Darwin, is handy for visiting Litchfield National Park, then continuing on to Kakadu National Park, Nitmaluk National Park, the Douglas Daly region, including the thermal springs, and Katherine. **Pros:** Australian cattle station experience; lots of birdlife around the billabongs; family-run and friendly staff. **Cons:** one-hour drive from Darwin; own transport essential; limited dining options. ✉ *Haynes Rd., Adelaide River* ☎ *08/8976–7009* ⊕ *www.mtbundy.com.au* 🛏 *3 cottages* 🔧 *In-room: no TV. In-hotel: pool, laundry facilities* ⚙ *Breakfast.*

$$$ 🏨 **Novotel Atrium.** Vying for the title of Darwin's prettiest hotel, the
★ Atrium has five floors served by glass elevators opening onto a central, vine-hung atrium. **Pros:** tropical garden in the atrium; some rooms have views over Darwin Harbour; close to shopping precinct. **Cons:** atrium can mean rooms are noisy; standard rooms are small, especially bathrooms. ✉ *100 Esplanade* ☎ *08/8941–0755* ⊕ *www.novotel.com* 🛏 *138 rooms, 2 suites* 🔧 *In-room: Internet. In-hotel: restaurant, bar, pool, parking.*

$$$ ⛱ **Sky City Darwin.** Shaped like pyramids with square tops, this casino and the smaller adjoining hotel are two of the most distinctive structures in the city. **Pros:** close to Mindil Beach Sunset Markets; excellent lagoon-style swimming pool; watch sunset while dining. **Cons:** casino operates 24 hours, so nights can be noisy; convention center attracts big groups. ⊠ *Gilruth Ave., Mindil Beach* ☎ *08/8943-8888, 1800/891118* 📠 *08/8943-8999* ⊕ *www.skycitydarwin.com. au* ⇥ *101 rooms, 16 suites* ⚐ *In-room: safe, Internet. In-hotel: restaurant, bar, golf course, pool, tennis court, gym, beach, parking* ⍟ *Some meals.*

THE INDIGENOUS ARTS SCENE

Start at the Museum and Art Gallery of the Northern Territory for a comprehensive understanding of indigenous art and artifacts. Then head to one of many art and craft outlets in and around Darwin to purchase an authentic and unique piece of art. In many indigenous communities throughout the tropical Outback—including Maningrida, Oenpelli, Tiwi islands, and Yirrikala—you can buy direct from the artist.

NIGHTLIFE AND THE ARTS

BARS AND LOUNGES   **Bogarts Bar and Grill.** Named after Humphrey, this small bar and restaurant is adorned with posters and memorabilia in a shabby chic kind of way, complete with couches and fantastic atmosphere. A favorite cocktail haunt for locals. ⊠ *52 Gregory St., Parap* ☎ *08/8981-3561.*

Monsoons. Monsoons is in the restored and remodeled original Darwin cinema building. It has an 80-foot-long granite bar with 20 different beers on tap and wines from Australia and New Zealand. The kitchen serves up African- and Eastern-influenced seafood, pastas, and meats. ⊠ *46 Mitchell St., City Center* ☎ *08/8941-7171.*

Shenannigans Irish Pub. Shenannigans Irish Pub has Guinness on tap, along with Kilkenny and Harp. Traditional Irish pub food is served, with meat roasts on Sunday. ⊠ *69 Mitchell St., City Center* ☎ *08/8981-2100.*

Ski Club. This is "the" place to go for a sunset beer in the tropics, and it's right next to the Museum and Art Gallery of the Northern Territory. Its plastic white chairs and tables add to the laid-back, "old Darwin" vibe. There's also a pool and live music on weekends. ⊠ *20 Conacher St., Fannie Bay* ☎ *08/8981-6630.*

Throb. Throb, a wild and wicked nightclub renowned for its floor shows and drag acts, is Darwin's premier gay nightclub. Open Friday and Saturday only, the shows start around 1:30 am and the fun doesn't end until 4 am. Cover charge is A$10–A$15. ⊠ *64 Smith St., City Center* ☎ *08/8942-3435.*

Top End Hotel. For a beer and live music, visit the Top End Hotel, a Darwin landmark, which has the city's biggest beer garden, a sports bar, a nightclub, and a band room. ⊠ *Daly and Mitchell Sts., Bicentennial Park* ☎ *08/8981-6511.*

CASINO   **SkyCity Darwin Casino.** SkyCity Darwin Casino is one of Darwin's most popular evening spots. The 460 gaming machines are open 24 hours,

10

while gaming tables are open from noon until 4 am Thursday and Sunday and until 6 am Friday and Saturday. ☒ *Gilruth Ave., Mindil Beach* ☎ *08/8943–8888* ⊕ *www.skycitydarwin.com.au.*

CINEMA   **Deckchair Cinema.** At this outdoor, 350-seat movie theater you can catch a flick beneath the stars against a backdrop of harbor lights. On show are Australian and major-release foreign films, screened every night April–November. Gates open at 6:30 for the sunset, and picnic baskets are permitted, although there are a snack kiosk and bar. The first movie screens at 7:30. ☒ *Jervois Rd. off Kitchener Dr., Wharf Precinct* ☎ *08/8981–0700* ⊕ *www.deckchaircinema.com* ☒ *A$15* ⊘ *Apr.–Nov. 6:30 pm.*

THEATERS AND   **Darwin Entertainment Centre.** The Darwin Entertainment Centre, behind
CONCERTS   the Carlton Hotel, has a large theater that stages concerts, dance, and drama. It also doubles as booking office for other big touring concerts in town—especially those at the Amphitheatre, one of Australia's best outdoor concert venues (entrance next to Botanic Gardens on Gardens Road). Check their Web site or the *Northern Territory News* or the *Sunday Territorian* for current shows. ☒ *93 Mitchell St., City Center* ☎ *08/8980–3333 box office, 08/8980–3366 general inquiries* ⊕ *www. darwinentertainment.com.au.*

SHOPPING

MARKETS   **Mindil Beach Sunset Market.** The Mindil Beach Sunset Market is an extravaganza that takes place every Thursday 5 pm–10 pm and every Sunday 4 pm–9 pm from April to October. Come in the late afternoon to snack at a choice of 60 stalls offering food from more than 25 different countries; shop at more than 200 artisans' booths; and enjoy singers, dancers, and musicians. Or join the other Darwinites with a bottle of wine to watch the sun plunge into the harbor. ☒ *Beach Rd., Mindil Beach* ☎ *08/8981–3454* ⊕ *www.mindil.com.au.*

Nightcliff Market. Nightcliff Market takes place Sunday 8 am–2 pm in Nightcliff Village, with craft and food stalls and entertainers. ☒ *Progress Dr., Nightcliff* ☎ *0414/368773.*

Parap Markets. North of downtown, the Parap Markets are open Saturday 8 am–2 pm and have a great selection of ethnic Asian food. ☒ *Parap Sq., Parap* ☎ *0438/882373, 08/8942–0805.*

Rapid Creek Markets. The Rapid Creek Markets, open Sundays 6:30 am–1:30 pm, are Darwin's oldest and have fresh food produce, as well as locally made handicrafts. ☒ *Rapid Creek Shopping Centre, Trower Rd., Rapid Creek* ☎ *08/8948–4866.*

KAKADU NATIONAL PARK

Begins 117 km (73 mi) east of Darwin.

Fodor's Choice   **Kakadu National Park.** Kakadu National Park is a jewel among the
★   many Top End parks, and many come to the region just to experience this tropical wilderness. Beginning east of Darwin, and covering some 19,800 square km (7,645 square mi), the park protects a large system of unspoiled rivers and creeks, as well as a rich Aboriginal heritage that extends back to the earliest days of humankind.

The superb gathering of Aboriginal rock art is one of Kakadu's major highlights. Two main types of Aboriginal artwork can be seen here. The Mimi style, which is the oldest, is believed to be up to 20,000 years old. Aborigines believe that Mimi spirits created the red-ocher stick figures to depict hunting scenes and other pictures of life at the time. The more recent artwork, known as X-ray painting, dates back fewer than 9,000 years and depicts freshwater animals—especially fish, turtles, and geese—living in floodplains created after the last ice age.

Most of the region is virtually inaccessible during the wet season. As the dry season progresses, billabongs (water holes) become increasingly important to the more than 280 species of birds that inhabit the park. Huge flocks often gather at Yellow Water, South Alligator River, and Magela Creek. Scenic flights over the wetlands and Arnhem Land escarpment provide unforgettable moments in any season.

GETTING HERE AND AROUND

From Darwin it's a two- to three-hour drive along the Arnhem Highway east to the entrance to the park at Bowali Visitor Center. Although four-wheel-drive vehicles are not necessary to travel to the park, they are required for many of the unpaved roads within, including the track to Jim Jim Falls. Entry is free, but you must buy a $25 National Park permit, which is good for 14 days.

SAFETY AND PRECAUTIONS

If you are driving, watch out for road trains—large trucks up to 160 feet in length with up to four trailers behind a prime mover. They are common on Northern Territory roads, and you should give them plenty of room. Avoid driving after dark outside towns because of the high likelihood of straying animals—kangaroos and cattle in particular. It is a good idea to always tell someone of your plans if your intend traveling to remote places; the same applies when bushwalking. Always make sure you have adequate water and food.

TIMING

The best time to visit is between May and September during the Dry. The shortest time you should allow is a three-day, two-night itinerary from Darwin. This will provide opportunities to visit the major sights— a cruise on the East Alligator River; Ubirr, a major Aboriginal rock-art site; a flight-seeing flight from Jabiru airport; Nourlangie Rock, another Aboriginal rock-art site; the Warradjan Aboriginal Cultural Centre, to learn about traditional Aboriginal people; and a sunset cruise on Yellow Water Billabong to see birds, crocodiles, and other wildlife. On the return to Darwin, you can visit Mamukala Wetlands for an abundance of birds and wildlife. A five-day itinerary will give you time to visit Jim Jim Falls and Twin Falls, a four-wheel-drive excursion.

TOURS

During the Dry, park rangers conduct free walks and tours at several popular locations. You can pick up a program at the entry station or at either of the visitor centers.

Intrepid Connections. Intrepid Connections provides camping and accommodation tours in Kakadu of two to five days, departing from Dar-

10

win. ⊠ *Level 3, Harrington St., The Rocks, Sydney* ☎ *02/8252–5300* ⊕ *www.connections.travel.*

Far Out Adventures. Far Out Adventures runs customized tours of Kakadu, as well as other regions of the Top End, for small groups. ⌂ *Box 1772, Howard Springs 0835* ☎ *04/2715–2288* ⊕ *www.farout.com.au.*

☾ ★ **The Gagudju Lodge Cooinda.** The Gagudju Lodge Cooinda arranges magical boat tours of Yellow Water, the major water hole in Kakadu, where innumerable birds and crocodiles gather. There are six tours throughout the day; the first (6:45 am) is the coolest— both in terms of temperature and activity. Tours, which run most of the year, cost A\$66 for 90 minutes and A\$97 for two hours, and include breakfast. ☎ *08/8979–0145* ⊕ *www.gagudju-dreaming.com.*

Kakadu Air. Kakadu Air makes scenic hour (A\$225) and half-hour (A\$130) flights out of Jabiru. In the Dry the flight encompasses the northern region, including Arnhem Land escarpment, Nourlangie and Mamakala Wetlands, East Alligator River, and Jabiru Township. During the Wet only, a similarly priced half-hour or one-hour flight takes in the Jim Jim and Twin falls. Heli tours are also available. ☎ *1800/089–113, 08/8941–9611* ⊕ *www.kakaduair.com.au.*

ESSENTIALS

Bank and Currency Exchange Westpac Bank ⊠ *Town Plaza, Jabiru* ☾ *9:30–4 Mon.–Thurs.; 9:30–5 Fri.*

Medical Emergencies Jabiru Community Health Centre ☎ *08/8979–2018* ☾ *8:30 am to 4 pm, plus 24-hour emergencies.* Royal Darwin Hospital. The nearest hospital is Royal Darwin Hospital. ⊠ *Rocklands Dr. at Floreyr Ave., Tiwi* ☎ *08/8922–8888.*

Police Jabiru Police Station ⌂ *Tasman Crescent, Jabiru* ☎ *13–1444.*

Visitor Information Kakadu National Park ⌂ *Box 71, Jabiru 0886* ☎ *08/8938–1120* ⊕ *www.environment.gov.au/parks/kakadu/.* Tourism Top End ⊠ *6 Bennett St., Darwin0800* ☎ *08/8980–6000* ⊕ *www.tourismtopend.com.au.*

Bowali Visitor Centre. Bowali Visitor Centre has state-of-the-art audiovisual displays and traditional exhibits that give an introduction to the park's ecosystems and its bird population, the world's most diverse. ⊠ *Arnhem and Kakadu Hwys.* ☎ *08/8938–1120* ⌷ *Free* ☾ *Daily 8–5.*

Warradjan Aboriginal Cultural Centre. Warradjan Aboriginal Cultural Centre, named after the pig-nose turtle unique to the Top End, provides an excellent experience of local Bininj (pronounced *bin*-ing) tribal culture. Displays take you through the Aboriginal Creation period, following the path of the creation ancestor Rainbow Serpent through the ancient landscape of Kakadu. ⊠ *5 km (3 mi) off Kakadu Hwy. on road to Gagudju Lodge, Cooinda* ☎ *08/8979–0145* ⊠ *Free* ⊙ *Daily 9–5.*

EXPLORING

Jim Jim Falls. The best way to gain a true appreciation of the natural beauty of Kakadu is to visit the waterfalls running off the escarpment. Some 39 km (24 mi) south of the park headquarters along the Kakadu Highway, a track leads off to the left toward Jim Jim Falls, 60 km (37 mi) away (about a two-hour drive). The track is unpaved, and you'll need a four-wheel-drive vehicle to navigate it. From the parking lot you have to walk 1 km (½ mi) over boulders to reach the falls and the plunge pools they have created at the base of the escarpment. After May, the water flow over the falls may cease, and the unpaved road is closed in the Wet.

Nourlangie Rock. Like the main Kakadu escarpment, Nourlangie Rock is a remnant of an ancient plateau that is slowly eroding, leaving sheer cliffs rising high above the floodplains. The main attraction is the **Anbangbang Gallery,** an excellent frieze of Aboriginal rock paintings. ⊠ *19 km (12 mi) from park headquarters on Kakadu Hwy.; turn left toward Nourlangie Rock, then follow paved road, accessible yr-round, 11 km (7 mi) to parking area* ⊠ *Free* ⊙ *Daily 7 am–sunset.*

Twin Falls. As you approach the Twin Falls, the ravine opens up dramatically to reveal a beautiful sandy beach scattered with palm trees, as well as the crystal waters of the falls spilling onto the end of the beach. This spot is a bit difficult to reach, but the trip is rewarding. Take the Jim Jim Falls Road, turn off just before the parking lot, and travel 10 km (6 mi) farther to the Twin Falls parking lot. A regular boat shuttle (A$12.50) operates a return service up the Twin Falls gorge, and then you need to walk over boulders, sand, and a boardwalk to the falls. Saltwater crocodiles may be in the water in the gorge, so visitors are urged not to enter the water. The round-trip, including the boat shuttle, takes around two hours.

Ubirr. Ubirr has an impressive display of Aboriginal paintings scattered through six shelters in the rock. The main gallery contains a 49-foot frieze of X-ray paintings depicting animals, birds, and fish. A 1-km (½-mi) path around the rock leads to all the galleries. It's just a short clamber to the top for wonderful views over the surrounding wetlands, particularly at sunset. Stop in at the Border Store and Cafe on your way in; they do lunch and a post-sunset dinner and sell arts and crafts. ⊠ *43 km (27 mi) north of park headquarters along paved road* ☎ *08/8979–2474 for the Border Store and Cafe* ⊠ *Free* ⊙ *Apr.–Nov., daily 8:30–sunset; Dec.–Mar., daily 2–sunset.*

10

WHERE TO STAY

For expanded hotel reviews, visit Fodors.com.

There are several lodges in the park, and campgrounds at Merl, Muirella Park, Mardugal, and Gunlom have toilets, showers, and water. Sites are A$10 per night. Alcohol is not available in Jabiru, so stock up in Darwin.

Gunlom Falls in the Kakadu National Park.

$$$ 🏨 **Aurora Kakadu.** This comfortable hotel, its buildings reminiscent of lilypads, has doubles and family rooms that sleep up to five. **Pros:** fauna is abundant; tropical garden setting; free bottled water in rooms. **Cons:** some distance from park attractions; limited amenities in rooms; thin walls; own transport essential. ⊠ *On Arnhem Hwy., 2½ km (1½ mi) before the highway crosses the South Alligator River* ⏏ *Box 221, Winnellie 0822* ☎ *08/8979–0166, 1800/818–845* ⊕ *www.auroraresorts. com.au* ↵ *138 rooms, 36 powered sites, 250 tent sites* ♨ *In-hotel: restaurant, pool, tennis court, laundry facilities, parking.*

$$$$ 🏨 **Gagudju Crocodile Holiday Inn.** Shaped like a crocodile, this unusual hotel with spacious rooms is the best of the area's accommodation options. **Pros:** friendly, helpful staff; Aboriginal artwork on sale; Jabiru village in walking distance. **Cons:** pool area is small; ground-floor rooms can have "critters." ⊠ *1 Flinders St., Jabiru* ☎ *08/8979–9000, 13/8388* ⊕ *www.gagudju-dreaming.com* ↵ *110 rooms* ♨ *In-hotel: restaurant, bar, pool, parking.*

$$$$ 🏨 **Gagudju Lodge Cooinda.** Near Yellow Water, this facility has light, airy lodgings looking out over tropical gardens. **Pros:** center for Yellow Water Cruises; close to Aboriginal cultural center. **Cons:** 30 minutes from Jabiru shops; limited amenities in rooms; limited dining options. ⊠ *Kakadu Hwy., 2 km (1 mi) toward Yellow Water Wetlands, Cooinda* ☎ *08/8979–0145, 1800/500401* ⊕ *www.gagudjulodgecooinda.com.au* ↵ *48 rooms* ♨ *In-hotel: restaurant, bar, pool, parking.*

THE KIMBERLEY

Perched on the northwestern hump of the loneliest Australian state, only half as far from Indonesia as it is from Sydney, the Kimberley remains a frontier of sorts. The first European explorers, dubbed by one of their descendants as "cattle kings in grass castles," ventured into the heart of the region in 1879 to establish cattle stations. They subsequently became embroiled in one of the country's longest-lasting conflicts between white settlers and Aborigines, led by Jandamarra of the Bunuba people.

ANCIENT ART AND NATURE

Almost the size of West Virginia, Kakadu National Park is an ancient landform, with wetlands, gorges, waterfalls, and rugged escarpments. It also has one of the highest concentrations of accessible Aboriginal rock-art sites in the world. Take a tour with an Aboriginal guide from one of the cultural centers near Jabiru or Cooinda. The art sites date back 20,000 years.

The Kimberley remains sparsely populated, with only 35,000 people living in an area of 351,200 square km (135,600 square mi). That's about 12 square km (4½ square mi) per person. The region is dotted with cattle stations and raked with craggy ochre ranges, croc-infested rivers, tropical forests, and towering cliffs. Several of the country's most spectacular national parks are here, including Purnululu (Bungle Bungle) National Park, a vast area of bizarrely shaped and colored rock formations that became widely known to white Australians only in 1983. Facilities in this remote region are few, but if you're looking for a genuine outback experience, the Kimberley represents the opportunity of a lifetime.

This section begins in Kununurra, just over the northwestern border of the Northern Territory, in Western Australia.

KUNUNURRA

516 km (322 mi) west of Katherine, 840 km (525 mi) southwest of Darwin.

Kununurra is the eastern gateway to the Kimberley. With a population of 6,000, it's a modern, planned town developed in the 1960s for the nearby Lake Argyle and Ord River irrigation scheme. It's a convenient base from which to explore local attractions such as Mirima National Park (a mini–Bungle Bungle on the edge of town), Lake Argyle, and the River Ord. The town is also one starting point for adventure tours of the Kimberley; the other option is to start from Broome.

GETTING HERE AND AROUND

Distances in this part of the continent are colossal. Flying is the fastest and easiest way to get to the Kimberley. Both Skywest and Air North have extensive air networks throughout the Top End, linking Kununurra to Broome, Perth, and Darwin.

From Darwin to Kununurra and the eastern extent of the Kimberley it's 827 km (513 mi). The route runs from Darwin to Katherine along the

Stuart Highway, and then along the Victoria Highway to Kununurra. The entire road is paved but quite narrow in parts—especially so, it may seem, when a road train (an extremely long truck convoy) is coming the other way. Drive with care. Fuel and supplies can be bought at small settlements along the way, but you should always keep supplies in abundance and expect to pay a pretty penny.

SAFETY AND PRECAUTIONS

Driving long distances through the Kimberley can be an adventure, but also carries risks. For drivers not used to the conditions, and not taking adequate rest breaks, the combination of warm sun through the windscreen, long, straight sections of road, the soothing hum of wheels and lack of traffic, can have a hypnotic effect. Take regular breaks every two hours to walk and have a stretch, and get plenty of sleep the night before. If you are feeling sleepy, stop immediately and take a break. Many vehicle crashes in this area are vehicle versus animal, often a kangaroo or straying cattle. Dusk and dawn are when animals are most active. If you see an animal on the road in front of you, brake firmly in a straight line and sound your horn. Do not swerve: it is safer to stay on the road.

TIMING

You should allow at least five days to see Kununurra and the East Kimberley, including your arrival and departure days. That will allow enough to visit the Ord River and cruise Lake Argyle, take a scenic flight to the Bungle Bungles and hike the area with a guide, and take a four-wheel-drive excursion to El Questro Wilderness Park. Winter—May to September—is the most popular time to visit, as days are warm and there is little rain. October to April is the wet season, and temperatures can be a lot higher—up to 45°C.

TOURS

Alligator Airways. Alligator Airways operates fixed-wing floatplanes from Lake Kununurra and land-based flights from Kununurra Airport. A two-hour scenic flight over the Bungle Bungles and other sights costs A$275. ☏ 08/9168–1333 ⊕ *www.alligatorairways.com.au.*

APT Kimberley Wilderness Adventures. APT Kimberley Wilderness Adventures conducts tours from Broome and Kununurra, which include excursions along Gibb River Road and into Purnululu National Park. A two-day tour from Kununurra includes the Mitchell Plateau and Mitchell Falls, with an overnight in a wilderness camp. ☏ 08/9191–8200, 1800/889–389 ⊕ *www.kimberleywilderness.com.au.*

East Kimberley Tours. East Kimberley Tours' most popular day tour includes an eye-popping flight to Purnululu National Park, a four-wheel-drive tour to the famous "beehive domes" and Cathedral Gorge, lunch, and a return scenic flight over Argyle Diamond mine. The tour costs A$660. Overnight fly-in, fly-out tours to the park cost from A$1,480. ☏ 08/9168–2213 ⊕ *www.eastkimberleytours.com.au.*

Lake Argyle Cruises. Lake Argyle Cruises operates excellent trips on Australia's largest expanse of freshwater, the man-made Lake Argyle. Tours, which start with a bus trip, run daily March to October. It's A$70 for the two-hour morning cruise, A$155 for the six-hour cruise, and A\$85 for the sunset cruise (which starts around 2:45). ✉ *Box 710, Kununurra, Western Australia 6743* ☎ *08/9168–7687* ⊕ *www.lakeargylecruises.com.*

Slingair Heliwork WA. Slingair conducts both fixed-wing and helicopter flights from Kununurra and Purnululu National Park. A 30-minute helicopter flight costs A\$325 from their helipad in the Purnululu National Park. An alternative 2-hour fixed-wing flight over the Bungle Bungle and Lake Argyle is A\$295. There are loads of options for coasting over the region with a bird's eye view, but a standout is the Kimberley Coastal five-hour scenic flight, covering the magnificent King George Falls, Berkeley River, an indigenous community, and other local sites and

> ## DROUGHT DOWN SOUTH
>
> The Top End's wet season drenches the region with more than 50 inches of rain. Just a tiny fraction is captured in Lake Argyle at Kununurra (with 21 times the water volume of Sydney Harbour) and later used to irrigate crops. Meanwhile, in Australia's more densely populated and heavily farmed southern states, a severe drought and declining annual rainfall—some say caused by global climate change—has sparked a major debate: How to bring the Top End's water south, or how to convince people to move north.

including a ground tour of Aboriginal-owned Home Valley Station and some locations from the film *Australia*. The cost is A\$629 and includes lunch and swimming. ☎ *08/9169–1300* ⊕ *www.slingair.com.au.*

ESSENTIALS

Banks and Currency Exchange Bankwest, Commonwealth Bank, Westpac, and National Australia banks all have branches in Kununurra.

Medical Emergencies **Kununurra District Hospital** ✉ *96 Coolibah Dr., Kununurra, Western Australia* ☎ *08/9166–4222.*

Police **Kununurra Police Station** ✉ *94 Coolibah Dr., Kununurra, Kununurra, Western Australia* ☎ *08/9166–4530.*

Taxis Alex Taxi ☎ *13–1008, 0417/960–675.* **Kununurra Yellow Taxi** ☎ *08/9168–2356.* Spud's Taxis ☎ *08/9168–2553.*

Visitor Information **Kununurra Visitor Centre** ✉ *75 Coolibah Dr., Kununurra, Western Australia* ☎ *08/9168–1177, 1800/586–868* ⊕ *www.kununurratourism.com.*

WHERE TO STAY

For expanded hotel reviews, visit Fodors.com.

\$\$ 🏨 **All Seasons Kununurra.** Set in tropical gardens, the brightly furnished rooms provide a comfortable base from which to explore the eastern Kimberley. **Pros:** walking distance to downtown; colorful Aboriginal art theme in rooms; swimming pool in tropical gardens setting. **Cons:** limited amenities in rooms; limited dining options. ✉ *Victoria Hwy. and Messmate Way, Kununurra, Western Australia* ☎ *08/9168–4000, 1300/656565* ⊕ *www.accorhotels.com.au* ➳ *60 rooms* ⚭ *In-room: Internet. In-hotel: restaurant, bar, pool, laundry facilities, parking* 🍴 *Some meals.*

10

$$$ 🏨 **Kununurra Country Club Resort.** In the center of town, this hotel is encircled by its own little rain forest of tropical gardens. **Pros:** complimentary airport shuttle; poolside dining and bars; easy walk to downtown. **Cons:** tour groups stay here; Wi-Fi is intermittent. ✉ *47 Coolibah Dr., Kununurra, Western Australia* ☎ *08/9168–1024* ⊕ *www.kununurracountryclub. com.au* ☞ *90 rooms* ⚲ *In-room: a/c, Internet, Wi-Fi. In-hotel: restaurant, bar, pool, laundry facilities, parking.*

$$ 🏨 **Kununurra Lakeside Resort.** On the shores of Lake Kununurra sits this understated, tranquil resort, where you can see stunning sunsets over the water (especially toward the end of the Dry), and watch for fruit bats flying overhead. **Pros:** lakeside location; crocodile spotting at night; abundant fauna. **Cons:** no Internet; own transport essential. ✉ *50 Casuarina Way, off Victoria Hwy., Kununurra, Western Australia* 🏠 *Box 1129, Casuarina Way, Kununurra, Western Australia 6743* ☎ *08/9169–1092, 1800/786692* ⊕ *www.lakeside.com.au* ☞ *42 rooms* ⚲ *In-room: a/c, kitchen. In-hotel: restaurant, bar, pool, laundry facilities.*

OFF THE BEATEN PATH

El Questro Wilderness Park. With 1 million acres, El Questro Wilderness Park is a working ranch in some of the most rugged country in Australia. Besides providing an opportunity to see Outback station life, El Questro has a full complement of such recreational activities as fishing, swimming, and horse and helicopter rides, and offers individually tailored walking and four-wheel-drive tours. At **Zebedee Springs,** a short walk off the graded road leads you through dense Livingstonia palms to a series of thermal pools for soaking and relaxing. Four independent accommodation facilities are on-site, each different in style and budget: the luxury Homestead; the safari-style tented cabins at Emma Gorge Resort; and air-conditioned Riverside Bungalows and Riverside Campgrounds at the Station Township. Each has a restaurant, and rates (minimum two nights) at the Homestead include drinks and food, laundry, and activities. Round-trip transportation from Kununurra is available from A\$220 per person. ✉ *100 km (60 mi) west of Kununurra, via Great Northern Hwy.; take Gibb River Rd. for 42 km (14 mi) from the highway exit, Kununurra, Western Australia* 🏠 *Box 909, Kununurra, Western Australia 6743* ☎ *08/9169–1777, 08/9161–4388 Emma Gorge Resort, 1300/233–432* ⊕ *www.elquestro.com.au* ✉ *El Questro Wilderness Park permit (required) A\$18 for 1- to 7-day pass with access to gorge walks, thermal springs, fishing holes, rivers, and use of the Emma Gorge Resort swimming pool* ☞ *6 suites, 60 tented cabins, 12 bungalows, 28 campsites, 6 lodge cabins* ☉ *Daily Apr.–Oct. Entry to Zebedee Springs closes at noon. Closed Nov.–Mar.*

A FANTASY LANDSCAPE

For millions of years nature has savaged the rocks of Purnululu National Park with water and wind, creating one of the most unusual landscapes in the world. Traveling into the area is a remarkable experience—the timelessness of the ancient rocks draws you back across the millennia. All around, the conically weathered formations cluster together like a meeting of some metamorphic executives.

PURNULULU (BUNGLE BUNGLE) NATIONAL PARK

252 km (156 mi) southwest Kununurra.

Fodor's Choice ★ **Purnululu (Bungle Bungle) National Park.** Purnululu (Bungle Bungle) National Park covers nearly 3,120 square km (1,200 square mi) in the southeast corner of the Kimberley. Australians of European descent first "discovered" its great beehive-shaped domes—their English name is the Bungle Bungle—in 1983, proving how much of this vast continent remains outside of "white" experience. The local Kidja Aboriginal tribe, who knew about these scenic wonders long ago, called the area Purnululu, meaning sandstone.

The striking, black-and-orange-stripe mounds seem to bubble up from the landscape. Climbing on them is not permitted, because the sandstone layer beneath their thin crust of lichen and silica is fragile, and would quickly erode without protection. Walking tracks follow rocky, dry creek beds. One popular walk leads hikers along the **Piccaninny Creek** to **Piccaninny Gorge,** passing through gorges with towering 328-foot cliffs to which slender fan palms cling.

GETTING HERE AND AROUND

The Bungle Bungle are 252 km (156 mi) south of Kununurra along the Great Northern Highway. A very rough, 55-km (34-mi) unpaved road, negotiable only in a four-wheel-drive vehicle, is the last stretch of road leading to the park from the turnoff near the Turkey Creek–Warmum Community. That part of the drive can take 2–3 hours, depending on the condition of the road. It's farther on to one of the three campgrounds, two public and one used by tour operators that is also available to self-drivers who prefer hot showers, flushing toilets, and regular beds. The most-visited section of the park is in the south, where there are rough walking trails to the main sights.

SAFETY AND PRECAUTIONS

The park is usually open from April to December (depending on whether the road is passable after the Wet), however temperatures in April, October, November, and December can be blisteringly hot. If you travel in these months, make sure you have plenty of water and be sun-smart.

TIMING

Purnululu National Park can be visited in a day from Kununurra, but only with a flight and safari package. There are also tours available that include overnight camping, but the road trip from Kununurra takes the best part of a day. Driving yourself to the park is not recommended, as the last section is a very rough track suitable only for four-wheel-drive vehicles; it has been kept deliberately so to limit visitation. If you do decide to drive in yourself, be aware that there are few facilities in the park's public campgrounds; you need to take in all your own food and camping equipment.

ESSENTIALS

Visitor Information Kununurra Visitor Centre ☎ *08/9168–1177, 1800/586–868.* **Purnululu Visitor Centre** ✉ *Park entrance, Kununurra, Western Australia* ☎ *08/9168–7300* ☼ *Daily 8–12 and 1–4:30.*

10

EXPLORING

The most popular walking trails are in the south of the park, where the famous "beehives" are located. From Piccaninny Creek car park you can hike in to **Cathedral Gorge**; the walk takes about an hour. Take a 20-minute detour on the **Domes Walk** to see more of the famous sandstone "beehives." If you have more time, you can follow the **Piccaninny Creek** walk into **Piccaninny Gorge**, following an eroded riverbed and sandstone ledges. This will take all day, but you can return at any time. In the north of the park there are walks to **Echidna Gorge** (about one hour), where dinosaur-era livistonia palms cling to the cliffs and the gorge narrows to about three feet across, and **Mini Palms Gorge**, a rock-strewn gorge again filled with livistonia palms. At the end there is a viewing platform overlooking the valley. Allow an hour for this walk.

WORD OF MOUTH

"Australia is easy to do on your own. However, if you are adventurous and interested in seeing some of the wilder, more isolated parts of the Australian Outback, doing a camping tour is a very good way to go. My wife and I did such a trip several years ago across the vast, empty and ruggedly beautiful Kimberly region in NW Australia—one of best, if not the best, vacations we've taken."

—RalphR

WHERE TO STAY

Although there are two designated campsites in the area, neither has many facilities. Both the Bellburn Creek and Walardi campgrounds have simple chemical toilets; fresh drinking water is at both campgrounds. Kununurra Visitor Centre has information about the campsites. The two tour operators who fly clients in from Kununurra, Broome, and Halls Creek and drive them around in four-wheel-drive vehicles, have comfortable bush camps that regular visitors can also pay to use and eat at. April through December, the most popular tours include an overnight stay. The mounds are closed from January through March.

GEIKIE GORGE NATIONAL PARK

Geikie Gorge National Park. Geikie Gorge is part of a 350-million-year-old reef system formed from fossilized layers of algae—evolutionary precursors of coral reefs—when this area was still part of the Indian Ocean. The limestone walls you see today were cut and shaped by the mighty Fitzroy River; during the Wet, the normally placid waters roar through the region. The walls of the gorge are stained red from iron oxide, except where they have been leached of the mineral and turned white by the floods, which have washed as high as 52 feet from the bottom of the gorge.

When the Indian Ocean receded, it stranded a number of sea creatures, which managed to adapt to their altered conditions. Geikie is one of the few places in the world where freshwater barramundi, mussels, stingrays, and prawns swim. The park is also home to the freshwater archerfish, which can spit water as far as a yard to knock insects out of the air. Aborigines call this place Kangu, meaning "big fishing hole."

Although there's a 5-km (3-mi) walking trail along the west side of the gorge, the opposite side is off-limits because it's a wildlife sanctuary.

National Park Ranger Station. The best way to see the gorge is aboard one of the thrice-daily 90-minute boat tours led by a ranger from the National Park Ranger Station, departing at 8, 9:30, and 3. The rangers are extremely knowledgeable, and helpful in pointing out the vegetation, strange limestone formations, and the many freshwater crocodiles along the way. You may also see part of the noisy fruit-bat colony that inhabits the region. The park is open for day visits daily from 6:30 am to 6:30 pm between April and November. Entry is restricted during the Wet, from December to March, when the Fitzroy River floods. ☎ 08/9191–5121, 08/9191–5112 ⊕ www. dec.wa.gov.au.

BROOME

1,032 km (640 mi) southwest of Kununurra via Halls Creek, 1,544 km (957 mi) southwest of Katherine, 1,859 km (1,152 mi) southwest of Darwin.

Broome is the holiday capital of the Kimberley. It's the only town in the region with sandy beaches, and is the base from which most strike out to see more of the region. In some ways, with its wooden sidewalks and charming Chinatown, it still retains the air of its past as a boisterous shantytown. However, with tourism increasing every year it is becoming noticeably upscale.

Long ago, Broome depended on pearling for its livelihood. By the early 20th century 300 to 400 sailing boats employing 3,000 men provided most of the world's mother-of-pearl shell. Many of the pearlers were Japanese, Malay, and Filipino, and the town is still a wonderful multicultural center today with the modern pearling industry very much at its heart. Each August during the famous Shinju Matsuri (Festival of the Pearl), Broome commemorates its early pearling years and heritage. The 10-day festival features many traditional Japanese ceremonies. Because of the popularity of the festival, advance bookings for accommodations are highly recommended. Several tour operators have multiday cruises out of Broome along the magnificent Kimberley coast. The myriad deserted islands and beaches, with 35-foot tides that create horizontal waterfalls and whirlpools, make it an adventurer's delight.

Broome marks the end of the Kimberley. From here it's another 2,250 km (1,395 mi) south to Perth, or 1,859 km (1,152 mi) back to Darwin.

GETTING HERE AND AROUND

Distances in this part of the continent are colossal. Flying is the fastest and easiest way to get to the Kimberley.

Qantas and its subsidiaries fly to Broome from Brisbane, Sydney, Melbourne, and Adelaide via Perth. Direct flights from Sydney, Melbourne, and Brisbane are twice a week. Air North has an extensive air network

10

throughout the Top End, linking Broome to Kununurra and Darwin. Virgin Blue also services Broome from Perth and Adelaide. Skywest flies to Broome from Perth and Kununurra. Broome's newly renovated airport is right next to the center of town, on the northern side. Though it's called Broome International Airport, there are no scheduled overseas flights, but charter flights and private flights arrive there. Approvals are in place for international flights in the future.

SAFETY AND PRECAUTIONS

From November to April there is a possibility of cyclones off the Kimberley coast. It is important that visitors are aware of the procedures to follow in the event of a cyclone alert. These procedures are provided in all accommodations and are also at the Broome Visitor Centre or the Shire of Broome office. Call ☎ *1300/659–210* for cyclone watch and warning messages, or go online at ⊕ *www.bom.gov.au.*

November to April is also when mosquitoes are at their most prevalent. To avoid the discomfort of mosquito bites and any risk of infection, it is advisable to cover up at dawn and dusk and apply insect repellent, which is supplied in most hotels. Sandflies become more active in Broome on high tides; use the same prevention methods.

Tropical waters can contain various stingers. The two types of dangerous jellyfish are the chironex box jellyfish (a large but almost transparent jellyfish up to 12 inches across with ribbonlike tentacles from each of the four corners) and Irukandji (a tiny transparent jellyfish less than 1 inch across with four thin tentacles). Both are found during the summer months of November to May. Take care when swimming (wear protective clothing—a wet suit or lycra stinger suit to reduce exposure to potential stings) and obey signs displayed on the beaches at all times. Medical attention (pour vinegar onto the sting and call 000 for an ambulance) should be sought in case someone is stung.

Saltwater crocodiles live in estuaries throughout the Kimberley, and freshwater Johnsons crocodiles hang out in freshwater gorges and lakes. Look for warning signs. Even if not signposted, advice from a reliable local authority should always be sought before swimming in rivers and waterholes.

TIMING

Ideally, you need at least five days in Broome and the West Kimberley, including your arrival and departure days. This will give you time to go swimming and sunbathing on Cable Beach, take a camel ride or go kayaking, then cruise on a restored pearl lugger. A scenic flight will show you the pristine Kimberley coastline and the horizontal waterfalls of Buccaneer Archipeligo. A day tour will get you to Cape Leveque or Windjana Gorge. To go farther afield, join a four-wheel-drive safari; a two-day tour will show you the gorges of the area, including Geikie Gorge.

The most popular time to visit is from May to October, during the dry season.

CLOSE UP

Broome By Camelback

Broome has for many years been a place where people enjoy camel rides—especially along the broad, desertlike sands of Cable Beach. Three tour companies in town now offer camel "adventures" on a daily basis; they're a great way to see the coast and get a taste of history.

Broome Camel Safaris. Broome Camel Safaris operates Monday–Saturday, and offers 30-minute rides (A$30) or one-hour sunset rides (A$65). ☎ *0419/916–101* ⊕ *www. broomecamelsafaris.com.au.*

Red Sun Camels. Red Sun Camels runs both morning and sunset rides every day on Cable Beach. The morning ride lasts for 40 minutes and costs A$50; the pre-sunset ride runs for 30 minutes and costs A$40; the sunset ride takes an hour and costs A$70. ☎ *08/9193–7423, 1800/184–488* ⊕ *www.redsuncamels.com.au.*

Ships of the Desert. Ships of the Desert leads its camels in the morning and twice in the evening. Morning tours run for 40 minutes and cost A$40; half-hour afternoon strolls cost A$30, and the shadow-throwing sunset tour lasts an hour and costs A$65. ☎ *04/1995–4022* ⊕ *www.shipsofthedesert.com.au.*

TOURS

APT Kimberley Wilderness Adventures conducts tours from Broome, which include excursions along Gibb River Road and into Purnululu National Park. Their 13-day Kimberley Complete tour includes the gorges along the Gibb River Road, the Aboriginal culture of the Mitchell Plateau, a scenic flight over the Mitchell Falls, Purnululu National Park, and an Aboriginal-guided tour through Geikie Gorge. The price is from A$6,995.

Broome Sightseeing Tours has a two-hour Broome town tour (A$50) that includes visits to Cable Beach, Gantheaume Point, Chinatown, Roebuck Bay, Sun Pictures, and the Japanese cemetery. It ends at Pearl Luggers in time for the attraction's next tour. A combination ticket must be prebought to access cheaper rates for both tours.

Pearl Sea Coastal Cruises has multiday Kimberley adventures along the region's magnificent coastline in their luxury *Kimberley Quest 11* cruiser. All meals and excursions (including fishing trips) are included in the cost of A$8,345 for 7 days to A$12,095 for 13 days. Cruising season runs from March to September.

Astro Tours organizes entertaining, informative night-sky tours of the Broome area. Two-hour shows (offered four nights a week) cost A$75, including transfers from your hotel, folding-stool seating, hot beverages, and cookies. The company also offers four-wheel-drive Outback stargazing adventures farther afield.

ESSENTIALS

Banks and Currency Exchange Banks with branches and ATMs in Broome include ANZ, Bankwest, Commonwealth, National Australia Bank, and Westpac.

Medical Emergencies Broome District Hospital ⊠ *Robinson St., Broome, Western Australia* ☎ *08/9194–2222.*

Tour Operators **APT Kimberley Wilderness Adventures** ☎ *03/9277–8555, 1300/278–278.* **Astro Tours** ✆ *Box 2537, Broome, Western Australia 6725* ☎ *08/9193–5362* ⊕ *www.astrotours.net.* **Broome Sightseeing Tours** ☎ *08/9192–0000.* **Pearl Sea Coastal Cruises** ✆ *Box 2838, Broome, Western Australia 6725* ☎ *08/9193–6131* ⊕ *www.kimberleyquest.com.au.*

Visitor Information **Broome Visitor Centre** ⊠ *1 Hamersley St., Broome, Western Australia* ☎ *08/9195–2200* ⊕ *www.broomevisitorcentre.com.au.*

CITY CENTER

Though not native to Australia, camels played a large part in exploring and opening up the country's big, dry, and empty interior. In the 1800s, around 20,000 camels were imported from the Middle East to use for cross-country travel—along with handlers (many from Afghanistan) who cared for them.

When railways and roads became the prime methods of transport in the early 20th century, many camels were simply set free in the desert. A steady population of wild camels—some 1,000,000 of them—now roams across the Australian Outback.

Cultured Pearling Monument. The life-size bronze statues of the Cultured Pearling Monument are near Chinatown. The monument depicts three pioneers of the cultured pearling industry that is so intertwined with the city's development and history. ⊠ *Carnarvon St., Broome, Western Australia.*

Japanese Cemetery. More than 900 pearl divers are buried in the Japanese Cemetery, on the road out to Broome's deepwater port. The graves testify to the contribution of the Japanese to the development of the industry in Broome, as well as to the perils of pearl gathering in the industry's early days. ⊠ *Port Dr., Broome, Western Australia.*

★ **Pearl Luggers.** The Pearl Luggers historical displays shed light on the difficulties and immense skill involved in pearl harvesting. It has two restored luggers along with other such pearling equipment as diving suits and an A$100,000 pearl you can hold. Get an insight into the risky lives of pearl divers, who spent years aboard pearling luggers and diving for pearl shells, on the regular tours (allow 1 hour). Tours run on the hour April–September, and at 10 and 3 October–March; more on demand. This is a must-see for those interested in Broome's history. ⊠ *31 Dampier Terr., Broome, Western Australia* ☎ *08/9192–0000* ⊕ *www.pearlluggers.com.au* ✒ *A$20* ⊗ *daily, 9–5.*

☪ **Sun Pictures.** Opened in 1916, Sun Pictures is the world's oldest operating ★ outdoor movie theater. Here silent movies—accompanied by a pianist—were once shown to the public. These days current releases are shown in the very pleasant outdoors. Historical tours of the theater are also available weekdays at 10:30 am and 1 pm for A$5 per person. ⊠ *8 Carnarvon St., Broome, Western Australia* ☎ *08/9192–1077, 08/9192–3738* ⊕ *www.broomemovies.com.au* ✒ *A$16.50* ⊗ *Daily 6:30 pm–11 pm.*

☪ **The Malcolm Douglas Wilderness Wildlife Park.** Entering via the jaws of a giant crocodile, you discover the Kimberley's native species in a variety of habitats in this huge park. From rare western quolls and bilbies to dingoes, flying foxes, barking owls and several types of kangaroo, and

Camel riding on Cable Beach, Broome.

of course hundreds of crocodiles, the park will keep you entertained for hours. Don't miss the nocturnal sanctuary, which houses endangered species that are part of an important breeding program. Beware the replica croc at the entry—many people have been fooled and frightened by its lifelike appearance. Tours run at 11, 1, and 3 in the Dry; croc feeding is at 3 pm. ⊠ *Great Northern Hwy., Broome, Western Australia* ✛ *Go 18 km out of Broome on the Great Northern Highway and see the sign pointing to the right.* ☎ *08/9193 6580* ⊕ *www.malcolmdouglas.com.au* 🎫 *A$35* ☉ *Weekdays 10–5, weekends 2–5.*

AROUND BROOME

Broome Bird Observatory. The Broome Bird Observatory, a nonprofit research, education, and accommodation facility, provides the perfect opportunity to see many of the Kimberley's 310 bird species, some of which migrate annually from Siberia. On the shores of Roebuck Bay, 25 km (15 mi) east of Broome, the observatory has a prolific number of migratory waders. The observatory offers a variety of daily guided tours, costing A$70 per person from the observatory. Pickup from Broome can also be arranged. A full-day tour costs A$150 from the observatory and A$195 from Broome. Start times depend on the day of the week and the tides and season, but are typically from 8 am to 3 pm. ⊠ *Crab Creek Rd., 15 km (9 mi) from Broome Hwy., Broome, Western Australia* ☎ *08/9193–5600* ⊕ *www.broomebirdobservatory.com* 🎫 *A$5 recommended donation for day visitors* ☉ *Reservations essential.*

Willie Creek Pearl Farm. You can watch demonstrations of the cultured pearling process—including the seeding of a live oyster and a boat ride to the marine farm—at Willie Creek Pearl Farm, 38 km (23½ mi) north of Broome. Drive out to the farm yourself (you must make reservations first and a 4WD is recommended), or join a four-hour tour bus leaving from town. There's also the option of taking a scenic helicopter ride while on the property. ⊠ *Drive 9 km (5½ mi) east from Broome on Broome Hwy., turn left onto Cape Leveque Rd. for 15 km (9 mi), turn left onto Manari Rd. for 5 km (3 mi), turn left and follow signs for 2½ km (1½ mi). Allow about 1 hr, Broome, Western Australia* ☎ *08/9192–0000* ⊕ *www.williecreekpearls.com.au* ✉ *A$50, bus tour A$90* ⏱ *Guided tours daily every hour 9–3; less often in the wet season, Oct.–Mar.*

WHERE TO STAY

For expanded hotel reviews, visit Fodors.com.

$$$$ ⊞ **Cable Beach Club Resort and Spa.** A few minutes out of town opposite
★ the broad, beautiful Cable Beach, this resort is the area's most luxurious accommodation. **Pros:** walk to Cable Beach; minigolf; reading room; peaceful, tropical atmosphere; distinctive architecture; separate swimming pool for adults. **Cons:** no shopping nearby; must have car to reach town. ⊠ *Cable Beach Rd., Broome, Western Australia* ☎ *08/9192–0400* ⊕ *www.cablebeachclub.com* ⤳ *176 rooms, 45 bungalows, 7 villas, 3 suites* ⅃ *In-room: a/c, kitchen, Wi-Fi. In-hotel: restaurant, bar, pool, tennis court, gym, spa, beach, parking.*

$$$$ ⊞ **Eco Beach.** This wilderness retreat peers over a cliff edge and gazes
★ into the ocean, giving the impression it's incredibly remote while only being about an hour and a half drive—or a shorter helicopter flight—away. ⊠ *Roebuck Bay, Broome, Western Australia* ☎ *08/9193–8015* ⊕ *www.ecobeach.com.au* ⤳ *29 eco tents, 24 villas (garden or ocean views), 2 beach houses.*

$$$$ ⊞ **McAlpine House.** Originally built for a pearling master, this luxury
★ guesthouse in tropical gardens is full of exquisite Javanese teak furniture. **Pros:** restored pearling master's residence; luxurious suites; intimate, private spaces; complimentary airport transfers. **Cons:** limited leisure facilities. ⊠ *84 Herbert St., Broome, Western Australia* ☎ *08/9192–0510, 1800/746–282* ✉ *reservations@mcalpinehouse.com* ⊕ *www.mcalpinehouse.com* ⤳ *8 rooms; one 5 bedroom villa, rented whole* ⅃ *In-hotel: restaurant, bar, pool, laundry facilities, parking, some age restrictions* ⅋ *Breakfast.*

$$$ ⊞ **Moonlight Bay Suites.** Rooms with great Roebuck Bay views and a
★ five-minute stroll from Chinatown add luxury and convenience to this complex of lovely self-contained apartments. **Pros:** next to a good brewery and restaurant; watch "Stairway to the Moon" (dependent on tides); handy to central shopping area. **Cons:** limited gym; need car to get to Cable Beach. ⊠ *51 Carnarvon St., Broome, Western Australia* ⊡ *Box 198, Broome, Western Australia 6725* ☎ *08/9195–5200, 1800/818 878* ⊕ *www.broomeaccommodation.com.au* ⤳ *59 apartments* ⅃ *In-room: kitchen, Internet. In-hotel: restaurant, pool, gym, spa, laundry facilities, parking.*

$$$ ⊞ **Pintcada Cable Beach.** This glam resort seduces with its stunning pool,
★ spa facilities, and chic bar that sit at the heart of the luxurious rooms and suites.**Pros:** 25-meter pool; great food; all rooms have private

balcony or courtyard. **Cons:** 10-minute walk to beach; parking-lot-facing rooms are noisy. ✉ *10 Murray Rd., Cable Beach, Broome, Western Australia* ☎ *08/9193–8340, 1800/746282* ↵ *72 rooms* ⚿ *In-room: a/c, Internet, Wi-Fi. In-hotel: restaurant, bar, pool, gym, spa, parking* ✵ *Some meals.*

SHOPPING

Broome has an abundance of jewelry stores.

Kailis Australian Pearls. Kailis Australian Pearls specializes in high-quality, expensive pearls and jewelry. ✉ *Shop 3, 23 Dampier Terr., Broome, Western Australia* ☎ *08/9192–2061* ⊕ *www.kailisaustralianpearls.com.au.*

Linneys. Linneys sells high-end jewelry. They also have an outlet at Cable Beach Club Resort and Spa. ✉ *25 Dampier Terr., Broome, Western Australia* ☎ *08/9192–2430* ⊕ *www.linneys.com.*

Paspaley Pearling. Family-owned Paspaley Pearling, in Chinatown, sells pearls and stylish local jewelry. ✉ *2 Short St., Broome, Western Australia* ☎ *08/9192–2203.*

WESTERN AUSTRALIA

Updated by
Jo Castro

Western Australia—sprawling across more than 1 million square mi, one-third of Australia—is a stunningly diverse place, with rugged interior deserts, endless, untrammeled white-sand beaches, a northern tropical wilderness and a temperate forested south.

It took more than 200 years after Dutch seafarer Dirk Hartog first landed on the coast of "New Holland" in 1616 in today's Shark Bay before British colonists arrived to establish the Swan River Colony (now Perth) in 1829.

Progress was slow for half a century, but the discovery of gold around Kalgoorlie and Coolgardie in the 1890s brought people and wealth, especially to the fledgling city of Perth; much later, in the 1970s, the discovery of massive mineral deposits throughout the state began an economic upswing that still continues.

Today Western Australia produces much of Australia's mineral, energy, and agricultural wealth. Perth, the capital city and home to nearly 75% of the state's 2.3 million residents, is a modern, pleasant metropolis with an easygoing, welcoming attitude. However, at 3,200 km (2,000 mi) from any other major city in the world, it has fondly been dubbed "the most isolated city on earth." The remoteness, though, is part of what makes Western Australia so awe-inspiring. The scenery here is magnificent; whether you travel through the rugged gorges and rock formations of the north; the green pastures, vineyards, and hardwood forests of the south; or the coastline's vast, pristine beaches, you'll be struck by how much space there is here. If the crowds and crush of big-city life aren't your thing, this is the Australia you may never want to leave.

10

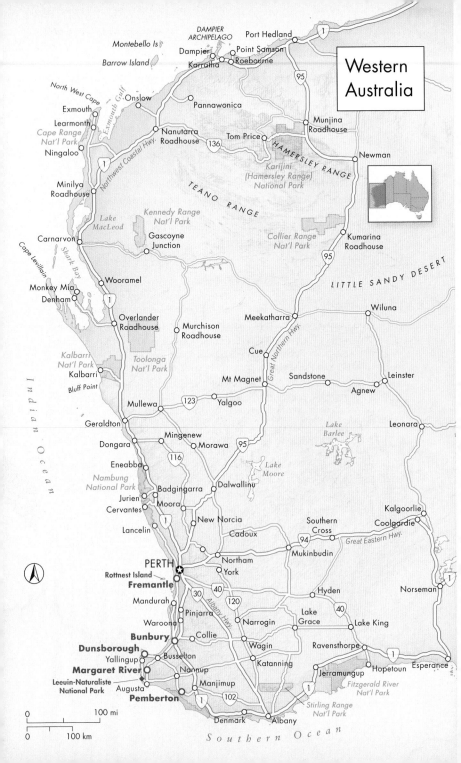

PERTH

Buoyed by mineral wealth and foreign investment, Perth now has high-rise buildings dotting the skyline, and an influx of immigrants gives the city a healthy diversity. Some of Australia's finest sandy beaches, sailing, and fishing are on the city's doorstep, and seaside villages and great beaches lie just north of Fremantle. The main business thoroughfare is St. George's Terrace, an elegant street with a number of the city's most appealing sights. Perth's literal highlight is King's Park, 1,000 acres of greenery atop Mt. Eliza, which affords panoramic city views.

GETTING HERE

The main gateway to Western Australia is Perth's busy airport. It has two separate terminals—the domestic terminal (by far the busiest, especially during the early morning and late afternoon rush hours) is about 11 km (7 mi) from Perth's central business district, while the international terminal is about 16 km (10 mi) away. A shuttle bus (A$10) connects the two terminals if you need to transfer.

Taxis are at the airport 24 hours a day. Trips to the city cost about A$33 and take around a half-hour. Airport City Shuttles (☎ 08/9277–7958) operates frequent coach services from both terminals to Perth city hotels, and between the airport terminals. The cost between terminals is A$8, and to downtown Perth is A$15 from the domestic terminal and A$18 from the international terminal (unless prepaid with your air ticket).

Fewer people arrive by road or rail from the east. Crossing the Nullarbor Plain from the eastern states is one of the great rail journeys of the world. Great Southern Railways' *Indian Pacific* makes three-day runs from Sydney on Saturday and Wednesday and two-day runs from Adelaide on Sunday and Thursday. The train arrives at the East Perth Terminal in the central business district.

Greyhound Australia has long-distance coaches to Perth from eastern states capitals, arriving at the Public Transport Center, West Parade, East Perth. From Adelaide, the trip takes about 24 hours. If you are driving, the Eyre Highway crosses the continent from Port Augusta in South Australia to Western Australia's transportation gateway, Norseman. From there, take the Coolgardie–Esperance Highway north to Coolgardie and the Great Eastern Highway on to Perth. Driving to Perth—2,580 km (1,600 mi) and 30 hours from Adelaide, and 4,032 km (2,500 mi) and 56 hours from Sydney—is an arduous journey, which should be undertaken only with a car (and mental faculties) in top condition. Spare tires and drinking water are essential. Service stations and motels are spaced at regular intervals along the route.

GETTING AROUND

Driving in Perth is relatively easy; just remember to stay on the left-hand side of the road, and give way to traffic on your right. Friday afternoons are especially busy, as Perth natives head away from the city to country destinations, mostly in the South West. Country roads are generally well maintained and have little traffic. All major car-rental companies have branches at the international and domestic airport terminals.

10

The Perth central business district and suburban areas are well connected by Transperth buses. The main terminals are at the Esplanade Bus Port on Mounts Bay Road and at Wellington Street Bus Station. Buses run daily 6 am–11:30 pm, with reduced service on weekends and holidays. Rides within the city center are free. CAT (Central Area Transit) buses circle the city center, running approximately every 10 minutes weekdays 7–6 and Saturday 9–5. Routes and timetables are available from Transperth. (⊕ *www.transperth.wa.go.au* ☎ *13–62–13)*

THE SWAN RIVER

Perth sits astride the Swan River. Though not a great river by global standards, it is the focus of many of the city's festivities, from weekend sailing and boating to annual fireworks spectaculars. For the visitor, it's best to start exploring the riverside at the cluster of boat sheds, cafés, jetties, and ticket offices at the bottom of Barrack Street. From here you can take trips up- or downriver.

Transperth tickets are valid for two hours and can be used on Transperth trains and ferries. Transperth ferries make daily runs from 6:50 am to 7:15 pm between Barrack Street Jetty in Perth to Mends Street, across the Swan River in South Perth. Reduced service runs on weekends and holidays.

Transperth trains also provide a quick way to get around the city. From Perth, lines run east–west to Midland and Fremantle, north to Clarkson, southeast to Armadale, and south to Mandurah. Perth to Fremantle takes about 30 minutes, while Perth to Mandurah takes 50 minutes. Central-city train stations are in Wellington Street and Perth Underground at the corner of Williams and Murray streets. Tickets must be purchased at vending machines before boarding.

TransWA trains cover routes in Western Australia, including the *Prospector* to Kalgoorlie, the *Australind* to Bunbury, and the *Avonlink* to Northam. TransWA also has coach services to towns not serviced by passenger trains.

South West Coachlines. South West Coachlines has daily coach services from Perth Central Bus Station at the Esplanade Bus Port on Mounts Bay Road to South-West towns, including Dunsborough. Services may vary according to season. ☎ *08/9261–7600* ⊕ *www.southwestcoachlines.com.au.*

SAFETY AND PRECAUTIONS

You'll find Perth a safe city to visit; there aren't any "no-go" neighborhoods, though there are some precautions you should take. Pickpocketing isn't a particular risk, but it's best to keep your personal belongings close, especially in busy shopping areas. Don't leave valuables—such as cameras—in the car when parked overnight at hotels or motels, or when visiting attractions. For your personal safety, avoid walking alone, especially late at night. There are instances of assault on Transperth trains and at suburban train stations, despite security guards and closed-circuit television monitors. A strong police presence—both on foot and on horse—usually ensures that late-night hot spots like Northbridge and Fremantle—are safe, though there are long lines for taxis, especially in the early morning hours when the night-club crowds start to go home. Alcohol and impatience are a troublesome combination. It's best to try and avoid Northbridge when the clubs start to close around 2 am.

TIMING

Perth and surroundings can be visited in two or three days, if you're short on time and plan to explore farther afield. Spend the first day in central Perth, visiting Kings Park, the Western Australian Museum, the Hay Street and Murray Street shopping malls and, perhaps, the Swan Bells Tower. On the second day, head to Fremantle, about 30 minutes by train, where you can spend the day exploring this heritage port city or even take a day-trip to Rottnest Island by ferry (30 minutes each way from Fremantle). An upriver cruise to the Swan Valley that includes a visit to a winery and lunch makes for a relaxing day. The third day offers a choice of one-day tours to attractions such as Nambung National Park—with its weird limestone formation—Margaret River, to visit its renowned wineries, or the Treetop Walk deep in the southern forests near Walpole (be aware this is a very long 14½-hour tour).

TOURS

Australian Pinnacle Tours conduct day tours of Perth and its major attractions. You can also take a day tour of outer sights like Nambung National Park and the Pinnacles, Wave Rock near Hyden, and the Treetop Walk near Walpole. Australian Pacific Touring has trips from Perth to Monkey Mia. The Perth Tram Company has hop-on, hop-off circle trips around central Perth and to Kings Park on either a wooden replica tram or a double-decker, open-top bus. Tickets ($30) are valid for two days and you can get on and off as you choose. Book online and get 10% discount. If you stay on, the full tour takes 90 minutes by bus and two hours by tram.

Rottnest Express runs excursions to Rottnest Island one or two times daily from Perth and four times daily from Fremantle, depending on the season.

Captain Cook Cruises has trips on the Swan River, traveling from Perth to the Indian Ocean at Fremantle. Cruises cost A$25–A$149 and *may* include meals and wine. Oceanic Cruises offers whale-watching in season, September–November. Golden Sun Cruises also has tours upriver to the vineyards, as well as trips to Fremantle. Springtime in Western Australia (September–November) is synonymous with wildflowers, as 8,000 species blanket an area that stretches 645 km (400 mi) north and 403 km (250 mi) south of Perth. Tours of these areas are popular, and early reservations are essential. ■ TIP➜ If you hire a car, check with local visitor centers to find out where the flowers are blooming.

10

ESSENTIALS

Banks and Currency Exchange Banks with dependable check-cashing and money-changing services include ANZ, Westpac, Commonwealth, and National Australia Bank. ATMs—which accept Cirrus, Plus, Visa, and MasterCard—are ubiquitous.

Boat Tours Captain Cook Cruises ✉ *Pier 3, Barrack Sq. Jetty, CBD, Perth, Western Australia* ☎ *08/9325–3341* ⊕ *www.captaincookcruises.com.au.* **Golden Sun**

Cruises ✉ *Pier 4, Barrack Sq. Jetty, CBD, Perth, Western Australia* ☎ *08/9325–9916* ⊕ *www.goldensuncruises.com.au.* **Rottnest Express** ✉ *Pier 2, Barrack St. Jetty, CBD, Perth, Western Australia* ☎ *1300/467688* ⊕ *www.rottnestexpress. com.au.* **Swan Jet Adventures** ✉ *Jetty 4, Barrack St Jetty, CBD, Perth, Western Australia* ☎ *08/9225–4166* ⊕ *www.swanjet.com.*

Medical Emergencies **Royal Perth Hospital** ✉ *Victoria Sq., East Perth, Perth, Western Australia* ☎ *08/9224–2244, 000 Emergency, 1800/022 222 Health Direct for medical advice.*

Orientation and Wildflower Tours **Australian Pacific Touring** ☎ *1300/243 137* ⊕ *www.aptouring.com.au.* **Australian Pinnacle Tours** ☎ *08/8132–8288, 1300/551–687* ⊕ *www.pinnacletours.com.au.* **Perth Tram Company** ☎ *08/9322–2006* ⊕ *www.perthtram.com.au.*

Police **Police** ☎ *13–1444 assistance, 08/9222–1111 general inquiries, 000 emergency.*

Taxis Cab fare between 6 am and 6 pm weekdays is an initial A$3.80 plus A$1.55 every 1 km (½ mi). From 6 pm to 6 am and on weekends the rate rises to A$5.60 plus A$1.55 per 1 km (½ mi). **Black & White** ☎ *13–1008.* **Swan Taxis** ☎ *13–1330.*

Visitor Information **Western Australia Visitor Centre** ✉ *Forrest Pl. at Wellington St., CBD, Perth, Western Australia* ☎ *08/9483–1111, 1300/361351, 61/89483–1111 from outside Australia.*

EXPLORING

Because of its relative colonial youth, Perth has an advantage over most other capital cities in that it was laid out with foresight and elegance. Streets were planned so that pedestrian traffic could flow smoothly from one avenue to the next, and this compact city remains easy to negotiate on foot. Most of the points of interest are in the downtown area close to the banks of the Swan River, while shopping arcades and pedestrian malls are a short stroll away.

The city center (CBD, or Central Business District), a pleasant blend of old and new, runs along Perth's major business thoroughfare, St. George's Terrace, as well as on parallel Hay and Murray streets.

WHAT TO SEE
TOP ATTRACTIONS

Art Gallery of Western Australia. Founded in 1895, the Art Gallery of Western Australia is home to more than 17,000 treasures, including one of the best collections of Indigenous art in Australia. Other works include Australian and international paintings, sculpture, prints, crafts, and decorative arts. Free guided tours run at 11 am and 1 pm Monday, Wednesday, Thursday, and Sunday, and at 2 pm on Friday and 1 pm on Saturday. The 12:30 pm Friday's Focus tour examines one particular artwork. Admission to the Gallery is free, although donations are encouraged. An entry charge may apply to special exhibitions. ✉ *Perth Cultural Centre, James St., at corner of Beaufort and Roe Sts., CBD, Perth, Western Australia* ☎ *08/9492–6600* ⊕ *www.artgallery.wa.gov. au* ⌨ *Free* ⊗ *Wed.–Mon. 10–5; Closed Good Friday and Anzac Day.*

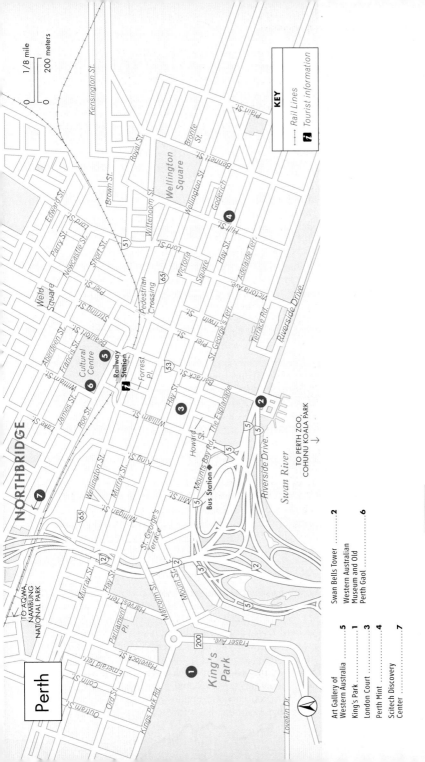

Perth

NORTHBRIDGE

TO AQWA,
NAMBUNG
NATIONAL PARK

King's Park

Swan River

TO PERTH ZOO,
COHUNU KOALA PARK →

KEY

— Rail Lines
🛈 Tourist Information

Art Gallery of
Western Australia **5**
King's Park **1**
London Court **3**
Perth Mint **4**
Scitech Discovery
Center **7**

Swan Bells Tower **2**
Western Australian
Museum and Old
Perth Gaol **6**

⟳ **King's Park.** Once a gathering place
★ for Aboriginal people, and established as a public space in 1890,
this 1,000-acre park overlooking
downtown Perth is one of the city's
most-visited attractions. Both tourists and locals enjoy picnics, parties, and weddings in the gardens,
as well as regular musical and theater presentations and the summer
Moonlight Cinema. In spring the
gardens blaze with orchids, kangaroo paw, banksias, and other wildflowers, making it ideal for a walk
in the bushland. The steel-and-tim-

> **THE VIEW FROM
> KING'S PARK**
>
> The best spot is the manicured
> eastern edge of the park, over-
> looking Perth's Central Business
> District and the Swan River. Pic-
> ture-perfect lookout points have
> the city in the background, as
> well as many of the city's most-
> treasured memorials, including the
> most recent to local victims of the
> 2002 terrorist bombing in Bali.

ber **Lotterywest Federation Walkway** takes you into the treetops and
the 17-acre botanic garden of Australian flora. The **Synergy Parkland**
details Western Australia's fossil and energy history. The **Lotterywest
Family Area** has a playground for youngsters. Free walking tours take
place daily at 10 am and 2 pm, and details on seasonal and themed
tours are available from the information kiosk near Fraser's Restaurant.
✉ *Fraser Ave. at King's Park Rd., West Perth, Perth, Western Australia* ☎ *08/9480–3634* ⊕ *www.bgpa.wa.gov.au* 🗲 *Free* ☉ *Daily 24 hrs.*

Perth Mint. All that glitters is gold at the Perth Mint, one of the oldest
mints in the world still operating from its original premises. Established
in 1899, it first refined gold from Western Australia's newly discovered
goldfields, striking gold sovereigns and half sovereigns for the British
Empire. Today it still produces Australia's legal tender in pure gold,
silver, and platinum bullion and commemorative coins for investors and
collectors. Visitors can have a hands-on experience at the Mint—watch
molten gold being poured in time-honored fashion to form a 6 kilogram
solid gold bar; see the world's largest collection of gold investment bars
from more than 30 countries; handle more than $400,000 worth of
gold bullion; and see Australia's best collection of natural gold nuggets, including the 369 ounce Golden Beauty, one of the largest natural
nuggets in the world. You can also engrave your own medallion and
discover the value of your weight in gold. ✉ *310 Hay St., CBD, Perth,
Western Australia* ☎ *08/9421–7223* ⊕ *www.perthmint.com.au* 🗲 *A$15*
☉ *Open 7 days 9–5 except on some public holidays; guided talk every
half-hour from 9:30–3:30; gold pour every hour from 10–4.*

⟳ **Western Australian Museum and Old Perth Gaol.** The state's largest and most
comprehensive museum includes some of Perth's oldest structures, such
as the Old Perth Gaol. Built of stone in 1856, this was Perth's first and
only prison until 1888. After being decommissioned as a jail it became
Perth's first museum. Get a feeling for Perth's criminal past and have
a coffee at the café in the courtyard close to where executions once
took place. Today it is part of a much larger museum where exhibitions include "Diamonds to Dinosaurs," which uses fossils, rocks, and
gemstones to take you back 3.5 billion years. "Katta Djinoong: First
Peoples of Western Australia" has a fascinating collection of primitive

King's park with downtown Perth in the distance.

tools and lifestyle artifacts used thousands of years ago by Australia's Aboriginals. ⊠ *Perth Cultural Centre, James and William Sts., CBD, Perth, Western Australia* ☎ *08/9212–3700* ⊕ *www.museum.wa.gov.au* ✉ *Free* ⏱ *Thurs.–Tues. 9:30–5.*

WORTH NOTING

🅒 **AQWA: Aquarium of Western Australia.** Huge aquariums filled with some 400 different species of local sea creatures from along the 12,000 km of Western Australia's coastline are the fascinating draws of this boutique aquarium north of Perth. Sharks, stingrays, turtles, and thousands of fish swim overhead as you take the moving walkway beneath a clear acrylic tunnel. You can even snorkel or scuba dive with the sharks at 1 pm and 3 pm daily. The newest exhibit is the coral reef—one of the largest living coral reef displays in the world. Check it out from above and then below in the underwater gallery. Other highlights include the rare seadragons and DANGERzone, featuring a deadly line up of sea creatures. ⊠ *Hillarys Boat Harbour, 91 Southside Dr., Hillarys, Perth, Western Australia* ⊹ *AQWA is a 20-minute drive north of Perth's CBD via the Mitchell Freeway, turn left at Hepburn Ave. and continue to Hillarys Boat Harbour. Or, take the northern Joondalup train line. Alight at Warwick station and take bus No. 423* ☎ *08/9447–7500* ⊕ *www. aqwa.com.au* ✉ *A$28.00; shark experience A$159, plus A$20 snorkel or A$40 scuba equipment rental* ⏱ *Daily 10–5.*

🅒 **Cohunu Koala Park.** The 30-acre Cohunu (pronounced co-*hu*-na) lets you cuddle with a koala. But the other native animals, such as emus, dingoes, wallabies, kangaroos, and wombats are worth visiting, too. A miniature steam railway operates mostly on weekends and school and public holidays. ✉ *Lot 802, Nettleton Road, Byford, Perth, Western Australia* ✛ *Cohuna is a 40-minute drive south of Perth's CBD. Take the South Western Hwy. to Byford, turn left at Nettleton Rd. for 500 meters* 📠 *08/9526–2966* ∰ *www.cohunu.com.au* ✉ *A$15* ☉ *Daily 10–4, koala cuddle with photo souvenir A$25, daily 10–4.*

London Court. Gold-mining entrepreneur Claude de Bernales built this outdoor shopping arcade in 1937. Today it's a magnet for anyone with a camera wanting to recapture the atmosphere and architecture of Tudor England, and for those looking for Australian souvenirs. Along its length are statues of Sir Walter Raleigh and Dick Whittington, the legendary lord mayor of London. Above the arcade costumed mechanical knights joust with one another when the clock strikes the quarter hour. ✉ *Between St. George's Terr. and Hay St., CBD, Perth, Western Australia.*

♺ **Perth Zoo.** Five minutes from Perth's CBD and more than 111 years old, Perth Zoo has established itself as a Western Australian icon. Expect lush gardens and the different native habitats of various animals from around the world. Walk among Australian animals in an environment depicting the diversity of Australia's native landscape. Discover the Reptile Encounter, Rainforest Retreat, and the Australian Bushwalk. For something a little more exotic, there's the African Savannah, with rhinoceros, giraffe, lions, cheetahs, and baboons, and the Asian Rainforest, with elephants, red pandas, tigers, otters, and a colony of Sumatran orangutans. Perth Zoo supports vital conservation both on-site and in the wild, and offers a fun and informative day out for young and old. A one-hour guided tour around the zoo on an electric Zebra Car, seating seven passengers and the driver, costs A$3.50. ✉ *20 Labouchere Rd., South Perth, Perth, Western Australia* ✛ *Catch the number 30 or 31 bus at Esplanade Busport or take a ferry ride across the Swan River from the bottom of Barrack St. and then a 10-minute walk following the signs* 📠 *08/9474–0444, 08/9474–3551* ∰ *www.perthzoo.wa.gov. au* ✉ *A$21* ☉ *Daily 9–5.*

♺ **Scitech Discovery Centre.** Interactive science and technology displays educate and entertain visitors of all ages. There are more than 100 hands-on general science exhibits, as well as in-depth feature exhibitions. Daily science and puppet shows present science in an entertaining way, and the space shows in the planetarium should stretch your imagination as they take you to the far edges of the known Universe. ✉ *City West Centre, Sutherland St., West Perth, Perth, Western Australia* 📠 *08/9215–0700* ∰ *www.scitech.org.au* ✉ *A$14* ☉ *Weekends, school holidays, and public holidays 10–5; weekdays 9:30–4.*

The Bell Tower. An interesting mix of 14th-century history and contemporary Australian architecture, the modern Bell Tower is home to the antique Swan Bells. Comprising one of the world's largest musical instruments, the 12 ancient bells installed in the tower are originally from St. Martin-in-the-Fields Church of London, England. The same bells rang to celebrate the destruction of the Spanish Armada in 1588, the homecoming of Captain James Cook in 1771, and the coronation of every British monarch. The tower contains fascinating displays on the history of the bells and bell ringing, and provides stunning views of the Perth skyline. A new product included in the entry price is the innovatory "video postcard," which streams to You Tube and lets you say "hi" to family and friends around the world. Head to the lofty heights of the observation deck on Level 6 for the Wow factor. ⊠ *Barrack Sq., Barrack St. at Riverside Dr., CBD, Perth, Western Australia* ☎ *08/6210–0444* ⊕ *www.thebelltower. com.au* ☜ *A$13* ◷ *Daily 10–3:45; close varies by season; bell-handling demonstrations (single bell) Wed. and Fri. 11:30 am–12:30 pm; full bell ringing Mon., Tues., Thurs., and weekends noon–1 pm. Flat, closed shoes must be worn for access to the observation deck; strollers, large bags, backpacks, and bulky items are not permitted in the tower.*

> ## CITY-DWELLING WATERBIRDS
>
> When a series of lakes was created with construction of the freeways and the Narrows Bridge across the Swan River in 1959, city planners probably didn't realize that these bodies of water would become an oasis for waterbirds. It's a pleasant stroll or bike ride along the riverside, west from the Barrack Street jetties. Laze on the grassy banks, or relax under a tree and check out the different species of waterbirds, including the famous black swan, egret, and red-necked stint, migrating from as far afield as Siberia.

OFF THE BEATEN PATH

Batavia Coast. A drive along this part of the coast, which starts at Greenhead, 285 km (178 mi) north of Perth, and runs up to Kalbarri, takes you past white sands and emerald seas, and some lovely small towns. Among them are the fig-shaded, seaside village of **Dongara** and the more northerly **Central Greenough Historical Settlement,** whose restored colonial buildings—including a jail with original leg irons—date from 1858. A few miles north is **Geraldton,** whose skyline is dominated by the beautiful Byzantine St. Francis Xavier Cathedral. Also of note is the HMAS Sydney II Memorial, recognized as the only national War Mermorial outside of Canberra. The huge Batavia Coast Marina has a pedestrian plaza and shopping arcades, and the Western Australian Museum houses a collection of artifacts from the *Batavia,* which was shipwrecked in 1629.

Nambung National Park. Set on the Swan coastal plain 245 km (152 mi) north of Perth, now accessible in just under two hours along a scenic coastal drive, Nambung National Park surrounds its most famous attraction: the **Pinnacles Desert.** Over the years, wind and drifting sand have sculpted eerie limestone forms that loom as high as 15 feet. These "pinnacles" are actually the fossilized roots of ancient coastal plants fused with sand, and you can walk among them along a 1.2 km (0.7 mi) return walk that starts at the parking area. There's also a 3-km (2-mi) one-way Pinnacles Desert Loop scenic drive (not suitable for large RVs or buses). August through October the heath blazes with wildflowers. ■TIP➔ Note the "No's:" No dogs, no bins, no drinking water, although water is available to purchase at the interpretative centre and gift shop. Entrance fees are A$11 per car. Call ☎ *08/9652–7043 or 9652–1911* for more information.

10

BEACHES

Perth's beaches and waterways are among the city's greatest attractions.

★ Traveling north from Fremantle, the first beach you come to is **Leighton,** where windsurfers and astonishing wave-jumpers ride boards against the surf and hurl themselves airborne.

★ **Cottesloe** and **North Cottesloe** attract families. **Trigg,** a top surf site and arguably Perth's best beach, overlooks an emerald-green bay.

★ **Scarborough** is favored by teenagers and young adults. **Swanbourne** (between North Cottesloe and City Beach) is a "clothing-optional" beach.

OUTDOOR ACTIVITIES

BICYCLING Perth's climate and its network of excellent trails make cycling a safe and enjoyable way to discover the city. But beware: summer temperatures can exceed 40°C (100°F) in the shade. A bicycle helmet is required by law, and carrying water is prudent. About Bike Hire, which rents bikes for A$36 a day or A$80 a week, is open daily 9–5 with extended hours in high season. Free brochures detailing trails, including stops at historic spots, are available from the Western Australia Visitor Centre. Rentals are available at

About Bike Hire ⊠ *Behind Causeway Car Park, Riverside Dr., Perth, Western Australia* ☎ *08/9221–2665* ⊕ *www.aboutbikehire.com.au.*

GOLF Perth has numerous public golf courses, all of which rent out clubs.

Western Australia Golf Association. The Western Australia Golf Association has details on golf courses in the state and a program of events. ☎ *08/9367–2490* ⊕ *www.golfwa.com.au.*

SURFING Western Australians take to the surf from a young age—and with world-famous surfing beaches right on the city's doorstep, it's no wonder. The most popular year-round beaches for body and board surfing are Scarborough and Trigg, where swells usually reach 6–9 feet, and occasionally rear up to 12 feet. There are also more than a dozen beaches heading north from Leighton (near Fremantle), including the Cables Artificial Reef (near Leighton) and Watermans (in the northern suburbs of Perth). Cottesloe is favored by novice surfers and children.

If you venture outside the city, Rottnest also has good surf, and if you head south on the coast, you'll find more than 20 surf locations from Cape Naturaliste to Cape Leeuwin. The Main Break at Margaret River is the best known, where waves often roll in at more than 12–15 feet, setting the scene for the annual Margaret River Pro, a world-qualifying series event held in April at Surfers Point. Western Australia's top board surfers head to Scarborough in August for the final round of the state competition. Wet suits are de rigueur for the winter months (May–September), when the surf is usually at its best.

Big Wave Surf School. Big Wave Surf School has a range of classes available, starting at A$30 for a one-hour casual class, Saturday only at 11:45 ☎ *08/9524–7671* ⊕ *www.surfingschool.com.au.*

WATER SPORTS **Funcats Surfcat Hire.** If you want to enjoy the Swan River at a leisurely pace, rent a catamaran or a sailboard from Funcats Surfcat Hire. It costs A$35 per hour. Funcats operates from October to April. ⊠ *Coode St. Jetty, South Perth, Perth, Western Australia* ☎ *0408/926003.*

South Perth Parasailing. Parasailing is available from Mill Point Road on the South Perth shore of the Swan River every day, weather and winds permitting. It's A$80 for a single for 10 minutes and A$140 for a 10 minutes tandem. Contact South Perth Parasailing. ⊠ *Mill Point Rd., South Perth, Perth, Western Australia* ☏ *0408/382595* ⊕ *www. southperthparasailing.com.au.*

WHERE TO EAT

Northbridge, northwest of the railway station, is *the* dining and nightclubbing center of Perth, and reasonably priced restaurants are everywhere. Elsewhere around Perth are seafood and international restaurants, many with stunning views over the Swan River or city, and cantilevered windows that make for a seamless transition between indoor and alfresco dining.

CATCHING WAVES

Western Australians have a love affair with the beach. During the summer months you'll find thousands of them lazing on sandy beaches, swimming, and surfing. There are popular beaches on Perth's doorstep, but serious board surfers will head south to the rugged coastline from Cape Naturaliste to Cape Leeuwin. Favorite surf breaks are Surfer's Point, Lefthanders, Three Bears, Grunters, the Bombie, Moses Rock, the Guillotine, the Farm, Barnyards, Suicides, and Supertubes. There are some 50 recognized surf breaks along this coast. Check out ⊕ *www.surf-forecast.com* for up-to-date surf reports.

For those on a budget, the noisy fun of a dim sum lunch at one of Perth's many traditional Asian teahouses (especially in Northbridge) is cheap and delicious. Along with a refreshing cup of green tea, you can enjoy steamed pork buns, fried chicken feet, and egg tarts served at your table from the trolley. Food halls in Perth, Northbridge, and Fremantle are other budget options. These one-stop eateries cater to diverse tastes; not all are the same, but you can usually take your pick from stalls selling vegetarian items, roast meats, fresh fruits and juices, Aussie burgers, and fried chicken. Some also serve Southeast Asian, Indian, Japanese, Korean, and Thai cuisine, usually for about A$10.

Use the coordinate (⊕ B2) at the end of each listing to locate a site on the corresponding map.

$$$
AUSTRALIAN
✕**Bluewater Grill.** Bustling with locals, Bluewater Grill serves up modern Australian cuisine with an emphasis on fresh seafood and quality steaks; try the pan-fried snapper, seared salmon, or chunky fillets fresh from the grill. Just 7 km from the center of Perth, in the affluent suburb of Applecross—once home to the late actor Heath Ledger—the heritage restaurant is on the south side of the Swan River at Heathcote Reserve, looking back to the city skyline across a yacht club that's home to some of the most palatial boats in the state. Sip world-class local wine on the pleasant alfresco area on a balmy summer's day and imagine Captain James Stirling landing here with his fleet in 1827. ⊠ *56 Duncraig Rd., Applecross, Perth, Western Australia* ☏ *08/9315 7700* ⊕ *www. bluewatergrill.com.au* ☾ *Open weekdays noon–3, 6–10, weekends 8–11, noon–3, 6–10* ⊕ *D2.*

$$ ✕ **CBD Restaurant and Bar.** The trendiest place in Perth's West End, this
AUSTRALIAN spot has an unusual leaf-shape bar where both diners and drinkers
congregate. The menu changes regularly, but could include pot-roast
chicken, red braised pork belly, and lamb-shank curry. There's a pizza
oven as well, with pizzas from A$23. A big selection of table wine and
"stickies" (dessert wines) is available by the glass. Late hours bring in
the nightcap crowd after shows at the adjacent His Majesty's Theatre.
✉ *Hay and King Sts., CBD, Perth, Western Australia* ☎ *08/9263–1859*
⊕ *www.rydges.com/perth* ✛ *C3.*

$$$ ✕ **Coco's Riverside Bar and Restaurant.** Overlooking the Swan River in
AUSTRALIAN South Perth you can't miss Coco's Riverside Bar and Restaurant as
you step off the ferry heading toward the Zoo. A varied menu includes
interesting mains such as Kalbarri pink snapper fillet, Szechuan-spiced
calamari with green papaya, soy-and-sesame pickled daikon and nam
jin, or char-grilled O'Reilly's lot sirloin with Madeira jus.While you gaze
at the fabulous view across the river to Perth's CBD, ponder your choice
of wine from the extensive list that includes many of the best labels from
the Margaret River region. ✉ *Southshore Centre, 85 Esplanade, South
Perth, Perth, Western Australia* ☎ *08/9474–3030* ⊕ *www.cocosperth.
com.au* ⌒ *Reservations essential* ✛ *D4.*

$$ ✕ **Dusit Thai Restaurant.** Come here for authentic Thai food, lovingly
THAI prepared and served among traditional sculptures and artwork. Starters
include *kra thong tong* (stir-fried diced prawns, minced chicken, and
sweet corn on deep-fried tartlets); or *gai hor bai-toey* (marinated breast
of chicken wrapped in Padang leaves and deep-fried). Main-course spe-
cialties include *gang keo-wan* (green curry chicken) and *gang-pa* (hot
and spicy red curry without coconut milk, served with green beans,
bamboo strips, and basil leaves). Attentive service placing accent on
detail—note the linen serviettes elaborately folded liked winged birds.
Dusit Thai has been in Northbridge for over 22 years. ✉ *249 James
St., Northbridge, Perth, Western Australia* ☎ *08/9328–7647* ⊕ *www.
dusitthai.com.au* ⊗ *No lunch. Closed Mon.* ✛ *A3.*

$$$ ✕ **Fraser's Restaurant.** In fair weather the large outdoor area at this newly
AUSTRALIAN refurbished King's Park restaurant fills with people enjoying food and
views of the city and Swan River. The ever-changing menu highlights
fresh Western Australian produce. Look for panfried goat-cheese gnocchi; Amelia Park lamb rack with chickpeas or perhaps line-caught snapper fillet, with potato puree and salsa verde with fennel. The adjacent
Botanical Cafe (*08/9482–0122*) is busy and more casual, serving breakfast, lunch, and dinner daily. ✉ *Fraser Ave., King's Park, West Perth,
Perth, Western Australia* ☎ *08/9481–7100* ⊕ *www.frasersrestaurant.
com.au* ⌒ *Reservations essential* ✛ *D1.*

$$$ ✕ **Jackson's Restaurant.** A long list of awards over the past two decades
AUSTRALIAN has established Jackson's Restaurant as one of Perth's top dining estab-
lishments. Chef Neal Jackson began his career in London, but it was in
the tiny Western Australian town of Donnybrook, in the South West,
that he burst onto the local scene. Over 17 years he impressed South
West diners before establishing Jackson's in Perth, where since 1998
he continues to impress by creating innovative and intensely flavored
foods. Current à la carte choices from the menu include baldivis rabbit,

The Pinnacles of Nambung National Park, Western Australia.

prosciutto, baby carrots, and cheesy potato mash, or another favorite, the charred Angus sirloin steak, with oysters, black bean, and snow peas. There are excellent vegetarian choices as well, such as tacu tacu, sweet sour and hot sauce, stir-fried lettuce, lotus seeds, and wolfberries. The Dego—a nine-course degustation menu—costs A$125. ⊠ *483 Beaufort St., Highgate, Perth, Western Australia* ☎ *08/9328–1177* ⊕ *www.jacksonsrestaurant.com.au* ☉ *Closed Sun.* ✛ *A5.*

$$
ASIAN

✕ **Joe's Oriental Diner.** On the street level of the Hyatt Regency Hotel on Adelaide Terrace, Joe's serves a wide range of dishes from China, Indonesia, Thailand, Malaysia, and Singapore. The rattan-and-bamboo interior is reminiscent of the many noodle houses throughout Southeast Asia, and meals are prepared in the spectacular open kitchen. Hearty soups and delicious noodle dishes, like *laksa* (rice noodles in a spicy coconut-milk broth with chicken, bean curd, fish cakes, fish balls, and prawns), are the standouts. Each dish carries a chili coding indicating its relative spiciness—so you won't breathe fire unless you want to. ⊠ *Hyatt Regency, 99 Adelaide Terr., CBD, Perth, Western Australia* ☎ *08/9225–1268* ⊕ *www.joesorientaldiner.com.au* ☉ *Closed Sun. No lunch Sat.* ✛ *D6.*

$$$$
FRENCH
Fodor's Choice
★

✕ **Loose Box.** Perth's finest French restaurant in semi-rural Mundaring is run by owner-chef Alain Fabregues, who has received France's highest culinary honor, the Meilleur Ouvrier de France, as well as a French knighthood—Chevalier Dans L'Ordre National du Merite—for his contribution to French culture and cuisine. His degustation menu applies classical French culinary principles to Australia's best seasonal bounty: there's *le blinis d'oiseaux au Raifort* (quail, duck, and chicken folded with kipfler potato in blinis of chives and olives) and *le nougat glacé* (French traditional nougat, made with honey, pistachio, and hazelnut,

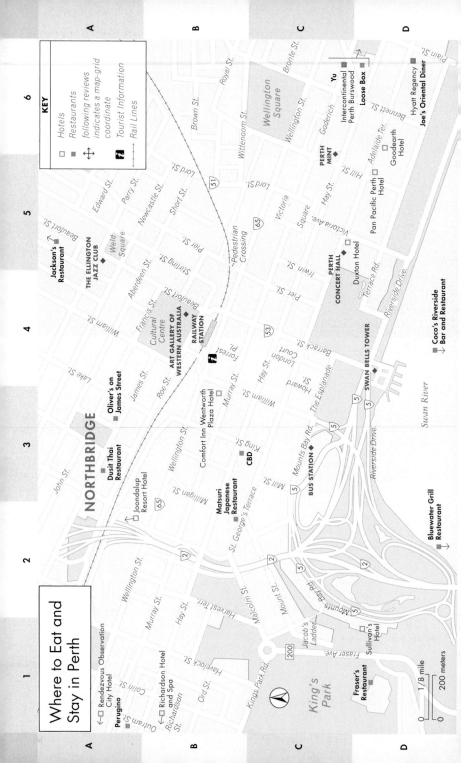

Where to Eat and Stay in Perth

KEY

- □ Hotels
- ■ Restaurants
- ✦ following reviews indicates a map-grid coordinate
- 🛈 Tourist Information
- ┼┼ Rail Lines

NORTHBRIDGE

King's Park

Wellington Square

Cultural Centre

ART GALLERY OF WESTERN AUSTRALIA

RAILWAY STATION

PERTH MINT

PERTH CONCERT HALL

SWAN BELLS TOWER

BUS STATION

CBD

Swan River

Rendezvous Observation City Hotel

Perugino

Richardson Hotel and Spa

Jackson's Restaurant

THE ELLINGTON JAZZ CLUB

Oliver's on James Street

Dusit Thai Restaurant

Joondalup Resort Hotel

Matsuri Japanese Restaurant

Comfort Inn Wentworth Plaza Hotel

Sullivan's Hotel

Fraser's Restaurant

Bluewater Grill Restaurant

Duxton Hotel

Pan Pacific Perth Hotel

Intercontinental Perth Burswood

Yu

Loose Box

Gooderath Hotel

Hyatt Regency

Joe's Oriental Diner

Coco's Riverside Bar and Restaurant

Weld Square

Pedestrian Crossing

1/8 mile

200 meters

served chilled on a strawberry coulis with caramel strands). There is no à la carte option. Each room (the restaurant used to be a house) is cozy, intimate, and warm. Accommodation is available, if you just can't bring yourself to leave. ✉ *6825 Great Eastern Hwy., Mundaring, Western Australia* ☎ *08/9295–1787* ⊕ *www.loosebox.com.au* ⚲ *Reservations essential* ◷ *Wed.–Sat. for dinner, Sun. for lunch. Closed approx. 3 wks over Christmas and New Year* ✛ *D6.*

$ ╳**Matsuri Japanese Restaurant.** Discerning diners fill every table most JAPANESE nights at this contemporary glass-and-steel restaurant. At the base of an office tower, Perth's most popular casual Japanese dining spot is famous for its fresh, flavorful,

EATING OUT

While there are plenty of high-end restaurants in Perth, it's also possible to eat on the cheap. Northbridge has a plethora of competitively priced restaurants, especially along James Street, and especially at lunchtime. A dim sum lunch at a traditional Asian teahouse is inexpensive and delicious. Food halls in Perth, Northbridge, and Fremantle are another budget option. These one-stop eateries cater to diverse tastes; not all are the same, but you can usually take your pick from stalls selling all sorts of delicious food, usually for about A$10.

and authentic cuisine. Served with steamed rice, miso soup, salad, and green tea, the sushi and sashimi are an excellent value. House specialties include delicately light tempura vegetables and *una don* (grilled eel in teriyaki sauce). ✉ *Lower level 1, QV1 Bldg., 250 St. George's Terr., CBD, Perth, Western Australia* ☎ *08/9322–7737* ⊕ *www.matsuri.com. au* ◷ *No lunch Sat. Closed Sun.* ✛ *B2.*

$$ ╳**Oliver's on James Street.** Watch the Northbridge world pass by from this EUROPEAN funky restaurant and pizzeria on James Street next to Cinema Paradiso, ★ an independent, foreign film cinema. Locals, tourists, and movie buffs flock to this popular eatery. If you have a Paradiso movie ticket (www. lunapalace.com.au) you'll get a 10% discount on your meal. Alive with laughter and conversation, Oliver's offers indoor and al fresco casual fine dining. Choose from a large selection of wood-fired pizza's prepared right in front of you by British-born head chef and proprietor, Wayne Willsher, or select from the main menu with options ranging from char-grilled steaks to freshly grilled fish. For an interesting selection, try the Tapas Plate, small items to share that may include sautéed chorizo, salt and pepper calamari, tempura prawns, and wild mushroom or Pecorino arancini. ✉ *160 James St., Northbridge, Perth, Western Australia* ☎ *08/9228–8725* ⊕ *www.oliversonjamesstreet.com.au* ◷ *No lunch Mon.–Thurs.*

$$ ╳**Perugino.** Chef Giuseppe Pagliaricci takes an imaginative yet simple ITALIAN approach to the cuisine of his native Umbria. Only the freshest produce ★ is used for such creations as *filetto in crosta* (an eye fillet of beef double crumbed, pan-fried, and served in a bed of porcini mushrooms); or *nodini di vitello con salsa d'asparagi* (loin of veal panfried and served in a fresh asparagus sauce). The six-course degustation menu highlights the best of the house. ✉ *77 Outram St., West Perth, Perth, Western Australia* ☎ *08/9321–5420* ⊕ *www.perugino.com.au* ⚲ *Reservations essential* ◷ *Closed Sun. and Mon. No lunch Sat.* ✛ *A1.*

10

$$ ✕ **Yu.** Some of the best Chinese food in the city is cooked up at this
CHINESE   elegant restaurant in the Burswood Entertainment Complex. Cantonese
flavors predominate under the guidance of chef de cuisine Pat Cheong,
with signature dishes Peking duck, fillet steak with Szechuan or Can-
tonese sauce, Portuguese crab, and sea-salt prawns. The setting is that
of a Cantonese manor, with woodcarvings and silk tapestries, and an
entrance over a "bridge" across marble floors laden with gold coins.
Nine-course banquet menus start at A$70. ⊠ *InterContinental Perth
Burswood, Great Eastern Hwy. at Bolton Ave., Burswood, Perth, West-
ern Australia* ☎ *08/9362–7551* ⊕ *www.yurestaurant.com.au* ✛ *D6.*

WHERE TO STAY

Businesspeople from around the world are flocking to Western Aus-
tralia, and consequently hotel rooms in Perth are at an unprecedented
premium. Few new hotels have been built, so hotels are frequently at
capacity, and prices are up. ■ TIP➜ The wise will book early.

For expanded hotel reviews, visit Fodors.com.

*Use the coordinate (✛ B2) at the end of each listing to locate a site on
the corresponding map.*

$$ 🏨 **Comfort Inn Wentworth Plaza Hotel.** This Federation-era inn is one
Fodor'sChoice   of Perth's most centrally located hotels; it's across the road from the
★   Perth Railway Station and a block from the Hay Street Mall. **Pros:**
few minutes' walk to city-center shopping malls and arcades; heritage-
style rooms with different configurations. **Cons:** no private en suites
with some rooms; no on-site parking; central Perth location, so can be
lively day and night. ⊠ *300 Murray St., CBD, Perth, Western Australia*
☎ *08/9338 5000, 1800/355109* ⊕ *www.wentworthplazahotel.com.au*
⤳ *59 rooms* ⚇ *In-hotel: restaurant, bar* ✛ *B3.*

$$$$ 🏨 **Duxton Hotel.** Adjacent to the Perth Concert Hall, this elegant hotel is
★   in the business district, within easy walking distance of the city center.
Pros: few minutes' walk to city-center shopping malls; popular restaurant with alfresco terrace; some rooms have river views. **Cons:** few
evening dining options nearby; parking fee applies. ⊠ *1 St. George's
Terr., CBD, Perth, Western Australia* ☎ *08/9261–8000, 1800/681118*
⊕ *www.duxtonhotels.com/perth* ⤳ *291 rooms, 15 suites* ⚇ *In-room:
Wi-Fi. In-hotel: restaurant, bar, pool, gym, parking* ✛ *C5.*

$$$ 🏨 **Goodearth Hotel.** Tourist accommodation at a reasonable price can be
hard to find close to Perth's CBD, which is why this business-district,
full-service apartment-style hotel is favored not only by regional West-
ern Australians and their families, but also by tourists conscious of
their dollars. ⊠ *195 Adelaide Terr., CBD, Perth, Western Australia*
☎ *08/9492–7777* ⊕ *www.goodearthhotel.com.au* ⤳ *181 rooms* ⚇ *In-
room: kitchen, Wi-Fi. In-hotel: restaurant, bar, spa, laundry facilities,
parking* ✛ *D6.*

$$$$ 🏨 **Hyatt Regency.** Within walking distance of Perth's central business
★   district, this hotel overlooking the Swan River is one of Perth's best.
Pros: river views from many rooms; evening nibbles and drinks in the
executive lounge; five restaurants in hotel. **Cons:** primarily a busi-
ness market hotel with corporate decor; few dining options nearby.
⊠ *99 Adelaide Terr., CBD, Perth, Western Australia* ☎ *08/9225–1234*

⊕ *www.perth.hyatt.com* ⤳ *367 rooms, 32 suites* ⌂ *In-room: safe, Internet. In-hotel: restaurant, bar, pool, tennis court, gym, business center, parking* ⛱ *Breakfast* ✛ *D6.*

$$$$
Fodor's Choice
★

Intercontinental Perth Burswood. From the 10-story glass atrium atop its pyramid-shape exterior to its 18-hole golf course, and the 2011 multimillion-dollar refurbishment, everything about the Burswood conveys luxury. **Pros:** impressive lobby rises the full height of the building complete with sails; extensive, all-you-can-eat buffet for breakfast, lunch and dinner. **Cons:** adjacent casino and nightclub attracts a boisterous crowd; Thursday through Saturday nights notable for partygoers; atrium-style lobby creates noise to some rooms. ⊠ *Great Eastern Hwy. at Bolton Ave., Burswood, Perth, Western Australia* ☎ *08/9362–7777, 1800/999667* ⊕ *www.burswood.com.au* ⤳ *399 rooms, 14 suites* ⌂ *In-room: safe, Internet. In-hotel: restaurant, bar, golf course, pool, tennis court, gym, spa, parking* ✛ *D6.*

$$$
★

Joondalup Resort Hotel. Although it's 30 km (19 mi) from Perth's business district, a drive that takes about 25 minutes, this palm-shaded building—which resembles a southern plantation owner's mansion—is a comfortable place to relax for a few days, especially if you like golf or want to see the kangaroos that roam freely across the golf course. **Pros:** international-standard golf course; country-club atmosphere; some rooms have golf-course views. **Cons:** in suburban area; conventions can make venues crowded. ⊠ *Country Club Blvd., Connolly, Perth, Western Australia* ☎ *08/9400–8888, 1800/803488* ⊕ *www.joondalupresort. com.au* ⤳ *66 rooms, 4 suites* ⌂ *In-room: safe, Wi-Fi. In-hotel: restaurant, bar, golf course, pool, tennis court, gym, parking* ✛ *A2.*

$$$$
Rendezvous Observation City Hotel. Watch the sun dip into the Indian Ocean from this beachside resort where large rooms are decorated in contemporary styles and many have ocean views and private balconies. **Pros:** great views of the Indian Ocean; walk straight on to Scarborough Beach; movies on demand. **Cons:** few other attractions nearby; limited shopping facilities. ⊠ *Esplanade, Scarborough Beach, Perth, Western Australia* ☎ *08/9245–1000, 1800/067680* ⊕ *www.rendezvoushotels. com* ⤳ *327 rooms, 6 suites* ⌂ *In-room: Internet. In-hotel: restaurant, bar, pool, tennis court, gym, spa, beach, parking* ✛ *A1.*

$$$$
The Richardson Hotel and Spa. Tucked away in a quiet, leafy, tree-lined street in West Perth, the Richardson offers a discrete and indulgent stay without forgoing any of the amenities of the bigger downtown hotels. **Pros:** large rooms and suites; complimentary Internet; Nespresso coffee machines and evening turn-down service in all rooms; convenient meal packs in rooms; modest minibar prices; balconies off all rooms. **Cons:** views mostly of surrounding buildings; Subiaco and shopping area 5–10 minutes walk away. ⊠ *32 Richardson St., Perth, Perth, Western Australia* ☎ *08/9217–8888* ⊕ *www.therichardson.com.au* ⤳ *54 rooms, 20 suites* ⌂ *In-room: safe, kitchen, Internet, Wi-Fi. In-hotel: restaurant, bar, pool, gym, spa, parking* ✛ *B1.*

$$$$
Pan Pacific Perth Hotel. Sweeping views over the Swan River from many guest rooms are a feature of this 23-story, five-star hotel, a handy 10-minute walk from downtown. **Pros:** many rooms have river views; gym with steam rooms open 24 hours; Wi-Fi is complimentary in public

10

areas. **Cons:** in an office area; limited nighttime dining options nearby, high-speed Internet access charges apply in guest rooms. ✉ *207 Adelaide Terr., CBD, Perth, Western Australia* ☎ *08/9224–7777* ⊕ *www.panpacific.com/perth* ⏎ *468 rooms, 18 suites* ⌂ *In-room: safe, Internet. In-hotel: restaurant, bar, pool, gym, parking* ✛ *D5.*

$$$ 🔲 **Sullivan's Hotel.** A friendly, family-run hotel opposite waterfront parkland at the foot of King's Park, Sullivan's is handy to the center of Perth and King's Park; it's a 10-minute walk to the city center, less to the Barrack Street jetties and the Swan River. **Pros:** good-value beds for the area; close to King's Park; free public bus service at front. **Cons:** no night service for free public bus service; parking subject to availability. ✉ *166 Mounts Bay Rd., CBD, Perth, Western Australia* ☎ *08/9321–8022* ⊕ *www.sullivans.com.au* ⏎ *71 rooms* ⌂ *In-room: kitchen, Wi-Fi. In-hotel: restaurant, bar, pool, laundry facilities, parking* ✛ *D1.*

> ### ROCKIN' IN PERTH
>
> Thanks to pop, rock, and metal bands like Eskimo Joe, the John Butler Trio, the Waifs, Karnivool, Little Birdy, the Panda Band, and the Sleepy Jackson—who all started in Perth—the music scene here is thriving. Despite their isolation from the rest of Australia, Western Australian musos are turning out some top-notch material. Music commentators claim there isn't a "Perth sound" as such, just a talented bunch of artists writing and performing original music. Check out ⊕ *www.xpressmag.com.au* for an up-to-date guide on live shows.

NIGHTLIFE AND THE ARTS

Details on cultural events in Perth are published in the comprehensive Saturday edition of the *West Australian*. A free weekly, *X-Press Magazine*, lists music, concerts, movies, entertainment reviews, and who's playing at pubs, clubs, and hotels. *SCOOP* magazine (⊕ *www.scooptraveller.com.au*), published quarterly, is an excellent guide to the essential Western Australian lifestyle.

THE ARTS

BOCS Ticketing. BOCS Ticketing is the main booking hotline in Perth for the performing arts. ☎ *08/9484–1133, 1800/193 300* ⊕ *www.bocsticketing.com.au.*

Perth International Arts Festival (PIAF). Local talent dominates the arts scene in Perth, although the acclaimed Perth International Arts Festival (PIAF), held February in venues throughout the city, attracts international music, dance, and theater stars. This is Australia's oldest and biggest annual arts festival, and it's been running for more than 50 years. As part of the festival, the Lotterywest Festival Films screens films outdoors December–March. ☎ *08/6488–5555 for information and bookings* ⊕ *www.perthfestival.com.au.*

BALLET   **West Australian Ballet Company.** The West Australian Ballet Company is a world-class ballet company with a diverse repertoire that includes new, full-length story ballets, cutting-edge contemporary dance, and classic and neoclassic ballets. The company has earned an international reputation for excellence due to its overall innovation and creativity, and performances are held throughout Perth, including His Majesty's Theatre, the Quarry Amphitheatre, and the State Theatre Centre. ⊠ *825 Hay St., CBD, Perth, Western Australia* ☎ *08/9214–0707* ⊕ *www.waballet.com.au.*

CONCERTS **Perth Concert Hall.** The Perth Concert Hall, a modern building overlooking the Swan River, stages regular recitals by the excellent West Australian Symphony Orchestra, as well as Australian and international performers. Adding to the appeal of the fine auditorium is the 3,000-pipe organ surrounded by a 160-person choir gallery. ⊠ *5 St. George's Terr., CBD, Perth, Western Australia* ☎ *08/9484–1133* ⊕ *www.perthconcerthall.com.au.*

OPERA **West Australian Opera Company.** The West Australian Opera Company presents three seasons annually—in April, August, and November—at His Majesty's Theatre. They also perform Opera in the Park in Perth's Supreme Court Gardens each February. The company's repertoire includes classic opera, Gilbert and Sullivan operettas, and occasional musicals. ⊠ *825 Hay St., CBD, Perth, Western Australia* ☎ *08/9278–8999* ⊕ *www.waopera.asn.au.*

THEATER **Burswood Theatre.** The Burswood Theatre has regular theatrical and musical productions from around Australia. ⊠ *Great Eastern Hwy., Burswood, Perth, Western Australia* ☎ *13–2849, 9362–7685* ⊕ *www.burswood.com.au.*

His Majesty's Theatre. The opulent Edwardian His Majesty's Theatre, opened in 1904, is loved by all who step inside. Home to the West Australian Opera Company and the West Australian Ballet Company, it hosts most theatrical productions in Perth. ⊠ *825 Hay St., CBD, Perth, Western Australia* ☎ *08/9484–1133* ⊕ *www.hismajestystheatre.com.au.*

Quarry Amphitheatre. For outdoor performances, the Quarry Amphitheatre is popular, particularly during the Perth International Arts Festival. ⊠ *Waldron Drive (left off Oceanic Dr.), City Beach, Perth, Western Australia* ☎ *08/9385–7144* ⊕ *www.quarryamphitheatre.com.au.*

Regal Theatre. The Regal Theatre hosts local and visiting performances. ⊠ *474 Hay St., at Rokeby Rd., Subiaco, Perth, Western Australia* ☎ *1300/795012* ⊕ *www.regaltheatre.com.au.*

State Theatre Centre of Western Australia. The State Theatre Centre of Western Australia features the 575 seat Heath Ledger Theatre and Studio Underground, a flexible performance space, while the Courtyard is a multipurpose outdoor events space. The State Theatre Centre presents contemporary performing arts, both theater and dance, and is the home of the Perth Theatre Company and Black Swan State Theatre Company. ⊠ *174–176 William St., Northbridge, Perth, Western Australia* ☎ *9484–1133* ⊕ *www.statetheatrecentrewa.com.au.*

NIGHTLIFE

Most luxury hotels in Perth have upscale nightclubs that appeal to the over-thirty crowd. Apart from these, however, nightlife in the city center is virtually nonexistent. Twentysomethings most often head to Northbridge, Subiaco, or Fremantle. Pubs and bars generally close by 11 pm, which is when the crowds start arriving at the nightclubs; these tend to stay open until around 5 am.

The London Court shopping mall facade at Hay Walking Street, Perth.

BARS

Brass Monkey. The Brass Monkey is in a huge, old, crimson-painted building with antique verandas, and is allegedly one of the oldest and most photographed pubs in WA. Twenty-one different beers on tap will keep hops aficionadas happy, and live stand-up comedy every Wednesday night may appeal to the fun-loving. There's no cover charge. ⊠ *William and James Sts., Northbridge, Perth, Western Australia* ☎ *08/9227–9596* ⊕ *www.thebrassmonkey.com.au.*

Queen's Tavern. Queen's Tavern has an excellent outdoor beer garden. The upstairs bar has a relaxed lounge vibe, with DJs on Friday, Saturday, and Sunday. ⊠ *520 Beaufort St., Highgate, Perth, Western Australia* ☎ *08/9328–7267.*

Subiaco Hotel. The Subiaco Hotel attracts a lively after-work crowd during the week, with live rock bands on Saturday in Bianca's Bar, live jazz on Wednesday in the Courtyard, R&B on Friday in Bianca's Bar, and live bands in the Courtyard on Saturday. ⊠ *465 Hay St., Subiaco, Perth, Western Australia* ☎ *08/9381–3069.*

JAZZ AND BLUES

Charles Hotel. Try the Charles Hotel for live blues performances on Tuesday night, live jazz every Monday night, and live stand-up comedy on Thursday. ⊠ *509 Charles St., North Perth, Perth, Western Australia* ☎ *08/9444–1051.*

Universal Bar. The Universal Bar has live jazz and blues Wednesday–Sunday from late afternoon till late. ⊠ *221 William St., Northbridge, Perth, Western Australia* ☎ *08/9227–6771.*

The Ellington Jazz Club. Inspired by the New York jazz scene, the Ellington is *the* place for jazz in Perth. Catch live music seven nights a week in an intimate and sophisticated setting. A tapas menu is available. General entry is $15 weekdays or $20 weekends for a table or $10 at the bar. National and international acts command a higher entry fee—check the Web site for details. ⊠ *191 Beaufort St., Northbridge, Perth, Western Australia* ☎ *08/9228–1088* ⊕ *www.ellingtonjazz.com.au* ☉ *Mon.– Thurs. 7 pm–1 am, Fri. and Sat. 7 pm–3 am, Sun. 6 pm–midnight.*

NIGHTCLUBS **Eve.** Eve is a glitzy, two-story venue done up with stainless steel and retro fittings. Wednesday through Sunday, the five bars, cozy lounge areas, stage, and dance floor with sound-and-light show reverberate to the sounds of renowned DJ's spinning the latest dance tunes. Doors open at 9 pm. Free entry Friday through Sunday before 10 pm. ⊠ *Intercontinental Perth Burswood, Great Eastern Hwy. at Bolton Ave., Burswood, Perth, Western Australia* ☎ *08/9362–7699.*

Hip-e Club. The Hip-e Club, a Perth legend and one of the funkiest nightclubs in Leederville, plays the latest commercial hits and favorite retro remixes. The famed student/backpacker night takes place on Tuesdays. Be there or be square. ⊠ *663 Newcastle St., Leederville, Perth, Western Australia* ☎ *08/9227–8899.*

SHOPPING

Shopping in Perth, with its pedestrian-friendly central business district, vehicle-free malls, and many covered arcades, is a delight. Hay Street Mall and Murray Street Mall are the main city shopping areas, linked by numerous arcades with small shops. In the suburbs, top retail strips include Napoleon Street in Cottesloe (for clothing and cooking items), Hampden Road in Nedlands (for crafts), and Beaufort Street in Mount Lawley (for antiques).

MALLS AND ARCADES **Forrest Place.** Forrest Place, flanked by the post office and the Forrest Chase Shopping Plaza, is the largest mall area in the city.

David Jones. David Jones department store opens onto the Murray Street pedestrian mall. ☎ *08/9210–4000*

Myer. Myer is a popular department store that carries all manner of goods and sundries. ⊠ *Murray St. Mall at Forrest Pl., Perth, Western Australia* ☎ *08/9265–5600*

Hay Street Mall. The Hay Street Mall, running parallel to Murray Street and linked by numerous arcades, is another extensive shopping area. Make sure you wander through the arcades that connect Hay and Murray streets, such as **Carillion Arcade,** which have many more shops.

AUSTRALIAN Australian souvenirs and knickknacks are on sale at small shops throughout the city and suburbs.

Purely Australian Clothing Company. Purely Australian Clothing Company carries the most comprehensive selection of Oz-abilia in Perth. There are also stores at Perth International Airport. ⊠ *35–36 London Court, CBD, Perth, Western Australia* ☎ *08/9325–4328* ⊕ *www.purelyaustralian.com.*

R.M. Williams. R.M. Williams sells everything for the Australian bushman, including moleskin pants, hand-tooled leather boots, and Akubra hats. ⊠ *Shop 38 Carillon City, Hay St. Mall, CBD, Perth, Western Australia* ☎ *08/9321–7786* ⊕ *www.rmwilliams.com.au.*

10

CRAFTS **Creative Native.** You can find authentic Aboriginal artifacts at Creative Native ; their selection of Aboriginal art is extensive. Each piece of original artwork comes with a certificate of authenticity. ⊠ *Shop 58, Forrest Chase, Forrest Pl., CBD, Perth, Western Australia* ☎ *08/9221–5800* ⊕ *www.creativenative.com.au.*

Indigenart–Mossenson Galleries. Featuring an innovative program of solo, group, and curated exhibitions by emerging and established artists and communities, Indigenart-Mossenson Galleries is one of Australia's leading commercial galleries specializing in Indigenous art. ⊠ *115 Hay St., Subiaco, Perth, Western Australia* ☎ *08/9388–2899* ⊕ *www. indigenart.com.au.*

Maalinup Aboriginal Gallery. Find authentic Aboriginal art, gifts, and souvenirs, including soaps, bath, and beauty products, some featuring Australian native plants, oils, and clays, made on-site. Maalinup Aboriginal Gallery is owned and operated by local Aboriginal people. ⊠ *10070 W. Swan Rd., Henley Brook, Western Australia* ☎ *08/9296–0711* ⊕ *www. maalinup.com.au* ☿ *Wed.–Sun., and Mon. Closed public holidays.*

FREMANTLE

About 19 km (12 mi) southwest of Perth.

The port city of Fremantle is a jewel in Western Australia's crown, largely because of its colonial architectural heritage. Freo (as the locals call it) is also a city where locals know each other, and there are plenty of interesting (and sometimes eccentric) residents. Modern Fremantle is a far cry from the barren, sandy plain that greeted the first wave of English settlers back in 1829 at the newly constituted Swan River Colony. Most were city dwellers, and after five months at sea in sailing ships they landed on salt-marsh flats that sorely tested their fortitude. Living in tents with packing cases for chairs, they found no edible crops, and the nearest freshwater was a distant 51 km (32 mi)—and a tortuous trip up the salty waters of the Swan. As a result they soon moved the settlement upriver to the vicinity of present-day Perth.

Fremantle remained the principal port, and many attractive limestone buildings were built to service the port traders. Australia's 1987 defence of the America's Cup—held in waters off Fremantle—triggered a major restoration of the colonial streetscapes. In the leafy suburbs nearly every other house is a restored 19th-century gem.

Like all great port cities, Freo is cosmopolitan, with mariners from all parts of the world strolling the streets—including 20,000 U.S. Navy personnel on rest and recreation throughout the year.

It's also a good jumping-off point for a day trip to Rottnest Island, where lovely beaches, rocky coves, and unique wallaby-like inhabitants called quokkas make their home.

GETTING HERE AND AROUND

Bus information for service from Perth is available from Transperth (☎ *13–6213* ⊕ *www.transperth.wa.gov.au*). Their Central Area Bus Service (CAT) provides free transportation around Fremantle in orange buses. The route begins and ends outside the Fremantle Bus/Train

Terminus, and stops include the Arts Centre, the cappuccino strip, and the Fremantle Market. CAT buses run every 10 minutes weekdays 7:30–6:30, and 10–6:30 on weekends and public holidays.

Trains bound for Fremantle depart from Perth approximately every 20–30 minutes from the Perth Central Station on Wellington Street. You can travel from Perth to Fremantle (or vice versa) in about 30 minutes. Tickets must be purchased at the ticket vending machines prior to travel. It is illegal to travel without a ticket.

If you are driving from downtown Perth, the most direct route is via Stirling Highway, from the foot of Kings Park; it will take about 35 minutes, depending on traffic.

SAFETY AND PRECAUTIONS

Fremantle is a safe destination, and is popular with families, particularly on weekends and during the school holidays. It also has a lively night-life, and late-night crowds leaving pubs and clubs can—and do—cause problems. Taxis are in high demand late at night when other public transport stops operating.

TIMING

Fremantle can easily be visited in a day from Perth, though if you want to trip over to Rottnest Island you will have to add an extra day. Most of the sights are clustered in a relatively small area close to the Fishing Boat Harbour, and you can take a walking tour or take a hop-on, hop-off tour tram.

TOURS

Fremantle Tram Tours. Fremantle Tram Tours runs hop-on, hop-off tours (A$22) around the city daily from 9:45 am to approximately 3:30 pm, with six stops all close to the major sights. A tour around Fremantle is a great way to get to know each area of the port city. A full-day tour is the Triple Tour, which includes a guided tour of Fremantle, a cruise on the Swan River to Perth, and a sightseeing tour in Perth. The tour finishes in Perth, but you can catch a train or bus back to Fremantle. The cost is A$56, not including your return to Fremantle. On Friday nights, "ghostly tours" take in suspected haunted premises, with a dinner of fish-and-chips included. The cost is A$56 per person. ⌂ *Box 1081, Fremantle, Western Australia 6959* ☎ *08/9433–6674* ⊕ *www.fremantletrams.com.*

ESSENTIALS

Banks and Currency Exchange Banks with dependable check-cashing and money-changing services include ANZ, Westpac, Commonwealth, Bendigo, Bank of Queensland, and National Australia Bank. **UAE Australia** ✉ *62 South Terr., Fremantle, Fremantle, Western Australia* ☎ *1300/705050* ⊕ *www.xpressmoney.com.au* ⊘ *Mon.–Sat. 9:30–5, Sun. 10–5.*

Medical Emergencies Fremantle Hospital ✉ *Alma St., Fremantle, Western Australia* ☎ *08/9431–3333 Fremantle Hospital, 000 Emergency, 1800/022 222 Health Direct/Medical Advice.*

Police Police ☎ *13–1444 assistance, 08/9222–1111 general inquiries, 000 emergency.*

10

Taxis Cab fare between 6 am and 6 pm weekdays is an initial A$3.80 plus A$1.55 every 1 km (½ mi). From 6 pm to 6 am and on weekends the rate rises to $5.60 plus A$1.55 per 1 km (½ mi). **Black & White** ✆ 13–1008. **Swan Taxis** ✆ 13–1330.

Visitor Information Fremantle Visitor Centre ⊠ *Kings Sq. at High St., Fremantle, Western Australia* ✆ *08/9431–7878* ⊕ *www.fremantlewa.com.au* ⊙ *Weekdays 9–5, Sat. 10–3, Sun. 11:30–2:30.*

EXPLORING

An ideal place to start a leisurely stroll is South Terrace, known as the Fremantle cappuccino strip. Wander alongside locals through sidewalk cafés or browse in bookstores, art galleries, and souvenir shops. No matter how aimlessly you meander, you'll invariably end up where you began. From South Terrace walk down to the Fishing Boat Harbour where there's always activity—commercial and pleasure craft bob about, and along the timber boardwalk is a cluster of outdoor eateries and a microbrewery.

Between Phillimore Street and Marine Terrace in the West End is a collection of some of the best-preserved heritage buildings in the state. The Fremantle Railway Station on Elder Place is another good spot to start a walk. Maps and details for 11 different self-guided walks are available at the Fremantle Visitor Center; a popular heritage walk is the Convict Trail, passing by 18 different sights and locations from Fremantle's convict past.

TOP ATTRACTIONS

Fremantle Prison. The former Fremantle Prison, built in 1855, is where 44 inmates met their fate on the prison gallows between 1888 and 1964. Tours feature the classic-art cell, where a superb collection of drawings by convict James Walsh decorates his quarters. Reservations are essential for the 90-minute Torchlight Tours (evening tours by flashlight). For the 2½-hour Tunnel Tour, visitors are provided with hard hats, overalls, boots, and headlamps before descending 65 feet into the labyrinthine tunnels that run beneath the prison; some of the tour is by boat in underground waterways. Reservations are essential. ⊠ *1 The Terrace, Fremantle, Western Australia* ✆ *08/9336–9200* ⊕ *www. fremantleprison.com.au* 🖃 *A$18.50, including a 75-min tour; Torchlight Tour A$25, Tunnel Tour A$59* ⊙ *Daily 10–5 with tour every 30 minutes, last tour at 5 pm. Torchlight Tours Wed. and Fri., regularly from 6:30 pm; last tour usually 9 pm. Tunnel Tour at 9, 9:45, 10:40, 12:20, 1:40, 2:40, 3:25.*

Fremantle Market. The Fremantle Market, established in 1897 and housed in a classic Victorian building, sells everything. You'll find paintings, incense, and antiques in the Hall, and vegetables, sausages, and even Chinese takeout in the Yard. Around 150 stalls attract an eclectic mix of locals and tourists. On weekends and public holidays the market can get crowded, but a small café and the Market Bar are nice places to take a break and watch the street musicians. ⊠ *South Terr. at Henderson St., Fremantle, Western Australia* ✆ *08/9335–2515* ⊕ *www.fremantlemarkets.com.au* ⊙ *Fri. 9–8 Hall, 8–8 Yard; weekends and Mon. public holidays 9–6 Hall, 8–6 Yard.*

Western Australian Maritime Museum. The Western Australian Maritime
Museum, which resembles an upside-down boat, sits at the edge of Fremantle Harbour. It houses *Australia 11,* winner of the 1983 America's
Cup, and has hands-on, rotating exhibits that are great fun for chil-
dren. You can also take one-hour guided tours of the adjacent subma-
rine *Ovens,* a former Royal Australian Navy World War II submarine.
Tours depart from the maritime museum every 30 minutes; reserva-
tions are recommended during school holidays. Another attraction is
the Welcome Wall, a record of all those who immigrated to Western
Australia via ship during the major postwar migration. The Shipwreck
Gallery houses the recovered remains of Dutch wrecks, including the
Batavia (wrecked offshore in 1629), and the 1872 SS *Xantho* steamer.
⊠ *Maritime Museum: west end of Victoria Quay; Shipwreck Gallery:
Cliff St., Fremantle, Western Australia* ☎ *08/9431–8444 museum,
08/9431–8444 gallery* ⊕ *www.museum.wa.gov.au/maritime* ✆ *Mu-
seum A$10 day pass, Ovens A$8, museum and Ovens A$15, Shipwreck
Gallery entry free, donation preferred.* ☉ *Daily 9:30–5* ☉ *Christmas
Week and Good Friday.*

WORTH NOTING

King's Square. Bounded by High, Queen, and William streets, King's
Square is at the heart of the central business district. Shaded by 100-
year-old Moreton Bay fig trees, it's a perfect place for a rest. Medieval-
style benches complete the picture of European elegance. From October
to April the Square hosts a lively market as well as bands and street
performers. Bordering the square are **St. John's Anglican Church** and
the **town hall.**

Round House. A landmark of early Fremantle atop the limestone cliff
known as Arthur's Head, the Round House was built in 1831 by convicts to house other convicts. This curious, 12-sided building is the
state's oldest surviving structure. From its ramparts great vistas span
out from High Street to the Indian Ocean. Underneath, a tunnel was
carved through the cliffs in the mid-1800s to give ships lying at anchor
offshore easy access from town. From the tunnel you can walk to Bathers Beach where there used to be a whaling station, and listen out for the
firing of the cannon at 1 pm daily. Volunteer guides are on duty during
opening hours. ⊠ *West end of High St., Fremantle, Western Australia*
☎ *08/9336–6897* ✆ *Donation suggested* ☉ *Daily 10:30–3:30.*

Fremantle Arts Centre. Like most of Fremantle, the fine, Gothic Revival
Fremantle Arts Centre (FAC) was built by convicts in the 19th century.
First used as a lunatic asylum, by 1900 it was overcrowded and nearly
shut down. It became a home for elderly women until 1942, when the
U.S. Navy turned it into its local headquarters. As one of Australia's
leading arts organisations, FAC offers a diverse cultural program year-
round. Dynamic exhibitions, a gift shop, and an expansive live music
and special events program feature throughout the year. ⊠ *1 Finnerty
St., Fremantle, Western Australia* ☎ *08/9432–9555* ⊕ *www.fac.org.au*
✆ *Free* ☉ *Daily 10–5.*

Fodor's Choice ★

10

WHERE TO EAT

$ **✕ Cicerello's.** No visit to Fremantle
SEAFOOD is complete without a stop at this
locally famous and widely beloved
fish-and-chips shop. Housed in a
boathouse-style building fronting
the famous Fishing Boat Harbour,
this joint serves the real thing: freshly
caught oysters, mussels, crabs, fish,
lobsters, and chips, all wrapped up
in butcher paper (no cardboard
boxes or plastic plates here). While
you eat, you can check out the huge
aquarium, where more than 50 species of Fremantle marine life swim.
Cicerello's also has a restaurant in
Mandurah. ⊠ *Fisherman's Wharf,
44 Mews Rd., Fremantle, Western
Australia* ☎ *08/9335–1911* ⊕ *www.
cicerellos.com.au* ▭ *No credit cards*
⊠ *73 Mandurah Terrace, Mandurah, Western Australia* ☎ *08/9535–
9777* ▭ No *credit cards.*

THE CUP

In 1848, Britain's Queen Victoria
authorized the creation of a solid
silver cup for a yacht race that
would be "open to all nations."
In 1851, the New York Yacht
Club challenged 16 English
yachts and won with the boat
America. The U.S. continued to
win for 132 years straight until
the upstart *Australia 11* won 4–3
in sensational style, and the Cup
came to Fremantle. Australia was
euphoric. Fremantle spruced up
for the defense of the Cup in
1987, but the fairy tale ended in
a 4–0 loss to the San Diego Yacht
Club entrant. Today *Australia 11*
is a centerpiece display at the WA
Maritime Museum.

$$$ **✕ The Essex.** This 1886 cottage, unobtrusively situated on a quiet street
SEAFOOD away from the crowds, is one of the best places for upscale dining in
★ Western Australia. Its elegant, candle-lighted dining room is decorated
with thick carpets and antiques. The fresh local seafood is excellent.
Head chef Noel Friend offers an extensive menu, including Essex fish
and mussel chowder, blue manna crab cakes, and saffron king prawns.
The fillet Rossini wrapped in proscuitto, with a rich duck-liver pâté
and a cabernet jus is something to look out for, while surf and turf
with Harvey fillet and Pemberton marron is definitely a keeper. Por-
tions are generous, and the extensive wine list includes some of Aus-
tralia's best vintages. ⊠ *20 Essex St., Fremantle, Western Australia*
☎ *08/9335–5725* ⊕ *www.essexrestaurant.com.au* ☉ *Closed for lunch
on Mon., Tues., and Sat.*

$$ **✕ Gino's Café.** There are 21 different ways to take your coffee at this cap-
ITALIAN puccino-strip property with an alfresco terrace. Among the most popu-
lar drinks are the house coffee (Gino's Blend), and the Baby Chino—a
froth of milk dusted with chocolate powder that young children love.
Gino's opens at 6 am to serve coffee, then cooks breakfasts from 7:00.
For lunch and dinner, more than two dozen different pasta dishes are
available, including a superb penne alla vodka with chicken. ⊠ *South
Terrace at Collie St., Fremantle, Western Australia* ☎ *08/9336–1464*
⊕ *www.ginoscafe.com.au.*

$$ **✕ Joe's Fish Shack.** Fremantle's quirkiest restaurant looks like everyone's
SEAFOOD vision of a run-down, weather-beaten Maine diner. With uninterrupted
harbor views, authentic nautical bric-a-brac, and great food, you can't go
wrong. Recommendations include the salt-and-pepper squid, stuffed tiger
prawns, and chili mussels. An outdoor dining area provides restaurant

Kookaburra 12-metre yachts are tack-training for the Americas Cup.

food at take-out prices. ⊠ *42 Mews Rd., Fremantle, Western Australia* 🕾 *08/9336–7161* ⊕ *www.joesfishshack.com.au* 🕙 *11am till late, 7 days.*

$$ **✕ Char Char Bull.** Waterfront Fremantle is renowned for its seafood res-
STEAKHOUSE taurants, and going to a harborside restaurant for steak seems almost
★ irreverent—a bit like going to Italy for a curry—but meat lovers will
revel in the juicy steak selection at Char Char Bull. This elegant res-
taurant, with full table service, specializes in char-grilled prime beef
selected from year-old, grass-fed Murray Greys. Choose from tender
filet mignon, tenderloin, sirloin, and rib eye cooked exactly how you
like it, with all the trimmings. If you just can't go a day without fish,
oysters, barramundi, salt-and-pepper squid, prawns, and mussels also
feature on the menu. Make reservations and try to get a table out on
the deck. ⊠ *44 Mews Rd., Fishing Boat Harbour, Fremantle, Western
Australia* 🕾 *08/9430–5005* ⊕ *www.charcharbull.com.au.*

WHERE TO STAY

For expanded hotel reviews, visit Fodors.com.

$$$$ 🛏 **Esplanade Hotel Fremantle.** Part of a colonial-era hotel, this establish-
ment has provided accommodation for more than a century. **Pros:** cen-
tral to Fremantle attractions; tropical garden setting around heated
pool; 3 outdoor spas; ample dining and shopping options nearby.
Cons: sea views are limited to some rooms; functions can make venues
crowded; parking for a fee; rooms facing resort pool may encounter car-
park noise. ⊠ *Marine Terrace at Essex St., Fremantle, Western Australia*
🕾 *08/9432–4000, 1800/998201* ⊕ *www.esplanadehotelfremantle.com.
au* 🛏 *293 rooms, 7 suites* ⚐ *In-room: safe, Internet. In-hotel: restau-
rant, bar, pool, gym, laundry facilities, parking.*

$$ ▦ **Fothergills of Fremantle.** Antiques, Italian pottery, sculptures, bronzes, and paintings adorn these three, two-story, 1892 limestone terrace houses opposite the old Fremantle prison. **Pros:** Heritage decor throughout; personalized service. **Cons:** comfy shoes required for the walk to central Fremantle; limited facilities on-site. ✉ *18–22 Ord St., Fremantle, Western Australia* ☎ *08/9335–6784* ⊕ *www.fothergills.net.au* ⟳ *7 rooms* ♿ *In-room: safe. In-hotel: laundry facilities* ⦿ *Breakfast.*

$$$ ▦ **Port Mill Bed & Breakfast.** Discreetly concealed in a picture-postcard
★   courtyard reminiscent of Tuscany, this diminutive bed-and-breakfast is built from limestone and landscaped with an abundance of flowers, and a tinkling little fountain. ✉ *3/17 Essex St., Fremantle, Western Australia* ☎ *08/9433–3832* ⊕ *www.portmillbb.com.au* ⟳ *4 rooms* ♿ *In-room: Wi-Fi. In-hotel: some age restrictions* ⦿ *Breakfast.*

NIGHTLIFE

There's nothing more pleasant than relaxing in the evening at one of the sidewalk tables on the cappuccino strip. This area, along South Terrace, opens at 6 am and closes around 3 am.

Clink. Fremantle's swankiest nightclub, the Clink, is open Wednesday and Friday–Sunday The industrial-style decor reflects the building's heritage—it used to be the police station with prison cells. ✉ *14–16 South Terr., Fremantle, Western Australia* ☎ *08/9336–1919* ⊕ *www. theclink.com.au.*

Dome Cafe. Dome Cafe is a big, airy space that gets a little frantic during busy periods. ✉ *13 South Terr., Fremantle, Western Australia* ☎ *08/9336–3040.*

Fly By Night Musicians Club. Don't be put off by the rather nondescript entry to this venue. Once an artillery drill hall and now a National Trust heritage property, it's home to a thriving arts scene and has a great tradition of music and dance. Many local bands and soloists owe their big breaks to Fly By Night Musicians Club, a smoke-free venue. Plenty of parking opposite. ✉ *1 Holdsworth St., at Parry St., Fremantle, Western Australia* ☎ *08/9430–5976* ⊕ *www.flybynight.org.*

Little Creatures. Little Creatures is a funky bar and restaurant surrounded by a gleaming state-of-the-art microbrewery. The industrial-style warehouse building, which overlooks Fremantle's busy harbor, cuts into a courtyard. The pale ale is quite good. It's open weekdays 10 am–midnight; weekends 9 am–midnight. ✉ *40 Mews Rd., Fremantle, Western Australia* ☎ *08/9430–5555* ⊕ *www.littlecreatures.com.au.*

Metropolis Concert Club Fremantle. In the heart of Fremantle's cappuccino strip, Metropolis Concert Club Fremantle, a nonstop techno and funk dance venue, is a great place to go on a Friday or Saturday night. ✉ *58 South Terr., Fremantle, Western Australia* ☎ *08/9336–1880* ⊕ *www. metropolisfremantle.com.au.*

Rosie O'Grady's. Away from the waterfront, Rosie O'Grady's is as Irish as it gets in the heart of Fremantle. Locals come for the numerous draft beers and filling food, as well as nightly live music. ✉ *23 William St., Fremantle, Western Australia* ☎ *08/9335–1645.*

Sail and Anchor Pub. Thanks to its selection of home-brewed beers, the Sail and Anchor Pub is an award-winning and popular watering hole. A shady courtyard beer garden makes a fair-weather gathering place, and the bistro serves up no-nsense pub grub. ⊠ *64 South Terrace, Fremantle, Western Australia* ☎ *08/9431–1666* ⊕ *www.sailandanchor.com.au.*

SHOPPING

Into Camelot. Going to a glittering fancy dress ball or a dress-up-costume party? Into Camelot, a medieval-style dress shop, sells romantic wedding gowns and cloaks, custom-made pirate costumes, and evening wear for all occasions. Classic Saxon and Celtic jewelry, and masks (feathered and plain) are sold at affordable prices. ⊠ *Shop 9, South Terrace Piazza, Fremantle, Western Australia* ☎🖬 *08/9335–4698* ⊕ *www. intocamelot.com.au.*

Kakulas Sisters. A strong supporter of WA produce, this unique produce shop still overflows with fragrances and sacks of goodies from across the globe. Delectable items such as Brazilian quince and guava pastries, Tasmanian honey, Japanese teas, locally produced pestos and olives, and European hard cheeses ensure that homesick visitors can enjoy a slice, sliver, or smell of home. ⊠ *29–31 Market St., Fremantle, Western Australia* ☎ *08/9430–4445.*

Pickled Fairy & Other Myths. A fairy theme pervades the Pickled Fairy & Other Myths, making it a delight for children and elves. All staff are dressed as fairies, and kids get sprinkled with magic dust and a wish. Fairy dresses, fairy books, and mystical magical knickknacks make this a treasure trove of potential presents for lucky little girls, or anyone with a numinous streak. ⊠ *Shop 7B, South Terrace Piazza, Fremantle, Western Australia* ☎ *08/9430–5827* ⊕ *www.pickledfairy.com.au.*

ROTTNEST ISLAND

19 km (12 mi) west of Fremantle.

An easy 25-minute cruise from Fremantle, or about 1 hour down the Swan River from Perth, sunny, quirky Rottnest Island makes an ideal day trip. The island has an interesting past. Though records of human occupation date back 6,500 years, when Aboriginal people inhabited the area, European settlement only dates back to 1829. Since then the island has been used for a variety of purposes, including attempts at agriculture, as a boy's reformatory, and for military purposes in both the Great War and World War II. The Rottnest Museum is a great place to get the history of the place, and you can take a train trip and tour to Oliver Hill to see gun emplacements from World War II.

Of course most West Australians go to the island for the beaches, the swimming, and the laid-back atmosphere on Perth's doorstep.

GETTING HERE AND AROUND

Rottnest Air Taxi. Speedy air service to Rottnest Island flies from Perth's Jandakot airport with Rottnest Air Taxi. Round-trip fare is from A$75 per person, and the service operates daily, weather permitting. Flight time is around 15 minutes. Telephone for flight times. ☎ *08/9292–5027, 1800/500006.*

10

Oceanic Cruises. Oceanic Cruises runs to Rottnest Island from Fremantle, as well as from Perth. Also offers whale watching trips from September to November. ☎ *08/9432–0825* ⊕ *www.oceaniccruises.com.au.*

Rottnest Express. Rottnest Express runs ferries to Rottnest Island from Fremantle, as well as from Perth. ☎ *1300/467688* ⊕ *www.rottnestexpress.com.au.*

Rottnest Fast Ferries. Rottnest Fast Ferries runs boats from Hillarys Boat Harbour. The ferries take approximately 45 minutes from Hillarys to Rottnest, with hotel pickups from Perth available. Round-trip prices, including entry to Rottnest are from $82. Bike hire on Rottnest, and whale-watching tours from $67 (mid-September to early December) also available. ☎ *08/9246–1039* ⊕ *rottnestfastferries.com.au* ⊗ *Closed June, July (except school holidays), and August.*

There are no taxis on Rottnest Island.

SAFETY AND PRECAUTIONS

Be sun-smart, especially from October through April. Even on cloudy days people unused to being outdoors for any length of time can suffer severe sunburn. Wear a hat, long-sleeved shirt, and high-strength sunscreen. If you are a weak or novice swimmer, always swim with a friend; there are no lifesavers (lifeguards) on Rottnest beaches.

TIMING

Rottnest Island can be visited in a day. An early ferry gets you to the island with plenty of time to tour the main attractions or beaches, returning to Fremantle or Perth in the late afternoon. Staying an extra day or two gives you time to laze at a beach or go surfing or diving.

TOURS

Bayseeker Bus. The Bayseeker Bus, which runs a continuous hop-on, hop-off island circuit, picks up and drops off passengers at the most beautiful bays and beaches. Day tickets are A$13 and can be purchased from the Rottnest Island Visitor Centre. Buses run from 8:30 to 3:30, hourly in winter and half-hourly in summer. ⊠ *Thomson Bay, Rottnest Island, Western Australia* ☎ *08/9372–9732* ⊕ *www.rottnestisland.com.*

The Oliver Hill Train. The Oliver Hill Train, known as the *Captain Hussey,* is an ideal way to see the island. The route from the Main Settlement to Oliver Hill is run daily at 11:30, 1:30, and 2:30, and connects with a guided tour of the historic Oliver Hill gun battery. The fare is A$26 and includes the guided tour. The train fare without the guided tours is A$18.00. Tickets are available at the visitor information center. ⊠ *Thomson Bay, Rottnest Island, Western Australia* ☎ *08/9372–9732.*

Discovery Tour. For those not keen on biking or hop-on, hop-off buses, the Rottnest Island Authority runs a 90-minute Discovery Tour that gives an overview of the island's activities, history, environment, and wildlife. Highlights of the tour are the Wadjemup Lighthouse and the remote West End. Tours depart daily from the Main Bus Stop at 11:20, 1:40, and 1:50 (times subject to ferry services.) Tours cost A$33. Tickets available from the visitor center. ⊠ *Thompson Bay, Rottnest Island, Western Australia* ☎ *9372–9732.*

The Rottnest Island Authority also runs a narrated 90-minute coach tour of the island's highlights, including convict-built cottages, World War II gun emplacements, salt lakes, and the remote West End. Tours depart daily from Main Bus Stop. The Oliver Hill Railway made its debut in the mid-1990s, utilizing 6 km (4 mi) of reconstructed railway line to reach the island's World War II gun batteries. Information is available from the Rottnest Island Visitor Information Centre.

ESSENTIALS

Banks and Currency Exchange
Bankwest. Bankwest has an ATM adjacent to the Rottnest Island Authority office at the Main Settlement.
☎ 13–1718 ⊕ www.bankwest.com.au.

Medical Emergencies The Rottnest Nursing Post ✉ Thomson Bay, Rottnest Island, Western Australia ☎ 08/9292–5030 ⊙ Daily 8:30–5.

Police The police station is in Somerville Drive in the Main Settlement.

Visitor Information Rottnest Island Visitor Information Centre ✉ Adjacent to Dome Café, Thomson Bay beachfront, Rottnest Island, Western Australia ☎ 08/9372–9732 ⊕ www.rottnestisland.com ⊙ Sat.–Thurs. 7:30– 6:15, Fri. 7:30–7:30.

EXPLORING

The most convenient way to get around Rottnest is by bicycle, as private cars are not allowed on the island. A bicycle tour of the island covers 26 km (16 mi) and can take as little as three hours, although you really need an entire day to enjoy the beautiful surroundings

Heading south from Thomson Bay, between Government House and Herschell Lakes, you'll find the Quokka Walk and a man-made causeway where you'll find a few quokka colonies. Continue south and to Oliver Hill and the Wadjemup Light House, where tours are run every half hour from 11 am until 2:30 pm. As you continue to Bickley Bay you can spot the wreckage of ships—the oldest dates from 1842—that came to rest on Rottnest's rocky coastline.

Follow the main road past Porpoise, Salmon, Strickland, and Wilson bays to West End, the westernmost point on the island and another graveyard for unfortunate vessels. Heading back to Thomson Bay, the road passes a dozen rocky inlets and bays. Parakeet Bay, the prettiest, is at the northernmost tip of the island.

Rottnest Bike Hire. You can rent bikes from A$27 per day, with a returnable deposit of A$25 per bike. Tandem bikes and pedal cars can also be rented. Also for hire: snorkel sets, paddleboards, surfboards,

---

MARSUPIALS, NOT RATS

Quokkas were among the first Australian mammals ever seen by Europeans. In 1658, the Dutch Captain Willem De Vlamingh described them as rats, but in fact they are marsupials, carrying their young in a pouch. Once common around Perth, quokkas are now confined to isolated pockets on the mainland, but still thrive on their namesake Rottnest Island, where they are safe from predators (mainly foxes). Their cute, furry faces and small, round bodies make them very photogenic.

10

Snorkelling at the Basin on Rottnest Island, Western Australia.

bodyboards, wet suits, and beach cricket and soccer essentials. It's open daily 8:30–5:30, though hours vary according to the season. ✉ *Thomson Bay, Rottnest Island, Western Australia* ☎ *08/9292–5105.*

Rottnest Museum. At the Thomson Bay settlement, visit the Rottnest Museum, which includes mementos of the island's turbulent past. Displays show local geology, natural and social history, and maritime lore. It's open daily 10:45–3:30. **Wadjemup Lighthouse Tours**—find out what goes on within the confines of a working lighthouse and climb to the top of this Heritage structure for fabulous 360-degree views. Tours depart daily at 11 am every half hour until 2:30 pm, and cost A$7. ✉ *Digby Dr., Thomson Bay, Rottnest Island, Western Australia* ☎ *08/9372–9732* ✉ *Donation suggested.*

BEACHES

There are some 63 beaches on Rottnest Island, suitable for swimming, surfing, snorkeling, and diving. The most popular include Fish Hook Bay, Geordie Bay, Little Armstrong, Little Parakeet, Little Salmon Bay, Parakeet, Parker Point, Ricey Beach, Salmon Bay, Stark Bay, Strickland Bay, the Basin, and West End.

Surfers and bodyboarders will head for Stark Bay, Strickland Bay, Geordie Bay, Parakeet Bay, Salmon Bay, and West End, while swimmers will enjoy sandy white beaches at Pinkies Beach and the Basin. Beach spots for snorkeling and diving include Salmon Bay, Parker Point, the Basin, and Little Armstrong. The Basin, Parker Point, Stark Bay, Strickland Bay, Rocky Bay, City of York Bays, Green Island, and Geordie Bay have public toilets but no other amenities.

WHERE TO STAY

Accommodation on the island ranges from basic camping sites to self-contained holiday villas and hotels. Space is at a premium during the summer months, Easter, and school holidays. November can be busy because of the so-called "schoolies week," when high-school students celebrate the end of five years of high school. Outside these times, accommodation is easier to find. Check ⊕ *www.rottnestisland.com* for details.

For expanded hotel reviews, visit Fodors.com.

$$$ 🍴 **Rottnest Lodge.** This hotel started out as a colonial barracks some 150 years ago, but now it's the island's largest hotel. **Pros:** centrally located; some rooms have lake views; some rooms ideal for families. **Cons:** not on beachfront; limited leisure facilities. ⊠ *Kitson St., Rottnest Island, Western Australia* ☎ *08/9292–5161* ⊕ *www.rottnestlodge.com.au* 🛏 *78 rooms, 2 suites* ᾱ *In-hotel: restaurant, bar, pool.*

THE SOUTH WEST WINE REGION

The South West—Western Australia's most popular destination, with more than 1.5 million visitors annually—should not be missed if you are coming to this state, a fact well known by Perth residents, who flock here year-round for the wines, beaches, and marine wildlife, forests, locally produced crafts and artisan products, and the country vistas.

The region stretches from the port city of Bunbury—about two hours south of Perth by freeway and highway—through Busselton, Dunsborough, and on to Margaret River, a further 1½ hours south.

Margaret River is, perhaps, best known for its wines, but the South West has wineries from well north of Bunbury to the south coast. Busselton, Dunsborough, and Margaret River are all suitable places to stay if you want to visit wineries; Busselton and Dunsborough works for those who prefer calm family beaches (Margaret River is not on the coast).

The best surfing beaches are on the coast between Cape Naturaliste and Cape Leeuwin.

All major South West towns have visitor centers that can arrange tours, book accommodations, and provide free information.

EN
ROUTE
Bunbury is a great stopover point where you can visit the Dolphin Discovery Centre, swim with wild dolphins (in season), or wade in shallow waters with them under the watchful eye of center volunteers and biologists. About 100 bottlenose dolphins make their permanent home in and around the waters of Koombana Bay off Bunbury, making your chances of seeing them in their natural habitat very high. You can also take a dolphin cruise with Naturaliste Charters.

Bunbury Visitor Centre ⊠ *Carmody Pl., Bunbury, Rottnest Island, Western Australia* ☎ *08/9792–7205* ⊕ *www.visitbunbury.com.au* ☉ *Weekdays 9–5; weekends 9:30–4:30, 10–2 sundays and public holidays.*

Dolphin Discovery Centre. Get up close to wild dolphins at the Dolphin Discovery Centre. Two-hundred dolphins have been identified in Koombana Bay—swim with them, book an eco-cruise, or stay on the beach and wade into the interaction zone. Enjoy the discovery center with

10

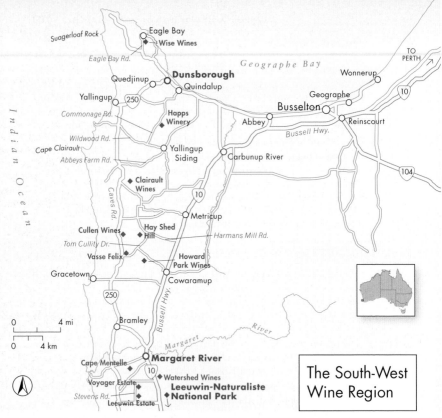

The South-West
Wine Region

its new, unique digital dolphinarium, interpretive panels and theater, as well as a café and gift shop. ■TIP→ Call first to book the weather-dependent swim and eco-cruises. Dolphin encounters are not guaranteed. ⊠ *Koombana Dr., Western Australia* ☎ *08/9791–3088* ⊕ *www. dolphindiscovery.com.au* ◪ *Discovery Centre & Interaction Zone A$10, Swim Encounter A$185, Eco-Cruise A$53* ⊘ *Oct.–May, daily 8–4; June–Sept., daily 9–2.*

Naturaliste Charters ☎ *0419–186–133, 0417–186–133* ⊕ *www.whales-australia.com.*

DUNSBOROUGH

252 km (157 mi) south of Perth.

The attractive seaside town of Dunsborough is perfect for a few days of swimming, sunning, and fishing—which is why it's become a popular holiday destination for many Perth families. Onshore attractions include Meelup Beach, a protected cove with calm swimming water, and the nearby wineries of Margaret River. Offshore, you can dive on the wreck of the HMAS *Swan*, the former Royal Australian Navy ship deliberately sunk in Geographe Bay at the end of its useful life, or take a cruise to see migrating humpback and southern right whales September–December.

⚠ November sees so-called "schoolies week," when teenage students boisterously celebrate the end of five years of high school. Dunsborough is a popular destination.

GETTING HERE AND AROUND

From Perth take the Kwinana Freeway south; it joins the Forrest Highway and then Highway 1 down the coast to Bunbury. Switch to Highway 10 through Busselton, then Caves Road to Dunsborough. If you drive from Perth, it will take around 3 hours. Alternatively, **South West Coachlines** (☎ 08/9261 7600 ⊕ *southwestcoachlines.com.au*) has daily coach services from Perth Central Bus Station at the Esplanade Bus Port on Mounts Bay Road to South West towns, including Dunsborough. Once here, a rental car is recommended, as there is limited public transport, and some accommodations are in bushland or beach settings away from the towns.

Dunsborough Car Rentals. Dunsborough Car Rentals has late-model vehicles available at reasonable rates for touring the Margaret River region. ✉ *201 Geographe Bay Rd., Quindalup, Dunsborough, Western Australia* ☎ *1800/449007* ⊕ *www.dunsboroughcarrentals.com.au.*

SAFETY AND PRECAUTIONS

The calm waters of Geographe Bay are home to a jellyfish with a nasty sting—colloquially named "stingers." They are not deadly but they are painful, and a sting occasionally requires hospitalization. They are hard to spot—the main body of the stinger is translucent and only about 2 inches across, and they trail hard-to-see black tentacles that are the cause for concern. They like warmer, very calm water, so still days in summer are when you are most likely to encounter them as they drift close to shore. Rubbing a sting is not recommended; try bathing in vinegar.

Mosquitoes carrying Ross River virus are more prevalent in summer, and especially along the South West coast and in swamplands. Ross River virus is not life-threatening, but can leave victims with weeks of fatigue, aching limbs, and painful joints. The only solution is to avoid being bitten by mosquitoes—cover up and use a repellent, especially around dawn and dusk, when mosquitoes are most active.

TIMING

Dunsborough (and the surrounding area) deserves at least two days, preferably three. Western Australian school holidays, especially the summer break over Christmas and New Year's Day, and Easter, are usually booked solid by Perth holidaymakers with families. One week in November is also crowded for "schoolies week." The summer months (December–March) are best for swimming and beaches, while the heaviest surfing conditions are often best during the winter months (May–September) when wet suits are required.

TOURS

Busselton Jetty and Underwater Observatory. At almost two km, the 146-year-old Busselton Jetty is the longest timber jetty in the southern hemisphere. You can visit the Interpretive Center and Heritage Museum at the start of the jetty, then either catch the train or walk the 1.8 km to the Underwater Observatory, one of only seven in the world, where tours for up to 40 people are run every hour. The cylinder observatory structure allows visitors to walk down a spiral staircase to some 8.5 meters below the water, observing the marine life through 11 large acrylic windows at different levels. The warm Leeuwin Current and the sheltering effect of the jetty above has created a unique microclimate rich with colorful tropical and sub-tropical corals, sponges, fish, and invertebrates. ■TIP→ Booking is essential. ✉ *Beachfront, Busselton, Dunsborough, Western Australia* ☎ *08/9754–0900* ⊕ *www. busseltonjetty.com.au* 💲 *40 minute Underwater Observatory Tour, return train ride, and jetty day pass A$28.00; jetty only A$2.50; One way train A$10, Interpretive Centre & Heritage Museum, free* ⊙ *Interpretive Center & Heritage Museum, May–Aug., daily 9–5; Sep.–Apr., daily 8:30–6. Underwater Observatory & Jetty Train Tour, May–Aug., on the hour 10–3; Sept.–Apr., on the hour 9–4.*

Cape Dive. Cape Dive has dive tours to the wreck of the HMAS *Swan*, deliberately scuttled in 30 meters of water off Dunsborough to become an artificial reef and dive wreck. They also offer dives around the Busselton Jetty, where an abundance of corals and marine life have made their homes on the pylons. ✉ *222 Naturaliste Terr., Dunsborough, Western Australia* ☎ *08/9756–8778* ⊕ *www.capediveexperience.com* ⊙ *Daily 9–5.*

Cellar d'Or Winery Tours. Cellar d'Or Winery Tours has daily tours of Margaret River region wineries from A$82 per person. The tours include pickup at your accommodation, wine tastings at five wineries, platter lunch, beer tasting, chocolate sampling, cheese and local produce tasting, and morning and afternoon coffee and tea. ☎ *0428/179729* ⊕ *www.cellardortours.com.au.*

ESSENTIALS

All major credit cards are widely accepted at restaurants, lodgings, and shops. Mastercard and Visa are always taken; American Express and Diners Club are less acceptable, and the merchant may add a small surcharge.

Medical Emergencies Busselton Hospital ✉ *Mill Rd., Busselton, Dunsborough, Western Australia* ☎ *08/9754–0333, 000.*

Police Police ☎ *13–1444 assistance, 08/9222–1111 general inquiries.*

Taxi Dunsborough Taxis ☎ *08/9756–8688.*

Visitor Information Busselton Visitor Centre. All tours are bookable via the Visitor Centre Web sites. ✉ *38 Peel Terrace, Busselton, Dunsborough, Western Australia* ☎ *08/9752–5800* ⊕ *www.geographebay.com* ⊙ *Mon.–Fri. 9–5, Sat._Sun. and public holidays, 9:30–4:30. Closed Christmas day.* **Dunsborough Visitor Centre** ✉ *Shop 14, Dunsborough Park Shopping Centre, Dunsborough, Western Australia* ☎ *08/9752–5800* ⊕ *www.geographebay.com* ⊙ *Mon.–Fri. 9–5, Sat.–Sun. and public holidays 9:30–4:30.*

OUTDOOR ACTIVITIES

The north-facing coastline of Geographe Bay from Busselton to Cape Naturaliste—unique in Western Australia because of its aspect—provides long sandy beaches and coves readily accessible from Dunsborough. From Dunsborough village, simply walk about 500 meters down to the sandy beach, which stretches east and west for miles. Heading toward Cape Naturaliste, the coastline changes into sandy bays and coves bracketed by rocky headlands. Meelup Beach is popular with families; its sister beach, Castle Rock, just around the headland, is a little quieter. Another charming sheltered beach is Eagle Bay, closer to the cape, with multimillion-dollar homes perched along the hillside. The only facilities you will find at these beaches are public toilets.

EXPLORING THE WINERIES

★ **Clairault Wines.** One of the few family-owned wineries in the region is also one of the region's best, known for its award-winning Cabernet Merlot, Cabernet Sauvignon, and Chardonnay. Set in a natural bush-land about 18 km (11 mi) south of Dunsborough, the cellar door is in a modern style with polished timber floors, natural stone, and walls of glass overlooking the bushland. The spacious restaurant (open Thurs.–Mon., noon–3:30) has glass doors that open on to a large timber deck in warm weather, while two huge stone fireplaces warm the tables in winter. The winery and restaurant are popular for weddings, especially during the spring and fall months. ⊠ *Caves Rd., Wilyabrup, Western Australia* ☎ *08/9755–6225* ⊕ *www.clairault.com.au* ☽ *Daily 10–5.*

Happs Pottery & Winery. Hand-made mudbricks, recycled timbers, and stained-glass windows point back to the origins of this family-owned and -built winery that is one of the pioneers in the Margaret River wine region. A few kilometers from Dunsborough you'll find a friendly welcome, a huge range of wines to taste (33 at last reckoning) and—unique in this area—a pottery gallery in the same building. Erl Happ began the pottery in 1975, then planted his first vines in 1978, going against local wisdom by planting Merlot. Later, a second vineyard was established near Karridale some 90 km (55 mi) to the south, with 31 varieties of grape, its wines produced under the Three Hills label. Free tastings allow you to try some wines only available at the cellar door, such as Fuchsia and preservative-free wines. His daughter-in-law Jacquie runs the pottery, his wife Roslyn has created a much photographed garden courtyard, and son Myles works at the home studio, producing what is described as the biggest collection of pottery in the area. ⊠ *575 Commonage Rd., Dunsborough, Western Australia* ☎ *08/9755–3300* ⊕ *www.happs.com.au* ☽ *Daily 10–5.*

Wise Wines. The view from the hilltop overlooking Geographe Bay is almost as good as the wines at this northernmost winery in the region, about a 15-minute drive from Dunsborough toward Cape Naturaliste. This family-owned boutique vineyard has a history of producing award-winning Chardonnay, though other wines have received accolades as well. Try the Sea Urchin or Bead Sparkling wines, or the single-vineyard Eagle Bay. The adjacent Wise Vineyard restaurant is open for breakfast and lunch as well as dinner on Friday and Saturday nights. If you can't bear to leave, five secluded timber cottages with names such as Teahouse, Potter's Cottage, and Doll's House are available. ⊠ *80 Eagle Bay Rd., Dunsborough, Western Australia* ☎ *08/9756–8627 cellar door* ⊕ *www.wisewine.com.au* ☽ *Daily 10–5.*

10

NEED A BREAK? When you have had your fill of wineries, or just need something for your sweet tooth, head on down to Simmo's, about a five-minute drive from Dunsborough.

Simmo's Ice Creamery and Fun Park. Simmo's Ice Creamery and Fun Park is an institution for families and sweet tooths whatever the season. Their menu includes up to 60 different flavored ice creams and sorbets, made fresh daily, to have in cones, waffles, and sundaes. There's coffee to go, and—for the kids—a great fun park with games including an 18 hole mini-golf course. You can have a picnic in the shady grounds and meet Edward, the ice cream–eating emu. Irishmen Gordon and Garth Simpson set up Simmos in 1993, using family recipes. ⊠ *161 Commonage Rd., Dunsborough, Western Australia* ☎ *08/9755-3745* ⊕ *www.simmos.com. au* ⊙ *Daily 10:30–5.*

WHERE TO EAT AND STAY

$$$
AUSTRALIAN
★
✕ **Wise Vineyard Restaurant.** Verdant bushland, manicured vineyards, and expansive views all the way down to Geographe Bay are show-stopping features of this modern restaurant. Expect the unexpected and be pleasantly surprised by culinary creations. Here the accent is on the use of fresh local produce. Look out for citrus salmon ceviche, crispy sesame swordfish, or the Amelia Park lamb with Israeli couscous; The chef experiments with flavors using ingredients like lemon myrtle, lilli pilli berries, or eucalyptus leaves in some dishes. Spend the night in rustic self-contained, timber settler's cottages nestled on the edge of a jarrah forest. They offer bucketloads of charm, like pot-bellied stoves and seating areas to watch the wildlife pass by. Don't be alarmed by the thump of a possum lumbering across the roof at night. ⊠ *80 Eagle Bay Rd., Dunsborough, Western Australia* ☎ *08/9755-3331* ⊕ *www. wisefood.com* ⌂ *Reservations essential* ⊙ *No dinner Sun.–Thurs.*

$$$
🏨 **Broadwater Beach Resort Busselton.** Sunny public areas and extensive sports facilities make this one of the best accommodation choices on the Geographe Bay beach strip, especially for families with energetic children. **Pros:** walk straight onto beach; apartments ideal for families; numerous leisure facilities. **Cons:** own transport essential; limited dining options nearby; no shopping (except convenience shopping) nearby. ⊠ *Bussell Highway and Holgate Rds., Busselton, Western Australia* ☎ *08/9754-1633* ⊕ *www.broadwaters.com.au* ⌸ *65 rooms* ⌂ *In-room: kitchen. In-hotel: restaurant, bar, pool, tennis court, beach, parking.*

$
🏨 **Dunsborough Central Motel.** This motel for the dollar-conscious provides comfortable accommodations and proximity to town and the beach. **Pros:** good-value beds for the area; guest laundry; close to shops and dining options. **Cons:** not on the beachfront; no restaurant; no Internet except by request ⊠ *50 Dunn Bay Rd., Dunsborough, Western Australia* ☎ *08/9756-7711* ⊕ *www.dunsboroughmotel.com.au* ⌸ *48 rooms* ⌂ *In-room: kitchen. In-hotel: pool, spa, parking.*

$$$$
🏨 **Quay West Bunker Bay Resort.** Sprawling down the hillside of the Cape Naturaliste Ridge in bushland, Bunker Bay Resort occupies a rare location with north-facing views of the calm blue waters of

Geographe Bay. **Pros:** large rooms; quiet environment; walk straight onto the beach. **Cons:** limited sea views from rooms; own transport essential; no shopping nearby. ✉ *Bunker Bay Rd. off Cape Naturaliste Rd., Dunsborough, Western Australia* ☎ *1800/010449, 08/ 9756–9100* ⊕ *www.mirvachotels. com.au* ☞ *150 villas* ☖ *In-room: kitchen, Internet. In-hotel: restaurant, bar, pool, tennis court, gym, spa, parking.*

LEEUWIN–NATURALISTE NATIONAL PARK

The northernmost part of the park is 266 km (165 mi) south of Perth, 25 km (16 mi) northwest of Dunsborough.

Fodor's Choice **Leeuwin-Naturaliste National Park.** Leeuwin-Naturaliste National Park lies ★ along one of Western Australia's most spectacular coastlines, from Cape Naturaliste on Geographe Bay in the north to Augusta, close to Cape Leeuwin in the south. The park is not a composite destination, rather a narrow patchwork of protected areas along the coast, intersected by beach access roads and small beachside villages.

The mostly-unspoiled coastal vistas are as awe-inspiring as any in the world—on a calm day the view northwards from Yallingup past Sugarloaf Rock towards Cape Naturaliste is nature at its best. Farther south, between Cowaramup Bay and Karridale, scenic lookouts allow you to access coastal cliffs and rocky shoreline that bears the brunt of giant ocean swells generated across thousands of miles of the Indian Ocean.

In addition to the scenic attractions of the coast, the park sits over limestone ridges where numerous caves have formed over the millennia, leached out by dripping water; a number of these caves are open to the public, including Lake, Mammoth, Jewel, and Ngilgi. Boranup Karri Forest, near Karridale, is the largest "patch," and creates a contrast to the coast—the distinctive, pale-bark hardwood giants reach 190 feet or more and dominate the hills and valleys of this area. This is the farthest west that karri trees grow in Western Australia, and, interestingly, Boranup is a regrowth forest; it was cut over by loggers more than 100 years ago, and 1961 wildfire destroyed many trees.

10

GETTING HERE AND AROUND

From Perth take the Kwinana Freeway south; it joins the Forrest Highway and then Highway 1 to Bunbury, switch to Highway 10 through Busselton to Dunsborough. Because of its patchwork boundaries, Leeuwin-Naturaliste National Park can be accessed at many points along the coast. Caves Road, a secondary road from Dunsborough to Augusta, provides the best access—all the side roads to the best coastal spots come off this road. Only on a section through the Boranup Karri Forest does Caves Road actually travel through the park for any distance. Marked trails are available from most of the coastal carparks; they vary from an easy 1-km (½-mi) trail from the carpark at Cape Naturaliste Lighthouse to a challenging 20-km (12-mi) full-day hike between Cosy Corner and Skippy Rock, near Augusta.

SAFETY AND PRECAUTIONS

Although the temptation is to climb all over the rocky outcrops, such as Canal Rocks, Sugarloaf Rock, and Skippy Rock, be aware of "king waves" that rise up with little warning from the ocean. Occasionally people have been swept from the rocks to their deaths. Take note of the warning signs; at a few locations lifebuoys have been stationed for just such incidents.

TIMING

Any time of the year is suitable for visiting the park. You can picnic, go for a scenic drive, explore the caves, and go fishing, surfing, and bushwalking year-round. The summer months are best for swimming and snorkeling, while whale-watching months are usually from June-December.

TOURS

Bushtucker Tours. Bushtucker Tours has canoe, cave, and bush-tucker tours daily from Margaret River. The tours give you an opportunity to see inaccessible parts of the Margaret River, Aboriginal sites, and caves while canoeing sections of the river down to the mouth at Surfers Point. A short walk shows you the rich variety of "bush tucker" Aboriginals would have eaten, while lunch includes a selection of authentic bush-tucker foods. The tours take about four hours. Winery and brewery tours are also available. ☎ 08/9757–9084 ⊕ www.bushtuckertours.com.

EXPLORING

Cape Naturaliste Lighthouse. At the northern end of the park stands Cape Naturaliste Lighthouse, open daily 9–4:30 (last entry at 4); school and public holidays daily 9–5 (last entry at 4:30). Fully guided tours of the lighthouse cost A$15. A 1½-km-long (1-mi-long) trail leads from Cape Naturaliste to Canal Rocks, passing rugged cliffs, quiet bays, and curving beaches. This is also the start of the 138-km (86-mi) Cape-to-Cape Walk. Four major cave systems are easily accessible. The Cave Works display center at Lake Cave acts as a central booking office for Cape Naturaliste Lighthouse and the cave system that includes Jewel, Lake and Mammoth caves—individual cave tours cost A$20 each. A pass for all four sites including the lighthouse costs A$60, while the Grand Tour Pass for three caves costs A$48. Cave Works is open daily from 9–5.

    CaveWorks. The CaveWorks display center at Lake Cave presents a good introduction to the whole cave system. CaveWorks is open daily from 9–5. ☎ 08/9757–7411 ✉ caveworks@margaretriver.com

    Jewel. Jewel, the southernmost of the system, has one of the longest straw stalactites in any tourist cave in the world. It's open daily with tours every hour 9:30 am–3:30 pm. ☎ 08/9757–7411

    Lake. Lake, centered around a tranquil, eerie-looking underground lake, is also open daily with tours every hour 9:30–3:30. Tour cost at both Jewel and Lake caves is A$20.00. ☎ 08/9757–7411

Mammoth. Mammoth, which has ancient fossil remains of extinct animals, is open daily 9–5, with the last entry at 4. Self-guided tours cost A$20. ☎ 08/9757–7411

Ngilgi. Ngilgi Cave, near Yallingup, is a main site for adventure caving. Semi-guided cave tours take about 1 hour, cost A$19.50, and run every half hour from 10 to 3:30 and 9:30 to 4 during school holidays. Adventure caving tours operate at 9:30 am weekdays. Prebooking at least 48 hours in advance is highly recommended. Adventure tours cost from A$44 to A$142, and vary from two to four hours in length, depending on the tour. ☎ 08/9755–2152

Cape Leeuwin Lighthouse. The view from the top of the Cape Leeuwin Lighthouse, the tallest lighthouse on mainland Australia and only a 10-minute drive south of Augusta, allows you to witness the meeting of the Southern and the Indian oceans. In some places this alliance results in giant swells that crash against the rocks. In others, small coves are blessed with calm waters ideal for swimming. The lighthouse precinct is open daily 8:45–5, entry is A$5. Guided tours to the top of the lighthouse cost A$15 and run daily every 40 minutes. The last tour is at 4:20 pm. ☎ 08/9758–1920 ⊕ www.margaretriver. com ☎ 08/9157–7411.

Metricup Bird Park. You'll soon be wearing a coat of many colors as friendly rainbow lorikeets attach themselves to your head, neck, arms, and hands in the open aviary. Wander around the leafy farmland setting, alive with squawking, and interact with a colorful mix of Australian native parrots including Rex, a rare Baudin cockatoo. Large walk-through avaries contain about 64 varieties of birds—a rare opportunity to view them up close. Not for the bird-phobic, but highly entertaining for bird-lovers and kids. ■TIP→ Pay attention to any signs that warn: "I bite." Gift shop, tea, coffee, and barbecue facilities available. ☎ 08/9755–7085 ☎ A$10 ۞ Closed Fri.

Natural Olive Oil Soap Factory. This surprising little cottage industry smack dab in the middle of vineyards and olive trees is an aromatherapy feast. Here you'll find a chemical-free range of soaps and body-care products hand blended with natural organic ingredients, as well as yummy olives, tapenades, duckahs, and pestos—all without preservatives or artificial additives. A place for gastronomes and purists. Sniff, rub, scrub, pamper, and taste to your heart's content! ☒ 135 Puzey Rd., Wilyabrup, Margaret River ☎ 08/9755–6111 ⊕ www.oliveoilsoapfactory.com.au ☎ Free ۞ Daily 10–5.

CAMPING

Campgrounds with toilets and barbecues are at Conto (Conto Road off Caves Road) and Boranup (southern end of Boranup Drive, off Caves Road) and cost A$7 per adult per night. For more information on camping in the state, visit www.naturebase.net.

MARGARET RIVER

★ 181 km (112 mi) south of Perth, 38 km (24 mi) south of Cape Naturaliste.

The town of Margaret River is considered the center of the South West's wine region, though vineyards and wineries stretch from well north of Bunbury to the south coast. Nevertheless, close to Margaret River are

Canal Rocks near Yallingup, Leeuwin-Naturaliste National Park, Western Australia.

over 100 wineries offering tastings and sales of some of the world's best wines. The region is often compared to France's Bordeaux for its similar climate and soils; it's gaining huge national and international acclaim for its exceptional red and white vintages, the most notable labels touting Chardonnay, Sauvignon Blanc, or Sauvignon Blanc–Semillon, and Cabernet-Merlot blends.

GETTING HERE AND AROUND

From Perth take Kwinana Freeway south; it joins Forrest Highway and then Highway 1 to Bunbury. Switch to Highway 10 through Busselton and on to Margaret River. Your best option is to rent a car in Perth, Bunbury, or possibly Busselton. Public transport is nonexistent around the area, and using taxis will soon blow the budget. The best accommodation—farmstays, bushland chalets, and boutique hotels—as well as the wineries, the beaches, and other attractions, are outside the town, and you need your own transportation to reach them.

SAFETY AND PRECAUTIONS

You are unlikely to have any personal safety concerns in the Margaret River area, except, perhaps, on the roads. Many of the roads leading to the wineries, the beaches, and your accommodation are narrow and winding, though traffic is usually light. While the roads are mostly paved, driveways into properties are often gravel roads, which need to be negotiated with care. As a precaution, you should avoid leaving expensive items, such as cameras, in your car when parked at attractions or overnight at accommodation.

TIMING

Margaret River is a year-round destination, with each season bringing its pleasures. Summer is generally busier, especially December and January, as families from Perth arrive during the school holidays. Winter (May–September) brings rain and cooler temperatures, but the paddocks are green and there are not too many days when the rain doesn't ease to showers with lengthy fine breaks in between. If you are traveling from Perth, you can easily spend a week in the region; at the least, try to schedule several days to truly appreciate the area's attractions.

TOURS

Margaret River Visitor Centre is the best starting point if you want to do a tour. They will find the right tour for you, make the booking, and arrange pickup at your accommodation if necessary. Tour operators in the area offer tours as diverse as wineries and food tasting, horse-back riding, surfing, bushwalks, whale-watching, scenic flights, mountain biking, river cruises, rock climbing, and abseiling.

ESSENTIALS

Banks and Currency Exchange Banks where you can exchange money and cash traveler's checks, including ANZ, Westpac, National Australia, Bankwest, and the Commonwealth Bank, are open weekdays, generally 9:30–4. There are ATMs (which accept Cirrus, Plus, Visa, and MasterCard), and all major credit cards are widely accepted at restaurants, lodgings, and shops.

Medical Emergencies Margaret River Hospital ⊠ Farrelly St., Margaret River, Western Australia ☎ 08/9757–0400, 000.

Police Police ☎ 13–1444 assistance, 08/9222–1111 general inquiries, 000 Emergency.

Taxi Margaret River Taxis ☎ 08/9757–3444.

Visitor Information Margaret River Visitor Centre. Margaret River Visitor Centre has extensive information on the region. The friendly staff will answer all your questions, and can book accommodation, tours, and activities at no additional cost. ⊠ 100 Bussell Hwy., Margaret River, Western Australia ☎ 08/9780–5911 ⊕ www.margaretriver.com ◷ Daily 9–5.

EXPLORING THE WINERIES

Cape Mentelle. One of the "founding five" wineries in the area, Cape Mentelle planted its first vines in 1970 on a 16-hectare block just outside Margaret River. Today it's still one of the most notable wineries. The adobe-style rammed-earth building and tasting rooms, so typical of the buildings in the Margaret River district, are as handsome and memorable as the wine. The winery produces Chardonnay, Sauvignon Blanc/Semillon, Botrytis Viognier (dessert wine), Cabernet/Merlot, Cabernet Sauvignon, Shiraz, and Zinfandel wines. They also offer private tours and tastings (A$25), and a degustation tour and tasting (A$70) on Monday, Wednesday, and Saturday at 11:30 am. In summer enjoy a balmy evening of food, wine, and film at "Movies in the vineyard." ⊠ Wallcliffe Rd., 3 km (2 mi) west of Margaret River, Margaret River, Western Australia ☎ 08/9757–0888 ⊕ www.capementelle.com.au ◷ Daily 10–4:30.

10

Cullen Wines. The late industry patriarchs Dr. Kevin Cullen and Diane Cullen established this winery in 1971. Today their daughter Vanya is MD of the operation and chief winemaker. It's one of the few vineyards and wineries in Australia to produce wines using biodynamic practices. Their flagship wines—Sauvignon Blanc/Semillon, Chardonnay, Merlot, and Cabernet Sauvignon/Merlot—can be sampled at their charming, small tasting room. The granite-and-timber building includes a small restaurant, where a wall of glass provides great views across the vineyards. The restaurant serves only organic or biodynamically grown foods. ■ TIP➜ Enjoy lunch outside under the pepper tree in summertime. ⊠ *Caves and Harman S Rds., Wilyabrup, Margaret River, Western Australia* ☎ *08/9755–5277, 08/9755–5656* ⊕ *www.cullenwines.com. au* ⊙ *Daily 10–4:30.*

Hay Shed Hill. Winemaker Michael Kerrigan—formerly chief winemaker at neighboring Howard Park and Madfish Wines—has taken the reins at Hay Shed Hill with the view of producing "modern wines from old vines." The hands-on approach in using the best grapes from the 30-year-old plantings at Hay Shed Hill has won show awards and lavish endorsements by wine writers. The tasting room breaks from the usual Margaret River vernacular architecture—no rammed earth, timber, and stone here, rather a lovely white-painted clapboard building, polished concrete floors, and pitched ceiling. As the name suggests, the building is the original hayshed on what was a dairy farm. The adjacent winery has now been turned into a pleasant café (open 9–3:30) overlooking the vineyards, where you can get a casual breakfast or lunch—pizzas, curries, and cold meat and cheese platters. Also available is a large selection of Australian and imported cheeses from Spain, France, Italy, and the UK. ⊠ *511 Harmans Mill Rd., Wilyabrup, Margaret River, Western Australia* ☎ *08/9755–6046* ⊕ *hayshedhill.com.au* ⊙ *Daily 10–5.*

Howard Park Wines. Feng shui principles were used to design the spacious tasting room at Howard Park's Margaret River winery (they also have another operation at Denmark in the Great Southern Region). The polished timber ceiling soars up 30 feet above a generous bar, capable of handling a couple of coachloads of visitors at once. Floor-to-ceiling windows allow in plenty of light as well as giving views over the property, and even the door has specific measurements to allow good luck to flow through. Wines produced under the Howard Park label include Riesling, Chardonnay, Sauvignon Blanc, and Cabernet Sauvignon. They also have a second range called Madfish (named after a small bay near Denmark on the south coast), which is extremely popular. ⊠ *Miamup Rd., Cowaramup, Margaret River, Western Australia* ☎ *08/9756–5200* ⊕ *www.howardparkwines.com.au* ⊙ *Daily 10–5.*

★ **Leeuwin Estate.** Their Art Series wines—especially the Chardonnay and Cabernet Sauvignon—have a deserved reputation as some of the best in the country. Tastings and guided tours (A$12.50) are conducted on the property daily at 11 am, noon, and 3 pm, and the restaurant has daily lunch and Saturday dinner. In February the estate holds a series of concerts, and many international superstars—including John Farnham, Tom Jones, Diana Ross, Sting, and the late Ray Charles—have performed there against a backdrop of floodlighted karri trees. ⊠ *Stevens Rd. off Gnaraway Rd., Margaret River, Western Australia* ☎ *08/9759–0000* ⊕ *www.leeuwinestate.com.au* ☽ *Daily 10–5.*

Vasse Felix. Here you'll find a busy cellar door, excellent upstairs restaurant overlooking the vineyards, landscaped grounds, and an art gallery that houses regular exhibitions from the celebrated Holmes à Court Collection, featuring works from prominent Australian artists. The estate aims to produce "the best possible wine," and winemaker Virginia Willcock is at the helm, making Semillon, Sauvignon Blanc/Semillon, Chardonnay, Cabernet Merlot, Shiraz, and Cabernet Sauvignon Wines are made from vines planted as far back as 1967, when pioneer Dr. Tom Cullity established Vasse Felix as the first commercial winery in the area. The award-winning, fine-dining restaurant with its feature Gyrofocus fireplace is warmly welcoming in winter—make sure to book in advance for a table on the outside balcony during summertime. ■ TIP➔ Try a set two-course menu at $48 or the three-course menu at $58; it's your chance to "trust the chefs and allow them to experiment with new ideas," says executive chef, Aaron Carr. ⊠ *Tom Cullity Dr. and Caves Rds., Cowaramup, Western Australia* ☎ *08/9756–5000 cellar door, 08/9756–5050 restaurant* ⊕ *www.vassefelix.com.au* ☽ *Daily 10–5.*

OUTDOOR ACTIVITIES

HIKING Marked trails through the Leeuwin-Naturaliste National Park provide many opportunities for hiking through the natural bushland and on coastal walks, with vistas along untouched rugged cliffs, rocky outcrops, and sandy bays. The **Cape-to-Cape Walk Track** runs 138 km (86 mi) from Cape Naturaliste to Cape Leeuwin, but can be broken into shorter sections. You will find the start points generally at beachside carparks. **Canal Rocks to Wyadup** is a two-hour return walk from the car park on Canal Rocks Road; a one-hour walk via beach, rocks, and bushland begins at the Leeuwin Waterwheel, near Cape Leeuwin Lighthouse in Augusta; and, a four-hour walk with expansive coastal views starts at the Hamelin Bay boat ramp and heads to Cosy Corner.

Away from the coast, a popular short walk is from the historic homestead of **Ellensbrook** (Ellensbrook Road, off Caves Road, 13 km [8 mi] from Margaret River). The walk takes about 40 minutes to the **Meekadarabee Falls,** known to Aboriginal people as the "bathing place of the moon," and is best in winter and spring.

Brochures and maps on all walk trails in the region are available from the Margaret River Visitor Centre.

WHERE TO EAT

$$$ ⨉ **Flutes Restaurant.** The pastoral setting—over the dammed waters of
AUSTRALIAN Wilyabrup Brook and encircled by olive groves in the midst of the Brookland Valley Vineyard—is almost as compelling as the food. The modern Australian cuisine produced by executive chef François Morvan makes use of prime local produce and includes the ever-popular Chinese-style duck and mushroom spring rolls. You're unlikely to be disappointed by the slow-cooked lamb shank with quince and saffron couscous, or the salmon and northwest prawn linguini with capers, dill, and Chardonnay cream sauce. Everything goes down well with a glass

10

of one of Brookland Valley's award-winning wines. ■TIP➜ Reserve a seat by the window, or on the wooden deck that juts out over the picturesque dam. ✉ *Caves Rd., 5 km (3 mi) south of Metricup Rd., Wilyabrup, Margaret River, Western Australia* ☎ *08/9755–6250* ⊕ *www.flutes.com. au* ⚐ *Reservations essential* ⊙ *Daily from noon. Cellar Door 10–5.*

$$

AUSTRALIAN

Fodor's Choice

★

✕ **Lamont's Margaret River.** As you wind down a country road into a wooded valley, you'll see Lamont's jutting over a dam, and from the moment you step inside this popular, family-owned restaurant and winery you'll be spoiled for choice. The menu comes in three sizes, allowing you to graze or feast as you wish—so supersize-up from tapas to entrée or main if you like the look of something. The signature dish is the local marron, served grilled with spiced chickpea salad and saffron aioli. Another popular bet is the home-cured gravlax with toasted coriander seeds and mandarin oil, and the Pavlova is famed, far and wide. Chef Kate Lamont is CEO and ambassaador for Lamont's (check out her cookbooks and cooking classes). You can pop in for wine tasting at the cellar door without eating at the restaurant. ✉ *Lot 1, Gunyulgup Valley Dr., Yallingup, Western Australia* ☎ *08/9755–2434* ⊕ *www.lamonts.com.au* ⊙ *Thurs.–Mon. 11–5, lunch and wine tasting. Dinner Fri., Sat nights.*

$

ECLECTIC

☾

✕ **Sea Gardens Café Restaurant.** Loved by locals for its laid-back breakfasts and sunset bistro-style dinners, Sea Gardens Café Restaurant is synonymous with the Margaret River scene. It's one of only two restaurants south of Busselton with ocean views and definitely a place to see and be seen: actress Emma Thompson and comedian Ben Elton have been spotted here. At Seadies (as it's affectionately known) you can expect casual dining—gourmet pizzas made by chef Gilles England-Brassy and delectably naughty cakes made by Rachel, his wife. People flock for the chicken burgers, chicken-liver parfait, beer-battered fish-and-chips, and crème brûlées. ■TIP➜ Go for the sunset, or early for the Bombie brekkie (named after the surf break opposite) and ask Giles for his binoculars to check out the surfers or the whales. ✉ *9 Mitchell Dr., Prevelly, Western Australia* ☎ *9757 3074* ⊕ *www.seagardens.com.au* ⊙ *Daily 7:30 am–8:30 pm.*

$$

CONTEMPORARY

✕ **Voyager Estate.** Formal gardens planted with more than 1,000 roses surround the elegant white lines of the vernacular Cape Dutch building that houses Voyager Estate restaurant, cellar door, and gift shop. The large restaurant with antique wooden furniture, brass chandeliers, and soaring cathedral ceilings exudes timeless elegance and sophistication, which is echoed in the innovative menu that makes use of locally sourced produce. Seared scallops with Gorgonzola pannacotta, pear and walnut chutney, and toasted walnut bread, paired with a 2007 Voyager Estate Chardonnay are a lunchtime favorite, while the Margaret River venison with roasted pumpkin pappardelle, beetroot puree, sautéed spinach, and chocolate infused jus is a popular signature dish. A children's menu is available. ■TIP➜ Book an estate tour in the safari-style bus with a private wine tasting and five-course degustation menu with wine pairings for $140. ✉ *Stevens Rd., Margaret River, Western Australia* ☎ *9757 6354* ⊕ *www.voyagerestate.com.au* ⊙ *Daily. Cellar door 10 am–5 pm, restaurant 10 am–4:30 pm.*

$$ × **Watershed.** Families are welcomed at this large vineyard restaurant
AUSTRALIAN and café with its impressive modern architecture; big windows and a
🕲 wraparound deck offer uninterrupted views and give the impression
★ that you are floating above the vines. The main restaurant menu changes
each season; benchmark choices like the local fig and brik pastry cones
with goat's curd and balsamic gel, and the crisp pork belly with plum,
lychee, and master stock are seasonal show-stoppers. The adjacent café
has an enclosed children's playground and caters to children and casual
dining. While the cellar door and restaurant are top-notch in terms of
design and construction, it's the seriously award winning wines that
keep your attention. ■ **TIP➜** Try the signature dish—the chef's Taste Plate
consisting of five almost too-gorgeous-to-eat morsels for A$42. ⊠ *Bussell
Hwy. and Darch Rd., Margaret River, Western Australia* 🕾 *08/9758–
8633* ⊕ *www.watershedwines.com.au* ⊘ *Closed for dinner.*

WHERE TO STAY

$$$ 🏨 **Basildene Manor.** Each of the rooms in this grand, circa-1912 house
has been lovingly refurbished, though history still looms large in the
main homestead. **Pros:** large, heritage decor rooms; lavish breakfast;
quiet location. **Cons:** own transport essential; no lunch or dinner; dining options 1.5 km away. ⊠ *100 Wallcliffe Rd., Margaret River, Western Australia* 🕾 *08/9757–3140* ⊕ *www.basildene.com.au* ⤴ *17 rooms*
⟳ *In-room: a/c, safe, Internet, Wi-Fi. In-hotel: restaurant, pool, tennis
court, laundry facilities, business center, parking* ⦿ *Breakfast.*

$$$$ 🏨 **Cape Lodge.** The Cape Dutch architecture perfectly suits this elegant
Fodor's Choice lodge in the midst of Margaret River wine country. **Pros:** intimate coun-
★ try estate atmosphere; large, luxurious rooms; highly regarded restaurant. **Cons:** no shopping nearby; limited dining options nearby; own
transport essential; tired-looking outside entry to some suites is unin-
spiring. ⊠ *3341 Caves Rd., Yallingup, Western Australia* 🕾 *08/9755–
6311* ⊕ *www.capelodge.com.au* ⤴ *22 suites, 5-bedroom residence*
⟳ *In-room: safe, Wi-Fi. In-hotel: restaurant, bar, pool, tennis court,
business center, parking, some age restrictions* ⦿ *Breakfast.*

$$$$ 🏨 **Forest Rise Eco Retreat.** King-size beds, fluffy gowns, dreamy candle-lit
Fodor's Choice spas with huge windows looking up to the forest canopy, and, oh-so-
★ private verandas make this retreat a sanctuary. ⊠ *231 Yelverton Rd.,
Yelverton, Margaret River, Western Australia* 🕾 *08/9755–7110* ⤴ *10
chalets, 1 homestead.*

$$ 🏨 **Gilgara Retreat.** This stunning property, a replica of an 1870 sta-
tion homestead, sits amid 23 gently rolling, bucolic acres. **Pros:** private
lounge with log fire; Mediterranean breakfast included for Main House
guests; lots of birds. **Cons:** standard Main House rooms are small; no
shopping nearby; Wi-Fi for a fee. ⊠ *Caves and Carter Rds., Margaret
River, Western Australia* 🕾 *08/9757–2705* ⊕ *www.gilgara.com.au* ⤴ *5
rooms, 8 suites* ⟳ *In-room: kitchen, no TV. In-hotel: laundry facilities,
parking, some age restrictions* ⦿ *Breakfast.*

$$$ 🏨 **Heritage Trail Lodge.** Nestled among the trees, this luxury retreat is
only about ½ km (¼ mi) from Margaret River township. **Pros:** walk-
ing trails nearby; minutes walk to shops and restaurants; bushland
setting. **Cons:** no leisure facilities; children discouraged, two rooms
face highway, meaning traffic noise during day. ⊠ *31 Bussell Hwy.,*

10

Margaret River, Western Australia ☎ *08/9757–9595* ⊕ *www.heritage-trail-lodge.com.au* ⇋ *10 suites* ⚬ *In-hotel: laundry facilities, parking* ❘⊙❘ *Breakfast.*

$$ 🖵 **Riverglen Chalets.** In a magical woodland setting, Riverglen Chalets
☾ consists of self-contained timber cabins interspersed among 7 acres of
forest and gardens just a 10-minute stroll along the river into Margaret River township. **Pros:** secluded chalets; breakfast hampers supplied
on request; some outdoor spas; communal games room. **Cons:** some
road noise during the day; bathroom amenities do not include hair
shampoo. ⊠ *Bussell Hwy. and Carters Rd., Margaret River, Western Australia* ☎ *08/9757–2101* ⊕ *www.riverglenchalets.com.au* ⇋ *14
chalets sleeping 2–8 persons* ⚬ *In-room: kitchen. In-hotel: laundry
facilities, parking.*

EN
ROUTE
Nannup. Rustic timber cottages and historic buildings characterize
the small, lovely town of Nannup, 100 km (62 mi) east of Margaret River. Several scenic drives wind through the area, including the
Blackwood River Tourist Drive, a 10-km (6-mi) ride along a section
of river surrounded by hills with karri and jarrah forests. You can
also canoe on the Blackwood River and wander through the Blythe
Gardens. At various times of the year look out for Nannup's popular
festivals; music, flower and garden, art and photography, and the festival of country gardens that offers an artist's palette of WA's spring
and autumn colors.

   Holberry House. If you'd like to spend the night, check out Holberry House, a charming colonial B&B with exposed beams and stone
fireplaces, overlooking the Blackwood Valley. The gardens are peppered with statues and sculptures set amongst a woodland of jarrrah
trees through which Mount Folly Creek flows. For a small (courtesy)
donation at the main gate you can explore the extensive gardens without overnighting at the B&B. ■TIP➜ Ask about the facts and myths
surrounding the legend of the Nannup Tiger. ☎ *08/9756–1276* ⊕ *www.
holberryhouse.com* ⊕ *www.nannupwa.com.*

Travel Smart
Australia

WORD OF MOUTH

"I recently spent 12 days driving from Sydney
up to Cairns (tried to save money by not flying)
and found that I didn't have a lot of time to see
everything I wanted as a result! The first thing I'd
say is not to underestimate how big Australia is!"
— kristieb

GETTING HERE AND AROUND

Australia is divided into six states and two territories—Northern Territory (NT) and Australian Capital Territory (ACT)—similar to the District of Columbia. Tasmania, the smallest state, is an island off mainland Australia's southeast point.

▌ AIR TRAVEL

Air Pass Information Aussie Airpass
☎ 1800/227–4500 in U.S., 13–1313 in Australia ⊕ www.qantas.com.au. Regional Express
☎ 13–1713 ⊕ www.rex.com.au. Visit Australia and New Zealand Pass ⊕ www.oneworld.com.

Sydney is Australia's main international hub, though it is also easy to get international flights to Melbourne, Brisbane, Cairns, and Perth. You can catch nonstop or one-stop flights to Australia from New York (21 hours via Los Angeles); Chicago (19 hours via Los Angeles); Los Angeles (14 hours nonstop); Vancouver (17 hours via Honolulu); Toronto (20 hours via Los Angeles); and London (20–24 hours via Hong Kong, Singapore, or Bangkok).

Since Pacific-route flights from the United States to Australia cross the international dateline, you lose a day, but regain it on the journey home.

Airlines and Airports Airline and Airport Links.com. Airline and Airport Links.com has links to many of the world's airlines and airports. ⊕ www.airlineandairportlinks.com.

Airline Security Issues Transportation Security Administration. Transportation Security Administration has answers for almost every question that might come up.
⊕ www.tsa.gov.

AIRPORTS

Sydney Airport (SYD) is Australia's main air hub and the first port of call for more than half of the country's visitors. Terminal 1 is for all international flights, Qantas domestic flights operate out of Terminal 3, and Terminal 2 is for all other domestic flights (including Qantaslink and Jetstar). A rail link connects the terminals underground, and frequent shuttle buses run between them aboveground. There is an excellent range of shops and restaurants in the international terminal.

Brisbane International Airport (BNE) is southern Queensland's main airport and rivals Sydney's in quality and services. There are separate domestic and international terminals—the latter was recently expanded. Cairns International Airport (CNS), in north Queensland, is the hub for northern Queensland and visits to the Great Barrier Reef.

Melbourne Airport (MEL) is sometimes known as "Tullamarine," after a neighboring suburb. International flights leave from Terminal 2; Qantas and Jetstar use Terminal 1 for their domestic operations. Virgin Blue makes up the bulk of the other domestic flights, which go from Terminal 3. Tiger Airways flies from Terminal 4.

South Australia's main airport is Adelaide International (ADL). Domestic flights and a few services to nearby Asian cities land at Darwin International Airport (DRW) in the Northern Territory. The hub for the Red Centre is Alice Springs Airport (ASP), which only receives domestic flights. Perth International Airport (PER) is the gateway to Western Australia. International flights operate from Terminal 1; Qantas domestic flights leave from Terminal 2; Terminal 3 is for Alliance Airlines, Ozjet, Skywest Airlines, and Virgin Blue.

Airport Information Adelaide Airport
☎ 08/8308–9211 ⊕ www.aal.com.au. Alice Springs Airport ☎ 08/8951–1211 ⊕ www.alicespringsairport.com.au. Brisbane International Airport ☎ 07/3406–3000 ⊕ www.bne.com.au. Cairns Airport ☎ 07/4080–6703 ⊕ www.cairnsairport.com. Darwin International Airport ☎ 08/8920–1811 ⊕ www.darwinairport.com.au. Melbourne Airport
☎ 03/9297–1600 ⊕ www.melbourneairport.

com.au. **Perth Airport** ☎ 08/9478–8888
⊕ www.perthairport.com.au. **Sydney Airport**
☎ 02/9667–9111 ⊕ www.sydneyairport.com.au.

FLIGHTS
TO AUSTRALIA

Qantas is Australia's flagship carrier. It operates direct flights to Sydney from New York, San Francisco, and Los Angeles, and from Los Angeles to Melbourne and Brisbane. There are connecting Qantas flights to many other North American cities, and direct flights from various Australian airports to many Asian and European destinations. It's part of the oneworld alliance, and has excellent standards of safety and comfort. Qantas flights aren't always the cheapest, but their Aussie Airpass includes three stops within Australia for the same price as your ticket from North America.

Jetstar is a low-cost local airline owned by Qantas, and has flights from Sydney, Melbourne, Brisbane, Cairns, Perth, Adelaide, and Darwin to Bali, Japan, New Zealand, Singapore, Thailand, Vietnam, and Honolulu. Other budget carriers, Pacific Blue and Polynesian Blue (part of Virgin Blue), fly to Tonga, Samoa, Fiji, Vanuatu, New Zealand, Indonesia, and the Cook Islands. Singapore Airlines–owned budget airline Tiger Airways flies from Perth to Singapore.

Airline Contacts Air New Zealand
☎ 1800/262–1234 in U.S., 13/2476
⊕ www.airnewzealand.com.au. **British Airways** ☎ 1800/247–9297 in U.S., 1300/767177 in Australia ⊕ www.britishairways.com. **Cathay Pacific** ☎ 1800/233–2742 in U.S., 13–1747 in Australia ⊕ www.cathaypacific.com. **Qantas** ☎ 1800/227–4500 in U.S., 13–1313 in Australia ⊕ www.qantas.com. **United** ☎ 1800/538–2929 in U.S., 13–1777 in Australia ⊕ www.united.com. **V Australia** ☎ 1800/444–0260 in US, 13-8287 in Australia ⊕ www.vaustralia.com.au.

WITHIN AUSTRALIA

Australia's large distances mean that flying is the locals' favorite way of getting from one city to another. In general, safety standards on domestic flights are high, flights are punctual, and there's plenty of timetable choice. On routes between popular destinations like Sydney, Melbourne, and Brisbane there are often several flights each hour.

Airline Contacts Airnorth ☎ 1800/627–474 ⊕ www.airnorth.com.au. **Jetstar** ☎ 13–1538 ⊕ www.jetstar.com. **Qantas** ☎ 13–1313 ⊕ www.qantas.com.au. **Regional Express** ☎ 13–1713 ⊕ www.rex.com.au. **Skywest** ☎ 1300/660–088 ⊕ www.skywest.com.au. **Tiger Airways** ☎ 03/9999–2888 ⊕ www. tigerairways.com. **Virgin Blue** ☎ 13–6789 ⊕ www.virginblue.com.au.

▌BOAT TRAVEL

Organized boat tours from the Queensland mainland are the only way to visit the Great Barrier Reef. Cairns is the number-one point of departure, but boats also leave from Mackay, Airlie Beach, Townsville, and Port Douglas. Boats also run between the Whitsunday Islands. The Great Barrier Reef Marine Park Authority Web site has helpful advice on how to choose a tour operator, and lists which companies are ecotourism-certified.

The daily ferries *Spirit of Tasmania I* and *II* take 10 hours to connect Melbourne with Devonport on Tasmania's north coast. Make reservations as early as possible, particularly during the busy December and January school holidays.

Sealink Ferries transport passengers and vehicles between Cape Jervis on the South Australian coastline south of Adelaide, and Penneshaw on Kangaroo Island.

You can find out about ferry and cruise schedules for these and other scenic rides at most state tourism offices and on their Web sites. All operators accept major credit cards and cash.

Information Great Barrier Reef Marine Park Authority ☎ 07/4750–0700 ⊕ www.gbrmpa.gov.au. **Sealink Ferries** ☎ 13–1301 ⊕ www.sealink.com.au. **Spirit of Tasmania** ☎ 1800/634–906 ⊕ www.spiritoftasmania.com.au.

▌BUS TRAVEL

Bus travel in Australia is comfortable and well organized. Long-distance buses, also called "coaches," have air-conditioning, on-board toilets, reclining seats, and even attendants and videos on longer routes. By law, all are required to provide seat belts, and you are required to use them. Smoking is prohibited on all buses.

Australia's national bus network is run by Greyhound Australia (no connection to Greyhound in the United States), which serves far more destinations than any plane or train services. However, Australia is a vast continent, and bus travel here requires plenty of time. The journey from Sydney to Melbourne takes 15 hours, Adelaide to Perth takes 39 hours, and Brisbane to Cairns takes 30 hours. If you plan to visit specific regions, it could be worthwhile considering flying to a major hub, then using buses to explore the region when you get there.

Oz Experience is a private bus company aimed at budget travelers. They work in a similar way to Greyhound, and their routes take in both major cities and adventure destinations. They have a great selection of routes—you buy a pass, and then have unlimited stopovers along that route. You book onto each section by telephone as you travel. Oz Experience also has a hostel booking service, and will take you to the door of your hostel for no extra cost. For example, their Bruce Pass takes you along the coast between Melbourne and Cairns and costs A$575.

You can book passes and individual tickets on Greyhound and Oz Experience buses online through their Web sites, over the telephone, or in person at their desks in bus terminals.

Bus Information Greyhound Australia
☎ 1300/473–946 ⊕ www.greyhound.com.au.
Oz Experience ☎ 1800/555–287
⊕ www.ozexperience.com.

▌CAR TRAVEL

Endless highways, fabulous scenery, bizarre little towns in the middle of nowhere: Australia is road-trip paradise. Even if you don't have time for major exploring, traveling by car can be a great way to explore a particular region at your own pace. Traffic in city centers can be terrible, so keep the car for the open road.

Driving is generally easy in Australia, once you adjust to traveling on the left side of the road. Road conditions on busy coastal highways usually pose few problems, though remote roads (even big highways) and routes through the desert are often a different story. When you're preparing a driving itinerary, it's vital to bear in mind the huge distances involved and calculate travel time and stopovers accordingly.

Most rental companies in Australia accept driving licenses from other countries, including the United States, provided that the information on the license is clear and in English. Otherwise, an International Driver's Permit is required (but they'll still want to see your regular license, too).

GASOLINE

Gas is known in Australia as "petrol." Self-service petrol stations are plentiful near major cities and in rural towns. In remote regions they can be few and far between, so fill up whenever you can. In really out-of-the-way places, carrying a spare petrol can is a good idea. Smaller petrol stations often close at night and on Sunday, though in major cities and on main highways there are plenty of stations open round the clock.

PARKING

On-street parking is usually plentiful in Australian cities, except in the traffic-heavy CBD (downtown area) of the big capitals. Electronic meters are the norm—you pay in advance, and there's usually a maximum stay, which you should respect, as Australian parking inspectors are very vigilant. Paid parking lots are also common, and are usually clearly signposted. Outside the capitals, on-street parking is usually free, as are the lots outside malls and supermarkets.

RENTING A CAR

Australia's cities have good public transport, so there's not much point in renting a car if you're staying in an urban area, especially one popular with tourists. Step outside city limits, and a car is practically a necessity.

Rates for economy cars (a Hyundai Getz, Excel, or Accent or a Nissan Pulsar, for example) with unlimited mileage start at A$58 a day (plus fees).

Intercity highways are usually in good condition, but remoter roads—even those that look important on maps—are often unpaved or full of potholes. You can manage short distances on these in a car (for example, an access road to an attraction a few miles from the highway). For longer stretches and any outback driving, a 4WD is necessary, as insurance generally doesn't cover damage to other types of cars traveling such roads. Only rent a 4WD if you're competent to drive one on tough surfaces like sand and bogs: rescue vehicles take a long time to get to the middle of nowhere.

Rental companies have varying policies and charges for unusual trips, such as lengthy cross-state expeditions around the Top End and Western Australia. Ask about additional mileage, fuel, and insurance charges if you're planning to cover a lot of ground.

Another popular way to see Australia is to rent a camper van (motor home). Nearly all have a toilet, shower, and cooking facilities; utensils and bed linen are usually included, too. Smaller vans for two can be rented for A$40–A$150 a day with unlimited mileage (there's usually a five-day minimum).

In Australia you must be 21 to rent a car, and rates may be higher if you're under 25. There is no upper age limit for rental so long as you have a valid international driver's license. Most companies charge extra for each additional driver. It's compulsory for children to use car seats, so be sure to notify your agency when you

BUYING A CAR

For road trips longer than a couple of months, renting costs add up, so buying a car or van (and selling it at the end of your trip) might be more economical. Most camper-van agencies have a sales department; Kings Cross Car Market and Travellers Auto Barn are two reputable agencies that specialize in selling to and rebuying from visitors.

book—most charge around A$8 per day for a baby or booster seat.

Your driver's license may not be recognized outside your home country. You may not be able to rent a car without an International Driving Permit (IDP), which can be used only in conjunction with a valid driver's license and which translates your license into 10 languages. Check the AAA Web site for more info as well as for IDPs ($15) themselves.

Car Rental Resources Automobile Associations **Australian Automobile Association** ☎ 02/6247–7311 ⊕ www.aaa.asn.au. **American Automobile Association** (*AAA*). In the US, the American Automobile Association is a good resource for rental options abroad. Most contact with the organization is through state and regional members. ☎ 315/797–5000 ⊕ www.aaa.com. **National Automobile Club** ☎ 650/294–7000 ⊕ www.thenac.com.

Local Rental Agencies Red Spot Rentals ☎ 61/2/8303–2222 ⊕ www.redspotrentals. com.au. **Wicked Campers** ☎ 61/7/3217–0100, 1800/246869 in Australia ⊕ www. wickedcampers.com.au.

Major Agencies Alamo ☎ 1877/222–9075 in US ⊕ www.alamo.com. **Avis** ☎ 1800/331–1212 in US, 136-333 in Australia ⊕ www. avis.com.au. **Budget** ☎ 800/472–3325 in US, 1300/362848 in Australia ⊕ www.budget. com. **Hertz** ☎ 800/654–3001, 13-3039 in Australia ⊕ www.hertz.com. **National Car Rental** ☎ 877/222–9058 ⊕ www.nationalcar. com. **Thrifty** ☎ 800/847–4389, 1300/367227 in Australia ⊕ www.thrifty.com.

Local Car Purchase Agencies **Kings Cross Car Market** ☎ *1800/808-188 in Australia* ⊕ *www.carmarket.com.au.* **Travellers Auto Barn** ☎ *61/2/9360-1500, 1800/674374 in Australia* ⊕ *www.travellers-autobarn.com.au.*

ROAD CONDITIONS

Except for some expressways in and around the major cities, most highways are two-lane roads with frequent passing lanes but no barrier separating the two directions of traffic. Main roads are usually paved and well maintained, though lanes are narrower than in the United States.

Outside big urban areas roundabouts are far more common than traffic lights—some towns have dozens of them. Remember that when driving on the left you go around a roundabout clockwise and give way to traffic entering from the left and already on the roundabout.

Potential road hazards multiply in rural areas. Driving standards, which are generally high in Australia, become more lax. Road surfaces deteriorate, becoming potholed or uneven. Fine sand sometimes fills the holes, making them hard to see. Windshield cracks caused by small stones are practically routine. Flash floods are also common during the summer months in northern Australia: when in doubt, turn back or seek advice from the police before crossing.

Animals—kangaroos and livestock, primarily—are common causes of road accidents, especially at night. If you see an animal near the edge of the road, slow down immediately, as they may just decide to step out in front of you. If they do, hitting the animal is generally preferable to swerving, as you can lose control of your car and roll. However, braking too suddenly into the animal can send it through your windshield. Ideally, you should report any livestock you kill to the nearest ranch, and should check dead kangaroos for joeys (babies carried in their pouches): if you find one, wrap it up and take it to the nearest vet.

"Road trains" are another Outback hazard: they're truck convoys made of several connected trailers, totaling up to 170 feet. They take a *long* time to brake, so keep your distance and overtake them only with extreme caution.

Outback driving can be very exhausting and potentially dangerous. Avoid driving alone, and rest often. Carry plenty of water with you (4–5 liters per person per day)—high temperatures make dehydration a common problem on the road. Don't count on your cell phone working in the middle of nowhere, and if an emergency occurs never ever leave your vehicle: it's visible, and provides you shelter from the sun and cold. Stick by the side of the road: sooner or later, someone will come along.

ROADSIDE EMERGENCIES

000. If you have an emergency requiring an ambulance, the fire department, or the police, dial 000.

Many major highways now have telephones for breakdown assistance; you can also use your cell phone if you have one. Otherwise, flag down and ask a passing motorist to call the nearest motoring service organization for you. Most Australian drivers will be happy to assist, particularly in country areas.

Each state has its own motoring organization that provides assistance for vehicle breakdowns. When you rent a vehicle, check that you are entitled to assistance from the relevant motoring organization free of charge. A toll-free nationwide number is available for roadside assistance.

Emergency Services **Emergency Services** ☎ *000.* **Motoring Organization Hotline** ☎ *13-1111.*

RULES OF THE ROAD

Speed limits vary from state to state. As a rough guide, 50–60 kilometers per hour (kph) is the maximum in populated areas, reduced to 40 kph near schools. On open roads limits range from 100 to 130 kph—the equivalent of 62–80 mph. Limits are usually signposted clearly and regularly, and

FROM	TO	DISTANCE	MAIN HIGHWAY NAMES
Sydney	Melbourne	873 km (542 mi) /1,043 km (648 mi)	Hume/Princes
Sydney	Brisbane	982 km (610 mi)	Pacific
Brisbane	Cairns	1,699 km (1,056 mi)	Bruce
Melbourne	Adelaide	732 km (455 mi) /912 km (567 mi)	Dukes/Pacific
Adelaide	Perth	2,716 km (1,688 mi)	Eyre and Great Eastern
Adelaide	Alice Springs	1,544 km (959 mi)	Stuart
Alice Springs	Darwin	1,503 km (934 mi)	Stuart
Darwin	Cairns	2,885 km (1,793 mi)	Bruce, Flinders, Barkley, and Stuart

are enforced by police speed checks and—in state capitals—by automatic cameras.

Drunk driving, once a big problem in Australia, is controlled obsessively. The legal limit is 0.05% blood-alcohol level, and penalties are so high that many Aussies just don't drink if they're driving. Seat belts are mandatory nationwide. Children must be restrained in a seat appropriate to their size. Car-rental agencies can install these for about A$30 per week, with 24 hours' notice. It is illegal to use a mobile-phone handset when driving.

Traffic circles, called "roundabouts," are widely used at intersections; cars that have already entered the circle have the right-of-way. At designated intersections in Melbourne's central business district you must get into the left lane to make a right-hand turn—this is to facilitate crossing streetcar lines. Watch for the sign "right-hand turn from left lane only." Everywhere, watch for sudden changes in speed limits.

The Australian Automobile Association has a branch in each state, known as the National Roads and Motorists Association (NRMA) in New South Wales and Canberra, the Automobile Association in the Northern Territory (AANT), and the Royal Automobile Club (RAC) in all other states. It's affiliated with AAA worldwide, and offers reciprocal services to American members, including emergency road service, road maps, copies of each state and territory's Highway Code, and discounts on car rental and accommodations.

▮ CRUISE SHIP TRAVEL

Coral Princess Cruises runs 3–7 night cruises along the Great Barrier Reef; their Across the Top trip continues to Darwin. There's also a cruise between Darwin and Broome.

Pacific Dawn, Australia's biggest cruise liner, sails various 1–2 week Pacific and New Zealand cruises out of Brisbane. It's owned by P&O, known in the rest of the world as Princess Cruises. From late 2010 their *Pacific Pearl* will cruise the Pacific from Sydney.

Princess Cruises' huge *Sapphire Princess* sails between New Zealand and Australia at the end of its 33-day cruise from Seattle, Washington. The smaller *Dawn Princess* visits Papua New Guinea, Vanuatu, and New Caledonia on its 18-day return cruise to Sydney.

Regent Seven Seas' *Seven Seas Mariner* docks at several points on Australia's south and east coast on cruises from Asia to Sydney and Auckland. Crystal Cruises' Kangaroos and Kiwis voyage—aboard *Crystal Serenity*—starts in Sydney and calls at Melbourne and Hobart before ending in Auckland. *Crystal Symphony* goes up past Brisbane, Cairns, the Barrier Reef, Darwin, and Indonesia to Singapore. Silversea's *Silver Whisper* has a similar route, and also runs between Australia and New Zealand.

Cunard's *Queen Elizabeth* sails from New York and Santiago to Sydney, and calls at Australian ports on round-the-world cruises, too. So do its *Queen Mary 2* and *Queen Victoria*.

▎ TRAIN TRAVEL

Australia has a network of long-distance trains providing first- and economy-class service along the east and south coasts, across the south of the country from Sydney to Perth, and through the middle of the country between Adelaide and Darwin.

Most long-distance trains are operated by various state-government-owned enterprises. The luxurious exceptions to the rule are the *Ghan, Indian Pacific,* and *Overland*, all run by the private company Great Southern Rail. Rail Australia is the umbrella organization for all of these services outside the country.

The state-owned trains are usually punctual and comfortable. Economy class has reclining seats, and on longer routes there are sleeper classes. Second-class sleepers have shared bathrooms and sometimes you share your cabin with strangers, too. In first class you have the cabin to yourself and a small en suite bathroom. Meals are sometimes included. Comfort levels increase in Premium Red Service on the *Overland*, and Gold and Platinum Service on the *Ghan* and *Indian Pacific* and in the *Sunlander's* Queenslander class. The high-speed *Tilt Train* is aimed at business travelers, and has business-class-style reclining seats.

Information Countrylink ☎ *13-2232* ⊕ *www.countrylink.info.* **Great Southern Rail** ☎ *13-2147* ⊕ *www.gsr.com.au.* **Queensland Rail** ☎ *13-1617* ⊕ *www.qr.com.au.* **Rail Australia** ☎ *13-2147* ⊕ *www.railaustralia.com.au.*

ESSENTIALS

▮ ACCOMMODATIONS

Australia operates a rating system of one to five stars. Five-star hotels include on-site dining options, concierge and valet services, a business center, and, of course, very luxurious rooms. Four stars denote an exceptional property that probably just doesn't have all the extras they need for five. Three stars means quality fittings and service. We list the best lodgings for each price category. The available facilities are specified, but we don't indicate whether they cost extra. Always ask about additional costs when pricing your hotel room.

APARTMENT AND HOUSE RENTALS

Judging from the huge number of short-term rental properties in Australia, locals prefer doing their own thing to being in a hotel. It's easy for you to do likewise. Serviced apartments are the norm in big cities, and you can often rent one for only a night or two. Booking agency Move and Stay has an enormous range of properties, usually aimed at executives. Medina has top-end apartments and apart-hotels in all the big cities. Quest owns apartment complexes all around the country. Furnished Properties focuses on the Sydney area, and have reasonable rates.

In beach areas "units" are the thing: they're usually small detached houses or bungalows, often with a communal area with laundry facilities and a swimming pool. Maid service is usually optional here. In summer, units at popular beach resorts will often be booked months in advance, so make reservations in plenty of time. To find beach units online, you usually need to search for agencies dealing with a specific area rather than a nationwide company.

Contacts Furnished Properties ☎ 612/9518–8828 ⊕ www.furnishedproperties. com.au. Medina Hotel Apartments ☎ 612/9356–5061 ⊕ www.medina.com.au. Move and Stay ⊕ www.moveandstay.com.au.

Quest Serviced Apartments ☎ 61/3/9645–8357, 1800/334033 ⊕ www.questapartments. com.au. Villas & Apartments Abroad ☎ 212/213–6435 ⊕ www.vaanyc.com. Villas International ☎ 415/499–9490, 800/221–2260 ⊕ www.villasintl.com.

BED AND BREAKFASTS

B&Bs are a big deal in Australia, and are popular in both urban and rural areas. The classic Aussie B&B is a family-run affair: expect clean, homey rooms, private bathrooms, and bountiful breakfasts. A room for two usually ranges from A$80 to A$200 a night. The word "boutique" in conjunction with a B&B implies a higher level of luxury—decorative, gastronomic, or both—and facilities, but all at a higher price.

The Bed & Breakfast Book, Australia lists a number of excellent properties. OzBedandBreakfast.com has comprehensive listings that include boutique properties. Australian Bed and Breakfast has listings of B&Bs, farm stays, cottages, and more, all over the country.

Local tourist-information centers throughout Australia also have lists of B&Bs in their area.

Reservation Services Australian Bed and Breakfast. Australian Bed and Breakfast has links to Web sites for each state. ⊕ www. australianbedandbreakfast.com.au. The Bed & Breakfast Book. The Bed & Breakfast Book publishes a yearly guide to Australian B&Bs and has online listings. ⊕ www.bbbook.com. au. Bed & Breakfast.com. Bed & Breakfast. com has resources at their Web site and sends out an online newsletter. ☎ 512/322–2710, 800/462–2632 ⊕ www.bedandbreakfast.com. Bed & Breakfast Farmstay Association of New South Wales & ACT ☎ 1300/888862, 02/4367–5505 ⊕ www.bedandbreakfast. org.au. Bed & Breakfast Inns Online ☎ 310/280–4363, 800/215–7365 ⊕ www. bbonline.com. Oz Bed and Breakfast ⊕ www. ozbedandbreakfast.com.

HOME AND FARM STAYS

Home and farm stays combine B&B-style accommodation with the chance to join in farm activities or explore the countryside. Some hosts run day trips, as well as horseback riding, hiking, and fishing trips. Accommodations vary from modest shearers' cabins to elegant homesteads; some include breakfast in the room price, others an evening meal. Families are usually welcomed. For two people the cost varies from A$100 to A$250 nightly. *Many of the B&B sites above also have farm stay listings.*

Reservation Services Australian Farm Stay. Australian Farm Stay is a private company dealing with luxury farm stays. ⊕ *www.australianfarmstay.com.au.*

HOME EXCHANGES

With a direct home exchange you stay in someone else's home while they stay in yours. Some outfits also deal with vacation homes, so you're not actually staying in someone's full-time residence, just their vacant weekend place.

Although home exchanges aren't popular choice in Australia, there are still many options available, particularly on the east coast.

Exchange Clubs Home Exchange.com. Home Exchange.com charges $99.95 for a 1-year online listing and use of the site. ☎ 800/877–8723 ⊕ *www.homeexchange. com.* **HomeLink International.** HomeLink International charges $115 yearly for Web-only membership; $175 includes Web access and two catalogs. ☎ 800/638–3841 ⊕ *www. homelink.org.* **Intervac U.S.** charges $99.99 for Web-only membership. ☎ 800/756–4663 ⊕ *www.intervacus.com.*

HOSTELS

Australian hostels are among the world's best. Often called "backpackers," hostels generally have a mix of dormitory and private accommodation, with well-equipped communal facilities, including a kitchen, laundry, and living area. In-house bars and travel agencies are popular, too. Owners and staff are often veteran Aussie backpackers who know from experience what budget travelers are looking for—they're lots of fun and full of useful advice. Guests are mostly globetrotters in their twenties and thirties, but families and older people are also common.

If you think "hostelling" is synonymous with "roughing it," think again. So-called luxury or boutique hostels and hostel resorts are a growing Australian trend, especially in tourist hot spots like Cairns. These mix high-quality dorms with floors of nicely furnished private rooms with en suite bathrooms. Prices are much lower than at hotels, and you still get the hostel vibe in the communal areas, which usually include a swimming pool.

Information Base Backpacking Hostels ☎ 1800/242–273 within Australia, 61/2/8268–6000 ⊕ *www.stayatbase.com.* **Hostelling International Australia** ⊕ *www. yha.com.au.* **Hostelling International—USA** ☎ 301/495–1240 ⊕ *www.hiusa.org.* **Hostels. com** ⊕ *www.hostels.com.* **Hostel World. com** ⊕ *www.hostelworld.com.* **Travellers' Point** ⊕ *www.travellerspoint.com.* **VIP Backpackers** ☎ 61/7/3395–6111 ⊕ *www. vipbackpackers.com.*

▌COMMUNICATIONS

INTERNET

Internet access is widely available to travelers in Australia. Top-end hotels always have some sort of in-room access for laptop users—Wi-Fi is becoming the norm, otherwise there are data ports. Note that sometimes you are charged a hefty premium for using this service. Hostels are also well connected and charge reasonable rates. Many have free Wi-Fi, others have large on-site cybercafés, or, at worst, some terminals for guests to use.

Australia's main telephone network, Telstra, has wireless hot spots all over the country. McDonalds and Starbucks (iiNet customers only) have free Wi-Fi. Alternatively, you can pay using Telstra Phone-Away calling cards: there's no connection charge and online time costs A$0.20 per minute. Connections can be slow, however. You can buy a card at newsagents, Australia Post, convenience stores, or online. Telstra's Web site also has hot spot listings.

Contacts Cybercafes. Cybercafes lists more than 4,000 Internet cafés worldwide. ⊕ *www.cybercafes.com*. Telstra ⊕ *www.telstra.com.au*.

PHONES

The country code for Australia is 61. To call Australia from the United States, dial the international access code (011), followed by the country code (61), the area or city code without the initial zero (e.g., 2), and the eight-digit phone number.

CALLING WITHIN AUSTRALIA

Australia's phone system is efficient and reliable. You can make local and long-distance calls from your hotel—usually with a surcharge—or from any public phone. There are public phones in shopping areas, on suburban streets, at train stations, and outside rural post offices—basically, they're everywhere. You can use coins or phone cards in most public phones; credit-card phones are common at airports.

All regular telephone numbers in Australia have eight digits. There are five area codes: 02 (for New South Wales and Australian Capital Territory), 03 (Victoria and Tasmania), 04 (for cell phones), 07 (for Queensland), and 08 (for Western Australia, South Australia, and Northern Territory). Toll-free numbers begin with 1800, and numbers starting with 13 or 1300 are charged at local rates anywhere in the country.

Calls within the same area code are charged as local: A0.50¢ for an unlimited amount of time. Long-distance call rates vary by distance, and are timed. When you're calling long distance within Australia, remember to include the area code, even when you're calling from a number with the same area code. For example, when calling Canberra from Sydney, both of which have an 02 prefix, you still need to include the area code when you dial.

Directory Assistance Local Directory Assistance ☎ *1223.*

CALLING OUTSIDE AUSTRALIA

To call overseas from Australia, dial 0011, then the country code and the number. Kiosks and groceries in major cities sell international calling cards. You can also use credit cards on public phones.

The country code for the United States is 1.

You can use AT&T, Sprint, and MCI services from Australian phones, though some pay phones require you to put coins in to make the call. Using a prepaid calling card is generally cheaper.

Access Codes AT&T Direct ☎ *1800/881–011 from Telstra phones, 1800/551–155 from Optus phones.* MCI WorldPhone ☎ *1800/881–100 from Telstra phones, 1800/551–111 from Optus phones.* Skype ⊕ *www.skype.com.* Sprint International Access ☎ *1800/881–877 from Telstra phones, 1800/551–110 from Optus phones.*

Useful Numbers International Call Cost Information ☎ *1300/362–162.* International Directory Assistance ☎ *1225.*

CALLING CARDS

It's worth buying a phone card in Australia even if you plan to make just a few calls.

Telstra, Australia's main telephone company, has three different calling cards. Their simply named Phonecard is a prepaid card you can use for local, long-distance, or international calls from public pay phones. There are many other calling cards in Australia as well, often with better rates than Telstra's. Gotalk and onesuite.com are two popular examples, but there are many more. The best way to find one is to ask in a convenience store or newsagent's: they usually have a selection on hand, and you can compare rates to the country you're calling to. Note that many companies don't even print their access numbers on cards any more, but instead give you a slip of paper.

Contacts Gotalk ⊕ *www.gotalk.com.au.* **onesuite.com** ⊕ *www.onesuite.com.* **Telstra** ⊕ *www.telstra.com.au.*

MOBILE PHONES

If you have a multiband phone (some countries use different frequencies from the ones used in the United States) and your service provider uses the world-standard GSM network (as do T-Mobile, Cingular, and Verizon), you can probably use your phone abroad. Roaming fees can be steep, however: 99¢ a minute is considered reasonable. And overseas you normally pay the toll charges for incoming calls. It's almost always cheaper to send a text message than to make a call, since text messages have a very low set fee (often less than 5¢).

If you just want to make local calls, consider buying a new SIM card (note that your provider may have to unlock your phone for you to use a different SIM card) and a prepaid service plan in the destination. You'll have a local number and can make local calls at local rates. If your trip is extensive, you could also simply buy a new cell phone in your destination, as the initial cost will be offset over time.

■ TIP→ If you travel internationally frequently, save one of your old mobile phones or buy a cheap one on the Internet; ask your cell-phone company to unlock it for you, and take it with you as a travel phone, buying a new SIM card with pay-as-you-go service in each destination.

Nearly all Australian mobile phones use the GSM network. If you have an unlocked tri-band phone and intend to make calls to Australian numbers, it makes sense to buy a prepaid Australian SIM card on arrival—rates will be much better than using your U.S. network. Alternatively, you can rent a phone or a SIM card from companies like Vodafone. Rates start at A$5 per day for a handset and A$1 a day for a SIM. You can also buy a cheap, pay-as-you-go handset from Telstra, Virgin Mobile, or Optus. Cell-phone stores are abundant, and staff are used to assessing tourists' needs.

Contacts Cellular Abroad. Cellular Abroad rents and sells GMS phones and sells SIM cards that work in many countries. ☎ *800/287-5072* ⊕ *www.cellularabroad.com.* **Mobal.** Mobal rents mobiles and sells GSM phones (starting at $49) that will operate in 140 countries. Per-call rates vary throughout the world. ☎ *888/888-9162* ⊕ *www.mobal.com.* **Optus** ⊕ *www.optus.com.au.* **Planet Fone.** Planet Fone rents cell phones, but the per-minute rates are expensive. ☎ *888/988-4777* ⊕ *www. planetfone.com.* **Telstra** ⊕ *www.telstra.com. au.* **Virgin Mobile** ⊕ *www.virginmobile.com.au.* **Vodafone.** Vodafone rents phones from stands in many airports. ⊕ *www.vodarent.com.au.*

▮ CUSTOMS AND DUTIES

Australian customs regulations are unlike any other. As an island long isolated from the rest of the world, Australia is free from many pests and diseases endemic in other places, and it wants to stay that way. Customs procedures are very thorough, and it can take up to an hour to clear them.

All animals are subject to quarantine. Many foodstuffs and natural products are forbidden, including meat, dairy products, fresh fruit and vegetables, and all food served on aircraft. Most canned or preserved foods may be imported, but you have to declare them on your customs statement and have them inspected, along with wooden artifacts and seeds.

Airport sniffer dogs patrol arrivals areas, and even an innocent dried flower forgotten between the pages of a book could incur a serious fine. If in doubt, declare something—the worst-case scenario is that it will be taken from you, without a fine.

Otherwise, nonresidents over 18 may bring in 250 cigarettes (or 250 grams of cigars or tobacco) and 2¼ liters of alcohol. Adults can bring in other taxable goods (that is, luxury items like perfume) to the value of A$900.

Information **Australian Customs Services.** Australian Customs Services is a good resource for information about duty-free allowances. ⊕ *www.customs.gov.au.* **Australian Quarantine and Inspection Services.** Australian Quarantine and Inspection Services tells you exactly what you can and cannot bring into Australia. ⊕ *www.daff.gov.au/aqis/travel/ entering-australia.*

U.S. Information **U.S. Customs and Border Protection** ⊕ *www.cbp.gov.*

▌ EATING OUT

Fresh ingredients, friendly service, innovative flavor combinations, and great value for your money mean that eating out Down Under is usually a happy experience.

Australia's British heritage is evident in the hearty food served in pubs, roadhouses, and country hotels. It all seems to taste much better than food in Britain, though. Roast meat and potatoes; fish-and-chips; pasties and pies swimming in gravy; flaky sausage rolls; sticky teacakes and fluffy scones—all these things are cheap and tasty counter staples. They give the big fast-food franchises a serious run for their money.

Some Australian restaurants serve prix-fixe dinners, but most are à la carte. The restaurants we list are the best in each price category.

MEALS AND MEALTIMES
Australians eat relatively early. Breakfast is typically between 7 and 10 am, and eating it out (usually at a café) is popular. Options range from toast or cereal through fruit and yogurt and muffins, pastries, and hotcakes to a full fry-up—eggs, bacon, sausages, baked beans, hash browns, tomatoes, and mushrooms. Morning coffee and afternoon tea are popular in-between meals.

For most locals lunch is usually lighter than dinner: a salad or a sandwich, say, usually between 11:30 am and 2:30 pm. Dinner is the main meal and begins around 6:30. In the cities, dining options are available outside these hours, but the choices are far more restricted in the countryside and smaller towns, where even take-aways close at 8:30 pm.

Unless otherwise noted, the restaurants listed in this guide are open daily for lunch and dinner.

PAYING
At most restaurants you ask for the bill at the end of the meal. At sandwich bars, burger joints, and take-aways you pay up front. Visa, MasterCard, and American Express are widely accepted in all but the simplest eateries.

For guidelines on tipping, see Tipping below.

RESERVATIONS AND DRESS
Regardless of where you are, it's a good idea to make a reservation if you can. In some places (Sydney, for example) it's expected. We only mention them specifically when reservations are essential (there's no other way you'll ever get a table) or when they are not accepted. For popular restaurants, book as far ahead as you can (often 30 days), and reconfirm as soon as you arrive. (Large parties should always call ahead to check the reservations policy.) We mention dress only when men are required to wear a jacket or a jacket and tie.

▌ ELECTRICITY

The electrical current in Australia is 240 volts, 50 cycles alternating current (AC), so most American appliances can't be used without a transformer. Wall outlets take slanted three-prong plugs and plugs with two flat prongs set in a V.

Consider making a small investment in a universal adapter, which has several types of plugs in one lightweight, compact unit. Most laptops and mobile-phone chargers are dual voltage (i.e., they operate equally well on 110 and 220 volts), so require only an adapter. These days the same is true of small appliances such as hair dryers. Always check labels and manufacturer instructions to be sure. Don't use 110-volt outlets marked "for shavers only" for high-wattage appliances such as hair dryers.

Contacts Steve Kropla's Help for World Travelers. Steve Kropla's Help for World Travelers has information on electrical and telephone plugs around the world. ⊕ www.kropla.com. Walkabout Travel Gear. Walkabout Travel Gear has a good coverage of electricity under "adapters." ⊕ www.walkabouttravelgear.com.

▌ HEALTH

The most common types of illnesses are caused by contaminated food and water. If you have problems, mild cases of traveler's diarrhea may respond to Imodium (known generically as loperamide) or Pepto-Bismol. Be sure to drink plenty of fluids; if you can't keep fluids down, seek medical help immediately.

Infectious diseases can be airborne or passed via mosquitoes and ticks and through direct or indirect physical contact with animals or people. Some, including Norwalk-like viruses that affect your digestive tract, can be passed along through contaminated food. Condoms can help prevent most sexually transmitted diseases, but they aren't absolutely reliable, and their quality varies from country to country. Speak with your physician and/or check the CDC or World Health Organization Web sites for health alerts, particularly if you're pregnant, traveling with children, or have a chronic illness.

OVER-THE-COUNTER REMEDIES
Familiar brands of nonprescription medications are available in pharmacies. Note that Tylenol is usually called paracetomol in Australia.

SHOTS AND MEDICATIONS
Unless you're arriving from an area that has been infected with yellow fever, typhoid, or cholera, you don't need to get any shots or carry medical certificates to enter Australia.

Australia is relatively free from diseases prevalent in many countries. In the far north there have been occasional localized outbreaks of dengue and Ross River fever—just take the usual precautions against mosquito bites (cover up your arms and legs and use ample repellent), and you should be fine.

SPECIFIC ISSUES IN AUSTRALIA
Australian health care is excellent, with highly trained medical professionals and well-equipped hospitals. Hygiene standards are also high and well monitored, so you can drink tap water and eat fresh produce without worrying. You may take a four weeks' supply of prescribed medication into Australia (more with a doctor's certificate)—if you run out, pharmacies require a prescription from an Australian doctor. The quickest way to find one is to ask your hotel or look under "M" (for Medical Practitioner) in the Yellow Pages.

Sunburn and sunstroke are the greatest health hazards when visiting Australia. Remember that there's a big hole in the ozone layer over Australia, so even on cloudy days the rays of light coming through are harmful. Stay out of the sun at midday and, regardless of whether you normally burn, follow the locals' example and slather on the sun cream. Protect your eyes with good-quality sunglasses, and try to cover up with a long-sleeve shirt, a hat, and pants or a beach wrap whenever possible. Keep in mind that you'll burn more easily at higher altitudes and in the water.

Dehydration is another serious danger, especially in the Outback. It's easy to avoid: carry plenty of water and drink it often.

Australia is free of malaria, but several cases of Ross River and dengue fevers have been reported in recent years. The best way to prevent both is to avoid being bitten: cover up your arms and legs, and use ample repellent, especially during summer months and in the north of the country. No rural scene is complete without bush flies, a major annoyance. These tiny pests, found throughout Australia, are especially attracted to the eyes and mouth in search of the fluids that are secreted there. Some travelers resort to wearing a face net, which can be suspended from a hat with a drawstring device.

Some of the world's deadliest creatures call Australia home. The chances of running into one are low, but wherever you go, pay close heed to any warnings given by hotel staff, tour operators, lifeguards, or locals in general. In the Outback you need to worry about snakes and spiders. On the coast there's everything from sharks through deadly octopi and stonefish to jellyfish to reckon with. In northern Australia, rivers, lakes, billabongs, and even flooded streams are home to estuarine crocodiles, known to attack and kill humans. The best advice we can give you is to always be cautious, and check, check, and double-check the situation at each stop on your visit with the appropriate authority.

As if deadly sea critters weren't enough, Australian coastal waters are also home to seriously strong currents known as "rips." These kill tens of swimmers every year. Pay close attention to the flags raised on beaches, and only swim in areas patrolled by lifeguards. If you get caught in a rip, the standard advice is never to swim against it, as you rapidly become exhausted. Instead, try to relax and float parallel to the shore: eventually the current will subside and you will be able to swim back to the shore, albeit farther down the coast.

▋ HOLIDAYS

New Year's Day, January 1; **Australia Day,** January 26; **Good Friday,** April 6, 2012, and March 29, 2013; **Easter Monday,** April 8, 2012, and March 31, 2013; **Anzac Day,** April 25; **Christmas,** December 25; **Boxing Day,** December 26. There are also several state- and territory-specific public holidays.

▋ MAIL

All regular mail services are run by the efficient Australia Post, which has offices all over the country. Post offices are usually open only during business hours weekdays, but stamps are available from newsagents at other times. Postboxes for regular mail in Australia are usually bright red; express postboxes are yellow. Postage rates are A0.55¢ for domestic letters, A$2.10 per 50-gram (28.35 grams = 1 ounce) airmail letter, and A$1.40 for airmail postcards to North America—allow a week for letters and postcards to arrive.

Contact Australia Post
⊕ *www.auspost.com.au.*

SHIPPING PACKAGES

Rates for large parcels shipped from Australia depend on their weight, shape, and contents. Printed papers (including books) are cheaper to send than clothes, for example. Sending parcels through Australia Post is usually reliable. It's worth paying the extra for recorded delivery, as you can track the parcel and claim insurance if it gets lost. Many stores—particularly upmarket ones—can ship your purchases for you, for a price.

Sending a 1-kilogram (2-pound) parcel to the United States with Australia Post costs A$18.80 by seamail, and A$27.30 by airmail. If you're shipping items in excess of 50 kilograms (110 pounds), it's often less expensive to send goods by sea via a shipping agent. Shipping time to the United States is 10–12 weeks.

Both DHL and Federal Express operate fast, reliable express courier services from

Australia. Rates are around A$120 for a 1-kilogram (2-pound) parcel to the United States, including door-to-door service. Delivery time between Sydney and New York is approximately three days.

Express Services DHL Worldwide Express
☎ *13–1406* ⊕ *www.dhl.com.au.* **Federal Express** ☎ *13–2610* ⊕ *www.fedex.com/au.*

▌ MONEY

The most expensive part of your trip to Australia will probably be getting there. Australian hotels are generally cheaper than similar establishments in North America, as is food.

Australians use debit cards wherever possible to pay for things—you can use your credit card, or pay cash, always in Australian dollars. ATMs are ubiquitous; it's very hard to change traveler's checks.

Prices for goods and services can be volatile at times. A 10% Goods and Services Tax (or GST—similar to V.A.T. in other countries) applies to most activities and goods, though some unprocessed foods are exempt.

Prices throughout this guide are given for adults. Substantially reduced fees are almost always available for children, students, and sometimes for senior citizens.

■**TIP→** Banks never have every foreign currency on hand, and it may take as long as a week to order. If you're planning to exchange funds before leaving home, don't wait until the last minute.

ATMS AND BANKS

Your own bank will probably charge a fee for using ATMs abroad; the foreign bank you use may also charge a fee. Nevertheless, you'll usually get a better rate of exchange at an ATM than you will at a currency-exchange office or even when changing money in a bank. And extracting funds as you need them is a safer option than carrying around a large amount of cash.

■**TIP→** PIN numbers with more than four digits are not recognized at ATMs in many countries. If yours has five or more, remember to change it before you leave.

For most travelers to Australia, ATMs are the easiest—and often cheapest—way to obtain Australia dollars. Australia's biggest banks are Westpac, ANZ, the Commonwealth Bank of Australia, and the National Australia Bank. Their ATMs all accept Cirrus and Plus cards. Smaller state-based banks are also common, but may not accept foreign cards. Major cities often have branches of international banks like Citibank or HSBC.

Before traveling, check if your bank has an agreement with any Australian banks for reduced ATM fees. For example, Bank of America customers can use Westpac ATMs to withdraw cash without incurring a fee.

CREDIT CARDS

It's a good idea to inform your credit-card company before you travel, especially if you're going abroad and don't travel internationally very often. Otherwise, the credit-card company might put a hold on your card owing to unusual activity—not a good thing halfway through your trip. Record all your credit-card numbers—as well as the phone numbers to call if your cards are lost or stolen—in a safe place, so you're prepared should something go wrong. Both MasterCard and Visa have general numbers you can call (collect if you're abroad) if your card is lost, but you're better off calling the number of your issuing bank, since MasterCard and Visa usually just transfer you to your bank; your bank's number is usually printed on your card.

If you plan to use your credit card for cash advances, you'll need to apply for a PIN at least two weeks before your trip. Although it's usually cheaper (and safer) to use a credit card abroad for large purchases (so you can cancel payments or be reimbursed if there's a problem), note that some credit-card companies *and* the banks that issue them add substantial percentages to all foreign transactions, whether they're in a foreign currency or not. Check on these fees before leaving home, so there won't be any surprises when you get the bill.

■ TIP➔ Before you charge something, ask the merchant whether he or she plans to do a dynamic currency conversion (DCC). In such a transaction the credit-card *processor* (shop, restaurant, or hotel, not Visa or MasterCard) converts the currency and charges you in dollars. In most cases you'll pay the merchant a 3% fee for this service in addition to any credit-card company and issuing-bank foreign-transaction surcharges.

Dynamic currency conversion programs are becoming increasingly widespread. Merchants who participate in them are supposed to ask whether you want to be charged in dollars or the local currency, but they don't always do so. And even if they do offer you a choice, they may well avoid mentioning the additional surcharges. The good news is that you *do* have a choice. And if this practice really gets your goat, you can avoid it entirely thanks to American Express; with its cards, DCC simply isn't an option.

Most Australian establishments take credit cards: Visa and MasterCard are the most widely accepted, American Express and Diners Club aren't always accepted outside the cities. Just in case, bring enough cash to cover your expenses if you're visiting a national park or a remote area.

Reporting Lost Cards **American Express** ☎ 800/992–3404 in the U.S., 336/393–1111 collect from abroad, 1300/132639 in Australia ⊕ www.americanexpress.com. **Diners Club** ☎ 800/234–6377 in the U.S., 303/799–1504 collect from abroad, 1300/360060 in Australia ⊕ www.dinersclub.com. **MasterCard** ☎ 800/627–8372 in the U.S., 636/722–7111 collect from abroad, 1800/120113 in Australia ⊕ www.mastercard.com. **Visa** ☎ 800/847–2911 in the U.S., 410/581–9994 collect from abroad, 1800/125440 in Australia ⊕ www.visa.com.

CURRENCY AND EXCHANGE

Australia has its own dollar—assume all prices you see in Australia are quoted in Australian dollars. The currency operates on a decimal system, with the dollar (A$) as the basic unit and 100 cents (¢) equaling A$1. Bills, differentiated by color and size, come in A$100, A$50, A$20, A$10, and A$5 denominations, and are made of plastic rather than paper—you can even take them swimming with you. Coins are minted in A$2, A$1, A0.50¢, A0.20¢, A0.10¢, and A0.05¢ denominations.

At this writing, the exchange rate was about A$1.187 to the U.S. dollar.

■ TIP➔ Even if a currency-exchange booth has a sign promising no commission, rest assured that there's some kind of huge, hidden fee. (Oh . . . that's right. The sign didn't say no *fee*.) And as for rates, you're almost always better off getting foreign currency at an ATM or exchanging money at a bank.

▮ PACKING

If Crocodile Dundee is your idea of an Aussie style icon, think again: Melburnians and Sydneysiders are as fashion-conscious as New Yorkers. In the big cities, slop around in shorts and you might as well wear an "I'm a tourist" badge. Instead, pack nicer jeans, Capri pants, skirts, or dress shorts for urban sightseeing. A jacket and tie or posh dress are only necessary if you plan on some seriously fine dining.

Things are a bit different out of town. No Aussie would be seen dead on the beach without their "thongs," as flip-flops are confusingly called here. Wherever you are, your accessories of choice are high-quality sunglasses and a hat with a brim—the sun is strong *and* dangerous. Carry insect repellent and avoid lotions or perfume in the tropics, as they attract mosquitoes and other insects.

A light sweater or jacket will keep you comfy in autumn, but winter in the southern states demands a heavier coat—ideally a raincoat with a zip-out wool lining.

You should pack sturdy walking boots if you're planning any bushwalking, otherwise sneakers or flats are fine.

Australian pharmacies stock all the usual hygiene products (including tampons and condoms) and toiletries, plus a whole lot of fabulous local brands often not available overseas. There's also a mind-boggling range of sunscreens and insect repellents, so have no qualms about bringing everything in travel-size bottles and stocking up when you arrive. Oral contraceptive pills are usually prescription-only, though emergency contraceptive pills are available over the counter. Grocery stores and supermarkets frown on your using too many plastic bags—carry a foldable canvas tote and you'll blend in perfectly.

▋ PASSPORTS AND VISAS

To enter Australia for up to 90 days you need a valid passport and a visa (New Zealand nationals are the exception). These days, instead of a visa label or stamp in your passport, citizens of the United States (and many other countries) can get an Electronic Travel Authority (ETA). This is an electronically stored travel permit. It saves you time both when you apply—the process is all online—and when you arrive in Australia.

To obtain an ETA for Australia you must: 1) hold an ETA-eligible passport; 2) be visiting Australia for tourism, family, or business; 3) stay less than three months; 4) be in good health; and 5) have no criminal convictions. The Visitor ETA allows you as many visits of up to 90 days as you like within a 12-month period, but remember that no work in the country is allowed. If you're visiting Australia on business, a Short Validity Business ETA might be more appropriate. Technically, both are free of charge, but you need to pay a A$20 service charge by credit card. Children traveling on a parent's passport also need an ETA. You can apply for the ETA yourself or your travel agent can do it for you.

If you don't meet the ETA requirements or need a different kind of visa, you should contact your nearest Australian diplomatic office well in advance of your trip, as processing other visas takes time. Equally, if you plan to stay longer than three months you must obtain a paper visa (there's a A$105 fee). If you travel to Australia on an under-three-month ETA and later decide to extend your visit, then you must apply for a visa at the nearest Australian Immigration regional office (there's a A$250 fee).

At present, Australia doesn't require a notarized letter of permission if only one parent is traveling with a child, but it's always best to err on the side of caution and take along such a letter if you can.

▋ TAXES

Everyone leaving Australia pays an A$47 departure tax, euphemistically known as a Passenger Movement Charge. It's included in your airline ticket price. There's also a 10% V.A.T. equivalent known as Goods and Services Tax (GST), which is included in displayed prices. There is a G.S.T. refund for visitors on purchases totaling more than A$300 made in one store. You need to keep the receipts for these and present them at the Australian Customs Services booths that are after passport control in international airports. The tax is refunded to a credit card, even if you paid cash for the purchases. Allow an extra 30 minutes for this process.

▋ TIME

Without daylight saving time, Sydney is 14 hours ahead of New York and Toronto; 15 hours ahead of Chicago and Dallas; and 17 hours ahead of Los Angeles.

Australia has three major time zones. Eastern Standard Time (EST) applies in Tasmania, Victoria, New South Wales, and Queensland; Central Standard Time applies in South Australia and Northern Territory; and Western Standard Time applies in Western Australia. Central Standard Time is ½ hour behind EST, and Western Standard Time is 2 hours behind EST.

Within the EST zone, each state chooses a slightly different date on which to commence or end daylight saving—except for Queensland, where the powerful farm lobby has prevented the state from introducing daylight saving at all, since it would make the cows wake up an hour earlier. Western Australia and Northern Territory also decline to recognize daylight saving, which means that at certain times of the year Australia can have as many as six different time zones.

Time Zones Timeanddate.com. Timeanddate.com can help you figure out the correct time anywhere. ⊕ *www.timeanddate.com.*

▋ TOURS

SPECIAL-INTEREST TOURS
ABORIGINAL ART
Australian Aboriginal Fine Art Gallery of New York runs collectors' art tours to Australia every year. Pilot and art lover Helen Read flies you and guides you on Didgeri Air Art Tours' small-group tours. Aboriginal Travel has several Aboriginal art tours, including a five-day collectors tour and shorter rock-art tours. The Wayward Bus Touring Company was purchased by Adventure Tours and now operates under that name; Adventure Tours runs a host of trips, many of which are Aboriginal-culture centric; the most art-focused is in Kakadu. Kimberley Dreams runs a 12-day Aboriginal art tour through the Kimberley Region in northern Western Australia.

Contacts Aboriginal Travel ☎ *61/8/8234–8324* ⊕ *www.aboriginaltravel.com.* Didgeri Air Art Tours ☎ *61/8/8948-5055* ⊕ *www.didgeri.com.au.* Kimberley Dreams ☎ *61/8/8942-0971* ⊕ *www.kimberleys.com.au.* Adventure Tours Australia ☎ *61/8132-8230* ⊕ *www.adventuretours.com.au.*

BIKING
Remote Outback Cycle (ROC) Tours combine biking with 4WD transportation and camping on remote desert tours. Epic Adventures runs a month-long transcontinental bike ride through Australia's Red Centre. You get biking, hiking, and water sports on the Great Barrier Reef in Backroads' multisport family Australian tour.

▋TIP➜ Most airlines accommodate bikes as luggage, provided they're dismantled and boxed.

Contacts Backroads ☎ *800/462-2848* ⊕ *www.backroads.com.* Epic Adventures ☎ *61/1300/948911* ⊕ *www.ecotrek.com.au.* ROC Tours ☎ *61/1/300948911* ⊕ *www.ecotrek.com.au.*

BIRD-WATCHING
Kirrama Wildlife Tours runs several tours a year in northern and southwestern Australia—they range from 6 to 16 days. There are around five small-group tours run every year by Kimberley Birdwatching: some are camping-based, others involve farmstays. Follow That Bird is a Sydney-based company that runs shorter tours in southeastern Australia.

Contacts Follow That Bird ☎ *61/2/9973-1865* ⊕ *www.followthatbird.com.au.* Kimberley Birdwatching ☎ *61/8/9192-1246* ⊕ *www.kimberleybirdwatching.com.au.* Kirrama Wildlife Tours ☎ *61/7/4065-5181* ⊕ *www.kirrama.com.au.*

CULTURE
Desert Tracks, owned by the Aboriginal Pitjantjatjara people, operates 3- and 5-day cultural tours in desert Northern Territory and South Australia. Learning is the focus of Smithsonian Journeys' small-group tours, which are led by university professors—their 26-day Great Trains, Wineries & Cultures tour covers a lot of Australia—and New Zealand, too. Local experts also lead National Geographic's Around the World trip, which takes in the Great Barrier Reef, but all that knowledge doesn't come cheap, nor does the private air transport they use.

Contacts **Desert Tracks** ☎ *04/3950–0419*
⊕ *www.deserttracks.com.au.* **National
Geographic Expeditions** ☎ *888/966–8687*
⊕ *www.nationalgeographicexpeditions.com.*
Smithsonian Journeys ☎ *877/338–8687*
⊕ *www.smithsonianjourneys.org.*

DIVING

Dive Directory and Diversion Dive Travel
run multiday live-aboard diving tours on
the Great Barrier Reef. Local flighsteeing
company Daintree Air's Ultimate Dive
package includes 18 dives in nine days—
the Great Barrier Reef, Coral Sea, and a
wreck dive are included.

Contacts **Daintree Air** ☎ *1800/246–206
within Australia, 61/7/4034–9300*
⊕ *www.daintreeair.com.au.* **Dive Directory**
☎ *61/7/4046–7303* ⊕ *www.dive-australia.
com.* **Diversion Dive Travel** ☎ *1800/607–913
within Australia, 617/4039–0200*
⊕ *www.diversionoz.com.*

ECO-TOURS AND SAFARIS

Oz Tours and Wayoutback are certified
eco-tour operators that run camping and
accommodated safaris in northern Australia. Sacred Earth Safaris and Odyssey Tours
and Safaris specialize in tented 4WD tours
around Australia's Top End. Outback Private Tours takes you back to nature without sacrificing creature comforts.

Contacts **Odyssey Tours and Safaris**
☎ *08/8952-6811.* **Outback Private Tours**
☎ *08/8593-0412* ⊕ *www.outbackprivatetours.
com.au.* **Oz Tours** ☎ *1800/079–006 within
Australia, 61/7/4055–9535* ⊕ *www.oztours.
com.au.* **Sacred Earth Safaris** ☎ *61/8/8981–
8420* ⊕ *www.sacredearthsafaris.com.au.* **Wayoutback** ☎ *1300/551–510 within Australia,
61/8/8952–4324* ⊕ *www.wayoutback.com.*

FLIGHTSEEING

Bill Peach Journeys has 10 different aircruising packages in Australia; the longest lasts 12 days and covers more than
10,000 km (6,200 mi). Daintree Air is a
Queensland-based flightseeing company
with several multiday packages.

Contacts **Bill Peach Journeys** ☎ *612/9693–
2233* ⊕ *www.billpeachjourneys.com.au.* **Daintree Air** ☎ *1800/246–206 within Australia,
61/7/4034–9300* ⊕ *www.daintreeair.com.au.*

FOOD AND WINE

Artisans of Leisure's nine-day Food and
Wine Australia tour divides time between
vineyards, markets, and seriously luxurious hotels.

Contacts **Artisans of Leisure** ☎ *800/214–
8144* ⊕ *www.artisansofleisure.com.*

HIKING

Auswalk has a huge range of hiking expeditions all over Australia. There are group
departures and customized self-guided
tours. You can mix hiking with other
adventure activities with one of Australian Walking Holidays' guided trips.

Contacts **Auswalk** ☎ *613/5356–4971*
⊕ *www.auswalk.com.au.*

INDEX

PHOTO CREDITS

1, Southern Grampians Shire/Tourism Victoria. 3, Pictor/age fotostock. **Chapter 1: Experience Australia:** 6-7, Konrad Wothe/age fotostock. 8, Kelly Kealy. 9 (left), Scott Sherrin, Fodors.com member. 9 (right), Robert Imhoff, Fodors.com member. 12 (left), Garry Moore/Tourism Tasmania . 12 (top right), Annie Doyle, Fodors.com member. 12 (bottom right), Gary Ott, Fodors.com member. 13 (left), Carol Matz, Fodors.com member. 13 (right), tab hauser, Fodors.com member. 14 (left), jonathanvlarocca/Flickr. 14 (right), The Rainforest Habitat Port Douglas. 15 (left), Tourism Australia. 15 (right), Barry Skipsey/Tourism NT. 16, Ashley M. Greig, Fodors.com member. 17 (left), Cindy Wichser, Fodors.com member. 17 (right), ms_go, Fodors.com member. 18, Oliver Strewe/Tourism Australia. 19, Jamie Mac-Fadyen/Tourism Australia. 20, Liz and Wade Davis, Fodors.com member. 21, Marilyn Mayers, Fodors.com member. 30 (top), Peter Eve/Tourism NT. 30 (bottom), Alma Webou/Short St. Gallery. 31 (top), Penny Tweedie/Alamy. 31 (bottom), Peter Eve/Tourism NT. 32 (top left), emmettanderson/Flickr. 32 (top right), safaris/Flickr. 32 (bottom), David B. Simmonds/Tourism Australia. 33 (top left), Thomas Schoch/wikipedia.org. 33 (top right), Jochen Schlenker/age fotostock. 33 (bottom), Paul Blackmore/Tourism Australia. 34, Sheila Smart/Alamy. 36 (top left), Lydia Balbal /Short St. Gallery. 36 (top right), Courtesy of Kara Napangardi Ross and Warlukurlangu Artists Aboriginal Corporation www.warlu.com. 36 (right center), Daniel Walbidi/Short St. Gallery. 36 (right bottom), Barry Skipsey/Tourism NT. 37 (top), Penny Tweedie/Alamy. 37 (bottom), Iconsinternational.Com/Alamy. 38 (left), Penny Tweedie/Alamy. 38 (right), Donald Moko/Short St. Gallery. 39 (top), Steve Strike/Tourism Australia/Tourism NT. 39 (bottom), Weaver Jack/Short St. Gallery. **Chapter 2: Sydney:** 41, ARCO/Schulz, I/age fotostock. 42, wizalt711, Fodors.com member. 43 (top), Mayitaazul, Fodors.com member. 43 (bottom), Kelly Kealy. 44, Robert Wallace/Tourism Australia. 45 (top), Carol Matz, Fodors.com member. 45 (bottom), archana bhartia/Shutterstock. 46, Gary Ott, Fodors.com member. 47 (top), Anson Smart. 47 (bottom), Mark Bean/Pier Restaurant. 48, varkster, Fodors.com member. 56, Carly Miller, Fodors.com member. 60, ImageState/Alamy. 66-67, Jose Fuste Raga/age fotostock. 70, Norman Price/Alamy. 75, Gary Ott, Fodors.com member. 79, Walter Bibikow/age fotostock. 84, David Coleman/Alamy. 90, R1/Alamy. 95, Jose Fuste Raga/age fotostock. 104, Tony Yeates/Tourism Australia. 105, Ming Pao Weekly/Tourism Australia. 106 (top), Oliver Strewe/Tourism Australia. 106 (bottom), Ron Hohenhaus/iStockphoto. 107 (top), Tony Yeates/Tourism Australia. 107 (bottom), CuboImages srl/Alamy. 108 (top), Murray Hilton/Sean's Panaroma. 108 (bottom), Matthew Cole/iStockphoto. 109 (top), Basquali Skamaachi/Tourism Australia. 109 (bottom), Dallas Events Inc/Shutterstock. 110 (top), Bon Appetit/Alamy. 110 (bottom), Christopher Meder - Photography/Shutterstock. 111 (top), Graham Monro /Tourism Australia. 111 (bottom), Tom Keating/Tourism Australia. 114, Anson Smart. 121, MAISANT Ludovic/age fotostock. 125, Dattatreya/Alamy. 130, Oliver Gerhard/age fotostock. 136, Dominic Harcourt Webs/age fotostock. **Chapter 3: New South Wales:** 139, Don Fuchs/Tourism NSW. 140, Scott Sherrin, Fodors.com member. 141 (top), Sharyn Cairns/Tourism NSW. 141 (bottom), Mucky, Fodors.com member. 142, Melanie Ball. 149 (top), Susan Wright/Tourism NSW. 149 (bottom), Chris Jones/Tourism NSW. 150 (left), Kitch Bain/Shutterstock. 150 (right), Darren Tieste/Tourism Australia. 151, Don Fuchs/Tourism NSW. 152, Jeff Davies/Shutterstock. 154, Vivian Zinc/Tourism Australia. 155, Chris Jones/Tourism NSW. 156 (left), LOOK Die Bildagentur der Fotografen GmbH/Alamy. 156 (top right), Keiichi Hiki/iStockphoto. 156 (bottom right), Inc/Shutterstock. 163, Oliver Strewe/Tourism. 171, Sydney Seaplanes/Tourism NSW. 175, David Wall/Alamy. 188, Grenville Turner/ Tourism NSW. 188, Sally Mayman/Tourism NSW. 194, Chris Howarth/Australia/Alamy. 198, Rob Walls/Alamy. 203, Wiskerke/Alamy. **Chapter 4: Melbourne:** 207, Mark Chew/Tourism Victoria. 208, Mojo Advertising Partners/Tourism Victoria. 209 (left), David Hannah/Tourism Victoria. 209 (right), sheldon Meyers, Fodors.com member. 210, Neale Cousland/Shutterstock. 219, sgusky, Fodors.com member. 220, JoseFuste Raga/age fotostock. 226, Richard Nebesky/age fotostock. 236, David Wall/Alamy. 242, Andrew Watson/age fotostock. 247, Tim Webster/Tourism Victoria. Chapter 5: Victoria: 251, Peter Dunphy/Tourism Victoria. 252, Southern Grampians Shire/Tourism Victoria. 253 (top), Tourism Victoria. 253 (bottom), lisargold, Fodors.com member. 254 and 255(top), Melanie Ball. 255 (bottom), Mark Watson/Tourism Victoria. 256, Southern Grampians Shire/Tourism Victoria. 263, lisargold, Fodors.com member.266, David Wall/Alamy. 269, Ern Mainka/Alamy. 274, Nick Osborne/Shutterstock. 275, kwest/Shutterstock. 276 (top left), iStockphoto. 276 (bottom left), Oliver Strewe/Tourism. 276 (right), Chris Kapa/Tourism Australia. 277 (top), kwest/Shutterstock. 277 (2nd from top), Phillip Minnis/iStockphoto. 277 (3rd from top), kwest/Shutterstock. 277 (4th from top), Vidler Steve/age fotostock. 277 (5th from top), Alison Griffiths/Campbell's Winery, Rutherglen. 277 (6th from top), giovannirivolta/age fotostock. 277 (7th from top and bottom), Claver Carroll/age fotostock. 278 (top), Tom Keating/Tourism Australia. 278 (bottom), kwest/Shutterstock. 279 (top), Oliver Strewe/Tourism Australia. 279 (bottom), Shoot/age fotostock. 280, Doug Pearson/age fotostock. 281 (top and bottom), Milton Wordley/Photolibrary. 289, Mark

Watson/Tourism Victoria. 295, David Wall/Alamy. 301, Darroch Donald/Alamy. 309, Bill Bachman/ Alamy. 314, CuboImages srl/Alamy. 319, Ern Mainka/Alamy. **Chapter 6: Tasmania:** 321, Mago World Image/age fotostock. 323 (top), logicaldog, Fodors.com member. 323 (bottom left), Gary Ott, Fodors. com member. 323 (bottom right), Masha1, Fodors.com member. 324, Matthew Newton /Tourism Tasmania. 325 (top), Paul Sinclair/Tourism Tasmania. 325 (bottom), Jochen Schlenker/age fotostock. 326, Joe Shemesh /Tourism Tasmania. 335 (top), Tourism Tasmania. 335 (bottom), Rachael Bowes/Alamy. 336 (top), Tourism Tasmania. 336 (bottom), Lyndon Giffard/Alamy. 337 (top), Tourism Tasmania. 337 (bottom), Alistair Scott/Alamy. 338 (top), David Moore/Alamy. 338 (center), David Parker/Alamy. 338 (bottom), Nick Osborne/Tourism Tasmania. 339 (top), Alistair Scott/Alamy. 339 (bottom), David Parker/Alamy. 340, Christian Kober/age fotostock. 346, Chris Bell/Tourism Tasmania. 349, Gary Ott, Fodors.com member. 356, Gabi Mocatta/Tourism Tasmania. **Chapter 7: Brisbane and its Beaches:** 359, Alan Jensen/Tourism Queensland. 360, Scott Sherrin, Fodors.com member. 361, Allison Kleine, Fodors. com member. 362 and 363 (top and bottom), Dreamworld. 364, Alan Jensen/Tourism Queensland. 365 (top), Ezra Patchett/Tourism Queensland. 365 (bottom), Peter Lik/Tourism Queensland. 366, Murray Waite & Assoc./Tourism Queensland. 367 (top), Alan Jensen/Tourism Queensland. 367 (bottom), Murray Waite & Assoc/Tourism Queensland. 368, ROSS EASON/Tourism Queensland. 377, Michael Schmid/Flickr. 378, Bjanka Kadic/Alamy. 388, Andrew Holt/Alamy. 397, Dattatreya/Alamy. 403, Murray Waite & Associates/Tourism Queensland. 409, jenwhitby, Fodors.com member. 414, ROSS EASON/Tourism Queensland. 418, Ezra Patchett/Tourism Queensland. 423, Darren Jew/Tourism Queensland. 426, Gary Bell/Tourism Queensland. **Chapter 8: The Great Barrier Reef:** 435, Lincoln J. Fowler/Tourism Australia Copyright. 436 (top), carla184, Fodors.com member. 436 (bottom), sgusky, Fodors.com member. 437, David Menkes, Fodors.com member. 438, Tourism Queensland. 439 (top), Daydream Island/Tourism Queensland. 439 (bottom), Murray Waite & Associates/Tourism Queensland. 440, Media Link Pty Ltd/Tourism Queensland. 441 (top and bottom), Peter Lik/Tourism Queensland. 442, Jess Moss. 443 (top and bottom), Daintree Eco Lodge & Spa. 444, Stuart Ireland/Spirit of Freedom. 450, Mark Nissen/ Tourism Queensland. 455, Skyrail Rainforest Cableway, Cairns, Tropical North Queensland, Australia. 462, Rowanne, Fodors.com member. 466, Robert Francis/age fotostock. 471, The Rainforest Habitat Port Douglas. 479, edoardo hahn/age fotostock. 480, Voyages Hotels & Resorts. 485, poimuffin, Fodors.com member. 494, Tourism Queensland. 499, Paul Ewart/ Tourism Queensland. 508, Arco Images GmbH/Alamy. 512, Pictor/age fotostock. 513 (top), Tourism Queensland. 514, Ulla Lohmann/age fotostock. 515 (top left and bottom left), John Rumney/marineencounters.com. au. 515 (top right), Richard Ling/wikipedia.org. 515 (bottom right), JUNIORS BILDARCHIV/age fotostock. 516 (top), Tourism Queensland. 516 (bottom), Tourism Australia. 517, Reinhard Dirscherl/ age fotostock. 518 (top left), Pro Dive Cairns. 518 (top right), Murray Waite & Associates/Tourism Queensland. 518 (bottom), Pro Dive Cairns. 519, Darren Jew/Tourism Queensland. 520 (left), Visual&Written SL/Alamy. 520 (right), Per-Andre Hoffmann/age fotostock. 521 (left), Gary Bell/age fotostock. 521 (right), JTB Photo/age fotostock. 524, Don Fuchs/age fotostock. 533, Chris McLennan/ Tourism Queensland. 536, Reinhard Dirscherl/age fotostock. **Chapter 9: Adelaide and South Australia:** 541, Wayne Lynch/age fotostock. 542, cyndyq, Fodors.com member. 543 (top left), David Menkes, Fodors.com member. 543 (bottom left), Ira Starr, Fodors.com member. 543 (right), David Menkes, Fodors.com member. 544, Chris Kapa/Tourism Australia. 551, David Moore/Alamy. 552, Paul Kingsley/Alamy. 561, V H/age fotostock. 569, Tom Keating/Tourism Australia. 576, South Australian Tourism Commission. 584, Robert Francis/age fotostock. 588, Rich_B_Florida, Fodors.com member. 590, Matt Netthiem/SATC. 593, Ira Starr, Fodors.com member. 597, Craig Ingram/SATC. **Chapter 10: Outback Adventures:** 601, Steve Strike/Tourism Australia. 602, Jane Horlings, Fodors.com member. 603, reginaca, Fodors.com member. 604, David Silva/Tourism NT. 605 (top), Anson Smart/Tourism Australia. 605 (bottom), Andrew Frolows/Tourism Australia. 606, robertpaulyoung/Flickr. 607 (top), iStockphoto. 607 (bottom), Juergen Hasenkopf/Alamy. 608, Rowanne, Fodors.com member. 619, Chris McLennan/Connections/Tourism Australia. 622, Steve Strike/Tourism Australia/Tourism NT. 627, David Wall/age fotostock. 633, Corey Leopold/wikipedia.org. 637, Gary Ott, Fodors.com member. 645, Peter Eve/Tourism NT. 648, Sylvain Grandadam/age fotostock. 654, Jennifer Fry/age fotostock. 660-61, Gunter Lenz/age fotostock. 667, Darren Tieste/Tourism Australia. 677, Michael Willis/Alamy. 683, Martin Rugner/age fotostock. 690, Ingo Jezierski/age fotostock. 697, Kos Picture Source Ltd/ Alamy. 702, Jon Arnold Images Ltd/Alamy. 712, Jochen Schlenker/age fotostock.

ABOUT OUR WRITERS

Fleur Bainger has tackled the croc-infested estuaries of Arnhem Land, swum with gigantic whale sharks in Ningaloo Marine Park, and lurked through the domes of the Bungle Bungles by moonlight in the name of her art. After spending years combing the outback for ABC radio (Australia), the travel junkie cum freelance journalist now also writes print and online features for the likes of *Australian Traveller*, *Taste*, *Outback* and *OUTthere* magazines.

Tim Baker is a freelance journalist and jack of all trades when it comes writing, researching and editing for multiple Australian publications. He is a local resident of South Australia and researching his own backyard for Fodor's Australia has given him a brand new appreciation for his home state.

Melanie Ball discovered her love of writing about travel somewhere between London and Johannesburg on an overland expedition uck in 1986. Her search for all ings olorful, edible, offbeat, adventurous ar d simply fun has since taken her from Ethiopia to England and around Australia, and descriptions and photographs of her adventure have appeared in many Australian newspapers and magazines.

A gypsy heart and a geologist husband brought travel writer **Johanna Castro** from South Africa to Western Australia. Exploring and writing about the region became a passion which led on to the opportunity to update Fodor's Western Australian chapter. Johanna's lived in 11 different countries and contributed to over 40 publications worldwide including, *The West Australian*, *A Place in the Sun*, *Traveller*, and *Flying Springbok*.

Tess Curran is a Byron Bay-born, Brisbane-raised journalist and editor, who has contributed to over a dozen titles nationally and internationally. She currently works as the deputy editor of the national eco-fashion magazine *Peppermint*, where her interests include food, fashion, travel,

design, photography, and the world around her.

Sydney-based **Barry Lorne Freedman** has written and photographed travel for international publications in Canada, the U.S. and Australia, including the 2011 Travel supplement in *GQ Australia*. His professional passion for travel led to stints in Tokyo, Mexico City, Quebec City, and Inuvik, an Arctic town. Currently, he is working on travel and fashion for Australia's first online lifestyle magazine, *supply-mag.com*.

A journalist and travel writer for 20 years, **Caroline Gladstone** has traveled across Australia, around the world, and on the high seas. Caroline writes for newspapers and magazines in Australia including the *Sunday Telegraph*, the *Sun Herald*, *The Australian*, *Luxury Travel*, *Cruise Passenger* magazine, and many more. Cruising is her specialty and she's sailed on and dined in dozens of ships of all shapes and sizes. She's also an expert on French Polynesia and co-authored the Fodor's inaugural guide to Tahiti and French Polynesia.

Amy Taylor-Kabbaz has spent most of her life in the Wine and Festival State, as a freelance writer for various magazines and newspapers, blogger of "The Mummy Monologues," and senior producer for the award-winning 891 ABC Adelaide radio program. Being married to a former cocktail bartender of the year and hospitality man-about-town also helped greatly in the research for this publication.

Merran White, a former national travel editor for Australia's *CitySearch*, has worked with Time Out Guides in London, Conde Nast Traveler's *www.concierge.com*, Australia's *Vacations & Travel*, P&O Cruises publications, and Virgin Blue's inflight magazine *Voyeur*. She's authored two books for solo women travelers, and spends her vacations beachcombing, scuba diving, and communing with the wildlife.